2015 North American
Coins & Prices

A GUIDE TO U.S., CANADIAN AND MEXICAN COINS

24TH EDITION

David C. Harper, Editor

Harry Miller & Thomas Michael, Market Analysts

The World's Best-Selling Coin Books

10-6-14

Published by

Krause Publications, a division of F+W Media, Inc.
700 East State Street • Iola, WI 54990-0001
715-445-2214 • 888-457-2873
www.krausebooks.com

To order books or other products call toll-free 1-800-258-0929
or visit us online at www.shopnumismaster.com

ISSN 1935-0562
ISBN-13: 978-1-4402-4166-6
ISBN-10: 1-4402-4166-X

Cover Design by Jana Tappa
Designed by Sandi Carpenter
Edited by George Cuhaj

Printed in the United States of America

Contents

1

"A Small Beginning"
The U.S. Mint grew from a modest start

By Robert R. Van Ryzin

It was a "small beginning" but a significant one. In July 1792, a site for the new U.S. Mint not yet having been secured, 1,500 silver half dismes were struck on a small screw press nestled in the cellar of a Philadelphia building owned by sawmaker John Harper. Though some have since categorized these early emissions of the fledgling U.S. Mint as patterns, it is clear that first President George Washington – who is said to have deposited the silver from which the coins were struck – considered this small batch of half dismes the first official U.S. coins.

It is true that this limited coinage, the first since passage of the act establishing the Mint on April 2, 1792, pales by comparison to modern U.S. Mint presses. Today's machines can churn out up to 750 coins a minute, striking as many as four coins at a time and boasting yearly mintages in the billions. But it is also true that these first small pieces – struck from silver and stamped with a plump Liberty on the obverse and a scrawny eagle in flight on the reverse – have tremendous historical importance.

For within what Washington would declare in his 1792 address to Congress as a "small beginning" were the seeds of a monetary system that has lasted more than 200 years and has become the study and admiration of many.

Before the U.S. Mint

Collectors today can trace much of the nation's development and learn of its struggles and growth through its coinage: from a cumbersome system first proposed by Robert Morris, a Revolutionary War financier and first superintendent of finance, to the refinements tendered by Thomas Jefferson and Alexander Hamilton, which firmly placed the nation on an easily understood decimal system of coinage.

At first there was little coinage in circulation, except for foreign coins that arrived through trade or in the purses of the first settlers. Despite a dire need for coinage in the Colonies, Great Britain considered it a royal right and granted franchises sparingly. Much of the Colonial economy, therefore, revolved around barter, with food staples, crops, and goods serving as currency. Indian wampum or bead money also was used, first in the fur trade and later as a form of money for Colonial use.

Copper pieces were produced around 1616 for the Sommer Islands (now Bermuda), but coinage within the American Colonies apparently didn't begin until 1652, when John Hull struck silver threepence, sixpence and shillings under authority of the General Court of Massachusetts. This coinage continued, with design changes (willow, oak and pine trees), through 1682. Most of the coins were dated 1652, apparently to avoid problems with England.

In 1658 Cecil Calvert, second Lord Baltimore, commissioned coins to be struck in England for use in Maryland. Other authorized and unauthorized coinages – including those of Mark Newby, John Holt, William Wood, and Dr. Samuel Higley – all became part of the landscape of circulating coins. In the 1780s this hodgepodge of coinage was augmented by influxes of counterfeit British halfpenny coins and various state coinages.

In terms of the latter, the Articles of Confederation had granted individual states the right to produce copper coins. Many states found this to be appealing, and merchants in the mid-1780s traded copper coins of Vermont, Connecticut, Massachusetts, New Jersey, and New York. Not all were legal issues; various entrepreneurs used this as an invitation to strike imitation state coppers and British halfpence. Mutilated and worn foreign coins also circulated in abundance. Included among these were coins of Portugal, Great Britain and France, with the large majority of the silver arriving from Spain.

The accounting system used by the states was derived from the British system of pounds, shillings and pence. Each state was allowed to set its own rates at which foreign gold and silver coins would trade in relation to the British pound.

In 1782 Robert Morris, newly named superintendent of finance, was appointed to head a committee to determine the values and weights of the gold and silver coins in circulation. Asked simply to draw up a table of values, Morris took the opportunity to propose the establishment of a federal mint. In his Jan. 15, 1782, report (largely prepared by his assistant, Gouverneur Morris), Morris noted that the exchange rates between the states were complicated.

He observed that a farmer in New Hampshire would be hard-pressed if asked to determine the value of a bushel of wheat in South Carolina. Morris recorded that an amount of wheat worth four shillings in his home state of New Hampshire would be worth 21 shillings and eightpence under the accounting system used in South Carolina.

Robert Morris devised a complicated plan for a national coinage based on a common denominator of 1,440.

Morris claimed these difficulties plagued not only farmers, but that "they are perplexing to most Men and troublesome to all." Morris further pressed for the adoption of an American coin to solve the problems of the need for small change and debased foreign coinages in circulation.

In essence, what he was advocating was a monometallic system based on silver. He said that gold and silver had fluctuated throughout history. Because these fluctuations resulted in the more valuable metal leaving the country, any nation that adopted a bimetallic coinage was doomed to have its gold or silver coins disappear from circulation.

Gouverneur Morris calculated the rate at which the Spanish dollar traded to the British pound in the various states. Leaving out South Carolina, because it threw off his calculations, Gouverneur Morris arrived at a common denominator of 1,440. Robert Morris, therefore, recommended a unit of value of 1/1,440, equivalent to a quarter grain of silver. He suggested the striking of a silver 100-unit coin, or cent; a silver 500-unit coin, or quint; a silver 1,000-unit coin, or mark; and two copper coins, one of eight units and the other of five units.

On Feb. 21, 1782, the Grand Committee of Congress approved the proposal and directed Morris to press forward and report with a plan to establish a mint. Morris had already done so. Apparently feeling confident that Congress would like his coinage ideas, Morris (as shown by his diary) began efforts at the physical establishment prior to his January 1782 report. He had already engaged Benjamin Dudley to acquire necessary equipment for the mint and hoped to have sample coins available to submit with his original report to Congress.

Things went awry, however.

By Dec. 12, 1782, 10 months after Congress had approved his plan, Morris still could not show any samples of his coins. He was forced, ironically, to suggest that Congress draw up a table of rates for foreign coins to be used until his report was ready. It was not until April 2, 1783, that Morris was able to note in his diary that the first of his pattern coins were being struck.

"I sent for Mr. Dudley who delivered me a piece of Silver Coin," he wrote, "being the first that has been struck as an American Coin."

He also recorded that he had urged Dudley to go ahead with production of the silver patterns.

It wasn't until April 23, 1783, that Morris was able to send his Nova Constellatio patterns to Congress and suggest that he was ready to report on establishing a mint. Apparently nothing came of Morris' efforts. Several committees looked into the matter, but nothing was accomplished. Dudley was eventually discharged as Morris' hopes dimmed.

Thomas Jefferson was the next to offer a major plan. Jefferson liked the idea of a decimal system of coinage, but disliked Morris' basic unit of value. As chairman of the Currency Committee, Jefferson reviewed Morris' plan and formulated his own ideas.

To test public reaction, Jefferson gave his "Notes on Coinage" to The Providence Gazette, and Country Journal, which published his plan in its July 24, 1784, issue. Jefferson disagreed with Morris' suggestion for a 1/1,440 unit of value and instead proposed a decimal coinage based on the dollar, with the lowest unit of account being the mil, or 1/1,000.

"The most easy ratio of multiplication and division is that by ten," Jefferson wrote. "Every one knows the facility of Decimal Arithmetic."

Jefferson argued that although Morris' unit would have eliminated the unwanted fraction that occurred when merchants converted British farthings to dollars, this was of little significance. After all, the original idea of establishing a mint was to get rid of foreign currencies.

Morris' unit, Jefferson said, was too cumbersome for use in normal business transactions. According to Jefferson, under Morris' plan a horse valued at 80 Spanish dollars would require a notation of six figures and would be shown as 115,200 units.

Jefferson' coinage plan suggested the striking of a dollar, or unit; half dollar, or five-tenths; a double tenth, or fifth of a dollar, equivalent to a pistereen; a tenth, equivalent to a Spanish bit; and a one-fifth copper coin, relating to the British farthing. He also wanted a gold coin of $10, corresponding to the British double guinea; and a copper one-hundredth coin, relating to the British halfpence.

In reference to his coinage denominations, Jefferson said, it was important that the coins "coincide in value with some of the known coins so nearly, that the people may by quick reference in the mind, estimate their value."

Thomas Jefferson proposed that the United States adopt a decimal system of coinage.

More than a year, however, passed without any further action on his plan or that proposed by Morris. In a letter to William Grayson, a member of the Continental Congress, Washington expressed concern for the establishment of a national coinage system, terming it "indispensably necessary." Washington also complained of the coinage in circulation: "A man must travel with a pair of scales in his pocket, or run the risk of receiving gold at one-fourth less than it counts."

A plan at last

On May 13, 1785, the 13-member Grand Committee, to whom Jefferson's plan had been submitted, filed its report, generally favoring Jefferson's coinage system. The committee did, however, make slight alterations, including the elimination of the gold $10 coin, the addition of a gold $5 coin, and the dropping of Jefferson's double tenth, which it replaced with a quarter dollar. The committee also added a coin equal to 1/200th of a dollar (half cent). On July 6, 1785, Congress unanimously approved the Grand Committee's plan. It failed, however, to set a standard weight for the silver dollar or to order plans drawn up for a mint.

These two factors led to new proposals.

On April 8, 1786, the Board of Treasury, which had been reinstated after Morris' resignation as superintendent of finance two years prior, tendered three distinct coinage proposals based on varying weights and bimetallic ratios for the silver dollar. The first of these three plans (the one passed by Congress on Aug. 8, 1786) required the silver dollar to contain 375.64 grains of pure silver. The board's proposal varied from earlier coinage plans in that it advocated a higher bimetallic ratio of 15.256-to-1 and differing charges to depositors for coining of gold and silver. It called for minting of gold $5 and $10 coins, and silver denominations of the dime, double dime, half dollar, and dollar. In copper were a cent and half cent. The proposal came during the peak of state coinages and influxes of debased coppers, which, as the board reported, were being "Imported into or manufactured in the Several States."

Concerned over the need to control state coinages and foreign coppers, the board suggested that, within nine months of passage of its proposal, the legal-tender status of all foreign coppers be repealed and that values be set at which the state coppers would circulate. The board obviously expected immediate action and ordered a supply of copper that was being stored in Boston to be brought to New York in the hope that it might soon be coined. Their hopes, however, rested on the positive and quick action of Congress, something that hadn't occurred with the other proposals and would not occur this time.

Opposition to the mint was beginning to surface. Several members of Congress expressed their belief that the supply of foreign gold and silver coins in circulation was sufficient to preclude any need for a mint. They also argued that the problem with debased coppers could be solved by contracting with private individuals to strike the nation's cents and half cents.

Several proposals were offered for a contract coinage. On April 21, 1787, the board accepted a proposal by James Jarvis to strike 300 tons of copper coin at the federal standard. Jarvis, however, delivered slightly less than 9,000 pounds of his contract. The contract was voided the following year for his failure to meet scheduled delivery times, but helped to delay further action on a mint. Concerted action on a coinage system and a mint would wait until the formation of the new government.

Alexander Hamilton, named in September 1789 to head the new Treasury, offered three different methods by which the new nation could achieve economic stability, including the funding of the national debt, establishment of the Bank of North America, and the founding of the U.S. Mint. On Jan. 21, 1791, Hamilton submitted to Congress a "Report on the Establishment of a Mint." It was compiled through his study of European economic theories and the earlier works of Morris and Jefferson, along with the 1786 report of the Board of Treasury.

Hamilton agreed with Jefferson that the dollar seemed to be best suited to serve as the basic unit, but believed it necessary to establish a proper weight and fineness for the new coin. To do so, Hamilton had several Spanish coins assayed to determine the fine weight of the Spanish dollar. He also watched the rate at which Spanish dollars traded for fine gold (24 3/4 grains per dollar) on the world market.

From his assays and observations he determined that the Spanish dollar contained 371 grains of silver. He then multiplied 24 3/4 by 15 (the gold value of silver times his suggested bimetallic ratio) and arrived at 371 1/4 as the proper fine silver weight for the new silver dollar.

In regard to his findings, Hamilton admitted that Morris had made similar assays and had arrived at a weight of 373 grains for the Spanish dollar. Hamilton attributed the discrepancy to the differing equipment used in making the assays. He failed, however, to observe that silver coins were traded in the world market at actual weight rather than the weight at time of issue. The Spanish dollar contained 376 grains of pure silver when new, 4 3/4 grains more than Hamilton's proposed silver dollar.

Hamilton also wanted a bimetallic ratio of 15-to-1, in contrast to the Board of Treasury's 15.6-to-1 ratio. Hamilton said his ratio was closer to Great Britain's, which would be important for trade, and Holland's, which would be important for repaying loans from that country.

His report suggested the striking of a gold $10; gold dollar; silver dollar; silver tenth, or disme; and copper one-hundredth and half-hundredth. Hamilton felt the last of these, the half cent, was necessary because it would enable merchants to lower their prices, which would help the poor.

Congress passed the act establishing the U.S. Mint in April 1792. It reinstated several coin denominations left out by Hamilton and dropped his gold dollar. In gold, the act authorized at $10 coin, or "eagle"; a $5 coin, or "half eagle"; and a $2.50 coin, or "quarter eagle." In silver were to be a dollar, half dollar, quarter dollar, disme, and half disme, and in copper a cent and half cent.

Though it established a sound system of U.S. coinage, the act failed to address the problem of foreign coins in circulation. It was amended in February 1793 to cancel their legal-tender status within three years of the Mint's opening.

Coinage begins

Coinage totals at the first mint were understandably low. Skilled coiners, assayers and others who could handle the mint's daily operations were in short supply in the United States. Also in want were adequate equipment and supplies of metal for coinage. Much of the former had to be built or imported. Much of the latter was also imported or salvaged from various domestic sources, including previously struck tokens and coins, and scrap metal.

Coinage began in earnest in 1793 with the striking of half cents and cents at the new mint located at Seventh Street between Market and Arch streets in Philadelphia. Silver coinage followed in 1794, with half dimes, half dollars and dollars. Gold coinage did not begin until 1795 with the minting of the first $5 and $10 coins. Silver dimes and quarters and gold $2.50 coins did not appear until 1796.

Production at the first U.S. mint, in Philadelphia, was minuscule by today's standards.

Under the bimetallic system of coinage by which gold and silver served as equal representations of the unit of value, much of the success and failure of the nation's coinage to enter and remain in circulation revolved around the supply and valuation of precious metals. One need only to gain a cursory knowledge of such movements to understand what role precious metals played in development of U.S. coinage. That role, to a large extent, determined why some coins today are rare and why some passed down from generation to generation are still plentiful and of lower value to collectors.

From the Mint's beginning, slight miscalculations in the proper weight for the silver dollar and a proper bimetallic ratio led gold and silver to disappear from circulation. The U.S. silver dollar traded at par with Spanish and Mexican dollars, but because the U.S. coin was lighter, it was doomed to export.

A depositor at the first mint could make a profit at the mint's expense by sending the coins to the West Indies. There they could be traded at par for the heavier Spanish or Mexican eight reales, which were then shipped back to the United States for recoinage. As a result, few early silver dollars entered domestic circulation; most failed to escape the melting pots.

Gold fared no better. Calculations of the bimetallic ratio by which silver traded for gold on the world market were also askew at first and were always subject to fluctuations. Gold coins either disappeared quickly after minting or never entered circulation, languishing in bank vaults. These problems led President Jefferson to halt coinage of the gold $10 and silver dollar.

The gold $10 reappeared in 1838 at a new, lower-weight standard. The silver dollar, not coined for circulation since 1803, returned in 1836 with a limited mintage. Full-scale coinage waited until 1840.

Nor was the coinage of copper an easy matter for the first mint. Severe shortages of the metal led the Mint to explore various avenues of obtaining sufficient supplies for striking cents and half cents.

Witness, for example, the half-cent issues of 1795 and 1797 struck over privately issued tokens of the New York firm of Talbot, Allum & Lee because of a shortage of copper for the federal issue. Rising copper prices and continued shortages forced the Mint to lower the cent's weight from 208 grains to 168 grains in 1795.

By that same year Congress had begun to investigate the Mint. Complaints about high costs and low production had been raised. Suggestions that a contract coinage might be more suitable for the new nation surfaced again, despite bad experiences with previous attempts.

The Mint survived this and another investigation, but the problems of fluctuating metal supplies continued to plague the nation. In 1798, because of the coinage shortage, the legal-tender status of foreign coins was restored. Several more extensions were given during the 1800s, ending with the withdrawal of legal-tender status for Spanish coins in 1857.

In the 1830s great influxes of silver from foreign mints raised the value of gold in relation to silver, which made it necessary for the Mint to lower the standard weight of all gold coins in 1834. It also led to the melting of great numbers of gold coins of the old specifications.

By the 1850s discovery of gold in California had again made silver the dearer metal. All silver quickly disappeared from circulation. Congress reacted in 1853 by lowering the weight of the silver half dime, dime, quarter, and half dollar, hoping to keep silver in circulation. A new gold coin of $20 value was introduced to absorb a great amount of the gold from Western mines.

Not long after, silver was discovered in Nevada. By the mid-1870s the various mines that made up what was known as the Comstock Lode (after its colorful early proprietor, Henry P. Comstock) had hit the mother lode. Large supplies of silver from the Comstock, combined with European demonetization, caused a severe drop in its value, which continued through the close of the 19th century.

It was believed that the introduction of a heavier, 420-grain silver dollar in 1873, known as the Trade dollar, would create a market for much of the Comstock silver, bolster its price, and at the same time wrest control from Great Britain of lucrative trade with the Orient. It didn't. Large numbers of Trade dollars eventually flooded back into the United States, where they were, ironically, accepted only at a discount to the lesser-weight Morgan dollars.

The latter had been introduced in 1878 as a panacea to the severe economic problems following the Civil War. Those who proudly carried the banner of free silver contended that by taking the rich output of the Comstock mines and turning it into silver dollars, a cheaper, more plentiful form of money would become available. In its wake, they believed, would be a much needed economic recovery.

The Free Silver Movement gained its greatest support during the late 19th century when William Jennings Bryan attempted to gain the White House on a plank largely based on restoration of the free and unlimited coinage of the standard 412.5-grain silver dollar. He failed. Silver failed. Shortly thereafter the United States officially adopted a gold standard.

Silver continued to be a primary coinage metal until 1964, when rising prices led the Mint to remove it from the dime and quarter. Mintage of the silver dollar had ended in 1935. The half dollar continued to be coined through 1970 with a 40-percent-silver composition. It, too, was then debased.

Gold coinage ended in 1933 and exists today only in commemorative issues and American Eagle bullion coins with fictive face values. A clad composition of copper and nickel is now the primary coinage metal. Even the cent is no longer all copper; a copper-coated zinc composition has been used since 1982.

Precious-metal supplies were also linked to the opening of additional mints, which served the parent facility in Philadelphia. The impact of gold discoveries in the 1820s in the southern Appalachian Mountains was directly tied to the construction of branch mints in Dahlonega, Ga., and Charlotte, N.C., in 1838. These new mints struck only gold coins. New Orleans also became the site of a branch mint in the same year as Dahlonega and Charlotte. It took in some of the outflow of gold from Southern mines, but also struck silver coins.

Discovery of gold in California in the late 1840s created a gold rush, and from it sprang a great western migration. Private issues of gold coinage, often of debased quality, were prevalent, and the cost of shipping the metal eastward for coinage at Philadelphia was high. A call for an official branch mint was soon heard and heeded in 1852 with the authorization of the San Francisco Mint, which began taking deposits in 1854.

The discovery of silver in the Comstock Lode led to yet another mint. Located only a short distance via Virginia & Truckee Railroad from the fabulous Comstock Lode, the Carson City mint began receiving bullion in early 1870.

Denver, also located in a mineral-rich region, became the site of an assay office in 1863 when the government purchased the Clark, Gruber & Co. private mint. It became a U.S. branch mint in 1906. In addition to the Denver and Philadelphia mints, San Francisco and a facility in West Point, N.Y., continue to serve as U.S. mints, but the others have left behind a rich legacy.

The collector taking a more extended journey into the history of U.S. coinage can find plenty of interesting tales – some as tall as the day is long and others factually based – all of which are part of the rich and ever-changing panoply of U.S. coinage history. There are stories of denominations that failed, great discoveries, great rarities, great collectors, and, for those with an artistic bent, a rich field of pattern coins to be explored and a wealth of much-heralded designs by famous sculptors such as Augustus Saint-Gaudens, Adolph Weinman, James Earle Fraser, and others.

For those who are drawn to the hobby by the allure of age-old relics of days gone by, or by coins handed down through the family, or even by dreams of great wealth, coin collecting has much to offer. The history of the U.S. Mint, with its small but ever so important beginning, is the starting point.

2

The Grading Factor
How to classify a coin's condition

By Arlyn G. Sieber

Grading is one of the most important factors in buying and selling coins as collectibles. Unfortunately, it's also one of the most controversial. Since the early days of coin collecting in the United States, buying through the mail has been a convenient way for collectors to acquire coins. As a result, there has always been a need in numismatics for a concise way to classify the amount of wear on a coin and its condition in general.

A look back

In September 1888, Dr. George Heath, a physician in Monroe, Mich., published a four-page pamphlet titled *The American Numismatist*. Publication of subsequent issues led to the founding of the American Numismatic Association, and *The Numismatist*, as it's known today, is the association's official journal. Heath's first issues were largely devoted to selling world coins from his collection. There were no formal grades listed with the coins and their prices, but the following statement by Heath indicates that condition was a consideration for early collectors:

"The coins are in above average condition," Heath wrote, "and so confident am I that they will give satisfaction, that I agree to refund the money in any unsatisfactory sales on the return of the coins."

As coin collecting became more popular and The Numismatist started accepting paid advertising from others, grading became more formal. The February 1892 issue listed seven "classes" for the condition of coins (from worst to best): mutilated, poor, fair, good, fine, uncirculated, and proof. Through the years, the hobby has struggled with developing a grading system that would be accepted by all and could apply to all coins. The hobby's growth was accompanied by a desire for more grades, or classifications, to more precisely define a coin's condition. The desire for more precision, however, was at odds with the basic concept of grading: to provide a concise method for classifying a coin's condition.

For example, even the conservatively few classifications of 1892 included fudge factors.

"To give flexibility to this classification," *The Numismatist* said, "such modification of fine, good and fair, as 'extremely,' 'very,' 'almost,' etc., are used to express slight variations from the general condition."

The debate over grading continued for decades in *The Numismatist*. A number of articles and letters prodded the ANA to write grading guidelines and endorse them as the association's official standards. Some submitted specific suggestions for terminology and accompanying standards for each grade. But grading remained a process of "instinct" gained through years of collecting or dealing experience.

A formal grading guide in book form finally appeared in 1958, but it was the work of two individuals rather than the ANA. *A Guide to the Grading of United States Coins* by Martin R. Brown and John W. Dunn was a breakthrough in the great grading debate. Now collectors had a reference that gave them specific guidelines for specific coins and could be studied and restudied at home.

The first editions of Brown and Dunn carried text only, no illustrations. For the fourth edition, in 1964, publication was assumed by Whitman Publishing Co. of Racine, Wis., and line drawings were added to illustrate the text.

The fourth edition listed six principal categories for circulated coins (from worst to best): good, very good, fine, very fine, extremely fine, and about uncirculated. But again, the desire for more precise categories were evidenced. In the book's introduction, Brown and Dunn wrote, "Dealers will sometimes advertise coins that are graded G-VG, VG-F, F-VF, VF-XF. Or the description may be ABT. G. or VG plus, etc. This means that the coin in question more than meets minimum standards for the lower grade but is not quite good enough for the higher grade."

When the fifth edition appeared, in 1969, the "New B & D Grading System" was introduced. The six principal categories for circulated coins were still intact, but variances within those categories were now designated by up to four letters: "A," "B," "C" or "D." For example, an EF-A coin was "almost about uncirculated." An EF-B was "normal extra fine" within the B & D standards. EF-C had a "normal extra fine" obverse, but the reverse was "obviously not as nice as obverse due to poor strike or excessive wear." EF-D had a "normal extra fine" reverse but a problem obverse.

But that wasn't the end. Brown and Dunn further listed 29 problem points that could appear on a coin – from No. 1 for an "edge bump" to No. 29 for "attempted re-engraving outside of the Mint." The number could be followed by the letter "O" or "R" to designate whether the problem appeared on the obverse or reverse and a Roman numeral corresponding to a clock face to designate where the problem appears on the obverse or reverse. For example, a coin described as "VG-B-9-O-X" would grade "VG-B"; the "9" designated a "single rim nick"; the "O" indicated the nick was on the obverse; and the "X" indicated it appeared at the 10 o'clock position, or upper left, of the obverse.

The authors' goal was noble – to create the perfect grading system. They again, however, fell victim to the age-old grading-system problem: Precision comes at the expense of brevity. Dealer Kurt Krueger wrote in the January 1976 issue of *The Numismatist*, "Under the new B & D system, the numismatist must contend with a minimum of 43,152 different grading combinations! Accuracy is apparent, but simplicity has been lost." As a result, the "New B & D Grading System" never caught on in the marketplace.

The 1970s saw two important grading guides make their debut. The first was *Photograde* by James F. Ruddy. As the title implies, Ruddy uses photographs instead of line drawings to show how coins look in the various circulated grades. Simplicity is also a virtue of Ruddy's book. Only seven circulated grades are listed (about good, good, very good, fine, very fine, extremely fine, and about uncirculated), and the designations stop there.

In 1977 the longtime call for the ANA to issue grading standards was met with the release of *The Official A.N.A. Grading Standards for United States Coins*. Like Brown and Dunn, the first edition of the ANA grading guide used line drawings to illustrate coins in various states of wear. But instead of using adjectival descriptions, the ANA guide adopted a numerical system for designating grades.

The numerical designations were based on a system used by Dr. William H. Sheldon in his book *Early American Cents*, first published in 1949. He used a scale of 1 to 70 to designate the grades of large cents.

"On this scale," Sheldon wrote, "1 means that the coin is identifiable and not mutilated – no more than that. A 70-coin is one in flawless Mint State, exactly as it left the dies, with perfect mint color and without a blemish or nick." (Sheldon's scale also had its pragmatic side. At the time, a No. 2 large cent was worth about twice a No. 1 coin; a No. 4 was worth about twice a No. 2, and so on up the scale.)

With the first edition of its grading guide, the ANA adopted the 70-point scale for grading all U.S. coins. It designated 10 categories of circulated grades: AG-3, G-4, VG-8, F-12, VF-20, VF-30, EF-40, EF-45, AU-50, and AU-55. The third edition, released in 1987, replaced the line drawings with photographs, and another circulated grade was added: AU-58. A fourth edition was released in 1991.

Grading circulated U.S. coins

Dealers today generally use either the ANA guide or Photograde when grading circulated coins for their inventories. (Brown and Dunn is now out of print.) Many local coin shops sell both books. Advertisers in *Numismatic News*, *Coins* magazine, and *Coin Prices* must indicate which standards they are using in grading their coins. If the standards are not listed, they must conform to ANA standards.

Following are some general guidelines, accompanied by photos, for grading circulated U.S. coins. Grading even circulated pieces can be subjective, particularly when attempting to draw the fine line between, for example, AU-55 and AU-58. Two longtime collectors or dealers can disagree in such a case.

But by studying some combination of the following guidelines, the ANA guide, and Photograde, and by looking at a lot of coins at shops and shows, collectors can gain enough grading knowledge to buy circulated coins confidently from dealers and other collectors. The more you study, the more knowledge and confidence you will gain. When you decide which series of coins you want to collect, focus on the guidelines for that particular series. Read them, reread them, and then refer back to them again and again.

AU-50

AU-50 (about uncirculated): Just a slight trace of wear, result of brief exposure

Indian cent

Lincoln cent

Buffalo nickel

Jefferson nickel

Mercury dime

Standing Liberty quarter

Washington quarter

Walking Liberty half dollar

Morgan dollar

Barber coins

to circulation or light rubbing from mishandling, may be evident on elevated design areas. These imperfections may appear as scratches or dull spots, along with bag marks or edge nicks. At least half of the original mint luster generally is still evident.

XF-40

Indian cent

Lincoln cent

Buffalo nickel

Jefferson nickel

Mercury dime

Standing Liberty quarter

Washington quarter   *Walking Liberty half dollar*

Morgan dollar   *Barber coins*

XF-40 (extremely fine): The coin must show only slight evidence of wear on the highest points of the design, particularly in the hair lines of the portrait on the obverse. The same may be said for the eagle's feathers and wreath leaves on the reverse of most U.S. coins. A trace of mint luster may still show in protected areas of the coin's surface.

VF-20

Indian cent

Lincoln cent

Buffalo nickel

Jefferson nickel

Mercury dime

Standing Liberty quarter

Washington quarter   *Walking Liberty half dollar*

Morgan dollar   *Barber coins*

VF-20 (very fine): The coin will show light wear at the fine points in the design, though they may remain sharp overall. Although the details may be slightly smoothed, all lettering and major features must remain sharp.

Indian cent: All letters in "Liberty" are complete but worn. Headdress shows considerable flatness, with flat spots on the tips of the feathers.

Lincoln cent: Hair, cheek, jaw, and bow-tie details will be worn but clearly separated, and wheat stalks on the reverse will be full with no weak spots.

Buffalo nickel: High spots on hair braid and cheek will be flat but show some detail, and a full horn will remain on the buffalo.

Jefferson nickel: Well over half of the major hair detail will remain, and the pillars on Monticello will remain well defined, with the triangular roof partially visible.

Mercury dime: Hair braid will show some detail, and three-quarters of the detail will remain in the feathers. The two diagonal bands on the fasces will show completely but will be worn smooth at the middle, with the vertical lines sharp.

Standing Liberty quarter: Rounded contour of Liberty's right leg will be flattened, as will the high point of the shield.

Washington quarter: There will be considerable wear on the hair curls, with feathers on the right and left of the eagle's breast showing clearly.

Walking Liberty half dollar: All lines of the skirt will show but will be worn on the high points. Over half the feathers on the eagle will show.

Morgan dollar: Two-thirds of the hair lines from the forehead to the ear must show. Ear should be well defined. Feathers on the eagle's breast may be worn smooth.

Barber coins: All seven letters of "Liberty" on the headband must stand out sharply. Head wreath will be well outlined from top to bottom.

F-12

Indian cent

Lincoln cent

Buffalo nickel

Jefferson nickel

Mercury dime

Standing Liberty quarter

Washington quarter

Walking Liberty half dollar

Morgan dollar

Barber coins

F-12 (fine): Coins show evidence of moderate to considerable but generally even wear on all high points, though all elements of the design and lettering remain bold. Where the word "Liberty" appears in a headband, it must be fully visible. On 20th century coins, the rim must be fully raised and sharp.

VG-8

Indian cent

Lincoln cent

Buffalo nickel

Jefferson nickel

Mercury dime

Standing Liberty quarter

Washington quarter

Walking Liberty half dollar

Morgan dollar

Barber coins

VG-8 (very good): The coin will show considerable wear, with most detail points worn nearly smooth. Where the word "Liberty" appears in a headband, at least three letters must show. On 20th century coins, the rim will start to merge with the lettering.

G-4

Indian cent

Lincoln cent

Buffalo nickel

Jefferson nickel

Mercury dime

Standing Liberty quarter

Washington quarter   Walking Liberty half dollar

Morgan dollar   Barber coins

G-4 (good): Only the basic design remains distinguishable in outline form, with all points of detail worn smooth. The word "Liberty" has disappeared, and the rims are almost merging with the lettering.

About good or fair: The coin will be identifiable by date and mint but otherwise badly worn, with only parts of the lettering showing. Such coins are of value only as fillers in a collection until a better example of the date and mintmark can be obtained. The only exceptions would be rare coins

Collectors have a variety of grading services from which to choose. This set of Arkansas half dollars that appeared in an Early American History Auctions sale used two of the services.

Grading uncirculated U.S. coins

The subjectivity of grading and the trend toward more classifications becomes more acute when venturing into uncirculated, or mint-state, coins. A minute difference between one or two grade points can mean a difference in value of hundreds or even thousands of dollars. In addition, the standards are more difficult to articulate in writing and illustrate through drawings or photographs. Thus, the possibilities for differences of opinion on one or two grade points increase in uncirculated coins.

Back in Dr. George Heath's day and continuing through the 1960s, a coin was either uncirculated or it wasn't. Little distinction was made between uncirculated coins of varying condition, largely because there was little if any difference in value. When *Numismatic News* introduced its value guide in 1962 (the forerunner of today's *Coin Market* section in the *News*), it listed only one grade of uncirculated for Morgan dollars.

But as collectible coins increased in value and buyers of uncirculated coins became more picky, distinctions within uncirculated grade started to surface. In 1975 *Numismatic News* still listed only one uncirculated grade in *Coin Market*, but added this note: "Uncirculated and proof specimens in especially choice condition will also command proportionately higher premiums than these listed."

The first edition of the ANA guide listed two grades of uncirculated, MS-60 and MS-65, in addition to the theoretical but non-existent MS-70 (a flawless coin). MS-60 was described as "typical uncirculated" and MS-65 as "choice uncirculated." *Numismatic News* adopted both designations for *Coin Market*. In 1981, when the second edition of the ANA grading guide was released, MS-67 and MS-63 were added. In 1985 *Numismatic News* started listing six grades of uncirculated for Morgan dollars: MS-60, MS-63, MS-65, MS-65+, and MS-63 prooflike.

Then in 1986, a new entity appeared that changed the nature of grading and trading uncirculated coins ever since. A group of dealers led by David Hall of Newport Beach, Calif., formed the Professional Coin Grading Service. For a fee, collectors could submit a coin through an authorized PCGS dealer and receive a professional opinion of its grade.

The concept was not new; the ANA had operated an authentication service since 1972 and a grading service since 1979. A collector or dealer could submit a coin directly to the service and receive a certificate giving the service's opinion on authenticity and grade. The grading service was the source of near constant debate among dealers and ANA officials. Dealers charged that ANA graders were too young and inexperienced, and that their grading was inconsistent.

Grading stability was a problem throughout the coin business in the early 1980s, not just with the ANA service. Standards among uncirculated grades would tighten during a bear market and loosen during a bull market. As a result, a coin graded MS-65 in a bull market may have commanded only MS-63 during a bear market.

PCGS created several innovations in the grading business in response to these problems:

1. Coins could be submitted through PCGS-authorized dealers only.

2. Each coin would be graded by at least three members of a panel of "top graders," all prominent dealers in the business. (Since then, however, PCGS does not allow its graders to also deal in coins.)

3. After grading, the coin would be encapsulated in an inert, hard-plastic holder with a serial number and the grade indicated on the holder.

4. PCGS-member dealers pledged to make a market in PCGS-graded coins and honor the grades assigned.

5. In one of the most far-reaching moves, PCGS said it would use all 11 increments of uncirculated on the 70-point numerical scale: MS-60, MS-61, MS-62, MS-63, MS-64, MS-65, MS-66, MS-67, MS-68, MS-69, and MS-70.

The evolution of more uncirculated grades had reached another milestone.

Purists bemoaned the entombment of classic coins in the plastic holders and denounced the 11 uncirculated grades as implausible. Nevertheless, PCGS was an immediate commercial success. The plastic holders were nicknamed "slabs," and dealers couldn't get coins through the system fast enough.

In subsequent years, a number of similar services have appeared. Among them, one of the original PCGS "top graders," John Albanese, left PCGS to found the Numismatic Guaranty Corp (NGC). The ANA grading service succumbed to "slab mania" and introduced its own encapsulated product.

There now are numerous other reputable private third-party grading services. PCGS and NGC are the oldest and remain the leaders. In 1990 the ANA sold its grading service to a private company. It operates under the ANACS acronym.

How should a collector approach the buying and grading of uncirculated coins? Collecting uncirculated coins worth thousands of dollars implies a higher level of numismatic expertise by the buyer. Those buyers without that level of expertise should cut their teeth on more inexpensive coins, just as today's experienced collectors did. Inexperienced collectors can start toward that level by studying the guidelines for mint-state coins in the ANA grading guide and looking at lots of coins at shows and shops.

Study the condition and eye appeal of a coin and compare it to other coins of the same series. Then compare prices. Do the more expensive coins look better? If so, why? Start to make your own judgments concerning relationships between condition and value.

According to numismatic legend, a collector walked up to a crusty old dealer at a show one time and asked the dealer to grade a coin the collector had with him. The dealer looked at the coin and said, "I grade it a hundred dollars." Such is the bottom line to coin grading.

Grading U.S. proof coins

Because proof coins are struck by a special process using polished blanks, they receive their own grading designation. A coin does not start out being a proof and then become mint state if it becomes worn. Once a proof coin, always a proof coin.

In the ANA system, proof grades use the same numbers as circulated and uncirculated grades, and the amount of wear on the coin corresponds to those grades. But the number is preceded by the word "proof." For example, Proof-65, Proof-55, Proof-45, and so on. In addition, the ANA says a proof coin with many marks, scratches or other defects should be called an "impaired proof."

Grading world coins

The state of grading non-U.S. issues is similar to U.S. coin grading before Brown and Dunn. There is no detailed, illustrated guide that covers the enormous scope and variety of world coins; collectors and dealers rely on their experience in the field and knowledge of the marketplace.

The *Standard Catalog of World Coins* gives the following guidelines for grading world coins, which apply to the Canadian and Mexican value listings in this book:

In grading world coins, there are two elements to look for: (1) overall wear and (2) loss of design details, such as strands of hair, feathers on eagles, designs on coats of arms, and so on. Grade each coin by the weaker of the two sides. Age, rarity or type of coin should not be considered in grading.

Grade by the amount of overall wear and loss of detail evident in the main design on each side. On coins with a moderately small design element that is prone to early wear, grade by that design alone.

In the marketplace, adjectival grades are still used for Mexican coins. The numerical system for Canadian coins is now commonplace:

Uncirculated, MS-60: No visible signs of wear or handling, even under a 30X microscope. Bag marks may be present.

Almost uncirculated, AU-50: All detail will be visible. There will be wear on only the highest points of the coin. There will often be half or more of the original mint luster present.

Extremely fine, XF-40: About 95 percent of the original detail will be visible. Or, on a coin with a design that has no inner detail to wear down, there will be light wear over nearly the entire coin. If a small design is used as the grading area, about 90 percent of the original detail will be visible. This latter rule stems from the logic that a smaller amount of detail needs to be present because a small area is being used to grade the whole coin.

Very fine, VF-20: About 75 percent of the original detail will be visible. Or, on a coin with no inner detail, there will be moderate wear over the entire coin. Corners of letters and numbers may be weak. A small grading area will have about 60 percent of the original detail.

Fine, F-12: About 50 percent of the original detail will be visible. Or, on a coin with no inner detail, there will be fairly heavy wear over the entire coin. Sides of letters will be weak. A typically uncleaned coin will often appear dirty or dull. A small grading area will have just under 50 percent of the original detail.

Very good, VG-8: About 25 percent of the original detail will be visible. There will be heavy wear on the entire coin.

Good, G-4: Design will be clearly outlined but with substantial wear. Some of the larger detail may be visible. The rim may have a few weak spots of wear.

About good, AG-3: Typically only a silhouette of a large design will be visible. The rim will be worn down into the letters, if any.

Where to write for more information

American Numismatic Association: 818 N. Cascade Ave.,
    Colorado Springs, CO 80903-3279.
Independent Coin Grading Co.: 7901 E. Belleview Ave., Suite 50,
    Englewood, CO 80111.
Numismatic Guaranty Corp: P.O. Box 4776, Sarasota, FL 34230.
Professional Coin Grading Service: P.O. Box 9458,
    Newport Beach, CA 92658.
Sovereign Entities Grading Service: 401 Chestnut St., Suite 103,
    Chattanooga, TN 37402-4924.

Visit the Krause Publications website
www.numismaster.com

3

Get a Map
How to organize a collection

By David C. Harper

Do you have a jar full of old coins? Did a favorite relative give you a few silver dollars over the years? Or did you just come across something unusual that you set aside?

All three circumstances make good beginnings for collecting coins. It may surprise you, but this is how just about everybody starts in the hobby. It is a rare collector who decides to start down the hobby road without first having come into a few coins one way or another.

What these random groupings lack is organization. It is organization that makes a collection. But think about it another way: Organization is the map that tells you where you can go in coin collecting and how you can get there.

Have you ever been at a large fair or a huge office building and seen the maps that say "you are here"? Did you ever consider that, over time, thousands of other people have stood on the same spot? This is true in numismatics also. Figuratively, you are standing on the same spot on which the writers of this book stood at some point in their lives.

At a fair, the map helps you consider various ways of seeing all the sights. In coin collecting, too, there are different ways to organize a collection. The method you choose helps you see the hobby sights you want to see.

It should be something that suits you. Remember, do what you want to do. See what you want to see. But don't be afraid to make a mistake; there aren't any. Just as one can easily retrace steps at a fair, one can turn around and head in another direction in the coin-collecting hobby. Besides, when you start off for any given point, often you see something along the way that was unplanned but more interesting. That's numismatics.

There are two major ways to organize a collection: by type, and by date and mintmark. These approaches work in basically the same fashion for coins of the

United States, Canada and Mexico. Naturally, there are differences. But to establish the concepts, let's focus first on U.S. coins.

United States

Let's take collecting by type first. Look at your jar of coins, or take the change out of your pocket. You find Abraham Lincoln and the Lincoln Memorial on most cents and four commemorative reverse designs in 2009. You find Thomas Jefferson and his home, Monticello, on most nickels, but special reverse designs were produced in 2004 and 2005 and a new obverse began in 2006. Franklin D. Roosevelt and a torch share the dime. George Washington and an eagle (or since 1999, designs honoring states and the District of Columbia and territories) appear on the quarter. John F. Kennedy and the presidential seal are featured on the half dollar. Sacagawea paired with an eagle or a woman planting and Presidents paired with the Statue of Liberty are on dollars.

Each design is called a "type." If you took one of each and put them in a holder, you would have a type set of recent coins.

With just these six denominations, you can study various metallic compositions. You can evaluate their states of preservation and assign a grade to each. You can learn about the artists who designed the coins, and you can learn of the times in which these designs were created.

As you might have guessed, many different coin types have been used in the United States over the years. You may remember seeing some of them circulating. These designs reflect the hopes and aspirations of people over time. Putting all of them together forms a wonderful numismatic mosaic of American history.

George Washington did not mandate that his image appear on the quarter. Quite the contrary. He would have been horrified. When he was president, he headed off those individuals in Congress who thought the leader of the country should have his image on its coins. Washington said it smacked of monarchy and would have none of it.

Almost a century and a half later, during the bicentennial of Washington's birth in 1932, a nation searching for its roots during troubled economic times decided that it needed his portrait on its coins as a reminder of his great accomplishments and as reassurance that this nation was the same place it had been in more prosperous days.

In its broadest definition, collecting coins by type requires that you obtain an example of every design that was struck by the U.S. Mint since it was founded in 1792. That's a tall order. You would be looking for denominations like the half cent, two-cent piece, three-cent piece, and 20-cent piece, which have not been produced in more than a century. You would be looking for gold coins ranging in face value from $1 to $50 and current bullion coins.

But even more important than odd-sounding denominations or high face values is the question of rarity. Some of the pieces in this multi-century type set are rare and expensive. That's why type collectors often divide the challenge into more digestible units.

Type collecting can be divided into 18th, 19th, 20th and 21st century units. The 21st century set is rapidly growing. Starting type collectors can focus on 20th century coin designs, which are easily obtainable. The fun and satisfaction of putting the 20th century set together then creates the momentum to continue backward in time.

In the process of putting a 20th century type set together, one is also learning how to grade, learning hobby jargon, and discovering how to obtain coins from dealers, the U.S. Mint, and other collectors. All of this knowledge is then refined as the collector increases the challenge to himself.

This book is designed to help. How many dollar types were struck in the 20th century? Turn to the U.S. price-guide section and check it out. We see the Morgan dollar, Peace dollar, Eisenhower dollar, and Anthony dollar. Hobbyists could also add the Ike dollar with the Bicentennial design of 1976 and the silver American Eagle bullion coin struck since 1986. One can also find out their approximate retail prices from the listings.

The beauty of type collecting is that one can choose the most inexpensive example of each type. There is no need to select a 1903-O Morgan when the 1921 will do just as well. With the 20th century type set, hobbyists can dodge some truly big-league prices.

As a collector's hobby confidence grows, he can tailor goals to fit his desires. He can take the road less traveled if that is what suits him. Type sets can be divided by denomination. You can choose more than two centuries of one-cent coins. You can take just obsolete denominations or copper, silver or gold denominations.

You can even collect by size. Perhaps you would like to collect all coin types larger than 30 millimeters or all coins smaller than 20 millimeters. Many find this freedom of choice stimulating.

Type collecting has proven itself to be enduringly popular over the years. It provides a maximum amount of design variety while allowing collectors to set their own level of challenge.

The second popular method of collecting is by date and mintmark. What this means, quite simply, is that a collector picks a given type – Jefferson nickels, for example – and then goes after an example of every year, every mintmark, and every type of manufacture that was used with the Jefferson design.

Looking at this method of collecting brings up the subject of mintmarks. The "U.S. Mint" is about as specific as most non-collectors get in describing the government agency that provides everyday coins. Behind that label are the various production facilities that actually do the work.

In the more than two centuries of U.S. coinage, there have been eight such facilities. Four are still in operation. Those eight in alphabetical order are Carson City, Nev., which used a "CC" mintmark to identify its work; Charlotte, N.C. ("C"); Dahlonega, Ga. ("D"); Denver (also uses a "D," but it opened long after the Dahlonega Mint closed, so there was never any confusion); New Orleans ("O"); Philadelphia (because it was the primary mint, it used no mintmark for much of its history, but currently uses a "P"); San Francisco ("S"); and West Point, N.Y. ("W").

A basic type set of
20th century dollar
coins would consist of
(from top) a Morgan
type, Peace type,
Eisenhower type and
Anthony type.

A person contemplating the collecting of Jefferson nickels by date and mint-mark will find that three mints produced them: San Francisco, Denver and Philadelphia. Because the first two are branch mints serving smaller populations, their output has tended over time to be smaller than that of Philadelphia. This fact, repeated in other series, has helped give mintmarks quite an allure to collectors. It provides one of the major attractions in collecting coins by date and mintmark.

The key date for Jeffersons is the 1950-D when using mintages as a guide. In that year, production was just 2.6 million pieces. Because collectors of the time were aware of the coin's low mintage, many examples were saved. As a result, prices are reasonable.

The Depression-era 1939-D comes in as the most valuable regular-issue Jefferson nickel despite a mintage of 3.5 million – almost 1 million more than the 1950-D. The reason: Fewer were saved for later generations of coin collectors.

Date and mintmark collecting teaches hobbyists to use mintage figures as a

Jefferson nickels have been produced at the (from top) Philadephia, Denver and San Francisco Mints. Note the Denver and San Francisco mintmarks to the right of Monticello.

The wartime nickels of 1942-1945 marked the first time a "P" mintmark, for Philadelphia, was used.

guide but to take them with a grain of salt. Rarity, after all, is determined by the number of surviving coins, not the number initially created.

The Jefferson series is a good one to collect by date and mintmark, because the mintmarks have moved around, grown in size, and expanded in number.

When the series was first introduced, the Jefferson nickel was produced at the three mints previously mentioned. In 1942, because of a diversion of certain metals to wartime use, the coin's alloy of 75 percent copper and 25 percent nickel was changed. The new alloy was 35 percent silver, 56 percent copper, and 9 percent manganese.

To denote the change, the mintmarks were moved and greatly enlarged. The pre-1942 mintmarks were small and located to the right of Monticello; the wartime mintmarks were enlarged and placed over the dome. What's more, for the first time in American history, the Philadelphia Mint used a mintmark ("P").

The war's end restored the alloy and mintmarks to their previous status. The "P" disappeared. This lasted until the 1960s, when a national coin shortage saw all mintmarks removed for three years (1965-1967) and then returned, but in a different location. Mintmarks were placed on the obverse, to the right of Jefferson's portrait near the date in 1968. In 1980 the "P" came back in a smaller form and is still used.

Another consideration arises with date and mintmark collecting: Should the hobbyist include proof coins in the set? This can be argued both ways. Suffice to say that anyone who has the desire to add proof coins to the set will have a larger one. It is not necessary nor is it discouraged.

Some of the first proof coins to carry mintmarks were Jefferson nickels. When proof coins were made in 1968 after lapsing from 1965 to 1967, production oc-curred at San Francisco instead of Philadelphia. The "S" mintmark was placed on the proof coins of that year, including the Jefferson nickel, to denote the change. Since that time, mintmarks used on proof examples of various denominations have included the "P," "D," "S," and "W."

For all of the mintmark history that is embodied in the Jefferson series, prices are reasonable. For a first attempt at collecting coins by date and mintmark, it pro-vides excellent background for going on to the more expensive and difficult types. After all, if you are ever going to get used to the proper handling of a coin, it is far better to experiment on a low-cost coin than a high-value rarity.

In 1968 the mintmarks reappeared on U.S. coins and production of proof coins resumed, this time at the San Francisco Mint. On the nickels, the mintmark moved from the reverse to the obverse below the date.

As one progresses in date and mintmark collecting and type collecting, it is important to remember that all of the coins should be of similar states of preservation. Sets look slapdash if one coin is VG and another is MS-65 and still another is VF. Take a look at the prices of all the coins in the series before you get too far, figure out what you can afford, and then stick to that grade or range of grades.

Sure, there is a time-honored practice of filling a spot with any old example until a better one comes along. That is how we got the term "filler." But if you get a few placeholders, don't stop there. By assembling a set of uniform quality, you end up with a more aesthetically pleasing collection.

The date and mintmark method used to be the overwhelmingly dominant form of collecting. It still has many adherents. Give it a try if you think it sounds right for you.

Before we leave the discussion of collecting U.S. coins, it should be pointed out that the two major methods of organizing a collection are simply guidelines. They are not hard-and-fast rules that must be followed without questions. Collecting should be satisfying to the hobbyist. It should never be just one more item in the daily grind. Take the elements of these collecting approaches that you like or invent your own.

It should also be pointed out that U.S. coinage history does not start with 1792, nor do all of the coins struck since that time conform precisely to the two major organizational approaches. But these two areas are good places to start.

There are coins and tokens from the American Colonial period (1607-1776) that are just as fascinating and collectible as regular U.S. Mint issues. There are federal issues struck before the Mint was actually established. See the Colonial price-guide section in this book.

There are special coins called commemoratives, which have been struck by the U.S. Mint since 1892 to celebrate some aspect of American history or a contemporary event. They are not intended for circulation. There was a long interruption between 1954 and 1982, but currently annual commemoratives are being offered for sale directly to collectors by the Mint.

Collecting commemoratives has always been considered something separate from collecting regular U.S. coinage. It is, however, organized the same way. Commemoratives can be collected by date and mintmark or by type.

Current commemoratives can be purchased from the U.S. Mint. Check the U.S.

Mint Web site at www.usmint.gov. Hobbyists who order from the U.S. Mint's Web site receive notices of product availability by e-mail. Hobbyists will get the various solicitations for not only commemoratives, but regular proof sets and mint sets and proof American Eagle bullion coins. Buying coins from the Mint can be considered a hobby pursuit in its own right. Some collectors let the Mint organize their holdings for them. They buy complete sets and put them away. They never buy anything from anywhere else.

Admittedly, this is a passive form of collecting, but there are individuals around the world who enjoy collecting at this level without ever really going any deeper. They like acquiring every new issue as it comes off the Mint's presses.

Once done, there is a certain knowledge that one has all the examples of the current year. Obviously, too, collectors by date and mintmark of the current types would have to buy the new coins each year, but, of course, they do not stop there.

Varieties and errors make up another area. Under this heading come the coins the Mint did not intend to make. There are all kinds of errors. Many of them are inexpensive. Check out the U.S. Minting Varieties and Errors section in the price guide. If you want to pursue it further, there are specialty books that deal with the topic in more detail.

Canada

Starting point for the national coinage of Canada is popularly fixed at 1858. In that year a large cent was first produced for use in Upper and Lower Canada (Ontario and Quebec). These prices were intended to supplant local copper coinage, which in turn had been attempts to give various regions a medium of exchange.

What was circulating in Canada at the time was a hodgepodge of world issues. The large cent predates a unified national government by nine years, but it is considered the beginning of national issues nevertheless.

There are many similarities between the United States and Canada and their respective monetary systems. Both continent-sized nations thought in terms of taming the frontier, new settlements, and growth. Both came to use the dollar as the unit of account because of the pervasiveness of the Spanish milled dollar in trade. For each, the dollar divides into 100 cents.

However, Canada had a far longer colonial history. Many of its residents resisted the tide that carried the United States to independence and worked to preserve their loyalties to the British crown. As a result, Canada was firmly a part of the British Empire. So even today with its constitution (the British North America Act transferred from Westminster to Ottawa in 1982), parliamentary democracy, and a national consciousness perhaps best symbolized by the maple leaf, Canada retains a loyalty to the crown in the person of Queen Elizabeth II of the United Kingdom. Canada is a member of the British Commonwealth of Nations.

The effect of this on coins is obvious. Current issues carry the queen's effigy. How Canada got its coins in the past was also influenced. The fledgling U.S. government set about creating its own mint as one of its earliest goals, despite that

Canadian coins have depicted (from top) Queen Victoria, King Edward VII, King George V, King George VI and Queen Elizabeth II.

better-quality pieces could be purchased abroad at lower cost. Canada found that ties to mints located in England were logical and comfortable.

The Royal Canadian Mint was not established until 1908, when it was called the Ottawa branch of the British Royal Mint, and it was not given its present name until 1931. Both events are within living memory. Canadian coins, therefore, have a unique mixture of qualities. They are tantalizingly familiar to U.S. citizens yet distinctly different.

The coinage of a monarchy brings its own logic to the organization of a collection. Type collecting is delineated by the monarch. United Canada has had six. The first was Queen Victoria, whose image appeared on those large cents of 1858. Her reign began in 1837 and lasted until 1901.

She was followed by Edward VII, 1901-1910; George V, 1910-1936; Edward VIII, 1936; George VI, 1936-1952; and Queen Elizabeth II, 1952-present. All but Edward VIII had coins struck for circulation in Canada. The collectible monarchs, therefore, number five, but the longer reigns inspired changes of portraits over time to show the aging process at work. Legends also changed. When George VI ceased being emperor of India, Canada's coins were modified to recognize the change.

Like U.S. coins, sizes and alloys were altered to meet new demands placed on the coinage. However, the separateness of each nation might best be summed up this way: Though the United States abolished its large cent in 1857, Canada's was just getting under way in 1858. The United States put an end to the silver dollar in 1935, the very year Canada finally got its series going.

And Canada, the nickel-mining giant, used a small-sized silver five-cent coin until 1921, almost 50 years after the half dime was abolished in the United States. But whereas the Civil War was the major cause of the emergence of modern U.S. coinage as specified by the Coinage Act of 1873, World War I influenced the alterations that made Canada's coins what they are today.

It might be assumed that change in the monarch also signaled a change in the reverse designs of the various denominations. A check of the Canadian price guide section shows this is not necessarily the case. Current designs paired with Queen Elizabeth II basically date back to the beginning of her father's reign. The familiar maple-leaf cent, beaver five-cent piece, schooner 10-cent, caribou 25-cent, and coat-of-arms 50-cent have been running for more than 50 years. Significant changes were made to the 50-cent coin in 1959, but the reverse design remains the coat of arms.

So where does that leave type collectors? It puts them in a situation similar to categorizing the various eagles on U.S. coins. They can be universalists and accept the broadest definitions of type, or they can narrow the bands to whatever degree suits them best.

By checking the price-guide section, date and mintmark collectors will quickly note that their method of organization more or less turns into collecting by date. Though currently there are three mints in Canada – Hull, Quebec; Ottawa, Ontario; and Winnipeg, Manitoba – they don't use mintmarks. Historically, few mintmarks were employed.

Ottawa used a "C" on gold sovereigns of 1908-1919 and on some exported colonial issues. The private Heaton Mint in Birmingham, England, used an "H" on coins it supplied to Canada from 1871 to 1907.

But the coins supplied to Canada by the British Royal Mint and later by its Ottawa branch did not carry any identifying mark. Collectors who confine their activities to the more recent issues need never think about a mintmark.

It would be easy to slant a presentation on Canadian issues to stress similarities or differences to U.S. issues. One should remember that the monetary structures of each evolved independently, but each was always having an impact on the other.

Common events, such as World War II, had a similar impact. For example, the Canadian five-cent coin changed in much the same way as the U.S. nickel. In Canada, nickel was removed and replaced first by a tombac (brass) alloy and then by chromium-plated steel. Peace brought with it a return to the prewar composition.

To see an example of differences between the United States and Canada, take the Canadian approach to the worldwide trend of removing silver from coinage. Canada made its move in 1968, three years after the United States. Instead of choosing a copper-nickel alloy as a substitute for silver, Canada looked to its own vast natural resources and employed pure nickel.

Canada also seems more comfortable with its coinage than the United States. Whereas the United States often feared confusion and counterfeiting from making the least little changes in its coins, Canada has long embraced coinage to communicate national events, celebrations and culture. Its silver-dollar series actually began as a celebration of George V's 25 years on the throne.

Succeeding years saw additional commemorative $1 designs interspersed with the regular Voyageur design. When the centennial of national confederation was observed in 1967, all of the denominations were altered for one year. The United States only reluctantly tried out the idea on three of its denominations for the nation's Bicentennial.

Ultimately, Canada began an annual commemorative dollar series in 1971. It issued coins for the 1976 Montreal Olympic Games and again in 1988 for the Calgary Olympic Games. Bullion coins were created to market its gold, silver and platinum output. A commemorative series of gold $100 coins was also undertaken. Canada, too, issues special proof, prooflike and specimen sets, similar to the United States.

Hobbyists who would like to be informed of new issues should write Royal Canadian Mint, P.O. Box 457, Station A, Ontario K1A 8V5, Canada. The mint also maintains special toll-free lines. In the United States, hobbyists may telephone the Royal Canadian Mint at 1-800-268-6468. In Canada, the number is 1-800-267-1871. You can get on the mailing list by using these numbers and you can buy currently available coins. (See Chapter 6 for Web information.)

When collecting Canada, another thing to remember is the importance varieties play in the nation's various series. Certainly, a type collector has no need to dwell on this information, but the date and mintmark collector may puzzle over the many extra identifying abbreviations in the price guide for certain coins. These varieties

Like the U.S. Mint, the Royal Canadian Mint offers sets of coins in a variety of finishes to the collector market.

should not be confused with the U.S. variety-and-error category.

Here the varieties are not mistakes; they are deliberately created and issued variations of the standard design. We see Voyageur dollars on which the number of water lines changes. Other dollars count the number of beads.

These differences are minor. Though they were deliberately done to meet varying mint needs, they were not intended to be set apart in the public mind. The hobby, however, likes to look at things under a microscope.

Some varieties were indeed intended to be deliberately and noticeably different. An example of this occurs with 1947-dated issues. A maple leaf was placed on the 1947-dated cent through 50-cent issues. This indicated the coin was struck after George VI lost his title of emperor of India, as proclaimed in the Latin legend, but that the design had not yet been altered to reflect this. All of these varieties are considered integral parts of the Canadian series, and they are listed as such.

Do not construe any of this to mean there is no collecting of varieties and errors of the type common in the United States. There is. Collecting Royal Canadian Mint mistakes is just as active, just as interesting, and just as rewarding. After all, mint errors are universal. The methods of manufacture are the same. So the mistakes can be classified in the same manner.

Canada's numismatic listings also include items from various provinces issued before they were part of the confederation. The largest portion of this section is devoted to Newfoundland, because it retained a separate status far longer than the other provinces – until 1949, in fact.

Advice given to collectors of U.S. coins also applies to collectors of Canadian coins: Do what interests you. Do what you can afford. Create sets of uniform grade.

The rules of rarity transcend national boundaries. The only thing to keep in mind is the relative size of the collecting population. Because Canada has only a tenth of the U.S. population, it stands to reason that the number of collectors in that nation is but a fraction of the U.S. number. A mintage that seems to indicate scarcity for U.S. coin, therefore, could indicate something quite common in Canada. Don't forget that mintage is just a guide. The same factors that caused loss of available specimens or preserved unusually large quantities were at work in Canada, too.

Mexico

Coinage produced in Mexico dates to the establishment of a mint in Mexico City in 1536, more than 250 years before a federal mint was set up in the United States and more than 300 years before Canada circulated its own coins. The output of those extra centuries alone would make organizing a Mexican coin collection more challenging than a collection of U.S. or Canadian coins. But there are numerous other factors involved.

You say you like the kings and queens on Canada's coins? Mexico has kings, too – nearly 300 years' worth, plus a couple of emperors. You say the ideals of liberty embodied by the great men and women on U.S. coins is more your cup of tea? Mexico's coins also feature men and women committed to liberty.

In addition, Mexico is the crossroads of civilizations and empires. The great pyramid-building society of southern Mexico and Central America met its end at the hands of the Spanish conquistadors led initially by Hernando Cortez. The great Aztec empire was looted and overturned in 1519-1521 in the name of Spain.

The great natural resources of the area then supported successive Spanish kings in their grand dreams of dominating Europe. Through the doors of the Mexico City Mint and later facilities scattered about the country passed legendary quantities of silver. Even today the country ranks at the top of the list of silver producers.

But while Spain could dominate Mexico for a long time, the basic ideals of liberty and human dignity eventually motivated the people to throw off the foreign yoke. Unfortunately, victory was often neither complete nor wisely led. And in more recent years, the scourge of inflation had exacted a high toll on the currency itself. The numismatic consequences of a long history punctuated by periods of turmoil are an abundance of denominations, metals and types.

It is tempting for a would-be collector of Mexican coins to forget about anything that happened in the country prior to its monetary reform of 1905. By starting at that point, a hobbyist can happily overlook anything other than a decimal monetary system in which 100 centavos equal 1 peso. That system is as modern as any. The coins' striking quality is high. Legends are easy to read and understand, and the variety of issues is wide but not overwhelming.

There always is a certain logic to begin the collecting of any country with recent issues. The costs of learning are minimized, and as one becomes comfortable, a level of confidence can be built up sufficient to prompt diving further into the past.

The issues of 1905 to date also more easily fit into the mold of type collecting and collecting by date and mintmark. To take type collecting, for example, let's look at the peso. In 1905 it was a silver-dollar-sized coin with a silver-dollar-sized quantity of bullion in it, 0.786 ounces. In 1918 it was reduced to 0.4663 ounces; in 1920, 0.3856 ounces; in 1947, 0.2250 ounces; 1950, 0.1285 ounces; 1957, 0.0514 ounces; and in 1970 silver was eliminated completely in favor of a copper-nickel alloy.

At almost every one of those steps, the design changed, too. After sinking to 3,300 to the U.S. dollar, monetary reform dropped three zeroes in 1993. The new

One thousand of these equaled one new peso as 1993 began.

peso, equal to 1,000 old ones, is now about 14 to the U.S. dollar.

By beginning with 1905, a date and mintmark collector misses out on issues of the various branch mints that were located around the country. Regular issues were all struck in Mexico City. Yearly output was reasonably regular for the various denominations, so date sets are extensive.

There have been rumblings since the early 1980s that Mexico would abandon the peso because of its greatly reduced value. The government, however, has been working hard to retain it since the monetary reform. So far it has succeeded.

One thing the government cannot do, however, is turn the clock back to a time when the fractional denominations of 1, 2, 5, 10, 20, 25, and 50 centavos were relatively high face values. However, it is stimulating to assemble sets because they offer a range of rarities. They are neither so expensive that it would prevent a collector from acquiring them at some point, but neither are they so common that you can walk into a shop, write a check, and come away with all of the 20th century sets complete. Check out the price guide section and see.

Gold in the post-1905 era is basically so much bullion. There are some scarcer pieces and some strikingly beautiful designs, such as the Centenario, a gold 50-peso coin containing 1.2 ounces of bullion. It was first struck in 1921 to mark 100 years of independence. Because Mexico actively restruck its gold coins, however, it is virtually impossible to tell an original issue from the newer version.

The result is a retail price structure based on metallic content. Gold, however, does not conjure up the images that silver does. Silver is the magic word for Mexico. That, of course, means the peso.

The modern Mexico City Mint also strikes commemoratives and collector sets from time to time. These are generally marketed to collectors through private firms, details of which are published in hobby newspapers like World Coin News. Mexico, like the United States and Canada, also issues gold and silver bullion coins.

These also are marketed through arrangements with private firms. Interestingly, Mexico's many gold-coin restrikes were the bullion coins of their day. They had the advantage of ready identification, and they were legally tradable according to gold-coin regulations that existed in the United States from 1933 through 1974.

It is appropriate that we conclude discussion of the modern period on the concept of bullion, because bullion is at the root of Mexico's numismatic history. That is a period to which we now turn.

Mexico also strikes commemorative coins for the collector market. They are available through private firms in the United States.

When Cortez toppled the Aztec Empire, for a time the wealth returning to Spain was merely that taken by the victors from the vanquished. But the business of permanently administering a vast area in the name of the Spanish king, exploiting its natural resources, and funneling the proceeds to Spain quite soon involved the establishment of a mint in Mexico City. This was undertaken in 1536, just 15 years after the end of Aztec dominion.

At first, the authorized coins were low denominations: silver quarter, half, 1, 2, 3, and 4 reales, and copper 2 and 4 maravedis. To understand their face values and how they related to each other, let's take the common reference point of a silver dollar. The silver dollar is 8 reales, and you might recognize the nickname for the denomination of "piece of eight" from pirate lore. The eighth part, the silver real, was divided into 34 copper maravedis. That means the 8 reales was worth 272 copper maravedis.

The copper coinage was hated and soon abolished, not to reappear until 1814. The silver coins were fine as far as they went. When the mines of Mexico began producing undreamed of quantities of metal, however, it was the 8 reales that took center stage. This occurred after 1572. The piece of eight became the standard form for shipping silver back to Spain.

Mexico City's output was prodigious. Minting standards were crude. All denominations produced are called "cobs," because they are basically little more than irregular-looking lumps of metal on which bits and pieces of design can be seen. The only constant was weight, fineness, and the appearance of assayer's initials (which guaranteed the weight and fineness). Not showing those initials was cause for severe punishment.

Designs showed the arms of the monarch on one side, a cross on the other, appropriate legends, and an indication of denomination. The period of cob issues lasted until 1732. Rulers of the period start with Charles and Johanna, 1516-1556; Philip II, 1556-1598; Philip III, 1598-1621; Philip IV, 1621-1665; Charles II, 1665-1700; Philip V, 1700-1724 and 1724-1746; and Luis I, 1724.

Modern mint machinery began turning out coins in 1732. Quality was similar to today. The arms design was continued. It was not until 1772 that the monarch's portrait began appearing. The honor of this numismatic debut belongs to Charles III. Kings of this period are Ferdinand VI, 1746-1759; Charles III, 1760-1788; Charles IV, 1788-1808; and Ferdinand VII, 1808-1821. The Standard Catalog of Mexican Coins by Colin R. Bruce II and Dr. George W. Vogt is recommended to those who want to study this period in greater depth.

The revolutionary period begins in 1810, when a parish priest, Miguel Hidalgo y Costilla, issued the call for independence. The first attempts to achieve this were violently suppressed. Hidalgo was executed, but independence did come in 1821.

With revolt against central authority came a dispersal of the right to strike coins. Mexico City continued as the major facility, but other operations began. The list of these over the next century is lengthy. Mintmarks and assayer initials proliferated.

The old colonial coinage standard survived the period. The 8 reales and its parts carried on. A slight reduction in bullion content had been ordered by the king in 1760, but otherwise things continued as they were. Gold was coined during the colonial period beginning in 1679 based on an 8-escudo piece, which divided into eighths just like the 8 reales. Gold, however, was not as important as silver.

Mexico's first emperor came shortly after independence. He was a leader in the struggle that set Mexico free from Spain. Augustin de Iturbide, originally an officer in the service of Spain, was proclaimed emperor in 1822. He abdicated in 1823 and was executed in 1824.

The second emperor had a reign almost as short as the first. Maximilian I, emperor only because he had a French army to secure the throne, reigned from 1863 to 1867. He was shot by a firing squad when the French left.

He is remembered numismatically because he decided to decimalize the coinage. The centavo and peso were born. Soon afterward, the republic was re-established. Further monetary changes were minor thereafter until 1905.

Collectors focusing on Mexico can devote much time to the study of the quasi-official issues of rebels during the periods of instability. They can look at hacienda tokens, which were issued by large farms or ranches that employed hundreds or thousands of people. Or they can pick whichever period in Mexico's history that fascinates them most. Whatever collectors of Mexico eventually settle on, they will find it rewarding.

Where to write for more information:

World Coin News: 700 E. State St., Iola, WI 54990.

4

American Eagles Fly High
Coins a hit with collectors, investors alike

By David C. Harper

Gold has been the stuff of dreams since King Midas. Large silver coins capture the imagination. You don't have to be a collector to appreciate either metal. When you combine dreams of wealth with collector appeal you arrive at the current conception of gold and silver American Eagle coins. While they are not exactly all things to all people, they definitely are two aspects to the appeal of these coins.

American Eagles are bullion coins. A "bullion coin" is a coin with a design that is widely recognized as containing a known quantity of precious metal in convenient troy weights and standard purity called fineness. To distinguish it in legal terms from a medal or a bar, bullion coins are recognized by the issuing government as legal tender and have face values. It is this face value, or denomination, that makes the object a coin rather than a medal. It also endows it with the full recognition and backing of the issuing government. In the case of the American Eagles, this face value has no relationship to the present metallic value of the coin. This is because face values are unchanging and the price of the metal in each coin changes in trading every business day. That is the nature of bullion and bullion trading. Combine the legal-tender status of a coin with the bullion aspect of the precious metal market and you get a "bullion coin."

What makes a coin qualify for the term of bullion coin is the fact that it contains an even troy weight, starting with 1 troy ounce, or convenient fractions like half ounce, quarter ounce and tenth ounce.

The need for a convenient troy weight bullion coin was first recognized in 1967 by South Africa, then the world's top miner of gold bullion. At that time the existing gold coin supply was a hodgepodge of many historical issues with the British sovereign, American $20 gold piece, Austrian 100 coronas and Mexican 50 pesos the most widely traded gold coins.

But there was a problem. The international gold market quoted the price of gold by the troy ounce, which was fixed by international agreement at $35 a troy ounce. None of the commonly traded coins contained an even troy ounce weight. To determine the gold value of each coin was like doing your math homework. The sovereign contains 0.2355 ounce of gold. Multiply that by $35. You get $8.2425 worth of gold. If you happened to own 67 of them, you would have to further multiply $8.2425 by 67 to determine the value of your holdings. In this case, it would be $552.2475. This was before personal computers. These calculations had to be done by hand. Ugh.

The weight of the U.S. $20 gold coin, also called a double eagle, was close to a troy ounce, but close doesn't cut it when determining value. The weight of 0.9675 troy ounces still has to be multiplied by the price of an ounce to determine the value of the coin. This also is true of the .9802 troy ounce weight of the 100 coronas and the 1.2056 ounce weight of the 50 pesos. Further complicating this was the fact that Austria and Mexico were supplying the bullion market with additional coins all carrying dates from the past. In Austria's case the new coins continued to have a 1915 date and Mexico's was 1947. The United States was not striking any new coins and the bulk of the supply of Great Britain's sovereigns were struck before 1914, although some new sovereigns with current dates were struck from time to time.

If you think this is confusing, it was, but gold buyers could put up with it because the price of gold did not change. It had been set by the United States in 1934 and enshrined in the international Bretton Woods treaty of 1944. The United States promised to supply enough gold to the market to keep that price point fixed. Until 1968 it worked, but then the free market was opened up in London and gold began to change value on a daily basis. New coin value calculations became a daily requirement around the world.

South Africa recognized a market need and created the Krugerrand in 1967. The weight of the gold in it was 1 troy ounce. If the price of gold ended trading on a given day at $35.27, well then, that's what the value of the Krugerrand was as well. The need for math was greatly reduced. It was a market winner. Mintages rose from 40,000 in the first year to 211,018 by 1970. By 1973 mintage was 859,000. In 1974 mintage skyrocketed to 3,203,000 pieces. South Africa dominated the market for new gold coins.

The United States began to notice in 1974 when for the first time since 1933 it became legal for Americans to own gold. For 41 years wedding rings and tooth fillings were the only legal avenues for owning gold for average Americans. Krugerrands flooded the country. Because South Africa practiced racial segregation called apartheid, there were soon calls to ban the importation of Krugerrands until that government's policy changed. In 1985 the ban went into effect.

This opened the possibility of the United States taking over the market for gold bullion coins. Production began for both gold and silver American Eagles.

At left is the enhanced uncirculated 2013 silver American Eagle. At right is a gold American Eagle.

Both were wildly popular in the first few years. Investors bought the regular issues and collectors bought proof versions. However, whereas South Africa rode the wave of rising metals prices throughout the 1970s, helping fuel demand for its coins, the years after 1986 saw gold and silver prices slip. Gold was around $425 an ounce when the Eagles were introduced and silver was $5.75. More than 13 years later at the end of 1999, gold was $288.50 and silver was $5.41. Even though the United States took over the market, the market had shrunk and mintages fell.

The decline in precious metals prices proved not to be all bad. Some collectors got used to the idea of obtaining bullion coins as collectibles rather than solely on the basis of bullion content. They got into the habit of building sets of the coins. Collectors enjoyed huge profits on the coins they faithfully acquired when precious metals skyrocked, with gold rising to nearly $1,900 an ounce and silver nearly $50 an ounce by 2011. Soon more investors were attracted to the market.

Mintages exploded with higher precious metals, especially for the silver American Eagle. Mintages of the silver American Eagle rose from 8 million to 10 million a year in the early years of the 21st century and then decisively exceeded the 1987 record mintage of 11,442,335 in 2008 when 19,583,500 were made. Mintages kept going higher. In 2009, 28,766,500 were made. In 2010, output reached 34,662,500. A new record of 39,868,500 was set in 2011. Output then backed off some in 2012 to 33,742,500. Gold's upward mintage trajectory while dramatic merely returned annual output levels to what occurred in the first few years of American Eagle production in the 1980s, but then paying as much as $1,900 for a 1-ounce coin might make that understandable. A silver 1-ounce coin is much more affordable for both collectors and investors.

What will the future bring for the American Eagle bullion coin series? The newest trend in the series are special collector issues. Since 2006 the U.S. Mint has created reverse proofs (design elements are mirror-like while the empty fields are frosted as opposed to the standard proof where design elements like Miss Liberty are frosted and the empty fields are mirror-like). The U.S. Mint has also created mintmarked burnished uncirculated coins and is expanding the number of mintmarks being regularly used. The latest arrival was the enhanced uncirculated silver American Eagle, which alternated frosted finish with polished finish in the stripes of Miss Liberty's skirt. Other design elements will have the usual heavy frosted finish and the field will be lightly frosted rather than mirror-like. The question as this edition goes to press is whether enhanced uncirculated coins will become popular with collectors.

Clearly the fluctuating level of collector and investor interest in American Eagle bullion coins will alternately emphasize the influence of one or the other, but long-term support from both kinds of buyers should keep the gold and silver American Eagle bullion coins as the most popular bullion coins in the world.

Introduction to Pricing

The following value guide is divided into six sections:
1. U.S. minting varieties and errors.
2. Colonial coins, issued prior to the establishment of the United States
3. U.S. issues of 1792.
4. U.S. issues of 1793-present.
5. Canadian coins.
6. Mexican coins.

Value listings

Values listed in the following price guide are average retail prices. These are the approximate prices collectors can expect to pay when purchasing coins from dealers. They are not offers to buy or sell. The pricing section should be considered a guide only; actual selling prices will vary.

The values were compiled by Krause Publications' independent staff of market analysts. They derived the values listed by monitoring auction results, business on electronic dealer trading networks, and business at major shows, and in consultation with a panel of dealers. For rare coins, when only a few specimens of a particular date and mintmark are known, a confirmed transaction may occur only once every several years. In those instances, the most recent auction result is listed.

Grading

Values are listed for coins in various states of preservation, or grades. Standards used in determining grades for U.S. coins are those set by the American Numismatic Association. See Chapter 2 for more on grading.

Dates and mintmarks

The dates listed are the individual dates that appear on each coin. The letter that follows the date is the mintmark and indicates where the coin was struck: "C" — Charlotte, N.C. (1838-1861); "CC" — Carson City, Nev. (1870-1893); "D" — Dahlonega, Ga. (1838-1861), and Denver (1906-present); "O" New Orleans (1838-1909); "P" — Philadelphia (1793-present); "S" San Francisco (1854-present); and "W" — West Point, N.Y. (1984-present). Coins without mintmarks were struck at Philadelphia.

A slash mark in a date indicates an overdate. This means a new date was engraved on a die over an old date. For example, if the date is listed as "1899/8," an 1898 die had a 9 engraved over the last 8 in the date. Portions of the old numeral are still visible on the coin.

A slash mark in a mintmark listing indicates an overmintmark (example: "1922-P/D"). The same process as above occurred, but this time a new mintmark was engraved over an old.

See the "U.S. Minting Varieties and Errors" section for more information on overdates and overmintmarks.

Price charts

Pricing data for the selected charts in the U.S. section were taken from the January issues of *Coin Prices* for the years indicated.

Mexican coin mintages

Quantities minted of each date are indicated when that information is available.

Precious-metal content

Throughout this book precious-metal content is indicated in troy ounces. One troy ounce equals 480 grains, or 31.103 grams.

Abbreviations

AGW. Actual gold weight.

APW. Actual platinum weight.

ASW. Actual silver weight.

BV. Bullion value. This indicates the coin's current value is based on the amount of its precious-metal content and the current price for that metal.

Est. Indicates the exact mintage is not known and the figure listed is an estimate.

G. Grams.

Inc. Abv. Indicates the mintage for the date and mintmark listed is included in the previous listing.

KM#. Indicates "Krause-Mishler number." This sequential cataloging numbering system originated with the *Standard Catalog of World Coins* and provides collectors with a means for identifying coins.

Leg. Legend.

Mkt value. Market value.

MM. Millimeters.

Obv. Obverse.

P/L. Indicates "prooflike," a type of finish used on some Canadian coins.

Rev. Reverse.

Spec. Indicates "specimen," a type of finish used on some Canadian coins.

U.S. Minting Varieties and Errors

Introduction

By Alan Herbert

The P.D.S. cataloging system used here to list minting varieties was originally compiled by Alan Herbert in 1971. PDS stands for the three main divisions of the minting process, "planchet," "die" and "striking." Two more divisions cover collectible modifications after the strike, as well as non-collectible alterations, counterfeits and damaged coins.

This listing includes 445 classes, each a distinct part of the minting process or from a specific non-mint change in the coin. Classes from like causes are grouped together. The PDS system applies to coins of the world, but is based on U.S. coinage with added classes for certain foreign minting practices.

Price ranges are based on a U.S. coin in MS-60 grade (uncirculated.) The ranges may be applied in general to foreign coins of similar size or value although collector values are not usually as high as for U.S. coins. Prices are only a guide as the ultimate price is determined by a willing buyer and seller.

To define minting varieties, "A coin which exhibits a variation of any kind from the normal, as a result of any portion of the minting process, whether at the planchet stage, as a result of a change or modification of the die, or during the striking process. It includes those classes considered to be intentional changes, as well as those caused by normal wear and tear on the dies or other minting equipment and classes deemed to be "errors.""

The three causes are represented as follows:
1. (I) = Intentional Changes
2. (W) = Wear and Tear
3. (E) = Errors
Note: A class may show more than one cause and could be listed as (IWE).

Rarity level

The rarity ratings are based on the following scale:
1 - Very Common. Ranges from every coin struck down to 1,000,000.
2 - Common. From 1,000,000 down to 100,000.
3 - Scarce. From 100,000 down to 10,000.
4 - Very Scarce. From 10,000 down to 1,000.
5 - Rare. From 1,000 down to 100.
6 - Very Rare. From 100 down to 10.
7 - Extremely Rare. From 10 down to 1.

Unknown: If there is no confirmed report of a piece fitting a particular class, it is listed as Unknown. Reports of finds by readers would be appreciated in order to update future presentations.

An Unknown does not mean that your piece automatically is very valuable. Even a Rarity 7 piece, extremely rare, even unique, may have a very low collector value because of a lack of demand or interest in that particular class.

Classes, definitions and price ranges are based on material previously offered in Alan Herbert's book, The Official Price Guide to Minting Varieties and Errors and in Coin Prices Magazine.

Pricing information has also been provided by John A. Wexler and Ken Potter, with special pricing and technical advice from Del Romines.

Also recommended is the Cherrypicker's Guide to Rare Die Varieties by Bill Fivaz and J.T. Stanton. Check your favorite coin shop, numismatic library or book seller for availability of the latest edition.

For help with your coin questions, to report significant new finds and for authentication of your minting varieties, include a loose first class stamp and write to Alan Herbert, 700 E. State St., Iola, WI 54990-0001. Don't include any numismatic material until you have received specific mailing instructions from me.

Quick check index

If you have a coin and are not sure where to look for the possible variety:

If your coin shows doubling, first check V-B-I.

Then try II-A, II-B, II-C, II-I (4 & 5), III-J, III-L, or IV-C.

If part of the coin is missing, check III-B, III-C, or III-D.

If there is a raised line of coin metal, check II-D, II-G.

If there is a raised area of coin metal, check II-E, II-F, or III-F.

If the coin is out of round, and too thin, check III-G.

If coin appears to be the wrong metal, check III-A, III-E, III-F-3 and III-G.

If the die appears to have been damaged, check II-E, II-G. (Damage to the coin itself usually is not a minting variety.)

If the coin shows incomplete or missing design, check II-A, II-E, III-B-3, III-B-5 or III-D.

If only part of the planchet was struck, check III-M.

If something was struck into the coin, check III-J and III-K.

If something has happened to the edge of the coin, check II-D-6, II-E-10, III-I, III-M and III-O.

If your coin shows other than the normal design, check II-A or II-C.

If a layer of the coin metal is missing, or a clad layer is missing, check III-B and III-D.

If you have an unstruck blank, or planchet, check I-G.

If your coin may be a restrike, check IV-C.

If your coin has a counterstamp, countermark, additional engraving or apparent official modifications, check IV-B and V-A-8.

Do not depend on the naked eye to examine your coins. Use a magnifying lens whenever possible, as circulation damage, wear and alterations frequently can be mistaken for legitimate minting varieties.

Division I: planchet varieties

The first division of the PDS System includes those minting varieties that occur in the manufacture of the planchet upon which the coins will ultimately be struck and includes classes resulting from faulty metallurgy, mechanical damage, faulty processing, or equipment or human malfunction prior to the actual coin striking.

Planchet alloy mix (I-A)

This section includes those classes pertaining to mixing and processing the various metals which will be used to make a coin alloy.

I-A-1 Improper Alloy Mix (WE), Rarity Level: 3-4 . . . . Values: $5 to $10

I-A-2 Slag Inclusion Planchet (WE), Rarity Level: 5-6 . . . . Values: $25 up

Damaged and defective planchets (I-B)

To be a class in this section the blank, or planchet, must for some reason not meet the normal standards or must have been damaged in processing. The classes cover the areas of defects in the melting, rolling, punching and processing of the planchets up to the point where they are sent to the coin presses to be struck.

I-B-1 Defective Planchet (WE), Rarity Level: 6 ....Values: $25 up
I-B-2 Mechanically Damaged Planchet (WE), Rarity Level: – .... Values: No Value
(See values for the coin struck on a mechanically damaged planchet.)
I-B-3 Rolled Thin Planchet (WE), Rarity Level: 6 - *(Less rare on half cents of 1795, 1797 and restrikes of 1831-52.)*..Values: $10 up
I-B-4 Rolled Thick Planchet (WE), Rarity Level: 7 - *(Less rare in Colonial copper coins. Notable examples occur on the restrike half cents of 1840-52.)* ....Values: $125 up
I-B-5 Tapered Planchet (WE), Rarity Level: 7 ....Values: $25 up
I-B-6 Partially Unplated Planchet (WE), Rarity Level: 6........................Values: $15 up
I-B-7 Unplated Planchet (WE), Rarity Level: 6-7........................Values: $50 up
I-B-8 Bubbled Plating Planchet (WE), Rarity Level: 1 .... Values: No Value
I-B-9 Included Gas Bubble Planchet (WE), Rarity Level: 6-7........................Values: $50 up
I-B-10 Partially Unclad Planchet (WE), Rarity Level: 6 ....Values: $20 up
I-B-11 Unclad Planchet (WE), Rarity Level: 6-7 ....Values: $50 up
I-B-12 Undersize Planchet (WE), Rarity Level: 7........................Values: $250 up
I-B-13 Oversize Planchet (WE), Rarity Level: 7........................Values: $250 up
I-B-14 Improperly Prepared Proof Planchet (WE), Rarity Level: 7........................Values: $100 up
I-B-15 Improperly Annealed Planchet (WE), Rarity Level: - .... Values: No Value
I-B-16 Faulty Upset Edge Planchet (WE), Rarity Level: 5-6........................Values: $10 up
I-B-17 Rolled-In Metal Planchet (WE), Rarity Level: 6-7........................Values: $50 up
I-B-18 Weld Area Planchet (WE), Rarity Level: Unknown ....Values: No Value Established
(See values for the coins struck on weld area planchets.)
I-B-19 Strike Clip Planchet (WE), Rarity Level: 7........................Values: $150 up
I-B-20 Unpunched Center-Hole Planchet (WE), Rarity Level: 5-7........................ Values: $5 and up
I-B-21 Incompletely Punched Center-Hole Planchet (WE), Rarity Level: 6-7........................Values: $15 up
I-B-22 Uncentered Center-Hole Planchet (WE), Rarity Level: 6-7........................ Values: $10 up
I-B-23 Multiple Punched Center-Hole Planchet (WE), Rarity Level: 7........................Values: $35 up
I-B-24 Unintended Center-Hole Planchet (WE), Rarity Level: Unknown ....Values: -
I-B-25 Wrong Size or Shape Center-Hole Planchet (IWE), Rarity Level: 5-7........................Values: $10 up

Clipped planchets (I-C)

Clipped blanks, or planchets, occur when the strip of coin metal fails to move forward between successive strokes of the gang punch to clear the previously punched holes, in the same manner as a cookie cutter overlapping a previously cut hole in the dough. The size of the clip is a function of the amount of overlap of the next punch.

The overlapping round punches produce a missing arc with curve matching the outside circumference of the blanking punch. Straight clips occur when the punch overlaps the beginning or end of a strip which has had the end sheared or sawed off. Ragged clips occur in the same manner when the ends of the strip have been left as they were rolled out.

The term "clip" as used here should not be confused with the practice of clipping or shaving small pieces of metal from a bullion coin after it is in circulation.

I-C-1 Disc Clip Planchet (WE), Rarity Level: 3-5 ....Values: $5 up
I-C-2 Curved Clip Planchet - (To 5%) (WE), Rarity Level: 5-6 ....Values: $5 up
I-C-3 Curved Clip Planchet - (6 to 10%) (WE), Rarity Level: 6........................Values: $10 up
I-C-4 Curved Clip Planchet - (11 to 25%) (WE), Rarity Level: 5-6........................ Values: $15 up
I-C-5 Curved Clip Planchet - (26 to 60%) (WE), Rarity Level: 6-7........................ Values: $25 up
I-C-6 Double Curved Clip Planchet (WE), Rarity Level: 6........................Values: $10 up
I-C-7 Triple Curved Clip Planchet (WE), Rarity Level: 5-6 ....Values: $25 up
I-C-8 Multiple Curved Clip Planchet (WE), Rarity Level: 6-7 ....Values: $35 up
I-C-9 Overlapping Curved Clipped Planchet (WE), Rarity Level: 6-7 ....Values: $50 up
I-C-10 Incompletely Punched Curved Clip Planchet (WE), Rarity Level: 6 ....Values: $35 up
I-C-11 Oval Curved Clip Planchet (WE), Rarity Level: 6-7 ....Values: $50 up
I-C-12 Crescent Clip Planchet - (61% or more) (WE), Rarity Level: 7 ....Values: $200 up

I-C-13 Straight Clip Planchet (WE), Rarity Level: 6. . . . . .Values: $30 up
I-C-14 Incompletely Sheared Straight Clip Planchet (WE), Rarity Level: 6 . . . . .Values: $50 up
I-C-15 Ragged Clip Planchet (WE), Rarity Level: 6-7 . . . . .Values: $35 up
I-C-16 Outside Corner Clip Planchet (E), Rarity Level: -. . . . . Values: No Value
I-C-17 Inside Corner Clip Planchet (E), Rarity Level: - . . . . Values: No Value
I-C-18 Irregularly Clipped Planchet (E) Rarity Level: - . . . . .Values: Value not established
I-C-19 Incompletely Punched Scalloped or Multi-Sided Planchet (E), Rarity Level: 7 . . . . .Values: $25 up

Laminated, split, or broken planchet (I-D)

For a variety of reasons the coin metal may split into thin layers (delaminate) and either split completely off the coin, or be retained. Common causes are included gas or alloy mix problems. Lamination cracks usually enter the surface of the planchet at a very shallow angle or are at right angles to the edge. The resulting layers differ from slag in that they appear as normal metal.

Lamination cracks and missing metal of any size below a split planchet are too common in the 35 percent silver 1942-1945 nickels to be collectible or have any significant value.

I-D-1 Small Lamination Crack Planchet (W), Rarity Level: 4-5 . . . . .Values: $1 up
I-D-2 Large Lamination Crack Planchet (W), Rarity Level: 3-4 . . . . .Values: $5 up
I-D-3 Split Planchet (W), Rarity Level: 5-6 . . . . .Values: $15 up
I-D-4 Hinged Split Planchet (W), Rarity Level: 6-7 . . . . .Values: $75 up
I-D-5 Clad Planchet With a Clad Layer Missing (W), Rarity Level: 5-6. . . . . .Values: $35 up
I-D-6 Clad Planchet With Both Clad Layers Missing (W), Rarity Level: 6-7 . . . . .Values: $75 up
I-D-7 Separated Clad Layer (W), Rarity Level: 5 . . . . .Values: $25 up
I-D-8 Broken Planchet (WE), Rarity Level: 3-4 . . . . .Values: $5 up

Wrong stock planchet (I-E)

The following classes cover those cases where the wrong coin metal stock was run through the blanking press, making blanks of the correct diameter, but of the wrong thickness, alloy or metal or a combination of the wrong thickness and the wrong metal.

I-E-1 Half Cent Stock Planchet (IE), Rarity Level: Unknown . . . . .Values: No Value Established
I-E-2 Cent Stock Planchet (IE), Rarity Level: Unknown . . . . .Values: No Value Established
I-E-3 Two Cent Stock Planchet (E), Rarity Level: Unknown .Values: No Value Established
I-E-4 Three Cent Silver Stock Planchet (E), Rarity Level: Unknown. . . . . .Values: No Value Established
I-E-5 Three Cent Nickel Stock Planchet (E), Rarity Level: Unknown . . . . .Values: No Value Established
I-E-6 Half Dime Stock Planchet (E), Rarity Level: Unknown . . . . .Values: No Value Established
I-E-7 Dime Stock Planchet (E), Rarity Level: 7 . . . . .Values: $200 up
I-E-8 Twenty Cent Stock Planchet (E), Rarity Level: Unknown. . . . . .Values: No Value Established
I-E-9 Quarter Stock Planchet (E), Rarity Level: Unknown .Values: No Value Established
I-E-10 Half Dollar Stock Planchet (E), Rarity Level: Unknown. . . . . .Values: No Value Established
I-E-11 Dollar Stock Planchet (E), Rarity Level: 7. . . . . .Values: $300 up
I-E-12 Token or Medal Stock Planchet (E), Rarity Level: Unknown . . . . .Values: No Value Established
I-E-13 Wrong Thickness Spoiled Planchet (IWE), Rarity Level: Unknown. . . . . . . .Values: No Value Established
I-E-14 Correct Thickness Spoiled Planchet (IWE), Rarity Level: Unknown . . . . . . .Values: No Value Established
I-E-15 Cut Down Struck Token Planchet (IWE), Rarity Level: Unknown . . . . .Values: No Value Established
I-E-16 Experimental or Pattern Stock Planchet (IE), Rarity Level: Unknown . . . . . .Values: No Value Established
I-E-17 Proof Stock Planchet (IE), Rarity Level: Unknown .Values: No Value Established
I-E-18 Adjusted Specification Stock Planchet (IE), Rarity Level: 7. . . . . .Values: $25 up
I-E-19 Trial Strike Stock Planchet (IE), Rarity Level: Unknown . . . . .Values: No Value Established
I-E-20 U.S. Punched Foreign Stock Planchet (E), Rarity Level: 7 . . . . Values: $75 up
I-E-21 Foreign Punched Foreign Stock Planchet (E), Rarity Level: 7. . . . . .Values: $75 up
I-E-22 Non-Standard Coin Alloy Planchet (IE), Rarity Level: 7 . . . . Values: Unknown

Extra metal on a blank, or planchet (I-F)

True extra metal is only added to the blank during the blanking operation. This occurs as metal is scraped off the sides of the blanks as they are driven down through the thimble, or lower die in the blanking press. The metal is eventually picked up by a blank passing through, welded to it by the heat of friction.

A second form of extra metal has been moved to this section, the sintered coating planchet, the metal deposited on the planchet in the form of dust during the annealing operation.

I-F-1 Extra Metal on a Type 1 Blank (W), Rarity Level: 7 . . . . Values: $50 up
I-F-2 Extra Metal on a Type 2 Planchet (W), Rarity Level: 6-7 . . . . Values: $75 up
I-F-3 Sintered Coating Planchet (W), Rarity Level: 7 . . . . Values: $75 up

Normal or abnormal planchets (I-G)

This section consists of the two principal forms – the blank as it comes from the blanking press – and in the form of a planchet after it has passed through the upsetting mill. It also includes a class for purchased planchets and one for planchets produced by the mint.

I-G-1 Type I Blank (IWE), Rarity Level: 3-5 . . . . Values: $2 up
I-G-2 Type II Planchet (IWE), Rarity Level: 3-4 . . . . Values: 50 up
I-G-3 Purchased Planchet (I), Rarity Level: 1 . . . . Values: No Value
I-G-4 Mint Made Planchet (I), Rarity Level: 1 . . . . Values: No Value
I-G-5 Adjustment-Marked Planchet (I), Rarity Level: Unknown . . . . Values: No Value
I-G-6 Hardness Test-Marked Planchet (I), Rarity Level: - . . . . Values: No Value Established
Note: There are no classes between I-G-6 and I-G-23
I-G-23 Proof Planchet (IE), Rarity Level: 6-7 . . . . Values: $1 up

Coin metal strip (I-H)

When the coin metal strip passes through the blanking press it goes directly to a chopper. This cuts the remaining web into small pieces to be sent back to the melting furnace. Pieces of the web or the chopped up web may escape into the hands of collectors.

I-H-1 Punched Coin Metal Strip (IWE), Rarity Level: 4-6 . . . . Values: $5 up,
   depending on size, denomination and number of holes showing
I-H-2 Chopped Coin Metal Strip (IE), Rarity Level: 3-5. . . . . Values: $5 up

The die varieties

Division II

Die varieties may be unique to a given die, but will repeat for the full life of the die unless a further change occurs. Anything that happens to the die will affect the appearance of the struck coin. This includes all the steps of the die making:

- Cutting a die blank from a tool steel bar.
- Making the design.
- Transferring it to a model.
- Transferring it to the master die or hub.
- The hubbing process of making the die.
- Punching in the mintmark.
- Heat treating of the die.

The completed dies are also subject to damage in numerous forms, plus wear and tear during the striking process and repair work done with abrasives. All of these factors can affect how the struck coin looks.

Engraving varieties (II-A)

In all cases in this section where a master die, or master hub is affected by the class, the class will affect all the working hubs and all working dies descending from it.

Identification as being on a master die or hub depends on it being traced to two or more of the working hubs descended from the same master tools.

II-A-1 Overdate (IE), Rarity Level: 1-7 . . . . .Values: $1 up
II-A-2 Doubled Date (IE), Rarity Level: 1-7 . . . . .Values: $1 up
II-A-3 Small Date (IE), Rarity Level: 2-5 . . . . .Values: $1 up
II-A-4 Large Date (IE), Rarity Level: 2-5 . . . . .Values: $1 up
II-A-5 Small Over Large Date (IE), Rarity Level: 4-6 . . . . .Values: $15 up
II-A-6 Large Over Small Date (IE), Rarity Level: 3-5 . . . . .Values: $10 up
II-A-7 Blundered Date (E), Rarity Level: 6-7 . . . . .Values: $50 up
II-A-8 Corrected Blundered Date (IE), Rarity Level: 3-5. . . . . .Values: $5 up
II-A-9 Wrong Font Date Digit (IE), Rarity Level: 5-6 . . . . .Values: Minimal
II-A-10 Worn, Broken or Damaged Punch (IWE), Rarity Level: 5-6 . . . . .Values: $5 up
II-A-11 Expedient Punch (IWE), Rarity Level: 5-6 . . . . .Values: $10 up
II-A-12 Blundered Digit (E), Rarity Level: 4-5 . . . . .Values: $50 up
II-A-13 Corrected Blundered Digit (IE), Rarity Level: 3-6 . . . . .Values: $10 up
II-A-14 Doubled Digit (IWE), Rarity Level: 2-6 . . . . .Values: $2 up
II-A-15 Wrong Style or Font Letter or Digit (IE), Rarity Level: 3-5. . . . . .Values: Minimal
II-A-16 One Style or Font Over Another (IE), Rarity Level: 4-6 . . . . .Values: $10 up
II-A-17 Letter Over Digit (E), Rarity Level: 6-7 . . . . .Values: $25 up
II-A-18 Digit Over Letter (E), Rarity Level: 6-7 . . . . .Values: $25 up
II-A-19 Omitted Letter or Digit (IWE), Rarity Level: 4-6. . . . . .Values: $5 up
II-A-20 Blundered Letter (E), Rarity Level: 6-7 . . . . .Values: $50 up
II-A-21 Corrected Blundered Letter (IE), Rarity Level: 1-3. . . . . .Values: $10 up
II-A-22 Doubled Letter (IWE), Rarity Level: 2-6. . . . . .Values: $2 up
II-A-23 Blundered Design Element (IE), Rarity Level: 6-7 . . . . .Values: $50 up
II-A-24 Corrected Blundered Design Element (IE), Rarity Level: 3-5. . . . . .Values: $10 up
II-A-25 Large Over Small Design Element (IE), Rarity Level: 4-6 . . . . .Values: $2 up
II-A-26 Omitted Design Element (IWE), Rarity Level: 5-7 . . . . .Values: $10 up
II-A-27 Doubled Design Element (IWE), Rarity Level: 2-6. . . . . .Values: $2 up
II-A-28 One Design Element Over Another (IE), Rarity Level: 3-6 . . . . .Values: $5 up
II-A-29 Reducing Lathe Doubling (WE), Rarity Level: 6-7. . . . . .Values: $50 up
II-A-30 Extra Design Element (IE), Rarity Level: 3-5 . . . . .Values: $10 up
II-A-31 Modified Design (IWE), Rarity Level: 1-5 . . . . Values: No Value up
II-A-32 Normal Design (I), Rarity Level: 1. . . . . Values: No Extra Value
II-A-33 Design Mistake (IE), Rarity Level: 2-6. . . . . .Values: $1 up
II-A-34 Defective Die Design (IWE), Rarity Level: 1. . . . . Values: No Value
II-A-35 Pattern (I), Rarity Level: 6-7 . . . . .Values: $100 up
II-A-36 Trial Design (I), Rarity Level: 5-7 . . . . .Values: $100 up
II-A-37 Omitted Designer's Initial (IWE), Rarity Level: 3-7 . . . . .Values: $1 up
II-A-38 Layout Mark (IE), Rarity Level: 5-7 . . . . .Values: Minimal
II-A-39 Abnormal Reeding (IWE), Rarity Level: 2-5. . . . . .Values: $1 up
II-A-40 Modified Die or Hub (IWE), Rarity Level: 1-5 . . . . .Values: No Value up
II-A-41 Numbered Die (I), Rarity Level: 3-5 . . . . .Values: $5 up
II-A-42 Plugged Die (IW), Rarity Level: 5-6 . . . . .Values: Minimal
II-A-43 Cancelled Die (IE), Rarity Level: 3-6. . . . . Values: No Value up
II-A-44 Hardness Test Marked Die (IE), Rarity Level: 7 . . . . .Values: $100 up
II-A-45 Coin Simulation (IE), Rarity Level: 6-7 . . . . Values: $100 up, but may be illegal to own
II-A-46 Punching Mistake (IE), Rarity Level: 2-6. . . . . .Values: $1 up
II-A-47 Small Over Large Design (IE), Rarity Level: 4-6 . . . . .Values: $5 up
II-A-48 Doubled Punch (IE), Rarity Level: 5-7. . . . . .Values: $5 up
II-A-49 Mint Display Sample (I) Rarity Level: 7. . . . . Values not established
II-A-50 Center Dot, Stud or Circle (IE) Rarity Level: 7, much more common on early cents. . Values not established

Hub doubling varieties (II-B)

Rotated hub doubling   *Hub break*

This section includes eight classes of hub doubling. Each class is from a different cause, described by the title of the class. At the latest count over 2,500 doubled dies have been reported in the U.S. coinage, the most famous being examples of the 1955, 1969-S and 1972 cent dies.

II-B-I Rotated Hub Doubling (WE), Rarity Level: 3-6 . . . . Values: $1 up
II-B-II Distorted Hub Doubling (WE), Rarity Level: 3-6 . . . . Values: $1 up
II-B-III Design Hub Doubling (IWE), Rarity Level: 3-6 . . . . Values: $1 up to five figure amounts
II-B-IV Offset Hub Doubling (WE), Rarity Level: 4-6 . . . . Values: $15 up
II-B-V Pivoted Hub Doubling (WE), Rarity Level: 3-6 . . . . Values: $10 up
II-B-VI Distended Hub Doubling (WE), Rarity Level: 2-5 . . . . Values: $1 up
II-B-VII Modified Hub Doubling (IWE), Rarity Level: 2-5 . . . . Values: $1 up
II-B-VIII Tilted Hub Doubling (WE), Rarity Level: 4-6 . . . . Values: $5 up

Mintmark varieties (II-C)

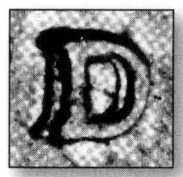

Double   *Triple*

Mintmarks are punched into U.S. coin dies by hand (Up to 1985 for proof coins, to 1990 for cents and nickels and 1991 for other denominations). Variations resulting from mistakes in the punching are listed in this section. Unless exceptionally mispunched, values are usually estimated at 150 percent of numismatic value. Slightly tilted or displaced mintmarks have no value.

II-C-1 Doubled Mintmark (IE), Rarity Level: 2-6 . . . . Values: 50 cents up
II-C-2 Separated Doubled Mintmark (IE), Rarity Level: 5-6 . . . . Values: $15 up
II-C-3 Over Mintmark (IE), Rarity Level: 3-6 . . . . Values: $2 up
II-C-4 Tripled Mintmark (IE), Rarity Level: 3-5 . . . . Values: 50 cents up
II-C-5 Quadrupled Mintmark (IE), Rarity Level: 4-6 . . . . Values: $1 up
II-C-6 Small Mintmark (IE), Rarity Level: 2-5 . . . . Values: No Extra Value up
II-C-7 Large Mintmark (IE), Rarity Level: 2-5 . . . . Values: No Extra Value up
II-C-8 Large Over Small Mintmark (IE), Rarity Level: 2-5 . . . . Values: $2 up
II-C-9 Small Over Large Mintmark (IE), Rarity Level: 3-6 . . . . Values: $5 up
II-C-10 Broken Mintmark Punch (W), Rarity Level: 5-6 . . . . Values: $5 up
II-C-11 Omitted Mintmark (IWE), Rarity Level: 4-7 . . . . Values: $125 up
II-C-12 Tilted Mintmark (IE), Rarity Level: 5-7 . . . . Values: $5 up
II-C-13 Blundered Mintmark (E), Rarity Level: 4-6 . . . . Values: $5 up

II-C-14 Corrected Horizontal Mintmark (IE), Rarity Level: 4-6 . . . . .Values: $5 up
II-C-15 Corrected Upside Down Mintmark (IE), Rarity Level: 4-6 . . . . .Values: $5 up
II-C-16 Displaced Mintmark (IE), Rarity Level: 4-6 . . . . .Values: $5 to $10
II-C-17 Modified Mintmark (IWE), Rarity Level: 1-4 . . . . Values: No Extra Value up
II-C-18 Normal Mintmark (I), Rarity Level: 1 . . . . .Values: No Extra Value
II-C-19 Doubled Mintmark Punch (I), Rarity Level: 6-7 . . . . Values: No Extra Value up
II-C-20 Upside Down Mintmark (E) Rarity Level 6-7 . . . . .Values: $5 up
II-C-21 Horizontal Mintmark (E) Rarity Level 6-7 . . . . .Values: $5 up
II-C-22 Wrong Mintmark (E) Rarity Level 6-7 . . . . Values $15 up
(Example has a D mintmark in the date, but was used at Philadelphia.)

Die, collar and hub cracks (II-D)

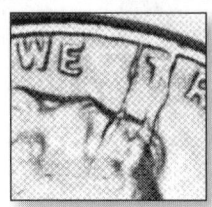

Die cracks

Cracks in the surface of the die allow coin metal to be forced into the crack during the strike, resulting in raised irregular lines of coin metal above the normal surface of the coin. These are one of the commonest forms of die damage and wear, making them easily collectible.

Collar cracks and hub cracks are added to this section because the causes and effects are similar or closely associated.

Die cracks, collar cracks and hub cracks are the result of wear and tear on the tools, with intentional use assumed for all classes.

II-D-1 Die Crack (W), Rarity Level: 1-3 . . . . .Values: 10 to $1, $25 up on a proof coin
with a rarity level of 6-7
II-D-2 Multiple Die Cracks (W), Rarity Level: 1-3 . . . . Values: 25 cents to $2
II-D-3 Head-To-Rim Die Crack (Lincoln Cent) (W), Rarity Level: 2-6 . . Values: 25 to $10 for multiple die cracks
II-D-4 Split Die (W), Rarity Level: 5-6 . . . . .Values: $10 up
II-D-5 Rim-To-Rim Die Crack (W), Rarity Level: 2-5 . . . . .Values: $1 up
II-D-6 Collar Crack (W), Rarity Level: 4-6 . . . . .Values: $10 up
II-D-7 Hub Crack (W), Rarity Level: 3-5 . . . . .Values: $1-$2

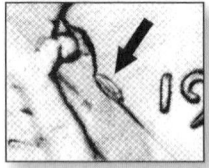

Small die break II-E-2

Clogged letter II-E-1

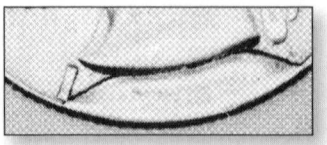

Major die break, date missing, II-E-5

Rim die break II-E-4

Die breaks (II-E)

Breaks in the surface of the die allow coin metal to squeeze into the resulting holes, causing raised irregular areas above the normal surface of the coin. Die chips and small die breaks are nearly as common as the die cracks, but major die breaks, which extend in from the edge of the coin, are quite rare on the larger coins.

If the broken piece of the die is retained, the resulting design will be above or below the level of the rest of the surface.

II-E-1 Die Chip (W), Rarity Level: 1-2 . . . . Values: 10 to $1
II-E-2 Small Die Break (W), Rarity Level: 1-3 . . . . Values: 10 to $2
II-E-3 Large Die Break (W), Rarity Level: 3-5 . . . . Values: $1 to $50 and up
II-E-4 Rim Die Break (W), Rarity Level: 2-3 . . . . Values: 25 cents to $5
II-E-5 Major Die Break (WE), Rarity Level: 3-6 . . . . Values: $5 to $100 and up
II-E-6 Retained Broken Die (W), Rarity Level: 3-5 . . . . Values: $1 to $10 and up
II-E-7 Retained Broken Center of the Die (W), Rarity Level: 6-7 . . . . Values: $100 up
II-E-8 Laminated Die (W), Rarity Level: 3-5 . . . . Values: 10 cents to $5
II-E-9 Chipped Chrome Plating (W), Rarity Level: 4-5 . . . . Values: $10 to $25 on proofs
II-E-10 Collar Break (W), Rarity Level: 4-6 . . . . Values: $5 to $25 and up
II-E-11 Broken Letter or Digit on an Edge Die (W), Rarity Level: 4-6 . . . . Values: Minimal.
II-E-12 "Bar" Die Break (W), Rarity Level: 3-5 . . . . Values: 25 to $20
II-E-13 Hub Break (W), Rarity Level: 4-6 . . . . Values: 50 to $10 and up

"BIE" varieties (II-F)

A series of small die breaks or die chips in the letters of "LIBERTY" mostly on the wheat-reverse Lincoln cent are actively collected. The name results from the resemblance to an "I" between the "B" and "E" on many of the dies, but they are found between all of the letters in different cases. Well over 1,500 dies are known and cataloged. Numerous more recent examples are known.

II-F-1 ILI Die Variety (W), Rarity Level: 4-5 . . . . Values: 25 cents to $10
II-F-2 LII Die Variety (W), Rarity Level: 3-5 . . . . Values: 50 cents to $15
II-F-3 IIB Die Variety (W), Rarity Level: 3-5 . . . . Values: 50 cents to $15
II-F-4 BIE Die Variety (W), Rarity Level: 3-5 . . . . Values: $1 to $20
II-F-5 EIR Die Variety (W), Rarity Level: 3-5 . . . . Values: 50 to $15
II-F-6 RIT Die Variety (W), Rarity Level: 4-5 . . . . Values: $2 to $25
II-F-7 TIY Die Variety (W), Rarity Level: 4-5 . . . . Values: $5 to $30
II-F-8 TYI Die Variety (W), Rarity Level: 4-5 . . . . Values: $2 to $25

Worn and damaged dies, collars and hubs (II-G)

Many dies are continued deliberately in service after they have been damaged, dented, clashed or show design transfer, since none of these classes actually affect anything but the appearance of the coin. The root cause is wear, but intent or mistakes may enter the picture.

II-G-1 Dented Die, Collar or Hub (IWE), Rarity Level: 3-5 . . . . Values: 25 to $5
II-G-2 Damaged Die, Collar or Hub (IWE), Rarity Level: 3-5 . . . . Values: 25 to $5
II-G-3 Worn Die, Collar or Hub (IWE), Rarity Level: 2-3 . . . . Values: No Extra Value to Minimal Value
II-G-4 Pitted or Rusted Die, Collar or Hub (IWE), Rarity Level: 3-4 . . . . Values: No Extra Value, marker only
II-G-5 Heavy Die Clash (IWE), Rarity Level: 4-5 . . . . Values: $1 to $10 and up
II-G-6 Heavy Collar Clash (IWE), Rarity Level: 3-4 . . . . Values: $1 to $5 and up
II-G-7 Heavy Design Transfer (IWE), Rarity Level: 3-4 . . . . Values: 10 cents to $1

Die progressions (II-H)

The progression section consists of three classes. These are useful as cataloging tools for many different die varieties, but especially the die cracks and die breaks which may enlarge, lengthen or increase in number.

II-H-1 Progression (W), Rarity Level: 3-5 . . . . Values: $1 up

II-H-2 Die Substitution (IW), Rarity Level: 2-4 . . . . Values: No Extra Value to Minimal Value
II-H-3 Die Repeat (I), Rarity Level: 2-4 . . . . Values: No Extra Value to Minimal Value

Die scratches, polished and abraded dies (II-I)

This section consists of those classes having to do with the use of an abrasive in some form to intentionally polish proof dies, or repair the circulating die surface. Several classes that previously were referred to as "polished" now are listed as "abraded."

II-I-1 Die Scratch (IW), Rarity Level: 1-2. . . . . .Values: No Extra Value to 10 cents to 25 cents, as a marker
II-I-2 Polished (proof) Die (IW), Rarity Level: 1. . . . . .Values: No Extra Value
II-I-3 Abraded (Circulation) Die (IW), Rarity Level: 1-2. . . . . .Values: No Extra Value up to $10
II-I-4 Inside Abraded Die Doubling (IW), Rarity Level: 1-3 . . . . Values: No Extra Value to $1
II-I-5 Outside Abraded Die Doubling (IW), Rarity Level: 1-3. . . . . Values: No Extra Value to $1
II-I-6 Lathe Marks (IW), Rarity Level: 5-7 . . . . .Values: No Extra Value, marker only

Striking varieties
Division III

Once the dies are made and the planchets have been prepared, they are struck by a pair of dies and become a coin. In this division, we list the misstrikes resulting from human or mechanical malfunction in the striking process. These are one-of-a-kind varieties, but there may be many similar coins that fall in a given class.

Multiples and combinations of classes must be considered on a case by case basis. The first several sections match the planchet sections indicated in the title.

Struck on defective alloy mix planchets (III-A)

This section includes those classes of coins struck on planchets that were made from a defective alloy.

III-A-1 Struck on an Improper Alloy Mix Planchet (IE), Rarity Level: 2-3 . . . . Values: 10 cents to $2
III-A-2 Struck on a Planchet With Slag Inclusions(IE), Rarity Level: 5-6 . . . . .Values: $10 up

Struck on damaged, defective or abnormal planchet (III-B)

Struck on a defective planchet III-B-1   *Struck on a tapered planchet III-B-5*

Coins get struck on many strange objects. The more common, of course, are planchets that have been damaged in some way in the production process. In most of the classes in this section, intent is at least presumed, if not specifically listed as a cause.

III-B-1 Struck on a Defective Planchet (IWE), Rarity Level: 4-6. . . . . .Values: $5 to $10 and up
III-B-2 Struck on a Mechanically Damaged Planchet (IWE), Rarity Level: 5-6. . . . . . .Values: $10 to $20 and up
III-B-3 Struck on a Rolled Thin Planchet (IWE), Rarity Level: 5-6. . . . . .Values: $2 to $5 and up
III-B-4 Struck on a Rolled Thick Planchet (IWE), Rarity Level: 5-6 . . . . .Values: $35 to $50 and up
III-B-5 Struck on a Tapered Planchet (WE), Rarity Level: 4-6 . . . . .Values: $2 to $5 and up
III-B-6 Struck on a Partially Unplated Planchet (WE), Rarity Level: 5 . . . . .Values: $10 up
III-B-7 Struck on an Unplated Planchet (WE), Rarity Level: 6-7 . . . . Values: $100 up
III-B-8 Struck on a Bubbled Plating Planchet (IWE), Rarity Level: 1 . . . . Values: No Value
III-B-9 Struck on an Included Gas Bubble Planchet (WE), Rarity Level: 5-6 . . . . .Values: $5 up
III-B-10 Struck on a Partially Unclad Planchet (WE), Rarity Level: 5-6 . . . . .Values: $5 up

III-B-11 Struck on an Unclad Planchet (WE), Rarity Level: 4-5 . . . . .Values: $5 and up
III-B-12 Struck on an Undersize Planchet (WE), Rarity Level: 4-6 . . . . .Values: Minimal
III-B-13 Struck on an Oversize Planchet (WE), Rarity Level: 6-7 . . . . Values: Minimal
III-B-14 Struck on an Improperly Prepared Proof Planchet (IWE), Rarity Level: 3-5 . . . . .Values: $5 up
III-B-15 Struck on an Improperly Annealed Planchet (IWE), Rarity Level: 4-5 . . . . .Values: $5 up
III-B-16 Struck on a Faulty Upset Edge Planchet (IWE), Rarity Level: 4-5 . . . . .Values: $1 to $2
III-B-17 Struck on a Rolled In Metal Planchet (WE), Rarity Level: 4-6 . . . . .Values: $2 up
III-B-18 Struck on a Weld Area Planchet (WE), Rarity Level: 6 . . . . .Values: $25 to $50
III-B-19 Struck on a Strike Clip Planchet (W), Rarity Level: 6-7 . . . . .Values: $25 up
III-B-20 Struck on an Unpunched Center Hole Planchet (WE), Rarity Level: 4-6 . . . . Values: $1 and up
III-B-21 Struck on an Incompletely Punched Center Hole Planchet (WE), Rarity Level: 6-7 . . . . . .Values: $5 up
III-B-22 Struck on an Uncentered Center Hole Planchet (WE), Rarity Level: 6-7 . . . . .Values: $10 up
III-B-23 Struck on a Multiple Punched Center Hole Planchet (WE), Rarity Level: 7 . . . . .Values: $25 up
III-B-24 Struck on an Unintended Center Hole Planchet (WE), Rarity Level: 6-7 . . . . Values: $25 up
III-B-25 Struck on a Wrong Size or Shape Center Hole Planchet (WE), Rarity Level: 5-7 . . . . .Values: $5 up
III-B-26 Struck on Scrap Coin Metal (E), Rarity Level: 4-6 . . . . .Values: $10 up
III-B-27 Struck on Junk Non Coin Metal (E), Rarity Level: 4-6 . . . . .Values: $15 up
III-B-28 Struck on a False Planchet (E), Rarity Level: 3-5 . . . . .Values: $35 up
III-B-29 Struck on Bonded Planchets (E), Rarity Level: 6-7 . . . . .Values: $50 up

Struck on a clipped planchet (III-C)

Ragged edge clip III-C-15

Multiple clip III-C-8

Incomplete curved clip III-C-10

Coins struck on clipped blanks, or planchets, exhibit the same missing areas as they did before striking, modified by the metal flow from the strike which rounds the edges and tends to move metal into the missing areas. Values for blanks will run higher than planchets with similar clips.

III-C-1 Struck on a Disc Clip Planchet (WE), Rarity Level: 4-5 . . . . Values: $1 on regular coins,
$20 and up for clad coins
III-C-2 Struck on a Curved Clip Planchet - to 5% (WE), Rarity Level: 3-5 . . . . Values: 50 cents up
III-C-3 Struck on a Curved Clip Planchet - (6 to 10%) (WE), Rarity Level: 4-5 . . . . .Values: $1 up
III-C-4 Struck on a Curved Clip Planchet - (11 to 25%) (WE), Rarity Level: 4-5 . . . . .Values: $2 up
III-C-5 Struck on a Curved Clip Planchet - (26 to 60%) (WE), Rarity Level: 4-6 . . . . .Values: $10 up
III-C-6 Struck on a Double Curved Clip Planchet (WE), Rarity Level: 3-4 . . . . .Values: $2 up
III-C-7 Struck on a Triple Curved Clip Planchet (WE), Rarity Level: 4-5 .Values: $5 up
III-C-8 Struck on a Multiple Curved Clip Planchet (WE), Rarity Level: 4-6 . . . . .Values: $5 up
III-C-9 Struck on an Overlapping Curved Clipped Planchet (WE), Rarity Level: 5-6 . . . . .Values: $15 up
III-C-10 Struck on an Incomplete Curved Clip Planchet (WE), Rarity Level: 4-5 . . . . .Values: $10 up
III-C-11 Struck on an Oval Clip Planchet (WE), Rarity Level: 5-6 . . . . .Values: $20 up
III-C-12 Struck on a Crescent Clip Planchet - (61% or more) (WE), Rarity Level: 6-7 . . . . .Values: $100 up
III-C-13 Struck on a Straight Clip Planchet (E), Rarity Level: 4-6 . . . . .Values: $10 up

III-C-14 Struck on an Incomplete Straight Clip Planchet (WE), Rarity Level: 5-6 . . . . .Values: $20 up
III-C-15 Struck on a Ragged Clip Planchet (E), Rarity Level: 4-6 . . . . .Values: $15 up
III-C-16 Struck on an Outside Corner Clip Planchet (E), Rarity Level: 7 . . . . .Values: $100 up
III-C-17 Struck on an Inside Corner Clip Planchet (E), Rarity Level: Unknown outside mint. . . . . .Values:
III-C-18 Struck on an Irregularly Clipped Planchet (E), Rarity Level: 6-7 . . . . Values: $20 up.
III-C-19 Struck on an Incompletely Punched Scalloped or Multi-Sided Planchet (E), Rarity Level: 7
. . . . Values: $20 up.

Struck on a laminated, split or broken planchet (III-D)

Lamination crack III-D-1   *Layer peeled off III-D-2*   *Split planchet III-D-3*

This section has to do with the splitting, cracking or breaking of a coin parallel to the faces of the coin, or at least very nearly parallel, or breaks at right angles to the faces of the coin.

Lamination cracks and missing metal of any size below a split planchet are too common in the 35-percent silver 1942-1945 nickels to be collectible or have any significant value.

III-D-1 Struck on a Small Lamination Crack Planchet (W), Rarity Level: 3-4. . . . . .Values: 10 up
III-D-2 Struck on a Large Lamination Crack Planchet (W), Rarity Level: 3-6. . . . . .Values: $1 up
III-D-3 Struck on a Split Planchet (W), Rarity Level: 4-6. . . . . .Values: $5 up
III-D-4 Struck on a Hinged Split Planchet (W), Rarity Level: 5-6. . . . . .Values: $35 up
III-D-5 Struck on a Planchet With a Clad Layer Missing (W), Rarity Level: 4-5. . . . . .Values: $15 up
III-D-6 Struck on a Planchet With Both Clad Layers Missing (W), Rarity Level: 4-5 . . . . .Values: $25 up
III-D-7 Struck on a Separated Clad Layer or Lamination (W), Rarity Level: 6-7. . . . . .Values: $75 up
III-D-8 Struck on a Broken Planchet Before the Strike (W), Rarity Level: 3-5 . . . . .Values: $10 up
III-D-9 Broken Coin During or After the Strike (W), Rarity Level: 4-6 . . . . .Values: $20 up
III-D-10 Struck Coin Fragment Split or Broken During or After the Strike (W), Rarity Level: 3-5. . . Values: $5 up
III-D-11 Reedless Coin Broken During or After the Strike (W), Rarity Level: Unknown . . . . .Values: -

Struck on wrong stock planchets (III-E)

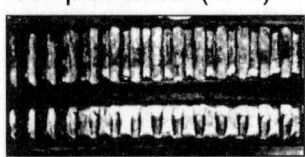

Quarter on dime stock
III-E-7 (lower coin edge)

These classes cover those cases where the wrong stock was run through the blanking press, making planchets of the correct diameter, but of the wrong thickness, alloy or metal or a combination of incorrect thickness and metal.

III-E-1 Struck on a Half Cent-Stock Planchet (IE), Rarity Level: Unknown. . . . . . . .Values: No Value Established
III-E-2 Struck on a Cent-Stock Planchet (IE), Rarity Level: Unknown . . . . .Values: No Value Established
III-E-3 Struck on a Two-Cent-Stock Planchet (E), Rarity Level: Unknown . . . . .Values: -
III-E-4 Struck on a Three-Cent-Silver Stock Planchet (E), Rarity Level: Unknown . . . . .Values: -
III-E-5 Struck on a Three-Cent-Nickel Stock Planchet (E), Rarity Level: Unknown . . . . .Values: -
III-E-6 Struck on a Half Dime-Stock Planchet (E), Rarity Level: Unknown. . . . . .Values: -
III-E-7 Struck on a Dime-Stock Planchet (E), Rarity Level: 5-6 . . . . .Values: $20 up

III-E-8 Struck on a Twenty-Cent-Stock Planchet (E), Rarity Level: Unknown . . . . .Values: -
III-E-9 Struck on a Quarter-Stock Planchet (E), Rarity Level: 6 . . . . .Values: $50 up
III-E-10 Struck on a Half Dollar-Stock Planchet (E), Rarity Level: 6-7 .Values: $100 up
III-E-11 Struck on a Dollar-Stock Planchet (E), Rarity Level: 6-7 . . . . .Values: $300 up
III-E-12 Struck on a Token/Medal-Stock Planchet (E), Rarity Level: 7 . . . . .Values: No Value Established
III-E-13 Struck on a Wrong Thickness Spoiled Planchet (IWE), Rarity Level: 7 . . . . .Values: $50 up
III-E-14 Struck on a Correct Thickness Spoiled Planchet (IWE), Rarity Level: Unknown. Values: No Value Established
III-E-15 Struck on a Cut Down Struck Token (IWE), Rarity Level: 6-7 . . . . .Values: $50 up
III-E-16 Struck on an Experimental or Pattern-Stock Planchet (IE), Rarity Level: 7 . . . . .Values: $50 up
III-E-17 Struck on a Proof-Stock Planchet (IE), Rarity Level: 7 . . . . .Values: $100 up
III-E-18 Struck on an Adjusted Specification-Stock Planchet (IE), Rarity Level: 3-7. Values: No Value to $5 and up
III-E-19 Struck on a Trial Strike-Stock Planchet (IE), Rarity Level: Unknown. . . . . . .Values: No Value Established
III-E-20 U.S. Coin Struck on a Foreign-Stock Planchet. (E), Rarity Level: 5 . . . . .Values: $35 up
III-E-21 Foreign Coin Struck on a Foreign-Stock Planchet (E), Rarity Level: 5-6 . . . . .Values: $25 up
III-E-22 Struck on a Non-Standard Coin Alloy (IE), Rarity Level: 4-7 . . . . .Values: $20 up

Extra metal (III-F)

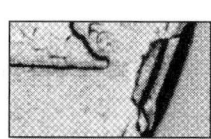

Extra metal on a
struck coin (III-F-2)

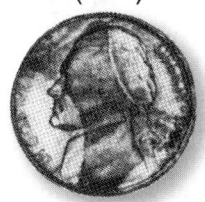

Sintered coating III-F-3

The term "extra metal" for the purpose of this section includes both extra metal added to the blank during the blanking operation and metal powder added to the planchet during the annealing operation.

III-F-1 Struck on a Type 1 Blank With Extra Metal (W), Rarity Level: Unknown . . . . .Values: -
III-F-2 Struck on a Type 2 Planchet With Extra Metal (W), Rarity Level: 4-5 . . . . .Values: $10 up
III-F-3 Struck on a Sintered Coating Planchet (W), Rarity Level: 6-7 . : .Values: $35 up

Struck on normal or abnormal blanks, or planchets (III-G)

Half on dime
planchet III-G-10

Cent on dime
planchet III-G-10

Half on quarter
planchet III-G-10

This section includes coins struck on either a blank, as it comes from the blanking press, or as a planchet that has passed through the upsetting mill. Added to this section are those planchets that are normal until they are struck by the wrong dies. These differ from the wrong stock planchets because the wrong stock planchets are already a variety before they are struck.

III-G-1 Struck on a Type 1 Blank (IWE), Rarity Level: 4-6 . . . . .Values: $10 up
III-G-2 Struck on a Type 2 Planchet (I), Rarity Level: 1 . . . . .Values: No Extra Value
III-G-3 Struck on a Purchased Planchet (I), Rarity Level: 1 . . . . .Values: No Extra Value
III-G-4 Struck on a Mint-Made Planchet (I), Rarity Level: 1 . . . . .Values: No Extra Value
III-G-5 Struck on an Adjustment-Marked Planchet (I), Rarity Level: 4-7 . . . . Values: Minimal, and may
reduce value of coin in some cases
III-G-6 Struck on a Hardness Test-Marked Planchet (I), Rarity Level: 6-7 . . . . .Values: $10 up

III-G-7 Wrong Planchet or Metal on a Half Cent Planchet (IE), Rarity Level: 5-7............Values: $100 up
III-G-8 Wrong Planchet or Metal on a Cent Planchet (IE), Rarity Level: 3-6 ....Values: $25 up
III-G-9 Wrong Planchet or Metal on a Nickel Planchet (E), Rarity Level: 4-6................Values: $35 up
III-G-10 Wrong Planchet or Metal on a Dime Planchet (E), Rarity Level: 4-6 ....Values: $50 up
III-G-11 Wrong Planchet or Metal on a Quarter Planchet (E), Rarity Level: 4-6..............Values: $100 up
III-G-12 Wrong Planchet or Metal on a Half Dollar Planchet (E), Rarity Level: 6-7 ....Values: $500 up
III-G-13 Wrong Planchet or Metal on a Dollar Planchet (E), Rarity Level: 7 ....Values: $500 up
III-G-14 Wrong Planchet or Metal on a Gold Planchet (E), Rarity Level: 7 ....Values: $1000 up
III-G-15 Struck on a Wrong Series Planchet (IE), Rarity Level: 6-7......................Values: $1500 up
III-G-16 U.S. Coin Struck on a Foreign Planchet (E), Rarity Level: 5-7....................Values: $35 up
III-G-17 Foreign Coin Struck on a U.S. Planchet (E), Rarity Level: 6-7..................Values: $50 up
III-G-18 Foreign Coin Struck on a Wrong Foreign Planchet (E), Rarity Level: 6-7 ....Values: $50 up
III-G-19 Struck on a Medal Planchet (E), Rarity Level: 6-7............................Values: $100 up
III-G-20 Medal Struck on a Coin Planchet (IE), Rarity Level: 3-5 ....Values: $10 up
III-G-21 Struck on an Official Sample Planchet (IE), Rarity Level: Unknown......Values: No Value Established
III-G-22 Struck Intentionally on a Wrong Planchet (I), Rarity Level: 6-7 .. Values: Mainly struck as Presentation
    Pieces, full numismatic value
III-G-23 Non-Proof Struck on a Proof Planchet (IE), Rarity Level: 6-7 ....Values: $500 up

Struck on coin metal strip (III-H)

Pieces of the coin metal strip do manage at times to escape into the coin press.
III-H-1 (See I-H-1 Punched Coin Metal Strip), Rarity Level: Impossible......................Values: -
III-H-2 Struck on Chopped Coin Metal Strip (E), Rarity Level: 6-7 ....Values: $25 up

Die adjustment strikes (III-I)

As the dies are set up and adjusted in the coin press, variations in the strike occur until the dies are properly set. Test strikes are normally scrapped, but on occasion reach circulation.

III-I-1 Die Adjustment Strike (IE), Rarity Level: 5-6..................................Values: $35 up
III-I-2 Edge Strike (E), Rarity Level: 5-6 ....Values: $10 to $20 and up
III-I-3 Weak Strike (W), Rarity Level: 1..Values: No Extra Value
III-I-4 Strong Strike (IWE), Rarity Level: 1......................Values: No value except for the premium
    that might be paid for a well struck coin
III-I-5 Jam Strike (IE), Rarity Level: 7 ....Values: $50 up
III-I-6 Trial Piece Strike (I), Rarity Level: 6-7......................................Values: $100 up
III-I-7 Edge-Die Adjustment Strike (I), Rarity Level: 5-7 ....Values: $5 up
III-I-8 Uniface Strike (I), Rarity Level 7 ....Values: $50 up

Indented, brockage and counter-brockage strikes (III-J)

Indented strike
III-J-1

Counter-brockage strike
III-J-11

Capped die strike
III-J-15

Indented and uniface strikes involve an extra unstruck planchet between one of the dies and the planchet being struck. Brockage strikes involve a struck coin between one of the dies and the planchet and a counter-brockage requires a brockage coin between one of the dies and the planchet.

A cap, or capped die strike results when a coin sticks to the die and is squeezed around it in the shape of a bottle cap.

III-J-1 Indented Strike (W), Rarity Level: 3-6...Values: $5 up
III-J-2 Uniface Strike (W), Rarity Level: 3-5 ....Values: $15 up
III-J-3 Indented Strike By a Smaller Planchet (WE), Rarity Level: 5-7 ....Values: $100 up

III-J-4 Indented Second Strike (W), Rarity Level: 3-5 . . . . Values: $10 up, about the same as a regular double strike of comparable size

III-J-5 Partial Brockage Strike (W), Rarity Level: 3-6. . . . . Values: $15 up

III-J-6 Full Brockage Strike (W), Rarity Level: 3-6. . . . . Values: $5 up

III-J-7 Brockage Strike of a Smaller Coin (WE), Rarity Level: 6-7 . . . . Values: $200 up

III-J-8 Brockage Strike of a Struck Coin Fragment (WE), Rarity Level: 4-6 . . . . Values: $5 up

III-J-9 Brockage Second Strike (WE), Rarity Level: 3-5. . . . . Values: $5 up

III-J-10 Partial Counter-Brockage Strike (WE), Rarity Level: 3-5. . . . . Values: $10 up

III-J-11 Full Counter-Brockage Strike (WE), Rarity Level: 5-7. . . . . Values: $100 up

III-J-12 Counter-Brockage Second Strike (WE), Rarity Level: 4-6. . . . . Values: $10 up

III-J-13 Full Brockage-Counter-Brockage Strike (WE), Rarity Level: 6-7. Values: $150 up

III-J-14 Multiple Brockage or Counter-Brockage Strike (WE), Rarity Level: 5-7 . . . . Values: $100 up

III-J-15 Capped Die Strike (WE), Rarity Level: 6-7 . . . . Values: $500 up

III-J-16 Reversed Capped Die Strike (WE), Rarity Level: 7 . . . . Values: $1,000 up

Struck through abnormal objects (III-K)

Struck through cloth
III-K-1

Struck through a filled die
III-K-4

Struck through a
dropped filling III-K-5

This section covers most of the objects or materials that might come between the planchet and the die and be struck into the surface of the coin. Unless noted, the materials - even the soft ones - are driven into the surface of the coin.

III-K-1 Struck Through Cloth (IWE), Rarity Level: 3-6. . . . . Values: $35 up

III-K-2 Struck Through Wire (IWE), Rarity Level: 3-6 . . . . Values: $5 up

III-K-3 Struck Through Thread (IWE), Rarity Level: 3-6. . . . . Values: $5 up

III-K-4 Struck Through Dirt-and-Grease-Filled Die (IWE), Rarity Level: 1-4

. . . . Values: 10 cents to 25 cents up, but no value on a worn or circulated coin

III-K-5 Struck Through a Dropped Filling (IWE), Rarity Level: 5-6 . . . . Values: $10 up

III-K-6 Struck Through Wrong Metal Fragments (IWE), Rarity Level: 4-6 . . . . Values: $1 up

III-K-7 Struck Through an Unstruck Planchet Fragment (IWE), Rarity Level: 3-5 . . . . Values: $1 up

III-K-8 Struck Through a Rim Burr (IWE), Rarity Level: 3-5. . . . . Values: $1 to $2 and up

III-K-9 Struck Through plit-Off Reeding (IWE), Rarity Level: 5-6. . . . . Values: $25 up

III-K-10 Struck Through a Feed Finger (IWE), Rarity Level: 5-7 . . . . Values: $25 to $50 and up

III-K-11 Struck Through Miscellaneous Objects (IWE), Rarity Level: 4-6 . . . . Values: $1 up

III-K-12 Struck Through Progression (IWE), Rarity Level: 4-6 . . . . Values: $1 up

Note: Some 1987 through 1994 quarters are found without mintmarks, classed as III-K-4, a Filled Die. Values depend on market conditions. Filled dies have value ONLY on current, uncirculated grade coins.

Double strikes (III-L)

Only coins that receive two or more strikes by the die pair fall in this section and are identified by the fact that both sides of the coin are affected. Unless some object interferes, an equal area of both sides of the coin will be equally doubled.

The exception is the second strike with a loose die, which will double only one side of a coin, but is a rare form usually occurring only on proofs. A similar effect is flat field doubling from die chatter.

III-L-1 Close Centered Double Strike (WE), Rarity Level: 4-6 . . . . Values: $15 up

III-L-2 Rotated Second Strike Over a Centered First Strike (WE), Rarity Level: 4-6. . . . . Values: $15 up

III-L-3 Off-Center Second Strike Over a Centered First Strike (WE), Rarity Level: 4-6. . . . . Values: $15 up

Off-center second strike over centered first strike III-L-3

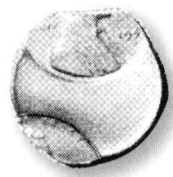

Non-overlapping double strike III-L-8

Multiple strike III-L-16

Chain strike III-L-10

III-L-4 Off-Center Second Strike Over an Off-Center First Strike (WE), Rarity Level: 4-6. . . . . . . .Values: $10 up
III-L-5 Off-Center Second Strike Over a Broadstrike (WE), Rarity Level: 5-6 . . . . .Values: $20 up
III-L-6 Centered Second Strike Over an Off-Center First Strike (WE), Rarity Level: 5-6. . . . . .Values: $50 up
III-L-7 Obverse Struck Over Reverse (WE), Rarity Level: 5-6. . . . . .Values: $25 up
III-L-8 Nonoverlapping Double Strike (WE), Rarity Level: 5-6. . . . . .Values: $20 up
III-L-9 Struck Over a Different Denomination or Series (WE), Rarity Level: 6 . . . . Values: $300 and up
III-L-10 Chain Strike (WE), Rarity Level: 6 . . . . . Values: $300 up for the pair of coins that were struck together
III-L-11 Second-Strike Doubling From a Loose Die (W), Rarity Level: 6-7 . . . . .Values: $200 up
III-L-12 Second-Strike Doubling From a Loose Screw Press Die (W), Rarity Level: 5-6 . . . . . .Values: $100 up
III-L-13 Second Strike on an Edge Strike (WE), Rarity Level: 5-6 . . . . .Values: $20 up
III-L-14 Folded Planchet Strike (WE), Rarity Level: 5-7. . . . . .Values: $100 up
III-L-15 Triple Strike (WE), Rarity Level: 6-7. . . . . .Values: $100 up
III-L-16 Multiple Strike (WE), Rarity Level: 6-7. . . . . .Values: $200 up
III-L-17 U.S. Coin Struck Over a Struck Foreign Coin (WE), Rarity Level: 6-7 . . . . .Values: $300 up
III-L-18 Foreign Coin Struck Over a Struck U.S. Coin (WE), Rarity Level: 6-7 . . . . .Values: $400 up
III-L-19 Foreign Coin Struck Over a Struck Foreign Coin (WE), Rarity Level: 7 . . . . .Values: $500 up
III-L-20 Double Strike on Scrap or Junk (E), Rarity Level: 6 . . . . .Values: $50 up
III-L-21 Struck on a Struck Token or Medal (E), Rarity Level: 5-6 . . . . .Values: $100 up
III-L-22 Double-Struck Edge Motto or Design (E), Rarity Level: 6-7 . . . . .Values: $200 up
III-L-23 One Edge Motto or Design Struck Over Another (E), Rarity Level: 7. . . . . .Values: $300 up
III-L-24 Flat Field Doubling (W), Rarity Level: 2-3 . . . . .Values: $1 to $5
III-L-25 Territorial Struck over Struck U.S. Coin: (I) Rarity Level: 6-7 .Values: $200 up
III-L-26 Pattern Struck over Struck U.S. Coin: (I) Rarity Level: 6-7 . . . . .Values: $200 up
III-L-27 Pattern Struck over Struck Pattern:(I) Rarity Level 6-7 . . . . .Values: $200 up
III-L-28 Pattern Struck Over Foreign Coin:(I) Rarity Level 6-7 . . . . Values - $200 up

Collar striking varieties (III-M)

The collar is often referred to as the "Third Die," and is involved in a number of forms of misstrikes. The collar normally rises around the planchet, preventing it from squeezing sideways between the dies and at the same time forming the reeding on reeded coins.

If the collar is out of position or tilted, a partial collar strike results; if completely missing, it causes a broadstrike; if the planchet is not entirely between the dies, an off-center strike.

Flanged partial collar III-M-1

Struck off center
10 to 30 percent III-M-7

Struck off center
31 to 70 percent III-M-8

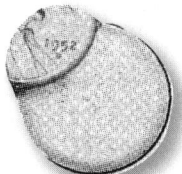

Struck off center
71 percent or more
III-M-9

III-M-1 Flanged Partial Collar Strike (WE), Rarity Level: 5-6. . . . . Values: $20 up
III-M-2 Reversed Flanged Partial Collar Strike (WE), Rarity Level: 6-7 . . . . Values: $35 up
III-M-3 Tilted Partial Collar Strike (WE), Rarity Level: 5-6 . . . . Values: $20 up
III-M-4 Centered Broadstrike (WE), Rarity Level: 5-6 . . . . Values: $5 up
III-M-5 Uncentered Broadstrike (WE), Rarity Level: 5 . . . . Values: $3 up
III-M-6 Reversed Broadstrike (WE), Rarity Level: 6 . . . . Values: $10 up
III-M-7 Struck Off-Center 10-30% (W), Rarity Level: 3-6 . . . . Values: $3 up
III-M-8 Struck Off-Center 31-70% (W), Rarity Level: 4-6 . . . . Values: $5 up
III-M-9 Struck Off-Center 71% or More (W), Rarity Level: 3-5 . . . . Values: $2 up
III-M-10 Rotated Multi-sided Planchet Strike (W), Rarity Level: 5-6 . . . . Values: $10 up
III-M-11 Wire Edge Strike (IWE), Rarity Level: 1-2 . . . . Values: No Extra Value
III-M-12 Struck With the Collar Too High (WE), Rarity Level: 6-7 . . . . Values: $20 up
III-M-13 Off-Center Slide Strike (W), Rarity Level: 3-6 . . . . Values: $4 up

Misaligned and rotated (die) strike varieties (III-N)

Misaligned die III-N-1

Normal rotation

90 degrees

180 degrees

One (rarely both) of the dies may be Offset Misaligned, off to one side, or may be tilted (Vertically Misaligned). One die may either have been installed so that it is turned in relation to the other die, or may turn in the holder, or the shank may break allowing the die face to rotate in relation to the opposing die.

Vertical misaligned dies are rarely found, and, like rotated dies, find only limited collector interest. Ninety- and 180-degree rotations are the most popular. Rotations of 14 degrees or less have no value. The 1989-D Congress dollar is found with a nearly

180-degree rotated reverse, currently retailing for around $2,000. Only about 30 have been reported to date.

III-N-1 Offset Die Misalignment Strike (WE), Rarity Level: 3-5 . . . . .Values: $2 up
III-N-2 Vertical Die Misalignment Strike (WE), Rarity Level: 4-6. . . . . .Values: $1 up
III-N-3 Rotated Die Strike - 15 to 45 Degrees (IWE), Rarity Level: 4-6 . . . . .Values: $2 up
III-N-4 Rotated Die Strike - 46 to 135 Degrees (IWE), Rarity Level: 5-6 .Values: $10 up
III-N-5 Rotated Die Strike - 136 to 180 Degrees (IWE), Rarity Level: 5-6 . . . . .Values: $25 up

Lettered and design edge strike varieties (III-O)

Overlapping edge letters III-O-1

Early U.S. coins and a number of foreign coins have either lettered edges or designs on the edge of the coin. Malfunctions of the application of the motto or design to the edge fall in this section.

III-O-1 Overlapping Edge Motto or Design (WE), Rarity Level: 3-4 . . . . Values: $5 to $10 and up
III-O-2 Wrong Edge Motto or Design (WE), Rarity Level: 5-6-7 . . . . .Values: $50 up
III-O-3 Missing Edge Motto, Design or Security Edge (IWE), Rarity Level: 5-6-7 . . . . .Values: $50 up
III-O-4 Jammed Edge Die Strike (W), Rarity Level: 6. . . . . .Values: $10 up
III-O-5 Misplaced Segment of an Edge Die (E), Rarity Level: 4-7 . . . . .Values: $25 up
III-O-6 Reeded Edge Struck Over a Lettered Edge (IE), Rarity Level: 3-6 . . . . Values: No Extra Value up

Defective strikes and mismatched dies (III-P)

The final section of the Striking Division covers coins that are not properly struck for reasons other than those in previous classes, such as coins struck with mismatched (muled) dies. The mismatched die varieties must be taken on a case by case basis, while the other classes presently have little collector demand or premium.

III-P-1 Defective Strike (WE), Rarity Level: 1. . . . . .Values: No Extra Value
III-P-2 Mismatched Die Strike (E), Rarity Level: 4-7 . . . . .Values: $25 up
III-P-3 Single-Strike Proof (WE), Rarity Level: 4-5 . . . . .Values: Minimal
III-P-4 Single Die-Proof Strike (IE), Rarity Level: 5-6 . . . . .Values: $100 up
III-P-5 Reversed Die Strike (I), Rarity Level: 4-5 . . . . .Values: No Extra Value to Minimal

Official Mint modifications
Division IV

Several mint-produced varieties occur after the coin has been struck, resulting in the addition of the fourth division to my PDS System. Since most of these coins are either unique or are special varieties, each one must be taken on a case by case basis. All classes listed here are by definition intentional.

I have not listed values as the coins falling in these classes, which are sold through regular numismatic channels, are cataloged with the regular issues or are covered in specialized catalogs in their particular area.

Matte proofs (IV-A)

Matte proofs IV-A-1

Matte proofs as a section include several of the forms of proof coins that have the striking characteristics of a mirror proof but have been treated AFTER striking to give them a grainy, non-reflective surface.

IV-A-1 Matte Proof (I), Rarity Level: 3-5 . . . . Values: Normal Numismatic Value
IV-A-2 Matte Proof on One Side (I), Rarity Level: 7 . . . . Values: Normal Numismatic Value
IV-A-3 Sandblast Proof (I), Rarity Level: 4-6 . . . . Values: Normal Numismatic Value

Additional engraving (IV-B)

Counterstamp IV-B-3

This section includes any added markings that are placed on the struck coin and struck coins that later were cut into pieces for various purposes. The warning is repeated: Anything done to a coin after the strike is extremely difficult t o authenticate and is much easier to fake than a die struck coin.

IV-B-1 Counterstamp and Countermark (I), Rarity Level: 3-6 . . . . Values: Normal Numismatic Value
IV-B-2 Perforated and Cut Coins (I), Rarity Level: 4-6 . . . . Values: Normal Numismatic Value

Restrikes (IV-C)

Restrike with new dies IV-C-7

Restrikes cover a complicated mixture of official use of dies from a variety of sources. Whether or not some were officially sanctioned is always a problem for the collector.

IV-C-1) Restrike on the Same Denomination Planchet (I), Rarity Level: 4-6. . .Values: Normal Numismatic Value
IV-C-2 Restrike on a Different Denomination or Series Planchet (I), Rarity Level: 4-6
. . . . .Values: Normal Numismatic Value
IV-C-3 Restrike on a Foreign Coin (I), Rarity Level: 6-7 . . . . .Values: Normal Numismatic Value
IV-C-4 Restrike on a Token or Medal (I), Rarity Level: 5-6 . . . . .Values: Normal Numismatic Value
IV-C-5 Restruck With the Original Dies (I), Rarity Level: 4-6 . . . . .Values: Normal Numismatic Value
IV-C-6 Restruck With Mismatched Dies (I), Rarity Level: 4-6 . . . . .Values: Normal Numismatic Value
IV-C-7 Copy Strike With New Dies (I), Rarity Level: 3-5 . . . . .Values: Normal Numismatic Value
IV-C-8 Fantasy Strike (I), Rarity Level: 4-6 . . . . .Values: Normal Numismatic Value

After strike modifications

Division V

This division includes both modifications that have value to collectors – and those that don't. I needed a couple of divisions to cover other things that happen to coins to aid in cataloging them. This avoids the false conclusion that an unlisted coin is quite rare, when the exact opposite is more likely to be the case.

Collectible modifications after strike (V-A)

Mint modification V-A-8

This section includes those classes having to do with deliberate modifications of the coin done with a specific purpose or intent that makes them of some value to collectors. Quite often these pieces were made specifically to sell to collectors, or at least to the public, under the guise of being collectible.

V-A-1 Screw Thaler, Rarity Level: 5-6 . . . . Values: Normal Numismatic Value
V-A-2 Love Token, Rarity Level: 3-6 . . . . Values: $10 up
V-A-3 Satirical or Primitive Engraving, Rarity Level: 6-7 . . . . Values: $5 up
V-A-4 Elongated Coin, Rarity Level: 2-7 . . . . Values: 50 cents to $1 and up
V-A-5 Coin Jewelry, Rarity Level: 2-5 . . . . Values: $1 up
V-A-6 Novelty Coin, Rarity Level: 1-3 . . . . Values: No Value up to $5 to $10
V-A-7 Toning, Rarity Level: 3-6 . . . . Values: No value up, depending on coloration. Easily faked
V-A-8 Mint Modification, Rarity Level: 4-7 . . . . Values: $5 up. Easily faked
V-A-9 Mint Packaging Mistake, Rarity Level: 5-7 . . . . Values: Nominal $1. Very easily faked

Alterations and damage after the strike (V-B)

Machine doubling damage V-B-1

This section includes those changes in a coin that have no collector value. In most cases, their effect on the coin is to reduce or entirely eliminate any collector value - and in the case of counterfeits they are actually illegal to even own.

V -B-1 Machine Doubling Damage: *NOTE: Machine doubling damage is defined as: "Damage to a coin after the strike, due to die bounce or chatter or die displacement, showing on the struck coin as scrapes on the sides of the design elements, with portions of the coin metal in the relief elements either displaced sideways or downward, depending on the direction of movement of the loose die."* Machine doubling damage, or MDD, is by far the most common form of doubling found on almost any coin in the world. Rarity Level: 0 . . . . Values: Reduces the coin's value
V-B-2 Accidental or Deliberate Damage, Rarity Level: 0 . . . . Values: Reduces the coin's value
V-B-3 Test Cut or Mark, Rarity Level: 0 . . . . Values: Reduces value of coin to face or bullion value
V-B-4 Alteration, Rarity Level: 0 . . . . Values: Reduces value to face or bullion value
V-B-5 Whizzing, Rarity Level: 0 . . . . . . Values: Reduces value sharply and may reduce it to face or bullion value
V-B-6 Counterfeit, Copy, Facsimile, Forgery or Fake, Rarity Level: 0 . . Values: No Value and may be illegal to own
V-B-7 Planchet Deterioration. Very common on copper-plated zinc cents. Rarity level: 0 . . . . . Values: No Value

COLONIAL COINAGE

MARYLAND
Lord Baltimore

PENNY (DENARIUM)

KM# 1 • **Copper** • **Obv. Legend:** CAECILIVS Dns TERRAE MARIAE

Date	Good	VG	Fine	VF	XF
(1659) 9 known	—	—	65,000	120,000	200,000

Note: Stack's Auction 5-04, Proof realized $241,500

4 PENCE (GROAT)

KM# 2 • **Silver** • **Obv:** Large bust **Obv. Legend:** CAECILIVS Dns TERRAE MARIAE **Rev:** Large shield

Date	AG	Good	VG	Fine	VF	XF
(1659)	1,250	1,950	3,500	6,250	13,500	22,000

KM# 3 • **Silver** • **Obv:** Small bust **Obv. Legend:** CAECILIVS Dns TERRAE MARIAE **Rev:** Small shield

Date	AG	Good	VG	Fine	VF	XF
(1659) unique	—	—	—	—	—	—

Note: Norweb $26,400

6 PENCE

KM# 4 • **Silver** • **Obv:** Small bust **Obv. Legend:** CAECILIVS Dns TERRAE MARIAE **Note:** Known in two other rare small-bust varieties and two rare large-bust varieties.

Date	AG	Good	VG	Fine	VF	XF
(1659)	850	1,400	2,400	5,000	9,500	15,000

SHILLING

KM# 6 • **Silver** • **Obv. Legend:** CAECILIVS Dns TERRAE MARIAE **Note:** Varieties exist; one is very rare.

Date	AG	Good	VG	Fine	VF	XF	Unc
(1659)	1,100	1,850	3,250	6,000	13,500	20,000	—

MASSACHUSETTS
New England

3 PENCE

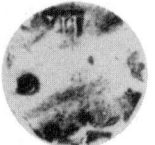

KM# 1 • **Silver** • **Obv:** NE **Rev:** III

Date	AG	Good	VG	Fine	VF	XF
(1652) Unique	—	—	—	—	—	—

Note: Massachusetts Historical Society specimen

6 PENCE

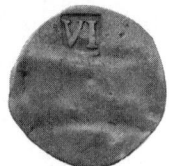

KM# 2 • **Silver** • **Obv:** NE **Rev:** VI

Date	Good	VG	Fine	VF	XF
(1652) 8 known	28,000	60,000	115,000	225,000	—

Note: Garrett $75,000

SHILLING

KM# 3 • **Silver** • **Obv:** NE **Rev:** XII

Date	AG	Good	VG	Fine	VF	XF
(1652)	—	37,500	75,000	150,000	250,000	—

Oak Tree

2 PENCE

KM# 7 • Silver • Note: Small 2 and large 2 varieites exist

Date	AG	Good	VG	Fine	VF	XF	Unc
1662	—	500	900	2,000	3,850	6,500	15,000

3 PENCE

KM# 8 • Silver • Note: Two types of legends.

Date	AG	Good	VG	Fine	VF	XF	Unc
1652	350	650	1,250	3,000	6,500	12,000	—

6 PENCE

KM# 9 • Silver • Note: Three types of legends.

Date	AG	Good	VG	Fine	VF	XF	Unc
1652	400	900	1,350	3,500	8,000	17,500	35,000

SHILLING

KM# 10 • Silver • Note: Two types of legends.

Date	AG	Good	VG	Fine	VF	XF	Unc
1652	375	750	1,250	3,000	6,000	11,500	27,500

Pine Tree

3 PENCE

KM# 11 • Silver • Obv: Tree without berries

Date	AG	Good	VG	Fine	VF	XF	Unc
1652	250	500	750	1,650	3,250	6,500	18,500

KM# 12 • Silver • Obv: Tree with berries

Date	AG	Good	VG	Fine	VF	XF	Unc
1652	250	500	750	1,650	3,500	6,750	19,500

6 PENCE

KM# 13 • Silver • Obv: Tree without berries; "spiney tree"

Date	AG	Good	VG	Fine	VF	XF	Unc
1652	400	700	1,400	2,000	4,000	7,000	22,000

KM# 14 • Silver • Obv: Tree with berries

Date	AG	Good	VG	Fine	VF	XF	Unc
1652	300	600	1,000	1,850	3,750	6,500	20,000

SHILLING

KM# 15 • Silver • Note: Large planchet. Many varieties exist; some are very rare.

Date	AG	Good	VG	Fine	VF	XF	Unc
1652	375	700	1,100	2,200	4,500	7,750	22,500

KM# 16 • Silver • Note: Small planchet; large dies. All examples are thought to be contemporary fabrications.

Date	AG	Good	VG	Fine	VF	XF	Unc
1652	—	—	—	—	—	—	—

KM# 17 • Silver • Note: Small planchet; small dies. Many varieties exist; some are very rare.

Date	AG	Good	VG	Fine	VF	XF	Unc
1652	285	550	850	1,750	3,750	7,250	25,000

Willow Tree

3 PENCE

KM# 4 • Silver •

Date	AG	Good	VG	Fine	VF	XF
1652 3 known	—	—	—	—	—	—

6 PENCE

KM# 5 • Silver •

Date	AG	Good	VG	Fine	VF	XF
1652						
14 known	9,500	18,500	30,000	60,000	135,000	225,000

SHILLING

KM# 6 • Silver •

Date	AG	Good	VG	Fine	VF	XF
1652	10,000	20,000	35,000	85,000	165,000	250,000

NEW JERSEY
St. Patrick or Mark Newby

FARTHING

KM# 1 • Copper • Obv. Legend: FLOREAT REX **Rev. Legend:** QUIESCAT PLEBS

Date	AG	Good	VG	Fine	VF	XF	Unc
(1682)	70.00	125	285	775	2,750	6,500	—

Note: One very rare variety is known with reverse legend: QUIESAT PLEBS

KM# 1a • Silver • Obv. Legend: FLOREAT REX **Rev. Legend:** QUIESCAT PLEBS

Date	AG	Good	VG	Fine	VF	XF
(1682)	800	1,750	2,750	5,500	9,500	17,500

HALFPENNY

KM# 2 • Copper • Obv. Legend: FLOREAT REX **Rev. Legend:** ECCE GREX

Date	AG	Good	VG	Fine	VF	XF	Unc
(1682)	180	365	850	1,650	4,000	12,500	—

EARLY AMERICAN TOKENS
American Plantations

1/24 REAL

KM# Tn5.1 • Tin • Obv. Legend: ET HIB REX

Date	AG	Good	VG	Fine	VF	XF	Unc
(1688)	125	200	300	450	850	2,000	—

KM# Tn5.3 • Tin • Rev: Horizontal 4

Date	AG	Good	VG	Fine	VF	XF	Unc
(1688)	275	400	900	1,750	4,250	6,750	—

KM# Tn5.4 • Tin • Obv. Legend: ET HB REX

Date	AG	Good	VG	Fine	VF	XF	Unc
(1688)	—	250	450	850	1,900	3,250	11,500

KM# Tn6 • Tin • Rev: Arms of Scotland left, Ireland right

Date	AG	Good	VG	Fine	VF	XF	Unc
(1688)	450	750	1,250	2,150	5,000	7,750	—

KM# Tn5.2 • Tin • Obv: Rider's head left of "B" in legend **Note:** Restrikes made in 1828 from two obverse dies.

Date	AG	Good	VG	Fine	VF	XF	Unc
(1828)	75.00	110	175	275	500	1,000	—

Elephant

KM# Tn1.1 • 15.5500 g., Copper • Note: Thick planchet.

Date	AG	Good	VG	Fine	VF	XF	Unc
(1664)	125	200	300	550	1,000	1,750	4,500

KM# Tn1.2 • Copper • Note: Thin planchet.

Date	AG	Good	VG	Fine	VF	XF	Unc
(1664)	175	300	500	900	3,000	5,500	12,500

KM# Tn2 • Copper • Rev: Diagonals tie shield

Date	AG	Good	VG	Fine	VF	XF	Unc
(1664)	250	450	650	2,250	7,000	11,500	35,000

KM# Tn3 • Copper • Rev: Sword right side of shield

Date	AG	Good	VG	Fine	VF	XF
(1664) 3 known	—	—	—	—25,000	—
Note: Norweb $1,320					

KM# Tn4 • Copper • Rev. Legend: LON DON

Date	AG	Good	VG	Fine	VF	XF	Unc
(1684)	340	650	1,000	2,250	4,250	8,000	20,000

KM# Tn7 • Copper • Rev. Legend: NEW ENGLAND

Date	Good	VG	Fine	VF	XF
(1694) 2 known	—	55,000	85,000	110,000	160,000
Note: Norweb $25,300					

KM# Tn8.1 • Copper • Rev. Legend: CAROLINA (PROPRIETORS)

Date	AG	Good	VG	Fine	VF	XF
(1694) 5 known	—	—	4,750	7,500	15,000	25,000
Note: Norweb $35,200						

KM# Tn8.2 • Copper • Rev. Legend: CAROLINA (PROPRIETORS, O over E)

Date	AG	Good	VG	Fine	VF	XF
1694	1,300	2,500	4,500	7,000	12,500	20,000
Note: Norweb $17,600						

Gloucester

KM# Tn15 • Copper • Obv. Legend: GLOVCESTER COVRTHOVSE VIRGINIA **Rev. Legend:** RIGHAVLT DAWSON.ANNO.DOM.1714.

Date	AG	Good	VG	Fine	VF	XF
(1714) 2 known	—	—	—	—	—	—
Note: Garrett $36,000						

Hibernia-Voce Populi

KM# Tn21.1 • Copper • Note: Large letters

Date	AG	Good	VG	Fine	VF	XF	Unc
1760	145	250	375	750	1,850	3,500	11,500

KM# Tn21.2 • Copper • Note: Small letters

Date	AG	Good	VG	Fine	VF	XF
1760	—	—	3,250	6,500	25,000	60,000
Note: Norweb $5,940.						

HALFPENNY

KM# Tn22 • Copper •

Date	AG	Good	VG	Fine	VF	XF	Unc
1700 Extremely rare	—	—	—	—	—	—	—

Note: Date is in error; ex-Roper $575. Norweb $577.50. Stack's Americana, VF, $2,900

Date	AG	Good	VG	Fine	VF	XF	Unc
1760	40.00	75.00	145	185	365	675	2,500
1760	50.00	80.00	135	195	425	775	3,500

Note: legend VOOE POPULI

Date	AG	Good	VG	Fine	VF	XF	Unc
1760 P below bust	65.00	120	200	375	750	1,750	8,250
1760 P in front of bust	55.00	110	180	325	650	1,450	6,500

Higley or Granby

KM# Tn16 • Copper • Obv. Legend: CONNECTICVT **Rev. Legend:** THE VALVE OF THREE PENCE

Date	AG	Good	VG	Fine	VF	XF
1737		—10,000	18,500	40,000	85,000	—

Note: Garrett $16,000

KM# Tn17 • Copper • Obv. Legend: THE VALVE OF THREE PENCE **Rev. Legend:** I AM GOOD COPPER

Date		Good	VG	Fine	VF	XF
1737 2 known		11,000	20,000	42,500	87,500	—

Note: ex-Norweb $6,875

KM# Tn18.1 • Copper • Obv. Legend: VALUE ME AS YOU PLEASE **Rev. Legend:** I AM GOOD COPPER

Date	AG	Good	VG	Fine	VF	XF
1737	6,500	10,000	18,500	42,000	87,500	—

KM# Tn18.2 • Copper • Obv. Legend: VALVE.ME.AS.YOU.PLEASE. **Rev. Legend:** I AM GOOD COPPER.

Date	AG	Good	VG	Fine	VF	XF
1737 3 known	—	—	—	—	—	275,000

KM# Tn19 • Copper • Rev: Broad axe

Date		Good	VG	Fine	VF	XF
(1737)		10,000	20,000	45,000	125,000	—

Note: Garrett $45,000

Date		Good	VG	Fine	VF	XF
1739 5 known		—	—	—	—	—

Note: Eliasberg $12,650. Oechsner $9,900. Steinberg (holed) $4,400.

KM# Tn20 • Copper • Obv. Legend: THE WHEELE GOES ROUND **Rev:** J CUT MY WAY THROUGH

Date	AG	Good	VG	Fine	VF	XF
(1737) unique	—	—	—	150,000	—	—

Note: Roper $60,500

New Yorke

KM# Tn9 • Brass • Obv. Legend:
NEW.YORK.IN.AMERICA

Date	AG	Good	VG	Fine	VF	XF
1700	1,800	3,750	7,250	17,500	28,000	60,000

KM# Tn9a • White Metal • Obv. Legend:
NEW.YORK.IN.AMERICA

Date	AG	Good	VG	Fine	VF	XF
1700 4 known	—	—	7,750	22,500	32,500	75,000

Pitt

FARTHING

KM# Tn23 • Copper •

Date	AG	Good	VG	Fine	VF	XF
1766	—	3,750	7,000	11,500	28,500	42,500

HALFPENNY

KM# Tn24 • Copper •

Date	AG	Good	VG	Fine	VF	XF	Unc
1766	145	275	450	750	1,650	3,000	9,500

KM# Tn24a • Silver Plated Copper •

Date	AG	Good	VG	Fine	VF	XF	Unc
1766	—	—	—	2,250	5,000	12,500

ROYAL PATENT COINAGE

Hibernia

FARTHING

KM# 20 • Copper • Note: Pattern.

Date	AG	Good	VG	Fine	VF	XF	Unc
1722	135	250	400	600	1,250	3,250	11,500

KM# 24 • Copper • Obv: 1722 obverse Obv. Legend: ...D:G:REX.

Date	AG	Good	VG	Fine	VF	XF	Unc
1723	20.00	75.00	120	170	300	550	1,250

KM# 25 • Copper • Obv. Legend: DEI • GRATIA • REX •

Date	AG	Good	VG	Fine	VF	XF	Unc
1723	25.00	45.00	60.00	180	300	550	950
1724	—	90.00	125	225	700	1,750	4,250

KM# 25a • Silver •

Date	AG	Good	VG	Fine	VF	XF	Unc
1723	—	—	1,600	2,250	4,200	6,500	12,000

HALFPENNY

KM# 21 • Copper • Obv: Bust right Obv. Legend: GEORGIUS • DEI • GRATIA • REX • **Rev:** Harp left, head left **Rev. Legend:** • HIBERNIA • 1722 •

Date	AG	Good	VG	Fine	VF	XF	Unc
1722	50.00	90.00	110	160	325	700	1,750

KM# 22 • Copper • Obv: Bust right **Obv. Legend:** GEORGIVS D: G: REX **Rev:** Harp left, head right **Rev. Legend:** • HIBERNIÆ • **Note:** "Rocks Reverse" pattern.

Date	AG	Good	VG	Fine	VF	XF	Unc
1722	—	—	—	5,000	7,500	12,500	—

KM# 23.1 • Copper • Rev: Harp right

Date	AG	Good	VG	Fine	VF	XF	Unc
1722	35.00	60.00	80.00	120	285	600	1,750
Note: 850							
1723	20.00	35.00	45.00	75.00	190	285	850
1723/22	35.00	60.00	80.00	150	400	850	2,500
1724	25.00	50.00	90.00	160	400	850	2,500

KM# 23.2 • Copper • Obv: DEII error in legend

Date	AG	Good	VG	Fine	VF	XF	Unc
1722	75.00	125	160	325	750	1,500	3,000

KM# 26 • Copper • Rev: Large head **Note:** Rare. Generally mint state only. Probably a pattern.

Date	AG	Good	VG	Fine	VF	XF	Unc
1723	—	—	—	—	—	—	—

KM# 27 • Copper • Rev: Continuous legend over head

Date	AG	Good	VG	Fine	VF	XF	Unc
1724	45.00	80.00	150	300	900	1,850	4,500

Rosa Americana

HALFPENNY

KM# 1 • Copper • Obv. Legend: D • G • REX •

Date	AG	Good	VG	Fine	VF	XF	Unc
1722	20.00	50.00	140	250	525	1,050	4,000

KM# 2 • Copper • Obv: Uncrowned rose **Obv. Legend:** ... • DEI • GRATIA • REX • **Note:** Several varieties exist.

Date	AG	Good	VG	Fine	VF	XF	Unc
1722	50.00	90.00	135	250	450	975	3,500
1723		385	700	850	1,750	3,600	—	—

KM# 3 • Copper • Rev. Legend: VTILE DVLCI

Date	AG	Good	VG	Fine	VF	XF	Unc
1722	250	450	850	2,200	3,800	7,500	—

KM# 9 • Copper • Rev: Crowned rose

Date	AG	Good	VG	Fine	VF	XF	Unc
1723	45.00	85.00	110	165	425	1,100	4,500

PENNY

KM# 4 • Copper • Rev. Legend: UTILE DULCI **Note:** Several varieties exist.

Date	AG	Good	VG	Fine	VF	XF	Unc
1722	60.00	100.00	135	240	450	950	3,750

KM# 5 • Copper • Note: Several varieties exist. Also known in two rare pattern types with long hair ribbons, one with V's for U's on the obverse.

Date	AG	Good	VG	Fine	VF	XF	Unc
1722	18.00	35.00	150	275	750	1,450	6,000

KM# 10 • Copper • Note: Several varieties exist.

Date	AG	Good	VG	Fine	VF	XF	Unc
1723	40.00	75.00	110	175	425	900	3,600

KM# 12 • Copper • Note: Pattern.

Date	AG	Good	VG	Fine	VF	XF
1724 2 known	—	—	—	—	—	—

KM# 13 • Copper • Rev. Legend: ROSA: SINE: SPINA •

Date	AG	Good	VG	Fine	VF	XF
(1724) 5 known	—	—	—	—	—	—

Note: Stack's Bowers 5-05, VF ralized $21,850; Norweb $2,035

KM# 14 • Copper • Obv: George II **Note:** Pattern.

Date	AG	Good	VG	Fine	VF	XF
1727 2 known	—	—	—	—	—	—

2 PENCE

KM# 6 • Copper • Rev: Motto with scroll

Date	AG	Good	VG	Fine	VF	XF	Unc
(1722)	80.00	150	200	425	750	1,650	7,000

KM# 7 • Copper • Rev: Motto without scroll

Date	AG	Good	VG	Fine	VF	XF
(1722) 3 known	—	—	—	—	—	—

KM# 8.1 • Copper • Obv. Legend: ...REX • **Rev:** Dated

Date	AG	Good	VG	Fine	VF	XF	Unc
1722	70.00	125	175	275	750	1,500	5,500

KM# 8.2 • Copper • Obv. Legend: ...REX

Date	AG	Good	VG	Fine	VF	XF	Unc
1722	70.00	125	175	275	775	1,600	6,000

KM# 11 • Copper • Obv: No stop after REX **Rev:** Stop after 1723 **Note:** Several varieties exist.

Date	AG	Good	VG	Fine	VF	XF	Unc
1723	65.00	125	175	300	550	1,200	3,500

KM# 15 • Copper • Note: Pattern. Two varieties exist; both extremely rare.

Date	AG	Good	VG	Fine	VF	XF	Unc
1724	—	—	—	—	—	—	—

Note: Stack's Bowers 5-05 choice AU realized $25,300. Ex-Garrett $5,775. Stack's Americana, XF, $10,925

KM# 16 • **Copper** • **Obv:** Bust left **Rev:** Crowned rose **Note:** Pattern.

Date	AG	Good	VG	Fine	VF	XF
1733 4 known	—	—	—	—	—	—

Note: Stacks-Bowers 5-05, Gem Proof realized $63,250; Norweb $19,800

Virginia Halfpenny

KM# Tn25.1 • **Copper** • **Rev:** Small 7s in date.
Note: Struck on Irish halfpenny planchets.

Date	Good	VG	Fine	VF	XF	Unc	Proof
1773	—	—	—	—	—	—	—22,000

KM# Tn25.2 • **Copper** • **Obv. Legend:**
GEORGIVS •... **Rev:** Varieties with 7 or 8 strings in harp

Date	AG	Good	VG	Fine	VF	XF	Unc
1773	30.00	50.00	70.00	110	235	425	1,000

KM# Tn25.3 • **Copper** • **Obv. Legend:**
GEORGIVS... **Rev:** Varieties with 6, 7 or 8 strings in harp

Date	AG	Good	VG	Fine	VF	XF	Unc
1773	35.00	60.00	75.00	135	275	525	1,350

KM# Tn25.4 • **Copper** • **Obv. Legend:**
GEORGIVS... **Rev:** 8 harp strings, dot on cross

Date	AG	Good	VG	Fine	VF	XF	Unc
1773	—	—	—	—	—	—	—

Note: ex-Steinberg $2,600

KM# Tn26 • **Silver** • **Note:** So-called "shilling" silver proofs.

Date	AG	Good	VG	Fine	VF	XF
1774 6 known	—	—	—	—	—	—

Note: Garrett $23,000

REVOLUTIONARY COINAGE
Continental "Dollar"

KM# EA1 • **Pewter** • **Obv. Legend:**
CURRENCY.

Date	Good	VG	Fine	VF	XF	Unc
1776	7,500	9,350	12,000	21,000	32,500	70,000

KM# EA2 • **Pewter** • **Obv. Legend:**
CURRENCY, EG FECIT.

Date	Good	VG	Fine	VF	XF	Unc
1776	8,000	10,500	13,500	25,000	37,500	80,000

KM# EA2a • **Silver** • **Obv. Legend:**
CURRENCY, EG FECIT.

Date	Good	VG	Fine	VF	XF	Unc
1776 2 known	—	—	300,000	450,000	—	—

KM# EA3 • **Pewter** • **Obv. Legend:**
CURRENCEY

Date	Good	VG	Fine	VF	XF	Unc
1776 extremely rare	—	—	—	—	150,000	—

KM# EA4 • **Pewter** • **Obv. Legend:**
CURRENCY. **Rev:** Floral cross.

Date	Good	VG	Fine	VF	XF	Unc
1776 3 recorded	—	—	—	—	400,000	—

Note: Norweb $50,600. Johnson $25,300

KM# EA5 • Pewter • Obv. Legend: CURENCY.

Date	Good	VG	Fine	VF	XF	Unc
1776	7,500	9,500	12,000	22,500	33,500	75,000

KM# EA5a • Brass • Obv. Legend: CURENCY. **Note:** Two varieties exist.

Date	Good	VG	Fine	VF	XF	Unc
1776	22,500	28,500	40,000	75,000	135,000	—

KM# EA5b • Silver • Obv. Legend: CURENCY.

Date	Good	VG	Fine	VF	XF	Unc
1776						
2 known	—	—	285,000	425,000	—	—

Note: Stacks-Bowers 5-05, VF realized $345,000; Romano $99,000

STATE COINAGE
CONNECTICUT

KM# 1 • Copper • Obv: Bust facing right.

Date	AG	Good	VG	Fine	VF	XF
1785	35.00	55.00	90.00	200	650	1,750

KM# 2 • Copper • Obv: "African head."

Date	AG	Good	VG	Fine	VF	XF
1785	55.00	85.00	150	600	1,500	3,800

KM# 3.1 • Copper • Obv: Mailed bust facing left.

Date	AG	Good	VG	Fine	VF	XF
1785	125	220	375	750	1,800	3,850
1786	30.00	50.00	90.00	175	500	1,400
1787	30.00	50.00	85.00	160	450	1,350
1788	30.00	50.00	80.00	160	435	1,150

KM# 3.3 • Copper • Obv: Perfect date. **Rev. Legend:** IN DE ET.

Date	AG	Good	VG	Fine	VF	XF
1787	50.00	80.00	125	350	750	1,850

KM# 3.4 • Copper • Obv. Legend: CONNLC.

Date	AG	Good	VG	Fine	VF	XF
1788	44.00	65.00	130	265	700	2,150

KM# 4 • Copper • Obv: Small mailed bust facing left. **Rev. Legend:** ETLIB INDE.

Date	AG	Good	VG	Fine	VF	XF
1786	45.00	90.00	175	400	1,100	2,750

KM# 5 • Copper • Obv: Small mailed bust facing right. **Rev. Legend:** INDE ET LIB.

Date	AG	Good	VG	Fine	VF	XF
1786	60.00	100.00	175	450	2,000	4,250

KM# 6 • Copper • Obv: Large mailed bust facing right.

Date	AG	Good	VG	Fine	VF	XF
1786	55.00	90.00	160	400	1,750	3,750

KM# 7 • Copper • Obv: "Hercules head."

Date	AG	Good	VG	Fine	VF	XF
1786	60.00	110	220	600	2,500	5,800

KM# 8.1 • Copper • Obv: Draped bust.

Date	AG	Good	VG	Fine	VF	XF
1786	50.00	100.00	200	500	1,250	2,850

KM# 8.2 • Copper • Obv: Draped bust. **Note:** Many varieties.

Date	AG	Good	VG	Fine	VF	XF
1787	28.00	42.00	70.00	115	325	775

KM# 8.3 • Copper • Obv. Legend: AUCIORI.

Date	AG	Good	VG	Fine	VF	XF
1787	30.00	55.00	90.00	175	450	1,100

KM# 8.4 • Copper • Obv. Legend: AUCTOPI.

Date	AG	Good	VG	Fine	VF	XF
1787	35.00	65.00	110	200	650	1,650

KM# 8.5 • Copper • Obv. Legend: AUCTOBI.

Date	AG	Good	VG	Fine	VF	XF
1787	35.00	65.00	110	200	625	1,550

KM# 8.6 • Copper • Obv. Legend: CONNFC.

Date	AG	Good	VG	Fine	VF	XF
1787	32.00	60.00	95.00	185	525	1,100

KM# 8.7 • Copper • Obv. Legend: CONNLC.

Date	AG	Good	VG	Fine	VF	XF
1787	60.00	90.00	180	375	950	3,000

KM# 8.8 • Copper • Rev. Legend: FNDE.

Date	AG	Good	VG	Fine	VF	XF
1787	35.00	55.00	85.00	175	525	1,650

KM# 8.9 • Copper • Rev. Legend: ETLIR.

Date	AG	Good	VG	Fine	VF	XF
1787	32.00	50.00	75.00	160	475	1,275

KM# 8.10 • Copper • Rev. Legend: ETIIB.

Date	AG	Good	VG	Fine	VF	XF
1787	35.00	50.00	75.00	160	485	1,300

KM# 9 • Copper • Obv: Small head. **Rev. Legend:** ETLIB INDE.

Date	AG	Good	VG	Fine	VF	XF
1787	65.00	110	180	425	1,750	4,300

KM# 10 • Copper • Obv: Small head. **Rev. Legend:** INDE ET LIB.

Date	AG	Good	VG	Fine	VF	XF
1787	75.00	135	200	525	2,300	4,600

KM# 11 • Copper • Obv: Medium bust. **Note:** Two reverse legend types exist.

Date	AG	Good	VG	Fine	VF	XF
1787	60.00	90.00	150	400	1,750	3,450

KM# 12 • Copper • Obv: "Muttonhead" variety. **Note:** Extremely rare with legend INDE ET LIB.

Date	AG	Good	VG	Fine	VF	XF
1787	60.00	90.00	175	575	2,550	5,200

KM# 13 • Copper • Obv: "Laughing head"

Date	AG	Good	VG	Fine	VF	XF
1787	35.00	60.00	120	240	650	1,800

KM# 14 • Copper • Obv: "Horned head"

Date	AG	Good	VG	Fine	VF	XF
1787	30.00	50.00	80.00	165	450	1,200

KM# 15 • Copper • Rev. Legend: IND ET LIB

Date	AG	Good	VG	Fine	VF	XF
1787/8	100.00	150	250	750	2,000	5,000
1787/1887	85.00	150	225	600	1,750	4,750

KM# 16 • Copper • Obv. Legend: CONNECT. **Rev. Legend:** INDE ET LIB. **Note:** Two additional scarce reverse legend types exist.

Date	AG	Good	VG	Fine	VF	XF
1787	35.00	50.00	120	240	675	1,750

KM# 22.1 • Copper • Obv: Draped bust facing left. **Rev. Legend:** INDE ET LIB.

Date	AG	Good	VG	Fine	VF	XF
1788	49.50	75.00	140	325	750	1,800

KM# 22.2 • Copper • Rev. Legend: INDLET LIB.

Date	AG	Good	VG	Fine	VF	XF
1788	60.00	90.00	195	425	875	1,950

KM# 20 • Copper • Obv: Mailed bust facing right.

Date	AG	Good	VG	Fine	VF	XF
1788	28.00	45.00	90.00	200	650	1,650

KM# 21 • Copper • Obv: Small mailed bust facing right.

Date	AG	Good	VG	Fine	VF	XF
1788	850	1,650	3,750	5,500	12,500	22,500

MASSACHUSETTS

HALFPENNY

KM# 17 • Copper •

Date	Good	VG	Fine	VF	XF	Unc
1776 unique	—	—	200,000	—	—	—

Note: Garrett $40,000

PENNY

KM# 22.3 • Copper • Obv. Legend: CONNEC. **Rev. Legend:** INDE ET LIB.

Date	AG	Good	VG	Fine	VF	XF
1788	58.00	85.00	190	400	875	1,850

KM# 22.4 • Copper • Obv. Legend: CONNEC. **Rev. Legend:** INDL ET LIB.

Date	AG	Good	VG	Fine	VF	XF
1788	58.00	85.00	190	400	925	2,250

KM# 18 • Copper •

Date	Good	VG	Fine	VF	XF	Unc
1776 unique	—	—	—	—	—	—

HALF CENT

KM# 19 • **Copper** • **Note:** Varieties exist; some are rare.

Date	AG	Good	VG	Fine	VF	XF	Unc
1787	60.00	90.00	140	225	575	1,000	3,250
1788	70.00	115	175	275	600	1,100	3,500

CENT

KM# 20.1 • **Copper** • **Rev:** Arrows in right talon

Date	Good	VG	Fine	VF	XF	Unc
1787 7 known	9,000	22,500	45,000	—	—	350,000

Note: Ex-Bushnell-Brand $8,800. Garrett $5,500

KM# 20.2 • **Copper** • **Rev:** Arrows in left talon

Date	AG	Good	VG	Fine	VF	XF	Unc
1787	60.00	90.00	165	240	650	1,350	6,800

KM# 20.3 • **Copper** • **Rev:** "Horned eagle" die break

Date	AG	Good	VG	Fine	VF	XF	Unc
1787	70.00	110	190	275	775	1,550	7,750

KM# 20.4 • **Copper** • **Rev:** Without period after Massachusetts

Date	AG	Good	VG	Fine	VF	XF	Unc
1788	70.00	105	190	260	675	1,600	6,250

KM# 20.5 • **Copper** • **Rev:** Period after Massachusetts, normal S's

Date	AG	Good	VG	Fine	VF	XF	Unc
1788	60.00	90.00	170	235	600	1,350	5,750

KM# 20.6 • **Copper** • **Rev:** Period after Massachusetts, S's like 8's

Date	AG	Good	VG	Fine	VF	XF	Unc
1788	50.00	75.00	135	200	575	1,250	5,400

NEW HAMPSHIRE

KM# 1 • **Copper** •

Date	AG	Good	VG	Fine	VF	XF
1776 extremely rare	—	—	—	—	—	—

Note: Garrett $13,000

NEW JERSEY

KM# 8 • Copper • Obv: Date below draw bar.

Date	AG	Good	VG	Fine	VF	XF
1786 extremely rare	—	—	—	75,000	135,000	—

Note: Garrett $52,000

KM# 9 • Copper • Obv: Large horse head, date below plow, no coulter on plow.

Date	AG	Good	VG	Fine	VF	XF	Unc
1786	450	850	1,500	3,000	8,500	22,500	—

KM# 10 • Copper • Rev: Narrow shield, straight beam.

Date	AG	Good	VG	Fine	VF	XF	Unc
1786	38.00	60.00	140	210	550	1,350	—

KM# 11.1 • Copper • Rev: Wide shield, curved beam. **Note:** Varieties exist.

Date	AG	Good	VG	Fine	VF	XF	Unc
1786	45.00	75.00	150	225	600	2,000	—

KM# 11.2 • Copper • Obv: Bridle variety (die break). **Note:** Reverse varieties exist.

Date	AG	Good	VG	Fine	VF	XF	Unc
1786	45.00	70.00	145	235	650	2,400	—

KM# 12.1 • Copper • Rev: Plain shield. **Note:** Small planchet. Varieties exist.

Date	AG	Good	VG	Fine	VF	XF	Unc
1787	35.00	55.00	110	200	500	950	—

KM# 12.2 • Copper • Rev: Shield heavily outlined. **Note:** Small planchet.

Date	AG	Good	VG	Fine	VF	XF	Unc
1787	38.00	60.00	120	215	550	1,150	—

KM# 13 • Copper • Obv: "Serpent head."

Date	AG	Good	VG	Fine	VF	XF	Unc
1787	55.00	85.00	200	375	1,650	4,200	—

KM# 14 • Copper • Rev: Plain shield. **Note:** Large planchet. Varieties exist.

Date	AG	Good	VG	Fine	VF	XF	Unc
1787	45.00	60.00	135	240	750	1,650	—

KM# 15 • Copper • Rev. Legend: PLURIBS.

Date	AG	Good	VG	Fine	VF	XF	Unc
1787	85.00	150	275	500	1,500	3,250	—

KM# 16 • Copper • Obv: Horse's head facing right. **Note:** Varieties exist.

Date	AG	Good	VG	Fine	VF	XF	Unc
1788	42.00	60.00	115	190	700	1,275	—

KM# 17 • Copper • Rev: Fox before legend. **Note:** Varieties exist.

Date	AG	Good	VG	Fine	VF	XF	Unc
1788	75.00	145	295	575	2,150	4,750	—

KM# 18 • Copper • Obv: Horse's head facing left. **Note:** Varieties exist.

Date	AG	Good	VG	Fine	VF	XF	Unc
1788	235	425	900	1,650	4,800	13,000	—

NEW YORK

KM# 1 • Copper • Obv: Bust right **Obv. Legend:** NON VI VIRTUTE VICI. **Rev. Legend:** NEO-EBORACENSIS

Date	AG	Good	VG	Fine	VF	XF
1786	3,250	5,000	7,500	15,000	35,000	—

KM# 2 • Copper • Obv: Eagle on globe facing right. **Obv. Legend:** EXCELSIOR **Rev. Legend:** E. PLURIBUS UNUM

Date	AG	Good	VG	Fine	VF	XF
1787	1,400	2,250	3,850	7,000	17,500	33,500

KM# 3 • Copper • Obv: Eagle on globe facing left. **Obv. Legend:** EXCELSIOR **Rev. Legend:** E. PLURIBUS UNUM

Date	AG	Good	VG	Fine	VF	XF
1787	1,250	2,000	3,500	6,500	16,500	32,000

KM# 4 • Copper • Obv. Legend: EXCELSIOR **Rev:** Large eagle, arrows in right talon. **Rev. Legend:** E. PLURIBUS UNUM

Date	Good	VG	Fine	VF	XF
1787	4,500	9,000	16,500	35,000	55,000

Note: Norweb $18,700

KM# 5 • Copper • Obv: George Clinton. **Rev. Legend:** EXCELSIOR

Date	AG	Good	VG	Fine	VF	XF
1787	5,000	9,000	15,500	35,000	75,000	185,000

KM# 6 • Copper • Obv: Indian. **Obv. Legend:** LIBERNATUS LIBERTATEM DEFENDO **Rev:** New York arms. **Rev. Legend:** EXCELSIOR

Date	AG	Good	VG	Fine	VF	XF
1787	4,500	7,500	12,500	30,000	65,000	160,000

KM# 7 • Copper • Obv: Indian. **Obv. Legend:**
LIBERNATUS LIBERTATEM DEFENDO **Rev:**
Eagle on globe. **Rev. Legend:** NEO EBORACUS
EXCELSIOR

Date	AG	Good	VG	Fine	VF	XF
1787	6,500	11,500	17,500	37,500	75,000	145,000

KM# 8 • Copper • Obv: Indian. **Rev:** George III.

Date	AG	Good	VG	Fine	VF	XF
1787 3 Known	—	—75,000	—	—	—

KM# 9 • Copper • Obv: Bust right **Obv.
Legend:** NOVA EBORAC. **Rev:** Figure seated
right. **Rev. Legend:** VIRT.ET.LIB.

Date	AG	Good	VG	Fine	VF	XF	Unc
1787	75.00	115	220	360	1,150	2,700	—

KM# 10 • Copper • Obv: Bust right **Obv.
Legend:** NOVA EBORAC **Rev:** Figure seated left.
Rev. Legend: VIRT.ET.LIB.

Date	AG	Good	VG	Fine	VF	XF	Unc
1787	60.00	100.00	200	325	825	1,750	—

KM# 11 • Copper • Obv: Small head, star
above. **Obv. Legend:** NOVA EBORAC. **Rev:**
Figure seated left **Rev. Legend:** VIRT.ET.LIB.

Date	AG	Good	VG	Fine	VF	XF	Unc
1787	2,450	3,750	5,500	9,500	22,500	—	—

KM# 12 • Copper • Obv: Large head, two
quatrefoils left. **Obv. Legend:** NOVA EBORAC.
Rev: Figure seated left **Rev. Legend:** VIRT.ET.LIB.

Date	AG	Good	VG	Fine	VF	XF	Unc
1787	350	600	1,250	2,500	7,750	15,000	—

Machin's Mill

KM# 13 • Copper • Note: Crude, lightweight
imitations of the British Halfpenny were struck at
Machin's Mill in large quantities bearing the
obverse legends: GEORGIVS II REX, GEORGIVS
III REX, and GEORGIUS III REX, with the
BRITANNIA reverse. There are many different
mulings. Plain crosses in the shield of Britannia
are noticeable on high grade pieces, unlike
common British made imitations, which usually
have outlined crosses in the shield. Some
Machin's Mill varieties are very rare.

Date	AG	Good	VG	Fine	VF	XF
(1747-1788)	40.00	75.00	145	325	800	2,250

Note: Prices are for most common within date ranges.
Examples are dated: 1747, 1771, 1772, 1774, 1775, 1776,
1777, 1778, 1784, 1785, 1786, 1787 and 1788. Other dates
may exist

VERMONT

KM# 1 • Copper • Rev. Legend: IMMUNE
COLUMBIA

Date	AG	Good	VG	Fine	VF	XF
(1785)	4,000	6,000	9,500	13,750	35,000	—

KM# 2 • Copper • Obv: Sun rising over field with plow **Obv. Legend:** VERMONTIS. RES. PUBLICA. **Rev:** Eye, with rays and stars **Rev. Legend:** QUARTA. DECIMA. STELLA.

Date	AG	Good	VG	Fine	VF	XF
1785	140	300	750	1,650	5,250	12,500

KM# 3 • Copper • Obv: Sun rising over field with plow **Obv. Legend:** VERMONTS. RES. PUBLICA. **Rev:** Eye, with rays and stars **Rev. Legend:** QUARTA. DECIMA. STELLA.

Date	AG	Good	VG	Fine	VF	XF
1785	150	285	600	1,250	3,150	7,500

KM# 4 • Copper • Obv: Sun rising over field with plow **Obv. Legend:** VERMONTENSIUM.RES.PUBLICA **Rev:** Eye, with pointed rays and stars **Rev. Legend:** QUARTA. DECIMA. STELLA.

Date	AG	Good	VG	Fine	VF	XF
1786	140	235	425	775	2,000	4,400

KM# 5 • Copper • Obv: "Baby head." **Obv. Legend:** AUCTORI: VERMON: **Rev:** Seated figure left **Rev. Legend:** ET:LIB: INDE

Date	AG	Good	VG	Fine	VF	XF
1786	200	350	650	1,750	4,800	12,500

KM# 6 • Copper • Obv: Bust facing left. **Obv. Legend:** VERMON: AUCTORI: **Rev:** Seated figure left **Rev. Legend:** INDE ETLIB

Date	AG	Good	VG	Fine	VF	XF
1786	115	175	350	825	2,850	5,000
1787 extremely rare	—	4,500	10,000	22,500	42,500	—

KM# 7 • Copper • Obv: Bust facing right. **Obv. Legend:** VERMON. AUCTORI. **Rev:** Seated figure left **Rev. Legend:** INDE ETLIB **Note:** Varieties exist.

Date	AG	Good	VG	Fine	VF	XF	Unc
1787	70.00	150	260	575	1,450	3,000	—

KM# 8 • Copper • Obv: Bust right **Obv. Legend:** VERMON AUCTORI **Rev:** Seated figure left **Note:** Britannia mule.

Date	AG	Good	VG	Fine	VF	XF	Unc
1787	65.00	120	170	300	700	1,650	—

KM# 9.2 • Copper • Obv: Bust right. "C" backward in AUCTORI. **Rev:** Seated figure left

Date	AG	Good	VG	Fine	VF	XF
1788 extremely rare	—	4,200	7,000	17,500	38,000	—

Note: Stack's Americana, Fine, $9,775

KM# 10 • **Copper** • **Obv:** Bust right **Rev:** Seated figure left **Rev. Legend:** .ET LIB. .INDE.

Date	AG	Good	VG	Fine	VF	XF
1788	200	325	675	1,450	4,750	13,500

KM# 11 • **Copper** • **Obv:** Bust right **Rev:** Seated figure left **Note:** George III Rex mule.

Date	AG	Good	VG	Fine	VF	XF
1788	325	575	950	5,000	12,500	12,000

KM# 9.1 • **Copper** • **Obv:** Bust right **Obv. Legend:** VERMON. AUCTORI. **Rev:** Seated figure left **Rev. Legend:** INDE . ET LIB. **Note:** Varieties exist.

Date	AG	Good	VG	Fine	VF	XF
1788	65.00	125	200	450	950	2,250

EARLY AMERICAN TOKENS

Albany Church "Penny"

KM# Tn54.1 • **Copper** • **Obv:** Without "D" above church. **Note:** Uniface.

Date	AG	Good	VG	Fine	VF	XF
5 known	—	—	10,000	25,000	45,000	75,000

 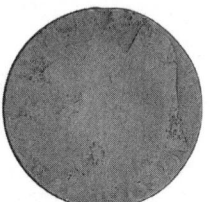

KM# Tn54.2 • **Copper** • **Obv:** With "D" above church. **Note:** Uniface.

Date	AG	Good	VG	Fine	VF	XF
rare	—	—	9,000	22,500	42,500	67,500

Auctori Plebis

KM# Tn50 • **Copper** • **Obv:** Bust left **Obv. Legend:** AUCTORI: PLEBIS: **Rev:** Seated figure left **Rev. Legend:** INDEP: ET. LIBER

Date	AG	Good	VG	Fine	VF	XF	Unc
1787	—	100.00	165	340	700	1,650	15,000

Bar "Cent"

KM# Tn49 • **Copper** • **Obv:** USA monogram **Rev:** Horizontal bars

Date	Good	VG	Fine	VF	XF	Unc
(1785)	1,400	1,750	3,100	6,250	9,500	27,500

Castorland "Half Dollar"

KM# Tn87.1 • **Silver** • **Obv. Legend:** FRANCO.AMERICANA COLONIA **Edge:** Reeded.

Date	AG	Good	VG	Fine	VF	XF	Unc
1796	—	—	—	—	—	4,500	13,500

KM# Tn87.1a • Copper • Obv. Legend:
FRANCO.AMERICANA COLONIA **Edge:** Reeded.

Date	Good	VG	Fine	VF	XF	Unc
1796 3 known	—	—	—	—	3,500	—

KM# Tn87.1b • Brass • Obv. Legend:
FRANCO.AMERICANA COLONIA **Edge:** Reeded.

Date	Good	VG	Fine	VF	XF	Unc
1796	—	—	—	—	225	650

KM# Tn87.2 • Copper • Obv. Legend:
FRANCO.AMERICANA COLONIA **Edge:** Plain.
Note: Thin planchet.

Date	Good	VG	Fine	VF	XF	Unc
1796 unique	—	—	—	—	—	—

KM# Tn87.3 • Silver • Obv. Legend:
FRANCO.AMERICANA COLONIA **Edge:** Reeded.
Note: Thin planchet. Restrike.

Date	Good	VG	Fine	VF	XF	Unc	Proof
1796	—	—	—	—	—	1,250	—

KM# Tn87.4 • Silver • Obv. Legend:
FRANCO.AMERICANA COLONIA **Edge:** Lettered.
Edge Lettering: ARGENT. **Note:** Thin planchet.
Restrike.

Date	Good	VG	Fine	VF	XF	Unc	Proof
1796	—	—	—	—	—	150	—

KM# Tn87.3a • Copper • Obv. Legend:
FRANCO.AMERICANA COLONIA **Edge:** Reeded.
Note: Thin planchet. Restrike.

Date	Good	VG	Fine	VF	XF	Unc	Proof
1796	—	—	—	—	—	350	—

KM# Tn87.5 • Copper • Obv. Legend:
FRANCO.AMERICANA COLONIA **Edge:** Lettered.
Edge Lettering: CUIVRE. **Note:** Thin planchet.
Restrike.

Date	Good	VG	Fine	VF	XF	Unc	Proof
1796	—	—	—	—	—	100.00	—

Chalmers

3 PENCE

KM# Tn45 • Silver •

Date	AG	Good	VG	Fine	VF	XF
1783	650	1,150	2,200	4,250	9,500	17,500

6 PENCE

KM# Tn46.1 • Silver • Rev: Small date

Date	AG	Good	VG	Fine	VF	XF
1783	900	1,650	2,750	6,750	16,500	28,500

KM# Tn46.2 • Silver • Rev: Large date

Date	AG	Good	VG	Fine	VF	XF
1783	775	1,450	2,250	6,000	14,500	27,500

SHILLING

KM# Tn47.1 • Silver • Rev: Birds with long worm

Date	AG	Good	VG	Fine	VF	XF
1783	450	775	1,350	2,750	6,000	11,500

KM# Tn47.2 • Silver • Rev: Birds with short worm

Date	AG	Good	VG	Fine	VF	XF
1783	450	750	1,250	2,350	5,500	11,000

KM# Tn48 • Silver • Rev: Rings and stars

Date	AG	Good	VG	Fine	VF	XF
1783 4 known	—	—	—	—	200,000	—

Note: Garrett $75,000

Copper Company of Upper Canada

HALFPENNY

KM# Tn86 • Copper • Obv. Legend: BRITISH
SETTLEMENT KENTUCKY

Date	Good	VG	Fine	VF	XF	Unc	Proof
1796	—	—	—	—	—	—	10,000

Franklin Press

KM# Tn73 • Copper • Obv: Printing press **Obv. Legend:** SIC ORITUR DOCTRINA SURGETQUE LIBERTAS **Edge:** Plain.

Date	AG	Good	VG	Fine	VF	XF	Unc
1794	30.00	75.00	110	150	285	450	1,350

Kentucky Token

KM# Tn70.1 • Copper • Obv. Legend: UNANIMITY IS THE STRENGTH OF SOCIETY **Rev. Legend:** E. PLURIBUS UNUM **Edge:** Plain. **Note:** 1793 date is circa.

Date	AG	Good	VG	Fine	VF	XF	Unc
(1793)	12.00	25.00	40.00	150	200	375	1,210

KM# Tn70.2 • Copper • Obv. Legend: UNANIMITY IS THE STRENGTH OF SOCIETY **Rev. Legend:** E. PLURIBUS UNUM **Edge:** Engrailed.

Date	AG	Good	VG	Fine	VF	XF	Unc
(1793)	35.00	75.00	125	200	500	950	3,400

KM# Tn70.3 • Copper • Obv. Legend: UNANIMITY IS THE STRENGTH OF SOCIETY **Rev. Legend:** E. PLURIBUS UNUM **Edge:** Lettered. **Edge Lettering:** PAYABLE AT BEDWORTH.

Date	AG	Good	VG	Fine	VF	XF
(1793) unique	—	—	—	—	—	1,980

KM# Tn70.4 • Copper • Obv. Legend: UNANIMITY IS THE STRENGTH OF SOCIETY **Rev. Legend:** E. PLURIBUS UNUM **Edge:** Lettered. **Edge Lettering:** PAYABLE AT LANCASTER.

Date	AG	Good	VG	Fine	VF	XF	Unc
(1793)	14.00	28.00	45.00	65.00	225	400	1,250

KM# Tn70.5 • Copper • Obv. Legend: UNANIMITY IS THE STRENGTH OF SOCIETY **Rev. Legend:** E. PLURIBUS UNUM **Edge:** Lettered. **Edge Lettering:** PAYABLE AT I.FIELDING.

Date	AG	Good	VG	Fine	VF	XF
(1793) unique	—	—	—	—	—	—

KM# Tn70.6 • Copper • Obv. Legend: UNANIMITY IS THE STRENGTH OF SOCIETY **Rev. Legend:** E. PLURIBUS UNUM **Edge:** Lettered. **Edge Lettering:** PAYABLE AT W. PARKERS.

Date	AG	Good	VG	Fine	VF	XF
(1793) unique	—	—	—	— 20,000	—	

KM# Tn70.7 • Copper • Obv. Legend: UNANIMITY IS THE STRENGTH OF SOCIETY **Rev. Legend:** E. PLURIBUS UNUM **Edge:** Ornamented branch with two leaves.

Date	AG	Good	VG	Fine	VF	XF
(1793) unique	—	—	—	—	—	—

Mott Token

KM# Tn52.1 • Copper • Obv: Clock **Rev:** Eagle with shield **Note:** Thin planchet.

Date	AG	Good	VG	Fine	VF	XF	Unc
1789	50.00	80.00	150	300	550	1,200	1,750

KM# Tn52.2 • Copper • Obv: Clock **Rev:** Eagle with shield **Note:** Thick planchet. Weight generally about 170 grams.

Date	AG	Good	VG	Fine	VF	XF	Unc
1789	60.00	95.00	175	325	525	100.00	—

KM# Tn52.3 • Copper • Obv: Clock **Rev:** Eagle with shield **Edge:** Fully engrailed. **Note:** Specimens struck with perfect dies are scarcer and generally command higher prices.

Date	AG	Good	VG	Fine	VF	XF	Unc
1789	90.00	160	325	450	700	1,750	4,800

Myddelton Token

KM# Tn85 • Copper • Obv. Legend: BRITISH SETTLEMENT KENTUCKY **Rev. Legend:** PAYABLE BY P.P.P.MYDDELTON.

Date	Good	VG	Fine	VF	XF	Unc	Proof
1796	—	—	—	—	—	—	37,500

KM# Tn85a • Silver •

Date	Good	VG	Fine	VF	XF	Unc	Proof
1796	—	—	—	—	—	—	28,000

New York Theatre

KM# Tn90 • Copper • Obv: Theater building
Obv. Legend: THE.THEATRE.AT.NEW.YORK.
AMERICA **Rev:** Ships at sea, viewed from dock
Rev. Legend: MAY.COMMERCE.FLOURISH
Note: 1796 date is circa.

Date	Good	VG	Fine	VF	XF	Unc
1796	—	—	—	7,500	10,000	26,500

North American

HALFPENNY

KM# Tn30 • Copper • Obv: Seated figure left,
with harp **Obv. Legend:** NORTH AMERICAN
TOKEN **Rev:** Ship **Rev. Legend:** COMMERCE

Date	AG	Good	VG	Fine	VF	XF	Unc
1781	32.00	50.00	70.00	140	300	750	3,250

Rhode Island Ship

KM# Tn27a • Brass • Obv: Without wreath
below ship.

Date	AG	Good	VG	Fine	VF	XF	Unc
1779	—	—	325	550	1,000	2,000	7,500

KM# Tn27b • Pewter • Obv: Without wreath
below ship.

Date	AG	Good	VG	Fine	VF	XF	Unc
1779	—	—	—	—	5,500	8,500	18,500

KM# Tn28a • Brass • Obv: Wreath below ship.

Date	AG	Good	VG	Fine	VF	XF	Unc
1779	—	—	—	675	1,100	2,100	7,750

KM# Tn28b • Pewter • Obv: Wreath below ship.

Date	AG	Good	VG	Fine	VF	XF	Unc
1779	—	—	—	—	5,500	9,000	20,000

KM# Tn29 • Brass • Obv: VLUGTENDE below
ship

Date	AG	Good	VG	Fine	VF	XF
1779 unique	—	—	—	—	—	35,000

Note: Garrett $16,000

Standish Barry

3 PENCE

KM# Tn55 • Silver • Obv: Bust left **Obv. Legend:**
BALTIMORE • TOWN • JULY • 4 • 90 • **Rev:**
Denomination **Rev. Legend:** STANDISH BARRY •

Date	AG	Good	VG	Fine	VF	XF	Unc
1790	—	—	15,000	23,500	55,000	—	—

Talbot, Allum & Lee

CENT

KM# Tn71.1 • Copper • Rev: NEW YORK
above ship **Edge:** Lettered. **Edge Lettering:**
PAYABLE AT THE STORE OF

Date	AG	Good	VG	Fine	VF	XF	Unc
1794	32.00	50.00	85.00	165	275	550	2,000

KM# Tn71.2 • Copper • Rev: NEW YORK above ship **Edge:** Plain. **Note:** Size of ampersand varies on obverse and reverse dies.

Date	AG	Good	VG	Fine	VF	XF
1794 4 known	—	—	—	—	10,000	24,000

KM# Tn72.1 • Copper • Rev: Without NEW YORK above ship **Edge:** Lettered. **Edge Lettering:** PAYABLE AT THE STORE OF

Date	AG	Good	VG	Fine	VF	XF	Unc
1794	200	375	600	1,250	3,750	7,500	22,000

KM# Tn72.2 • Copper • Edge: Lettered. **Edge Lettering:** WE PROMISE TO PAY THE BEARER ONE CENT.

Date	AG	Good	VG	Fine	VF	XF	Unc
1795	30.00	50.00	75.00	135	250	400	1,200

KM# Tn72.3 • Copper • Edge: Lettered. **Edge Lettering:** CURRENT EVERYWHERE.

Date	Good	VG	Fine	VF	XF	Unc
1795 unique	—	—	—	—	—	—

KM# Tn72.4 • Copper • Edge: Olive leaf.

Date	Good	VG	Fine	VF	XF	Unc
1795 unique	—	—	—	—	15,000	—

Note: Norweb $4,400

KM# Tn72.5 • Copper • Edge: Plain.

Date	Good	VG	Fine	VF	XF	Unc
1795 plain edge; 2 known	—	—	—	—	—	—
1795 Lettered edge; unique	—	—	—	—	15,000	—

Note: Edge: Cambridge Bedford Huntington.X.X.; Norweb, $3,960

Washington Pieces

KM# Tn35 • Copper • Obv. Legend: GEORGIVS TRIUMPHO.

Date	AG	Good	VG	Fine	VF	XF	Unc
1783	—	95.00	135	285	650	1,150	—

KM# Tn36 • Copper • Obv: Large military bust. **Note:** Varieties exist.

Date	AG	Good	VG	Fine	VF	XF	Unc
1783	—	—	50.00	90.00	185	450	2,600

KM# Tn37.1 • Copper • Obv: Small military bust. **Edge:** Plain.

Date	AG	Good	VG	Fine	VF	XF	Unc
1783	—	—	70.00	95.00	220	525	3,800

Note: One proof example is known. Value: $25,000

KM# Tn37.2 • Copper • Obv: Small military bust. **Edge:** Engrailed.

Date	AG	Good	VG	Fine	VF	XF	Unc
1783	—	75.00	110	150	300	750	4,250

KM# Tn38.1 • Copper • Obv: Draped bust, no button on drapery, small letter.

Date	AG	Good	VG	Fine	VF	XF	Unc
1783	—	40.00	60.00	95.00	185	400	2,250

KM# Tn38.2 • Copper • Obv: Draped bust, button on drapery, large letter.

Date	AG	Good	VG	Fine	VF	XF	Unc
1783	—	85.00	110	150	325	625	4,500

KM# Tn38.4 • Copper • Edge: Engrailed. **Note:** Restrike.

Date	Good	VG	Fine	VF	XF	Unc	Proof
1783	—	—	—	—	—	—	800

KM# Tn38.4a • Copper • Note: Bronzed. Restrike.

Date	Good	VG	Fine	VF	XF	Unc	Proof
1783	—	—	—	—	—	—	—

KM# Tn83.3 • Copper • Obv: Large modern lettering. **Edge:** Plain. **Note:** Restrike.

Date	Good	VG	Fine	VF	XF	Unc	Proof
1783	—	—	—	—	—	—	950

KM# Tn83.4b • Silver • Note: Restrike.

Date	Good	VG	Fine	VF	XF	Unc	Proof
1783	—	—	—	—	—	—	1,750

KM# Tn83.4c • Gold • Note: Restrike.

Date	AG	Good	VG	Fine	VF	XF
1783 2 known	—	—	—	—	—	—

KM# Tn60.1 • Copper • Obv. Legend: WASHINGTON PRESIDENT. **Edge:** Plain.

Date	AG	Good	VG	Fine	VF	XF
1792	850	1,450	3,000	7,500	18,500	—

Note: Steinberg $12,650. Garrett $15,500.

KM# Tn60.2 • Copper • Obv. Legend: WASHINGTON PRESIDENT. **Edge:** Lettered. **Edge Lettering:** UNITED STATES OF AMERICA.

Date	AG	Good	VG	Fine	VF	XF	Unc
1792	—	—	—	—	—	—	—

KM# Tn61.1 • Copper • Obv. Legend: BORN VIRGINIA. **Note:** Varieties exist.

Date	AG	Good	VG	Fine	VF	XF	Unc
(1792)	500	1,000	2,000	4,000	7,500	12,000	—

KM# Tn61.2 • Silver • Edge: Lettered. **Edge Lettering:** UNITED STATES OF AMERICA.

Date	AG	Good	VG	Fine	VF	XF
(1792) 2 known	—	—	—	—	—	—

KM# Tn61.1a • Silver • Edge: Plain.

Date	AG	Good	VG	Fine	VF	XF
(1792) 4 known	—	—	—	—	—	200,000

Note: Roper $16,500

KM# Tn62 • Silver • Rev: Heraldic eagle. 1792 half dollar. **Note:** Mule.

Date	AG	Good	VG	Fine	VF	XF
(1792) 3 known	—	—	—	—	50,000	75,000

KM# Tn77.1 • Copper • Obv. Legend: LIBERTY AND SECURITY. **Edge:** Lettered. **Note:** "Penny."

Date	AG	Good	VG	Fine	VF	XF	Unc
(1795)	70.00	110	165	300	500	850	3,500

KM# Tn77.2 • Copper • Edge: Plain. **Note:** "Penny."

Date	AG	Good	VG	Fine	VF	XF
(1795) extremely rare	—	—	—	—	—	—

KM# Tn77.3 • Copper • Note: "Penny." Engine-turned borders.

Date	Good	VG	Fine	VF	XF	Unc
(1795) 12 known	275	450	650	1,250	2,400	7,500

KM# Tn78 • Copper • Note: Similar to "Halfpenny" with date on reverse.

Date	Good	VG	Fine	VF	XF	Unc
1795 very rare	—	—	—	—	—	—

Note: Roper $6,600

HALFPENNY

KM# Tn56 • Copper • Obv. Legend: LIVERPOOL HALFPENNY

Date	AG	Good	VG	Fine	VF	XF	Unc
1791	40.00	70.00	1,000	125	300	550	3,250

KM# Tn66.1 • Copper • Rev: Ship **Edge:** Lettered.

Date	AG	Good	VG	Fine	VF	XF	Unc
1793	25.00	45.00	85.00	225	450	825	3,500

KM# Tn66.2 • Copper • Rev: Ship **Edge:** Plain.

Date	Good	VG	Fine	VF	XF	Unc
1793 5 known	—	—	— 15,000	—	—	

KM# Tn75.1 • Copper • Obv: Large coat buttons **Rev:** Grate **Edge:** Reeded.

Date	AG	Good	VG	Fine	VF	XF	Unc
1795	—	— 70.00	110	200	400	900	

KM# Tn75.2 • Copper • Rev: Grate **Edge:** Lettered.

Date	AG	Good	VG	Fine	VF	XF	Unc
1795	90.00	140	210	275	400	800	2,800

KM# Tn75.3 • Copper • Obv: Small coat buttons **Rev:** Grate **Edge:** Reeded.

Date	AG	Good	VG	Fine	VF	XF	Unc
1795	50.00	75.00	120	190	275	585	2,650

KM# Tn76.1 • Copper • Obv. Legend: LIBERTY AND SECURITY. **Edge:** Plain.

Date	AG	Good	VG	Fine	VF	XF	Unc
1795	18.00	35.00	60.00	160	350	700	3,250

KM# Tn76.2 • Copper • Edge: Lettered. **Edge Lettering:** PAYABLE AT LONDON ...

Date	AG	Good	VG	Fine	VF	XF	Unc
1795	40.00	65.00	90.00	140	300	650	3,000

KM# Tn76.3 • Copper • Edge: Lettered. **Edge Lettering:** BIRMINGHAM ...

Date	AG	Good	VG	Fine	VF	XF	Unc
1795	55.00	85.00	125	175	350	800	3,600

KM# Tn76.4 • Copper • Edge: Lettered. **Edge Lettering:** AN ASYLUM ...

Date	AG	Good	VG	Fine	VF	XF	Unc
1795	18.00	35.00	60.00	275	600	1,600	6,500

KM# Tn76.5 • Copper • Edge: Lettered. **Edge Lettering:** PAYABLE AT LIVERPOOL ...

Date	Good	VG	Fine	VF	XF	Unc
1795 unique	—	—	—	—	—	—

KM# Tn76.6 • Copper • Edge: Lettered. **Edge Lettering:** PAYABLE AT LONDON-LIVERPOOL.

Date	Good	VG	Fine	VF	XF	Unc
1795 unique	—	—	—	—	—	—

KM# Tn81.1 • Copper • Rev. Legend: NORTH WALES **Edge:** Plain.

Date	AG	Good	VG	Fine	VF	XF	Unc
(ca.1795)	60.00	110	175	265	625	1,750	—

KM# Tn82 • Copper • Rev: Four stars at bottom **Rev. Legend:** NORTH WALES

Date	AG	Good	VG	Fine	VF	XF	Unc
(1795)	1,250	2,250	4,750	7,750	21,500	—	—

KM# Tn81.2 • Copper • Rev. Legend: NORTH WALES **Edge:** Lettered.

Date	AG	Good	VG	Fine	VF	XF	Unc
(1795)	350	550	1,150	1,750	5,500	9,500	—

CENT

KM# Tn39 • Copper • Obv: Draped Bust left **Obv. Legend:** WASHINGTON & INDEPENDENCE **Rev:** Denomination in wreath **Rev. Legend:** UNITY STATES OF AMERICA

Date	AG	Good	VG	Fine	VF	XF	Unc
1783	30.00	50.00	70.00	10.00	265	550	2,250

KM# Tn40 • Copper • Note: Double head.

Date	AG	Good	VG	Fine	VF	XF	Unc
(1783)	25.00	45.00	60.00	95.00	250	500	2,750

KM# Tn41 • Copper • Obv: "Ugly head." **Note:** 3 known in copper, 1 in white metal.

Date	AG	Good	VG	Fine	VF	XF
1784	—	120,000	—	—	—	—

Note: Roper $14,850

KM# Tn57 • Copper • Obv: Military bust left **Obv. Legend:** WASHINGTON PRESIDENT. **Rev:** Small eagle

Date	AG	Good	VG	Fine	VF	XF	Unc
1791	—	—	350	500	725	1,000	4,250

KM# Tn58 • Copper • Obv: Military bust left **Obv. Legend:** WASHINGTON PRESIDENT **Rev:** Large eagle

Date	AG	Good	VG	Fine	VF	XF	Unc
1791	—	200	325	485	650	900	3,200

KM# Tn65 • Copper • Obv: "Roman" head **Obv. Legend:** WASHINGTON PRESIDENT.

Date	AG	Good	VG	Fine	VF	XF	Unc
1792	—	—	—	—	—	—	—

HALF DOLLAR

KM# Tn59.1 • Copper • Edge: Lettered. **Edge Lettering:** UNITED STATES OF AMERICA

Date	AG	Good	VG	Fine	VF	XF
1792 2 known	—	—	—	—	—	75,000

Note: Roper $2,860. Benson, EF, $48,300

KM# Tn59.2 • Copper • Edge: Plain.

Date		Good	VG	Fine	VF	XF
1792 3 known		—	—	—	125,000	200,000

KM# Tn59.1a • Silver • Edge: Lettered. **Edge Lettering:** UNITED STATES OF AMERICA

Date	AG	Good	VG	Fine	VF	XF
1792 rare	—	—	—	—	40,000	65,000

Note: Roper $35,200

KM# Tn59.2a • Silver • Edge: Plain.

Date	AG	Good	VG	Fine	VF	XF	Unc
1792 rare	—	—	—	—	—	—	

KM# Tn59.1b • Gold • Edge: Lettered. **Edge Lettering:** UNITED STATES OF AMERICA

Date	AG	Good	VG	Fine	VF	XF
1792 unique	—	—	—	—	—	—

KM# Tn63.1 • Silver • Rev: Small eagle **Edge:** Plain.

Date	AG	Good	VG	Fine	VF	XF
1792	—	—	—	—	200,000	300,000

KM# Tn63.2 • Silver • Edge: Ornamented, circles and squares.

Date	VG	Fine	VF	XF	Unc
1792 5 known	—	—	100,000	175,000	400,000

KM# Tn63.1a • Copper • Edge: Plain.

Date	Good	VG	Fine	VF	XF	Unc
1792	4,000	6,500	12,500	32,000	65,000	—

Note: Garrett $32,000

KM# Tn63.3 • Silver • Edge: Two olive leaves.

Date	Good	VG	Fine	VF	XF	Unc
1792 unique	—	—	—	—	—	—

KM# Tn64 • Silver • Rev: Large heraldic eagle

Date	Good	VG	Fine	VF	XF
1792 unique	—	—	—	100,000	—

Note: Garrett $16,500

EARLY AMERICAN PATTERNS
Confederatio

KM# EA22 • Copper • Obv: Standing figure with bow & arrow **Obv. Legend:** INIMICA TYRANNIS • AMERICANA • **Rev:** Small circle of stars **Rev. Legend:** • CONFEDERATIO •

Date	AG	Good	VG	Fine	VF	XF	Unc
1785	—	—	—	—	50,000	95,000	—

KM# EA23 • Copper • Obv: Standing figure with bow & arrow **Obv. Legend:** INIMICA TYRANNIS • AMERICANA • **Rev:** Large circle of stars **Rev. Legend:** • CONFEDERATIO • **Note:** The Confederatio dies were struck in combination with 13 other dies of the period. All surviving examples of these combinations are extremely rare.

Date	AG	Good	VG	Fine	VF	XF
extremely rare	—	—	—	—	50,000	100,000

Immune Columbia

KM# EA20 • Copper • Obv: George III **Obv. Legend:** GEORGIVS III • REX • **Rev. Legend:** IMMUNE COLUMBIA •

Date	AG	Good	VG	Fine	VF	XF	Unc
1785	3,500	5,250	7,750	11,500	22,500	—	—

KM# EA21 • Copper • Obv: Head right **Obv. Legend:** VERMON AUCTORI **Rev. Legend:** IMMUNE COLUMBIA •

Date	AG	Good	VG	Fine	VF	XF	Unc
1785	—	6,000	9,500	12,500	35,000	—	—

KM# EA17a • Silver • Obv. Legend: IMMUNE COLUMBIA • **Rev:** Eye, with pointed rays & stars **Rev. Legend:** NOVA CONSTELLATIO

Date	AG	Good	VG	Fine	VF	XF	Unc
1785	—	—	—	—	45,000	75,000	—

KM# EA19a • Gold • Obv. Legend: IMMUNE COLUMBIA • **Rev:** Blunt rays **Rev. Legend:** NOVA CONSTELATIO •

Date	Good	VG	Fine	VF	XF	Unc
1785 unique	—	—	—	—	—	—

Note: In the Smithsonian Collection

KM# EA17 • Copper • Obv. Legend: IMMUNE COLUMBIA. **Rev:** Eye, with pointed rays & stars **Rev. Legend:** NOVA • CONSTELLATIO

Date	AG	Good	VG	Fine	VF	XF	Unc
1785	—	—	—	—	25,000	45,000	—

KM# EA18 • Copper • Obv. Legend: IMMUNE COLUMBIA • **Rev:** Eye, with pointed rays & stars. Extra star in reverse legend **Rev. Legend:** NOVA • CONSTELLATIO *

Date	AG	Good	VG	Fine	VF	XF
1785	—	—	—	—	25,000	45,000

Note: Caldwell $4,675

KM# EA19 • Copper • Obv. Legend: IMMUNE COLUMBIA • **Rev:** Blunt rays **Rev. Legend:** NOVA CONSTELATIO

Date	AG	Good	VG	Fine	VF	XF
1785 2 known	—	—	—	—	—	120,000

Note: Norweb $22,000

KM# EA28 • Copper • Obv. Legend: IMMUNIS COLUMBIA **Rev:** Eagle **Rev. Legend:** * E * PLURIBUS * UNUM *

Date	Good	VG	Fine	VF	XF
1786 3 known	—	—	—	50,000	90,000

KM# EA24 • Copper • Obv: Washington **Rev:** Stars in rayed circle **Rev. Legend:** • CONFEDERATIO •

Date	Good	VG	Fine	VF	XF
1786 3 known	—	—	—	60,000	—

Note: Garrett $50,000. Steinberg $12,650

KM# EA25 • Copper • Obv: Eagle, raw shield **Obv. Legend:** * E • PLURIBUS UNUM • **Rev:** Shield **Rev. Legend:** * E * PLURIBUS * UNUM *

Date	AG	Good	VG	Fine	VF	XF
1786 unique	—	—	—	—	—	—

Note: Garrett $37,500

KM# EA26 • Copper • Obv: Washington **Obv. Legend:** GEN • WASHINGTON • **Rev:** Eagle

Date	AG	Good	VG	Fine	VF	XF
1786 2 known	—	—	—	—	—	—

KM# EA27 • Copper • Obv. Legend: IMMUNIS COLUMBIA • **Rev:** Shield **Rev. Legend:** * E * PLURIBUS * UNUM *

Date	AG	Good	VG	Fine	VF	XF
1786						
extremely rare	—	—	—	—	40,000	60,000

Note: Rescigno, AU, $33,000. Steinberg, VF, $11,000

Nova Constellatio

KM# EA6.1 • Copper • Obv: Pointed rays **Obv. Legend:** NOVA • CONSTELLATIO • **Rev:** Small "U•S"

Date	AG	Good	VG	Fine	VF	XF	Unc
1783	50.00	70.00	100.00	225	440	950	3,750

KM# EA6.2 • Copper • Obv: Pointed rays **Obv. Legend:** NOVA • CONSTELLATIO • **Rev:** Large "US"

Date	AG	Good	VG	Fine	VF	XF	Unc
1783	55.00	75.00	110	250	600	1,400	7,000

KM# EA7 • Copper • Obv: Blunt rays **Obv. Legend:** NOVA • CONSTELATIO •

Date	AG	Good	VG	Fine	VF	XF	Unc
1783	50.00	75.00	110	250	575	1,350	5,000

KM# EA8 • Copper • Obv: Blunt rays **Obv. Legend:** NOVA • CONSTELATIO •

Date	AG	Good	VG	Fine	VF	XF	Unc
1785	50.00	75.00	110	260	650	1,550	6,500

KM# EA9 • Copper • Obv: Pointed rays **Obv. Legend:** NOVA • CONSTELATIO •

Date	AG	Good	VG	Fine	VF	XF	Unc
1785	—	—	100.00	225	450	1,000	3,600

KM# EA10 • Copper • Note: Contemporary circulating counterfeit. Similar to previously listed coin.

Date	AG	Good	VG	Fine	VF	XF
1786 extremely rare	—	—	—	—	—	—

5 UNITS

KM# EA12 • Copper • Obv: Eye, with pointed rays & stars **Obv. Legend:** NOVA CONSTELLATIO **Rev. Legend:** • LIBERTAS • JUSTITIA •

Date	AG	Good	VG	Fine	VF	XF
1783 unique	—	—	—	—	—	—

100 (BIT)

KM# EA13.1 • Silver • Obv: Eye, with pointed rays & stars **Obv. Legend:** NOVA

CONSTELLATIO **Rev. Legend:** • LIBERTAS • JUSTITIA • **Edge:** Leaf.

Date	AG	Good	VG	Fine	VF	XF
1783 2 known	—	—	—	—	—	—

Note: Garrett $97,500. Stack's auction, May 1991, $72,500

KM# EA13.2 • Silver • Obv: Eye, with pointed rays & stars **Obv. Legend:** NOVA CONSTELLATIO **Rev. Legend:** • LIBERTAS • JUSTITIA • **Edge:** Plain

Date	AG	Good	VG	Fine	VF	XF
1783 unique	—	—	—	—	—	—

500 (QUINT)

KM# EA14 • Silver • Obv: Eye with pointed rays & stars **Obv. Legend:** NOVA CONSTELLATIO **Rev. Legend:** • LIBERTAS • JUSTITIA •

Date	AG	Good	VG	Fine	VF	XF
1783 unique	—	—	—	—	—	250,000

Note: Garrett $165,000

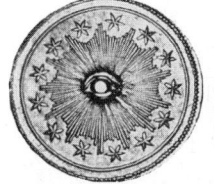

KM# EA15 • Silver • Obv: Eye, with rays & stars, no legend **Rev. Legend:** • LIBERTAS • JUSTITIA •

Date	AG	Good	VG	Fine	VF	XF
1783 unique	—	—	—	—	75,000	—

Note: Garrett $55,000

1000 (MARK)

KM# EA16 • Silver • Obv: Eye, with pointed rays & stars **Obv. Legend:** NOVA CONSTELLATIO **Rev. Legend:** • LIBERTAS • JUSTITIA •

Date	AG	Good	VG	Fine	VF	XF
1783 unique	—	—	—	—	—	350,000

Note: Garrett $190,000

EARLY FEDERAL COINAGE

Brasher

KM# Tn51.1 • Gold • Obv: Sunrise over mountains. **Rev:** Displayed eagle with shield on breast, EB counterstamp on wing.

Date	AG	Good	VG	Fine	VF	XF
1787 6 known	—	—	—	—	—	—

Note: Heritage FUN Sale, January 2005, AU-55, $2.415 million.

KM# Tn51.2 • Gold • Obv: Sun rise over mountains **Rev:** Displayed eagle with sheild on breast. EB counterstamp on breast.

Date	AG	Good	VG	Fine	VF	XF
1787 unique	—	—	—	—	—	—

Note: Heritage FUN Sale, January 2005, XF-45, $2.99 million. Foreign gold coins with the EB counterstamp exist. These are valued at over $5,000, with many much higher.

Fugio "Cent"

KM# EA30.1 • Copper • Obv: Club rays, round ends.

Date	AG	Good	VG	Fine	VF	XF	Unc
1787	225	325	450	950	2,000	3,850	—

KM# EA30.2 • Copper • Obv: Club rays, concave ends.

Date	AG	Good	VG	Fine	VF	XF	Unc
1787	1,500	2,500	4,500	900	27,500	—	—

KM# EA30.3 • Copper • Obv. Legend: FUCIO.

Date	AG	Good	VG	Fine	VF	XF
1787	—	2,000	3,000	7,000	25,000	35,000

KM# EA31.1 • Copper • Obv: Pointed rays. **Rev:** UNITED above, STATES below.

Date	AG	Good	VG	Fine	VF	XF
1787	600	950	1,500	3,250	80,000	11,500

KM# EA31.2 • Copper • Rev: UNITED STATES at sides of ring.

Date	AG	Good	VG	Fine	VF	XF	Unc
1787	110	175	275	550	900	1,800	3,500

KM# EA31.3 • Copper • Rev: STATES UNITED at sides of ring.

Date	AG	Good	VG	Fine	VF	XF	Unc
1787	110	190	275	550	850	1,650	3,500

KM# EA31.4 • Copper • Rev: Eight-pointed stars on ring.

Date	AG	Good	VG	Fine	VF	XF	Unc
1787	150	285	475	700	1,250	2,750	9,000

KM# EA31.5 • Copper • Rev: Raised rims on ring, large lettering in center.

Date	AG	Good	VG	Fine	VF	XF	Unc
1787	185	325	550	950	2,750	6,000	18,500

KM# EA32.1 • Copper • Obv: No cinquefoils, cross after date. **Obv. Legend:** UNITED STATES.

Date	AG	Good	VG	Fine	VF	XF	Unc
1787	300	485	750	1,450	3,850	6,700	—

KM# EA32.2 • Copper • Obv: No cinquefoils, cross after date. **Obv. Legend:** STATES UNITED.

Date	AG	Good	VG	Fine	VF	XF	Unc
1787	175	350	750	1,500	4,000	7,200	—

KM# EA32.3 • Copper • Obv: No cinquefoils, cross after date. **Rev:** Raised rims on ring.

Date	AG	Good	VG	Fine	VF	XF	Unc
1787	—	—	—	—	27,500	—	—

KM# EA33 • Copper • Obv: No cinquefoils, cross after date. **Rev:** With rays. **Rev. Legend:** AMERICAN CONGRESS.

Date	VG	Fine	VF	XF
1787 extremely rare	—	—	225,000	300,000

Note: Norweb $63,800

KM# EA34 • Brass • Note: New Haven restrike.

Date	AG	Good	VG	Fine	VF	XF	Unc
1787	—	—	—	—	—	450	1,000

KM# EA34a • Copper • Note: New Haven restrike.

Date	AG	Good	VG	Fine	VF	XF	Unc
1787	—	—	—	—	450	750	1,000

KM# EA34b • Silver • Note: New Haven restrike.

Date	Good	VG	Fine	VF	XF	Unc
1787(ca.1858)	—	—	—	—	2,750	4,000

KM# EA34c • Gold • Note: New Haven restrike.

Date	AG	Good	VG	Fine	VF	XF
1787(ca.1858) 2 known	—	—	—	—	—	—

Note: Norweb (holed) $1,430

ISSUES OF 1792

CENT

KM# PnE1 • Bi-Metallic, Silver center in Copper ring •

Date	Good	VG	Fine	VF	XF
1792 14 known	—	—	185,000	325,000	475,000

Note: Norweb, MS-60, $143,000; Heritage 4-12; MS61 $1.15 million

KM# PnF1 • Copper • Note: No silver center.

Date	Good	VG	Fine	VF	XF
1792 9 known	—	—	250,000	500,000	750,000

Note: Norweb, EF-40, $35,200; Benson, VG-10, $57,500

KM# PnG1 • Copper • Edge: Plain **Note:** Commonly called "Birch cent."

Date	AG	Good	VG	Fine	VF	XF
1792 unique	—	—	—	—	—	650,000

KM# PnH1 • Copper • Obv: One star in edge legend **Note:** Commonly called "Birch cent."

Date	AG	Good	VG	Fine	VF	XF
1792 2 known	—	—	—	—	—	600,000

Note: Norweb, EF-40, $59,400

KM# PnI1 • Copper • Obv: Two stars in edge legend **Note:** Commonly called "Birch cent."

Date	Good	VG	Fine	VF	XF
1792 8 known	—	—	200,000	400,000	550,000

Note: Hawn, strong VF, $57,750

KM# PnJ1 • White Metal • Rev: "G.W.Pt." below wreath tie **Note:** Commonly called "Birch cent."

Date	AG	Good	VG	Fine	VF	XF
1792 unique	—	—	—	—	—	—

Note: Garrett, $90,000

HALF DISME

KM# 5 • Silver •

Date	AG	VG	Fine	VF	XF	Unc
1792	25,000	35,000	55,000	90,000	125,000	450,000

KM# PnA1 • Copper •

Date		AG	Good	VG	Fine	VF	XF
1792	unique	—	—	—	—	—	—

Note: Heritage Auction, 4-06, 5p-67 realized $1,322,500

DISME

KM# PnB1 • Silver •

Date		Good	VG	Fine	VF	XF
1792	3 known	—	—	—	700,000	1,000,000

Note: Norweb, EF-40, $28,600

KM# PnC1 • Copper • Edge: Reeded

Date		VG	Fine	VF	XF	Unc
1792	14 known	—	—	150,000	250,000	500,000

Note: Hawn, VF, $30,800; Benson, EF-45, $109,250

KM# PnD1 • Copper • Edge: Plain

Date		Good	VG	Fine	VF	XF
1792	2 known	—	—	—	450,000	750,000

Note: Garrett, $45,000

QUARTER

KM# PnK1 • Copper • Edge: Reeded Note:
Commonly called "Wright quarter."

Date		AG	Good	VG	Fine	VF	XF
1792	2 known	—	—	—	—	—	—

KM# PnL1 • White Metal • Edge: Plain Note:
Commonly called "Wright quarter."

Date		AG	Good	VG	Fine	VF	XF
1792	4 known	—	—	—	—	175,000	—

Note: Norweb, VF-30 to EF-40, $28,600

KM# PnM1 • White Metal • Note: Commonly
called "Wright quarter."

Date		AG	Good	VG	Fine	VF	XF
1792	die trial	—	—	—	—	—	—

Note: Garrett, $12,000

UNITED STATES
CIRCULATION COINAGE

HALF CENT

Liberty Cap Half Cent
Head facing left obverse

KM# 10 • 6.74 g., **Copper**, 22 mm. • **Designer:** Henry Voigt

Date	Mintage	G4	VG8	F12	VF20	XF40	MS60
1793	35,334	3,900	6,100	10,750	15,500	27,000	72,000

Head facing right obverse

KM# 14 • **Copper**, 6.74 g. (1794-95) and 5.44 g. (1795-97), 23.5 mm. • **Designer:** Robert Scot (1794) and John Smith Gardner (1795) **Note:** The "lettered edge" varieties have TWO HUNDRED FOR A DOLLAR inscribed around the edge. The "pole" varieties have a pole upon which the cap is hanging, resting on Liberty's shoulder. The "punctuated date" varieties have a comma after the 1 in the date. The 1797 "1 above 1" variety has a second 1 above the 1 in the date.

Date		Mintage	G4	VG8	F12	VF20	XF40	MS60
1794	Normal Relief Head, lg letters	81,600	485	700	1,135	2,500	5,000	20,000
1794	High Relief Head, Lt wreath	Inc. above	485	700	1,135	2,500	5,000	20,000
1795	lettered edge, pole	25,600	535	750	1,450	2,900	5,400	17,500
1795	plain edge, no pole	109,000	485	775	1,400	2,750	5,250	16,000
1795	lettered edge, punctuated date	Inc. above	560	700	2,500	3,750	8,000	50,000
1795	plain edge, punctuated date	Inc. above	485	1,000	1,450	2,800	5,250	57,500
1796	pole	5,090	20,000	50,000	53,500	75,000	75,000	—
1796	no pole	1,390	32,000	42,500	47,500	75,000	—	—
1797	plain edge	119,215	485	750	125,000	200,000	6,500	57,500
1797	lettered edge	Inc. above	1,850	5,700	1,260	2,750	40,000	—
1797	1 above 1	Inc. above	505	750	10,000	25,000	5,000	50,000
1797	gripped edge	Inc. above	140,000	250,000	1,135	2,500	—	—

Draped Bust Half Cent
Draped bust right, date at angle below obverse   Value within thin wreath reverse

Stemless   Stems

KM# 33 • 5.44 g., **Copper**, 23.5 mm. • **Obv. Legend:** LIBERTY **Rev. Legend:** UNITED STATES OF AMERICA **Designer:** Robert Scot **Note:** The wreath on the reverse was redesigned slightly in 1802, resulting in "reverse of 1800" and "reverse of 1802" varieties. The "stems" varieties have stems extending from the wreath above and on both sides of the fraction on the reverse. On the 1804 "crosslet 4" variety, a serif appears at the far right of the crossbar on the 4 in the date. The "spiked chin" variety appears to have a spike extending from Liberty's chin, the result of a damaged die. Varieties of the 1805 strikes are distinguished by the size of the 5 in the date. Varieties of the 1806 strikes are distinguished by the size of the 6 in the date.

Date	Mintage	G4	VG8	F12	VF20	XF40	MS60
1800	211,530	75.00	90.00	160	205	600	5,500
1802/0 rev. 1800	14,366	23,500	55,000	—	—	—	—
1802/0 rev. 1802	Inc. above	875	2,000	6,500	9,000	—	—
1803	97,900	75.00	95.00	140	325	950	7,000
1804 plain 4, stemless wreath	1,055,312	60.00	80.00	125	215	385	1,400
1804 plain 4, stems	Inc. above	60.00	110	175	325	1,850	15,000
1804 crosslet 4, stemless	Inc. above	65.00	90.00	135	240	410	1,350
1804 crosslet 4, stems	Inc. above	62.00	90.00	160	260	450	1,500
1804 spiked chin	Inc. above	75.00	105	190	260	435	1,500
1805 small 5, stemless	814,464	65.00	90.00	140	240	410	3,500
1805 small 5, stems	Inc. above	1,850	2,350	5,400	8,000	35,000	—
1805 large 5, stems	Inc. above	85.00	125	135	305	650	3,000
1806 small 6, stems	356,000	500	475	750	1,350	5,750	—
1806 small 6, stemless	Inc. above	65.00	85.00	135	260	435	1,350
1806 large 6, stems	Inc. above	65.00	85.00	135	260	460	1,500
1807	476,000	75.00	95.00	190	275	485	1,400
1808/7	400,000	300	400	600	1,500	4,250	57,500
1808	Inc. above	95.00	130	175	295	600	5,000

Classic Head Half Cent

Classic head left, flanked by stars, date below obverse   Value within wreath reverse

KM# 41 • 5.44 g., **Copper**, 23.5 mm. • **Rev. Legend:** UNITED STATES OF AMERICA **Designer:** John Reich **Note:** Restrikes listed were produced privately in the mid-1800s. The 1831 restrikes have two varieties with different sized berries in the wreath on the reverse. The 1828 strikes have either 12 or 13 stars on the obverse.

Date	Mintage	G4	VG8	F12	VF20	XF40	MS60Brn
1809/6	1,154,572	60.00	95.00	100	125	300	1,000
1809	Inc. above	59.00	80.00	90.00	107	185	800
1809 circle in 0	—	76.00	95.00	150	375	750	5,100
1810	215,000	66.00	105	150	325	600	3,550
1811 Close Date	63,140	300	950	1,650	2,400	5,500	—
1811 Wide Date Inc. Above	—	290	725	1,550	2,550	4,750	—
1811 restrike, reverse of 1802, uncirculated	—	—	—	—	—	—	57,500
1825	63,000	56.00	75.00	85.00	110	155	950
1826	234,000	53.00	72.00	82.00	99.00	125	750
1828 13 stars	606,000	51.00	70.00	75.00	82.00	105	235
1828 12 stars	Inc. above	61.00	80.00	125	160	275	850
1829	487,000	53.00	73.00	82.00	102	125	500
1831 original	2,200	—	—	—	—	65,000	—
1831 1st restrike, lg. berries, reverse of 1836	—	—	—	—	—	—	6,500
1831 2nd restrike, sm. berries, reverse of 1840, proof	—	—	—	—	—	—	55,000
1832	154,000	51.00	70.00	75.00	82.00	105	235
1833	120,000	51.00	70.00	75.00	82.00	105	235
1834	141,000	51.00	70.00	75.00	82.00	105	235
1835	398,000	51.00	70.00	75.00	82.00	105	235
1836 original, proof	—	—	—	—	—	—	6,000
1836 restrike, reverse of 1840, proof	—	—	—	—	—	—	50,000

Braided Hair Half Cent

Head left, braided hair, within circle of stars, date below obverse
Value within wreath reverse

KM# 70 • 5.44 g., Copper, 23 mm. • **Rev. Legend:** UNITED STATES OF AMERICA **Designer:** Christian Gobrecht **Note:** 1840-1849 and 1852 strikes, both originals and restrikes, are known in proof only; mintages are unknown. The small-date varieties of 1849, both originals and restrikes are known in proof only. The restrikes were produced clandestinely by Philadelphia Mint personnel in the mid-1800s.

Date	G4	VG8	F12	VF20	XF40	AU50	MS60	PF60Brn
1840 original	—	—	—	—	3,000	3,500	—	—
1840 1st restrike	—	—	—	—	3,000	3,500	—	—
1840 2nd restrike	—	—	—	—	3,000	3,500	—	—
1841 original	—	—	—	—	3,000	3,500	—	—
1841 1st restrike	—	—	—	—	3,000	3,500	—	—
1841 2nd restrike	—	—	—	—	3,000	3,500	—	—
1842 original	—	—	—	—	3,000	3,500	—	—
1842 1st restrike	—	—	—	—	3,000	3,500	—	—
1842 2nd restrike	—	—	—	—	3,000	3,500	—	—
1843 original	—	—	—	—	3,000	3,500	—	—
1843 1st restrike	—	—	—	—	3,000	3,500	—	—
1843 2nd restrike	—	—	—	—	3,000	3,500	—	—
1844 original	—	—	—	—	3,000	3,500	—	—
1844 1st restrike	—	—	—	—	3,000	3,500	—	—
1844 2nd restrike	—	—	—	—	3,000	3,500	—	—
1845 original	—	—	—	—	3,000	3,500	—	—
1845 1st restrike	—	—	—	—	3,000	3,500	—	—
1845 2nd restrike	—	—	—	—	3,000	3,500	—	—
1846 original	—	—	—	—	3,000	3,500	—	—
1846 1st restrike	—	—	—	—	3,000	3,500	—	—
1846 2nd restrike	—	—	—	—	3,000	3,500	—	—
1847 original	—	—	—	—	3,000	3,500	—	—
1847 1st restrike	—	—	—	—	5,500	6,000	—	—
1847 2nd restrike	—	—	—	—	3,000	3,500	—	—
1848 original	—	—	—	—	3,000	3,500	—	—
1848 1st restrike	—	—	—	—	3,000	3,500	—	—
1848 2nd restrike	—	—	—	—	3,000	3,500	—	—
1849 original, small date	—	—	—	—	3,000	3,500	—	—
1849 1st restrike small date	—	—	—	—	3,000	3,500	—	—
1849 large date	58.00	76.00	82.00	92.00	150	200	300	—
1850	58.00	76.00	82.00	92.00	110	175	340	—
1851	54.00	71.00	77.00	84.00	96.00	155	220	—
1852 original	15,000	55,000	30,000	35,000	40,000	47,000	—	—
1852 1st restrike	1,000	1,500	1,850	2,600	3,000	3,500	—	—
1852 2nd restrike	1,000	1,500	1,850	2,600	3,000	3,500	—	—
1853	54.00	71.00	77.00	84.00	96.00	155	220	—
1854	54.00	71.00	77.00	84.00	96.00	155	220	—
1855	54.00	71.00	77.00	84.00	96.00	155	220	—
1856	54.00	71.00	77.00	84.00	96.00	165	220	—
1857	59.00	78.00	87.00	110	175	250	295	—

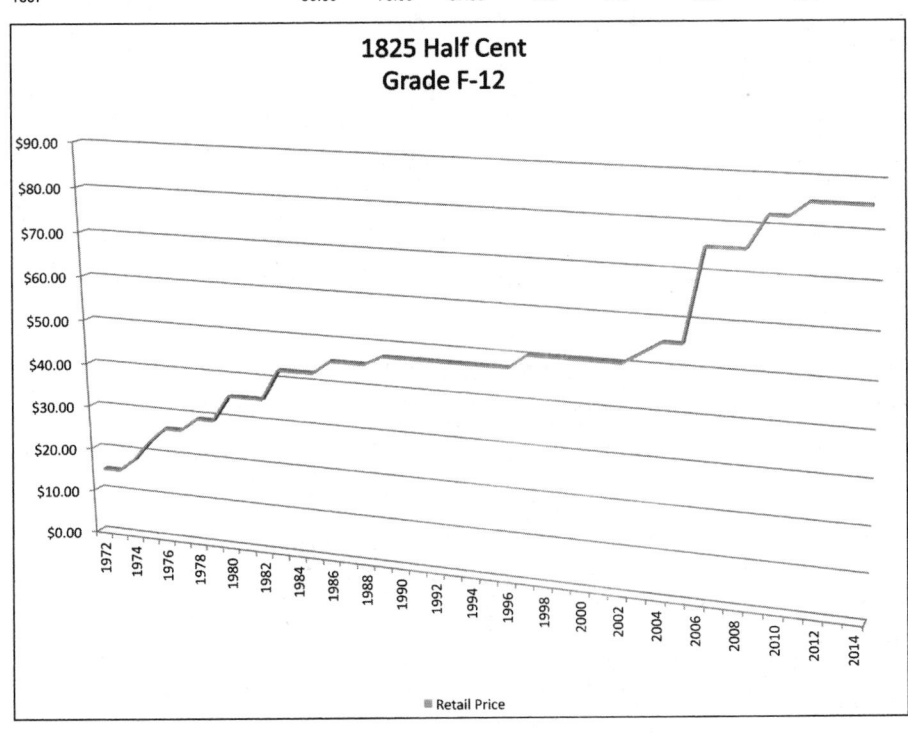

1825 Half Cent
Grade F-12

CENT

Flowing Hair Cent
Chain reverse

KM# 11 • 13.48 g., **Copper**, 26-27 mm. • **Designer:** Henry Voigt

Date		Mintage	G4	VG8	F12	VF20	XF40	MS60
1793	AMERI	36,103	9,950	14,850	25,500	45,500	96,000	245,000
1793	AMERICA	Inc. above	6,950	10,600	17,750	36,500	71,500	140,000
1793	periods after "LIBERTY	Inc. above	7,850	12,350	19,850	38,500	73,500	147,000

Wreath reverse

KM# 12 • 13.48 g., **Copper**, 26-28 mm. • **Designer:** Henry Voigt

Date		Mintage	G4	VG8	F12	VF20	XF40	MS60
1793	vine and bars edge	63,353	3,150	4,450	7,750	12,000	22,500	48,500
1793	lettered edge	Inc. above	3,450	5,150	8,850	14,000	25,500	56,000
1793	strawberry leaf; 4 known	—	350,000	550,000	875,000	—	—	—

Liberty Cap Cent

KM# 13 • **Copper**, 13.48 g., 29 mm. • **Designer:** Joseph Wright **Note:** The heavier pieces were struck on a thicker planchet. The Liberty design on the obverse was revised slightly in 1794, but the 1793 design was used on some 1794 strikes. A 1795 "lettered edge" variety has ONE HUNDRED FOR A DOLLAR and a leaf inscribed on the edge.

Date		Mintage	G4	VG8	F12	VF20	XF40	MS60
1793	cap	11,056	5,500	12,500	23,500	45,000	98,500	—
1794	NO FRACTION BAR	Inc. above	500	800	1,350	3,000	8,000	40,000
1794	head '93	918,521	1,550	2,600	4,250	9,850	21,500	85,000
1794	head '94	Inc. above	445	710	1,200	2,425	4,500	16,500
1794	head '95	Inc. above	530	775	1,265	2,775	5,000	20,000
1794	starred rev.	Inc. above	13,500	23,500	44,500	115,000	275,000	—
1795	Lettered Edge	Inc. above	515	650	1,375	3,200	4,500	16,500
1795	plain edge	501,500	375	610	1,050	1,775	3,800	12,500
1795	reeded edge	Inc. above	350,000	700,000	—	—	—	—
1795	Jefferson head plain edge	Inc. above	24,500	49,500	95,000	150,000	—	—
1795	Jefferson head lettered edge	Inc. above	75,000	95,000	155,000	250,000	—	—

KM# 13a • 10.89 g., **Copper**, 29 mm. • **Designer:** John Smith Gardner

Date	Mintage	G4	VG8	F12	VF20	XF40	MS60
1795 lettered edge, "One Cent" high in wreath	37,000	445	735	1,100	2,175	4,800	15,000
1796	109,825	425	610	1,650	3,850	9,500	36,500

Draped Bust Cent
Draped bust right, date at angle below obverse   Value within wreath reverse

 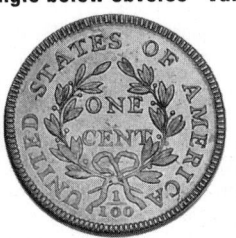

Stemless   Stems

KM# 22 • 10.98 g., **Copper**, 29 mm. • **Obv. Legend:** LIBERTY **Rev. Legend:** UNITED STATES OF AMERICA **Designer:** Robert Scot **Note:** The 1801 "3 errors" variety has the fraction on the reverse reading "1/000," has only one stem extending from the wreath above and on both sides of the fraction on the reverse, and UNITED in UNITED STATES OF AMERICA appears as "linited."

Date	Mintage	G4	VG8	F12	VF20	XF40	MS60
1796 reverse of 1794	363,375	300	450	1,050	2,800	6,850	—
1796 reverse of 1795	Inc. above	260	375	850	3,250	9,500	36,500
1796 reverse of 1797	Inc. above	240	350	1,050	2,150	4,250	11,000
1796 Liberty error	Inc. above	450	850	1,800	5,500	13,500	75,000
1797 reverse of 1795 plain edge	897,510	165	300	600	3,450	5,500	38,500
1797 reverse of 1795 gripped edge	Inc. above	185	425	850	1,450	4,750	—
1797 stems	Inc. above	165	325	450	1,275	2,650	9,000
1797 stemless	Inc. above	300	495	750	1,850	4,750	38,500
1797 reverse of 1795	—	—	—	—	—	—	9,500
1798 reverse of 1795	—	—	—	—	—	—	7,000
1798 reverse of 1796	Inc. above	150	250	600	1,750	3,600	9,500
1798 1st hair style	Inc. above	90.00	130	325	800	4,450	9,850
1798 2nd hair style	Inc. above	85.00	125	310	750	2,850	8,000
1798/7	1,841,745	200	325	650	2,100	5,100	22,000
1799	42,540	2,750	4,650	11,500	24,500	85,000	650,000
1799/98	Inc. above	2,600	4,300	11,000	34,000	110,000	—
1800	2,822,175	100	165	375	1,850	3,000	12,500
1800/798	Inc. above	85.00	225	550	1,550	4,000	—
1800/79	Inc. above	80.00	200	375	1,500	3,300	16,500
1801	1,362,837	75.00	100	250	700	2,025	7,750
1801 3 errors	Inc. above	225	500	1,150	2,400	6,850	35,000
1801 1/000	Inc. above	80.00	175	475	1,350	2,650	9,850
1801 100/000	Inc. above	150	325	850	1,650	4,200	12,500
1802	3,435,100	65.00	100	250	535	1,500	4,500
1802 stemless	Inc. above	68.00	95.00	200	515	1,800	5,000
1802 1/000	Inc. above	80.00	135	325	750	1,750	7,500
1803 small date, small fraction	2,471,353	65.00	100	225	425	1,200	3,850
1803 small date, large fraction	Inc. above	65.00	100	225	435	1,250	4,050
1803 large date, small fraction	Inc. above	4,600	11,500	14,500	42,000	75,000	—
1803 large date, large fraction	Inc. above	80.00	135	450	1,550	3,150	—
1803 1/100 over 1/1000	—	95.00	165	360	900	2,600	10,000
1803 Stemless wreath	—	80.00	150	350	650	2,100	6,950
1804	96,500	1,650	2,650	4,000	8,950	16,500	80,000
1804 Restrike of 1860	—	—	—	650	750	875	1,750
1805	941,116	60.00	90.00	245	425	1,600	4,650
1806	348,000	70.00	110	305	600	2,075	7,500
1807 small fraction	727,221	65.00	100	265	625	2,200	4,600
1807 large fraction	Inc. above	65.00	100	225	510	1,400	3,850
1807/6 large 7/6	Inc. above	65.00	175	225	625	1,700	—

Date	Mintage	G4	VG8	F12	VF20	XF40	MS60
1807/6 small 7/6	Inc. above	1,900	4,250	9,500	24,500	49,500	—
1807 Comet Variety	Inc. above	95.00	175	345	1,100	3,200	16,500

Classic Head Cent
Classic head left, flanked by stars, date below obverse   Value within wreath reverse

KM# 39 • 10.89 g., **Copper**, 29 mm. • **Rev. Legend:** UNITED STATES OF AMERICA **Designer:** John Reich

Date	Mintage	G4	VG8	F12	VF20	XF40	MS60
1808	1,109,000	121	160	535	700	1,850	9,500
1809	222,867	135	285	450	1,050	3,350	13,500
1810/09	1,458,500	90.00	160	515	910	1,850	10,500
1810	Inc. above	75.00	110	415	910	1,550	9,500
1811/10	218,025	175	300	700	1,950	4,650	60,000
1811	Inc. above	110	225	575	1,300	3,350	11,000
1812 small date	1,075,500	90.00	155	440	885	2,125	8,000
1812 large date	—	90.00	155	440	895	2,175	8,500
1813	418,000	60.00	175	400	800	1,950	9,000
1814 Plain 4	357,830	90.00	160	400	910	1,925	6,800
1814 Crosslet 4	Inc. above	90.00	155	390	885	1,825	6,650

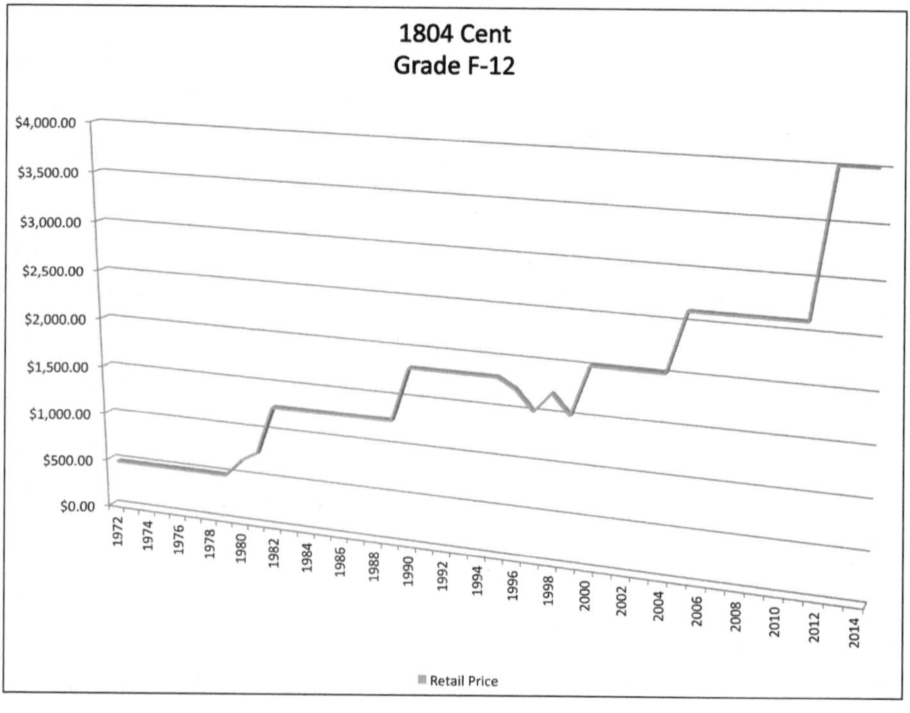

1804 Cent
Grade F-12

Retail Price

Coronet Cent

Coronet head left, within circle of stars, date below obverse   Value within wreath reverse

KM# 45 • 10.89 g., **Copper**, 28-29 mm. • **Rev. Legend:** UNITED STATES OF AMERICA **Designer:** Robert Scot

Date	Mintage	G4	VG8	F12	VF20	XF40	MS60
1816	2,820,982	31.00	42.00	60.00	117	245	1,350
1817 13 obverse stars	3,948,400	29.00	33.00	44.00	74.00	155	650
1817 15 obverse stars	Inc. above	35.00	56.00	90.00	225	675	2,650
1818	3,167,000	29.00	35.00	42.00	74.00	150	450
1819 Large date, 9/8	2,671,000	—	—	—	—	—	—
1819	—	31.00	38.00	46.00	116	315	1,000
1819/8	—	—	—	—	—	—	—
1819 Large date	Inc. above	29.00	33.00	42.00	78.00	183	600
1819 Small date	Inc. above	30.00	35.00	45.00	82.00	203	675
1820 Large date, 20/19	4,407,550	31.00	38.00	50.00	88.00	250	950
1820 Large date	—	33.00	39.00	60.00	117	335	1,600
1820 Small date	—	29.00	36.00	46.00	78.00	188	450
1821	389,000	45.00	72.00	200	525	1,375	7,500
1822	2,072,339	31.00	45.00	45.00	150	365	1,500
1823 Included in 1824 mintage	—	90.00	200	450	1,350	3,950	30,000
1823/22 Included in 1824 mintage	—	80.00	165	425	975	3,250	—
1823 Restrike	—	600	650	700	800	900	1,850
1824	1,262,000	31.00	35.00	46.00	210	450	1,950
1824/22	Inc. above	40.00	49.00	110	440	1,000	5,500
1825	1,461,100	30.00	35.00	45.00	125	400	2,150
1826	1,517,425	30.00	35.00	45.00	87.00	265	950
1826/25	Inc. above	40.00	55.00	95.00	275	1,200	4,250
1827	2,357,732	29.00	33.00	42.00	92.00	260	800
1828 Large date	2,260,624	29.00	33.00	44.00	87.00	225	900
1828 Small date	—	32.00	37.00	49.00	110	265	1,650
1829 Large letters	1,414,500	29.00	33.00	40.00	93.00	208	1,100
1829 Medium letters	Inc. above	32.00	45.00	90.00	275	675	5,250
1830 Large letters	1,711,500	25.00	29.00	36.00	70.00	188	650
1830 Medium letters	Inc. above	45.00	90.00	265	650	1,650	7,500
1831 Large letters	3,359,260	25.00	31.00	36.00	70.00	193	500
1831 Medium letters	—	29.00	34.00	41.00	76.00	225	950
1832 Large letters	2,362,000	25.00	31.00	36.00	70.00	158	525
1832 Medium letters	—	27.00	32.00	39.00	74.00	178	850
1833	2,739,000	25.00	31.00	36.00	70.00	158	475
1834 Large 8, stars and letters	1,855,100	75.00	120	145	250	625	2,350
1834 Large 8 & stars, medium letters	Inc. above	190	275	600	1,100	3,250	6,200
1834 Large 8, small stars, medium letters	Inc. above	25.00	29.00	36.00	70.00	158	650
1834 Small 8 & stars	Inc. above	25.00	29.00	36.00	70.00	145	750
1835 Large 8 & stars	3,878,400	25.00	31.00	39.00	74.00	168	1,000
1835 Head '36	—	25.00	31.00	39.00	74.00	158	550
1835 Small 8 & stars	—	25.00	29.00	36.00	70.00	158	650
1836	2,111,000	25.00	29.00	36.00	70.00	125	290
1837 Plain hair cords, medium letters	5,558,300	25.00	29.00	36.00	70.00	125	290
1837 Plain hair cords, small letters	Inc. above	25.00	31.00	39.00	74.00	133	485
1837 Head '38	Inc. above	25.00	31.00	39.00	74.00	125	250
1838	6,370,200	25.00	29.00	36.00	70.00	125	250
1839 Head '38, beaded hair cords	3,128,661	29.00	33.00	40.00	74.00	130	450
1839/36 Plain hair cords	Inc. above	300	600	1,250	2,450	6,800	75,000
1839 Silly head	Inc. above	35.00	40.00	50.00	90.00	165	900
1839 Booby head	Inc. above	34.00	38.00	47.00	85.00	153	875

Braided Hair Cent
Head left, braided hair, within circle of stars, date below obverse
Value within wreath reverse

KM# 67 • 10.89 g., **Copper**, 27.5 mm. • **Rev. Legend:** UNITED STATES OF AMERICA **Designer:** Christian Gobrecht **Note:** 1840 and 1842 strikes are known with both small and large dates, with little difference in value. A slightly larger Liberty head and larger reverse lettering were used beginning in 1843.

Date		Mintage	G4	VG8	F12	VF20	XF40	MS60
1839	Petite Head	3,128,661	29.00	33.00	47.00	62.50	100	825
1840	Large date	2,462,700	25.00	28.00	36.00	51.50	80.00	440
1840	Small date	Inc. above	30.00	35.00	42.00	53.50	90.00	550
1840	Small date over large 18	Inc. above	40.00	50.00	75.00	125	210	1,150
1841		1,597,367	25.00	28.00	36.00	51.50	79.00	450
1842	Small date	2,383,390	25.00	28.00	36.00	51.50	69.00	400
1842	Large date	Inc. above	28.00	32.00	42.00	57.50	100	365
1843	Petite Head, small date	2,425,342	25.00	28.00	35.00	51.50	69.00	360
1843	Petite Head, (rev '44)	Inc. above	27.00	30.00	37.00	51.50	79.00	550
1843	Mature Head	—	28.00	32.00	50.00	140	260	600
1844		2,398,752	25.00	28.00	36.00	51.50	69.00	375
1844/81		Inc. above	40.00	60.00	80.00	100	225	1,900
1845		3,894,804	25.00	28.00	33.00	51.50	69.00	300
1846	Small date	4,120,800	23.00	27.00	31.00	51.50	69.00	225
1846	MD	Inc. above	25.00	28.00	35.00	53.50	72.00	375
1846	TD	Inc. above	36.00	45.00	80.00	125	260	1,650
1847		6,183,669	23.00	27.00	31.00	47.50	65.00	250
1847/7		Inc. above	37.00	50.00	90.00	150	385	1,350
1848		6,415,799	25.00	28.00	33.00	47.50	61.00	215
1849		4,178,500	25.00	28.00	33.00	47.50	61.00	225
1850		4,426,844	25.00	28.00	33.00	39.50	61.00	225
1851		9,889,707	23.00	26.00	31.00	37.50	59.00	195
1851/81		Inc. above	36.00	45.00	60.00	90.00	175	700
1852		5,063,094	23.00	26.00	31.00	37.50	59.00	195
1853		6,641,131	23.00	26.00	31.00	37.50	59.00	195
1854		4,236,156	23.00	26.00	31.00	37.50	59.00	195
1855	Slanted 5's	1,574,829	43.00	56.00	65.00	74.50	95.00	245
1855	Upright 5's	Inc. above	23.00	26.00	33.00	37.50	59.00	195
1855	Slanted 5's Knob on Ear	Inc. above	27.00	34.00	46.00	70.00	99.00	450
1856	Slanted 5	2,690,463	23.00	26.00	31.00	37.50	59.00	195
1856	Upright 5	Inc. above	30.00	40.00	52.00	63.50	80.00	250
1857	Large date	333,456	90.00	125	175	235	310	600
1857	Small date	Inc. above	75.00	100	160	195	265	550

Flying Eagle Cent
Flying eagle above date obverse   Value within wreath reverse

Large
letters—
AM
touch at
bottom

Small
letters—
Space
between
AM

KM# 85 • 4.67 g., **Copper-Nickel**, 19 mm. • **Obv. Legend:** UNITED STATES OF AMERICA **Designer:** James B. Longacre **Note:** On the large-letter variety of 1858, the "A" and "M" in AMERICA are connected at their bases; on the small-letter variety, the two letters are separated.

Date		Mintage	G4	VG8	F12	VF20	XF40	AU50	MS60	MS65	Prf65
1856		Est. 2500	6,250	7,250	9,000	10,750	12,850	13,500	16,500	65,000	28,500
1857		17,450,000	27.50	39.00	40.00	47.00	140	210	425	3,500	29,000
1858/7		Inc. below	65.00	92.50	175	380	760	1,500	3,300	60,000	—
1858	large letters	24,600,000	28.00	41.00	43.50	56.00	160	230	445	3,850	24,500
1858	small letters	Inc. above	27.50	39.00	42.00	47.00	140	210	425	3,650	30,000

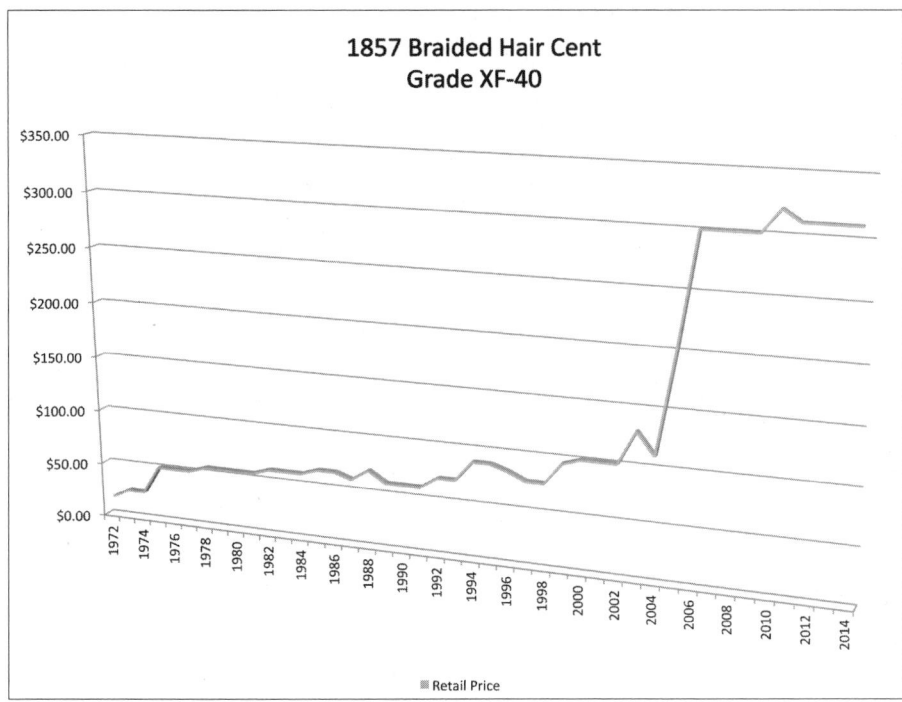

Indian Head Cent
Indian head with headdress left above date obverse   Value within wreath reverse

KM# 87 • 4.67 g., **Copper-Nickel**, 19 mm. • **Obv. Legend:** UNITED STATES OF AMERICA **Designer:** James B. Longacre

Date	Mintage	G4	VG8	F12	VF20	XF40	AU50	MS60	MS65	Prf65
1859	36,400,000	13.00	16.00	22.50	48.00	100	175	230	3,650	5,200

Indian head with headdress left above date obverse
Value within wreath, shield above reverse

KM# 90 • 4.67 g., **Copper-Nickel**, 19 mm. • **Obv. Legend:** UNITED STATES OF AMERICA **Designer:** James B. Longacre

Date		Mintage	G4	VG8	F12	VF20	XF40	AU50	MS60	MS65	Prf65
1860	Rounded Bust	20,566,000	11.00	15.00	22.00	46.00	68.00	110	190	965	3,600
1860		1,000	—	—	—	—	—	—	—	—	—
1860	Pointed Bust	Inc. above	20.00	30.00	42.00	60.00	100	160	300	6,000	—
1861		10,100,000	23.00	30.00	42.00	58.00	95.00	160	180	975	7,250
1862		28,075,000	11.50	11.50	12.50	15.00	28.00	60.00	80.00	1,050	2,350
1863		49,840,000	9.00	9.25	11.00	12.50	25.00	58.00	75.00	1,050	3,100
1864		13,740,000	20.00	28.50	35.00	72.00	125	175	220	1,400	3,200

Indian head with headdress left above date obverse
Value within wreath, shield above reverse

1864 "L"

KM# 90a • 3.11 g., **Bronze**, 19 mm. • Obv. **Legend:** UNITED STATES OF AMERICA **Designer:** James B. Longacre **Note:**
The 1864 "L" variety has the designer's initial in Liberty's hair to the right of her neck.

Date	Mintage	G4	VG8	F12	VF20	XF40	AU50	MS60	MS65	Prf65
1864	39,233,714	12.50	20.00	25.00	45.00	70.00	80.00	110	335	10,500
1864 L pointed bust	Inc. above	52.50	72.50	139	185	275	325	410	1,700	200,000
1865 plain 5	35,429,286	13.00	14.50	20.00	25.00	45.00	60.00	90.00	485	6,750
1865 fancy 5	Inc. above	12.50	14.00	18.50	23.00	40.00	55.00	85.00	465	—
1866	9,826,500	52.00	66.00	80.00	115	195	240	280	1,350	4,500
1867	9,821,000	52.00	72.00	110	120	195	240	285	1,350	6,100
1867/1867	Inc. above	65.00	85.00	130	190	275	385	565	1,950	—
1868	10,266,500	38.50	50.00	77.00	120	180	245	265	985	5,750
1869/9	6,420,000	190	375	525	750	865	1,000	1,250	2,350	—
1869	Inc. above	90.00	125	230	335	450	560	625	1,750	3,100
1870	5,275,000	62.00	118	225	285	410	510	600	1,400	2,650
1871	3,929,500	88.00	125	280	310	420	510	610	2,400	2,500
1872	4,042,000	110	180	345	425	625	750	840	3,850	4,250
1873 closed 3	11,676,500	30.00	52.00	95.00	135	235	300	400	2,850	2,950
1873 open 3	Inc. above	21.00	34.00	65.00	82.00	175	215	250	1,300	—
1873 Double Liberty die 1	Inc. above	275	450	950	1,500	2,400	4,250	7,500	—	—
1873 Double Liberty die 2	Inc. above	—	—	450	900	1,650	2,800	4,500	—	—
1874	14,187,500	15.00	22.50	46.00	65.00	112	150	225	700	2,850
1875	13,528,000	16.50	29.00	56.00	72.00	120	165	215	800	8,500
1876	7,944,000	30.00	39.50	74.00	130	230	295	325	975	2,600
1877	852,500	985	1,190	1,600	2,050	2,650	3,000	3,450	13,000	12,500
1878	5,799,850	27.00	35.00	68.00	135	245	290	350	875	1,375
1879	16,231,200	7.00	10.00	16.50	33.00	75.00	90.00	100	365	1,250
1880	38,964,955	3.50	5.50	6.50	11.00	28.00	48.00	66.00	360	1,250
1881	39,211,575	3.50	4.25	6.50	8.00	22.00	30.00	43.00	325	1,250
1882	38,581,100	3.50	4.25	5.00	10.00	22.00	30.00	40.00	325	1,450
1883	45,589,109	3.00	4.00	4.50	7.50	17.50	30.00	42.00	325	1,600
1884	23,261,742	3.50	4.50	7.00	12.50	29.00	40.00	60.00	460	1,250
1885	11,765,384	6.75	8.00	12.00	27.00	62.00	82.00	105	625	1,500
1886 Type 1 obverse	17,654,290	3.75	6.60	19.75	56.00	148	170	190	1,250	2,650
1886 Type 2 obverse	Inc. above	7.00	10.00	35.00	90.00	200	250	325	2,500	7,500
1887	45,226,483	2.50	3.00	4.00	7.00	19.00	28.00	50.00	400	6,200
1888	37,494,414	2.75	3.25	5.00	8.00	21.00	28.00	48.00	900	5,400
1889	48,869,361	2.25	2.75	3.50	6.00	12.00	26.00	40.00	400	1,900
1890	57,182,854	2.10	2.50	3.00	5.50	10.00	23.00	37.50	400	1,800
1891	47,072,350	2.25	2.75	3.25	5.50	13.00	23.00	37.00	400	2,150
1892	37,649,832	2.40	3.25	4.40	6.00	18.50	25.00	35.00	400	1,325
1893	46,642,195	2.10	2.75	3.25	5.50	10.00	22.00	30.00	340	1,250
1894	16,752,132	5.00	6.00	13.00	20.00	50.00	65.00	85.00	375	1,350
1894/94	Inc. above	24.00	34.00	80.00	150	275	440	800	8,000	—
1895	38,343,636	2.10	2.40	3.50	4.50	11.00	22.00	32.00	200	1,275
1896	39,057,293	1.95	2.50	3.25	4.75	13.00	26.00	34.00	225	1,900
1897	50,466,330	1.95	2.40	2.75	4.00	10.00	22.00	34.00	195	1,600
1898	49,823,079	1.95	2.40	2.75	4.00	10.00	22.00	34.00	195	1,275
1899	53,600,031	1.95	2.20	2.60	4.00	10.00	22.00	34.00	165	1,275
1900	66,833,764	1.95	2.20	2.50	4.00	12.00	23.00	34.00	175	1,275
1901	79,611,143	1.85	2.20	2.50	4.00	11.00	22.00	33.00	165	1,275
1902	87,376,722	1.85	2.20	2.50	4.00	10.00	22.00	32.00	165	1,325
1903	85,094,493	1.85	2.20	2.50	4.00	10.00	21.00	32.00	165	1,275
1904	61,328,015	1.75	2.20	2.50	4.00	10.00	21.00	32.00	165	1,275
1905	80,719,163	1.75	2.20	2.50	3.50	9.00	20.00	32.00	165	1,350
1906	96,022,255	1.75	2.20	2.50	3.50	9.00	21.00	32.00	165	1,275
1907	108,138,618	1.75	2.20	2.50	3.50	8.50	20.00	32.00	165	1,950
1908	32,327,987	1.75	2.30	2.50	3.50	9.00	20.00	32.00	165	1,275
1908 S	1,115,000	79.00	84.00	110	127	170	190	275	700	—
1909	14,370,645	11.00	13.50	14.00	15.50	19.00	30.00	38.00	155	1,275
1909 S	309,000	485	500	535	600	750	800	1,125	2,250	—

CENT

Lincoln Cent
Wheat Ears reverse

KM# 132 • 3.11 g., **Bronze**, 19 mm. • **Designer:** Victor D. Brenner **Note:** The 1909 "VDB" varieties have the designer's initials inscribed at the 6 o'clock position on the reverse. The initials were removed until 1918, when they were restored on the obverse • MS60 and MS63 prices are for brown coins and MS65 prices are for coins that are at least 90% original red.

Date	Mintage	G4	VG8	F12	VF20	XF40	AU50	MS60	MS65	Prf65
1909 VDB	27,995,000	11.50	12.00	12.50	13.50	14.00	16.50	24.00	95.00	2,750
1909 VDB Doubled Die Obverse	Inc. above	—	—	55.00	75.00	100	120	200	1,500	—
1909 S VDB	484,000	660	675	695	800	1,025	1,325	1,575	2,950	—
1909	72,702,618	3.65	3.50	4.35	4.75	5.50	12.50	14.50	85.00	625
1909 S	1,825,000	89.00	105	110	150	225	245	340	750	—
1909 S/S S over horizontal S	Inc. above	115	135	148	200	275	290	365	850	—
1910	146,801,218	0.50	0.60	0.75	1.00	4.25	10.00	17.50	120	610
1910 S	6,045,000	16.50	21.00	21.00	28.00	47.50	72.00	98.00	425	—
1911	101,177,787	0.45	0.60	1.60	2.35	6.75	11.00	18.50	175	525
1911 D	12,672,000	4.75	5.75	9.00	22.50	50.00	75.00	90.00	750	—
1911 S	4,026,000	49.00	53.00	55.00	59.00	75.00	105	175	1,100	—
1912	68,153,060	1.60	1.75	2.35	5.50	13.50	26.00	33.00	235	625
1912 D	10,411,000	6.50	9.25	10.00	26.00	70.00	110	165	800	—
1912 S	4,431,000	24.00	26.00	29.00	42.00	78.00	118	175	1,250	—
1913	76,532,352	0.80	1.00	1.45	3.20	18.50	28.50	34.50	240	625
1913 D	15,804,000	2.75	3.25	3.60	11.00	49.00	62.00	105	875	—
1913 S	6,101,000	13.50	16.50	21.00	31.00	57.00	110	195	2,100	—
1914	75,238,432	0.60	0.95	2.10	6.00	18.50	40.00	52.00	240	625
1914 D	1,193,000	190	200	245	365	760	1,475	2,000	9,500	—
1914 S	4,137,000	25.00	27.50	30.00	40.00	85.00	175	310	3,250	—
1915	29,092,120	2.25	2.90	4.00	18.00	60.00	70.00	82.00	375	625
1915 D	22,050,000	2.25	2.85	4.50	6.85	24.00	44.00	72.00	350	—
1915 S	4,833,000	21.00	24.50	28.50	32.00	70.00	96.00	190	2,600	—

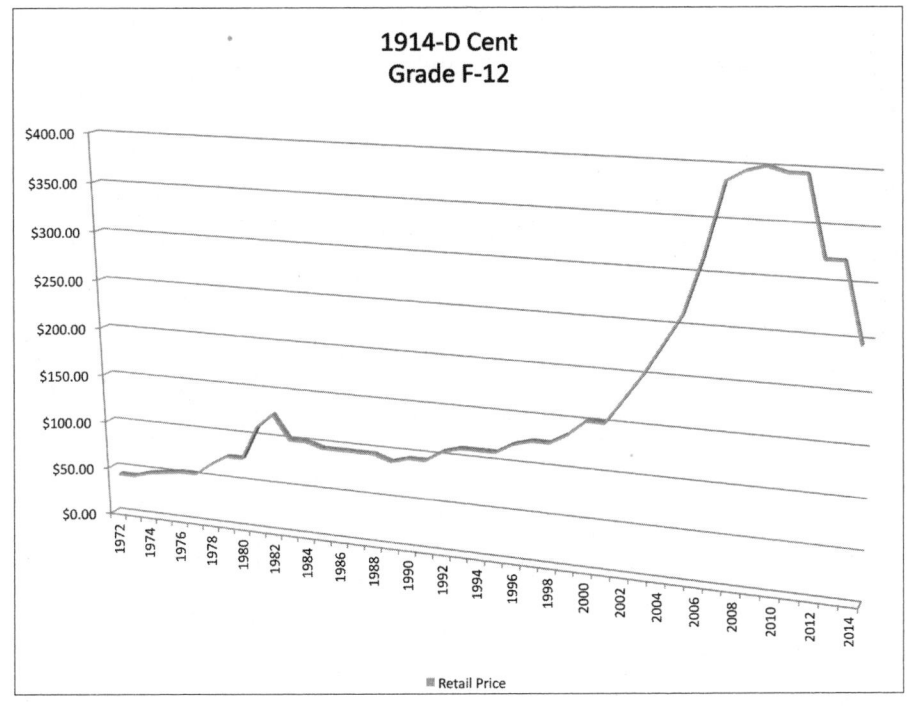

**1914-D Cent
Grade F-12**

Retail Price

Date	Mintage	G4	VG8	F12	VF20	XF40	AU50	MS60	MS65	Prf65
1916	131,833,677	0.45	0.55	0.85	2.40	8.00	14.50	19.00	135	650
1916 D	35,956,000	1.35	2.00	3.10	6.50	17.50	38.00	88.00	850	—
1916 S	22,510,000	1.65	3.25	4.40	9.50	27.50	48.00	105	1,100	—
1917	196,429,785	0.30	0.40	0.55	1.85	4.75	14.50	18.50	150	—
1917 Doubled Die Obverse	Inc. above	175	225	2.75	350	1,350	2,000	3,200	15,000	—
1917 D	55,120,000	1.00	1.50	2.85	5.00	36.50	44.00	72.00	850	—
1917 S	32,620,000	0.55	0.90	1.40	2.60	11.50	26.00	74.00	1,350	—
1918	288,104,634	0.30	0.40	0.50	1.00	4.40	10.00	13.50	185	—
1918 D	47,830,000	0.95	1.45	2.45	5.50	15.50	36.00	76.00	1,200	—
1918 S	34,680,000	0.40	0.90	1.45	3.65	11.00	33.00	70.00	1,750	—
1919	392,021,000	0.30	0.40	0.50	0.80	1.60	5.75	8.00	85.00	—
1919 D	57,154,000	0.80	1.20	1.60	4.85	12.75	35.00	60.00	775	—
1919 S	139,760,000	0.40	0.60	1.50	2.45	5.75	17.50	48.00	1,175	—
1920	310,165,000	0.25	0.35	0.75	1.25	2.80	7.50	15.50	225	—
1920 D	49,280,000	1.00	1.65	2.90	6.85	18.50	37.00	70.00	650	—
1920 S	46,220,000	0.60	0.80	1.50	2.75	13.00	34.50	105	2,150	—
1921	39,157,000	0.55	0.80	1.15	3.00	10.75	22.50	42.00	175	—
1921 S	15,274,000	1.50	2.00	3.50	6.25	36.50	68.00	110	1,100	—
1922 D	7,160,000	23.50	24.50	25.50	27.00	37.50	75.00	105	475	—
1922 D Weak Rev	Inc. above	22.00	23.00	24.00	25.50	34.00	65.00	95.00	400	—
1922 D Weak D	Inc. above	30.00	44.00	48.00	60.00	135	190	285	7,500	—
1922 No D Die 2 Strong Rev	Inc. above	550	580	730	925	2,050	4,250	10,500	85,000	—
1922 No D Die 3 Weak Rev	Inc. above	300	375	575	750	1,650	3,350	8,500	45,000	—
1923	74,723,000	0.40	0.60	0.85	1.50	5.75	10.50	13.50	160	—
1923 S	8,700,000	5.85	7.00	8.50	12.50	42.00	105	190	2,850	—
1924	75,178,000	0.25	0.35	0.45	1.00	5.25	11.00	17.50	120	—
1924 D	2,520,000	37.50	45.00	50.00	62.00	118	170	255	1,800	—
1924 S	11,696,000	1.25	1.50	2.75	5.35	34.50	68.00	110	2,350	—
1925	139,949,000	0.25	0.35	0.45	0.70	3.00	6.50	9.50	65.00	—
1925 D	22,580,000	1.00	1.65	3.10	6.25	15.50	30.00	62.00	625	—
1925 S	26,380,000	0.80	1.20	1.85	2.75	11.75	31.50	85.00	3,650	—
1926	157,088,000	0.25	0.35	0.45	0.60	1.65	5.25	7.50	70.00	—
1926 D	28,020,000	1.50	1.70	3.40	5.25	15.50	34.00	82.00	800	—
1926 S	4,550,000	9.00	10.00	11.75	16.50	35.00	72.00	140	5,500	—
1927	144,440,000	0.20	0.25	0.35	0.60	1.60	5.25	7.50	60.00	—
1927 D	27,170,000	1.15	1.70	2.25	3.35	7.50	25.00	60.00	525	—
1927 S	14,276,000	1.40	1.85	2.65	5.25	14.50	42.00	65.00	2,550	—
1928	134,116,000	0.20	0.25	0.35	0.60	1.45	4.00	7.50	82.00	—
1928 D	31,170,000	0.90	1.40	2.15	3.65	6.75	19.00	37.50	300	—
1928 S Small S	17,266,000	1.00	1.65	2.60	4.00	9.50	31.00	71.50	800	—
1928 S Large S	Inc. above	1.65	2.85	4.25	7.50	16.50	55.00	135	1,250	—
1929	185,262,000	0.20	0.25	0.35	0.55	2.75	5.25	7.00	55.00	—
1929 D	41,730,000	0.50	1.00	1.40	2.75	5.85	13.50	25.00	145	—
1929 S	50,148,000	0.60	1.10	1.85	2.80	6.75	14.75	20.00	100	—
1930	157,415,000	0.20	0.25	0.35	0.60	1.25	2.75	4.00	45.00	—
1930 D	40,100,000	0.25	0.35	0.60	0.90	2.00	5.50	11.00	55.00	—
1930 S	24,286,000	0.25	0.35	0.55	0.80	1.50	6.50	9.50	48.00	—
1931	19,396,000	0.65	0.75	1.10	2.00	4.00	9.50	19.00	85.00	—
1931 D	4,480,000	5.00	5.85	6.50	8.00	13.00	33.50	48.50	375	—
1931 S	866,000	60.00	66.00	71.00	77.00	135	140	160	350	—
1932	9,062,000	1.60	1.95	2.85	3.50	6.75	13.00	17.50	65.00	—
1932 D	10,500,000	1.50	1.90	2.50	2.85	4.15	11.00	18.50	65.00	—
1933	14,360,000	1.50	1.80	2.65	2.85	6.50	11.50	16.50	65.00	—
1933 D	6,200,000	3.50	4.25	5.65	7.50	13.50	19.00	24.00	60.00	—
1934	219,080,000	0.15	0.25	0.30	0.45	1.25	4.00	9.00	25.00	—
1934 D	28,446,000	0.35	0.50	0.80	1.25	5.50	9.00	20.00	30.00	—
1935	245,338,000	0.15	0.20	0.25	0.40	0.90	1.50	5.00	20.00	—
1935 D	47,000,000	0.20	0.30	0.40	0.55	0.95	2.50	5.50	20.00	—
1935 S	38,702,000	0.25	0.35	0.60	1.75	3.00	5.00	11.00	44.00	—
1936 (Proof in Satin Finish)	309,637,569	0.15	0.20	0.30	0.40	0.85	1.40	1.90	10.00	600
1936 Brilliant Proof	Inc. above	—	—	—	—	—	—	—	—	800
1936 DDO	Inc. above	—	—	25.00	50.00	80.00	125	175	1,000	—
1936 D	40,620,000	0.20	0.30	0.40	0.55	0.90	1.50	4.00	15.00	—
1936 S	29,130,000	0.20	0.30	0.45	0.60	1.50	2.25	5.00	18.00	—
1937	309,179,320	0.15	0.20	0.30	0.40	0.50	0.75	1.75	13.50	110
1937 D	50,430,000	0.20	0.30	0.40	0.60	0.80	1.20	2.65	15.00	—
1937 S	34,500,000	0.20	0.30	0.40	0.55	0.90	1.25	2.75	16.50	—
1938	156,696,734	0.15	0.20	0.30	0.40	0.50	1.20	2.25	18.00	90.00
1938 D	20,010,000	0.20	0.30	0.45	0.60	1.00	1.50	3.50	20.00	—
1938 S	15,180,000	0.30	0.40	0.50	0.70	1.00	1.75	3.00	15.00	—
1939	316,479,520	0.15	0.20	0.30	0.40	0.45	0.75	1.00	16.00	60.00
1939 D	15,160,000	0.35	0.45	0.50	0.60	0.95	1.75	3.00	18.00	—
1939 S	52,070,000	0.30	0.40	0.50	0.60	0.80	1.20	2.50	16.00	—
1940	586,825,872	0.10	0.20	0.30	0.35	0.45	0.75	1.00	12.00	65.00
1940 D	81,390,000	0.20	0.30	0.40	0.55	0.75	1.10	2.00	11.00	—
1940 S	112,940,000	0.20	0.30	0.40	0.55	0.70	1.25	2.50	12.50	—
1941	887,039,100	0.10	0.20	0.30	0.35	0.45	0.60	1.25	10.00	60.00

CENT

Date		Mintage	G4	VG8	F12	VF20	XF40	AU50	MS60	MS65	Prf65
1941	Doubled Die Obv	Inc. above	35.00	50.00	70.00	80.00	95.00	135	200	1,000	—
1941 D		128,700,000	0.20	0.30	0.40	0.55	0.90	1.35	2.20	12.50	—
1941 S		92,360,000	0.20	0.30	0.40	0.55	0.95	1.75	2.50	15.00	—
1942		657,828,600	0.10	0.20	0.30	0.35	0.40	0.55	0.85	11.00	65.00
1942 D		206,698,000	0.20	0.25	0.30	0.35	0.45	0.60	1.00	12.00	—
1942 S		85,590,000	0.25	0.35	0.45	0.85	1.25	2.50	5.00	18.00	—
1943	Copper planchet error	—	—	—	35,000	42,000	45,000	80,000	155,000	—	—
1943 S	Copper planchet error	—	—	—	125,000	150,000	185,000	275,000	—	—	—

KM# 132a • 2.70 g., **Zinc Coated Steel**, 19 mm. • **Designer:** Victor D. Brenner

Date	Mintage	G4	VG8	F12	VF20	XF40	AU50	MS60	MS65	Prf65
1943	684,628,670	0.20	0.30	0.35	0.45	0.60	0.85	1.25	18.00	—
1943 D	217,660,000	0.35	0.40	0.45	0.50	0.70	1.00	1.50	—	—
1943 D/D RPM	Inc. above	30.00	38.00	50.00	65.00	90.00	125	200	—	—
1943 S	191,550,000	0.40	0.45	0.50	0.65	0.90	1.40	4.00	28.00	—

KM# A132 • 3.11 g., **Brass**, 19 mm. • **Designer:** Victor D. Brenner **Note:** KM#132 design and composition resumed • MS60 prices are for brown coins and MS65 prices are for coins that are at least 90% original red.

Date	Mintage	XF40	MS65	Prf65
1944	1,435,400,000	0.30	8.00	—
1944 D	430,578,000	0.40	14.00	—
1944 D/S Type 1	Inc. above	220	3,750	—
1944 D/S Type 2	Inc. above	175	1,600	—
1944 S	282,760,000	0.35	8.00	—
1945	1,040,515,000	0.40	13.50	—
1945 D	226,268,000	0.40	8.00	—
1945 S	181,770,000	0.40	7.50	—
1946	991,655,000	0.25	13.50	—
1946 D	315,690,000	0.30	10.00	—
1946 S	198,100,000	0.30	13.50	—
1946 S/D	—	70.00	650	—
1947	190,555,000	0.45	18.50	—
1947 D	194,750,000	0.35	7.50	—
1947 S	99,000,000	0.35	8.00	—
1948	317,570,000	0.35	18.50	—
1948 D	172,637,000	0.40	12.00	—
1948 S	81,735,000	0.40	12.00	—
1949	217,775,000	0.40	18.00	—
1949 D	153,132,000	0.40	15.00	—
1949 S	64,290,000	0.50	10.00	—
1950	272,686,386	0.35	16.50	65.00
1950 D	334,950,000	0.35	12.50	—
1950 S	118,505,000	0.30	9.00	—
1951	295,633,500	0.40	16.50	62.00
1951 D	625,355,000	0.30	8.50	—
1951 S	136,010,000	0.40	9.00	—
1952	186,856,980	0.40	16.00	36.00
1952 D	746,130,000	0.30	8.50	—
1952 S	137,800,004	0.60	12.00	—
1953	256,883,800	0.25	18.00	37.00
1953 D	700,515,000	0.25	8.50	—
1953 S	181,835,000	0.40	8.00	—
1954	71,873,350	0.25	20.00	19.00
1954 D	251,552,500	0.25	8.50	—
1954 S	96,190,000	0.25	10.00	—
1955	330,958,000	0.25	9.00	14.00
1955 Doubled Die	Inc. above	1,900	37,500	—

Note: The 1955 "doubled die" has distinct doubling of the date and lettering on the obverse.

1955 D	563,257,500	0.20	8.00	—
1955 S	44,610,000	0.35	7.50	—
1956	421,414,384	0.20	12.00	5.00
1956 D	1,098,201,100	0.20	7.00	—
1957	283,787,952	0.20	7.50	4.00
1957 D	1,051,342,000	0.20	6.00	—

Date	Mintage	XF40	MS65	Prf65
1958	253,400,652	0.20	9.00	6.50
1958 D	800,953,300	0.20	7.00	—

Lincoln Memorial reverse

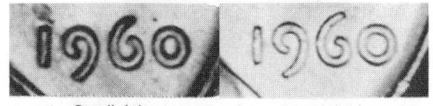

Small date | Large date

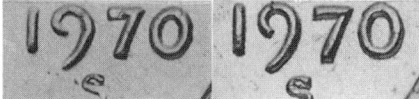

Small date | Large date

KM# 201 • 3.11 g., **Brass**, 19 mm. • **Rev. Designer:** Frank Gasparro **Note:** MS60 prices are for brown coins and MS65 prices are for coins that are at least 90% original red. The dates were modified in 1960, 1970 and 1982, resulting in large-date and small-date varieties for those years. The 1972 "doubled die" shows doubling of IN GOD WE TRUST. The 1979-S and 1981-S Type II proofs have a clearer mint mark than the Type I proofs of those years. Some 1982 cents have the predominantly copper composition; others have the predominantly zinc composition. They can be distinguished by weight.

Date	Mintage	XF40	MS65	Prf65
1959	610,864,291	—	15.00	10.00
1959 D	1,279,760,000	—	7.50	—
1960 small date, low 9	588,096,602	1.85	12.00	16.00
1960 large date, high 9	Inc. above	—	8.00	7.50
1960 small over large date	Inc. above	—	—	600
1960 D small date, low 9	1,580,884,000	—	10.00	—
1960 D large date, high 9	Inc. above	—	8.00	—
1960 D/D small over large date	Inc. above	—	300	—
1961	756,373,244	—	8.50	9.00
1961 D	1,753,266,700	—	18.00	—
1962	609,263,019	—	8.00	8.00
1962 D	1,793,148,400	—	14.00	—
1963	757,185,645	—	10.00	6.00
1963 D	1,774,020,400	—	12.00	—
1964	2,652,525,762	—	8.50	6.00
1964 D	3,799,071,500	—	10.00	—
1965	1,497,224,900	—	10.00	—
1965 SMS	Inc. above	—	7.50	—

Date	Mintage	XF40	MS65	Prf65
1966	2,188,147,783	—	10.00	—
1966 SMS	Inc. above	—	8.00	—
1967	3,048,667,100	—	12.00	—
1967 SMS	Inc. above	—	8.00	—
1968	1,707,880,970	—	12.00	—
1968 D	2,886,269,600	—	12.50	—
1968 S	261,311,510	—	10.00	4.50
1969	1,136,910,000	—	7.00	—
1969 D	4,002,832,200	—	10.00	—
1969 S	547,309,631	—	15.00	5.50
1969 S Doubled Die Obverse	Inc. above	10,000	125,000	100,000
1970	1,898,315,000	—	8.00	—
1970 D	2,891,438,900	—	6.00	—
1970 S small date, level 7	Inc. above	30.00	65.00	60.00
1970 S large date, low 7	Inc. above	—	15.00	5.00
1970 S Doubled Die Obverse	Inc. above	—	20,000	15,000
1971	1,919,490,000	—	20.00	—
1971 D	2,911,045,600	—	6.50	—
1971 S	528,354,192	—	7.50	5.50
1971 S Doubled Die Obverse	Inc. above	—	—	400
1972	2,933,255,000	—	6.00	—
1972 Doubled Die Obverse	Inc. above	290	785	—
1972 D	2,665,071,400	—	12.00	—
1972 S	380,200,104	—	26.50	5.50
1973	3,728,245,000	—	8.00	—
1973 D	3,549,576,588	—	11.00	—
1973 S	319,937,634	—	10.00	5.50
1974	4,232,140,523	—	12.00	—
1974 D	4,235,098,000	—	9.00	—
1974 S	412,039,228	—	12.00	5.00
1975	5,451,476,142	—	8.00	—
1975 D	4,505,245,300	—	13.50	—
1975 S	2,845,450	—	—	5.00
1976	4,674,292,426	—	14.00	—
1976 D	4,221,592,455	—	16.00	—
1976 S	4,149,730	—	—	6.00
1977	4,469,930,000	—	16.00	—
1977 D	4,149,062,300	—	16.00	—
1977 S	3,251,152	—	—	5.00
1978	5,558,605,000	—	16.00	—
1978 D	4,280,233,400	—	14.00	—
1978 S	3,127,781	—	—	5.00
1979	6,018,515,000	—	12.00	—
1979 D	4,139,357,254	—	8.00	—
1979 S type I, proof	3,677,175	—	—	5.00
1979 S type II, proof	—	—	—	10.00
1980	7,414,705,000	—	6.50	—
1980 D	5,140,098,660	—	12.00	—
1980 S	3,554,806	—	—	5.00
1981	7,491,750,000	—	8.50	—
1981 D	5,373,235,677	—	9.00	—
1981 S type I, proof	4,063,083	—	—	5.00
1981 S type II, proof	—	—	—	42.00
1982 large date	10,712,525,000	—	7.00	—
1982 small date	Inc. above	—	9.00	—
1982 D large date	6,012,979,368	—	7.50	—
1982 S	3,857,479	—	—	5.00

KM# 201a • 2.50 g., Copper Plated Zinc, 19 mm. • **Note:** MS60 prices are for brown coins and MS65 prices are for coins that are at least 90% original red.

Date	Mintage	XF40	MS65	Prf65
1982 large date	—	—	6.00	—
1982 small date	—	—	9.00	—
1982 D large date	—	—	8.00	—
1982 D small date	—	—	6.00	—

KM# 201b • Copper Plated Zinc, 19 mm. • **Note:** MS60 prices are for brown coins and MS65 prices are for coins that are at least 90% original red.

Date	Mintage	XF40	MS65	Prf65
1983	7,752,355,000	—	7.00	—
1983 Doubled Die	Inc. above	135	450	—
1983 D	6,467,199,428	—	5.50	—
1983 S	3,279,126	—	—	3.50
1984	8,151,079,000	—	7.50	—
1984 Doubled Die	Inc. above	100	325	—
1984 D	5,569,238,906	—	6.50	—
1984 S	3,065,110	—	—	3.50
1985	5,648,489,887	—	4.50	—
1985 D	5,287,399,926	—	4.50	—
1985 S	3,362,821	—	—	3.50
1986	4,491,395,493	—	5.00	—
1986 D	4,442,866,698	—	8.00	—
1986 S	3,010,497	—	—	3.50
1987	4,682,466,931	—	7.50	—
1987 D	4,879,389,514	—	5.50	—
1987 S	4,227,728	—	—	3.50
1988	6,092,810,000	—	10.00	—
1988 D	5,253,740,443	—	6.00	—
1988 S	3,262,948	—	—	3.50
1989	7,261,535,000	—	6.50	—
1989 D	5,345,467,111	—	6.50	—
1989 S	3,220,194	—	—	5.00
1990	6,851,765,000	—	5.00	—
1990 D	4,922,894,533	—	5.50	—
1990 S	3,299,559	—	—	3.50
1990 no S, Proof only	Inc. above	—	—	4,650
1991	5,165,940,000	—	6.50	—
1991 D	4,158,442,076	—	5.50	—
1991 S	2,867,787	—	—	3.50
1992	4,648,905,000	—	5.50	—
1992 D	4,448,673,300	—	5.50	—
1992 D Close AM, Proof Reverse Die	Inc. above	—	—	—
1992 S	4,176,560	—	—	3.50
1993	5,684,705,000	—	5.00	—
1993 D	6,426,650,571	—	4.50	—
1993 S	3,394,792	—	—	3.50
1994	6,500,850,000	—	6.00	—
1994 D	7,131,765,000	—	4.50	—
1994 S	3,269,923	—	—	3.50
1995	6,411,440,000	—	5.00	—
1995 Doubled Die Obverse	Inc. above	20.00	60.00	—
1995 D	7,128,560,000	—	4.50	—
1995 S	2,707,481	—	—	3.50
1996	6,612,465,000	—	4.50	—
1996 D	6,510,795,000	—	4.50	—
1996 S	2,915,212	—	—	3.50
1997	4,622,800,000	—	3.00	—
1997 D	4,576,555,000	—	3.50	—
1997 S	2,796,678	—	—	4.00
1998	5,032,155,000	—	3.00	—
1998 Wide AM, reverse from proof die	Inc. above	—	110	—
1998 D	5,255,353,500	—	3.00	—
1998 S	2,957,286	—	—	4.00
1999	5,237,600,000	—	3.00	—
1999 Wide AM, reverse from proof die	Inc. above	—	450	—
1999 D	6,360,065,000	—	3.00	—
1999 S	3,362,462	—	—	3.50
2000 Wide AM, reverse from proof die	Inc. above	—	45.00	—
2000	5,503,200,000	—	3.00	—
2000 D	8,774,220,000	—	3.00	—

Date	Mintage	XF40	MS65	Prf65
2000 S	4,063,361	—	—	3.50
2001	4,959,600,000	—	3.00	—
2001 D	5,374,990,000	—	3.00	—
2001 S	3,099,096	—	—	3.50
2002	3,260,800,000	—	3.00	—
2002 D	4,028,055,000	—	3.00	—
2002 S	3,157,739	—	—	3.50
2003	3,300,000,000	—	3.50	—
2003 D	3,548,000,000	—	3.50	—
2003 S	3,116,590	—	—	3.50
2004	3,379,600,000	—	3.50	—
2004 D	3,456,400,000	—	3.50	—
2004 S	2,992,069	—	—	3.50
2005	3,935,600,000	—	2.50	—
2005 Satin Finish	1,160,000	—	4.00	—
2005 D	3,764,450,000	—	2.50	—
2005 D Satin Finish	1,160,000	—	4.00	—
2005 S	3,273,000	—	—	3.50
2006	4,290,000,000	—	2.00	—
2006 Satin Finish	847,361	—	4.00	—
2006 D	3,944,000,000	—	2.50	—
2006 D Satin Finish	847,361	—	4.00	—
2006 S	2,923,105	—	—	3.50
2007	3,762,400,000	—	2.00	—
2007 Satin Finish	895,628	—	4.00	—
2007 D	3,638,800,000	—	2.00	—
2007 D Satin Finish	895,628	—	4.00	—
2007 S	2,577,166	—	—	3.50
2008	2,558,800,000	—	2.25	—
2008 Satin Finish	745,464	—	4.00	—
2008 D	2,849,600,000	—	2.25	—
2008 D Satin Finish	745,464	—	4.00	—
2008 S	2,169,561	—	—	4.50

Lincoln Bicentennial
Bust right obverse   Log cabin reverse

KM# 441 • 2.50 g., **Copper Plated Zinc**, 19 mm. • **Subject:** Early Childhood in Kenturcky **Rev. Designer:** Richard Masters and James Licaretz

Date	Mintage	XF40	MS65	Prf65
2009 P	284,400,000	—	1.50	—
2009 D	350,400,000	—	1.50	—

KM# 441a • 3.31 g., **Brass**, 19 mm. • **Rev. Designer:** Richard Masters and James Licaretz

Date	Mintage	XF40	MS65	Prf65
2009 P Satin finish	784,614	—	4.00	—
2009 D Satin finish	784,614	—	4.00	—
2009 S	2,995,615	—	—	4.00

Lincoln seated on log reverse

KM# 442 • 2.50 g., **Copper Plated Zinc**, 19 mm. • **Subject:** Formative years in Indiana **Rev. Designer:** Charles Vickers

Date	Mintage	XF40	MS65	Prf65
2009 P	376,000,000	—	1.50	—
2009 D	363,600,000	—	1.50	—

KM# 442a • 3.11 g., **Brass**, 19 mm. • **Rev. Designer:** Charles Vickers

Date	Mintage	XF40	MS65	Prf65
2009 P Satin finish	784,614	—	4.00	—
2009 D Satin finish	784,614	—	4.00	—
2009 S	2,995,615	—	—	4.00

Lincoln standing before
Illinois Statehouse reverse

KM# 443 • 2.50 g., **Copper Plated Zinc**, 19 mm. • **Subject:** Professional life in Illinois **Rev. Designer:** Joel Iskowitz and Don Everhart

Date	Mintage	XF40	MS65	Prf65
2009 P	316,000,000	—	1.50	—
2009 D	336,000,000	—	1.50	—

KM# 443a • 3.11 g., **Brass**, 19 mm. • **Rev. Designer:** Joel Iskowitz and Don Everhart

Date	Mintage	XF40	MS65	Prf65
2009 P Satin finish	784,614	—	4.00	—
2009 D Satin finish	784,614	—	4.00	—
2009 S	2,995,615	—	—	4.00

Capitol Building reverse

KM# 444 • 2.50 g., **Copper Plated Zinc Subject:** Presidency in Washington, DC **Rev. Designer:** Susan Gamble and Joseph Menna **Shape:** 19

Date	Mintage	XF40	MS65	Prf65
2009 P	129,600,000	—	1.50	—
2009 D	198,000,000	—	1.50	—

KM# 444a • 3.11 g., **Brass**, 19 mm. • **Subject:** Presidency in Washington, DC **Rev. Designer:** Susan Ganmble and Joseph Menna

Date	Mintage	XF40	MS65	Prf65
2009 P Satin finish	784,614	—	4.00	—
2009 D Satin finish	784,614	—	4.00	—
2009 S	2,995,615	—	—	4.00

Lincoln - Shield Reverse
Lincoln bust right obverse   Shield reverse

KM# 468 • 2.50 g., **Copper Plated Zinc**, 19 mm. • **Obv. Designer:** Victor D. Brenner **Rev. Designer:** Lyndall Bass and Joseph Menna

Date	Mintage	XF40	MS65	Prf65
2010 P	1,963,630,000	—	1.50	—
2010 P Satin finish	583,912	—	—	—
2010 D	2,047,200,000	—	1.50	—
2010 D Satin finish	583,912	—	—	—

CENT

Date	Mintage	XF40	MS65	Prf65	Date	Mintage	XF40	MS65	Prf65
2010 S	1,689,364	—	—	4.00	2013 D	3,319,600,000	—	1.50	—
2011 P	2,006,800,000	—	1.50	—	2013 S	1,237,926	—	—	4.00
2011 D	2147483647	—	1.50	—	2014 D	—	—	—	—
2011 S	1,673,010	—	—	4.00	2014 S	—	—	—	—
2012 P	3,132,000,000	—	1.50	—	2014 P	—	—	—	—
2012 D	2,883,200,000	—	1.50	—					
2012 S	1,237,415	—	—	4.00					
2013 P	3,750,400,000	—	1.50	—					

2 CENTS

Shield in front of crossed arrows, banner above, date below obverse
Value within wheat wreath reverse

Small motto   Large motto

KM# 94 • 6.22 g., **Copper-Tin-Zinc**, 23 mm. • **Rev. Legend:** UNITED STATES OF AMERICA **Designer:** James B. Longacre
Note: The motto IN GOD WE TRUST was modified in 1864, resulting in small-motto and large-motto varieties for that year.

Date		Mintage	G4	VG8	F12	VF20	XF40	AU50	MS60	MS65	Prf65
1864	small motto	19,847,500	140	210	285	425	650	725	1,125	3,000	45,000
1864	large motto	Inc. above	16.50	18.50	20.00	27.50	42.50	72.00	88.00	375	1,100
1865	fancy 5	13,640,000	16.50	18.50	20.00	27.50	42.50	72.00	88.00	375	—
1865	plain 5	Inc. above	16.50	18.50	21.00	29.00	45.00	75.00	92.00	400	650
1866		3,177,000	17.00	20.00	21.50	29.00	46.00	77.00	98.00	395	650
1867		2,938,750	18.00	21.00	36.00	46.00	60.00	96.00	125	395	650
1867	double die obverse	Inc. above	—	80.00	165	250	350	500	650	4,750	—
1868		2,803,750	18.00	22.00	37.50	47.50	65.00	105	135	465	650
1869		1,546,000	20.00	23.00	40.00	50.00	79.00	125	165	550	650
1869	repunched 18	Inc. above	35.00	45.00	75.00	150	325	550	—	—	—
1869/8	die crack	Inc. above	50	185	375	435	650	900	—	—	—
1870		861,250	31.00	42.00	60.00	82.00	135	190	280	550	650
1871		721,250	43.50	49.00	70.00	110	150	215	285	650	650
1872		65,000	400	550	700	900	1,200	1,800	3,150	5,500	850
1873	closed 3 proof only	Est. 600	1,250	1,400	1,535	1,650	1,750	2,000	—	—	3,850
1873	open 3 proof only	Est. 500	1,275	1,400	1,575	1,700	1,875	2,150	—	—	4,200

SILVER 3 CENTS

Silver 3 Cents - Type 1
Shield within star, no outlines in star obverse
Roman numeral in designed C, within circle of stars reverse

KM# 75 • 0.80 g., 0.750 **Silver**, 14 mm. • **Obv. Legend:** UNITED STATES OF AMERICA **Designer:** James B. Longacre

Date	Mintage	G4	VG8	F12	VF20	XF40	AU50	MS60	MS65	Prf65
1851	5,447,400	32.00	48.50	51.00	58.50	68.00	145	180	825	—
1851 O	720,000	38.50	58.50	61.00	95.00	160	275	500	3,100	—
1852	18,663,500	32.00	48.50	51.00	58.50	68.00	145	180	825	—
1853	11,400,000	32.00	48.50	51.00	58.50	68.00	145	180	825	—

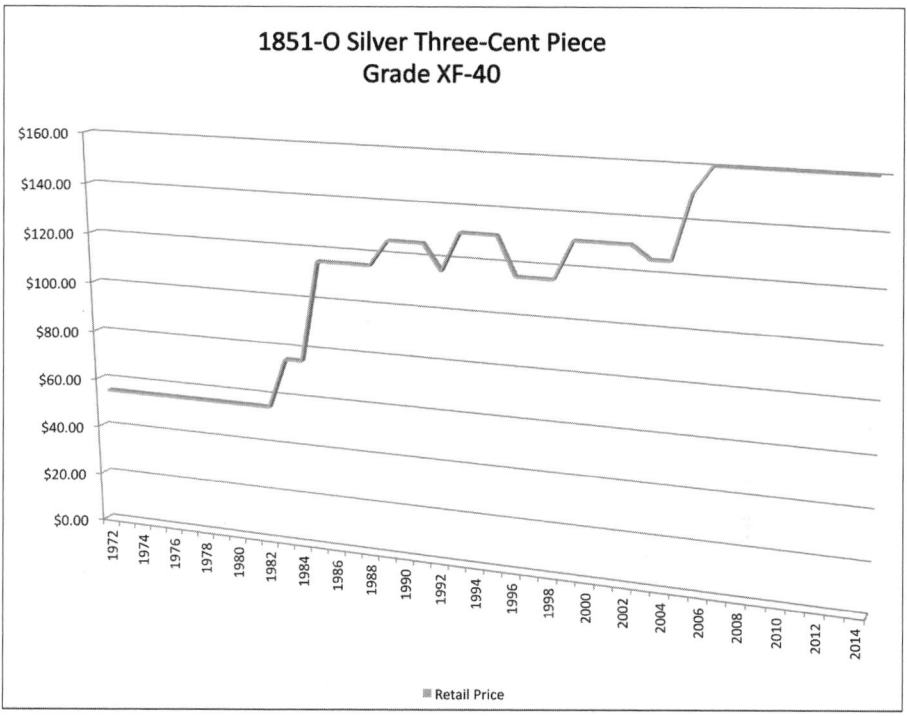

1851-O Silver Three-Cent Piece
Grade XF-40

◼ Retail Price

Silver 3 Cents - Type 2
Shield within star, three outlines in star obverse
Roman numeral in designed C, within circle of stars reverse

KM# 80 • 0.75 g., 0.900 **Silver**, 14 mm. • **Obv. Legend:** UNITED STATES OF AMERICA **Designer:** James B. Longacre

Date	Mintage	G4	VG8	F12	VF20	XF40	AU50	MS60	MS65	Prf65
1854	671,000	32.00	48.50	51.00	59.50	112	205	340	2,700	33,500
1855	139,000	44.00	57.50	75.00	125	200	325	520	7,400	15,000
1856	1,458,000	34.00	50.50	54.00	67.00	119	205	260	3,250	15,500
1857	1,042,000	34.00	50.50	54.00	67.00	112	223	285	2,375	13,500
1858	1,604,000	33.00	49.50	52.00	62.00	122	205	230	2,350	6,400

Silver 3 Cents - Type 3
Shield within star, two outlines in star obverse
Roman numeral in designed C, within circle of stars reverse

KM# 88 • 0.75 g., 0.900 **Silver**, 14 mm. • **Obv. Legend:** UNITED STATES OF AMERICA **Designer:** James B. Longacre

Date	Mintage	G4	VG8	F12	VF20	XF40	AU50	MS60	MS65	Prf65
1859	365,000	40.00	53.50	56.00	64.00	87.00	160	195	975	2,150
1860	287,000	40.00	53.50	56.00	64.00	83.00	160	195	1,050	4,000
1861	498,000	40.00	53.50	56.00	64.00	83.00	160	195	1,050	1,800
1862	343,550	46.00	55.50	58.00	66.00	88.00	180	235	935	1,400
1862/1	Inc. above	43.00	57.50	62.00	71.00	94.00	177	210	865	—
1863	21,460	375	420	450	485	520	725	825	2,250	1,350
1863/62 proof only; Rare	Inc. above	—	—	—	—	—	—	—	—	5,400

Date	Mintage	G4	VG8	F12	VF20	XF40	AU50	MS60	MS65	Prf65
1864	12,470	375	420	450	485	520	725	850	1,675	1,350
1865	8,500	475	525	550	620	665	700	875	1,650	1,350
1866	22,725	375	420	450	485	520	675	775	1,950	1,325
1867	4,625	475	525	575	625	675	725	850	2,750	1,300
1868	4,100	475	535	585	640	690	750	875	5,750	1,400
1869	5,100	475	535	585	640	690	750	875	2,450	1,400
1869/68 proof only; Rare	Inc. above	—	—	—	—	—	—	—	—	—
1870	4,000	450	460	525	600	665	750	950	5,650	1,350
1871	4,360	440	450	535	625	670	710	835	1,800	1,450
1872	1,950	465	485	550	645	690	750	875	5,500	1,350
1873 proof only	600	—	—	—	—	950	1,050	—	—	2,950

NICKEL 3 CENTS

Coronet head left, date below obverse   Roman numeral value within wreath reverse

KM# 95 • 1.94 g., **Copper-Nickel**, 17.9 mm. • **Obv. Legend:** UNITED STATES OF AMERICA **Designer:** James B. Longacre

Date	Mintage	G4	VG8	F12	VF20	XF40	AU50	MS60	MS65	Prf65
1865	11,382,000	15.50	16.50	17.50	22.50	37.50	60.00	100	550	6,500
1866	4,801,000	15.50	16.50	17.50	22.50	37.50	60.00	100	550	1,725
1867	3,915,000	15.50	16.50	17.50	22.50	37.50	60.00	100	670	1,575
1868	3,252,000	15.50	16.50	17.50	22.50	37.50	60.00	100	550	1,450
1869	1,604,000	16.50	17.50	19.50	25.50	40.50	61.00	120	730	1,050
1870	1,335,000	17.50	18.50	20.50	26.50	41.50	62.00	135	725	2,250
1871	604,000	17.50	19.00	22.50	27.50	42.50	64.00	155	740	1,200
1872	862,000	19.00	22.50	24.50	29.00	43.50	68.00	175	995	910
1873 Closed 3	1,173,000	16.50	18.50	22.50	25.50	40.50	62.00	145	1,050	1,125
1873 Open 3	Inc. above	16.50	18.50	22.50	26.00	41.50	68.00	180	4,500	—
1874	790,000	17.50	20.50	22.50	27.50	42.50	66.00	160	950	950
1875	228,000	19.00	22.50	27.50	30.50	45.50	82.00	190	750	1,500
1876	162,000	20.50	23.50	26.50	34.50	49.50	97.00	225	1,290	1,025
1877 proof	Est. 900	1,100	1,150	1,175	1,250	1,275	1,350	—	—	3,750
1878 proof	2,350	615	645	720	770	795	830	—	—	1,200
1879	41,200	70.00	80.00	96.00	110	122	180	320	750	690
1880	24,955	100	115	130	165	185	235	375	730	700
1881	1,080,575	15.50	16.50	19.00	23.50	39.50	60.00	100	585	680
1882	25,300	130	150	180	225	300	325	425	1,025	700
1883	10,609	200	225	265	305	375	425	480	4,850	690
1884	5,642	400	445	550	600	645	730	800	6,250	700
1885	4,790	470	520	645	700	745	775	900	12,000	720
1886 proof	4,290	320	330	345	385	385	420	—	—	715
1887/6 proof	7,961	350	390	415	450	460	515	—	—	940
1887	Inc. above	305	355	395	440	455	500	540	1,200	1,125
1888	41,083	54.00	63.00	70.00	80.00	100	170	315	650	690
1889	21,561	90.00	115	145	180	230	260	320	775	690

HALF DIME

Flowing Hair Half Dime

KM# 15 • 1.35 g., 0.892 **Silver** 0.04 oz. ASW, 16.5 mm. • **Designer:** Robert Scot

Date	Mintage	G4	VG8	F12	VF20	XF40	MS60
1794	86,416	1,325	1,625	2,150	3,125	7,325	19,000
1795	Inc. above	1,050	1,350	1,875	2,900	5,800	13,000

Draped Bust Half Dime
Draped bust right obverse   Small eagle reverse

KM# 23 • 1.35 g., 0.892 **Silver** 0.04 oz. ASW, 16.5 mm. • **Designer:** Robert Scot

Date	Mintage	G4	VG8	F12	VF20	XF40	MS60
1796	10,230	1,435	1,550	3,150	4,850	8,650	17,550
1796 LIKERTY	Inc. above	1,485	1,600	3,200	4,900	8,700	17,600
Note: In 1796 the word LIKERTY was spelled LIKERTY on a die.							
1796/5	Inc. above	1,555	1,700	3,300	5,000	8,800	17,700
1797 13 stars	44,527	2,100	2,650	4,250	5,950	9,750	30,750
1797 15 stars	Inc. above	1,385	1,500	3,100	4,800	8,600	17,500
1797 16 stars	Inc. above	1,535	1,750	3,350	5,050	8,850	17,750

Draped bust right, flanked by stars, date at angle below obverse   Heraldic eagle reverse

KM# 34 • 1.35 g., 0.892 **Silver** 0.04 oz. ASW, 16.5 mm. • **Obv. Legend:** LIBERTY **Rev. Legend:** UNITED STATES OF AMERICA **Designer:** Robert Scot

Date	Mintage	G4	VG8	F12	VF20	XF40	MS60
1800	24,000	1,000	1,250	1,875	2,550	6,500	13,500
1800 LIBEKTY	Inc. above	1,000	1,250	1,875	2,550	7,000	15,050
1801	33,910	1,225	1,500	2,125	2,800	6,750	17,750
1802	3,060	44,500	65,000	95,000	135,000	300,000	—
1803 Large 8	37,850	1,100	1,375	2,000	2,675	6,625	13,625
1803 Small 8	Inc. above	1,325	1,625	2,250	2,925	6,875	15,850
1805	15,600	1,225	1,525	2,350	3,025	9,900	31,000

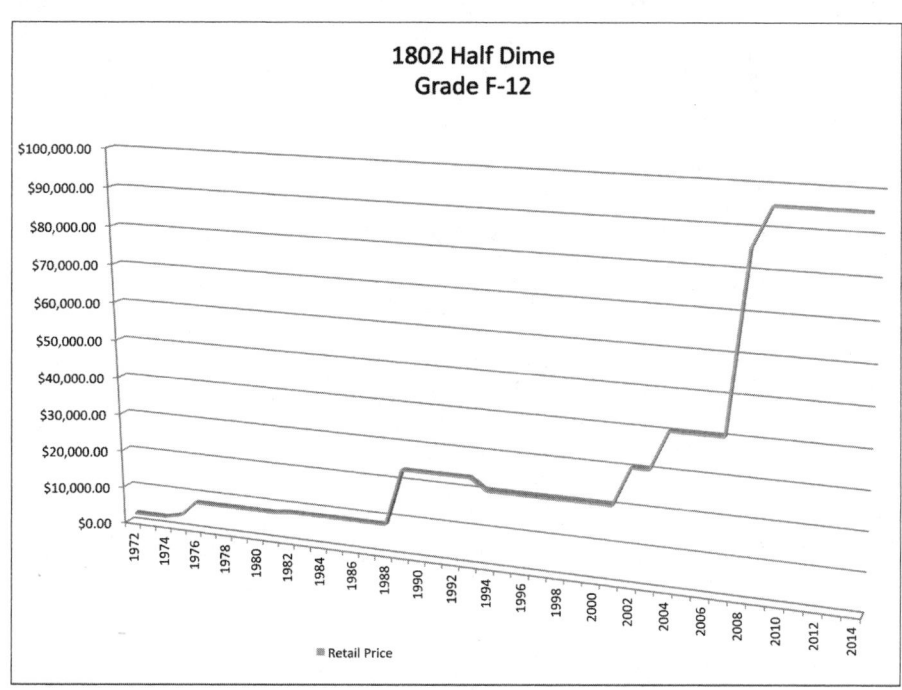

1802 Half Dime Grade F-12

HALF DIME

Liberty Cap Half Dime
Classic head left, flanked by stars, date below obverse
Eagle with arrows in talons, banner above reverse

KM# 47 • 1.35 g., 0.892 **Silver** 0.04 oz. ASW, 15.5 mm. • **Rev. Legend:** UNITED STATES OF AMERICA **Designer:** William Kneass

Date	Mintage	G4	VG8	F12	VF20	XF40	AU50	MS60	MS65
1829	1,230,000	60.00	75.00	85.00	148	190	275	365	2,750
1830	1,240,000	52.50	67.50	75.00	118	160	225	350	2,600
1831	1,242,700	52.50	67.50	75.00	118	160	225	350	2,600
1832	965,000	52.50	67.50	75.00	118	160	225	350	2,600
1833	1,370,000	52.50	67.50	75.00	118	160	225	350	2,600
1834	1,480,000	52.50	67.50	75.00	118	160	225	350	2,600
1835 large date and 5C.	2,760,000	52.50	75.00	87.00	133	175	245	350	2,600
1835 large date, small 5C.	Inc. above	52.50	67.50	75.00	118	160	225	410	3,800
1835 small date, large 5C.	Inc. above	52.50	67.50	75.00	118	160	225	375	3,500
1835 small date and 5C.	Inc. above	52.50	67.50	75.00	118	160	225	350	2,600
1836 large 5C.	1,900,000	52.50	67.50	75.00	118	160	225	350	2,600
1836 small 5C.	Inc. above	54.50	70.50	79.00	128	172	237	362	3,100
1837 large 5C.	2,276,000	52.50	67.50	83.00	136	175	245	395	3,800
1837 small 5C.	Inc. above	59.50	77.50	90.00	148	240	465	950	11,000

Seated Liberty Half Dime
Seated Liberty, no stars around border, date below obverse   Value within wreath reverse

KM# 60 • 1.34 g., 0.900 **Silver** 0.04 oz. ASW, 15.5 mm. • **Rev. Legend:** UNITED STATES OF AMERICA **Designer:** Christian Gobrecht **Note:** A design modification in 1837 resulted in small-date and large-date varieties for that year.

Date	Mintage	G4	VG8	F12	VF20	XF40	AU50	MS60	MS65
1837 small date	Inc. above	35.00	46.50	75.00	135	220	495	750	4,450
1837 large date	Inc. above	39.00	49.50	82.00	150	235	445	620	3,650
1838 O	70,000	110	130	250	475	975	1,450	2,500	29,500

Seated Liberty, stars around top 1/2 of border, date below obverse
Value within wreath reverse

KM# 62.1 • 1.34 g., 0.900 **Silver** 0.04 oz. ASW, 15.5 mm. • **Rev. Legend:** UNITED STATES OF AMERICA **Designer:** Christian Gobrecht **Note:** The two varieties of 1838 are distinguished by the size of the stars on the obverse. The 1839-O with reverse of 1838-O was struck from rusted reverse dies. The result is a bumpy surface on this variety's reverse.

Date	Mintage	G4	VG8	F12	VF20	XF40	AU50	MS60	MS65
1838 large stars	2,255,000	22.50	25.50	29.00	36.00	88.00	198	265	2,475
1838 small stars	Inc. above	26.50	31.50	46.00	115	189	299	595	3,950
1839	1,069,150	23.50	26.50	30.00	37.00	93.00	203	265	2,000
1839 O	1,034,039	27.50	30.50	34.00	41.00	88.00	198	715	6,850
1839 O reverse 1838O	Inc. above	500	700	1,200	1,750	3,000	—	—	—
1840	1,344,085	24.50	27.50	31.00	38.00	80.00	190	255	2,275
1840 O	935,000	29.50	32.50	38.00	48.00	138	368	1,235	—

Seated Liberty, stars around top 1/2 of border, date below obverse

KM# 62.2 • 1.34 g., 0.900 **Silver** 0.04 oz. ASW, 15.5 mm. • **Rev. Legend:** UNITED STATES OF AMERICA **Designer:** Christian Gobrecht **Note:** In 1840 drapery was added to Liberty's left elbow. Varieties for the 1848 Philadelphia strikes are distinguished by the size of the numerals in the date.

Date	Mintage	G4	VG8	F12	VF20	XF40	AU50	MS60	MS65
1840	Inc. above	21.50	18.00	75.00	135	210	350	490	3,850
1840 O	Inc. above	52.50	60.00	115	225	650	1,350	6,500	—
1841	1,150,000	18.50	21.50	23.50	31.00	60.50	127	180	1,325
1841 O	815,000	21.50	24.50	30.00	50.00	125	300	650	6,750
1842	815,000	18.50	21.50	23.50	28.00	57.50	127	175	1,750
1842 O	350,000	39.50	45.00	75.00	225	550	1,050	2,250	16,500
1843	1,165,000	18.50	21.50	23.50	28.00	57.50	122	175	1,365
1844	430,000	20.50	24.50	26.50	34.00	60.50	127	180	1,150
1844 O	220,000	80.00	110	210	600	1,300	2,650	5,400	27,500
1845	1,564,000	18.50	21.50	23.50	35.00	60.50	122	175	1,150
1845/1845	Inc. above	20.50	24.50	26.50	38.00	85.00	132	190	1,200
1846	27,000	410	550	850	1,250	2,475	3,600	11,500	—
1847	1,274,000	18.50	21.50	23.50	28.00	57.50	127	175	1,150
1848 medium date	668,000	20.50	24.50	26.50	34.00	67.50	137	215	3,150
1848 large date	Inc. above	24.00	28.00	48.00	65.00	145	275	635	4,250
1848 O	600,000	21.50	25.50	33.00	62.00	135	265	450	2,350
1849/8	1,309,000	28.50	35.00	47.50	67.50	140	250	785	2,950
1849/6	Inc. above	24.00	26.00	30.00	56.50	110	200	425	2,800
1849	Inc. above	20.50	18.50	27.50	52.50	67.50	137	190	1,825
1849 O	140,000	29.00	40.00	95.00	225	540	1,100	2,350	—
1850	955,000	20.50	24.50	26.50	34.00	62.50	127	190	1,300
1850 O	690,000	21.50	24.50	35.00	65.00	125	280	685	4,450
1851	781,000	17.50	21.50	23.50	28.00	59.90	122	175	1,350
1851 O	860,000	20.50	24.50	26.50	41.50	110	220	500	4,350
1852	1,000,500	17.50	21.50	23.50	28.00	59.50	122	175	1,150
1852 O	260,000	26.50	44.50	79.00	135	275	475	885	11,500
1853	135,000	40.00	60.00	90.00	175	300	525	850	2,850
1853 O	160,000	285	325	450	850	1,800	3,500	6,450	27,500

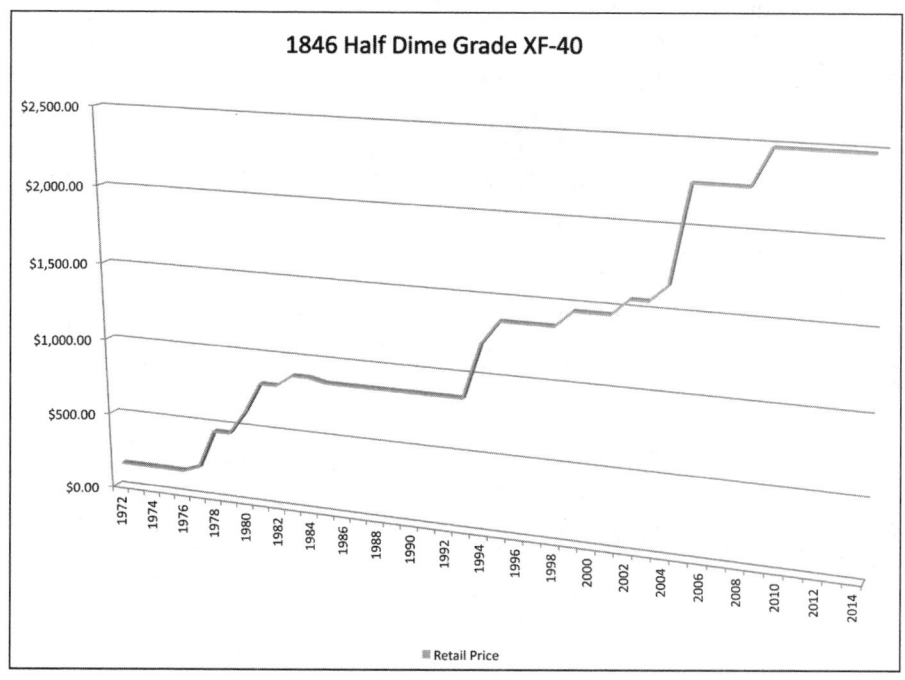

HALF DIME

Seated Liberty, stars around top 1/2 of border, arrows at date obverse
Value within wreath reverse

KM# 76 • 1.24 g., 0.900 **Silver** 0.04 oz. ASW **Rev. Legend:** UNITED STATES OF AMERICA **Designer:** Christian Gobrecht

Date	Mintage	G4	VG8	F12	VF20	XF40	AU50	MS60	MS65	Prf65
1853	13,210,020	17.75	21.50	22.50	28.00	58.00	135	195	1,410	—
1853 O	2,200,000	20.75	29.50	30.50	36.00	66.00	143	310	3,260	—
1854	5,740,000	17.75	21.50	24.50	30.00	60.00	137	205	1,410	15,000
1854 O	1,560,000	18.75	22.50	32.50	38.00	88.00	165	235	3,560	—
1855	1,750,000	18.75	22.50	24.50	30.00	60.00	137	200	1,810	15,000
1855 O	600,000	22.75	27.50	38.50	54.00	140	220	540	4,260	—

Seated Liberty, stars around top 1/2 of border, date below obverse
Value within wreath reverse

KM# A62.2 • 1.24 g., 0.900 **Silver** 0.04 oz. ASW **Rev. Legend:** UNITED STATES OF AMERICA **Designer:** Christian Gobrecht **Note:** On the 1858/inverted date variety, the date was engraved into the die upside down and then re-engraved right side up. Another 1858 variety has the date doubled.

Date	Mintage	G4	VG8	F12	VF20	XF40	AU50	MS60	MS65	Prf65
1856	4,880,000	17.50	21.00	23.00	27.00	52.50	115	175	1,200	15,000
1856 O	1,100,000	18.50	22.00	26.00	28.00	97.50	260	470	2,150	—
1857	7,280,000	17.50	21.00	23.00	27.00	52.50	115	175	1,050	5,600
1857 O	1,380,000	18.50	22.00	24.00	28.00	62.50	185	320	1,750	—
1858	3,500,000	17.50	21.00	23.00	27.00	52.50	115	175	1,150	5,500
1858 inverted date	Inc. above	30.00	43.50	62.50	100	225	300	675	3,950	—
1858 double date	Inc. above	45.00	60.00	90.00	175	285	425	800	—	—
1858 O	1,660,000	18.50	22.00	24.00	28.00	71.50	137	245	1,650	—
1859	340,000	19.50	23.00	25.00	29.00	54.50	117	225	1,350	4,000
1859 O	560,000	20.50	24.00	26.00	42.00	128	200	285	1,850	—

Seated Liberty, date below obverse   Value within wreath reverse

KM# 91 • 1.24 g., 0.900 **Silver** 0.04 oz. ASW **Obv. Legend:** UNITED STATES OF AMERICA **Designer:** Christian Gobrecht

Date	Mintage	G4	VG8	F12	VF20	XF40	AU50	MS60	MS65	Prf65
1860	799,000	17.00	20.00	23.00	26.00	47.00	77.00	155	825	1,550
1860 O	1,060,000	18.00	20.00	23.00	29.00	49.00	79.00	180	1,175	—
1861	3,361,000	17.00	20.00	22.00	25.00	45.00	75.00	155	825	1,600
1861/0	Inc. above	26.00	32.50	59.00	125	260	435	560	3,650	—
1862	1,492,550	21.00	25.00	34.00	44.00	64.00	94.00	164	825	1,550
1863	18,460	200	250	300	400	485	550	800	1,375	1,550
1863 S	100,000	35.00	45.00	70.00	95.00	165	300	750	3,450	—
1864	48,470	375	475	575	750	950	1,100	1,375	2,350	1,600
1864 S	90,000	60.00	75.00	115	175	250	450	785	3,750	—
1865	13,500	375	475	575	750	950	1,100	1,350	1,950	1,550
1865 S	120,000	30.00	40.00	60.00	85.00	145	375	975	5,450	—
1866	10,725	350	475	550	700	875	1,000	1,225	2,375	1,550
1866 S	120,000	30.00	40.00	60.00	85.00	145	285	485	5,000	—
1867	8,625	550	650	775	900	1,100	1,200	1,375	2,350	1,550
1867 S	120,000	30.00	40.00	60.00	85.00	150	325	850	3,850	—
1868	89,200	60.00	90.00	190	225	300	425	625	2,400	1,550
1868 S	280,000	21.00	25.00	35.00	42.00	59.00	125	335	3,250	—
1869	208,600	21.00	25.00	35.00	42.00	59.00	135	210	1,175	1,560
1869 S	230,000	19.00	24.00	30.00	35.00	55.00	125	320	4,150	—
1870	536,600	19.00	24.00	30.00	35.00	55.00	125	195	775	1,550

Date	Mintage	G4	VG8	F12	VF20	XF40	AU50	MS60	MS65	Prf65
1870 S unique	—	—	—	—	—	—	—	—	—	—
Note: 1870S, Superior Galleries, July 1986, brilliant uncirculated, $253,000.										
1871	1,873,960	17.00	20.00	22.00	25.00	45.00	75.00	145	775	1,550
1871 S	161,000	26.00	30.00	45.00	60.00	90.00	175	320	2,225	—
1872	2,947,950	17.00	20.00	22.00	25.00	45.00	75.00	145	775	1,550
1872 S mint mark in wreath	837,000	17.00	20.00	22.00	25.00	45.00	75.00	145	775	—
1872 S mint mark below wreath	Inc. above	18.00	21.00	24.00	27.00	47.00	80.00	145	775	—
1873	712,600	17.00	20.00	22.00	25.00	45.00	75.00	145	1,175	1,550
1873 S	324,000	21.00	25.00	30.00	42.00	62.00	90.00	160	775	—

5 CENTS

Shield Nickel
Draped garland above shield, date below obverse
Value within center of rays between stars reverse

KM# 96 • 5.00 g., **Copper-Nickel**, 20.5 mm. • **Obv. Legend:** IN GOD WE TRUST **Rev. Legend:** UNITED STATES OF AMERICA **Designer:** James B. Longacre

Date	Mintage	G4	VG8	F12	VF20	XF40	AU50	MS60	MS65	Prf65
1866	14,742,500	29.00	38.00	55.00	80.00	150	250	280	2,050	3,450
1867	2,019,000	37.00	45.50	63.50	90.00	180	280	330	3,850	75,000

Draped garland above shield, date below obverse
Value within circle of stars reverse

KM# 97 • 5.00 g., **Copper-Nickel Obv. Legend:** IN GOD WE TRUST **Rev. Legend:** UNITED STATES OF AMERICA

Date	Mintage	G4	VG8	F12	VF20	XF40	AU50	MS60	MS65	Prf65
1867	28,890,500	18.50	28.00	30.00	37.50	64.00	115	150	825	2,500
1868 Rev'67	28,817,000	18.50	28.00	30.00	37.50	64.00	115	150	675	1,325
1868 Rev'68	Inc. above	22.00	34.00	36.00	45.00	77.00	144	188	—	—
Note: Star points to center of A in STATES.										
1869	16,395,000	18.50	28.00	30.00	37.50	64.00	115	150	700	900
1870	4,806,000	27.00	35.00	54.00	69.00	100	150	210	1,600	1,060
1871	561,000	72.00	95.00	140	210	310	365	415	2,100	910
1872	6,036,000	39.00	48.00	85.00	96.00	135	180	235	1,350	715
1873 Open 3	4,550,000	29.00	39.00	54.00	68.00	80.00	135	230	1,950	—
1873 Closed 3	Inc. above	36.00	48.00	70.00	100	150	220	350	3,250	715
1874	3,538,000	31.00	45.00	74.00	94.00	120	165	245	1,400	800
1875	2,097,000	46.00	62.00	90.00	125	170	230	290	1,500	1,500
1876	2,530,000	40.00	54.00	84.00	125	165	200	255	1,350	825
1877 proof	Est. 900	—	—	—	2,100	2,150	2,300	—	—	4,850
1878 proof	2,350	—	—	—	1,100	1,250	1,450	—	—	2,100
1879	29,100	390	485	625	660	720	800	970	1,900	750
1879/8	Inc. above	—	—	—	—	—	—	—	—	825
1880	19,995	500	575	700	850	1,275	1,700	3,250	47,500	730
1881	72,375	260	340	430	500	600	675	735	1,800	700
1882	11,476,600	18.50	28.00	30.00	37.50	64.00	115	150	635	645
Note: Many exist with excess metal at numeral 2 & 3 these should not be confused with the following overdate.										
1883	1,456,919	18.50	28.00	32.00	39.50	67.00	135	160	750	645
Note: Many exist with excess metal at numeral 2 & 3 these should not be confused with the following overdate.										
1883/2	Inc. above	220	300	535	850	1,250	1,750	2,000	3,750	—

Liberty head left, within circle of stars, date below obverse
Roman numeral value within wreath, without CENTS below reverse

KM# 111 • 5.00 g., **Copper-Nickel**, 21.2 mm. • **Rev. Legend:** UNITED STATES OF AMERICA **Designer:** Charles E. Barber

Date	Mintage	G4	VG8	F12	VF20	XF40	AU50	MS60	MS65	Prf65
1883	5,479,519	7.00	7.75	8.50	8.75	9.25	12.00	25.50	215	1,075

Liberty Nickel
Liberty head left, within circle of stars, date below obverse
Roman numeral value within wreath, CENTS below reverse

KM# 112 • 5.00 g., **Copper-Nickel**, 21.2 mm. • **Rev. Legend:** UNITED STATES OF AMERICA

Date	Mintage	G4	VG8	F12	VF20	XF40	AU50	MS60	MS65	Prf65
1883	16,032,983	19.00	29.50	39.50	55.00	85.00	120	160	625	610
1884	11,273,942	22.50	33.50	39.50	59.00	92.00	135	190	1,675	610
1885	1,476,490	585	635	875	1,050	1,350	1,650	1,950	8,650	3,150
1886	3,330,290	285	335	400	500	685	850	1,950	7,250	1,950
1887	15,263,652	16.00	25.00	31.00	44.00	78.00	115	150	1,025	585
1888	10,720,483	28.00	44.00	68.00	130	185	250	295	1,500	585
1889	15,881,361	14.50	19.50	30.00	52.50	77.00	125	155	850	585
1890	16,259,272	10.50	20.50	26.00	39.50	68.50	115	165	1,365	585
1891	16,834,350	5.75	11.00	22.00	37.50	60.00	120	160	1,050	585
1892	11,699,642	6.50	11.00	22.50	39.00	65.00	120	165	1,300	585
1893	13,370,195	5.50	11.00	24.00	37.50	60.00	120	155	1,050	585
1894	5,413,132	16.50	31.00	98.00	165	230	295	350	1,500	585
1895	9,979,884	5.75	7.50	24.00	45.00	66.00	120	145	2,200	585
1896	8,842,920	9.00	21.00	41.50	68.50	98.00	150	205	1,950	585
1897	20,428,735	3.25	4.50	12.50	27.50	46.00	69.50	95.00	925	585
1898	12,532,087	2.15	4.25	11.00	23.50	40.00	68.50	130	1,025	585
1899	26,029,031	1.80	3.00	8.50	19.50	34.00	62.50	89.00	560	585
1900	27,255,995	1.60	2.50	8.50	19.00	34.00	69.50	84.00	650	585
1901	26,480,213	1.60	2.50	7.00	14.50	34.00	65.00	100	550	585
1902	31,480,579	1.60	2.50	4.00	15.00	32.00	65.00	102	550	585
1903	28,006,725	1.80	2.50	4.75	14.50	32.00	60.00	77.00	500	585
1904	21,404,984	1.60	2.40	4.75	11.50	30.00	65.00	96.00	500	585
1905	29,827,276	1.60	2.40	4.00	12.00	30.00	65.00	96.00	550	585
1906	38,613,725	1.80	2.40	4.00	11.50	30.00	65.00	96.00	650	585
1907	39,214,800	1.50	2.20	4.00	12.00	30.00	65.00	96.00	1,000	585
1908	22,686,177	1.80	2.20	4.00	12.00	30.00	68.00	104	1,100	585
1909	11,590,526	2.50	2.80	4.35	13.00	33.00	80.00	112	1,075	585
1910	30,169,353	1.50	1.85	4.00	10.00	30.00	52.00	62.00	550	585
1911	39,559,372	1.50	1.85	4.00	10.00	30.00	52.00	62.00	500	585
1912	26,236,714	1.50	1.85	4.00	10.00	30.00	52.00	62.00	570	585
1912 D	8,474,000	2.75	3.60	11.50	38.00	70.00	170	280	2,200	—
1912 S	238,000	165	190	220	480	810	1,300	1,475	5,900	—
1913 5 known	—	—	—	—	—	—	—	—	—	—

Note: 1913, Heritage Sale, January 2010, Proof-64 (Olsen), $3,737,500. Private treaty, 2007, (Eliasburg) Proof-66 $5 million.

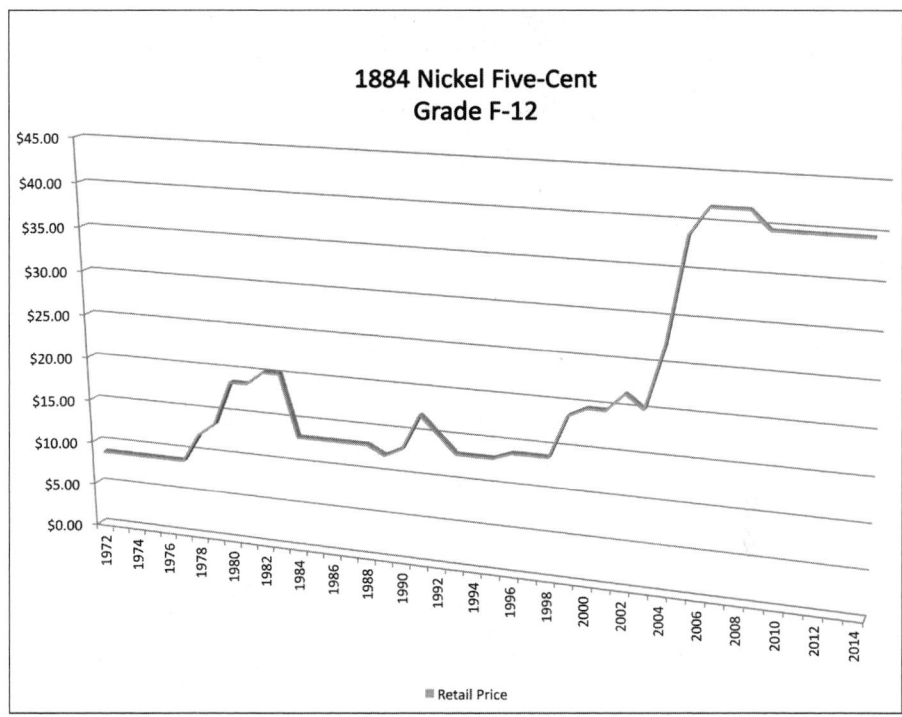

1884 Nickel Five-Cent
Grade F-12

Retail Price

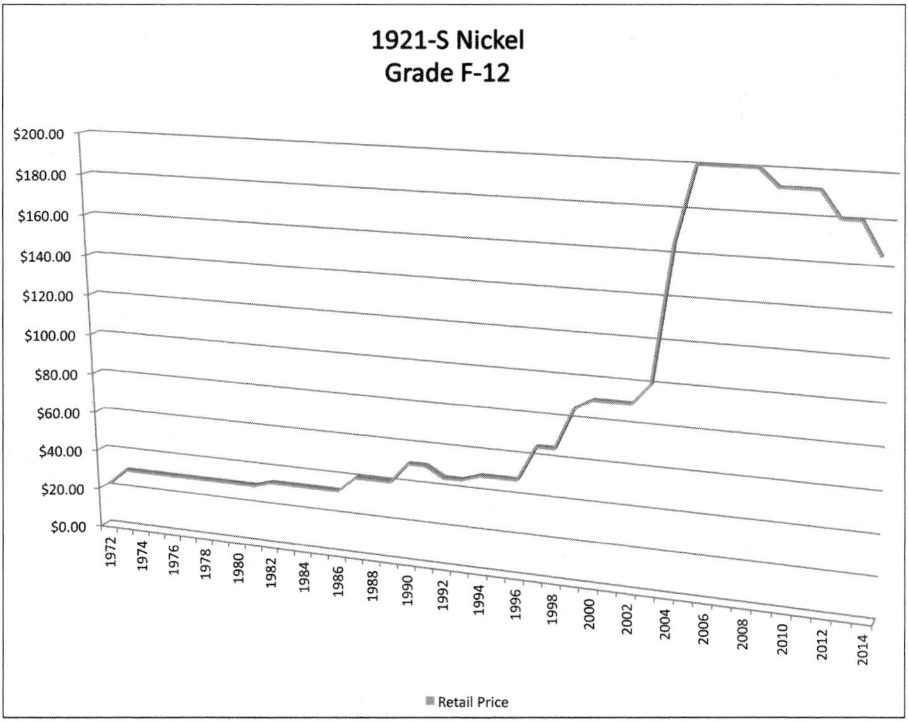

1921-S Nickel
Grade F-12

Retail Price

5 CENTS

Buffalo Nickel
American Bison standing on a mound reverse

KM# 133 • 5.00 g., **Copper-Nickel**, 21.2 mm. • **Designer:** James Earle Fraser

Date	Mintage	G4	VG8	F12	VF20	XF40	AU50	MS60	MS65	Prf65
1913	30,993,520	12.00	15.50	17.00	18.50	20.00	24.50	32.50	150	3,150
1913 D	5,337,000	16.00	19.50	21.00	28.00	35.00	55.00	60.00	300	—
1913 S	2,105,000	43.00	46.00	50.00	60.00	70.00	95.00	125	660	—

American Bison standing on a line reverse

1918/17D

KM# 134 • 5.00 g., **Copper-Nickel**, 21.2 mm. • **Designer:** James Earle Fraser **Note:** In 1913 the reverse design was modified so the ground under the buffalo was represented as a line rather than a mound. On the 1937D 3-legged variety, the buffalo's right front leg is missing, the result of a damaged die.

Date	Mintage	G4	VG8	F12	VF20	XF40	AU50	MS60	MS65	Prf65
1913	29,858,700	12.00	13.00	13.00	14.00	19.00	25.00	32.50	325	2,500
1913 D	4,156,000	125	155	156	160	210	235	285	1,150	—
1913 S	1,209,000	340	375	385	415	550	650	875	3,850	—
1914	20,665,738	20.00	22.00	23.00	25.00	27.50	35.00	47.00	420	2,250
1914/3	Inc. above	150	300	425	525	700	1,050	2,850	30,000	—
1914 D	3,912,000	90.00	110	145	180	295	375	456	1,450	—
1914/3 D	Inc. above	115	225	335	450	625	900	3,500	—	—
1914 S	3,470,000	26.00	35.00	42.00	56.00	90.00	145	165	2,000	—
1914/3 S	Inc. above	250	500	750	1,000	1,450	2,260	4,300	—	—
1915	20,987,270	7.00	8.00	8.50	11.00	20.00	37.50	50.00	325	2,100
1915 D	7,569,500	21.50	31.00	38.50	60.00	115	150	225	1,600	—
1915 S	1,505,000	49.00	68.00	105	155	315	490	625	3,000	—
1916	63,498,066	7.50	6.50	7.00	8.00	13.50	22.00	42.00	300	3,250
1916 2 Feathers	Inc. above	35.00	—	45.00	—	—	—	—	150	—
1916/16	Inc. above	3,950	5,200	8,750	11,000	16,500	34,500	49,500	375,000	—
1916 D	13,333,000	16.50	26.50	27.50	35.00	82.50	110	165	1,850	—
1916 S	11,860,000	11.00	14.00	22.50	33.00	75.00	125	195	1,900	—
1917	51,424,029	7.50	8.00	8.75	9.00	14.00	32.50	56.00	510	—
1917 2 Feathers	Inc. above	40.00	—	50.00	—	—	—	—	165	—
1917 D	9,910,800	26.00	31.00	52.50	75.00	135	255	345	2,650	—
1917 S	4,193,000	23.00	42.00	80.00	105	180	285	395	4,000	—
1917 S 2 Feathers	Inc. above	50.00	70.00	95.00	—	—	—	—	315	—
1918	32,086,314	7.00	7.25	8.00	15.00	31.00	48.50	105	1,400	—
1918/17 D	8,362,314	1,000	1,550	2,750	4,950	8,750	11,000	36,500	350,000	—
1918 D	Inc. above	22.50	39.00	63.00	120	220	330	420	3,750	—
1918 2 Feathers	Inc. above	50.00	—	95.00	—	—	—	—	315	—
1918 S	4,882,000	14.00	27.50	52.50	95.00	175	300	485	20,000	—
1919	60,868,000	2.60	3.50	3.90	7.00	13.50	32.00	57.00	465	—
1919 D	8,006,000	15.50	31.00	72.00	125	235	335	560	6,500	—
1919 S	7,521,000	8.00	21.00	48.00	100	225	360	535	16,500	—
1920	63,093,000	1.50	2.75	3.25	8.00	14.50	30.00	57.00	675	—
1920 D	9,418,000	8.50	19.00	35.00	110	260	340	550	5,250	—
1920 S	9,689,000	4.50	12.75	30.00	95.00	204	285	525	21,000	—
1921	10,663,000	4.00	7.75	8.50	25.00	49.00	70.00	115	775	—
1921 S	1,557,000	64.00	98.00	165	350	785	1,150	1,575	7,350	—
1923	35,715,000	1.70	3.25	4.25	7.00	13.50	36.00	58.00	575	—
1923 S	6,142,000	8.00	10.00	24.00	100	265	315	625	9,500	—
1924	21,620,000	1.50	2.40	4.50	9.00	18.50	40.00	70.00	825	—
1924 D	5,258,000	8.00	10.50	27.50	80.00	210	315	375	4,000	—
1924 S	1,437,000	16.50	32.00	85.00	325	1,050	1,700	2,300	11,500	—
1925	35,565,100	3.00	4.00	4.25	8.50	16.50	32.00	42.00	350	—
1925 D	4,450,000	10.00	22.00	35.00	70.00	160	265	425	4,650	—
1925 S	6,256,000	4.00	8.50	16.50	72.00	170	250	435	25,500	—
1926	44,693,000	1.50	2.00	2.80	5.40	11.50	22.00	30.00	210	—

Date	Mintage	G4	VG8	F12	VF20	XF40	AU50	MS60	MS65	Prf65
1926 D	5,638,000	10.00	17.50	28.50	95.00	170	285	335	4,650	—
1926 S	970,000	20.00	42.00	95.00	235	725	2,450	4,750	115,000	—
1927	37,981,000	1.40	1.75	2.50	4.50	12.50	22.00	35.00	275	—
1927 D	5,730,000	2.50	6.00	7.00	30.00	75.00	115	155	7,250	—
1927 S	3,430,000	1.50	2.50	4.00	32.00	80.00	160	490	17,000	—
1928	23,411,000	1.40	1.75	2.50	4.50	12.50	25.00	32.50	285	—
1928 D	6,436,000	1.90	2.50	3.50	14.50	40.00	46.50	53.00	645	—
1928 S	6,936,000	1.75	2.35	2.50	10.50	27.50	100	225	3,650	—
1929	36,446,000	1.40	1.75	2.25	4.50	13.00	21.00	35.00	315	—
1929 D	8,370,000	1.50	1.85	2.25	6.75	32.50	42.50	60.00	1,150	—
1929 S	7,754,000	1.50	1.85	2.00	2.50	12.50	25.00	49.50	435	—
1930	22,849,000	1.40	1.75	2.25	4.50	11.00	21.00	32.50	235	—
1930 S	5,435,000	1.50	2.00	2.75	4.50	14.50	37.50	65.00	400	—
1931 S	1,200,000	15.00	16.00	17.00	19.00	32.00	46.00	59.00	300	—
1934	20,213,003	1.00	1.30	2.25	4.50	11.00	19.00	47.50	320	—
1934 D	7,480,000	2.00	3.00	4.25	9.60	22.00	50.00	76.00	550	—
1935	58,264,000	0.90	1.20	1.50	1.90	3.50	7.00	25.50	125	—
1935 Double Die Rev.	Inc. above	50.00	75.00	125	250	675	1,800	4,000	75,000	—
1935 D	12,092,000	1.60	2.50	3.00	9.00	22.00	48.00	72.00	415	—
1935 S	10,300,000	1.35	1.75	2.00	2.50	3.75	17.50	48.50	225	—
1936	119,001,420	0.90	1.20	1.50	1.90	3.00	6.50	25.00	90.00	1,650
1936 Brilliant	Inc. above	—	—	—	—	—	—	—	—	2,450
1936 D	24,814,000	1.35	1.75	2.00	2.50	5.00	11.50	33.50	115	—
1936 D 3-1/2 leg	Inc. above	750	1,250	2,000	3,500	6,000	10,500	17,500	—	—
1936 D/S	Inc. above	—	—	10.00	16.00	25.00	—	—	—	—
1936 S	14,930,000	1.35	1.75	2.00	2.50	4.00	11.50	33.50	110	—
1937	79,485,769	0.90	1.20	1.50	1.90	3.00	6.50	25.00	52.50	2,100
1937 D	17,826,000	1.35	1.75	2.00	2.50	4.00	9.00	29.00	60.00	—
1937 D 3-legged	Inc. above	535	585	615	725	965	1,225	2,375	37,000	—
1937 S	5,635,000	1.35	1.75	2.00	2.50	4.00	9.50	27.50	58.00	—
1938 D	7,020,000	3.50	3.75	3.90	4.00	4.50	12.00	25.00	52.50	—
1938 D/D	Inc. above	3.75	4.50	6.00	8.00	10.00	18.50	35.00	100	—
1938 D/S	Inc. above	4.50	6.75	9.00	12.50	18.00	30.00	50.00	150	—

Jefferson Nickel
Monticello, mintmark to right side reverse

KM# 192 • 5.00 g., Copper-Nickel, 21.2 mm. • **Designer:** Felix Schlag **Note:** Some 1939 strikes have doubling of the word MONTICELLO on the reverse.

Date	Mintage	VG8	F12	VF20	XF40	MS60	MS65	65FS	Prf65
1938	19,515,365	0.50	0.75	1.00	2.25	7.50	18.00	125	—
1938 D	5,376,000	1.00	1.25	1.50	2.00	4.00	15.00	95.00	—
1938 S	4,105,000	1.75	2.00	2.50	3.00	5.25	12.00	165	—
1939 T I, wavy steps, Rev. of 1939	120,627,535	—	—	—	—	3.00	30.00	300	70.00
1939 T II, even steps, Rev. of 1940	Inc. above	—	0.20	0.25	0.30	4.00	45.00	50.00	130
1939 doubled MONTICELLO T II	Inc. above	40.00	60.00	90.00	165	300	1,250	2,000	—
1939 D T IT I, wavy steps, Rev. of 1939	3,514,000	—	—	10.00	17.50	75.00	160	275	—
1939 D T IIT II, even steps, Rev. of 1940	Inc. above	4.00	5.00	8.00	14.00	55.00	105	400	—
1939 S T IT I, wavy steps, Rev. of 1939	6,630,000	0.45	0.60	1.50	4.00	17.00	45.00	250	—
1939 S T IIT II, even steps, Rev. of 1940	Inc. above	—	—	—	5.00	24.00	250	275	—
1940	176,499,158	—	—	—	0.25	1.00	12.00	60.00	125
1940 D	43,540,000	—	0.20	0.30	0.40	1.50	2.75	25.00	—
1940 S	39,690,000	0.25	0.40	0.50	1.25	4.50	20.00	55.00	—
1941	203,283,720	—	—	—	0.20	0.75	20.00	55.00	—
1941 D	53,432,000	—	0.20	0.30	0.50	2.25	7.50	25.00	—
1941 S	43,445,000	0.25	0.40	0.50	1.35	5.00	14.00	60.00	—
1942	49,818,600	—	—	—	0.40	5.00	22.00	75.00	—
1942 D	13,938,000	1.00	1.75	3.00	5.00	38.00	65.00	85.00	—
1942 D D over horizontal D	Inc. above	35.00	60.00	100	165	750	10,000	25,000	—

Note: Fully Struck Full Step nickels command higher prices. Bright, Fully Struck coins command even higher prices. 1938 thru 1989 - 5 Full Steps. 1990 to date - 6 Full Steps. Without bag marks or nicks on steps.

5 CENTS

Monticello, mint mark above reverse

1943/2P

KM# 192a • 0.350 Copper-Silver-Manganese, 21.2 mm. • **Designer:** Felix Schlag **Note:** War-time composition nickels have the mint mark above MONTICELLO on the reverse.

Date	Mintage	VG8	F12	VF20	XF40	MS60	MS65	65FS	Prf65
1942 P	57,900,600	1.87	1.93	2.13	2.00	9.00	20.00	75.00	150
1942 S	32,900,000	1.87	1.93	2.13	2.45	8.00	19.00	170	—
1943 P	271,165,000	1.87	1.93	2.13	2.00	5.00	20.00	40.00	—
1943P DDO	Inc. above	—	—	32.00	54.00	125	575	1,100	—
1943/2 P	Inc. above	35.00	50.00	75.00	110	300	775	1,000	—
1943 D	15,294,000	2.12	2.18	2.38	2.05	4.00	18.00	40.00	—
1943 S	104,060,000	1.87	1.93	2.13	2.15	6.75	18.50	48.00	—
1944 P	119,150,000	1.87	1.93	2.13	2.15	10.00	28.00	75.00	—
1944 D	32,309,000	1.92	1.98	2.18	2.25	10.00	22.50	65.00	—
1944 S	21,640,000	1.92	1.98	2.18	2.15	8.50	20.00	185	—
1945 P	119,408,100	1.87	1.93	2.13	2.15	6.00	28.00	120	—
1945 D	37,158,000	1.97	2.03	2.28	2.30	5.50	20.00	40.00	—
1945 S	58,939,000	1.87	1.93	2.13	2.15	5.00	18.00	250	—

Pre-war design resumed reverse

KM# A192 • 5.00 g., **Copper-Nickel**, 21.2 mm. • **Edge:** Plain **Designer:** Felix Schlag

Date	Mintage	XF40	MS65	Prf65
1946	161,116,000	0.25	35.00	—
1946 D	45,292,200	0.35	22.00	—
1946 D/D	Inc. above	—	1,750	—
1946 S	13,560,000	0.40	15.00	—
1947	95,000,000	0.25	18.00	—
1947 D	37,822,000	0.30	18.00	—
1947 S	24,720,000	0.25	20.00	—
1948	89,348,000	0.25	25.00	—
1948 D	44,734,000	0.35	19.00	—
1948 S	11,300,000	0.50	15.00	—
1949	60,652,000	0.30	40.00	—
1949 D	36,498,000	0.40	18.00	—
1949 D/S	Inc. above	65.00	550	—
1949 S	9,716,000	0.90	25.00	—
1950	9,847,386	0.75	25.00	75.00
1950 D	2,630,030	10.00	25.00	—
1951	28,609,500	0.50	35.00	70.00
1951 D	20,460,000	0.50	22.00	—
1951 S	7,776,000	1.10	28.00	—
1952	64,069,980	0.25	35.00	42.00
1952 D	30,638,000	0.45	30.00	—
1952 S	20,572,000	0.25	30.00	—
1953	46,772,800	0.25	26.00	45.00
1953 D	59,878,600	0.25	25.00	—
1953 S	19,210,900	0.25	35.00	—
1954	47,917,350	—	37.50	20.00
1954 D	117,136,560	—	40.00	—
1954 S	29,384,000	0.20	35.00	—
1954 S/D	Inc. above	20.00	350	—
1955	8,266,200	0.45	25.00	13.50
1955 D	74,464,100	—	25.00	—
1955 D/S	Inc. above	25.00	300	—
1956	35,885,384	—	16.00	3.00
1956 D	67,222,940	—	26.00	—

Date	Mintage	XF40	MS65	Prf65
1957	39,655,952	—	35.00	2.50
1957 D	136,828,900	—	22.00	—
1958	17,963,652	0.20	36.00	8.00
1958 D	168,249,120	—	13.00	—
1959	28,397,291	—	22.00	1.40
1959 D	160,738,240	—	22.00	—
1960	57,107,602	—	30.00	1.25
1960 D	192,582,180	—	25.00	—
1961	76,668,244	—	40.00	1.00
1961 D	229,342,760	—	35.00	—
1962	100,602,019	—	24.00	1.00
1962 D	280,195,720	—	110	—
1963	178,851,645	—	4.00	1.00
1963 D	276,829,460	—	100	—
1964	1,028,622,762	—	5.00	1.00
1964 D	1,787,297,160	—	12.00	—
1965	136,131,380	—	12.00	—
1965 SMS	2,360,000	—	12.00	—
1966	156,208,283	—	10.00	—
1966 SMS	2,261,583	—	15.00	—
1967	107,325,800	—	8.00	—
1967 SMS	1,863,344	—	12.00	—
1968 none minted	—	—	—	—
1968 D	91,227,880	—	6.00	—
1968 S	103,437,510	—	5.00	0.75
1969 none minted	—	—	—	—
1969 D	202,807,500	—	5.00	—
1969 S	123,099,631	—	7.50	0.75
1970 none minted	—	—	—	—
1970 D	515,485,380	—	12.00	—
1970 S	241,464,814	—	30.00	0.75
1971	106,884,000	—	9.00	—
1971 D	316,144,800	—	4.50	—
1971 S	3,220,733	—	—	1.00
1972	202,036,000	—	4.00	—
1972 D	351,694,600	—	3.00	—
1972 S	3,260,996	—	—	1.00
1973	384,396,000	—	5.00	—
1973 D	261,405,000	—	4.00	—
1973 S	2,760,339	—	—	0.75
1974	601,752,000	—	12.00	—
1974 D	277,373,000	—	5.00	—
1974 S	2,612,568	—	—	0.75
1975	181,772,000	—	6.00	—
1975 D	401,875,300	—	6.00	—
1975 S	2,845,450	—	—	0.75
1976	367,124,000	—	8.00	—
1976 D	563,964,147	—	6.00	—

Date	Mintage	XF40	MS65	Prf65
1976 S	4,149,730	—	—	0.75
1977	585,376,000	—	8.50	—
1977 D	297,313,460	—	6.50	—
1977 S	3,251,152	—	—	0.75
1978	391,308,000	—	7.00	—
1978 D	313,092,780	—	5.00	—
1978 S	3,127,781	—	—	0.75
1979	463,188,000	—	8.50	—
1979 D	325,867,672	—	5.50	—
1979 S type I, proof	3,677,175	—	—	0.75
1979 S type II, proof	—	—	—	2.00
1980 P	593,004,000	—	6.50	—
1980 D	502,323,448	—	5.50	—
1980 S	3,554,806	—	—	0.75
1981 P	657,504,000	—	50.00	—
1981 D	364,801,843	—	6.00	—
1981 S type I, proof	4,063,083	—	—	2.00
1981 S type II, proof	—	—	—	2.50
1982 P	292,355,000	—	15.00	—
1982 D	373,726,544	—	14.00	—
1982 S	3,857,479	—	—	1.50
1983 P	561,615,000	—	9.00	—
1983 D	536,726,276	—	6.00	—
1983 S	3,279,126	—	—	1.50
1984 P	746,769,000	—	5.00	—
1984 D	517,675,146	—	4.75	—
1984 S	3,065,110	—	—	1.50
1985 P	647,114,962	—	4.75	—
1985 D	459,747,446	—	4.75	—
1985 S	3,362,821	—	—	1.50
1986 P	536,883,483	—	5.00	—
1986 D	361,819,140	—	4.75	—
1986 S	3,010,497	—	—	3.00
1987 P	371,499,481	—	5.00	—
1987 D	410,590,604	—	4.50	—
1987 S	4,227,728	—	—	1.25
1988 P	771,360,000	—	4.50	—
1988 D	663,771,652	—	5.00	—
1988 S	3,262,948	—	—	1.75
1989 P	898,812,000	—	4.50	—
1989 D	570,842,474	—	6.00	—
1989 S	3,220,194	—	—	1.50
1990 P	661,636,000	—	4.50	—
1990 D	663,938,503	—	5.50	—
1990 S	3,299,559	—	—	1.50
1991 P	614,104,000	—	4.50	—
1991 D	436,496,678	—	4.50	—
1991 S	2,867,787	—	—	1.50
1992 P	399,552,000	—	5.00	—
1992 D	450,565,113	—	4.00	—
1992 S	4,176,560	—	—	1.00
1993 P	412,076,000	—	4.00	—
1993 D	406,084,135	—	4.00	—
1993 S	3,394,792	—	—	1.00
1994 P	722,160,000	—	4.00	—
1994 P Special Uncirculed matte finish	167,703	—	—	—
1994 D	715,762,110	—	4.00	—
1994 S	3,269,923	—	—	1.00
1995 P	774,156,000	—	4.00	—
1995 D	888,112,000	—	4.50	—
1995 S	2,707,481	—	—	1.50
1996 P	829,332,000	—	4.00	—
1996 D	817,736,000	—	4.00	—
1996 S	2,915,212	—	—	1.50
1997 P	470,972,000	—	4.75	—
1997 P Special Uncirculated matte finish	25,000	—	—	—
1997 D	466,640,000	—	4.50	—
1997 S	1,975,000	—	—	1.50
1998 P	688,272,000	—	3.75	—
1998 D	635,360,000	—	3.75	—
1998 S	2,957,286	—	—	1.25
1999 P	1,212,000,000	—	3.75	—
1999 D	1,066,720,000	—	3.75	—
1999 S	3,362,462	—	—	1.25

Date	Mintage	XF40	MS65	Prf65
2000 P	846,240,000	—	3.75	—
2000 D	1,509,520,000	—	3.75	—
2000 S	4,063,361	—	—	1.00
2001 P	675,704,000	—	3.75	—
2001 D	627,680,000	—	3.75	—
2001 S	3,099,096	—	—	1.00
2002 P	539,280,000	—	3.75	—
2002 D	691,200,000	—	3.75	—
2002 S	3,157,739	—	—	1.00
2003 P	441,840,000	—	3.75	—
2003 D	383,040,000	—	3.75	—
2003 S	3,116,590	—	—	1.00

Jefferson - Westward Expansion - Lewis & Clark Bicentennial
Jefferson era peace medal design

KM# 360 • 5.00 g., **Copper-Nickel**, 21.2 mm. • **Obv. Designer:** Felix Schlag **Rev. Designer:** Norman E. Nemeth

Date	Mintage	MS65	Prf65
2004 P	361,440,000	—	—
2004 D	372,000,000	—	—
2004 S	2,992,069	—	5.00

Lewis and Clark's Keelboat reverse

KM# 361 • 5.00 g., **Copper-Nickel**, 21.2 mm. • **Obv. Designer:** Felix Schlag **Rev. Designer:** Al Maletsky

Date	Mintage	MS65	Prf65
2004 P	366,720,000	1.50	—
2004 D	344,880,000	1.50	—
2004 S	2,965,422	—	5.00

Thomas Jefferson large profile right obverse   American Bison right reverse

KM# 368 • 5.00 g., **Copper-Nickel**, 21.2 mm. • **Obv. Designer:** Joe Fitzgerald and Don Everhart II **Rev. Designer:** Jamie Franki and Norman E. Nemeth

Date	Mintage	MS65	Prf65
2005 P	448,320,000	1.50	—
2005 P Satin Finish	1,160,000	4.00	—
2005 D	487,680,000	1.50	—
2005 D Satin Finish	1,160,000	4.00	—
2005 S	3,344,679	—	6.50

5 CENTS

5 CENTS

Pacific coastline reverse

KM# 369 • 5.00 g., **Copper-Nickel**, 21.2 mm. • **Subject:** Ocean in View!, oh the joy! **Obv. Designer:** Joe Fitzgerald and Don Everhart **Rev. Designer:** Joe Fitzgerald and Donna Weaver

Date	Mintage	MS65	Prf65
2005 P	394,080,000	1.25	—
2005 P Satin Finish	1,160,000	4.00	—
2005 D	411,120,000	1.25	—
2005 D Satin Finish	1,160,000	4.00	—
2005 S	3,344,679	—	5.50

Jefferson head facing obverse
Monticello, enhanced design reverse

KM# 381 • 5.00 g., **Copper-Nickel**, 21.2 mm. • **Subject:** Jefferson facing head **Obv. Designer:** Jamie N. Franki

and Donna Weaver **Rev. Designer:** Felix Schlag and John Mercanti

Date	Mintage	MS65	Prf65
2006 P	693,120,000	2.50	—
2006 P Satin finish	847,361	4.00	—
2006 D	809,280,000	2.50	—
2006 D Satin finish	847,361	4.00	—
2006 S	3,054,436	—	5.00
2007 P	571,680,000	2.50	—
2007 P Satin finish	895,628	4.00	—
2007 D	626,160,000	2.50	—
2007 D Satin finish	895,628	4.00	—
2007 S	2,577,166	—	4.00
2008 P	279,840,000	2.50	—
2008 P Satin finish	745,464	4.00	—
2008 D	345,600,000	2.50	—
2008 D Satin finish	745,464	4.00	—
2008 S	2,169,561	—	4.00
2009 P	39,840,000	3.50	—
2009 P Satin finish	784,614	4.00	—
2009 D	46,800,000	1.75	—
2009 D Satin finish	784,614	4.00	—
2009 S	2,179,867	—	3.00
2010 P	260,640,000	1.50	—
2010 P Satin finish	—	4.00	—
2010 D	229,920,000	1.50	—
2010 D Satin finish	—	4.00	—
2010 S	1,689,216	—	3.00
2011 P	450,000,000	1.50	—
2011 D	540,240,000	1.50	—
2011 S	1,673,010	—	4.00
2012 P	464,640,000	1.50	—
2012 D	558,960,000	1.50	—
2012 S	1,237,415	—	4.00
2013 P	607,440,000	1.50	—
2013 D	615,600,000	1.50	—
2013 S	1,237,926	—	3.00

DIME

Draped Bust Dime
Draped bust right obverse
Small eagle reverse

KM# 24 • 2.70 g., 0.892 **Silver** 0.08 oz. ASW, 19 mm. • **Designer:** Robert Scot

Date	Mintage	G4	VG8	F12	VF20	XF40	MS60
1796	22,135	2,850	3,600	5,500	7,000	12,350	24,500
1797 13 stars	25,261	3,100	3,950	6,050	8,000	13,150	70,000
1797 16 stars	Inc. above	3,000	3,850	5,800	7,150	13,650	36,500

Draped bust right obverse   Heraldic eagle reverse

KM# 31 • 2.70 g., 0.892 **Silver** 0.08 oz. ASW, 19 mm. • **Obv. Legend:** LIBERTY **Rev. Legend:** UNITED STATES OF AMERICA **Designer:** Robert Scot **Note:** The 1805 strikes have either 4 or 5 berries on the olive branch held by the eagle.

Date	Mintage	G4	VG8	F12	VF20	XF40	MS60
1798 large 8	27,550	725	1,250	1,550	2,100	3,625	8,850
1798 small 8	Inc. above	975	1,450	2,350	3,250	6,000	53,500
1798/97 13 stars	Inc. above	2,150	3,850	5,650	8,850	13,850	59,000

Date	Mintage	G4	VG8	F12	VF20	XF40	MS60
1798/97 16 stars	Inc. above	775	1,125	1,800	2,650	4,600	10,500

Note: The 1798 overdates have either 13 or 16 stars under the clouds on the reverse; Varieties of the regular 1798 strikes are distinguished by the size of the 8 in the date

Date	Mintage	G4	VG8	F12	VF20	XF40	MS60
1800	21,760	700	1,075	1,400	2,700	4,350	37,500
1801	34,640	750	1,150	1,650	3,100	6,250	49,500
1802	10,975	1,750	2,650	3,500	4,750	10,000	37,500
1803	33,040	675	1,150	1,900	2,750	5,900	49,500
1804 13 stars	8,265	2,650	4,450	10,500	19,000	41,500	—
1804 14 stars	Inc. above	4,850	6,500	12,500	24,500	46,500	—
1805 5 berries	Inc. above	625	1,000	1,400	2,100	3,700	9,100
1805 4 berries	120,780	615	920	1,225	1,650	2,950	7,350
1807	165,000	575	900	1,200	1,650	2,950	6,850

Liberty Cap Dime
Draped bust left, flanked by stars, date below obverse
Eagle with arrows in talons, banner above, value below reverse

KM# 42 • 2.70 g., 0.892 **Silver** 0.08 oz. ASW, 18.8 mm. • **Rev. Legend:** UNITED STATES OF AMERICA **Designer:** John Reich **Note:** The 1820 varieties are distinguished by the size of the 0 in the date. The 1823 overdates have either large E's or small E's in UNITED STATES OF AMERICA on the reverse.

Date	Mintage	G4	VG8	F12	VF20	XF40	AU50	MS60	MS65
1809	51,065	140	220	450	700	1,500	2,850	4,500	24,500
1811/9	65,180	110	175	275	650	1,350	2,000	4,000	33,500
1814 small date	421,500	60.00	80.00	145	300	650	1,250	2,000	19,500
1814 large date	Inc. above	43.00	56.00	75.00	168	450	720	1,425	17,000
1814 large date with period	Inc. above	46.00	60.00	85.00	195	500	775	2,000	—
1814 STATESOF	Inc. above	70.00	88.00	160	335	750	1,400	2,350	24,500

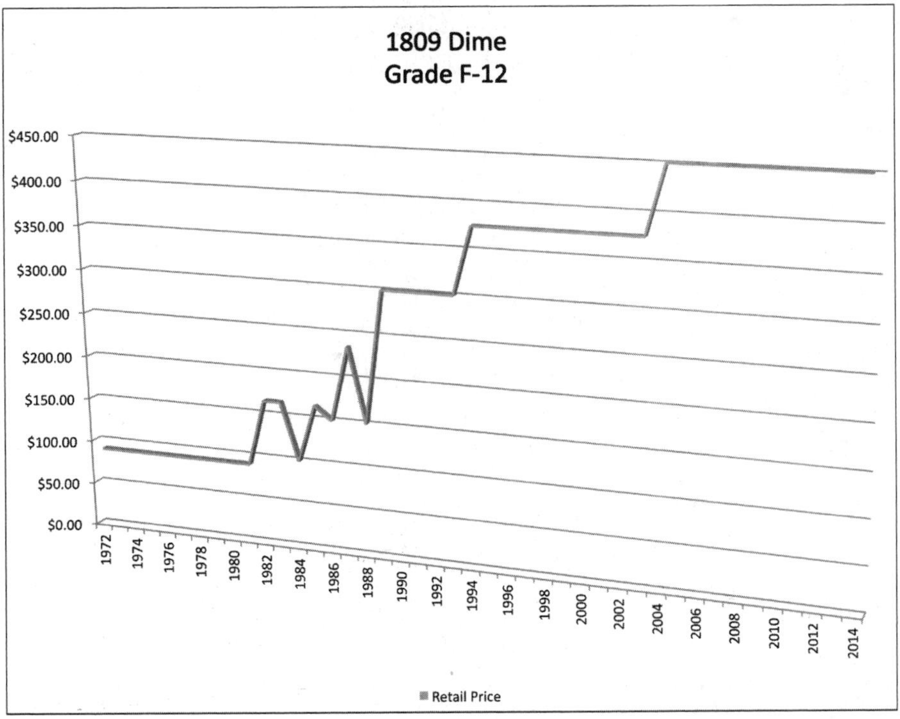

1809 Dime
Grade F-12

[Line chart showing Retail Price from 1972 to 2014. Y-axis ranges from $0.00 to $450.00 in $50.00 increments. The price starts around $90 in 1972, rises with fluctuations through the 1980s peaking around $200, settles around $275 in the early 1990s, rises to about $345, and steps up to around $415 by 2004 where it remains flat through 2014.]

■ Retail Price

DIME

Date	Mintage	G4	VG8	F12	VF20	XF40	AU50	MS60	MS65
1820 large O	942,587	42.00	54.00	71.00	155	445	715	1,410	14,750
1820 small O	Inc. above	43.00	56.00	75.00	170	465	800	1,675	17,250
1820 STATESOF	Inc. above	43.00	56.00	75.00	168	450	720	1,425	16,500
1821 large date	1,186,512	42.00	54.00	71.00	155	445	715	1,410	14,750
1821 small date	Inc. above	43.00	56.00	75.00	170	465	800	1,675	19,000
1822	100,000	1,000	1,850	3,250	4,500	6,250	7,850	13,500	70,000
1823/22 large E's	440,000	42.00	54.00	71.00	163	465	735	1,460	16,850
1823/22 small E's	Inc. above	42.00	54.00	71.00	163	465	735	1,460	15,600
1824/22	—	50.00	80.00	145	300	650	1,250	2,000	19,500
1825	510,000	39.00	50.00	65.00	145	425	675	1,350	14,850
1827	1,215,000	39.00	50.00	65.00	145	425	675	1,350	14,500
1827/7	Inc. above	250	—	—	750	1,100	1,500	—	—
1828 large date	125,000	70.00	110	175	375	750	1,250	3,100	17,250

Draped bust left, flanked by stars, date below obverse
Eagle with arrows in talons, banner above, value below reverse

KM# 48 • Silver, 18.5 mm. • **Rev. Legend:** UNITED STATES OF AMERICA **Designer:** John Reich **Note:** The three varieties of 1829 strikes and two varieties of 1830 strikes are distinguished by the size of "10C." on the reverse. On the 1833 "high 3" variety, the last 3 in the date is higher thatn the first 3. The two varieties of the 1834 strikes are distinguished by the size of the 4 in the date.

Date	Mintage	G4	VG8	F12	VF20	XF40	AU50	MS60	MS65
1828 small date	Inc. above	41.50	52.00	80.00	155	425	625	1,250	12,500
1829 very large 10C	770,000	60.00	75.00	120	235	550	800	1,500	—
1829 large 10C.	Inc. above	54.00	65.00	110	200	400	600	1,150	9,250
1829 medium 10C.	Inc. above	37.50	46.00	54.00	85.00	255	400	900	8,500
1829 small 10C.	Inc. above	37.50	46.00	56.00	90.00	270	460	920	8,700
1829 curl base 2	Inc. above	7,750	10,500	16,500	27,500	38,500	44,000	—	—
1830 large 10C.	510,000	37.50	46.00	56.00	85.00	255	440	900	8,500
1830 small 10C.	Inc. above	37.50	46.00	54.00	90.00	270	465	950	10,500
1830/29	Inc. above	53.50	79.00	120	220	430	815	1,625	—
1831	771,350	37.50	46.00	54.00	85.00	255	440	900	8,500
1832	522,500	37.50	46.00	54.00	85.00	255	440	900	8,500
1833	485,000	37.50	46.00	54.00	85.00	260	455	915	8,500
1833 last 3 high	Inc. above	37.50	46.00	54.00	85.00	260	455	945	11,000
1834 small 4	635,000	37.50	46.00	54.00	85.00	255	440	900	8,650
1834 large 4	Inc. above	37.50	46.00	54.00	85.00	255	440	900	8,500
1835	1,410,000	37.50	46.00	54.00	85.00	255	440	900	8,500
1836	1,190,000	37.50	46.00	54.00	85.00	255	440	900	8,500
1837	1,042,000	37.50	46.00	56.00	90.00	270	460	920	8,650

Seated Liberty Dime
Seated Liberty, date below obverse   Value within wreath reverse

KM# 61 • 2.67 g., 0.900 **Silver** 0.08 oz. ASW, 17.9 mm. • **Rev. Legend:** UNITED STATES OF AMERICA **Designer:** Christian Gobrecht

Date	Mintage	G4	VG8	F12	VF20	XF40	AU50	MS60	MS65
1837 flat top	Inc. above	44.00	58.00	110	285	515	700	1,050	6,500
1837 curly top	Inc. above	40.00	52.00	95.00	250	465	750	1,000	6,500
1838 O	406,034	47.50	70.00	125	375	725	1,250	3,500	21,000

DIME

Seated Liberty, stars around top 1/2 of border, date below obverse
Value within wreath reverse

No drapery at elbow

KM# 63.1 • 2.67 g., 0.900 **Silver** 0.08 oz. ASW, 17.9 mm. • **Obv. Designer:** Christian Gobrecht **Rev. Legend:** UNITED STATES OF AMERICA **Note:** The 1839-O with reverse of 1838-O variety was struck from rusted dies, it has a bumpy reverse surface.

Date		Mintage	G4	VG8	F12	VF20	XF40	AU50	MS60	MS65
1838	small stars	1,992,500	27.00	38.00	55.00	85.00	175	400	625	—
1838	large stars	Inc. above	22.00	25.50	34.50	45.00	135	260	375	8,500
1838	partial drapery	Inc. above	35.00	50.00	85.00	150	225	350	550	—
1839		1,053,115	19.00	23.50	28.50	40.00	125	245	315	3,000
1839 O		1,323,000	23.50	30.00	47.00	140	150	280	650	6,000
1839 O reverse 1838O		Inc. above	165	225	375	550	1,150	—	—	—
1840		1,358,580	19.00	24.50	28.50	40.00	125	245	315	4,000
1840 O		1,175,000	23.00	28.50	36.50	60.00	165	325	2,750	6,500

Seated Liberty, stars around top 1/2 of border, date below obverse
Value within wreath reverse

Drapery at elbow

KM# 63.2 • 2.67 g., 0.900 **Silver** 0.08 oz. ASW, 17.9 mm. • **Rev. Legend:** UNITED STATES OF AMERICA **Designer:** Christian Gobrecht **Note:** Drapery added to Liberty's left elbow

Date	Mintage	G4	VG8	F12	VF20	XF40	AU50	MS60	MS65
1840	Inc. above	32.00	50.00	90.00	175	300	400	2,400	—
1841	1,622,500	17.50	20.00	22.50	29.00	50.00	150	310	2,700
1841 O	2,007,500	23.50	28.50	33.00	41.50	90.00	250	1,500	5,000
1841 O large O	Inc. above	600	900	1,200	2,500	—	—	—	—
1842	1,887,500	16.50	18.00	22.00	28.50	47.00	150	280	2,700
1842 O	2,020,000	25.00	30.00	37.50	75.00	225	1,350	2,900	—
1843	1,370,000	16.50	18.00	22.00	28.50	47.00	150	280	3,000
1843/1843	Inc. above	16.00	18.50	22.50	30.00	75.00	200	295	—
1843 O	150,000	50.00	75.00	135	300	1,100	3,450	—	—
1844	72,500	200	300	375	600	1,350	1,850	3,000	—
1845	1,755,000	17.50	18.00	22.00	28.50	47.00	150	280	2,600
1845/1845	Inc. above	17.00	20.00	35.00	55.00	100	175	—	—
1845 O	230,000	32.00	48.00	90.00	225	650	1,350	—	—
1846	31,300	150	250	365	575	1,600	9,000	5,500	—
1847	245,000	19.50	30.00	40.00	70.00	125	350	950	9,000
1848	451,500	19.50	25.00	28.50	52.50	95.00	175	750	7,000
1849	839,000	19.50	21.50	25.00	37.50	55.00	150	500	4,000
1849 O	300,000	26.00	33.00	50.00	125	275	750	2,200	—
1850	1,931,500	19.50	21.50	24.50	34.50	50.00	150	280	5,900
1850 O	510,000	25.00	32.00	40.00	75.00	135	300	1,250	—
1851	1,026,500	19.50	21.50	24.50	32.50	50.00	150	335	5,000
1851 O	400,000	25.00	34.00	42.50	85.00	175	475	1,850	—
1852	1,535,500	16.50	18.00	20.00	26.50	45.00	150	280	2,550
1852 O	430,000	28.50	34.00	53.50	145	250	400	1,800	—
1853	95,000	95.00	145	220	300	425	575	750	—

Seated Liberty, stars around top 1/2 of border, arrows at date obverse
Value within wreath reverse

KM# 77 • 2.49 g., 0.900 **Silver** 0.07 oz. ASW **Rev. Legend:** UNITED STATES OF AMERICA **Designer:** Christian Gobrecht

Date	Mintage	G4	VG8	F12	VF20	XF40	AU50	MS60	MS65	Prf65
1853	12,078,010	16.00	18.00	19.00	25.00	44.00	145	260	2,500	31,500

Date	Mintage	G4	VG8	F12	VF20	XF40	AU50	MS60	MS65	Prf65
1853 O	1,100,000	18.00	20.00	24.00	45.00	125	285	900	—	—
1854	4,470,000	16.00	18.00	19.00	22.00	44.00	145	260	2,500	31,500
1854 O	1,770,000	17.00	20.00	22.00	26.00	60.00	160	600	—	—
1855	2,075,000	16.00	18.00	19.00	22.00	48.00	150	350	3,800	31,500

Seated Liberty, stars around top 1/2 of border, date below obverse
Value within wreath reverse

KM# A63.2 • 2.49 g., 0.900 **Silver** 0.07 oz. ASW **Rev. Legend:** UNITED STATES OF AMERICA **Designer:** Christian Gobrecht

Date	Mintage	G4	VG8	F12	VF20	XF40	AU50	MS60	MS65	Prf65
1856 small date	5,780,000	15.50	17.00	18.50	21.00	42.00	138	250	7,050	38,000
1856 large date	Inc. above	20.00	23.50	27.00	34.00	65.00	175	475	—	—
1856 O	1,180,000	19.00	22.00	23.50	32.00	70.00	225	625	5,250	—
1856 S	70,000	135	185	360	575	1,150	1,750	—	—	—
1857	5,580,000	15.50	17.00	18.50	21.00	42.00	138	250	2,600	3,400
1857 O	1,540,000	16.50	18.00	19.50	26.00	55.00	175	375	2,600	—
1858	1,540,000	15.50	17.00	18.50	21.00	42.00	138	260	2,600	3,400
1858 O	290,000	16.50	25.00	36.00	85.00	120	280	800	5,000	—
1858 S	60,000	135	200	265	475	1,000	1,650	—	—	—
1859	430,000	16.00	20.00	23.50	38.00	55.00	138	350	—	3,400
1859 O	480,000	16.00	20.00	25.00	40.00	80.00	240	550	—	—
1859 S	60,000	100	175	350	600	1,350	2,750	—	—	—
1860 S	140,000	37.50	55.00	70.00	145	325	625	—	—	—

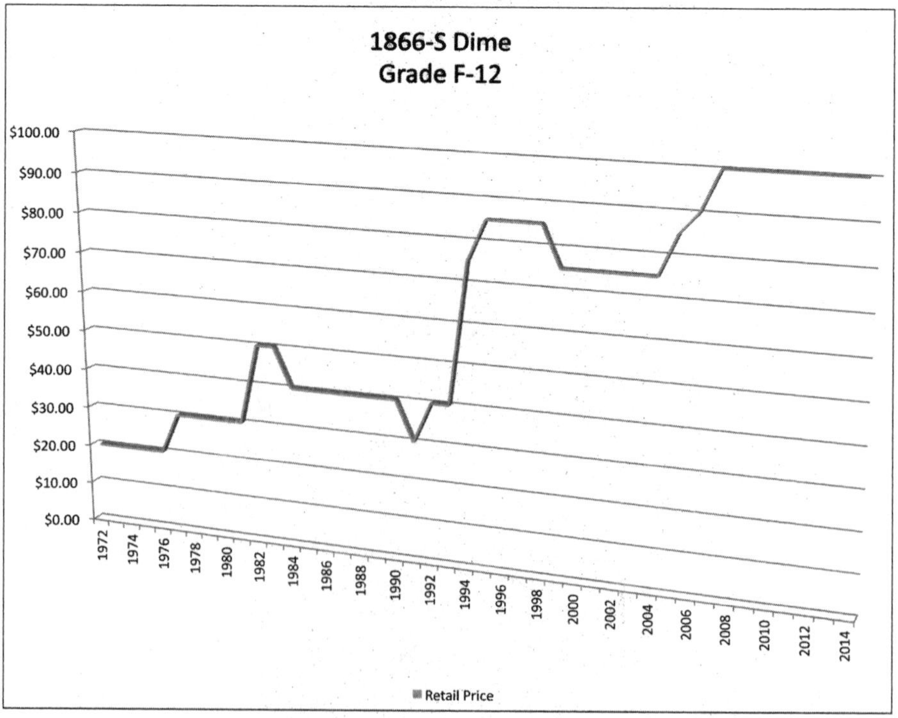

1866-S Dime
Grade F-12

[Line graph titled "1866-S Dime Grade F-12" with y-axis from $0.00 to $100.00 and x-axis years from 1972 to 2014, showing "Retail Price"]

UNITED STATES OF AMERICA replaced stars obverse   Value within wreath reverse

KM# 92 • 2.49 g., 0.900 **Silver** 0.07 oz. ASW **Obv. Legend:** UNITED STATES OF AMERICA **Obv. Designer:** Christian Gobrecht **Note:** The 1873 "closed-3" and "open-3" varieties are distinguished by the amount of space between the upper left and lower left serifs of the 3 in the date.

Date	Mintage	G4	VG8	F12	VF20	XF40	AU50	MS60	MS65	Prf65
1860	607,000	17.50	19.00	29.00	32.00	44.00	115	275	1,350	1,400
1860 O	40,000	400	600	900	1,950	3,650	6,500	8,500	—	—
1861	1,884,000	16.50	18.00	20.00	23.00	32.00	85.00	150	1,250	1,400
1861 S	172,500	55.00	90.00	150	200	400	650	1,400	—	—
1862	847,550	17.50	19.00	21.00	24.00	45.00	75.00	165	1,250	1,400
1862 S	180,750	45.00	60.00	95.00	175	300	675	1,000	—	—
1863	14,460	425	500	650	900	1,050	1,100	1,300	—	1,400
1863 S	157,500	45.00	55.00	75.00	145	250	500	1,200	—	—
1864	11,470	425	500	650	800	1,000	1,150	1,200	—	1,400
1864 S	230,000	35.00	45.00	75.00	120	225	375	1,200	—	—
1865	10,500	475	575	700	875	1,250	1,200	1,350	—	1,400
1865 S	175,000	45.00	55.00	85.00	200	350	775	—	—	—
1866	8,725	500	600	775	950	1,300	1,200	1,800	—	1,750
1866 S	135,000	50.00	65.00	100	150	275	400	1,900	—	—
1867	6,625	600	700	950	1,100	1,450	1,600	1,800	—	1,750
1867 S	140,000	45.00	80.00	135	200	365	675	1,200	—	—
1868	464,000	25.00	30.00	36.00	50.00	90.00	175	300	—	1,400
1868 S	260,000	32.00	38.00	50.00	115	175	275	600	—	—
1869	256,600	30.00	35.00	45.00	110	145	250	600	—	1,400
1869 S	450,000	25.00	30.00	40.00	55.00	90.00	160	400	—	—
1870	471,000	17.50	22.00	30.00	40.00	50.00	85.00	150	—	1,400
1870 S	50,000	300	375	500	650	850	1,050	2,000	—	—
1871	907,710	16.50	18.00	20.00	30.00	45.00	160	300	—	1,400
1871 CC	20,100	2,000	3,500	4,500	9,500	12,500	25,000	—	—	—
1871 S	320,000	35.00	55.00	85.00	135	195	325	900	—	—
1872	2,396,450	15.00	16.50	18.50	21.50	30.00	85.00	175	—	1,400
1872 CC	35,480	650	1,250	1,850	3,000	7,500	—	—	—	—
1872 S	190,000	40.00	65.00	85.00	165	250	400	1,100	—	—
1873 closed 3	1,568,600	16.50	18.00	20.00	24.00	32.50	75.00	200	—	1,400
1873 open 3	Inc. above	28.00	35.00	60.00	90.00	140	220	650	—	—
1873 CC	12,400	—	—	—	—	—	—	—	—	—

Note: 1873-CC, Heritage Sale, April 1999, MS-64, $632,500.

Seated Liberty, arrows at date obverse   Value within wreath reverse

KM# 105 • 2.50 g., 0.900 **Silver** 0.07 oz. ASW **Obv. Legend:** UNITED STATES OF AMERICA **Designer:** Christian Gobrecht

Date	Mintage	G4	VG8	F12	VF20	XF40	AU50	MS60	MS65	Prf65
1873	2,378,500	17.00	20.00	27.50	60.00	118	280	500	4,500	4,500
1873 CC	18,791	1,350	2,850	4,250	9,500	16,500	—	—	—	—
1873 S	455,000	22.00	30.00	40.00	80.00	200	425	1,500	—	—
1874	2,940,700	16.00	19.00	26.00	60.00	118	280	500	4,500	4,500
1874 CC	10,817	5,000	7,000	10,500	18,500	34,000	—	—	—	—
1874 S	240,000	50.00	60.00	85.00	150	265	450	1,500	—	—

Seated Liberty, date below obverse   Value within wreath reverse

KM# A92 • 2.50 g., 0.900 **Silver** 0.07 oz. ASW **Obv. Legend:** UNITED STATES OF AMERICA **Designer:** Christian Gobrecht **Note:** On the 1876-CC doubled-obverse variety, doubling appears in the words OF AMERICA in the legend.

Date	Mintage	G4	VG8	F12	VF20	XF40	AU50	MS60	MS65	Prf65
1875	10,350,700	16.00	17.50	19.50	22.50	32.00	80.00	145	2,250	4,600
1875 CC mint mark in wreath	4,645,000	29.00	32.00	36.00	52.00	68.00	130	190	2,700	—
1875 CC mint mark under wreath	Inc. above	32.00	34.00	40.00	58.00	90.00	165	235	3,000	—
1875 S mint mark in wreath	9,070,000	19.00	23.00	28.00	40.00	65.00	95.00	225	3,100	—
1875 S mint mark under wreath	Inc. above	16.00	18.00	20.00	22.50	32.00	80.00	145	1,100	—
1876 Type 1 rev	11,461,150	15.00	17.00	19.00	22.50	30.00	75.00	145	1,100	1,200
1876 Type 2 rev	Inc. above	19.00	25.00	30.00	40.00	60.00	120	200	—	—
1876 CC Type 1 rev	8,270,000	29.00	32.00	36.00	50.00	70.00	125	225	—	—
1876 CC Type 2 rev	Inc. above	32.00	34.00	48.00	65.00	90.00	175	300	—	—
1876 CC doubled die obverse	Inc. above	35.00	40.00	55.00	100	185	340	600	—	—
1876 S Type 1 rev	10,420,000	15.00	16.50	18.50	22.50	30.00	75.00	145	1,750	—
1876 S Type 2 rev	Inc. above	20.00	20.00	24.00	30.00	40.00	90.00	150	—	—
1877 Type 1 rev	7,310,510	15.00	16.50	18.50	22.50	30.00	75.00	145	1,100	1,200
1877 Type 2 rev	Inc. above	18.00	24.00	30.00	40.00	40.00	90.00	150	—	—
1877 CC Type 1 rev	7,700,000	35.00	42.00	48.00	70.00	90.00	175	300	1,100	—
1877 CC Type 2 rev	Inc. above	29.00	32.00	36.00	52.00	70.00	125	225	—	—
1877 S Type 1 rev	2,340,000	—	—	—	—	—	—	—	—	—
1877 S Type 2 rev	Inc. above	15.00	16.50	18.50	22.50	30.00	85.00	225	—	—
1878 Type 1 rev	1,678,800	28.00	35.00	50.00	65.00	100	175	—	—	—
1878 Type 2 rev	Inc. above	15.00	16.50	18.50	22.50	33.00	75.00	145	1,500	1,200
1878 CC Type 1 rev	200,000	100	135	175	285	450	600	—	—	—
1878 CC Type 2 rev	Inc. above	65.00	90.00	135	225	370	500	900	3,500	—
1879	15,100	275	310	375	500	625	700	800	1,750	1,500
1880	37,335	225	275	330	425	475	585	675	1,750	1,500
1881	24,975	240	300	350	450	500	610	700	2,500	1,600
1882	3,911,100	15.00	16.50	18.50	21.50	30.00	75.00	145	1,100	1,200
1883	7,675,712	15.00	16.50	18.50	21.50	30.00	75.00	145	1,100	1,200
1884	3,366,380	15.00	16.50	18.50	21.50	30.00	75.00	145	1,100	1,200
1884 S	564,969	26.00	33.00	42.00	55.00	125	280	650	—	—
1885	2,533,427	15.00	16.50	18.50	21.50	30.00	75.00	145	1,100	1,200
1885 S	43,690	475	575	850	1,400	2,400	3,350	5,000	—	—
1886	6,377,570	15.00	16.50	18.50	21.50	30.00	75.00	145	1,100	1,200
1886 S	206,524	30.00	45.00	65.00	125	150	175	600	—	—
1887	11,283,939	15.00	16.50	18.50	21.50	30.00	75.00	145	1,100	1,200
1887 S	4,454,450	15.00	16.50	18.50	21.50	30.00	75.00	145	1,100	—
1888	5,496,487	15.00	16.50	18.50	21.50	30.00	75.00	145	1,100	1,200
1888 S	1,720,000	15.00	16.50	18.50	25.50	35.00	90.00	200	—	—
1889	7,380,711	15.00	16.50	18.50	21.50	30.00	75.00	145	1,100	1,200
1889 S	972,678	15.00	18.50	25.00	45.00	70.00	150	475	4,500	—
1890	9,911,541	15.00	16.50	18.50	21.50	30.00	75.00	145	1,100	1,200
1890 S	1,423,076	15.00	16.50	24.00	44.00	85.00	145	400	4,900	—
1891	15,310,600	15.00	16.50	18.50	21.50	30.00	75.00	145	1,100	1,200
1891 O	4,540,000	16.00	17.50	20.50	25.50	35.00	90.00	175	1,750	—
1891 O /horizontal O	Inc. above	65.00	95.00	125	175	225	400	—	—	—
1891 S	3,196,116	15.00	17.00	19.00	21.50	30.00	75.00	175	1,650	—
1891 S/S	Inc. above	25.00	30.00	40.00	85.00	135	250	—	—	—

Barber Dime
Laureate head right, date at angle below obverse Value within wreath reverse

KM# 113 • 2.50 g., 0.900 Silver 0.07 oz. ASW, 17.9 mm. • Obv. Legend: UNITED STATES OF AMERICA Designer: Charles E. Barber

Date	Mintage	G4	VG8	F12	VF20	XF40	AU50	MS60	MS65	Prf65
1892	12,121,245	8.75	9.50	16.00	25.00	27.50	66.00	115	600	1,485
1892 O	3,841,700	11.00	15.00	36.00	58.00	78.00	96.00	150	1,275	—
1892 S	990,710	66.00	115	210	245	285	340	425	4,250	—
1893/2	3,340,792	135	155	175	225	300	325	675	6,000	—
1893	Inc. above	8.25	12.50	20.00	30.00	46.00	80.00	165	1,000	1,485
1893 O	1,760,000	31.00	45.00	135	168	195	250	315	2,950	—
1893 S	2,491,401	14.00	25.00	39.00	50.00	92.50	155	300	3,750	—
1894	1,330,972	25.00	45.00	122	165	190	235	310	1,150	1,485
1894 O	720,000	70.00	105	215	280	425	650	1,550	15,500	—
1894 S	24	—	—	—	—	—	—	—	2,500,000	—
Note: 1894S, Eliasberg Sale, May 1996, Prf-64, $451,000.										
1895	690,880	85.00	180	355	480	565	650	750	2,650	1,485
1895 O	440,000	385	575	900	1,350	2,500	3,650	6,000	24,500	—
1895 S	1,120,000	43.50	60.00	135	210	240	320	500	7,500	—
1896	2,000,762	11.50	23.00	58.00	82.00	100	120	155	1,450	1,485
1896 O	610,000	80.00	155	305	375	465	700	975	9,500	—

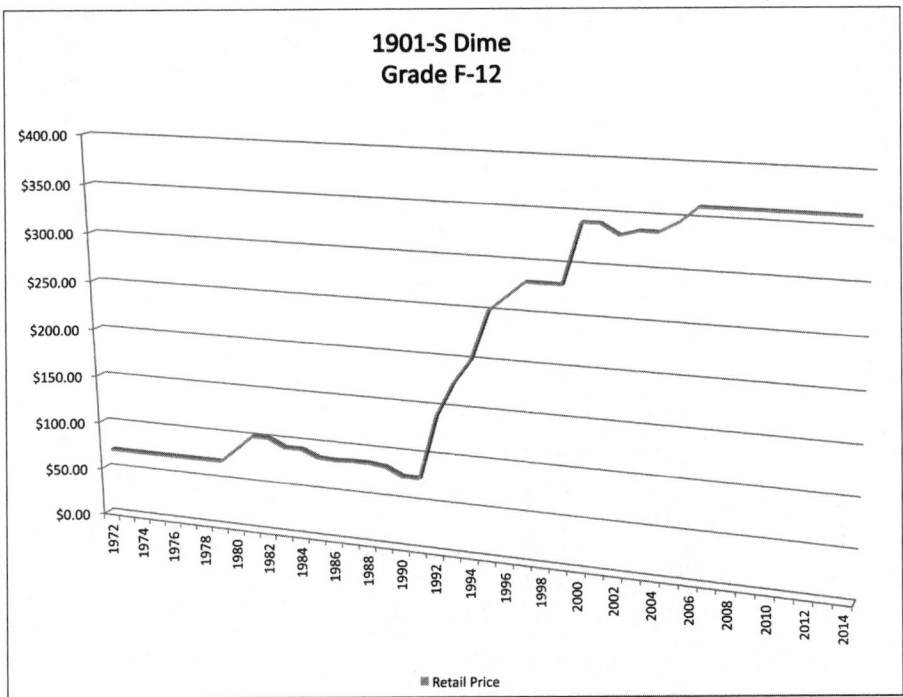

**1901-S Dime
Grade F-12**

■ Retail Price

DIME

Date	Mintage	G4	VG8	F12	VF20	XF40	AU50	MS60	MS65	Prf65
1896 S	575,056	85.00	160	310	345	385	525	775	4,650	—
1897	10,869,264	4.00	5.00	8.00	15.00	32.00	76.00	135	600	1,485
1897 O	666,000	69.50	115	290	385	480	600	975	4,450	—
1897 S	1,342,844	21.00	45.00	98.00	130	185	265	435	3,950	—
1898	16,320,735	4.00	5.00	15.00	28.00	71.00	135	600	1,485
1898 O	2,130,000	13.50	27.50	95.00	150	210	285	450	3,850	—
1898 S	1,702,507	8.50	15.00	36.00	52.00	78.00	160	370	3,750	—
1899	19,580,846	4.00	5.00	7.50	12.00	26.00	71.00	120	600	1,485
1899 O	2,650,000	10.00	19.50	72.00	115	150	230	415	4,450	—
1899 S	1,867,493	9.00	16.00	36.00	39.00	48.50	105	300	3,550	—
1900	17,600,912	4.00	5.00	7.00	11.00	26.00	66.00	115	630	1,485
1900 O	2,010,000	19.50	38.50	122	168	225	355	595	5,350	—
1900 S	5,168,270	5.00	6.25	12.50	19.50	32.00	75.00	155	1,850	—
1901	18,860,478	4.00	5.00	6.50	10.00	27.50	66.00	115	645	1,485
1901 O	5,620,000	4.00	5.50	16.00	27.50	68.00	175	450	4,350	—
1901 S	593,022	80.00	150	360	475	520	675	985	5,350	—
1902	21,380,777	4.00	5.00	6.55	8.00	25.00	66.00	115	645	1,485
1902 O	4,500,000	4.00	5.50	15.00	32.50	62.50	145	350	4,500	—
1902 S	2,070,000	8.00	21.00	58.00	95.00	135	195	375	3,950	—
1903	19,500,755	4.00	5.00	6.55	8.00	27.00	66.00	115	1,100	1,485
1903 O	8,180,000	4.00	5.50	14.50	23.50	54.00	110	250	4,850	—
1903 S	613,300	84.00	130	350	500	750	840	1,100	3,150	—
1904	14,601,027	5.00	5.50	7.30	9.75	28.00	66.00	115	1,650	1,485
1904 S	800,000	45.00	75.00	175	245	335	465	725	4,500	—
1905	14,552,350	4.50	5.25	7.00	9.75	28.00	66.00	115	625	1,485
1905 O	3,400,000	4.25	10.00	36.50	57.50	100	155	285	1,650	—
1905 O micro O	Inc. above	35.00	50.00	75.00	140	235	375	1,750	12,500	—
1905 S	6,855,199	4.00	5.00	9.00	18.50	43.50	96.00	210	975	—
1906	19,958,406	3.50	3.90	4.30	7.25	25.00	61.00	110	625	1,485
1906 D	4,060,000	4.00	5.00	7.00	15.00	35.00	78.00	175	1,650	—
1906 O	2,610,000	5.50	13.00	50.00	78.00	105	135	195	1,150	—
1906 S	3,136,640	4.50	6.60	13.00	24.00	49.00	110	240	1,350	—
1907	22,220,575	3.50	3.90	4.30	7.25	25.00	61.00	110	590	1,485
1907 D	4,080,000	4.00	5.40	10.50	11.00	43.50	115	275	2,350	—
1907 O	5,058,000	4.50	7.50	35.00	50.00	63.50	110	210	1,350	—
1907 S	3,178,470	4.50	5.50	17.00	27.50	68.50	150	410	2,450	—
1908	10,600,545	3.50	3.90	4.30	7.25	25.00	61.00	110	590	1,485
1908 D	7,490,000	3.50	3.90	6.00	9.75	32.00	66.00	125	990	—
1908 O	1,789,000	5.25	11.00	46.00	68.00	93.00	150	290	1,350	—

Date	Mintage	G4	VG8	F12	VF20	XF40	AU50	MS60	MS65	Prf65
1908 S	3,220,000	4.75	6.60	12.00	22.00	49.00	175	310	2,350	—
1909	10,240,650	3.50	3.90	4.30	7.25	25.00	61.00	110	590	1,485
1909 D	954,000	7.25	18.50	60.00	100	135	225	485	2,850	—
1909 O	2,287,000	4.00	7.25	13.00	23.00	50.00	92.50	185	1,650	—
1909 S	1,000,000	8.75	19.50	92.00	135	182	315	525	2,850	—
1910	11,520,551	3.50	3.90	4.30	9.75	25.00	61.00	110	590	1,485
1910 D	3,490,000	3.75	4.00	9.50	19.00	49.00	100	210	1,650	—
1910 S	1,240,000	5.25	9.00	52.50	74.00	112	195	425	2,450	—
1911	18,870,543	3.50	3.90	4.30	7.00	25.00	61.00	110	590	1,485
1911 D	11,209,000	3.50	3.90	4.30	7.00	27.00	61.00	110	590	—
1911 S	3,520,000	4.25	5.10	9.50	18.50	39.50	105	195	1,050	—
1912	19,350,700	3.50	3.90	4.30	7.00	25.00	61.00	110	590	1,485
1912 D	11,760,000	3.50	3.90	4.30	7.00	25.00	61.00	110	710	—
1912 S	3,420,000	3.75	4.90	5.60	12.50	34.00	92.50	155	775	—
1913	19,760,622	3.50	3.90	4.30	7.00	25.00	61.00	110	590	1,485
1913 S	510,000	35.00	50.00	120	190	240	325	480	1,375	—
1914	17,360,655	3.50	3.90	4.30	7.00	25.00	61.00	110	590	1,485
1914 D	11,908,000	3.50	3.90	4.30	7.00	25.00	61.00	110	590	—
1914 S	2,100,000	3.75	4.90	8.50	17.50	39.50	78.00	150	1,250	—
1915	5,620,450	3.50	3.90	5.00	7.00	25.00	61.00	110	590	1,485
1915 S	960,000	7.50	11.50	36.00	49.50	68.50	135	250	1,550	—
1916	18,490,000	3.50	3.90	4.30	8.00	25.00	61.00	110	590	—
1916 S	5,820,000	3.75	4.90	5.30	8.50	28.50	66.00	115	685	—

Mercury Dime

Mint mark   1942/41

KM# 140 • 2.50 g., 0.900 **Silver** 0.07 oz. ASW, 17.8 mm. • **Designer:** Adolph A. Weinman **Note:** All specimens listed as -65FSB are for fully struck MS-65 coins with fully split and rounded horizontal bands on the fasces.

Date	Mintage	G4	VG8	F12	VF20	XF40	MS60	MS65	MS65FSB	PF65
1916	22,180,080	3.75	4.75	6.00	7.00	10.50	29.00	110	165	—
1916 D	264,000	785	1,450	2,500	3,950	6,350	13,950	25,000	48,500	—
1916 S	10,450,000	4.00	5.00	9.25	15.00	25.00	44.00	200	800	—

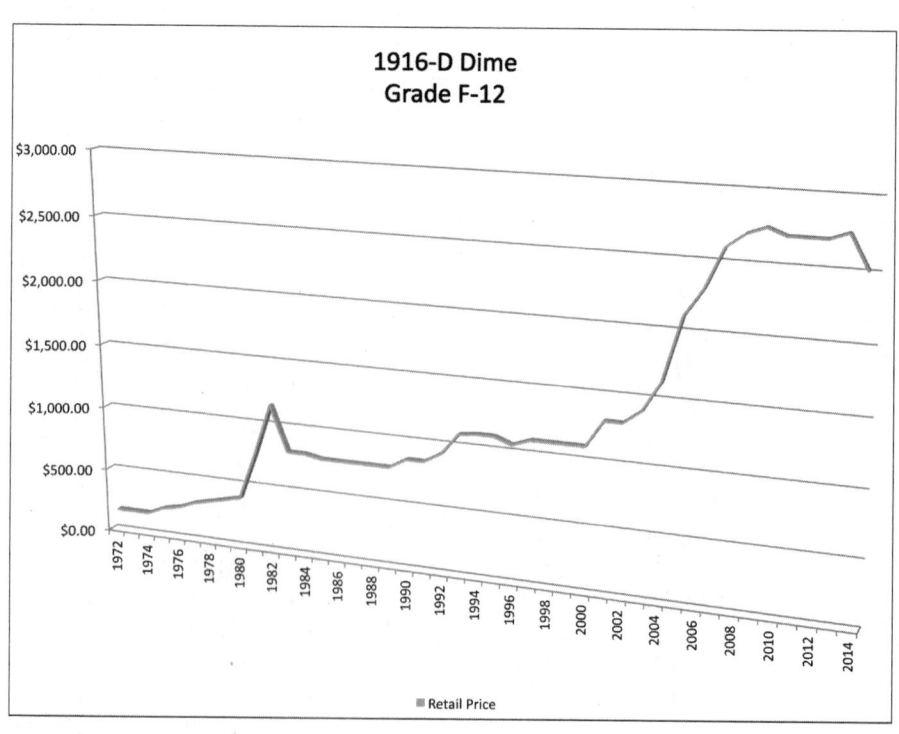

1916-D Dime
Grade F-12

Date	Mintage	G4	VG8	F12	VF20	XF40	MS60	MS65	MS65FSB	PF65
1917	55,230,000	3.00	3.50	4.40	5.50	8.00	27.00	155	375	—
1917 D	9,402,000	4.30	6.00	12.50	26.00	52.50	120	1,050	5,650	—
1917 S	27,330,000	3.00	3.60	4.20	7.50	15.00	60.00	450	1,265	—
1918	26,680,000	3.00	4.30	5.75	12.00	34.00	67.00	350	1,325	—
1918 D	22,674,800	3.00	4.20	6.50	13.00	32.00	100	575	27,500	—
1918 S	19,300,000	3.00	3.60	4.00	11.00	24.00	90.00	650	7,450	—
1919	35,740,000	3.00	3.50	4.00	5.50	12.00	36.00	335	685	—
1919 D	9,939,000	3.00	6.00	13.50	31.00	46.00	175	1,450	38,500	—
1919 S	8,850,000	3.00	4.20	10.50	20.00	42.00	175	1,250	14,350	—
1920	59,030,000	3.00	3.50	4.00	4.50	8.50	28.00	235	540	—
1920 D	19,171,000	3.00	4.20	4.75	9.00	24.00	110	600	4,750	—
1920 S	13,820,000	3.00	3.60	7.00	10.00	21.00	110	1,250	8,250	—
1921	1,230,000	55.00	77.00	110	245	540	1,150	3,000	4,350	—
1921 D	1,080,000	68.00	—	185	365	650	1,250	3,050	5,200	—
1923	50,130,000	3.00	3.50	4.00	4.50	7.00	27.00	120	340	—
1923 S	6,440,000	3.00	4.20	8.25	20.00	75.00	150	1,250	7,450	—
1924	24,010,000	3.00	3.50	4.00	4.50	13.50	40.00	165	500	—
1924 D	6,810,000	3.50	4.60	9.00	23.50	63.00	165	975	1,365	—
1924 S	7,120,000	3.00	3.60	4.00	12.00	59.00	205	1,050	16,750	—
1925	25,610,000	3.00	3.50	4.00	5.50	11.00	28.00	210	990	—
1925 D	5,117,000	4.50	4.60	12.75	46.50	135	335	1,650	3,500	—
1925 S	5,850,000	3.00	3.60	7.75	18.50	85.00	180	1,200	4,650	—
1926	32,160,000	3.00	3.50	3.50	4.25	5.75	26.00	240	525	—
1926 D	6,828,000	3.50	4.00	5.00	12.50	32.00	125	520	2,500	—
1926 S	1,520,000	11.75	13.50	29.00	70.00	275	865	2,850	6,750	—
1927	28,080,000	3.00	3.50	4.00	4.25	6.00	26.00	150	350	—
1927 D	4,812,000	3.50	5.00	7.75	27.00	88.00	165	1,200	8,500	—
1927 S	4,770,000	3.00	3.60	5.50	13.00	30.00	270	1,350	7,600	—
1928	19,480,000	3.00	3.50	4.00	4.25	4.75	28.00	128	345	—
1928 D	4,161,000	3.70	4.60	11.50	27.50	62.50	165	840	2,750	—
1928 S Large S	7,400,000	4.00	5.10	7.50	12.00	40.00	225	750	6,500	—
1928 S Small S	Inc. above	3.00	3.50	4.00	6.50	19.00	130	400	2,000	—
1929	25,970,000	3.00	3.50	4.00	4.25	4.50	24.00	65.00	175	—
1929 D	5,034,000	3.00	3.60	4.00	8.00	15.00	32.00	75.00	225	—
1929 S	4,730,000	3.00	3.50	4.00	5.00	7.50	32.50	115	560	—
1929 S Doubled Die Obv	Inc. above	5.00	9.00	16.00	25.00	40.00	95.00	335	1,150	—
1930	6,770,000	3.00	3.50	3.60	4.25	7.00	26.00	110	575	—
1930 S	1,843,000	3.00	3.60	4.80	6.50	19.00	85.00	220	685	—
1931	3,150,000	3.00	3.50	4.00	8.00	12.50	33.00	135	800	—
1931 D	1,260,000	8.50	10.00	15.00	21.00	48.00	110	285	375	—
1931 Doubled Die Obv & Rev	Inc. above	—	—	—	50.00	70.00	135	485	650	—
1931 S	1,800,000	4.00	5.00	5.50	11.00	23.50	110	275	2,500	—
1931 S Doubled Die Obv	Inc. above	7.50	10.00	13.00	25.00	35.00	140	425	3,850	—
1934	24,080,000	1.80	1.80	1.90	2.55	6.50	28.00	44.00	130	—
1934 D	6,772,000	2.50	2.60	3.60	7.50	14.00	54.00	78.00	320	—
1935	58,830,000	1.80	1.85	1.90	2.25	4.25	10.00	30.00	68.00	—
1935 D	10,477,000	2.20	2.25	2.30	6.50	13.00	37.00	88.00	500	—
1935 S	15,840,000	2.20	2.30	2.40	2.95	5.50	24.00	39.00	360	—
1936	87,504,130	1.80	1.85	1.90	2.00	2.60	9.00	27.50	84.00	1,950
1936 Doubled Die Obv	Inc. above	—	—	8.00	15.00	25.00	50.00	165	—	—
1936 D	16,132,000	2.20	2.25	2.30	4.25	8.50	28.00	55.00	290	—
1936 S	9,210,000	—	2.25	2.30	2.65	6.00	25.00	35.00	88.00	—
1937	56,865,756	1.80	1.85	1.90	2.25	3.75	8.00	25.00	52.00	800
1937 Doubled Die Obv	Inc. above	—	—	—	6.00	9.00	20.00	95.00	175	—
1937 D	14,146,000	2.20	2.25	2.30	2.75	6.00	22.50	45.00	105	—
1937 S	9,740,000	2.20	2.25	2.30	2.65	5.50	22.00	37.50	190	—
1937 S Doubled Die Obv	Inc. above	—	—	—	5.00	8.00	28.00	125	275	—
1938	22,198,728	1.80	1.85	1.90	2.25	3.75	13.50	27.00	80.00	480
1938 D	5,537,000	2.20	2.25	2.30	5.00	6.00	18.50	34.00	62.00	—
1938 S	8,090,000	2.20	2.25	2.30	2.65	5.00	21.50	42.00	160	—
1939	67,749,321	1.80	1.85	1.90	2.05	2.60	9.00	26.00	170	425
1939 Doubled Die Obv	Inc. above	—	—	—	4.00	6.00	14.00	35.00	450	—
1939 D	24,394,000	1.80	1.90	2.02	2.35	3.50	7.50	27.50	49.00	—
1939 S	10,540,000	2.15	2.20	2.37	2.75	6.75	27.00	50.00	765	—
1940	65,361,827	1.65	1.70	1.77	2.05	2.46	6.00	30.00	48.00	325
1940 D	21,198,000	1.80	1.90	2.02	2.35	3.86	8.00	32.00	48.00	—
1940 S	21,560,000	1.80	1.90	1.97	2.35	3.86	8.50	33.00	95.00	—
1941	175,106,557	1.65	1.70	1.77	2.05	2.46	6.00	30.00	46.00	325
1941 Doubled Die Obv	Inc. above	—	—	—	10.00	16.00	55.00	165	295	—
1941 D	45,634,000	1.80	1.90	1.97	2.35	2.86	10.00	24.00	46.00	—
1941 D Doubled Die Obv	Inc. above	—	—	—	9.00	14.00	30.00	125	250	—
1941 S Small S	43,090,000	1.80	1.90	1.97	2.35	2.86	7.00	30.00	46.00	—
1941 S Large S	Inc. above	4.00	5.00	8.00	15.00	25.00	110	250	425	—
1941 S Doubled Die Rev	Inc. above	4.00	4.50	5.00	5.50	6.00	18.00	60.00	85.00	—
1942	205,432,329	1.65	1.70	1.77	2.05	2.46	6.00	24.00	46.00	325
1942/41	Inc. above	485	490	510	555	675	2,650	14,500	35,000	—

DIME

Date	Mintage	G4	VG8	F12	VF20	XF40	MS60	MS65	MS65FSB	PF65
1942 D	60,740,000	1.80	1.90	1.97	2.35	2.86	8.00	28.00	46.00	—
1942/41 D	Inc. above	465	475	500	535	640	2,700	10,000	26,500	—
1942 S	49,300,000	1.80	1.90	1.97	2.35	2.86	9.75	24.00	145	—
1943	191,710,000	1.65	1.70	1.77	2.05	2.46	6.00	30.00	50.00	—
1943 D	71,949,000	1.80	1.90	1.97	2.35	2.86	7.75	30.00	47.00	—
1943 S	60,400,000	1.80	1.90	1.97	2.35	2.86	9.50	27.50	66.00	—
1944	231,410,000	1.65	1.70	1.77	2.05	2.46	6.00	24.00	75.00	—
1944 D	62,224,000	1.80	1.90	1.97	2.35	2.86	7.50	24.00	46.00	—
1944 S	49,490,000	1.80	1.90	1.97	2.35	2.86	7.50	30.00	50.00	—
1945	159,130,000	1.65	170	1.77	2.05	2.46	6.00	24.00	97.50	—
1945 D	40,245,000	1.80	1.90	1.97	2.35	2.86	6.50	24.00	46.50	—
1945 S	41,920,000	1.80	1.90	1.97	2.35	2.86	7.00	24.00	105	—
1945 S micro S	Inc. above	3.25	4.00	6.00	9.00	13.00	28.00	110	685	—

Roosevelt Dime

  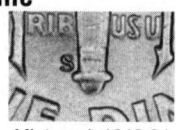

Mint mark 1946-64

KM# 195 • 2.50 g., 0.900 **Silver** 0.07 oz. ASW, 17.9 mm. • **Designer:** John R. Sinnock

Date	Mintage	G4	VG8	F12	VF20	XF40	AU50	MS60	MS65	Prf65
1946	225,250,000	—	—	—	—	1.80	2.10	2.40	13.50	—
1946 D	61,043,500	—	—	—	—	1.80	2.30	2.40	13.50	—
1946 S	27,900,000	—	—	—	—	1.80	2.30	2.40	18.50	—
1947	121,520,000	—	—	—	—	1.80	2.00	3.50	15.00	—
1947 D	46,835,000	—	—	—	—	1.80	2.00	4.50	16.00	—
1947 S	34,840,000	—	—	—	—	1.80	2.00	3.50	15.00	—
1948	74,950,000	—	—	—	—	1.80	2.00	3.30	14.00	—
1948 D	52,841,000	—	—	—	—	1.80	2.00	5.00	15.00	—
1948 S	35,520,000	—	—	—	—	1.80	2.00	4.50	17.00	—
1949	30,940,000	—	—	1.60	1.70	3.00	8.50	16.00	65.00	—
1949 D	26,034,000	—	—	1.60	1.70	2.60	5.50	9.00	25.00	—
1949 S	13,510,000	—	—	1.60	3.50	8.00	15.00	35.00	65.00	—
1950	50,181,500	—	—	—	1.70	1.80	3.50	7.00	32.00	55.00
1950 D	46,803,000	—	—	—	—	—	2.00	3.50	15.00	—
1950 S	20,440,000	—	—	1.60	1.70	3.75	9.00	23.00	68.00	—
1951	102,937,602	—	—	—	—	—	2.20	2.40	11.00	60.00
1951 D	56,529,000	—	—	—	—	—	2.10	2.40	11.00	—
1951 S	31,630,000	—	—	—	1.70	1.80	4.00	10.00	34.00	—
1952	99,122,073	—	—	—	—	—	2.00	2.40	22.00	35.00
1952 D	122,100,000	—	—	—	—	—	2.00	2.40	11.00	—
1952 S	44,419,500	—	—	—	1.70	2.20	2.50	5.50	16.00	—
1953	53,618,920	—	—	—	—	—	2.00	2.40	12.00	42.00
1953 D	136,433,000	—	—	—	—	—	2.00	2.80	11.00	—
1953 S	39,180,000	—	—	—	—	—	2.40	3.00	12.50	—
1954	114,243,503	—	—	—	—	—	2.00	2.40	10.00	18.00
1954 D	106,397,000	—	—	—	—	—	2.00	2.40	15.00	—
1954 S	22,860,000	—	—	—	—	—	2.00	2.50	10.00	—
1955	12,828,381	—	—	—	1.70	1.80	2.00	2.40	8.50	17.00
1955 D	13,959,000	—	—	—	1.70	1.80	2.00	2.40	8.50	—
1955 S	18,510,000	—	—	—	1.70	1.80	2.00	2.40	8.00	—
1956	109,309,384	—	—	—	—	—	2.00	2.40	9.50	8.00
1956 D	108,015,100	—	—	—	—	—	2.00	2.50	9.00	—
1957	161,407,952	—	—	—	—	—	2.00	2.40	8.50	5.00
1957 D	113,354,330	—	—	—	—	—	2.00	2.40	7.50	—
1958	32,785,652	—	—	—	—	—	2.00	2.40	11.00	6.00
1958 D	136,564,600	—	—	—	—	—	2.00	2.40	10.00	—
1959	86,929,291	—	—	—	—	—	2.00	2.40	8.00	4.50
1959 D	164,919,790	—	—	—	—	—	2.00	2.40	8.50	—
1960	72,081,602	—	—	—	—	—	2.00	2.40	8.50	4.50
1960 D	200,160,400	—	—	—	—	—	2.00	2.40	7.50	—
1961	96,758,244	—	—	—	—	—	2.00	2.40	8.00	4.00
1961 D	209,146,550	—	—	—	—	—	2.00	2.40	6.50	—
1962	75,668,019	—	—	—	—	—	2.00	2.40	6.50	4.00
1962 D	334,948,380	—	—	—	—	—	2.00	2.40	7.00	—
1963	126,725,645	—	—	—	—	—	2.00	2.40	7.50	3.75
1963 D	421,476,530	—	—	—	—	—	2.00	2.40	7.00	—
1964	933,310,762	—	—	—	—	—	2.00	2.40	7.50	3.75
1964 D	1,357,517,180	—	—	—	—	—	2.00	2.40	7.00	—

DIME

Mint mark 1968- present

KM# 195a • 2.27 g., **Copper-Nickel Clad Copper**, 17.91 mm. • **Designer:** John R. Sinnock **Note:** The 1979-S and 1981-S Type II proofs have clearer mint marks than the Type I proofs of those years. On the 1982 no-mint-mark variety, the mint mark was inadvertently left off.

Date	Mintage	MS65	Prf65
1965	1,652,140,570	6.00	—
1965 SMS	—	2.00	—
1966	1,382,734,540	6.50	—
1966 SMS	—	2.25	—
1967	2,244,007,320	7.00	—
1967 SMS	—	3.50	—
1968	424,470,000	6.50	—
1968 D	480,748,280	6.50	—
1968 S	3,041,506	—	4.00
1968 no S error	—	—	7,500
1969	145,790,000	7.00	—
1969 D	563,323,870	6.00	—
1969 S	2,934,631	—	4.00
1970	345,570,000	5.50	—
1970 D	754,942,100	5.00	—
1970 S	2,632,810	—	4.00
1970 S No S	—	—	1,300
1971	162,690,000	10.00	—
1971 D	377,914,240	8.00	—
1971 S	3,220,733	—	4.00
1972	431,540,000	7.50	—
1972 D	330,290,000	8.50	—
1972 S	3,260,996	—	4.00
1973	315,670,000	6.00	—
1973 D	455,032,426	5.50	—
1973 S	2,760,339	—	4.00
1974	470,248,000	5.50	—
1974 D	571,083,000	4.50	—
1974 S	2,612,568	—	4.00
1975	585,673,900	4.50	—
1975 D	313,705,300	4.50	—
1975 S	2,845,450	—	4.00
1976	568,760,000	4.50	—
1976 D	695,222,774	4.50	—
1976 S	4,149,730	—	4.00
1977	796,930,000	4.50	—
1977 D	376,607,228	8.00	—
1977 S	3,251,152	—	4.00
1978	663,980,000	5.00	—
1978 D	282,847,540	4.50	—
1978 S	3,127,781	—	4.00
1979	315,440,000	5.50	—
1979 D	390,921,184	5.00	—
1979 S type I	3,677,175	—	5.00
1979 S type II	—	—	2.00
1980 P	735,170,000	6.00	—
1980 D	719,354,321	5.00	—
1980 S	3,554,806	—	4.00
1981 P	676,650,000	4.00	—
1981 D	712,284,143	4.00	—
1981 S type I	—	—	4.00
1981 S type II	—	—	6.50
1982 P	519,475,000	8.50	—
1982 no mint mark	Inc. above	300	—
1982 D	542,713,584	3.20	—
1982 S	3,857,479	—	4.00
1983 P	647,025,000	6.00	—

Date	Mintage	MS65	Prf65
1983 D	730,129,224	4.00	—
1983 S	3,279,126	—	4.00
1984 P	856,669,000	4.00	—
1984 D	704,803,976	3.50	—
1984 S	3,065,110	—	4.00
1985 P	705,200,962	5.00	—
1985 D	587,979,970	3.50	—
1985 S	3,362,821	—	4.00
1986 P	682,649,693	3.50	—
1986 D	473,326,970	3.50	—
1986 S	3,010,497	—	4.00
1987 P	762,709,481	4.50	—
1987 D	653,203,402	4.50	—
1987 S	4,227,728	—	4.00
1988 P	1,030,550,000	5.50	—
1988 D	962,385,488	5.50	—
1988 S	3,262,948	—	3.00
1989 P	1,298,400,000	4.00	—
1989 D	896,535,597	5.00	—
1989 S	3,220,194	—	4.00
1990 P	1,034,340,000	4.50	—
1990 D	839,995,824	5.50	—
1990 S	3,299,559	—	4.00
1991 P	927,220,000	5.00	—
1991 D	601,241,114	5.00	—
1991 S	2,867,787	—	3.00
1992 P	593,500,000	4.50	—
1992 D	616,273,932	4.50	—
1992 S	2,858,981	—	4.00
1993 P	766,180,000	3.50	—
1993 D	750,110,166	4.50	—
1993 S	2,633,439	—	7.00
1994 P	1,189,000,000	4.00	—
1994 D	1,303,268,110	5.50	—
1994 S	2,484,594	—	5.00
1995 P	1,125,500,000	4.00	—
1995 D	1,274,890,000	4.50	—
1995 S	2,010,384	—	20.00
1996 P	1,421,163,000	3.00	—
1996 D	1,400,300,000	5.00	—
1996 W	1,457,949	24.00	—
1996 S	2,085,191	—	3.50
1997 P	991,640,000	4.00	—
1997 D	979,810,000	3.00	—
1997 S	1,975,000	—	14.00
1998 P	1,163,000,000	2.75	—
1998 D	1,172,250,000	2.75	—
1998 S	2,078,494	—	4.00
1999 P	2,164,000,000	2.75	—
1999 D	1,397,750,000	2.75	—
1999 S	2,557,897	—	4.00
2000 P	1,842,500,000	2.75	—
2000 D	1,818,700,000	2.75	—
2000 S	3,097,440	—	1.00
2001 P	1,369,590,000	2.75	—
2001 D	1,412,800,000	2.75	—
2001 S	2,249,496	—	3.75
2002 P	1,187,500,000	2.75	—
2002 D	1,379,500,000	3.00	—
2002 S	2,268,913	—	2.50
2003 P	1,085,500,000	3.00	—
2003 D	986,500,000	3.00	—
2003 S	2,076,165	—	2.60
2004 P	1,328,000,000	3.00	—
2004 D	1,159,500,000	3.00	—
2004 S	1,804,396	—	4.75
2005 P	1,412,000,000	2.75	—
2005 P Satin Finish	—	4.00	—
2005 D	1,423,500,000	2.75	—
2005 D Satin Finish	—	4.00	—
2005 S	2,275,000	—	2.60
2006 P	1,381,000,000	2.50	—
2006 P Satin Finish	—	4.00	—
2006 D	1,447,000,000	2.50	—
2006 D Satin Finish	—	4.00	—
2006 S	2,000,428	—	2.50
2007 P	1,047,500,000	2.00	—

DIME

Date	Mintage	MS65	Prf65
2007 P Satin Finish	—	3.00	—
2007 D	1,042,000,000	2.00	—
2007 D Satin Finish	—	3.00	—
2007 S	1,702,116	—	2.50
2008 P	391,000,000	1.25	—
2008 Satin Finish	—	2.50	—
2008 D	624,500,000	1.25	—
2008 D Satin Finish	—	2.50	—
2008 S	1,405,674	—	2.50
2009 P	96,500,000	1.25	—
2009 P Satin Finish	—	1.00	—
2009 D	49,500,000	1.25	—
2009 D Satin Finish	—	1.00	—
2009 S	1,482,502	—	2.50
2010 P	557,000,000	4.00	—
2010 P Satin Finish	—	2.00	—
2010 D	562,000,000	4.00	—
2010 D Satin Finish	—	2.00	—
2010 S	1,103,815	—	2.50
2011 P	748,000,000	4.00	—
2011 D	754,000,000	4.00	—
2011 S	1,098,835	—	2.50
2012 P	808,000,000	4.00	—
2012 D	868,000,000	4.00	—
2012 S	841,972	—	2.50
2013 P	1,086,500,000	4.00	—
2013 D	1,025,500,000	4.00	—
2013 S	821,031	—	2.50

KM# 195b • 2.50 g., 0.900 **Silver** 0.07 oz. ASW, 17.9 mm. • **Designer:** John R. Sinnock

Date	Mintage	Prf65
1992 S	1,317,579	5.00
1993 S	761,353	7.00
1994 S	785,329	7.00
1995 S	838,953	8.00
1996 S	830,021	7.00
1997 S	821,678	14.00
1998 S	878,792	7.00
1999 S	804,565	7.00
1999 S	1,317,579	7.00
1999 S	761,353	7.00
1999 S	785,329	7.00
1999 S	838,953	7.00
2000 S	965,921	5.50
2001 S	849,600	5.00
2002 S	888,826	5.00
2003 S	1,090,425	4.75
2004 S	1,175,934	5.00
2005 S	1,069,679	5.00
2006 S	1,054,008	4.50
2007 S	875,050	6.00
2008 S	763,887	6.50
2009 S	697,365	6.75
2010 S	585,401	6.75
2011 S	574,175	6.75
2012 S	395,443	6.75
2013 S	821,031	6.75

DIME

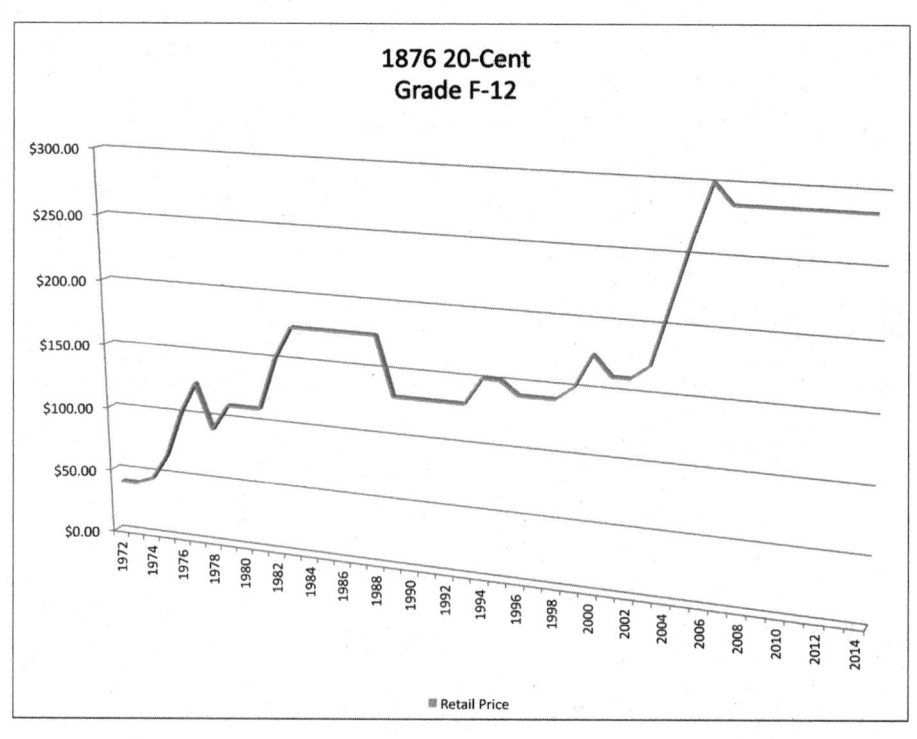

1876 20-Cent
Grade F-12

■ Retail Price

20 CENTS

Seated Liberty within circle of stars, date below obverse
Eagle with arrows in talons, value below reverse

KM# 109 • 5.00 g., 0.900 **Silver** 0.14 oz. ASW, 22 mm. • **Rev. Legend:** UNITED STATES OF AMERICA **Designer:** William Barber

Date	Mintage	G4	VG8	F12	VF20	XF40	AU50	MS60	MS65	Prf65
1875	39,700	165	210	270	325	415	550	835	5,500	9,500
1875 S Clear S	Inc. above	110	120	135	200	235	350	600	5,500	—
1875 S	1,155,000	100	110	120	175	210	320	500	4,900	—
Note: 1875-S exists as a branch mint proof										
1875 S over horizontal S	Inc. above	100	110	120	175	210	320	500	4,900	—
Note: Also known as filled S										
1875 S as	Inc. above	—	120	130	150	225	260	375	1,300	—
1875 CC	133,290	335	385	475	600	775	1,150	1,650	10,000	—
1876	15,900	185	225	285	350	410	535	800	5,600	9,400
1876 CC	10,000	—	—	—	—	—	60,000	—	—	175,000
Note: Only one circulated example known. Eliasberg Sale, April 1997, MS-65, $148,500. Heritage 1999 ANA, MS-63, $86,500.										
1877 proof only	510	—	—	2,700	2,900	3,300	3,500	—	—	10,000
1878 proof only	600	—	—	2,000	2,300	2,400	2,800	—	—	9,500

QUARTER

Draped Bust Quarter
Draped bust right obverse Small eagle reverse

KM# 25 • 6.74 g., 0.892 **Silver** 0.19 oz. ASW, 27.5 mm. • **Designer:** Robert Scot

Date	Mintage	G4	VG8	F12	VF20	XF40	AU50	MS60	MS65
1796	6,146	12,000	17,500	25,500	36,500	55,000	59,000	83,000	410,000

Draped bust right, flanked by stars, date at angle below obverse Heraldic eagle reverse

KM# 36 • 6.74 g., 0.892 **Silver** 0.19 oz. ASW, 27.5 mm. • **Obv. Legend:** LIBERTY **Rev. Legend:** UNITED STATES OF AMERICA **Designer:** Robert Scot

Date	Mintage	G4	VG8	F12	VF20	XF40	AU50	MS60	MS65
1804	6,738	5,500	6,750	9,250	14,500	32,500	56,500	92,500	425,000
1805	121,394	555	690	1,085	1,965	3,900	6,000	11,500	95,000
1806/5	206,124	585	725	1,160	2,365	4,200	6,300	12,500	100,000
1806	Inc. above	525	650	985	1,865	4,100	5,850	11,000	116,000
1807	220,643	525	650	985	1,865	4,100	5,850	11,500	117,500

QUARTER

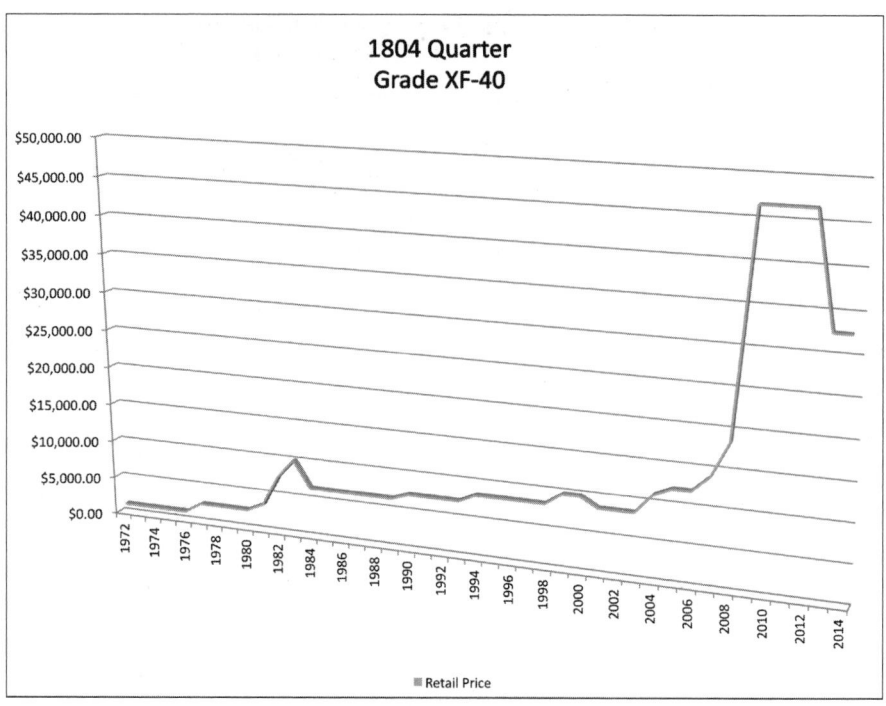

Liberty Cap Quarter

Draped bust left, flanked by stars, date below obverse
Eagle with arrows in talons, banner above, value below reverse

KM# 44 • 6.74 g., 0.892 **Silver** 0.19 oz. ASW, 27 mm. • **Rev. Legend:** UNITED STATES OF AMERICA **Designer:** John Reich **Note:** Varieties of the 1819 strikes are distinguished by the size of the 9 in the date. Varieties of the 1820 strikes are distinguished by the size of the 0 in the date. One 1822 variety and one 1828 variety have "25" engraved over "50" in the denomination. The 1827 restrikes were produced privately using dies sold as scrap by the U.S. Mint.

Date		Mintage	G4	VG8	F12	VF20	XF40	AU50	MS60	MS65
1815		89,235	120	160	250	550	1,725	2,250	4,600	39,000
1818/15		361,174	120	180	310	750	1,650	2,600	5,000	31,000
1818		Inc. above	110	135	215	515	1,675	2,400	4,550	30,000
1819	small 9	144,000	95.00	135	215	595	1,875	2,525	4,550	35,000
1819	large 9	Inc. above	95.00	145	225	655	1,975	2,600	5,550	42,500
1820	small 0	127,444	95.00	135	215	515	1,675	2,400	4,550	35,000
1820	large 0	Inc. above	95.00	140	220	800	1,950	3,150	5,500	42,500
1821		216,851	115	160	240	540	1,675	2,350	4,350	30,000
1822		64,080	150	240	350	850	1,800	3,000	4,250	38,500
1822	25/50C.	Inc. above	2,750	6,500	7,850	11,000	18,500	25,000	36,500	125,000
1823/22		17,800	35,000	35,000	48,500	70,000	85,000	110,000	150,000	—
1824/2		—	950	1,350	2,250	4,000	5,850	9,000	22,500	—
1825/22		168,000	170	275	400	2,250	5,500	8,800	18,500	40,000
1825/23		Inc. above	160	235	375	700	1,875	2,600	4,650	35,000
1825/24		Inc. above	140	225	350	650	1,650	2,500	4,550	32,500
1827	original curl base 2	4,000	—	—	—	70,000	75,000	80,000	—	—
1827	restrike, square base 2	Inc. above	—	—	—	—	—	—	—	—
1828		102,000	95.00	135	215	515	1,575	2,300	4,350	30,000
1828	25/50C.	Inc. above	500	850	1,550	1,900	3,000	4,250	9,500	—

Draped bust left, flanked by stars, date below obverse
Eagle with arrows in talons, value below reverse

KM# 55 • 0.892 **Silver**, 24.3 mm. • **Rev. Legend:** UNITED STATES OF AMERICA **Designer:** William Kneass **Note:** Varieties of the 1831 strikes are distinguished by the size of the lettering on the reverse.

Date		Mintage	G4	VG8	F12	VF20	XF40	AU50	MS60	MS65
1831	small letter rev.	398,000	68.00	120	145	185	425	850	1,875	29,000
1831	large letter rev.	Inc. above	90.00	135	165	220	470	895	1,920	29,000
1832		320,000	68.00	110	135	170	400	825	1,850	31,000
1833		156,000	80.00	120	145	185	435	860	1,885	26,500
1834		286,000	68.00	110	135	170	400	825	1,850	29,000
1834	No period after C	Inc. above	75.00	120	149	190	430	870	1,925	27,500
1834	0 over 0	Inc. above	—	—	—	—	—	—	—	—
1835		1,952,000	68.00	110	135	170	400	875	1,900	26,500
1836		472,000	68.00	110	135	170	400	825	1,850	29,000
1837		252,400	68.00	110	135	170	400	825	1,850	26,500
1838		832,000	68.00	110	135	170	400	825	1,850	29,000

Seated Liberty Quarter

Seated Liberty, stars around top 1/2 of border, date below obverse
Eagle with arrows in talons, value below reverse

KM# 64.1 • 6.68 g., 0.900 **Silver** 0.19 oz. ASW, 24.3 mm. • **Rev. Legend:** UNITED STATES OF AMERICA **Designer:** Christian Gobrecht

Date	Mintage	G4	VG8	F12	VF20	XF40	AU50	MS60	MS65
1838	Inc. above	35.00	42.00	53.00	120	450	860	1,625	36,500
1839	491,146	37.00	46.00	58.00	126	465	885	1,700	38,000
1840 O	425,200	40.00	54.00	75.00	145	485	925	1,650	48,500

Drapery added to Liberty's left elbow, stars around top 1/2 of border obverse
Eagle with arrows in talons, value below reverse

KM# 64.2 • 6.68 g., 0.900 **Silver** 0.19 oz. ASW, 24.3 mm. • **Rev. Legend:** UNITED STATES OF AMERICA **Designer:** Christian Gobrecht

Date		Mintage	G4	VG8	F12	VF20	XF40	AU50	MS60	MS65
1840		188,127	31.00	36.50	55.00	100	225	325	900	14,500
1840 O		Inc. above	45.00	55.00	90.00	200	350	525	1,100	17,500
1841		120,000	52.00	75.00	95.00	190	275	400	850	11,000
1841 O		452,000	34.00	43.50	58.00	125	285	375	750	10,000
1842	small date	88,000	—	—	—	—	—	—	—	—
1842	large date	Inc. above	80.00	140	235	325	390	750	1,550	14,500
1842 O	small date	769,000	500	1,000	1,750	2,650	4,500	9,000	20,000	—
1842 O	large date	Inc. above	33.00	44.50	55.00	95.00	275	400	1,350	—
1843		645,600	28.00	31.50	34.00	45.00	85.00	185	400	6,750
1843 O		968,000	33.00	44.50	100	325	450	825	2,000	—

Date	Mintage	G4	VG8	F12	VF20	XF40	AU50	MS60	MS65
1844	421,200	28.00	31.50	34.00	45.00	95.00	215	450	8,250
1844 O	740,000	33.00	44.50	58.00	90.00	200	350	1,100	8,250
1845	922,000	28.00	31.50	34.00	45.00	110	200	475	6,650
1846	510,000	30.00	33.50	36.00	48.00	200	275	500	10,000
1847	734,000	28.00	31.50	34.00	45.00	85.00	200	450	6,650
1847 O	368,000	36.00	55.00	100	200	950	1,850	4,850	—
1848	146,000	38.00	52.00	90.00	175	275	465	1,075	14,500
1849	340,000	30.00	33.50	38.00	75.00	145	290	700	15,000
1849 O	—	550	800	1,300	2,450	4,000	8,500	18,500	—
1850	190,800	31.00	44.50	75.00	135	180	360	850	11,000
1850 O	412,000	36.00	44.50	85.00	150	245	575	1,550	15,000
1851	160,000	37.50	65.00	125	200	285	400	875	9,000
1851 O	88,000	200	350	550	950	1,650	3,250	5,850	—
1852	177,060	45.00	62.00	85.00	185	285	400	750	6,200
1852 O	96,000	210	300	600	1,250	2,850	4,250	11,000	—
1853 recut date	44,200	750	800	1,050	1,250	1,750	2,650	3,850	13,500

Seated Liberty, arrows at date obverse Rays around eagle reverse

KM# 78 • 6.22 g., 0.900 **Silver** 0.18 oz. ASW, 24.3 mm. • **Rev. Legend:** UNITED STATES OF AMERICA **Designer:** Christian Gobrecht

Date	Mintage	G4	VG8	F12	VF20	XF40	AU50	MS60	MS65	Prf65
1853	15,210,020	27.50	31.00	34.00	44.00	170	425	1,025	17,000	175,000
1853/4	Inc. above	40.00	70.00	110	200	400	650	1,750	55,000	—
1853 O	1,332,000	35.50	45.00	54.00	85.00	300	1,000	2,850	35,000	—

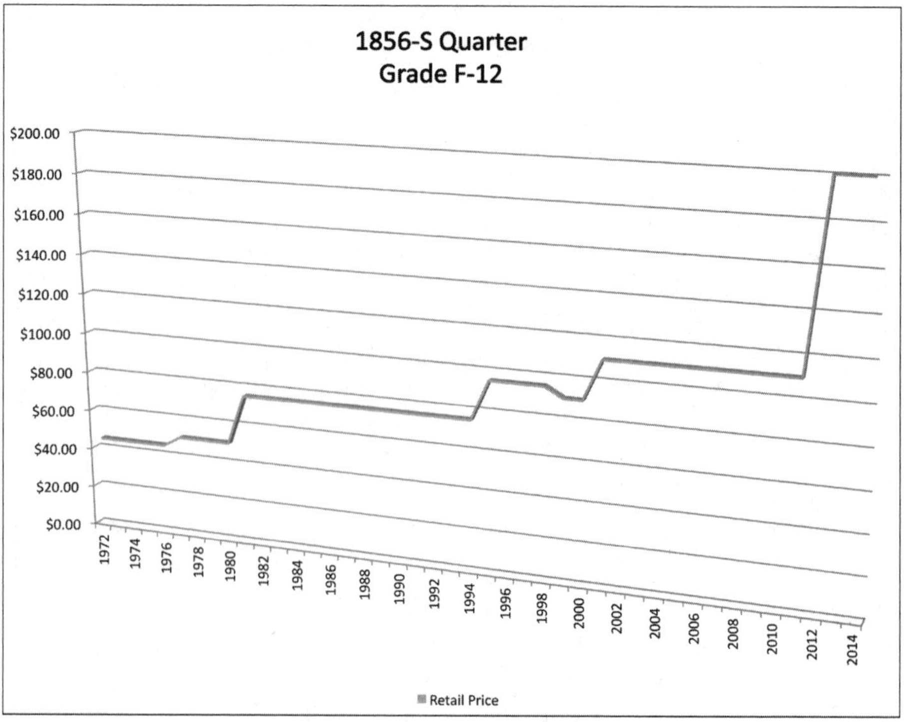

1856-S Quarter
Grade F-12

(Line chart: Retail Price from 1972 to 2014, ranging from about $45.00 in 1972, rising in steps to about $180.00 in 2014.)

■ Retail Price

Seated Liberty, arrows at date obverse
Eagle with arrows in talons, value below reverse

KM# 81 • 6.22 g., 0.900 **Silver** 0.18 oz. ASW, 24.3 mm. • **Rev. Legend:** UNITED STATES OF AMERICA **Designer:** Christian Gobrecht

Date	Mintage	G4	VG8	F12	VF20	XF40	AU50	MS60	MS65	Prf65
1854	12,380,000	27.50	31.00	33.00	42.00	77.50	255	610	8,900	37,500
1854 O	1,484,000	29.50	40.00	45.00	60.00	125	300	950	10,000	—
1854 O huge O	Inc. above	800	1,400	2,650	4,350	7,400	12,500	—	—	—
1855	2,857,000	27.50	31.00	33.00	42.00	77.50	255	610	9,400	37,500
1855 O	176,000	40.00	55.00	115	250	475	975	2,900	—	—
1855 S	396,400	48.00	60.00	120	225	550	1,150	2,400	45,000	—

Seated Liberty, date below obverse
Eagle with arrows in talons, value below reverse

KM# A64.2 • 6.22 g., 0.900 **Silver** 0.18 oz. ASW, 24.3 mm. • **Rev. Legend:** UNITED STATES OF AMERICA **Designer:** Christian Gobrecht

Date	Mintage	G4	VG8	F12	VF20	XF40	AU50	MS60	MS65	Prf65
1856	7,264,000	28.00	31.50	34.00	45.00	75.00	185	330	4,350	18,500
1856 O	968,000	30.00	43.50	50.00	60.00	115	260	925	9,350	—
1856 S	286,000	60.00	120	200	350	1,600	2,450	5,000	—	—
1856 S/S	Inc. above	175	320	550	1,250	2,450	6,000	—	—	—
1857	9,644,000	28.00	31.50	34.00	45.00	75.00	185	330	4,000	11,500
1857 O	1,180,000	35.00	33.50	50.00	47.00	175	420	950	—	—
1857 S	82,000	100	150	250	400	700	1,350	2,900	—	—
1858	7,368,000	28.00	31.50	34.00	45.00	75.00	185	350	4,000	8,500
1858 O	520,000	34.00	41.50	50.00	60.00	110	325	1,300	24,000	—
1858 S	121,000	75.00	120	250	800	2,850	4,750	13,500	—	—
1859	1,344,000	30.00	33.50	36.00	47.00	80.00	185	350	7,750	7,000
1859 O	260,000	36.00	33.50	50.00	65.00	185	400	1,100	13,500	—
1859 S	80,000	150	250	400	900	3,250	15,500	—	—	—
1860	805,400	32.00	35.50	38.00	49.00	85.00	195	375	4,500	5,650
1860 O	388,000	36.00	44.00	52.00	70.00	120	360	950	13,000	—
1860 S	56,000	750	1,350	2,500	6,600	14,500	24,500	—	—	—
1861	4,854,600	30.00	33.50	36.00	47.00	80.00	195	360	3,350	5,650
1861 S	96,000	175	325	750	1,850	4,100	9,750	—	—	—
1862	932,550	32.00	35.50	44.00	53.00	90.00	190	350	4,450	5,650
1862 S	67,000	65.00	130	250	475	880	1,400	3,500	—	—
1863	192,060	48.00	57.00	75.00	140	250	360	650	4,850	5,650
1864	94,070	80.00	100	130	225	400	450	775	5,000	5,650
1864 S	20,000	450	650	1,150	2,150	3,450	4,850	12,500	—	—
1865	59,300	85.00	95.00	150	235	340	450	850	6,950	5,650
1865 S	41,000	105	180	255	400	825	1,250	2,800	15,000	—
1866 unique	—	—	—	—	—	—	—	—	—	—

Seated Liberty, date below obverse   "In God We Trust" above eagle reverse

QUARTER

KM# 98 • 6.22 g., 0.900 **Silver** 0.18 oz. ASW, 24.3 mm. • **Rev. Legend:** UNITED STATES OF AMERICA **Designer:** Christian Gobrecht **Note:** The 1873 closed-3 and open-3 varieties are distinguished by the amount of space between the upper left and lower left serifs in the 3.

Date	Mintage	G4	VG8	F12	VF20	XF40	AU50	MS60	MS65	Prf65
1866	17,525	450	600	750	1,050	1,400	1,700	2,350	6,950	2,750
1866 S	28,000	295	390	750	1,400	1,950	2,600	3,500	17,500	—
1867	20,625	260	325	500	850	1,325	1,575	1,950	—	2,550
1867 S	48,000	250	450	850	1,350	2,850	7,000	13,500	—	—
1868	30,000	150	200	275	385	500	675	900	7,350	2,650
1868 S	96,000	100	185	325	450	775	1,350	2,850	15,000	—
1869	16,600	300	450	560	700	935	1,150	1,600	7,500	2,650
1869 S	76,000	100	185	325	475	840	1,325	2,650	15,500	—
1870	87,400	55.00	65.00	130	190	275	360	850	6,500	2,650
1870 CC	8,340	10,000	16,000	21,000	29,500	40,000	60,000	—	—	—
1871	119,160	33.00	47.50	60.00	125	300	425	725	8,500	2,500
1871 CC	10,890	3,450	7,500	11,500	16,000	26,500	40,000	66,500	350,000	—
1871 S	30,900	500	750	1,650	2,400	3,750	5,250	7,400	35,000	—
1872	182,950	30.00	55.00	75.00	110	270	400	1,100	8,500	2,550
1872 CC	22,850	1,450	2,000	3,250	6,000	13,000	21,000	44,500	—	—
1872 S	83,000	850	1,250	2,250	3,350	5,000	6,750	8,750	100,000	—
1873 closed 3	212,600	250	425	550	800	1,850	2,500	7,500	—	2,650
1873 open 3	Inc. above	32.00	47.50	62.00	130	175	200	450	8,250	—
1873 CC 6 known	4,000	—	75,000	—	—	100,000	124,000	150,000	650,000	—

Note: 1873CC, Heritage, April 1999, MS-62, $106,375.

Seated Liberty, arrows at date obverse "In God We Trust" above eagle reverse

KM# 106 • 6.25 g., 0.900 **Silver** 0.18 oz. ASW, 24.3 mm. • **Rev. Legend:** UNITED STATES OF AMERICA **Designer:** Christian Gobrecht

Date	Mintage	G4	VG8	F12	VF20	XF40	AU50	MS60	MS65	Prf65
1873	1,271,700	28.00	32.00	37.50	62.00	195	425	850	4,400	8,000
1873 CC	12,462	5,000	9,500	12,500	18,500	26,500	48,500	100,000	175,000	—
1873 S	156,000	35.00	45.00	85.00	175	325	525	1,450	20,000	—
1874	471,900	28.00	32.00	37.50	62.00	195	425	850	4,500	8,000
1874 S	392,000	33.00	37.00	52.00	110	275	485	900	3,750	—

Seated Liberty, date below obverse "In God We Trust" above eagle reverse

KM# A98 • 6.25 g., 0.900 **Silver** 0.18 oz. ASW, 24.3 mm. • **Rev. Legend:** UNITED STATES OF AMERICA **Designer:** Christian Gobrecht **Note:** The 1876-CC fine-reeding variety has a more finely reeded edge.

Date	Mintage	G4	VG8	F12	VF20	XF40	AU50	MS60	MS65	Prf65
1875	4,293,500	27.50	31.50	33.50	40.00	67.50	155	290	1,800	2,350
1875 CC	140,000	95.00	160	270	450	900	1,250	3,800	30,000	—
1875 S	680,000	40.00	50.00	67.00	110	190	275	575	3,350	—
1876	17,817,150	27.50	31.50	33.50	40.00	67.50	155	290	1,850	2,350
1876 CC Ty1 rev. sm wide CC	4,944,000	60.00	80.00	95.00	125	185	310	600	5,500	—
1876 CC Ty1 rev. sm close CC	Inc. above	55.00	73.00	87.50	110	175	275	500	4,250	—
1876 CC Ty1 rev. tall CC	Inc. above	48.00	65.00	75.00	95.00	160	235	450	4,000	—
1876 CC Ty2 rev. sm CC	Inc. above	48.00	65.00	75.00	95.00	160	235	450	4,150	—
1876 CC Ty2 rev tall CC	Inc. above	58.00	75.00	90.00	115	180	300	550	4,400	—
1876 S	8,596,000	27.50	31.50	33.50	40.00	67.50	155	290	2,350	—
1877	10,911,710	27.50	31.50	33.50	40.00	67.50	155	290	1,800	2,350
1877 CC	4,192,000	50.00	68.00	80.00	100	165	235	450	2,600	—
1877 S	8,996,000	27.50	31.50	33.50	40.00	67.50	155	290	1,850	—
1877 S over horizontal S	Inc. above	34.00	44.00	85.00	175	285	335	650	4,750	—
1878	2,260,800	27.50	31.50	33.50	40.00	67.50	165	310	3,000	2,350
1878 CC	996,000	58.00	75.00	90.00	140	300	265	550	3,650	—
1878 S	140,000	150	225	345	500	785	1,150	1,950	—	—

Date	Mintage	G4	VG8	F12	VF20	XF40	AU50	MS60	MS65	Prf65
1879	14,700	180	235	255	325	375	485	600	2,000	2,350
1880	14,955	155	215	275	325	375	435	575	2,100	2,350
1881	12,975	200	250	280	350	400	455	550	2,250	2,350
1882	16,300	210	260	290	350	400	435	600	2,150	2,350
1883	15,439	200	240	280	365	400	465	585	2,800	2,350
1884	8,875	235	285	475	550	600	650	725	2,150	2,350
1885	14,530	165	225	340	280	400	475	610	2,900	2,350
1886	5,886	335	450	550	750	850	925	1,050	3,250	2,350
1887	10,710	225	300	385	450	500	550	700	2,500	2,350
1888	10,833	200	275	325	425	475	520	660	2,000	2,350
1888 S	1,216,000	27.50	31.50	33.50	40.00	67.50	165	340	4,000	—
1889	12,711	185	275	300	350	425	475	600	1,900	2,350
1890	80,590	60.00	75.00	100	135	200	300	440	1,900	2,350
1891	3,920,600	27.50	31.50	33.50	42.00	67.50	155	290	1,800	2,350
1891 O	68,000	240	400	500	1,350	2,350	3,500	4,850	28,500	—
1891 S	2,216,000	28.50	32.50	35.50	43.00	73.00	165	295	2,100	—

Barber Quarter
Laureate head right, flanked by stars, date below obverse   Heraldic eagle reverse

KM# 114 • 6.25 g., 0.900 **Silver** 0.18 oz. ASW, 24.3 mm. • **Obv. Legend:** IN GOD WE TRUST **Rev. Legend:** UNITED STATES OF AMERICA **Designer:** Charles E. Barber

Date	Mintage	G4	VG8	F12	VF20	XF40	AU50	MS60	MS65	Prf65
1892	8,237,245	11.00	14.50	30.00	65.00	100	167	285	—	2,450
1892 Type 2 Rev	Inc. above	10.50	12.00	26.00	46.00	72.00	122	220	1,350	2,450
1892 O	2,640,000	22.00	30.00	55.00	90.00	155	245	400	—	—
1892 O Type 2 Rev	Inc. above	15.00	22.50	44.50	64.00	100	160	290	1,600	—
1892 S	964,079	50.00	75.00	135	200	300	480	650	—	—
1892 S Type 2 Rev	Inc. above	35.00	59.00	95.00	145	205	320	475	4,500	—
1893	5,484,838	10.50	12.50	32.00	39.00	70.00	122	220	1,550	2,450

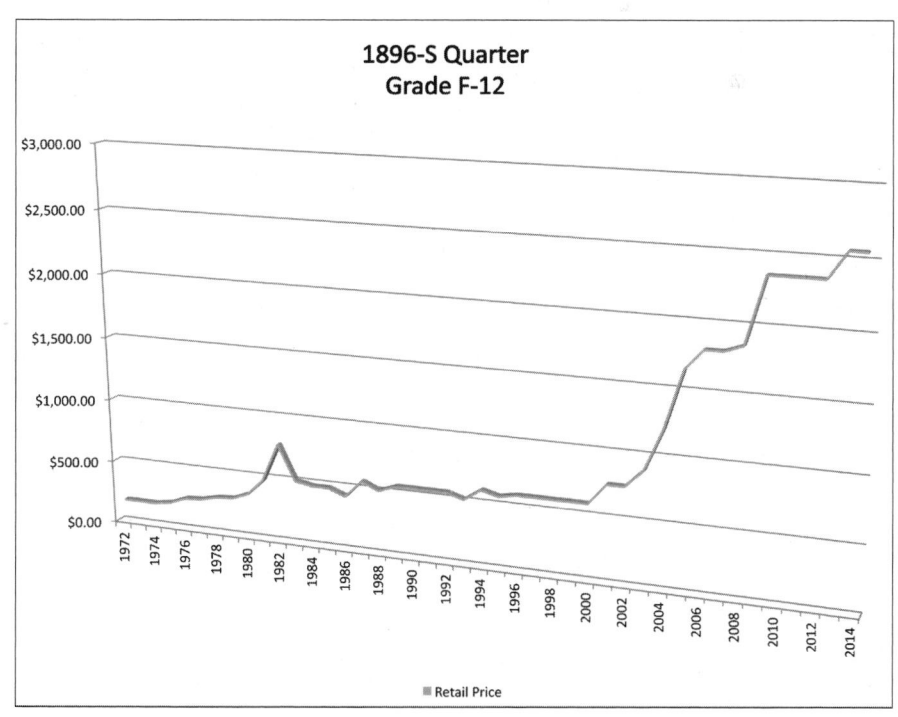

1896-S Quarter
Grade F-12

QUARTER

Date	Mintage	G4	VG8	F12	VF20	XF40	AU50	MS60	MS65	Prf65
1893 O	3,396,000	13.50	22.00	44.00	75.00	165	285	390	—	—
1893 O MM far right	Inc. above	12.00	15.50	32.00	60.00	120	175	265	1,850	—
1893 S	1,454,535	26.00	47.50	82.00	158	255	390	635	—	—
1893 S MM far right	Inc. above	21.00	38.00	69.00	128	195	320	450	6,350	—
1894	3,432,972	11.00	12.00	32.50	48.00	93.50	140	235	1,300	2,450
1894 O	2,852,000	12.50	24.00	50.00	95.00	165	285	415	—	—
1894 O MM far right	Inc. above	12.50	18.50	44.00	82.00	142	220	325	2,000	—
1894 S	2,648,821	12.00	17.00	50.00	95.00	180	265	410	—	—
1894 S MM far right	Inc. above	11.00	13.50	37.50	72.00	130	195	295	2,650	—
1895	4,440,880	10.50	13.00	30.00	39.00	78.00	135	235	1,650	2,450
1895 O	2,816,000	17.50	27.50	60.00	92.00	175	290	525	—	—
1895 O MM far right	Inc. above	12.50	19.50	46.00	77.50	145	230	390	2,650	—
1895 S	1,764,681	28.00	40.00	85.00	165	235	375	560	—	—
1895 S MM far right	Inc. above	22.00	36.00	77.00	128	190	300	425	3,650	—
1896	3,874,762	10.50	12.00	25.00	41.50	82.00	135	225	1,150	2,450
1896 O	1,484,000	62.00	95.00	200	365	625	775	815	6,950	—
1896 S	188,039	845	1,625	2,550	4,000	5,350	6,250	9,750	50,000	—
1897	8,140,731	10.50	12.00	21.50	33.50	70.00	122	220	1,450	2,450
1897 O	1,414,800	45.00	75.00	200	390	420	625	900	3,550	—
1897 S	542,229	130	160	320	475	625	925	1,400	6,850	—
1898	11,100,735	10.50	12.00	22.50	35.00	75.00	122	220	1,150	2,450
1898 O	1,868,000	16.00	28.50	75.00	165	300	430	665	8,950	—
1898 S	1,020,592	12.50	19.00	50.00	74.00	100	220	385	7,950	—
1899	12,624,846	10.50	12.00	22.50	35.00	75.00	120	220	1,150	2,450
1899 O	2,644,000	14.00	21.00	38.50	72.00	145	290	425	2,850	—
1899 S	708,000	18.00	28.50	70.00	95.00	145	275	410	3,650	—
1900	10,016,912	10.50	12.00	23.50	36.00	71.50	130	220	1,550	2,450
1900 O	3,416,000	16.00	29.00	69.50	120	175	345	575	3,750	—
1900 S	1,858,585	10.50	15.00	38.00	50.00	80.00	135	375	4,950	—
1901	8,892,813	30.00	36.00	45.00	75.00	88.00	200	215	1,550	2,450
1901 O	1,612,000	70.00	112	215	385	625	820	1,065	5,450	—
1901 S	72,664	5,200	9,500	18,500	26,500	31,000	38,000	41,500	77,500	—
1902	12,197,744	8.70	9.40	19.50	32.50	65.00	121	220	1,100	2,450
1902 O	4,748,000	10.50	16.00	52.50	89.00	150	245	485	4,000	—
1902 S	1,524,612	14.50	22.00	55.00	92.00	170	260	525	3,600	—
1903	9,670,064	8.70	9.40	20.00	34.00	70.00	121	220	2,150	2,450
1903 O	3,500,000	10.50	13.50	41.50	65.00	130	260	435	4,850	—
1903 S	1,036,000	15.50	26.00	46.00	89.00	150	285	435	2,450	—
1904	9,588,813	8.70	9.80	20.00	35.00	69.00	120	230	1,200	2,450
1904 O	2,456,000	32.00	45.00	90.00	165	235	460	850	2,650	—
1905	4,968,250	30.00	36.00	50.00	65.00	72.00	125	220	1,500	2,450
1905 O	1,230,000	44.00	62.50	125	245	265	365	500	6,850	—
1905 S	1,884,000	32.00	42.00	72.00	105	115	220	345	3,650	—
1906	3,656,435	8.70	9.40	18.50	32.50	95.00	121	215	1,100	2,450
1906 D	3,280,000	8.70	9.70	25.00	42.50	69.00	155	230	1,675	—
1906 O	2,056,000	10.50	13.50	40.00	60.00	112	200	290	1,150	—
1907	7,192,575	8.70	9.40	17.00	32.50	62.00	121	215	1,100	2,450
1907 D	2,484,000	8.70	9.50	29.00	50.00	76.00	175	240	2,650	—
1907 O	4,560,000	10.50	13.50	19.00	38.50	66.00	135	215	1,950	—
1907 S	1,360,000	10.50	18.50	47.50	75.00	135	275	465	5,650	—
1908	4,232,545	8.70	9.40	18.50	33.50	66.00	121	215	1,100	2,450
1908 D	5,788,000	8.70	9.40	17.50	35.00	66.00	117	250	1,100	—
1908 O	6,244,000	8.70	12.50	17.50	38.50	72.00	120	215	1,100	—
1908 S	784,000	18.50	40.00	90.00	165	295	500	775	4,750	—
1909	9,268,650	8.70	9.40	17.50	33.50	63.00	117	215	1,100	2,450
1909 D	5,114,000	8.70	9.50	22.00	41.50	85.00	160	215	1,350	—
1909 O	712,000	42.00	110	310	485	650	1,000	1,525	8,750	—
1909 S	1,348,000	10.50	15.00	37.50	57.50	90.00	200	300	2,250	—
1910	2,244,551	8.70	10.00	30.00	46.00	78.00	140	215	1,100	2,450
1910 D	1,500,000	8.90	11.00	47.50	72.00	130	260	375	1,875	—
1911	3,720,543	8.70	9.40	19.50	33.50	72.50	125	225	1,100	2,450
1911 D	933,600	31.00	44.00	160	310	460	650	900	5,750	—
1911 S	988,000	10.50	13.00	53.00	92.00	210	300	385	1,425	—
1912	4,400,700	8.70	9.40	17.50	33.50	55.00	117	215	1,100	2,485
1912 S	708,000	10.50	13.00	46.00	84.00	130	230	400	1,675	—
1913	484,613	16.00	26.00	75.00	190	390	535	900	4,450	2,485
1913 D	1,450,800	12.50	14.50	38.50	58.50	90.00	185	275	1,200	—
1913 S	40,000	1,800	2,450	5,350	7,950	10,500	13,250	15,500	31,500	—
1914	6,244,610	8.70	9.40	17.00	32.00	55.00	117	215	1,100	2,550
1914 D	3,046,000	8.70	9.40	17.00	28.00	55.00	117	215	1,100	—
1914 S	264,000	125	210	425	610	885	1,025	1,400	3,450	—
1915	3,480,450	8.70	9.40	17.00	28.00	61.00	117	215	1,100	2,485
1915 D	3,694,000	8.70	9.40	17.00	28.00	61.00	117	215	1,100	—
1915 S	704,000	28.00	42.00	63.50	92.00	110	220	285	1,200	—
1916	1,788,000	8.70	9.40	17.00	28.00	55.00	117	215	1,100	—
1916 D	6,540,800	8.70	9.40	17.00	28.00	55.00	117	215	1,100	—
1916 D/D	Inc. above	12.00	15.00	26.00	50.00	100	150	400	—	—

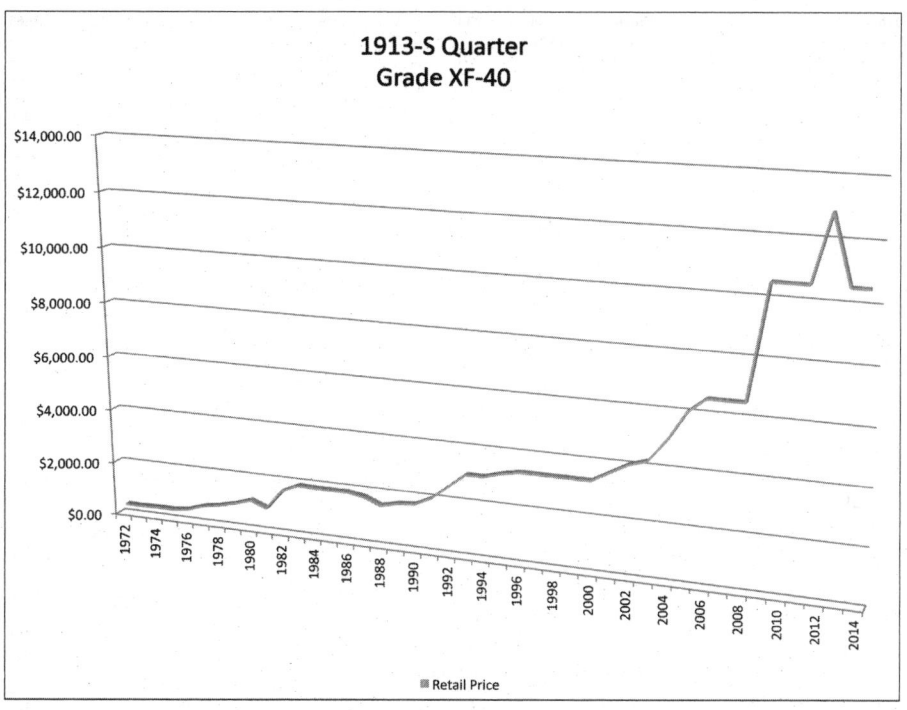

1913-S Quarter
Grade XF-40

■ Retail Price

Standing Liberty Quarter
Right breast exposed; Type 1 obverse

Right breast exposed

KM# 141 • 6.25 g., 0.900 Silver 0.18 oz. ASW, 24.3 mm. • **Designer:** Hermon A. MacNeil

Date	Mintage	G4	VG8	F12	VF20	XF40	AU50	MS60	MS65	65FH
1916	52,000	2,850	5,650	6,900	9,000	9,500	12,000	14,000	25,000	36,500
1917	8,792,000	—	50.00	63.50	85.00	120	182	230	695	850
1917 D	1,509,200	28.00	67.50	90.00	130	200	240	310	1,225	1,650
1917 S	1,952,000	30.00	75.00	105	155	220	280	340	1,150	3,200

Standing Liberty Quarter

Right breast covered; Type 2 obverse Three stars below eagle reverse

Right breast covered   Mint mark

KM# 145 • 6.25 g., 0.900 Silver 0.18 oz. ASW, 24.3 mm. • **Designer:** Hermon A. MacNeil

Date	Mintage	G4	VG8	F12	VF20	XF40	AU50	MS60	MS65	65FH
1917	13,880,000	25.00	35.00	52.00	72.00	97.50	135	200	600	900
1917 D	6,224,400	40.00	45.00	86.00	120	155	210	265	1,550	3,350
1917 S	5,522,000	40.00	45.00	88.00	115	148	200	255	1,085	3,650
1918	14,240,000	17.00	21.00	27.50	30.00	43.00	75.00	150	510	1,750

QUARTER

Date	Mintage	G4	VG8	F12	VF20	XF40	AU50	MS60	MS65	65FH
1918 D	7,380,000	26.00	36.00	68.50	75.00	135	190	275	1,750	4,850
1918 S	11,072,000	17.00	21.00	30.00	35.00	50.00	85.00	170	1,150	10,500
1918/17 S	Inc. above	1,550	2,250	3,650	4,850	7,500	11,750	15,000	90,000	320,000
1919	11,324,000	33.00	44.00	58.50	70.00	80.00	118	170	510	1,275
1919 D	1,944,000	85.00	110	200	400	595	775	950	2,875	37,500
1919 S	1,836,000	80.00	105	170	285	490	675	735	3,850	31,500
1920	27,860,000	15.00	18.00	24.00	37.00	50.00	88.00	150	510	1,850
1920 D	3,586,400	48.00	65.00	82.00	120	160	220	335	2,050	6,850
1920 S	6,380,000	19.00	25.00	28.00	37.00	57.00	155	225	2,250	24,000
1921	1,916,000	165	210	400	635	810	1,100	1,650	3,850	5,500
1923	9,716,000	15.00	18.00	33.00	37.00	43.00	95.00	155	550	3,850
1923 S	1,360,000	300	425	665	1,000	1,550	2,000	2,600	5,250	7,500
1924	10,920,000	15.00	18.00	23.00	35.00	46.00	110	185	525	1,550
1924 D	3,112,000	56.00	68.00	105	135	185	235	295	540	4,350
1924 S	2,860,000	27.00	32.00	43.00	60.00	120	220	310	1,650	5,650
1925	12,280,000	7.90	8.90	10.50	18.00	44.00	88.00	170	520	950
1926	11,316,000	7.90	8.50	9.60	14.00	36.00	72.50	168	495	1,650
1926 D	1,716,000	6.50	10.00	25.00	47.50	92.00	135	170	465	25,000
1926 S	2,700,000	8.20	8.80	11.50	24.00	105	215	325	1,850	26,000
1927	11,912,000	7.90	8.50	9.60	11.00	28.00	72.50	125	515	1,150
1927 D	976,400	14.00	19.00	30.00	73.50	145	210	250	565	2,450
1927 S	396,000	35.00	48.00	110	295	925	2,600	4,500	11,000	185,000
1928	6,336,000	7.90	8.50	9.60	12.00	28.00	72.50	125	515	1,850
1928 D	1,627,600	8.40	9.00	10.60	20.00	42.50	84.00	130	465	4,950
1928 S Large S	2,644,000	9.90	11.00	15.00	25.00	65.00	115	200	—	—
1928 S Small S	Inc. above	8.20	8.80	10.30	16.50	38.00	75.00	130	525	900
1929	11,140,000	7.90	8.50	9.60	12.00	28.00	72.50	125	465	795
1929 D	1,358,000	8.40	9.00	10.60	16.00	38.50	77.50	130	465	5,850
1929 S	1,764,000	8.20	8.80	10.10	15.00	34.00	77.50	130	465	795
1930	5,632,000	7.90	8.50	9.60	11.00	28.00	72.50	125	465	795
1930 S	1,556,000	8.20	8.80	9.60	11.50	34.00	77.50	130	465	845

Washington Quarter

Mint mark 1932-64

KM# 164 • 6.25 g., 0.900 **Silver** 0.18 oz. ASW, 24.3 mm. • **Designer:** John Flanagan

Date	Mintage	G4	VG8	F12	VF20	XF40	AU50	MS60	MS65	Prf65
1932	5,404,000	5.00	5.10	5.20	5.30	9.50	14.50	25.00	300	—
1932 D	436,800	115	125	140	180	290	440	1,150	12,500	—
1932 S	408,000	125	140	150	165	225	260	465	4,000	—
1934 Medium Motto	31,912,052	5.00	5.60	5.90	6.30	7.60	10.50	26.00	100	—
1934 Heavy Motto	Inc. above	4.80	4.90	9.00	12.50	18.00	30.00	50.00	265	—
1934 Light motto	Inc. above	5.40	6.20	10.00	12.00	15.00	26.00	45.00	340	—
1934 Doubled Die Obverse	Inc. above	75.00	100	165	200	320	450	850	4,250	—
1934 D Medium Motto	3,527,200	4.80	4.90	11.50	18.50	29.00	85.00	235	825	—
1934 D Heavy Motto	Inc. above	5.00	7.50	12.50	20.00	34.00	100	265	1,350	—
1935	32,484,000	4.80	5.00	5.30	5.80	7.30	10.00	20.00	110	—
1935 D	5,780,000	5.50	5.80	6.50	16.50	33.50	125	245	595	—
1935 S	5,660,000	5.00	5.20	6.20	7.30	15.50	36.50	95.00	310	—
1936	41,303,837	4.80	5.00	5.30	5.80	7.30	9.50	26.00	100	1,550
1936 D	5,374,000	5.50	5.80	10.50	26.00	52.00	255	585	975	—
1936 S	3,828,000	5.20	5.50	6.20	6.70	14.50	48.50	108	345	—
1937	19,701,542	4.80	5.00	5.30	7.20	10.00	16.50	22.00	90.00	475
1937 Double Die Obverse	Inc. above	75.00	100	235	340	450	850	1,850	11,500	—
1937 D	7,189,600	5.00	5.20	6.20	6.60	16.50	38.00	67.50	150	—
1937 S	1,652,000	5.50	5.80	6.60	22.00	34.00	95.00	160	430	—
1938	9,480,045	5.00	5.20	6.20	6.60	18.00	49.00	90.00	215	350
1938 S	2,832,000	5.50	5.70	5.90	9.75	22.50	55.00	108	215	—
1939	33,548,795	4.80	5.00	5.30	5.80	6.90	7.00	15.50	55.00	250
1939 D	7,092,000	5.00	5.20	5.80	7.30	12.00	19.50	42.00	122	—
1939 S	2,628,000	5.50	6.20	8.30	12.00	26.00	60.00	105	275	—
1940	35,715,246	4.80	5.00	5.30	5.80	6.80	7.50	17.50	53.50	160
1940 D	2,797,600	5.00	5.20	5.30	12.50	26.00	65.00	130	300	—
1940 S	8,244,000	5.00	5.20	5.30	5.40	9.00	16.50	28.50	52.00	—
1941	79,047,287	—	—	—	—	5.00	5.20	9.50	36.00	175
1941 Double Die Obv.	Inc. above	—	—	—	20.00	40.00	50.00	65.00	120	—
1941 D	16,714,800	—	—	—	5.50	6.60	15.00	33.00	66.00	—
1941 S	16,080,000	—	—	—	5.70	5.80	12.50	30.00	65.00	—

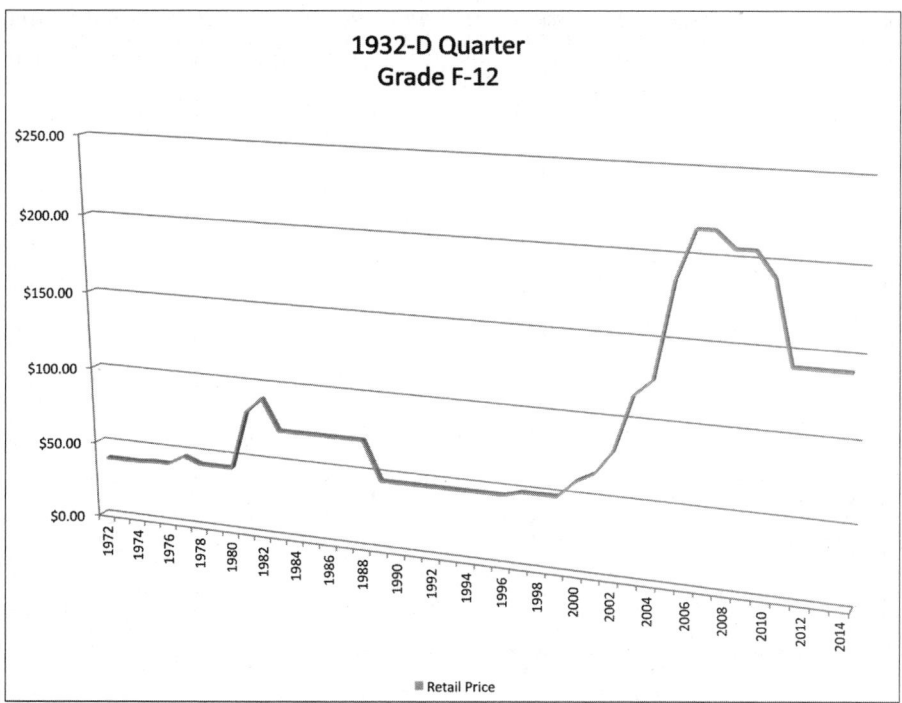

1932-D Quarter
Grade F-12

■ Retail Price

QUARTER

Date	Mintage	G4	VG8	F12	VF20	XF40	AU50	MS60	MS65	Prf65
1941 Lg S	Inc. above	—	5.80	12.00	20.00	30.00	50.00	100	350	—
1942	102,117,123	—	—	—	—	4.90	5.10	6.60	29.00	135
1942 D	17,487,200	—	—	—	5.50	6.70	11.00	18.00	38.00	—
1942 D Double Die Obv.	Inc. above	—	115	250	440	650	1,350	2,150	5,000	—
1942 D Double Die Rev.	Inc. above	—	22.00	40.00	60.00	75.00	150	350	1,850	—
1942 S	19,384,000	—	—	—	5.60	11.00	22.50	70.00	135	—
1943	99,700,000	—	—	—	—	4.90	5.10	6.60	39.00	—
1943 Double Die Obv.	Inc. above	—	12.00	20.00	35.00	50.00	90.00	175	450	—
1943 D	16,095,600	—	—	—	5.70	6.80	16.50	29.00	50.00	—
1943 S	21,700,000	—	—	5.40	5.80	6.20	14.50	27.00	51.50	—
1943 S Double Die Obv.	Inc. above	30.00	60.00	80.00	110	150	265	400	1,200	—
1943 Trumpet tail S	Inc. above	10.00	15.00	25.00	40.00	60.00	100	175	675	—
1944	104,956,000	—	—	—	—	4.90	5.10	5.70	29.00	—
1944 D	14,600,800	—	—	—	5.40	5.50	11.00	19.00	38.50	—
1944 S	12,560,000	—	—	—	5.40	5.50	9.50	14.50	31.00	—
1945	74,372,000	—	—	—	—	4.90	5.10	5.70	34.00	—
1945 D	12,341,600	—	—	—	5.50	7.50	11.00	18.00	37.00	—
1945 S	17,004,001	—	—	—	5.30	5.40	5.60	8.50	32.00	—
1946	53,436,000	—	—	—	—	4.90	5.10	5.70	38.00	—
1946 D	9,072,800	—	—	—	5.40	6.00	6.20	9.75	40.00	—
1946 S	4,204,000	—	—	—	5.40	6.00	6.20	6.90	34.00	—
1947	22,556,000	—	—	—	—	6.00	6.20	11.50	39.00	—
1947 D	15,338,400	—	—	—	5.40	5.90	6.10	11.00	39.00	—
1947 S	5,532,000	—	—	—	5.40	5.90	6.10	9.25	28.00	—
1948	35,196,000	—	—	—	5.40	5.90	6.10	5.90	30.00	—
1948 D	16,766,800	—	—	—	5.40	6.00	6.40	13.00	45.00	—
1948 S	15,960,000	—	—	—	5.40	5.90	6.10	6.70	40.00	—
1949	9,312,000	—	—	—	5.50	6.50	15.00	36.00	62.00	—
1949 D	10,068,400	—	—	—	5.30	6.00	9.50	16.50	48.00	—
1950	24,971,512	—	—	—	—	5.50	7.00	10.00	30.00	65.00
1950 D	21,075,600	—	—	—	—	5.00	5.20	5.90	32.00	—
1950 D/S	Inc. above	30.00	37.00	45.00	75.00	140	225	350	5,000	—
1950 S	10,284,004	—	—	—	—	5.60	7.50	13.50	34.00	—
1950 S/D	Inc. above	32.00	44.00	65.00	125	180	285	400	1,250	—
1950 S/S	Inc. above	6.00	7.00	8.00	10.00	14.00	18.00	35.00	135	—
1951	43,505,602	—	—	—	—	4.90	5.10	8.00	27.00	60.00
1951 D	35,354,800	—	—	—	—	5.10	5.70	8.50	26.00	—
1951 S	9,048,000	—	—	4.70	5.60	7.50	11.00	21.00	40.00	—
1952	38,862,073	—	—	—	—	4.90	5.80	9.10	28.00	46.00
1952 D	49,795,200	—	—	—	—	4.90	5.10	6.70	32.00	—

Date	Mintage	G4	VG8	F12	VF20	XF40	AU50	MS60	MS65	Prf65
1952 S	13,707,800	—	—	—	5.50	5.60	11.00	15.00	32.00	—
1953	18,664,920	—	—	—	—	5.50	6.40	10.00	25.00	44.00
1953 D	56,112,400	—	—	—	—	4.90	5.10	6.20	22.00	—
1953 S	14,016,000	—	—	—	—	4.90	5.10	6.50	28.00	—
1954	54,645,503	—	—	—	—	4.90	5.10	5.70	24.00	18.00
1954 D	42,305,500	—	—	—	—	4.90	5.10	5.70	24.00	—
1954 S	11,834,722	—	—	—	—	4.90	5.10	6.20	22.00	—
1955	18,558,381	—	—	—	—	4.90	5.10	5.70	26.00	22.00
1955 D	3,182,400	—	—	—	—	5.60	6.00	6.70	24.00	—
1956	44,813,384	—	—	—	—	4.90	5.10	5.70	22.00	15.00
1956 Double Bar 5	Inc. above	—	5.60	5.70	5.80	6.50	9.00	20.00	125	—
1956 Type B rev, proof rev die	Inc. above	—	—	8.00	12.00	18.00	25.00	35.00	275	—
1956 D	32,334,500	—	—	—	—	4.90	5.10	5.70	15.00	—
1957	47,779,952	—	—	—	—	4.90	5.10	5.70	14.00	12.00
1957 Type B rev, proof rev die	Inc. above	—	—	—	5.60	10.00	20.00	40.00	125	—
1957 D	77,924,160	—	—	—	—	4.90	5.10	5.70	16.00	—
1958	7,235,652	—	—	—	—	4.90	5.10	5.70	12.00	12.00
1958 Type B rev, proof rev die	Inc. above	—	—	—	5.60	10.00	16.00	24.00	90.00	—
1958 D	78,124,900	—	—	—	—	4.90	5.10	5.70	15.00	—
1959	25,533,291	—	—	—	—	4.90	5.10	5.70	12.00	12.00
1959 Type B rev, proof rev die	Inc. above	—	—	—	5.80	8.00	12.00	18.00	65.00	—
1959 D	62,054,232	—	—	—	—	4.90	5.10	5.70	18.00	—
1960	30,855,602	—	—	—	—	4.90	5.10	5.70	14.00	12.00
1960 Type B rev, proof rev die	Inc. above	—	—	—	5.10	10.00	16.00	24.00	90.00	—
1960 D	63,000,324	—	—	—	—	4.90	5.10	5.70	14.00	—
1961	40,064,244	—	—	—	—	4.90	5.10	5.70	15.00	12.00
1961 Type B rev, proof rev die	Inc. above	—	—	—	5.80	10.00	14.00	20.00	200	—
1961 D	83,656,928	—	—	—	—	4.90	5.10	5.70	20.00	—
1962	39,374,019	—	—	—	—	4.90	5.10	5.70	15.00	12.00
1962 Type B rev, proof rev die	Inc. above	—	—	—	8.00	12.00	15.00	30.00	175	—
1962 D	127,554,756	—	—	—	—	4.90	5.10	5.70	22.00	—
1963	77,391,645	—	—	—	—	4.90	5.10	5.70	12.00	12.00
1963 Type B rev, proof rev die	Inc. above	—	—	—	5.80	5.90	8.00	15.00	50.00	—
1963 D	135,288,184	—	—	—	—	4.90	5.10	5.70	15.00	—
1964	564,341,347	—	—	—	—	4.90	5.10	5.70	12.00	12.00
1964 Type B rev, proof rev die	Inc. above	—	—	—	5.80	9.00	10.00	18.00	75.00	—
1964 SMS	Inc. above	—	—	—	—	—	250	750	1,400	—
1964 D	704,135,528	—	—	—	—	4.90	5.10	5.70	12.00	—
1964 D Type C rev, clad rev die	Inc. above	—	—	—	40.00	55.00	75.00	125	450	—

KM# 164a • 5.67 g., **Copper-Nickel Clad Copper**, 24.3 mm. • **Designer:** John Flanagan

Date	Mintage	MS65	Prf65
1965	1,819,717,540	10.00	—
1965 SMS	2,360,000	9.00	—
1966	821,101,500	7.50	—
1966 SMS	2,261,583	9.00	—
1967	1,524,031,848	10.00	—
1967 SMS	1,863,344	9.00	—
1968	220,731,500	10.00	—
1968 D	101,534,000	7.00	—
1968 S	3,041,506	—	2.00
1969	176,212,000	14.00	—
1969 D	114,372,000	8.00	—
1969 S	2,934,631	—	2.25
1970	136,420,000	12.00	—
1970 D	417,341,364	6.00	—
1970 S	2,632,810	—	2.00
1971	109,284,000	12.00	—
1971 D	258,634,428	6.00	—
1971 S	3,220,733	—	2.00
1972	215,048,000	7.50	—
1972 D	311,067,732	6.00	—
1972 S	3,260,996	—	2.00
1973	346,924,000	8.00	—
1973 D	232,977,400	7.00	—
1973 S	2,760,339	—	1.75
1974	801,456,000	6.00	—
1974 D	353,160,300	8.00	—
1974 S	2,612,568	—	2.10
1975 none minted	—	—	—
1975 D none minted	—	—	—
1975 S none minted	—	—	—

Colonial drummer, torch at top left within ring of stars reverse

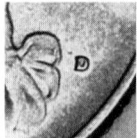

Mint mark
1968-present

KM# 204 • 5.67 g., **Copper-Nickel Clad Copper**, 24.3 mm. • **Rev. Designer:** Jack L. Ahr

Date	Mintage	MS60	MS65	PF65
1976	809,784,016	0.50	7.00	—
1976 D	860,118,839	0.50	8.00	—
1976 S	4,149,730	—	—	3.25

KM# 204a • 5.75 g., **Silver Clad**, 24.3 mm. • **Rev. Designer:** Jack L. Ahr

Date	Mintage	MS60	MS65	PF65
1976 S	4,908,319	1.85	6.00	—
1976 S	3,998,621	1.85	6.00	4.50

Eagle, regular design resumed reverse

KM# A164a • 5.67 g., **Copper-Nickel Clad Copper**, 24.3 mm. • **Edge:** Reeded **Note:** KM#164 design and composition resumed. The 1979-S and 1981 Type II proofs have clearer mint marks than the Type I proofs for those years.

Date	Mintage	MS65	Prf65
1977	468,556,000	7.50	—
1977 D	256,524,978	8.00	—
1977 S	3,251,152	—	2.75
1978	521,452,000	6.00	—
1978 D	287,373,152	7.00	—
1978 S	3,127,781	—	2.75
1979	515,708,000	8.00	—
1979 D	489,789,780	7.00	—
1979 S T-I	3,677,175	—	2.50
1979 S T-II	Inc. above	—	4.00
1980 P	635,832,000	8.00	—
1980 D	518,327,487	8.50	—
1980 S	3,554,806	—	2.75
1981 P	601,716,000	7.50	—
1981 D	575,722,833	6.50	—
1981 S T-I	4,063,083	—	2.75
1981 S T-II	Inc. above	—	7.50
1982 P	500,931,000	28.00	—
1982 D	480,042,788	15.00	—
1982 S	3,857,479	—	4.00
1983 P	673,535,000	50.00	—
1983 D	617,806,446	30.00	—
1983 S	3,279,126	—	3.00
1984 P	676,545,000	14.50	—
1984 D	546,483,064	12.50	—
1984 S	3,065,110	—	3.00
1985 P	775,818,962	12.50	—
1985 D	519,962,888	10.00	—
1985 S	3,362,821	—	3.00
1986 P	551,199,333	11.00	—
1986 D	504,298,660	15.00	—
1986 S	3,010,497	—	3.00
1987 P	582,499,481	10.50	—
1987 D	655,594,696	8.50	—
1987 S	4,227,728	—	3.00
1988 P	562,052,000	10.00	—
1988 D	596,810,688	7.50	—
1988 S	3,262,948	—	3.00
1989 P	512,868,000	16.00	—
1989 D	896,535,597	7.50	—
1989 S	3,220,194	—	3.00
1990 P	613,792,000	12.00	—
1990 D	927,638,181	6.00	—
1990 S	3,299,559	—	4.50
1991 P	570,968,000	10.00	—
1991 D	630,966,693	12.00	—
1991 S	2,867,787	—	3.00
1992 P	384,764,000	20.00	—
1992 D	389,777,107	12.00	—
1992 S	2,858,981	—	3.00
1993 P	639,276,000	7.50	—
1993 D	645,476,128	8.50	—
1993 S	2,633,439	—	3.00
1994 P	825,600,000	8.00	—
1994 D	880,034,110	8.00	—

Date	Mintage	MS65	Prf65
1994 S	2,484,594	—	3.00
1995 P	1,004,336,000	7.50	—
1995 D	1,103,216,000	6.50	—
1995 S	2,117,496	—	6.00
1996 P	925,040,000	7.50	—
1996 D	906,868,000	11.00	—
1996 S	1,750,244	—	4.00
1997 P	595,740,000	22.50	—
1997 D	599,680,000	17.00	—
1997 S	2,055,000	—	9.00
1998 P	896,268,000	14.00	—
1998 D	821,000,000	18.00	—
1998 S	2,086,507	—	9.00

KM# A164b • 6.25 g., 0.9000 **Silver**, 0.1808 oz. ASW, 24.3 mm.

	Mintage		Prf65
1992S	1,317,579		6.80
1993S	761,353		6.80
1994S	785,329		8.00
1995S	838,953		8.00
1996S	775,021		8.00
1997S	741,678		8.00
1998S	878,792		6.80

50 State Quarters
Delaware

KM# 293 • 5.67 g., **Copper-Nickel Clad Copper**, 24.3 mm.

Date	Mintage	MS63	MS65	Prf65
1999P	373,400,000	1.00	5.00	—
1999D	401,424,000	1.00	7.00	—
1999S	3,713,359	—	—	3.50

KM# 293a • 6.25 g., 0.900 **Silver**, 0.18 oz. ASW 24.3 mm.

Date	Mintage	MS63	MS65	Prf65
1999S	804,565	—	—	20.00

Pennsylvania

KM# 294 • 5.67 g., **Copper-Nickel Clad Copper**, 24.3 mm.

Date	Mintage	MS63	MS65	Prf65
1999P	349,000,000	1.00	5.00	—
1999D	358,332,000	1.00	4.00	—
1999S	3,713,359	—	—	3.50

KM# 294a • 6.25 g., 0.900 **Silver**, 0.18 oz. ASW 24.3 mm.

Date	Mintage	MS63	MS65	Prf65
1999S	804,565	—	—	20.00

QUARTER

New Jersey

KM# 295 • 5.67 g., **Copper-Nickel Clad Copper**, 24.3 mm.

Date	Mintage	MS63	MS65	Prf65
1999P	363,200,000	1.00	5.00	—
1999D	299,028,000	1.00	4.00	—
1999S	3,713,359	—	—	3.50

KM# 295a • 6.25 g., 0.900 **Silver**, 0.18 oz. ASW 24.3 mm.

Date	Mintage	MS63	MS65	Prf65
1999S	804,565	—	—	20.00

Georgia

KM# 296 • 5.67 g., **Copper-Nickel Clad Copper**, 24.3 mm.

Date	Mintage	MS63	MS65	Prf65
1999P	451,188,000	1.00	4.50	—
1999D	488,744,000	1.00	4.50	—
1999S	3,713,359	—	—	3.50

KM# 296a • 6.25 g., 0.900 **Silver**, 0.18 oz. ASW 24.3 mm.

Date	Mintage	MS63	MS65	Prf65
1999S	804,565	—	—	20.00

Connecticut

KM# 297 • 5.67 g., **Copper-Nickel Clad Copper**, 24.3 mm.

Date	Mintage	MS63	MS65	Prf65
1999P	688,742,000	0.80	6.00	—
1999D	657,480,000	0.80	5.00	—
1999S	3,713,359	—	—	3.50

KM# 297a • 6.25 g., 0.900 **Silver**, 0.18 oz. ASW 24.3 mm.

Date	Mintage	MS63	MS65	Prf65
1999S	804,565	—	—	20.00

Massachusetts

KM# 305 • 5.67 g., **Copper-Nickel Clad Copper**, 24.3 mm.

Date	Mintage	MS63	MS65	Prf65
2000P	629,800,000	0.80	7.00	—
2000D	535,184,000	0.80	8.00	—
2000S	4,078,747	—	—	3.00

KM# 305a • 6.25 g., 0.900 **Silver**, 0.18 oz. ASW 24.3 mm.

Date	Mintage	MS63	MS65	Prf65
2000S	965,921	—	—	9.00

Maryland

KM# 306 • 5.67 g., **Copper-Nickel Clad Copper**, 24.3 mm.

Date	Mintage	MS63	MS65	Prf65
2000P	678,200,000	0.80	6.00	—
2000D	556,526,000	0.80	6.00	—
2000S	4,078,747	—	—	3.00

KM# 306a • 6.25 g., 0.900 **Silver**, 0.18 oz. ASW 24.3 mm.

Date	Mintage	MS63	MS65	Prf65
2000S	965,921	—	—	9.00

South Carolina

KM# 307 • 5.67 g., **Copper-Nickel Clad Copper**, 24.3 mm.

Date	Mintage	MS63	MS65	Prf65
2000P	742,756,000	0.80	6.00	—
2000D	566,208,000	0.80	9.00	—
2000S	4,078,747	—	—	3.00

KM# 307a • 6.25 g., 0.900 **Silver**, 0.18 oz. ASW 24.3 mm.

Date	Mintage	MS63	MS65	Prf65
2000S	965,921	—	—	9.00

QUARTER

New Hampshire

KM# 308 • 5.67 g., **Copper-Nickel Clad Copper**, 24.3 mm.

Date	Mintage	MS63	MS65	Prf65
2000P	673,040,000	0.80	8.00	—
2000D	495,976,000	0.80	9.00	—
2000S	4,078,747	—	—	3.00

KM# 308a • 6.25 g., 0.900 **Silver**, 0.18 oz. ASW 24.3 mm.

Date	Mintage	MS63	MS65	Prf65
2000S	965,921	—	—	9.00

Virginia

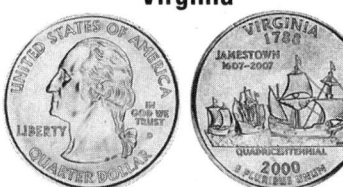

KM# 309 • 5.67 g., **Copper-Nickel Clad Copper**, 24.3 mm.

Date	Mintage	MS63	MS65	Prf65
2000P	943,000,000	0.80	6.50	—
2000D	651,616,000	0.80	6.50	—
2000S	4,078,747	—	—	3.00

KM# 309a • 6.25 g., 0.900 **Silver**, 0.18 oz. ASW 24.3 mm.

Date	Mintage	MS63	MS65	Prf65
2000S	965,921	—	—	9.50

New York

KM# 318 • 5.67 g., **Copper-Nickel Clad Copper**, 24.3 mm.

Date	Mintage	MS63	MS65	Prf65
2001P	655,400,000	0.80	5.50	—
2001D	619,640,000	0.80	5.50	—
2001S	3,094,140	—	—	4.00

KM# 318a • 6.25 g., 0.900 **Silver**, 0.18 oz. ASW 24.3 mm.

Date	Mintage	MS63	MS65	Prf65
2001S	889,697	—	—	9.50

North Carolina

KM# 319 • 5.67 g., **Copper-Nickel Clad Copper**, 24.3 mm.

Date	Mintage	MS63	MS65	Prf65
2001P	627,600,000	1.00	5.50	—
2001D	427,876,000	1.00	6.50	—
2001S	3,094,140	—	—	4.00

KM# 319a • 6.25 g., 0.900 **Silver**, 0.18 oz. ASW 24.3 mm.

Date	Mintage	MS63	MS65	Prf65
2001S	889,697	—	—	9.50

Rhode Island

KM# 320 • 5.67 g., **Copper-Nickel Clad Copper**, 24.3 mm.

Date	Mintage	MS63	MS65	Prf65
2001P	423,000,000	0.80	5.50	—
2001D	447,100,000	0.80	6.00	—
2001S	3,094,140	—	—	4.00

KM# 320a • 6.25 g., 0.900 **Silver**, 0.18 oz. ASW 24.3 mm.

Date	Mintage	MS63	MS65	Prf65
2001S	889,697	—	—	9.50

Vermont

KM# 321 • 5.67 g., **Copper-Nickel Clad Copper**, 24.3 mm.

Date	Mintage	MS63	MS65	Prf65
2001P	423,400,000	0.80	6.50	—
2001D	459,404,000	0.80	6.50	—
2001S	3,094,140	—	—	4.00

KM# 321a • 6.25 g., 0.900 **Silver**, 0.18 oz. ASW 24.3 mm.

Date	Mintage	MS63	MS65	Prf65
2001S	889,697	—	—	9.50

Kentucky

KM# 322 • 5.67 g., **Copper-Nickel Clad Copper**, 24.3 mm.

Date	Mintage	MS63	MS65	Prf65
2001P	353,000,000	1.00	6.50	—
2001D	370,564,000	1.00	7.00	—
2001S	3,094,140	—	—	4.00

KM# 322a • 6.25 g., 0.900 **Silver**, 0.18 oz. ASW 24.3 mm.

Date	Mintage	MS63	MS65	Prf65
2001S	889,697	—	—	9.50

Tennessee

KM# 331 • 5.67 g., **Copper-Nickel Clad Copper**, 24.3 mm.

Date	Mintage	MS63	MS65	Prf65
2002P	361,600,000	1.40	6.50	—
2002D	286,468,000	1.40	7.00	—
2002S	3,084,245	—	—	2.30

KM# 331a • 6.25 g., 0.900 **Silver**, 0.18 oz. ASW 24.3 mm.

Date	Mintage	MS63	MS65	Prf65
2002S	892,229	—	—	8.50

Ohio

KM# 332 • 5.67 g., **Copper-Nickel Clad Copper**, 24.3 mm.

Date	Mintage	MS63	MS65	Prf65
2002P	217,200,000	0.80	5.50	—
2002D	414,832,000	0.80	5.50	—
2002S	3,084,245	—	—	2.30

KM# 332a • 6.25 g., 0.900 **Silver**, 0.18 oz. ASW 24.3 mm.

Date	Mintage	MS63	MS65	Prf65
2002S	892,229	—	—	8.50

Louisiana

KM# 333 • 5.67 g., **Copper-Nickel Clad Copper**, 24.3 mm.

Date	Mintage	MS63	MS65	Prf65
2002P	362,000,000	0.80	5.50	—
2002D	402,204,000	0.80	6.00	—
2002S	3,084,245	—	—	2.30

KM# 333a • 6.25 g., 0.900 **Silver**, 0.18 oz. ASW 24.3 mm.

Date	Mintage	MS63	MS65	Prf65
2002S	892,229	—	—	8.50

Indiana

KM# 334 • 5.67 g., **Copper-Nickel Clad Copper**, 24.3 mm.

Date	Mintage	MS63	MS65	Prf65
2002P	362,600,000	0.80	5.00	—
2002D	327,200,000	0.80	5.00	—
2002S	3,084,245	—	—	2.30

KM# 334a • 6.25 g., 0.900 **Silver**, 0.18 oz. ASW 24.3 mm.

Date	Mintage	MS63	MS65	Prf65
2002S	892,229	—	—	8.50

Mississippi

KM# 335 • 5.67 g., **Copper-Nickel Clad Copper**, 24.3 mm.

Date	Mintage	MS63	MS65	Prf65
2002P	290,000,000	0.80	5.00	—
2002D	289,600,000	0.80	5.00	—
2002S	3,084,245	—	—	2.30

KM# 335a • 6.25 g., 0.900 **Silver**, 0.18 oz. ASW 24.3 mm.

Date	Mintage	MS63	MS65	Prf65
2002S	892,229	—	—	8.50

QUARTER

Illinois

KM# 343 • 5.67 g., **Copper-Nickel Clad Copper**, 24.3 mm.

Date	Mintage	MS63	MS65	Prf65
2003P	225,800,000	1.10	5.00	—
2003D	237,400,000	1.10	5.00	—
2003S	3,408,516	—	—	2.30

KM# 343a • 6.25 g., 0.900 **Silver**, 0.18 oz. ASW 24.3 mm.

Date	Mintage	MS63	MS65	Prf65
2003S	1,257,555	—	—	8.50

Alabama

KM# 344 • 5.67 g., **Copper-Nickel Clad Copper**, 24.3 mm.

Date	Mintage	MS63	MS65	Prf65
2003P	225,000,000	0.65	5.00	—
2003D	232,400,000	0.65	5.00	—
2003S	3,408,516	—	—	2.30

KM# 344a • 6.25 g., 0.900 **Silver**, 0.18 oz. ASW 24.3 mm.

Date	Mintage	MS63	MS65	Prf65
2003S	1,257,555	—	—	8.50

Maine

KM# 345 • 5.67 g., **Copper-Nickel Clad Copper**, 24.3 mm.

Date	Mintage	MS63	MS65	Prf65
2003P	217,400,000	0.65	5.00	—
2003D	213,400,000	0.65	5.00	—
2003S	3,408,516	—	—	2.30

KM# 345a • 6.25 g., 0.900 **Silver**, 0.18 oz. ASW 24.3 mm.

Date	Mintage	MS63	MS65	Prf65
2003S	1,257,555	—	—	8.50

Missouri

KM# 346 • 5.67 g., **Copper-Nickel Clad Copper**, 24.3 mm.

Date	Mintage	MS63	MS65	Prf65
2003P	225,000,000	0.65	5.00	—
2003D	228,200,000	0.65	5.00	—
2003S	3,408,516	—	—	2.30

KM# 346a • 6.25 g., 0.900 **Silver**, 0.18 oz. ASW 24.3 mm.

Date	Mintage	MS63	MS65	Prf65
2003S	1,257,555	—	—	8.50

Arkansas

KM# 347 • 5.67 g., **Copper-Nickel Clad Copper**, 24.3 mm.

Date	Mintage	MS63	MS65	Prf65
2003P	228,000,000	0.65	5.00	—
2003D	229,800,000	0.65	5.00	—
2003S	3,408,516	—	—	2.30

KM# 347a • 6.25 g., 0.900 **Silver**, 0.18 oz. ASW 24.3 mm.

Date	Mintage	MS63	MS65	Prf65
2003S	1,257,555	—	—	8.50

Michigan

KM# 355 • 5.67 g., **Copper-Nickel Clad Copper**, 24.3 mm.

Date	Mintage	MS63	MS65	Prf65
2004P	233,800,000	0.65	5.00	—
2004D	225,800,000	0.65	5.00	—
2004S	2,740,684	—	—	2.30

KM# 355a • 6.25 g., 0.900 **Silver**, 0.18 oz. ASW 24.3 mm.

Date	Mintage	MS63	MS65	Prf65
2004S	1,775,370	—	—	8.50

Florida

KM# 356 • 5.67 g., **Copper-Nickel Clad Copper**, 24.3 mm.

Date	Mintage	MS63	MS65	Prf65
2004P	240,200,000	0.65	5.00	—
2004D	241,600,000	0.65	5.00	—
2004S	2,740,684	—	—	2.30

KM# 356a • 6.25 g., 0.900 **Silver**, 0.18 oz. ASW 24.3 mm.

Date	Mintage	MS63	MS65	Prf65
2004S	1,775,370	—	—	8.50

Texas

KM# 357 • 5.67 g., **Copper-Nickel Clad Copper**, 24.3 mm.

Date	Mintage	MS63	MS65	Prf65
2004P	278,800,000	0.65	5.00	—
2004D	263,000,000	0.65	5.00	—
2004S	2,740,684	—	—	2.30

KM# 357a • 6.25 g., 0.900 **Silver**, 0.18 oz. ASW 24.3 mm.

Date	Mintage	MS63	MS65	Prf65
2004S	1,775,370	—	—	8.50

Iowa

KM# 358 • 5.67 g., **Copper-Nickel Clad Copper**, 24.3 mm.

Date	Mintage	MS63	MS65	Prf65
2004P	213,800,000	0.65	5.00	—
2004D	251,800,000	0.65	5.00	—
2004S	2,740,684	—	—	2.30

KM# 358a • 6.25 g., 0.900 **Silver**, 0.18 oz. ASW 24.3 mm.

Date	Mintage	MS63	MS65	Prf65
2004S	—	—	—	8.50

Wisconsin

KM# 359 • 5.67 g., **Copper-Nickel Clad Copper**, 24.3 mm.

Date	Mintage	MS63	MS65	Prf65
2004P	226,400,000	0.65	5.00	—
2004D	226,800,000	0.65	5.00	—
2004D Extra Leaf Low	Est. 9000	135	190	—
2004D Extra Leaf High	Est. 3000	175	285	—
2004S	—	—	—	2.30

KM# 359a • 6.25 g., 0.900 **Silver**, 0.18 oz. ASW 24.3 mm.

Date	Mintage	MS63	MS65	Prf65
2004S	1,775,370	—	—	8.50

Minnesota

KM# 371 • 5.67 g., **Copper-Nickel Clad Copper**, 24.3 mm.

Date	Mintage	MS63	MS65	Prf65
2005P	226,400,000	0.65	5.00	—
2005P Satin Finish	Inc. above	1.50	4.50	—
2005D	226,800,000	0.65	5.00	—
2005D Satin Finish	Inc. above	1.50	4.50	—
2005S	3,262,960	—	—	2.30

KM# 371a • 6.25 g., 0.900 **Silver**, 0.18 oz. ASW 24.3 mm.

Date	Mintage	MS63	MS65	Prf65
2005S	1,679,600	—	—	8.50

Oregon

KM# 372 • 5.67 g., **Copper-Nickel Clad Copper**, 24.3 mm.

Date	Mintage	MS63	MS65	Prf65
2005P	316,200,000	0.65	5.00	—
2005P Satin Finish	Inc. above	1.50	4.50	—
2005D	404,000,000	0.65	5.00	—
2005D Satin Finish	Inc. above	1.50	4.50	—
2005S	3,262,960	—	—	2.30

KM# 372a • 6.25 g., 0.900 **Silver**, 0.18 oz. ASW 24.3 mm.

Date	Mintage	MS63	MS65	Prf65
2005S	1,679,600	—	—	8.50

QUARTER

Kansas

KM# 373 • 5.67 g., **Copper-Nickel Clad Copper**, 24.3 mm.

Date	Mintage	MS63	MS65	Prf65
2005P	263,400,000	0.65	5.00	—
2005P Satin Finish	Inc. above	1.50	4.50	—
2005D	300,000,000	0.65	5.00	—
2005D Satin Finish	Inc. above	1.50	4.50	—
2005S	3,262,960	—	—	2.30

KM# 373a • 6.25 g., 0.900 **Silver**, 0.18 oz. ASW 24.3 mm.

Date	Mintage	MS63	MS65	Prf65
2005S	1,679,600	—	—	8.50

West Virginia

KM# 374 • 5.67 g., **Copper-Nickel Clad Copper**, 24.3 mm.

Date	Mintage	MS63	MS65	Prf65
2005P	365,400,000	0.65	5.00	—
2005P Satin Finish	Inc. above	1.50	4.50	—
2005D	356,200,000	0.65	5.00	—
2005D Satin Finish	Inc. above	1.50	4.50	—
2005S	3,262,960	—	—	2.30

KM# 374a • 6.25 g., 0.900 **Silver**, 0.18 oz. ASW 24.3 mm.

Date	Mintage	MS63	MS65	Prf65
2005S	1,679,600	—	—	8.50

California

KM# 370 • 5.67 g., **Copper-Nickel Clad Copper**, 24.3 mm.

Date	Mintage	MS63	MS65	Prf65
2005P	257,200,000	0.65	5.00	—
2005P Satin Finish	Inc. above	1.50	4.50	—
2005D	263,200,000	0.65	5.00	—
2005D Satin Finish	Inc. above	1.50	4.50	—
2005S	3,262,960	—	—	2.30

KM# 370a • 6.25 g., 0.900 **Silver**, 0.18 oz. ASW 24.3 mm.

Date	Mintage	MS63	MS65	Prf65
2005S	1,679,600	—	—	8.50

Nevada

KM# 382 • 5.67 g., **Copper-Nickel Clad Copper**, 24.3 mm.

Date	Mintage	MS63	MS65	Prf65
2006P	277,000,000	0.65	5.00	—
2006P Satin Finish	Inc. above	1.50	4.50	—
2006D	312,800,000	0.65	5.00	—
2006D Satin Finish	Inc. above	1.50	4.50	—
2006S	2,862,078	—	—	2.30

KM# 382a • 6.25 g., 0.900 **Silver**, 0.18 oz. ASW 24.3 mm.

Date	Mintage	MS63	MS65	Prf65
2006S	1,571,839	—	—	8.50

Nebraska

KM# 383 • 5.67 g., **Copper-Nickel Clad Copper**, 24.3 mm.

Date	Mintage	MS63	MS65	Prf65
2006P	318,000,000	0.65	5.00	—
2006P Satin Finish	Inc. above	1.50	4.50	—
2006D	273,000,000	0.65	5.00	—
2006D Satin Finish	Inc. above	1.50	4.50	—
2006S	2,862,078	—	—	2.30

KM# 383a • 6.25 g., 0.900 **Silver**, 0.18 oz. ASW 24.3 mm.

Date	Mintage	MS63	MS65	Prf65
2006S	1,571,839	—	—	8.50

Colorado

KM# 384 • 5.67 g., **Copper-Nickel Clad Copper**, 24.3 mm.

Date	Mintage	MS63	MS65	Prf65
2006P	274,800,000	0.65	5.00	—
2006P Satin Finish	Inc. above	1.50	4.50	—
2006D	294,200,000	0.65	5.00	—
2006D Satin Finish	Inc. above	1.50	4.50	—
2006S	2,862,078	—	—	2.30

KM# 384a • 6.25 g., 0.900 **Silver**, 0.18 oz. ASW 24.3 mm.

Date	Mintage	MS63	MS65	Prf65
2006S	1,571,839	—	—	8.50

QUARTER

QUARTER

North Dakota

KM# 385 • 5.67 g., **Copper-Nickel Clad Copper**, 24.3 mm.

Date	Mintage	MS63	MS65	Prf65
2006P	305,800,000	0.65	5.00	—
2006P Satin Finish	Inc. above	1.50	4.50	—
2006D	359,000,000	0.65	5.00	—
2006D Satin Finish	Inc. above	1.50	4.50	—
2006S	2,862,078	—	—	2.30

KM# 385a • 6.25 g., 0.900 **Silver**, 0.18 oz. ASW 24.3 mm.

Date	Mintage	MS63	MS65	Prf65
2006S	1,571,839	—	—	8.50

South Dakota

KM# 386 • 5.67 g., **Copper-Nickel Clad Copper**, 24.3 mm.

Date	Mintage	MS63	MS65	Prf65
2006P	245,000,000	0.65	5.00	—
2006P Satin Finish	Inc. above	1.50	4.50	—
2006D	265,800,000	0.65	5.00	—
2006D Satin Finish	Inc. above	1.50	4.50	—
2006S	2,862,078	—	—	2.30

KM# 386a • 6.25 g., 0.900 **Silver**, 0.18 oz. ASW 24.3 mm.

Date	Mintage	MS63	MS65	Prf65
2006S	1,571,839	—	—	8.50

Montana

KM# 396 • 5.67 g., **Copper-Nickel Clad Copper**, 24.3 mm.

Date	Mintage	MS63	MS65	Prf65
2007P	257,000,000	0.65	5.00	—
2007P Satin Finish	—	1.50	4.50	—
2007D	256,240,000	0.65	5.00	—
2007D Satin Finish	—	1.50	4.50	—
2007S	2,374,778	—	—	2.30

KM# 396a • 6.25 g., 0.900 **Silver**, 0.18 oz. ASW 24.3 mm.

Date	Mintage	MS63	MS65	Prf65
2007S	1,299,878	—	—	8.50

Washington

KM# 397 • 5.67 g., **Copper-Nickel Clad Copper**, 24.3 mm.

Date	Mintage	MS63	MS65	Prf65
2007P	265,200,000	0.65	5.00	—
2007P Satin Finish	—	1.50	4.50	—
2007D	280,000,000	0.65	5.00	—
2007D Satin Finish	—	1.50	4.50	—
2007S	2,374,778	—	—	2.30

KM# 397a • 6.25 g., 0.900 **Silver**, 0.18 oz. ASW 24.3 mm.

Date	Mintage	MS63	MS65	Prf65
2007S	1,299,878	—	—	8.50

Idaho

KM# 398 • 5.67 g., **Copper-Nickel Clad Copper**, 24.3 mm.

Date	Mintage	MS63	MS65	Prf65
2007P	294,600,000	0.65	5.00	—
2007P Satin finish	—	1.50	4.50	—
2007D	286,800,000	0.65	5.00	—
2007D Satin finish	—	1.50	4.50	—
2007S	2,374,778	—	—	2.30

KM# 398a • 6.25 g., 0.900 **Silver**, 0.18 oz. ASW 24.3 mm.

Date	Mintage	MS63	MS65	Prf65
2007S	1,299,878	—	—	8.50

Wyoming

KM# 399 • 5.67 g., **Copper-Nickel Clad Copper**, 24.3 mm.

Date	Mintage	MS63	MS65	Prf65
2007P	243,600,000	0.65	5.00	—
2007P Satin finish	—	1.50	4.50	—
2007D	320,800,000	0.65	5.00	—
2007 Satin finish	—	1.50	4.50	—
2007S	2,374,778	—	—	2.30

KM# 399a • 6.25 g., 0.900 **Silver**, 0.18 oz. ASW 24.3 mm.

Date	Mintage	MS63	MS65	Prf65
2007S	1,299,878	—	—	8.50

Utah

KM# 400 • 5.67 g., **Copper-Nickel Clad Copper**, 24.3 mm.

Date	Mintage	MS63	MS65	Prf65
2007P	255,000,000	0.65	5.00	—
2007P Satin finish	—	1.50	4.50	—
2007D	253,200,000	0.65	5.00	—
2007D Satin finish	—	1.50	4.50	—
2007S	2,374,778	—	—	2.30

KM# 400a • 6.25 g., 0.900 **Silver**, 0.18 oz. ASW

Date	Mintage	MS63	MS65	Prf65
2007S	1,299,878	—	—	8.50

Oklahoma

KM# 421 • 5.67 g., **Copper-Nickel Clad Copper**, 24.3 mm.

Date	Mintage	MS63	MS65	Prf65
2008P	222,000,000	0.65	5.00	—
2008P Satin finish	—	1.50	4.50	—
2008D	194,600,000	0.65	5.00	—
2008D Satin finish	—	1.50	4.50	—
2008S	2,100,000	—	—	2.30

KM# 421a • 6.25 g., 0.900 **Silver**, 0.18 oz. ASW 24.3 mm.

Date	Mintage	MS63	MS65	Prf65
2008S	1,200,000	—	—	8.50

New Mexico

KM# 422 • 5.67 g., **Copper-Nickel Clad Copper**, 24.3 mm.

Date	Mintage	MS63	MS65	Prf65
2008P	244,200,000	0.65	5.00	—
2008P Satin finish	—	1.50	4.50	—
2008D	244,400,000	0.65	5.00	—
2008D Satin finish	—	1.50	4.50	—
2008S	2,100,000	—	—	2.30

KM# 422a • 6.25 g., 0.900 **Silver**, 0.18 oz. ASW 24.3 mm.

Date	Mintage	MS63	MS65	Prf65
2008S	1,200,000	—	—	8.50

Arizona

KM# 423 • 5.67 g., **Copper-Nickel Clad Copper**, 24.3 mm.

Date	Mintage	MS63	MS65	Prf65
2008P	244,600,000	0.65	5.00	—
2008P Satin finish	—	1.50	4.50	—
2008D	265,000,000	0.65	5.00	—
2008D Satin finish	—	1.50	4.50	—
2008S	2,100,000	—	—	2.30

KM# 423a • 6.25 g., 0.900 **Silver**, 0.18 oz. ASW 24.3 mm.

Date	Mintage	MS63	MS65	Prf65
2008S	1,200,000	—	—	8.50

Alaska

KM# 424 • 5.67 g., **Copper-Nickel Clad Copper**, 24.3 mm.

Date	Mintage	MS63	MS65	Prf65
2008P	251,800,000	0.65	5.00	—
2008P Satin finish	—	1.50	4.50	—
2008D	254,000,000	0.65	5.00	—
2008D Satin finish	—	1.50	4.50	—
2008S	2,100,000	—	—	2.30

KM# 424a • 6.25 g., 0.900 **Silver**, 0.18 oz. ASW 24.3 mm.

Date	Mintage	MS63	MS65	Prf65
2008S	1,200,000	—	—	8.50

Hawaii

KM# 425 • 5.67 g., **Copper-Nickel Clad Copper**, 24.3 mm.

Date	Mintage	MS63	MS65	Prf65
2008P	254,000,000	0.65	5.00	—
2008P Satin finish	—	1.50	4.50	—
2008D	263,600,000	0.65	5.00	—
2008D Satin finish	—	1.50	4.50	—
2008S	2,100,000	—	—	2.30

KM# 425a • 6.25 g., 0.900 **Silver**, 0.18 oz. ASW 24.3 mm.

Date	Mintage	MS63	MS65	Prf65
2008S	1,200,000	—	—	8.50

QUARTER

QUARTER

DC and Territories
District of Columbia

KM# 445 • 5.67 g., **Copper-Nickel Clad Copper**, 24.3 mm. **Rev. Designer:** Don Everhart

Date	Mintage	MS63	MS65	Prf65
2009P	83,600,000	0.75	5.00	—
2009D	88,800,000	0.75	5.00	—
2009S	2,113,478	—	—	3.75

KM# 445a • 6.25 g., 0.900 **Silver**, 0.18 oz. ASW 24.3 mm.

Date	Mintage	MS63	MS65	Prf65
2009S	996,548	—	—	7.75

Puerto Rico

KM# 446 • 5.67 g., **Copper-Nickel Clad Copper**, 24.3 mm. **Rev. Designer:** Joseph Menna

Date	Mintage	MS63	MS65	Prf65
2009P	53,200,000	0.75	5.00	—
2009D	86,000,000	0.75	5.00	—
2009S	2,113,478	—	—	3.75

KM# 446a • 6.25 g., 0.900 **Silver**, 0.18 oz. ASW 24.3 mm.

Date	Mintage	MS63	MS65	Prf65
2009S	996,548	—	—	7.75

Guam

KM# 447 • 5.67 g., **Copper-Nickel Clad Copper**, 24.3 mm. **Rev. Designer:** James Licaretz

Date	Mintage	MS63	MS65	Prf65
2009P	45,000,000	0.75	5.00	—
2009D	42,600,000	0.75	5.00	—
2009S	2,113,478	—	—	3.75

KM# 447a • 6.25 g., 0.900 **Silver**, 0.18 oz. ASW 24.3 mm.

Date	Mintage	MS63	MS65	Prf65
2009S	996,548	—	—	7.75

American Samoa

KM# 448 • 5.67 g., **Copper-Nickel Clad Copper**, 24.3 mm. **Rev. Designer:** Charles Vickers

Date	Mintage	MS63	MS65	Prf65
2009P	42,600,000	0.75	5.00	—
2009D	39,600,000	0.75	5.00	—
2009S	2,113,478	—	—	3.75

KM# 448a • 6.25 g., 0.900 **Silver**, 0.18 oz. ASW 24.3 mm.

Date	Mintage	MS63	MS65	Prf65
2009S	996,548	—	—	7.75

US Virgin Islands

KM# 449 • 5.67 g., **Copper-Nickel Clad Copper**, 24.3 mm. **Rev. Designer:** Joseph Menna

Date	Mintage	MS63	MS65	Prf65
2009P	41,000,000	0.75	5.00	—
2009D	41,000,000	0.75	5.00	—
2009S	2,113,478	—	—	3.75

KM# 449a • 6.25 g., 0.900 **Silver**, 0.18 oz. ASW 24.3 mm.

Date	Mintage	MS63	MS65	Prf65
2009S	996,548	—	—	7.75

Northern Mariana Islands

KM# 466 • 5.67 g., **Copper-Nickel Clad Copper**, **Rev. Designer:** Pheve Hemphill

Date	Mintage	MS63	MS65	Prf65
2009P	35,200,000	0.75	5.00	—
2009D	37,600,000	0.75	5.00	—
2009S	2,113,478	—	—	3.75

KM# 466a • 6.25 g., 0.900 **Silver**, 0.18 oz. ASW

Date	Mintage	MS63	MS65	Prf65
2009S	996,548	—	—	7.75

America the Beautiful
Hot Springs, Ark.

KM# 469 • 5.67 g., **Copper-Nickel Clad Copper**, 24.3 mm.

Date	Mintage	MS63	MS65	Prf65
2010P	35,600,000	0.75	5.00	—
2010D	34,000,000	0.75	5.00	—
2010S	1,401,903	—	—	3.75

KM# 469a • 6.25 g., **0.900 Silver**, 0.18 oz. ASW

Date	Mintage	MS63	MS65	Prf65
2010S	859,435	—	—	7.75

Yellowstone National Park

KM# 470 • 5.67 g., **Copper-Nickel Clad Copper**, 24.3 mm. **Rev. Designer:** Don Everhart

Date	Mintage	MS63	MS65	Prf65
2010P	33,600,000	0.75	5.00	—
2010D	34,800,000	0.75	5.00	—
2010S	1,402,756	—	—	3.75

KM# 470a • 6.25 g., **0.900 Silver**, 0.18 oz. ASW

Date	Mintage	MS63	MS65	Prf65
2010S	859,435	—	—	7.75

Yosemite National Park

KM# 471 • 5.67 g., **Copper-Nickel Clad Copper**, 24.3 mm. **Rev. Designer:** Joseph Menna and Phebe Hemphill

Date	Mintage	MS63	MS65	Prf65
2010P	35,200,000	0.75	5.00	—
2010D	34,800,000	0.75	5.00	—
2010S	1,400,215	—	—	3.75

KM# 471a • 6.25 g., **0.900 Silver**, 0.18 oz. ASW

Date	Mintage	MS63	MS65	Prf65
2010S	859,435	—	—	7.75

Grand Canyon National Park

KM# 472 • 5.67 g., **Copper-Nickel Clad Copper**, 24.3 mm. **Rev. Designer:** Phebe Hemphill

Date	Mintage	MS63	MS65	Prf65
2010P	34,800,000	0.75	5.00	—
2010D	35,400,000	0.75	5.00	—
2010S	1,399,970	—	—	3.75

KM# 472a • 6.25 g., **0.900 Silver**, 0.18 oz. ASW

Date	Mintage	MS63	MS65	Prf65
2010S	859,435	—	—	7.75

Mount Hood National Park

KM# 473 • 5.67 g., **Copper-Nickel Clad Copper**, 24.3 mm. **Rev. Designer:** Phebe Hemphill

Date	Mintage	MS63	MS65	Prf65
2010P	34,400,000	0.75	5.00	—
2010D	34,400,000	0.75	5.00	—
2010S	1,397,101	—	—	3.75

KM# 473a • 6.25 g., **0.900 Silver**, 0.18 oz. ASW

Date	Mintage	MS63	MS65	Prf65
2010S	859,435	—	—	7.75

Gettysburg National Military Park

KM# 494 • 5.67 g., **Copper-Nickel Clad Copper**, 24 mm. **Rev. Designer:** Joel Iskowitz and Phebe Hemphill

Date	Mintage	MS63	MS65	Prf65
2011P	30,800,000	0.75	5.00	—
2011D	30,400,000	0.75	5.00	—
2011S	1,271,553	—	—	3.75

KM# 494a • 6.25 g., **0.900 Silver**, 0.18 oz. ASW

Date	Mintage	MS63	MS65	Prf65
2011S	722,076	—	—	7.75

QUARTER

QUARTER

Glacier National Park

KM# 495 • 5.67 g., **Copper-Nickel Clad Copper**, 24 mm.
Rev. Designer: Barbara Fox and Charles L. Vickers

Date	Mintage	MS63	MS65	Prf65
2011P	30,400,000	0.75	5.00	—
2011D	31,200,000	0.75	5.00	—
2011S	1,268,452	—	—	3.75

KM# 495a • 6.25 g., 0.900 **Silver**, 0.18 oz. ASW

Date	Mintage	MS63	MS65	Prf65
2011S	722,076	—	—	7.75

Olympic National Park

KM# 496 • 5.67 g., **Copper-Nickel Clad Copper**, 24 mm. • **Series:** America the Beautiful **Subject:** Olympic National Park

Date	Mintage	MS63	MS65	Prf65
2011 P	30,400,000	—	—	—
2011 D	30,600,000	—	—	—
2011 S	1,267,361	—	—	—

KM# 496a • 6.25 g., 0.900 **Silver**, 0.18 oz. ASW

Date	Mintage	MS63	MS65	Prf65
2011S	722,076	—	—	7.75

Vicksburg National Military Park

KM# 497 • 5.67 g., **Copper-Nickel Clad Copper**, 24 mm.
Rev. Designer: Thomas Cleveland and Joseph Menna

Date	Mintage	MS63	MS65	Prf65
2011P	30,800,000	0.75	5.00	—
2011D	33,400,000	0.75	5.00	—
2011S	1,267,691	—	—	3.75

KM# 497a • 6.25 g., 0.900 **Silver**, 0.18 oz. ASW

Date	Mintage	MS63	MS65	Prf65
2011S	722,076	—	—	7.75

Chickasaw National Recreation Area

KM# 498 • 5.67 g., **Copper-Nickel Clad Copper**, 24 mm.
Rev. Designer: Donna Weaver and Jim Licaretz

Date	Mintage	MS63	MS65	Prf65
2011P	73,800,000	0.75	5.00	—

Date	Mintage	MS63	MS65	Prf65
2011D	69,400,000	0.75	5.00	—
2011S	1,266,010	—	—	3.75

KM# 498a • 6.25 g., 0.900 **Silver**, 0.18 oz. ASW

Date	Mintage	MS63	MS65	Prf65
2011S	722,076	—	—	7.75

El Yunque National Forest

KM# 519 • 5.67 g., **Copper-Nickel Clad Copper**, 24.3 mm. **Rev. Designer:** Gary Whitley and Michael Gaudioso

Date	Mintage	MS63	MS65	Prf65
2012P	25,800,000	0.75	5.00	—
2012D	25,800,000	0.75	5.00	—
2012S	1,010,361	—	7.50	—
2012S	1,679,240	—	—	3.75

KM# 519a • 6.25 g., 0.900 **Silver**, 0.18 oz. ASW 24.3 mm.

Date	Mintage	MS63	MS65	Prf65
2012S	557,891	—	—	7.75

Chaco Culture National Historic Park

KM# 520 • 5.71 g., **Copper-Nickel Clad Copper**, 24.3 mm.

Date	Mintage	MS63	MS65	Prf65
2012P	22,000,000	0.75	8.00	—
2012D	22,000,000	0.75	8.00	—
2012S	960,049	—	10.00	—
2012S	1,389,020	—	—	4.00

KM# 520a • 6.25 g., 0.900 **Silver**, 0.18 oz. ASW 24.3 mm.

Date	Mintage	MS63	MS65	Prf65
2012S	557,891	—	—	7.75

Acadia National Park

KM# 521 • 5.67 g., **Copper-Nickel Clad Copper**, 24.3 mm. **Rev. Designer:** Barbara Fox and Joseph Menna

Date	Mintage	MS63	MS65	Prf65
2012P	24,800,000	0.75	5.00	—
2012D	21,606,000	0.75	5.00	—
2012S	960,409	—	7.50	—
2012S	1,409,120	—	—	3.75

KM# 521a • 6.25 g., 0.900 **Silver**, 0.18 oz. ASW 24.3 mm.

Date	Mintage	MS63	MS65	Prf65
2012S	557,891	—	—	7.75

Hawai'i Volcanoes National Park

KM# 522 • 5.67 g., **Copper-Nickel Clad Copper**, 24.3 mm. **Rev. Designer:** Charles L. Vickers

Date	Mintage	MS63	MS65	Prf65
2012P	46,200,000	0.75	5.00	—
2012D	78,600,000	0.75	5.00	—
2012S	961,272	—	7.50	—
2012S	1,407,520	—	—	3.75

KM# 522a • 6.25 g., 0.900 **Silver**, 0.18 oz. ASW 24.3 mm.

Date	Mintage	MS63	MS65	Prf65
2012S	557,891	—	—	7.75

Denali National Park

KM# 523 • 5.67 g., **Copper-Nickel Clad Copper**, 24.3 mm.

Date	Mintage	MS63	MS65	Prf65
2012P	135,400,000	0.75	5.00	—
2012D	166,600,000	0.75	5.00	—
2012S	957,856	—	7.50	—
2012S	1,401,920	—	—	3.75

KM# 523a • 6.25 g., 0.900 **Silver**, 0.18 oz. ASW 24.3 mm.

Date	Mintage	MS63	MS65	Prf65
2012S	557,891	—	—	7.75

White Mountain National Forest

KM# 542 • 5.67 g., **Copper-Nickel Clad Copper**, 24.3 mm.

Date	Mintage	MS63	MS65	Prf65
2013P	68,800,000	0.75	5.00	—
2013D	107,600,000	0.75	5.00	—
2013S	950,080	—	7.50	—
2013S	—	—	—	3.75

KM# 542a • 6.25 g., 0.900 **Silver**, 0.18 oz. ASW 24.3 mm.

Date	Mintage	MS63	MS65	Prf65
2013S	579,409	—	—	7.75

Perry's Victory and International Peace Memorial

KM# 543 • 5.67 g., **Copper-Nickel Clad Copper**, 24.3 mm. **Rev. Designer:** Don Everhart

Date	Mintage	MS63	MS65	Prf65
2013P	107,800,000	0.75	0.50	—
2013D	131,600,000	0.75	5.00	—
2013S	913,563	—	7.50	—
2013S	—	—	—	3.75

KM# 543a • 6.25 g., 0.900 **Silver**, 0.18 oz. ASW 24.3 mm.

Date	Mintage	MS63	MS65	Prf65
2013S	579,409	—	—	7.75

Great Basin National Park

KM# 544 • 5.67 g., **Copper-Nickel Clad Copper**, 24.3 mm. **Rev. Designer:** Ronald D. Sanders and Renata Gordon

Date	Mintage	MS63	MS65	Prf65
2013P	122,400,000	0.75	5.00	—
2013D	141,400,000	0.75	5.00	—
2013S	911,525	—	7.50	—
2013S	—	—	—	3.75

KM# 544a • 6.25 g., 0.900 **Silver**, 0.18 oz. ASW 24.3 mm.

Date	Mintage	MS63	MS65	Prf65
2013S	579,409	—	—	7.75

Fort McHenry National Monument and Historic Shrine

KM# 545 • 5.67 g., **Copper-Nickel Clad Copper**, 24.3 mm. **Rev. Designer:** Joseph Menna

Date	Mintage	MS63	MS65	Prf65
2013P	120,000,000	0.75	5.00	—
2013D	151,400,000	0.75	5.00	—
2013S	911,451	—	7.50	—
2013S	—	—	—	3.75

KM# 545a • 6.25 g., 0.900 **Silver**, 0.18 oz. ASW 24.3 mm.

Date	Mintage	MS63	MS65	Prf65
2013S	579,409	—	—	7.75

QUARTER

QUARTER

Mount Rushmore National Memorial

KM# 546 • 5.67 g., **Copper-Nickel Clad Copper**, 24.3 mm. **Rev. Designer:** Joseph Menna

Date	Mintage	MS63	MS65	Prf65
2013P	231,800,000	0.75	5.00	—
2013D	272,400,000	0.75	5.00	—
2013S	920,695	—	7.50	—
2013S	—	—	—	3.75

KM# 546a • 6.25 g., 0.900 **Silver**, 0.18 oz. ASW 24.3 mm.

Date	Mintage	MS63	MS65	Prf65
2013S	579,409	—	—	7.75

Great Smokey Mountains National Park

KM# 566 • 5.67 g., **Copper-Nickel Clad Copper**, 24.3 mm.

Date	Mintage	MS63	MS65	Prf65
2014P	—	0.75	5.00	—
2014D	—	0.75	5.00	—
2014S	—	—	7.50	—

KM# 566a • 6.25 g., 0.900 **Silver** 0.18 oz. ASW, 24.3 mm. • **Series:** America the Beautiful **Subject:** Great Smokey Mountains National Park

Date	Mintage	MS63	MS65	Prf65
2014 S	—	—	—	7.75

Shenandoah National Park

KM# 567 • 5.67 g., **Copper-Nickel Clad Copper**, 24.3 mm.

Date	Mintage	MS63	MS65	Prf65
2014P	—	0.75	5.00	—
2014D	—	0.75	5.00	—
2014S	—	—	7.50	—

KM# 567a • 6.25 g., 0.900 **Silver** 0.18 oz. ASW, 24.3 mm. • **Series:** America the Beautiful **Subject:** Shenandoah National Park

Date	Mintage	MS63	MS65	Prf65
2014 S	—	—	—	7.75

Arches National Park

KM# 568 • 5.67 g., **Copper-Nickel Clad Copper**, 24.3 mm.

Date	Mintage	MS63	MS65	Prf65
2014P	—	0.75	5.00	—
2014D	—	0.75	5.00	—
2014S	—	—	7.50	—

KM# 568a • 6.25 g., 0.900 **Silver** 0.18 oz. ASW, 24.3 mm. • **Series:** America the Beautiful **Subject:** Arches National Park

Date	Mintage	MS63	MS65	Prf65
2014 S	—	—	—	7.75

Great Sand Dunes National Park

KM# 569 • 5.67 g., **Copper-Nickel Clad Copper**, 24.3 mm.

Date	Mintage	MS63	MS65	Prf65
2014P	—	0.75	5.00	—
2014D	—	0.75	5.00	—
2014S	—	—	7.50	—

KM# 569 • 6.25 g., 0.900 **Silver** 0.18 oz. ASW, 24.3 mm. • **Series:** America the Beautiful **Subject:** Great Sand Dunes National Park

Date	Mintage	MS63	MS65	Prf65
2014 S	—	—	—	7.75

Everglades National Park

KM# 570 • 5.67 g., **Copper-Nickel Clad Copper**, 24.3 mm.

Date	Mintage	MS63	MS65	Prf65
2014P	—	0.75	5.00	—
2014D	—	0.75	5.00	—
2014S	—	—	7.50	—

KM# 570a • 6.25 g., 0.900 **Silver** 0.18 oz. ASW, 24.3 mm. • **Series:** America the Beautiful **Subject:** Everglades National Park

Date	Mintage	MS63	MS65	Prf65
2014 S	—	—	—	7.75

HALF DOLLAR

Flowing Hair Half Dollar

KM# 16 • 13.48 g., 0.892 **Silver** 0.38 oz. ASW, 32.5 mm. • **Designer:** Robert Scot **Note:** The 1795 "recut date" variety had the date cut into the dies twice, so both sets of numbers are visible on the coin. The 1795 "3 leaves" variety has three leaves under each of the eagle's wings on the reverse.

Date		Mintage	G4	VG8	F12	VF20	XF40	MS60
1794		23,464	2,850	5,750	8,850	19,500	37,500	225,000
1795		299,680	1,025	1,450	2,850	4,850	13,850	46,500
1795	recut date	Inc. above	1,040	1,470	2,895	5,200	14,250	46,500
1795	3 leaves	Inc. above	2,600	3,150	5,350	8,350	17,500	59,500

Draped Bust Half Dollar
Draped bust right obverse   Small eagle reverse

KM# 26 • 13.48 g., 0.892 **Silver** 0.38 oz. ASW, 32.5 mm. • **Designer:** Robert Scot

Date		Mintage	G4	VG8	F12	VF20	XF40	MS60
1796	15 obverse stars	3,918	36,500	46,000	62,000	73,500	118,000	300,000
1796	16 obverse stars	Inc. above	39,500	50,000	67,000	79,500	128,000	320,000
1797		Inc. above	36,700	46,300	62,500	74,300	121,000	310,000

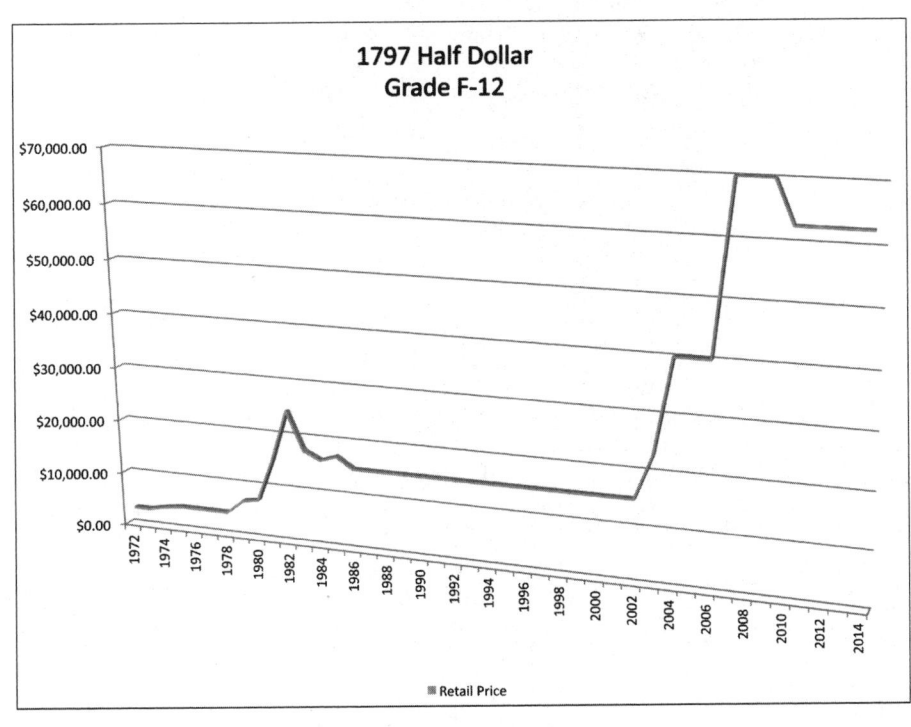

Draped bust right, flanked by stars, date at angle below obverse   Heraldic eagle reverse

KM# 35 • 13.48 g., 0.892 **Silver** 0.38 oz. ASW, 32.5 mm. • **Obv. Legend:** LIBERTY **Rev. Legend:** UNITED STATES OF AMERICA **Designer:** Robert Scot **Note:** The two varieties of the 1803 strikes are distinguished by the size of the 3 in the date. The several varieties of the 1806 strikes are distinguished by the style of 6 in the date, size of the stars on the obverse, and whether the stem of the olive branch held by the reverse eagle extends through the claw.

Date		Mintage	G4	VG8	F12	VF20	XF40	MS60
1801		30,289	850	1,250	2,550	4,250	10,500	50,000
1802		29,890	900	1,350	2,750	4,500	11,000	52,000
1803	small 3	188,234	255	325	425	825	2,325	17,250
1803	large 3	Inc. above	195	235	295	715	1,925	14,750
1805		211,722	195	235	295	685	1,865	10,750
1805/4		Inc. above	270	385	570	1,515	3,325	30,000
1806	knobbed 6, large stars	839,576	195	235	295	665	1,825	—
1806	knobbed 6, small stars	Inc. above	195	235	295	680	2,025	13,500
1806	knobbed 6, stem not through claw	Inc. above	20,000	35,000	42,000	57,500	95,000	—
1806	pointed-top 6, stem not through claw	Inc. above	195	235	295	665	1,825	15,250
1806	pointed-top 6, stem through claw	Inc. above	195	235	295	665	1,825	9,750
1806/5		Inc. above	215	270	355	775	2,050	10,075
1806	/inverted 6	Inc. above	255	355	845	1,615	4,375	28,500
1807		301,076	195	235	295	665	1,825	9,750

Capped Bust
Draped bust left, flanked by stars, date at angle below obverse
"50 C." below eagle reverse

KM# 37 • 13.48 g., 0.892 **Silver** 0.38 oz. ASW, 32.5 mm. • **Rev. Legend:** UNITED STATES OF AMERICA **Designer:** John Reich **Note:** There are three varieties of the 1807 strikes. Two are distinguished by the size of the stars on the obverse. The third was struck from a reverse die that had a 5 cut over a 2 in the "50C" denomination. Two varieties of the 1811 are distinguished by the size of the 8 in the date. A third has a period between the 8 and second 1 in the date. One variety of the 1817 has a period between the 1 and 7 in the date. Two varieties of the 1820 are distinguished by the size of the date. On the 1823 varieties, the "broken 3" appears to be almost separated in the middle of the 3 in the date; the "patched 3" has the error reparied; the "ugly 3" has portions of its detail missing. The 1827 "curled-2" and "square-2" varieties are distinguished by the numeral's base -- either curled or square. Among the 1828 varieties, "knobbed 2" and "no knob" refers to whether the upper left serif of the digit is rounded. The 1830 varieties are distinguished by the size of the 0 in the date. The four 1834 varieties are distinguished by the sizes of the stars, date and letters in the inscriptions. The 1836 "50/00" variety was struck from a reverse die that has "50" recut over "00" in the denomination.

Date		Mintage	G4	VG8	F12	VF20	XF40	AU50	MS60	MS65
1807	small stars	750,500	125	175	350	750	1,900	6,500	9,850	54,000
1807	large stars	Inc. above	115	165	300	660	1,750	5,650	8,900	—
1807	50/20 C.	Inc. above	85.00	125	195	450	1,500	3,150	6,500	30,000
1807	bearded goddess	—	450	775	1,500	3,350	6,850	22,500	—	—
1808		1,368,600	67.00	84.00	97.00	145	350	550	1,800	20,000
1808/7		Inc. above	90.00	110	135	240	440	1,850	5,400	32,500
1809	IIIIIII edge	Inc. above	85.00	110	140	210	450	850	4,000	—
1809	Normal edge	1,405,810	65.00	82.00	94.00	140	375	750	1,500	12,650
1809	XXXX edge	Inc. above	80.00	105	135	185	550	950	4,450	—

Date	Mintage	G4	VG8	F12	VF20	XF40	AU50	MS60	MS65
1810	1,276,276	64.00	81.00	91.00	135	265	650	1,950	19,500
1811 small 8	1,203,644	70.00	80.00	88.00	125	350	800	2,350	28,500
1811 large 8	Inc. above	80.00	107	119	175	425	1,000	2,400	28,500
1811 dated 18.11	Inc. above	78.00	100	110	165	650	1,250	3,500	28,500
1812	1,628,059	64.00	81.00	88.00	114	254	440	1,350	13,450
1812/1 small 8	Inc. above	80.00	97.00	119	200	500	1,350	2,500	—
1812/1 large 8	Inc. above	1,650	2,450	4,500	6,750	12,000	21,000	—	—
1812 Single leaf below wing	Inc. above	750	950	1,250	2,400	4,000	6,800	12,500	—
1813	1,241,903	64.00	81.00	88.00	114	184	480	1,400	12,650
1813 50/UNI reverse	1,241,903	74.00	101	124	179	650	1,350	3,650	27,500
1814	1,039,075	64.00	81.00	88.00	124	285	650	1,650	11,450
1814/3	Inc. above	100	165	245	300	850	1,650	3,250	—
1814 E/A in States	Inc. above	85.00	110	150	225	385	950	3,950	—
1814 Single leaf below wing	Inc. above	75.00	97.00	124	194	575	1,350	2,250	—
1815/2	47,150	1,100	1,550	2,250	3,650	5,500	7,950	14,500	85,000
1817	1,215,567	67.00	84.00	91.00	119	195	450	1,300	11,650
1817/3	Inc. above	115	175	280	525	1,150	2,350	4,850	—
1817/4	—	60,000	80,000	150,000	200,000	240,000			
1817 dated 181.7	Inc. above	100	87.00	94.00	104	575	1,350	3,950	27,500
1817 Single leaf below wing	Inc. above	75.00	98.00	124	209	550	2,100	2,750	—
1818	1,960,322	64.00	81.00	88.00	119	225	440	1,350	11,250
1818/7 Large 8	Inc. above	100	115	145	190	325	950	1,850	17,500
1818/7 Small 8	Inc. above	98.00	110	130	150	250	850	1,650	16,500
1819	2,208,000	64.00	81.00	88.00	119	175	430	1,350	13,650
1819/8 small 9	Inc. above	75.00	92.00	109	184	290	650	1,900	11,650
1819/8 large 9	Inc. above	85.00	105	150	275	385	850	2,000	25,650
1820 Curl Base 2, small date	751,122	70.00	85.00	96.00	124	285	950	2,250	11,650
1820 Square Base 2 with knob, large date	Inc. above	72.00	90.00	104	139	400	800	2,400	13,150
1820 Square Base 2 without knob, large date	Inc. above	72.00	90.00	104	154	475	1,100	2,500	26,500
1820 E's without Serifs	Inc. above	260	450	900	2,150	3,500	5,500	—	—
1820/19 Square Base 2	Inc. above	110	130	165	240	775	1,650	3,250	25,000
1820/19 Curled Base 2	Inc. above	95.00	115	140	200	650	1,450	2,900	24,500
1821	1,305,797	58.00	76.00	89.00	101	185	575	1,350	11,250
1822	1,559,573	58.00	76.00	89.00	101	180	450	1,250	10,950
1822/1	Inc. above	83.00	100	129	275	385	800	1,900	—
1823	1,694,200	58.00	76.00	89.00	101	175	425	1,150	11,150
1823 broken 3	Inc. above	68.00	88.00	104	139	500	1,500	3,200	—
1823 patched 3	Inc. above	73.00	94.00	119	159	550	950	2,000	15,150
1823 ugly 3	Inc. above	78.00	99.00	129	184	750	1,750	4,200	—
1824	3,504,954	58.00	76.00	89.00	101	175	360	1,075	10,150
1824/21	Inc. above	63.00	82.00	99.00	126	275	650	2,000	15,650
1824/4	Inc. above	61.00	80.00	91.00	114	225	500	1,350	—
1824 1824/various dates	Inc. above	60.00	79.00	91.00	104	300	875	2,000	15,150
1825	2,943,166	58.00	76.00	89.00	101	175	385	1,050	10,150
1826	4,004,180	58.00	76.00	89.00	101	175	385	1,050	10,150
1827 curled 2	5,493,400	61.00	81.00	99.00	134	185	485	1,400	12,650
1827 square 2	Inc. above	58.00	76.00	89.00	101	175	385	1,050	10,150
1827/6	Inc. above	85.00	95.00	120	155	265	650	1,450	11,650
1828 curled-base 2, no knob	3,075,200	58.00	76.00	89.00	101	175	385	1,150	11,150
1828 curled-base 2, knobbed 2	Inc. above	78.00	99.00	129	184	245	460	1,300	—
1828 small 8s, square-base 2, large letters	Inc. above	60.00	80.00	99.00	124	175	385	1,050	12,650
1828 small 8s, square-base 2, small letters	Inc. above	58.00	76.00	89.00	106	250	750	1,900	—
1828 large 8s, square-base 2	Inc. above	58.00	76.00	89.00	101	175	385	1,050	11,150
1829	3,712,156	55.00	72.00	79.00	89.00	159	350	1,000	10,150
1829 Large letters	Inc. above	59.00	79.00	89.00	104	180	420	1,250	12,650
1829/7	Inc. above	78.00	99.00	129	174	200	475	1,250	12,650
1830 Small O rev	4,764,800	55.00	72.00	79.00	89.00	159	350	1,000	10,150
1830 Large O	Inc. above	60.00	78.00	88.00	109	189	550	2,000	13,150
1830 Large letter rev	Inc. above	1,500	2,250	3,000	3,750	4,800	9,800	—	—
1831	5,873,660	55.00	72.00	79.00	89.00	159	350	1,000	10,150
1832 small letters	4,797,000	55.00	72.00	79.00	89.00	159	350	1,000	10,150
1832 large letters	Inc. above	58.00	75.00	85.00	99.00	175	410	1,350	12,650
1833	5,206,000	55.00	72.00	79.00	89.00	159	360	1,000	10,150
1834 small date, large stars, small letters	6,412,004	55.00	74.00	81.00	91.00	163	360	1,025	10,400
1834 small date, small stars, small letters	Inc. above	55.00	74.00	81.00	9.00	163	360	1,025	10,400
1834 large date, small letters	Inc. above	55.00	74.00	81.00	91.00	163	360	1,025	10,400
1834 large date, large letters	Inc. above	55.00	72.00	79.00	89.00	159	350	1,000	10,150
1835	5,352,006	55.00	72.00	79.00	89.00	159	350	1,000	10,150
1836	6,545,000	55.00	72.00	79.00	89.00	159	350	1,000	10,150
1836	Inc. above	80.00	95.00	120	265	450	1,000	2,500	—
1836 50/00	Inc. above	93.00	112	129	165	300	800	1,750	19,500

Bust Half Dollar
Draped bust left, flanked by stars, date at angle below obverse
"50 Cents" below eagle reverse

KM# 58 • 13.48 g., 0.892 **Silver** 0.38 oz. ASW, 30 mm. • **Rev. Legend:** UNITED STATES OF AMERICA **Edge:** Reeded.
Designer: Christian Gobrecht

Date	Mintage	G4	VG8	F12	VF20	XF40	AU50	MS60	MS65
1836	1,200	850	1,075	1,600	2,000	3,350	4,400	8,850	66,500

Draped bust left, flanked by stars, date at angle below obverse
"50 Cents" below eagle reverse

KM# 58a • 13.36 g., 0.900 **Silver** 0.38 oz. ASW, 30 mm. • **Rev. Legend:** UNITED STATES OF AMERICA **Edge:** Reeded.
Designer: Christian Gobrecht

Date	Mintage	G4	VG8	F12	VF20	XF40	AU50	MS60	MS65
1837	3,629,820	58.00	73.00	80.00	115	200	345	1,100	24,500

Draped bust left, flanked by stars, date below obverse　HALF DOL. below eagle reverse

KM# 65 • 13.36 g., 0.900 **Silver** 0.38 oz. ASW, 30 mm. • **Rev. Legend:** UNITED STATES OF AMERICA **Designer:**
Christian Gobrecht

Date	Mintage	G4	VG8	F12	VF20	XF40	AU50	MS60	MS65
1838	3,546,000	58.00	70.00	82.00	120	205	420	1,200	17,500
1838 O proof only	Est. 20	—	—	—	—	250,000	300,000	—	—
1839	1,392,976	60.00	76.00	92.00	130	245	410	1,350	39,500
1839 O	116,000	240	325	425	650	1,350	2,350	4,500	46,500

Seated Liberty Half Dollar
Seated Liberty, date below obverse　Half Dol." below eagle reverse

KM# 68 • 13.36 g., 0.900 **Silver** 0.38 oz. ASW, 30.6 mm. • **Rev. Legend:** UNITED STATES OF AMERICA **Designer:**
Christian Gobrecht

Date	Mintage	G4	VG8	F12	VF20	XF40	AU50	MS60	MS65
1839 no drapery from elbow	Inc. above	55.00	95.00	365	580	1,275	2,875	6,900	200,000
1839 drapery	Inc. above	52.00	60.00	75.50	110	225	345	1,000	25,000
1840 small letters	1,435,008	54.00	60.00	70.00	108	170	325	600	7,500

HALF DOLLAR

Date	Mintage	G4	VG8	F12	VF20	XF40	AU50	MS60	MS65
1840 reverse 1838	Inc. above	150	185	310	385	850	1,350	3,500	30,000
1840 O	855,100	52.00	62.00	76.00	115	250	440	1,050	—
1841	310,000	52.00	65.00	110	165	235	375	1,200	6,850
1841 O	401,000	50.00	65.00	75.00	110	265	375	1,250	7,000
1842 small date	2,012,764	48.00	60.00	80.00	135	200	325	1,300	13,500
1842 medium date	Inc. above	44.00	60.00	74.50	90.00	152	300	750	8,800
1842 O small date	957,000	650	950	1,550	2,450	4,650	7,750	25,000	—
1842 O medium date	Inc. above	44.00	60.00	76.00	90.00	175	350	1,250	10,500
1843	3,844,000	49.00	55.00	71.50	89.00	125	245	500	4,500
1843 O	2,268,000	60.00	65.00	73.50	89.00	165	320	550	—
1844	1,766,000	52.50	55.00	71.50	89.00	160	210	525	4,500
1844 O	2,005,000	46.00	55.00	71.50	90.00	165	320	675	—
1844/1844 O	Inc. above	500	850	1,150	1,400	3,000	6,250	10,000	—
1845	589,000	49.00	65.00	79.50	125	220	365	1,250	12,000
1845 O	2,094,000	46.00	60.00	71.50	89.00	165	325	700	9,400
1845 O no drapery	Inc. above	48.00	70.00	90.00	165	350	650	1,450	—
1846 medium date	2,210,000	46.00	60.00	77.00	86.00	175	340	900	9,000
1846 tall date	Inc. above	47.00	61.00	90.00	135	350	550	750	12,000
1846 /horizontal 6	Inc. above	160	250	325	550	775	1,350	3,800	—
1846 O medium date	2,304,000	49.00	60.00	79.50	86.00	220	300	1,100	12,000
1846 O tall date	Inc. above	200	325	425	675	1,750	2,450	6,650	—
1847/1846	1,156,000	2,000	2,750	4,000	5,500	10,000	13,500	23,500	—
1847	Inc. above	44.00	52.00	67.50	80.00	125	245	450	9,000
1847 O	2,584,000	54.00	65.00	71.50	86.00	160	355	640	7,000
1848	580,000	54.00	75.00	110	185	275	485	1,050	9,000
1848 O	3,180,000	46.00	55.00	71.50	86.00	210	375	850	9,000
1849	1,252,000	49.00	70.00	79.50	90.00	165	365	1,250	15,000
1849 O	2,310,000	54.00	65.00	71.50	90.00	175	325	750	9,000
1850	227,000	275	325	450	585	700	1,000	2,200	—
1850 O	2,456,000	50.00	57.00	73.50	95.00	185	275	950	9,000
1851	200,750	375	475	850	850	1,350	1,650	3,000	—
1851 O	402,000	49.00	65.00	125	135	225	325	1,500	9,000
1852	77,130	425	500	700	925	1,100	1,350	2,350	—
1852 O	144,000	70.00	160	210	350	750	1,650	3,850	26,000
1853 O mintage unrecorded	—	—	250,000	—	—	600,000	—	—	—

Seated Liberty, arrows at date obverse   Rays around eagle reverse

KM# 79 • 12.44 g., 0.900 **Silver** 0.36 oz. ASW **Rev. Legend:** UNITED STATES OF AMERICA **Designer:** Christian Gobrecht

Date	Mintage	G4	VG8	F12	VF20	XF40	AU50	MS60	MS65	Prf65
1853	3,532,708	36.50	48.00	72.00	97.50	270	615	1,500	24,500	175,000
1853 O	1,328,000	48.50	56.50	81.00	124	325	695	2,250	29,500	—

Seated Liberty, arrows at date obverse   HALF DOL. below eagle reverse

KM# 82 • 12.44 g., 0.900 **Silver** 0.36 oz. ASW **Rev. Legend:** UNITED STATES OF AMERICA **Designer:** Christian Gobrecht

Date	Mintage	G4	VG8	F12	VF20	XF40	AU50	MS60	MS65	Prf65
1854	2,982,000	36.50	48.00	60.00	73.50	145	305	585	8,500	37,500
1854 O	5,240,000	36.50	48.00	60.00	73.50	145	305	610	8,000	—
1855	759,500	38.50	50.00	64.00	87.00	375	575	1,250	9,000	39,500
1855/4	Inc. above	65.00	75.00	135	175	400	600	2,350	17,500	37,000

Date	Mintage	G4	VG8	F12	VF20	XF40	AU50	MS60	MS65	Prf65
1855 O	3,688,000	39.50	55.00	65.00	78.50	145	305	650	8,000	—
1855 S	129,950	350	575	800	1,600	3,650	6,850	19,500	—	—

Seated Liberty, date below obverse   HALF DOL. below eagle reverse

KM# A68 • 12.44 g., 0.900 Silver 0.36 oz. ASW **Rev. Legend:** UNITED STATES OF AMERICA **Designer:** Christian Gobrecht

Date	Mintage	G4	VG8	F12	VF20	XF40	AU50	MS60	MS65	Prf65
1856	938,000	44.00	57.00	67.50	84.00	135	245	550	6,500	12,500
1856 O	2,658,000	49.00	57.00	67.50	95.00	135	245	450	12,500	—
1856 S	211,000	85.00	110	175	275	750	1,500	6,500	19,000	—
1857	1,988,000	44.00	52.00	67.50	84.00	125	245	450	5,150	12,500
1857 O	818,000	49.00	55.00	71.00	85.00	150	275	1,150	12,500	—
1857 S	158,000	90.00	125	185	400	1,050	1,650	4,500	19,000	—
1858	4,226,000	44.00	52.00	67.50	84.00	125	245	450	6,500	12,500
1858 O	7,294,000	49.00	57.00	67.50	84.00	125	245	485	12,500	—
1858 S	476,000	50.00	65.00	90.00	140	365	475	1,350	12,500	—
1859	748,000	40.00	57.00	72.00	90.00	145	245	600	6,600	5,500
1859 O	2,834,000	44.00	62.00	67.50	84.00	125	245	450	6,500	—
1859 S	566,000	45.00	68.00	79.50	100	275	375	950	12,500	—
1860	303,700	48.00	56.00	71.50	100	150	325	750	6,500	5,500
1860 O	1,290,000	44.00	56.00	67.50	84.00	135	260	450	5,150	—
1860 S	472,000	49.00	70.00	72.50	88.00	215	335	850	12,500	—
1861	2,888,400	54.00	60.00	67.50	84.00	130	255	485	5,150	5,500
1861 O	2,532,633	60.00	68.00	77.00	88.00	175	285	650	5,150	—
1861 O CSA Obv, cracked die	Inc. above	55.00	65.00	74.50	110	170	325	875	9,500	—
1861 S	939,500	250	350	600	750	1,200	2,350	—		—
1862	253,550	56.00	69.00	92.50	120	235	425	650	5,150	5,500
1862 S	1,352,000	54.00	62.00	67.50	80.00	125	265	485	9,000	—
1863	503,660	59.00	73.00	92.50	145	240	350	750	5,150	5,500
1863 S	916,000	52.00	69.00	82.50	105	220	295	600	9,000	—
1864	379,570	64.00	75.00	97.50	150	275	400	750	5,150	5,500
1864 S	658,000	56.00	69.00	81.50	145	250	350	1,250	9,000	—
1865	511,900	52.00	71.00	88.00	100	265	375	1,000	5,150	5,500
1865 S	675,000	56.00	68.00	82.50	100	250	450	900	9,000	—
1866 proof, unique	—	—	—	—	—	—	—	—	—	—
1866 S	60,000	485	650	925	1,250	2,550	3,500	6,500	68,000	—

Seated Liberty, date below obverse   IN GOD WE TRUST above eagle reverse

KM# 99 • 12.44 g., 0.900 Silver 0.36 oz. ASW **Rev. Legend:** UNITED STATES OF AMERICA **Designer:** Christian Gobrecht

Date	Mintage	G4	VG8	F12	VF20	XF40	AU50	MS60	MS65	Prf65
1866	745,625	54.00	72.50	82.00	95.00	175	300	565	4,800	3,750
1866 S	994,000	48.50	62.50	80.00	85.00	200	275	650	5,000	—
1867	449,925	53.50	67.50	88.00	165	275	290	450	4,800	3,750
1867 S	1,196,000	47.50	61.50	80.00	100	200	285	775	7,000	—
1868	418,200	58.50	70.00	105	185	275	350	750	7,100	3,750
1868 S	1,160,000	48.50	55.50	70.00	95.00	175	285	550	7,000	—
1869	795,900	48.50	64.50	78.00	95.00	165	275	550	4,600	3,750
1869 S	656,000	50.00	66.50	80.00	95.00	210	325	850	7,000	—
1870	634,900	47.50	59.50	70.00	98.00	165	250	625	7,000	3,750
1870 CC	54,617	1,450	2,650	4,500	7,250	16,000	30,000	110,000	—	—

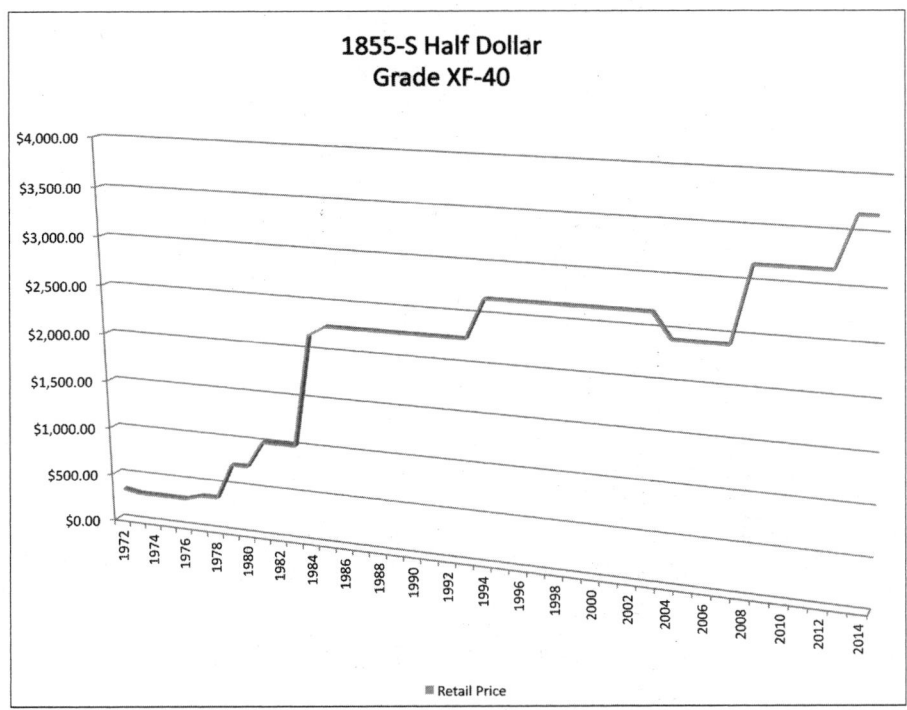

1855-S Half Dollar
Grade XF-40

■ Retail Price

Date	Mintage	G4	VG8	F12	VF20	XF40	AU50	MS60	MS65	Prf65
1870 S	1,004,000	43.50	59.50	72.00	110	200	425	1,250	7,000	—
1871	1,204,560	41.00	51.50	71.00	85.00	160	285	650	7,000	3,750
1871 CC	153,950	375	650	950	1,450	3,350	6,000	22,500	—	—
1871 S	2,178,000	48.50	60.00	68.00	88.00	175	275	675	7,000	—
1872	881,550	48.50	59.50	68.00	88.00	185	310	575	2,850	3,750
1872 CC	272,000	210	265	500	950	2,350	4,850	16,500	50,000	—
1872 S	580,000	48.50	62.00	86.00	135	300	375	1,150	7,000	—
1873 closed 3	801,800	48.50	57.50	83.00	115	165	280	675	4,500	3,750
1873 open 3	Inc. above	3,550	4,450	5,600	7,250	10,000	13,500	30,000	—	—
1873 CC	122,500	275	440	650	1,150	2,350	6,500	17,500	80,000	—
1873 S no arrows	5,000	—	—	—	—	—	—	—	—	—

Note: 1873S no arrows, no specimens known to survive.

Seated Liberty, arrows at date obverse
IN GOD WE TRUST above eagle reverse

KM# 107 • 12.50 g., 0.900 **Silver** 0.36 oz. ASW **Rev. Legend:** UNITED STATES OF AMERICA **Designer:** Christian Gobrecht

Date	Mintage	G4	VG8	F12	VF20	XF40	AU50	MS60	MS65	Prf65
1873	1,815,700	48.00	62.00	78.00	105	265	470	925	17,500	9,000
1873 CC	214,560	275	400	650	1,100	2,350	3,900	11,500	42,000	—
1873 S	233,000	55.00	130	175	245	475	850	3,850	40,000	—
1874	2,360,300	44.00	56.00	72.00	90.00	250	455	900	15,500	9,000
1874 CC	59,000	775	1,550	2,200	3,650	5,400	9,750	12,500	—	—
1874 S	394,000	54.00	70.00	85.00	225	365	685	2,500	20,000	—

HALF DOLLAR

Seated Liberty, date below obverse   IN GOD WE TRUST above eagle reverse

KM# A99 • 12.50 g., 0.900 **Silver** 0.36 oz. ASW **Rev. Legend:** UNITED STATES OF AMERICA **Designer:** Christian Gobrecht

Date	Mintage	G4	VG8	F12	VF20	XF40	AU50	MS60	MS65	Prf65
1875	6,027,500	38.50	49.50	66.00	88.00	128	225	450	3,500	3,375
1875 CC	1,008,000	55.00	85.00	135	225	325	500	1,450	8,350	—
1875 S	3,200,000	38.50	49.50	66.00	95.00	130	210	390	2,700	—
1876	8,419,150	38.50	49.50	66.00	88.00	118	210	390	5,300	3,775
1876 CC	1,956,000	52.00	65.00	100	140	265	375	1,250	4,200	—
1876 S	4,528,000	36.50	47.50	66.00	88.00	118	210	390	2,700	—
1877	8,304,510	36.50	47.50	66.00	88.00	118	210	390	2,700	3,825
1877 CC	1,420,000	52.00	75.00	110	140	265	350	1,150	3,250	—
1877 S	5,356,000	36.50	47.50	66.00	88.00	118	210	390	2,700	—
1878	1,378,400	38.50	57.50	100	130	150	210	485	3,650	3,900
1878 CC	62,000	900	1,300	2,350	2,750	3,750	6,500	12,500	43,500	—
1878 S	12,000	28,500	42,000	49,500	60,000	75,000	95,000	135,000	175,000	—
1879	5,900	275	310	375	450	540	575	775	3,650	3,150
1880	9,755	260	300	350	425	510	600	800	3,750	3,150
1881	10,975	270	325	345	425	500	565	750	4,000	3,150
1882	5,500	340	410	460	600	650	675	850	3,850	3,150
1883	9,039	325	390	480	560	625	650	1,000	3,950	3,150
1884	5,275	385	425	500	610	700	685	1,000	3,850	3,150
1885	6,130	390	450	485	575	660	700	825	3,850	3,150
1886	5,886	400	550	630	725	850	875	1,150	3,900	3,150
1887	5,710	475	600	700	800	875	950	1,100	3,900	3,150
1888	12,833	280	310	365	410	525	550	800	3,900	3,150
1889	12,711	275	315	400	465	510	575	800	3,900	3,150
1890	12,590	275	310	365	415	500	550	800	3,850	3,150
1891	200,600	55.00	75.00	125	140	165	240	480	3,850	3,150

Barber Half Dollar

Laureate head right, flanked by stars, date below obverse   Heraldic eagle reverse

KM# 116 • 12.50 g., 0.900 **Silver** 0.36 oz. ASW, 30.6 mm. • **Obv. Legend:** IN GOD WE TRUST **Rev. Legend:** UNITED STATES OF AMERICA **Designer:** Charles E. Barber

Date	Mintage	G4	VG8	F12	VF20	XF40	AU50	MS60	MS65	Prf65
1892	935,245	29.50	44.00	73.50	120	200	385	560	3,100	3,750
1892 O	390,000	310	420	515	600	675	700	850	3,950	—
1892 O micro O	Inc. above	2,250	3,950	5,000	7,000	11,500	17,500	24,000	80,000	—
1892 S	1,029,028	250	330	425	550	650	700	985	4,400	—
1893	1,826,792	22.00	36.00	78.00	150	205	385	575	4,250	3,750
1893 O	1,389,000	36.00	70.00	130	230	360	435	700	8,250	—
1893 S	740,000	165	240	550	750	1,000	1,525	1,275	22,000	—
1894	1,148,972	32.50	54.00	115	220	280	395	560	3,050	3,750
1894 O	2,138,000	25.00	36.00	95.00	180	320	420	610	5,600	—
1894 S	4,048,690	24.00	30.00	75.00	130	195	400	575	8,350	—
1895	1,835,218	22.00	28.00	72.00	165	195	400	595	4,050	3,750
1895 O	1,766,000	40.00	68.00	130	195	285	425	650	5,950	—
1895 S	1,108,086	32.00	56.00	140	255	345	440	635	6,350	—
1896	950,762	22.50	30.00	88.00	160	265	395	625	5,000	3,750

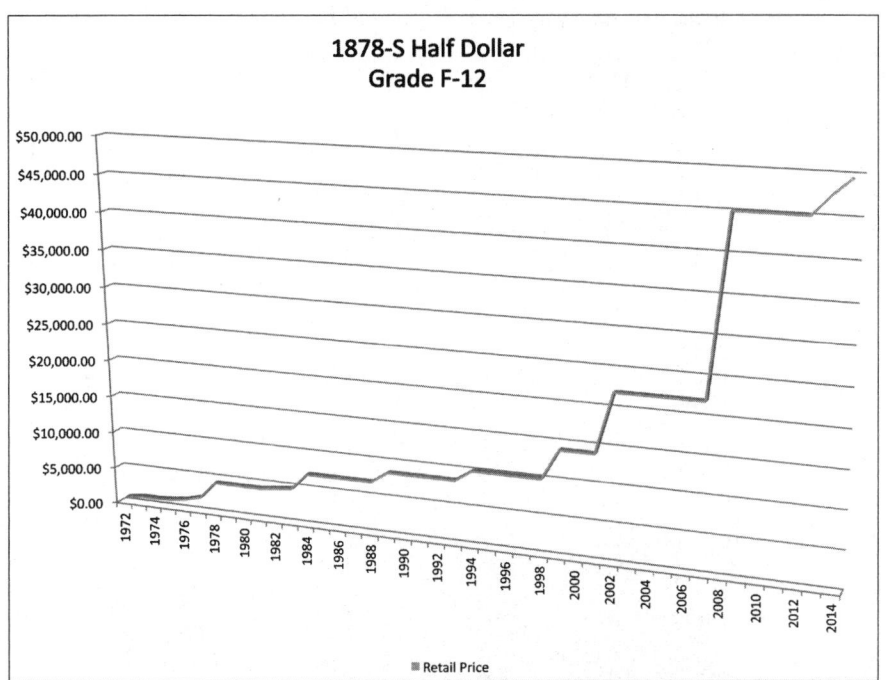

1878-S Half Dollar
Grade F-12

Retail Price

Date	Mintage	G4	VG8	F12	VF20	XF40	AU50	MS60	MS65	Prf65
1896 O	924,000	48.00	65.00	210	350	650	1,050	2,450	19,500	—
1896 S	1,140,948	120	160	235	400	560	850	1,575	9,750	—
1897	2,480,731	21.50	26.00	47.50	105	200	385	560	3,150	3,750
1897 O	632,000	170	240	510	835	1,050	1,350	2,700	7,350	—
1897 S	933,900	155	230	410	600	925	1,275	2,600	7,250	—
1898	2,956,735	20.50	24.00	43.50	105	200	395	560	3,150	3,750
1898 O	874,000	37.50	100	240	400	575	640	1,250	8,950	—
1898 S	2,358,550	29.00	52.50	95.00	175	340	440	985	9,400	—
1899	5,538,846	19.50	24.00	43.50	105	200	405	560	3,350	3,750
1899 O	1,724,000	26.00	37.50	85.00	180	300	435	700	8,000	—
1899 S	1,686,411	25.00	45.00	92.00	165	275	395	660	5,750	—
1900	4,762,912	19.50	24.50	43.50	105	200	395	560	3,650	3,750
1900 O	2,744,000	21.50	22.50	62.00	190	315	425	900	13,500	—
1900 S	2,560,322	19.50	24.50	46.50	105	215	390	660	8,250	—
1901	4,268,813	19.50	24.50	45.00	99.00	200	385	560	3,750	3,750
1901 O	1,124,000	21.50	29.50	85.00	235	400	500	1,500	14,850	—
1901 S	847,044	34.00	55.00	175	375	825	1,300	2,350	16,500	—
1902	4,922,777	19.50	24.50	45.00	99.00	200	385	560	3,750	3,750
1902 O	2,526,000	19.50	24.50	55.00	115	240	410	850	9,850	—
1902 S	1,460,670	21.50	28.50	66.00	165	285	420	825	7,500	—
1903	2,278,755	19.50	24.50	47.50	105	215	395	560	7,000	3,750
1903 O	2,100,000	19.50	24.50	55.00	135	225	425	665	8,750	—
1903 S	1,920,772	21.50	24.50	60.00	145	265	455	675	4,850	—
1904	2,992,670	19.50	24.50	43.50	99.00	200	395	560	4,100	3,750
1904 O	1,117,600	21.50	33.00	90.00	250	435	610	1,375	11,000	—
1904 S	553,038	42.00	100	325	775	1,450	2,450	9,850	38,500	—
1905	662,727	23.50	34.00	95.00	195	270	410	650	5,650	3,750
1905 O	505,000	30.00	44.50	130	245	340	460	760	4,400	—
1905 S	2,494,000	21.50	26.50	50.00	135	240	410	675	8,750	—
1906	2,638,675	16.50	24.50	38.50	105	200	385	550	3,150	3,750
1906 D	4,028,000	16.50	24.50	41.50	113	195	375	550	3,650	—
1906 O	2,446,000	16.50	24.50	44.00	105	210	400	600	5,850	—
1906 S	1,740,154	19.50	26.50	57.50	135	230	420	600	4,650	—
1907	2,598,575	16.50	22.50	36.50	99.00	195	375	550	3,600	3,750
1907 D	3,856,000	16.50	22.50	36.50	99.00	195	375	550	2,950	—
1907 O	3,946,000	16.50	22.50	38.50	99.00	195	375	550	3,050	—
1907 S	1,250,000	22.00	25.00	85.00	190	385	675	1,275	12,000	—
1908	1,354,545	15.50	22.50	36.50	99.00	195	375	550	3,350	3,750
1908 D	3,280,000	15.50	22.50	36.50	99.00	195	375	550	2,950	—
1908 O	5,360,000	15.50	22.50	36.50	99.00	195	385	550	2,950	—

Date	Mintage	G4	VG8	F12	VF20	XF40	AU50	MS60	MS65	Prf65
1908 S	1,644,828	17.00	29.50	75.00	175	285	475	875	5,500	—
1909	2,368,650	16.50	24.00	39.50	105	195	375	550	2,950	3,750
1909 O	925,400	19.70	23.50	58.00	185	440	725	1,500	4,850	—
1909 S	1,764,000	16.50	23.50	37.50	105	215	395	600	3,950	—
1910	418,551	20.00	30.00	95.00	180	365	485	675	3,750	3,750
1910 S	1,948,000	19.00	27.50	42.50	105	200	395	640	6,250	—
1911	1,406,543	15.50	22.50	36.50	99.00	195	375	550	2,950	3,750
1911 D	695,080	16.50	24.00	43.50	115	195	385	575	3,750	—
1911 S	1,272,000	17.00	24.50	42.00	105	210	385	600	5,350	—
1912	1,550,700	15.50	22.50	36.50	99.00	195	375	550	3,450	3,750
1912 D	2,300,800	15.50	22.50	36.50	99.00	195	375	550	2,950	—
1912 S	1,370,000	17.70	22.00	43.50	115	210	425	600	4,250	—
1913	188,627	77.00	88.00	235	400	615	875	1,600	4,950	3,900
1913 D	534,000	19.00	22.50	44.00	105	200	395	575	3,750	—
1913 S	604,000	21.00	25.00	53.50	125	260	425	710	4,000	—
1914	124,610	145	170	335	525	775	1,000	1,475	7,850	4,100
1914 S	992,000	17.50	22.50	41.00	105	210	395	575	4,250	—
1915	138,450	100	140	285	410	650	920	1,350	5,850	4,100
1915 D	1,170,400	15.50	22.50	36.50	99.00	195	375	550	2,950	—
1915 S	1,604,000	19.50	24.50	43.50	118	210	390	575	2,950	—

Walking Liberty Half Dollar
Liberty walking left wearing U.S. flag gown, sunrise at left obverse
Eagle advancing left reverse

Obverse mint mark
1916-1917

KM# 142 • 12.50 g., 0.900 **Silver** 0.36 oz. ASW, 30.6 mm. • **Designer:** Adolph A. Weinman **Note:** The mint mark appears on the obverse below the word "Trust" on 1916 and some 1917 issues. Starting with some 1917 issues and continuing through the remainder of the series, the mint mark was changed to the reverse, at about the 8 o'clock position near the rim.

Date	Mintage	G4	VG8	F12	VF20	XF40	AU50	MS60	MS65	Prf65
1916	608,000	52.00	55.00	95.00	170	235	320	345	1,850	—
1916 D	1,014,400	48.50	55.00	80.00	135	210	255	360	2,350	—
1916 S	508,000	105	135	280	440	600	720	1,050	6,400	—
1917	12,292,000	12.20	14.20	18.00	22.00	42.00	72.00	130	1,175	—
1917 D obv. mint mark	765,400	23.50	33.00	80.00	155	235	335	625	8,250	—
1917 S obv. mint mark	952,000	27.00	44.00	135	365	700	1,100	2,200	22,500	—
1917 D rev. mint mark	1,940,000	16.00	18.00	45.00	135	275	550	940	17,500	—
1917 S rev. mint mark	5,554,000	15.00	17.00	19.00	32.00	65.00	155	350	15,000	—
1918	6,634,000	16.00	17.00	19.00	64.00	150	245	565	4,100	—
1918 D	3,853,040	18.00	22.00	40.00	90.00	225	500	1,300	27,500	—
1918 S	10,282,000	15.00	17.00	18.00	34.00	75.00	190	485	22,500	—
1919	962,000	26.00	32.50	78.50	265	535	875	1,325	7,500	—
1919 D	1,165,000	25.00	38.50	95.00	320	765	2,200	5,950	140,000	—
1919 S	1,552,000	20.00	27.50	72.00	310	825	1,750	3,450	19,000	—
1920	6,372,000	17.00	18.00	20.00	42.00	75.00	155	350	4,750	—
1920 D	1,551,000	17.00	19.00	65.00	240	460	900	1,550	17,500	—
1920 S	4,624,000	16.00	18.00	19.00	90.00	235	510	850	17,500	—
1921	246,000	165	210	315	750	2,150	3,150	6,300	22,000	—
1921 D	208,000	295	370	575	900	2,700	4,450	9,600	32,500	—
1921 S	548,000	45.00	65.00	200	775	4,150	4,450	18,250	110,000	—
1923 S	2,178,000	16.00	17.00	27.50	110	450	1,150	1,600	19,500	—
1927 S	2,392,000	14.50	16.00	17.50	46.00	165	425	990	13,000	—
1928 S Large S	1,940,000	18.50	22.00	28.00	110	325	650	1,850	—	—
1928 S Small S	Inc. above	16.00	18.00	19.00	66.00	195	475	1,000	13,500	—
1929 D	1,001,200	13.00	16.00	18.00	42.50	98.00	195	400	3,250	—
1929 S	1,902,000	13.00	16.00	17.00	28.50	115	220	425	3,250	—
1933 S	1,786,000	15.70	16.50	17.50	22.00	62.00	260	650	3,500	—
1934	6,964,000	12.70	14.00	16.00	18.00	23.00	25.00	85.00	400	—
1934 D	2,361,400	13.00	15.00	17.00	19.50	36.00	88.00	150	1,350	—
1934 S	3,652,000	13.00	14.00	16.00	17.50	32.00	100	385	3,500	—
1935	9,162,000	10.70	11.20	13.50	16.00	22.00	26.00	45.00	275	—
1935 D	3,003,800	13.00	14.00	16.00	20.00	33.00	66.00	140	2,200	—
1935 S	3,854,000	12.20	13.00	15.00	17.50	45.00	95.00	285	2,250	—
1936	12,617,901	10.70	11.20	11.50	13.60	21.00	26.00	38.00	220	3,000

Date	Mintage	G4	VG8	F12	VF20	XF40	AU50	MS60	MS65	Prf65
1936 D	4,252,400	11.70	12.20	12.50	16.00	23.00	52.00	78.00	400	—
1936 S	3,884,000	11.70	12.20	12.50	16.00	30.00	58.00	140	850	—
1937	9,527,728	9.70	10.50	10.70	12.60	20.00	26.00	38.00	200	900
1937 D	1,676,000	11.70	12.20	12.70	13.60	34.00	105	220	665	—
1937 S	2,090,000	11.70	12.20	12.50	13.10	26.00	62.00	168	620	—
1938	4,118,152	9.70	10.70	11.10	12.60	21.00	38.00	66.00	325	750
1938 D	491,600	60.00	71.00	100	110	185	250	475	1,500	—
1939	6,820,808	9.70	10.20	10.50	11.10	20.00	24.00	41.00	175	650
1939 D	4,267,800	10.20	10.70	11.00	12.10	20.00	26.00	45.00	150	—
1939 S	2,552,000	10.70	11.20	11.50	13.90	25.00	76.00	155	300	—
1940	9,167,279	9.70	10.20	10.50	10.60	19.00	24.00	35.00	120	600
1940 S	4,550,000	9.70	10.50	10.70	12.10	20.00	21.00	50.00	335	—
1941	24,207,412	9.70	10.20	10.50	10.60	18.00	23.00	34.00	119	575
1941 D	11,248,400	9.70	10.50	11.00	11.10	19.00	24.00	39.00	160	—
1941 S Small S	8,098,000	9.70	10.50	11.00	11.10	22.00	28.00	74.00	750	—
1941 S Large S	Inc. above	12.20	13.20	15.50	20.00	35.00	60.00	—	—	—
1942	47,839,120	9.70	10.20	10.50	10.60	18.00	23.00	34.00	119	575
1942 D	10,973,800	9.70	10.50	10.70	11.10	19.00	24.00	37.00	310	—
1942 S	12,708,000	9.70	10.50	10.70	11.10	19.00	25.00	37.00	350	—
1943	53,190,000	9.70	10.20	10.50	10.60	18.00	23.00	34.00	119	—
1943 D	11,346,000	9.70	10.50	10.70	11.10	19.00	25.00	42.00	200	—
1943 D Double Die Obverse	Inc. above	12.00	15.00	17.00	19.00	22.00	30.00	58.00	450	—
1943 S	13,450,000	9.70	10.50	10.70	11.10	19.00	24.00	42.00	250	—
1944	28,206,000	9.70	10.20	10.50	10.60	18.00	23.00	34.00	119	—
1944 D	9,769,000	9.70	10.50	10.70	11.10	19.00	24.00	37.00	165	—
1944 S	8,904,000	9.70	10.20	10.70	11.10	19.00	26.00	42.00	400	—
1945	31,502,000	9.70	10.50	10.50	10.60	18.00	23.00	34.00	119	—
1945 D	9,966,800	9.70	10.50	10.70	11.10	19.00	24.00	36.00	119	—
1945 S	10,156,000	9.70	10.20	10.70	11.10	19.00	24.00	36.00	135	—
1946	12,118,000	9.70	—	10.50	10.60	18.00	23.00	34.00	155	—
1946 Double Die Reverse	Inc. above	16.00	24.00	35.00	50.00	85.00	175	325	3,200	—
1946 D	2,151,000	10.20	10.70	11.00	12.60	26.00	42.00	48.00	119	—
1946 S	3,724,000	9.70	10.50	10.70	11.10	21.00	35.00	44.00	140	—
1947	4,094,000	9.70	10.20	10.50	11.10	19.00	26.00	48.00	165	—
1947 D	3,900,600	10.20	10.70	10.70	11.00	12.60	19.00	32.00	48.00	119

Franklin Half Dollar

Franklin bust right obverse   Liberty Bell, small eagle at right reverse

Mint mark

KM# 199 • 12.50 g., 0.900 **Silver** 0.36 oz. ASW, 30.6 mm. • **Designer:** John R. Sinnock

Date	Mintage	G4	VG8	F12	VF20	XF40	AU50	MS60	MS65	65FBL
1948	3,006,814	—	9.40	9.50	10.10	10.70	10.90	11.80	75.00	190
1948 D	4,028,600	—	9.40	9.50	10.10	10.20	10.60	10.80	125	260
1949	5,614,000	—	—	—	—	11.20	14.00	38.50	120	250
1949 D	4,120,600	—	—	—	9.90	12.20	25.00	43.50	900	1,750
1949 S	3,744,000	—	—	—	10.10	16.50	30.00	62.50	160	700
1950	7,793,509	—	—	—	—	9.50	13.00	26.00	110	285
1950 D	8,031,600	—	—	—	—	10.50	10.70	22.00	425	900
1951	16,859,602	—	—	—	—	9.20	12.20	12.40	75.00	340
1951 D	9,475,200	—	—	—	—	13.50	17.50	26.00	170	540
1951 S	13,696,000	—	—	—	9.50	10.20	15.00	23.50	125	750
1952	21,274,073	—	—	—	—	9.40	12.20	12.60	70.00	210
1952 D	25,395,600	—	—	—	—	9.40	12.20	12.60	130	450
1952 S	5,526,000	—	—	9.50	12.10	16.00	32.00	52.00	140	1,500
1953	2,796,920	—	—	9.50	9.60	10.00	16.00	25.00	140	1,000
1953 D	20,900,400	—	—	—	—	9.20	9.40	9.60	150	400
1953 S	4,148,000	—	—	—	9.50	10.20	18.50	25.00	65.00	16,000
1954	13,421,503	—	—	—	—	9.20	9.40	9.60	75.00	225
1954 D	25,445,580	—	—	—	—	9.20	9.40	9.60	110	235
1954 S	4,993,400	—	—	—	—	9.60	10.20	10.70	42.00	440
1955	2,876,381	—	15.50	16.00	17.50	18.00	18.50	20.00	70.00	140
1955 Bugs Bunny	Inc. above	—	20.00	22.00	23.00	25.00	26.00	28.00	120	750
1956 Type 1 rev.	4,701,384	—	9.10	9.20	9.30	9.60	10.40	11.00	55.00	125
1956 Type 2 rev.	Inc. above	—	—	—	—	—	—	—	—	—

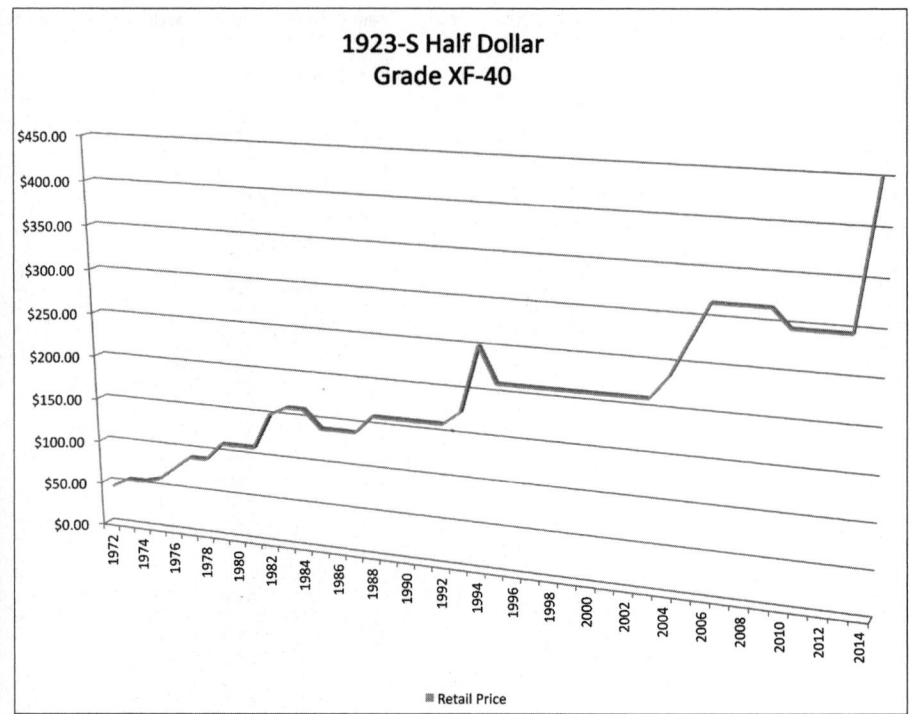

1923-S Half Dollar
Grade XF-40
$450.00
$400.00
$350.00
$300.00
$250.00
$200.00
$150.00
$100.00
$50.00
$0.00
1972
1974
1976
1978
1980
1982
1984
1986
1988
1990
1992
1994
1996
1998
2000
2002
2004
2006
2008
2010
2012
2014
Retail Price

1953 Half Dollar
Grade MS-60
$45.00
$40.00
$35.00
$30.00
$25.00
$20.00
$15.00
$10.00
$5.00
$0.00
1972
1974
1976
1978
1980
1982
1984
1986
1988
1990
1992
1994
1996
1998
2000
2002
2004
2006
2008
2010
2012
2014
Retail Price

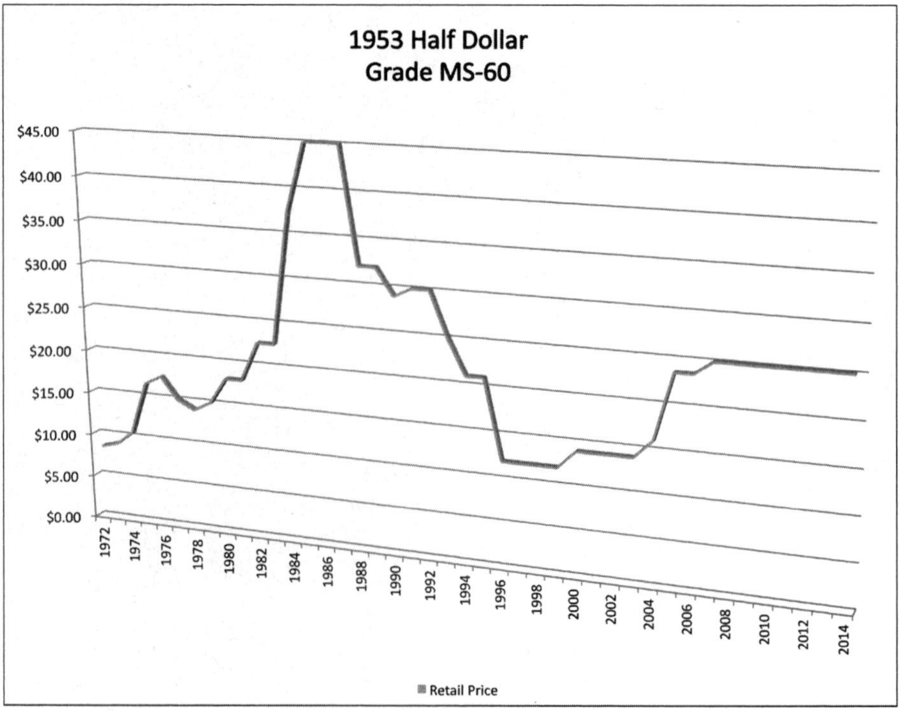

Date	Mintage	G4	VG8	F12	VF20	XF40	AU50	MS60	MS65	65FBL
1957 Type 1 rev.	6,361,952	—	—	—	—	9.20	10.40	11.30	63.00	95.00
1957 Type 2 rev.	Inc. above	—	—	—	—	—	—	—	—	—
1957 D	19,966,850	—	—	—	—	9.20	10.40	11.10	60.00	100
1958 Type 1 rev.	4,917,652	—	—	—	—	9.20	10.40	11.10	55.00	110
1958 Type 2 rev.	Inc. above	—	—	—	—	9.90	20.00	26.00	—	—
1958 D	23,962,412	—	—	—	—	9.20	10.40	11.10	55.00	80.00
1959 Type 1 rev.	7,349,291	—	—	—	—	9.20	10.40	11.10	110	250
1959 Type 2 rev.	Inc. above	—	—	—	—	9.70	16.00	30.00	115	—
1959 D	13,053,750	—	—	—	—	9.20	10.40	11.10	125	215
1960 Type 1 rev.	7,715,602	—	—	—	—	9.20	10.40	11.10	110	340
1960 Type 2 rev.	Inc. above	—	—	—	—	—	—	—	—	—
1960 D	18,215,812	—	—	—	—	9.20	10.40	11.10	400	1,350
1961 Type 1 rev.	11,318,244	—	—	—	—	9.20	10.40	11.10	125	1,300
1961 Type 2 rev.	Inc. above	—	—	—	—	25.00	—	—	—	—
1961 Double die rev.	Inc. above	—	—	—	—	—	—	—	—	—
1961 D	20,276,442	—	—	—	—	9.20	10.40	11.10	155	875
1962 Type 1 rev.	12,932,019	—	—	—	—	9.20	10.40	11.10	145	1,850
1962 Type 2 rev.	Inc. above	—	—	—	—	—	—	—	—	—
1962 D	35,473,281	—	—	—	—	9.20	10.40	11.10	175	800
1963 Type 1 rev.	25,239,645	—	—	—	—	9.20	10.40	11.10	55.00	1,200
1963 Type 2 rev.	Inc. above	—	—	—	—	—	—	—	—	—
1963 D	67,069,292	—	—	—	—	9.20	10.40	11.10	75.00	165

Kennedy Half Dollar

Mint mark 1964

KM# 202 • 12.50 g., 0.900 **Silver** 0.36 oz. ASW, 30.6 mm. • **Obv. Designer:** Gilroy Roberts **Rev. Designer:** Frank Gasparro **Edge:** Reeded

Date	Mintage	MS60	MS65	PF65
1964	277,254,766	12.50	22.00	15.00
1964 Accented Hair	Inc. above	—	—	40.00
1964 D	156,205,446	12.70	24.00	—

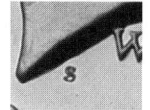

Mint mark 1968 - present

KM# 202a • 11.50 g., 0.400 **Silver** 0.15 oz. ASW, 30.6 mm. • **Obv. Designer:** Gilroy Roberts **Rev. Designer:** Frank Gasparro **Edge:** Reeded

Date	Mintage	MS60	MS65	PF65
1965	65,879,366	6.10	14.50	—
1965 SMS	2,360,000	—	15.00	—
1966	108,984,932	6.10	22.50	—
1966 SMS	2,261,583	—	17.00	—
1967	295,046,978	6.10	18.50	—
1967 SMS	1,863,344	—	18.00	—
1968 D	246,951,930	6.10	16.50	—
1968 S	3,041,506	—	—	8.56
1969 D	129,881,800	6.10	20.00	—
1969 S	2,934,631	—	—	8.56
1970 D	2,150,000	8.50	40.00	—
1970 S	2,632,810	—	—	12.00

KM# 202b • 11.34 g., **Copper-Nickel Clad Copper**, 30.6 mm. • **Obv. Designer:** Gilroy Roberts **Rev. Designer:** Frank Gasparro

Date	Mintage	MS60	MS65	PF65
1971	155,640,000	1.00	17.50	—
1971 D	302,097,424	1.00	12.00	—
1971 S	3,244,183	—	—	5.00
1972	153,180,000	1.00	15.50	—
1972 D	141,890,000	1.00	14.50	—
1972 S	3,267,667	—	—	5.00
1973	64,964,000	1.00	20.00	—
1973 D	83,171,400	—	12.00	—
1973 S	2,769,624	—	—	5.00
1974	201,596,000	1.00	25.00	—
1974 D	79,066,300	1.00	17.00	—
1974 D DDO	Inc. above	32.00	165	—
1974 S	2,617,350	—	—	5.00
1975 none minted		—	—	—
1975 D none minted		—	—	—
1975 S none minted		—	—	—

Independence Hall reverse

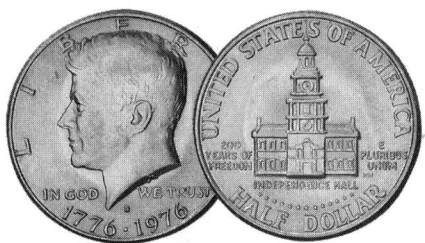

KM# 205 • 11.20 g., **Copper-Nickel**, 30.6 mm. • **Obv. Designer:** Gilroy Roberts **Rev. Designer:** Seth Huntington

Date	Mintage	MS60	MS65	PF65
1976	234,308,000	1.00	16.50	—
1976 D	287,565,248	1.00	14.00	—
1976 S	7,059,099	—	—	5.00

Bicentennial design,
Independence Hall reverse

KM# 205a • 11.50 g., 0.400 **Silver** 0.15 oz. ASW, 30.6 mm. • **Rev. Designer:** Seth Huntington

Date	Mintage	MS60	MS65	PF65
1976 S	4,908,319	—	12.00	8.70
1976 S	3,998,621	—	—	8.70

Regular design resumed reverse

KM# A202b • 11.34 g., **Copper-Nickel Clad Copper**, 30.61 mm. • **Edge:** Reeded **Note:** KM#202b design and composition resumed. The 1979-S and 1981-S Type II proofs have clearer mint marks than the Type I proofs of those years.

Date	Mintage	MS65	Prf65
1977	43,598,000	12.50	—
1977 D	31,449,106	16.50	—
1977 S	3,251,152	—	4.50
1978	14,350,000	12.00	—
1978 D	13,765,799	15.00	—
1978 S	3,127,788	—	5.00
1979	68,312,000	13.50	—
1979 D	15,815,422	13.50	—
1979 S Type I	3,677,175	—	5.00
1979 S Type II	Inc. above	—	18.00
1980 P	44,134,000	12.50	—
1980 D	33,456,449	17.50	—
1980 S	3,547,030	—	5.00
1981 P	29,544,000	9.00	—
1981 D	27,839,533	12.00	—
1981 S Type I	4,063,083	—	5.00
1981 S Type II	Inc. above	—	18.50
1982 P	10,819,000	18.50	—
1982 P no initials FG	Inc. above	110	—
1982 D	13,140,102	20.00	—
1982 S	38,957,479	—	5.00
1983 P	34,139,000	22.50	—
1983 D	32,472,244	12.50	—
1983 S	3,279,126	—	5.00
1984 P	26,029,000	12.00	—
1984 D	26,262,158	18.00	—
1984 S	3,065,110	—	6.00
1985 P	18,706,962	16.50	—
1985 D	19,814,034	12.50	—
1985 S	3,962,138	—	5.00
1986 P	13,107,633	17.50	—
1986 D	15,336,145	14.00	—
1986 S	2,411,180	—	6.00
1987 P	2,890,758	16.50	—
1987 D	2,890,758	12.50	—
1987 S	4,407,728	—	5.00
1988 P	13,626,000	16.50	—
1988 D	12,000,096	10.00	—
1988 S	3,262,948	—	5.00
1989 P	24,542,000	13.00	—
1989 D	23,000,216	13.00	—
1989 S	3,220,194	—	5.00

Date	Mintage	MS65	Prf65
1990 P	22,780,000	17.50	—
1990 D	20,096,242	20.00	—
1990 S	3,299,559	—	5.00
1991 P	14,874,000	12.50	—
1991 D	15,054,678	16.00	—
1991 S	2,867,787	—	5.00
1992 P	17,628,000	10.00	—
1992 D	17,000,106	10.00	—
1992 S	2,858,981	—	5.00
1993 P	15,510,000	12.00	—
1993 D	15,000,006	10.00	—
1993 S	2,633,439	—	5.00
1994 P	23,718,000	12.00	—
1994 D	23,828,110	8.50	—
1994 S	2,484,594	—	5.00
1995 P	26,496,000	10.00	—
1995 D	26,288,000	8.00	—
1995 S	2,010,384	—	12.00
1996 P	24,442,000	10.00	—
1996 D	24,744,000	10.00	—
1996 S	2,085,191	—	9.00
1997 P	20,882,000	14.00	—
1997 D	19,876,000	13.50	—
1997 S	1,975,000	—	10.00
1998 P	15,646,000	12.50	—
1998 D	15,064,000	12.50	—
1998 S	2,078,494	—	7.00
1999 P	8,900,000	11.00	—
1999 D	10,682,000	10.00	—
1999 S	2,557,897	—	8.00
2000 P	22,600,000	12.00	—
2000 D	19,466,000	12.00	—
2000 S	3,082,944	—	5.00
2001 P	21,200,000	10.00	—
2001 D	19,504,000	9.00	—
2001 S	2,235,000	—	5.00
2002 P	3,100,000	10.00	—
2002 D	2,500,000	10.50	—
2002 S	2,268,913	—	5.00
2003 P	2,500,000	6.00	—
2003 D	2,500,000	6.00	—
2003 S	2,076,165	—	5.00
2004 P	2,900,000	4.50	—
2004 D	2,900,000	4.50	—
2004 S	1,789,488	—	6.00
2005 P	3,800,000	6.00	—
2005 P Satin finish	1,160,000	8.00	—
2005 D	3,500,000	5.00	—
2005 D Satin finish	1,160,000	10.00	—
2005 S	2,275,000	—	5.00
2006 P	2,400,000	4.50	—
2006 P Satin finish	847,361	12.00	—
2006 D	2,000,000	4.50	—
2006 D Satin finish	847,361	14.00	—
2006 S	1,934,965	—	6.00
2007 P	2,400,000	4.50	—
2007 P Satin finish	—	8.00	—
2007 D	2,400,000	4.50	—
2007 D Satin finish	—	8.00	—
2007 S	1,702,116	—	6.00
2008 P	1,700,000	4.50	—
2008 P Satin finish	—	8.50	—
2008 D	1,700,000	4.50	—
2008 D Satin finish	—	8.50	—
2008 S	1,405,674	—	9.00
2009 P	1,900,000	4.50	—
2009 P Satin finish	—	8.50	—
2009 D	1,900,000	4.50	—
2009 D Satin finish	—	8.50	—
2009 S	1,482,502	—	6.00
2010 P	1,800,000	4.50	—
2010 P Satin finish	—	8.50	—
2010 D	1,700,000	4.50	—
2010 D Satin finish	—	8.50	—
2010 S	1,103,815	—	13.00
2011 P	1,750,000	4.50	—
2011 D	1,700,000	4.50	—

HALF DOLLAR

Date	Mintage	MS65	Prf65
2011 S	1,098,835	—	9.00
2012 P	1,800,000	4.50	—
2012 D	1,700,000	4.50	—
2012 S	841,972	—	9.00
2013 P	5,000,000	4.50	—
2013 D	4,600,000	4.50	—
2013 S	821,031	—	9.00

Date	Mintage	MS65	Prf65
1992S	1,317,579	—	13.20
1993S	761,353	—	15.20
1994S	785,329	—	13.20
1995S	838,953	—	46.00
1996S	830,021	—	15.20
1997S	821,678	—	35.00
1998S Matte Finish	62,350	225	—
1998S	878,792	—	13.20
1999S	804,565	—	15.20
2000S	965,921	—	13.20
2001S	849,600	—	13.20
2002S	888,816	—	13.20
2003S	1,040,425	—	13.20
2004S	1,175,935	—	13.20
2005S	1,069,679	—	14.20
2006S	988,140	—	14.20
2007S	1,384,797	—	15.70
2008S	620,684	—	14.20
2009S	697,365	—	13.20
2010S	585,401	—	14.20
2011S	574,175	—	14.20
2012S	395,443	—	14.20
2013S	451,342	—	14.20

KM# A202c • 12.50 g., 0.900 **Silver** 0.36 oz. ASW, 30.6 • **Designer:** Gilroy Roberts

DOLLAR

Flowing Hair Dollar

KM# 17 • 26.96 g., 0.892 **Silver** 0.77 oz. ASW, 39-40 mm. • **Designer:** Robert Scot **Note:** The two 1795 varieties have either two or three leaves under each of the eagle's wings on the reverse.

Date	Mintage	F12	VF20	XF40	AU50	MS60	MS63
1794	1,758	120,000	170,000	245,000	365,000	575,000	950,000
1795 2 leaves	203,033	4,450	7,800	16,150	25,500	80,500	196,500
1795 3 leaves	Inc. above	4,200	7,250	14,500	22,500	69,500	182,500
1795 Silver plug	Inc. above	9,850	13,950	28,500	48,500	115,000	235,000

Draped Bust Dollar
Small eagle reverse

KM# 18 • 26.96 g., 0.892 **Silver** 0.77 oz. ASW, 39-40 mm. • **Designer:** Robert Scot

Date	Mintage	F12	VF20	XF40	AU50	MS60	MS63
1795 Off-center bust	Inc. above	3,850	5,850	12,500	17,000	52,000	126,000
1795 Centered bust	—	3,900	5,950	12,700	17,250	52,500	126,000

DOLLAR

Date	Mintage	F12	VF20	XF40	AU50	MS60	MS63
1796 small date, small letters	72,920	4,100	6,300	13,750	18,500	70,000	—
1796 small date, large letters	Inc. above	3,875	6,400	13,700	19,400	—	—
1796 large date, small letters	Inc. above	4,250	6,750	14,350	19,200	57,000	136,000
1797 9 stars left, 7 stars right, small letters	7,776	5,200	9,000	18,850	36,500	—	—
1797 9 stars left, 7 stars right, large letters	Inc. above	4,250	6,850	13,950	20,300	55,500	—
1797 10 stars left, 6 stars right	Inc. above	4,050	6,350	13,600	18,500	53,500	125,000
1798 13 stars	327,536	4,150	6,300	13,750	21,000	85,000	—
1798 15 stars	Inc. above	4,700	7,450	16,150	25,500	95,000	—

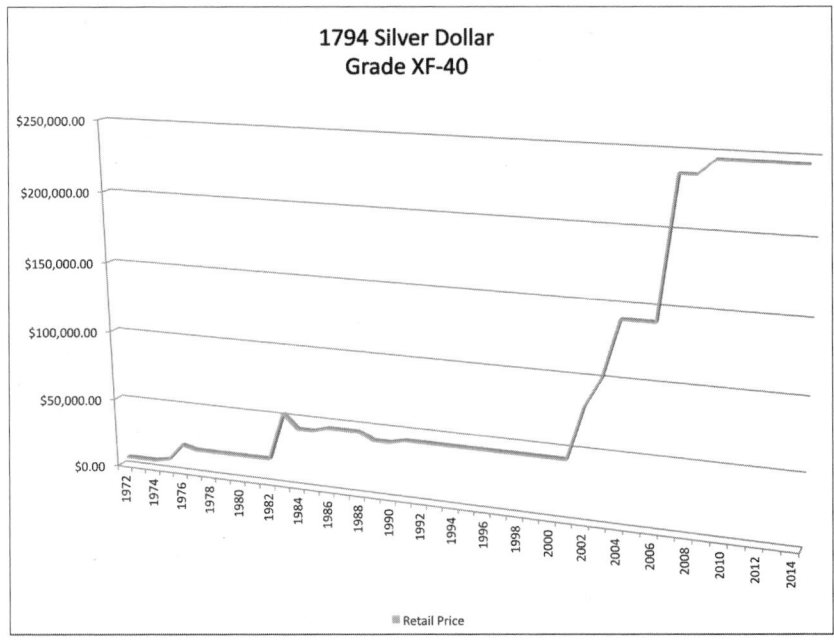

**1794 Silver Dollar
Grade XF-40**

■ Retail Price

Draped bust right, flanked by stars, date below obverse   Heraldic eagle reverse

KM# 32 • 26.96 g., 0.892 **Silver** 0.77 oz. ASW, 39-40 mm. • **Obv. Legend:** LIBERTY **Rev. Legend:** UNITED STATES OF AMERICA **Designer:** Robert Scot **Note:** The 1798 "knob 9" variety has a serif on the lower left of the 9 in the date. The 1798 varieties are distinguished by the number of arrows held by the eagle on the reverse and the number of berries on the olive branch. On the 1798 "high-8" variety, the 8 in the date is higher than the other numerals. The 1799 varieties are distinguished by the number and positioning of the stars on the obverse and by the size of the berries in the olive branch on the reverse. On the 1700 "irregular date" variety, the first 9 in the date is smaller than the other numerals. Some varieties of the 1800 strikes had letters in the legend cut twice into the dies; as between the numerals in the date are wider than other varieties and the 8 is lower than the other numerals. The 1800 "small berries" variety refers to the size of the berries in the olive branch on the reverse. The 1800 "12 arrows" and "10 arrows" varieties refer to the number of arrows held by the eagle. The 1800 "Americai" variety appears to have the faint outline of an "I" after "America" in the reverse legend. The "close" and "wide" varieties of the 1802 refer to the amount of space between the numerals in the date. The 1800 large-3 and small-3 varieties are distinguished by the size of the 3 in the date.

Date	Mintage	F12	VF20	XF40	AU50	MS60	MS63
1798 knob 9, 4 stripes	423,515	1,785	2,735	5,550	9,850	21,750	95,000
1798 knob 9, 10 arrows	Inc. above	1,785	2,735	5,550	9,850	21,750	87,000

Date	Mintage	F12	VF20	XF40	AU50	MS60	MS63
1798 knob 9, 5 stripes	Inc. above	—	—	—	—	—	124,500
1798 pointed 9, 4 berries	Inc. above	1,785	2,735	5,550	9,850	21,750	43,500
1798 5 berries, 12 arrows	Inc. above	1,785	2,735	5,550	9,850	21,750	43,500
1798 high 8	Inc. above	1,785	2,735	5,550	9,850	21,750	43,500
1798 13 arrows	Inc. above	1,785	2,735	5,550	9,850	21,750	43,500
1799/98 13-star reverse	Inc. above	2,000	2,950	4,300	8,600	23,500	45,000
1799/98 15-star reverse	Inc. above	1,875	2,850	4,000	8,300	24,500	47,500
1799 irregular date, 13-star reverse	Inc. above	1,825	3,000	3,900	8,200	23,500	45,000
1799 irregular date, 15-star reverse	Inc. above	1,825	3,200	5,550	9,850	21,500	42,500
1799 perfect date, 7- and 6-star obverse, no berries	Inc. above	1,750	2,700	3,850	8,150	18,500	42,500
1799 perfect date, 7- and 6-star obverse, small berries	Inc. above	1,750	2,700	3,850	8,150	18,500	42,500
1799 perfect date, 7- and 6-star obverse, medium large berries	Inc. above	1,750	2,700	3,850	8,150	18,500	42,500
1799 perfect date, 7- and 6-star obverse, extra large berries	Inc. above	1,750	2,700	3,850	8,150	18,500	51,500
1799 8 stars left, 5 stars right on obverse	Inc. above	1,825	2,800	3,900	8,200	24,000	45,000
1800 R" in "Liberty" double cut	220,920	1,825	2,775	5,550	9,850	21,500	45,000
1800 first "T" in "States" double cut	Inc. above	1,800	2,750	5,550	9,850	21,500	45,000
1800 both letters double cut	Inc. above	1,800	2,750	5,550	9,850	21,500	45,000
1800 T' in "United" double cut	Inc. above	1,800	2,750	5,550	9,850	21,500	45,000
1800 very wide date, low 8	Inc. above	1,800	2,750	5,550	9,850	21,500	—
1800 small berries	Inc. above	1,850	2,800	3,900	8,200	22,000	48,500
1800 dot date	Inc. above	2,000	3,000	4,300	8,600	21,500	45,000
1800 12 arrows	Inc. above	1,825	3,200	5,550	9,850	31,000	—
1800 10 arrows	Inc. above	1,825	3,200	5,550	9,850	—	—
1800 Americai	Inc. above	2,000	3,300	4,300	8,600	21,500	49,000
1801	54,454	2,050	3,200	4,000	8,300	25,000	—
1801 proof restrike	—	—	—	—	—	—	—
1802/1 close	Inc. above	2,000	3,300	4,300	8,600	20,500	—
1802/1 wide	Inc. above	2,000	3,300	4,300	8,600	20,500	—
1802 close, perfect date	Inc. above	1,850	2,800	3,900	8,200	20,500	—
1802 wide, perfect date	Inc. above	1,825	2,775	3,950	8,250	21,500	—
1802 proof restrike, mintage unrecorded	—	—	—	—	—	—	—
1803 large 3	85,634	1,875	3,000	4,000	8,300	20,500	47,500
1803 small 3	Inc. above	2,000	3,300	4,300	8,600	21,500	48,500
1803 proof restrike, mintage unrecorded	—	—	—	—	—	—	—
1804 15 known	—	—	—	—	3,000,000	—	—

Note: 1804, Childs Sale, Aug. 1999, Prf-68, $4,140,000.

Gobrecht Dollar

"C Gobrecht F." in base obverse
Eagle flying left amid stars reverse

KM# 59.1 • 26.73 g., 0.900 **Silver** 0.77 oz. ASW, 38.1 mm. • **Obv. Designer:** Christian Gobrecht **Rev. Legend:** UNITED STATES OF AMERICA **Edge:** Plain.

Date	Mintage	VF20	XF40	AU50	PF60
1836	1,000	11,500	14,850	18,000	25,500

"C. Gobrecht F." in base obverse
Eagle flying in plain field reverse

KM# 59.2 • 26.73 g., 0.900 **Silver** 0.77 oz. ASW, 38.1 mm. • **Obv. Designer:** Christian Gobrecht. **Edge:** Plain.

Date	Mintage	VF20	XF40	AU50	PF60
1836 Restrike	—	—	—	17,500	24,000

"C. Gobrecht F." in base obverse

KM# 59a.1 • 26.73 g., 0.900 **Silver** 0.77 oz. ASW, 38.1 mm. • **Obv. Legend:** Eagle flying left amid stars. **Edge:** Plain.

Date	Mintage	VF20	XF40	AU50	PF60
1836	600	—	—	—	—

"C. Gobrecht F." in base obverse
Eagle flying left amid stars reverse

KM# 59a.2 • 26.73 g., 0.900 **Silver** 0.77 oz. ASW, 38.1 mm. • **Edge:** Reeded.

Date	Mintage	VF20	XF40	AU50	PF60
1836 Restrike	—	—	—	—	—

Designer's name omitted in base obverse
Eagle in plain field reverse

KM# 59a.3 • 26.73 g., 0.900 **Silver** 0.77 oz. ASW, 38.1 mm. • **Edge:** Reeded.

Date	Mintage	VF20	XF40	AU50	PF60
1839	300	—	—	27,500	38,000

Designer's name omitted in base obverse   Eagle in plain field reverse

KM# 59a.4 • 26.73 g., 0.900 **Silver** 0.77 oz. ASW, 38.1 mm.

Date	Mintage	VF20	XF40	AU50	PF60
1839 Restrike	—	—	—	26,500	36,500

Note: All other combinations are restrikes of the late 1850's.

Seated Liberty Dollar
Seated Liberty, date below obverse   No motto above eagle reverse

KM# 71 • 26.73 g., 0.900 **Silver** 0.77 oz. ASW, 38.1 mm. • **Rev. Legend:** UNITED STATES OF AMERICA **Designer:** Christian Gobrecht

Date	Mintage	G4	VG8	F12	VF20	XF40	AU50	MS60	MS63	MS65	Prf65
1840	61,005	290	320	340	420	680	1,075	4,000	21,500	—	—
1841	173,000	265	295	315	395	610	1,000	2,950	5,500	100,000	—
1842	184,618	265	295	315	395	630	925	2,650	4,700	—	—
1843	165,100	265	295	315	395	465	925	2,750	9,000	—	—
1844	20,000	280	313	360	455	785	1,250	6,450	15,000	100,000	—
1845	24,500	300	335	385	455	900	1,750	10,500	26,500	—	75,000
1846	110,600	275	313	345	490	650	1,100	2,750	5,200	98,000	125,000
18460	59,000	285	330	370	480	775	1,325	8,750	20,000	—	—
1847	140,750	265	295	315	395	465	900	2,950	7,500	100,000	—
1848	15,000	325	385	515	795	1,250	1,700	4,100	12,500	100,000	—
1849	62,600	275	305	350	420	600	1,000	3,200	7,950	100,000	155,000
1850	7,500	465	545	380	845	1,750	2,650	7,850	15,000	—	80,000
18500	40,000	335	400	515	750	1,550	3,950	12,850	34,500	—	—
1851	1,300	4,000	4,850	5,750	7,750	18,000	27,000	43,500	68,500	150,000	225,000
1851 Restrike	—	—	—	—	—	—	—	—	—	—	90,000
1852	1,100	3,500	4,150	5,200	7,000	15,000	26,000	38,500	60,000	150,000	200,000
1852 Restrike	—	—	—	—	—	—	—	—	—	—	70,000
1853	46,110	335	400	550	660	1,100	1,425	4,000	7,950	100,000	90,000
1853 Restrike	—	—	—	—	—	—	—	—	—	—	—
1854	33,140	1,100	1,450	2,000	2,850	4,500	5,750	8,500	13,500	100,000	80,000
1855	26,000	900	1,150	1,500	2,150	3,750	4,950	8,850	31,500	—	55,000
1856	63,500	400	450	650	775	1,650	2,850	4,350	11,500	—	39,500
1857	94,000	450	525	675	800	1,500	1,850	3,650	9,000	95,000	39,500
1858 proof o nly	Est. 800	3,200	3,600	4,000	4,800	7,250	8,850	—	—	—	42,500
Note: Later restrike.											
1859	256,500	285	335	400	515	655	1,000	2,850	5,850	95,000	17,500
18590	360,000	265	295	315	395	465	800	2,250	4,150	56,000	—
1859S	20,000	330	390	515	750	1,550	3,500	15,000	36,500	—	—
1860	218,930	275	310	380	510	660	900	2,550	5,500	90,000	15,700
18600	515,000	265	295	315	395	465	800	2,250	3,850	56,000	—
1861	78,500	600	750	900	985	1,750	1,975	2,950	5,650	90,000	15,700
1862	12,090	440	600	850	945	1,450	1,650	3,250	5,750	90,000	15,700
1863	27,660	375	525	575	660	985	1,400	3,250	6,000	90,000	18,000
1864	31,170	350	410	500	565	920	1,375	3,350	6,400	90,000	15,700
1865	47,000	300	350	420	585	1,050	1,750	3,250	6,250	90,000	15,700
1866 2 known without motto	—	—	—	—	—	—	—	—	—	—	—

Seated Liberty, date below obverse IN GOD WE TRUST above eagle reverse

KM# 100 • 26.73 g., 0.900 **Silver** 0.77 oz. ASW, 38.1 mm. • **Rev. Legend:** UNITED STATES OF AMERICA **Designer:**
Christian Gobrecht **Note:** In 1866 the motto was added to the reverse above the eagle.

Date	Mintage	G4	VG8	F12	VF20	XF40	AU50	MS60	MS63	MS65	Prf65
1866	49,625	320	350	440	590	795	1,250	2,400	5,000	85,000	16,000
1867	47,525	315	345	405	565	670	895	2,435	5,050	85,000	16,000
1868	162,700	325	355	395	535	650	920	3,500	7,350	85,000	16,000
1869	424,300	290	320	370	490	640	985	2,400	5,000	85,000	16,000
1870	416,000	280	320	350	430	595	970	2,300	4,950	67,500	16,000
1870CC	12,462	475	600	825	1,375	3,650	8,250	27,500	44,500	—	—
1870S 12-15 known	—	150,000	235,000	350,000	600,000	850,000	1,350,000	1,850,000	2,500,000	—	—
Note: 1870S, Eliasberg Sale, April 1997, EF-45 to AU-50, $264,000.											
1871	1,074,760	270	300	330	410	545	970	2,300	4,950	67,500	16,000
1871CC	1,376	2,000	2,850	4,750	7,450	14,500	25,000	68,500	175,000	—	—
1872	1,106,450	270	300	330	410	495	820	2,300	4,850	67,500	16,000
1872CC	3,150	900	1,400	2,850	4,300	4,850	13,500	28,500	120,000	385,000	—
1872S	9,000	310	365	550	700	2,000	4,500	11,000	26,000	—	—
1873	293,600	275	310	340	420	510	840	2,350	4,900	67,500	16,000
1873CC	2,300	6,250	7,250	11,500	19,000	31,500	43,500	125,000	225,000	625,000	—
1873S none known	700	—	—	—	—	—	—	—	—	—	—

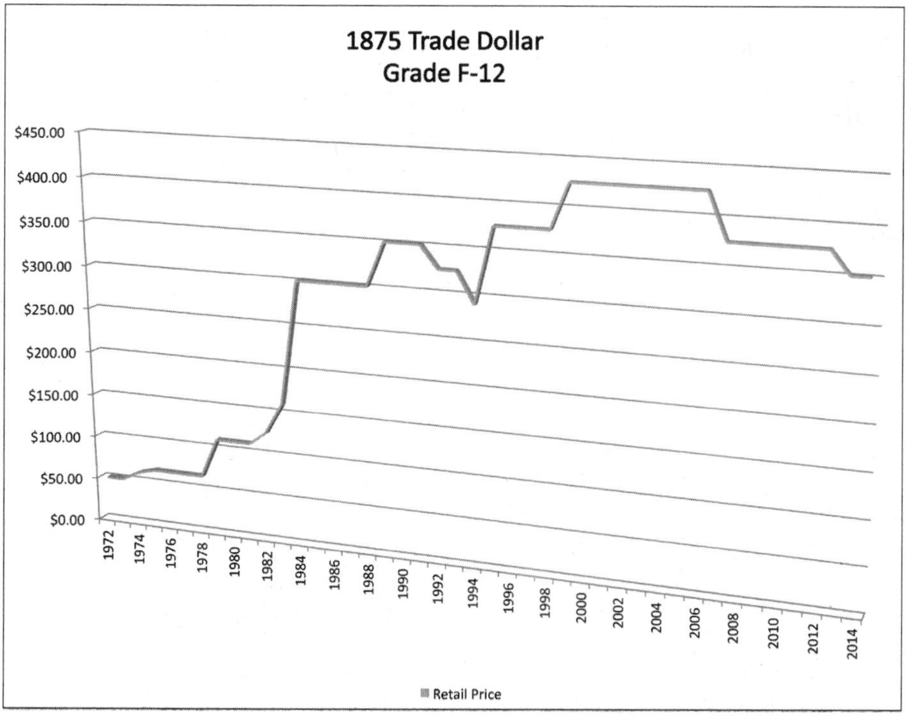

1875 Trade Dollar
Grade F-12

(line chart titled "1875 Trade Dollar, Grade F-12"; y-axis from $0.00 to $450.00; x-axis years 1972–2014; legend: Retail Price)

Trade Dollar
Seated Liberty, IN GOD WE TRUST in base above date obverse
TRADE DOLLAR below eagle reverse

KM# 108 • 27.22 g., 0.900 **Silver** 0.78 oz. ASW, 38.1 mm. • **Rev. Legend:** UNITED STATES OF AMERICA. **Designer:** William Barber

Date	Mintage	G4	VG8	F12	VF20	XF40	AU50	MS60	MS65	Prf65
1873	397,500	115	155	165	185	280	360	1,200	15,500	10,250
1873 CC	124,500	245	295	335	460	875	1,875	10,000	120,000	—
1873 S	703,000	115	155	160	210	280	355	1,475	18,500	—
1874	987,800	125	155	160	185	280	365	1,100	18,250	10,250
1874 CC	1,373,200	255	295	335	385	625	775	3,450	33,000	—
1874 S	2,549,000	115	155	160	170	280	340	1,125	17,500	—
1875	218,900	145	185	350	425	550	800	2,450	18,000	15,000
1875 CC	1,573,700	235	275	315	350	525	800	2,650	38,500	—
1875 S	4,487,000	105	155	155	160	260	330	1,050	12,500	—
1875 S/CC	Inc. above	210	285	365	560	925	1,450	4,650	59,000	—
1876	456,150	115	155	160	170	280	340	1,100	12,500	10,250
1876 CC	509,000	245	285	310	365	585	985	8,000	76,500	—
1876 CC DDR	Inc. above	—	—	375	650	1,250	2,000	8,500	—	—
1876 S	5,227,000	105	145	150	160	255	330	1,050	17,500	—
1877	3,039,710	115	155	160	170	265	340	1,150	23,500	10,250
1877 CC	534,000	255	295	335	425	700	825	2,650	59,000	—
1877 S	9,519,000	105	145	150	160	255	330	1,050	12,500	—
1878 proof only	900	—	—	—	1,200	1,300	1,500	—	—	11,000
1878 CC	97,000	425	625	935	1,475	2,750	4,000	13,500	112,500	—
1878 S	4,162,000	105	145	150	160	225	330	1,050	12,500	—
1879 proof only	1,541	—	—	—	1,175	1,275	1,400	—	—	10,250
1880 proof only	1,987	—	—	—	1,150	1,250	1,350	—	—	10,250
1881 proof only	960	—	—	—	1,200	1,300	1,400	—	—	10,250
1882 proof only	1,097	—	—	—	1,175	1,275	1,375	—	—	10,250
1883 proof only	979	—	—	—	1,200	1,300	1,400	—	—	10,250
1884 proof only	10	—	—	—	—	—	100,000	—	—	650,000

Note: 1884, Eliasberg Sale, April 1997, Prf-66, $396,000.

Date	Mintage	G4	VG8	F12	VF20	XF40	AU50	MS60	MS65	Prf65
1885 proof only	5	—	—	—	—	—	—	—	—	3,000,000

Note: 1885, Eliasberg Sale, April 1997, Prf-65, $907,500.

Morgan Dollar
Laureate head left, date below flanked by stars obverse   Eagle within 1/2 wreath reverse

8 Tail feathers   7 Tail feathers   7/8 Tail feathers

KM# 110 • 26.73 g., 0.900 **Silver** 0.77 oz. ASW, 38.1 mm. • **Obv. Legend:** E • PLURIBUS • UNUM **Rev. Legend:** UNITED STATES OF AMERICA **Designer:** George T. Morgan **Note:** 65DMPL" values are for coins grading MS-65 deep-mirror prooflike. The 1878 "8 tail feathers" and "7 tail feathers" varieties are distinguished by the number of feathers in the eagle's tail. On the "reverse of 1878" varieties, the top of the top feather in the arrows held by the eagle is straight across and the eagle's breast is concave. On the "reverse of 1879 varieties," the top feather in the arrows held by the eagle is slanted and the eagle's breast is convex. The 1890-CC "tail-bar" variety has a bar extending from the arrow feathers to the wreath on the reverse, the result of a die gouge. The Pittman Act of 1918 authorized the melting of 270 Million pieces of various dates. They were not indivudually recorded.

Date	Mintage	VG8	F12	VF20	XF40	AU50	MS60	MS63	MS64	MS65	65DMPL	Prf65
1878 8 tail feathers	750,000	47.50	55.00	61.00	66.50	90.00	172	300	500	1,625	23,500	8,350
1878 7 over 8 tail feathers	9,759,550	31.50	42.20	50.30	50.00	51.00	110	220	535	2,650	24,500	185,000
1878 7 tail feathers, reverse of 1878	Inc. above	40.50	42.20	50.30	52.00	71.50	188	300	500	2,425	17,000	—
1878 7 tail feathers, reverse of 1879	Inc. above	31.50	42.20	50.30	51.00	52.50	90.00	150	2,750	1,150	11,500	11,500
1878CC	2,212,000	115	120	125	137	180	440	510	620	1,950	10,800	—
1878S	9,744,000	31.50	33.20	36.30	40.60	52.00	66.00	105	120	345	10,350	—
1879	14,807,100	29.50	31.20	34.30	36.60	41.40	61.00	100	160	895	17,250	7,550
1879CC	756,000	145	155	315	755	2,400	4,675	8,000	11,500	31,500	49,000	—
1879CC capped CC	Inc. above	145	182	250	640	1,850	4,500	6,800	10,150	43,000	63,500	—
1879O	2,887,000	31.90	40.80	43.80	46.50	48.50	95.00	270	595	4,450	28,500	—
1879S reverse of 1878	9,110,000	34.50	37.20	44.30	51.00	71.00	192	645	1,560	6,000	24,000	—
1879S reverse of 1879	Inc. above	29.50	31.20	34.30	36.60	41.40	58.00	70.00	88.50	215	1,450	—
1880	12,601,335	29.50	31.20	34.30	38.90	41.90	54.00	83.00	160	800	6,350	7,550
1880CC reverse of 1878	591,000	175	210	245	300	355	575	745	1,160	2,375	21,500	—
1880CC 80/79 reverse of 1878	Inc. above	190	230	270	335	410	640	850	1,750	4,000	—	—
1880CC 8/7 reverse of 1878	Inc. above	170	200	235	290	360	600	750	1,300	2,800	—	—
1880CC reverse of 1879	Inc. above	170	200	240	285	345	550	660	710	1,265	9,850	—
1880CC 8/7 high 7 reverse of 1879	Inc. above	175	205	245	290	355	525	685	775	1,800	—	—
1880CC 8/7 low 7 reverse of 1879	Inc. above	175	205	245	290	355	525	665	775	1,800	10,500	—
1880O	5,305,000	32.80	36.20	40.30	41.60	43.40	90.00	415	2,000	29,500	70,000	—
1880S	8,900,000	29.50	34.20	34.30	36.60	41.40	55.00	67.00	85.00	215	1,025	—
1880S 8/7 crossbar	—	33.50	36.20	41.30	45.00	75.00	90.00	265	335	450	—	—
1881	9,163,975	29.50	31.20	34.30	36.60	39.40	58.50	83.00	170	700	21,750	7,650
1881CC	296,000	375	385	410	425	460	525	635	635	935	3,050	—
1881O	5,708,000	29.50	31.20	34.30	36.60	39.40	53.00	77.50	1+5	1,375	35,000	—
1881S	12,760,000	29.50	31.20	34.30	36.60	41.40	55.00	64.00	82.00	220	1,100	—
1882	11,101,100	29.50	31.20	34.30	36.60	39.40	55.50	70.00	155	570	6,800	7,550
1882CC	1,133,000	92.00	96.00	110	130	155	220	285	305	575	2,000	—
1882O	6,090,000	29.80	31.20	34.30	37.60	41.40	54.00	83.00	135	600	4,950	—
1882O/S	Inc. above	46.00	47.00	55.00	67.50	99.50	245	775	1,925	61,500	65,000	—
1882S	9,250,000	29.50	31.20	34.30	36.60	42.40	56.00	73.00	82.00	227	4,100	—
1883	12,291,039	29.50	31.20	34.30	36.60	41.40	56.00	77.50	110	225	1,675	7,500
1883CC	1,204,000	92.00	96.00	110	128	148	215	248	270	570	1,450	—
1883O	8,725,000	29.50	36.20	42.30	44.60	44.60	52.00	61.00	86.00	227	1,550	—
1883S	6,250,000	29.50	32.20	37.80	41.60	145	965	2,750	5,950	51,500	94,500	—
1884	14,070,875	29.50	31.20	34.30	36.60	39.40	54.00	77.50	110	375	4,350	7,550
1884CC	1,136,000	138	145	150	170	174	215	250	275	583	1,485	—
1884O	9,730,000	29.50	31.20	34.30	36.60	39.40	52.00	63.00	80.00	247	1,100	—
1884S	3,200,000	29.50	31.70	36.30	43.00	310	8,850	37,000	110,000	235,000	220,000	—
1885	17,787,767	29.50	31.20	34.30	36.60	39.40	52.00	70.00	80.00	215	1,050	7,550
1885O	9,185,000	29.50	31.20	34.30	36.60	39.40	51.00	63.00	80.00	227	1,075	—
1885S	1,497,000	21.00	28.00	40.00	64.00	110	275	365	745	2,325	42,500	—
1885CC	—	575	590	605	610	615	775	880	925	1,155	2,650	—

DOLLAR

Date	Mintage	VG8	F12	VF20	XF40	AU50	MS60	MS63	MS64	MS65	65DMPL	Prf65
1886	19,963,886	29.50	31.20	34.30	36.60	39.40	52.00	63.00	80.00	226	1,400	7,550
1886O	10,710,000	29.50	31.20	34.80	44.60	78.00	1,015	3,575	10,650	190,000	300,000	—
1886S	750,000	54.00	62.50	85.00	120	145	395	540	870	3,375	30,000	—
1887	20,290,710	29.50	31.20	34.30	36.60	39.40	52.00	63.00	80.00	226	1,430	7,550
1887/6	Inc. above	33.00	34.70	38.80	55.00	165	420	565	800	2,300	44,750	—
1887O	11,550,000	29.50	31.20	36.30	39.60	42.40	71.50	175	425	2,550	12,000	—
1887/6O	—	33.00	34.70	38.80	65.00	190	495	2,050	4,800	29,500	—	—
1887S	1,771,000	30.00	31.70	37.80	40.60	45.90	145	335	755	2,875	29,500	—
1888	19,183,833	29.50	34.20	39.30	41.10	40.40	54.00	68.00	80.00	255	3,000	7,500
1888O	12,150,000	29.50	31.20	34.30	38.60	45.40	66.00	77.50	117	655	4,850	—
1888O Hot Lips	Inc. above	55.00	125	250	600	3,000	—	—	—	—	—	—
1888S	657,000	115	190	210	225	235	365	530	65.00	3,550	16,500	—
1889	21,726,811	29.50	31.20	34.30	36.60	39.40	53.00	67.00	90.00	385	4,050	7,550
1889CC	350,000	660	940	1,300	3,150	8,100	26,250	52,000	85,000	320,000	—	—
1889O	11,875,000	29.80	31.20	36.30	38.60	41.40	200	400	1,000	8,350	18,000	—
1889S	700,000	51.00	60.00	65.00	82.00	125	275	395	685	2,350	38,500	—
1890	16,802,590	29.50	31.20	34.30	36.60	39.40	54.00	94.00	170	2,100	19,750	7,550
1890CC	2,309,041	85.00	96.00	105	140	220	535	990	1,500	5,350	15,500	—
1890CC tail bar	Inc. above	155	175	225	400	700	1,450	3,600	5,500	—	—	—
1890O	10,701,000	30.00	31.70	36.30	38.60	41.40	80.00	110	335	2,700	10,000	—
1890S	8,230,373	29.80	31.50	34.80	38.60	41.40	66.00	110	330	1,300	10,500	—
1891	8,694,206	30.00	32.20	35.30	38.60	45.40	71.00	225	950	8,900	27,500	7,550
1891CC	1,618,000	85.00	96.00	105	135	215	550	800	1,360	5,300	34,500	—
1891CC Spitting Eagle	Inc. above	105	115	135	185	260	485	850	1,450	5,500	—	—
1891O	7,954,529	30.00	31.60	34.80	38.60	41.90	210	400	885	8,550	37,500	—
1891S	5,296,000	30.00	31.70	35.30	38.60	42.90	80.00	155	360	1,925	21,500	—
1892	1,037,245	37.00	38.70	42.30	55.00	88.00	365	550	1,265	5,500	20,500	7,500
1892CC	1,352,000	190	210	245	485	725	1,565	2,425	3,450	9,500	39,500	—
1892O	2,744,000	33.00	35.20	40.30	42.50	77.00	305	445	1,225	8,150	52,500	—
1892S	1,200,000	33.20	38.70	136	290	1,650	44,500	72,500	112,500	205,000	225,000	—
1893	378,792	245	250	260	300	400	780	1,125	2,450	8,950	66,000	7,500
1893CC	677,000	255	310	660	1,455	2,575	5,750	9,350	17,600	70,000	90,000	—
1893O	300,000	195	235	360	555	850	3,450	6,950	17,600	210,000	235,000	—
1893S	100,000	3,000	4,150	5,750	9,500	23,200	143,000	245,000	365,000	715,000	735,000	—
1894	110,972	1,200	1,235	1,320	1,375	1,825	3,650	5,200	10,150	38,500	78,000	7,500
1894O	1,723,000	55.00	57.00	59.00	105	310	1,160	5,100	12,100	68,500	61,500	—
1894S	1,260,000	62.00	65.00	110	155	485	965	1,400	2,450	7,200	26,000	—
1895 proof only	12,880	21,500	29,500	36,500	38,000	40,000	—	—	—	—	—	75,000
1895O	450,000	315	350	480	595	1,225	15,500	57,500	79,000	165,000	—	—
1895S	400,000	465	525	900	1,325	1,865	4,350	7,000	10,800	28,000	42,500	—
1896	9,967,762	29.50	31.20	34.30	36.60	39.40	52.00	67.00	84.00	265	1,450	7,550
1896O	4,900,000	30.00	32.20	35.30	44.10	155	1,625	8,500	44,000	180,000	180,000	—
1896S	5,000,000	34.00	35.70	60.00	235	895	2,500	3,975	5,675	19,500	110,000	—
1897	2,822,731	29.50	31.20	34.30	38.60	41.90	53.00	73.00	99.00	365	3,950	7,550
1897O	4,004,000	30.00	32.20	36.30	52.60	93.50	950	4,400	15,900	70,000	72,500	—
1897S	5,825,000	30.00	32.20	35.30	38.60	44.90	83.00	137	172	635	3,250	—
1898	5,884,735	29.50	31.20	34.30	37.10	39.90	52.50	67.00	90.00	265	1,350	7,550
1898O	4,440,000	29.50	31.20	34.30	37.10	39.90	54.50	63.50	80.00	215	1,175	—
1898S	4,102,000	34.00	35.70	36.80	55.00	93.50	270	510	685	2,500	18,000	—
1899	330,846	170	182	195	205	220	265	335	415	935	2,650	7,550
1899O	12,290,000	29.50	31.20	34.30	36.60	39.40	54.50	70.00	83.00	215	1,650	—
1899S	2,562,000	34.00	35.70	38.80	61.00	155	440	550	845	2,365	26,000	—
1900	8,880,938	29.50	31.20	34.30	36.60	39.40	52.50	67.00	87.00	243	42,500	7,550
1900O	12,590,000	29.50	31.20	34.30	36.60	39.40	56.50	67.00	79.00	226	6,250	—
1900O/CC	Inc. above	39.50	55.00	62.50	100	190	305	810	965	2,260	19,000	—
1900S	3,540,000	33.50	36.70	39.80	44.10	88.00	320	415	690	1,875	38,500	—
1901	6,962,813	43.00	48.50	57.50	105	280	3,000	17,250	55,000	375,000	—	7,850
1901 doubled die reverse	Inc. above	275	450	900	2,000	3,850	—	—	—	—	—	—
1901O	13,320,000	31.90	34.60	38.70	39.60	41.40	53.00	71.00	90.00	215	10,000	—
1901S	2,284,000	32.00	35.20	39.80	61.00	200	560	880	1,190	3,800	24,500	—
1902	7,994,777	31.50	34.20	41.30	47.60	48.40	66.00	132	180	480	19,500	7,550
1902O	8,636,000	29.50	31.20	34.30	36.60	39.40	54.50	61.00	84.00	251	16,000	—
1902S	1,530,000	99.00	105	148	210	275	425	690	910	3,000	15,000	—
1903	4,652,755	47.00	48.00	49.00	52.00	52.00	66.00	82.50	120	345	36,850	7,550
1903O	4,450,000	325	350	375	390	398	435	485	510	690	6,150	—
1903S	1,241,000	95.00	130	210	365	1,925	4,950	6,875	8,575	11,750	40,000	—
1903S Micro S	Inc. above	135	225	450	1,150	3,000	—	—	—	—	—	—
1904	2,788,650	31.50	35.20	39.30	46.10	48.40	105	265	600	2,850	86,500	7,550
1904O	3,720,000	36.00	47.00	52.50	55.00	57.00	59.50	63.00	82.00	215	1,385	—
1904S	2,304,000	43.00	48.50	87.00	230	525	2,585	4,950	5,665	10,350	24,500	—
1921	44,690,000	27.10	29.40	32.60	34.10	38.30	46.50	55.00	66.00	175	11,500	—
1921D	20,345,000	—	—	—	—	—	50.00	77.00	117	395	10,000	—
1921S	21,695,000	—	—	—	—	—	50.00	81.50	165	1,925	31,000	—

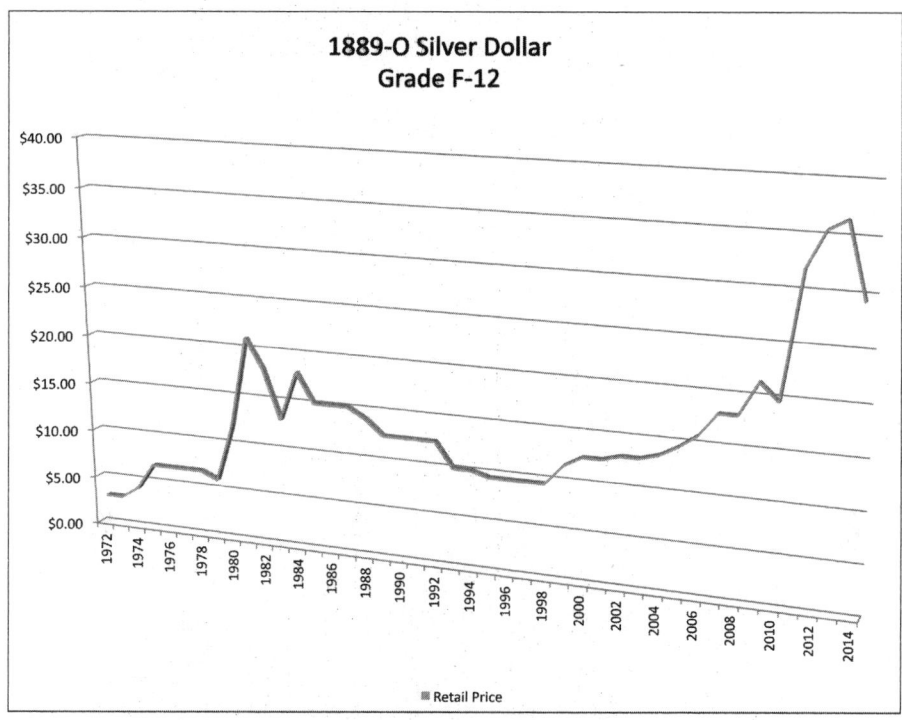

1889-O Silver Dollar
Grade F-12

Retail Price

Peace Dollar
Liberty Head left obverse   Eagle facing right perched on rock reverse

KM# 150 • 26.73 g., 0.900 **Silver** 0.77 oz. ASW, 38.1 mm. • **Designer:** Anthony DeFrancisci

Date	Mintage	G4	VG8	F12	VF20	XF40	AU50	MS60	MS63	MS64	MS65
1921	1,006,473	95.00	120	126	133	143	165	300	460	904	2,425
1922	51,737,000	22.40	24.60	25.10	31.40	32.20	34.10	44.00	48.50	63.00	160
1922 D	15,063,000	22.60	24.80	25.40	31.70	32.50	35.00	52.00	79.00	132	670
1922 S	17,475,000	22.60	24.80	25.40	31.70	32.50	35.00	52.00	90.00	340	2,650
1923	30,800,000	22.40	24.60	25.10	31.40	32.20	34.10	44.00	48.50	63.00	160
1923 D	6,811,000	22.60	24.80	25.40	31.70	32.50	38.10	75.00	150	420	1,350
1923 S	19,020,000	22.60	24.80	25.40	31.70	32.50	35.00	50.00	88.00	520	6,600
1924	11,811,000	22.40	24.60	25.40	31.40	32.20	34.10	44.00	48.50	63.00	183
1924 S	1,728,000	22.40	25.60	28.10	35.40	41.50	64.00	245	510	1,560	9,750
1925	10,198,000	22.40	24.60	25.10	31.40	32.20	34.10	46.00	53.00	63.00	172
1925 S	1,610,000	23.30	25.50	26.00	32.30	33.10	43.00	105	300	1,155	25,000
1926	1,939,000	23.50	25.70	26.20	32.70	33.50	34.10	55.00	99.00	132	630
1926 D	2,348,700	23.50	25.70	26.00	32.30	32.20	36.10	93.50	215	430	1,085
1926 S	6,980,000	23.00	25.20	25.70	32.00	32.80	37.10	59.00	110	330	1,185
1927	848,000	24.70	27.80	30.10	37.40	38.20	50.00	85.00	195	635	3,200
1927 D	1,268,900	24.70	27.80	30.10	37.40	38.20	80.00	220	410	1,130	5,150
1927 S	866,000	24.70	27.80	30.10	37.40	38.20	80.00	205	605	1,320	9,900
1928	360,649	345	375	380	385	390	405	540	970	1,300	4,900

DOLLAR

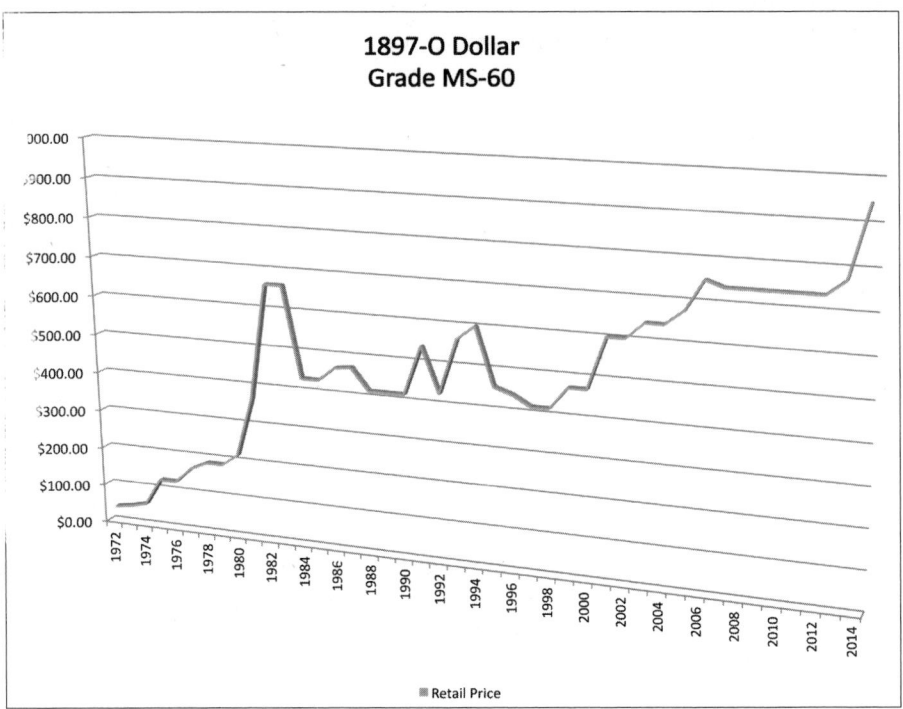

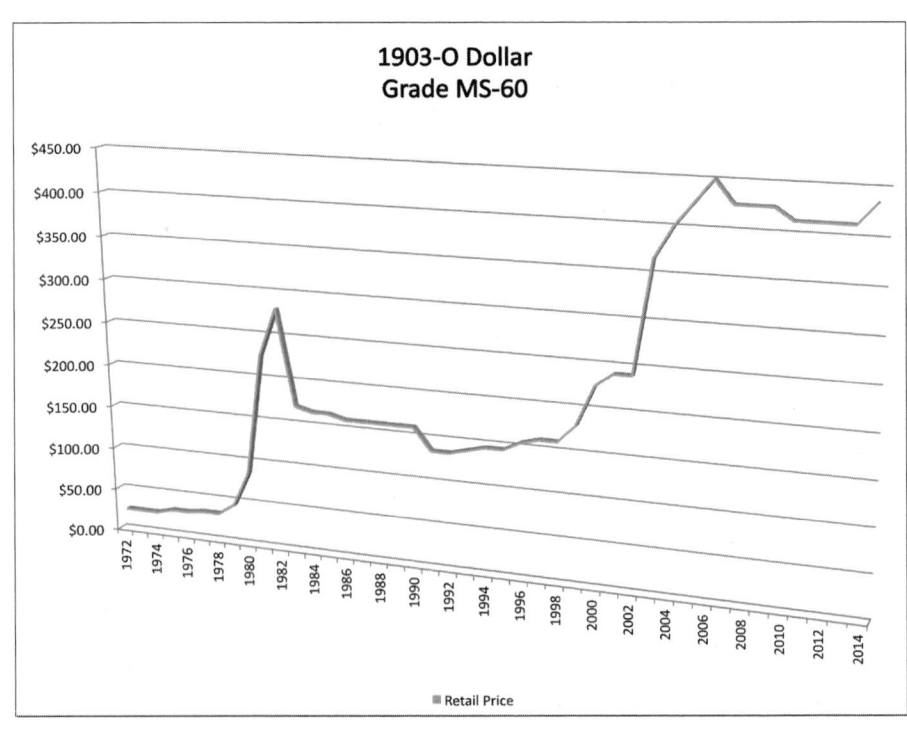

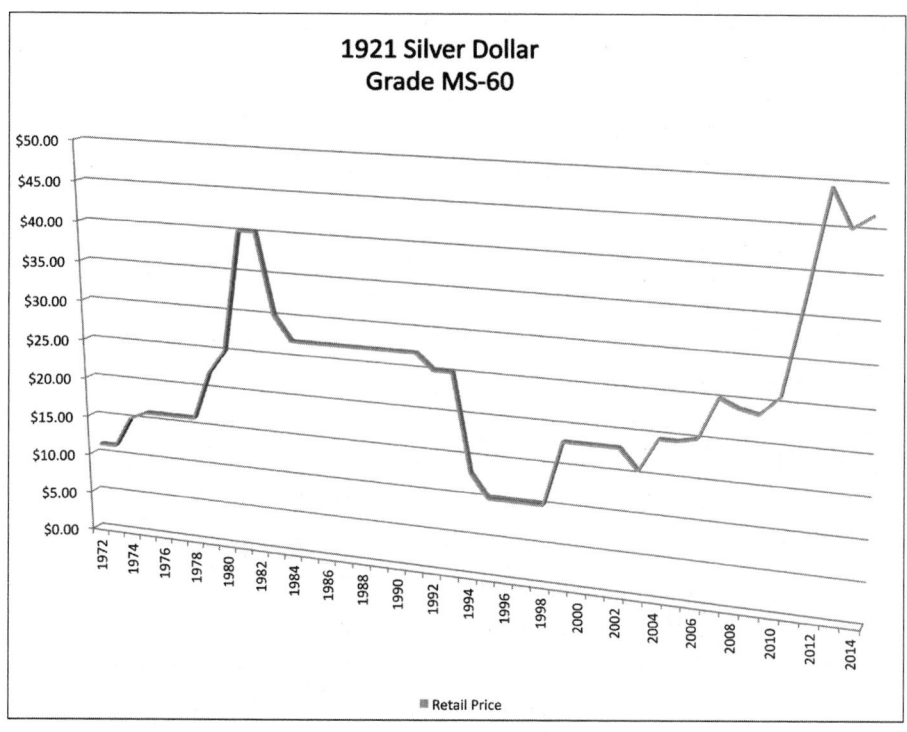

1921 Silver Dollar
Grade MS-60
$50.00
$45.00
$40.00
$35.00
$30.00
$25.00
$20.00
$15.00
$10.00
$5.00
$0.00
1972
1974
1976
1978
1980
1982
1984
1986
1988
1990
1992
1994
1996
1998
2000
2002
2004
2006
2008
2010
2012
2014
Retail Price

1927-S Dollar
Grade MS-60
$500.00
$450.00
$400.00
$350.00
$300.00
$250.00
$200.00
$150.00
$100.00
$50.00
$0.00
1972
1974
1976
1978
1980
1982
1984
1986
1988
1990
1992
1994
1996
1998
2000
2002
2004
2006
2008
2010
2012
2014
Retail Price

DOLLAR

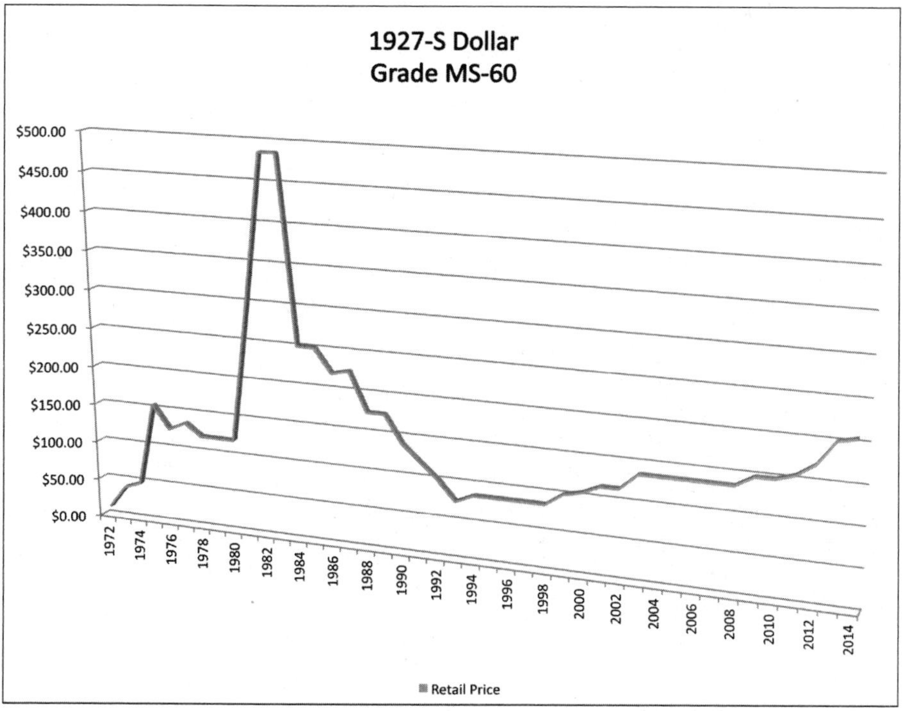

DOLLAR

Date	Mintage	G4	VG8	F12	VF20	XF40	AU50	MS60	MS63	MS64	MS65
1928 S	1,632,000	34.00	35.00	40.00	42.50	48.00	66.00	178	555	1,240	24,000
1934	954,057	35.00	44.00	45.00	46.00	47.50	51.00	122	215	420	800
1934 D Large D	1,569,500	36.00	45.00	46.00	50.00	54.00	65.00	180	600	925	3,000
1934 D Small D	Inc. above	35.00	44.00	45.00	46.00	47.50	50.00	160	385	630	2,175
1934 S	1,011,000	38.00	45.00	53.00	80.00	180	510	2,325	4,200	5,500	9,650
1935	1,576,000	35.00	44.00	45.00	46.00	47.50	57.50	85.00	135	280	825
1935 S 3 Rays	1,964,000	35.00	44.00	45.00	46.00	47.50	99.50	300	510	710	1,650
1935 S 4 Rays	—	36.00	45.00	46.00	50.00	58.00	122	365	600	850	1,850

Eisenhower Dollar

Date	Mintage	MS63	MS65	Prf65
1971 S Peg Leg "R" Variety	Inc. above	8.00	—	17.00
1971 S Partial Peg Leg "R" Variety	Inc. above	9.00	—	18.00
1972 S	2,193,056	—	7.50	—
1972 S	1,811,631	6.50	—	9.00
1973 S	1,833,140	—	7.50	—
1973 S	1,005,617	30.00	—	45.00
1974 S	1,720,000	—	7.50	—
1974 S	1,306,579	6.50	—	11.00

Bicentennial design, moon behind Liberty Bell reverse

KM# 203 • 22.80 g., **Copper-Nickel Clad Copper**, 38 mm.
• **Designer:** Frank Gasparro

Date	Mintage	MS63	MS65	Prf65
1971	47,799,000	—	5.00	—
1971 D	68,587,424	—	4.00	—
1972 Low Relief	75,890,000	—	18.00	—
1972 High Relief	Inc. above	—	100	—
1972 Modified High Relief	Inc. above	—	25.00	—
1972 D	92,548,511	—	8.00	—
1973	2,000,056	—	12.00	—
1973 D	2,000,000	—	12.00	—
1973 S	2,769,624	7.00	—	12.00
1974	27,366,000	—	9.00	—
1974 D	35,466,000	—	7.50	—
1974 S	2,617,350	6.00	—	11.00

Type I
Squared "T"

Type II
Slant-top "T"

KM# 206 • 22.68 g., **Copper-Nickel Clad Copper**, 38.1 mm. • **Rev. Designer:** Dennis R. Williams **Note:** In 1976 the lettering on the reverse was changed to thinner letters, resulting in the Type II variety for that year. The Type I variety was minted 1975 and dated 1976.

Date	Mintage	MS63	MS65	Prf65
1976 type I	117,337,000	—	12.00	—
1976 type II	Inc. above	—	7.50	—
1976 D type I	103,228,274	—	10.00	—
1976 D type II	Inc. above	—	7.00	—
1976 S type I	2,909,369	5.00	—	10.00
1976 S type II	4,149,730	5.00	—	9.00

KM# 203a • 24.59 g., 0.400 **Silver** 0.31 oz. ASW, 38.1 mm. • **Designer:** Frank Gasparro

Date	Mintage	MS63	MS65	Prf65
1971 S	6,868,530	6.50	7.50	11.00
1971 S	4,265,234	—	—	—

KM# 206a • 24.59 g., 0.400 **Silver** 0.31 oz. ASW **Rev. Designer:** Dennis R. Williams

Date	Mintage	MS63	MS65	Prf65
1976 S	4,908,319	11.50	7.50	14.00
1976 S	3,998,621	—	—	—

Regular design resumed

KM# A203 • Copper-Nickel Clad Copper, 38.1 mm. •

Date	Mintage	MS63	MS65	Prf65
1977	12,596,000	—	5.50	—
1977 D	32,983,006	—	8.00	—
1977 S	3,251,152	5.00	—	9.00
1978	25,702,000	—	6.50	—
1978 D	33,012,890	—	6.50	—
1978 S	3,127,788	5.50	—	9.00

Susan B. Anthony Dollar

Susan B. Anthony bust right obverse Eagle landing on moon, symbolic of Apollo manned moon landing reverse

KM# 207 • 8.10 g., Copper-Nickel Clad Copper, 26.5 mm. • **Edge:** Reeded **Designer:** Frank Gasparro **Note:** The 1979-S and 1981-S Type II coins have a clearer mint mark than the Type I varieties for those years.

Date	Mintage	MS63	MS65	Prf65
1979 P Near date	360,222,000	30.00	90.00	—
1979 P	Inc. above	2.50	12.50	—
1979 D	288,015,744	2.50	12.50	—
1979 S Proof, Type I	3,677,175	—	—	6.00
1979 S Proof, Type II	Inc. above	—	—	85.00
1979 S	109,576,000	2.50	13.50	—
1980 P	27,610,000	2.50	12.00	—
1980 D	41,628,708	2.50	12.00	—
1980 S	20,422,000	5.00	20.00	—
1980 S Proof	3,547,030	—	—	5.00
1981 P	3,000,000	5.00	18.00	—
1981 D	3,250,000	5.00	13.50	—
1981 S	3,492,000	5.00	30.00	—
1981 S Proof, Type I	4,063,083	—	—	7.00
1981 S Proof, Type II	Inc. above	—	—	225
1999 P	29,592,000	3.00	10.00	—
1999 P Proof	Est. 750000	—	—	22.00
1999 D	11,776,000	3.00	10.00	—

Sacagawea Dollar

Sacagawea bust right, with baby on back obverse Eagle in flight left reverse

KM# 310 • 8.07 g., Copper-Zinc-Manganese-Nickel Clad Copper, 26.5 mm. • **Obv. Designer:** Glenda Goodacre **Rev. Designer:** Thomas D. Rodgers

Date	Mintage	MS63	MS65	Prf65
2000 P	767,140,000	2.00	7.50	—
2000 P Goodacre Presentation	5,000	—	575	—
2000 D	518,916,000	2.00	11.00	—

Date	Mintage	MS63	MS65	Prf65
2000 D from Millennium Set	5,500	10.00	50.00	—
2000 S	4,048,000	—	—	5.00
2001 P	62,468,000	2.25	6.00	—
2001 D	70,909,500	2.25	8.00	—
2001 S	3,084,000	—	—	16.00
2002 P	3,865,610	3.00	9.00	—
2002 D	3,732,000	2.75	10.00	—
2002 S	3,157,739	—	—	10.00
2003 P	3,090,000	4.50	10.00	—
2003 D	3,090,000	4.75	12.00	—
2003 S	3,116,590	—	—	8.00
2004 P	2,660,000	3.50	6.00	—
2004 D	2,660,000	4.00	8.00	—
2004 S	2,992,069	—	—	7.50
2005 P	2,520,000	3.00	9.00	—
2005 P Satin Finish	1,160,000	5.00	9.00	—
2005 D	2,520,000	3.00	10.00	—
2005 D Satin Finish	1,160,000	5.00	9.00	—
2005 S	3,273,000	—	—	6.00
2006 P	4,900,000	3.25	6.00	—
2006 P Satin Finish	847,361	4.50	9.00	—
2006 D	2,800,000	3.50	10.00	—
2006 D Satin Finish	847,361	4.00	6.00	—
2006 S	3,054,436	—	—	9.00
2007 P	3,640,000	2.25	5.50	—
2007 P Satin Finish	895,628	4.00	6.00	—
2007 D	3,920,000	2.25	7.50	—
2007 D Satin Finish	895,628	4.00	6.00	—
2007 S	2,577,166	—	—	6.50
2008 P	1,820,000	2.00	7.00	—
2008 P Satin Finish	745,464	4.00	6.00	—
2008 D	1,820,000	3.50	10.00	—
2008 D Satin Finish	745,464	4.00	6.00	—
2008 S	2,169,561	—	—	16.00

Native American Dollar

Planting crops reverse

KM# 467 • 8.07 g., Copper-Zinc-Manganese-Nickel Clad Copper, 26.5 mm. • **Obv. Designer:** Glenda Goodacre **Rev. Designer:** Norm Nemeth **Edge Lettering:** E PLURIBUS UNUM, date, mint mark **Note:** Date and mint mark on edge

Date	Mintage	MS63	MS65	Prf65
2009 P	37,380,000	2.00	5.00	—
2009 P Satin finish	784,614	4.00	7.00	—
2009 D	33,880,000	2.00	5.00	—
2009 D Satin finish	784,614	4.00	7.00	—
2009 S	2,179,867	—	—	6.00

Hiawatha belt reverse

KM# 474 • 8.07 g., Copper-Zinc-Manganese-Nickel Clad

Copper, 26.5 mm. • **Obv. Designer:** Glenda Goodacre
Rev. Designer: Thomas Cleveland and Charles L. Vickers
Edge Lettering: E PLURIBUS UNUM, date, mint mark
Note: Date and mint mark on edge

Date	Mintage	MS63	MS65	Prf65
2010 P	32,060,000	2.00	5.00	—
2010 P Satin Finish	583,897	4.00	7.00	—
2010 D	48,720,000	2.00	5.00	—
2010 D Satin Finish	583,897	4.00	7.00	—
2010 S	1,689,364	—	—	12.50

Peace Pipe reverse

KM# 503 • 8.07 g., **Copper-Zinc-Manganese-Nickel Clad Copper**, 26.5 mm. • **Obv. Designer:** Glenna Goodacre
Rev. Designer: Richard Masters and Joseph Menna **Edge Lettering:** E PLURIBUS UNUM, date, mint mark **Note:** Date and mint mark on edge

Date	Mintage	MS63	MS65	Prf65
2011 P	29,400,000	2.00	5.50	—
2011 D	48,160,000	2.00	5.00	—
2011 S	1,453,276	—	—	8.00

Horse reverse

KM# 528 • 8.07 g., **Copper-Zinc-Manganese-Nickel Clad Copper**, 26.5 mm. • **Obv. Designer:** Glenda Goodacre
Rev. Designer: Thomas Cleveland and Phebe Hemphill
Edge Lettering: E PLURIBUS UNUM, date, mint mark
Note: Date and mint mark on edge

Date	Mintage	MS63	MS65	Prf65
2012 P	2,800,000	2.00	7.00	—
2012 D	3,080,000	2.00	7.00	—
2012 S	1,189,445	—	—	12.50

Delaware Treaty of 1778

KM# 551 • 8.07 g., **Copper-Zinc-Manganese-Nickel Clad Copper**, 26.5 mm. • **Edge:** E PLURIBUS UNUM, date, mint mark **Note:** Date and mint mark on edge.

Date	Mintage	MS63	MS65	Prf65
2013 P	1,820,000	2.00	7.00	—
2013 D	1,820,000	2.00	7.00	—
2013 S	1,192,690	—	—	12.50

Native Hospitality

KM# 575 • 8.07 g., **Copper-Zinc-Manganese-Nickel Clad Copper**, 26.5 mm. •

Date	Mintage	MS63	MS65	Prf65
2014 P	—	2.00	7.00	—
2014 D	—	2.00	7.00	—
2014 S	—	—	—	12.50

Presidential Dollars
George Washington

KM# 401 • 8.07 g., **Copper-Zinc-Manganese-Nickel Clad Copper**, 26.5 mm. **Obv. Designer:** Joseph Menna **Rev. Designer:** Don Everhart **Edge Lettering:** IN GOD WE TRUST date, mint mark E PLURIBUS UNUM **Note:** Date and mint mark incuse on edge.

Date	Mintage	MS63	MS65	Prf65
2007P	176,680,000	2.00	3.00	—
2007P Satin Finish	895,628	2.00	4.00	—
Plain edge error	Inc. above	175	275	—
2007D	163,680,000	2.00	3.00	—
2007D Satin Finish	895,628	2.00	4.00	—
2007S	3,883,103	—	—	3.00

John Adams

KM# 402 • 8.07 g., **Copper-Zinc-Manganese-Nickel Clad Copper**, 26.5 mm. **Obv. Designer:** Joel Iskowitz and Charles Vickers **Rev. Designer:** Don Everhart **Edge Lettering:** IN GOD WE TRUST date, mint mark E PLURIBUS UNUM **Note:** Date and mint mark incuse on edge.

Date	Mintage	MS63	MS65	Prf65
2007P	112,420,000	2.00	3.00	—
2007P Double edge lettering	Inc. above	45.00	65.00	—
2007D Plain edge error	Inc. above	60.00	70.00	—
2007P Satin Finish	895,628	2.00	4.00	—
2007D	112,140,000	2.00	3.00	—
2007D Satin Finish	895,628	2.00	4.00	—
2007S	3,877,409	—	—	3.00

Thomas Jefferson

KM# 403 • 8.07 g., Copper-Zinc-Manganese-Nickel Clad Copper, 26.5 mm. **Obv. Designer:** Joseph Menna **Rev. Designer:** Don Everhart **Edge Lettering:** IN GOD WE TRUST date, mint mark E PLURIBUS UNUM **Note:** Date and mint mark incuse on edge.

Date	Mintage	MS63	MS65	Prf65
2007P	100,800,000	2.00	3.00	—
2007P Satin Finish	895,628	2.00	4.00	—
2007D	102,810,000	2.00	3.00	—
2007D Satin Finish	895,628	2.00	4.00	—
2007S	3,877,573	—	—	3.00

James Madison

KM# 404 • 8.07 g., Copper-Zinc-Manganese-Nickel Clad Copper, 26.5 mm. **Obv. Designer:** Joel Iskowitz and Don Everhart **Rev. Designer:** Don Everhart **Edge Lettering:** IN GOD WE TRUST date, mint mark E PLURIBUS UNUM **Note:** Date and mint mark incuse on edge.

Date	Mintage	MS63	MS65	Prf65
2007P	84,560,000	2.00	3.00	—
2007P Satin Finish	895,628	2.00	4.00	—
2007D	87,780,000	2.00	3.00	—
2007D Satin Finish	895,628	2.00	4.00	—
2007S	3,876,829	—	—	3.00

James Monroe

KM# 426 • 8.07 g., Copper-Zinc-Manganese-Nickel Clad Copper, 26.5 mm. **Obv. Designer:** Joseph Menna **Rev. Designer:** Don Everhart **Edge Lettering:** IN GOD WE TRUST date, mint mark E PLURIBUS UNUM

Date	Mintage	MS63	MS65	Prf65
2008P	64,260,000	2.00	3.00	—
2008P Satin Finish	745,464	2.00	4.00	—
2008D	60,230,000	2.00	3.00	—
2008D Satin Finish	745,464	2.00	4.00	—
2008S	3,000,000	—	—	4.00

John Quincy Adams

KM# 427 • 8.07 g., Copper-Zinc-Manganese-Nickel Clad Copper, 26.5 mm. **Obv. Designer:** Don Everhart **Rev. Designer:** Don Everhart **Edge Lettering:** IN GOD WE TRUST date, mint mark E PLURIBUS UNUM **Note:** Date and mint mark incuse on edge.

Date	Mintage	MS63	MS65	Prf65
2008P	57,540,000	2.00	3.00	—
2008P Satin Finish	745,464	2.00	4.00	—
2008D	57,720,000	2.00	3.00	—
2008D Satin Finish	745,464	2.00	4.00	—
2008S	3,000,000	—	—	4.00

Andrew Jackson

KM# 428 • 8.07 g., Copper-Zinc-Manganese-Nickel Clad Copper, 26.5 mm. **Obv. Designer:** Joel Iskowitz and Jim Licaretz **Rev. Designer:** Don Everhart **Edge Lettering:** IN GOD WE TRUST date, mint mark E PLURIBUS UNUM **Note:** Date and mint mark incuse on edge.

Date	Mintage	MS63	MS65	Prf65
2008P	61,180,000	2.00	3.00	—
2008P Satin Finish	745,464	2.00	4.00	—
2008D	61,070,000	2.00	3.00	—
2008D Satin Finish	745,464	2.00	4.00	—
2008S	3,000,000	—	—	4.00

Martin van Buren

KM# 429 • 8.07 g., Copper-Zinc-Manganese-Nickel Clad Copper, 26.5 mm. **Obv. Designer:** Joel Iskowitz and Phebe Hemphill **Rev. Designer:** Don Everhart **Edge Lettering:** IN GOD WE TRUST date, mint mark E PLURIBUS UNUM **Note:** Date and mint mark incuse on edge.

Date	Mintage	MS63	MS65	Prf65
2008P	51,520,000	2.00	3.00	—
2008P Satin Finish	745,464	2.00	4.00	—
2008D	50,960,000	2.00	3.00	—
2008D Satin Finish	745,464	2.00	4.00	—
2008S	3,000,000	—	—	4.00

DOLLAR

William Henry Harrison

KM# 450 • 8.07 g., Copper-Zinc-Manganese-Nickel Clad Copper, 26.5 mm. **Obv. Designer:** Joseph Menna **Rev. Designer:** Don Everhart **Edge Lettering:** E PLURIBUS UNUM, date, mint mark **Note:** Date and mint mark on edge

Date	Mintage	MS63	MS65	Prf65
2009P	43,260,000	2.00	3.00	—
2009P Satin Finish	784,614	2.00	4.00	—
2009D	55,160,000	2.00	3.00	—
2009P Satin Finish	784,614	2.00	4.00	—
2009S	2,224,827	—	—	3.00

John Tyler

KM# 451 • 8.07 g., Copper-Zinc-Manganese-Nickel Clad Copper, 26.5 mm. **Obv. Designer:** Phebe Hemphill **Rev. Designer:** Don Everhart **Edge Lettering:** E PLURIBUS UNUM, date, mint mark **Note:** Date and mint mark on edge.

Date	Mintage	MS63	MS65	Prf65
2009P	43,540,000	2.00	3.00	—
2009P Satin Finish	784,614	2.00	4.00	—
2009D	43,540,000	2.00	3.00	—
2009D Satin Finish	784,614	2.00	4.00	—
2009S	2,224,827	—	—	3.00

James K. Polk

KM# 452 • 8.07 g., Copper-Zinc-Manganese-Nickel Clad Copper, 26.5 mm. **Obv. Designer:** Susan Gamble and Charles Vickers **Rev. Designer:** Don Everhart **Edge Lettering:** E PLURIBUS UNUM, date, mint mark **Note:** Date and mint mark on edge

Date	Mintage	MS63	MS65	Prf65
2009P	46,620,000	2.00	3.00	—
2009P Satin Finish	784,614	2.00	4.00	—
2009D	41,720,000	2.00	3.00	—
2009D Satin Finish	784,614	2.00	4.00	—
2009S	2,224,827	—	—	3.00

Zachary Taylor

KM# 453 • 8.07 g., Copper-Zinc-Manganese-Nickel Clad Copper, 26.5 mm. **Obv. Designer:** Don Everhart **Rev. Designer:** Don Everhart **Edge Lettering:** E PLURIBUS UNUM, date, mint mark **Note:** Date and mint mark on edge.

Date	Mintage	MS63	MS65	Prf65
2009P	41,580,000	2.00	3.00	—
2009P Satin Finish	784,614	2.00	4.00	—
2009D	36,680,000	2.00	3.00	—
2009D Satin Finish	784,614	2.00	4.00	—
2009S	2,224,827	—	—	3.00

Millard Filmore

KM# 475 • 8.07 g., Copper-Zinc-Manganese-Nickel Clad Copper, 26.5 mm. **Obv. Designer:** Don Everhart **Rev. Designer:** Don Everhart **Edge Lettering:** E PLURIBUS UNUM, date, mint mark **Note:** Date and mint mark on edge.

Date	Mintage	MS63	MS65	Prf65
2010P	37,520,000	2.00	3.00	—
2010P Satin Finish	583,897	2.00	4.00	—
2010D	36,960,000	2.00	3.00	—
2010D Satin Finish	583,897	2.00	4.00	—
2010S	2,224,827	—	—	4.00

Franklin Pierce

KM# 476 • 8.07 g., Copper-Zinc-Manganese-Nickel Clad Copper, 26.5 mm. **Obv. Designer:** Susan Gamble and Charles L. Vickers **Rev. Designer:** Don Everhart **Edge Lettering:** E PLURIBUS UNUM, date, mint mark **Note:** Date and mint mark on edge.

Date	Mintage	MS63	MS65	Prf65
2010P	38,220,000	2.00	3.00	—
2010P Satin Finish	583,897	2.00	4.00	—
2010D	38,360,000	2.00	3.00	—
2010D Satin Finish	583,897	2.00	4.00	—
2010S	2,224,827	—	—	4.00

James Buchanan

KM# 477 • 8.07 g., **Copper-Zinc-Manganese-Nickel Clad Copper**, 26.5 mm. **Obv. Designer:** Phebe Hemphill **Rev. Designer:** Don Everhart **Edge Lettering:** E PLURIBUS UNUM, date, mint mark **Note:** Date and mint mark on edge.

Date	Mintage	MS63	MS65	Prf65
2010P	36,820,000	2.00	3.00	—
2010P Satin Finish	583,897	2.00	4.00	—
2010D	36,540,000	2.00	3.00	—
2010D Satin Finish	583,897	2.00	4.00	—
2010S	2,224,827	—	—	4.00

Abraham Lincoln

KM# 478 • 8.07 g., **Copper-Zinc-Manganese-Nickel Clad Copper**, 26.5 mm. **Obv. Designer:** Don Everhart **Rev. Designer:** Don Everhart **Edge Lettering:** E PLURIBUS UNUM, date, mint mark **Note:** Date and mint mark on edge.

Date	Mintage	MS63	MS65	Prf65
2010P	49,000,000	2.00	3.00	—
2010P Satin Finish	583,897	2.00	4.00	—
2010D	48,020,000	2.00	3.00	—
2010D Satin Finish	583,897	2.00	4.00	—
2010S	2,224,827	—	—	4.00

Andrew Johnson

KM# 499 • 8.07 g., **Copper-Zinc-Manganese-Nickel Clad Copper**, 26.5 mm. **Obv. Designer:** Don Everhart **Rev. Designer:** Don Everhart **Edge Lettering:** E PLURIBUS UNUM, date, mint mark **Note:** Date and mint mark on edge.

Date	Mintage	MS63	MS65	Prf65
2011P	35,560,000	2.00	3.00	—
2011D	37,100,000	2.00	3.00	—
2011S	1,706,916	—	—	4.00

Ulysses S. Grant

KM# 500 • 8.07 g., **Copper-Zinc-Manganese-Nickel Clad Copper**, 26.5 mm. **Obv. Designer:** Don Everhart **Rev. Designer:** Don Everhart **Edge Lettering:** E PLURIBUS UNUM, date, mint mark **Note:** Date and mint mark on edge.

Date	Mintage	MS63	MS65	Prf65
2011P	38,080,000	2.00	3.00	—
2011D	37,940,000	2.00	3.00	—
2011S	1,706,916	—	—	4.00

Rutherford B. Hayes

KM# 501 • 8.07 g., **Copper-Zinc-Manganese-Nickel Clad Copper**, 26.5 mm. **Obv. Designer:** Don Everhart **Rev. Designer:** Don Everhart **Edge Lettering:** E PLURIBUS UNUM, date, mint mark **Note:** Date and mint mark on edge.

Date	Mintage	MS63	MS65	Prf65
2011P	37,660,000	2.00	3.00	—
2011D	36,820,000	2.00	3.00	—
2011S	1,706,916	—	—	4.00

James Garfield

KM# 502 • 8.07 g., **Copper-Zinc-Manganese-Nickel Clad Copper**, 26.5 mm. **Obv. Designer:** Phebe Hemphill **Rev. Designer:** Don Everhart **Edge Lettering:** E PLURIBUS UNUM, date, mint mark **Note:** Date and mint mark on edge.

Date	Mintage	MS63	MS65	Prf65
2011P	37,100,000	2.00	3.00	—
2011D	37,100,000	2.00	3.00	—
2011S	1,706,916	—	—	4.00

Chester A. Arthur

KM# 524 • 8.07 g., **Copper-Zinc-Manganese-Nickel Clad Copper**, 26.5 mm. **Obv. Designer:** Don Everhart **Rev. Designer:** Don Everhart **Edge Lettering:** E PLURIBUS UNUM, date, mintmark **Note:** Date and mintmark on edge

Date	Mintage	MS63	MS65	Prf65
2012P	6,020,000	2.00	3.00	—
2012D	4,060,000	2.00	3.00	—
2012S	—	—	—	5.00

Grover Cleveland, first term

KM# 525 • 8.07 g., **Copper-Zinc-Manganese-Nickel Clad Copper**, 26.5 mm. **Obv. Designer:** Don Everhart **Rev. Designer:** Don Everhart **Edge Lettering:** E PLURIBUS UNUM, date, mintmark **Note:** Date and mint mark on edge

Date	Mintage	MS63	MS65	Prf65
2012P	5,460,000	2.00	3.00	—
2012D	4,060,000	2.00	3.00	—
2012S	1,438,710	—	—	5.00

Benjamin Harrison

KM# 526 • 8.07 g., **Copper-Zinc-Manganese-Nickel Clad Copper**, 26.5 mm. **Obv. Designer:** Phebe Hemphill **Rev. Designer:** Don Everhart **Edge Lettering:** E PLURIBUS UNUM, date, mintmark **Note:** Date at mint mark on edge

Date	Mintage	MS63	MS65	Prf65
2012P	5,640,001	2.00	3.00	—
2012D	4,200,000	2.00	3.00	—
2012S	1,438,710	—	—	5.00

Grover Cleveland, second term

KM# 527 • 8.07 g., **Copper-Zinc-Manganese-Nickel Clad Copper**, 26.5 mm. **Obv. Designer:** Don Everhart **Rev. Designer:** Don Everhart **Edge Lettering:** E PLURIBUS UNUM, date, mintmark **Note:** Date and mint mark on edge

Date	Mintage	MS63	MS65	Prf65
2012P	10,680,000	2.00	3.00	—
2012D	3,920,000	2.00	3.00	—
2012S	1,438,710	—	—	5.00

William McKinley

KM# 547 • 8.07 g., **Copper-Zinc-Manganese-Nickel Clad Copper**, 26.5 mm. **Edge:** E PLURIBUS UNUM, date, mint mark **Note:** Date and mint mark on edge.

Date	Mintage	MS63	MS65	Prf65
2013P	4,760,000	2.00	3.00	—
2013D	3,365,100	2.00	3.00	—
2013S	1,449,415	—	—	5.00

Theodore Roosevelt

KM# 548 • 8.07 g., **Copper-Zinc-Manganese-Nickel Clad Copper**, 26.5 mm. **Edge:** E PLURIBUS UNUM, date, mint mark **Note:** Date and mint mark on edge.

Date	Mintage	MS63	MS65	Prf65
2013P	5,310,700	2.00	3.00	—
2013D	3,920,000	2.00	3.00	—
2013S	1,449,415	—	—	5.00

William Howard Taft

KM# 549 • 8.07 g., **Copper-Zinc-Manganese-Nickel Clad Copper**, 26.5 mm. **Edge:** E PLURIBUS UNUM, date, mint mark **Note:** Date and mint mark on edge.

Date	Mintage	MS63	MS65	Prf65
2013P	4,760,000	2.00	3.00	—
2013D	3,360,000	2.00	3.00	—
2013S	1,449,415	—	—	5.00

Woodrow Wilson

KM# 550 • 8.07 g., **Copper-Zinc-Manganese-Nickel Clad Copper**, 26.5 mm. **Edge:** E PLURIBUS UNUM, date, mint mark **Note:** Date and mint mark on edge.

Date	Mintage	MS63	MS65	Prf65
2013P	4,620,000	2.00	3.00	—
2013D	3,360,000	2.00	3.00	—
2013S	1,449,415	—	—	5.00

Warren G. Harding

KM# 571 • 8.07 g., **Copper-Zinc-Manganese-Nickel Clad Copper**, 26.5 mm. **Note:** Date and mint mark on edge.

Date	Mintage	MS63	MS65	Prf65
2014P	—	2.00	3.00	—
2014D	—	2.00	3.00	—
2014S	—	—	—	5.00

Calvin Coolidge

KM# 572 • 8.07 g., **Copper-Zinc-Manganese-Nickel Clad Copper**, 26.5 mm. **Note:** Date and mint mark on edge.

Date	Mintage	MS63	MS65	Prf65
2014P	—	2.00	5.00	—
2014D	—	2.00	5.00	—
2014S	—	—	—	5.00

Herbert Hoover

KM# 573 • 8.07 g., **Copper-Zinc-Manganese-Nickel Clad Copper**, 26.5 mm. **Note:** Date and mint mark on edge.

Date	Mintage	MS63	MS65	Prf65
2014P	—	2.00	3.00	—
2014D	—	2.00	3.00	—
2014S	—	—	—	5.00

Franklin D. Roosevelt

KM# 574 • 8.07 g., **Copper-Zinc-Manganese-Nickel Clad Copper**, 26.5 mm. **Note:** Date and mint mark on edge.

Date	Mintage	MS63	MS65	Prf65
2014P	—	2.00	3.00	—
2014D	—	2.00	3.00	—
2014S	—	—	—	5.00

DOLLAR

DOLLAR

$1

GOLD
Liberty Head - Type 1
Liberty head left within circle of stars obverse
Value, date within 3/4 wreath reverse

KM# 73 • 1.67 g., 0.900 **Gold** 0.05 oz. AGW, 13 mm. • **Rev. Legend:** UNITED STATES OF AMERICA **Designer:** James B. Longacre **Note:** On the "closed wreath" varieties of 1849, the wreath on the reverse extends closer to the numeral 1.

Date	Mintage	F12	VF20	XF40	AU50	MS60
1849 open wreath	688,567	175	225	265	300	650
1849 small head, no L	—	—	—	—	—	—
1849 closed wreath	Inc. above	175	210	245	270	335
1849C closed wreath	11,634	800	950	1,450	2,400	8,850
1849C open wreath	Inc. above	135,000	240,000	320,000	475,000	600,000
1849D open wreath	21,588	1,050	1,300	1,875	2,600	6,000
1849O open wreath	215,000	195	235	310	390	800
1850	481,953	175	210	245	270	335
1850C	6,966	900	1,150	1,600	2,350	9,000
1850D	8,382	1,050	1,250	1,725	2,950	12,500
1850O	14,000	200	275	390	775	3,300
1851	3,317,671	175	210	245	270	335
1851C	41,267	840	1,150	1,500	1,700	3,150
1851D	9,882	1,000	1,250	1,675	2,500	5,650
1851O	290,000	160	195	240	265	775
1852	2,045,351	175	210	245	270	335
1852C	9,434	845	1,040	1,400	1,700	5,100
1852D	6,360	1,025	1,250	1,675	2,300	10,000
1852O	140,000	130	175	260	385	1,400
1853	4,076,051	175	210	245	270	335
1853C	11,515	900	1,100	1,400	2,000	5,600
1853D	6,583	1,040	1,250	1,700	2,650	9,700
1853O	290,000	135	160	235	270	665
1854	736,709	175	210	245	270	335
1854D	2,935	1,050	1,400	2,350	6,000	13,000
1854S	14,632	260	360	525	775	2,450

Indian Head - Type 2
Indian head with headdress left obverse   Value, date within wreath reverse

KM# 83 • 1.67 g., 0.900 **Gold** 0.05 oz. AGW, 15 mm. • **Obv. Legend:** UNITED STATES OF AMERICA **Designer:** James B. Longacre

Date	Mintage	F12	VF20	XF40	AU50	MS60
1854	902,736	250	280	410	535	1,680
1855	758,269	250	280	410	535	1,680
1855C	9,803	975	1,450	3,750	11,500	33,000
1855D	1,811	3,250	4,750	9,800	22,000	48,000
1855O	55,000	345	440	600	1,500	7,800
1856S	24,600	525	820	1,325	2,500	8,650

Indian Head - Type 3
Indian head with headdress left obverse   Value, date within wreath reverse

KM# 86 • 1.67 g., 0.900 **Gold** 0.05 oz. AGW, 15 mm. • **Obv. Legend:** UNITED STATES OF AMERICA **Designer:** James B. Longacre **Note:** The 1856 varieties are distinguished by whether the 5 in the date is slanted or upright. The 1873 varieties are distinguished by the amount of space between the upper left and lower left serifs in the 3.

Date	Mintage	F12	VF20	XF40	AU50	MS60	PF65
1856 upright 5	1,762,936	225	260	310	335	510	—
1856 slanted 5	Inc. above	220	250	285	300	360	55,000
1856 D	1,460	2,350	3,650	5,800	8,000	32,000	—
1857	774,789	210	245	285	300	360	32,000
1857 C	13,280	900	1,150	1,750	3,750	13,250	—
1857 D	3,533	1,000	1,300	2,300	4,400	11,000	—
1857 S	10,000	260	520	650	1,300	6,200	—
1858	117,995	210	245	285	300	360	28,500
1858 D	3,477	1,025	1,250	1,600	2,850	10,000	—
1858 S	10,000	300	400	575	1,450	5,350	—
1859	168,244	210	245	285	300	360	17,000
1859 C	5,235	885	1,050	1,700	4,250	9,850	—
1859 D	4,952	1,050	1,500	2,100	3,250	10,500	—
1859 S	15,000	210	265	525	1,250	5,500	—
1860	36,668	210	245	285	300	360	16,500
1860 D	1,566	2,150	2,500	4,200	7,000	19,500	—
1860 S	13,000	300	380	500	750	2,900	—
1861	527,499	210	245	285	300	360	14,850
1861 D mintage unrecorded	—	4,950	7,000	11,000	21,000	41,500	—
1862	1,361,390	210	245	285	300	360	15,000
1863	6,250	370	500	925	2,100	3,900	18,000
1864	5,950	290	370	475	825	1,050	18,000
1865	3,725	290	370	590	750	1,600	18,000
1866	7,130	300	385	470	685	1,025	18,000
1867	5,250	325	420	525	675	1,160	17,500
1868	10,525	265	290	415	500	1,025	19,000
1869	5,925	315	460	530	725	1,150	17,000
1870	6,335	255	290	410	500	875	16,000
1870 S	3,000	300	475	785	1,250	2,650	—
1871	3,930	260	290	390	480	750	18,000
1872	3,530	260	295	400	480	975	18,500
1873 closed 3	125,125	325	425	825	950	1,650	—
1873 open 3	Inc. above	210	245	285	300	360	—
1874	198,820	210	245	285	300	360	30,000
1875	420	1,650	2,350	4,650	5,200	10,000	32,500
1876	3,245	240	300	360	475	725	16,750
1877	3,920	210	210	340	460	725	18,000
1878	3,020	195	250	365	480	675	15,500
1879	3,030	210	225	285	330	525	14,000
1880	1,636	235	180	300	300	475	14,000
1881	7,707	235	270	300	300	460	11,500
1882	5,125	245	275	300	300	460	10,500
1883	11,007	235	265	300	300	460	11,000
1884	6,236	235	265	—	300	460	10,000
1885	12,261	235	265	300	300	460	10,000
1886	6,016	235	265	300	300	460	10,000
1887	8,543	235	265	300	300	460	10,000
1888	16,580	235	265	300	300	460	10,000
1889	30,729	235	265	300	300	390	10,000

$2.50 (QUARTER EAGLE)

GOLD
Liberty Cap
Liberty cap on head, right, flanked by stars obverse   Heraldic eagle reverse

KM# 27 • 4.37 g., 0.916 Gold 0.13 oz. AGW, 20mm. • **Obv. Legend:** LIBERTY **Rev. Legend:** UNITED STATES OF AMERICA **Designer:** Robert Scot **Note:** The 1796 "no stars" variety does not have stars on the obverse. The 1804 varieties are distinguished by the number of stars on the obverse.

Date		Mintage	F12	VF20	XF40	MS60
1796	no stars	963	55,000	71,500	100,000	245,000
1796	stars	432	26,500	32,500	65,000	185,000
1797		427	20,000	25,000	45,000	125,000
1798	close date	1,094	6,250	8,650	16,500	60,000
1798	wide date	Inc. above	5,250	7,650	15,500	57,500
1802/1		3,035	4,250	6,650	14,500	34,500
1804	13-star reverse	3,327	45,000	65,000	125,000	—
1804	14-star reverse	Inc. above	4,550	7,150	15,500	46,500
1805		1,781	4,250	6,650	14,500	37,000
1806/4		1,616	4,250	6,650	15,000	38,000
1806/5		Inc. above	6,250	8,650	21,500	95,000
1807		6,812	4,250	6,650	14,500	34,500

Turban Head
Turban on head left flanked by stars obverse   Banner above eagle reverse

KM# 40 • 4.37 g., 0.916 Gold 0.13 oz. AGW, 20mm. • **Rev. Legend:** UNITED STATES OF AMERICA **Designer:** John Reich

Date	Mintage	F12	VF20	XF40	MS60
1808	2,710	26,500	36,500	54,500	175,000

Turban on head left within circle of stars obverse   Banner above eagle reverse

KM# 46 • 4.37 g., 0.916 Gold 0.13 oz. AGW, 18.5mm. • **Rev. Legend:** UNITED STATES OF AMERICA **Designer:** John Reich

Date	Mintage	F12	VF20	XF40	MS60
1821	6,448	6,250	8,250	12,350	32,500
1824/21	2,600	6,250	8,250	12,250	32,000
1825	4,434	6,250	8,250	12,250	30,000
1826/25	760	6,750	9,000	13,000	80,000
1827	2,800	6,350	8,450	12,750	31,500

Turban on head left within circle of stars obverse   Banner above eagle reverse

KM# 49 • 4.37 g., 0.916 Gold 0.13 oz. AGW, 18.2mm. • **Rev. Legend:** UNITED STATES OF AMERICA **Designer:** John Reich

Date	Mintage	F12	VF20	XF40	MS60
1829	3,403	5,400	6,950	9,950	21,500
1830	4,540	5,400	6,950	9,950	21,500
1831	4,520	5,400	6,950	9,950	22,000
1832	4,400	5,400	6,950	9,950	21,500
1833	4,160	5,400	6,950	9,950	22,000
1834	4,000	9,000	12,450	20,000	49,500

Classic head
Classic head left within circle of stars obverse   No motto above eagle reverse

KM# 56 • 4.18 g., 0.899 Gold 0.12 oz. AGW, 18.2mm. • **Rev. Legend:** UNITED STATES OF AMERICA **Designer:** William Kneass

Date	Mintage	F12	VF20	XF40	MS60
1834	112,234	260	475	675	3,300
1835	131,402	260	475	675	3,200
1836	547,986	260	475	675	3,100
1837	45,080	280	500	800	4,000
1838	47,030	260	500	625	3,200
1838 C	7,880	950	1,700	3,000	27,000
1839	27,021	260	500	900	5,500
1839 C	18,140	880	1,500	2,650	26,500
1839/8	Inc. above	—	—	—	—
1839 D	13,674	880	1,750	3,450	24,000
1839 O	17,781	400	700	1,100	7,250

Coronet Head
Coronet head left within circle of stars obverse   No motto above eagle reverse

1848 "Cal." reverse

KM# 72 • 4.18 g., 0.900 **Gold** 0.12 oz. AGW, 18mm. • **Rev. Legend:** UNITED STATES OF AMERICA **Designer:** Christian Gobrecht

Date	Mintage	F12	VF20	XF40	AU50	MS60	PF65
1840	18,859	275	375	900	2,950	6,000	—
1840 C	12,822	1,250	1,400	1,600	6,000	13,000	—
1840 D	3,532	2,500	3,200	8,700	15,500	35,000	—
1840 O	33,580	325	400	825	2,100	11,000	—
1841	—	—	48,000	100,000	—	—	—
1841 C	10,281	1,100	1,500	2,000	3,500	18,500	—
1841 D	4,164	1,350	2,100	4,750	11,000	25,000	—
1842	2,823	1,100	900	2,600	6,500	20,000	140,000
1842 C	6,729	1,250	1,700	3,500	8,000	27,000	—
1842 D	4,643	1,300	2,100	4,000	11,750	—	—
1842 O	19,800	325	390	1,200	2,500	14,000	—
1843	100,546	275	345	450	915	3,000	140,000
1843 C small date, Crosslet 4	26,064	1,500	2,400	5,500	9,000	29,000	—
1843 C large date, Plain 4	Inc. above	1,200	1,600	2,200	3,500	8,800	—
1843 D small date, Crosslet 4	36,209	1,350	1,800	2,350	3,250	10,500	—
1843 O small date, Crosslet 4	288,002	285	315	375	400	1,700	—
1843 O large date, Plain 4	76,000	295	370	465	1,600	8,000	—
1844	6,784	350	400	850	2,000	7,500	140,000

$2.50

$2.50

Date	Mintage	F12	VF20	XF40	AU50	MS60	PF65
1844 C	11,622	1,050	1,600	2,600	7,000	20,000	—
1844 D	17,332	1,100	1,650	2,200	3,200	7,800	—
1845	91,051	325	395	360	600	1,275	140,000
1845 D	19,460	1,100	1,900	2,600	3,900	15,000	—
1845 O	4,000	575	1,050	2,300	9,000	20,000	—
1846	21,598	320	365	500	950	6,000	140,000
1846 C	4,808	1,100	1,575	3,500	8,950	18,750	—
1846 D	19,303	1,000	1,400	2,000	3,000	12,000	—
1846 O	66,000	350	385	400	1,150	6,500	—
1847	29,814	275	350	360	825	3,800	—
1847 C	23,226	900	1,800	2,300	3,500	7,250	—
1847 D	15,784	950	1,650	2,250	3,250	10,500	—
1847 O	124,000	275	365	400	1,000	4,000	—
1848	7,497	340	500	850	2,400	7,000	125,000
1848 CAL.	1,389	35,000	40,000	45,000	50,000	55,000	—
1848 C	16,788	950	1,600	2,100	3,800	13,750	—
1848 D	13,771	1,100	2,000	2,500	4,500	12,000	—
1849	23,294	295	375	475	1,000	2,600	—
1849 C	10,220	975	1,475	2,150	5,150	23,500	—
1849 D	10,945	1,050	2,000	2,500	4,500	18,000	—
1850	252,923	265	310	360	385	1,100	—
1850 C	9,148	800	1,500	2,000	3,600	13,500	—
1850 D	12,148	950	1,700	2,350	3,450	1,600	—
1850 O	84,000	300	345	485	1,300	4,500	—
1851	1,372,748	265	300	330	345	495	—
1851 C	14,923	900	1,650	2,250	3,450	9,850	—
1851 D	11,264	1,000	1,800	2,500	3,850	12,000	—
1851 O	148,000	300	335	370	900	4,450	—
1852	1,159,681	265	300	330	345	495	—
1852 C	9,772	975	1,500	2,050	4,250	16,500	—
1852 D	4,078	1,100	1,650	2,950	7,000	17,500	—
1852 O	140,000	300	335	365	1,000	5,000	—
1853	1,404,668	265	300	330	345	495	—
1853 D	3,178	1,250	1,975	3,450	4,850	18,000	—
1854	596,258	265	300	330	345	495	—
1854 C	7,295	1,100	1,450	2,450	4,750	13,500	—
1854 D	1,760	2,100	3,350	6,950	11,500	27,500	—
1854 O	153,000	300	335	365	420	1,600	—
1854 S	246	95,000	175,000	300,000	—	—	—
1855	235,480	270	305	335	350	495	—
1855 C	3,677	1,050	1,675	3,250	6,350	19,500	—
1855 D	1,123	2,100	3,350	7,500	16,500	50,000	—
1856	384,240	270	305	335	350	515	75,000
1856 C	7,913	985	1,600	2,500	4,000	14,500	—
1856 D	874	3,850	6,500	12,850	30,000	72,500	—
1856 O	21,100	300	345	750	1,350	7,500	—
1856 S	71,120	300	335	425	950	4,350	—
1857	214,130	270	305	335	350	515	75,000
1857 D	2,364	1,025	1,650	2,775	3,700	13,200	—
1857 O	34,000	300	335	425	1,050	4,450	—
1857 S	69,200	300	335	365	875	5,350	—
1858	47,377	275	310	340	395	1,250	59,000
1858 C	9,056	965	1,500	2,100	3,350	9,250	—
1859	39,444	275	310	350	425	1,250	61,000
1859 D	2,244	1,150	1,850	3,100	3,950	18,500	—
1859 S	15,200	310	365	950	2,350	5,000	—
1860	22,675	275	310	340	450	1,150	58,000
1860 C	7,469	985	1,475	2,175	3,100	20,000	—
1860 S	35,600	310	365	625	1,150	3,850	—
1861	1,283,878	270	305	335	350	850	31,500
1861 S	24,000	320	400	900	3,250	7,250	—
1862	98,543	310	340	600	1,950	5,150	32,500
1862/1	Inc. above	650	875	1,850	3,450	7,500	—
1862 S	8,000	650	875	2,050	4,200	17,500	—
1863	30	—	—	—	—	—	95,000
1863 S	10,800	465	475	1,475	3,150	13,500	—
1864	2,874	3,750	5,450	11,500	22,500	47,500	27,000
1865	1,545	2,950	4,750	7,750	18,000	37,500	30,000
1865 S	23,376	320	335	595	1,450	4,400	—
1866	3,110	775	1,250	3,150	5,750	11,500	25,000
1866 S	38,960	365	400	625	1,500	5,950	—
1867	3,250	350	395	850	1,150	4,750	27,000
1867 S	28,000	300	335	575	1,600	4,100	—
1868	3,625	300	335	395	640	1,625	27,000
1868 S	34,000	270	305	365	1,050	3,850	—
1869	4,345	300	335	435	685	2,750	24,500
1869 S	29,500	300	365	445	800	4,000	—

Date	Mintage	F12	VF20	XF40	AU50	MS60	PF65
1870	4,555	290	375	550	900	4,150	33,500
1870 S	16,000	270	345	465	1,000	4,900	—
1871	5,350	295	360	385	850	3,100	36,500
1871 S	22,000	270	345	415	550	2,350	—
1872	3,030	305	450	800	1,250	4,650	33,500
1872 S	18,000	275	340	485	1,150	4,350	—
1873 closed 3	178,025	270	330	375	395	435	42,500
1873 open 3	Inc. above	270	325	355	375	405	—
1873 S	27,000	280	345	395	900	2,800	—
1874	3,940	285	345	425	850	2,250	42,500
1875	420	1,950	3,500	5,500	11,000	24,000	70,000
1875 S	11,600	270	330	375	850	3,950	—
1876	4,221	285	345	675	1,250	3,350	27,500
1876 S	5,000	285	345	625	1,150	2,850	—
1877	1,652	310	395	875	1,250	3,250	35,000
1877 S	35,400	265	325	355	415	750	—
1878	286,260	265	320	345	370	410	35,000
1878 S	178,000	265	320	345	375	415	—
1879	88,990	270	325	355	385	435	26,000
1879 S	43,500	270	340	365	765	2,500	—
1880	2,996	275	345	385	750	1,400	26,000
1881	691	950	2,150	3,150	5,250	9,850	26,500
1882	4,067	270	330	375	550	1,050	23,500
1883	2,002	280	395	750	1,350	3,350	23,500
1884	2,023	275	375	440	750	1,600	23,500
1885	887	400	750	1,850	2,650	4,850	22,500
1886	4,088	275	340	375	650	1,150	23,500
1887	6,282	275	340	365	500	850	17,500
1888	16,098	270	335	365	450	520	18,000
1889	17,648	270	335	365	450	535	20,500
1890	8,813	275	340	365	500	600	18,500
1891	11,040	—	—	—	—	—	17,500
1891	Inc. above	275	335	365	475	585	—
1892	2,545	275	330	365	500	950	15,500
1893	30,106	270	330	355	375	400	15,500
1894	4,122	275	330	365	440	800	18,000
1895	6,199	265	325	355	400	525	16,750
1896	19,202	265	325	350	370	400	16,750
1897	29,904	270	325	350	370	400	16,750
1898	24,165	265	325	345	365	385	15,000
1899	27,350	265	325	345	365	385	15,000
1900	67,205	265	325	345	365	385	15,000
1901	91,322	265	325	345	365	385	15,000
1902	133,733	265	320	345	365	385	15,000
1903	201,257	265	320	345	365	385	15,000
1904	160,960	265	320	345	365	385	15,000
1905	217,944	265	320	345	365	385	15,000
1906	176,490	265	320	345	365	385	15,000
1907	336,448	265	320	345	365	385	15,000

Indian Head

KM# 128 • 4.18 g., 0.900 Gold 0.12 oz. AGW, 18mm. • **Designer:** Bela Lyon Pratt

Date	Mintage	VF20	XF40	AU50	MS60	MS63	MS65	Prf65
1908	565,057	320	325	355	425	915	2,800	30,000
1909	441,899	320	325	355	435	1,650	6,540	50,000
1910	492,682	320	325	355	425	1,550	7,500	40,000
1911	704,191	320	325	355	425	930	8,500	30,000
1911D D strong D	55,680	2,750	3,800	4,650	8,150	18,750	65,000	—
1911 1D weak D	Inc. above	1,150	1,950	2,850	4,950	—	—	—
1912	616,197	320	325	360	450	1,750	11,850	30,000
1913	722,165	320	325	355	425	855	7,500	30,000
1914	240,117	325	325	415	610	4,950	34,500	35,000
1914D	448,000	320	325	365	440	1,500	36,500	—
1915	606,100	320	325	350	425	890	6,500	37,500
1925D	578,000	320	325	350	415	640	2,200	—
1926	446,000	320	325	350	415	640	2,200	—
1927	388,000	320	325	350	415	640	2,200	—
1928	416,000	320	325	350	415	640	2,200	—
1929	532,000	320	325	365	445	730	7,000	—

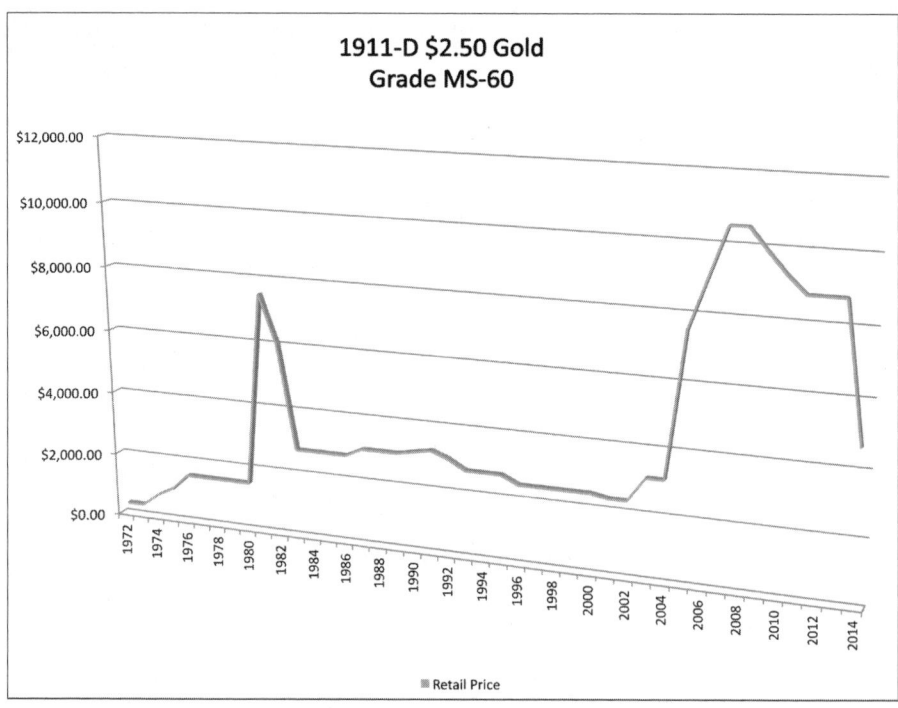

1911-D $2.50 Gold
Grade MS-60

Retail Price

$3

GOLD

Indian head with headdress, left obverse   Value, date within wreath reverse

KM# 84 • 5.02 g., 0.900 Gold 0.14 oz. AGW, 20.5mm. • **Obv. Legend:** UNITED STATES OF AMERICA **Designer:** James B. Longacre **Note:** The 1873 "closed-3" and "open-3" varieties are distinguished by the amount of space between the upper left and lower left serifs of the 3 in the date.

Date	Mintage	VF20	XF40	AU50	MS60	MS65	Prf65
1854	138,618	860	1,150	1,290	2,650	19,500	175,000
1854D	1,120	8,300	16,500	35,000	77,500	—	—
1854O	24,000	1,150	2,650	5,000	50,000	—	—
1855	50,555	840	1,175	1,750	3,200	44,000	150,000
1855S	6,600	1,055	2,750	6,950	25,000	—	—
1856	26,010	830	1,125	1,650	3,250	45,000	115,000
1856S	34,500	930	1,600	2,650	12,500	—	—
1857	20,891	830	1,125	1,415	3,500	44,000	105,000
1857S	14,000	980	2,775	5,350	21,000	—	—
1858	2,133	980	1,900	3,650	9,300	50,000	95,000
1859	15,638	930	1,725	1,975	3,250	32,500	60,000
1860	7,155	930	1,625	2,150	3,600	33,000	60,000
1860S	7,000	980	2,450	8,650	26,000	—	—
1861	6,072	955	2,550	3,650	6,900	37,500	60,000
1862	5,785	955	2,350	3,650	6,900	44,500	60,000
1863	5,039	930	2,350	3,650	6,900	34,500	60,000
1864	2,680	980	2,350	3,650	6,900	39,500	60,000
1865	1,165	1,275	2,700	6,500	11,700	55,000	60,000
1866	4,030	1,000	1,500	2,250	3,500	38,500	60,000
1867	2,650	1,025	1,550	2,650	3,600	39,500	60,000

Date	Mintage	VF20	XF40	AU50	MS60	MS65	Prf65
1868	4,875	875	1,475	2,125	3,350	33,000	60,000
1869	2,525	1,150	1,550	2,350	4,300	50,000	60,000
1870	3,535	1,030	1,625	2,450	4,400	—	60,000
1870S unique	—	—	4,000,000	—	—	—	—
Note: H. W. Bass Collection. AU50, cleaned. Est. value, $1,250,000.							
1871	1,330	1,030	1,575	2,375	4,000	42,500	60,000
1872	2,030	930	1,525	2,250	3,850	4,500	60,000
1873 closed 3, mintage unknown	—	4,000	9,000	16,000	27,500	—	95,000
1873 open 3, proof only	25	—	—	—	—	—	90,000
1874	41,820	830	1,125	1,265	2,250	16,750	62,500
1875 proof only	20	20,000	28,000	47,500	—	—	225,000
1876	45	6,000	11,500	18,000	—	—	97,500
1877	1,488	1,350	3,150	7,500	23,000	—	65,000
1878	82,324	830	1,125	1,265	2,250	14,500	65,000
1879	3,030	880	1,325	2,000	3,200	22,500	50,000
1880	1,036	950	2,100	3,375	4,700	27,000	42,000
1881	554	1,400	3,350	6,750	12,000	38,500	36,500
1882	1,576	955	1,475	2,350	3,600	30,000	35,500
1883	989	1,000	1,625	2,950	3,800	34,500	35,500
1884	1,106	1,285	2,000	2,800	3,650	34,500	35,500
1885	910	1,300	2,050	3,450	5,200	38,500	34,500
1886	1,142	1,250	2,250	2,875	5,000	47,500	34,500
1887	6,160	930	1,550	2,175	3,250	22,500	34,500
1888	5,291	980	1,525	2,125	3,150	15,000	34,500
1889	2,429	955	1,475	2,000	3,200	22,500	34,500

$5 (HALF EAGLE)

GOLD
Liberty Cap
Liberty Cap on head, right, flanked by stars obverse   Small eagle reverse

KM# 19 • 8.75 g., 0.916 Gold 0.26 oz. AGW

Date	Mintage	F12	VF20	XF40	MS60
1795	8,707	19,500	25,000	31,000	79,500
1796/95	6,196	20,500	25,350	32,750	84,500
1797 15 obverse stars	Inc. above	23,000	27,500	42,250	—
1797 16 obverse stars	Inc. above	21,000	25,850	41,000	210,000
1798	—	112,000	185,000	350,000	—

Large Heraldic eagle reverse

KM# 28 • 8.75 g., 0.916 Gold 0.26 oz. AGW, 25mm. • Obv. Legend: LIBERTY Rev. Legend: UNITED STATES OF AMERICA Designer: Robert Scot

Date	Mintage	F12	VF20	XF40	MS60
1795	Inc. above	10,000	16,500	22,500	85,000
1797/95	3,609	10,850	17,500	24,000	155,000
1797 15 star obv.; Unique	—	—	—	—	—
Note: Smithsonian collection					
1797 16 star obv.; Unique					
Note: Smithsonian collection					

Date	Mintage	F12	VF20	XF40	MS60
1798 small 8	24,867	4,850	6,650	10,100	—
1798 large 8, 13-star reverse	Inc. above	4,050	5,050	8,350	33,500
1798 large 8, 14-star reverse	Inc. above	5,050	6,650	10,950	—
1799 small reverse stars	7,451	3,850	4,900	11,100	21,500
1799 large reverse stars	Inc. above	3,950	4,750	14,200	31,700
1800	37,628	3,850	4,650	7,100	15,850
1802/1	53,176	3,850	4,650	7,100	15,850
1803/2	33,506	3,850	4,650	7,100	15,850
1804 small 8	30,475	3,850	4,650	7,100	15,850
1804 small 8 over large 8	Inc. above	3,950	4,850	7,600	17,850
1805	33,183	3,850	4,650	7,100	15,850
1806 pointed 6	64,093	3,850	4,650	7,100	17,750
1806 round 6	Inc. above	3,850	4,650	7,100	15,850
1807	32,488	3,850	4,650	7,100	15,850

Turban Head

Caped draped bust, left, flanked by stars obverse   Heraldic eagle reverse

 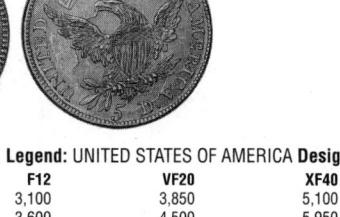

KM# 38 • 8.75 g., 0.916 Gold 0.26 oz. AGW, 25mm. • **Rev. Legend:** UNITED STATES OF AMERICA **Designer:** John Reich

Date	Mintage	F12	VF20	XF40	MS60
1807	51,605	3,100	3,850	5,100	13,850
1808	55,578	3,600	4,500	5,950	18,850
1808/7	Inc. above	3,100	3,850	5,100	13,850
1809/8	33,875	3,100	3,850	5,100	13,850
1810 small date, small 5	100,287	17,500	32,500	48,500	125,000
1810 small date, large 5	Inc. above	3,100	3,850	5,100	16,250
1810 large date, small 5	Inc. above	17,500	37,500	60,000	135,000
1810 large date, large 5	Inc. above	3,100	3,850	5,100	13,850
1811 small 5	99,581	3,100	3,850	5,100	13,850
1811 tall 5	Inc. above	3,100	3,850	5,100	13,850
1812	58,087	3,100	3,850	5,100	13,850

Caped head, left, within circle of stars obverse

KM# 43 • 8.75 g., 0.916 Gold 0.26 oz. AGW, 25mm. • **Rev. Legend:** UNITED STATES OF AMERICA **Designer:** John Reich

Date	Mintage	F12	VF20	XF40	MS60
1813	95,428	3,150	3,850	6,250	13,250
1814/13	15,454	5,000	6,250	8,250	19,000
1815	635	32,500	50,000	200,000	245,000
Note: 1815, private sale, Jan. 1994, MS-61, $150,000					
1818	48,588	5,000	6,450	13,500	20,000
1818 5D over 50 Inc. Above	—	5,500	6,450	10,500	23,500
1819	51,723	8,800	16,500	50,000	64,000
1819 5D over 50 Inc. Above	—	5,500	11,000	35,000	64,000
1820 curved-base 2, small letters	263,806	5,250	6,600	12,850	22,500
1820 curved-base 2, large letters	Inc. above	5,100	6,400	12,000	20,000
1820 square-base 2	Inc. above	5,000	6,250	11,500	19,000
1821	34,641	12,000	22,000	43,000	115,000
1822 3 known	—	500,000	90,000	1,250,000	1,000,000
1823	14,485	5,500	6,250	13,500	27,500
1824	17,340	5,500	10,500	32,000	38,000
1825/21	29,060	5,750	9,500	25,000	39,500
1825/24	Inc. above	—	—	550,000	750,000
Note: 1825/4, Bowers & Merena, March 1989, XF, $148,500.					
1826	18,069	5,500	7,800	16,500	30,000

Date	Mintage	F12	VF20	XF40	MS60
1827	24,913	6,000	10,000	23,500	34,500
1828/7	28,029	15,000	28,500	66,000	125,000
Note: 1828/7, Bowers & Merena, June 1989, XF, $20,900.					
1828	Inc. above	6,000	13,000	30,000	60,000
1829 large planchet	57,442	15,000	28,500	65,000	125,000
Note: 1829 large planchet, Superior, July 1985, MS-65, $104,500.					
1829 small planchet	Inc. above	37,500	54,000	86,500	140,000
Note: 1829 small planchet, private sale, 1992 (XF-45), $89,000.					
1830 small "5D.	126,351	16,500	33,500	50,000	70,000
1830 large "5D.	Inc. above	16,500	33,500	50,000	70,000
1831	140,594	16,500	33,500	50,000	70,000
1832 curved-base 2, 12 stars	157,487	50,000	80,000	175,000	—
1832 square-base 2, 13 stars	Inc. above	16,500	33,500	50,000	70,000
1833 large date	Inc. above	16,500	33,500	50,000	70,000
1833 small date	193,630	17,500	35,500	60,000	90,000
1834 plain 4	50,141	16,500	33,500	50,000	70,000
1834 crosslet 4	Inc. above	17,500	35,500	60,000	80,000

Classic Head

Classic head, left, within circle of stars obverse   No motto above eagle reverse

KM# 57 • 8.36 g., 0.899 Gold 0.24 oz. AGW, 22.5mm. • **Rev. Legend:** UNITED STATES OF AMERICA **Designer:** William Kneass

Date	Mintage	F12	VF20	XF40	MS60	Prf65
1834 plain 4	540	585	795	1,350	4,750	—
1834 crosslet 4	1,050	1,850	3,150	6,500	25,000	—
1835	540	585	795	1,400	4,900	—
1836	540	585	795	1,400	4,750	—
1837	540	585	845	1,625	5,000	—
1838	540	585	975	1,850	5,400	—
1838C	1,475	4,150	8,750	13,000	42,500	—
1838D	1,375	2,100	4,650	10,250	31,000	—

Coronet Head

Coronet head, left, within circle of stars obverse   No motto above eagle reverse

KM# 69 • 8.36 g., 0.900 Gold 0.24 oz. AGW, 21.6mm. • **Rev. Legend:** UNITED STATES OF AMERICA **Designer:** Christian Gobrecht **Note:** Varieties for 1843 are distinguished by the size of the numerals in the date. One 1848 variety has "Cal." incsribed on the reverse, indicating it was made from California gold. The 1873 "closed-3" and "open-3" varieties are distinguished by the amount of space between the upper left and lower left serifs in the 3 in the date.

Date	Mintage	F12	VF20	XF40	MS60	Prf65
1839	450	540	655	1,100	3,850	—
1839/8 curved date	552	582	611	619	2,250	—
1839 C	1,250	1,900	3,200	5,750	20,000	—
1839 D	1,350	1,950	4,250	7,000	24,500	—
1840	440	540	645	1,100	3,300	—
1840 C	1,200	1,775	2,900	6,400	22,000	—
1840 D	1,200	1,750	3,000	5,800	15,000	—
1840 O	450	540	825	1,775	10,000	—
1841	450	500	875	1,550	4,850	—
1841 C	1,200	1,750	2,150	3,000	14,500	—
1841 D	1,300	1,775	2,350	3,150	12,500	—
1841 O 2 known	—	—	—	—	—	—
1842 small letters	450	490	1,000	2,750	13,500	—
1842 large letters	480	660	1,850	2,700	11,000	—

$5

Date	Mintage	F12	VF20	XF40	MS60	Prf65
1842 C small date	5,500	9,400	17,500	35,000	90,000	—
1842 C large date	1,050	1,650	2,150	2,950	15,000	—
1842 D small date	1,350	1,850	2,475	3,100	13,500	—
1842 D large date	1,650	2,350	5,950	12,500	48,000	—
1842 O	725	1,000	3,650	8,900	22,000	—
1843	440	490	565	595	1,825	—
1843 C	1,250	1,600	2,200	3,400	10,500	—
1843 D	1,250	1,750	2,250	3,000	10,600	—
1843 O small letters	470	610	1,400	2,100	17,500	—
1843 O large letters	450	604	1,050	1,800	11,000	—
1844	440	490	565	595	2,000	—
1844 C	1,300	1,700	2,750	5,200	185,800	—
1844 D	1,500	1,700	2,200	3,000	10,000	—
1844 O	474	524	595	650	4,000	—
1845	440	490	565	595	2,100	—
1845 D	1,300	1,800	2,275	3,000	10,500	—
1845 O	474	520	725	2,450	8,750	—
1846	440	510	565	595	2,350	—
1846 C	1,350	1,700	2,600	5,600	18,500	—
1846 D	1,250	1,750	2,250	3,250	11,500	—
1846 O	474	540	900	2,800	11,000	—
1847	440	490	565	595	1,850	—
1847 C	1,350	1,725	2,150	3,100	10,000	—
1847 D	1,400	1,800	2,250	3,000	9,000	—
1847 O	550	1,800	5,800	8,750	24,500	—
1848	440	490	565	595	1,900	—
1848 C	1,400	1,750	2,150	2,950	17,000	—
1848 D	1,450	1,800	2,250	3,100	12,750	—
1849	440	490	565	595	2,450	—
1849 C	1,500	1,750	2,200	3,000	10,000	—
1849 D	1,550	1,850	2,300	3,100	12,500	—
1850	440	510	565	925	3,350	—
1850 C	1,350	1,750	2,100	3,000	10,500	—
1850 D	1,450	1,800	2,250	3,600	24,500	—
1851	440	490	565	615	2,400	—
1851 C	1,300	1,700	2,150	3,000	11,750	—
1851 D	1,400	1,700	2,250	3,100	13,000	—
1851 O	280	590	1,400	3,600	12,500	—
1852	440	490	565	595	1,850	—
1852 C	1,350	1,750	2,100	3,000	6,250	—
1852 D	1,450	1,850	2,250	2,900	10,500	—
1853	440	490	565	595	1,850	—
1853 C	1,500	1,750	2,150	3,000	7,750	—
1853 D	1,550	1,850	2,250	3,100	8,250	—
1854	440	490	565	595	2,000	—
1854 C	1,400	1,750	2,150	3,400	12,500	—
1854 D	1,400	1,850	2,250	3,100	9,000	—
1854 O	470	520	595	1,300	7,500	—
1854 S	—	—	—	250,000	—	—

Note: 1854S, Bowers & Merena, Oct. 1982, AU-55, $170,000.

Date	Mintage	F12	VF20	XF40	MS60	Prf65
1855	440	490	565	595	2,000	—
1855 C	1,400	1,750	2,150	3,000	13,500	—
1855 D	1,500	1,850	2,300	3,100	1,500	—
1855 O	460	625	1,950	4,150	20,000	—
1855 S	470	620	900	2,100	15,500	—
1856	440	490	565	595	2,300	—
1856 C	1,450	1,750	2,100	3,000	20,000	—
1856 D	1,475	1,850	2,250	3,450	11,000	—
1856 O	470	650	1,200	4,750	14,000	—
1856 S	450	550	615	1,150	7,350	—
1857	440	490	565	595	2,000	123,500
1857 C	1,400	1,750	2,150	3,000	8,400	—
1857 D	1,500	1,850	2,300	3,200	12,000	—
1857 O	470	640	1,350	4,200	15,000	—
1857 S	450	500	615	1,000	9,000	—
1858	450	500	625	675	3,500	190,000
1858 C	1,400	1,750	2,150	3,000	9,500	—
1858 D	1,500	1,850	2,275	3,150	11,000	—
1858 S	490	750	2,200	5,000	31,000	—
1859	450	520	575	800	6,500	—
1859 C	1,400	1,750	2,150	3,150	11,000	—
1859 D	1,600	1,900	2,300	3,100	10,500	—
1859 S	615	1,125	3,250	4,750	26,000	—
1860	450	500	575	1,000	4,000	100,000
1860 C	1,500	1,900	2,400	3,450	12,000	—
1860 D	1,500	1,950	2,450	3,350	13,000	—
1860 S	500	1,050	2,000	5,250	23,000	—

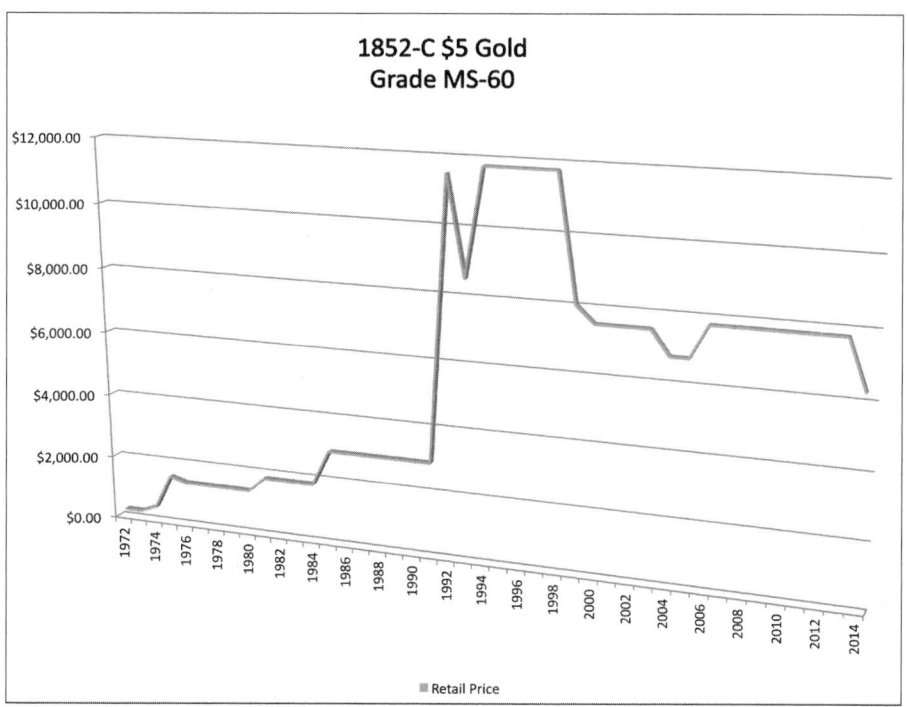

1852-C $5 Gold
Grade MS-60

Date	Mintage	F12	VF20	XF40	MS60	Prf65
1861	440	510	575	605	1,850	100,000
1861 C	1,500	2,250	4,850	7,000	23,000	—
1861 D	3,000	7,900	18,500	28,000	63,500	—
1861 S	500	975	4,100	6,000	—	—
1862	490	675	3,650	4,950	19,000	96,000
1862 S	1,500	2,900	5,500	8,750	40,000	—
1863	1,450	2,150	4,000	9,800	32,000	90,000
1863 S	600	1,325	7,250	8,650	35,500	—
1864	540	675	1,800	3,750	13,500	72,000
1864 S	2,300	4,450	20,000	27,500	50,000	—
1865	500	1,450	6,750	10,000	21,000	82,500
1865 S	475	1,200	2,400	4,850	16,000	—
1866 S	750	1,700	4,000	11,500	36,000	—

Coronet head, left, within circle of stars obverse   IN GOD WE TRUST above eagle reverse

KM# 101 • 8.36 g., 0.900 Gold 0.24 oz. AGW, 21.6mm. • **Rev. Legend:** UNITED STATES OF AMERICA **Designer:** Christian Gobrecht

Date	Mintage	VF20	XF40	AU50	MS60	MS63	MS65	Prf65
1866	6,730	750	1,650	3,500	16,500	—	—	70,000
1866S	34,920	900	2,600	8,800	25,000	—	—	—
1867	6,920	500	1,500	3,300	11,500	—	—	70,000
1867S	29,000	1,400	2,900	8,000	34,500	—	—	—
1868	5,725	650	1,000	3,500	11,500	—	—	70,000
1868S	52,000	486	1,550	4,000	20,000	—	—	—
1869	1,785	925	2,400	3,500	17,500	34,000	—	65,000
1869S	31,000	500	1,750	4,000	26,000	—	—	—
1870	4,035	800	2,000	2,850	18,000	—	—	75,000
1870CC	7,675	5,250	15,000	30,000	110,000	137,500	200,000	—

$5

Date	Mintage	VF20	XF40	AU50	MS60	MS63	MS65	Prf65
1870S	17,000	950	2,600	8,250	29,000	—	—	—
1871	3,230	900	1,700	3,300	12,500	—	—	70,000
1871CC	20,770	1,250	3,000	12,000	60,000	—	—	—
1871S	25,000	500	950	2,950	13,000	—	—	—
1872	1,690	850	1,925	3,000	15,000	18,000	—	60,000
1872CC	16,980	1,250	5,000	20,000	60,000	—	—	—
1872S	36,400	537	800	3,400	13,500	—	—	—
1873 closed 3	49,305	472	486	500	1,200	6,500	24,000	70,000
1873 open 3	63,200	467	477	487	850	3,650	—	—
1873CC	7,416	2,600	12,500	27,500	60,000	—	—	—
1873S	31,000	525	1,400	3,250	21,000	—	—	—
1874	3,508	660	1,675	2,500	13,000	26,000	—	66,000
1874CC	21,198	850	1,700	9,500	36,000	—	—	—
1874S	16,000	640	2,100	4,800	22,500	—	—	—
1875	220	34,000	45,000	60,000	190,000	—	—	185,000
1875CC	11,828	1,400	4,500	11,500	52,000	—	—	—
1875S	9,000	715	2,250	5,000	16,500	32,500	—	—
1876	1,477	1,100	2,500	4,125	11,000	14,500	55,000	60,000
1876CC	6,887	1,450	5,000	14,000	46,500	82,500	165,000	—
1876S	4,000	2,000	3,600	9,500	30,000	—	—	—
1877	1,152	900	2,750	4,000	13,750	29,000	—	75,000
1877CC	8,680	1,000	3,300	11,000	52,500	—	—	—
1877S	26,700	499	650	1,400	9,200	—	—	—
1878	131,740	469	480	524	550	2,000	—	50,000
1878CC	9,054	3,100	7,200	20,000	60,000	—	—	—
1878S	144,700	467	475	3,000	675	4,250	—	—
1879	301,950	467	475	485	520	2,000	12,000	55,000
1879CC	17,281	1,000	1,500	3,150	22,000	—	—	—
1879S	426,200	469	480	524	950	3,300	—	—
1880	3,166,436	462	470	480	500	840	7,500	54,000
1880CC	51,017	625	815	1,375	9,900	—	—	—
1880S	1,348,900	462	470	480	490	800	5,750	—
1881	5,708,802	462	470	480	500	775	4,800	54,000
1881/80	Inc. above	465	600	750	1,500	4,500	—	—
1881CC	13,886	650	1,500	7,000	22,500	60,000	—	—
1881S	969,000	462	470	480	500	775	7,150	—
1882	2,514,568	462	470	480	500	800	6,150	54,000
1882CC	82,817	625	625	900	7,500	40,000	—	—
1882S	969,000	462	470	480	510	800	4,500	—
1883	233,461	479	487	497	530	1,200	—	40,000
1883CC	12,958	625	1,100	3,200	18,000	—	—	—
1883S	83,200	479	478	490	1,000	2,950	—	—
1884	191,078	479	480	497	650	2,250	—	35,000
1884CC	16,402	625	975	3,000	17,000	—	—	—
1884S	177,000	479	487	497	490	2,000	—	—
1885	601,506	462	470	480	505	825	4,800	35,000
1885S	1,211,500	462	470	480	510	790	4,000	—
1886	388,432	462	470	480	510	1,125	5,600	44,000
1886S	3,268,000	462	470	480	510	815	4,500	—
1887	87	—	14,500	20,000	—	—	—	120,000
1887S	1,912,000	462	470	480	510	800	4,800	—
1888	18,296	477	485	497	550	1,500	—	29,000
1888S	293,900	467	475	547	1,200	4,000	—	—
1889	7,565	576	584	557	1,150	2,400	—	30,000
1890	4,328	499	507	550	2,200	6,500	—	27,000
1890CC	53,800	576	584	615	1,600	7,500	55,000	—
1891	61,413	469	480	524	640	2,000	5,400	29,000
1891CC	208,000	561	565	800	1,350	3,500	28,500	—
1892	753,572	462	470	480	530	1,350	7,000	30,000
1892CC	82,968	562	584	750	1,500	6,500	33,500	—
1892O	10,000	524	1,000	1,375	3,300	15,000	—	—
1892S	298,400	462	470	485	525	2,850	—	—
1893	1,528,197	462	470	480	510	1,150	3,900	34,000
1893CC	60,000	596	634	825	1,550	6,650	—	—
1893O	110,000	477	581	585	950	5,950	—	—
1893S	224,000	462	470	485	510	1,040	9,000	—
1894	957,955	462	470	480	500	905	2,600	35,000
1894O	16,600	479	487	570	1,300	5,500	—	—
1894S	55,900	489	487	575	2,900	10,000	—	—
1895	1,345,936	462	470	480	495	905	4,500	29,000
1895S	112,000	467	487	497	3,150	6,500	26,000	—
1896	59,063	462	470	485	510	1,650	4,500	30,000
1896S	155,400	469	480	524	1,150	6,000	24,500	—
1897	867,883	462	470	480	495	905	4,500	35,000
1897S	354,000	462	470	485	865	5,150	—	—
1898	633,495	462	470	480	500	905	6,000	30,000
1898S	1,397,400	462	470	480	495	1,310	—	—

Date	Mintage	VF20	XF40	AU50	MS60	MS63	MS65	Prf65
1899	1,710,729	462	470	480	495	890	3,600	30,000
1899S	1,545,000	462	470	480	495	1,260	9,600	—
1900	1,405,730	462	470	480	495	890	3,600	30,000
1900S	329,000	462	470	480	500	1,260	14,000	—
1901	616,040	462	470	480	495	890	3,650	27,000
1901S	3,648,000	462	470	480	495	890	3,600	—
1902	172,562	462	470	480	495	890	4,400	27,000
1902S	939,000	462	470	480	495	890	3,600	—
1903	227,024	462	470	480	500	905	4,000	27,000
1903S	1,855,000	462	470	480	495	890	3,600	—
1904	392,136	462	470	480	495	890	3,600	27,000
1904S	97,000	469	480	524	885	4,000	9,600	—
1905	302,308	462	470	480	500	905	4,000	27,000
1905S	880,700	462	470	480	495	3,350	9,600	—
1906	348,820	462	470	480	495	890	3,600	26,000
1906D	320,000	462	470	480	495	905	3,200	—
1906S	598,000	462	470	480	500	1,190	4,400	—
1907	626,192	462	470	480	495	890	3,400	23,000
1907D	888,000	462	470	480	495	890	3,400	—
1908	421,874	462	470	485	510	905	3,400	—

Indian Head

KM# 129 • 8.36 g., 0.900 Gold 0.24 oz. AGW, 21.6mm. • **Designer:** Bela Lyon Pratt

Date	Mintage	VF20	XF40	AU50	MS60	MS63	MS65	Prf65
1908	578,012	390	415	435	575	1,850	12,350	25,500
1908D	148,000	390	415	435	575	2,000	36,500	—
1908S	82,000	465	540	1,150	2,350	7,000	21,500	—
1909	627,138	390	415	435	555	1,850	13,350	36,000
1909D	3,423,560	390	415	435	555	1,600	12,350	—
1909O	34,200	4,850	6,500	10,000	31,500	75,000	550,000	—
1909S	297,200	420	455	495	1,350	13,250	51,000	—
1910	604,250	390	415	435	555	1,650	13,600	37,000
1910D	193,600	390	415	435	575	4,175	38,500	—
1910S	770,200	430	470	505	975	8,500	49,500	—
1911	915,139	390	415	435	555	1,475	13,350	28,500
1911D	72,500	625	825	1,600	6,850	41,500	265,000	—
1911S	1,416,000	400	450	490	600	5,850	43,000	—
1912	790,144	390	415	435	555	1,475	13,350	28,500
1912S	392,000	435	480	580	1,675	14,500	142,500	—
1913	916,099	390	415	435	555	1,475	13,350	28,000
1913S	408,000	430	475	620	1,450	13,250	120,000	—
1914	247,125	390	415	435	575	2,250	15,500	28,500
1914D	247,000	390	415	435	575	2,550	23,500	—
1914S	263,000	435	470	530	1,375	14,350	105,000	—
1915	588,075	390	415	435	555	1,475	14,350	39,000
1915S	164,000	445	490	615	1,950	17,000	110,000	—
1916S	240,000	415	450	515	770	6,750	33,500	—
1929	662,000	11,750	14,750	18,000	29,000	48,500	88,500	—

$5

$10 (EAGLE)

GOLD
Liberty Cap
Small eagle reverse

KM# 21 • 17.50 g., 0.916 Gold 0.51 oz. AGW, 33mm. • **Designer:** Robert Scot

Date	Mintage	F12	VF20	XF40	MS60
1795 13 leaves	5,583	28,500	33,850	48,500	122,500
1795 9 leaves	Inc. above	30,000	45,000	73,500	250,000
1796	4,146	27,500	36,000	50,000	135,000
1797 small eagle	3,615	31,500	40,000	55,000	200,000

Liberty cap on head, right, flanked by stars obverse Heraldic eagle reverse

KM# 30 • 17.50 g., 0.916 Gold 0.51 oz. AGW, 33mm. • **Obv. Legend:** LIBERTY **Rev. Legend:** UNITED STATES OF AMERICA **Designer:** Robert Scot

Date	Mintage	F12	VF20	XF40	MS60
1797 large eagle	10,940	9,800	12,850	21,400	58,500
1798/97 9 stars left, 4 right	900	13,500	19,000	34,500	127,500
1798/97 7 stars left, 6 right	842	28,500	38,500	87,500	235,000
1799 large star obv	37,449	9,350	10,750	18,200	37,500
1799 small star obv	Inc. above	9,350	10,750	18,200	37,500
1800	5,999	9,500	10,750	18,350	39,500
1801	44,344	9,250	10,900	17,400	37,500
1803 extra star	15,017	9,600	11,850	19,550	67,500
1803 large stars rev	Inc. above	9,250	11,400	17,800	37,500
1804 crosslet 4	3,757	16,500	22,750	31,500	92,500
1804 plain 4	—	—	—	—	400,000

Coronet Head
Old-style head, left, wthin circle of stars obverse   No motto above eagle reverse

KM# 66.1 • 16.72 g., 0.900 Gold 0.48 oz. AGW, 27mm. • **Rev. Legend:** UNITED STATES OF AMERICA **Designer:** Christian Gobrecht

Date	Mintage	F12	VF20	XF40	MS60	Prf65
1838	1,750	2,650	6,850	15,000	43,500	1,500,000
1839/8 Type of 1838	1,100	1,450	5,850	10,500	28,500	1,500,000
1839 large letters	800	1,150	2,150	5,500	32,000	

New-style head, left, within circle of stars obverse No motto above eagle reverse

KM# **66**.2 • 16.72 g., 0.900 Gold 0.48 oz. AGW, 27mm. • **Rev. Legend:** UNITED STATES OF AMERICA **Designer:** Christian Gobrecht

Date	Mintage	F12	VF20	XF40	MS60	Prf65
1839 small letters	975	1,550	6,850	9,500	75,000	—
1840	994	1,059	1,333	1,450	11,500	—
1841	974	1,049	1,233	1,200	9,000	—
1841 O	1,750	3,450	6,950	19,500	—	—
1842 small date	974	1,049	1,158	1,350	15,000	—
1842 large date	974	1,049	1,148	1,250	9,500	—
1842 O	974	1,059	1,463	2,850	22,500	—
1843	974	1,049	1,263	1,550	16,750	—
1843 O	974	1,059	1,218	1,300	12,000	—
1844	800	1,350	3,200	6,000	16,750	—
1844 O	974	1,059	1,403	2,850	15,000	—
1845	1,009	1,219	1,343	2,100	17,500	—
1845 O	994	1,059	875	2,750	16,500	—
1845 O repunched	1,069	1,419	3,850	5,950	—	—
1846	1,019	1,289	1,250	5,250	—	—
1846 O	974	1,059	1,150	3,900	—	—
1846/5	1,069	1,419	1,135	—	—	—
1847	974	1,049	1,093	1,153	3,450	—
1847 O	974	1,049	1,093	1,218	6,500	—
1848	974	1,049	1,158	900	5,000	—
1848 O	1,049	1,239	1,850	3,300	17,750	—
1849	974	1,049	1,093	1,153	3,400	—
1849 O	1,049	1,239	2,450	5,700	27,500	—
1850 large date	974	1,049	1,093	1,153	4,500	—
1850 small date	1,049	1,239	1,150	1,850	8,500	—
1850 O	994	1,074	1,275	3,200	19,500	—
1851	974	1,049	1,093	1,218	5,150	—
1851 O	974	1,059	1,148	1,050	6,650	—
1852	974	1,049	1,093	1,218	5,250	—
1852 O	1,049	1,219	1,650	3,750	27,500	—
1853	994	1,059	1,093	1,163	3,600	—
1853/2	994	1,074	1,428	1,850	14,950	—
1853 O	974	1,074	1,158	1,100	14,500	—
1854	974	1,049	1,118	1,278	6,250	—
1854 O small date	994	1,074	1,398	1,850	11,000	—
1854 O large date	1,049	1,214	925	2,000	9,450	—
1854 S	974	1,049	1,118	1,498	10,500	—
1855	974	1,049	1,093	1,153	4,750	—
1855 O	994	1,074	2,100	6,100	28,000	—
1856	974	1,049	1,093	1,163	4,250	—
1856 O	1,049	1,374	2,150	4,000	18,500	—
1856 S	974	1,049	1,168	1,100	9,000	—
1857	994	1,074	1,050	2,000	13,500	—
1857 O	1,149	1,800	3,650	4,450	—	—
1857 S	994	1,059	1,050	2,100	11,500	—
1858	3,000	5,200	8,250	13,500	35,000	—
1858 O	974	1,049	1,418	1,700	10,000	—
1858 S	900	1,600	3,950	6,950	—	—
1859	994	1,074	1,278	1,450	10,500	—
1859 O	2,000	4,250	10,500	20,000	—	—
1859 S	1,450	2,600	5,250	13,500	—	—
1860	1,019	1,114	1,328	1,300	8,450	175,000
1860 O	1,039	1,214	1,850	3,000	13,750	—
1860 S	1,400	2,950	6,400	14,750	—	—
1861	974	1,049	1,093	1,153	6,250	170,000
1861 S	690	1,600	3,750	6,250	—	—
1862	1,049	1,204	1,200	2,500	—	170,000

$10

$10

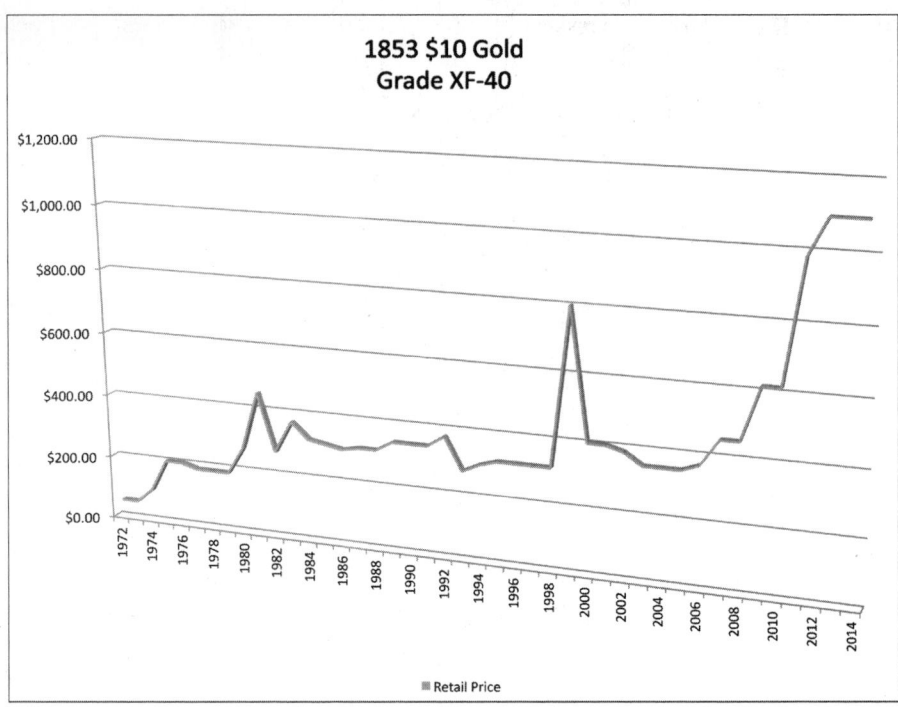

1853 $10 Gold
Grade XF-40

■ Retail Price

Date	Mintage	F12	VF20	XF40	MS60	Prf65
1862 S	700	2,000	3,450	5,750	—	—
1863	2,400	4,000	10,000	17,500	52,500	165,000
1863 S	700	1,600	3,750	8,800	29,500	—
1864	775	1,800	4,950	7,150	18,000	165,000
1864 S	2,600	5,100	17,500	27,500	—	—
1865	900	1,950	4,850	6,600	34,500	165,000
1865 S	1,700	4,850	12,500	18,000	—	—
1865 S over inverted 186	1,300	3,450	8,750	16,000	50,000	—
1866 S	1,000	2,650	5,950	12,000	—	—

IN GOD WE TRUST above eagle reverse

KM# 102 • 16.72 g., 0.900 Gold 0.48 oz. AGW, 27mm. • **Rev. Legend:** UNITED STATES OF AMERICA **Designer:** Christian Gobrecht

Date	Mintage	VF20	XF40	AU50	MS60	MS63	MS65	Prf65
1866	3,780	1,175	2,600	5,000	45,000	—	—	120,000
1866S	11,500	1,600	3,850	8,000	—	—	—	—
1867	3,140	1,550	2,750	5,000	35,000	—	—	—
1867S	9,000	2,350	6,650	9,850	—	—	—	—
1868	10,655	880	1,200	2,000	19,000	—	—	120,000
1868S	13,500	1,350	2,400	3,900	—	—	—	—
1869	1,855	1,550	3,000	5,150	36,000	—	—	—
1869S	6,430	1,450	2,700	5,750	30,000	60,000	—	—
1870	4,025	1,200	1,650	3,750	20,000	—	—	—
1870CC	5,908	32,500	50,000	85,000	—	—	—	—
1870S	8,000	1,250	2,850	6,500	33,500	—	—	—

Date	Mintage	VF20	XF40	AU50	MS60	MS63	MS65	Prf65
1871	1,820	1,500	3,000	4,850	28,000	—	—	120,000
1871CC	8,085	2,600	6,400	22,500	65,000	—	—	—
1871S	16,500	1,300	2,200	5,500	—	—	—	—
1872	1,650	2,400	5,000	8,700	25,000	42,500	—	90,000
1872CC	4,600	5,250	9,850	26,500	—	—	—	—
1872S	17,300	880	1,175	1,900	19,500	—	—	—
1873 closed 3	825	4,500	20,000	24,000	55,000	—	—	—
1873CC	4,543	6,000	23,500	32,000	—	—	—	—
1873S	12,000	1,150	2,650	4,850	27,500	—	—	—
1874	53,160	850	925	913	1,750	6,750	42,500	120,000
1874CC	16,767	2,850	4,650	12,000	52,500	100,000	200,000	—
1874S	10,000	1,275	2,950	6,500	—	—	—	—
1875	120	110,000	225,000	300,000	—	—	—	—
Note: 1875, Akers, Aug. 1990, Proof, $115,000.								
1875CC	7,715	4,250	9,850	25,000	75,000	150,000	—	—
1876	732	3,950	8,500	18,500	60,000	—	—	—
1876CC	4,696	3,850	10,500	21,500	—	—	—	—
1876S	5,000	1,300	3,750	7,500	—	—	—	—
1877	817	3,350	6,350	10,000	37,500	—	—	—
1877CC	3,332	2,400	6,750	15,000	—	—	—	—
1877S	17,000	832	1,050	2,450	20,000	—	—	—
1878	73,800	820	868	925	1,050	7,000	30,000	—
1878CC	3,244	3,850	8,650	19,000	—	—	—	—
1878S	26,100	1,000	1,150	2,050	14,000	29,500	—	—
1879	384,770	823	868	905	1,000	5,000	14,500	83,000
1879/78	Inc. above	830	880	1,100	1,250	2,850	—	—
1879CC	1,762	8,350	12,500	42,500	75,000	—	—	—
1879O	1,500	2,150	8,000	10,850	—	—	—	—
1879S	224,000	823	868	935	1,150	6,500	35,000	—
1880	1,644,876	805	830	875	980	2,000	25,000	—
1880CC	11,190	955	1,250	2,450	17,500	—	—	—
1880O	9,200	925	1,450	2,450	10,000	—	—	—
1880S	506,250	805	830	875	930	2,600	25,000	—
1881	3,877,260	805	830	875	910	1,350	15,000	63,000
1881CC	24,015	951	1,300	1,950	6,850	36,500	—	—
1881O	8,350	807	868	1,375	10,000	35,000	—	—
1881S	970,000	805	830	875	920	3,450	—	—
1882	2,324,480	805	830	875	910	1,200	19,500	63,000
1882CC	6,764	985	1,900	3,250	—	—	—	—
1882O	10,820	833	1,010	1,250	6,500	42,500	—	—
1882S	132,000	833	868	913	992	3,650	20,000	—
1883	208,740	805	830	875	920	1,500	40,000	63,000
1883CC	12,000	1,005	1,250	2,600	22,500	—	—	—
1883O	800	4,400	12,000	37,500	—	—	—	—
1883S	38,000	833	868	913	1,650	10,500	23,500	—
1884	76,905	833	868	913	1,000	4,200	15,000	53,000
1884CC	9,925	1,025	1,600	2,500	12,850	60,000	—	—
1884S	124,250	805	830	875	925	6,500	—	—
1885	253,527	805	830	875	910	3,000	23,000	57,500
1885S	228,000	805	830	875	910	4,400	—	—
1886	236,160	805	830	875	910	3,500	—	63,000
1886S	826,000	805	830	875	920	1,500	—	—
1887	53,680	833	868	925	975	6,500	—	95,000
1887S	817,000	805	830	875	920	2,000	17,500	—
1888	132,996	833	868	925	1,000	7,500	—	—
1888O	21,335	833	868	925	1,200	5,750	—	—
1888S	648,700	805	830	875	910	1,500	—	—
1889	4,485	863	1,025	1,075	3,500	10,000	—	53,000
1889S	425,400	805	830	875	920	1,650	53,000	—
1890	58,043	843	888	933	1,000	4,500	20,000	46,000
1890CC	17,500	1,085	1,145	1,350	4,000	20,000	—	—
1891	91,868	863	908	953	988	2,650	20,000	48,000
1891CC	103,732	1,085	1,145	1,350	2,300	7,500	85,000	—
1892	797,552	805	830	875	910	1,500	9,100	48,000
1892CC	40,000	1,085	1,145	1,200	4,000	30,000	—	—
1892O	28,688	863	888	933	986	8,000	—	—
1892S	115,500	833	892	937	972	2,700	—	—
1893	1,840,895	805	830	875	910	1,200	8,500	46,000
1893CC	14,000	1,085	1,230	2,100	8,500	—	—	—
1893O	17,000	833	868	955	1,190	5,000	—	—
1893S	141,350	833	868	925	985	2,500	20,000	—
1894	2,470,778	805	830	875	910	1,100	16,000	46,000
1894O	107,500	833	868	970	1,100	6,000	28,000	—
1894S	25,000	833	892	1,050	3,850	—	—	—
1895	567,826	805	830	875	910	1,075	11,500	43,500
1895O	98,000	833	868	925	1,200	6,500	—	—
1895S	49,000	833	880	890	2,400	9,500	—	—

$10

$10

Date	Mintage	VF20	XF40	AU50	MS60	MS63	MS65	Prf65
1896	76,348	805	830	875	920	1,500	10,000	43,500
1896S	123,750	833	863	935	1,600	10,000	35,000	—
1897	1,000,159	805	830	875	910	1,085	7,000	—
1897O	42,500	833	868	913	1,110	6,500	28,000	—
1897S	234,750	833	863	908	1,020	5,750	22,500	—
1898	812,197	805	830	875	910	1,350	8,000	43,500
1898S	473,600	833	830	875	920	3,300	18,500	—
1899	1,262,305	805	830	875	910	1,035	3,350	43,500
1899O	37,047	833	868	915	1,000	7,500	35,000	—
1899S	841,000	805	830	875	920	1,850	14,000	—
1900	293,960	805	830	875	920	1,250	5,500	43,500
1900S	81,000	833	868	913	980	6,500	25,000	—
1901	1,718,825	805	830	875	910	1,035	3,350	43,500
1901O	72,041	833	868	913	1,050	3,500	12,500	—
1901S	2,812,750	805	830	875	910	1,035	3,350	—
1902	82,513	805	830	875	930	1,600	9,000	43,500
1902S	469,500	805	830	875	910	1,135	6,000	—
1903	125,926	805	830	875	920	2,450	7,000	43,500
1903O	112,771	833	868	913	1,020	1,260	17,500	—
1903S	538,000	805	830	875	920	1,035	3,350	—
1904	162,038	805	830	875	920	1,750	8,000	46,000
1904O	108,950	833	868	913	1,020	3,000	22,500	—
1905	201,078	805	830	875	920	1,085	8,500	43,500
1905S	369,250	833	863	920	1,100	6,000	30,000	—
1906	165,497	805	830	875	920	1,500	10,500	43,500
1906D	981,000	805	830	875	910	1,100	7,000	—
1906O	86,895	833	868	913	1,060	4,800	15,000	—
1906S	457,000	833	863	913	960	4,500	15,000	—
1907	1,203,973	805	830	875	910	1,035	5,000	43,500
1907D	1,030,000	805	830	875	920	1,700	14,000	—
1907S	210,500	833	863	935	975	5,450	17,500	—

Indian Head
No motto next to eagle reverse

KM# 125 • 16.72 g., 0.900 Gold 0.48 oz. AGW, 27mm. • **Designer:** Augustus Saint-Gaudens **Note:** 1907 varieties are distinguished by whether the edge is rolled or wired, and whether the legend E PLURIBUS UNUM has periods between each word.

Date	Mintage	VF20	XF40	AU50	MS60	MS63	MS65	Prf65
1907 wire edge, periods before and after legend	500	13,850	17,500	21,000	26,500	44,500	72,500	—
1907 same, without stars on edge, unique	—	—	—	—	—	—	—	—
1907 rolled edge, periods	42	26,000	38,500	49,000	66,500	113,000	265,000	—
1907 without periods	239,406	1,013	1,030	1,052	1,215	3,400	10,500	—
1908 without motto	33,500	998	1,015	1,037	1,200	4,650	15,500	—
1908D without motto	210,000	998	1,015	1,037	1,240	7,000	37,500	—

IN GOD WE TRUST left of eagle reverse

KM# 130 • 16.72 g., 0.900 Gold 0.48 oz. AGW, 27mm. • **Designer:** Augustus Saint-Gaudens

Date	Mintage	VF20	XF40	AU50	MS60	MS63	MS65	Prf65
1908	341,486	993	1,010	1,032	1,185	2,450	12,250	75,000
1908D	836,500	998	1,030	1,052	1,205	7,000	29,000	—
1908S	59,850	1,008	1,085	1,150	2,950	11,500	25,500	—

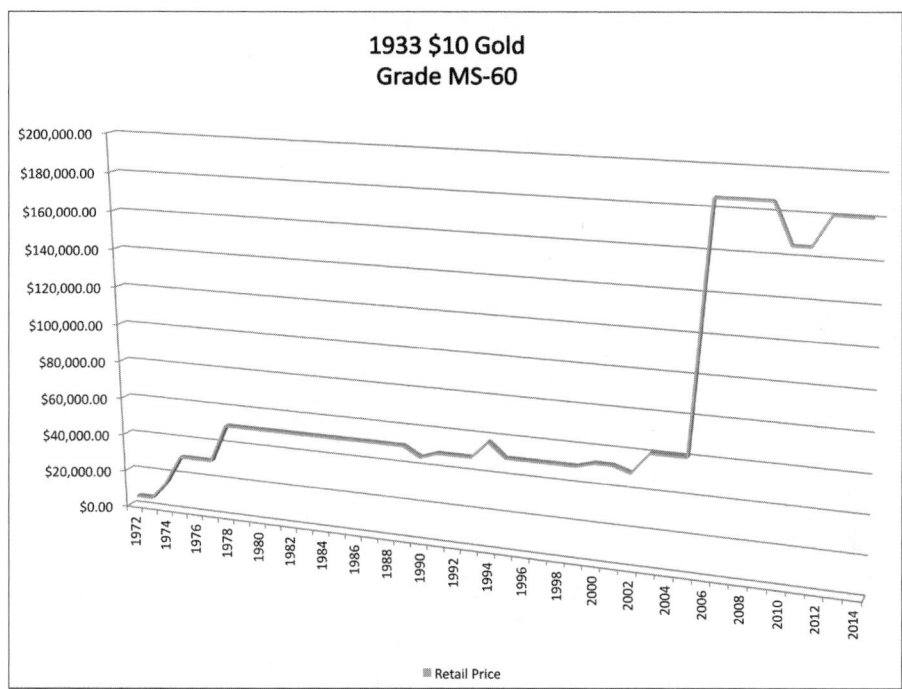

1933 $10 Gold
Grade MS-60

Date	Mintage	VF20	XF40	AU50	MS60	MS63	MS65	Prf65
1909	184,863	993	1,010	1,032	1,165	3,950	18,500	80,000
1909D	121,540	998	1,015	1,037	1,230	6,100	36,500	—
1909S	292,350	998	1,015	1,037	1,375	6,350	19,000	—
1910	318,704	993	1,010	1,032	1,155	1,500	12,750	76,500
1910D	2,356,640	988	1,005	1,032	1,155	1,500	10,250	—
1910S	811,000	998	1,015	1,037	1,500	8,850	54,500	—
1911	505,595	988	1,005	1,027	1,170	1,550	10,000	75,000
1911D	30,100	1,200	1,400	1,700	9,000	31,000	140,000	—
1911S	51,000	1,028	1,150	1,200	2,050	10,000	21,500	—
1912	405,083	993	1,010	1,032	1,155	1,475	12,000	75,000
1912S	300,000	998	1,015	1,037	1,600	7,300	46,000	—
1913	442,071	993	1,010	1,032	1,155	1,500	11,000	75,000
1913S	66,000	1,043	1,200	1,300	4,650	31,500	125,000	—
1914	151,050	993	1,010	1,032	1,065	2,250	12,000	75,000
1914D	343,500	993	1,010	1,032	1,155	2,550	18,000	—
1914S	208,000	1,003	1,165	1,250	1,400	7,750	33,500	—
1915	351,075	993	1,010	1,032	1,155	2,000	12,000	75,000
1915S	59,000	1,043	1,075	1,200	3,150	15,500	58,500	—
1916S	138,500	1,028	1,045	1,100	1,425	6,350	26,500	—
1920S	126,500	12,500	16,850	19,750	37,000	88,500	275,000	—
1926	1,014,000	988	1,005	1,027	1,150	1,300	3,600	—
1930S	96,000	8,500	11,250	14,850	23,500	46,500	79,500	—
1932	4,463,000	988	1,005	1,027	1,150	1,300	3,600	—
1933	312,500	—	140,000	160,000	180,000	225,000	600,000	—

$20

$20 (DOUBLE EAGLE)

GOLD
Liberty Head
Coronet head, left, within circle of stars obverse
TWENTY D. belo eagle, no motto above eagle reverse

KM# 74.1 • 33.44 g., 0.900 Gold 0.96 oz. AGW, 34mm. • **Rev. Legend:** UNITED STATES OF AMERICA **Designer:** James B. Longacre

Date	Mintage	VF20	XF40	AU50	MS60	MS63	MS65	Prf65
1849 unique, in Smithsonian collection	1	—	—	—	—	—	—	—
1850	1,170,261	2,295	2,475	3,800	11,500	46,500	175,000	—
1850O	141,000	2,345	4,350	9,800	45,000	—	—	—
1851	2,087,155	2,175	2,235	2,550	5,000	22,500	—	—
1851O	315,000	2,410	4,200	6,150	23,000	—	—	—
1852	2,053,026	2,175	2,225	2,550	4,950	18,500	—	—
1852O	190,000	2,365	3,850	6,000	22,500	—	—	—
1853	1,261,326	2,335	2,235	2,550	5,000	27,500	—	—
1853/2	Inc. above	2,415	2,465	5,000	34,500	—	—	—
1853O	71,000	2,425	3,650	7,950	32,500	—	—	—
1854 SD	757,899	2,175	2,225	2,550	9,750	—	—	—
1854 LD	Inc. above	2,575	3,350	6,000	30,000	—	—	—
1854O	3,250	125,000	250,000	375,000	—	—	—	—
1854S	141,468	23,315	3,400	7,500	17,500	26,000	90,000	—
1855	364,666	2,175	2,225	2,550	8,850	66,500	—	—
1855O	8,000	10,500	19,500	42,500	110,000	—	—	—
1855S	879,675	2,315	2,475	2,800	6,750	15,500	—	—
1856	329,878	2,175	2,225	2,550	8,400	28,000	—	—
1856O	2,250	175,000	275,000	400,000	550,000	1,100,000	—	—
1856S	1,189,750	2,315	2,475	2,800	5,900	15,000	35,000	—
1857	439,375	2,175	2,225	2,550	4,250	24,500	—	—
1857O	30,000	2,390	4,250	9,400	37,500	115,000	—	—
1857S	970,500	2,315	2,475	2,900	4,750	9,300	12,850	—
1858	211,714	2,175	2,225	2,550	6,750	34,500	—	—
1858O	35,250	2,515	5,000	11,000	42,000	—	—	—
1858S	846,710	2,295	2,495	3,000	8,500	—	—	—
1859	43,597	2,360	2,450	6,950	28,000	—	—	280,000
1859O	9,100	5,000	18,500	40,000	110,000	—	—	—
1859S	636,445	2,175	2,225	2,550	8,000	35,000	—	—
1860	577,670	2,315	2,475	2,800	5,500	18,000	63,500	—
1860O	6,600	4,350	14,500	35,000	120,000	—	—	—
1860S	544,950	2,175	2,225	3,090	7,350	18,500	48,000	—
1861	2,976,453	2,200	2,325	2,650	6,750	19,500	70,000	275,000
1861O	17,741	4,200	21,000	37,500	88,000	—	—	—
1861S	768,000	2,250	2,575	2,925	10,500	37,500	—	—

Paquet design, TWENTY D. below eagle reverse

KM# 93 • 33.44 g., 0.900 Gold 0.96 oz. AGW **Rev. Legend:** UNITED STATES OF AMERICA **Note:** In 1861 the reverse was redesigned by Anthony C. Paquet, but it was withdrawn soon after its release. The letters in the inscriptions on the Paquet-reverse variety are taller than on the regular reverse.

Date	Mintage	VF20	XF40	AU50	MS60	MS63	MS65	Prf65
1861 2 Known	—	—	—	—	—	—	—	—
Note: 1861 Paquet reverse, Bowers & Merena, Nov. 1988, MS-67, $660,000.								
1861S	—	22,000	55,000	92,500	275,000	—	—	—
Note: Included in mintage of 1861S, KM#74.1								

KM# A74.1 • 33.44 g., 0.900 Gold 0.96 oz. AGW

Date	Mintage	VF20	XF40	AU50	MS60	MS63	MS65	Prf65
1862	92,133	2,315	4,850	10,000	17,500	36,500	—	250,000
1862S	854,173	2,300	2,425	2,800	12,400	60,000	—	—
1863	142,790	2,415	3,100	7,900	19,500	55,000	—	250,000
1863S	966,570	2,300	2,430	2,755	8,350	28,500	—	—
1864	204,285	2,315	2,465	3,250	21,500	—	—	250,000
1864S	793,660	2,300	2,425	2,735	8,850	32,000	125,000	—
1865	351,200	2,315	2,450	2,840	6,200	23,500	90,000	250,000
1865S	1,042,500	2,300	2,430	2,750	5,350	13,500	28,000	—
1866S	Inc. below	2,750	11,500	37,500	—	—	—	—

Longacre design resumed reverse

KM# 74.2 • 33.44 g., 0.900 Gold 0.96 oz. AGW, 34mm. • **Rev. Legend:** UNITED STATES OF AMERICA **Designer:** James B. Longacre

Date	Mintage	VF20	XF40	AU50	MS60	MS63	MS65	Prf65
1866	698,775	1,810	1,980	2,155	11,000	65,000	—	200,000
1866S	842,250	1,810	1,990	3,350	15,500	—	—	—
1867	251,065	1,810	2,000	2,155	4,650	40,000	—	200,000
1867S	920,750	1,810	1,990	2,175	15,000	—	—	—
1868	98,600	1,850	2,100	3,450	17,500	60,000	—	200,000
1868S	837,500	1,810	1,960	2,150	14,500	—	—	—
1869	175,155	1,820	1,950	2,175	7,250	40,000	350,000	210,000
1869S	686,750	1,810	1,980	2,075	7,100	45,000	—	—
1870	155,185	1,830	1,980	2,300	10,500	55,000	—	215,000
1870CC	3,789	215,000	275,000	410,000	—	—	—	—
1870S	982,000	1,810	1,935	2,110	5,450	—	—	—
1871	80,150	1,820	1,935	2,100	7,950	55,000	—	—
1871CC	17,387	10,000	25,000	50,000	97,500	300,000	650,000	—
1871S	928,000	1,810	1,950	2,150	4,750	25,000	—	—
1872	251,880	1,810	1,980	2,180	4,000	24,500	—	—
1872CC	26,900	2,750	6,500	11,500	38,500	—	—	—
1872S	780,000	1,810	1,980	2,155	3,700	23,500	—	—
1873 closed 3	Est. 208925	1,810	2,040	2,215	3,500	—	—	200,000
1873 open 3	Est. 1500900	1,810	1,980	1,960	2,425	12,200	235,000	—
1873CC	22,410	3,250	9,000	14,500	37,500	150,000	—	—
1873S closed 3	1,040,600	1,700	1,950	2,150	2,400	30,000	—	—
1873S open 3	Inc. above	1,810	1,980	2,155	2,375	—	—	—
1874	366,800	1,810	1,980	1,950	2,325	20,000	—	—
1874CC	115,085	2,350	2,850	5,250	16,500	—	—	—
1874S	1,214,000	1,700	1,950	1,950	2,175	24,500	—	—
1875	295,740	1,810	1,980	2,155	2,380	11,000	—	—
1875CC	111,151	2,450	4,250	3,450	6,400	33,500	—	—
1875S	1,230,000	1,700	1,950	1,950	2,175	16,850	—	—
1876	583,905	1,700	1,970	1,950	2,175	13,500	—	—
1876CC	138,441	2,350	3,250	4,750	9,850	50,000	—	—
1876S	1,597,000	1,700	1,950	1,950	2,175	12,200	235,000	—

$20

TWENTY DOLLARS below eagle reverse

KM# 74.3 • 33.44 g., 0.900 Gold 0.96 oz. AGW **Rev. Legend:** UNITED STATES OF AMERICA

Date	Mintage	VF20	XF40	AU50	MS60	MS63	MS65	Prf65
1877	397,670	1,520	1,700	1,720	1,775	16,000	35,000	—
1877CC	42,565	2,350	3,450	5,650	19,500	—	—	—
1877S	1,735,000	1,510	1,570	1,720	1,775	17,500	35,000	—
1878	543,645	1,530	1,670	1,800	1,965	15,000	—	—
1878CC	13,180	3,000	11,500	18,500	36,000	—	—	—
1878S	1,739,000	1,510	1,545	1,720	1,775	20,500	—	—
1879	207,630	1,590	1,725	175	1,845	20,500	—	—
1879CC	10,708	3,350	10,000	16,500	37,500	—	—	—
1879O	2,325	16,500	32,000	40,000	105,000	—	—	—
1879S	1,223,800	1,510	1,545	1,720	2,450	40,000	—	—
1880	51,456	1,620	1,750	1,825	7,250	25,000	—	110,000
1880S	836,000	1,510	1,545	1,720	1,795	42,500	125,000	—
1881	2,260	12,500	21,000	34,500	98,500	—	—	110,000
1881S	727,000	1,510	1,545	1,655	1,845	22,500	—	—
1882	630	11,800	39,500	88,000	135,000	225,000	—	130,000
1882CC	39,140	2,350	3,250	4,550	11,000	85,000	—	—
1882S	1,125,000	1,580	1,545	1,635	1,915	18,500	—	—
1883 proof only	92	—	—	27,500	—	—	—	195,000
1883CC	59,962	2,350	3,200	4,850	8,750	45,000	—	—
1883S	1,189,000	1,510	1,545	1,745	1,845	8,500	—	—
1884 proof only	71	—	—	35,000	—	—	—	225,000
1884CC	81,139	2,350	3,000	4,600	7,950	32,500	—	—
1884S	916,000	1,510	1,545	1,645	1,785	6,150	55,000	—
1885	828	8,450	24,500	39,500	75,000	125,000	—	115,000
1885CC	9,450	2,650	6,500	9,850	23,500	—	—	—
1885S	683,500	1,510	1,545	1,655	1,785	5,700	—	—
1886	1,106	21,000	36,000	70,000	135,000	160,000	—	105,000
1887	121	—	—	40,000	—	—	—	142,500
1887S	283,000	1,510	1,545	1,645	1,845	16,500	40,000	—
1888	226,266	1,510	1,545	1,665	1,895	10,000	36,500	93,500
1888S	859,600	1,510	1,545	1,645	1,785	4,850	45,000	—
1889	44,111	1,670	1,800	1,990	2,450	16,500	—	105,000
1889CC	30,945	2,600	4,250	5,000	10,500	24,000	—	—
1889S	774,700	1,510	1,545	1,645	1,795	5,950	—	—
1890	75,995	1,510	1,570	1,770	1,845	10,000	—	100,000
1890CC	91,209	2,350	2,650	3,950	6,000	40,000	—	—
1890S	802,750	1,510	1,545	1,645	1,785	6,650	—	—
1891	1,442	9,250	15,000	22,500	75,000	145,000	—	108,000
1891CC	5,000	6,000	12,500	17,500	28,500	—	—	—
1891S	1,288,125	1,510	1,545	1,645	1,785	3,000	—	—
1892	4,523	2,000	4,100	6,750	16,500	35,000	75,000	90,000
1892CC	27,265	2,350	2,850	4,350	9,000	46,500	—	—
1892S	930,150	1,510	1,545	1,700	1,775	3,500	34,500	—
1893	344,339	1,510	1,565	1,710	1,815	2,750	12,500	95,000
1893CC	18,402	2,350	3,000	7,000	9,850	45,000	—	—
1893S	996,175	1,470	1,500	1,595	1,620	3,950	45,000	—
1894	1,368,990	1,470	1,500	1,595	1,620	2,350	25,000	85,000
1894S	1,048,550	1,470	1,500	1,595	1,620	2,850	25,000	—
1895	1,114,656	1,470	1,500	1,595	1,620	1,875	22,000	82,500
1895S	1,143,500	1,470	1,500	1,595	1,620	1,875	16,500	—
1896	792,663	1,470	1,500	1,595	1,620	1,875	30,000	200,000
1896S	1,403,925	1,470	1,500	1,595	1,620	1,875	23,500	—
1897	1,383,261	1,470	1,500	1,595	1,620	1,975	30,000	200,000
1897S	1,470,250	1,470	1,500	1,595	1,620	1,875	21,500	—
1898	170,470	1,475	1,530	1,695	1,920	5,300	—	200,000
1898S	2,575,175	1,475	1,500	1,595	1,620	1,875	9,500	—
1899	1,669,384	1,470	1,500	1,595	1,620	1,875	10,500	200,000
1899S	2,010,300	1,470	1,500	1,595	1,620	2,075	21,500	—
1900	1,874,584	1,470	1,500	1,595	1,620	1,910	5,750	200,000
1900S	2,459,500	1,470	1,500	1,595	1,620	1,875	25,000	—

Date	Mintage	VF20	XF40	AU50	MS60	MS63	MS65	Prf65
1901	111,526	1,470	1,500	1,595	1,620	2,010	6,850	200,000
1901S	1,596,000	1,470	1,500	1,595	1,620	3,850	22,000	—
1902	31,254	1,470	1,695	1,855	2,030	13,000	37,500	200,000
1902S	1,753,625	1,470	1,500	1,595	1,620	2,900	23,500	—
1903	287,428	1,470	1,500	1,595	1,620	1,910	4,250	200,000
1903S	954,000	1,470	1,500	1,595	1,620	2,340	13,500	—
1904	6,256,797	1,470	1,500	1,595	1,620	1,875	3,725	200,000
1904S	5,134,175	1,470	1,500	1,595	1,620	1,875	6,000	—
1905	59,011	1,475	1,520	1,630	1,920	14,500	65,000	200,000
1905S	1,813,000	1,470	1,500	1,595	1,620	4,000	25,000	—
1906	69,690	1,381	1,505	1,650	1,800	7,700	31,500	200,000
1906D	620,250	1,470	1,500	1,595	1,620	3,700	23,500	—
1906S	2,065,750	1,470	1,500	1,595	1,620	2,650	24,500	—
1907	1,451,864	1,470	1,500	1,595	1,620	1,975	8,800	200,000
1907D	842,250	1,470	1,500	1,595	1,620	3,500	7,500	—
1907S	2,165,800	1,470	1,500	1,595	1,620	3,000	27,000	—

Saint-Gaudens High Relief

Roman numerals in date obverse No motto below eagle reverse

KM# 126 • 33.44 g., 0.900 Gold 0.96 oz. AGW, 34mm. • **Edge:** Plain. **Designer:** Augustus Saint-Gaudens

Date	Mintage	VF20	XF40	AU50	MS60	MS63	MS65	Prf65
MCMVII high relief, unique, AU-55, 150,000	—	—	—	—	—	—	—	—
MCMVII high relief, wire rim	11,250	7,650	9,350	11,000	14,350	24,500	47,500	—
MCMVII high relief, flat rim	Inc. above	7,900	9,850	12,000	15,600	26,000	49,000	—

Saint-Gaudens

Arabic numberals in date obverse   No motto eagle reverse

KM# 127 • 33.44 g., 0.900 Gold 0.96 oz. AGW, 34mm. • **Edge:** Lettered; large letters. **Designer:** Augustus Saint-Gaudens

Date	Mintage	VF20	XF40	AU50	MS60	MS63	MS65	Prf65
1907 large letters on edge, unique	—	—	—	—	—	—	—	—
1907 small letters on edge	361,667	1,500	1,525	1,620	1,665	1,920	4,600	—
1908	4,271,551	1,490	1,515	1,600	1,625	1,710	2,150	—
1908D	663,750	1,500	5,125	1,610	1,650	1,820	11,800	—

Saint-Gaudens

Roman numerals in date obverse No motto below eagle reverse

KM # Pn1874 • 33.4360 g.,0.9000 Gold, 0.9675 oz. AGW, 34mm. • **Designer:** Augustus Saint-Gaudens Edge Desc:Plain. **Notes:** The "Roman numerals" varieties for 1907 use Roman numerals for the date instead of Arabic numerals. The lettered-edge varieties have "E Pluribus Unum" on the edge, with stars between the words.

Date	Mintage	VF20	XF40	AU50	MS60	MS63	MS65	Prf65
1907 extremely high relief, unique	—	—	—	—	—	—	—	—
1907 extremely high relief, lettered edge	—	—	—	—	—	—	—	—

Note: 1907 extremely high relief, lettered edge, Prf-68, private sale, 1990, $1,500,000.

$20

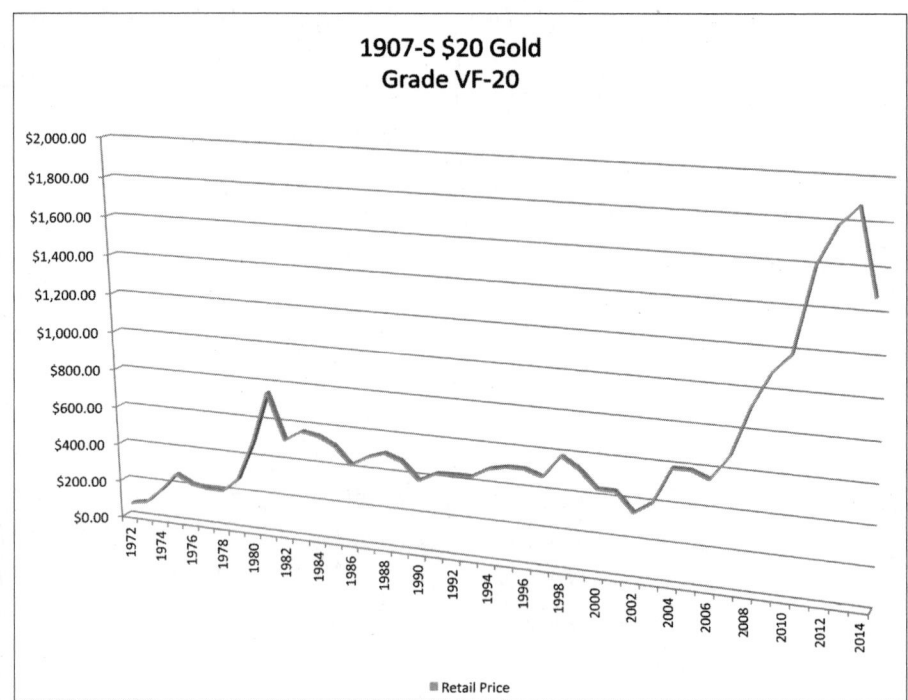

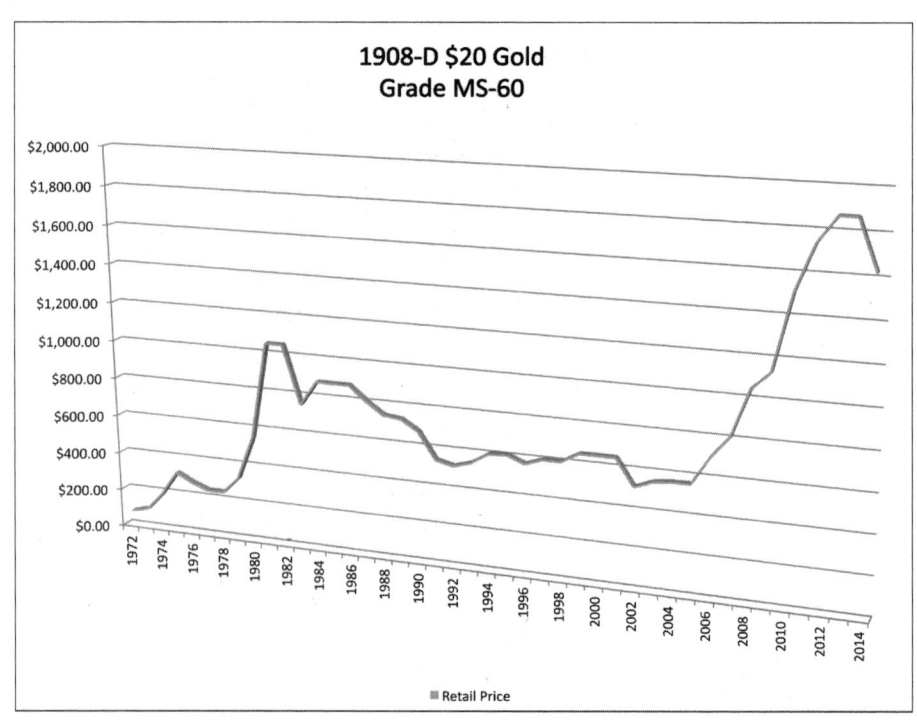

IN GOD WE TRUST below eagle reverse

KM# 131 • 33.44 g., 0.900 Gold 0.96 oz. AGW, 34mm. • **Designer:** Augustus Saint-Gaudens

Date	Mintage	VF20	XF40	AU50	MS60	MS63	MS65	Prf65
1908	156,359	1,495	1,520	1,610	1,675	2,300	28,000	76,500
1908 Roman finish	—	PRF64 Rare						
1908D	349,500	1,500	1,525	1,620	1,665	1,840	7,000	—
1908S	22,000	2,450	3,150	4,850	10,650	24,500	52,500	—
1909/8	161,282	1,500	1,525	1,660	1,850	6,250	52,000	—
1909	Inc. above	1,510	1,545	1,630	1,725	3,150	46,000	92,500
1909D	52,500	1,540	1,565	1,755	3,100	8,950	57,500	—
1909S	2,774,925	1,500	1,525	1,620	1,645	1,795	7,000	—
1910	482,167	1,495	1,520	1,610	1,675	1,810	9,000	84,500
1910D	429,000	1,495	1,520	1,610	1,650	1,780	3,450	—
1910S	2,128,250	1,500	1,525	1,625	1,655	1,845	11,350	—
1911	197,350	1,500	1,525	1,630	1,665	2,900	23,500	76,500
1911D	846,500	1,495	1,520	1,610	1,650	1,780	2,950	—
1911S	775,750	1,495	1,520	1,610	1,655	1,780	6,850	—
1912	149,824	1,500	1,525	1,625	1,690	2,050	31,000	76,500
1913	168,838	1,500	1,525	1,625	1,695	3,250	53,500	82,500
1913D	393,500	1,495	1,520	1,610	1,650	1,860	7,850	—
1913S	34,000	1,550	1,575	1,660	2,000	4,350	36,500	—
1914	95,320	1,510	1,535	1,660	1,275	3,900	25,000	81,500
1914D	453,000	1,495	1,520	1,610	1,650	1,790	3,450	—
1914S	1,498,000	1,495	1,520	1,610	1,650	1,780	3,150	—
1915	152,050	1,500	1,525	1,620	1,655	2,650	28,000	125,000
1915S	567,500	1,495	1,520	1,610	1,650	1,780	3,000	—
1916S	796,000	1,500	1,525	1,620	1,690	1,810	3,250	—
1920	228,250	1,490	1,515	1,600	1,650	2,450	118,000	—
1920S	558,000	14,500	18,500	28,500	53,000	105,000	355,000	—
1921	528,500	35,000	43,500	56,500	125,000	300,000	975,000	—
1922	1,375,500	1,490	1,515	1,600	1,625	1,730	6,850	—
1922S	2,658,000	1,610	1,150	1,300	2,450	5,650	63,500	—
1923	566,000	1,490	1,515	1,600	1,625	1,730	8,000	—
1923D	1,702,250	1,500	1,525	1,610	1,635	1,730	2,260	—
1924	4,323,500	1,490	1,515	1,600	1,625	1,710	2,150	—
1924D	3,049,500	1,713	1,738	2,100	3,950	11,200	115,000	—
1924S	2,927,500	1,665	1,750	2,200	3,800	12,250	180,000	—
1925	2,831,750	1,490	1,515	1,600	1,625	1,710	2,150	—
1925D	2,938,500	1,665	2,100	2,375	4,450	11,500	148,000	—
1925S	3,776,500	1,900	2,850	4,850	9,850	23,500	210,000	—
1926	816,750	1,490	1,515	1,600	1,625	1,710	2,150	—
1926D	481,000	10,000	15,500	19,350	27,500	35,000	235,000	—
1926S	2,041,500	1,693	1,550	1,725	3,050	5,650	37,500	—
1927	2,946,750	1,490	1,515	1,600	1,625	1,710	2,150	—
1927D	180,000	155,000	200,000	245,000	325,000	1,500,000	1,950,000	—
1927S	3,107,000	6,850	8,850	13,250	26,750	54,000	160,000	—
1928	8,816,000	1,490	1,515	1,600	1,625	1,710	2,150	—
1929	1,779,750	10,000	13,500	15,500	19,300	38,500	112,000	—
1930S	74,000	35,000	41,000	49,500	72,500	105,000	235,000	—
1931	2,938,250	10,500	13,500	20,500	31,500	63,500	120,000	—
1931D	106,500	8,850	11,500	21,500	42,500	83,500	140,000	—
1932	1,101,750	12,500	14,500	17,850	26,500	73,500	110,000	—
1933	445,500	—	—	—	—	—	9,000,000	—

Note: Sotheby/Stack's Sale, July 2002. Thirteen known, only one currently available.

MINT SETS

Mint, or uncirculated, sets contain one uncirculated coin of each denomination from each mint produced for circulation that year. Values listed here are only for those sets sold by the U.S. Mint. Sets were not offered in years not listed. In years when the Mint did not offer the sets, some private companies compiled and marketed uncirculated sets. Mint sets from 1947 through 1958 contained two examples of each coin mounted in cardboard holders, which caused the coins to tarnish. Beginning in 1959, the sets have been packaged in sealed Pliofilm packets and include only one specimen of each coin struck for that year (both P & D mints). Listings for 1965, 1966 and 1967 are for "special mint sets," which were of higher quality than regular mint sets and were prooflike. They were packaged in plastic cases. The 1970 large-date and small-date varieties are distinguished by the size of the date on the coin. The 1976 three-piece set contains the quarter, half dollar and dollar with the Bicentennial design. The 1971 and 1972 sets do not include a dollar coin; the 1979 set does not include an S-mint-marked dollar. Mint sets issued prior to 1959 were double sets (containing two of each coin) packaged in cardboard with a paper overlay. Origional sets will always be toned and can bring large premiums if nicely preserved with good color.

Date	Sets Sold	Issue Price	Mkt Val	Date	Sets Sold	Issue Price	Mkt Val
1947 Est. 5,000	—	4.87	2,950	1980 Susan B. Anthony	—	—	6.50
1948 Est. 6,000	—	4.92	1,800	PDS Souvenir Set			
1949 Est. 5,200	—	5.45	2,400	1981 Type I	2,908,145	11.00	9.35
1950 None issued	—	—	—	1981 Susan B. Anthony	—	—	22.00
1951	8,654	6.75	1,950	PDS Souvenir Set			
1952	11,499	6.14	1,650	1982 & 1983 None issued	—	—	—
1953	15,538	6.14	1,325	1982 Souvenir set	—	—	59.00
1954	25,599	6.19	670	1983 Souvenir set	—	—	65.00
1955 flat pack	49,656	3.57	475	1984	1,832,857	7.00	3.65
1956	45,475	3.34	450	1985	1,710,571	7.00	3.60
1957	32,324	24.50	680	1986	1,153,536	7.50	6.85
1958	50,314	4.43	415	1987	2,890,758	7.00	3.85
1959	187,000	2.40	55.00	1988	1,646,204	7.00	4.40
1960 large date	260,485	2.40	44.00	1989	1,987,915	7.00	3.10
1961	223,704	2.40	46.50	1990	1,809,184	7.00	3.30
1962	385,285	2.40	44.00	1991	1,352,101	7.00	4.15
1963	606,612	2.40	39.00	1992	1,500,143	7.00	3.10
1964	1,008,108	2.40	38.50	1993	1,297,094	8.00	4.40
1965 Special Mint Set	2,360,000	4.00	9.60	1994	1,234,813	8.00	3.30
1966 Special Mint Set	2,261,583	4.00	9.10	1995	1,038,787	8.00	3.60
1967 Special Mint Set	1,863,344	4.00	9.35	1996	1,457,949	8.00	20.00
1968	2,105,128	2.50	5.50	1997	950,473	8.00	4.40
1969	1,817,392	2.50	7.10	1998	1,187,325	8.00	3.60
1970 large date	2,038,134	2.50	18.50	1999 9 piece	1,421,625	14.95	5.50
1970 small date	Inc. above	2.50	62.50	2000	1,490,160	14.95	6.85
1971	2,193,396	3.50	3.30	2001	1,066,900	14.95	6.85
1972	2,750,000	3.50	2.75	2002	1,139,388	14.95	6.60
1973	1,767,691	8.00	11.75	2003	1,002,555	14.95	8.80
1974	1,975,981	6.75	6.10	2004	844,484	16.95	8.00
1975	1,921,488	6.00	6.60	2005	—	16.95	7.00
1976 3 coins	4,908,319	9.00	16.75	2006	—	16.95	8.00
1976	1,892,513	6.00	7.50	2007	—	—	26.50
1977	2,006,869	7.00	6.60	2008	—	—	59.50
1978	2,162,609	7.00	7.15	2009 18 piece clad set	—	—	25.00
1979 Type I	2,526,000	8.00	5.50	2010 28 piece clad set	—	—	29.70
1979 Susan B Anthony PDS	—	—	6.50	2010 14 piece clad	—	—	26.50
Souvenir Set				2011 14 piece clad set	532,059	—	32.00
1980	2,815,066	9.00	6.10	2012 14 piece clad set	365,298	—	72.00

PROOF SETS

Proof coins are produced through a special process involving specially selected, highly polished planchets and dies. They usually receive two strikings from the coin press at increased pressure. The result is a coin with mirrorlike surfaces and, in recent years, a cameo effect on its raised design surfaces. Proof sets have been sold off and on by the U.S. Mint since 1858. Listings here are for sets from what is commonly called the modern era, since 1936. Values for earlier proofs are included in regular date listings. Sets were not offered in years not listed. Since 1968, proof coins have been produced at the San Francisco Mint; before that they were produced at the Philadelphia Mint. In 1942 the five-cent coin was struck in two compositions. Some proof sets for that year contain only one type (five-coin set); others contain both types. Two types of packaging were used in 1955 -- a box and a flat, plastic holder. The 1960 large-date and small-date sets are distinguished by the size of the date on the cent. Some 1968 sets are missing the mint mark on the dime, the result of an error in the preparation of an obverse die. The 1970 large-date and small-date sets are distinguished by the size of the date on the cent. Some 1970 sets are missing the mint mark on the dime, the result of an error in the preparation of an obverse die. Some 1971 sets are missing the mint mark on the five-cent piece, the result of an error in the preparation of an obverse die. The 1976 three-piece set contains the quarter, half dollar and dollar with the Bicentennial designs. The 1979 and 1981 Type II sets have clearer mint marks than the Type I sets for those years. Some 1983 sets are missing the mint mark on the dime, the result of an error in the preparation of an obverse die. Prestige sets contain the five regular-issue coins plus a commemorative silver dollar from that year. Sets issued prior to 1956 came in transparent envelopes stapled together in a small square box. In mid 1955 sets were changed to a flat clear cellophane envelope. In 1968 sets were changed to a clear hard plastic case as they still are currently issued.

Date	Sets Sold	Issue Price	Mkt Val	Date	Sets Sold	Issue Price	Mkt Val
Date			Value	1941	15,287	—	1,450
1936	3,837	1.89	7,500	1942 6 coins	21,120	1.89	1,475
1937	5,542	1.89	4,350	1942 5 coins	Inc. above	1.89	1,250
1938	8,045	1.89	1,900	1950	51,386	2.10	545
1939	8,795	—	1,800	1951	57,500	2.10	575
1940	11,246	—	1,385	1952	81,980	2.10	225

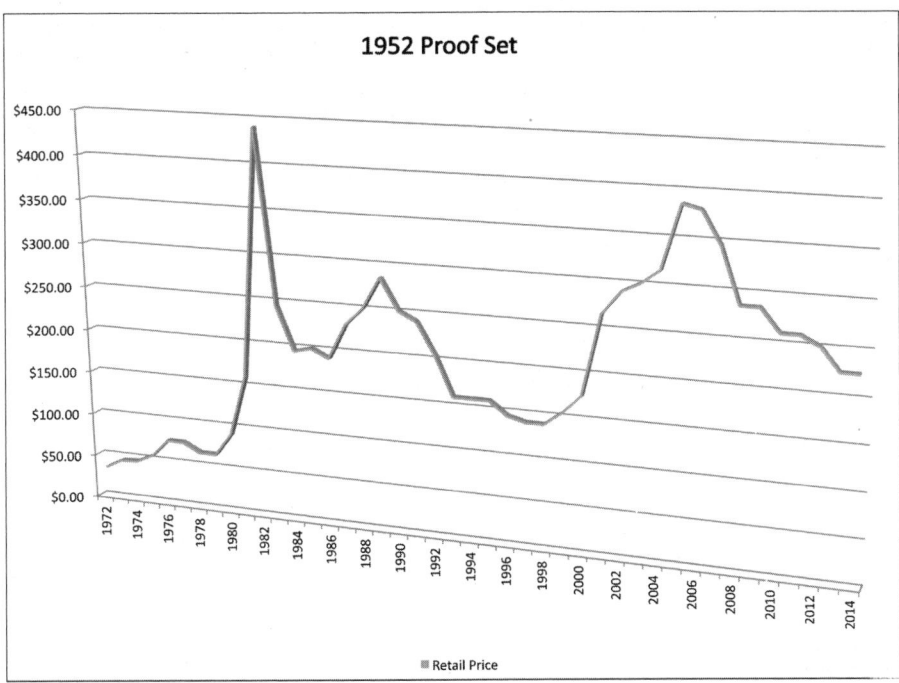

1952 Proof Set

■ Retail Price

Date	Sets Sold	Issue Price	Mkt Val	Date	Sets Sold	Issue Price	Mkt Val
1953	128,800	2.10	210	1976S 3 coins	3,998,621	13.00	24.25
1954	233,300	2.10	107	1976S	4,149,730	7.00	8.00
1955 box	378,200	2.10	93.50	1977S	3,251,152	9.00	7.70
1955 flat pack	Inc. above	2.10	119	1978S	3,127,788	9.00	7.15
1956	669,384	2.10	54.00	1979S Type I	3,677,175	9.00	8.00
1957	1,247,952	2.10	30.00	1979S Type II	Inc. above	9.00	68.5
1958	875,652	2.10	38.00	1980S	3,547,030	10.00	5.2
1959	1,149,291	2.10	32.50	1981S Type I	4,063,083	11.00	5.9
1960 large date	1,691,602	2.10	29.50	1981S Type II	Inc. above	11.00	2.
1960 small date	Inc. above	2.10	33.50	1982S	3,857,479	11.00	3.0
1961	3,028,244	2.10	28	1983S	3,138,765	11.00	3.6
			28.00	1983S Prestige Set	140,361	59.00	44.0
1962	3,218,019	2.10	26.50	1983S no mint mark dime	Inc. above	11.00	660
1964	3,950,762	2.10	27.50	1984S	2,748,430	11.00	4.10
1965 Special Mint Set	—	—	—	1984S Prestige Set	316,680	59.00	27.00
1966 Special Mint Set	—	—	—	1985S	3,362,821	11.00	3.30
1967 Special mint set	—	—	—	1986S	2,411,180	11.00	5.25
2003 X#207, 208, 209.2	—	44.00	28.75	1986S Prestige Set	599,317	48.50	30.00
2008 14 piece clad set	—	—	67.00	1987S	3,972,233	11.00	4.40
2011 6 quarter set	—	—	18.25	1987S Prestige Set	435,495	45.00	26.00
2012 8 piece Limited Edition	—	—	225	1988S	3,031,287	11.00	5.50
1795 XPn1-XPn3	—	—	—	1988S Prestige Set	231,661	45.00	27.50
1836 XPn4, 10-11	—	—	—	1989S	3,009,107	11.00	3.60
1863 XPn12-14	—	—	—	1989S Prestige Set	211,087	45.00	32.00
1871 XPn15-17	—	—	—	1990S	2,793,433	11.00	6.15
1879 XPn18-20	—	—	—	1990S no S 1¢	3,555	11.00	4,400
1879 XPn21-23	—	—	—	1990S Prestige Set	506,126	45.00	28.00
1968S	3,041,509	5.00	6.35	1990S Prestige Set, no S 1¢	Inc. above	45.00	5,100
1968S no mint mark dime	Inc. above	5.00	16,500	1991S	2,610,833	11.00	4.40
1969S	2,934,631	5.00	6.10	1991S Prestige Set	256,954	59.00	41.50
1970S large date	2,632,810	5.00	9.35	1992S	2,675,618	12.00	4.40
1970S small date	Inc. above	5.00	84.50	1992S Prestige Set	183,285	59.00	40.00
1970S no mint mark dime	Inc. above	5.00	820	1992S Silver	1,009,585	21.00	21.50
1971S	3,224,138	5.00	3.30	1992S Silver premier	308,055	37.00	24.50
1971S no mint mark nickel	1,655	5.00	1,350	1993S	2,337,819	12.50	3.85
Est. 1,655				1993S Prestige Set	224,045	57.00	52.00
1972S	3,267,667	5.00	4.20	1993S Silver	570,213	21.00	30.00
1973S	2,769,624	7.00	6.60	1993S Silver premier	191,140	37.00	34.00
1974S	2,617,350	7.00	9.00	1994S	2,308,701	13.00	3.85
1975S	2,909,369	7.00	8.80	1994S Prestige Set	175,893	57.00	45.00
1975S no mint mark dime	Inc. above	7.00	275,000	1994S Silver	636,009	21.00	24.50

PROOF SETS

Date	Sets Sold	Issue Price	Mkt Val	Date	Sets Sold	Issue Price	Mkt Val
1994S Silver premier	149,320	37.50	31.00	2005S Silver 5 quarter set	—	23.95	21.70
1995S	2,010,384	12.50	11.00	2006S 10 piece clad	—	22.95	8.25
1995S Prestige Set	107,112	57.00	77.00	2006S 5 quarter set	—	15.95	3.65
1995S Silver	549,878	21.00	42.00	2006S Silver 10 piece	—	37.95	37.50
1995S Silver premier	130,107	37.50	59.00	2006S Silver 5 quarter set	—	23.95	21.70
1996S	2,085,191	16.00	7.00	2006S American Legacy	—	—	81.00
1996S Prestige Set	55,000	57.00	315	2007S 5 quarter set	—	13.95	3.85
1996S Silver	623,655	21.00	30.00	2007S Silver 5 quarter set	—	22.95	21.70
1996S Silver premier	151,366	37.50	33.50	2007S 14 piece clad	—	—	16.50
1997S	1,975,000	12.50	9.50	2007S Silver 14 piece	—	—	47.50
1997S Prestige Set	80,000	57.00	55.00	2007S Presidental $ set	—	—	6.65
1997S Silver	605,473	21.00	27.00	2007S American Legacy	—	—	120
1997S Silver premier	136,205	37.50	39.50	2008S 5 quarter clad set	—	22.95	48.50
1998S	2,078,494	12.50	10.25	2008S 5 quarter silver set	—	—	24.20
1998S Silver	638,134	21.00	25.50	2008S 14 piece silver set	734,045	—	59.50
1998S Silver premier	240,658	26.50	31.00	2008S Presidental $ set	—	—	11.85
1999S 9 piece	2,557,899	19.95	9.00	2008S American Legacy	—	—	120
1999S 5 quarter set	1,169,958	13.95	6.15	2009S 18 piece clad set	1,477,967	—	27.50
1999S Silver	804,565	31.95	132	2009S 18 piece silver set	694,406	—	57.50
2000S 10 piece	3,097,442	19.95	5.00	2009S Presidental $ set	627,925	—	9.60
2000S 5 quarter set	995,803	13.95	3.60	2009S Lincoln Chronicle	—	—	122
2000S Silver	965,421	31.95	39.18	2009S Lincoln 4 piece	—	—	11.00
2001S 10 piece	2,249,498	19.95	13.75	2009S 6 quarter clad set	—	—	8.60
2001S 5 quarter set	774,800	13.95	7.50	2009S 6 quarter silver set	—	—	25.20
2001S Silver	849,600	31.95	52.50	2010S 14 piece clad set	1,103,950	—	55.00
2002S 10 piece	2,319,766	19.95	6.85	2010S 14 piece silver set	583,912	—	66.00
2002S 5 quarter set	764,419	13.95	3.85	2010S Presidential $ set	535,463	—	18.25
2002S Silver	892,229	31.95	45.00	2010S 6 quarter set	276,335	—	26.50
2003S 10 piece	2,175,684	16.75	5.75	2010S 5 quarter silver set	274,003	—	29.70
2003S 5 quarter set	1,225,507	13.95	3.00	2011S 5 quarter silver set	147,005	—	34.50
2003S Silver	1,142,858	31.95	32.20	2011S 14 piece silver set	572,247	—	83.50
2004S 11 piece	1,804,396	22.95	8.80	2011S 5 quarter clad set	151,434	—	14.50
2004S 5 quarter set	987,960	23.95	3.75	2011S Presidential $ set	299,161	—	27.50
2004S Silver 11 piece	1,187,673	37.95	33.20	2011S 14 piece clad set	1,095,318	—	46.50
2004S Silver 5 quarter set	594,137	—	23.70	2012S 5 quarter silver set	—	—	45.00
2005S American Legacy	—	—	84.50	2012S 14 piece silver set	—	—	225
2005S American Legacy	—	—	77.50	2012S 6 quarter set	—	—	18.25
2005S 11 piece	—	22.95	5.00	2012S 14 piece clad set	—	—	115
2005S 5 quarter set	—	15.95	2.75	2012S Presidential $ set	—	—	62.00
2005S Silver 11 piece	—	37.95	34.70				

UNCIRCULATED ROLLS

Listings are for rolls containing uncirculated coins. Large date and small date varieties for 1960 and 1970 apply to the one cent coins.

Date	Cents	Nickels	Dimes	Quarters	Halves	Date	Cents	Nickels	Dimes	Quarters	Halves
1934	585	3,500	2,350	1,650	2,350	1943	60.00	275	470	365	725
1934D	2,650	4,350	2,950	9,000	—	1943D	170	210	610	2,000	1,775
1934S	—	—	—	—	—	1943S	310	325	650	2,100	1,365
1935	885	1,700	1,450	1,725	1,250	1944	30.00	720	460	280	715
1935D	750	3,150	2,950	8,850	4,000	1944D	38.00	680	635	725	1,250
1935S	2,500	1,725	1,950	4,650	6,500	1944S	120	565	660	950	1,300
1936	285	1,450	885	1,300	1,750	1945	125	375	410	325	730
1936D	400	1,450	1,700	—	2,750	1945D	110	315	500	1,000	1,000
1936S	885	1,800	1,675	6,250	3,500	1945S	80.00	270	525	575	950
1937	250	1,100	710	1,250	1,150	1946	39.00	80.00	140	365	1,025
1937D	250	1,200	1,550	3,450	5,000	1946D	36.50	75.00	140	380	900
1937S	335	1,285	1,650	4,850	3,450	1946S	185	50.00	140	275	900
1938	665	535	1,100	3,100	1,850	1947	220	58.00	215	735	1,000
1938D Buffalo	—	1,065	—	—	—	1947D	46.50	72.00	275	385	1,000
1938D	710	485	1,000	—	—	1947S	39.00	72.00	210	415	—
1938S	440	355	1,350	3,250	—	1948	72.50	55.00	188	270	450
1939	180	160	630	1,040	1,250	1948D	175	155	325	645	425
1939D	535	3,850	610	1,875	1,975	1948S	165	80.00	255	475	—
1939S	265	2,750	1,900	3,200	2,350	1949	180	330	1,200	2,350	1,300
1940	225	145	535	1,850	975	1949D	125	215	550	1,285	1,475
1940D	265	120	780	5,350	—	1949S	140	138	2,350	—	2,250
1940S	300	265	675	1,275	1,200	1950	115	120	525	395	750
1941	170	215	430	475	750	1950D	42.00	385	200	440	875
1941D	335	330	710	2,750	1,200	1950S	78.00	—	1,550	850	—
1941S	360	295	535	2,450	3,000	1951	165	230	140	435	390
1942	140	315	465	450	690	1951D	26.50	285	140	325	800
1942P	—	600	—	—	—	1951S	60.00	265	690	1,350	750
1942D	140	2,550	740	1,060	1,350	1952	165	145	140	535	385
1942S	585	525	1,050	5,350	1,475	1952D	26.50	260	140	300	230

Date	Cents	Nickels	Dimes	Quarters	Halves
1952S	300	42.00	290	1,000	1,585
1953	42.00	24.50	140	635	490
1953D	22.50	17.00	140	280	280
1953S	35.00	39.00	140	280	850
1954	39.00	57.50	140	280	280
1954D	22.50	24.00	140	280	280
1954S	22.50	39.50	140	280	400
1955	24.50	19.00	140	280	300
1955D	19.00	7.00	170	280	—
1955S	27.50	—	140	—	—
1956	10.50	7.50	140	280	280
1956D	12.50	9.25	140	280	—
1957	10.00	12.50	140	280	280
1957D	9.50	4.75	140	280	280
1958	10.50	6.50	140	280	280
1958D	9.75	5.50	140	280	280
1959	2.50	5.00	140	280	280
1959D	2.10	5.25	140	280	280
1960 large date	1.60	4.40	140	280	280
1960 small date	220	—	—	—	—
1960D large date	1.60	5.00	140	280	280
1960D small date	2.85	—	—	—	—
1961	1.60	4.25	140	280	280
1961D	1.90	4.50	140	280	280
1962	1.65	5.25	140	280	280
1962D	1.65	5.50	140	280	280
1963	1.50	4.25	140	280	280
1963D	1.65	4.75	140	280	280
1964	1.50	3.50	140	280	280
1964D	1.60	3.50	140	280	280
1965	2.25	8.75	8.00	25.00	120
1966	3.75	6.00	10.00	53.00	120
1967	4.50	9.75	8.50	25.00	120
1968	1.75	—	8.50	25.00	—
1968D	1.70	6.00	9.50	33.00	120
1968S	1.90	6.25	—	—	—
1969	7.75	—	44.00	100	—
1969D	2.00	6.25	21.50	82.00	120
1969S	3.75	6.75	—	—	—
1970	2.10	—	8.00	26.00	—
1970D	2.10	4.00	7.75	16.00	235
1970S	3.00	4.50	—	—	—
1970S small date	2,650	—	—	—	—
1971	17.00	26.50	16.00	50.00	26.00
1971D	3.00	7.50	9.50	19.50	15.50
1971S	4.00	—	—	—	—
1972	2.00	6.50	11.00	23.00	32.00
1972D	6.00	5.75	10.00	21.50	23.00
1972S	4.75	—	—	—	—
1973	1.75	6.25	10.50	22.00	25.50
1973D	1.75	6.25	9.00	23.00	18.00
1973S	3.00	—	—	—	—
1974	1.75	4.50	7.50	18.50	15.00
1974D	1.75	5.75	7.75	17.50	21.00
1974S	3.50	—	—	—	—
1975	3.75	12.50	8.75	—	—
1975D	1.75	5.25	15.50	—	—
1976	1.75	13.50	21.00	17.50	18.00
1976D	2.50	11.00	18.00	17.50	15.50
1977	1.75	6.25	9.75	16.50	21.50
1977D	2.85	5.75	8.50	17.50	24.00
1978	3.00	4.50	7.25	16.00	32.00
1978D	10.00	5.00	8.00	16.50	46.50
1979	1.75	4.75	8.75	17.00	22.50
1979D	3.00	5.75	8.00	22.50	22.50
1980	1.75	4.25	8.00	16.50	20.50
1980D	2.50	4.50	7.50	16.50	20.50
1981	1.75	4.25	7.50	16.50	16.50
1981D	1.85	4.25	8.00	16.50	19.00
1982 Large date	2.50	—	—	—	—
1982 Small date	25.00	325	270	250	98.00
1982D Large date	4.00	54.00	66.00	165	80.00
1982 Copper plated Zinc	8.00	—	—	—	—
1982 Small date, copper plated zinc	3.00	—	—	—	—
1982D Large date, copper plated zinc	35.00	—	—	—	—
1982D Small date, copper plated zinc	2.50	—	—	—	—
1983	7.50	90.00	235	945	80.00
1983D	17.50	39.00	39.00	410	120
1984	5.50	22.00	8.50	17.00	26.00
1984D	14.50	6.50	21.00	29.00	37.00
1985	4.25	10.00	9.75	31.00	76.00
1985D	9.75	8.00	9.25	22.00	44.00
1986	20.00	8.75	25.00	85.00	75.00
1986D	31.50	24.50	22.50	210	90.00
1987	6.50	6.00	7.75	15.50	52.00
1987D	13.50	4.50	8.75	15.50	52.00
1988	6.25	5.50	9.75	39.00	75.00
1988D	12.50	9.00	9.25	22.50	45.00
1989	3.25	5.50	12.00	19.50	42.00
1989D	3.50	8.75	12.50	17.00	25.00
1990	4.00	11.50	14.50	20.00	39.00
1990D	5.85	13.75	10.00	25.00	52.00
1991	2.60	12.00	10.00	29.00	37.50
1991D	11.50	12.00	11.00	31.00	33.00
1992	3.00	46.00	8.00	42.00	21.00
1992D	5.00	9.00	8.00	27.50	50.00
1993	3.25	13.50	9.50	39.00	64.00
1993D	7.50	17.50	13.00	36.00	17.00
1994	2.00	7.75	12.00	42.00	15.00
1994D	2.00	8.00	12.00	47.50	20.00
1995	1.85	10.50	16.50	15.00	17.00
1995D	2.00	20.00	19.50	53.00	40.00
1996	2.25	8.75	11.00	19.00	17.00
1996D	2.85	8.25	11.50	27.50	19.00
1997	2.75	14.50	29.00	22.50	20.00
1997D	3.35	60.00	11.00	39.00	16.50
1998	2.00	13.75	9.75	17.00	20.00
1998D	1.85	14.00	12.00	18.00	16.50
1999P	2.35	5.50	8.50	—	20.00
1999D	2.25	6.25	8.50	—	19.00
2000P	2.50	6.25	7.75	—	15.00
2000D	1.75	4.75	7.00	—	17.00
2001P	3.75	4.75	7.75	—	16.50
2001D	2.00	6.50	7.25	—	16.00
2002P	2.00	4.00	7.25	—	20.00
2002D	3.25	4.10	7.25	—	20.00
2003P	3.35	7.50	7.00	—	22.50
2003D	2.00	3.50	7.00	—	19.50
2004P Peace Medal Nickel	1.75	6.75	7.00	—	30.00
2004D Peace Medal Nickel	2.50	7.00	7.00	—	30.00
2004P Keel-boat Nickel	—	4.00	—	—	—
2004D Keel-boat Nickel	—	3.50	—	—	—
2005P Bison Nickel	1.75	3.25	7.00	—	21.00
2005D Bison Nickel	2.75	3.25	7.00	—	21.00
2005P Ocean in view Nickel	—	3.25	—	—	—
2005D Ocean in view Nickel	—	3.25	—	—	—
2006P	2.75	3.25	8.50	—	29.00
2006D	1.75	3.25	8.50	—	29.00
2007P	1.75	3.50	8.00	—	21.00
2007D	1.75	3.50	7.75	—	21.00

Date	Cents	Nickels	Dimes	Quarters	Halves
2008P	1.75	3.75	8.00	—	24.50
2008D	1.75	3.75	7.50	—	25.50
2009P Log Cabin	2.00	23.00	13.50	—	18.50
2009D Log Cabin	2.15	13.50	13.50	—	18.50
2009P Log Splitter	1.75	—	—	—	—
2009D Log Splitter	1.75	—	—	—	—
2009P Professional	1.75	—	—	—	—
2009D Professional	1.75	—	—	—	—
2009P President	2.00	—	—	—	—
2009D President	2.00	—	—	—	—

50 STATE QUARTERS UNCIRCULATED ROLLS

Listings are for rolls containing uncirculated coins.

Date	Philadelphia	Denver
1999 Delaware	15.00	15.50
1999 Pennsylvania	16.00	16.50
1999 New Jersey	16.00	15.50
1999 Georgia	28.00	30.00
1999 Connecticut	26.00	27.00
2000 Massachusetts	14.00	15.00
2000 Maryland	14.00	15.50
2000 South Carolina	15.50	15.50
2000 New Hampshire	13.50	14.50
2000 Virginia	14.50	14.50
2001 New York	14.00	14.00
2001 North Carolina	14.50	15.00
2001 Rhode Island	14.00	15.50
2001 Vermont	14.50	14.50
2001 Kentucky	16.50	18.50
2002 Tennessee	30.00	39.50
2002 Ohio	21.50	21.50
2002 Louisiana	14.00	14.00
2002 Indiana	14.50	15.50
2002 Mississippi	16.50	16.50
2003 Illinois	39.00	45.00
2003 Alabama	17.00	18.50
2003 Maine	14.50	15.50
2003 Missouri	14.50	14.75
2003 Arkansas	14.50	15.50
2004 Michigan	13.75	14.50
2004 Florida	13.75	14.50
2004 Texas	14.00	15.00
2004 Iowa	14.00	14.50
2004 Wisconsin	15.50	16.50
2005 California	21.00	22.50
2005 Minnesota	17.50	17.50
2005 Oregon	13.75	13.75
2005 Kansas	13.75	14.50
2005 West Virginia	13.50	13.75
2006 Nevada	13.75	13.75
2006 Nebraska	13.75	14.00
2006 Colorado	13.75	14.00
2006 North Dakota	13.75	14.50
2006 South Dakota	13.75	13.75
2007 Montana	14.00	17.00
2007 Washington	18.00	18.75
2007 Idaho	15.50	15.50
2007 Wyoming	14.75	15.00
2007 Utah	15.00	14.50
2008 Oklahoma	13.75	13.75
2008 New Mexico	14.00	15.50
2008 Arizona	15.50	13.75
2008 Alaska	13.50	13.75
2008 Hawaii	13.50	13.50

COMMEMORATIVE COINAGE 1892-1954

All commemorative half dollars of 1892-1954 have the following specifications: diameter — 30.6 millimeters; weight — 12.500 grams; composition — 0.900 silver, 0.3617 ounces actual silver weight. Values for PDS sets contain one example each from the Philadelphia, Denver and San Francisco mints. Type coin prices are the most inexpensive single coin available from the date and mint mark combinations listed.1892-1954

QUARTER

KM# 115 COLUMBIAN EXPOSITION Weight: 6.25 g. **Composition:** 0.900 Silver, 0.18 oz. ASW **Diameter:** 24.3mm. **Obv.** Queen Isabella bust left **Rev:** Female kneeling with distaff and spindle

Date	Mintage	AU50	MS60	MS63	MS64	MS65
1893	24,214	450	525	650	950	2,750

HALF DOLLAR

KM# 117 COLUMBIAN EXPOSITION Weight: 12.50 g. **Composition:** 0.900 Silver, 0.36 oz. ASW **Diameter:** 30.6mm. **Obv.** Christopher Columbus bust right **Rev:** Santa Maria sailing left, two globes below **Obv. Designer:** Charles E. Barber **Rev. Designer:** George T. Morgan

Date	Mintage	AU50	MS60	MS63	MS64	MS65
1892	950,000	18.50	28.00	80.00	135	525
1893	1,550,405	17.00	28.00	75.00	145	465

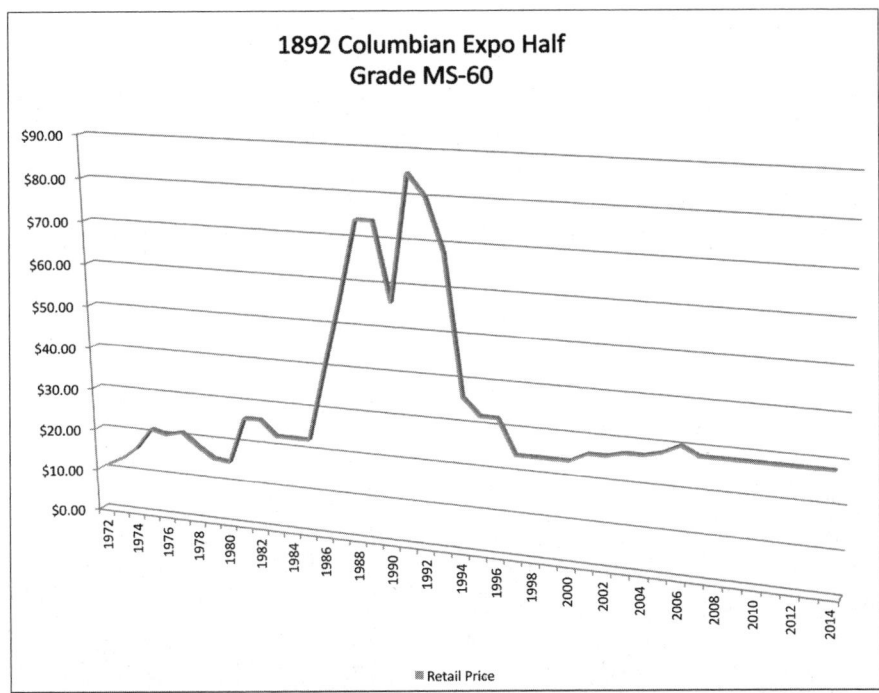

1892 Columbian Expo Half
Grade MS-60

KM# 135 PANAMA-PACIFIC EXPOSITION Weight: 12.50 g. **Composition:** 0.900 Silver, 0.36 oz. ASW **Diameter:** 30.6mm. **Obv.** Columbia standing, sunset in background **Rev:** Eagle standing on shield **Designer:** Charles E. Barber

Date	Mintage	AU50	MS60	MS63	MS64	MS65
1915 S	27,134	465	535	825	1,250	2,650

KM# 143 ILLINOIS CENTENNIAL-LINCOLN Weight: 12.50 g. **Composition:** 0.900 Silver, 0.36 oz. ASW **Diameter:** 30.6mm. **Obv.** Abraham Lincon bust right **Rev:** Eagle standing left **Obv. Designer:** George T. Morgan **Rev. Designer:** John R. Sinnock

Date	Mintage	AU50	MS60	MS63	MS64	MS65
1918	100,058	135	150	165	200	565

KM# 146 MAINE CENTENNIAL Weight: 12.50 g. **Composition:** 0.900 Silver, 0.36 oz. ASW **Diameter:** 30.6mm. **Obv.** Arms of the State of Maine **Rev:** Legend within wreath **Designer:** Anthony de Francisci

Date	Mintage	AU50	MS60	MS63	MS64	MS65
1920	50,028	130	165	185	250	500

KM# 147.1 PILGRIM TERCENTENARY Weight: 12.50 g. **Composition:** 0.900 Silver, 0.36 oz. ASW **Diameter:** 30.6mm. **Obv.** William Bradford half-length left **Rev:** Mayflower sailing left **Designer:** Cyrus E. Dallin

Date	Mintage	AU50	MS60	MS63	MS64	MS65
1920	152,112	80.00	100	110	120	375

KM# 147.2 PILGRIM TERCENTENARY Weight: 12.50 g. **Composition:** 0.900 Silver, 0.36 oz. ASW **Diameter:** 30.6mm. **Obv.** William Bradford half-length left, 1921 added at left **Rev:** Mayflower sailing left **Designer:** Cyrus E. Dallin

Date	Mintage	AU50	MS60	MS63	MS64	MS65
1921	20,053	170	200	220	235	515

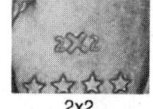

2x2

KM# 148.1 ALABAMA CENTENNIAL Weight: 12.50 g. **Composition:** 0.900 Silver, 0.36 oz. ASW **Diameter:** 30.6mm. **Obv.** William W. Bibb and T.E. Kilby conjoint busts left. "2x2" at right above stars **Rev:** Ealge left on shield **Designer:** Laura G. Fraser **Note:** Fake 2x2" counterstamps exist.

Date	Mintage	AU50	MS60	MS63	MS64	MS65
1921	6,006	315	330	525	675	1,600

KM# 148.2 ALABAMA CENTENNIAL Weight: 12.50 g. **Composition:** 0.900 Silver, 0.36 oz. ASW **Diameter:** 30.6mm. **Obv.** William W. Bibb and T.E. Kilby conjoint busts left **Rev:** Eagle standing left on shield **Obv. Designer:** Laura G. Fraser

Date	Mintage	AU50	MS60	MS63	MS64	MS65
1921	59,038	190	215	525	685	1,800

KM# 149.1 MISSOURI CENTENNIAL Weight: 12.50 g. **Composition:** 0.900 Silver, 0.36 oz. ASW **Diameter:** 30.6mm. **Obv.** Frontiersman in coonskin cap left **Rev:** Frontiersman and Native American standing left **Designer:** Robert Aitken

Date	Mintage	AU50	MS60	MS63	MS64	MS65
1921	15,428	400	600	885	1,275	3,650

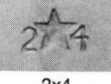

2x4

KM# 149.2 MISSOURI CENTENNIAL Weight: 12.50 g. **Composition:** 0.900 Silver, 0.36 oz. ASW **Diameter:** 30.6mm. **Obv.** Frontiersman in coonskin cap left, 2(star)4 in field at left **Rev:** Frontiersman and Native American standing left **Designer:** Robert Aitken **Note:** Fake "2*4" counterstamps exist.

Date	Mintage	AU50	MS60	MS63	MS64	MS65
1921	5,000	620	720	1,050	1,500	3,450

KM# 151.1 GRANT MEMORIAL Weight: 12.50 g. **Composition:** 0.900 Silver, 0.36 oz. ASW **Diameter:** 30.6mm. **Obv.** Grant bust right **Rev:** Birthplace in Point Pleasant, Ohio **Designer:** Laura G. Fraser

Date	Mintage	AU50	MS60	MS63	MS64	MS65
1922	67,405	120	125	155	250	700

KM# 151.2 GRANT MEMORIAL Weight: 12.50 g.
Composition: 0.900 Silver, 0.36 oz. ASW **Diameter:**
30.6mm. **Obv.** Grant bust left, star above the word
GRANT **Rev:** Birthplace in Point Pleasant, Ohio **Designer:**
Laura G. Fraser **Note:** Fake star" counterstamps exist.

Date	Mintage	AU50	MS60	MS63	MS64	MS65
1922	4,256	925	1,275	1,750	3,450	7,850

KM# 153 MONROE DOCTRINE CENTENNIAL Weight:
12.50 g. **Composition:** 0.900 Silver, 0.36 oz. ASW
Diameter: 30.6mm. **Obv.** James Monroe and John
Quincy Adams conjoint busts left **Rev:** Western
Hemisphere portraied by two female figures **Designer:**
Chester Beach

Date	Mintage	AU50	MS60	MS63	MS64	MS65
1923 S	274,077	56.00	72.50	125	250	1,950

KM# 154 HUGUENOT-WALLOON TERCENTENARY
Weight: 12.50 g. **Composition:** 0.900 Silver, 0.36
oz. ASW **Diameter:** 30.6mm. **Obv.** Huguenot leader
Gaspard de Coligny and William I of Orange conjoint
busts right **Rev:** Nieuw Nederland sailing left **Designer:**
George T. Morgan

Date	Mintage	AU50	MS60	MS63	MS64	MS65
1924	142,080	135	145	150	215	385

KM# 155 CALIFORNIA DIAMOND JUBILEE Weight: 12.50
g. **Composition:** 0.900 Silver, 0.36 oz. ASW **Diameter:**
30.6mm. **Obv.** Fourty-Niner kneeling panning for gold
Rev: Grizzly bear walking left **Designer:** Jo Mora

Date	Mintage	AU50	MS60	MS63	MS64	MS65
1925 S	86,594	195	225	270	485	900

KM# 156 LEXINGTON-CONCORD SESQUICENTENNIAL
Weight: 12.50 g. **Composition:** 0.900 Silver, 0.36 oz.
ASW **Diameter:** 30.6mm. **Obv.** Concord's Minute Man
statue **Rev:** Old Belfry at Lexington **Designer:** Chester
Beach

Date	Mintage	AU50	MS60	MS63	MS64	MS65
1925	162,013	95.00	105	110	145	615

KM# 157 STONE MOUNTAIN MEMORIAL Weight: 12.50
g. **Composition:** 0.900 Silver, 0.36 oz. ASW **Diameter:**
30.6mm. **Obv.** Generals Robert E. Lee and Thomas
"Stonewall" Jackson mounted left. **Rev:** Eagle on rock at
right **Designer:** Gutzon Borglum

Date	Mintage	AU50	MS60	MS63	MS64	MS65
1925	1,314,709	62.00	67.50	80.00	190	315

KM# 158 FORT VANCOUVER CENTENNIAL Weight:
12.50 g. **Composition:** 0.900 Silver, 0.36 oz. ASW
Diameter: 30.6mm. **Obv.** John McLoughlin bust left

Rev: Frontiersmen standing with musket, Ft. Vancouver in background **Designer:** Laura G. Fraser

Date	Mintage	AU50	MS60	MS63	MS64	MS65
1925	14,994	320	360	420	475	1,250

KM# 159 OREGON TRAIL MEMORIAL Weight: 12.50 g. **Composition:** 0.900 Silver, 0.36 oz. ASW **Diameter:** 30.6mm. **Obv.** Native American standing in full headdress and holding bow, US Map in background **Rev:** Conestoga wagon pulled by oxen left towards sunset **Designer:** James E. and Laura G. Fraser

Date	Mintage	AU50	MS60	MS63	MS64	MS65
1926	47,955	135	165	175	195	315
1926 S	83,055	135	165	180	195	320
1928	6,028	220	245	275	285	375
1933 D	5,008	365	380	385	390	465
1934 D	7,006	195	205	215	220	365
1936	10,006	165	190	205	220	340
1936 S	5,006	175	190	210	235	350
1937 D	12,008	175	200	210	225	325
1938	6,006	155	170	205	210	335
1938 D	6,005	155	170	205	220	335
1938 S	6,006	155	170	205	215	335
1939	3,004	510	585	600	620	675
1939 D	3,004	510	585	610	620	675
1939 S	3,005	510	585	590	600	665

KM# 160 U.S. SESQUICENTENNIAL Weight: 12.50 g. **Composition:** 0.900 Silver, 0.36 oz. ASW **Diameter:** 30.6mm. **Obv.** George Washington and Calvin Coolidge conjoint busts right **Rev:** Liberty Bell **Designer:** John R. Sinnock

Date	Mintage	AU50	MS60	MS63	MS64	MS65
1926	141,120	85.00	110	118	465	4,800

KM# 162 VERMONT SESQUICENTENNIAL Weight: 12.50 g. **Composition:** 0.900 Silver, 0.36 oz. ASW **Diameter:** 30.6mm. **Obv.** Ira Allen bust right **Rev:** Catamount advancing left **Obv. Designer:** Charles Keck

Date	Mintage	AU50	MS60	MS63	MS64	MS65
1927	28,142	250	275	290	335	880

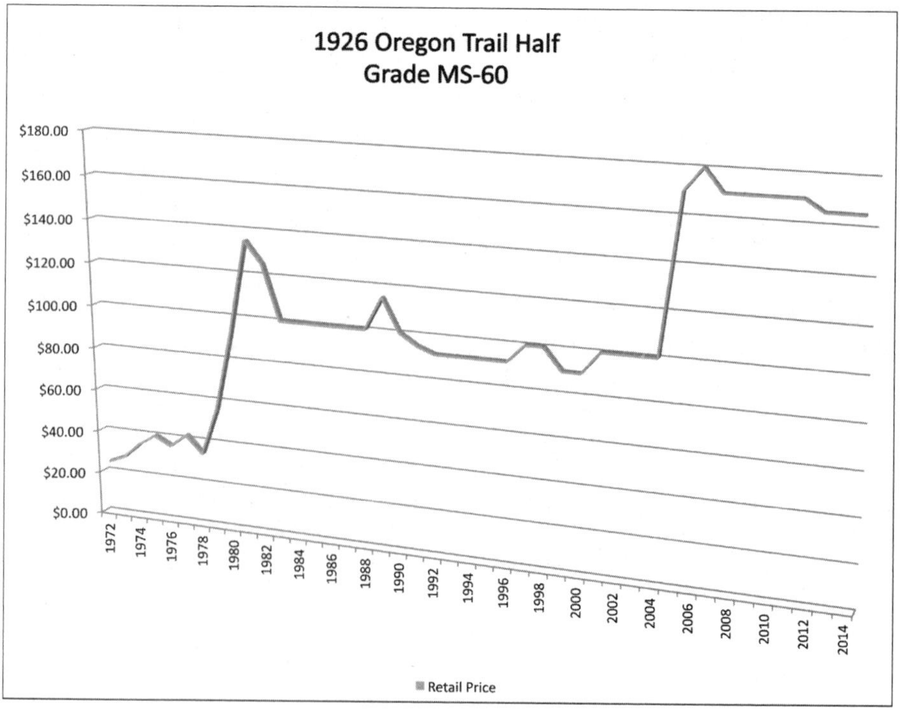

1926 Oregon Trail Half
Grade MS-60

■ Retail Price

KM# 163 HAWAIIAN SESQUICENTENNIAL Weight: 12.50 g. **Composition:** 0.900 Silver, 0.36 oz. ASW **Diameter:** 30.6mm. **Obv.** Captain James Cook bust left **Rev:** Native Hawaiian standing over view of Diamond Head **Designer:** Juliette May Fraser and Chester Beach **Note:** Counterfeits exist.

Date	Mintage	AU50	MS60	MS63	MS64	MS65
1928	10,008	1,785	2,650	3,350	3,775	6,200

KM# 165.2 DANIEL BOONE BICENTENNIAL Weight: 12.50 g. **Composition:** 0.900 Silver, 0.36 oz. ASW **Diameter:** 30.6mm. **Obv.** Daniel Boone bust left **Rev:** Daniel Boone and Native American standing, "1934" added above the word "PIONEER. **Designer:** Augustus Lukeman

Date	Mintage	AU50	MS60	MS63	MS64	MS65
1935	10,008	125	135	140	145	260
1935 D	2,003	360	390	425	450	835
1935 S	2,004	360	390	425	450	815
1936	12,012	120	125	135	140	250
1936 D	5,005	130	135	145	155	295
1936 S	5,006	130	135	145	155	285
1937	9,810	135	135	138	145	260
1937 D	2,506	320	375	385	400	515
1937 S	2,506	320	375	385	400	540
1938	2,100	340	380	390	400	535
1938 D	2,100	340	380	390	410	525
1938 S	2,100	340	380	390	400	565

KM# 167 TEXAS CENTENNIAL Weight: 12.50 g. **Composition:** 0.900 Silver, 0.36 oz. ASW **Diameter:** 30.6mm. **Obv.** Eagle standing left, large star in background **Rev:** Winged Victory kneeling beside Alamo Mission, small busts of Sam Houston and Stephen Austin at sides **Designer:** Pompeo Coppini

Date	Mintage	AU50	MS60	MS63	MS64	MS65
1934	61,463	135	140	150	165	300
1935	9,994	140	145	155	160	300

Date	Mintage	AU50	MS60	MS63	MS64	MS65
1935 D	10,007	140	145	155	160	300
1935 S	10,008	140	145	155	160	300
1936	8,911	140	145	155	160	310
1936 D	9,039	140	145	155	160	310
1936 S	9,055	140	145	155	160	325
1937	6,571	140	145	155	160	310
1937 D	6,605	140	145	155	160	300
1937 S	6,637	140	145	155	160	300
1938	3,780	235	250	260	305	425
1938 D	3,775	240	255	265	305	415
1938 S	3,814	235	250	260	305	415

KM# 168 ARKANSAS CENTENNIAL Weight: 12.50 g. **Composition:** 0.900 Silver, 0.36 oz. ASW **Diameter:** 30.6mm. **Obv.** Liberty and Indian Chief's conjoint heads left **Rev:** Eagle with outstretched wings and Flag of Arkansas in background **Designer:** Edward E. Burr

Date	Mintage	AU50	MS60	MS63	MS64	MS65
1935	13,012	90.00	100	110	120	215
1935 D	5,505	105	110	120	130	250
1935 S	5,506	105	110	120	130	250
1936	9,660	90.00	100	110	120	225
1936 D	9,660	105	110	120	130	255
1936 S	9,662	105	110	120	130	255
1937	5,505	105	115	120	135	275
1937 D	5,505	105	115	120	130	265
1937 S	5,506	105	115	120	135	290
1938	3,156	155	180	190	200	590
1938 D	3,155	160	180	190	200	580
1938 S	3,156	160	180	190	200	640
1939	2,104	320	375	380	400	940
1939 D	2,104	320	375	380	400	910
1939 S	2,105	320	375	380	400	925

KM# 165.1 DANIEL BOONE BICENTENNIAL Weight: 12.50 g. **Composition:** 0.900 Silver, 0.36 oz. ASW **Diameter:** 30.6mm. **Obv.** Daniel Boone bust left **Rev:** Daniel Boone and Native American standing **Designer:** Augustus Lukeman

Date	Mintage	AU50	MS60	MS63	MS64	MS65
1934	10,007	120	125	135	140	250
1935	10,010	120	125	135	140	250
1935 D	5,005	130	135	145	155	295
1935 S	5,005	130	135	145	155	285

KM# 166 MARYLAND TERCENTENARY Weight: 12.50
g. **Composition:** 0.900 Silver, 0.36 oz. ASW **Diameter:**
30.6mm. **Obv.** Lord Baltimore, Cecil Calvert bust right
Rev: Maryland state arms **Designer:** Hans Schuler

Date	Mintage	AU50	MS60	MS63	MS64	MS65
1934	25,015	150	175	185	200	375

**KM# 171 SAN DIEGO-PACIFIC INTERNATIONAL
EXPOSITION Weight:** 12.50 g. **Composition:** 0.900 Silver,
0.36 oz. ASW **Diameter:** 30.6mm. **Obv.** Seated female
with bear at her side **Rev:** State of California exposition
building **Designer:** Robert Aitken

Date	Mintage	AU50	MS60	MS63	MS64	MS65
1935 S	70,132	95.00	98.00	105	110	240
1936 D	30,092	100	120	125	135	275

KM# 169 CONNECTICUT TERCENTENARY Weight: 12.50
g. **Composition:** 0.900 Silver, 0.36 oz. ASW **Diameter:**
30.6mm. **Obv.** Eagle standing left **Rev:** Charter oak tree
Designer: Henry Kreiss

Date	Mintage	AU50	MS60	MS63	MS64	MS65
1935	25,018	240	265	275	325	500

KM# 170 HUDSON, N.Y., SESQUICENTENNIAL Weight:
12.50 g. **Composition:** 0.900 Silver, 0.36 oz. ASW
Diameter: 30.6mm. **Obv.** Hudson's ship, the Half Moon
sailing right **Rev:** Seal of the City of Hudson **Designer:**
Chester Beach

Date	Mintage	AU50	MS60	MS63	MS64	MS65
1935	10,008	750	875	1,050	1,550	2,100

KM# 172 OLD SPANISH TRAIL Weight: 12.50 g.
Composition: 0.900 Silver, 0.36 oz. ASW **Diameter:**
30.6mm. **Obv.** Long-horn cow's head facing **Rev:** The
1535 route of Cabeza de Vaca's expedition and a yucca
tree **Designer:** L.W. Hoffecker **Note:** Counterfeits exist.

Date	Mintage	AU50	MS60	MS63	MS64	MS65
1935	10,008	1,250	1,375	1,650	1,750	2,000

**KM# 173 ALBANY, N.Y., CHARTER ANNIVERSARY
Weight:** 12.50 g. **Composition:** 0.900 Silver, 0.36 oz.
ASW **Diameter:** 30.6mm. **Obv.** Beaver knawing on
maple branch **Rev:** Standing figures of Thomas Dongan,
Peter Schyuyler and Robert Livingston **Designer:**
Gertrude K. Lathrop

Date	Mintage	AU50	MS60	MS63	MS64	MS65
1936	17,671	300	310	330	350	440

**KM# 174 SAN FRANCISCO-OAKLAND BAY BRIDGE
Weight:** 12.50 g. **Composition:** 0.900 Silver, 0.36 oz.
ASW **Diameter:** 30.6mm. **Obv.** Grizzly bear facing **Rev:**
Oakland Bay Bridge **Designer:** Jacques Schnier

Date	Mintage	AU50	MS60	MS63	MS64	MS65
1936	71,424	155	160	165	185	365

KM# 175 BRIDGEPORT, CONN., CENTENNIAL Weight:
12.50 g. **Composition:** 0.900 Silver, 0.36 oz. ASW
Diameter: 30.6mm. **Obv.** P.T. Barnum bust left **Rev:**
Eagle standing right **Designer:** Henry Kreiss

Date	Mintage	AU50	MS60	MS63	MS64	MS65
1936	25,015	130	140	150	175	320

KM# 176 CINCINNATI MUSIC CENTER Weight: 12.50
g. **Composition:** 0.900 Silver, 0.36 oz. ASW **Diameter:**
30.6mm. **Obv.** Stephen Foster bust right **Rev:** Kneeling
female with lyre **Designer:** Constance Ortmayer

Date	Mintage	AU50	MS60	MS63	MS64	MS65
1936	5,005	295	310	335	410	725
1936 D	5,005	295	310	335	410	750
1936 S	5,006	295	310	335	410	750

KM# 177 CLEVELAND-GREAT LAKES EXPOSITION
Weight: 12.50 g. **Composition:** 0.900 Silver, 0.36 oz.
ASW **Diameter:** 30.6mm. **Obv.** Moses Cleaveland bust
left **Rev:** Dividers and map of the Great Lakes **Designer:**
Brenda Putnam

Date	Mintage	AU50	MS60	MS63	MS64	MS65
1936	50,030	110	115	120	160	215

KM# 178 COLUMBIA, S.C., SESQUICENTENNIAL
Weight: 12.50 g. **Composition:** 0.900 Silver, 0.36
oz. ASW **Diameter:** 30.6mm. **Obv.** Figure of Justice

between capitols of 1786 and 1936 **Rev:** Palmetto tree
Designer: A. Wolfe Davidson

Date	Mintage	AU50	MS60	MS63	MS64	MS65
1936	9,007	250	265	270	275	310
1936 D	8,009	260	270	280	285	340
1936 S	8,007	260	270	280	285	340

KM# 179 DELAWARE TERCENTENARY Weight: 12.50
g. **Composition:** 0.900 Silver, 0.36 oz. ASW **Diameter:**
30.6mm. **Obv.** Old Swedes Church in Wilmington **Rev:**
Kalmar Nyckel sailing left **Designer:** Carl L. Schmitz

Date	Mintage	AU50	MS60	MS63	MS64	MS65
1936	20,993	255	265	275	290	465

KM# 180 ELGIN, ILL., CENTENNIAL Weight: 12.50 g.
Composition: 0.900 Silver, 0.36 oz. ASW **Diameter:**
30.6mm. **Obv.** Pioneer head left **Rev:** Statue group
Designer: Trygve Rovelstad

Date	Mintage	AU50	MS60	MS63	MS64	MS65
1936	20,015	195	205	215	225	355

KM# 181 BATTLE OF GETTYSBURG 75TH ANNIVERSARY
Weight: 12.50 g. **Composition:** 0.900 Silver, 0.36 oz.
ASW **Diameter:** 30.6mm. **Obv.** Union and Confederate
veteran conjoint busts right **Rev:** Double blased fasces
seperating two shields **Designer:** Frank Vittor

Date	Mintage	AU50	MS60	MS63	MS64	MS65
1936	26,928	435	460	485	565	925

KM# 182 LONG ISLAND TERCENTENARY Weight: 12.50 g. **Composition:** 0.900 Silver, 0.36 oz. ASW **Diameter:** 30.6mm. **Obv.** Dutch settler and Native American conjoint head right **Rev:** Dutch sailing vessel **Designer:** Howard K. Weinman

Date	Mintage	AU50	MS60	MS63	MS64	MS65
1936	81,826	85.00	92.00	98.00	105	325

KM# 183 LYNCHBURG, VA., SESQUICENTENNIAL Weight: 12.50 g. **Composition:** 0.900 Silver, 0.36 oz. ASW **Diameter:** 30.6mm. **Obv.** Sen. Carter Glass bust left **Rev:** Liberty standing, old Lynchburg courthouse at right **Designer:** Charles Keck

Date	Mintage	AU50	MS60	MS63	MS64	MS65
1936	20,013	220	230	265	275	365

KM# 184 NORFOLK, VA., BICENTENNIAL Weight: 12.50 g. **Composition:** 0.900 Silver, 0.36 oz. ASW **Diameter:** 30.6mm. **Obv.** Seal of the City of Norfolk **Rev:** Royal Mace of Norfolk **Designer:** William M. and Marjorie E. Simpson

Date	Mintage	AU50	MS60	MS63	MS64	MS65
1936	16,936	425	435	445	460	575

KM# 185 RHODE ISLAND TERCENTENARY Weight: 12.50 g. **Composition:** 0.900 Silver, 0.36 oz. ASW **Diameter:** 30.6mm. **Obv.** Roger Williams in canoe hailing Native American **Rev:** Shield with anchor **Designer:** Arthur G. Carey and John H. Benson

Date	Mintage	AU50	MS60	MS63	MS64	MS65
1936	20,013	98.00	105	110	120	290
1936 D	15,010	100	110	120	125	305
1936 S	15,011	100	110	120	130	320

KM# 186 ROANOKE ISLAND, N.C. Weight: 12.50 g. **Composition:** 0.900 Silver, 0.36 oz. ASW **Diameter:** 30.6mm. **Obv.** Sir Walter Raleigh bust left **Rev:** Ellinor Dare holding baby Virginia, two small ships flanking **Designer:** William M. Simpson

Date	Mintage	AU50	MS60	MS63	MS64	MS65
1937	29,030	220	225	235	245	315

KM# 187 ARKANSAS CENTENNIAL Weight: 12.50 g. **Composition:** 0.900 Silver, 0.36 oz. ASW **Diameter:** 30.6mm. **Obv.** Eagle with wings outstreatched, Arkansas flag in backgorund **Rev:** Sen. Joseph T. Robinson bust right **Obv. Designer:** Henry Kreiss **Rev. Designer:** Edward E. Burr

Date	Mintage	AU50	MS60	MS63	MS64	MS65
1936	25,265	140	175	210	220	385

KM# 188 WISCONSIN TERRITORIAL CENTENNIAL Weight: 12.50 g. **Composition:** 0.900 Silver, 0.36 oz. ASW **Diameter:** 30.6mm. **Obv.** Badger from the Territorial seal **Rev:** Pick axe and mound of lead ore **Designer:** David Parsons

Date	Mintage	AU50	MS60	MS63	MS64	MS65
1936	25,015	215	240	255	265	365

KM# 189 YORK COUNTY, MAINE, TERCENTENARY
Weight: 12.50 g. **Composition:** 0.900 Silver, 0.36 oz.
ASW **Diameter:** 30.6mm. **Obv.** Stockade **Rev:** York
County seal **Designer:** Walter H. Rich

Date	Mintage	AU50	MS60	MS63	MS64	MS65
1936	25,015	210	215	225	235	340

KM# 190 BATTLE OF ANTIETAM 75TH ANNIVERSARY
Weight: 12.50 g. **Composition:** 0.900 Silver, 0.36 oz.
ASW **Diameter:** 30.6mm. **Obv.** Generals Robert E. Lee
and George McClellan conjoint busts left **Rev:** Burnside
Bridge **Designer:** William M. Simpson

Date	Mintage	AU50	MS60	MS63	MS64	MS65
1937	18,028	695	735	750	775	950

KM# 191 NEW ROCHELLE, N.Y. Weight: 12.50 g.
Composition: 0.900 Silver, 0.36 oz. ASW **Diameter:**
30.6mm. **Obv.** John Pell and a calf **Rev:** Fleur-de-lis
from the seal of the city **Designer:** Gertrude K. Lathrop

Date	Mintage	AU50	MS60	MS63	MS64	MS65
1938	15,266	375	385	425	440	600

KM# 198 BOOKER T. WASHINGTON Weight: 12.50 g.
Composition: 0.900 Silver, 0.36 oz. ASW **Diameter:**
30.6mm. **Obv.** Booker T. Washington bust right **Rev:**
Cabin and NYU's Hall of Fame **Designer:** Isaac S.

Hathaway **Note:** Actual mintages are higher, but unsold
issues were melted to produce Washington Carver
issues.

Date	Mintage	AU50	MS60	MS63	MS64	MS65
1946	1,000,546	14.00	18.00	21.00	23.00	64.00
1946 D	200,113	16.50	20.00	32.00	37.00	72.00
1946 S	500,729	15.00	18.50	23.00	27.00	66.00
1947	100,017	30.00	36.00	56.00	65.00	80.00
1947 D	100,017	32.00	38.00	62.00	70.00	100
1947 S	100,017	32.00	38.00	59.00	65.00	76.00
1948	8,005	46.00	64.00	77.00	80.00	84.00
1948 D	8,005	46.00	62.00	77.00	80.00	84.00
1948 S	8,005	46.00	65.00	78.00	82.00	88.00
1949	6,004	67.00	82.00	85.00	96.00	115
1949 D	6,004	67.00	82.00	85.00	96.00	115
1949 S	6,004	67.00	82.00	85.00	102	105
1950	6,004	46.00	68.00	72.00	82.00	90.00
1950 D	6,004	46.00	68.00	75.00	82.00	88.00
1950 S	512,091	18.00	20.00	24.00	26.00	65.00
1951	51,082	17.00	22.00	24.00	26.00	65.00
1951 D	7,004	47.00	68.00	80.00	85.00	90.00
1951 S	7,004	47.00	68.00	80.00	84.00	88.00

KM# 197 IOWA STATEHOOD CENTENNIAL Weight: 12.50
g. **Composition:** 0.900 Silver, 0.36 oz. ASW **Diameter:**
30.6mm. **Obv.** First Capitol building at Iowa City **Rev:**
Iowa state seal **Designer:** Adam Pietz

Date	Mintage	AU50	MS60	MS63	MS64	MS65
1946	100,057	100	105	108	112	160

**KM# 200 BOOKER T. WASHINGTON AND GEORGE
WASHINGTON CARVER Weight:** 12.50 g. **Composition:**
0.900 Silver, 0.36 oz. ASW **Diameter:** 30.6mm. **Obv.**
Booker T. Washington and George Washington Carver
conjoint busts right **Rev:** Map of the United States
Designer: Isaac S. Hathaway

Date	Mintage	AU50	MS60	MS63	MS64	MS65
1951	110,018	18.00	20.00	25.00	44.00	290
1951 D	10,004	42.00	50.00	80.00	82.00	140
1951 S	10,004	42.00	50.00	80.00	86.00	90.00
1952	2,006,292	17.00	18.00	24.00	42.00	83.00
1952 D	8,006	40.00	50.00	80.00	85.00	190
1952 S	8,006	40.00	50.00	80.00	84.00	185
1953	8,003	40.00	50.00	80.00	85.00	260
1953 D	8,003	40.00	50.00	80.00	85.00	175
1953 S	108,020	17.00	18.00	24.00	42.00	120
1954	12,006	39.00	48.00	70.00	75.00	200
1954 D	12,006	39.00	48.00	70.00	80.00	83.00
1954 S	122,024	17.00	18.00	24.00	42.00	83.00

DOLLAR

KM# 118 LA FAYETTE Weight: 26.73 g. **Composition:** 0.900 Silver, 0.77 oz. ASW **Diameter:** 38.1mm. **Obv.** George Washington and Marquis de La Fayette conjoint busts right **Rev:** La Fayette on horseback left **Designer:** Charles E. Barber

Date	Mintage	AU50	MS60	MS63	MS64	MS65
1900	36,026	550	950	1,875	3,250	11,500

KM# 119 LOUISIANA PURCHASE EXPOSITION - JEFFERSON Weight: 1.67 g. **Composition:** 0.900 Gold, 0.05 oz. AGW, **Diameter:** 15mm. **Obv.** Jefferson bust left **Rev:** Legend and laurel branch **Designer:** Charles E. Barber

Date	Mintage	AU50	MS60	MS63	MS64	MS65
1903	17,500	600	660	925	1,450	2,150

KM# 120 LOUISIANA PURCHASE EXPOSITION - MCKINLEY Weight: 1.67 g. **Composition:** 0.900 Gold, 0.05 oz. AGW, **Diameter:** 15mm. **Obv.** William McKinley bust left **Rev:** Legend and laurel branch **Obv. Designer:** Charles E. Barber

Date	Mintage	AU50	MS60	MS63	MS64	MS65
1903	17,500	590	650	800	1,400	2,100

KM# 121 LEWIS AND CLARK EXPOSITION Weight: 1.67 g. **Composition:** 0.900 Gold, 0.05 oz. AGW, **Diameter:** 15mm. **Obv.** Lewis bust left **Rev:** Clark bust left **Obv. Designer:** Charles E. Barber

Date	Mintage	AU50	MS60	MS63	MS64	MS65
1904	10,025	950	1,100	1,850	3,650	7,900
1905	10,041	975	1,450	2,250	3,950	15,000

KM# 136 PANAMA-PACIFIC EXPOSITION Weight: 1.67 g. **Composition:** 0.900 Gold, 0.05 oz. AGW, **Diameter:** 15mm. **Obv.** Canal laborer bust left **Rev:** Value within two dolphins **Obv. Designer:** Charles Keck

Date	Mintage	AU50	MS60	MS63	MS64	MS65
1915 S	15,000	565	625	775	1,100	1,700

KM# 144 MCKINLEY MEMORIAL Weight: 1.67 g. **Composition:** 0.900 Gold, 0.05 oz. AGW, **Diameter:** 15mm. **Obv.** William McKinley head left **Rev:** Memorial building at Niles, Ohio **Obv. Designer:** Charles E. Barber **Rev. Designer:** George T. Morgan

Date	Mintage	AU50	MS60	MS63	MS64	MS65
1916	9,977	520	600	685	1,000	1,750
1917	10,000	575	700	900	1,475	2,250

KM# 152.1 GRANT MEMORIAL Weight: 1.67 g. **Composition:** 0.900 Gold, 0.05 oz. AGW, **Diameter:** 15mm. **Obv.** U.S. Grant bust right **Rev:** Birthplace **Obv. Designer:** Laura G. Fraser **Note:** Without an incuse "star" above the word GRANT on the obverse.

Date	Mintage	AU50	MS60	MS63	MS64	MS65
1922	5,000	1,875	1,900	2,350	3,650	4,900

  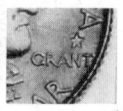 Star

KM# 152.2 GRANT MEMORIAL Weight: 1.67 g. **Composition:** 0.900 Gold, 0.05 oz. AGW, **Diameter:** 15mm. **Obv.** U.S. Grant bust right **Rev:** Birthplace **Obv. Designer:** Laura G. Fraser **Note:** Variety with an incuse "star" above the word GRANT on the obverse.

Date	Mintage	AU50	MS60	MS63	MS64	MS65
1922	5,016	1,650	1,775	2,100	2,150	3,100

$2.50 (QUARTER EAGLE)

KM# 137 PANAMA-PACIFIC EXPOSITION Weight: 4.18 g. **Composition:** 0.900 Gold, 0.12 oz. AGW, **Diameter:** 18mm. **Obv.** Columbia holding cadueus while seated on a hippocamp **Rev:** Eagle standing left **Obv. Designer:** Charles E. Barber **Rev. Designer:** George T. Morgan

Date	Mintage	AU50	MS60	MS63	MS64	MS65
1915 S	6,749	1,550	1,950	4,100	5,650	6,750

KM# 161 U.S. SESQUICENTENNIAL Weight: 4.18 g.
Composition: 0.900 Gold, 0.12 oz. AGW, **Diameter:**
18mm. **Obv.** Liberty standing holding torch and scroll
Rev: Independence Hall **Obv. Designer:** John R. Sinnock

Date	Mintage	AU50	MS60	MS63	MS64	MS65
1926	46,019	425	500	800	1,375	3,450

$50

KM# 138 PANAMA-PACIFIC EXPOSITION ROUND
Weight: 83.59 g. **Composition:** 0.900 Gold, 2.40 oz.
AGW, **Diameter:** 44mm. **Obv.** Minerva bust helmeted
left **Rev:** Owl pearched on California pin branch **Obv.**
Designer: Robert Aitken **Shape:** Round

Date	Mintage	AU50	MS60	MS63	MS64	MS65
1915 S	483	46,500	57,500	90,000	105,000	160,000

KM# 139 PANAMA-PACIFIC EXPOSITION OCTAGONAL
Weight: 83.59 g. **Composition:** 0.900 Gold, 2.40 oz.
AGW, **Diameter:** 44mm. **Obv.** Minerva bust helmeted
left **Rev:** Owl perched on California pine branch **Obv.**
Designer: Robert Aitken **Shape:** Octagon

Date	Mintage	AU50	MS60	MS63	MS64	MS65
1915 S	645	50,000	52,500	84,500	98,000	146,000

COMMEMORATIVE COINAGE 1982-PRESENT

All commemorative silver dollar coins of 1982-present have the following specifications: diameter — 38.1 millimeters;
weight — 26.730 grams; composition — 0.900 silver, 0.7736 ounces actual silver weight. All commemorative $5 coins of
1982-present have the following specificiations: diameter — 21.6 millimeters; weight — 8.359 grams; composition: 0.900
gold, 0.242 ounces actual gold weight. Note: In 1982, after a hiatus of nearly 20 years, coinage of commemorative half
dollars resumed. Those designated with a 'W' were struck at the West Point Mint. Some issues were struck in copper-nickel.
Those struck in silver have the same size, weight and composition as the prior commemorative half-dollar series.

HALF DOLLAR

KM# 208 • ObvDesc: George Washington on horseback
facing • **RevDesc:** Mount Vernon • 12.50 g., 0.900
Silver 0.36 oz. ASW 30.6mm • **Obv. Designer:** Elizabeth
Jones • **Rev. Designer:** Matthew Peloso

Date	Mintage	MS63	MS65	Prf65
1982D	2,210,458	—	13.70	—
1982S	4,894,044	—	—	13.70

COMMEMORATIVES

KM# 212 • ObvDesc: Statue of Liberty and sunrise • **RevDesc:** Emigrant family looking toward mainland • 11.34 g.**Copper-Nickel Clad Copper • Obv. Designer:** Edgar Z. Steever • **Rev. Designer:** Sherl Joseph Winter

Date	Mintage	MS63	MS65	Prf65
1986D	928,008	—	3.25	—
1986S	6,925,627	—	—	3.50

KM# 224 • ObvDesc: Statue of Freedom head • **RevDesc:** Capitol building • 11.34 g.**Copper-Nickel Clad Copper • Obv. Designer:** Patricia L. Verani • **Rev. Designer:** William Woodward and Edgar Z. Steever

Date	Mintage	MS63	MS65	Prf65
1989D	163,753	—	7.50	—
1989S	762,198	—	—	7.50

KM# 228 • RevDesc: Mount Rushmore portraits • 11.34 g.**Copper-Nickel Clad Copper • Obv. Designer:** Marcel Jovine • **Rev. Designer:** T. James Ferrell

Date	Mintage	MS63	MS65	Prf65
1991D	172,754	—	17.50	—
1991S	753,257	—	—	16.00

KM# 233 • ObvDesc: Torch and laurel • **RevDesc:** Female gymnast and large flag • 11.34 g.**Copper-Nickel**

Clad Copper • Obv. Designer: William Cousins • **Rev. Designer:** Steven M. Bieda

Date	Mintage	MS63	MS65	Prf65
1992P	161,607	—	8.50	—
1992S	519,645	—	—	8.50

KM# 237 • ObvDesc: Columbus standing on shore • **RevDesc:** Nina, Pinta and Santa Maria sailing right • 11.34 g.**Copper-Nickel Clad Copper • Obv. Designer:** T. James Ferrell • **Rev. Designer:** Thomas D. Rogers, Sr.

Date	Mintage	MS63	MS65	Prf65
1992D	135,702	—	11.50	—
1992S	390,154	—	—	8.75

KM# 240 • ObvDesc: James Madison writing, Montpelier in background • **RevDesc:** Statue of Liberty torch • 12.50 g., 0.900 **Silver** 0.36 oz. ASW • **Obv. Designer:** T. James Ferrell • **Rev. Designer:** Dean McMullen

Date	Mintage	MS63	MS65	Prf65
1993W	193,346	—	19.00	—
1993S	586,315	—	—	19.00

KM# 243 • ObvDesc: Three portraits, plane above, large V in background • **RevDesc:** Pacific island battle scene • 11.34 g.**Copper-Nickel Clad Copper • Obv. Designer:** George Klauba and T. James Ferrell • **Rev. Designer:** William J. Leftwich and T. James Ferrell

Date	Mintage	MS63	MS65	Prf65
NDP	317,396	—	—	16.50
NDP	197,072	—	17.00	—

KM# 246 • ObvDesc: Soccer player with ball •
RevDesc: World Cup 94 logo • 11.34 g.**Copper-Nickel
Clad Copper** • **Obv. Designer:** Richard T. LaRoche •
Rev. Designer: Dean McMullen

Date	Mintage	MS63	MS65	Prf65
1994D	168,208	—	8.25	—
1994P	609,354	—	—	8.00

KM# 254 • ObvDesc: Drummer and fenceline
• **RevDesc:** Canon overlooking battlefield • 11.34
g.**Copper-Nickel Clad Copper** • **Obv. Designer:** Don
Troiani • **Rev. Designer:** T. James Ferrell

Date	Mintage	MS63	MS65	Prf65
1995S	119,510	—	36.50	—
1995S	330,099	—	—	33.50

KM# 257 • ObvDesc: Three players, one jumping for a
shot • **RevDesc:** Hemisphere and Atlanta Olympics logo
• 11.34 g.**Copper-Nickel Clad Copper** • **Obv. Designer:**
Clint Hansen and Al Maletsky • **Rev. Designer:** T. James
Ferrell

Date	Mintage	MS63	MS65	Prf65
1995S	171,001	—	17.00	—
1995S	169,655	—	—	18.00

KM# 262 • ObvDesc: Baseball batter at plate, catcher

and umpire • **RevDesc:** Hemisphere and Atlanta
Olympics logo • 11.34 g.**Copper-Nickel Clad Copper**
• **Obv. Designer:** Edgar Z. Steever • **Rev. Designer:** T.
James Ferrell

Date	Mintage	MS63	MS65	Prf65
1995S	164,605	—	19.50	—
1995S	118,087	—	—	17.50

KM# 271 • ObvDesc: Two female soccer players •
RevDesc: Atlanta Olympics logo • 11.34 g.**Copper-
Nickel Clad Copper**

Date	Mintage	MS63	MS65	Prf65
1996S	52,836	—	130	—
1996S	122,412	—	—	88.00

KM# 267 • ObvDesc: Swimmer right in butterfly stroke •
RevDesc: Atlanta Olympics logo • 11.34 g.**Copper-Nickel
Clad Copper** • **Obv. Designer:** William J. Krawczewicz
and Edgar Z. Steever • **Rev. Designer:** Malcolm Farley
and Thomas D. Rogers, Sr.

Date	Mintage	MS63	MS65	Prf65
1996S	49,533	—	140	—
1996S	114,315	—	—	31.00

KM# 323 • ObvDesc: Capitol sillouete, 1800 structure
in detail • **RevDesc:** Legend within circle of stars •
11.34 g.**Copper-Nickel Clad Copper** • **Obv. Designer:**
Dean McMullen • **Rev. Designer:** Alex Shagin and Marcel
Jovine

Date	Mintage	MS63	MS65	Prf65
2001P	99,157	—	14.50	—
2001P	77,962	—	—	15.50

COMMEMORATIVES

KM# 348 • ObvDesc: Wright Monument at Kitty Hawk • **RevDesc:** Wright Flyer in flight • 11.34 g.**Copper-Nickel Clad Copper • Obv. Designer:** John Mercanti • **Rev. Designer:** Donna Weaver

Date	Mintage	MS63	MS65	Prf65
2003P	57,726	—	15.00	—
2003P	111,569	—	—	17.00

KM# 438 • ObvDesc: Two eaglets in nest with egg • **RevDesc:** Eagle Challenger facing right, American Flag in background • 11.34 g.**Copper-Nickel Clad Copper**, 30.6 • **Obv. Designer:** Susan Gamble and Joseph Menna • **Rev. Designer:** Donna Weaver and Charles Vickers

Date	Mintage	MS63	MS65	Prf65
2008S	120,180	—	12.50	—
2008S	222,577	—	—	14.00

KM# 506 • ObvDesc: Army contributions during peacetime, surveying, building a flood wall and space exploration • **RevDesc:** Continental soldier with musket • 11.34 g.**Copper-Nickel Clad Copper**, 30.6 • **Obv. Designer:** Donna Weaver and Charles L. Vickers • **Rev. Designer:** Thomas Cleveland and Joseph Menna

Date	Mintage	MS63	MS65	Prf65
2011D	39,461	—	69.00	—
2011S	68,349	—	—	35.00

KM# 554 • 5-Star General **Silver**, 30.6

Date	Mintage	MS63	MS65	Prf65
2013P	38,097	—	50.00	—
2013S	47,337	—	—	60.00

KM# 576 • 11.34 g.Copper-Nickel Clad Copper, 30.6mm. • **Subject:** Baseball Hall of Fame

Date	Mintage	MS63	MS65	PRF65
2014	—	—	50.00	—
2014	—	—	—	60.00

DOLLAR

KM# 209 • ObvDesc: Trippled discus thrower and five star logo • **RevDesc:** Eagle bust left • 26.73 g., 0.900 **Silver** 0.77 oz. ASW, 38.1mm • **Obv. Designer:** Elizabeth Jones

Date	Mintage	MS63	MS65	Prf65
1983P	294,543	—	34.80	—
1983D	174,014	—	34.70	—
1983S	174,014	—	34.80	—
1983S	1,577,025	—	—	36.80

KM# 210 • ObvDesc: Statues at exterior of Los Angeles Memorial Coliseum • **RevDesc:** Eagle standing on rock • 26.73 g., 0.900 **Silver** 0.77 oz. ASW, 38.1 • **Obv. Designer:** Robert Graham

Date	Mintage	MS63	MS65	Prf65
1984P	217,954	—	34.80	—
1984D	116,675	—	35.30	—
1984S	116,675	—	35.30	—
1984S	1,801,210	—	—	36.80

KM# 220 • ObvDesc: Feather pen and document • **RevDesc:** Group of people • 26.73 g., 0.900 **Silver** 0.77 oz. ASW, 38.1 • **Obv. Designer:** Patricia L. Verani

Date	Mintage	MS63	MS65	Prf65
1987P	451,629	—	34.80	—
1987S	2,747,116	—	—	36.80

KM# 214 • ObvDesc: Statue of Liberty and Ellis Island great hall • **RevDesc:** Statue of Liberty torch • 26.73 g., 0.900 **Silver** 0.77 oz. ASW, 38.1 • **Obv. Designer:** John Mercanti • **Rev. Designer:** John Mercanti and Matthew Peloso

Date	Mintage	MS63	MS65	Prf65
1986P	723,635	—	34.80	—
1986S	6,414,638	—	—	36.80

KM# 222 • ObvDesc: Olympic torch and Statue of Liberty torch within laurel wreath • **RevDesc:** Olympic rights within olive wreath • 26.73 g., 0.900 **Silver** 0.77 oz. ASW, 38.1 • **Obv. Designer:** Patricia L. Verani • **Rev. Designer:** Sherl Joseph Winter

Date	Mintage	MS63	MS65	Prf65
1988D	191,368	—	34.80	—
1988S	1,359,366	—	—	36.80

COMMEMORATIVES

KM# 225 • ObvDesc: Statue of Freedom in clouds and sunburst • **RevDesc:** Mace from the House of Represeatives • 26.73 g., 0.900 **Silver** 0.77 oz. ASW, 38.1

Date	Mintage	MS63	MS65	Prf65
1989D	135,203	—	34.80	—
1989S	762,198	—	—	36.80

KM# 229 • ObvDesc: Mount Rushmore portraits, wreath below • **RevDesc:** Great seal in rays, United States map in background • 26.73 g., 0.900 **Silver** 0.77 oz. ASW, 38.1 • **Obv. Designer:** Marika Somogyi and Chester Martin • **Rev. Designer:** Frank Gasparro

Date	Mintage	MS63	MS65	Prf65
1991P	133,139	—	39.80	—
1991S	738,419	—	—	42.80

KM# 227 • ObvDesc: Two Eisenhower profiles, as general, left, as President, right • **RevDesc:** Eisenhower home at Gettysburg • 26.73 g., 0.900 **Silver** 0.77 oz. ASW, 38.1 • **Obv. Designer:** John Mercanti • **Rev. Designer:** Marcel Jovine and John Mercanti

Date	Mintage	MS63	MS65	Prf65
1990W	241,669	—	34.80	—
1990P	1,144,461	—	—	36.80

KM# 231 • ObvDesc: Solder advancing right up a hill; planes above, ships below • **RevDesc:** Map of Korean peninsula, eagle's head • 26.73 g., 0.900 **Silver** 0.77 oz. ASW, 38.1 • **Obv. Designer:** John Mercanti • **Rev. Designer:** T. James Ferrell

Date	Mintage	MS63	MS65	Prf65
1991D	213,049	—	37.80	—
1991P	618,488	—	—	36.80

KM# 232 • ObvDesc: USO banner • **RevDesc:** Eagle pearched right atop globe • 26.73 g., 0.900 **Silver** 0.77 oz. ASW, 38.1 • **Obv. Designer:** Robert Lamb • **Rev. Designer:** John Mercanti

Date	Mintage	MS63	MS65	Prf65
1991D	124,958	—	37.80	—
1991S	321,275	—	—	38.80

KM# 236 • ObvDesc: White House's north portico • **RevDesc:** John Hoban bust left, main entrance doorway • 26.73 g., 0.900 **Silver** 0.77 oz. ASW, 38.1 • **Obv. Designer:** Edgar Z. Steever • **Rev. Designer:** Chester Y. Martin

Date	Mintage	MS63	MS65	Prf65
1992D	123,803	—	37.80	—
1992W	375,851	—	—	38.80

KM# 234 • ObvDesc: Baseball pitcher, Nolan Ryan as depicted on card • **RevDesc:** Shield flanked by stylized wreath, olympic rings above • 26.73 g., 0.900 **Silver** 0.77 oz. ASW, 38.1 • **Obv. Designer:** John R. Deecken and Chester Y. Martin • **Rev. Designer:** Marcel Jovine

Date	Mintage	MS63	MS65	Prf65
1992D	187,552	—	37.80	—
1992S	504,505	—	—	38.80

KM# 238 • ObvDesc: Columbus standing with banner, three ships in background • **RevDesc:** Half view of Santa Maria on left, Space Shuttle Discovery on right • 26.73 g., 0.900 **Silver** 0.77 oz. ASW, 38.1 • **Obv. Designer:** John Mercanti • **Rev. Designer:** Thomas D. Rogers, Sr.

Date	Mintage	MS63	MS65	Prf65
1992D	106,949	—	40.80	—
1992P	385,241	—	—	37.80

COMMEMORATIVES

KM# 241 • ObvDesc: James Madison bust right, at left •
RevDesc: Montpelier home • 26.73 g., 0.900 **Silver** 0.77
oz. ASW, 38.1 • **Obv. Designer:** William Krawczewicz
and Thomas D. Rogers, Sr. • **Rev. Designer:** Dean
McMullen and Thomas D. Rogers, Sr.

Date	Mintage	MS63	MS65	Prf65
1993D	98,383	—	37.80	—
1993S	534,001	—	—	38.80

KM# 247 • ObvDesc: Two players with ball • **RevDesc:**
World Cup 94 logo • 26.73 g., 0.900 **Silver** 0.77 oz. ASW,
38.1 • **Obv. Designer:** Dean McMullen and T. James
Ferrell • **Rev. Designer:** Dean McMullen

Date	Mintage	MS63	MS65	Prf65
1994D	81,698	—	38.80	—
1994S	576,978	—	—	36.80

KM# 244 • ObvDesc: Soldier on Normandy beach •
RevDesc: Insignia of the Supreme Headquarters of the
AEF above Eisenhower quote • 26.73 g., 0.900 **Silver**
0.77 oz. ASW, 38.1

Date	Mintage	MS63	MS65	Prf65
1993D	94,708	—	36.80	—
1993W	342,041	—	—	40.80

KM# 249 • ObvDesc: Jefferson's head left • **RevDesc:**
Monticello home • 26.73 g., 0.900 **Silver** 0.77 oz. ASW,
38.1

Date	Mintage	MS63	MS65	Prf65
1993P	266,927	—	36.80	—
1993S	332,891	—	—	40.80

KM# 250 • ObvDesc: Outstretched hand touching names on the Wall, Washington Monument in background • **RevDesc:** Service Medals • 26.73 g., 0.900 **Silver** 0.77 oz. ASW, 38.1 • **Obv. Designer:** John Mercanti • **Rev. Designer:** Thomas D. Rogers, Sr.

Date	Mintage	MS63	MS65	Prf65
1994W	57,317	—	79.00	—
1994P	226,262	—	—	63.00

KM# 252 • ObvDesc: Five uniformed women left • **RevDesc:** Memorial at Arlington National Cemetery • 26.73 g., 0.900 **Silver** 0.77 oz. ASW, 38.1 • **Obv. Designer:** T. James Ferrell • **Rev. Designer:** Thomas D. Rogers, Sr.

Date	Mintage	MS63	MS65	Prf65
1994W	53,054	—	38.80	—
1994P	213,201	—	—	38.80

KM# 251 • ObvDesc: Eagle in flight left within circle of barbed wire • **RevDesc:** National Prisioner of War Museum • 26.73 g., 0.900 **Silver** 0.77 oz. ASW, 38.1 • **Obv. Designer:** Thomas Nielson and Alfred Maletsky • **Rev. Designer:** Edgar Z. Steever

Date	Mintage	MS63	MS65	Prf65
1994W	54,790	—	84.00	—
1994P	220,100	—	—	39.80

KM# 253 • ObvDesc: Capitol dome, Statue fo Freedom surrounded by stars • **RevDesc:** Eagle on shield, flags flanking • 26.73 g., 0.900 **Silver** 0.77 oz. ASW, 38.1 • **Obv. Designer:** William C. Cousins • **Rev. Designer:** John Mercanti

Date	Mintage	MS63	MS65	Prf65
1994D	68,352	—	38.80	—
1994S	279,416	—	—	40.80

COMMEMORATIVES

KM# 255 • ObvDesc: Soldier giving water to wounded soldier • **RevDesc:** Chamberlain quote and battlefield monument • 26.73 g., 0.900 **Silver** 0.77 oz. ASW, 38.1 • **Obv. Designer:** Don Troiani and Edgar Z. Steever • **Rev. Designer:** John Mercanti

Date	Mintage	MS63	MS65	Prf65
1995P	45,866	—	65.00	—
1995S	437,114	—	—	54.00

KM# 259 • ObvDesc: Blind runner • **RevDesc:** Two clasped hands, Atlanta Olympic logo above • 26.73 g., 0.900 **Silver** 0.77 oz. ASW, 38.1 • **Obv. Designer:** Jim C. Sharpe and Thomas D. Rogers, Sr. • **Rev. Designer:** William J. Krawczewicz and T. James Ferrell

Date	Mintage	MS63	MS65	Prf65
1995D	28,649	—	67.00	—
1995P	138,337	—	—	45.00

KM# 260 • ObvDesc: Two gymnasts, female on floor exercise and male on rings • **RevDesc:** Two clasped hands, Atlanta Olympic logo above • 26.73 g., 0.900 **Silver** 0.77 oz. ASW, 38.1 • **Obv. Designer:** James C. Sharpe and Thomas D. Rogers, Sr. • **Rev. Designer:** William J. Krawczewicz and T. James Ferrell

Date	Mintage	MS63	MS65	Prf65
1995D	42,497	—	55.00	—
1995P	182,676	—	—	36.80

KM# 263 • ObvDesc: Three cyclists approaching • **RevDesc:** Two clasped hands, Atlanta Olympic logo above • 26.73 g., 0.900 **Silver** 0.77 oz. ASW, 38.1 • **Obv. Designer:** John Mercanti • **Rev. Designer:** William J. Krawczewicz and T. James Ferrell

Date	Mintage	MS63	MS65	Prf65
1995D	19,662	—	135	—
1995P	118,795	—	—	45.00

KM# 264 • ObvDesc: Two runners on a track, one crossing finish line • **RevDesc:** Two clasped hands, Atlanta Olympic logo above • 26.73 g., 0.900 **Silver** 0.77 oz. ASW, 38.1 • **Obv. Designer:** John Mercanti • **Rev. Designer:** William J. Krawczewicz and T. James Ferrell

Date	Mintage	MS63	MS65	Prf65
1995D	24,796	—	88.00	—
1995P	136,935	—	—	38.80

KM# 268 • ObvDesc: Wheelchair racer approaching with uplifted arms • **RevDesc:** Atlanta Olympics logo • 26.73 g., 0.900 **Silver** 0.77 oz. ASW, 38.1 • **Obv. Designer:** James C. Sharpe and Alfred F. Maletsky • **Rev. Designer:** Thomas D. Rogers, Sr.

Date	Mintage	MS63	MS65	Prf65
1996D	14,497	—	305	—
1996P	84,280	—	—	71.00

KM# 266 • ObvDesc: Eunice Schriver head left; founder of the Special Olympics • **RevDesc:** Special Olympics Logo on an award medal, rose, quote from Schriver • 26.73 g., 0.900 **Silver** 0.77 oz. ASW, 38.1 • **Obv. Designer:** Jamie Wyeth and T. James Ferrell • **Rev. Designer:** Thomas D. Rogers, Sr.

Date	Mintage	MS63	MS65	Prf65
1995W	89,301	—	40.80	—
1995P	351,764	—	—	41.80

KM# 269 • ObvDesc: Female tennis player • **RevDesc:** Atlanta Olympics logo • 26.73 g., 0.900 **Silver** 0.77 oz. ASW, 38.1 • **Obv. Designer:** James C. Sharpe and T. James Ferrell • **Rev. Designer:** Thomas D. Rogers, Sr.

Date	Mintage	MS63	MS65	Prf65
1996D	15,983	—	245	—
1996P	92,016	—	—	83.00

COMMEMORATIVES

KM# A272 • Obv. Desc.: High jumper • 26.73 g., 0.900 **Silver** 0.77 oz. ASW • **Obv. Designer:** T. James Ferrell • **Rev. Designer:** Thomas D. Rogers, Sr.

Date	Mintage	MS63	MS65	Prf65
1996D	15,697	—	310	—
1996P	124,502	—	—	43.00

KM# 272 • Obv. Desc.: Four man crew rowing left • **Rev. Desc.:** Atlanta Olympic logo • 26.73 g., 0.900 **Silver** 0.77 oz. ASW, 38.1 • **Obv. Designer:** Bart Forbes and T. James Ferrell • **Rev. Designer:** Thomas D. Rogers, Sr.

Date	Mintage	MS63	MS65	Prf65
1996D	16,258	—	290	—
1996P	151,890	—	—	62.00

KM# 275 • Obv. Desc.: Female standing with lamp and shield • **Rev. Desc.:** Legend within wreath • 26.73

g., 0.900 **Silver** 0.77 oz. ASW, 38.1 • **Obv. Designer:** Thomas D. Rogers, Sr. • **Rev. Designer:** William C. Cousins

Date	Mintage	MS63	MS65	Prf65
1996S	101,543	—	—	51.00
1996S	23,500	—	170	—

KM# 276 • Obv. Desc.: Original Smithsonian building, the "Castle" designed by James Renwick • **Rev. Desc.:** Female seated with torch and scroll on globe • 26.73 g., 0.900 **Silver** 0.77 oz. ASW, 38.1 • **Obv. Designer:** Thomas D. Rogers, Sr. • **Rev. Designer:** John Mercanti

Date	Mintage	MS63	MS65	Prf65
1996D	31,230	—	122	—
1996P	129,152	—	—	49.00

KM# 278 • Obv. Desc.: National Botanic Gardens Conservatory building • **Rev. Desc.:** Rose • 26.73 g., 0.900 **Silver** 0.77 oz. ASW, 38.1 • **Obv. Designer:** Edgar Z. Steever • **Rev. Designer:** William C. Cousins

Date	Mintage	MS63	MS65	Prf65
1997P	57,272	—	42.00	—
1997P	264,528	—	—	42.00

KM# 279 • Obv. Desc.: Jackie Robinson sliding into base • **Rev. Desc.:** Anniversary logo • 26.73 g., 0.900 **Silver** 0.77 oz. ASW, 38.1 • **Obv. Designer:** Alfred Maletsky • **Rev. Designer:** T. James Ferrell

Date	Mintage	MS63	MS65	Prf65
1997S	30,007	—	72.00	—
1997S	110,495	—	—	90.00

KM# 281 • Obv. Desc.: Male and female officer admiring name on monument • **Rev. Desc.:** Rose on a plain shield • 26.73 g., 0.900 **Silver** 0.77 oz. ASW, 38.1

Date	Mintage	MS63	MS65	Prf65
1997P	28,575	—	135	—
1997P	110,428	—	—	78.00

KM# 287 • Obv. Desc.: Kennedy bust facing • **Rev. Desc.:** Eagle on sheild, Senate Seal • 26.73 g., 0.900 **Silver** 0.77 oz. ASW, 38.1 • **Obv. Designer:** Thomas D. Rogers, Sr. • **Rev. Designer:** James M. Peed and Thomas D. Rogers, Sr.

Date	Mintage	MS63	MS65	Prf65
1998S	106,422	—	47.50	—
1998S	99,020	—	—	47.50

KM# 288 • Obv. Desc.: Crispus Attucks bust right • **Rev. Desc.:** Family standing • 26.73 g., 0.900 **Silver** 0.77 oz. ASW, 38.1 • **Obv. Designer:** John Mercanti • **Rev. Designer:** Edward Dwight and Thomas D. Rogers, Sr.

Date	Mintage	MS63	MS65	Prf65
1998S	37,210	—	145	—
1998S	75,070	—	—	89.00

COMMEMORATIVES

KM# 298 • Obv. Desc.: Madison bust right, at left •
Rev. Desc.: Montpelier home • 26.73 g., 0.900 **Silver**
0.77 oz. ASW, 38.1 • **Obv. Designer:** Tiffany & Co.
and T. James Ferrell • **Rev. Designer:** Tiffany & Co. and
Thomas D. Rogers, Sr.

Date	Mintage	MS63	MS65	Prf65
1999P	22,948	—	38.30	—
1999P	158,247	—	—	38.30

KM# 299 • Obv. Desc.: Old Faithful gyser erupting •
Rev. Desc.: Bison and vista as on National Parks shield
• 26.73 g., 0.900 **Silver** 0.77 oz. ASW, 38.1 • **Obv.
Designer:** Edgar Z. Steever • **Rev. Designer:** William C.
Cousins

Date	Mintage	MS63	MS65	Prf65
1999P	82,563	—	44.00	—
1999P	187,595	—	—	40.30

KM# 311 • Obv. Desc.: Open and closed book, torch
in background • **Rev. Desc.:** Skylight dome above the
main reading room • 26.73 g., 0.900 **Silver** 0.77 oz.
ASW • **Obv. Designer:** Thomas D. Rogers, Sr. • **Rev.
Designer:** John Mercanti

Date	Mintage	MS63	MS65	Prf65
2000P	52,771	—	40.80	—
2000P	196,900	—	—	38.30

KM# 313 • Obv. Desc.: Ericson bust helmeted right
• **Rev. Desc.:** Viking ship sailing left • 26.73 g., 0.900
Silver 0.77 oz. ASW • **Obv. Designer:** John Mercanti •
Rev. Designer: T. James Ferrell

Date	Mintage	MS63	MS65	Prf65
2000P	28,150	—	69.00	—
2000P	58,612	—	—	62.50
2000 Iceland	15,947	—	—	26.80

KM# 324 • Obv. Desc.: Original and current Capital facades • **Rev. Desc.:** Eagle with sheild and ribbon • 26.73 g., 0.900 **Silver** 0.77 oz. ASW • **Obv. Designer:** Marika Somogyi • **Rev. Designer:** John Mercanti

Date	Mintage	MS63	MS65	Prf65
2001P	66,636	—	40.80	—
2001P	143,793	—	—	40.80

KM# 336 • Obv. Desc.: Salt Lake City Olympic logo • **Rev. Desc.:** Stylized skyline with mountains in background • 26.73 g., 0.900 **Silver** 0.77 oz. ASW, 38.1 • **Obv. Designer:** John Mercanti • **Rev. Designer:** Donna Weaver

Date	Mintage	MS63	MS65	Prf65
2002P	35,388	—	40.80	—
2002P	142,873	—	—	38.30

KM# 325 • Obv. Desc.: Native American bust right • **Rev. Desc.:** Bison standing left • 26.73 g., 0.900 **Silver** 0.77 oz. ASW

Date	Mintage	MS63	MS65	Prf65
2001D	197,131	—	165	—
2001P	272,869	—	—	169

KM# 338 • Obv. Desc.: Cadet Review flagbearers, Academy buildings in background • **Rev. Desc.:** Academy emblems - Corinthian helmet and sword • 26.73 g., 0.900 **Silver** 0.77 oz. ASW, 38.1 • **Obv. Designer:** T. James Ferrell • **Rev. Designer:** John Mercanti

Date	Mintage	MS63	MS65	Prf65
2002W	103,201	—	38.30	—
2002W	288,293	—	—	39.80

KM# 349 • Obv. Desc.: Orville and Wilbur Wright busts left • **Rev. Desc.:** Wright Flyer over dunes • 26.75 g., 0.900 **Silver** 0.77 oz. ASW, 38.1 • **Obv. Designer:** T. James Ferrell • **Rev. Designer:** Norman E. Nemeth

Date	Mintage	MS63	MS65	Prf65
2003P	53,761	—	40.80	—
2003P	193,086	—	—	46.80

KM# 363 • Obv. Desc.: Lewis and Clark standing • **Rev. Desc.:** Jefferson era clasped hands peace medal • 26.73 g., 0.900 **Silver** 0.77 oz. ASW

Date	Mintage	MS63	MS65	Prf65
2004P	90,323	—	40.80	—
2004P	288,492	—	—	46.80

KM# 362 • Obv. Desc.: Edison half-length figure facing holding light bulb • **Rev. Desc.:** Light bulb and rays • 23.73 g., 0.900 **Silver** 0.68 oz. ASW • **Obv. Designer:** Donna Weaver • **Rev. Designer:** John Mercanti

Date	Mintage	MS63	MS65	Prf65
2004P	68,031	—	40.80	—
2004P	213,409	—	—	41.80

KM# 375 • Obv. Desc.: Marshall bust left • **Rev. Desc.:** Marshall era Supreme Court Chamber • 26.73 g., 0.900 **Silver** 0.77 oz. ASW, 38.1 • **Obv. Designer:** John Mercanti • **Rev. Designer:** Donna Weaver

Date	Mintage	MS63	MS65	Prf65
2005P	48,953	—	37.30	—
2005P	141,993	—	—	35.80

KM# 376 • Obv. Desc.: Flag Raising at Mt. Suribachi on Iwo Jima • **Rev. Desc.:** Marine Corps emblem • 26.73 g., 0.900 **Silver** 0.77 oz. ASW, 38.1 • **Obv. Designer:** Norman E. Nemeth • **Rev. Designer:** Charles Vickers

Date	Mintage	MS63	MS65	Prf65
2005P	130,000	—	48.00	—
2005P	370,000	—	—	52.50

KM# 388 • Obv. Desc.: Bust 3/4 right, signature in oval below • **Rev. Desc.:** Continental Dollar of 1776 in center • 26.73 g., 0.900 **Silver** 0.77 oz. ASW, 38.1 • **Obv. Designer:** Don Everhart II • **Rev. Designer:** Donna Weaver

Date	Mintage	MS63	MS65	Prf65
2006P	58,000	—	40.80	—
2006P	142,000	—	—	51.00

KM# 387 • Obv. Desc.: Youthful Franklin flying kite • **Rev. Desc.:** Revolutionary era "JOIN, or DIE" snake cartoon illustration • 26.73 g., 0.900 **Silver** 0.77 oz. ASW, 38.1 • **Obv. Designer:** Norman E. Nemeth • **Rev. Designer:** Charles Vickers

Date	Mintage	MS63	MS65	Prf65
2006P	58,000	—	40.80	—
2006P	142,000	—	—	45.00

KM# 394 • Obv. Desc.: 3/4 view of building • **Rev. Desc.:** Reverse of 1880s Morgan silver dollar • 26.73 g., 0.900 **Silver** 0.77 oz. ASW, 38.1 • **Obv. Designer:** Sherl J. Winter • **Rev. Designer:** George T. Morgan

Date	Mintage	MS63	MS65	Prf65
2006S	65,609	—	40.80	—
2006S	255,700	—	—	40.80

COMMEMORATIVES

KM# 405 • Obv. Desc.: Two settlers and Native American • **Rev. Desc.:** Three ships • 26.73 g., 0.900 **Silver** 0.77 oz. ASW, 38.1 • **Obv. Designer:** Donna Weaver and Don Everhart II • **Rev. Designer:** Susan Gamble and Charles Vickers

Date	Mintage	MS63	MS65	Prf65
2007P	79,801	—	40.80	—
2007P	258,802	—	—	38.30

KM# 439 • Obv. Desc.: Eagle with flight, mountain in background at right • **Rev. Desc.:** Great Seal of the United States • 26.73 g., 0.900 **Silver** 0.77 oz. ASW, 38.1 • **Obv. Designer:** Joel Iskowitz and Don Everhart II • **Rev. Designer:** James Licaretz

Date	Mintage	MS63	MS65	Prf65
2008P	110,073	—	44.00	—
2008P	243,558	—	—	38.30

KM# 418 • Obv. Desc.: Children's feet walking left with adult feet in military boots • **Rev. Desc.:** Little Rock's Central High School • 26.73 g., 0.900 **Silver** 0.77 oz. ASW, 38.1 • **Obv. Designer:** Richard Masters and Charles Vickers • **Rev. Designer:** Don Everhart II

Date	Mintage	MS63	MS65	Prf65
2007P	66,093	—	40.80	—
2007P	124,618	—	—	43.00

KM# 454 • Obv. Desc.: 3/4 portrait facing right • **Rev. Desc.:** Part of Gettysburg Address within wreath • 26.73 g., 0.900 **Silver** 0.77 oz. ASW, 38.1 • **Obv. Designer:** Justin Kunz and Don Everhart II • **Rev. Designer:** Phebe Hemphill

Date	Mintage	MS63	MS65	Prf65
2009P	125,000	—	55.00	—
2009P	375,000	—	—	55.00

KM# 455 • Obv. Desc.: Louis Braille bust facing • **Rev. Desc.:** School child reading book in Braille, BRL in Braille code above • 26.73 g., 0.900 **Silver** 0.77 oz. ASW, 38.1 • **Obv. Designer:** Joel Iskowitz and Phebe Hemphill • **Rev. Designer:** Susan Gamble and Joseph Menna

Date	Mintage	MS63	MS65	Prf65
2009P	82,639	—	38.50	—
2009P	135,235	—	—	38.30

KM# 480 • Obv. Desc.: Cub Scout, Boy Scout and Venturer saluting • **Rev. Desc.:** Boy Scouts of America logo0.900 **Silver** • **Obv. Designer:** Donna Weaver • **Rev. Designer:** Jim Licaretz

Date	Mintage	MS63	MS65	Prf65
2010P	105,020	—	38.50	—
2010P	244,963	—	—	42.00

KM# 479 • Obv. Desc.: Soldier's feet, crutches • **Rev. Desc.:** Legend within wreath0.900 **Silver** • **Obv. Designer:** Don Everhart II • **Rev. Designer:** Thomas Cleveland and Joseph Menna

Date	Mintage	MS63	MS65	Prf65
2010W	77,859	—	40.80	—
2010W	189,881	—	—	42.30

KM# 504 • Obv. Desc.: Medal of Honor designs for Army, Navy and Air Force awards • **Rev. Desc.:** Army infantry doldier carrying another to safety • 26.73 g., 0.900 **Silver** 0.77 oz. ASW, 38.1 • **Obv. Designer:** James Licaretz • **Rev. Designer:** Richard Masters and Phebe Hemphill

Date	Mintage	MS63	MS65	Prf65
2011S	44,769	—	46.50	—
2011S	112,850	—	—	43.50

COMMEMORATIVES

KM# 507 • Obv. Desc.: Male and femlae soldier heads looking outward • **Rev. Desc.:** Seven core values of the Army, Eagle from the great seal • 26.73 g., 0.900 **Silver** 0.77 oz. ASW, 38.1 • **Obv. Designer:** Richard Masters and Michael Gaudioso • **Rev. Designer:** Susan Gamble and Don Everhart, II

Date	Mintage	MS63	MS65	Prf65
2011S	43,512	—	45.00	—
2011S	119,829	—	—	43.50

KM# 529 • Obv. Desc.: Infantry soldier advancing left • **Rev. Desc.:** Crossed rifles insignia • 26.73 g., 0.900 **Silver** 0.77 oz. ASW, 38.1 • **Obv. Designer:** Joel Iskowitz and Michael Gaudioso • **Rev. Designer:** Ronald D. Sanders and Norman E. Nemeth

Date	Mintage	MS63	MS65	Prf65
2012	—	—	50.00	—
2012	—	—	—	60.00

KM# 530 • Obv. Desc.: Liberty waving 15 star and stripe flag, Ft. McHenry in background • **Rev. Desc.:** Modern American Flag • 26.73 g., 0.900 **Silver** 0.77 oz. ASW, 38.1 • **Obv. Designer:** Joel Iskowitz and Phebe Hemphill • **Rev. Designer:** William C Burgard III and Don Everhart

Date	Mintage	MS63	MS65	Prf65
2012	—	—	50.00	—
2012	—	—	—	60.00

KM# 552 • Obv. Desc.: Three busts right • **Rev. Desc.:** Trefoil logoSilver, 38.1

Date	Mintage	MS63	MS65	Prf65
2013W	37,461	—	50.00	—
2013W	86,353	—	—	60.00

KM# 553 Star Generals Marshall & Eisenhower • **Silver**, 38.1

Date	Mintage	MS63	MS65	Prf65
2013W	34,639	—	50.00	—
2013S	69,290	—	—	60.00

KM# 577 • Silver ASW **Subject:** Baseball Hall of Fame

Date	Mintage	MS63	MS65	Prf65
2014	—	—	50.00	—
2014	—	—	—	60.00

KM# 579 • Silver ASW **Subject:** Civil Rights

Date	Mintage	MS63	MS65	Prf65
2014	—	—	50.00	—
2014	—	—	—	60.00

$5 (HALF EAGLE)

KM# 215 • Obv. Desc.: Statue of Liberty head right • **Rev. Desc.:** Eagle in flight left • 8.36 g., 0.900 **Gold** 0.24 oz. AGW, 21.6

Date	Mintage	MS63	MS65	Prf65
1986W	95,248	—	442	—
1986W	404,013	—	—	442

KM# 221 • Obv. Desc.: Eagle left with quill pen in talon • **Rev. Desc.:** Upright quill pen • 8.36 g., 0.900 **Gold** 0.24 oz. AGW, 21.6

Date	Mintage	MS63	MS65	Prf65
1987W	214,225	—	442	—
1987W	651,659	—	—	442

KM# 223 • Obv. Desc.: Nike head wearing olive wreath
• Rev. Desc.: Stylized olympic couldron • 8.36 g., 0.900
Gold 0.24 oz. AGW, 21.6 • **Obv. Designer:** Elizabeth
Jones • **Rev. Designer:** Marcel Jovine

Date	Mintage	MS63	MS65	Prf65
1988W	62,913	—	442	—
1988W	281,456	—	—	442

KM# 239 • Obv. Desc.: Columbus' profile left, at right,
map of Western Hemisphere at left • **Rev. Desc.:** Arms
of Spain, and parchment map • 8.36 g., 0.900 **Gold** 0.24
oz. AGW, 21.6 • **Obv. Designer:** T. James Ferrell • **Rev.
Designer:** Thomas D. Rogers, Sr.

Date	Mintage	MS63	MS65	Prf65
1992W	24,329	—	442	—
1992W	79,730	—	—	442

KM# 226 • Obv. Desc.: Capitol dome • **Rev. Desc.:**
Eagle atop of the canopy from the Old Senate Chamber •
8.36 g., 0.900 **Gold** 0.24 oz. AGW, 21.6

Date	Mintage	MS63	MS65	Prf65
1989W	46,899	—	442	—
1989W	164,690	—	—	442

KM# 242 • Obv. Desc.: Madison at left holding
document • **Rev. Desc.:** Eagle above legend, torch and
laurel at sides • 8.36 g., 0.900 **Gold** 0.24 oz. AGW, 21.6 •
Obv. Designer: Scott R. Blazek • **Rev. Designer:** Joseph
D. Peña

Date	Mintage	MS63	MS65	Prf65
1993W	22,266	—	442	—
1993W	78,651	—	—	442

KM# 230 • Obv. Desc.: Eagle in flight towards Mount
Rushmore • **Rev. Desc.:** Legend at center • 8.36 g.,
0.900 **Gold** 0.24 oz. AGW, 21.6 • **Obv. Designer:** John
Mercanti • **Rev. Designer:** Robert Lamb and William C.
Cousins

Date	Mintage	MS63	MS65	Prf65
1991W	31,959	—	442	—
1991W	111,991	—	—	442

KM# 245 • Obv. Desc.: Soldier with expression of
victory • **Rev. Desc.:** Morse code dot-dot-dot-dash for
V, large in background; V for Victory • 8.36 g., 0.900 **Gold**
0.24 oz. AGW, 21.6 • **Obv. Designer:** Charles J. Madsen
and T. James Ferrell • **Rev. Designer:** Edward S. Fisher
and T. James Ferrell

Date	Mintage	MS63	MS65	Prf65
1993W	23,089	—	442	—
1993W	65,461	—	—	442

KM# 235 • Obv. Desc.: Sprinter, U.S. Flag in
background • **Rev. Desc.:** Heraldic eagle, olympic rings
above • 8.36 g., 0.900 **Gold** 0.24 oz. AGW, 21.6 • **Obv.
Designer:** James C. Sharpe and T. James Ferrell • **Rev.
Designer:** James M. Peed

Date	Mintage	MS63	MS65	Prf65
1992W	27,732	—	442	—
1992W	77,313	—	—	442

KM# 248 • Obv. Desc.: World Cup trophy • **Rev. Desc.:**
World Cup 94 logo • 8.36 g., 0.900 **Gold** 0.24 oz. AGW,
21.6 • **Obv. Designer:** William J. Krawczewicz • **Rev.
Designer:** Dean McMullen

Date	Mintage	MS63	MS65	Prf65
1994W	22,464	—	442	—
1994W	89,619	—	—	442

KM# 256 • Obv. Desc.: Bugler on horseback right • **Rev. Desc.:** Eagle on shield • 8.36 g., 0.900 Gold 0.24 oz. AGW, 21.6

Date	Mintage	MS63	MS65	Prf65
1995W	55,246	—	—	442
1995W	12,735	—	950	—

KM# 261 • Obv. Desc.: Torch runner, Atlanta skyline and logo in background • **Rev. Desc.:** Eagle advancing right • 8.36 g., 0.900 Gold 0.24 oz. AGW, 21.6

Date	Mintage	MS63	MS65	Prf65
1995W	14,675	—	885	—
1995W	57,442	—	—	442

KM# 265 • Obv. Desc.: Atlanta Stadium and logo • **Rev. Desc.:** Eagle advancing right • 8.36 g., 0.900 Gold 0.24 oz. AGW, 21.6 • **Obv. Designer:** Marvel Jovine and William C. Cousins • **Rev. Designer:** Frank Gasparro

Date	Mintage	MS63	MS65	Prf65
1995W	10,579	—	2,500	—
1995W	43,124	—	—	442

KM# 270 • Obv. Desc.: Torch bearer lighting cauldron • **Rev. Desc.:** Atlanta Olympics logo flanked by laurel • 8.36 g., 0.900 Gold 0.24 oz. AGW, 21.6 • **Obv. Designer:** Frank Gasparro and T. James Ferrell • **Rev. Designer:** William J. Krawczewicz and Thomas D. Rogers, Sr.

Date	Mintage	MS63	MS65	Prf65
1996W	9,210	—	2,600	—
1996W	38,555	—	—	442

KM# 274 • Obv. Desc.: Flag bearer advancing • **Rev. Desc.:** Atlanta Olympic logo flanked by laurel • 8.36 g., 0.900 Gold 0.24 oz. AGW, 21.6 • **Obv. Designer:** Patricia Verani and John Mercanti • **Rev. Designer:** William J. Krawczewicz and Thomas D. Rogers, Sr.

Date	Mintage	MS63	MS65	Prf65
1996W	9,174	—	2,600	—
1996W	32,886	—	—	442

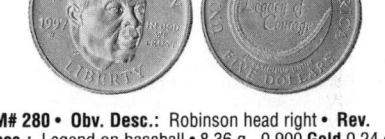

KM# 277 • Obv. Desc.: Smithson bust left • **Rev. Desc.:** Sunburst museum logo • 8.36 g., 0.900 Gold 0.24 oz. AGW, 21.6 • **Obv. Designer:** Alfred Maletsky • **Rev. Designer:** T. James Ferrell

Date	Mintage	MS63	MS65	Prf65
1996W	9,068	—	850	—
1996W	29,474	—	—	442

KM# 280 • Obv. Desc.: Robinson head right • **Rev. Desc.:** Legend on baseball • 8.36 g., 0.900 Gold 0.24 oz. AGW, 21.6 • **Obv. Designer:** William C. Cousins • **Rev. Designer:** James M. Peed

Date	Mintage	MS63	MS65	Prf65
1997W	5,202	—	2,900	—
1997W	24,072	—	—	590

KM# 282 • Obv. Desc.: Roosevelt bust right • **Rev. Desc.:** Eagle shield • 8.36 g., 0.900 Gold 0.24 oz. AGW, 21.6 • **Obv. Designer:** T. James Ferrell • **Rev. Designer:** James M. Peed and Thomas D. Rogers, Sr.

Date	Mintage	MS63	MS65	Prf65
1997W	11,894	—	1,275	—
1997W	29,474	—	—	442

COMMEMORATIVES

KM# 300 • Obv. Desc.: Washington's head right • **Rev. Desc.:** Eagle with wings outstretched • 8.36 g., 0.900 **Gold** 0.24 oz. AGW, 21.6

Date	Mintage	MS63	MS65	Prf65
1999W	22,511	—	452	—
1999W	41,693	—	—	447

KM# 326 • Obv. Desc.: Column at right • **Rev. Desc.:** First Capital building • 8.54 g., 0.900 **Gold** 0.25 oz. AGW

Date	Mintage	MS63	MS65	Prf65
2001W	6,761	—	1,750	—
2001W	27,652	—	—	442

KM# 337 • Obv. Desc.: Salt Lake City Olympics logo • **Rev. Desc.:** Stylized cauldron • 8.36 g., 0.900 **Gold** 0.24 oz. AGW, 21.6

Date	Mintage	MS63	MS65	Prf65
2002W	10,585	—	452	—
2002W	32,877	—	—	442

KM# 395 • Obv. Desc.: Front entrance façade • **Rev. Desc.:** Eagle as on 1860's $5. Gold • 8.36 g., 0.900 **Gold** 0.24 oz. AGW • **Obv. Designer:** Charles Vickers and Joseph Menna • **Rev. Designer:** Christian Gobrecht

Date	Mintage	MS63	MS65	Prf65
2006S	16,230	—	442	—
2006S	41,517	—	—	442

KM# 406 • Obv. Desc.: Settler and Native American • **Rev. Desc.:** Jamestown Memorial Church ruins • 8.36 g., 0.900 **Gold** 0.24 oz. AGW • **Obv. Designer:** John

Mercanti • **Rev. Designer:** Susan Gamble and Norman Nemeth

Date	Mintage	MS63	MS65	Prf65
2007W	18,843	—	442	—
2007W	47,050	—	—	442

KM# 440 • Obv. Desc.: Two eagles on branch • **Rev. Desc.:** Eagle with shield • 8.36 g., 0.900 **Gold** 0.24 oz. AGW, 21.6 • **Obv. Designer:** Susan Gamble adn Phebe Hemphill • **Rev. Designer:** Don Everhart II

Date	Mintage	MS63	MS65	Prf65
2008W	13,467	—	457	—
2008W	59,269	—	—	442

KM# 505 • Obv. Desc.: 1861 Medal of Honor design for the Navy • **Rev. Desc.:** Minerva standing with shield and Union flag, field artillery canon flanking • 8.36 g., 0.900 **Gold** 0.24 oz. AGW, 21.1 • **Obv. Designer:** Joseph Menna • **Rev. Designer:** Joel Iskowitz and Michael Gaudioso

Date	Mintage	MS63	MS65	Prf65
2011S	18,012	—	—	500
2011S	8,251	—	585	—

KM# 508 • Obv. Desc.: Five Soldiers of different eras • **Rev. Desc.:** Elements from the Army's emblem • 8.36 g., 0.900 **Gold** 0.24 oz. AGW, 21.1 • **Obv. Designer:** Joel Iskowitz and Phebe Hemphill • **Rev. Designer:** Joseph Menna

Date	Mintage	MS63	MS65	Prf65
2011P	8,062	—	585	—
2011W	17,173	—	—	495

KM# 531 • Obv. Desc.: Naval battle scene from the War of 1812. American ship in foreground, damaged British ship in background • **Rev. Desc.:** 15 stars and 15 stripes, opening words to the Star-Spangled Banner: O say can you see. • 8.36 g., 0.900 **Gold** 0.24 oz. AGW, 21.1 • **Obv. Designer:** Donna Weaver • **Rev. Designer:** Joseph Menna

Date	Mintage	MS63	MS65	Prf65
2012	—	—	585	—
2012	—	—	—	600

KM# 555 • Gold AGW **Subject:** Douglas McArthur

Date	Mintage	MS63	MS65	Prf65
2013P	5,658	—	585	—
2013S	15,843	—	—	600

KM# 578 • Gold AGW **Subject:** Baseball Hall of Fame

Date	Mintage	MS63	MS65	Prf65
2014	—	—	—	585

$10 (EAGLE)

KM# 211 • **Obv. Desc.:** Male and female runner with torch • **Rev. Desc.:** Heraldic eagle • 16.72 g., 0.900 **Gold** 0.48 oz. AGW, 27 • **Obv. Designer:** James M. Peed and John Mercanti • **Rev. Designer:** John Mercanti

Date	Mintage	MS63	MS65	Prf65
1984W	75,886	—	883	—
1984W	381,085	—	—	893
1984P	33,309	—	—	893
1984D	34,533	—	—	893
1984S	48,551	—	—	893

KM# 312 • **Obv. Desc.:** Torch and partial facade • **Rev. Desc.:** Stylized eagle within laurel wreath • 16.26 g., **Bi-Metallic:** Platinum center in gold ring • **Obv. Designer:** John Mercanti • **Rev. Designer:** Thomas D. Rogers, Sr.

Date	Mintage	MS63	MS65	Prf65
2000W	6,683	—	4,500	—
2000W	27,167	—	—	1,300

KM# 350 • **Obv. Desc.:** Orvile and Wilbur Wright busts facing • **Rev. Desc.:** Wright flyer and eagle • 16.72 g., 0.900 **Gold** 0.48 oz. AGW • **Obv. Designer:** Donna Weaver • **Rev. Designer:** Norman Nemeth

Date	Mintage	MS63	MS65	Prf65
2003P	10,129	—	1,050	—
2003W	21,846	—	—	893

$20 (DOUBLE EAGLE)

KM# 464 • **Obv. Desc.:** Ultra high relief Liberty holding torch, walking forward • **Rev. Desc.:** Eagle in flight left, sunrise in background • 31.11 g., 0.999 **Gold** 0.99 oz. AGW, 27

Date	Mintage	MS63	MS65	Prf65
2009	115,178	1,275	2,475	—

MODERN COMMEMORATIVE COIN SETS

Olympic, 1983-1984

Date	Value
1983 collectors 3 coin set: 1983 PDS uncirculated dollars; KM209.	104
1983 & 1984 3 coin set: 1983 and one 1984 uncirculated dollar and 1984W uncirculated gold $10; KM209, 210, 211.	952
1983S & 1984S 3 coin set: proof 1983 and 1984 dollar and 1984W gold $10; KM209, 210, 211.	956
1983 & 1984 6 coin set in a cherrywood box: 1983S and 1984S uncirculated and proof dollars, 1984W uncirculated and proof gold $10; KM209, 210, 211.	1,909
1983S & 1984S 2 coin set: proof dollars.	74.00
1984 collectors 3 coin set: 1984 PDS uncirculated dollars; KM210.	105

Statue of Liberty

Date	Value
1986 2 coin set: uncirculated silver dollar and clad half dollar; KM212, 214.	38.00
1986 2 coin set: proof silver dollar and clad half dollar; KM212, 214.	40.00
1986 3 coin set: uncirculated silver dollar, clad half dollar and gold $5; KM212, 214, 215.	480
1986 3 coin set: proof silver dollar, clad half dollar and gold $5; KM212, 214, 215.	483
1986 6 coin set: 1 each of the proof and uncirculated issues; KM212, 214, 215.	963

Constitution

Date	Value
1987 2 coin set: uncirculated silver dollar and gold $5; KM220, 221.	477
1987 2 coin set: proof silver dollar and gold $5; KM220, 221.	479
1987 4 coin set: silver dollar and $5 gold proof and uncirculated issues; KM220, 221.	958

Olympic, 1988

Date	Value
1988 2 coin set: uncirculated silver dollar and gold $5; KM222, 223.	477
1988 2 coin set: proof silver dollar and gold $5; KM222, 223.	479
1988 4 coin set: silver dollar and $5 gold proof and uncirculated issues; KM222, 223.	958

Congress

Date	Value
1989 2 coin set: uncirculated silver dollar and clad half dollar; KM224, 225.	42.00
1989 2 coin set: proof silver dollar and clad half dollar; KM224, 225.	44.00
1989 3 coin set: uncirculated silver dollar, clad half and gold $5; KM224, 225, 226.	485
1989 3 coin set: proof silver dollar, clad half and gold $5; KM224, 225, 226.	487
1989 6 coin set: 1 each of the proof and uncirculated issues; KM224, 225, 226.	973

Mt. Rushmore

Date	Value
1991 2 coin set: uncirculated half dollar and silver dollar; KM228, 229.	57.00
1991 2 coin set: proof half dollar and silver dollar; KM228, 229.	60.00
1991 3 coin set: uncirculated half dollar, silver dollar and gold $5; KM228, 229, 230.	500
1991 3 coin set: proof half dollar, silver dollar and gold $5; KM228, 229, 230.	502
1991 6 coin set: 1 each of proof and uncirculated issues; KM228, 229, 230.	1,004

Olympic, 1992

Date	Value
1992 2 coin set: uncirculated half dollar and silver dollar; KM233, 234.	46.00
1992 2 coin set: proof half dollar and silver dollar; KM233, 234.	47.00
1992 3 coin set: uncirculated half dollar, silver dollar and gold $5; KM233, 234, 235.	489
1992 3 coin set: proof half dollar, silver dollar and gold $5; KM233, 234, 235.	490
1992 6 coin set: 1 each of proof and uncirculated issues; KM233, 234, 235.	978

Columbus Quincentenary

Date	Value
1992 2 coin set: uncirculated half dollar and silver dollar; KM237, 238.	52.00
1992 2 coin set: proof half dollar and silver dollar; KM237, 238.	47.00
1992 3 coin set: uncirculated half dollar, silver dollar and gold $5; KM237, 238, 239.	495
1992 3 coin set: proof half dollar, silver dollar and gold $5; KM237, 238, 239.	489
1992 6 coin set: 1 each of proof and uncirculated issues; KM237, 238, 239.	985

Jefferson

Date	Value
1993 Jefferson: dollar, 1994 matte proof nickel and $2 note; KM249, 192.	109

Madison / Bill of Rights

Date	Value
1993 2 coin set: uncirculated half dollar and silver dollar; KM240, 241.	57.00
1993 2 coin set: proof half dollar and silver dollar; KM240, 241.	58.00
1993 3 coin set: uncirculated half dollar, silver dollar and gold $5; KM240, 241, 242.	499

Date	Value
1993 3 coin set: proof half dollar, silver dollar and gold $5; KM240, 241, 242.	500
1993 6 coin set: 1 each of proof and uncirculated issues; KM240, 241, 242.	999
1993 Coin and stamp set; KM#240 and 20c stamp	21.00

World War II

Date	Value
1993 2 coin set: uncirculated half dollar and silver dollar; KM243, 244.	54.00
1993 2 coin set: proof half dollar and silver dollar; KM243, 244.	57.00
1993 3 coin set: uncirculated half dollar, silver dollar and gold $5; KM243, 244, 245.	496
1993 3 coin set: proof half dollar, silver dollar and gold $5; KM243, 244, 245.	500
1993 6 coin set: 1 each of proof and uncirculated issues; KM243, 244, 245.	1,000

U.S. Veterans

Date	Value
1994 3 coin set: uncirculated POW, Vietnam, Women dollars; KM250, 251, 252.	202
1994 3 coin set: proof POW, Vietnam, Women dollars; KM250, 251, 252.	142

World Cup

Date	Value
1994 2 coin set: uncirculated half dollar and silver dollar; KM246, 247.	48.00
1994 2 coin set: proof half dollar and silver dollar; KM246, 247.	45.00
1994 3 coin set: uncirculated half dollar, silver dollar and gold $5; KM246, 247, 248.	490
1994 3 coin set: proof half dollar, silver dollar and gold $5; KM246, 247, 248.	487
1994 6 coin set: 1 each of proof and uncirculated issues; KM246, 247, 248.	983

Olympic, 1995-96

Date	Value
1995 4 coin set: uncirculated basketball half, $1 gymnast & blind runner, $5 torch runner; KM257, 259, 260, 261.	1,024
1995 4 coin set: proof basketball half, $1 gymnast & blind runner, $5 torch runner; KM257, 259, 260, 261.	533
1995P 2 coin set: proof $1 gymnast & blind runner; KM259, 260.	82.00
1995P 2 coin set: proof $1 track & field, cycling; KM263, 264.	84.00
1995-96 4 coin set: proof halves, basketball, baseball, swimming, soccer; KM257, 262, 271.	75.00
1995 & 96 8 coins in cherry wood case: proof silver dollars: blind runner, gymnast, cycling, track & field, wheelchair, tennis, rowing, high jump; KM259, 260, 263, 264, 268, 269, 272, 272A.	425
1995 & 96 16 coins in cherry wood case: bu and proof silver dollars: blind runner, gymnast, cycling, track & field, wheelchair, tennis, rowing, high jump; KM259, 260, 263, 264, 268, 269, 272, 272A.	10,400
1995 & 96 16 coins in cherry wood case: proof half dollars: basketball, baseball, swimming, soccer, KM257, 262, 267, 271. Proof silver dollars: blind runner, gymnast, cycling, track & field, wheelchair, tennis, rowing, high jump, KM259, 260, 263, 264, 268, 269, 272, 272A. Proof $5 gold: torch runner, stadium, cauldron, flag bearer, KM 261, 265, 270, 274.	2,370
1995 & 96 32 coins in cherry wood case: bu & proof half dollars: basketball, baseball, swimming, soccer, KM257, 262, 267, 271. BU & proof silver dollars: blind runner, gymnast, cycling, track & field, wheelchair, tennis, rowing, high jump, KM259, 260, 263, 264, 268, 269, 272, 272A. BU & proof $5 gold: torch runner, stadium, cauldron, flag bearer, KM261, 265, 270, 274.	12,800
1996P 2 coin set: proof $1 wheelchair & tennis; KM268, 269.	154
1996P 2 coin set: proof $1 rowing & high jump; KM272, 272A.	105
1996 Young collector 4 coin set; Half dollars: KM#257, 262, 267, 271	205

Civil War

Date	Value
1995 2 coin set: uncirculated half and dollar; KM254, 255.	102
1995 2 coin set: proof half and dollar; KM254, 255.	88.00
1995 3 coin set: uncirculated half, dollar and gold $5; KM254, 255, 256.	1,055
1995 3 coin set: proof half, dollar and gold $5; KM254, 255, 256.	530
1995 6 coin set: 1 each of proof and uncirculated issues; KM254, 255, 256.	1,585
1995 Civil War Young Collectors set KM#245	37.50

Smithsonian

Date	Value
1996 2 coin set: proof dollar and $5 gold; KM276, 277.	495
1996 4 coin set: proof and B.U. ; KM276, 277.	1,465

Franklin Delano Roosevelt

Date	Value
1997W 2 coin set: uncirculated and proof; KM282.	3,500

Jackie Robinson

Date	Value
1997 2 coin set: proof dollar & $5 gold; KM279, 280.	680
1997 4 coin set: proof & BU; KM279, 280.	3,660
1997 legacy set.	650

Botanic Garden

Date	Value
1997 2 coin set: dollar, Jefferson nickel and $1 note; KM278, 192.	220

Black Patriots

Date	Value
1998S 2 coin set: uncirculated and proof; KM288.	220

Kennedy

Date	Value
1998 2 coin set: proof; KM287.	88.00
1998 2 coin collectors set: Robert Kennedy dollar and John Kennedy half dollar; KM287, 202b. Matte finished.	225

Dolley Madison

Date	Value
1999 2 coin set: proof and uncirculated silver dollars; KM298.	76.00

Yellowstone National Park

Date	Value
1999 2 coin set: proof and uncirculated silver dollars; KM299.	84.00

George Washington

Date	Value
1999 2 coin set: proof and uncirculated gold $5; KM300.	900

Millennium Coin & Currency

Date	Value
2000 2 coin set: uncirculated Sacagewea $1, silver Eagle & $1 note.	67.50

Leif Ericson

Date	Value
2000 2 coin set: proof and uncirculated silver dollars; KM313.	85.00

American Buffalo

Date	Value
2001 2 coin set: 90% silver unc. & proof $1.; KM325.	330
2001 coin & currency set 90% unc. dollar & replicas of 1899 $5 silver cert.; KM325.	180

Capitol Visitor Center

Date	Value
2001 3 coin set: proof half, silver dollar, gold $5; KM323, 324, 326.	495

Winter Olympics - Salt Lake City

Date	Value
2002 2 coin set: proof 90% silver dollar KM336 & $5.00 Gold KM337.	465
2002 4 coin set: 90% silver unc. & proof $1, KM336 & unc. & proof gold $5, KM337.	925

Thomas Alva Edison

Date	Value
2004 Uncirculated silver dollar and light bulb.	55.00

Lewis and Clark Bicentennial

Date	Value
2004 Coin and pouch set.	65.00
2004 coin and currency set: Uncirculated silver dollar, two 2005 nickels, replica 1901 $10 Bison note, silver plated peace medal, three stamps & two booklets.	58.00
2004 Westward Journey Nickel series coin and medal set: Proof Sacagawea dollar, two 2005 proof nickels and silver plated peace medal.	40.00

Chief Justice John Marshall

Date	Value
2005 Coin and Chronicles set: Uncirculated silver dollar, booklet and BEP intaglio portrait.	57.00

U.S. Marine Corps

Date	Value
2005 Uncirculated silver dollar and stamp set.	63.00

Benjamin Franklin Tercentennary

Date	Value
2006 Coin and Chronicles set: Uncirculated "Scientist" silver dollar, four stamps, Poor Richards Almanac and intaglio print.	49.00

Central High School Desegregation

Date	Value
2007 Little Rock Dollar and medal set, KM#418	47.80

American Bald Eagle

Date	Value
2008 Proof half dollar, dollar and $5 gold, KM438, KM439, KM440	490
2008 Bald Eagle young collector's set; Half Dollar, KM#438	23.00

Louis Braille

Date	Value
2009 Braille Education set, KM#455	43.50

AMERICA EAGLE SILVER BULLION

SILVER DOLLAR

KM# 273 • **Obv. Desc.:** Liberty walking left • **Rev. Desc.:** Eagle with shield • 31.11 g., 0.9993 **Silver** 0.99 oz. ASW, 40.6 • **Obv. Designer:** Adolph A. Weinman • **Rev. Designer:** John Mercanti

Date	Mintage	MS65	Prf65
1986	5,393,005	38.30	—
1986S	1,446,778	—	66.00
1987	11,442,335	30.50	—
1987S	904,732	—	66.00
1988	5,004,646	30.50	—
1988S	557,370	—	66.00
1989	5,203,327	—	—
1989S	617,694	—	66.00
1990	5,840,110	30.50	—
1990S	695,510	—	66.00
1991	7,191,066	30.50	—
1991S	511,924	—	66.00
1992	5,540,068	30.50	—
1992S	498,543	—	66.00
1993	6,763,762	33.50	—
1993P	405,913	—	98.00
1994	4,227,319	44.00	—
1994P	372,168	—	180
1995	4,672,051	40.00	—
1995P	407,822	—	90.00
1995W 10th Anniversary	30,102	—	4,450
1996	3,603,386	70.00	—
1996P	498,293	—	82.00
1997	4,295,004	39.50	—
1997P	440,315	—	95.00
1998	4,847,547	34.00	—
1998P	450,728	—	69.00
1999	7,408,640	30.50	—
1999P	549,330	—	66.00
2000	9,239,132	32.30	—
2000P	600,743	—	59.00
2001	9,001,711	30.30	—
2001W	746,398	—	56.00
2002	10,539,026	30.30	—
2002W	647,342	—	66.00
2003	8,495,008	26.80	—
2003W	747,831	—	80.00
2004	8,882,754	26.80	—
2004W	801,602	—	66.00
2005	8,891,025	26.80	—
2005W	816,663	—	56.00
2006	10,676,522	26.80	—
2006W Burnished Unc.	468,000	85.00	—
2006W	1,093,600	—	56.00
2006P Reverse Proof	Est. 250000	—	265
2006 20th Aniv. 3 pc. set	—	—	415
2007	9,028,036	26.80	—
2007W Burnished Unc.	690,891	26.80	—
2007W	821,759	—	56.00
2008	20,583,000	26.80	—
2008W Burnished Unc.	Est. 550000	71.50	—
2008W Reverse of '07, U in United with rounded bottom.	Est. 47000	555	—
2008	713,353	—	56.00
2009	30,459,000	26.80	—
2010	34,764,500	26.80	—
2010	—	—	56.00
2011	39,764,500	25.80	—
2011P Reverse Proof	100,000	—	305
2011S Burnished Unc.	100,000	285	—
2011W Burnished Unc.	—	50.00	—
2011W	850,000	—	59.00
2012	—	25.80	—
2012 Reverse Proof	—	—	125
2012S	60,203	23.80	59.00
2012W Burnished Unc.	33,742,500	60.00	—
2013	178,941	23.80	—
2013W Enhanced Finish	—	—	—
2013W	—	—	60.00
2013 Enhanced Finish	—	93.50	—
2013W Enhanced Finish Reverse Proof	—	—	88.00

AMERICA THE BEAUTIFUL SILVER BULLION

SILVER QUARTER

KM# 489 • Rev. Desc.: Park Headquarters and fountain • 155.55 g., 0.999 **Silver** 4.96 oz. ASW • **Rev. Designer:** Don Everhart II and Joseph Menna

Date	Mintage	MS65	MS69
2010	33,000	290	360
2010P Vapor Blast finish	27,000	250	375

KM# 490 • Rev. Desc.: Old Faithful geyser and bison • 155.55 g., 0.999 **Silver** 4.96 oz. ASW • **Rev. Designer:** Don Everhart II

Date	Mintage	MS65	MS69
2010	33,000	275	360
2010P Vapor Blast finish	27,000	240	325

KM# 491 • Rev. Desc.: El Capitan, largest monolith of granite in the world • 155.55 g., 0.999 **Silver** 4.96 oz. ASW • **Rev. Designer:** Joseph Menna and Phebe Hemphill

Date	Mintage	MS65	MS69
2010	33,000	275	385
2010P Vapor blast finish	27,000	225	260

KM# 492 • Rev. Desc.: Grabarues above the Nankoweap Delta in Marble Canyon near the Colorado River • 155.55 g., 0.999 **Silver** 4.96 oz. ASW • **Rev. Designer:** Phebe Hemphill

Date	Mintage	MS65	MS69
2010	33,000	250	325
2010P Vapor blast finish	26,019	225	325

KM# 493 • Rev. Desc.: Mt. Hood with Lost Lake in the foreground • 155.55 g., 0.999 **Silver** 4.96 oz. ASW • **Rev. Designer:** Phebe Hemphill

Date	Mintage	MS65	MS69
2010	33,000	275	360
2010P Vapor blast finish	25,318	200	260

KM# 513 • Rev. Desc.: 72nd Pennsylvania Infantry Monumnet on the battle line of the Union Army at Cemetery Ridge • 155.55 g., 0.999 **Silver** 4.96 oz. ASW • **Rev. Designer:** Joel Iskowitz and Phebe Hemphill

Date	Mintage	MS65	MS69
2011	126,700	200	260
2011P Vapor blast finish	24,625	190	240

KM# 514 • Rev. Desc.: Northeast slope of Mount Reynolds • 155.55 g., 0.999 **Silver** 4.96 oz. ASW • **Rev. Designer:** Barbara Fox and Charles L. Vickers

Date	Mintage	MS65	MS69
2011	126,700	200	260
2011P Vapor blast finish	20,503	190	240

KM# 515 • Rev. Desc.: Roosevelt elk on a gravel river bar along the Hoh River, Mount Olympus in the background • 155.55 g., 0.999 **Silver** 4.96 oz. ASW • **Rev. Designer:** Susan Gambel and Michael Gaudioso

Date	Mintage	MS65	MS69
2011	85,900	200	260
2011P Vapor blast finish	17,988	190	240

KM# 516 • Rev. Desc.: U.S.S. Cairo on the Yazoo River • 155.55 g., 0.999 **Silver** 4.96 oz. ASW • **Rev. Designer:** Thomas Cleveland and Joseph menna

Date	Mintage	MS65	MS69
2011	39,500	200	260
2011P Vapor blast finish	18,181	190	240

KM# 517 • Rev. Desc.: Limestone Lincoln Bridge • 155.55 g., 0.999 **Silver** 4.96 oz. ASW • **Rev. Designer:** Donna Weaver and James Licaretz

Date	Mintage	MS65	MS69
2011	29,700	200	260
2011P Vapor blast finish	16,386	190	240

KM# 536 • Rev. Desc.: Coquin tree frog and Puerto Rico parrot • 155.55 g., 0.999 **Silver** 4.96 oz. ASW

Date	Mintage	MS65	MS69
2012	21,900	200	260
2012P Vapor blast finish	15,271	190	240

KM# 537 • Rev. Desc.: Two elevated kivas at Chetro Ketl complex • 155.52 g., 0.999 **Silver** 4.96 oz. ASW

Date	Mintage	MS65	MS69
2012	20,000	200	260
2012P Vapor blast finish	12,679	190	240

KM# 538 • Rev. Desc.: Bass Harbor Head Lighthouse • 155.52 g., 0.999 **Silver** 4.96 oz. ASW

Date	Mintage	MS65	MS69
2012	25,400	200	260
2012P Vapor blast finish	13,196	190	240

KM# 539 • Rev. Desc.: Volcano erupting • 155.52 g., 0.999 **Silver** 4.96 oz. ASW

Date	Mintage	MS65	MS69
2012	20,000	200	260
2012P Vapor blast finish	13,789	190	240

KM# 540 • Rev. Desc.: Dall sheep and Mount McKinley • 155.55 g., 0.999 **Silver** 4.96 oz. ASW

Date	Mintage	MS65	MS69
2012	20,000	200	260
2012P Vapor blast finish	10,180	190	240

KM# 556 • Rev. Desc.: Mountain vista • 155.55 g., 0.999 **Silver** 4.96 oz. ASW

Date	Mintage	MS65	MS69
2013	—	200	260
2013P Vapor blast finish	—	190	240

KM# 557 • Rev. Desc.: Perry standing and Memorial column • 155.55 g., 0.999 **Silver** 4.96 oz. ASW

Date	Mintage	MS65	MS69
2013	—	200	260
2013 Vapor blast finsih	—	190	240

KM# 558 • Rev. Desc.: Ancient weatherworn tree • 155.55 g., 0.999 **Silver** 4.96 oz. ASW

Date	Mintage	MS65	MS69
2013	—	200	260
2013 Vapor blast finish	—	190	240

KM# 559 • Rev. Desc.: Fort McHenry and flag • 155.55 g., 0.999 **Silver** 4.96 oz. ASW

Date	Mintage	MS65	MS69
2013	—	200	260
2013	—	190	240

KM# 560 • Rev. Desc.: Presidential head sculpture on Mt. Rushmore • 155.55 g., 0.999 **Silver** 4.96 oz. ASW

Date	Mintage	MS65	MS69
2013	—	200	260
2013 Vapor blast finish	—	190	240

KM# 580 • Rev. Desc.: Smokey Mountains • 155.55 g., 0.999 **Silver** 4.96 oz. ASW

Date	Mintage	MS65	MS69
2014	—	200	260
2014P Vapor blast finish	—	190	240

KM# 581 • Rev. Desc.: Shenandoah National Park • 155.55 g., 0.999 **Silver** 4.96 oz. ASW

Date	Mintage	MS65	MS69
2014	—	200	260
2014P Vapor blast finish	—	190	240

KM# 582 • Rev. Desc.: Arches National Park • 155.55 g., 0.999 **Silver** 4.96 oz. ASW

Date	Mintage	MS65	MS69
2014	—	200	260
2014P Vapor blast finish	—	190	240

KM# 583 • Rev. Desc.: Great Sand Dunes National Park • 155.55 g., 0.999 **Silver** 4.96 oz. ASW

Date	Mintage	MS65	MS69
2014	—	200	260
2014P Vapor blast finish	—	190	240

KM# 584 • Rev. Desc.: Everglades National Park • 155.55 g., 0.999 **Silver** 4.96 oz. ASW

Date	Mintage	MS65	MS69
2014	—	200	260
2014P Vapor blast finish	—	190	240

AMERICAN EAGLE GOLD BULLION

GOLD $5

KM# 216 • 3.39 g., 0.9167 Gold 0.10 oz. AGW, 16.5 • Obv. Designer: Augustus Saint-Gaudens • **Rev. Designer:** Miley Busiek

Date	Mintage	MS65	Prf65
MCMLXXXVI -1986	912,609	190	—
MCMLXXXVII -1987	580,266	190	—
MCMLXXXVIII -1988	159,500	200	—
MCMLXXXVIII P	143,881	—	190
MCMLXXXIX -1989	264,790	185	—
MCMLXXXIX P	84,647	—	180
MCMXC -1990	210,210	195	—
MCMXC P	99,349	—	225
MCMXCI -1991	165,200	215	—
MCMXCI P	70,334	—	210
1992	209,300	162	—
1992P	64,874	—	205
1993	210,709	200	—
1993P	45,960	—	192
1994	206,380	205	—
1994W	62,849	—	192
1995	223,025	205	—
1995W	62,667	—	205
1996	401,964	165	—
1996W	57,047	—	192
1997	528,515	195	—
1997W	34,977	—	192
1998	1,344,520	165	—
1998W	39,395	—	192
1999	2,750,338	168	—
1999W	48,428	—	192
1999W Unfinished Proof die	Est. 6000	900	—

Note: The 1999 W issues are standard matte finished gold that were struck with unfinished proof dies.

Date	Mintage	MS65	Prf65
2000	569,153	165	—
2000W	49,971	—	192
2001	269,147	165	—
2001W	37,530	—	192
2002	230,027	205	—
2002W	40,864	—	192
2003	245,029	195	—
2003W	40,027	—	192
2004	250,016	195	—
2004W	35,131	—	225
2005	300,043	195	—
2005W	49,265	—	225
2006	285,006	195	—
2006W Burnished Unc.	20,643	200	—
2006W	47,277	—	192
2007	190,010	195	—
2007W Burnished Unc.	22,501	210	—
2007W	58,553	—	192

Date	Mintage	MS65	Prf65
2008	305,000	165	—
2008W Burnished Unc.	12,657	360	—
2008W	Est. 29000	—	192
2009	27,000	165	—
2010	435,000	165	—
2010W	54,285	—	192
2011	350,000	185	—
2011W	42,697	—	192
2012W	—	165	—
2012W	20,740	—	—
2013W	—	165	—
2013	21,879	—	225

GOLD $10

KM# 217 • 8.48 g., 0.9167 Gold 0.25 oz. AGW, 22 • Obv. Designer: Augustus Saint-Gaudens • **Rev. Designer:** Miley Busiek

Date	Mintage	MS65	Prf65
MCMLXXXVI -1986	726,031	550	—
MCMLXXXVII -1987	269,255	550	—
MCMLXXXVIII -1988	49,000	660	—
MCMLXXXVIII P	98,028	—	449
MCMLXXXIX -1989	81,789	660	—
MCMLXXXIX P	54,170	—	510
MCMXC -1990	41,000	780	—
MCMXC P	62,674	—	495
MCMXCI -1991	36,100	780	—
MCMXCI P	50,839	—	470
1992	59,546	605	—
1992P	46,269	—	439
1993	71,864	605	—
1993P	33,775	—	510
1994	72,650	605	—
1994W	47,172	—	469
1995	83,752	605	—
1995W	47,526	—	439
1996	60,318	429	—
1996W	38,219	—	605
1997	108,805	381	—
1997W	29,805	—	429
1998	309,829	381	—
1998W	29,503	—	429
1999	564,232	381	—
1999W	34,417	—	429
1999W Unfinished Proof die	Est. 6000	1,600	—

Note: The 1999 W issues are standard matte finished gold that were struck with unfinished proof dies.

Date	Mintage	MS65	Prf65
2000	128,964	361	—
2000W	36,036	—	429

Date	Mintage	MS65	Prf65
2001	71,280	605	—
2001W	25,613	—	429
2002	62,027	605	—
2002W	29,242	—	429
2003	74,029	381	—
2003W	30,292	—	429
2004	72,014	381	—
2004W	28,839	—	429
2005	72,015	381	—
2005W	37,207	—	429
2006	60,004	381	—
2006W Burnished Unc.	15,188	715	—
2006W	36,127	—	429
2007	34,004	610	—
2007W Burnished Unc.	12,786	660	—
2007W	46,189	—	429
2008	Est. 58000	381	—
2008W Burnished Unc.	8,883	1,675	—
2008W	28,000	—	429
2009	110,000	381	—
2010	86,000	381	—
2010W	44,507	—	429
2011	80,000	381	—
2011W	28,782	—	429
2012	—	381	—
2012W	13,375	—	—
2013	—	381	—
2013	12,642	—	475

Date	Mintage	MS65	Prf65
2001	48,047	1,550	—
2001W	23,240	—	868
2002	70,027	1,050	—
2002W	26,646	—	868
2003	79,029	722	—
2003W	28,270	—	868
2004	98,040	722	—
2004W	27,330	—	868
2005	80,023	722	—
2005W	34,311	—	868
2006	66,004	725	—
2006W Burnished Unc.	15,164	1,155	—
2006W	34,322	—	868
2007	47,002	1,115	—
2007W Burnished Unc.	11,458	1,650	—
2007W	44,025	—	1,028
2008	61,000	725	—
2008W Burnished Unc.	15,683	1,650	—
2008W	27,800	—	855
2009	55,000	725	—
2010	81,000	722	—
2010W	44,527	—	868
2011	70,000	722	—
2011W	26,781	—	868
2012W	—	722	—
2013W	12,570	722	—
2013	—	—	975

GOLD $25

KM# 218 • 16.97 g., 0.9167 **Gold** 0.50 oz. AGW, 27
• **Obv. Designer:** Augustus Saint-Gaudens • **Rev.
Designer:** Miley Busiek

Date	Mintage	MS65	Prf65
MCMLXXXVI -1986	599,566	1,065	—
MCMLXXXVII -1987	131,255	1,320	—
MCMLXXXVII (1987)P	143,398	—	868
MCMLXXXVIII -1988	45,000	2,050	—
MCMLXXXVIII (1988)P	76,528	—	898
MCMLXXXIX -1989	44,829	2,150	—
MCMLXXXIX (1989)P	44,798	—	1,015
MCMXC -1990	31,000	2,475	—
MCMXC (1990)P	51,636	—	1,000
MCMXCI -1991	24,100	3,650	—
MCMXCI (1991)P	53,125	—	1,015
1992	54,404	1,520	—
1992P	40,976	—	878
1993	73,324	1,050	—
1993P	31,130	—	1,050
1994	62,400	1,035	—
1994W	44,584	—	868
1995	53,474	1,700	—
1995W	45,388	—	868
1996	39,287	1,725	—
1996W	35,058	—	868
1997	79,605	1,050	—
1997W	26,344	—	868
1998	169,029	722	—
1998W	25,374	—	868
1999	263,013	722	—
1999W	30,427	—	888
2000	79,287	995	—
2000W	32,028	—	868

GOLD $50

KM# 219 • 33.93 g., 0.9167 **Gold** 0.99 oz. AGW, 32.7
• **Obv. Designer:** Augustus Saint-Gaudens • **Rev.
Designer:** Miley Busiek

Date	Mintage	MS65	Prf65
MCMLXXXVI -1986	1,362,650	1,380	—
MCMLXXXVI (1986)W	446,290	—	1,666
MCMLXXXVII -1987	1,045,500	1,380	—
MCMLXXXVII (1987)W	147,498	—	1,666
MCMLXXXVIII -1988	465,000	1,380	—
MCMLXXXVIII (1988)W	87,133	—	1,666
MCMLXXXIX -1989	415,790	1,380	—
MCMLXXXIX (1989)W	54,570	—	1,666
MCMXC -1990	373,219	1,380	—
MCMXC (1990)W	62,401	—	1,926
MCMXCI -1991	243,100	1,380	—
MCMXCI (1991)W	50,411	—	1,966
1992	275,000	1,380	—
1992W	44,826	—	1,631
1993	480,192	1,380	—
1993W	34,369	—	2,081
1994	221,663	1,380	—
1994W	46,674	—	1,731
1995	200,636	1,380	—
1995W	46,368	—	1,731
1995W 10th Anniversary	—	—	—
1996	189,148	1,380	—

Date	Mintage	MS65	Prf65
1996W	36,153	—	1,731
1997	664,508	1,380	—
1997W	28,034	—	1,731
1998	1,468,530	1,380	—
1998W	25,886	—	1,731
1999	1,505,026	1,380	—
1999W	31,427	—	1,931
1999W Die error	—	3,300	—

Note: The 1999 W issues are standard matte finished gold that were struck with unfinished proof dies.

Date	Mintage	MS65	Prf65
2000	433,319	1,380	—
2000W	33,007	—	1,631
2001	143,605	1,380	—
2001W	24,555	—	1,631
2002	222,029	1,380	—
2002W	27,499	—	1,631
2003	416,032	1,380	—
2003W	28,344	—	1,631
2004	417,149	1,380	—
2004W	28,215	—	1,631
2005	356,555	1,380	—
2005W	35,246	—	1,631

Date	Mintage	MS65	Prf65
2006	237,510	1,380	—
2006W Burnished Unc.	45,912	1,885	—
2006W	47,000	—	1,631
2006W Reverse Proof	10,000	—	2,800
2007	140,016	1,393	—
2007W Burnished Unc.	18,609	1,980	—
2007W	51,810	—	1,740
2008W	710,000	1,380	—
2008W Burnished Unc.	11,908	2,100	—
2008W Reverse of '07	—	—	—
2008W	29,000	—	2,150
2009	122,000	1,380	—
2010	1,125,000	1,380	—
2010W	59,480	—	1,631
2011	857,000	1,380	—
2011 Burnished Unc.	8,729	2,350	—
2011W	48,306	—	1,631
2012W	—	1,380	—
2012 Burnished Unc.	5,829	2,975	—
2013W	24,753	1,380	—
2013	—	—	1,850

AMERICAN EAGLE PLATINUM BULLION

PLATINUM $10

KM# 283 • Rev. Desc.: Eagle flying right over sunrise • 3.11 g., 0.9995 **Platinum** 0.10 oz. APW, 17 • **Obv. Designer:** John Mercanti • **Rev. Designer:** Thomas D. Rogers Sr

Date	Mintage	MS65	Prf65
1997	70,250	187	—
1997W	36,996	—	188
1998	39,525	187	—
1999	55,955	187	—
2000	34,027	187	—
2001	52,017	187	—
2002	23,005	187	—
2003	22,007	187	—
2004	15,010	187	—
2005	14,013	187	—
2006	11,001	187	—
2006W Burnished Unc.	—	425	—
2007	13,003	285	—
2007W Burnished Unc.	—	280	—
2008	17,000	187	—
2008 Burnished Unc.	—	390	—

KM# 289 • Rev. Desc.: Eagle in flight over New England costal lighthouse • 3.11 g., 0.9995 **Platinum** 0.10 oz. APW • **Obv. Designer:** John Mercanti

Date	Mintage	MS65	Prf65
1998W	19,847	—	188

KM# 301 • Rev. Desc.: Eagle in flight over Southeastern Wetlands • 3.11 g., 0.9995 **Platinum** 0.10 oz. APW • **Obv. Designer:** John Mercanti

Date	Mintage	MS65	Prf65
1999W	19,133	—	188

KM# 314 • Rev. Desc.: Eagle in flight over Heartland • 3.11 g., 0.9995 **Platinum** 0.10 oz. APW • **Obv. Designer:** John Mercanti

Date	Mintage	MS65	Prf65
2000W	15,651	—	188

KM# 327 • Rev. Desc.: Eagle in flight over Southwestern cactus desert • 3.11 g., 0.9995 **Platinum** 0.10 oz. APW, 17 • **Obv. Designer:** John Mercanti

Date	Mintage	MS65	Prf65
2001W	12,174	—	188

KM# 339 • Rev. Desc.: Eagle fishing in America's Northwest • 3.11 g., 0.9995 **Platinum** 0.10 oz. APW, 17 • **Obv. Designer:** John Mercanti

Date	Mintage	MS65	Prf65
2002W	12,365	—	188

KM# 351 • Rev. Desc.: Eagle pearched on a Rocky Mountain Pine branch against a flag backdrop • 3.11 g., 0.9995 **Platinum** 0.10 oz. APW, 17 • **Obv. Designer:** John Mercanti • **Rev. Designer:** Al Maletsky

Date	Mintage	MS65	Prf65
2003W	9,534	—	250

KM# 364 • Rev. Desc.: Chester French, 1907. The sculpture is outside the N.Y. Customs House, now part of the Smithsonian's Museum of the American Indian • 3.11 g., 0.9995 **Platinum** 0.10 oz. APW, 17 • **Obv. Designer:** John Mercanti

Date	Mintage	MS65	Prf65
2004W	7,161	—	445

KM# 377 • Rev. Desc.: Eagle with cornucopiae • 3.11 g., 0.9995 **Platinum** 0.10 oz. APW, 17 • **Obv. Designer:** John Mercanti • **Rev. Designer:** Donna Weaver

Date	Mintage	MS65	Prf65
2005W	8,104	—	265

KM# 389 • Rev. Desc.: Liberty seated writing between two columns • 3.11 g., 0.9995 **Platinum** 0.10 oz. APW, 17 • **Obv. Designer:** John Mercanti

Date	Mintage	MS65	Prf65
2006W	10,205	—	188

KM# 414 • Rev. Desc.: Eagle with shield • 3.11 g., 0.9995 **Platinum** 0.10 oz. APW, 17 • **Obv. Designer:** John Mercanti

Date	Mintage	MS65	Prf65
2007W	8,176	—	188

KM# 434 • Rev. Desc.: Justice standing before eagle • 3.11 g., 0.9995 **Platinum** 0.10 oz. APW, 17 • **Obv. Designer:** John Mercanti

Date	Mintage	MS65	Prf65
2008W	8,176	—	495

KM# 460 • 3.11 g., 0.9995 **Platinum** 0.10 oz. APW, 17 • **Obv. Designer:** John Mercanti

Date	Mintage	MS65	Prf65
2009W	5,600	—	—

PLATINUM $25

KM# 284 • Rev. Desc.: Eagle in flight over sunrise • 7.79 g., 0.9995 **Platinum** 0.25 oz. APW, 22 • **Obv. Designer:** John Mercanti • **Rev. Designer:** Thomas D. Rogers Sr

Date	Mintage	MS65	Prf65
1997	27,100	432	—
1997W	18,628	—	470
1998	38,887	432	—
1999	39,734	432	—
2000	20,054	432	—
2001	21,815	432	—
2002	27,405	432	—
2003	25,207	432	—
2004	18,010	432	—
2005	12,013	432	—
2006	12,001	432	—
2006W Burnished Unc.	—	590	—
2007	8,402	432	—
2007W Burnished Unc.	—	590	—
2008	—	402	—
2008 Burnished Unc.	22,800	665	—

KM# 290 • Rev. Desc.: Eagle in flight over New England costal lighthouse • 7.79 g., 0.9995 **Platinum** 0.25 oz. APW • **Obv. Designer:** John Mercanti

Date	Mintage	MS65	Prf65
1998W	14,873	—	470

KM# 302 • Rev. Desc.: Eagle in flight over Southeastern Wetlands • 7.79 g., 0.9995 **Platinum** 0.25 oz. APW • **Obv. Designer:** John Mercanti

Date	Mintage	MS65	Prf65
1999W	13,507	—	470

KM# 315 • Rev. Desc.: Eagle in flight over Heartland
• 7.79 g., 0.9995 **Platinum** 0.25 oz. APW. • **Obv.
Designer:** John Mercanti

Date	Mintage	MS65	Prf65
2000W	11,995	—	470

KM# 328 • Rev. Desc.: Eagle in flight over
Southwestern cactus desert • 7.79 g., 0.9995 **Platinum**
0.25 oz. APW, 22 • **Obv. Designer:** John Mercanti

Date	Mintage	MS65	Prf65
2001W	8,847	—	470

KM# 340 • Rev. Desc.: Eagle fishing in America's
Northwest • 7.79 g., 0.9995 **Platinum** 0.25 oz. APW, 22 •
Obv. Designer: John Mercanti

Date	Mintage	MS65	Prf65
2002W	9,282	—	470

KM# 352 • Rev. Desc.: Eagle pearched on a Rocky
Mountain Pine branch against a flag backdrop. • 7.79 g.,
0.9995 **Platinum** 0.25 oz. APW, 22 • **Obv. Designer:**
John Mercanti • **Rev. Designer:** Al Maletsky

Date	Mintage	MS65	Prf65
2003W	7,044	—	470

KM# 365 • Rev. Desc.: Chester French, 1907. The
sculpture is outside the N.Y. Customs House, now part of
the Smithsonian's Museum of the American Indian • 7.79
g., 0.9995 **Platinum** 0.25 oz. APW, 22 • **Obv. Designer:**
John Mercanti

Date	Mintage	MS65	Prf65
2004W	5,193	—	1,000

KM# 378 • Rev. Desc.: Eagle with cornucopiae • 7.79
g., 0.9995 **Platinum** 0.25 oz. APW, 22 • **Obv. Designer:**
John Mercanti • **Rev. Designer:** Donna Weaver

Date	Mintage	MS65	Prf65
2005W	6,592	—	610

KM# 390 • Rev. Desc.: Liberty seated writing between
two columns • 7.79 g., 0.9995 **Platinum** 0.25 oz. APW,
22 • **Obv. Designer:** John Mercanti

Date	Mintage	MS65	Prf65
2006W	7,813	—	470

KM# 415 • Rev. Desc.: Eagle with shield • 7.79 g.,
0.9995 **Platinum** 0.25 oz. APW, 22 • **Obv. Designer:**
John Mercanti

Date	Mintage	MS65	Prf65
2007W Polished Freedom	6,017	—	470
2007W Frosted Freedom, Rare	—	—	—

KM# 435 • Rev. Desc.: Justice standing before eagle
• 7.79 g., 0.9995 **Platinum** 0.25 oz. APW, 22 • **Obv.
Designer:** John Mercanti

Date	Mintage	MS65	Prf65
2008W	6,017	—	715

KM# 461 • 7.79 g., 0.9995 **Platinum** 0.25 oz. APW, 22 •
Obv. Designer: John Mercanti

Date	Mintage	MS65	Prf65
2009W	3,800	—	—

BULLION COINS

PLATINUM $50

KM# 285 • Rev. Desc.: Eagle flying right over sunrise • 15.55 g., 0.9995 **Platinum** 0.50 oz. APW, 27 • **Obv. Designer:** John Mercanti • **Rev. Designer:** Thomas D. Rogers Sr

Date	Mintage	MS65	Prf65
1997	20,500	864	—
1997W	15,432	—	935
1998	32,419	864	—
1999	32,309	864	—
2000	18,892	864	—
2001	12,815	864	—
2002	24,005	864	—
2003	17,409	864	—
2004	13,236	864	—
2005	9,013	864	—
2006	9,602	864	—
2006W Burnished Unc.	—	990	—
2007	7,001	864	—
2007W Burnished Unc.	—	925	—
2008	14,000	864	—
2008W Burnished Unc.	—	1,200	—

KM# 291 • Rev. Desc.: Eagle in flight over New England costal lighthouse • 15.55 g., 0.9995 **Platinum** 0.50 oz. APW • **Obv. Designer:** John Mercanti

Date	Mintage	MS65	Prf65
1998W	13,836	—	935

KM# 303 • Rev. Desc.: Eagle in flight over Southeastern Wetlands • 15.55 g., 0.9995 **Platinum** 0.50 oz. APW • **Obv. Designer:** John Mercanti

Date	Mintage	MS65	Prf65
1999W	11,103	—	935

KM# 316 • Rev. Desc.: Eagle in flight over Heartland • 15.55 g., 0.9995 **Platinum** 0.50 oz. APW • **Obv. Designer:** John Mercanti

Date	Mintage	MS65	Prf65
2000W	11,049	—	935

KM# 329 • Rev. Desc.: Eagle in flight over Southwestern cactus desert • 15.55 g., 0.9995 **Platinum** 0.50 oz. APW, 27 • **Obv. Designer:** John Mercanti

Date	Mintage	MS65	Prf65
2001W	8,254	—	935

KM# 341 • Rev. Desc.: Eagle fishing in America's Northwest • 15.55 g., 0.9995 **Platinum** 0.50 oz. APW, 27 • **Obv. Designer:** John Mercanti

Date	Mintage	MS65	Prf65
2002W	8,772	—	935

KM# 353 • Rev. Desc.: Eagle pearched on a Rocky Mountain Pine branch against a flag backdrop. • 15.55 g., 0.9995 **Platinum** 0.50 oz. APW, 27 • **Obv. Designer:** John Mercanti • **Rev. Designer:** Al Maletsky

Date	Mintage	MS65	Prf65
2003W	7,131	—	935

KM# 366 • Rev. Desc.: Chester French, 1907. The sculpture is outside the N.Y. Customs House, now part of the Smithsonian's Museum of the American Indian • 15.55 g., 0.9995 **Platinum** 0.50 oz. APW, 27 • **Obv. Designer:** John Mercanti

Date	Mintage	MS65	Prf65
2004W	5,063	—	1,550

BULLION COINS

KM# 379 • Rev. Desc.: Eagle with cornucopiae • 15.55 g., 0.9995 **Platinum** 0.50 oz. APW, 27 • **Obv. Designer:** John Mercanti • **Rev. Designer:** Donna Weaver

Date	Mintage	MS65	Prf65
2005W	5,942	—	1,175

KM# 391 • Rev. Desc.: Liberty seated writing between two columns • 15.55 g., 0.9995 **Platinum** 0.50 oz. APW, 27 • **Obv. Designer:** John Mercanti

Date	Mintage	MS65	Prf65
2006W	7,649	—	935

KM# 416 • Rev. Desc.: Eagle with shield • 15.55 g., 0.9995 **Platinum** 0.50 oz. APW, 27 • **Obv. Designer:** John Mercanti

Date	Mintage	MS65	Prf65
2007W Reverse Proof	22,873	—	885
2007W Frosted Freedom, Rare	—	—	—

KM# 436 • Rev. Desc.: Justice standing before eagle • 15.55 g., 0.9995 **Platinum** 0.50 oz. APW, 27 • **Obv. Designer:** John Mercanti

Date	Mintage	MS65	Prf65
2008W	22,873	—	1,225

KM# 462 • 15.55 g., 0.9995 **Platinum** 0.50 oz. APW, 27 • **Obv. Designer:** John Mercanti

Date	Mintage	MS65	Prf65
2009	3,600	—	—

PLATINUM $100

KM# 286 • Rev. Desc.: Eagle in flight over sun rise • 31.11 g., 0.9995 **Platinum** 0.99 oz. APW, 33 • **Obv. Designer:** John Mercanti • **Rev. Designer:** Thomas D. Rogers Sr

Date	Mintage	MS65	Prf65
1997W	15,885	—	1,777
1997	56,000	1,608	—
1998	133,002	1,608	—
1999	56,707	1,608	—
2000	10,003	1,608	—
2001	14,070	1,608	—
2002	11,502	1,608	—
2003	8,007	1,608	—
2004	7,009	1,608	—
2005	6,310	1,608	—
2006	6,000	1,608	—
2006W Burnished Unc.	—	2,200	—
2007W	—	1,651	—
2007 Burnished Unc.	7,202	2,100	—
2008	21,800	1,608	—
2008W Burnished Unc.	—	2,300	—
2011	—	—	—

KM# 292 • Rev. Desc.: Eagle in flight over New England costal lighthouse • 31.11 g., 0.9995 **Platinum** 0.99 oz. APW • **Obv. Designer:** John Mercanti

Date	Mintage	MS65	Prf65
1998W	14,912	—	1,760

KM# 304 • Rev. Desc.: Eagle in flight over Southeastern Wetlands • 31.11 g., 0.9995 **Platinum** 0.99 oz. APW • **Obv. Designer:** John Mercanti

Date	Mintage	MS65	Prf65
1999W	12,363	—	1,760

KM# 317 • Rev. Desc.: Eagle in flight over Heartland
• 31.11 g., 0.9995 **Platinum** 0.99 oz. APW • **Obv.
Designer:** John Mercanti

Date	Mintage	MS65	Prf65
2000W	12,453	—	1,760

KM# 330 • Rev. Desc.: Eagle in flight over
Southwestern cactus desert • 31.11 g., 0.9995 **Platinum**
0.99 oz. APW, 33 • **Obv. Designer:** John Mercanti

Date	Mintage	MS65	Prf65
2001W	8,969	—	1,760

KM# 342 • Rev. Desc.: Eagle fishing in America's
Northwest • 31.11 g., 0.9995 **Platinum** 0.99 oz. APW, 33
• **Obv. Designer:** John Mercanti

Date	Mintage	MS65	Prf65
2002W	9,834	—	1,760

KM# 354 • Rev. Desc.: Eagle pearched on a Rocky
Mountain Pine branch against a flag backdrop • 31.11
g., 0.9995 **Platinum** 0.99 oz. APW, 33 • **Obv. Designer:**
John Mercanti • **Rev. Designer:** Al Maletsky

Date	Mintage	MS65	Prf65
2003W	8,246	—	1,777

KM# 367 • Rev. Desc.: Inspired by the sculpture
"America" by Daniel Chester French, 1907. The sculpture
is outside the N.Y. Customs House, now part of the
Smithsonian's Museum of the American Indian • 31.11
g., 0.9995 **Platinum** 0.99 oz. APW, 33 • **Obv. Designer:**
John Mercanti • **Rev. Designer:** Donna Weaver

Date	Mintage	MS65	Prf65
2004W	6,007	—	2,119

KM# 380 • Rev. Desc.: Eagle with cornucopiae • 31.11
g., 0.9995 **Platinum** 0.99 oz. APW, 33 • **Obv. Designer:**
John Mercanti • **Rev. Designer:** Donna Weaver

Date	Mintage	MS65	Prf65
2005W	6,602	—	2,400

KM# 392 • Rev. Desc.: Liberty seated writing between
two columns • 31.11 g., 0.9995 **Platinum** 0.99 oz. APW,
33 • **Obv. Designer:** John Mercanti

Date	Mintage	MS65	Prf65
2006W	9,152	—	1,760

KM# 417 • Rev. Desc.: Eagle with shield • 31.11 g., 0.9995 **Platinum** 0.99 oz. APW, 33 • **Obv. Designer:** John Mercanti

Date	Mintage	MS65	Prf65
2007W Freedom Frosted	8,363	—	1,760
2007W Freedom Polished	—	—	50,000

KM# 437 • Rev. Desc.: Justice standing before eagle • 31.11 g., 0.9995 **Platinum** 0.99 oz. APW, 33 • **Obv. Designer:** John Mercanti

Date	Mintage	MS65	Prf65
2008W	8,363	—	3,000

KM# 463 • Rev. Desc.: Four portraits • 31.10 g., 0.9995 **Platinum** 0.99 oz. APW, 33 • **Obv. Designer:** John Mercanti

Date	Mintage	MS65	Prf65
2009W Proof	4,900	—	2,260

KM# 488 • Rev. Desc.: Statue of Justice holding scales • 31.11 g., 0.999 **Platinum** 0.99 oz. APW, 33 • **Obv. Designer:** John Mercanti

Date	Mintage	MS65	Prf65
2010W	—	—	2,160

KM# 518 • Rev. Desc.: Female with dove, walking in field • 31.11 g., 0.9995 **Platinum** 0.99 oz. APW, 33

Date	Mintage	MS65	Prf65
2011W	10,299	—	2,100

KM# 541 • Rev. Desc.: Colonial soldier and flag • 31.11 g., 0.9995 **Platinum** 0.99 oz. APW

Date	Mintage	MS65	Prf65
2012	—	—	1,793

KM# 585 • Rev. Desc.: Female and gears of industry • 31.11 g., 0.9995 **Platinum** 0.99 oz. APW, 33

Date	Mintage	MS65	Prf65
2013	—	—	

BISON BULLION COINAGE

GOLD $5

KM# 411 • Obv. Desc.: Indian Head right • **Rev. Desc.:** Bison • 3.11 g., 0.9999 **Gold** 0.10 oz. AGW

Date	Mintage	MS65	Prf65
2008W	17,429	600	—
2008W	18,884	—	660

GOLD $10

KM# 412 • Obv. Desc.: Indian Head right • **Rev. Desc.:** Bison • 7.79 g., 0.9999 **Gold** 0.25 oz. AGW

Date	Mintage	MS65	Prf65
2008W	9,949	1,375	—
2008W	13,125	—	1,550

GOLD $25

KM# 413 • Obv. Desc.: Indian Head right • **Rev. Desc.:** Bison • 15.55 g., 0.999 **Gold** 0.50 oz. AGW

Date	Mintage	MS65	Prf65
2008W	16,908	1,350	—
2008W	12,169	—	1,850

GOLD $50

KM# 393 • Obv. Desc.: Indian head right • **Rev. Desc.:** Bison standing left on mound • 31.11 g., 0.9999 **Gold** 0.99 oz. AGW, 32 • **Designer:** James E. Fraser

Date	Mintage	MS65	Prf65
2006	337,012	1,380	—
2006W Proof	246,267	—	1,535
2007	136,503	1,380	—
2007W Proof	58,998	—	1,535
2008	189,500	1,380	—
2008W Burnished	18,863	—	3,200
2008W Moy Family Chop, Proof	—	—	3,950
2009	200,000	1,380	—
2009W Proof	49,306	—	1,505
2010	209,000	1,380	—
2010W Proof	49,263	—	1,535
2011W	174,500	—	1,535
2011 Proof	28,693	1,380	—
2012	132,000	—	—
2012W Proof	19,765	—	2,000
2013W	—	—	—
2013 Reverse Proof	47,836	1,380	1,950

FIRST SPOUSE GOLD COINAGE

GOLD $10

KM# 407 • Obv. Desc.: Bust 3/4 facing • **Rev. Desc.:** Martha Washington seated sewing • 15.55 g., 0.9999 **Gold** 0.50 oz. AGW, 23.5 • **Obv. Designer:** Joseph Menna • **Rev. Designer:** Susan Gamble and Don Everhart

Date	Mintage	MS65	Prf65
2007W	17,661	710	—
2007W	19,169	—	710

KM# 408 • Obv. Desc.: Bust 3/4 facing • **Rev. Desc.:** Abigail Adams seated at desk writing to John during the Revolutionary War • 15.55 g., 0.9999 **Gold** 0.50 oz. AGW, 26.5 • **Obv. Designer:** Joseph Menna • **Rev. Designer:** Thomas Cleveland and Phebe Hemphill

Date	Mintage	MS65	Prf65
2007W	17,142	—	710
2007W	17,149	710	—

KM# 409 • Obv. Desc.: Bust design from coinage • **Rev. Desc.:** Jefferson's tombstone • 15.55 g., 0.9999 **Gold** 0.50 oz. AGW, 26.5 • **Obv. Designer:** Robert Scot and Phebe Hemphill • **Rev. Designer:** Charles Vickers

Date	Mintage	MS65	Prf65
2007W	19,823	—	710
2007W	19,815	710	—

KM# 410 • Obv. Desc.: Bust 3/4 facing • **Rev. Desc.:** Dolley standing before painting of Washington, which she saved from the White House • 15.55 g., 0.9999 **Gold** 0.50 oz. AGW, 26.5 • **Obv. Designer:** Don Everhart • **Rev. Designer:** Joel Iskowitz and Don Everhart

Date	Mintage	MS65	Prf65
2007W	11,813	710	—
2007W	17,661	—	710

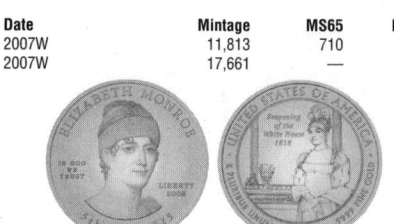

KM# 430 • Obv. Desc.: Bust 3/4 facing right • **Rev. Desc.:** Elizabeth standing before mirror • 15.55 g., 0.999 **Gold** 0.50 oz. AGW, 26.5 • **Obv. Designer:** Joel Iskowitz and Don Everhart • **Rev. Designer:** Donna Weaver and Charles Vickers

Date	Mintage	MS65	Prf65
2008W	4,519	975	—
2008W	7,933	—	950

KM# 431 • Obv. Desc.: Bust 3/4 facing right • **Rev. Desc.:** Lousia and son Charles before entrance • 15.55 g., 0.999 **Gold** 0.50 oz. AGW, 26.5 • **Obv. Designer:** Susan Gamble and Phebe Hemphill • **Rev. Designer:** Joseph Menna

Date	Mintage	MS65	Prf65
2008W	4,223	1,175	—
2008W	7,454	—	1,125

KM# 432 • Obv. Desc.: Capped and draped bust left • **Rev. Desc.:** Andrew Jackson on horseback right • 15.55 g., 0.999 **Gold** 0.50 oz. AGW, 26.5 • **Obv. Designer:** John Reich • **Rev. Designer:** Justin Kunz and Don Everhart

Date	Mintage	MS65	Prf65
2008W	4,281	1,575	—
2008W	7,454	—	1,325

KM# 433 • Obv. Desc.: Seated Liberty with shiled • **Rev. Desc.:** Youthful van Buren seated under tree, family tavern in distance • 15.55 g., 0.999 **Gold** 0.50 oz. AGW, 26.5 • **Obv. Designer:** Christian Gobrecht • **Rev. Designer:** Thomas Cleveland and James Licaretz

Date	Mintage	MS65	Prf65
2008W	3,443	1,500	—
2008W	6,187	—	1,525

KM# 456 • Obv. Desc.: Bust 3/4 left • **Rev. Desc.:** Anna reading to her three children • 15.55 g., 0.999 **Gold** 0.50 oz. AGW • **Obv. Designer:** Donna Weaver and Joseph Menna • **Rev. Designer:** Thomas Cleveland and Charles Vickers

Date	Mintage	MS65	Prf65
2009W	2,993	1,225	—
2009W	5,801	—	1,150

KM# 457 • Obv. Desc.: Bust facing • **Rev. Desc.:** Letitia and two children playing outside of Cedar Grove Plantation • 15.55 g., 0.999 **Gold** 0.50 oz. AGW • **Obv. Designer:** Phebe Hemphill • **Rev. Designer:** Susan Gamble and Norm Nemeth

Date	Mintage	MS65	Prf65
2009W	2,381	1,525	—
2009W	4,341	—	1,325

KM# 458 • Obv. Desc.: Bust facing • **Rev. Desc.:** Julia and John Tyler dancing • 15.55 g., 0.999 **Gold** 0.50 oz. AGW • **Designer:** Joel Iskowitz and Don Everhart

Date	Mintage	MS65	Prf65
2009W	2,188	1,650	—
2009W	3,878	—	1,800

KM# 459 • Obv. Desc.: Bust 3/4 right • **Rev. Desc.:** Sarah seated at desk as personal secretary to James Polk • 15.55 g., 0.999 **Gold** 0.50 oz. AGW • **Designer:** Phebe Hemphill

Date	Mintage	MS65	Prf65
2009W	1,893	1,300	—
2009W	3,512	—	1,100

KM# 465 • Obv. Desc.: Bust 3/4 left • **Rev. Desc.:**
Margaret Taylor nurses wounded soldier during the
Seminole War • 15.55 g., 0.999 **Gold** 0.50 oz. AGW •
Obv. Designer: Phebe Hemphill and Charles Vickers •
Rev. Designer: Mary Beth Zeitz and James Licaretz

Date	Mintage	MS65	Prf65
2009W	3,430	1,050	—
2009W	4,787	—	1,225

KM# 481 • Rev. Desc.: Abigail Fillmore placing books
on library shelf • 15.52 g., 0.999 **Gold** 0.50 oz. AGW •
Obv. Designer: Phebe Hemphill • **Rev. Designer:** Susan
Gamble and Joseph Menna

Date	Mintage	MS65	Prf65
2010W	3,482	1,300	—
2010W	6,130	—	1,025

KM# 482 • Rev. Desc.: Jane Pierce seated on porch •
15.52 g., 0.999 **Gold** 0.50 oz. AGW • **Obv. Designer:**
Donna Weaver and Don Everhart • **Rev. Designer:** Donna
Weaver and Charles Vickers

Date	Mintage	MS65	Prf65
2010W	3,338	1,000	—
2010W	4,775	—	1,225

KM# 483 • Rev. Desc.: Buchanan as clerk • 15.52
g., 0.999 **Gold** 0.50 oz. AGW, 26.5 • **Obv. Designer:**
Christian Gobrecht • **Rev. Designer:** Joseph Menna

Date	Mintage	MS65	Prf65
2010W	5,162	1,000	—
2010W	7,110	—	1,075

KM# 484 • Rev. Desc.: Mary Lincoln visiting soldiers
at hospital • 15.52 g., 0.999 **Gold** 0.50 oz. AGW • **Obv.
Designer:** Phebe Hemphill • **Rev. Designer:** Joel Iskowitz
and Pheve Hemphill

Date	Mintage	MS65	Prf65
2010W	3,965	1,000	—
2010W	6,861	—	975

KM# 509 • Obv. Desc.: Bust of Eliza Johnson • 15.55 g.,
0.999 **Gold** 0.50 oz. AGW

Date	Mintage	MS65	Prf65
2011W	2,915	1,075	—
2011W	3,907	—	1,075

KM# 510 • Obv. Desc.: Bust of Julia Grant • 15.55 g.,
0.999 **Gold** 0.50 oz. AGW, 26.5

Date	Mintage	MS65	Prf65
2011W	2,952	1,075	—
2011W	3,969	—	1,075

KM# 511 • Obv. Desc.: Bust of Lucy Hayes • 15.55 g.,
0.999 **Gold** 0.50 oz. AGW

Date	Mintage	MS65	Prf65
2011W	2,263	1,325	—
2011W	3,885	—	1,075

KM# 512 • Obv. Desc.: Bust of Lucretia Garfield • 15.55
g., 0.999 **Gold** 0.50 oz. AGW

Date	Mintage	MS65	Prf65
2011W	2,498	1,325	—
2011W	3,652	—	1,075

KM# 532 • Obv. Desc.: Alice Paul, suffragist • 15.55 g., 0.999 **Gold** 0.50 oz. AGW, 26.5

Date	Mintage	MS65	Prf65
2012W	2,798	1,050	—
2012W	3,506	—	1,075

KM# 533 • Obv. Desc.: Frances Cleveland • 15.55 g., 0.999 **Gold** 0.50 oz. AGW, 26.5

Date	Mintage	MS65	Prf65
2012W	2,454	1,050	—
2012W	3,158	—	1,075

KM# 534 • Obv. Desc.: Caroline Harrison • 15.55 g., 0.999 **Gold** 0.50 oz. AGW, 26.5

Date	Mintage	MS65	Prf65
2012W	2,436	1,050	—
2012W	3,046	—	1,075

KM# 535 • Obv. Desc.: Frances Cleveland • 15.55 g., 0.999 **Gold** 0.50 oz. AGW, 26.5

Date	Mintage	MS65	Prf65
2012W	2,425	1,050	—
2012W	3,104	—	1,075

KM# 561 • Obv. Desc.: Bust of Ida McKinley • 15.55 g., 0.999 **Gold** 0.50 oz. AGW

Date	Mintage	MS65	Prf65
2013W	—	800	—
2013W	—	—	825

KM# 562 • Obv. Desc.: Bust of Edith Roosevelt • 15.55 g., 0.999 **Gold** 0.50 oz. AGW

Date	Mintage	MS65	Prf65
2013W	—	800	—
2013W	—	—	825

KM# 563 • Obv. Desc.: Bust of Helen Taft • 15.55 g., 0.999 **Gold** 0.50 oz. AGW

Date	Mintage	MS65	Prf65
2013W	—	800	—
2013W	—	—	825

KM# 564 • Obv. Desc.: Bust of Ellen Wilson • 15.55 g., 0.999 **Gold** 0.50 oz. AGW

Date	Mintage	MS65	Prf65
2013W	—	800	—
2013W	—	—	825

KM# 565 • Obv. Desc.: Bust of Edith Wilson • 15.55 g., 0.999 **Gold** 0.50 oz. AGW

Date	Mintage	MS65	Prf65
2013W	—	800	—
2013W	—	—	825

CANADA
CONFEDERATION
CIRCULATION COINAGE

KM# 1 CENT
4.54 g., Bronze, **Obv.** Laureate head left **Rev:** Denomination and date within beaded circle, chain of leaves surrounds **Obv. Legend:** VICTORIA DEI GRATIA REGINA. CANADA **Rev. Legend:** ONE CENT **Edge:** plain

Date	Mintage	VG8	F12	VF20	XF40	AU50	MS60	MS63
1858	421,000	75.00	100	125	200	300	500	2,000
1859 Narrow 9	9,579,000	2.25	3.00	5.00	7.00	15.00	45.00	250
1859/8 Wide 9	Inc. above	30.00	45.00	60.00	125	225	350	1,800
1859 Double punched narrow 9 type I	Inc. above	200	250	350	550	850	1,300	5,000
1859 Double punched narrow 9 type II	Inc. above	55.00	75.00	125	175	300	550	3,000

KM# 7 CENT
5.67 g., Bronze, 25.5mm. **Obv.** Crowned head left within beaded circle **Obv. Designer:** Leonard C. Wyon **Rev:** Denomination and date within beaded circle, chain of leaves surrounds **Obv. Legend:** VICTORIA DEI GRATIA REGINA. CANADA **Edge:** Plain

Date	Mintage	VG8	F12	VF20	XF40	AU50	MS60	MS63
1876	4,000,000	3.00	4.00	6.00	9.00	27.00	45.00	250
1881	2,000,000	4.00	5.00	11.00	18.00	45.00	75.00	300
1882	4,000,000	3.00	3.50	4.00	7.50	23.00	40.00	250
1884	2,500,000	3.00	4.00	6.50	11.00	35.00	60.00	300
1886	1,500,000	4.00	7.00	13.00	20.00	55.00	95.00	450
1887	1,500,000	3.50	5.00	8.00	14.00	40.00	70.00	225
1888	4,000,000	3.00	4.00	5.00	7.50	22.00	40.00	175
1890	1,000,000	8.00	12.00	19.00	30.00	65.00	125	450
1891 Large date	1,452,000	8.00	11.00	17.00	35.00	80.00	150	450
1891 S.D.L.L.	Inc. above	65.00	125	200	300	500	1,000	4,000
1891 S.D.S.L.	Inc. above	60.00	95.00	125	200	270	450	1,750
1892	1,200,000	5.50	8.00	12.00	15.00	35.00	60.00	225
1893	2,000,000	3.00	4.00	5.00	9.50	27.00	45.00	200
1894	1,000,000	11.00	15.00	20.00	40.00	70.00	125	300
1895	1,200,000	5.00	9.50	13.00	16.00	35.00	60.00	225
1896	2,000,000	3.00	5.00	6.50	7.50	23.00	40.00	150
1897	1,500,000	3.00	5.00	6.50	9.00	27.00	45.00	200
1898	1,000,000	9.00	13.00	17.00	35.00	55.00	100	300
1899	2,400,000	3.00	3.50	5.00	7.00	26.00	45.00	150
1900	1,000,000	9.00	13.50	20.00	30.00	75.00	125	500
1900	2,600,000	3.00	3.50	5.00	7.50	18.50	30.00	95.00
1901	4,100,000	3.00	4.00	6.00	11.00	22.00	45.00	100

KM# 8 CENT
5.67 g., Bronze, 25.5mm. **Obv.** Kings bust right within beaded circle **Obv. Designer:** G. W. DeSaulles **Rev:** Denomination above date within circle, chain of leaves surrounds **Edge:** Plain

Date	Mintage	VG8	F12	VF20	XF40	AU50	MS60	MS63
1902	3,000,000	2.25	3.00	4.00	8.00	13.50	27.00	75.00
1903	4,000,000	2.25	3.00	4.00	8.00	15.00	30.00	90.00
1904	2,500,000	2.50	4.00	6.00	10.00	22.00	45.00	100
1905	2,000,000	4.00	6.00	9.00	13.00	27.00	55.00	150
1906	4,100,000	2.25	3.00	4.00	8.00	18.00	40.00	175
1907	2,400,000	2.50	3.00	5.00	10.00	19.50	40.00	175
1907H	800,000	15.00	21.00	30.00	55.00	90.00	175	600
1908	2,401,506	3.00	4.00	6.00	10.00	22.00	40.00	125
1908	—	PF60 350						
1909	3,973,339	2.00	3.00	4.00	7.00	15.00	30.00	100
1910	5,146,487	1.50	2.00	3.00	6.00	13.50	30.00	85.00

KM# 15 CENT
5.67 g., Bronze, 25.5mm. **Obv.** King's bust left **Obv. Designer:** E. B. MacKennal **Rev:** Denomination above date within beaded circle, chain of leaves surrounds **Edge:** Plain

Date	Mintage	VG8	F12	VF20	XF40	AU50	MS60	MS63
1911	4,663,486	0.80	1.50	2.25	3.50	13.50	25.00	70.00
1911	—	PF60 700						

KM# 21 CENT
5.67 g., Bronze, 25.5mm. **Obv.** King's bust left **Obv. Designer:** E. B. MacKennal **Rev:** Denomination above date within beaded circle, chain of leaves surrounds **Edge:** Plain

Date	Mintage	VG8	F12	VF20	XF40	AU50	MS60	MS63
1912	5,107,642	0.90	1.75	2.50	4.00	13.00	30.00	75.00
1913	5,735,405	0.90	1.75	2.50	5.00	13.00	27.50	95.00
1914	3,405,958	1.50	1.75	3.00	5.00	18.00	40.00	100
1915	4,932,134	0.90	1.50	2.50	5.00	13.00	35.00	95.00
1916	11,022,367	0.60	0.80	1.50	3.00	11.00	19.00	60.00
1917	11,899,254	0.60	0.80	1.00	2.50	5.00	16.00	55.00
1918	12,970,798	0.60	0.80	1.00	2.50	5.00	14.00	55.00
1919	11,279,634	0.60	0.80	1.00	2.50	5.00	14.00	55.00
1920	6,762,247	0.70	0.90	1.25	2.50	8.00	22.00	85.00

Dot below date

KM# 28 CENT
3.24 g., Bronze, 19.10mm. **Obv.** King's bust left **Obv. Designer:** E. B. MacKennal **Rev:** Denomination above date, leaves flank **Rev. Designer:** Fred Lewis **Edge:** Plain

Date	Mintage	VG8	F12	VF20	XF40	AU50	MS60	MS63
1920	15,483,923	0.20	0.45	0.95	1.75	5.00	15.00	50.00
1921	7,601,627	0.45	0.75	1.75	5.00	13.00	35.00	250
1922	1,243,635	13.00	16.00	25.00	45.00	100	200	1,200
1923	1,019,002	29.00	35.00	40.00	60.00	150	300	2,000
1924	1,593,195	6.00	7.00	12.00	20.00	55.00	125	850
1925	1,000,622	22.00	25.00	30.00	50.00	100	200	1,200
1926	2,143,372	4.00	5.00	7.00	16.00	45.00	95.00	650
1927	3,553,928	1.25	1.75	3.50	8.00	22.00	40.00	225
1928	9,144,860	0.15	0.30	0.65	1.50	8.00	20.00	90.00
1929	12,159,840	0.15	0.30	0.65	1.50	9.00	20.00	80.00

Date	Mintage	VG8	F12	VF20	XF40	AU50	MS60	MS63
1930	2,538,613	2.00	2.50	4.50	9.00	27.00	50.00	225
1931	3,842,776	0.65	1.00	2.50	6.00	22.00	40.00	200
1932	21,316,190	0.15	0.20	0.50	1.50	5.00	16.00	60.00
1933	12,079,310	0.15	0.30	0.50	1.50	5.00	16.00	55.00
1934	7,042,358	0.20	0.30	0.75	1.50	5.00	16.00	60.00
1935	7,526,400	0.20	0.30	0.75	1.50	5.00	16.00	50.00
1936	8,768,769	0.15	0.30	0.75	1.50	5.00	14.00	45.00
1936 dot below date; Rare	678,823	—	—	—	—	—	—	250,000

Note: Only one possible business strike is known to exist. No other examples (or possible business strikes) have ever surfaced.

| 1936 dot below date, specimen, 3 known | | — | — | — | — | — | — | — |

Note: At the David Akers auction of the John Jay Pittman collection (Part 1, 10-97), a gem specimen realized $121,000. At the David Akers auction of the John Jay Pittman collection (Part 3, 10-99), a near choice specimen realized $115,000.

Maple leaf

KM# 32 CENT
3.24 g., Bronze, 19.10m m. **Obv.** Head left **Obv. Designer:** T. H. Paget **Rev:** Maple leaf divides date and denomination **Rev. Designer:** George E. Kruger-Gray **Edge:** Plain

Date	Mintage	VG8	F12	VF20	XF40	AU50	MS60	MS63
1937	10,040,231	0.35	0.45	0.70	0.95	1.50	2.50	12.00
1938	18,365,608	0.10	0.20	0.30	0.70	1.50	2.50	13.00
1939	21,600,319	0.20	0.20	0.30	0.70	1.25	2.00	8.00
1940	85,740,532	—	0.10	0.25	0.50	0.90	2.50	8.00
1941	56,336,011	—	0.10	0.25	0.50	2.25	8.00	50.00
1942	76,113,708	—	0.10	0.25	0.50	1.75	7.00	50.00
1943	89,111,969	—	0.10	0.25	0.45	1.25	3.50	22.00
1944	44,131,216	—	0.10	0.30	0.60	2.25	11.00	70.00
1945	77,268,591	—	0.10	0.20	0.35	0.90	2.50	22.00
1946	56,662,071	—	0.10	0.20	0.35	0.90	2.50	12.00
1947	31,093,901	—	0.10	0.20	0.35	0.90	2.50	9.00
1947 maple leaf	47,855,448	—	0.15	0.20	0.35	0.90	2.50	9.00

KM# 41 CENT
3.24 g., Bronze, 19.10mm. **Obv.** Modified legend **Obv. Designer:** T. H. Paget **Rev. Designer:** George E. Kruger-Gray **Edge:** Plain

Date	Mintage	VG8	F12	VF20	XF40	AU50	MS60	MS63
1948	25,767,779	—	0.15	0.25	0.70	1.25	4.00	27.00
1949	33,128,933	—	—	0.15	0.35	0.90	2.50	9.00
1950	60,444,992	—	—	0.15	0.25	0.65	1.75	9.00
1951	80,430,379	—	—	0.15	0.20	0.45	1.75	14.00
1952	67,631,736	—	—	0.15	0.20	0.45	1.25	9.00

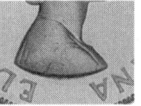

No strap   With strap

KM# 49 CENT
3.24 g., Bronze, 19.10mm. **Obv.** Laureate bust right **Obv. Designer:** Mary Gillick **Rev:** Maple leaf divides date and denomination **Rev. Designer:** George E. Kruger-Gray

Date	Mintage	VG8	F12	VF20	XF40	AU50	MS60	MS63
1953	67,806,016	—	—	—	0.25	0.45	0.80	2.50
Note: Without strap								
1953	Inc. above	0.50	1.00	1.50	2.50	7.00	12.00	60.00
Note: With strap								
1954	22,181,760	—	—	0.10	0.40	0.90	1.75	6.00
Note: With strap								
1954 Prooflike only	Inc. above	—	—	—	—	—	550	800
Note: Without strap								
1955	56,403,193	—	—	—	0.15	0.20	0.45	3.00
Note: With strap								
1955	Inc. above	100	150	175	250	400	600	2,000
Note: Without strap								
1956	78,658,535	—	—	—	0.15	0.20	0.30	2.00
1957	100,601,792	—	—	—	—	—	0.10	1.00
1958	59,385,679	—	—	—	—	—	0.10	1.00
1959	83,615,343	—	—	—	—	—	—	0.60
1960	75,772,775	—	—	—	—	—	—	0.60
1961	139,598,404	—	—	—	—	—	—	0.60

Date	Mintage	VG8	F12	VF20	XF40	AU50	MS60	MS63
1962	227,244,069	—	—	—	—	—	—	0.40
1963	279,076,334	—	—	—	—	—	—	0.40
1964	484,655,322	—	—	—	—	—	—	0.40

KM# 59.1 CENT
3.24 g., Bronze, 19.10mm. **Obv.** Queens bust right **Obv. Designer:** Arnold Machin **Rev:** Maple leaf divides date and denomination **Rev. Designer:** George E. Kruger-Gray **Edge:** Plain

Date	Mintage	VG8	F12	VF20	XF40	AU50	MS60	MS63
1965	304,441,082	—	0.10	0.20	0.40	0.70	1.00	5.00
Note: Small beads, pointed 5								
1965	Inc. above	—	—	—	—	—	—	0.40
Note: Small beads, blunt 5								
1965	Inc. above	1.75	3.00	4.50	7.50	12.50	18.00	45.00
Note: Large beads, pointed 5								
1965	Inc. above	—	—	—	—	—	—	0.40
Note: Large beads, blunt 5								
1966	184,151,087	—	—	—	—	—	—	0.40
1968	329,695,772	—	—	—	—	—	—	0.40
1969	335,240,929	—	—	—	—	—	—	0.40
1970	311,145,010	—	—	—	—	—	—	0.40
1971	298,228,936	—	—	—	—	—	—	0.40
1972	451,304,591	—	—	—	—	—	—	0.40
1973	457,059,852	—	—	—	—	—	—	0.40
1974	692,058,489	—	—	—	—	—	—	0.40
1975	642,318,000	—	—	—	—	—	—	0.40
1976	701,122,890	—	—	—	—	—	—	0.40
1977	453,762,670	—	—	—	—	—	—	0.40

KM# 65 CENT
3.24 g., Bronze, 19.10mm. **Subject:** Confederation Centennial **Obv.** Queen's bust right **Obv. Designer:** Arnold Machin **Rev:** Dove with wings spread, denomination above, two dates below **Rev. Designer:** Alex Coville

Date	Mintage	VG8	F12	VF20	XF40	AU50	MS60	MS63
1867-1967	345,140,645	—	—	—	—	—	—	0.40
Specimen	—	PF60 2.50						

KM# 59.2 CENT
3.24 g., Bronze, 19.10mm. **Obv.** Queen's bust right **Obv. Designer:** Arnold Machin **Rev:** Maple leaves **Rev. Designer:** George E. Kruger-Gray **Edge:** Plain **Note:** Thin planchet.

Date	Mintage	VG8	F12	VF20	XF40	AU50	MS60	MS63
1978	911,170,647	—	—	—	—	—	—	0.30
1979	754,394,064	—	—	—	—	—	—	0.30

KM# 127 CENT
2.80 g., Bronze, 19.10mm. **Obv.** Queen's bust right **Obv. Designer:** Arnold Machin **Rev. Designer:** George E. Kruger-Gray **Edge:** Plain **Note:** Reduced weight.

Date	Mintage	VG8	F12	VF20	XF40	AU50	MS60	MS63
1980	912,052,318	—	—	—	—	—	—	0.30
1981	1,209,468,500	—	—	—	—	—	—	0.30
1981	199,000	PF60 1.50						

KM# 132 CENT
2.50 g., Bronze, 19.10mm. **Obv.** Queen's bust right **Obv. Designer:** Arnold Machin **Rev:** Maple leaf divides date and denomination **Rev. Designer:** George E. Kruger-Gray **Edge:** Plain **Shape:** 10-sided **Note:** Reduced weight.

Date	Mintage		VG8	F12	VF20	XF40	AU50	MS60	MS63
1982	911,001,000		—	—	—	—	—	—	0.30
1982	180,908	PF60 1.50							
1983	975,510,000		—	—	—	—	—	—	0.30
1983	168,000	PF60 1.50							
1984	838,225,000		—	—	—	—	—	—	0.30
1984	161,602	PF60 1.50							
1985	771,772,500		0.95	1.75	2.50	3.50	6.00	10.00	19.00
Note: Pointed 5									
1985	Inc. above		—	—	—	—	—	—	0.30
Note: Blunt 5									
1985	157,037	PF60 1.50							
Note: Blunt 5									
1986	740,335,000		—	—	—	—	—	—	0.30
1986	175,745	PF60 1.50							
1987	774,549,000		—	—	—	—	—	—	0.30
1987	179,004	PF60 1.50							
1988	482,676,752		—	—	—	—	—	—	0.30
1988	175,259	PF60 1.50							
1989	1,077,347,200		—	—	—	—	—	—	0.30
1989	170,928	PF60 1.50							

KM# 181 CENT
2.50 g., Bronze, 19.10mm. **Obv.** Crowned Queen's head right **Obv. Designer:** Dora dePedery-Hunt **Rev:** Maple leaf divides date and denomination **Rev. Designer:** George E. Kruger-Gray **Edge:** Plain

Date	Mintage		MS63
1990	218,035,000		0.30
1990	140,649	PF60 2.50	
1991	831,001,000		0.30
1991	131,888	PF60 3.50	
1993	752,034,000		0.30
1993	145,065	PF60 2.00	
1994	639,516,000		0.30
1994	146,424	PF60 2.50	
1995	624,983,000		0.30
1995	—	PF60 2.50	
1996	445,746,000		0.30
1996	—	PF60 2.50	

KM# 204 CENT
Bronze, 19.10mm. **Subject:** Confederation 125 **Obv.** Crowned Queen's head right **Obv. Designer:** Dora dePedery-Hunt **Rev:** Maple leaf divides date and denomination **Rev. Designer:** George E. Kruger-Gray

Date	Mintage		MS63
1992	147,061	PF60 2.50	
1992	673,512,000		0.30

KM# 289 CENT
2.25 g., Copper Plated Steel, 19.05mm. **Obv.** Crowned head right **Obv. Designer:** Dora dePédery-Hunt **Rev:** Maple twig design **Rev. Designer:** George E. Kruger-Gray **Edge:** Round and plain

Date	Mintage			MS63
1997	549,868,000			0.30
1997	—	PF63 1.75	PF65 2.75	
1998	999,578,000			0.30
1998	—	PF63 2.00	PF65 3.00	
1998W	—			1.75
1999P	—			6.00
1999	1,089,625,000			0.30
1999	—	PF63 3.00	PF65 4.00	
1999W	—			—
2000	771,908,206			0.30
2000	—	PF63 3.00	PF65 4.00	
2000W	—			1.75
2001	919,358,000			0.30
2001P	—	PF63 3.50	PF65 5.00	
2003	92,219,775			0.30
2003P	—	PF63 3.50	PF65 5.00	
2003P	235,936,799			1.50

KM# 289a CENT
Bronze, 19.10mm.

Date	Mintage	MS63
1998	—	0.75

Note: In Specimen sets only

KM# 309 CENT
5.67 g., 0.925 Copper Plated Silver, 0.17 oz. **Subject:** 90th Anniversary Royal Canadian Mint - 1908-1998 **Obv. Designer:** Dora dePedery-Hunt **Rev. Designer:** G. W.

DeSaulles

Date	Mintage	MS63
1908-1998	25,000	16.00
Note: Antique finish		
1908-1998 Proof	—	—

KM# 332 CENT
5.67 g., 0.925 Silver, 0.17 oz. ASW **Subject:** 90th Anniversary Royal Canadian Mint - 1908-1998 **Obv.** Crowned Queen's head right, with "Canada" added to head **Obv. Designer:** Dora dePedery-Hunt **Rev:** Denomination above dates withn beaded circle, chain of leaves surrounds **Rev. Designer:** G. W. DeSaulles

Date	Mintage	
1908-1998	—	PF60 16.00
Note: Mirror finish		

KM# 445 CENT
2.25 g., Copper Plated Steel, 19.1mm. **Subject:** Elizabeth II Golden Jubilee **Obv.** Crowned head right, Jubilee commemorative dates 1952-2002 **Obv. Designer:** Dora dePédery-Hunt **Rev:** Denomination above maple leaves **Rev. Designer:** George E. Kruger-Gray **Edge:** Plain

Date	Mintage			MS63
1952-2002	716,366,000			0.75
1952-2002P	114,212,000			1.00
1952-2002P	32,642	PF63 4.00	PF65 5.00	

KM# 445a CENT
0.925 Silver, **Subject:** Elizabeth II Golden Jubilee **Obv.** Crowned head right, Jubilee commemorative dates 1952-2002 **Obv. Designer:** Dora dePédery-Hunt **Rev:** Denomination above maple leaves **Rev. Designer:** George E. Kruger-Gray

Date	Mintage		
1952-2002	21,537	PF63 2.50	PF65 3.00

KM# 468 CENT
2.50 g., Copper, **Subject:** 50th Anniversary of the Coronation of Elizabeth II **Obv.** 1953 Effigy of the Queen, Jubilee commemorative dates 1953-2003 **Obv. Designer:** Mary Gillick

Date	Mintage		
1953-2003	—	PF63 1.50	PF65 2.50

KM# 490 CENT
2.25 g., Copper Plated Zinc, 19.05mm. **Obv.** New effigy of Queen Elizabeth II right **Obv. Designer:** Susanna Blunt **Rev:** Two maple leaves **Edge:** Plain

Date	Mintage			MS63
2003	56,877,144			0.25
2004	653,317,000			0.25
2004	—	PF63 1.50	PF65 2.50	
2005	759,658,000			0.25
2005	—	PF63 1.50	PF65 2.50	
2006	886,275,000			0.25
2006	—	PF63 1.50	PF65 2.50	

KM# 490a CENT
2.25 g., Copper Plated Steel, 19.05mm. **Obv.** Bust right **Obv. Designer:** Susanna Blunt **Rev:** Two maple leaves **Rev. Designer:** G. E. Kruger-Gray

Date	Mintage			MS63
2003P	591,257,000			0.25
2003 WP	Inc. above			0.25
2004P	134,906,000			0.25
2005P	30,525,000			0.25
2006P	137,733,000			0.25
2006(ml)	Inc. above			0.25
2007(ml)	938,270,000			0.25
2007(ml)	—	PF63 2.00	PF65 2.50	
2008(ml)	787,625,000			0.25
2008(ml)	—	PF63 2.00	PF65 2.50	
2009(ml)	455,680,000			0.25
2009(ml)	—	PF63 2.00	PF65 2.50	
2010(ml)	—			0.25
2010(ml)	—	PF63 2.00	PF65 2.50	
2011(ml)	—			0.25
2011(ml)	—	PF63 2.00	PF65 2.50	
2012(ml)	—			0.25
2012(ml)	—	PF63 2.00	PF65 2.50	

KM# 490b CENT
2.25 g., Copper Plated Zinc, **Obv.** Head right **Rev:** Maple leaf, selectively gold plated **Note:** Bound into Annual Report.

Date	Mintage		
2003	7,746	PF63 25.00	PF65 35.00

KM# 1023 CENT
Copper, 19.1mm. **Obv.** George V bust left **Rev:** Value within wreath, dual dates below

Date	Mintage		
1935-2010	—	PF63 8.00	PF65 10.00

KM# 1153 CENT
5.67 g., Copper, 19.1mm. **Obv.** George V bust **Rev:** Value within wreath

Date	Mintage		
1911-2011	6,000	PF63 8.00	PF65 10.00

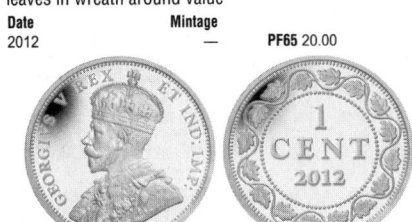

KM# 1342 CENT
Silver, 25.5mm. **Obv.** Edward VII bust right **Rev:** Small leaves in wreath around value

Date	Mintage	
2012	—	PF65 20.00

KM# 1343 CENT
Silver, 25.5mm. **Obv.** George V bust left **Rev:** Small leaves in wreath around value

Date	Mintage	
2012	—	PF65 20.00

KM# 1344 CENT

0.925 Silver, 19.1mm. **Obv.** Elizabeth II bust right **Rev:** Two maple leaves

Date	Mintage		
2012	—	PF65	20.00

KM# 1345 CENT

0.925 Silver, 19.1mm. **Obv.** Elizabeth II Malouf bust right **Rev:** Dove in flight

Date	Mintage		
2012	—	PF65	20.00

KM# 1427 CENT

157.60 g., 0.999 Silver, 5.03 oz. ASW 65mm. **Subject:** Farewell to the cent **Obv. Designer:** Susanna Blunt **Rev:** Two maple leaves **Rev. Designer:** G.E. Kruger-Gray

Date	Mintage		
2012	Est. 1500	PF65	500

KM# 1428 CENT

15.87 g., 0.999 Silver, 0.51 oz. ASW **Ruler:** Elizabeth II 34mm. **Obv. Designer:** Susanna Blunt **Rev:** Two maple leaves selectively gilt **Rev. Designer:** G.E. Kruger-Gray **Mint:** Royal Canadian Mint

Date	Mintage				
2013	Est. 3000	PF63	45.00	PF65	55.00

KM# 410 3 CENTS

3.11 g., 0.925 Silver, 0.09 oz. ASW 21.3mm. **Subject:** 1st Canadian Postage Stamp **Obv.** Crowned head right **Obv. Designer:** Dora dePédery-Hunt **Rev:** Partial stamp design **Rev. Designer:** Sandford Fleming **Edge:** Plain

Date	Mintage				
2001	59,573	PF63	11.00	PF65	12.50

   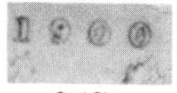

Round O's   Oval O's

KM# 2 5 CENTS

1.16 g., 0.925 Silver, 0.03 oz. ASW **Obv.** Head left **Rev:** Denomination and date within wreath, crown above **Obv. Legend:** VICTORIA DEI GRATIA REGINA. CANADA **Designer:** Leonard C. Wyon

Date	Mintage	VG8	F12	VF20	XF40	AU50	MS60	MS63
1858 Small date	1,500,000	19.00	30.00	45.00	80.00	150	250	550
1858 Large date over small date	Inc. above	150	225	350	550	1,000	1,500	3,500
1870	2,800,000	15.00	24.00	40.00	75.00	150	250	850
Note: Flat rim								
1870	Inc. above	15.00	24.00	40.00	75.00	150	250	600
Note: Wire rim								
1871	1,400,000	15.00	24.00	40.00	75.00	175	300	800
1872H	2,000,000	13.00	20.00	35.00	80.00	200	350	1,250
1874H Plain 4	800,000	22.00	45.00	90.00	150	300	450	1,000
1874H Crosslet 4	Inc. above	18.00	40.00	75.00	150	300	500	1,100
1875H Large date	1,000,000	300	500	800	1,400	3,000	5,000	15,000
1875H Small date	Inc. above	150	225	500	700	1,400	2,100	6,000
1880H	3,000,000	6.00	12.00	27.00	65.00	175	300	800
1881H	1,500,000	9.00	15.00	30.00	70.00	150	300	800
1882H	1,000,000	12.00	18.00	28.00	80.00	175	300	800
1883H	600,000	23.00	40.00	85.00	200	550	900	3,000
1884H	200,000	125	200	350	750	1,350	3,500	9,000
1885 Small 5	1,000,000	16.00	24.00	50.00	125	400	750	2,900
1885 Large 5	Inc. above	15.00	27.00	55.00	150	450	850	3,000
1885 Large 5 over small 5	Inc. above	65.00	125	200	500	1,650	4,000	—
1886 Small 6	1,700,000	9.00	15.00	30.00	60.00	225	400	1,300
1886 Large 6	Inc. above	11.00	18.00	40.00	70.00	225	425	1,500
1887	500,000	30.00	60.00	75.00	175	300	500	1,000
1888	1,000,000	6.00	9.00	18.00	50.00	100	175	450
1889	1,200,000	24.00	40.00	90.00	175	350	600	1,600
1890H	1,000,000	6.00	12.00	22.00	50.00	125	200	450
1891	1,800,000	6.00	9.00	15.00	30.00	90.00	150	400
1892	860,000	6.00	10.00	20.00	50.00	125	250	700
1893	1,700,000	6.00	9.00	14.00	30.00	100	175	500
1894	500,000	19.00	30.00	75.00	125	250	450	1,400
1896	1,500,000	6.00	9.00	14.00	35.00	100	175	450
1897	1,319,283	4.50	6.50	20.00	45.00	90.00	150	450
1898	580,717	12.00	20.00	40.00	90.00	200	350	950
1899	3,000,000	4.50	6.50	12.00	25.00	80.00	5.00	350
1900 Oval 0's	1,800,000	4.50	6.50	12.00	25.00	75.00	125	400

Date	Mintage	VG8	F12	VF20	XF40	AU50	MS60	MS63
1900 Round 0's	Inc. above	21.00	40.00	60.00	150	300	450	1,000
1901	2,000,000	6.00	8.00	16.00	35.00	80.00	175	500

KM# 9 5 CENTS
1.16 g., 0.925 Silver, 0.03 oz. ASW 15.5mm. **Obv. Designer:** G. W. DeSaulles **Rev. Designer:** Leonard C. Wyon

Date	Mintage	VG8	F12	VF20	XF40	AU50	MS60	MS63
1902	2,120,000	2.00	3.00	5.00	9.00	19.50	45.00	70.00
1902	2,200,000	2.00	4.00	7.00	14.00	27.00	45.00	80.00
Note: Large broad H								
1902	Inc. above	10.00	17.00	30.00	50.00	85.00	125	225
Note: Small narrow H								

KM# 13 5 CENTS
1.16 g., 0.925 Silver, 0.03 oz. ASW 15.5mm. **Obv.** King's bust right **Rev:** Denomination and date within wreath, crown at top

Date	Mintage	VG8	F12	VF20	XF40	AU50	MS60	MS63
1903	1,000,000	5.00	9.00	22.50	45.00	100	200	450
1903H	2,640,000	2.50	4.50	10.00	22.00	65.00	125	400
1904	2,400,000	3.00	5.00	9.00	30.00	90.00	225	650
1905	2,600,000	2.50	4.00	10.00	20.00	50.00	125	300
1906	3,100,000	2.50	3.00	7.00	17.00	45.00	125	250
1907	5,200,000	2.50	3.00	5.00	13.00	30.00	70.00	175
1908	1,220,524	7.00	13.00	30.00	50.00	85.00	125	225
1909 Round leaves	1,983,725	4.00	8.00	13.00	40.00	95.00	250	700
1909 Pointed leaves	Inc. above	16.00	24.00	55.00	125	250	700	1,700
1910 Pointed leaves	3,850,325	2.50	3.00	6.00	12.00	27.00	65.00	125
1910 Round leaves	Inc. above	18.00	24.00	45.00	125	225	550	1,700

KM# 16 5 CENTS
1.16 g., 0.925 Silver, 0.03 oz. ASW **Obv.** King's bust left **Obv. Designer:** E. B. MacKennal **Rev:** Denomination and date within wreath, crown above **Rev. Designer:** Leonard C. Wyon

Date	Mintage	VG8	F12	VF20	XF40	AU50	MS60	MS63
1911	3,692,350	2.50	4.00	7.00	12.00	40.00	80.00	125

KM# 22 5 CENTS
1.13 g., 0.925 Silver, 0.03 oz. ASW 15.5mm. **Obv.** King's bust left **Obv. Designer:** E. B. MacKennal **Rev:** Denomination and date within wreath, crown above **Rev. Designer:** Leonard C. Wyon

Date	Mintage	VG8	F12	VF20	XF40	AU50	MS60	MS63
1912	5,863,170	2.50	3.00	6.00	10.00	30.00	70.00	200
1913	5,488,048	2.50	3.00	5.00	8.00	18.00	35.00	70.00
1914	4,202,179	2.50	3.00	6.00	10.00	30.00	65.00	200
1915	1,172,258	14.00	20.00	35.00	65.00	175	350	800
1916	2,481,675	4.00	7.00	12.00	28.00	65.00	125	300
1917	5,521,373	2.25	3.00	4.00	9.00	22.00	40.00	100
1918	6,052,298	2.25	3.00	4.00	8.00	22.00	40.00	85.00
1919	7,835,400	2.25	3.00	4.00	8.00	18.00	35.00	80.00

KM# 22a 5 CENTS
1.17 g., 0.800 Silver, 0.03 oz. ASW 15.48mm. **Obv. Designer:** E. B. MacKennal **Rev. Designer:** Leonard C. Wyon

Date	Mintage	VG8	F12	VF20	XF40	AU50	MS60	MS63
1920	10,649,851	2.00	2.50	3.00	6.50	17.00	28.00	65.00
1921	2,582,495	4,500	6,000	7,000	9,000	12,500	16,000	28,000

Note: Approximately 460 known; balance remelted. Stack's A.G. Carter Jr. Sale (12-89) choice BU, finest known, realized $57,200

Far 6   Near 6

KM# 29 5 CENTS
4.60 g., Nickel, 21.2mm. **Obv.** King's bust left **Obv. Designer:** E. B. MacKennal **Rev:** Maple leaves divide denomination and date **Rev. Designer:** W. H. J. Blakemore

Date	Mintage	VG8	F12	VF20	XF40	AU50	MS60	MS63
1922	4,794,119	0.30	0.95	1.75	7.00	30.00	60.00	125
1923	2,502,279	0.40	1.25	5.50	16.00	60.00	150	350
1924	3,105,839	0.30	1.00	4.00	10.00	40.00	100	300
1925	201,921	70.00	90.00	150	300	700	1,600	5,000
1926 Near 6	938,162	3.00	7.00	16.00	75.00	225	450	1,600
1926 Far 6	Inc. above	150	175	300	600	1,100	2,000	6,000
1927	5,285,627	0.30	0.65	3.00	14.00	35.00	75.00	200
1928	4,577,712	0.30	0.65	3.00	14.00	35.00	65.00	125
1929	5,611,911	0.30	0.65	3.00	14.00	35.00	80.00	200
1930	3,704,673	0.30	1.25	3.00	15.00	45.00	100	250
1931	5,100,830	0.30	1.25	3.50	18.00	70.00	175	650
1932	3,198,566	0.30	1.00	3.50	16.00	50.00	150	500
1933	2,597,867	0.40	1.50	6.00	18.00	80.00	200	800
1934	3,827,304	0.30	1.00	3.00	16.00	50.00	150	500
1935	3,900,000	0.30	1.00	3.00	11.00	50.00	125	350
1936	4,400,450	0.30	0.65	1.75	9.00	30.00	60.00	150

KM# 33 5 CENTS
4.50 g., Nickel, 21.2mm. **Obv.** Head left **Obv. Designer:** T. H. Paget **Rev:** Beaver on rock divides denomination and date **Rev. Designer:** George E. Kruger-Gray

Date	Mintage	VG8	F12	VF20	XF40	AU50	MS60	MS63
1937 Dot	4,593,263	0.20	0.30	1.25	2.50	5.00	12.00	24.00
1938	3,898,974	0.30	0.90	2.00	7.00	40.00	80.00	175
1939	5,661,123	0.20	0.35	1.25	3.00	22.00	55.00	90.00
1940	13,920,197	0.20	0.30	0.75	2.25	9.00	20.00	55.00
1941	8,681,785	0.20	0.30	0.75	2.25	13.00	28.00	70.00
1942 Round	6,847,544	0.20	0.30	0.75	1.75	9.00	20.00	50.00

KM# 39 5 CENTS
Tombac, 21.2mm. **Obv.** Head left **Obv. Designer:** T. H. Paget **Rev:** Beaver on rock divides denomination and date **Rev. Designer:** George E. Kruger-Gray **Shape:** 12-sided

Date	Mintage	VG8	F12	VF20	XF40	AU50	MS60	MS63
1942	3,396,234	0.40	0.65	1.25	1.75	2.50	4.00	16.00

KM# 40 5 CENTS
Tombac, 21.2mm. **Subject:** Victory **Obv.** Head left **Obv. Designer:** T. H. Paget **Rev:** Torch on "V" divides date **Rev. Designer:** Thomas Shingles

Date	Mintage	VG8	F12	VF20	XF40	AU50	MS60	MS63
1943	24,760,256	0.20	0.30	0.40	0.80	1.75	3.50	12.00
1944	8,000	—	—	—	—	—	—	—
Note: 1 known								

5 CENTS

KM# 40a 5 CENTS
4.40 g., Chrome Plated Steel, 21.2mm. **Obv.** Head left **Rev:** Torch on "V" divides date

Date	Mintage	VG8	F12	VF20	XF40	AU50	MS60	MS63
1944	11,532,784	0.10	0.20	0.45	0.90	1.25	2.50	6.50
1945	18,893,216	0.10	0.20	0.40	0.80	1.25	2.50	6.50

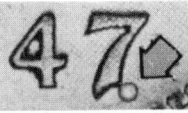

Maple leaf   Dot

KM# 39a 5 CENTS
4.50 g., Nickel, 21.2mm. **Obv.** Head left **Obv. Designer:** T. H. Paget **Rev:** Beaver on rock divides denomination and date **Rev. Designer:** George E. Kruger-Gray

Date	Mintage	VG8	F12	VF20	XF40	AU50	MS60	MS63
1946	6,952,684	0.10	0.25	0.50	2.00	8.00	16.00	40.00
1947	7,603,724	0.20	0.25	0.50	1.25	5.00	12.00	28.00
1947 Dot	Inc. above	18.00	22.00	35.00	75.00	125	200	400
1947 Maple leaf	9,595,124	0.20	0.25	0.45	1.25	5.00	12.00	25.00

KM# 42 5 CENTS
4.54 g., Nickel, 21.2mm. **Obv.** Head left, modified legend **Obv. Designer:** T. H. Paget **Rev:** Beaver on rock divides date and denomination **Rev. Designer:** George E. Kruger-Gray

Date	Mintage	VG8	F12	VF20	XF40	AU50	MS60	MS63
1948	1,810,789	0.40	0.50	1.00	3.00	10.50	20.00	40.00
1949	13,037,090	0.15	0.25	0.45	0.75	3.50	7.00	16.00
1950	11,970,521	0.15	0.25	0.45	0.75	3.50	7.00	16.00

KM# 42a 5 CENTS
Chromium and Nickel Plated Steel, 21.2mm. **Obv.** Head left **Obv. Designer:** T. H. Paget **Rev:** Beaver on rock divides date and denomination **Rev. Designer:** George E. Kruger-Gray

Date	Mintage	VG8	F12	VF20	XF40	AU50	MS60	MS63
1951	4,313,410	0.10	0.20	0.45	0.80	1.75	3.50	11.00
Note: Low relief; Second "A" in GRATIA points between denticles								
1951	Inc. above	550	750	1,200	1,800	2,400	3,500	
Note: High relief; Second "A" in GRATIA points to a denticle								
1952	10,891,148	0.10	0.20	0.45	0.80	1.75	3.50	8.00

KM# 48 5 CENTS
4.55 g., Nickel, 21.2mm. **Subject:** Nickel Bicentennial **Obv.** Head left **Obv. Designer:** T. H. Paget **Rev:** Buildings with center tower divide dates and denomination **Rev. Designer:** Stephen Trenka **Shape:** 12-sided

Date	Mintage	VG8	F12	VF20	XF40	AU50	MS60	MS63
1951	9,028,507	0.15	0.25	0.30	0.45	0.90	1.75	8.00

KM# 50 5 CENTS
Chromium and Nickel Plated Steel, 21.2mm. **Obv.** Laureate queen's bust, right **Obv. Designer:** Mary Gillick **Rev:** Beaver on rock divides date and denomination **Rev. Designer:** George E. Kruger-Gray **Shape:** 12-sided

Date	Mintage	VG8	F12	VF20	XF40	AU50	MS60	MS63
1953	16,635,552	—	0.20	0.40	0.90	1.75	3.00	7.00

5 CENTS

Date	Mintage	VG8	F12	VF20	XF40	AU50	MS60	MS63
Note: Without strap								
1953	Inc. above	175	250	350	550	900	1,600	3,500
Note: With strap, far leaf								
1953	Inc. above	300	450	700	900	1,100	1,300	3,500
Note: Without strap, near leaf								
1953	Inc. above	—	0.20	0.40	0.90	2.25	5.00	8.00
Note: With strap								
1954	6,998,662	—	0.25	0.50	1.00	2.50	6.00	12.00

KM# 50a 5 CENTS
4.59 g., Nickel, 21.2mm. **Obv.** Laureate queen's bust right **Obv. Designer:** Mary Gillick **Rev:** Beaver on rock divides date and denomination **Rev. Designer:** George E. Kruger-Gray

Date	Mintage	VG8	F12	VF20	XF40	AU50	MS60	MS63
1955	5,355,028	—	0.15	0.40	0.75	1.75	3.50	6.50
1956	9,399,854	—	0.15	0.30	0.45	1.25	2.50	5.00
1957	7,387,703	—	—	0.25	0.30	0.65	1.25	3.50
1958	7,607,521	—	—	0.25	0.30	0.65	1.25	3.50
1959	11,552,523	—	—	—	0.20	0.25	0.45	1.75
1960	37,157,433	—	—	—	0.20	0.25	0.45	1.75
1961	47,889,051	—	—	—	—	0.25	0.40	1.25
1962	46,307,305	—	—	—	—	0.20	0.40	1.25

KM# 57 5 CENTS
Nickel, 21.2mm. **Obv.** Laureate queen's bust right **Obv. Designer:** Mary Gillick **Rev:** Beaver on rock divides date and denomination **Rev. Designer:** George E. Kruger-Gray **Shape:** Round

Date	Mintage	VG8	F12	VF20	XF40	AU50	MS60	MS63
1963	43,970,320	—	—	—	—	0.15	0.30	0.80
1964	78,075,068	—	—	—	—	0.15	0.30	0.80
1964	—	18.00	20.00	21.00	24.00	30.00	40.00	125
Note: Extra water line								

KM# 60.1 5 CENTS
4.54 g., Nickel, 21.2mm. **Obv.** Queen's bust right **Obv. Designer:** Arnold Machin **Rev:** Beaver on rock divides date and denomination **Rev. Designer:** George E. Kruger-Gray

Date	Mintage	MS63
1965	84,876,018	0.80
1966	27,976,648	0.80
1968	101,930,379	0.80
1969	27,830,229	0.80
1970	5,726,010	1.75
1971	27,312,609	0.80
1972	62,417,387	0.80
1973	53,507,435	0.80
1974	94,704,645	0.80
1975	138,882,000	0.80
1976	55,140,213	0.80
1977	89,120,791	0.80
1978	137,079,273	0.80

KM# 66 5 CENTS
Nickel, 21.2mm. **Subject:** Confederation Centennial **Obv.** Queen's bust right **Obv. Designer:** Arnold Machin **Rev:** Snowshoe rabbit bounding left divides dates and denomination **Rev. Designer:** Alex Coville

Date	Mintage		
1867-1967	36,876,574	PF60 1.00	PF65 1.00

KM# 60.2 5 CENTS
Nickel, 21.2mm. **Obv.** Queen's bust right **Obv. Designer:** Arnold Machin **Rev:** Beaver on rock divides date and denomination **Rev. Designer:** George E. Kruger-Gray

Date	Mintage		MS63
1979	186,295,825		0.30
1980	134,878,000		0.30
1981	99,107,900		0.30
1981	199,000	PF60 1.50	PF65 1.50

KM# 60.2a 5 CENTS
4.60 g., Copper-Nickel, 21.2mm. **Obv.** Queen's bust right **Obv. Designer:** Arnold Machin **Rev:** Beaver on rock divides date and denomination **Rev. Designer:** George E. Kruger-Gray

Date	Mintage		MS63
1982	64,924,400		0.30
1982	180,908	PF60 1.50	PF65 1.50
1983	72,596,000		0.30

Date	Mintage					MS63
1983	168,000	PF60 1.50		PF65 1.50		
1984	84,088,000					0.30
1984	161,602	PF60 1.50		PF65 1.50		
1985	126,618,000					0.30
1985	157,037	PF60 1.50		PF65 1.50		
1986	156,104,000					0.30
1986	175,745	PF60 1.50		PF65 1.50		
1987	106,299,000					0.30
1987	179,004	PF60 1.50		PF65 1.50		
1988	75,025,000					0.30
1988	175,259	PF60 1.50		PF65 1.50		
1989	141,570,538					0.30
1989	170,928	PF60 1.50		PF65 1.50		

KM# 182 5 CENTS
4.60 g., Copper-Nickel, 19.55mm. **Obv.** Crowned head right **Obv. Designer:** Dora dePedery-Hunt **Rev:** Beaver on rock divides dates and denomination **Rev. Designer:** George E. Kruger-Gray **Edge:** Plain

Date	Mintage					MS63
1990	42,537,000					0.30
1990	140,649	PF63 2.00		PF65 2.50		
1991	10,931,000					0.55
1991	131,888	PF63 5.00		PF65 7.00		
1993	86,877,000					0.30
1993	143,065	PF63 2.00		PF65 2.50		
1994	99,352,000					0.30
1994	146,424	PF63 2.00		PF65 3.00		
1995	78,528,000					0.30
1995	—	PF63 2.00		PF65 2.50		
1996 Far 6	36,686,000					2.25
1996 Near 6	Inc. above					2.25
1996	—	PF63 5.00		PF65 6.00		
1997	27,354,000					0.30
1997	—	PF63 4.00		PF65 5.00		
1998	156,873,000					0.30
1998W	—					1.50
1998	—	PF63 4.00		PF65 5.00		
1999	124,861,000					0.30
1999W	—					—
1999	—	PF63 4.00		PF65 5.00		
2000	108,514,000					0.30
2000W	—					1.50
2000	—	PF63 4.00		PF65 5.00		
2001	30,035,000					12.50
2001P	—	PF63 8.00		PF65 10.00		
2003	—					0.30

KM# 205 5 CENTS
4.60 g., Copper-Nickel, 21.2mm. **Subject:** Confederation 125 **Obv.** Crowned head right **Obv. Designer:** Dora dePedery-Hunt **Rev:** Beaver on rock divides date and denomination **Rev. Designer:** George E. Kruger-Gray

Date	Mintage				MS63
1992	147,061	PF60 4.00		PF65 4.00	
1992	53,732,000				0.30

KM# 182a 5 CENTS
5.35 g., 0.925 Silver, 0.16 oz. ASW 21.2mm. **Obv.** Crowned head right **Obv. Designer:** Dora dePedery-Hunt **Rev:** Beaver on rock divides date and denomination **Rev. Designer:** George E. Kruger-Gray

Date	Mintage				
1996	—	PF63 7.00		PF65 8.00	
1997	—	PF63 7.00		PF65 8.00	
1998	—	PF63 7.00		PF65 8.00	
1998O	—	PF63 7.00		PF65 8.00	
1999	—	PF63 7.00		PF65 8.00	
2000	—	PF63 7.00		PF65 8.00	
2001	—	PF63 7.00		PF65 8.00	
2003	—	PF63 7.00		PF65 8.00	

KM# 182b 5 CENTS
3.90 g., Nickel Plated Steel, 21.2mm. **Obv.** Crowned head right **Obv. Designer:** Dora dePedery-Hunt **Rev:** Beaver on rock divides date and denomination **Rev. Designer:** George E. Kruger-Gray **Edge:** Plain

Date	Mintage	MS63
1999 P	Est. 20000	15.00
2000 P	Est. 2300000	3.50
2001 P	136,650,000	0.35
2003 P	32,986,921	0.35

KM# 310 5 CENTS
1.17 g., 0.925 Silver, 0.03 oz. ASW **Subject:** 90th Anniversary Royal Canadian Mint **Obv.** Crowned head right **Obv. Designer:** Dora dePedery-Hunt **Rev:** Denomination and date within wreath, crown above **Rev. Designer:** W. H. J. Blackmore

Date	Mintage		MS63
1908-1998	25,000		12.00
1908-1998	25,000	PF60 12.00	

KM# 400 5 CENTS
0.925 Silver, 21.2mm. **Subject:** First French-Canadian Regiment **Obv.** Crowned head right **Obv. Designer:** Dora dePedery-Hunt **Rev:** Regimental drums, sash and baton, denomination above, date at right **Rev. Designer:** R. C. M. Staff **Edge:** Plain

Date	Mintage	
2000	—	PF60 9.00

KM# 413 5 CENTS
5.35 g., 0.925 Silver, 0.16 oz. ASW 21.2mm. **Subject:**

5 CENTS

Royal Military College **Obv.** Crowned head right **Rev:** Marching cadets and arch **Rev. Designer:** Gerald T. Locklin **Edge:** Plain

Date	Mintage		
2001	—	PF63 7.00	PF65 8.00

KM# 446a 5 CENTS

5.35 g., 0.925 Silver, 0.16 oz. ASW 21.2mm. **Subject:** Elizabeth II Golden Jubilee **Obv.** Queen, Jubilee commemorative dates 1952-2002

Date	Mintage		
1952-2002	21,573	PF63 10.00	PF65 11.50

KM# 446 5 CENTS

3.95 g., Nickel Plated Steel, 21.2mm. **Subject:** Elizabeth II Golden Jubilee **Obv.** Crowned head right, Jubilee commemorative dates 1952-2002 **Obv. Designer:** Dora dePedery-Hunt **Rev. Designer:** George E. Kruger-Gray **Note:** Magnetic.

Date	Mintage		MS63
1952-2002P	135,960,000		0.45
1952-2002P	32,642	PF63 8.00	PF65 10.00

KM# 453 5 CENTS

5.35 g., 0.925 Silver, 0.16 oz. ASW 21.2mm. **Subject:** Vimy Ridge - WWI **Obv.** Crowned head right **Rev:** Vimy Ridge Memorial, allegorical figure and dates 1917-2002 **Rev. Designer:** S. A. Allward

Date	Mintage		
2002	—	PF63 10.00	PF65 11.50

KM# 491 5 CENTS

3.95 g., Nickel Plated Steel, 21.2mm. **Obv.** Bare head right **Obv. Designer:** Susanna Blunt **Rev:** Beaver divides date and denomination **Rev. Designer:** George E. Kruger-Gray **Note:** Magnetic.

Date	Mintage		MS63
2003P	61,392,180		0.45
2004P	132,097,000		0.45
2004P	—	PF63 1.50	PF65 2.50
2005P	89,664,000		0.45
2005P	—	PF63 1.50	PF65 2.50
2006P	139,308,000		0.50
2006P	—	PF63 1.50	PF65 2.50
2006(ml)	184,874,000		0.45
2006(ml)	—	PF63 1.50	PF65 2.50
2007(ml)	221,472,000		0.45
2007(ml)	—	PF63 1.50	PF65 2.50
2008(ml)	278,530,000		0.45
2008(ml)	—	PF63 1.50	PF65 2.50
2009(ml)	266,488,000		0.45
2009(ml)	—	PF63 1.50	PF65 2.50
2010(ml)	—		0.45
2010(ml)	—	PF63 1.50	PF65 2.50
2011(ml)	—		0.45
2011(ml)	—	PF63 1.50	PF65 2.50
2012(ml)	—		0.45
2012(ml)	—	PF63 1.50	PF65 2.50
2013(ml)	—		0.45
2013(ml)	—	PF63 1.50	PF65 2.50

KM# 469 5 CENTS

5.35 g., 0.925 Silver, 0.16 oz. ASW 21.2mm. **Subject:** 50th Anniversary of the Coronation of Elizabeth II **Obv.** Crowned head right, Jubilee commemorative dates 1953-2003 **Obv. Designer:** Mary Gillick

Date	Mintage		
1953-2003	21,573	PF63 10.00	PF65 11.50

KM# 491a 5 CENTS

5.35 g., 0.925 Silver, 0.16 oz. ASW 21.1mm. **Obv.** Crowned head right **Obv. Designer:** Susanna Blunt **Rev:** Beaver divides date and denomination **Edge:** Plain

Date	Mintage		
2004	—	PF63 5.00	PF65 6.50

KM# 506 5 CENTS

5.35 g., 0.925 Silver, 0.16 oz. ASW 21.3mm. **Obv.** Bare head right **Rev:** Victory " design of the KM-40 reverse **Edge:** Plain **Shape:** 12-sided

Date	Mintage		
1944-2004	20,019	PF63 13.00	PF65 15.00

KM# 627 5 CENTS

3.95 g., Nickel Plated Steel, 21.2mm. **Subject:** 60th Anniversary, Victory in Europe 1945-2005 **Obv.** Head right **Rev:** Large V **Edge:** Plain

Date	Mintage	MS63
2005P	59,269,192	4.50

KM# 758 5 CENTS

5.30 g., 0.925 Silver, 0.16 oz. ASW **Obv.** George VI head left **Rev:** Torch and large V

Date	Mintage		
2005	42,792	PF63 30.00	PF65 35.00

KM# 758a 5 CENTS

5.30 g., 0.925 Silver, 0.16 oz. ASW **Obv.** George VI head left **Rev:** Torch and large V **Note:** Bound into Annual Report.

Date	Mintage		
2005	6,065	PF63 35.00	PF65 40.00

KM# 491b 5 CENTS

4.60 g., Copper-Nickel, **Obv.** Bust right **Rev:** Beaver

Date	Mintage	MS63
2006	43,008,000	5.00

KM# 1024 5 CENTS

Nickel, 21.2mm. **Obv.** George V bust left **Rev:** Denomination and 1935-2010 anniversary dates, two maple leaves below

Date	Mintage		
1935-2010	—	PF63 12.00	PF65 15.00

KM# 1154 5 CENTS

1.56 g., 0.925 Silver, 0.05 oz. ASW 15.5mm. **Obv.** George V bust **Rev:** Value within wreath

Date	Mintage		
1911-2011	6,000	PF63 12.00	PF65 15.00

KM# 3   10 CENTS

2.32 g., 0.925 Silver, 0.07 oz. ASW 18.03mm. **Obv.** Head left **Rev:** Denomination and date within wreath, crown above **Obv. Legend:** VICTORIA DEI GRATIA REGINA. CANADA **Edge:** Reeded **Designer:** Leonard C. Wyon

Date	Mintage	VG8	F12	VF20	XF40	AU50	MS60	MS63
1858/5	Inc. below	900	1,400	2,100	4,000	8,000	12,000	—
1858	1,250,000	20.00	35.00	65.00	125	225	350	850
1870 Narrow 0	1,600,000	18.00	40.00	75.00	125	250	400	1,300
1870 Wide 0	Inc. above	35.00	65.00	125	225	400	600	2,100
1871	800,000	29.00	50.00	125	200	400	600	2,500
1871H	1,870,000	35.00	60.00	125	225	400	600	2,100
1872H	1,000,000	150	225	400	600	1,150	1,750	4,000
1874H	600,000	14.00	24.00	50.00	125	225	350	1,100
1875H	1,000,000	400	800	1,200	2,000	4,000	7,000	16,000
1880H	1,500,000	18.00	30.00	65.00	125	225	350	1,200
1881H	950,000	21.00	35.00	70.00	150	300	400	1,300
1882H	1,000,000	21.00	35.00	70.00	150	300	450	1,500
1883H	300,000	65.00	125	250	500	900	1,300	3,000
1884	150,000	300	500	950	1,700	3,500	6,000	20,000
1885	400,000	65.00	125	250	500	1,100	1,700	7,000
1886 Small 6	800,000	30.00	65.00	125	300	900	1,500	4,000
1886 Large 6	Inc. above	40.00	80.00	150	350	900	1,500	4,000
1887	350,000	65.00	125	225	450	1,050	1,700	4,000
1888	500,000	16.00	27.00	55.00	125	225	350	1,100
1889	600,000	750	1,200	2,000	4,000	8,500	13,000	35,000
1890H	450,000	21.00	45.00	90.00	200	350	500	1,100
1891 21 leaves	800,000	21.00	45.00	90.00	200	350	500	1,300
1891 22 leaves	Inc. above	21.00	45.00	90.00	200	350	500	1,200
1892/1	520,000	250	400	700	1,400	2,700	4,000	—
1892	Inc. above	20.00	35.00	75.00	150	300	450	1,200
1893 Flat-top 3	500,000	45.00	80.00	150	300	650	1,000	2,300
1893 Round-top 3	Inc. above	850	1,400	2,700	5,000	9,000	13,000	35,000
1894	500,000	45.00	80.00	150	250	450	750	1,800
1896	650,000	14.00	24.00	45.00	90.00	175	300	750
1898	720,000	14.00	24.00	45.00	90.00	175	300	750
1899 Small 9's	1,200,000	12.00	22.00	40.00	75.00	150	225	600
1899 Large 9's	Inc. above	24.00	45.00	85.00	150	300	500	1,200
1900	1,100,000	8.50	18.00	40.00	85.00	150	225	650
1901	1,200,000	13.00	24.00	50.00	100	150	250	850

KM# 10   10 CENTS

2.32 g., 0.925 Silver, 0.07 oz. ASW 18.03mm. **Obv.** Crowned bust right **Obv. Designer:** G. W. DeSaulles **Rev:** Denomination and date within wreath, crown above **Rev. Designer:** Leonard C. Wyon **Edge:** Reeded

Date	Mintage	VG8	F12	VF20	XF40	AU50	MS60	MS63
1902	720,000	9.00	18.00	35.00	100	200	450	1,200
1902H	1,100,000	4.00	9.00	20.00	45.00	90.00	150	350
1903	500,000	15.00	35.00	90.00	300	600	1,200	2,300
1903H	1,320,000	8.00	18.00	35.00	90.00	150	350	800
1904	1,000,000	12.00	27.50	50.00	150	225	400	1,000
1905	1,000,000	7.00	27.50	60.00	150	300	600	1,400
1906	1,700,000	7.00	13.00	35.00	80.00	150	350	900
1907	2,620,000	5.00	12.00	25.00	45.00	125	300	600
1908	776,666	9.00	27.50	60.00	150	200	300	600
1909	1,697,200	7.00	20.00	45.00	125	225	500	1,200
Note: Victorian leaves, similar to 1902-08 coins								
1909	Inc. above	11.00	30.00	60.00	150	350	750	1,800
Note: Broad leaves, similar to 1910-12 coins								
1910	4,468,331	4.00	9.00	20.00	40.00	80.00	150	400

KM# 17 10 CENTS

2.32 g., 0.925 Silver, 0.07 oz. ASW 23.5mm. **Obv.** Crowned bust left **Obv. Designer:** E. B. MacKennal **Rev:** Denomination and date within wreath, crown above **Rev. Designer:** Leonard C. Wyon **Edge:** Reeded

Date	Mintage	VG8	F12	VF20	XF40	AU50	MS60	MS63
1911	2,737,584	5.00	12.00	20.00	45.00	80.00	150	300

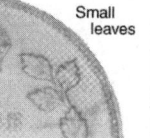

Small leaves

Large leaves

KM# 23 10 CENTS

2.32 g., 0.925 Silver, 0.07 oz. ASW 17.8mm. **Obv.** Crowned bust left **Obv. Designer:** E. B. MacKennal **Rev:** Denomination and date within wreath, crown above **Rev. Designer:** Leonard C. Wyon **Edge:** Reeded

Date	Mintage	VG8	F12	VF20	XF40	AU50	MS60	MS63
1912	3,235,557	2.50	5.00	11.00	35.00	90.00	250	650
1913	3,613,937	2.00	3.50	9.00	30.00	80.00	200	500
Note: Small leaves								
1913	Inc. above	125	225	450	1,350	3,000	8,500	27,500
Note: Large leaves								
1914	2,549,811	2.00	4.00	9.00	30.00	75.00	175	500
1915	688,057	7.00	16.00	40.00	125	225	500	950
1916	4,218,114	2.00	3.50	6.00	20.00	45.00	100	225
1917	5,011,988	2.00	3.50	4.00	12.00	40.00	75.00	125
1918	5,133,602	2.00	3.50	4.00	10.00	35.00	65.00	100
1919	7,877,722	2.00	3.50	4.00	10.00	35.00	65.00	100

KM# 23a 10 CENTS

2.33 g., 0.800 Silver, 0.06 oz. ASW 17.9mm. **Obv.** Crowned bust left **Obv. Designer:** E. B. MacKennal **Rev:** Denomination and date within wreath, crown above **Edge:** Reeded

Date	Mintage	VG8	F12	VF20	XF40	AU50	MS60	MS63
1920	6,305,345	2.00	2.75	3.50	12.00	40.00	75.00	125
1921	2,469,562	2.00	2.75	6.00	20.00	50.00	90.00	225
1928	2,458,602	2.00	2.75	4.00	12.00	40.00	80.00	150
1929	3,253,888	2.00	3.00	3.50	12.00	40.00	75.00	125
1930	1,831,043	2.00	3.50	4.50	14.00	45.00	80.00	175
1931	2,067,421	2.50	3.50	4.00	12.00	40.00	70.00	125
1932	1,154,317	2.00	3.00	9.00	23.00	60.00	125	250
1933	672,368	2.50	5.00	12.00	35.00	90.00	200	400
1934	409,067	4.00	7.00	22.00	60.00	150	350	650
1935	384,056	4.50	7.00	19.00	60.00	150	350	600
1936	2,460,871	2.00	2.50	3.00	9.00	30.00	60.00	100
1936 Specimen	—	—	—	—	—	—	—	150,000

Note: Dot on reverse. Specimen, 4 known; David Akers sale of John Jay Pittman collection, Part 1, 10-97, a gem specimen realized $120,000

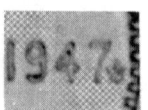

Maple leaf

KM# 34 10 CENTS

2.33 g., 0.800 Silver, 0.06 oz. ASW 18.03mm. **Obv.** Head left **Obv. Designer:** T. H. Paget **Rev:** Bluenose sailing left, date at right, denomination below **Rev. Designer:** Emanuel Hahn **Edge:** Reeded

Date	Mintage	VG8	F12	VF20	XF40	AU50	MS60	MS63
1937	2,500,095	BV	3.00	3.50	4.00	8.00	16.00	24.00
1938	4,197,323	BV	3.00	4.50	7.00	30.00	60.00	100

Date	Mintage	VG8	F12	VF20	XF40	AU50	MS60	MS63
1939	5,501,748	BV	3.00	3.50	6.00	22.00	50.00	90.00
1940	16,526,470	—	BV	3.00	4.00	9.00	20.00	40.00
1941	8,716,386	—	BV	3.00	7.00	22.00	50.00	100
1942	10,214,011	—	BV	3.00	5.00	18.00	40.00	60.00
1943	21,143,229	—	BV	3.00	4.00	9.00	20.00	35.00
1944	9,383,582	—	BV	3.00	5.00	12.00	28.00	45.00
1945	10,979,570	—	BV	3.00	4.00	9.00	20.00	35.00
1946	6,300,066	BV	3.00	4.00	5.00	15.00	30.00	45.00
1947	4,431,926	BV	2.00	3.00	7.00	18.00	40.00	60.00
1947	9,638,793	—	BV	3.00	4.00	7.00	15.00	20.00

Note: Maple leaf

KM# 43   10 CENTS
2.33 g., 0.800 Silver, 0.06 oz. ASW 18.03mm. **Obv.** Head left, modified legend **Obv. Designer:** T. H. Paget **Rev:** Bluenose sailing left, date at right, denomination below **Rev. Designer:** Emanuel Hahn

Date	Mintage	VG8	F12	VF20	XF40	AU50	MS60	MS63
1948	422,741	2.50	3.50	7.50	13.00	35.00	60.00	80.00
1949	11,336,172	—	BV	2.00	2.50	6.00	12.00	18.00
1950	17,823,075	—	BV	2.00	2.50	5.00	10.00	15.00
1951	15,079,265	—	—	BV	2.50	4.00	7.00	12.00
1951	—	—	6.00	8.00	12.00	18.00	40.00	65.00
Note: Doubled die								
1952	10,474,455	—	—	BV	2.50	4.00	6.00	10.00

KM# 51   10 CENTS
2.31 g., 0.800 Silver, 0.06 oz. ASW 18mm. **Obv.** Laureate bust right **Obv. Designer:** Mary Gllick **Rev:** Bluenose sailing left, date at right, denomination below **Rev. Designer:** Emanuel Hahn

Date	Mintage	VG8	F12	VF20	XF40	AU50	MS60	MS63
1953	Inc. above	—	BV	2.00	3.00	3.50	4.00	8.00
Note: With straps								
1953	17,706,395	—	—	BV	3.00	3.50	4.50	12.00
Note: Without straps								
1954	4,493,150	—	BV	2.00	3.00	7.00	12.00	20.00
1955	12,237,294	—	—	BV	2.00	3.00	4.50	8.00
1956	Inc. above	BV	3.50	4.00	7.00	9.50	15.00	24.00
Note: Dot below date								
1956	16,732,844	—	—	—	BV	2.00	3.00	6.00
1957	16,110,229	—	—	—	BV	2.25	3.50	4.00
1958	10,621,236	—	—	—	BV	2.25	3.50	4.00
1959	19,691,433	—	—	—	—	BV	3.00	4.00
1960	45,446,835	—	—	—	—	BV	3.00	4.00
1961	26,850,859	—	—	—	—	BV	3.00	4.00
1962	41,864,335	—	—	—	—	BV	2.00	2.50
1963	41,916,208	—	—	—	—	BV	2.00	2.50
1964	49,518,549	—	—	—	—	BV	2.00	2.50

KM# 61   10 CENTS
2.33 g., 0.800 Silver, 0.06 oz. ASW 18.03mm. **Obv.** Young bust right **Obv. Designer:** Arnold Machin **Rev:** Bluenose sailing left, date at right, denomination below

Date	Mintage	VG8	F12	VF20	XF40	AU50	MS60	MS63
1965	56,965,392	—	—	—	—	—	BV	2.50
1966	34,567,898	—	—	—	—	—	BV	2.50

KM# 67 10 CENTS

2.33 g., 0.800 Silver, 0.06 oz. ASW 18.03mm. **Subject:** Confederation Centennial **Obv.** Bust right **Rev:** Atlantic mackerel left, denomination above, dates below **Rev. Designer:** Alex Colville

Date	Mintage	VG8	F12	VF20	XF40	AU50	MS60	MS63
1867-1967	62,998,215	—	—	—	—	—	BV	2.50
1867-1967	— PF60 2.50							

KM# 67a 10 CENTS

2.33 g., 0.500 Silver, 0.04 oz. ASW 18.03mm. **Subject:** Confederation Centennial **Obv.** Young bust right **Rev:** Atlantic mackerel left, denomination above, dates below

Date	Mintage	VG8	F12	VF20	XF40	AU50	MS60	MS63
1867-1967	Inc. above	—	—	—	—	—	BV	2.00

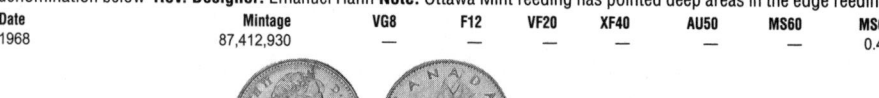

Ottawa

KM# 72 10 CENTS

2.33 g., 0.500 Silver, 0.04 oz. ASW 18.03mm. **Obv.** Bust right **Obv. Designer:** Arnold Machin **Rev:** Bluenose sailing left, date at right, denomination below **Rev. Designer:** Emanuel Hahn **Note:** Ottawa Mint reeding has pointed deep areas in the edge reeding.

Date	Mintage	VG8	F12	VF20	XF40	AU50	MS60	MS63
1968	70,460,000	—	—	—	—	—	BV	1.50

Ottawa

KM# 72a 10 CENTS

Nickel, 18.03mm. **Obv.** Young bust right **Obv. Designer:** Arnold Machin **Rev:** Bluenose sailing left, date at right, denomination below **Rev. Designer:** Emanuel Hahn **Note:** Ottawa Mint reeding has pointed deep areas in the edge reeding.

Date	Mintage	VG8	F12	VF20	XF40	AU50	MS60	MS63
1968	87,412,930	—	—	—	—	—	—	0.40

Philadelphia

KM# 73 10 CENTS

2.33 g., Nickel, 18.03mm. **Obv.** Young bust right **Obv. Designer:** Arnold Machin **Rev:** Bluenose sailing left, date at right, denomination below **Rev. Designer:** Emanuel Hahn **Note:** Philadelphia Mint reeding has flat deep areas in the edge reeding.

Date	Mintage	VG8	F12	VF20	XF40	AU50	MS60	MS63
1968	85,170,000	—	—	—	—	—	—	0.40
1969	—	—	10,000	12,000	16,000	20,000	25,000	—

Note: Large date, large ship, 10-20 known

KM# 77.1 10 CENTS

2.07 g., Nickel, 18.03mm. **Obv.** Young bust right **Obv. Designer:** Arnold Machin **Rev:** Redesigned smaller Bluenose sailing left, date at right, denomination below **Rev. Designer:** Emanuel Hahn **Edge:** Reeded

Date	Mintage	MS63
1969	55,833,929	0.50
1970	5,249,296	1.00
1971	41,016,968	0.50
1972	60,169,387	0.50
1973	167,715,435	0.50
1974	201,566,565	0.50
1975	207,680,000	0.50
1976	95,018,533	0.50
1977	128,452,206	0.50
1978	170,366,431	0.50

KM# 77.2 10 CENTS

2.07 g., Nickel, 18.03mm. **Obv.** Smaller young bust right **Obv. Designer:** Arnold Machin **Rev:** Redesigned smaller Bluenose sailing left, denomination below, date at right **Rev. Designer:** Emanuel Hahn **Edge:** Reeded

Date	Mintage		MS63
1979	237,321,321		0.35
1980	170,111,533		0.35
1981	123,912,900		0.35
1981	199,000	PF65 1.50	
1982	93,475,000		0.35
1982	180,908	PF65 1.50	
1983	111,065,000		0.35
1983	168,000	PF65 1.50	
1984	121,690,000		0.35
1984	161,602	PF65 1.50	

Date	Mintage		MS63
1985	143,025,000		0.35
1985	157,037	PF65 1.50	
1986	168,620,000		0.35
1986	175,745	PF65 1.50	
1987	147,309,000		0.35
1987	179,004	PF65 1.50	
1988	162,998,558		0.35
1988	175,259	PF65 1.50	
1989	199,104,414		0.35
1989	170,528	PF65 1.50	

KM# 183 10 CENTS
2.14 g., Nickel, 18.03mm. **Obv.** Crowned head right **Obv. Designer:** Dora dePedery-Hunt **Rev:** Bluenose sailing left, date at right, denomination below **Rev. Designer:** Emanuel Hahn **Edge:** Reeded

Date	Mintage		MS63
1990	65,023,000		0.35
1990	140,649	PF65 2.50	
1991	50,397,000		0.45
1991	131,888	PF65 4.00	
1993	135,569,000		0.35
1993	143,065	PF65 2.00	
1994	145,800,000		0.35
1994	146,424	PF65 2.50	
1995	123,875,000		0.35
1995	—	PF65 2.50	
1996	51,814,000		0.35
1996	—	PF65 2.50	
1997	43,126,000		0.35
1997	—	PF65 2.50	
1998	203,514,000		0.35
1998	—	PF65 2.50	
1998W	—		1.50
1999	258,462,000		0.35
1999	—	PF65 2.50	
2000	159,125,000		0.35
2000	—	PF65 2.50	
2000W	—		1.50

KM# 206 10 CENTS
Nickel, 18.03mm. **Subject:** Confederation 125 **Obv.** Crowned head right **Rev:** Bluenose sailing left, date at right, denomination below

Date	Mintage		MS63
1867-1992	174,476,000		0.35
1867-1992	147,061	PF60 3.00 PF65 3.00	

KM# 183a 10 CENTS
2.40 g., 0.925 Silver, 0.07 oz. ASW 18.03mm. **Obv.** Crowned head right **Rev:** Bluenose sailing left, date at right, denomination below

Date	Mintage		
1996	—	PF63 4.50	PF65 5.50
1997	—	PF63 4.50	PF65 5.50
1998	—	PF63 3.00	PF65 4.00
1998O	—	PF63 3.00	PF65 4.00
1999	—	PF63 4.00	PF65 5.00
2000	—	PF63 4.00	PF65 5.00
2001	—	PF63 4.00	PF65 5.00
2002	—	PF63 6.50	PF65 7.50
2003	—	PF63 6.50	PF65 7.50

KM# 299 10 CENTS
2.40 g., 0.925 Silver, 0.07 oz. ASW 18.03mm. **Subject:** John Cabot **Obv.** Crowned head right **Rev:** Ship with full sails divides dates, denomination below **Rev. Designer:** Donald H. Curley

Date	Mintage	
1997	—	PF60 17.50

KM# 311 10 CENTS
2.32 g., 0.925 Silver, 0.07 oz. ASW 18.03mm. **Subject:** 90th Anniversary Royal Canadian Mint **Obv.** Crowned head right **Rev:** Denomination and date within wreath, crown above

Date	Mintage	
1908-1998	—	PF60 10.00
Matte		
1908-1998	—	PF60 10.00

KM# 183b 10 CENTS
1.77 g., Nickel Plated Steel, 18.03mm. **Obv.** Crowned head right **Obv. Designer:** Dora dePedery-Hunt **Rev:** Bluenose sailing left, date at right, denomination below **Rev. Designer:** Emanuel Hahn **Edge:** Reeded

Date	Mintage	MS63
1999 P	Est. 20000	15.00
2000 P	Est. 200	1,000
2001 P	266,000,000	0.45
2003 P	162,398,000	0.20

KM# 409 10 CENTS
2.40 g., 0.925 Silver, 0.07 oz. ASW 18.03mm. **Subject:** First Canadian Credit Union **Obv.** Crowned head right **Rev:** Alphonse Desjardins' house (founder of the first credit union in Canada), dates at right, denomination below **Edge:** Reeded

Date	Mintage	
2000	—	PF60 8.00

KM# 412a 10 CENTS
2.40 g., 0.925 Silver, 0.07 oz. ASW 18mm. **Subject:** Year of the Volunteer **Obv.** Crowned head right **Rev:** Three portraits left above banner, radiant sun below **Edge:** Reeded

Date	Mintage		
2001P	40,634	PF63 8.00	PF65 9.00

10 CENTS

 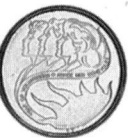

KM# 412 10 CENTS
1.77 g., Nickel Plated Steel, 18mm. **Subject:** Year of the
Volunteer **Obv.** Crowned head right **Rev:** Three portraits
left and radiant sun **Edge:** Reeded

Date	Mintage		MS63
2001P	224,714,000		4.50

KM# 447 10 CENTS
1.77 g., Nickel Plated Steel, 18mm. **Subject:** Elizabeth
II Golden Jubilee **Obv.** Crowned head right, Jubilee
commemorative dates 1952-2002

Date	Mintage		MS63
1952-2002P	252,563,000		1.00
1952-2002	32,642	PF63 1.50 PF65 2.50	

KM# 447a 10 CENTS
2.32 g., 0.925 Silver, 0.07 oz. ASW 18mm. **Subject:**
Elizabeth II Golden Jubilee **Obv.** Crowned head right,
Jubilee commemorative dates 1952-2002

Date	Mintage	
2002	21,537	PF63 11.00 PF65 12.50

KM# 470 10 CENTS
2.32 g., 0.925 Silver, 0.07 oz. ASW **Subject:** 50th
Anniversary of the Coronation of Elizabeth II **Obv.** Head
right **Rev:** Bluenose sailing left

Date	Mintage	
1953-2003	21,537	PF63 11.00 PF65 12.00

KM# 492 10 CENTS
1.77 g., Nickel Plated Steel, 18mm. **Obv.** Head right **Obv.**
Designer: Susanna Blunt **Rev:** Bluenose sailing left

Date	Mintage		MS63
2003P	—		1.25
2004P	211,924,000		0.60
2004P	—	PF63 1.50 PF65 2.50	
2005P	212,175,000		0.60
2005P	—	PF63 1.50 PF65 2.50	

Date	Mintage		MS63
2006P	312,122,000		0.60
2006P	—	PF63 1.50 PF65 2.50	
2007(ml) Straight 7	304,110,000		0.60
2007(ml) Curved 7	Inc. above		0.60
2007(ml)	—	PF63 1.50 PF65 2.50	
2008(ml)	467,495,000		0.60
2008(ml)	—	PF63 1.50 PF65 2.50	
2009(ml)	370,700,000		0.60
2009(ml)	—	PF63 1.50 PF65 2.50	
2010(ml)	—		0.60
2010(ml)	—	PF63 1.50 PF65 2.50	
2011(ml)	—		0.60
2011(ml)	—	PF63 1.50 PF65 2.50	
2012(ml)	—		0.60
2012(ml)	—	PF63 1.50 PF65 2.50	
2013(ml)	—		0.60
2013(ml)	—	PF63 1.50 PF65 2.50	

KM# 492a 10 CENTS
2.40 g., 0.925 Silver, 0.07 oz. ASW 18mm. **Obv.** Bare
head right **Obv. Designer:** Susanna Blunt **Rev:** Sailboat
Edge: Reeded

Date	Mintage	
2004	—	PF65 6.00

KM# 524 10 CENTS
2.40 g., 0.925 Silver, 0.07 oz. ASW 18mm. **Subject:** Golf,
Championship of Canada, Centennial. **Obv.** Head right

Date	Mintage	MS63
2004	39,486	12.50

KM# 1025 10 CENTS
Silver, 18.03mm. **Obv.** George V bust left **Rev:** Value
within wreath, dual dates below

Date	Mintage	
1935-2010	—	PF63 17.00 PF65 20.00

KM# 1155 10 CENTS
2.40 g., 0.925 Silver, 0.07 oz. ASW 18.03mm. **Obv.**
George V bust **Rev:** Value within wreath

Date	Mintage	
1911-2011	6,000	PF63 17.00 PF65 20.00

KM# 4 20 CENTS
4.65 g., 0.925 Silver, 0.14 oz. ASW **Obv.** Head left **Rev:** Denomination and date within wreath, crown above **Obv. Legend:**
VICTORIA DEI GRATIA REGINA. CANADA

Date	Mintage	VG8	F12	VF20	XF40	AU50	MS60	MS63
1858	750,000	60.00	100	125	225	500	900	2,500

KM# 5 25 CENTS

5.81 g., 0.925 Silver, 0.17 oz. ASW 23.88mm. **Obv.** Crowned head left **Obv. Designer:** Leonard C. Wyon **Rev:** Denomination and date within wreath, crown above **Obv. Legend:** VICTORIA DEI GRATIA REGINA / CANADA

Date	Mintage	VG8	F12	VF20	XF40	AU50	MS60	MS63
1870	900,000	22.00	45.00	85.00	200	450	750	2,000
1871	400,000	27.00	50.00	125	250	600	1,000	2,400
1871H	748,000	35.00	60.00	150	300	700	1,100	2,100
1872H	2,240,000	13.00	25.00	45.00	125	300	550	1,800
1872H	Inc. above	75.00	125	250	600	2,500	6,000	
Note: Inverted "A" for "V" in Victoria								
1874H	1,600,000	13.00	25.00	45.00	125	250	450	1,400
1875H	1,000,000	400	700	1,700	3,000	8,500	20,000	35,000
1880H Narrow 0	400,000	60.00	125	300	600	1,150	1,700	3,500
1880H Wide 0	Inc. above	150	350	600	1,400	2,900	4,500	8,000
1880H Narrow/ wide 0	Inc. above	100	225	400	950	1,850	2,800	—
1881H	820,000	30.00	55.00	125	300	750	1,300	4,000
1882H	600,000	30.00	65.00	125	300	750	1,200	3,000
1883H	960,000	20.00	40.00	85.00	200	400	600	1,700
1885	192,000	150	300	5,500	1,100	2,500	4,000	10,000
1886/3	540,000	90.00	200	400	750	1,550	2,400	4,500
1886	Inc. above	45.00	90.00	200	450	1,050	1,700	4,500
1887	100,000	150	300	550	1,200	3,000	7,500	12,500
1888	400,000	26.00	40.00	90.00	200	450	750	2,200
1889	66,324	175	350	650	1,400	2,900	4,500	13,000
1890H	200,000	30.00	60.00	150	300	650	1,000	2,300
1891	120,000	125	225	400	750	1,250	1,800	3,500
1892	510,000	20.00	40.00	85.00	200	450	750	2,300
1893	100,000	150	300	550	1,000	1,450	2,000	3,000
1894	220,000	30.00	65.00	150	300	550	850	2,000
1899	415,580	12.00	25.00	60.00	150	350	600	1,500
1900	1,320,000	11.00	20.00	50.00	125	300	550	1,200
1901	640,000	15.00	24.00	65.00	200	350	650	1,400

KM# 11 25 CENTS

5.81 g., 0.925 Silver, 0.17 oz. ASW 23.4mm. **Obv.** Crowned bust right **Obv. Designer:** G. W. DeSaulles **Rev:** Denomination and date within wreath, crown above

Date	Mintage	VG8	F12	VF20	XF40	AU50	MS60	MS63
1902	464,000	16.00	35.00	85.00	250	450	1,000	2,600
1902H	800,000	11.00	22.50	65.00	150	225	350	700
1903	846,150	20.00	40.00	100	300	600	1,100	2,600
1904	400,000	40.00	75.00	200	500	950	2,250	7,000
1905	800,000	20.00	45.00	150	400	800	2,000	6,000
1906 Large crown	1,237,843	14.00	30.00	75.00	250	450	800	2,400
1906 Small crown, Rare	Inc. above	3,500	5,500	12,000	19,000	24,000	30,000	40,000
1907	2,088,000	11.00	22.50	70.00	175	300	600	1,700
1908	495,016	27.50	50.00	100	250	400	550	1,000
1909	1,335,929	16.00	40.00	100	250	450	850	2,000

KM# 11a 25 CENTS

5.83 g., 0.925 Silver, 0.17 oz. ASW **Obv.** Crowned bust right **Rev:** Denomination and date within wreath, crown above

Date	Mintage	VG8	F12	VF20	XF40	AU50	MS60	MS63
1910	3,577,569	10.00	22.50	55.00	100	200	350	850

KM# 18 25 CENTS

5.83 g., 0.925 Silver, 0.17 oz. ASW **Obv.** Crowned bust left **Obv. Designer:** E. B. MacKennal **Rev:** Denomination and date within wreath, crown above **Obv. Legend:** GEORGIVS V REX ET IND IMP

Date	Mintage	VG8	F12	VF20	XF40	AU50	MS60	MS63
1911	1,721,341	12.00	20.00	55.00	125	175	350	650

KM# 24 25 CENTS

5.83 g., 0.925 Silver, 0.17 oz. ASW 23.5mm. **Obv.** Crowned bust left **Obv. Designer:** E. B. MacKennal **Rev:** Denomination and date within wreath, crown above **Obv. Legend:** GEORGIVS V DEI GRA REX ET IND IMP

Date	Mintage	VG8	F12	VF20	XF40	AU50	MS60	MS63
1912	2,544,199	9.00	15.00	30.00	70.00	200	400	1,500
1913	2,213,595	8.00	14.00	30.00	65.00	175	350	1,250
1914	1,215,397	9.00	17.00	40.00	80.00	250	650	2,100
1915	242,382	28.00	70.00	225	600	1,500	3,500	8,500
1916	1,462,566	7.50	12.00	25.00	50.00	100	250	800
1917	3,365,644	7.50	9.00	18.00	40.00	65.00	150	300
1918	4,175,649	5.00	9.00	14.00	35.00	55.00	125	225
1919	5,852,262	5.00	9.00	14.00	35.00	50.00	125	225

Dot below wreath

KM# 24a 25 CENTS

5.83 g., 0.800 Silver, 0.15 oz. ASW **Obv.** Crowned bust left **Obv. Designer:** E. B. MacKennal **Rev:** Denomination and date within wreath, crown below

Date	Mintage	VG8	F12	VF20	XF40	AU50	MS60	MS63
1920	1,975,278	5.00	9.00	18.00	40.00	90.00	200	550
1921	597,337	17.00	35.00	125	300	750	1,450	3,500
1927	468,096	40.00	70.00	125	300	650	1,000	2,100
1928	2,114,178	5.00	9.00	18.00	50.00	90.00	175	450
1929	2,690,562	5.00	9.00	18.00	45.00	90.00	150	400
1930	968,748	5.00	9.00	27.00	50.00	95.00	250	650
1931	537,815	5.00	10.00	30.00	65.00	100	300	650
1932	537,994	5.00	10.00	30.00	65.00	100	300	650
1933	421,282	5.00	10.00	35.00	85.00	125	250	450
1934	384,350	5.00	12.00	45.00	90.00	150	350	650
1935	537,772	5.00	10.00	35.00	65.00	125	200	400
1936	972,094	5.00	8.00	14.00	28.00	55.00	100	225
1936 Dot below wreath	153,322	40.00	95.00	225	450	750	1,050	2,400

Note: David Akers John Jay Pittman sale Part Three, 10-99, nearly Choice Unc. realized $6,900; considered a possible specimen example

Maple leaf after date

KM# 35 25 CENTS

5.83 g., 0.800 Silver, 0.15 oz. ASW 23.5mm. **Obv.** Head left **Obv. Designer:** T. H. Paget **Rev:** Caribou left, denomination above, date at right **Rev. Designer:** Emanuel Hahn

Date	Mintage	VG8	F12	VF20	XF40	AU50	MS60	MS63
1937	2,690,176	—	5.00	7.00	7.50	13.00	20.00	40.00
1938	3,149,245	—	5.00	8.00	15.00	35.00	80.00	150
1939	3,532,495	—	5.00	8.00	11.00	27.00	65.00	125
1940	9,583,650	—	—	4.00	5.00	10.00	20.00	40.00
1941	6,654,672	—	—	4.00	6.00	10.00	23.00	45.00
1942	6,935,871	—	—	4.00	6.00	10.00	24.00	45.00
1943	13,559,575	—	—	4.00	6.00	10.00	23.00	45.00
1944	7,216,237	—	4.00	5.00	6.00	15.00	30.00	65.00
1945	5,296,495	—	—	4.00	6.00	10.00	23.00	55.00
1946	2,210,810	—	4.00	6.00	12.00	30.00	55.00	100
1947	1,524,554	—	4.00	6.00	12.00	35.00	65.00	100
1947 Dot after 7	Inc. above	65.00	90.00	125	225	300	450	900
1947 Maple leaf after 7	4,393,938	—	—	4.00	6.00	11.00	20.00	30.00

KM# 44 25 CENTS
5.83 g., 0.800 Silver, 0.15 oz. ASW 23.5mm. **Obv.** Head left, modified legend **Obv. Designer:** T. H. Paget **Rev:** Caribou left, denomination above, date at right **Rev. Designer:** Emanuel Hahn

Date	Mintage	VG8	F12	VF20	XF40	AU50	MS60	MS63
1948	2,564,424	BV	4.00	6.00	12.00	30.00	70.00	125
1949	7,988,830	—	BV	4.00	8.00	10.50	15.00	30.00
1950	9,673,335	—	BV	4.00	8.00	10.00	12.00	23.00
1951	8,290,719	—	BV	4.00	7.00	9.00	11.00	18.00
1952	8,859,642	—	BV	4.00	7.00	8.50	10.00	17.00

KM# 52 25 CENTS
5.83 g., 0.800 Silver, 0.15 oz. ASW 23.8mm. **Obv.** Laureate bust right **Obv. Designer:** Mary Gillick **Rev:** Caribou left, denomination above, date at right **Rev. Designer:** Emanuel Hahn

Date	Mintage	VG8	F12	VF20	XF40	AU50	MS60	MS63
1953 Without strap	10,546,769	—	—	BV	4.00	6.00	8.00	15.00
1953 With strap	Inc. above	—	BV	4.00	6.00	8.50	11.00	27.50
1954	2,318,891	BV	4.00	5.00	11.00	18.00	30.00	60.00
1955	9,552,505	—	—	BV	6.00	7.50	9.00	17.00
1956	11,269,353	—	—	—	BV	5.50	8.00	12.00
1957	12,770,190	—	—	—	BV	5.50	8.00	10.00
1958	9,336,910	—	—	—	BV	5.50	8.00	10.00
1959	13,503,461	—	—	—	BV	BV	4.00	8.00
1960	22,835,327	—	—	—	BV	BV	4.00	8.00
1961	18,164,368	—	—	—	BV	BV	4.00	8.00
1962	29,559,266	—	—	—	BV	BV	4.00	8.00
1963	21,180,652	—	—	—	—	BV	BV	8.00
1964	36,479,343	—	—	—	—	BV	BV	8.00

KM# 62 25 CENTS
5.83 g., 0.800 Silver, 0.15 oz. ASW 23.8mm. **Obv.** Young bust right **Obv. Designer:** Arnold Machin **Rev:** Caribou left, denomination above, date at right **Rev. Designer:** Emanuel Hahn

Date	Mintage	VG8	F12	VF20	XF40	AU50	MS60	MS63
1965	44,708,869	—	—	—	—	BV	BV	8.00
1966	25,626,315	—	—	—	—	BV	BV	8.00

KM# 68   25 CENTS
5.83 g., 0.800 Silver, 0.15 oz. ASW 23.8mm. **Subject:** Confederation Centennial **Obv.** Young bust right **Rev:** Lynx striding left divides dates and denomination **Rev. Designer:** Alex Colville

Date	Mintage	VG8	F12	VF20	XF40	AU50	MS60	MS63
1867-1967	48,855,500	—	—	—	—	BV	BV	6.00

KM# 68a   25 CENTS
5.83 g., 0.500 Silver, 0.09 oz. ASW 23.8mm. **Subject:** Confederation Centennial **Obv.** Young bust right **Rev:** Lynx striding left divides dates and denomination

Date	Mintage	VG8	F12	VF20	XF40	AU50	MS60	MS63
1867-1967	Inc. above	—	—	—	—	BV	BV	4.50

KM# 62a   25 CENTS
5.83 g., 0.500 Silver, 0.09 oz. ASW 23.8mm. **Obv.** Young bust right **Obv. Designer:** Machin **Rev:** Caribou left, denomination above, date at right

Date	Mintage	MS63
1968	71,464,000	4.50

KM# 62b   25 CENTS
5.06 g., Nickel, 23.8mm. **Obv.** Young bust right **Obv. Designer:** Machin **Rev:** Caribou left, denomination above, date at right

Date	Mintage	MS63
1968	88,686,931	0.80
1969	133,037,929	0.80
1970	10,302,010	2.00
1971	48,170,428	0.80
1972	43,743,387	0.80
1974	192,360,598	0.80
1975	141,148,000	0.80
1976	86,898,261	0.80
1977	99,634,555	0.80
1978	176,475,408	0.80

KM# 81.1   25 CENTS
Nickel, 23.8mm.   **Subject:** Royal Candian Mounted Police Centennial **Obv.** Young bust right **Rev:** Mountie divides dates, denomination above **Rev. Designer:** Paul Cedarberg **Note:** 120 beads.

Date	Mintage	MS63
1873-1973	134,958,587	1.25

KM# 81.2   25 CENTS
Nickel, 23.8mm. **Subject:** RCMP Centennial **Obv.** Young bust right **Rev:** Mountie divides dates, denomination above **Note:** Large bust, 132 beads.

Date	Mintage	MS63
1873-1973	Inc. above	750

KM# 74   25 CENTS
5.07 g., Nickel, 23.88mm. **Obv.** Small young bust right **Obv. Designer:** Machin **Rev. Designer:** Emanuel Hahn

Date	Mintage		MS63
1979	131,042,905		0.75
1980	76,178,000		0.75
1981	131,580,272		0.75
1981	—	PF60 2.00	
1982	171,926,000		0.75
1982	180,908	PF60 2.00	
1983	13,162,000		1.50
1983	168,000	PF60 3.00	
1984	121,668,000		0.75
1984	161,602	PF60 2.00	
1985	158,734,000		0.75
1985	157,037	PF60 2.00	
1986	132,220,000		0.75
1986	175,745	PF60 2.00	
1987	53,408,000		1.25
1987	179,004	PF60 2.00	
1988	80,368,473		0.95
1988	175,259	PF60 2.00	
1989	119,796,307		0.75
1989	170,928	PF60 2.00	

KM# 184   25 CENTS
5.07 g., Nickel, 23.88mm. **Obv.** Crowned head right **Obv. Designer:** Dora dePedery-Hunt **Rev:** Caribou left, denomination above, date at right **Rev. Designer:** Emanuel Hahn

Date	Mintage			MS63
1990	31,258,000			0.90
1990	140,649	PF63 2.00	PF65 2.50	
1991	459,000			12.00
1991	131,888	PF63 17.00	PF65 20.00	

Date	Mintage			MS63
1993	73,758,000			0.70
1993	143,065	PF63 1.50	PF65 2.00	
1994	77,670,000			0.70
1994	146,424	PF63 2.00	PF65 3.00	
1995	89,210,000			0.70
1995	—	PF63 2.00	PF65 3.00	
1996	28,106,000			0.70
1996	—	PF63 5.00	PF65 6.00	
1997	—			0.70
1997	—	PF63 5.00	PF65 6.00	
1998W	—			5.00
1999	258,888,000			0.75
1999	—	PF63 5.00	PF65 6.00	
2000	434,087,000			0.75
2000	—	PF63 5.00	PF65 6.00	
2000W	—			5.00
2001	8,415,000			5.00
2001	—	PF63 6.50	PF65 7.50	

KM# 184a 25 CENTS
5.90 g., 0.925 Silver, 0.17 oz. ASW 23.88mm. **Obv.** Crowned head right **Rev:** Caribou left, denomination above, date at right

Date	Mintage		
1996	—	PF63 8.50	PF65 9.50
1997	—	PF63 8.50	PF65 9.50
1998	—	PF63 7.50	PF65 8.50
1998O	—	PF63 7.50	PF65 8.50
1999	—	PF63 7.50	PF65 8.50
2001	—	PF63 8.50	PF65 9.50
2003	—	PF63 8.50	PF65 9.50

KM# 184b 25 CENTS
4.40 g., Nickel Plated Steel, 23.88mm. **Obv.** Crowned head right **Rev:** Caribou left, denomination above, date at right

Date	Mintage		MS63
1999 P	Est. 20000		20.00
2000 P	—		5,500
Note: 3-5 known			
2001 P	55,773,000		0.95
2001 P	—	PF65 5.00	
2002 P	156,105,000		2.50
2002 P	—	PF65 5.00	
2003 P	87,647,000		2.50
2003 P	—	PF65 5.00	

KM# 207 25 CENTS
Nickel, 23.8mm. **Subject:** Confederation 125 **Obv.** Crowned head right **Obv. Designer:** Dora dePedery-Hunt **Rev:** Caribou left, denomination above, date at right **Rev. Designer:** Emanuel Hahn

Date	Mintage		MS63
1867-1992	147,061	PF65 20.00	
1867-1992	442,986		12.50

KM# 203 25 CENTS
5.00 g., Nickel, 23.9mm. **Subject:** New Brunswick **Obv.**

Crowned head right **Rev:** Covered bridge in Newton, denomination below **Series:** 125th Anniversary of Confederation **Rev. Designer:** Ronald Lambert

Date	Mintage	MS63
1992	12,174,000	0.70

KM# 203a 25 CENTS
5.83 g., 0.925 Silver, 0.17 oz. ASW 23.8mm. **Subject:** New Brunswick **Obv.** Crowned head right **Rev:** Covered bridge in Newton, denomination below **Series:** 125th Anniversary of Confederation

Date	Mintage	
1992	149,579	PF60 8.50

KM# 212 25 CENTS
Nickel, 23.8mm. **Subject:** Northwest Territories **Obv.** Crowned head right **Series:** 125th Anniversary of Confederation **Rev. Designer:** Beth McEachen

Date	Mintage	MS63
1992	12,582,000	0.70

KM# 212a 25 CENTS
5.83 g., 0.925 Silver, 0.17 oz. ASW 23.8mm. **Subject:** Northwest Territories **Obv.** Crowned head right **Series:** 125th Anniversary of Confederation

Date	Mintage	
1992	149,579	PF60 8.50

KM# 213 25 CENTS
Nickel, 23.8mm. **Subject:** Newfoundland **Rev:** Fisherman rowing a dory, denomination below **Series:** 125th Anniversary of Confederation **Rev. Designer:** Christopher Newhook

Date	Mintage	MS63
1992	11,405,000	0.70

KM# 213a 25 CENTS
5.83 g., 0.925 Silver, 0.17 oz. ASW 23.8mm. **Subject:** Newfoundland **Rev:** Fisherman rowing a dory, denomination below **Series:** 125th Anniversary of Confederation

Date	Mintage	
1992	149,579	PF60 8.50

KM# 214 25 CENTS
Nickel, 23.8mm. **Subject:** Manitoba **Obv.** Crowned head right **Series:** 125th Anniversary of Confederation **Rev. Designer:** Muriel Hope

Date	Mintage	MS63
1992	11,349,000	0.70

KM# 214a 25 CENTS
5.83 g., 0.925 Silver, 0.17 oz. ASW 23.8mm. **Subject:** Manitoba **Obv.** Crowned head right **Series:** 125th Anniversary of Confederation

Date	Mintage	
1992	149,579	PF60 8.50

KM# 220   25 CENTS
Nickel, 23.8mm. **Subject:** Yukon **Obv.** Crowned head right **Series:** 125th Anniversary of Confederation **Rev. Designer:** Libby Dulac

Date	Mintage	MS63
1992	10,388,000	0.70

KM# 220a   25 CENTS
5.83 g., 0.925 Silver, 0.17 oz. ASW 23.8mm. **Subject:** Yukon **Obv.** Crowned head right **Series:** 125th Anniversary of Confederation

Date	Mintage	
1992	149,579	PF60 8.50

KM# 221   25 CENTS
Nickel, 23.8mm. **Subject:** Alberta **Obv.** Crowned head right **Rev:** Rock formations in the badlands near Drumhelter, denomination below **Series:** 125th Anniversary of Confederation **Rev. Designer:** Mel Heath

Date	Mintage	MS63
1992	12,133,000	0.70

KM# 221a   25 CENTS
5.83 g., 0.925 Silver, 0.17 oz. ASW 23.8mm. **Subject:** Alberta **Obv.** Crowned head right **Rev:** Rock formations in the badlands near Drumhelter, denomination below **Series:** 125th Anniversary of Confederation **Rev. Designer:** Mel Heath

Date	Mintage	
1992	—	PF60 8.50

KM# 222   25 CENTS
Nickel, 23.8mm. **Subject:** Prince Edward Island **Obv.** Crowned head right **Series:** 125th Anniversary of Confederation **Rev. Designer:** Nigel Roe

Date	Mintage	MS63
1992	13,001,000	0.70

KM# 222a   25 CENTS
5.83 g., 0.925 Silver, 0.17 oz. ASW 23.8mm. **Subject:** Prince Edward Island **Obv.** Crowned head right **Series:** 125th Anniversary of Confederation **Rev. Designer:** Nigel Roe

Date	Mintage	
1992	149,579	PF60 8.50

KM# 223   25 CENTS
Nickel, 23.8mm. **Subject:** Ontario **Obv.** Crowned head right **Rev:** Jack pine, denomination below **Series:** 125th Anniversary of Confederation **Rev. Designer:** Greg Salmela

Date	Mintage	MS63
1992	14,263,000	0.70

KM# 223a   25 CENTS
5.83 g., 0.925 Silver, 0.17 oz. ASW 23.8mm. **Subject:** Ontario **Obv.** Crowned head right **Rev:** Jack pine, denomination below **Series:** 125th Anniversary of Confederation **Rev. Designer:** Greg Salmela

Date	Mintage	
1992	149,579	PF60 8.50

KM# 231   25 CENTS
5.03 g., Nickel, 23.8mm. **Subject:** Nova Scotia **Obv.** Crowned head right **Rev:** Lighthouse, denomination below **Series:** 125th Anniversary of Confederation **Rev. Designer:** Bruce Wood

Date	Mintage	MS63
1992	13,600,000	0.70

KM# 231a   25 CENTS
5.83 g., 0.925 Silver, 0.17 oz. ASW 23.8mm. **Subject:** Nova Scotia **Obv.** Crowned head right **Rev:** Lighthouse, denomination below **Series:** 125th Anniversary of Confederation **Rev. Designer:** Bruce Wood

Date	Mintage	
1992	149,579	PF60 8.50

KM# 232   25 CENTS
Nickel, 23.8mm. **Subject:** British Columbia **Obv.** Crowned head right, dates below **Rev:** Large rock, whales, denomination below **Series:** 125th Anniversary of Confederation **Rev. Designer:** Carla Herrera Egan

Date	Mintage	MS63
1992	14,001,000	0.70

KM# 232a   25 CENTS
5.83 g., 0.925 Silver, 0.17 oz. ASW 23.8mm. **Subject:** British Columbia **Obv.** Crowned head right, dates below **Rev:** Large rock, whales, denomination below **Series:** 125th Anniversary of Confederation **Rev. Designer:** Carla Herrera Egan

Date	Mintage	
1992	149,579	PF60 8.50

KM# 233 25 CENTS
Nickel, 23.8mm. **Subject:** Saskatchewan **Obv.** Crowned head right **Rev:** Buildings behind wall, grain stalks on right, denomination below **Series:** 125th Anniversary of Confederation **Rev. Designer:** Brian Cobb

Date	Mintage	MS63
1992	14,165,000	0.70

KM# 233a 25 CENTS
5.83 g., 0.925 Silver, 0.17 oz. ASW 23.8mm. **Subject:** Saskatchewan **Obv.** Crowned head right **Rev:** Buildings behind wall, grain stalks on right, denomination below **Series:** 125th Anniversary of Confederation **Rev. Designer:** Brian Cobb

Date	Mintage	
1992	149,579	**PF60** 8.50

KM# 234 25 CENTS
Nickel, 23.8mm. **Subject:** Quebec **Obv.** Crowned head right **Rev:** Boats on water, large rocks in background, denomination below **Series:** 125th Anniversary of Confederation **Rev. Designer:** Romualdas Bukauskas

Date	Mintage	MS63
1992	13,607,000	0.70

KM# 234a 25 CENTS
5.83 g., 0.925 Silver, 0.17 oz. ASW 23.8mm. **Subject:** Quebec **Obv.** Crowned head right **Rev:** Boats on water, large rocks in background, denomination below **Series:** 125th Anniversary of Confederation **Rev. Designer:** Romualdas Bukauskas

Date	Mintage	
1992	149,579	**PF60** 8.50

KM# 312 25 CENTS
0.925 Silver, 23.88mm. **Subject:** 90th Anniversary Royal Canadian Mint **Obv.** Crowned head right **Rev:** Denomination and date within wreath, crown above

Date	Mintage	
1998 Matte	—	**PF60** 15.00
1998	—	**PF60** 15.00

KM# 342 25 CENTS
5.07 g., Nickel, 23.8mm. **Subject:** January - A Country Unfolds **Obv.** Crowned head right **Rev:** Totem pole, portraits **Series:** Millennium **Rev. Designer:** P. Ka-Kin Poon

Date	Mintage	MS63
1999	12,181,200	0.65

KM# 342a 25 CENTS
5.83 g., 0.925 Silver, 0.17 oz. ASW 23.8mm. **Subject:** January **Obv.** Crowned head right **Rev:** Totem pole, portraits **Series:** Millennium **Rev. Designer:** P. Ka-kin Poon

Date	Mintage	
1999	113,645	**PF60** 9.50

KM# 343 25 CENTS
5.09 g., Nickel, 23.8mm. **Subject:** February - Etched in Stone **Obv.** Crowned head right **Rev:** Native petroglyphs **Series:** Millennium **Rev. Designer:** L. Springer

Date	Mintage	MS63
1999	14,469,250	0.65

KM# 343a 25 CENTS
5.83 g., 0.925 Silver, 0.17 oz. ASW 23.8mm. **Subject:** February **Obv.** Crowned head right **Rev:** Native petroglyphs **Series:** Millennium **Rev. Designer:** L. Springer

Date	Mintage	
1999	—	**PF60** 9.50

KM# 344 25 CENTS
5.07 g., Nickel, 23.8mm. **Subject:** March - The Log Drive **Obv.** Crowned head right **Rev:** Lumberjack **Series:** Millennium **Rev. Designer:** M. Lavoie

Date	Mintage	MS63
1999	15,033,500	0.65

KM# 344a 25 CENTS
5.83 g., 0.925 Silver, 0.17 oz. ASW 23.8mm. **Subject:** March **Obv.** Crowned head right **Rev:** Lumberjack **Series:** Millennium **Rev. Designer:** M. Lavoie

Date	Mintage	
1999	113,645	**PF60** 9.50

KM# 345   25 CENTS
5.07 g., Nickel, 23.8mm. **Subject:** April - Our Northern Heritage **Obv.** Crowned head right **Rev:** Owl, polar bear **Series:** Millennium **Rev. Designer:** Ken Ojnak Ashevac

Date	Mintage		MS63
1999	15,446,000		0.65

KM# 345a   25 CENTS
5.83 g., 0.925 Silver, 0.17 oz. ASW 23.8mm. **Subject:** April **Obv.** Crowned head right **Rev:** Owl, polar bear **Series:** Millennium **Rev. Designer:** Ken Ojnak Ashevac

Date	Mintage		
1999	113,645	**PF60**	9.50

KM# 346   25 CENTS
5.07 g., Nickel, 23.8mm. **Subject:** May - The Voyageures **Obv.** Crowned head right **Rev:** Voyageurs in canoe **Series:** Millennium **Rev. Designer:** S. Mineok

Date	Mintage		MS63
1999	15,566,100		0.65

KM# 346a   25 CENTS
5.83 g., 0.925 Silver, 0.17 oz. ASW 23.8mm. **Subject:** May **Obv.** Crowned head right **Rev:** Voyageurs in canoe **Series:** Millennium **Rev. Designer:** S. Mineok

Date	Mintage		
1999	113,645	**PF60**	9.50

KM# 347   25 CENTS
5.03 g., Nickel, 23.8mm. **Subject:** June - From Coast to Coast **Obv.** Crowned head right **Rev:** 19th-century locomotive **Series:** Millennium **Rev. Designer:** G. Ho **Edge:** Reeded

Date	Mintage		MS63
1999	20,432,750		0.65

KM# 347a   25 CENTS
5.83 g., 0.925 Silver, 0.17 oz. ASW 23.8mm. **Subject:** June **Obv.** Crowned head right **Rev:** 19th-century locomotive **Series:** Millennium **Rev. Designer:** G. Ho **Edge:** Reeded

Date	Mintage		
1999	113,645	**PF60**	9.50

KM# 348   25 CENTS
5.07 g., Nickel, 23.8mm. **Subject:** July - A Nation of People **Obv.** Crowned head right **Rev:** 6 stylized portraits **Series:** Millennium **Rev. Designer:** M. H. Sarkany

Date	Mintage		MS63
1999	17,321,000		0.65

KM# 348a   25 CENTS
5.83 g., 0.925 Silver, 0.17 oz. ASW 23.8mm. **Subject:** July **Obv.** Crowned head right **Rev:** 6 stylized portraits **Series:** Millennium **Rev. Designer:** M.H. Sarkany

Date	Mintage		
1999	113,645	**PF60**	9.50

KM# 349   25 CENTS
5.07 g., Nickel, 23.8mm. **Subject:** August - The Pioneer Spirit **Obv.** Crowned head right **Rev:** Hay harvesting **Series:** Millennium **Rev. Designer:** A. Botelho

Date	Mintage		MS63
1999	18,153,700		0.65

KM# 349a   25 CENTS
5.83 g., 0.925 Silver, 0.17 oz. ASW 23.8mm. **Subject:** August **Obv.** Crowned head right **Rev:** Hay harvesting **Series:** Millennium **Rev. Designer:** A. Botelho

Date	Mintage		
1999	113,645	**PF60**	9.50

KM# 350   25 CENTS
5.07 g., Nickel, 23.8mm. **Subject:** September - Canada Through a Child's Eye **Obv.** Crowned head right **Rev:** Childlike artwork **Series:** Millennium **Rev. Designer:** Claudia Bertrand

Date	Mintage		MS63
1999	31,539,350		0.65

KM# 350a   25 CENTS
5.83 g., 0.925 Silver, 0.17 oz. ASW 23.8mm. **Subject:** September **Obv.** Crowned head right **Rev:** Childlike artwork **Series:** Millennium **Rev. Designer:** Claudia Bertrand

Date	Mintage		
1999	113,645	**PF60**	9.50

KM# 351 25 CENTS
5.07 g., Nickel, 23.8mm. **Subject:** October - Tribute to the
First Nations **Obv.** Crowned head right **Rev:** Aboriginal
artwork **Series:** Millennium **Rev. Designer:** J. E. Read

Date	Mintage	MS63
1999	32,136,650	0.65

KM# 351a 25 CENTS
5.83 g., 0.925 Silver, 0.17 oz. ASW 23.8mm. **Subject:**
October **Obv.** Crowned head right **Rev:** Aboriginal artwork
Series: Millennium **Rev. Designer:** J.E. Read

Date	Mintage	
1999	113,645	PF60 9.50

KM# 352 25 CENTS
5.07 g., Nickel, 23.8mm. **Subject:** November - The
Airplane Opens the North **Obv.** Crowned head right **Rev:**
Bush plane with landing skis **Series:** Millennium **Rev.
Designer:** B. R. Brown

Date	Mintage	MS63
1999	27,162,800	0.65

KM# 352a 25 CENTS
5.83 g., 0.925 Silver, 0.17 oz. ASW 23.8mm. **Subject:**
November **Obv.** Crowned head right **Rev:** Bush plane
with landing skis **Series:** Millennium **Rev. Designer:** B.R.
Brown

Date	Mintage	
1999	113,645	PF60 9.50

KM# 353 25 CENTS
5.07 g., Nickel, 23.8mm. **Subject:** December - This is
Canada **Obv.** Crowned head right **Rev:** Eclectic geometric
design **Series:** Millennium **Rev. Designer:** J. L. P.
Provencher

Date	Mintage	MS63
1999	43,339,200	0.70

KM# 353a 25 CENTS
5.10 g., 0.925 Silver, 0.15 oz. ASW 23.8mm. **Subject:**
December **Obv.** Crowned head right **Rev:** Eclectic
geometric design **Series:** Millennium **Rev. Designer:**
J.L.P. Provencher

Date	Mintage	
1999	113,645	PF60 9.50

KM# 373 25 CENTS
Nickel, 23.8mm. **Subject:** Health **Obv.** Crowned head
right, denomination below **Rev:** Ribbon and caduceus,
date above **Rev. Designer:** Anny Wassef

Date	Mintage	MS63
2000	35,470,900	0.65

KM# 373a 25 CENTS
0.925 Silver, 23.8mm. **Subject:** Health **Obv.** Crowned
head right, denomination below **Rev:** Ribbon and
caduceus, date above **Rev. Designer:** Anny Wassef

Date	Mintage	
2000	—	PF60 9.50

KM# 374 25 CENTS
5.10 g., Nickel, 23.85mm. **Subject:** Freedom **Obv.**
Crowned head right, denomination below **Rev:** 2 children
on maple leaf and rising sun, date above **Rev. Designer:**
Kathy Vinish

Date	Mintage	MS63
2000	35,188,900	0.65

KM# 374a 25 CENTS
0.925 Silver, 23.8mm. **Subject:** Freedom **Obv.** Crowned
head right, denomination below **Rev:** 2 children on maple
leaf and rising sun, date above **Rev. Designer:** Kathy
Vinish

Date	Mintage	
2000	—	PF60 9.00

KM# 375 25 CENTS
Nickel, 23.8mm. **Subject:** Family **Obv.** Crowned head
right, denomination below **Rev:** Wreath of native carvings,
date above **Rev. Designer:** Wade Stephen Baker

Date	Mintage	MS63
2000	35,107,700	0.65

KM# 375a 25 CENTS
0.925 Silver, 23.8mm. **Subject:** Family **Obv.** Crowned
head right, denomination below **Rev:** Wreath of native
carvings, date above **Rev. Designer:** Wade Stephen Baker

Date	Mintage	
2000	—	PF60 9.50

KM# 376   25 CENTS
5.08 g., Nickel, 23.8mm. **Subject:** Community **Obv.**
Crowned head right, denomination below **Rev:** Map on
globe, symbols surround, date above **Rev. Designer:**
Michelle Thibodeau

Date	Mintage	MS63
2000	35,155,400	0.65

KM# 376a   25 CENTS
0.925 Silver, 23.8mm. **Subject:** Community **Obv.**
Crowned head right, denomination below **Rev:** Map on
globe, symbols surround, date above **Rev. Designer:**
Michelle Thibodeau

Date	Mintage	
2000	—	PF60 9.00

KM# 377   25 CENTS
Nickel, 23.8mm. **Subject:** Harmony **Obv.** Crowned **Rev:**
Maple leaf, date above **Rev. Designer:** Haver Demirer

Date	Mintage	MS63
2000	35,184,200	0.65

KM# 377a   25 CENTS
0.925 Silver, 23.8mm. **Subject:** Harmony **Obv.** Crowned
head right, denomination below **Rev:** Maple leaf **Rev.**
Designer: Haver Demirer

Date	Mintage	
2000	—	PF60 9.00

KM# 378   25 CENTS
Nickel, 23.8mm. **Subject:** Wisdom **Obv.** Crowned head
right, denomination below **Rev:** Man with young child,
date above **Rev. Designer:** Cezar Serbanescu

Date	Mintage	MS63
2000	35,123,950	0.65

KM# 378a   25 CENTS
0.925 Silver, 23.8mm. **Subject:** Wisdom **Obv.** Crowned
head right, denomination below **Rev:** Man with young
child **Rev. Designer:** Cezar Serbanescu

Date	Mintage	
2000	—	PF60 9.00

KM# 379   25 CENTS
Nickel, 23.8mm. **Subject:** Creativity **Obv.** Crowned head
right, denomination below **Rev:** Canoe full of children,
date above **Rev. Designer:** Kong Tat Hui

Date	Mintage	MS63
2000	35,316,770	0.65

KM# 379a   25 CENTS
0.925 Silver, 23.8mm. **Subject:** Creativity **Obv.** Crowned
head right, denomination below **Rev:** Canoe full of children
Rev. Designer: Kong Tat Hui

Date	Mintage	
2000	—	PF60 9.00

KM# 380   25 CENTS
Nickel, 23.8mm. **Subject:** Ingenuity **Obv.** Crowned head
right, denomination below **Rev:** Crescent-shaped city
views, date above **Rev. Designer:** John Jaciw

Date	Mintage	MS63
2000	36,078,360	0.65

KM# 380a   25 CENTS
0.925 Silver, 23.8mm. **Subject:** Ingenuity **Obv.** Crowned
head right, denomination below **Rev:** Crescent-shaped city
views **Rev. Designer:** John Jaciw

Date	Mintage	
2000	—	PF60 9.00

KM# 381   25 CENTS
Nickel, 23.8mm. **Subject:** Achievement **Obv.** Crowned
head right, denomination below **Rev:** Rocket above jagged
design, date above **Rev. Designer:** Daryl Dorosz

Date	Mintage	MS63
2000	35,312,750	0.65

KM# 381a   25 CENTS
0.925 Silver, 23.8mm. **Subject:** Achievement **Obv.**
Crowned head right, denomination below **Rev:** Rocket
above jagged design **Rev. Designer:** Daryl Dorosz

Date	Mintage	
2000	—	PF60 9.00

KM# 382   25 CENTS
Nickel, 23.8mm. **Subject:** Natural legacy **Obv.** Crowned
head right, denomination below **Rev:** Environmental
elements, date above **Rev. Designer:** Randy Trantau

Date	Mintage	MS63
2000	36,236,900	0.65

KM# 382a 25 CENTS
0.925 Silver, 23.8mm. **Subject:** Natural legacy **Obv.** Crowned head right, denomination below **Rev:** Environmental elements **Rev. Designer:** Randy Trantau

Date	Mintage	
2000	—	PF60 9.00

KM# 383 25 CENTS
Nickel, 23.8mm. **Subject:** Celebration **Obv.** Crowned head right, denomination below **Rev:** Fireworks, children behind flag, date above **Rev. Designer:** Laura Paxton

Date	Mintage	MS63
2000	35,144,100	0.65

KM# 383a 25 CENTS
0.925 Silver, 23.8mm. **Subject:** Celebration **Obv.** Crowned head right, denomination below **Rev:** Fireworks, children behind flag **Rev. Designer:** Laura Paxton

Date	Mintage	
2000	—	PF60 9.00

KM# 384.1 25 CENTS
Nickel, 23.8mm. **Subject:** Pride **Obv.** Crowned head right, denomination below **Rev:** Large ribbon 2 in red with 3 small red maple leaves on large maple leaf, date above **Rev. Designer:** Donald F. Warkentin **Edge:** Reeded **Note:** Colorized version.

Date	Mintage	MS63
2000	49,399	6.50

KM# 384.2 25 CENTS
Nickel, 23.8mm. **Subject:** Pride **Obv.** Crowned head right, denomination below **Rev:** Large ribbon 2 with three small maple leaves on large maple leaf, date above **Rev. Designer:** Donald F. Warkentin

Date	Mintage	MS63
2000	50,666,800	0.65

KM# 384.2a 25 CENTS
0.925 Silver, 23.8mm. **Subject:** Pride **Obv.** Crowned head right, denomination below **Rev:** Ribbon 2 with 3 small maple leaves on large maple leaf **Rev. Designer:** Donald F. Warkentin

Date	Mintage	
2000	—	PF60 9.00

KM# 419 25 CENTS
4.40 g., Nickel Plated Steel, 23.9mm. **Subject:** Canada Day **Obv.** Crowned head right **Rev:** Maple leaf at center, children holding hands below **Rev. Designer:** Silke Ware **Edge:** Reeded

Date	Mintage	MS63
2001	96,352	7.00

KM# 448 25 CENTS
4.40 g., Nickel Plated Steel, 23.9mm. **Subject:** Elizabeth II Golden Jubilee **Obv.** Crowned head right **Rev:** Caribou left

Date	Mintage	MS63		
1952-2002P	152,485,000	2.00		
1952-2002P	32,642	PF63 5.00	PF65 6.00	

KM# 448a 25 CENTS
5.90 g., 0.925 Silver, 0.17 oz. ASW 23.9mm. **Subject:** Elizabeth II Golden Jubilee **Obv.** Crowned head right, Jubilee commemorative dates 1952-2002

Date	Mintage		
1952-2002	100,000	PF63 11.00	PF65 12.50

KM# 451 25 CENTS
4.40 g., Nickel Plated Steel, 23.9mm. **Rev:** Small human figures supporting large maple leaf

Date	Mintage	MS63
2002P	30,627,000	5.00

KM# 451a 25 CENTS
4.40 g., Nickel Plated Steel, 23.9mm. **Subject:** Canada Day **Obv.** Crowned head right **Rev:** Human figures supporting large red maple leaf **Edge:** Reeded

Date	Mintage	MS63
2002P	49,901	6.00

KM# 471 25 CENTS
5.90 g., 0.925 Silver, 0.17 oz. ASW 23.9mm. **Subject:** 50th Anniversary of the Coronation of Elizabeth II **Obv.** 1953 Effigy of the Queen, Coronation Jubilee dates 1953-2003 **Obv. Designer:** Mary Gillick

Date	Mintage		
1953-2003	21,537	PF63 11.00	PF65 12.50

KM# 474 25 CENTS
4.40 g., 0.925 Silver, 0.13 oz. ASW 23.9mm. **Subject:** Canada Day **Obv.** Queen's head right **Rev:** Polar bear and red colored maple leaves

Date	Mintage		
2003	63,511	PF63 11.00	PF65 12.00

KM# 493   25 CENTS
4.40 g., Nickel Plated Steel, 23.9mm.   **Obv.** Bare head
right   **Obv. Designer:** Susanna Blunt **Rev:** Caribou left,
denomination above, date at right

Date	Mintage			MS63
2003P	66,861,633			2.00
2003P W	—			—
2004P	177,466,000			2.50
2004P	—	PF63 4.00	PF65 5.00	
2005P	206,346,000			2.50
2005P	—	PF63 4.00	PF65 5.00	
2006P	423,189,000			2.50
2006P	—	PF63 4.00	PF65 5.00	
2006(ml)	—			2.50
2007(ml)	386,763,000			2.50
2007(ml)	—	PF63 4.00	PF65 5.00	
2008(ml)	387,222,000			2.50
2008(ml)	—	PF63 4.00	PF65 5.00	
2009(ml)	266,766,000			2.50
2009(ml)	—	PF63 4.00	PF65 5.00	
2010(ml)	—			2.50
2010(ml)	—	PF63 4.00	PF65 5.00	
2011(ml)	—			2.50
2011(ml)	—	PF63 4.00	PF65 5.00	
2012(ml)	—			2.50
2012(ml)	—	PF63 4.00	PF65 5.00	
2013(ml)	—			2.50
2013(ml)	—	PF63 4.00	PF65 5.00	

KM# 493a   25 CENTS
5.90 g., 0.925 Silver, 0.17 oz. ASW 23.9mm. **Obv.** Bare
head right   **Obv. Designer:** Suanne Blunt **Rev:** Caribou
Edge: Reeded

Date	Mintage		
2004	—	PF63 5.00	PF65 6.50

KM# 510   25 CENTS
4.40 g., Nickel Plated Steel, 23.9mm.   **Obv.** Bare head
right **Rev:** Red poppy in center of maple leaf **Edge:** Reeded

Date	Mintage	MS63
2004	28,500,000	5.00

KM# 510a   25 CENTS
5.90 g., 0.925 Silver, 0.17 oz. ASW 23.9mm. **Obv.** Bare
head right **Rev:** Poppy at center of maple leaf, selectively
gold plated **Edge:** Reeded **Note:** Housed in Annual Report.

Date	Mintage		
2004	12,677	PF63 18.00	PF65 20.00

KM# 525   25 CENTS
4.40 g., Nickel Plated Steel, 23.9mm.   **Obv.** Bare head
right **Rev:** Maple leaf, colorized

Date	Mintage	MS63
2004	16,028	8.00

KM# 628   25 CENTS
4.40 g., Nickel Plated Steel, 23.9mm.   **Subject:** First
Settlement, Ile Ste Croix 1604-2004 **Obv.** Bare head right
Rev: Sailing ship Bonne-Renommee

Date	Mintage	MS63
2004P	15,400,000	5.00

KM# 698   25 CENTS
4.40 g., Nickel Plated Steel, 23.88mm.   **Rev:** Santa,
colorized

Date	Mintage	MS63
2004	62,777	5.00

KM# 699   25 CENTS
4.40 g., Nickel Plated Steel, 23.9mm.   **Rev:** Moose head,
humorous **Series:** Canada Day

Date	Mintage	MS63
2004	44,752	5.00

KM# 529   25 CENTS
4.40 g., Nickel Plated Steel, 23.9mm.   **Subject:** WWII, 60th
Anniversary **Obv.** Head right **Rev:** Three soldiers and flag

Date	Mintage	MS63
1945-2005	3,500	20.00

KM# 530   25 CENTS
4.40 g., Nickel Plated Steel, 23.9mm.   **Subject:** Alberta
Obv. Head right **Rev:** Oil rig and sunset

Date	Mintage	MS63
2005P	20,640,000	7.00

KM# 531 25 CENTS
4.40 g., Nickel Plated Steel, 23.9mm. **Subject:** Canada Day **Obv.** Head right **Rev:** Beaver, colorized

Date	Mintage	MS63
2005P	58,370	8.50

KM# 532 25 CENTS
4.40 g., Nickel Plated Steel, 23.9mm. **Subject:** Saskatchewan **Obv.** Head right **Rev:** Bird on fencepost

Date	Mintage	MS63
2005P	19,290,000	7.00

KM# 533 25 CENTS
4.40 g., Nickel Plated Steel, 23.9mm. **Obv.** Head right **Rev:** Stuffed bear in Christmas stocking, colorized

Date	Mintage	MS63
2005P	72,831	10.00

KM# 535 25 CENTS
4.40 g., Nickel Plated Steel, 23.9mm. **Subject:** Year of the Veteran **Obv.** Head right **Rev:** Conjoined busts of young and veteran left **Edge:** Reeded

Date	Mintage	MS63
2005P	29,390,000	7.00

KM# 576 25 CENTS
4.40 g., Nickel Plated Steel, 23.9mm. **Subject:** Quebec Winter Carnival **Obv.** Head right **Rev:** Snowman, colorized

Date	Mintage	MS63
2006	8,200	10.00

KM# 534 25 CENTS
4.40 g., Nickel Plated Steel, 23.9mm. **Subject:** Toronto Maple Leafs **Obv.** Head right **Rev:** Colorized team logo

Date	Mintage	MS63
2006P	11,765	12.50

KM# 575 25 CENTS
4.40 g., Nickel Plated Steel, 23.9mm. **Subject:** Montreal Canadiens **Obv.** Head right **Rev:** Colorized logo

Date	Mintage	MS63
2006P	11,765	12.50

KM# 629 25 CENTS
4.40 g., Nickel Plated Steel, 23.9mm. **Obv.** Head right **Rev:** Medal of Bravery (maple leaf within wreath) **Edge:** Reeded

Date	Mintage	MS63
2006(ml)	20,045,111	2.50

KM# 632 25 CENTS
12.61 g., Nickel Plated Steel, 35mm. **Subject:** Queen Elizabeth II 80th Birthday **Rev:** Crown, colorized

Date	Mintage	MS63
1926-2006 Specimen	24,977	25.00

KM# 633 25 CENTS
4.43 g., Nickel Plated Steel, 23.9mm. **Subject:** Canada Day **Obv.** Crowned head right **Rev:** Boy marching with flag, colorized

Date	Mintage	MS63
2006P	30,328	6.00

KM# 634 25 CENTS
4.43 g., Nickel Plated Steel, 23.88mm. **Subject:** Breast Cancer **Rev:** Four ribbons, all colorized **Note:** Sold housed in a bookmark.

Date	Mintage	MS63
2006P	40,911	10.00

KM# 637 25 CENTS
4.43 g., Nickel Plated Steel, 23.88mm. **Subject:** Wedding **Rev:** Colorized bouquet of flowers

Date	Mintage	MS63
2006(ml)	10,318	5.00

KM# 642 25 CENTS
4.43 g., Nickel Plated Steel, 23.88mm. **Subject:** Ottawa Senators **Obv.** Head right **Rev:** Logo

Date	Mintage	MS63
2006P	11,765	12.50

KM# 644 25 CENTS
4.43 g., Nickel Plated Steel, 23.88mm. **Subject:** Calgary Flames **Obv.** Head right **Rev:** Logo

Date	Mintage	MS63
2006(ml)	1,082	12.50

KM# 645 25 CENTS
4.43 g., Nickel Plated Steel, 23.88mm. **Subject:** Edmonton Oilers **Obv.** Head right **Rev:** Logo

Date	Mintage	MS63
2006(ml)	2,214	12.50

25 CENTS

KM# 647 25 CENTS
4.43 g., Nickel Plated Steel, **Subject:** Santa and Rudolph
Rev: Colorized Santa in sled lead by Rudolph

Date	Mintage	MS63
2006P	99,258	5.00

KM# 638 25 CENTS
4.43 g., Nickel Plated Steel, 23.88mm. **Subject:** Birthday
Rev: Colorized balloons

Date	Mintage	MS63
2007(ml)	24,531	5.00

KM# 639 25 CENTS
4.43 g., Nickel Plated Steel, 23.88mm. **Subject:** Baby
birth **Rev:** Colorized baby rattle **Edge:** Reeded

Date	Mintage	MS63
2007(ml)	30,090	5.00

KM# 640 25 CENTS
4.43 g., Nickel Plated Steel, 23.88mm. **Subject:** Oh
Canada **Obv.** Head right **Rev:** Maple leaf, colorized

Date	Mintage	MS63
2006 (2007)(ml)	23,582	8.50

KM# 641 25 CENTS
4.43 g., Nickel Plated Steel, 23.88mm. **Subject:**
Congratulations **Obv.** Head right **Rev:** Fireworks, colorized

Date	Mintage	MS63
2006 (2007)(ml)	9,671	8.00

KM# 643 25 CENTS
4.43 g., Nickel Plated Steel, 23.88mm. **Subject:** Vancouver
Canucks **Obv.** Head right **Rev:** Logo

Date	Mintage	MS63
2007(ml)	1,526	12.50

KM# 682 25 CENTS
4.43 g., Nickel Plated Steel, **Subject:** Curling **Obv.** Head
right

Date	Mintage	MS63
2007	22,400,000	7.50
2008 Mule	—	—

KM# 683 25 CENTS
4.43 g., Nickel Plated Steel, **Subject:** Ice Hockey **Obv.**
Head right

Date	Mintage	MS63
2007	22,400,000	7.50
2008 Mule	—	—

KM# 684 25 CENTS
4.43 g., Nickel Plated Steel, 23.8mm. **Subject:** Paralympic
Winter Games **Obv.** Head right **Rev:** Wheelchair curling

Date	Mintage	MS63
2007	22,400,000	7.50
2008 Mule	—	—

KM# 685 25 CENTS
4.43 g., Nickel Plated Steel, **Subject:** Biathlon **Obv.** Head
right

Date	Mintage	MS63
2007	22,400,000	7.50
2008 Mule	—	—

KM# 686 25 CENTS
4.43 g., Nickel Plated Steel, 23.8mm. **Subject:** Alpine
Skiing **Obv.** Head right

Date	Mintage	MS63
2007	22,400,000	7.50
2008 Mule	—	—

KM# 701 25 CENTS
4.43 g., Nickel Plated Steel, 23.88mm. **Subject:** Birthday
Rev: Party hat, multicolor

Date	Mintage	MS63
2007	11,376	8.00

KM# 702 25 CENTS
4.43 g., Nickel Plated Steel, 23.88mm. **Subject:** Congratulations **Rev:** Trophy, multicolor

Date	Mintage	MS63
2007	—	8.00

KM# 703 25 CENTS
4.43 g., Nickel Plated Steel, 23.88mm. **Subject:** Wedding **Rev:** Cake, multicolor

Date	Mintage	MS63
2007	—	8.00

KM# 704 25 CENTS
4.43 g., Nickel Plated Steel, 23.88mm. **Subject:** Canada Day **Rev:** Mountie, colorized

Date	Mintage	MS63
2007(ml)	27,743	8.00

KM# 705 25 CENTS
4.43 g., Nickel Plated Steel, 23.88mm. **Subject:** Christmas **Rev:** Multicolor tree

Date	Mintage	MS63
2007	66,267	8.00

KM# 706 25 CENTS
12.61 g., Nickel Plated Steel, 35.0mm. **Subject:** Red-breasted Nuthatch **Obv.** Head right **Obv. Designer:** Susanna Blunt **Rev:** Nuthatch perched on pine branch multicolor **Obv. Legend:** ELIZABETH II - D • G • REGINA **Rev. Designer:** Arnold Nogy **Rev. Legend:** CANADA **Edge:** Plain

Date	Mintage	MS63
2007(ml) Specimen	11,909	295

KM# 707 25 CENTS
12.61 g., Nickel Plated Steel, 35mm. **Obv.** Elizabeth II **Rev:** Multicolor ruby-throated hummingbird and flower **Edge:** Plain

Date	Mintage	MS63
2007 Specimen	17,174	135

KM# 708 25 CENTS
12.61 g., Nickel Plated Steel, 35mm. **Subject:** Queen's 60th Wedding Anniversary **Rev:** Royal carriage in color

Date	Mintage	MS63
1947-2007 Specimen	15,235	25.00

KM# 713 25 CENTS
4.40 g., Nickel Plated Steel, **Rev:** Toronto Maple Leaf logo, colorized

Date	Mintage	MS63
2007(ml)	5,365	5.00

KM# 714 25 CENTS
4.40 g., Nickel Plated Steel, **Rev:** Ottawa Senators logo, colorized

Date	Mintage	MS63
2007(ml)	2,474	5.00

KM# 723 25 CENTS
4.40 g., Nickel Plated Steel, **Rev:** Montreal Canadiens logo, colorized

Date	Mintage	MS63
2007(ml)	4,091	5.00

KM# 1039 25 CENTS
4.43 g., Nickel Plated Steel, 23.9mm. **Subject:** Canada

Day **Rev:** Colorized moose head

Date	Mintage	MS63
2008	11,538	12.50

KM# 760   25 CENTS
4.43 g., Nickel Plated Steel, 23.88mm. **Subject:** Baby
Rev: Multicolor blue teddy bear

Date	Mintage	MS63
2008	29,639	8.00

KM# 761   25 CENTS
4.43 g., Nickel Plated Steel, 23.88mm. **Subject:** Birthday
Rev: Multicolor party hat

Date	Mintage	MS63
2008	11,376	8.00

KM# 762   25 CENTS
4.43 g., Nickel Plated Steel, 23.88mm. **Subject:**
Congratulations **Rev:** Multicolor trophy

Date	Mintage	MS63
2008	6,821	8.00

KM# 763   25 CENTS
4.43 g., Nickel Plated Steel, 23.88mm. **Subject:** Wedding
Rev: Multicolor wedding cake

Date	Mintage	MS63
2008	7,407	8.00

KM# 764   25 CENTS
4.43 g., Nickel Plated Steel, 23.88mm. **Subject:** Santa
Claus **Rev:** Multicolor Santa

Date	Mintage	MS63
2008	42,344	8.00

KM# 765   25 CENTS
4.43 g., Nickel Plated Steel, 23.9mm. **Subject:** Vancouver
Olympics **Rev:** Freestyle skiing

Date	Mintage	MS63
2008	—	2.00

KM# 766   25 CENTS
4.43 g., Nickel Plated Steel, 23.8mm. **Subject:** Vancouver
Olympics **Rev:** Figure skating

Date	Mintage	MS63
2008	—	2.00

KM# 768   25 CENTS
4.43 g., Nickel Plated Steel, 23.88mm. **Subject:** Vancouver
Olympics **Rev:** Snowboarding

Date	Mintage	MS63
2008	—	2.00

KM# 769   25 CENTS
4.43 g., Nickel Plated Steel, 23.88mm. **Subject:** Vancouver
Olympics **Rev:** Olympic mascot - Miga

Date	Mintage	MS63
2008	—	3.00

KM# 770   25 CENTS
4.43 g., Nickel Plated Steel, 23.88mm. **Subject:** Vancouver
Olympics **Rev:** Olympic mascot - Quatchi

Date	Mintage	MS63
2008	—	3.00

KM# 771   25 CENTS
4.43 g., Nickel Plated Steel, 23.88mm. **Subject:** Vancouver
Olympics **Rev:** Olympic mascot - Sumi

Date	Mintage	MS63
2008	—	3.00

KM# 772   25 CENTS
4.43 g., Nickel Plated Steel, 23.88mm. **Subject:** Oh
Canada **Rev:** Multicolor red flag

Date	Mintage	MS63
2008	—	8.00

KM# 773   25 CENTS
12.61 g., Nickel Plated Steel, 35mm. **Obv.** Bust right
Obv. Designer: Susanna Blunt **Rev:** Downy woodpecker in

tree, multicolor **Rev. Designer:** Arnold Nogy **Edge:** Plain **Note:** Prev. KM#717.

Date	Mintage	MS63
2008(ml) Specimen	14,282	275

KM# 774 25 CENTS
12.61 g., Nickel Plated Steel, 35mm. **Obv.** Bust right **Obv. Designer:** Susanna Blunt **Rev:** Northern cardinal perched on branch - multicolor **Rev. Designer:** Arnold Nogy **Edge:** Plain **Note:** Prev. KM#718.

Date	Mintage	MS63
2008(ml) Specimen	11,604	275

KM# 775 25 CENTS
4.43 g., Nickel Plated Steel, 23.8mm. **Subject:** End of WWI, 90th Anniversary **Rev:** Multicolor poppy

Date	Mintage	MS63
1918-2008	10,167	8.00

KM# 776 25 CENTS
12.61 g., Nickel Plated Steel, 35mm. **Subject:** Anne of Green Gables **Rev:** Image of young girl, multicolor **Rev. Designer:** Ben Stahl

Date	Mintage	MS63
1908-2008 Specimen	32,795	20.00

KM# 841 25 CENTS
4.43 g., Nickel Plated Steel, 23.8mm. **Subject:** Vancouver Olympics **Rev:** Bobsleigh

Date	Mintage	MS63
2008	—	3.00

KM# 1041 25 CENTS
4.43 g., Nickel Plated Steel, **Subject:** WWI **Rev:** Three military men standing over tomb

Date	Mintage	MS63
2008(ml)	10,167	12.50

KM# 840 25 CENTS
4.43 g., Nickel Plated Steel, 23.8mm. **Subject:** Valcouver 2010 Olympics **Rev:** Cross-country skiing

Date	Mintage	MS63
2009	—	3.00

KM# 842 25 CENTS
4.43 g., Nickel Plated Steel, 23.9mm. **Subject:** Edmonton Olympics **Rev:** Speed skating

Date	Mintage	MS63
2009	—	3.00

KM# 885 25 CENTS
4.40 g., Nickel Plated Steel, 23.88mm. **Subject:** Canada Day **Rev:** Animals in boat with flag **Rev. Legend:** Canada 25 cents

Date	Mintage	MS63
2009	11,091	5.00

KM# 886   25 CENTS
12.61 g., Nickel Plated Steel, 35mm.   **Subject:** Notre-Dame-Du-Saguenay **Obv.**   Bust right   **Obv. Designer:** Susanna Blunt **Rev:** Color photo of fjord and statue **Obv. Legend:** Elizabeth II DG Regina **Rev. Legend:** Canada 25 cents

Date	Mintage	MS63
2009 Specimen	16,653	25.00

KM# 915   25 CENTS
4.43 g., Nickel Plated Steel, 23.9mm.   **Subject:** Surprise Birthday **Obv.**   Bust right   **Obv. Designer:** Susanna Blunt **Rev:** Colorized

Date	Mintage	MS63
2009	9,663	12.50

KM# 916   25 CENTS
4.43 g., Nickel Plated Steel, 23.9mm.   **Subject:** Share the Excitement **Obv.**   Bust right   **Obv. Designer:** Susanna Blunt **Rev:** Colorized

Date	Mintage	MS63
2009	4,126	12.50

KM# 917   25 CENTS
4.43 g., Nickel Plated Steel, 23.9mm.   **Subject:** Share the Love **Obv.**   Bust right   **Obv. Designer:** Susanna Blunt **Rev:** Two doves, coolored

Date	Mintage	MS63
2009	7,571	12.50

KM# 918   25 CENTS
4.43 g., Nickel Plated Steel, 23.9mm.   **Subject:** Thank You **Obv.**   Bust right **Obv. Designer:** Susanna Blunt **Rev:** Colorized

Date	Mintage	MS63
2009	4,415	12.50

KM# 933   25 CENTS
4.40 g., Nickel Plated Steel, 23.9mm.   **Rev:** Santa Claus, multicolor

Date	Mintage	MS63
2009	—	16.50

KM# 934   25 CENTS
4.40 g., Nickel Plated Steel, 23.9mm.   **Rev:** Multicolor teddy bear, crescent moon

Date	Mintage	MS63
2009	25,182	16.50

KM# 935   25 CENTS
4.40 g., Nickel Plated Steel, 23.9mm.   **Subject:** Oh Canada **Rev:** Maple leaves, yellow color

Date	Mintage	MS63
2009	14,451	16.50

KM# 952   25 CENTS
4.40 g., Nickel Plated Steel, 23.9mm.   **Rev:** Sledge hockey

Date	Mintage	MS63
2009	—	3.00

KM# 1063 25 CENTS
Nickel Plated Steel, **Subject:** Men's Hockey **Rev:** Hockey player and maple leaf outline

Date	Mintage	MS63
2009	—	2.50

KM# 1063a 25 CENTS
Nickel Plated Steel, **Subject:** Men's Hockey **Rev:** Hockey player and maple leaf outline in red

Date	Mintage	MS63
2009	—	7.50

KM# 1064 25 CENTS
Nickel Plated Steel, 23.9mm. **Subject:** Women's Hockey **Rev:** Hockey player and maple leaf outline

Date	Mintage	MS63
2009	—	2.50

KM# 1064a 25 CENTS
Nickel Plated Steel, **Subject:** Women's Hockey **Rev:** Hockey player and male leaf outline in red

Date	Mintage	MS63
2009	—	7.50

KM# 1065 25 CENTS
Nickel Plated Steel, 23.9mm. **Subject:** Klassen - Female speed skater **Rev:** Skater and maple leaf outline

Date	Mintage	MS63
2009	—	2.50

KM# 1065a 25 CENTS
Nickel Plated Steel, **Subject:** Klassen - female skater **Rev:** Skater and maple leaf outline in red

Date	Mintage	MS63
2009	—	7.50

KM# 880 25 CENTS
4.40 g., Nickel Plated Steel, 23.88mm. **Subject:** Miga Mascot Vancouver Olympics **Rev:** Mica Mascot - color **Rev. Legend:** Vancouver 2010 25 cents

Date	Mintage	MS63
2010	14,654	3.00

KM# 881 25 CENTS
4.40 g., Nickel Plated Steel, 23.88mm. **Subject:** Quatchi Mascot - Vancouver Olympics **Obv.** Bust right **Rev:** Quatchi Mascot color **Rev. Legend:** Vancouver 2010 25 cents

Date	Mintage	MS63
2010	15,310	3.00

KM# 882 25 CENTS
4.40 g., Nickel Plated Steel, 23.88mm. **Subject:** Sumi Mascot **Rev:** Sumi Mascot color **Rev. Legend:** Vancouver 2010 25 cents

Date	Mintage	MS63
2010	15,333	3.00

KM# 953 25 CENTS
4.40 g., Nickel Plated Steel, 23.9mm. **Rev:** Ice hockey

Date	Mintage	MS63
2010	—	3.00

KM# 953a 25 CENTS
4.40 g., Nickel Plated Steel, 23.9mm. **Rev:** Ice Hockey - red enamel

Date	Mintage	MS63
2010	—	8.00

KM# 954 25 CENTS
4.40 g., Nickel Plated Steel, 23.9mm. **Rev:** Curling

Date	Mintage	MS63
2010	—	3.00

KM# 954a 25 CENTS
4.40 g., Nickel Plated Steel, 23.9mm. **Rev:** Curling red enamel

Date	Mintage	MS63
2010	—	8.00

KM# 955 25 CENTS
4.40 g., Nickel Plated Steel, 23.9mm. **Rev:** Wheelchair curling

Date	Mintage	MS63
2010	—	3.00

KM# 955a 25 CENTS
4.40 g., Nickel Plated Steel, 23.9mm. **Rev:** Wheelchair curling - red enamel

Date	Mintage	MS63
2010	—	8.00

KM# 956 25 CENTS
4.40 g., Nickel Plated Steel, 23.9mm. **Rev:** Biathlon

Date	Mintage	MS63
2010	—	3.00

KM# 956a 25 CENTS
4.40 g., Nickel Plated Steel, 23.9mm. **Rev:** Biathlon - red enamel

Date	Mintage	MS63
2010	—	8.00

KM# 957   25 CENTS
4.40 g., Nickel Plated Steel, 23.9mm. **Rev:** Alpine skiing

Date	Mintage	MS63
2010	—	3.00

KM# 957a   25 CENTS
4.40 g., Nickel Plated Steel, 23.9mm. **Rev:** Alpine skiing - red enamel

Date	Mintage	MS63
2010	—	8.00

KM# 958   25 CENTS
4.40 g., Nickel Plated Steel, 23.9mm. **Rev:** Snowboarding

Date	Mintage	MS63
2010	—	3.00

KM# 958a   25 CENTS
4.40 g., Nickel Plated Steel, 23.9mm. **Rev:** Snowboarding - red enamel

Date	Mintage	MS63
2010	—	8.00

KM# 959   25 CENTS
23.90 g., Nickel Plated Steel, 23.9mm. **Rev:** Free-style skiing

Date	Mintage	MS63
2010	—	3.00

KM# 959a   25 CENTS
4.40 g., Nickel Plated Steel, 23.9mm. **Rev:** Free-style skiing - red enamel

Date	Mintage	MS63
2010	—	8.00

KM# 960   25 CENTS
4.40 g., Nickel Plated Steel, 23.9mm. **Rev:** Alpine skiing

Date	Mintage	MS63
2010	—	3.00

KM# 960a   25 CENTS
4.40 g., Nickel Plated Steel, 23.9mm. **Rev:** Alpine skiing - red enamel

Date	Mintage	MS63
2010	—	8.00

KM# 988   25 CENTS
4.40 g., Nickel Plated Steel, 23.88mm. **Rev:** Blue baby carriage

Date	Mintage	MS63
2010	—	10.00

KM# 989   25 CENTS
4.40 g., Nickel Plated Steel, 23.9mm. **Rev:** Purple gift box

Date	Mintage	MS63
2010	—	10.00

KM# 991   25 CENTS
4.40 g., Nickel Plated Steel, 23.9mm. **Rev:** Three maple leaves

Date	Mintage	MS63
2010	—	12.50

KM# 992   25 CENTS
4.40 g., Nickel Plated Steel, 23.9mm. **Rev:** Three zinnias

Date	Mintage	MS63
2010	—	12.50

KM# 993   25 CENTS
4.43 g., Nickel Plated Steel, 23.9mm. **Rev:** Pink hearts and roses

Date	Mintage	MS63
2010	—	10.00

KM# 994   25 CENTS
12.61 g., Nickel Plated Steel, 35mm. **Rev:** Goldfinch, multicolor **Rev. Designer:** Arnold Nogy

Date	Mintage	MS63
2010 Specimen	Est. 14000	90.00

KM# 1001   25 CENTS
12.61 g., Nickel Plated Steel, 35mm. **Subject:** Blue Jay
Rev: Multicolor blue jay on yellow maple leaves

Date	Mintage	MS63
2010 Specimen	Est. 14000	90.00

KM# 1006   25 CENTS
0.50 g., 0.999 Gold, AGW 11mm. **Rev:** Caribou head left

Date	Mintage		
2010	15,000	PF63 70.00	PF65 80.00

KM# 1021   25 CENTS
Nickel Plated Steel, 23.9mm. **Rev:** Santa Claus in color

Date	Mintage	MS63
2010	—	15.00

KM# 1026   25 CENTS
Silver, 23.8mm. **Obv.** George V bust left **Rev:** Value within wreath, dual dates below

Date	Mintage		
1935-2010	—	PF63 22.00	PF65 25.00

KM# 1028   25 CENTS
4.40 g., Nickel Plated Steel, 23.9mm. **Rev:** Soldier standing, two red poppies, large maple leaf behind

Date	Mintage	MS63
2010	—	15.00

KM# 1110   25 CENTS
12.61 g., Nickel Plated Steel, 35mm. **Subject:** Royal Wedding **Rev:** Colored portraits left of William and Katherine

Date	Mintage	MS63
2011 Specimen	—	25.00

KM# 1156   25 CENTS
5.90 g., 0.925 Silver, 0.17 oz. ASW 23.8mm. **Obv.** George V bust **Rev:** Value within wreath

Date	Mintage		
1911-2011	6,000	PF63 22.00	PF65 25.00

KM# 1168a   25 CENTS
4.40 g., Nickel Plated Steel, 23.9mm. **Obv.** Bust right **Rev:** Stylized bison, green circle in background

Date	Mintage	MS63
2011	—	9.50

KM# 1169a   25 CENTS
4.40 g., Nickel Plated Steel, 23.9mm. **Obv.** Bust right **Rev:** Stylized falcon with yellow circle in background

Date	Mintage	MS63
2011	—	9.50

KM# 1170a   25 CENTS
4.40 g., Nickel Plated Steel, 23.9mm. **Obv.** Bust right **Rev:** Stylized orca whale with blue circle in background

Date	Mintage	MS63
2011	—	9.50

25 CENTS

KM# 1079   25 CENTS
12.61 g., Nickel Plated Steel, 35mm. **Rev:** Barn Swallow
in color **Rev. Designer:** Arnold Nagy

Date	Mintage	MS63
2011 Specimen	Est. 14000	55.00

KM# 1080   25 CENTS
4.43 g., Nickel Plated Steel, 23.88mm. **Subject:** Oh
Canada! **Rev:** Maple leaf and circular legend

Date	Mintage	MS63
2011	—	2.50

KM# 1081   25 CENTS
4.43 g., Nickel Plated Steel, 23.88mm. **Subject:** Wedding
Rev: Two rings

Date	Mintage	MS63
2011	—	2.50

KM# 1082   25 CENTS
4.43 g., Nickel Plated Steel, 23.88mm. **Subject:** Birthday
Rev: Year in four baloons

Date	Mintage	MS63
2011	—	2.50

KM# 1083   25 CENTS
4.43 g., Nickel Plated Steel, 23.88mm. **Subject:** New
Baby! **Rev:** Baby's feet

Date	Mintage	MS63
2011	—	2.50

KM# 1084   25 CENTS
4.43 g., Nickel Plated Steel, 23.88mm. **Rev:** Tooth Fairy

Date	Mintage	MS63
2011	—	2.50

KM# 1113   25 CENTS
12.61 g., Nickel Plated Steel, 35mm. **Rev:** Fantasy Furry
Woods creature in color

Date	Mintage	MS63
2011	—	20.00

KM# 1114   25 CENTS
12.61 g., Nickel Plated Steel, 35mm. **Rev:** Fantasy sea
serpent in color

Date	Mintage	MS63
2011	—	20.00

KM# 1115   25 CENTS
12.61 g., Nickel Plated Steel, 35mm. **Rev:** Tulip and
ladybug in color

Date	Mintage	MS63
2011	—	35.00

KM# 1116 25 CENTS
12.61 g., Nickel Plated Steel, 35mm. **Rev:** Black capped chickadee in color

Date	Mintage	MS63
2011 Specimen	—	55.00

KM# 1148 25 CENTS
4.43 g., Nickel Plated Steel, 23.9mm. **Obv.** Bust right **Rev:** Snowflake

Date	Mintage	MS63
2011	—	7.50

KM# 1168 25 CENTS
4.40 g., Nickel Plated Steel, 23.9mm. **Obv.** Bust right **Rev:** Stylized bison

Date	Mintage	MS63
2011	—	2.50

KM# 1169 25 CENTS
4.40 g., Nickel Plated Steel, 23.9mm. **Obv.** Bust right **Rev:** Stylized falcon

Date	Mintage	MS63
2011	—	2.50

KM# 1170 25 CENTS
4.40 g., Nickel Plated Steel, 23.9mm. **Obv.** Bust right

Rev: Stylized orca whale

Date	Mintage	MS63
2011	—	2.50

KM# 1171 25 CENTS
0.50 g., 0.999 Gold, AGW 11mm. **Obv.** Bust right **Rev:** Cougar head left

Date	Mintage		
2011	—	PF63 70.00	PF65 80.00

KM# 1172 25 CENTS
12.61 g., Copper Plated Silver, 35mm. **Obv.** Bust right **Rev:** Wayne Greskey in hockey helmet left

Date	Mintage	MS63
2011 Specimen	—	35.00

KM# 1192 25 CENTS
4.43 g., Nickel Plated Steel, 23.9mm. **Subject:** Canadian Broadcasting Company, 75th Anniversary **Obv.** Bust right **Rev:** Old-time radio microphone

Date	Mintage	MS63
2011	—	2.50

KM# 1193 25 CENTS
12.61 g., Nickel Plated Steel, 35mm. **Subject:** Mythical Creature - Mishepishu **Obv.** Bust right **Rev:** Horned lizard in color

Date	Mintage	MS63
2011	—	15.00

KM# 1322a 25 CENTS
4.43 g., Nickel Plated Steel, 23.9mm. **Subject:** War of 1812 - Brock **Rev:** Portrait at right, red maple leaf **Rev. Designer:** Bonnie Ross

Date	Mintage	MS63
2012	—	10.00

KM# 1227 25 CENTS
4.43 g., Nickel Plated Steel, 23.9mm. **Obv.** Bust right **Rev:** Tooth Fairy in flight

Date	Mintage	MS63
2012	—	2.50

KM# 1228 25 CENTS
4.43 g., Nickel Plated Steel, 23.9mm. **Subject:** Baby **Rev:** Baby's mobile

Date	Mintage	MS63
2012	—	2.50

KM# 1229 25 CENTS
4.43 g., Nickel Plated Steel, 23.9mm. **Subject:** Wedding **Rev:** Two wedding rings with small feet

Date	Mintage	MS63
2012	—	2.50

KM# 1230 25 CENTS
4.43 g., Nickel Plated Steel, 23.9mm. **Subject:** Birthday **Rev:** Cone with character face

Date	Mintage	MS63
2012	—	2.50

KM# 1231 25 CENTS
4.43 g., Nickel Plated Steel, 23.9mm. **Subject:** Oh, Canada ! **Rev:** Maple leaves with character faces

Date	Mintage	MS63
2012	—	2.50

KM# 1232 25 CENTS
4.43 g., Nickel Plated Steel, 23.88mm. **Subject:** Winnipeg Jets **Rev:** Jet superimposed on Maple leaf

Date	Mintage	MS63
2012	—	2.50

KM# 1233 25 CENTS
12.61 g., Nickel Plated Steel, 35mm. **Subject:** Titanic, 100th Anniversary **Obv.** Bust right **Rev:** Two views of Titanic, one at dockside, one nighttime at sea

Date	Mintage	MS63
2012	—	20.00

KM# 1247 25 CENTS
12.61 g., Nickel Plated Steel, 35mm. **Subject:** Coast Guard, 100th anniversary **Rev:** Rescue craft in rough seas

Date	Mintage	MS63
2012	—	30.00

KM# 1252 25 CENTS
12.61 g., Nickel Plated Steel, 35mm. **Subject:**
Pachyrhinosaurus Lakusta **Note:** Skelton glows in the dark.

Date	Mintage	MS63
2012	—	25.00

KM# 1253 25 CENTS
12.61 g., Nickel Plated Steel, 35mm. **Subject:** Rose
Breasted Grosbeak

Date	Mintage	MS63
2012	—	35.00

KM# 1265 25 CENTS
12.61 g., Nickel Plated Steel, 35mm. **Subject:** Aster and Bee

Date	Mintage	MS63
2012	—	35.00

KM# 1313 25 CENTS
0.50 g., Silver, 35mm. **Subject:** Grey Cup, 100th
Anniversary **Obv.** Bust right **Obv. Designer:** Susana Blunt
Rev: B.C. Lions logo in color

Date	Mintage	
2012	—	PF65 25.00

KM# 1314 25 CENTS
0.50 g., Copper-Nickel, 35mm. **Subject:** Grey Cup, 100th
Anniversary **Obv.** Bust right **Obv. Designer:** Susana Blunt
Rev: Calgary Stampeeders logo in color

Date	Mintage	
2012	—	PF65 25.00

KM# 1315 25 CENTS
0.50 g., Copper-Nickel, 35mm. **Subject:** Grey Cup, 100th
Anniversary **Obv.** Bust right **Obv. Designer:** Susana Blunt
Rev: Edmonton Eskimos logo in color

Date	Mintage	
2012	—	PF65 25.00

KM# 1316 25 CENTS
GREY CUP, 100TH ANNIVERSARY 0.50 g., Copper-
Nickel, **Ruler:** Elizabeth II 35mm. **Obv.** Bust right **Obv.**
Designer: Susana Blunt **Rev:** Hamilton Tiger-Cats logo in
color **Mint:** Royal Canadian Mint

Date	Mintage	
2012	—	PF65 25.00

KM# 1317 25 CENTS
0.50 g., Copper-Nickel, 35mm. **Subject:** Grey Cup, 100th
Anniversary **Obv.** Bust right **Obv. Designer:** Susana Blunt
Rev: Montreal Alouettes logo in color

Date	Mintage	
2012	—	PF65 25.00

KM# 1318 25 CENTS
0.50 g., Copper-Nickel, 35mm. **Subject:** Grey Cup, 100th
Anniversary **Obv.** Bust right **Obv. Designer:** Susana Blunt
Rev: Saskatchewan Roughriders logo in color

Date	Mintage	
2012	—	PF65 25.00

KM# 1319 25 CENTS
0.50 g., Copper-Nickel, 35mm. **Subject:** Grey Cup, 100th
Anniversary **Obv.** Bust right **Obv. Designer:** Susana Blunt
Rev: Toronto Argonauts logo in color

Date	Mintage	
2012	—	PF65 25.00

KM# 1320 25 CENTS
0.50 g., Copper-Nickel, 35mm. **Subject:** Grey Cup, 100th
Anniversary **Obv.** Bust right **Obv. Designer:** Susana Blunt
Rev: Winnipeg Blue Bombers logo in color

Date	Mintage	
2012	—	PF65 25.00

KM# 1321 25 CENTS
12.61 g., Nickel Plated Steel, 35mm. **Subject:** Calgary
Stampeed **Rev:** Cowboy on bucking horse in color

Date	Mintage	MS63
2012 Specimen	—	45.00

KM# 1322 25 CENTS
4.43 g., Nickel Plated Steel, 23.9mm. **Subject:** War of 1812
- Brock **Rev:** Porrait at right **Rev. Designer:** Bonnie Ross

Date	Mintage	MS63
2012	—	2.50

KM# 1324   25 CENTS
4.43 g., Nickel Plated Steel, 23.9mm.   **Subject:** War of
1812 - Tecumseh **Rev:** Portrait at right **Rev. Designer:**
Bonnie Ross

Date	Mintage	MS63
2012	—	2.50

KM# 1324a   25 CENTS
4.42 g., Nickel Plated Steel, 23.9mm.   **Subject:** War of
1812 - Tecumseh **Rev:** Portrait at right, red maple leaf
Rev. Designer: Bonnie Ross

Date	Mintage	MS63
2012	—	10.00

KM# 1326   25 CENTS
12.61 g., Nickel Plated Steel, 35mm.   **Rev:** Evening
Grosbeak in color

Date	Mintage	MS63
2012 Specimen	—	35.00

KM# 1341   25 CENTS
12.16 g., Copper-Nickel, 35mm.   **Subject:** Christmas
Lenticular **Rev:** Santa Claus with bag of presents **Rev.**
Designer: Tony Bianco

Date	Mintage	MS63
2012 Specimen	25,000	30.00

KM# 1351   25 CENTS
Nickel Plated Steel, 35mm.   **Subject:** Quetzalcoatlus **Rev:**
Dinosaur in color and as glow-in-the-dark skelton

Date	Mintage	MS63
2013	—	40.00

KM# 1353   25 CENTS
12.61 g., Copper-Nickel, 35mm.   **Rev:** Purple cone flower
and butterfly in color

Date	Mintage	MS63
2013 Specimen	17,500	30.00

KM# 1354   25 CENTS
12.61 g., Copper-Nickel, 35mm.   **Rev:** Male and female
mallards in color **Rev. Designer:** Trevor Tennant

Date	Mintage	MS63
2013 Specimen	17,500	30.00

KM# 1368   25 CENTS
4.43 g., Nickel Plated Steel, 23.9mm. **Subject:** Oh Canada
Rev: Maple Leaf

Date	Mintage		
2013	—	PF63 8.00	PF65 10.00

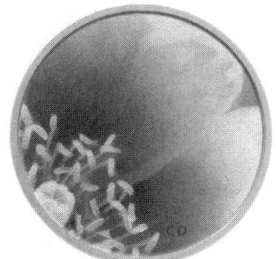

KM# 1491   25 CENTS
15.50 g., Copper-Nickel, 35mm. **Subject:** Eastern Prickly
Pear Cactus **Rev:** Partial flower in color **Rev. Designer:**
Claudio D'Angelo

Date	Mintage		
2013	17,500	PF63 20.00	PF65 25.00

KM# 1494   25 CENTS
0.50 g., 0.999 Gold, AGW 11mm. **Subject:** Rocky
Mountain Bighorn Sheep **Rev:** Head right

Date	Mintage		
2013	10,000	PF63 70.00	PF65 80.00

KM# 1373   25 CENTS
12.61 g., Nickel Plated Steel, 35mm. **Rev:** American
Robin in color

Date	Mintage	MS63
2013 Specimen	—	35.00

KM# 1380   25 CENTS
0.50 g., 0.9999 Gold, AGW 11mm. **Rev:** Hummingbird in
flight right **Rev. Designer:** Claudio D'Angelo

Date	Mintage		
2013	Est. 10000	PF63 70.00	PF65 80.00

KM# 1419   25 CENTS
4.43 g., Nickel Plated Steel, 23.9mm. **Subject:** Birthday
Rev: Birthday cake and candle

Date	Mintage		
2013	—	PF63 17.00	PF65 20.00

KM# 1420   25 CENTS
4.43 g., Nickel Plated Steel, 23.9mm. **Rev:** Two Rings

Date	Mintage		
2013	—	PF63 17.00	PF65 20.00

KM# 1443   25 CENTS
Copper-Nickel, 35mm. **Obv.** Bust right **Rev:** Barn owl in
flight left, in color

Date	Mintage		
2013	17,500	PF63 30.00	PF65 35.00

KM# 1460   25 CENTS
0.50 g., Nickel Plated Steel, 35mm. **Rev:** Baby carriage
- William and Catherine names around **Rev. Designer:**
Laurie McGaw

Date	Mintage	MS63
2013 Specimen	—	25.00

KM# 1465   25 CENTS
12.61 g., Nickel Plated Steel, 35mm. **Rev:** Christmas
wreath in color

Date	Mintage	MS63
2013	—	25.00

KM# 1572   25 CENTS
12.61 g., Nickel Plated Steel, 35mm. **Obv.** Bust right **Rev:**
Montreal Canadians logo in color

Date	Mintage	MS63
2014	—	10.00

KM# 1573   25 CENTS
12.61 g., Nickel Plated Steel, 35mm. **Obv.** Bust right **Rev:**
Canucks logo in color

Date	Mintage	MS63
2014	—	10.00

KM# 1574   25 CENTS
12.61 g., Nickel Plated Steel, 35mm. **Obv.** Bust right **Rev:** Calgary Flames logo in color

Date	Mintage	MS63
2014	—	10.00

KM# 1575   25 CENTS
12.61 g., Nickel Plated Steel, 35mm. **Obv.** Bust right **Rev:** Winnipeg Jets logo in color

Date	Mintage	MS63
2014	—	10.00

KM# 1576   25 CENTS
12.61 g., Nickel Plated Steel, 35mm. **Obv.** Bust right **Rev:** Toronto Maple Leafs logo in color

Date	Mintage	MS63
2014	—	10.00

KM# 1577   25 CENTS
12.61 g., Nickel Plated Steel, 35mm. **Obv.** Bust right **Rev:** Edmonton Oilers logo in color

Date	Mintage	MS63
2014	—	10.00

KM# 1602   25 CENTS
0.50 g., 0.999 Gold AGW 11mm. **Obv.** Bust right **Rev:** Chipmonk

Date	Mintage		
2014	—	PF63 70.00	PF65 80.00

KM# 1618   25 CENTS
12.61 g., Nickel Plated Steel, 35mm. **Obv.** Bust right **Rev:** Eastern Meadowlark in color

Date	Mintage	MS63
2014	—	35.00

KM# 1619 25 CENTS
12.61 g., Nickel Plated Steel, 35mm. **Obv.** Bust right **Rev:** Tikaalik creature in glow in the dark format

Date	Mintage	MS63
2014	—	25.00

KM# 1630 25 CENTS
12.61 g., Nickel Plated Steel, 35mm. **Obv.** Bust right **Rev:** Pintail ducks in color

Date	Mintage	MS63
2014	—	25.00

KM# 1631 25 CENTS
12.61 g., Nickel Plated Steel, **Ruler:** Elizabeth II 35mm. **Obv.** Bust right **Rev:** Eastern Meadow Lark in color **Mint:** Royal Canadian Mint

Date	Mintage	MS63
2014	—	35.00

KM# 6 50 CENTS
11.62 g., 0.925 Silver, 0.34 oz. ASW 29.72mm. **Obv.** VICTORIA DEI GRATIA REGINA. CANADA **Obv. Designer:** Leonard C. Wyon **Rev:** Denomination and date within wreath, crown above **Edge:** Reeded

Date	Mintage	VG8	F12	VF20	XF40	AU50	MS60	MS63
1870	450,000	900	1,400	2,400	5,000	13,500	25,000	40,000
1870 LCW	Inc. above	45.00	75.00	175	400	1,150	3,500	10,000
1871	200,000	75.00	150	350	650	2,000	7,000	15,000
1871	45,000	150	225	450	1,100	2,800	8,500	22,000
1872	80,000	55.00	95.00	200	450	1,350	4,000	10,500
1872 Inverted A for V in Victoria	Inc. above	500	700	1,900	5,000	10,500	25,000	—
1881	150,000	60.00	125	225	550	2,100	5,500	16,000
1888	60,000	225	400	750	1,400	4,000	9,500	22,000
1890	20,000	1,200	1,900	3,500	6,000	14,000	30,000	65,000
1892	151,000	70.00	125	350	650	2,500	9,000	21,000
1894	29,036	500	900	1,500	2,500	7,000	14,000	35,000
1898	100,000	75.00	150	350	750	2,800	9,000	26,000
1899	50,000	200	350	700	1,600	5,000	14,000	35,000
1900	118,000	60.00	100	200	500	1,800	5,000	10,500
1901	80,000	80.00	150	300	750	2,000	7,000	17,500

Victorian leaves

KM# 12 50 CENTS
11.62 g., 0.925 Silver, 0.34 oz. ASW 29.72mm. **Obv.** Crowned bust right **Obv. Designer:** G. W. DeSaulles **Rev:** Denomination and date within wreath, crown above **Edge:** Reeded

Date	Mintage	VG8	F12	VF20	XF40	AU50	MS60	MS63
1902	120,000	28.00	55.00	150	350	650	1,950	4,500
1903H	140,000	35.00	70.00	225	550	850	2,100	5,500
1904	60,000	200	350	750	1,500	2,700	5,000	14,500
1905	40,000	250	500	1,000	2,100	4,000	9,000	22,500
1906	350,000	24.00	45.00	150	400	800	1,950	4,500
1907	300,000	24.00	50.00	125	350	700	1,900	5,000
1908	128,119	40.00	95.00	250	600	850	1,500	2,800
1909	302,118	28.00	90.00	250	750	1,600	3,000	12,000
1910 Victoria leaves	649,521	35.00	70.00	175	550	1,050	2,400	7,500

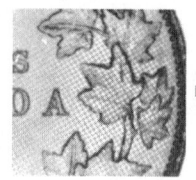

Edwardian leaves

KM# 12a 50 CENTS
11.62 g., 0.925 Silver, 0.34 oz. ASW 29.72mm. **Obv.** Crowned bust right **Obv. Designer:** G. W. DeSaulles **Rev:** Denomination and date within wreath **Edge:** Reeded

Date	Mintage	VG8	F12	VF20	XF40	AU50	MS60	MS63
1910 Edwardian leaves	Inc. above	23.00	40.00	100	400	650	1,550	4,500

KM# 19 50 CENTS
11.62 g., 0.925 Silver, 0.34 oz. ASW 29.72mm. **Obv.** Crowned bust left **Obv. Designer:** E. B. MacKennal **Rev:** Denomination and date within wreath, crown above **Edge:** Reeded

Date	Mintage	VG8	F12	VF20	XF40	AU50	MS60	MS63
1911	209,972	25.00	100	350	800	1,100	1,950	4,000

KM# 25 50 CENTS
11.62 g., 0.925 Silver, 0.34 oz. ASW 29.72mm. **Obv.** Crowned bust left, modified legend **Obv. Designer:** E. B. MacKennal **Rev:** Denomination and date within wreath, crown above **Edge:** Reeded

Date	Mintage	VG8	F12	VF20	XF40	AU50	MS60	MS63
1912	285,867	16.00	40.00	150	350	650	1,650	4,000
1913	265,889	16.00	40.00	175	400	800	1,900	6,500
1914	160,128	40.00	100	300	850	1,800	4,000	11,500
1916	459,070	15.00	24.00	75.00	200	400	950	2,900
1917	752,213	13.00	22.00	55.00	150	300	700	1,650
1918	754,989	13.00	20.00	40.00	125	250	600	1,400
1919	1,113,429	13.00	20.00	40.00	125	225	550	1,400

KM# 25a 50 CENTS
11.66 g., 0.800 Silver, 0.30 oz. ASW 29.72mm. **Obv.** Crowned bust left **Obv. Designer:** E. B. MacKennal **Rev:** Denomination and date within wreath, crown below **Edge:** Reeded

Date	Mintage	VG8	F12	VF20	XF40	AU50	MS60	MS63
1920	584,691	14.50	22.00	55.00	200	400	850	2,100
1921	—	35,000	40,000	50,000	55,000	60,000	70,000	125,000

Note: 75 to 100 known; David Akers John Jay Pittman sale, Part Three, 10-99, Gem Unc. realized $63,250

Date	Mintage	VG8	F12	VF20	XF40	AU50	MS60	MS63
1929	228,328	14.00	22.00	50.00	150	300	700	1,650
1931	57,581	25.00	50.00	100	300	600	1,200	2,400
1932	19,213	150	250	500	1,100	2,200	5,000	9,500
1934	39,539	30.00	50.00	125	300	550	950	1,950
1936	38,550	24.00	45.00	100	300	450	750	1,400

KM# 36 50 CENTS
11.66 g., 0.800 Silver, 0.30 oz. ASW 29.72mm. **Obv.** Head left **Obv. Designer:** T. H. Paget **Rev:** Crowned arms with supporters, denomination above, date below **Rev. Designer:** George E. Kruger-Gray **Edge:** Reeded

Date	Mintage	VG8	F12	VF20	XF40	AU50	MS60	MS63
1937	192,016	BV	13.00	14.00	18.00	25.00	40.00	95.00
1938	192,018	BV	15.00	20.00	40.00	85.00	175	450
1939	287,976	BV	13.00	15.00	28.00	60.00	100	300
1940	1,996,566	—	—	BV	14.00	19.00	35.00	75.00
1941	1,714,874	—	—	BV	14.00	19.00	35.00	75.00
1942	1,974,164	—	—	BV	14.00	19.00	35.00	75.00
1943	3,109,583	—	—	BV	14.00	19.00	35.00	75.00
1944	2,460,205	—	—	BV	14.00	19.00	35.00	75.00
1945	1,959,528	—	—	BV	14.00	19.00	35.00	95.00
1946	950,235	—	BV	13.00	18.00	35.00	80.00	175
1946 hoof in 6	Inc. above	28.00	40.00	60.00	225	600	1,650	4,500
1947 straight 7	424,885	—	BV	13.00	20.00	45.00	95.00	250
1947 curved 7	Inc. above	—	BV	13.00	30.00	65.00	125	350
1947 maple leaf, straight 7	38,433	28.00	40.00	55.00	100	150	250	400
1947 maple leaf, curved 7	Inc. above	1,500	1,950	2,500	3,500	4,000	6,000	13,000

KM# 45 50 CENTS
11.66 g., 0.800 Silver, 0.30 oz. ASW 29.72mm. **Obv.** Head left, modified legend **Obv. Designer:** T. H. Paget **Rev:** Crowned arms with supporters, denomination above, date below **Rev. Designer:** George E. Kruger-Gray **Edge:** Reeded

Date	Mintage	VG8	F12	VF20	XF40	AU50	MS60	MS63
1948	37,784	90.00	125	150	175	225	300	450
1949	858,991	—	—	BV	13.00	22.00	55.00	125
1949 hoof over 9	Inc. above	20.00	22.50	45.00	90.00	200	500	1,150
1950 no lines in 0	2,384,179	14.00	16.00	18.00	45.00	90.00	200	300
1950 lines in 0	Inc. above	—	—	BV	12.00	14.50	16.00	45.00
1951	2,421,730	—	—	—	BV	10.00	14.00	30.00
1952	2,596,465	—	—	—	BV	10.00	14.00	24.00

KM# 53 50 CENTS
11.66 g., 0.800 Silver, 0.30 oz. ASW 29.72mm. **Obv.** Laureate bust right **Obv. Designer:** Mary Gillick **Rev:** Crowned arms with supporters, denomination above, date below **Edge:** Reeded

Date	Mintage	VG8	F12	VF20	XF40	AU50	MS60	MS63
1953	1,630,429	—	—	—	BV	9.50	13.00	22.50
Note: small date								
1953	Inc. above	—	—	BV	12.00	15.00	28.00	55.00
Note: large date, straps								
1953	Inc. above	—	BV	12.00	20.00	45.00	95.00	225
Note: large date without straps								
1954	506,305	—	—	BV	14.00	19.50	28.00	50.00
1955	753,511	—	—	BV	12.00	15.00	19.00	30.00
1956	1,379,499	—	—	—	BV	BV	12.00	20.00
1957	2,171,689	—	—	—	BV	BV	12.00	13.00
1958	2,957,266	—	—	—	BV	BV	12.00	13.00

KM# 56 50 CENTS
11.66 g., 0.800 Silver, 0.30 oz. ASW 29.7mm. **Obv.** Luareate bust right **Obv. Designer:** Mary Gillick **Rev:** Crown divides date above arms with supporters, denomination at right **Rev. Designer:** Thomas Shingles **Edge:** Reeded

Date	Mintage	VG8	F12	VF20	XF40	AU50	MS60	MS63
1959	3,095,535	—	—	—	—	BV	BV	12.00
Note: horizontal shading								
1960	3,488,897	—	—	—	—	BV	BV	12.00
1961	3,584,417	—	—	—	—	BV	BV	12.00
1962	5,208,030	—	—	—	—	BV	BV	12.00
1963	8,348,871	—	—	—	—	BV	BV	12.00
1964	9,377,676	—	—	—	—	BV	BV	12.00

KM# 63 50 CENTS
11.66 g., 0.800 Silver, 0.30 oz. ASW 29.72mm. **Obv.** Young bust right **Obv. Designer:** Arnold Machin **Rev:** Crown divides date above arms with supporters, denomination at right **Rev. Designer:** Thomas Shingles **Edge:** Reeded

Date	Mintage	VG8	F12	VF20	XF40	AU50	MS60	MS63
1965	12,629,974	—	—	—	—	BV	BV	12.00
1966	7,920,496	—	—	—	—	BV	BV	12.00

KM# 69 50 CENTS
11.66 g., 0.800 Silver, 0.30 oz. ASW 29.72mm. **Subject:** Confederation Centennial **Obv.** Young bust right **Rev:** Seated wolf howling divides denomination at top, dates at bottom **Rev. Designer:** Alex Colville **Edge:** Reeded

Date	Mintage
1867-1967	4,211,392 **PF60** 14.00

KM# 75.1 50 CENTS

8.10 g., Nickel, 27.13mm. **Obv.** Young bust right **Obv. Designer:** Arnold Machin **Rev:** Crown divides date above arms with supporters, denomination at right **Rev. Designer:** Thomas Shingles **Edge:** Reeded

Date	Mintage	VG8	F12	VF20	XF40	AU50	MS60	MS63
1968	3,966,932	—	—	—	0.50	0.50	0.80	1.25
1969	7,113,929	—	—	—	0.50	0.50	0.80	1.25
1970	2,429,526	—	—	—	0.50	0.50	0.80	1.25
1971	2,166,444	—	—	—	0.50	0.50	0.80	1.25
1972	2,515,632	—	—	—	0.50	0.50	0.80	1.25
1973	2,546,096	—	—	—	0.50	0.50	0.80	1.25
1974	3,436,650	—	—	—	0.50	0.50	0.80	1.25
1975	3,710,000	—	—	—	0.50	0.50	0.80	1.25
1976	2,940,719	—	—	—	0.50	0.50	0.80	1.25

KM# 75.2 50 CENTS

8.10 g., Nickel, 27.13mm. **Obv.** Small young bust right **Obv. Designer:** Arnold Machin **Rev:** Crown divides date above arms with supporters, denomination at right **Rev. Designer:** Thomas Shingles **Edge:** Reeded

Date	Mintage	VG8	F12	VF20	XF40	AU50	MS60	MS63
1977	709,839	—	—	0.50	0.75	0.50	1.25	2.00

KM# 75.3 50 CENTS

8.10 g., Nickel, 27.13mm. **Obv.** Young bust right **Obv. Designer:** Arnold Machin **Rev:** Crown divides date above arms with supporters, denomination at right, redesigned arms **Rev. Designer:** Thomas Shingles **Edge:** Reeded

Date	Mintage	VG8	F12	VF20	XF40	AU50	MS60	MS63
1978	3,341,892	—	—	—	0.50	0.50	0.65	1.00
Note: square jewels								
1978	Inc. above	—	—	1.00	2.50	3.50	4.50	6.00
Note: round jewels								
1979	3,425,000	—	—	—	0.50	0.50	0.65	1.00
1980	1,574,000	—	—	—	0.50	0.50	0.65	1.00
1981	2,690,272	—	—	—	0.50	0.50	0.65	1.00
1981	199,000	PF60 3.00						
1982	2,236,674	—	—	—	30.00	45.00	65.00	95.00
Note: small beads								
1982	180,908	PF60 3.00						
Note: small beads								
1982	Inc. above	—	—	—	0.50	0.50	0.65	1.00
Note: large beads								
1983	1,177,000	—	—	—	0.50	0.50	0.65	1.00
1983	168,000	PF60 3.00						
1984	1,502,989	—	—	—	0.50	0.50	0.65	1.00
1984	161,602	PF60 3.00						
1985	2,188,374	—	—	—	0.50	0.50	0.65	1.00
1985	157,037	PF60 3.00						
1986	781,400	—	—	—	0.50	0.50	0.80	1.00
1986	175,745	PF60 3.00						
1987	373,000	—	—	—	0.50	0.50	0.80	1.00
1987	179,004	PF60 3.50						
1988	220,000	—	—	—	0.50	0.50	0.80	1.00
1988	175,259	PF60 3.00						
1989	266,419	—	—	—	0.50	0.50	0.80	1.00
1989	170,928	PF60 3.00						

KM# 185 50 CENTS

8.10 g., Nickel, 27.13mm. **Obv.** Crowned head right **Obv. Designer:** Dora dePedery-Hunt **Rev:** Crown divides date above arms with supporters, denomination at right **Rev. Designer:** Thomas Shingles **Edge:** Reeded

Date	Mintage		VG8	F12	VF20	XF40	AU50	MS60	MS63
1990	207,000		—	—	—	0.50	0.50	0.80	1.00
1990	140,649	PF60 5.00							
1991	490,000		—	—	—	0.50	0.55	0.85	1.00
1991	131,888	PF60 7.00							
1993	393,000		—	—	—	0.50	0.55	0.85	1.00
1993	143,065	PF60 3.00							
1994	987,000		—	—	—	0.50	0.50	0.75	1.00
1994	146,424	PF60 4.00							
1995	626,000		—	—	—	0.50	0.50	0.75	1.00
1995	—	PF60 4.00							
1996	—	PF60 4.00							
1996	458,000		—	—	—	0.50	0.50	0.65	1.00

KM# 208 50 CENTS

8.10 g., Nickel, 27.1mm. **Subject:** Confederation 125 **Obv.** Crowned head right **Obv. Designer:** Dora dePedery-Hunt **Rev:** Crown divides date above arms with supporters, denomination at right **Rev. Designer:** Thomas Shingles **Edge:** Reeded

Date	Mintage		MS63
1992	445,000		1.00
1992	147,061	PF60 5.00	

KM# 261 50 CENTS

9.34 g., 0.925 Silver, 0.28 oz. ASW **Obv.** Crowned head right **Rev:** Atlantic Puffin, denomination and date at right **Rev. Designer:** Sheldon Beveridge

Date	Mintage	
1995	—	PF60 24.00

KM# 262 50 CENTS

9.34 g., 0.925 Silver, 0.28 oz. ASW **Obv.** Crowned head right **Rev:** Whooping crane left, denomination and date at right **Rev. Designer:** Stan Witten

Date	Mintage	
1995	—	PF60 24.00

KM# 263 50 CENTS

9.34 g., 0.925 Silver, 0.28 oz. ASW **Obv.** Crowned head right **Rev:** Gray Jays, denomination and date at right **Rev. Designer:** Sheldon Beveridge

Date	Mintage	
1995	—	PF60 24.00

KM# 264 50 CENTS

9.34 g., 0.925 Silver, 0.28 oz. ASW **Obv.** Crowned head

right **Rev:** White-tailed ptarmigans, date and denomination at right **Rev. Designer:** Cosme Saffioti

Date	Mintage	
1995	—	PF60 22.00

KM# 283 50 CENTS
9.34 g., 0.925 Silver, 0.28 oz. ASW 27mm. **Obv.** Crowned head right **Rev:** Moose calf left, denomination and date at right **Rev. Designer:** Ago Aarand

Date	Mintage	
1996	—	PF60 20.00

KM# 284 50 CENTS
9.34 g., 0.925 Silver, 0.28 oz. ASW 27mm. **Obv.** Crowned head right **Rev:** Wood ducklings, date and denomination at right **Rev. Designer:** Sheldon Beveridge

Date	Mintage	
1996	—	PF60 20.00

KM# 285 50 CENTS
9.34 g., 0.925 Silver, 0.28 oz. ASW 27mm. **Obv.** Crowned head right **Rev:** Cougar kittens, date and denomination at right **Rev. Designer:** Stan Witten

Date	Mintage	
1996	—	PF60 20.00

KM# 286 50 CENTS
9.34 g., 0.925 Silver, 0.28 oz. ASW 27mm. **Obv.** Crowned head right **Rev:** Bear cubs standing, date and denomination at right **Rev. Designer:** Sheldon Beveridge

Date	Mintage	
1996	—	PF60 20.00

KM# 185a 50 CENTS
11.64 g., 0.925 Silver, 0.34 oz. ASW **Obv.** Crowned head right **Obv. Designer:** Dora dePedery-Hunt **Rev:** Crown

divides date above arms with supporters, denomination at right **Rev. Designer:** Thomas Shingles

Date	Mintage	
1996	—	PF60 13.00

KM# 290 50 CENTS
8.10 g., Nickel, 27.1mm. **Obv.** Crowned head right **Obv. Designer:** Dora dePedery-Hunt **Rev:** Redesigned arms **Rev. Designer:** Cathy Bursey-Sabourin **Edge:** Reeded

Date	Mintage			MS63
1997	387,000			1.00
1997	—	PF63 3.50	PF65 5.00	
1998	308,000			1.00
1998 Proof	—			—
1998W	—			2.00
1999	496,000			1.00
1999	—	PF63 3.50	PF65 5.00	
2000	559,000			1.00
2000	—	PF63 3.50	PF65 5.00	
2000W	—			1.50
2001P	—			1.50
2001P	—	PF63 3.50	PF65 5.00	
2003P	—			1.50
2003P	—	PF63 3.50	PF65 5.00	

KM# 292 50 CENTS
9.34 g., 0.925 Silver, 0.28 oz. ASW 27mm. **Obv.** Crowned head right **Rev:** Duck Toling Retriever, date and denomination at right **Rev. Designer:** Stan Witten

Date	Mintage	
1997	—	PF60 17.00

KM# 293 50 CENTS
9.34 g., 0.925 Silver, 0.28 oz. ASW **Obv.** Crowned head right **Rev:** Labrador leaping left, date and denomination at right **Rev. Designer:** Sheldon Beveridge

Date	Mintage	
1997	—	PF60 17.00

KM# 294 50 CENTS
9.34 g., 0.925 Silver, 0.28 oz. ASW **Obv.** Crowned head right **Rev:** Newfoundland right, date and denomination at right **Rev. Designer:** William Woodruff

Date	Mintage		
1997	—	PF60	17.00

KM# 295 50 CENTS
9.34 g., 0.925 Silver, 0.28 oz. ASW 27.1mm. **Obv.** Crowned head right **Rev:** Eskimo dog leaping forward, date and denomination at right **Rev. Designer:** Cosme Saffioti

Date	Mintage		
1997	—	PF60	17.00

KM# 290a 50 CENTS
11.66 g., 0.925 Silver, 0.34 oz. ASW 27.13mm. **Obv.** Crowned head right **Obv. Designer:** Dora dePedery-Hunt **Rev:** Redesigned arms **Rev. Designer:** Cathy Bursey-Sabourin **Edge:** Reeded

Date	Mintage		
1997	—	PF65	13.00
1998	—	PF65	13.00
1999	—	PF65	13.00
2000	—	PF65	13.00
2001	—	PF65	13.00
2003	—	PF65	13.00

KM# 313 50 CENTS
11.66 g., 0.925 Silver, 0.34 oz. ASW **Subject:** 90th Anniversary Royal Canadian Mint **Obv.** Crowned head right **Rev:** Denomination and date within wreath, crown above **Rev. Designer:** W. H. J. Blakemore

Date	Mintage		
1908-1998 Matte	—	PF60	15.00
1908-1998	—	PF60	15.00

KM# 318 50 CENTS
9.34 g., 0.925 Silver, 0.28 oz. ASW **Obv.** Crowned head right **Rev:** Killer Whales, date and denomination at right **Rev. Designer:** William Woodruff

Date	Mintage		
1998	—	PF60	17.00

KM# 319 50 CENTS
9.34 g., 0.925 Silver, 0.28 oz. ASW 27mm. **Obv.** Crowned head right **Rev:** Humpback whale, date and denomination at right **Rev. Designer:** Sheldon Beveridge

Date	Mintage		
1998	—	PF60	17.00

KM# 320 50 CENTS
9.34 g., 0.925 Silver, 0.28 oz. ASW **Obv.** Crowned head right **Rev:** Beluga whales, date and denomination at right **Rev. Designer:** Cosme Saffioti

Date	Mintage		
1998	—	PF60	17.00

KM# 321 50 CENTS
9.34 g., 0.925 Silver, 0.28 oz. ASW 27mm. **Obv.** Crowned head right **Rev:** Blue whale, date and denomination at right **Rev. Designer:** Stan Witten

Date	Mintage		
1998	—	PF60	17.00

KM# 327 50 CENTS
9.34 g., 0.925 Silver, 0.28 oz. ASW **Subject:** 110 Years Canadian Soccer **Obv.** Crowned head right **Rev:** Soccer players, dates above, denomination at right **Rev. Designer:** Stan Witten

Date	Mintage	
1998	—	PF60 13.00

KM# 314 50 CENTS
9.34 g., 0.925 Silver, 0.28 oz. ASW **Subject:** 110 Years Canadian Speed and Figure Skating **Obv.** Crowned head right **Rev:** Speed skaters, dates below, denomination above **Rev. Designer:** Sheldon Beveridge

Date	Mintage	
1998	—	PF60 13.00

KM# 315 50 CENTS
9.34 g., 0.925 Silver, 0.28 oz. ASW **Subject:** 100 Years Canadian Ski Racing **Obv.** Crowned head right **Rev:** Skiers, dates below, denomination upper left **Rev. Designer:** Ago Aarand

Date	Mintage	
1998	—	PF60 13.00

KM# 328 50 CENTS
9.34 g., 0.925 Silver, 0.28 oz. ASW **Subject:** 20 Years Canadian Auto Racing **Obv.** Crowned head right **Rev:** Race car divides date and denomination **Rev. Designer:** Cosme Saffioti

Date	Mintage	
1998	—	PF60 13.00

KM# 290b 50 CENTS
6.90 g., Nickel Plated Steel, 27.13mm. **Obv.** Crowned head right **Obv. Designer:** Dora dePedery-Hunt **Rev:** Redesigned arms **Rev. Designer:** Cathy Bursey-Sabourin **Edge:** Reeded

Date	Mintage	MS63
1999 P	Est. 20000	15.00
2000 P	Est. 50	3,500
Note: Available only in RCM presentation coin clocks		
2001 P	389,000	1.50
2003 P	—	5.00

KM# 333 50 CENTS
9.34 g., 0.925 Silver, 0.28 oz. ASW **Subject:** 1904 Canadian Open **Obv.** Crowned head right **Rev:** Golfers, date at right, denomination below **Rev. Designer:** William Woodruff

Date	Mintage	
1999	—	PF60 15.00

KM# 334 50 CENTS
9.34 g., 0.925 Silver, 0.28 oz. ASW **Subject:** First U.S.-Canadian Yacht Race **Obv.** Crowned head right **Rev:** Yachts, dates at left, denomination below **Rev. Designer:** Stan Witten

Date	Mintage	
1999	—	PF60 13.00

KM# 335 50 CENTS
9.34 g., 0.925 Silver, 0.28 oz. ASW **Obv.** Crowned head right **Rev:** Cymric cat, date below, denomination at bottom **Series:** Canadian Cats **Rev. Designer:** Susan Taylor

Date	Mintage	
1999	—	PF60 35.00

50 CENTS

KM# 336   50 CENTS
9.34 g., 0.925 Silver, 0.28 oz. ASW **Obv.** Crowned head right **Rev:** Tonkinese cat, date below, denomination at bottom **Series:** Canadian Cats **Rev. Designer:** Susan Taylor

Date	Mintage		
1999	—	PF60	35.00

KM# 337   50 CENTS
9.34 g., 0.925 Silver, 0.28 oz. ASW **Obv.** Crowned head right **Rev:** Cougar, date and denomination below **Series:** Canadian Cats **Rev. Designer:** Susan Taylor

Date	Mintage		
1999	—	PF60	35.00

KM# 338   50 CENTS
9.34 g., 0.925 Silver, 0.28 oz. ASW **Obv.** Crowned head right **Rev:** Lynx, date and denomination below **Series:** Canadian Cats **Rev. Designer:** Susan Taylor

Date	Mintage		
1999	—	PF60	35.00

KM# 371   50 CENTS
9.36 g., 0.925 Silver, 0.28 oz. ASW 27.1mm. **Subject:** Basketball **Obv.** Crowned head right **Rev:** Basketball players **Rev. Designer:** Sheldon Beveridge **Edge:** Reeded

Date	Mintage		
1999	—	PF60	11.00

KM# 372   50 CENTS
9.36 g., 0.925 Silver, 0.28 oz. ASW 27.1mm. **Obv.** Crowned head right **Rev:** Football players **Rev. Designer:** Cosme Saffioti **Edge:** Reeded

Date	Mintage		
1999	—	PF60	12.00

KM# 389   50 CENTS
9.35 g., 0.925 Silver, 0.28 oz. ASW **Obv.** Crowned head right **Rev:** Great horned owl, facing, date and denomination at right **Rev. Designer:** Susan Taylor

Date	Mintage		
2000	—	PF60	20.00

KM# 390   50 CENTS
9.35 g., 0.925 Silver, 0.28 oz. ASW **Obv.** Crowned head right **Rev:** Red-tailed hawk, dates and denomination at right

Date	Mintage		
2000	—	PF60	20.00

KM# 391   50 CENTS
9.35 g., 0.925 Silver, 0.28 oz. ASW **Obv.** Crowned head right **Rev:** Osprey, dates and denomination at right **Rev. Designer:** Susan Taylor

Date	Mintage		
2000	—	PF60	20.00

KM# 392   50 CENTS
9.35 g., 0.925 Silver, 0.28 oz. ASW **Obv.** Crowned head right **Rev:** Bald eagle, dates and denomination at right **Rev. Designer:** William Woodruff

Date	Mintage		
2000	—	PF60	20.00

KM# 393   50 CENTS
9.35 g., 0.925 Silver, 0.28 oz. ASW **Subject:** Steeplechase **Obv.** Crowned head right **Rev:** Steeplechase, dates and denomination below **Rev. Designer:** Susan Taylor

Date	Mintage		
1840-2000	—	PF60	12.00

KM# 394 50 CENTS
9.35 g., 0.925 Silver, 0.28 oz. ASW **Subject:** Bowling **Obv.** Crowned head right **Rev. Designer:** William Woodruff

Date	Mintage		
2000	—	**PF60** 12.00	

KM# 385 50 CENTS
9.35 g., 0.925 Silver, 0.28 oz. ASW **Subject:** Ice Hockey **Obv.** Crowned head right **Rev:** 4 hockey players **Rev. Designer:** Stanley Witten

Date	Mintage		
2000	—	**PF60** 12.00	

KM# 386 50 CENTS
9.35 g., 0.925 Silver, 0.28 oz. ASW **Subject:** Curling **Obv.** Crowned head right **Rev:** Motion study of curlers, dates and denomination below **Rev. Designer:** Cosme Saffioti

Date	Mintage		
1910-2000	—	**PF60** 12.00	

KM# 420 50 CENTS
9.30 g., 0.925 Silver, 0.27 oz. ASW 27.13mm. **Obv.** Crowned head right **Rev:** Snowman and Chateau Frontenac **Series:** Festivals - Quebec **Rev. Designer:** Sylvie Daigneault **Edge:** Reeded

Date	Mintage		
2001	58,123	**PF63** 7.50	**PF65** 8.50

KM# 421 50 CENTS
9.30 g., 0.925 Silver, 0.27 oz. ASW 27.13mm. **Obv.** Crowned head right **Rev:** Dancer, dog sled and snowmobiles **Series:** Festivals - Nunavut **Rev. Designer:** John Mardon **Edge:** Reeded

Date	Mintage		
2001	—	**PF63** 7.50	**PF65** 8.50

KM# 422 50 CENTS
9.30 g., 0.925 Silver, 0.27 oz. ASW 27.13mm. **Obv.** Crowned head right **Rev:** Sailor and musical people **Series:** Festivals - Newfoundland **Rev. Designer:** David Craig **Edge:** Reeded

Date	Mintage		
2001	58,123	**PF63** 7.50	**PF65** 8.50

KM# 423 50 CENTS
9.30 g., 0.925 Silver, 0.27 oz. ASW 27.13mm. **Obv.** Crowned head right **Rev:** Family, juggler and building **Series:** Festivals - Prince Edward Island **Rev. Designer:** Brenda Whiteway **Edge:** Reeded

Date	Mintage		
2001	58,123	**PF63** 7.50	**PF65** 8.50

KM# 424 50 CENTS
9.30 g., 0.925 Silver, 0.27 oz. ASW 27.13mm. **Obv.** Crowned head right **Rev:** Family scene **Series:** Folklore - The Sled **Rev. Designer:** Valentina Hotz-Entin **Edge:** Reeded

Date	Mintage		
2001	28,979	**PF63** 8.00	**PF65** 9.00

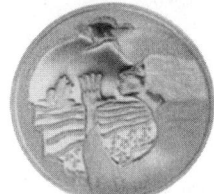

KM# 425 50 CENTS
9.30 g., 0.925 Silver, 0.27 oz. ASW 27.13mm. **Obv.** Crowned head right **Rev:** Woman shouting **Series:** Folklore - The Maiden's Cave **Rev. Designer:** Peter Kiss **Edge:** Reeded

Date	Mintage		
2001	28,979	**PF63** 8.00	**PF65** 9.00

KM# 426 50 CENTS
9.30 g., 0.925 Silver, 0.27 oz. ASW 27.13mm. **Obv.** Crowned head right **Rev:** Jumping children on seashore **Series:** Folklore - The Small Jumpers **Rev. Designer:** Miynki Tanobe **Edge:** Reeded

Date	Mintage		
2001	28,979	**PF63** 8.00	**PF65** 9.00

50 CENTS

KM# 509 50 CENTS
6.90 g., Nickel Plated Steel, 27.13mm. **Obv.** Crowned head right **Rev:** National arms **Edge:** Reeded

Date	Mintage	MS63
2001 P	—	1.50

KM# 459 50 CENTS
9.30 g., 0.925 Silver, 0.27 oz. ASW 27.13mm. **Obv.** Crowned head right **Rev:** The Shoemaker in Heaven **Series:** Folklore and Legends **Rev. Designer:** Francine Gravel

Date	Mintage		
2002	19,267	PF63 10.00	PF65 11.00

KM# 460 50 CENTS
9.30 g., 0.925 Silver, 0.27 oz. ASW 27.13mm. **Subject:** The Ghost Ship **Obv.** Crowned head right **Series:** Folklore and Legends **Rev. Designer:** Colette Boivin

Date	Mintage		
2002	19,267	PF63 10.00	PF65 11.00

KM# 461 50 CENTS
9.30 g., 0.925 Silver, 0.27 oz. ASW 27.13mm. **Subject:** The Pig That Wouldn't Get Over the Stile **Obv.** Crowned head right **Series:** Folklore and Legends **Rev. Designer:** Laura Jolicoeur

Date	Mintage		
2002	19,267	PF63 10.00	PF65 11.00

KM# 444 50 CENTS
6.90 g., Nickel Plated Steel, 27.13mm. **Subject:** Queen's Golden Jubilee **Obv.** Coronation crowned head right and monogram **Rev:** Canadian arms **Rev. Designer:** Bursey Sabourin **Edge:** Reeded

Date	Mintage	MS63
1952-2002P	14,440,000	2.50

KM# 444a 50 CENTS
9.30 g., 0.925 Silver, 0.27 oz. ASW 27.13mm. **Subject:** Elizabeth II Golden Jubilee **Obv.** Crowned head right, Jubilee commemorative dates 1952-2002

Date	Mintage		
1952-2002	100,000	PF63 15.00	PF65 17.50

KM# 444b 50 CENTS
9.30 g., 0.925 Silver Gilt, 0.27 oz. 27.13mm. **Subject:** Queen's Golden Jubilee **Obv.** Crowned head right and monogram **Rev:** Canadian arms **Edge:** Reeded **Note:** Special 24 karat gold-plated issue of KM#444.

Date	Mintage		
1952-2002	32,642	PF63 30.00	PF65 35.00

KM# 454 50 CENTS
9.30 g., 0.925 Silver, 0.27 oz. ASW 27.13mm. **Subject:** Nova Scotia Annapolis Valley Apple Blossom Festival **Obv.** Crowned head right **Rev. Designer:** Bonnie Ross

Date	Mintage		
2002	59,998	PF63 7.50	PF65 9.50

KM# 455 50 CENTS
9.30 g., 0.925 Silver, 0.27 oz. ASW 27.13mm. **Subject:** Stratford Festival **Obv.** Crowned head right **Rev:** Couple with building in background **Rev. Designer:** Laurie McGaw

Date	Mintage		
2002	59,998	PF63 7.50	PF65 9.50

KM# 456 50 CENTS
9.30 g., 0.925 Silver, 0.27 oz. ASW 27.13mm. **Subject:** Folklorama **Obv.** Crowned head right **Rev. Designer:** William Woodruff

Date	Mintage		
2002	59,998	PF63 7.50	PF65 9.50

KM# 457 50 CENTS
9.30 g., 0.925 Silver, 0.27 oz. ASW 27.13mm. **Subject:** Calgary Stampede **Obv.** Crowned head right **Rev. Designer:** Stan Witten

Date	Mintage		
2002	59,998	PF63 7.50	PF65 9.50

KM# 458 50 CENTS
9.30 g., 0.925 Silver, 0.27 oz. ASW 27.13mm. **Subject:** Squamish Days Logger Sports **Obv.** Crowned head right **Rev. Designer:** Jose Osio

Date	Mintage		
2002	59,998	PF63 7.50	PF65 9.50

KM# 472 50 CENTS
11.62 g., 0.925 Silver, 0.34 oz. ASW 27.13mm. **Subject:** 50th Anniversary of the Coronation of Elizabeth II **Obv.** Crowned head right, Jubilee commemorative dates 1952-2002 **Obv. Designer:** Mary Gillick

Date	Mintage		
2003	30,000	PF63 12.00	PF65 15.00

KM# 475 50 CENTS
9.30 g., 0.925 Silver, 0.27 oz. ASW 27.13mm. **Obv.** Crowned head right **Obv. Designer:** Dora dePédery-Hunt **Rev:** Golden daffodil **Rev. Designer:** Christie Paquet, Stan Witten

Date	Mintage		
2003	36,293	PF63 20.00	PF65 25.00

KM# 476 50 CENTS
9.30 g., 0.925 Silver, 0.27 oz. ASW 27.13mm. **Subject:** Yukon International Storytelling Festival **Obv.** Crowned head right **Obv. Designer:** Dora dePédery-Hunt **Rev. Designer:** Ken Anderson, Jose Oslo

Date	Mintage		
2003	—	PF63 10.00	PF65 11.00

KM# 477 50 CENTS
9.30 g., 0.925 Silver, 0.27 oz. ASW 27.13mm. **Subject:** Festival Acadien de Caraquet **Obv.** Crowned head right **Obv. Designer:** Dora dePédery-Hunt **Rev:** Sailboat and couple **Rev. Designer:** Susan Taylor, Hudson Design Group

Date	Mintage		
2003	—	PF63 10.00	PF65 11.00

KM# 478 50 CENTS
9.30 g., 0.925 Silver, 0.27 oz. ASW 27.13mm. **Subject:** Back to Batoche **Obv.** Crowned head right **Obv. Designer:** Dora dePédery-Hunt **Rev. Designer:** David Hannan, Stan Witten

Date	Mintage		
2003	—	PF63 10.00	PF65 11.00

KM# 479 50 CENTS
9.30 g., 0.925 Silver, 0.27 oz. ASW 27.13mm. **Subject:** Great Northern Arts Festival **Obv.** Crowned head right **Obv. Designer:** Dora dePédery-Hunt **Rev. Designer:** Dawn Oman, Susan Taylor

Date	Mintage		
2003	—	PF63 10.00	PF65 11.00

KM# 494 50 CENTS
6.90 g., Nickel Plated Steel, 27.13mm. **Obv.** Crowned head right **Obv. Designer:** Susanna Blunt **Rev:** National arms **Rev. Designer:** Cathy Bursey-Sabourin **Edge:** Reeded

Date	Mintage			MS63
2003P W	—			5.00
2003P W	—	PF63 6.50	PF65 7.50	
2004P	—			5.00
2004P	—	PF63 6.50	PF65 7.50	
2005P	200,000			1.50
2005P	—	PF63 4.00	PF65 5.00	
2006P	98,000			1.50
2006P	—	PF63 4.00	PF65 5.00	
2007(ml)	250,000			1.50
2007(ml)	—	PF63 4.00	PF65 5.00	
2008(ml)	211,000			1.50
2008(ml)	—	PF63 4.00	PF65 5.00	
2009(ml)	150,000			1.50
2009(ml)	—	PF63 4.00	PF65 5.00	
2010(ml)	—			1.50
2010(ml)	—	PF63 4.00	PF65 5.00	
2011(ml)	—			1.50
2011(ml)	—	PF63 4.00	PF65 5.00	
2012(ml)	—			1.50
2012(ml)	—	PF63 4.00	PF65 5.00	
2013(ml)	—			1.50
2013(ml)	—	PF63 4.00	PF65 5.00	

KM# 494a 50 CENTS
9.30 g., 0.925 Silver, 0.27 oz. ASW 27.13mm. **Obv.** Crowned head right **Obv. Designer:** Susanna Blunt **Rev:** Canadian coat of arms **Edge:** Reeded

Date	Mintage		
2004	—	PF63 6.00	PF65 7.50

KM# 526 50 CENTS
1.27 g., 0.9999 Gold, 0.04 oz. AGW 14mm. **Subject:** Moose **Obv.** Head right **Rev:** Moose head facing right

Date	Mintage	
2004	—	PF65 85.00

KM# 606 50 CENTS
9.30 g., 0.925 Silver, 0.27 oz. ASW 27.13mm. **Obv.** Head right **Obv. Designer:** Susanna Blunt **Rev:** Clouded Sulphur Butterfly, hologram **Rev. Designer:** Susan Taylor

Date	Mintage		
2004	15,281	PF63 40.00	PF65 45.00

KM# 712 50 CENTS
9.30 g., 0.925 Silver, 0.27 oz. ASW 27.13mm. **Rev:** Hologram of Tiger Swallowtail butterfly

Date	Mintage		
2004	20,462	PF63 42.00	PF65 45.00

KM# 536 50 CENTS
9.30 g., 0.925 Silver, 0.27 oz. ASW 27.13mm. **Subject:** Golden rose **Obv.** Head right **Obv. Designer:** Susanna Blunt **Rev. Designer:** Christie Paquet

Date	Mintage		
2005	17,418	PF63 35.00	PF65 40.00

KM# 537 50 CENTS
9.30 g., 0.925 Silver, 0.27 oz. ASW 27.13mm. **Obv.** Head right **Obv. Designer:** Susanna Blunt **Rev:** Great Spangled Fritillary butterfly, hologram **Rev. Designer:** Jianping Yan

Date	Mintage		
2005	20,000	PF63 45.00	PF65 50.00

KM# 538 50 CENTS
9.30 g., 0.925 Silver, 0.27 oz. ASW 27.13mm. **Subject:** Toronto Maple Leafs **Obv.** Head right **Obv. Designer:** Susanna Blunt **Rev:** Darryl Sittler

Date	Mintage	
2005 Specimen	25,000	PF65 16.00

KM# 539 50 CENTS
9.30 g., 0.925 Silver, 0.27 oz. ASW 27.13mm. **Subject:** Toronto Maple Leafs **Obv.** Head right **Obv. Designer:** Susanna Blunt **Rev:** Dave Keon

Date	Mintage	
2005 Specimen	25,000	PF65 16.00

KM# 540 50 CENTS
9.30 g., 0.925 Silver, 0.27 oz. ASW 27.13mm. **Subject:** Toronto Maple Leafs **Obv.** Head right **Obv. Designer:** Susanna Blunt **Rev:** Jonny Bover, goalie

Date	Mintage		
2005 Specimen	25,000	PF65 16.00	

KM# 541 50 CENTS
9.30 g., 0.925 Silver, 0.27 oz. ASW 27.13mm. **Subject:** Toronto Maple Leafs **Obv.** Head right **Obv. Designer:** Susanna Blunt **Rev:** Tim Horton

Date	Mintage		
2005 Specimen	25,000	PF65 16.00	

KM# 543 50 CENTS
9.30 g., 0.925 Silver, 0.27 oz. ASW **Subject:** WWII - Battle of Britain **Obv.** Head right **Rev:** Fighter plane in sky

Date	Mintage		
2005 Specimen	20,000	PF63 20.00	PF65 22.50

KM# 544 50 CENTS
9.30 g., 0.925 Silver, 0.27 oz. ASW 27.13mm. **Subject:** WWII - Battle of Scheldt **Obv.** Head right **Obv. Designer:** Susanna Blunt **Rev:** Four soldiers walking down road **Rev. Designer:** Peter Mossman

Date	Mintage	
2005 Specimen	20,000	PF65 19.00

KM# 545 50 CENTS
9.30 g., 0.925 Silver, 0.27 oz. ASW 27.13mm. **Subject:** WWII - Battle of the Atlantic **Obv.** Head right **Obv. Designer:** Susanna Blunt **Rev:** Merchant ship sinking **Rev. Designer:** Peter Mossman

Date	Mintage	
2005 Specimen	20,000	PF65 19.00

KM# 546 50 CENTS
9.30 g., 0.925 Silver, 0.27 oz. ASW 27.13mm. **Subject:** WWII - Conquest of Sicily **Obv.** Head right **Obv. Designer:** Susanna Blunt **Rev:** Tank among town ruins **Rev. Designer:** Peter Mossman

Date	Mintage	
2005 Specimen	20,000	PF65 19.00

KM# 547 50 CENTS
9.30 g., 0.925 Silver, 0.27 oz. ASW 27.13mm. **Subject:** WWII - Liberation of the Netherlands **Obv.** Head right **Obv. Designer:** Susanna Blunt **Rev:** Soldiers in parade, one holding flag **Rev. Designer:** Peter Mossman

Date	Mintage	
2005 Specimen	20,000	PF65 19.00

KM# 548 50 CENTS
9.30 g., 0.925 Silver, 0.27 oz. ASW 27.13mm. **Subject:** WWII - Raid of Dieppe **Obv.** Head right **Obv. Designer:** Susanna Blunt **Rev:** Three soldiers exiting landing craft **Rev. Designer:** Peter Mossman

Date	Mintage	
2005 Specimen	20,000	PF65 19.00

KM# 577 50 CENTS
9.30 g., 0.925 Silver, 0.27 oz. ASW 27.13mm. **Subject:** Montreal Canadiens **Obv.** Head right **Obv. Designer:** Susanna Blunt **Rev:** Guy LaFleur

Date	Mintage	
2005 Specimen	25,000	PF65 17.50

KM# 578 50 CENTS
9.30 g., 0.925 Silver, 0.27 oz. ASW 27.13mm. **Subject:** Montreal Canadiens **Obv.** Head right **Obv. Designer:** Susanna Blunt **Rev:** Jaque Plante

Date	Mintage	
2005 Specimen	25,000	PF65 17.50

KM# 579 50 CENTS
9.30 g., 0.925 Silver, 0.27 oz. ASW 27.13mm. **Subject:** Montreal Canadiens **Obv.** Head right **Obv. Designer:** Susanna Blunt **Rev:** Jean Beliveau

Date	Mintage	
2005 Specimen	25,000	PF65 17.50

KM# 580 50 CENTS
9.30 g., 0.925 Silver, 0.27 oz. ASW 27.13mm. **Subject:** Montreal Canadiens **Obv.** Head right **Obv. Designer:** Susanna Blunt **Rev:** Maurice Richard

Date	Mintage	
2005 Specimen	25,000	PF65 17.50

KM# 599 50 CENTS
9.30 g., 0.925 Silver, 0.27 oz. ASW 27.13mm. **Obv.** Head right **Obv. Designer:** Susanna Blunt **Rev:** Monarch butterfly, colorized **Rev. Designer:** Susan Taylor

Date	Mintage		
2005	20,000	PF63 45.00	PF65 50.00

KM# 494b 50 CENTS
6.90 g., Nickel Plated Steel, 27.13mm. **Rev:** State Arms, gilt **Note:** Housed in Mint Annual Report

Date	Mintage	MS63
2006	—	15.00

KM# 648 50 CENTS
9.30 g., 0.925 Silver, 0.27 oz. ASW **Subject:** Golden Daisy **Obv.** Head right

Date	Mintage		
2006	18,190	PF63 27.00	PF65 30.00

KM# 649 50 CENTS
9.30 g., 0.925 Silver, 0.27 oz. ASW 27.13mm. **Subject:** Short-tailed swallowtail **Obv.** Head right **Rev:** Colorized butterfly

Date	Mintage		
2006	24,568	PF63 42.00	PF65 45.00

KM# 650 50 CENTS
9.30 g., 0.925 Silver, 0.27 oz. ASW 27.13mm. **Obv.** Head right **Rev:** Butterfly, silvery blue hologram

Date	Mintage		
2006	16,000	PF63 42.00	PF65 45.00

KM# 651 50 CENTS
9.30 g., 0.925 Silver, 0.27 oz. ASW **Subject:** Cowboy **Obv.** Head right

Date	Mintage	MS63
2006	—	17.50

KM# 716 50 CENTS
9.30 g., 0.925 Silver, 0.27 oz. ASW **Rev:** Multicolor holiday ornaments

Date	Mintage	MS63
2006	16,989	17.50

KM# 715 50 CENTS
9.30 g., 0.925 Silver, 0.27 oz. ASW 27.12mm. **Rev:** Forget-me-not flower

Date	Mintage		
2007	22,882	PF63 35.00	PF65 40.00

KM# 778 50 CENTS
20.00 g., 0.925 Silver, 0.59 oz. ASW 34.06mm. **Subject:** Milk delivery **Obv.** Bust right **Rev:** Cow head and milk can **Shape:** Triangle

Date	Mintage		
2008	24,448	PF63 25.00	PF65 35.00

KM# 779 50 CENTS
9.30 g., 0.925 Silver, 0.27 oz. ASW 35mm. **Rev:** Multicolor snowman

Date	Mintage	MS63
2008	21,679	17.50

KM# 780 50 CENTS
9.30 g., 0.925 Silver, 0.27 oz. ASW 29.72mm. **Subject:** Ottawa Mint Centennial 1908-2008 **Obv.** Edward bust right **Rev:** Crowned value and dates within wreath

Date	Mintage	
2008	3,248	PF65 20.00

KM# 845 50 CENTS
9.30 g., 0.925 Silver, 0.27 oz. ASW 27.13mm. **Rev:** Calgary Flames lenticular design, old and new logos

Date	Mintage	MS63
2009	—	12.00

KM# 846 50 CENTS
9.30 g., 0.925 Silver, 0.27 oz. ASW 27.13mm. **Rev:** Edmonton Oiler's lenticular design, old and new logos

Date	Mintage	MS63
2009	—	12.00

KM# 847 50 CENTS
9.30 g., 0.925 Silver, 0.27 oz. ASW 27.13mm. **Rev:** Montreal Canadiens lenticular design, old and new logos

Date	Mintage	MS63
2009	—	12.00

KM# 848   50 CENTS
9.30 g.,   0.925 Silver, 0.27 oz. ASW 27.13mm.   **Rev:**
Ottawa Senators lenticular design, old and new logos

Date	Mintage	MS63
2009	—	12.00

KM# 849   50 CENTS
9.30 g.,   0.925 Silver, 0.27 oz. ASW 27.13mm.   **Rev:**
Toronto Maple Leafs lenticular design, old and new logos

Date	Mintage	MS63
2009	—	12.00

KM# 850   50 CENTS
9.30 g.,   0.925 Silver, 0.27 oz. ASW 27.13mm.   **Rev:**
Vancouver Canucks lenticular design, old and new logos

Date	Mintage	MS63
2009	—	12.00

KM# 857   50 CENTS
6.90 g., Nickel Plated Steel, 35mm. **Rev:** Calgary Flames
lenticular old and new logos

Date	Mintage	MS63
2009	—	25.00

KM# 858   50 CENTS
6.90 g., Nickel Plated Steel, 35mm. **Rev:** Edmonton Oilers
lenticular old and new logos

Date	Mintage	MS63
2009	—	25.00

KM# 859   50 CENTS
35.00 g., Nickel Plated Steel, 35mm.   **Rev:** Montreal
Canadians lenticular old and new logo

Date	Mintage	MS63
2009	—	25.00

KM# 860   50 CENTS
6.90 g., Nickel Plated Steel, 35mm. **Rev:** Ottawa Senators
lenticular old and new logos

Date	Mintage	MS63
2009	—	25.00

KM# 861   50 CENTS
6.90 g., Nickel Plated Steel, 35mm. **Rev:** Toronto Maple
Leafs lenticular old and new logos

Date	Mintage	MS63
2009	—	25.00

KM# 862   50 CENTS
6.90 g., Nickel Plated Steel, 35mm.   **Rev:** Vancouver
Canucks lenticular old and new logos

Date	Mintage	MS63
2009	—	25.00

KM# 887   50 CENTS
19.10 g., Copper-Nickel, 34.06mm.   **Subject:** Six-string
national guitar **Obv.** Bust right **Obv. Designer:** Susanna
Blunt **Rev:** Hologram with 6 "strings **Obv. Legend:**
Elizabeth II DG Regina **Rev. Legend:** 50 CENTS Canada
Shape: Triangle

Date	Mintage		MS63
2009	13,602	PF63 45.00 PF65 50.00	

KM# 936   50 CENTS
9.30 g., Nickel, **Rev:** Vancouver Canucks goalie jersey

Date	Mintage	MS63
2009	3,563	15.00

KM# 937   50 CENTS
6.90 g., Nickel Plated Steel, 35mm. **Rev:** Calgary Flames
player - colorized

Date	Mintage	MS63
2009	3,518	15.00

KM# 938   50 CENTS
6.90 g., Nickel Plated Steel, 35mm. **Rev:** Edmonton Oilers
player

Date	Mintage	MS63
2009	3,562	15.00

KM# 939   50 CENTS
6.90 g., Nickel Plated Steel, 35mm. **Rev:** Toronto Maple
Leafs player

Date	Mintage	MS63
2009	5,918	15.00

KM# 940   50 CENTS
6.90 g., Nickel Plated Steel, 35mm.   **Rev:** Montreal
Canadiens player

Date	Mintage	MS63
2009	9,865	15.00

KM# 941   50 CENTS
6.90 g., Nickel Plated Steel, 35mm. **Rev:** Ottawa Senators
player

Date	Mintage	MS63
2009	3,293	15.00

KM# 1035   50 CENTS
12.61 g., Brass Plated Steel, 35mm. **Subject:** Christmas
toy train **Rev:** movement from far to close

Date	Mintage	MS63
2009	19,103	17.50

50 CENTS

KM# 961 50 CENTS
6.90 g., Nickel Plated Steel, 35mm. **Rev:** Bob sleigh

Date	Mintage	MS63
2010	—	12.00

KM# 961a 50 CENTS
6.90 g., Nickel Plated Steel, 35mm. **Rev:** Bob sleigh - red enamel

Date	Mintage	MS63
2010	—	12.00

KM# 962 50 CENTS
6.90 g., Nickel Plated Steel, 35mm. **Rev:** Speed skating

Date	Mintage	MS63
2010	—	12.00

KM# 962a 50 CENTS
6.90 g., Nickel Plated Steel, 35mm. **Rev:** Speed skating - red enamel

Date	Mintage	MS63
2010	—	12.00

KM# 963 50 CENTS
6.90 g., Nickel Plated Steel, 35mm. **Rev:** Migaand Quatchi in bob sleigh

Date	Mintage	MS63
2010	2,119	12.00

KM# 964 50 CENTS
6.90 g., Nickel Plated Steel, 35mm. **Rev:** Miga in hockey

Date	Mintage	MS63
2010	5,275	12.00

KM# 965 50 CENTS
6.90 g., Nickel Plated Steel, 35mm. **Rev:** Quatchi in ice hockey

Date	Mintage	MS63
2010	5,614	12.00

KM# 966 50 CENTS
6.90 g., Nickel Plated Steel, 35mm. **Rev:** Sumi Para Sledge

Date	Mintage	MS63
2010	3,707	12.00

KM# 967 50 CENTS
6.90 g., Nickel Plated Steel, 35mm. **Rev:** Miga and Quatchi Figure-skating **Edge:** Reeded

Date	Mintage	MS63
2010	2,981	12.00

KM# 968 50 CENTS
6.90 g., Nickel Plated Steel, 35mm. **Rev:** Free-style mascot

Date	Mintage	MS63
2010	2,114	12.00

KM# 969 50 CENTS
6.90 g., Nickel Plated Steel, 35mm. **Rev:** Skeleton mascot

Date	Mintage	MS63
2010	1,672	12.00

KM# 970 50 CENTS
6.90 g., Nickel Plated Steel, 35mm. **Rev:** Parallel giant slalom mascot

Date	Mintage	MS63
2010	1,730	12.00

KM# 971 50 CENTS
6.90 g., Nickel Plated Steel, 35mm. **Rev:** Alpine skiing mascot

Date	Mintage	MS63
2010	2,309	12.00

KM# 972 50 CENTS
6.90 g., Nickel Plated Steel, 35mm. **Rev:** Para Olympic alpine skiing mascott

Date	Mintage	MS63
2010	1,902	12.00

KM# 973 50 CENTS
6.90 g., Nickel Plated Steel, 35mm. **Rev:** Snowboard mascot

Date	Mintage	MS63
2010	2,090	12.00

KM# 974 50 CENTS
6.90 g., Nickel Plated Steel, 35mm. **Rev:** Speed-skating mascott

Date	Mintage	MS63
2010	1,825	12.00

50 CENTS

KM# 986 50 CENTS
12.61 g., Brass Plated Steel, 35mm. **Rev:** Dasplerosaurus
Torosus - 3-D lenticular movement

Date	Mintage	MS63
2010	—	20.00

KM# 1015 50 CENTS
12.61 g., Brass Plated Steel, 35mm. **Rev:** Sinosauropteryx

Date	Mintage	MS63
2010	—	20.00

KM# 1016 50 CENTS
12.61 g., Brass Plated Steel, 35mm. **Rev:** Albertosaurus

Date	Mintage	MS63
2010	—	20.00

KM# 1043 50 CENTS
Nickel Plated Steel, 34mm. **Rev:** Santa Claus transforms
into Rudolf the red-nosed reindeer

Date	Mintage	MS63
2010	—	17.50

KM# 1157 50 CENTS
11.62 g., 0.925 Silver, 0.34 oz. ASW 29.72mm. **Obv.**
George V bust **Rev:** Value within wreath

Date	Mintage		
1911-2011	6,000	PF63 40.00	PF65 45.00

KM# 1180 50 CENTS
6.90 g., Nickel Plated Steel, 27.13mm. **Obv.** Bust right
Rev: Winnipeg Jets Logo, jet over maple leaf **Edge:**
Reeded

Date	Mintage	MS63
2011	—	15.00

KM# 1191 50 CENTS
12.61 g., Copper Plated Steel, 35mm. **Obv.** Bust right
Rev: Santa Claus checking list, and in sled over house

Date	Mintage	MS63
2011	—	27.50

KM# 1202 50 CENTS
1.27 g., 0.9999 Gold, 0.04 oz. AGW 13.92mm. **Rev:**
Wood Bison **Rev. Designer:** Corrine Hunt **Edge:** Reeded

Date	Mintage		
2011	Est. 2500	PF63 95.00	PF65 100

KM# 1204 50 CENTS
1.27 g., 0.9999 Gold, 0.04 oz. AGW 13.92mm. **Subject:**
Boreal Forest **Rev:** Bird and tree **Rev. Designer:** Corrine
Hunt **Edge:** Reeded

Date	Mintage		
2011	Est. 2500	PF63 95.00	PF65 100

KM# 1206 50 CENTS
1.27 g., 0.9999 Gold, 0.04 oz. AGW 13.92mm. **Rev:**
Peregrine Falcon perched on branch **Rev. Designer:**
Corrine Hunt

Date	Mintage		
2011	Est. 2500	PF63 95.00	PF65 100

KM# 1208 50 CENTS
1.27 g., 0.9999 Gold, 0.04 oz. AGW 13.92mm. **Rev:** Orca
Whale **Rev. Designer:** Corrine Hunt **Edge:** Reeded

Date	Mintage		
2011	Est. 2500	PF63 95.00	PF65 100

KM# 1234 50 CENTS
12.61 g., Nickel Plated Steel, 35mm. **Subject:** Titanic,
100th Anniversary **Obv.** Bust right **Rev:** Titanic sailing
forward towards iceberg, colored sea

Date	Mintage	
2012	—	PF65 65.00

KM# 1264 50 CENTS
GOLD RUSH 1.27 g., 0.999 Gold, 0.04 oz. AGW **Ruler:**
Elizabeth II 13.92mm. **Mint:** Royal Canadian Mint

Date	Mintage		
2012	—	PF63 90.00	PF65 100

KM# 1293 50 CENTS
9.30 g., 0.925 Silver, 0.27 oz. ASW 27.13mm. **Subject:**
Elizabeth II Diamond Jubilee **Rev:** Crowned monogram
within wreath in color

Date	Mintage	MS63
2012	—	30.00

KM# 1444 50 CENTS
12.51 g., Copper-Nickel, 35mm. **Subject:** 75th
Anniversary of Superman **Rev:** Superman lenticular
background - then and now **Rev. Designer:** Joe Shuster
and Jim Lee, DC Comics

Date	Mintage		
2013	—	PF63 25.00	PF65 30.00

KM# 1493 50 CENTS
1.27 g., 0.9999 Gold, 0.04 oz. AGW 13.92mm. **Rev:**
Starfish **Rev. Designer:** Emily Damstra

Date	Mintage		
2013	10,000	PF63 120	PF65 130

KM# 1496 50 CENTS
1.27 g., 0.9999 Gold, 0.04 oz. AGW 13.92mm. **Subject:**
Louisbourg, 300th Anniversary **Rev:** Ship, fort gate and
fish

Date	Mintage		
2013	1,000	PF63 120	PF65 130

KM# 1584 50 CENTS
1.27 g., 0.999 Gold, 0.04 oz. AGW 13.92mm. **Obv.** Bust
right **Rev:** Beaver left from 5 Cent coin

Date	Mintage		
2014	—	PF63 80.00	PF65 90.00

KM# 1585 50 CENTS
Silver Plated 35mm. **Subject:** 100 Blessings of Good
Fortune **Obv.** Bust right

Date	Mintage		
2014	—	PF63 45.00	PF65 50.00

KM# 1603 50 CENTS
1.27 g., 0.999 Gold, 0.04 oz. AGW 13.92mm. **Obv.** Bust
right **Rev:** Osprey head

Date	Mintage		
2014	—	PF63 90.00	PF65 100

50 CENTS

KM# 30 DOLLAR
23.33 g., 0.800 Silver, 0.60 oz. ASW 36mm. **Subject:** Silver Jubilee **Obv.** Bust left **Obv. Designer:** Percy Metcalfe **Rev:** Voyager, date and denomination below **Rev. Designer:** Emanuel Hahn

Date	Mintage	F12	VF20	XF40	AU50	MS60	MS63
1935	428,707	23.00	27.00	35.00	40.00	45.00	70.00
1935 Specimen	—	—	—	—	—	—	3,500

KM# 31 DOLLAR
23.33 g., 0.800 Silver, 0.60 oz. ASW 36mm. **Obv.** Crowned bust left **Obv. Designer:** E. B. MacKennal **Rev:** Voyageur, date and denomination below **Rev. Designer:** Emanuel Hahn

Date	Mintage	F12	VF20	XF40	AU50	MS60	MS63
1936	339,600	25.00	28.00	30.00	35.00	50.00	100
1936 Specimen	—	—	—	—	—	—	3,500

Maple leaf

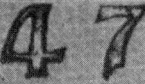 

Blunt 7   Pointed 7

KM# 37 DOLLAR

23.33 g., 0.800 Silver, 0.60 oz. ASW 36mm. **Obv.** Head left **Obv. Designer:** T. H. Paget **Rev:** Voyageur, date and denomination below **Rev. Designer:** Emanuel Hahn

Date	Mintage	F12	VF20	XF40	AU50	MS60	MS63
1937	207,406	25.00	28.00	32.00	40.00	50.00	95.00
1937 Mirror Specimen	1,295	—	—	—	—	—	900
1937 Matte Specimen	—	—	—	—	—	—	350
1938	90,304	35.00	45.00	70.00	85.00	100	250
1938 Specimen	—	—	—	—	—	—	7,000
1945	38,391	125	175	225	300	350	750
1945 Specimen	—	—	—	—	—	—	2,200
1946	93,055	26.00	40.00	55.00	75.00	100	400
1946 Specimen	—	—	—	—	—	—	2,000
1947 Pointed 7	Inc. below	80.00	125	175	225	400	2,000
1947 Pointed 7, Specimen	—	—	—	—	—	—	4,000
1947 Blunt 7	65,595	60.00	90.00	125	150	175	400
1947 Blunt 7, Specimen	—	—	—	—	—	—	5,000
1947 Maple leaf	21,135	150	200	225	300	400	800
1947 Maple leaf, Specimen	—	—	—	—	—	—	2,700

KM# 38 DOLLAR

23.33 g., 0.800 Silver, 0.60 oz. ASW 36mm. **Subject:** Royal Visit **Obv.** Head left **Obv. Designer:** T. H. Paget **Rev:** Tower at center of building, date and denomination below **Rev. Designer:** Emanuel Hahn

Date	Mintage	F12	VF20	XF40	AU50	MS60	MS63
1939	1,363,816	—	—	16.00	20.00	24.00	35.00
1939 Matte specimen	—	—	—	—	—	—	650
1939 Mirror specimen	—	—	—	—	—	—	1,100

KM# 46 DOLLAR

23.33 g., 0.800 Silver, 0.60 oz. ASW 36mm. **Obv.** Head left, modified left legend **Obv. Designer:** T. H. Paget **Rev:** Voyageur, date and denomination below **Rev. Designer:** Emanuel Hahn

Date	Mintage	F12	VF20	XF40	AU50	MS60	MS63
1948	18,780	750	950	1,300	1,400	1,700	3,000
1948 Specimen	—	—	—	—	—	—	4,500
1950	261,002	—	23.00	24.00	25.00	30.00	75.00

Date	Mintage	F12	VF20	XF40	AU50	MS60	MS63
Note: With 3 water lines							
1950 Specimen	—	—	—	—	—	—	1,500
Note: With 3 water lines							
1950 Matte Proof	—	**PF60** 10,000					
Note: With 4 water lines, 1 known							
1950	Inc. above	23.00	28.00	35.00	40.00	55.00	125
Note: Arnprior with 2-1/2 water lines							
1950 Specimen	—	—	—	—	—	—	2,100
Note: Amprior with 2-1/2 water lines							
1951	416,395	—	—	18.00	22.00	25.00	40.00
Note: With 3 water lines							
1951 Specimen	—	—	—	—	—	—	900
Note: With 3 water lines							
1951	Inc. above	40.00	60.00	90.00	125	225	450
Note: Arnprior with 1-1/2 water lines							
1951 Specimen	—	—	—	—	—	—	2,250
Note: Amprior with 1-1/2 water lines							
1952	406,148	—	—	BV	22.00	24.00	35.00
Note: With 3 water lines							
1952 Specimen	—	—	—	—	—	—	1,150
Note: With 3 water lines							
1952	Inc. above	BV	23.00	27.00	35.00	55.00	100
Note: Short water links							
1952 Specimen	—	—	—	—	—	—	1,400
Note: Short water lines							
1952	Inc. above	—	18.00	22.00	24.00	26.00	60.00
Note: Without water lines							
1952 Specimen	—	—	—	—	—	—	1,150
Note: Without water lines							

KM# 47 DOLLAR

23.33 g., 0.800 Silver, 0.60 oz. ASW 36mm. **Subject:** Newfoundland **Obv.** Head left **Obv. Designer:** T. H. Paget **Rev:** "The Matthew", John Cabot's ship, date and denomination below **Rev. Designer:** Thomas Shingles

Date	Mintage	F12	VF20	XF40	AU50	MS60	MS63
1949	672,218	BV	23.00	25.00	27.50	30.00	35.00
1949 Specimen	—	—	—	—	—	—	700
1949	—	**PF60** 2,600					

KM# 54 DOLLAR

23.33 g., 0.800 Silver, 0.60 oz. ASW 36mm. **Obv.** Laureate bust right **Obv. Designer:** Mary Gillick **Rev:** Voyageur, date and denomination below **Rev. Designer:** Emanuel Hahn **Note:** All genuine circulation strike 1955 Arnprior dollars have a die break running along the top of TI in the word GRATIA on the obverse.

Date	Mintage	F12	VF20	XF40	AU50	MS60	MS63
1953	1,074,578	**PF60** 1,600					
Note: Without strap, wire rim							
1953 Specimen	—	—	—	—	—	—	1,300
Note: Without strap, wire rim							
1953	Inc. above	—	—	—	BV	23.00	30.00
Note: With strap, flat rim							

Date	Mintage	F12	VF20	XF40	AU50	MS60	MS63
1953 Specimen	—	—	—	—	—	—	1,400
Note: With strap, flat rim							
1954	246,606	—	18.00	20.00	25.00	30.00	50.00
1955	268,105	—	16.00	18.00	24.00	30.00	50.00
Note: With 3 water lines							
1955	Inc. above	85.00	95.00	100	125	150	300
Note: Arnprior with 1-1/2 water lines* and die break							
1956	209,092	20.00	22.00	24.00	26.00	35.00	85.00
1957	496,389	—	—	—	21.00	23.00	26.00
Note: With 3 water lines							
1957	Inc. above	—	22.00	24.00	26.00	28.00	50.00
Note: With 1 water line							
1959	1,443,502	—	—	—	16.00	21.00	24.00
1960	1,420,486	—	—	—	BV	BV	24.00
1961	1,262,231	—	—	—	BV	BV	24.00
1962	1,884,789	—	—	—	BV	18.00	24.00
1963	4,179,981	—	—	—	BV	BV	24.00

KM# 55 DOLLAR
23.33 g., 0.800 Silver, 0.60 oz. ASW 36mm. **Subject:** British Columbia **Obv.** Laureate bust right **Obv. Designer:** Mary Gillick **Rev:** Totem Pole, dates at left, denomination below **Rev. Designer:** Stephan Trenka

Date	Mintage	F12	VF20	XF40	AU50	MS60	MS63
1858-1958	3,039,630	—	16.00	18.00	21.00	23.00	26.00

KM# 58 DOLLAR
23.33 g., 0.800 Silver, 0.60 oz. ASW 36mm. **Subject:** Charlottetown **Obv.** Laureate bust right **Rev:** Design at center, dates at outer edges, denomination below **Rev. Designer:** Dinko Voldanovic

Date	Mintage	F12	VF20	XF40	AU50	MS60	MS63
1864-1964	7,296,832	—	—	—	BV	BV	5.50
1864-1964 Specimen	—	—	—	—	—	—	250

Small beads

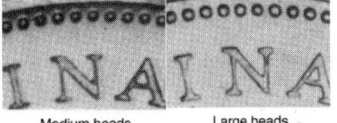

Medium beads   Large beads

KM# 64.1 DOLLAR
23.33 g., 0.800 Silver, 0.60 oz. ASW 36mm. **Obv.** Young bust right **Obv. Designer:** Arnold Machin **Rev:** Voyageur, date

and denomination below **Rev. Designer:** Emanual Hahn

Date	Mintage	F12	VF20	XF40	AU50	MS60	MS63
1965	10,768,569	**PF60** 400					
Note: Small beads, pointed 5							
(1965) Specimen	—	—	—	—	—	—	350
Note: Small beads, pointed 5							
1965	Inc. above	**PF60** 400					
Note: Small beads, blunt 5							
1965 Specimen	—	—	—	—	—	—	350
Note: Small beads, blunt 5							
1965	Inc. above	—	—	—	BV	BV	24.00
Note: Large beads, blunt 5							
1965 Specimen	—	—	—	—	—	—	300
Note: Large beads, blunt 5							
1965	Inc. above	—	—	—	BV	23.00	28.00
Note: Large beads, pointed 5							
1965 Specimen	—	—	—	—	—	—	550
Note: Large beads, pointed 5							
1965	Inc. above	—	BV	23.00	26.00	30.00	45.00
Note: Medium beads, pointed 5							
1966	9,912,178	—	—	—	BV	BV	24.00
Note: Large beads							
1966 Specimen	—	—	—	—	—	—	350
Note: Large beads							
1966	485	—	—	2,400	2,600	3,000	4,000
Note: Small beads							

Date	Mintage	MS63
Note: Small island		
1968 No Island	—	12.00
1968 Prooflike	—	4.50
Note: No island		
1968	Prooflike	30.00
Note: Doubled die; exhibits extra water lines		
1969	4,809,313	2.50
1969 Prooflike	594,258	1.75
1965 (1969) Specimen	—	1,200
1972	2,676,041	3.50
1972 Prooflike	405,865	2.25

KM# 70 DOLLAR
23.33 g., 0.800 Silver, 0.60 oz. ASW 36mm. **Subject:** Confederation Centennial **Obv.** Young bust right **Obv. Designer:** Arnold Machin **Rev:** Goose left, dates below, denomination above **Rev. Designer:** Alex Colville

Date	Mintage	MS63
1867-1967	6,767,496	24.00
1867-1967 Specimen	—	30.00

KM# 76.1 DOLLAR
15.64 g., Nickel, 32mm. **Obv.** Young bust right **Obv. Designer:** Arnold Machin **Rev:** Voyageur, date and denomination below **Rev. Designer:** Emanuel Hahn

Date	Mintage	MS63
1968	5,579,714	2.50
1968 Prooflike	1,408,143	1.75
1968 Small island	—	10.00
1968 Prooflike		7.50

KM# 78 DOLLAR
15.60 g., Nickel, 32mm. **Subject:** Manitoba **Obv.** Young bust right **Rev:** Pasque flower divides dates and denomination **Rev. Designer:** Raymond Taylor

Date	Mintage	MS63
1870-1970	4,140,058	3.50
1870-1970 Prooflike	645,869	2.25
1870-1970 Specimen	—	60.00

KM# 79 DOLLAR
15.70 g., Nickel, 32.1mm. **Subject:** British Columbia **Obv.** Young bust right **Rev:** Shield divides dates, denomination

below, flowers above **Rev. Designer:** Thomas Shingles

Date	Mintage	MS63
1871-1971	4,260,781	3.50
1871-1971 Prooflike	468,729	2.25
1871-1971 Specimen	—	75.00

Date	Mintage	MS63
1873-1973 Specimen	1,031,271	14.00
1873-1973 Specimen	—	20.00

Note: Dollar housed in special blue case with RCMP crest.

KM# 80 DOLLAR
23.33 g., 0.500 Silver, 0.37 oz. ASW 36mm. **Subject:** British Columbia **Obv.** Young bust right **Rev:** Crowned arms with supporters divide dates, maple at top divides denomination, crowned lion atop crown on shield **Rev. Designer:** Patrick Brindley

Date	Mintage	MS63
1871-1971 Specimen	585,674	14.00

KM# 64.2a DOLLAR
23.33 g., 0.500 Silver, 0.37 oz. ASW 36mm. **Obv.** Smaller young bust right **Obv. Designer:** Arnold Machin **Rev:** Voyageur **Rev. Designer:** Emanuel Hahn

Date	Mintage	MS63
1972 Specimen	341,598	13.00
1972	Inc. above	PF60 15.00

KM# 82 DOLLAR
Nickel, 32mm. **Subject:** Prince Edward Island **Obv.** Young bust right **Rev:** Building, inscription below divides dates, denomination above **Rev. Designer:** Terry Manning

Date	Mintage	MS63
1873-1973	3,196,452	3.00
1873-1973 (c) Prooflike	—	2.25

KM# 83 DOLLAR
23.33 g., 0.500 Silver, 0.37 oz. ASW 36mm. **Obv.** Young bust right **Rev:** Mountie left, dates below, denomination at right **Rev. Designer:** Paul Cedarberg

KM# 88a DOLLAR
23.33 g., 0.500 Silver, 0.37 oz. ASW 36mm. **Subject:** Winnipeg Centennial **Obv.** Young bust right **Rev:** Zeros frame pictures, dates below, denomination at bottom **Rev. Designer:** Paul Pederson and Patrick Brindley

Date	Mintage	MS63
1974-1974 Specimen	728,947	14.00

KM# 88 DOLLAR
Nickel, 32mm. **Subject:** Winnipeg Centennial **Obv.** Young bust right **Rev:** Zeros frame pictures, dates below, denomination at bottom **Rev. Designer:** Paul Pederson and Patrick Brindley

Date	Mintage	MS63
1874-1974	2,799,363	3.50
1874-1974 (c) Prooflike	—	2.50

KM# 97 DOLLAR
23.33 g., 0.500 Silver, 0.37 oz. ASW 36mm. **Subject:** Calgary **Obv.** Youmg bust right **Rev:** Figure on bucking horse, dates divided below, denomination above **Rev. Designer:** Donald D. Paterson

Date	Mintage	MS63
1875-1975 Specimen	930,956	14.00

KM# 76.2 DOLLAR

15.62 g., Nickel, 32mm. **Obv.** Smaller young bust right **Obv. Designer:** Arnold Machin **Rev:** Voyageur **Rev. Designer:** Emanuel Hahn

Date	Mintage	MS63
1975	3,256,000	1.50
1975 Prooflike	322,325	2.50
1976	2,498,204	1.50
1976 Prooflike	274,106	2.50

KM# 76.3 DOLLAR

Nickel, 32mm. **Obv.** Young bust right **Obv. Designer:** Arnold Machin **Rev:** Voyageur **Rev. Designer:** Emanuel Hahn **Note:** Only known in prooflike sets with 1976 obverse slightly modified.

Date	Mintage	MS63
1975	Inc. above	3.00

Note: mule with 1976 obv.

KM# 106 DOLLAR

23.33 g., 0.500 Silver, 0.37 oz. ASW 36mm. **Subject:** Parliament Library **Obv.** Young bust right **Rev:** Library building, dates below, denomination above **Rev. Designer:** Walter Ott and Patrick Brindley

Date	Mintage	MS63
1876-1976 Specimen	578,708	14.00
1876-1976	—	PF60 25.00

Note: Blue VIP case

KM# 117 DOLLAR

Nickel, 32mm. **Obv.** Young bust right **Obv. Designer:** Arnold Machin **Rev:** Voyageur modified **Rev. Designer:** Emanuel Hahn

Date	Mintage	MS63
1977	1,393,745	3.50
1977 Prooflike	—	2.50

KM# 118 DOLLAR

23.33 g., 0.500 Silver, 0.37 oz. ASW 36mm. **Subject:** Silver Jubilee **Obv.** Young bust right, dates below **Rev:** Throne, denomination below **Rev. Designer:** Raymond Lee

Date	Mintage	MS63
1952-1977 Specimen	744,848	14.00
1952-1977 Specimen	—	45.00

Note: Red VIP case

KM# 121 DOLLAR

23.33 g., 0.500 Silver, 0.37 oz. ASW 36mm. **Subject:** XI Commonwealth Games **Obv.** Young bust right **Rev:** Commonwealth games, logo at center **Rev. Designer:** Raymond Taylor

Date	Mintage	MS63
1978 Specimen	709,602	14.00

KM# 120.1 DOLLAR

15.50 g., Nickel, 32.1mm. **Obv.** Young bust right **Obv. Designer:** Arnold Machin **Rev:** Voyageur, date and denomination below **Rev. Designer:** Emanuel Hahn **Note:** Modified design.

Date	Mintage	MS63
1978	2,948,488	1.50
1979	2,954,842	1.50
1980	3,291,221	1.50

Date	Mintage		MS63
1981	2,778,900		1.50
1981	—	PF60 5.25	
1982	1,098,500		2.50
1982	180,908	PF60 5.25	
1983	2,267,525		4.00
1983	166,779	PF60 5.25	
1984	1,223,486		1.50
1984	161,602	PF60 6.00	
1985	3,104,092		3.50
1985	153,950	PF60 7.00	
1986	3,089,225		4.00
1986	176,224	PF60 7.50	
1987	287,330		5.00
1987	175,686	PF60 7.50	

KM# 124 DOLLAR
23.33 g., 0.500 Silver, 0.37 oz. ASW 36mm. **Subject:** Griffon **Obv.** Young bust right **Rev:** Ship, dates below, denomination above **Rev. Designer:** Walter Schluep

Date	Mintage	MS63
1979 Specimen	826,695	14.00

KM# 128 DOLLAR
23.33 g., 0.500 Silver, 0.37 oz. ASW 36mm. **Subject:** Arctic Territories **Obv.** Young bust right **Rev:** Bear right, date below, denomination above **Rev. Designer:** Donald D. Paterson

Date	Mintage	MS63
1980 Specimen	539,617	22.00

KM# 130 DOLLAR
23.33 g., 0.500 Silver, 0.37 oz. ASW 36mm. **Subject:** Transcontinental Railroad **Obv.** Young bust right **Rev:** Train engine and map, date below, denomination above **Rev. Designer:** Christopher Gorey

Date	Mintage		MS63
1981	699,494		14.00
1981	—	PF60 15.00	

KM# 133 DOLLAR
23.33 g., 0.500 Silver, 0.37 oz. ASW 36mm. **Subject:** Regina **Obv.** Young bust right **Rev:** Cattle skull divides dates and denomination below **Rev. Designer:** Huntley Brown

Date	Mintage		MS63
1882-1982	144,930		14.00
1882-1982	—	PF60 14.00	

KM# 134 DOLLAR
15.42 g., Nickel, 32mm. **Subject:** Constitution **Obv.** Young bust right **Rev:** Meeting of Government **Rev. Designer:** Ago Aarand

Date	Mintage	MS63
1867-1982	9,709,422	6.00

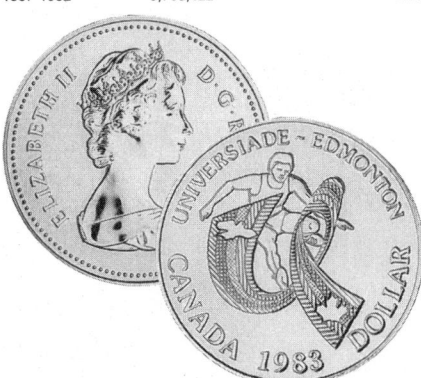

KM# 138 DOLLAR
23.33 g., 0.500 Silver, 0.37 oz. ASW 36mm. **Subject:** Edmonton University Games **Obv.** Young bust right **Rev:** Athlete within game logo, date and denomination below **Rev. Designer:** Carola Tietz

Date	Mintage		MS63
1983	159,450		14.00
1983	—	PF60 14.00	

KM# 141   DOLLAR
15.50 g., Nickel, 32mm. **Subject:** Jacques Cartier **Obv.** Young bust right **Rev:** Cross with shield above figures **Rev. Designer:** Hector Greville

Date	Mintage		MS63
1534-1984	7,009,323		3.50
1534-1984	—	PF60 6.00	

KM# 140   DOLLAR
23.33 g., 0.500 Silver, 0.37 oz. ASW 36mm. **Subject:** Toronto Sesquicentennial **Obv.** Young bust right **Rev. Designer:** D. J. Craig

Date	Mintage		MS63
1984	133,610		14.00
1984	—	PF60 14.00	

KM# 143   DOLLAR
23.33 g., 0.500 Silver, 0.37 oz. ASW 36mm. **Subject:** National Parks **Obv.** Young bust right **Rev:** Moose right, dates above, denomination below **Rev. Designer:** Karel Rohlicek

Date	Mintage		MS63
1885-1985	163,314		14.00
1885-1985	733,354	PF60 14.00	

KM# 120.2   DOLLAR
Nickel, 32.13mm. **Obv.** Young bust right **Rev:** Voyageur **Note:** Mule with New Zealand 50 cent, KM-37 obverse.

Date	Mintage	MS63
1985	—	3,000

KM# 149   DOLLAR
23.33 g., 0.500 Silver, 0.37 oz. ASW 36mm. **Subject:** Vancouver **Obv.** Young bust right **Rev:** Train left, dates divided below, denomination above **Rev. Designer:** Elliot John Morrison

Date	Mintage		MS63
1886-1986	125,949		14.00
1886-1986	—	PF60 14.00	

KM# 154   DOLLAR
23.33 g., 0.500 Silver, 0.37 oz. ASW 36mm. **Subject:** John Davis **Obv.** Young bust right **Rev:** Ship "John Davis" with masts, rock in background, dates below, denomination at bottom **Rev. Designer:** Christopher Gorey

Date	Mintage		MS63
1587-1987	118,722		14.00
1587-1987	—	PF60 14.00	

KM# 157   DOLLAR
7.00 g., Aureate-Bronze Plated Nickel, 26.5mm. **Obv.** Young bust right **Obv. Designer:** Arnold Machin **Rev:** Loon right, date and denomination below **Rev. Designer:** Robert R. Carmichael **Shape:** 11-sided

Date	Mintage		MS63
1987	205,405,000		2.25
1987	178,120	PF60 8.00	
1988	138,893,539		4.00
1988	175,259	PF60 6.75	
1989	184,773,902		4.00
1989	170,928	PF60 6.75	

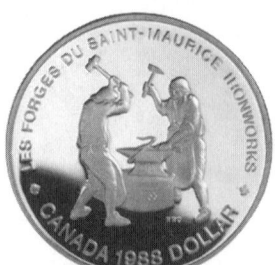

KM# 161   DOLLAR
23.33 g., 0.500 Silver, 0.37 oz. ASW 36mm. **Subject:** Ironworks **Obv.** Young bust right **Rev:** Ironworkers, date and denomination below **Rev. Designer:** Robert R. Carmichael

Date	Mintage	MS63
1988	106,872	14.00
1988	— PF60 17.50	

KM# 168 DOLLAR
23.33 g., 0.500 Silver, 0.37 oz. ASW 36mm. **Subject:** MacKenzie River **Obv.** Young bust right **Rev:** People in canoe, date above, denomination below **Rev. Designer:** John Mardon

Date	Mintage	MS63
1989	99,774	14.00
1989	— PF60 17.50	

KM# 186 DOLLAR
7.00 g., Aureate-Bronze Plated Nickel, 26.5mm. **Obv.** Crowned head right **Obv. Designer:** Dora dePedery-Hunt **Rev:** Loon right, date and denomination **Rev. Designer:** Robert R. Carmichael **Shape:** 11-sided

Date	Mintage			MS63
1990	68,402,000			4.00
1990	140,649	PF63 6.00	PF65 7.00	
1991	23,156,000			6.50
1991	131,888	PF63 12.00	PF65 13.00	
1993	33,662,000			3.00
1993	143,065	PF63 5.00	PF65 6.00	
1994	16,232,530			3.50
1994	104,485	PF63 6.00	PF65 7.00	
1995	27,492,630			4.50
1995	101,560	PF63 6.00	PF65 7.00	
1996	17,101,000			6.00
1996	112,835	PF63 6.50	PF65 7.50	
1997	—			6.00
1997	113,647	PF63 7.00	PF65 8.00	
1998	—			6.00
1998W Prooflike	—			10.00
1998	93,632	PF63 8.00	PF65 10.00	
1999	—			6.00
1999	95,113	PF63 7.00	PF65 8.00	
2000	—			6.00
2000W Prooflike	—			10.00
2000	90,921	PF63 7.00	PF65 8.00	
2001	—			6.00
2001	74,194	PF63 7.00	PF65 8.00	
2002	—			4.50
2002	65,315	PF63 6.50	PF65 7.50	
2003	—			5.50

Note: Mintage of 5,101,000 includes both KM186 and KM495 examples.

2003	—	PF63 10.00	PF65 12.00

KM# 170 DOLLAR
23.33 g., 0.500 Silver, 0.37 oz. ASW 36mm. **Subject:** Henry Kelsey **Obv.** Crowned head right **Rev:** Kelsey with natives, dates below, denomination above **Rev. Designer:** D. J. Craig

Date	Mintage	MS63
1690-1990	99,455	14.00
1690-1990	— PF60 20.00	

KM# 179 DOLLAR
23.33 g., 0.500 Silver, 0.37 oz. ASW 36mm. **Subject:** S.S. Frontenac **Obv.** Crowned head right **Rev:** Ship,"Frontenac," date and denomination below, **Rev. Designer:** D. J. Craig

Date	Mintage	MS63
1991	73,843	14.00
1991	195,424 PF60 25.00	

KM# 209 DOLLAR
Aureate, 26.5mm. **Subject:** Loon right, dates and denomination **Obv.** Crowned head right **Rev. Designer:** Robert R. Carmichael

Date	Mintage	MS63
1867-1992	4,242,085	4.00
1867-1992	147,061 PF60 8.00	

KM# 218 DOLLAR

Aureate, 26mm. **Subject:** Parliament **Obv.** Crowned head right, dates below **Rev:** Backs of three seated figures in front of building, denomination below **Rev. Designer:** Rita Swanson

Date	Mintage	MS63
1867-1992	23,915,000	5.00
1867-1992	— PF60 9.00	

KM# 210 DOLLAR

25.18 g., 0.925 Silver, 0.74 oz. ASW 36mm. **Subject:** Stagecoach service **Obv.** Crowned head right **Rev:** Stagecoach, date and denomination below **Rev. Designer:** Karsten Smith

Date	Mintage	MS63
1992	78,160	25.00
1992	187,612 PF60 25.00	

KM# 235 DOLLAR

25.18 g., 0.925 Silver, 0.74 oz. ASW 36mm. **Subject:** Stanley Cup hockey **Obv.** Crowned head right **Rev:** Hockey players between cups, dates below, denomination above **Rev. Designer:** Stewart Sherwood

Date	Mintage	MS63
1993	88,150	25.00
1993	— PF60 25.00	

KM# 248 DOLLAR

7.00 g., Aureate-Bronze Plated Nickel, 26mm. **Subject:** War Memorial **Obv.** Crowned head right, date below **Rev:** Memorial, denomination at right **Rev. Designer:** R. C. M. Staff

Date	Mintage	MS63
1994	20,004,830	2.25
1994	— PF60 7.50	

KM# 251 DOLLAR

25.18 g., 0.925 Silver, 0.74 oz. ASW 36mm. **Subject:** Last RCMP sled-dog patrol **Obv.** Crowned head right **Rev:** Dogsled, denomination divides dates below **Rev. Designer:** Ian Sparks

Date	Mintage	MS63
1969-1994	61,561	25.00
1969-1994	170,374 PF60 25.00	

KM# 258 DOLLAR

7.00 g., Aureate, 26mm. **Subject:** Peacekeeping Monument in Ottawa **Obv.** Crowned head right, date below **Rev:** Monument, denomination above right **Rev. Designer:** J. K. Harmon, R. G. Henriquez and C. H. Oberlander **Note:** Mintage included with KM#186.

Date	Mintage	MS63
1995	18,502,750	2.25
1995	— PF60 7.50	

KM# 259 DOLLAR

25.18 g., 0.925 Silver, 0.74 oz. ASW 36mm. **Subject:** Hudson Bay Company **Obv.** Crowned head right **Rev:** Explorers and ship, date and denomination below **Rev. Designer:** Vincent McIndoe

Date	Mintage	MS63
1995	61,819	25.00
1995	166,259 PF60 30.00	

KM# 274 DOLLAR
25.18 g., 0.925 Silver, 0.74 oz. ASW 36mm. **Subject:** McIntosh Apple **Obv.** Crowned head right **Rev:** Apple, dates and denomination below **Rev. Designer:** Roger Hill

Date	Mintage		MS63
1796-1996	58,834		25.00
1796-1996	133,779	**PF60** 25.00	

KM# 296 DOLLAR
25.18 g., 0.925 Silver, 0.74 oz. ASW 36mm. **Subject:** Loon Dollar 10th Anniversary **Obv.** Crowned head right **Rev:** Loon in flight left, dates above, denomination below **Rev. Designer:** Jean-Luc Grondin

Date	Mintage		
1987-1997	—	**PF60** 95.00	

KM# 282 DOLLAR
25.18 g., 0.925 Silver, 0.74 oz. ASW 36mm. **Subject:** 25th Anniversary Hockey Victory **Obv.** Crowned head right **Rev:** The winning goal by Paul Aenderson. Based on a painting by Andre l'Archeveque, dates at right, denomination at bottom **Rev. Designer:** Walter Burden

Date	Mintage		MS63
1972-1997	155,252		25.00
1972-1997	184,965	**PF60** 30.00	

KM# 306 DOLLAR
25.18 g., 0.925 Silver, 0.74 oz. ASW 36mm. **Subject:** 120th Anniversary Royal Canadian Mounted Police **Obv.** Crowned head right **Rev:** Mountie on horseback, dates at left, denomination above **Rev. Designer:** Adeline Halvorson **Note:** Individually cased prooflikes, proofs or specimens are from broken-up prooflike or specimen sets.

Date	Mintage		MS63
1873-1998	79,777		25.00
1873-1998	120,172	**PF60** 35.00	

KM# 291 DOLLAR
7.00 g., Aureate-Bronze Plated Nickel, 26mm. **Subject:** Loon Dollar 10th Anniversary **Obv.** Crowned head right **Rev:** Loon in flight left, dates above, denomination below **Rev. Designer:** Jean-Luc Grondin

Date	Mintage	MS63
1987-1997	—	22.00

KM# 355 DOLLAR
25.18 g., 0.925 Silver, 0.74 oz. ASW 36mm. **Subject:** International Year of Old Persons **Obv.** Crowned head right **Rev:** Figures amid trees, date and denomination below **Rev. Designer:** S. Armstrong-Hodgson

Date	Mintage		
1999	—	**PF60** 40.00	

DOLLAR

KM# 356 DOLLAR
25.18 g., 0.925 Silver, 0.74 oz. ASW 36mm. **Subject:** Discovery of Queen Charlotte Isle **Obv.** Crowned head right **Rev:** Ship and three boats, dates at right, denomination below **Rev. Designer:** D. J. Craig

Date	Mintage		MS63
1999	67,655		25.00
1999	126,435	**PF60** 35.00	

KM# 434 DOLLAR
25.18 g., 0.925 Silver, 0.74 oz. ASW 36mm. **Obv.** Crowned head right **Rev:** Recycled 1911 pattern dollar design: denomination, country name and dates in crowned wreath **Edge:** Reeded

Date	Mintage		
1911-2001	24,996	**PF63** 45.00	**PF65** 55.00

KM# 186a DOLLAR
Gilt, 26.5mm. **Subject:** Olympic Win

Date	Mintage		
2002	—	**PF63** 35.00	**PF65** 40.00

KM# 401 DOLLAR
25.18 g., 0.925 Silver, 0.74 oz. ASW 36mm. **Subject:** Voyage of Discovery **Obv.** Crowned head right **Rev:** Human and space shuttle, date above, denomination below **Rev. Designer:** D. F. Warkentine

Date	Mintage		MS63
2000	60,100		25.00
2000	114,130	**PF60** 30.00	

KM# 443 DOLLAR
25.18 g., 0.925 Silver, 0.74 oz. ASW 36mm. **Subject:** Queen's Golden Jubilee **Obv.** Crowned head right, with anniversary date at left **Obv. Designer:** Dora dePédery-Hunt **Rev:** Queen in her coach and a view of the coach, denomination below **Edge:** Reeded

Date	Mintage		MS63
1952-2002	65,140		28.50
1952-2002	29,688	**PF63** 30.00	**PF65** 40.00

KM# 443a DOLLAR
25.18 g., 0.925 Silver Gilt, 0.74 oz. 36mm. **Subject:** Queen's Golden Jubilee **Obv.** Crowned head right with anniversary date **Rev:** Queen in her coach and a view of the coach **Edge:** Reeded **Note:** Special 24 karat gold plated issue of KM#443.

Date	Mintage		
2002	32,642	**PF63** 40.00	**PF65** 45.00

KM# 462 DOLLAR
7.00 g., Aureate-Bronze Plated Nickel, **Obv.** Commemorative dates 1952-2002 **Obv. Designer:** Dora dePédery-Hunt **Rev:** Family of Loons

Date	Mintage	MS63
2002 Specimen	67,672	25.00

KM# 467a DOLLAR
Gold, AGW **Subject:** 50th Anniversary, Accession to the Throne **Obv.** Crowned head right **Note:** Sold on the internet.

Date	Mintage		
2002	1	**PF65** 55,500	

KM# 414 DOLLAR
25.18 g., 0.925 Silver, 0.74 oz. ASW 36mm. **Subject:** National Ballet **Obv.** Crowned head right **Rev:** Ballet dancers **Rev. Designer:** Scott McKowen **Edge:** Reeded

Date	Mintage		MS63
2001	—	**PF63** 25.00	**PF65** 35.00
2001	65,000		27.50

KM# 467 DOLLAR
7.00 g., Aureate-Bronze Plated Nickel, **Subject:** Elizabeth II Golden Jubilee **Obv.** Crowned head right, Jubilee commemorative dates 1952-2002 **Obv. Designer:** Dora dePédery-Hunt

Date	Mintage			MS63
2002	2,302,000			2.50
2002	—	PF63 7.00	PF65 8.00	

KM# 503 DOLLAR
25.18 g., 0.925 Silver, 0.74 oz. ASW 36mm. **Subject:** Queen Mother **Obv.** Crowned head right **Obv. Designer:** Dora de Pedery-Hunt **Rev:** Queen Mother facing

Date	Mintage	
2002	9,994	PF65 250

KM# 450 DOLLAR
25.18 g., 0.9999 Silver, 0.80 oz. ASW 36mm. **Subject:** Cobalt Mining Centennial **Obv.** Queens portrait right **Obv. Designer:** Dora dePédery-Hunt **Rev:** Mine tower and fox **Edge:** Reeded

Date	Mintage			MS63
2003	51,130			30.00
2003	88,536	PF63 35.00	PF65 45.00	

KM# 495 DOLLAR
7.00 g., Aureate-Bronze Plated Nickel, 26.5mm. **Obv.** Bare head right **Obv. Designer:** Susanna Blunt **Rev:** Loon right **Rev. Designer:** Robert R. Carmichael **Shape:** 11-sided

Date	Mintage			MS63
2003	5,102,000			5.50

Note: Mintage of 5,101,000 includes both KM 186 and 495 examples.

Date	Mintage			MS63
2003W	—			7.50
Prooflike				
2003	62,507	PF63 6.50	PF65 7.50	
2004	10,894,000			1.75
2004	—	PF63 10.00	PF65 12.00	
2005	44,375,000			3.00
2005	—	PF63 6.50	PF65 7.50	
2006	49,111,000			3.00
2006	—	PF63 6.50	PF65 7.50	
2006(ml)	49,111,000			3.00
2006(ml)	—	PF63 6.50	PF65 7.50	
2007(ml)	38,045,000			3.00
2007(ml)	—	PF63 6.50	PF65 7.50	

Date	Mintage			MS63
2008(ml)	29,561,000			3.00
2008(ml)	—	PF63 6.50	PF65 7.50	
2009(ml)	39,601,000			3.00
2009(ml)	—	PF63 6.50	PF65 7.50	
2010(ml)	—			3.00
2010(ml)	—	PF63 6.50	PF65 7.50	
2011(ml)	—			3.00
2011(ml)	—	PF63 6.50	PF65 7.50	
2012(ml)	—			3.00
2012(ml)	—	PF63 6.50	PF65 7.50	

KM# 473 DOLLAR
25.18 g., 0.9999 Silver, 0.80 oz. ASW **Subject:** 50th Anniversary of the Coronation of Elizabeth II **Obv.** 1953 effigy of the Queen, Jubilee dates 1953-2003 **Obv. Designer:** Mary Gillick **Rev:** Voyageur, date and denomination below

Date	Mintage		
1953-2003	21,537	PF63 35.00	PF65 45.00

KM# 480 DOLLAR
25.18 g., 0.9999 Silver, 0.80 oz. ASW **Subject:** Coronation of Queen Elizabeth II **Obv.** Head right **Rev:** Voyaguers **Rev. Designer:** Emanuel Hahn

Date	Mintage		
1953-2003	29,586	PF63 40.00	PF65 50.00

KM# 480a DOLLAR
Gold, AGW **Subject:** 50th Anniversary of Coronation **Obv. Designer:** Mary Gilick **Rev:** Voyageur **Note:** Sold on the internet.

Date	Mintage	
1953-2003	1	PF65 62,750

KM# 507 DOLLAR
7.00 g., Aureate-Bronze Plated Nickel, 26.5mm. **Obv.** Bare head right, date below **Obv. Designer:** Susanna Blunt **Rev:** Loon **Edge:** Plain **Shape:** 11-sided

Date	Mintage	
2004	25,105	PF65 75.00

KM# 511 DOLLAR
25.18 g., 0.9999 Silver, 0.80 oz. ASW 36mm. **Obv.** Elizabeth II **Rev:** Poppy on maple leaf **Edge:** Reeded

Date	Mintage		
2004	24,527	PF63 45.00	PF65 50.00

KM# 513 DOLLAR
7.00 g., Aureate-Bronze Plated Nickel, 26.5mm. **Subject:** Olympics **Obv.** Bare head right **Rev:** Maple leaf, Olympic flame and rings above loon **Edge:** Plain **Shape:** 11-sided

Date	Mintage	MS63
2004	6,526,000	8.00

KM# 513a DOLLAR
9.31 g., 0.925 Silver, 0.28 oz. ASW 26.5mm. **Subject:** Olympics **Obv.** Bare head right **Rev:** Multicolor maple leaf, Olympic flame and rings above loon **Edge:** Plain **Shape:** 11-sided

Date	Mintage		
2004	19,994	PF63 45.00	PF65 50.00

KM# 512 DOLLAR
25.18 g., 0.9999 Silver, 0.80 oz. ASW 36mm. **Subject:** First French Settlement in America **Obv.** Crowned head right **Rev:** Sailing ship **Edge:** Reeded

Date	Mintage		MS63
2004	42,582		30.00
2004 Fleur-dis-lis privy mark	8,315		60.00
2004	106,974	PF63 45.00	PF65 50.00

KM# 549 DOLLAR
25.18 g., 0.925 Silver, 0.74 oz. ASW 36.07mm. **Subject:** 40th Anniversary of National Flag **Obv.** Head right **Obv. Designer:** Susanna Blunt **Rev. Designer:** William Woodruff

Date	Mintage		MS63
2005	50,948		27.50
2005	95,431	PF63 35.00	PF65 40.00

KM# 549a DOLLAR
25.18 g., 0.925 Silver, 0.74 oz. ASW 36.07mm. **Subject:** 40th Anniversary of National Flag **Obv.** Head right

Date	Mintage	MS63
2005	62,562	75.00

KM# 549b DOLLAR
25.18 g., 0.925 Silver, 0.74 oz. ASW 36.07mm. **Subject:** 40th Anniversary National Flag **Rev:** National flag, colorized

Date	Mintage	
2005	4,898	PF65 350

KM# 552 DOLLAR
7.00 g., Aureate-Bronze Plated Nickel, 26.5mm. **Obv.**

Head right **Rev:** Terry Fox walking left

Date	Mintage	MS63
2005	1,290,900	3.50

KM# 553 DOLLAR
7.00 g., Aureate-Bronze Plated Nickel, **Subject:** Tuffed Puffin **Obv.** Head right **Obv. Designer:** Susanna Blunt

Date	Mintage		
2005	39,818	PF63 25.00	PF65 30.00

KM# 581 DOLLAR
9.31 g., 0.925 Silver, 0.28 oz. ASW **Subject:** Lullabies Loonie **Obv.** Head right **Obv. Designer:** Susanna Blunt **Rev:** Loon and moon, teddy bear in stars

Date	Mintage	MS63
2006	18,103	4.50

KM# 582 DOLLAR
7.00 g., Aureate-Bronze Plated Nickel, 26.5mm. **Subject:** Snowy owl **Obv.** Head right **Obv. Designer:** Susanna Blunt **Rev:** Snowy owl with year above

Date	Mintage	
2006 Specimen	39,935	PF65 30.00

KM# 583 DOLLAR
25.18 g., 0.925 Silver, 0.74 oz. ASW 36mm. **Obv.** Head right **Rev:** Victoria Cross

Date	Mintage		MS63
2006	27,254		25.00
2006	53,822	PF63 40.00	PF65 45.00

KM# 583a DOLLAR
25.18 g., 0.925 Silver, 0.74 oz. ASW 36mm. **Obv.** Head right **Rev:** Victoria Cross gilt

Date	Mintage		
2006	53,822	PF63 65.00	PF65 75.00

DOLLAR

KM# 630 DOLLAR
7.00 g., Aureate Bronze, 26.5mm. **Obv.** Bust right **Rev:** Loon splashing in water

Date	Mintage	MS63
2006	—	3.00

KM# 630a DOLLAR
9.31 g., 0.925 Silver, 0.28 oz. ASW 26.5mm. **Subject:** Olympic Games **Obv.** Crowned head right **Rev:** Loon in flight, colored olympic logo above

Date	Mintage	MS63
2006	19,956	30.00

KM# 654 DOLLAR
7.00 g., 0.925 Silver, 0.21 oz. ASW **Obv.** Head right **Rev:** Snowflake, colorized **Note:** Sold in a CD package.

Date	Mintage	MS63
2006(ml)	34,014	35.00

KM# 655 DOLLAR
7.00 g., 0.925 Silver, 0.21 oz. ASW **Subject:** Baby Rattle **Obv.** Head right **Rev:** Baby rattle

Date	Mintage	MS63
2006	3,207	20.00

KM# 655a DOLLAR
7.00 g., 0.925 Silver, 0.21 oz. ASW **Obv.** Bust right **Rev:** Baby Rattle, partially gilt

Date	Mintage	MS63
2006	1,911	15.00

KM# 656 DOLLAR
28.18 g., 0.925 Silver, 0.83 oz. ASW **Subject:** Medal of Bravery **Obv.** Head right

Date	Mintage		
2006	8,343	PF63 45.00	PF65 50.00

KM# 656a DOLLAR
28.18 g., 0.925 Silver, 0.83 oz. ASW **Subject:** Medal of Bravery **Obv.** Head right **Rev:** Maple leaf within wreath. Colorized.

Date	Mintage	
2006	4,999	PF65 150

KM# 1287 DOLLAR
7.00 g., Aureate Bronze, 26.5mm. **Rev:** Goose in flight

Date	Mintage	
2006	—	PF65 20.00

KM# 688 DOLLAR
7.00 g., Aureate-Bronze Plated Nickel, 26.5mm. **Obv.** Head right **Rev:** Trumpeter Swan

Date	Mintage	MS63
2007(ml)	40,000	20.00

KM# 653 DOLLAR
25.18 g., 0.925 Silver, 0.74 oz. ASW 36.07mm. **Subject:** Thayendanegea **Obv.** Head right **Rev:** Bust 3/4 facing right

Date	Mintage		MS63
2007	16,378		30.00
2007	—	PF63 37.00	PF65 40.00

KM# 653a DOLLAR
25.18 g., 0.925 Silver, 0.74 oz. ASW 36.07mm. **Subject:** Thayendanega **Rev:** Bust 3/4 right, partially gold plated

Date	Mintage	
2007	60,000	PF65 125

KM# 720 DOLLAR
25.18 g., 0.925 Silver, 0.74 oz. ASW 36.07mm. **Obv.** Bust right **Rev:** Thayendanega multicolor

Date	Mintage		
2007	4,760	PF63 110	PF65 120

KM# 700 DOLLAR
7.00 g., 0.925 Silver, 0.21 oz. ASW 23.88mm. **Rev:** Alphabet Letter Blocks

Date	Mintage		
2007	3,207	PF63 22.00	PF65 25.00

KM# 719 DOLLAR
25.18 g., 0.925 Silver, 0.74 oz. ASW 36.07mm. **Subject:** Celebration of the Arts **Rev:** Book, TV set, musical instruments, film montage **Rev. Designer:** Friedrich Peter **Edge:** Reeded

Date	Mintage		
2007	6,466	PF63 50.00	PF65 55.00

KM# A727 DOLLAR
7.00 g., Aureate-Bronze Plated Nickel, 26.5mm. **Subject:** Vancouver Olympic Games **Rev:** Loon splashing in water, Olympics logo at right

Date	Mintage	MS63
2007(ml)	19,973	3.00

KM# 724 DOLLAR
7.00 g., Nickel, 26.5mm. **Rev:** Ottawa Senators, multicolor logo in circle

Date	Mintage	MS63
2008	1,633	25.00

KM# 725 DOLLAR
7.00 g., Aureate-Bronze Plated Nickel, 26.5mm. **Obv.** Bust right **Rev:** Toronto Maple Leafs, multicolor logo in circle

Date	Mintage	MS63
2008	—	25.00

KM# 726 DOLLAR
7.00 g., Aureate-Bronze Plated Nickel, 26.5mm. **Obv.** Bust left **Rev:** Vancouver Canucks, logo in center

Date	Mintage	MS63
2008	1,302	25.00

KM# 767 DOLLAR
25.18 g., 0.925 Silver, 0.74 oz. ASW 36.07mm. **Rev:** Poppy at center of large maple leaf

Date	Mintage		
2008	—	PF63 40.00	PF65 50.00

KM# 781 DOLLAR
25.18 g., 0.925 Silver, 0.74 oz. ASW 36.07mm. **Subject:** Ottawa Mint Centennial 1908-2008 **Rev:** Maple leaf transforming into a common loon, gilt rim and 100 **Rev. Designer:** Jason Bowman

Date	Mintage		
2008	15,000	PF63 55.00	PF65 65.00

KM# 784 DOLLAR
7.00 g., Aureate-Bronze Plated Nickel, 26.5mm. **Rev:** Common elder

Date	Mintage	
2008 Specimen	21,227	PF65 50.00

KM# 785 DOLLAR
25.18 g., 0.925 Silver, 0.74 oz. ASW 36.07mm. **Subject:** Founding of Quebec 400th Anniversary **Rev:** Samuel de Champlain, ship and town view **Rev. Designer:** Susanne Duranceau

Date	Mintage		MS63
2008	35,000		25.00
2008	65,000	PF63 35.00	PF65 40.00

KM# 785a DOLLAR
25.18 g., 0.925 Silver, 0.74 oz. ASW 36.07mm. **Subject:** Founding of Quebec 400th Anniversary **Rev:** Samuel de Champlain selectively gold plated, ship, town view **Rev. Designer:** Susanne Duranceau

Date	Mintage		
2008	38,630	PF63 65.00	PF65 75.00

KM# 787 DOLLAR
7.00 g., Aureate-Bronze Plated Nickel, 26.5mm. **Subject:** Lucky Loonie **Rev:** Loon splashing and Olympic logo at right **Rev. Designer:** Steve Hepurn

Date	Mintage	MS63
2008	—	20.00

KM# 787a DOLLAR
9.31 g., 0.925 Silver, 0.28 oz. ASW 26.5mm. **Rev:** Loon splashing with Olympic logo and maple leaf in color above **Rev. Designer:** Steve Hepurn

Date	Mintage		
2008	52,987	**PF63** 22.00	**PF65** 25.00

KM# 791 DOLLAR
6.50 g., Nickel, 26.5mm. **Rev:** Edmonton Oilers

Date	Mintage	MS63
2008	—	25.00

KM# 792 DOLLAR
6.50 g., Nickel, 26.5mm. **Rev:** Montreal Canadiens

Date	Mintage	MS63
2008	—	25.00

KM# 793 DOLLAR
6.50 g., Nickel, 26.5mm. **Rev:** Ottawa Senators

Date	Mintage	MS63
2008	—	25.00

KM# 794 DOLLAR
6.50 g., Nickel, 26.5mm. **Rev:** Toronto Maple Leafs

Date	Mintage	MS63
2008	—	25.00

KM# 795 DOLLAR
6.50 g., Nickel, 26.5mm. **Rev:** Vancouver Canucks

Date	Mintage	MS63
2008	—	25.00

KM# 851 DOLLAR
33.65 g., Nickel, 26.5mm. **Rev:** Calgary Flames Road Jersey

Date	Mintage	MS63
2009	382	25.00

KM# 852 DOLLAR
33.65 g., Nickel, 26.5mm. **Rev:** Edmonton Oilers Road Jersey

Date	Mintage	MS63
2009	472	25.00

KM# 853 DOLLAR
33.65 g., Nickel, 26.5mm. **Rev:** Montreal Canadians Road Jersey

Date	Mintage	MS63
2009	4,857	25.00

DOLLAR

KM# 854 DOLLAR
33.65 g., Nickel, 26.5mm. **Rev:** Ottawa Senators Road Jersey

Date	Mintage	MS63
2009	387	25.00

KM# 855 DOLLAR
33.65 g., Nickel, 26.5mm. **Rev:** Toronto Maple Leafs Road Jersey

Date	Mintage	MS63
2009	1,328	25.00

KM# 856 DOLLAR
33.65 g., Nickel, 26.5mm. **Rev:** Vancouver Canucks Road Jersey

Date	Mintage	MS63
2009	794	25.00

KM# 864 DOLLAR
7.00 g., Aureate-Bronze Plated Nickel, 26.5mm. **Subject:** Montreal Canadiens, 100th Anniversary **Obv.** Bust right **Rev:** Montreal Canadiens logo and large 100 **Shape:** 11-sided

Date	Mintage	MS63
2009	—	25.00

KM# 865 DOLLAR
25.17 g., 0.925 Silver, 0.74 oz. ASW 36.07mm. **Subject:** Montreal Canadiens 100th Anniversary **Obv.** Bust right **Obv. Designer:** Susanna Blunt **Rev:** Montreal Canadiens logo partially gilt

Date	Mintage		
2009 Proof in black case	15,000	PF65	75.00
2009 Proof in acrillic stand	5,000	PF65	150

KM# 889 DOLLAR
25.18 g., 0.925 Silver, 0.74 oz. ASW 36.07mm. **Subject:** 100th Anniversary of flight in Canada **Obv.** Bust right **Obv. Designer:** Susanna Blunt **Rev:** Silhouette with arms spread, 3 planes, plane cutout **Obv. Legend:** Elizabeth II DG Regina **Rev. Designer:** Jason Bouwman **Rev. Legend:** Canada Dollar 1909-2009

Date	Mintage				MS63
2009	13,074				40.00
2009	52,549	PF63	40.00	PF65	50.00

KM# 889a DOLLAR
25.18 g., 0.925 Silver, 0.74 oz. ASW 36.07mm. **Obv.** Bust right **Rev:** Boy silouette with arms spread, 3 planes, plane shadow partially gilt

Date	Mintage				
2009(ml)	27,549	PF63	55.00	PF65	65.00

KM# 914 DOLLAR
7.00 g., Aureate-Bronze Plated Nickel, 26.5mm. **Obv.** Bust right **Obv. Designer:** Susanna Blunt **Rev:** Blue heron in flight

Date	Mintage	MS63
2009 Specimen	21,677	50.00

DOLLAR

KM# 883 DOLLAR
7.00 g., Aureate-Bronze Plated Nickel, 26.5mm. **Subject:**
Lucky Loonie **Obv.** Bust right **Rev:** Canadian Olympic logo
Obv. Legend: Elizabeth II DG Regina **Rev. Legend:** Canada
Dollar

Date	Mintage	MS63
2010	12,000	20.00

KM# 883a DOLLAR
9.31 g., 0.925 Silver, 0.28 oz. ASW 26.5mm. **Subject:**
Lucky Loonie **Obv.** Bust right **Rev:** Canadian Olympic
logo in color **Obv. Legend:** Elizabeth II DG Regina **Rev.**
Legend: Vancouver 2010 Canada Dollar **Shape:** 11-sided

Date	Mintage		
2010	40,000	PF63 45.00	PF65 55.00

KM# 1046 DOLLAR
Aureate-Bronze Plated Nickel, 26.5mm. **Subject:**
Roughriders **Rev:** S logo **Shape:** 11-sided

Date	Mintage	MS63
2010(ml)	—	7.50

KM# 975 DOLLAR
0.925 Silver, 36mm. **Rev:** Sun mask **Rev. Designer:** Xwa
lack Tun

Date	Mintage	
2010	1,278	PF65 200

KM# 995 DOLLAR
25.17 g., 0.925 Silver, 0.74 oz. ASW 36.07mm. **Rev:**
HMCS Sackville **Rev. Designer:** Yves Berube

Date	Mintage		
2010	—	PF63 45.00	PF65 55.00

KM# 995a DOLLAR
25.17 g., 0.925 Silver, 0.74 oz. ASW 36.07mm. **Subject:**
Navy Centennial **Rev:** HMCS Sackville, sea waves in gilt

Date	Mintage		
2010	—	PF63 100	PF65 110

KM# 996 DOLLAR
7.00 g., Aureate-Bronze Plated Nickel, 26.5mm. **Rev:**
Northern Harrier Hawk

Date	Mintage	MS63
2010	35,000	30.00
2010(ml)	—	PF63 40.00 PF65 50.00

KM# 1017 DOLLAR
7.00 g., Aureate-Bronze Plated Nickel, 26.5mm. **Rev:**
Male and female sailors saluting, HMCS Halifax and
anchor above

Date	Mintage	MS63
2010	—	5.00

KM# 1017a DOLLAR
7.00 g., Aureate Bronze, 26.5mm. **Rev:** Male and female
sailors saluting, HMCS Halifax in background and anchor
above

Date	Mintage		
2010	—	PF63 45.00	PF65 50.00

DOLLAR

KM# 1027 DOLLAR
25.18 g., 0.925 Silver, 0.74 oz. ASW 36.07mm. **Obv.** George V bust left **Rev:** Voyaguers, dual dates below

Date	Mintage		
2010	7,500	PF63 60.00	PF65 70.00

KM# 1050 DOLLAR
25.18 g., 0.925 Silver, 0.74 oz. ASW 36.07mm. **Rev:** Red poppy in large field of poppies **Edge:** Reeded

Date	Mintage		
2010	5,000	PF63 140	PF65 150

KM# 1086 DOLLAR
7.00 g., Aureate-Bronze Plated Nickel, 26.5mm. **Rev:** Great Grey Owl **Rev. Designer:** Arnold Nagy

Date	Mintage	MS63
2011	35,000	13.50

KM# 1087 DOLLAR
25.18 g., 0.925 Silver, 0.74 oz. ASW 36.07mm. **Subject:** Parks Canada, 100th Anniversary **Rev:** Female head looking downward into hands holding nature scene **Rev. Designer:** Luc Normandin

Date	Mintage			MS63
2011	—	PF63 50.00	PF65 60.00	
2011	25,000			50.00

KM# 1087a DOLLAR
25.18 g., 0.925 Silver, 0.74 oz. ASW 36.07mm. **Subject:** Parks Canada, 100th Anniversary **Rev:** Female head looking downward to hands holding nature scene, partially gilt **Rev. Designer:** Luc Normandin

Date	Mintage		
2011	45,000	PF63 65.00	PF65 75.00

KM# 1112 DOLLAR
25.17 g., 0.925 Silver, 0.74 oz. ASW 36.07mm. **Obv.** Crowned bust left of George V **Obv. Designer:** E. B. MacKennal **Rev:** Value and date within maple wreath **Rev. Designer:** W.H.J. Blakemore

Date	Mintage		
2011	Est. 15000	PF63 110	PF65 115

KM# 1166 DOLLAR
7.00 g., Aureate-Bronze Plated Nickel, 26.5mm. **Subject:** Canada Parks **Obv.** Bust right **Rev:** Stylized animals

Date	Mintage	MS63
2011	—	5.00

KM# 1225 DOLLAR

25.18 g., 0.925 Silver, 0.74 oz. ASW 36.07mm. **Subject:** War of 1812, 200th Anniversary **Obv.** Bust right **Rev:** Two soldiers and guide on patrol

Date	Mintage		MS63
2012	—	PF63 50.00 PF65 60.00	
2012	—		50.00

KM# 1225a DOLLAR

25.18 g., 0.925 Silver, 0.74 oz. ASW 36.07mm. **Subject:** War of 1812, 200th Anniversary **Obv.** Bust right, gilt rim **Rev:** Two solders and guide, partially gilt

Date	Mintage	
2012	—	PF63 55.00 PF65 65.00

KM# 1256 DOLLAR

6.27 g., Brass Plated Steel, 26.5mm. **Subject:** Lucky Loonie **Rev:** Loon and Olympic logo **Shape:** 11-sided

Date	Mintage	MS63
2012	—	10.00

KM# 1256a DOLLAR

12.16 g., 0.925 Silver, 0.36 oz. ASW 26.5mm. **Subject:** Lucky loonie **Rev:** Loon and olympic logo in color

Date	Mintage	
2012	—	PF63 30.00 PF65 35.00

KM# 1216 DOLLAR

9.31 g., 0.925 Silver, 0.28 oz. ASW 26.5mm. **Obv.** Bust right, SP/PA below **Rev:** Loon, 1987-2012 below

Date	Mintage	
2012 Specimen	—	PF65 55.00

KM# 1222 DOLLAR

7.00 g., Aureate-Bronze Plated Nickel, 26.5mm. **Obv.** Bust right **Rev:** Loon and two young, 1987-2012 dates

Date	Mintage	
2012 Specimen	—	PF65 40.00

KM# 1244 DOLLAR

25.18 g., 0.925 Silver, 0.74 oz. ASW 36.07mm. **Subject:** Calgary Stampede

Date	Mintage	
2012	—	PF63 45.00 PF65 55.00

KM# 1254 DOLLAR

7.89 g., 0.999 Silver, 0.25 oz. ASW 26.5mm. **Subject:** Loonie, 25th Anniversary **Rev:** Two loons and large 25

Date	Mintage	
1987-2012	15,000	PF63 32.00 PF65 35.00

KM# 1255 DOLLAR

6.27 g., Brass Plated Steel, 26.5mm. **Rev:** Loon with security feature above **Shape:** 11-sided

Date	Mintage		MS63
2012	—		5.00
2012	—	PF65 7.50	
2013	—		5.00
2013	—	PF65 7.50	

KM# 1274 DOLLAR
25.18 g., 0.925 Silver, 0.74 oz. ASW 36.07mm. **Subject:** Artistic Loonie **Rev:** Four Loons in color

Date	Mintage	
2012	—	PF65 125

KM# 1294 DOLLAR
6.27 g., Brass Plated Steel, 26.5mm. **Subject:** Grey Cup, 100th Anniversary **Obv.** Bust right **Shape:** 11-sided

Date	Mintage	MS63
2012	—	5.00

KM# 1295 DOLLAR
25.18 g., 0.925 Silver, 0.74 oz. ASW 36.07mm. **Subject:** Grey Cup, 100th Anniversary

Date	Mintage	
2012	—	PF63 75.00 PF65 85.00

KM# 1387 DOLLAR
23.17 g., 0.999 Silver, 0.74 oz. ASW 36.07mm. **Subject:** Arctic Exploration - 100th Anniversary **Rev:** Three explorers and dog sled team, Company Rose in background **Rev. Designer:** Bonnie Ross

Date	Mintage		MS63
2013	Est. 40000	PF63 50.00 PF65 60.00	
2013	20,000		55.00

KM# 1360 DOLLAR
7.00 g., Bronze Plated Nickel, 26.5mm. **Rev:** Blue wing teal standing on log **Rev. Designer:** Glen Loates

Date	Mintage	
2013	50,000	PF63 35.00 PF65 40.00

KM# 1387a DOLLAR
23.17 g., 0.999 Silver, 0.74 oz. ASW 36.07mm. **Subject:** Arctic Exploration - 100th Anniversary **Rev:** Map of North Pole, Arctic Explorers, Selectively Gilt **Rev. Designer:** Bonnie Ross

Date	Mintage	
2013	—	PF65 225

KM# 1388 DOLLAR
23.17 g., 0.999 Silver, 0.74 oz. ASW 36.07mm. **Subject:** End of 7 Years War - 250th Anniversary **Rev:** Soldiers and Settlers **Rev. Designer:** Tony Bianco

Date	Mintage	
2013	Est. 10000	PF63 60.00 PF65 70.00

KM# 1394 DOLLAR
25.11 g., 0.925 Silver, 0.74 oz. ASW 36.07mm. **Obv.** Elizabeth II, Mary Glick portrait

Date	Mintage	
2013	—	PF63 55.00 PF65 65.00

KM# 1464 DOLLAR
23.17 g., 0.925 Silver, 0.68 oz. ASW 36mm. **Subject:** Korean War Armistance, 60th Anniversary **Rev:** Hercules slaying Hydra **Rev. Designer:** Edward Carter Preston **Note:** Based on the design of the Korean Service Medal

Date	Mintage		
2013	10,000	PF63 65.00	PF65 75.00

KM# 1586 DOLLAR
25.18 g., 0.925 Silver, 0.74 oz. ASW 36.07mm. **Subject:** WWI **Obv.** Bust right **Rev:** Soldier and woman kissing, soldiers boarding train

Date	Mintage	MS63
2014	—	50.00
2014		PF63 55.00 PF65 65.00

KM# 1587 DOLLAR
7.00 g., Aluminum-Bronze, 26.5mm. **Subject:** Lucky Loon **Obv.** Bust right **Rev:** Loon, Olympic logo at left

Date	Mintage	MS63
2014	—	5.00

KM# 1588 DOLLAR
7.00 g., Aluminum-Bronze, 26.5mm. **Subject:** Baby loon **Obv.** Bust right **Rev:** Stork in flight left with baby bundle

Date	Mintage	MS63
2014	—	5.00

KM# 1591 DOLLAR
7.00 g., Aluminum-Bronze, **Subject:** Oh Canada Loonie **Obv.** Bust right **Rev:** Maple leaf

Date	Mintage	MS63
2014	—	5.00

KM# 1627 DOLLAR
6.27 g., Brass Plated Nickel, 26.5mm. **Subject:** Wedding **Rev:** Two birds

Date	Mintage	MS63
2014	—	20.00

KM# 1628 DOLLAR
6.27 g., Bronze Plated Nickel, 26.5mm. **Rev:** Ferruginous Hawk in flight right **Rev. Designer:** Trevor Tennant

Date	Mintage	MS63
2014 Specimen	50,000	50.00

KM# 1589 DOLLAR
7.00 g., Aluminum-Bronze, 26.5mm. **Subject:** Birthday Loon **Obv.** Bust right **Rev:** Party hats, decorations, presents

Date	Mintage	MS63
2014	—	5.00

KM# 652 DOLLAR (LOUIS)
1.50 g., 0.999 Gold, 0.05 oz. AGW 14.1mm. **Subject:** Gold Louis **Obv.** Bust right **Obv. Designer:** Susanna Blunt **Rev:** Crowned double L monogram within wreath

Date	Mintage		
2006	5,648	PF63 100	PF65 110

KM# 756 DOLLAR (LOUIS)
1.56 g., 0.999 Gold, 0.05 oz. AGW 14.1mm. **Obv.** Bust right **Obv. Designer:** Susanna Blunt **Rev:** Crown above two oval shields

Date	Mintage	
2007	4,023	PF65 110

KM# 834 DOLLAR (LOUIS)
1.56 g., 0.999 Gold, 0.05 oz. AGW 14.1mm. **Obv.** Bust right **Obv. Designer:** Susanna Blunt **Rev:** Crowned double L monogram, three lis around

Date	Mintage	
2008	3,793	PF65 110

KM# 270 2 DOLLARS
7.30 g., Bi-Metallic, 28mm. **Obv.** Crowned head right within circle, date below **Obv. Designer:** Dora dePedery-Hunt **Rev:** Polar bear right within circle, denomination

below **Rev. Designer:** Brent Townsend **Edge:** Segmented reeding

Date	Mintage			MS63
1996	375,483,000			5.00
1996	—	PF65 10.00		
1997	16,942,000			3.25
1998	4,926,000			3.25
1998W	Inc. above			3.25
1999	25,130,000			3.25
2000	29,847,000			3.25
2000W	Inc. above			3.25
2001	27,008,000			5.00
2001	74,944	PF63 11.00	PF65 12.50	
2002	11,910,000			5.00
2002	65,315	PF63 11.00	PF65 12.50	
2003	7,123,697			5.00
2003	62,007	PF63 11.00	PF65 12.50	

KM# 270a 2 DOLLARS
11.32 g., Bi-Metallic, 28mm. **Obv.** Crowned head right within circle, date below **Rev:** Polar bear right within circle, denomination below

Date	Mintage	
1996	—	PF60 375

KM# 270b 2 DOLLARS
25.00 g., 0.925 Bi-Metallic, 0.74 oz. 28mm. **Obv.** Crowned head right within circle, date below **Rev:** Polar bear right within circle, denomination below **Edge:** 4.5mm thick

Date	Mintage	
1996	10,000	PF60 55.00
1998 Proof	—	—

KM# 270c 2 DOLLARS
8.83 g., 0.925 Silver, 0.26 oz. ASW 28mm. **Obv.** Crowned head right within circle, date below **Rev:** Polar bear right within circle, denomination below **Note:** 1.9mm thick.

Date	Mintage	
1996	10,000	PF65 12.00
1997	—	PF65 10.00
1998O	—	PF65 12.00
1999	—	PF65 12.00
2000	—	PF65 12.00
2001	—	PF65 12.00

KM# 357 2 DOLLARS
7.30 g., Bi-Metallic, 28mm. **Subject:** Nunavut **Obv.** Crowned head right **Rev:** Inuit person with drum, denomination below **Rev. Designer:** G. Arnaktavyok **Edge:** Segmented reeding

Date	Mintage	MS63
1999	—	4.00

KM# 357a 2 DOLLARS
8.52 g., 0.925 Silver, 0.25 oz. ASW 28mm. **Subject:** Nunavut **Obv.** Crowned head right **Rev:** Drum dancer **Edge:** Interrupted reeding

Date	Mintage	
1999	39,873	PF60 15.00

KM# 357b 2 DOLLARS
Gold, AGW **Subject:** Nunavut **Obv.** Crowned head right **Rev:** Drum dancer

Date	Mintage	
1999	4,298	PF60 400

KM# 399 2 DOLLARS
7.30 g., Bi-Metallic, 28mm. **Subject:** Knowledge **Obv.** Crowned head right within circle, denomination below **Rev:** Polar bear and 2 cubs right within circle, date above **Rev. Designer:** Tony Bianco **Edge:** Segmented reeding

Date	Mintage	MS63
2000 Specimen	1,500	5.00

KM# 399a 2 DOLLARS
8.52 g., 0.925 Silver, 0.25 oz. ASW **Subject:** Knowledge **Obv.** Crowned head right within circle, denomination below **Rev:** Polar bear and 2 cubs within circle, date above

Date	Mintage	
2000	39,768	PF60 15.00

KM# 399b 2 DOLLARS
6.31 g., 0.916 Gold, 0.18 oz. AGW **Subject:** Knowledge **Obv.** Crowned head right within circle, denomination below **Rev:** Polar bear and two cubs right within circle, date above

Date	Mintage	
2000	5,881	PF60 350

KM# 449 2 DOLLARS
7.30 g., Bi-Metallic, 28mm. **Subject:** Elizabeth II Golden Jubilee **Obv.** Crowned head right, jubilee commemorative dates below **Edge:** Segmented reeding

Date	Mintage	MS63
1952-2002	27,020,000	4.00

KM# 449a 2 DOLLARS
8.83 g., 0.925 Silver, 0.26 oz. ASW 28mm. **Subject:** Elizabeth II Golden Jubilee **Obv.** Crowned head right, jubilee commemorative dates below

Date	Mintage		
1952-2002	100,000	PF63 12.00	PF65 14.00

KM# 270d 2 DOLLARS
8.83 g., 0.925 Silver, 0.26 oz. ASW **Subject:** 100th Anniversary of the Cobalt Silver Strike **Obv.** Crowned head right, within circle, date below **Rev:** Polar bear right, within circle, denomination below

Date	Mintage	
2003	100,000	PF65 25.00

KM# 496   2 DOLLARS
7.30 g., Bi-Metallic, 28mm. **Obv.** Head right **Obv. Designer:** Susanna Blunt **Rev:** Polar bear advancing right **Rev. Designer:** Brent Townsend **Edge:** Segmented reeding

Date	Mintage					MS63
2003	11,244,000					5.00
2003W	71,142					25.00
2004	12,908,000					5.00
2004	—	**PF63** 11.00	**PF65** 12.50			
2005	38,317,000					5.00
2005	—	**PF63** 11.00	**PF65** 12.50			
2006(ml)	35,319,000					5.00
2006(ml)	—	**PF63** 11.00	**PF65** 12.50			
2007(ml)	38,957,000					5.00
2007(ml)	—	**PF63** 11.00	**PF65** 12.50			
2008(ml)	18,400,000					5.00
2008(ml)	—	**PF63** 11.00	**PF65** 12.50			
2009(ml)	38,430,000					5.00
2009(ml)	—	**PF63** 11.00	**PF65** 12.50			
2010(ml)	—					5.00
2010(ml)	—	**PF63** 11.00	**PF65** 12.50			
2011(ml)	—					5.00
2011(ml)	—	**PF63** 11.00	**PF65** 12.50			
2012(ml)	—					5.00
2012(ml)	—	**PF63** 11.00	**PF65** 12.50			

KM# 496a   2 DOLLARS
10.84 g., 0.925 Bi-Metallic, 0.32 oz. 28mm. **Obv.** Head right **Obv. Designer:** Susanna Blunt **Rev:** Polar Bear **Edge:** Segmented reeding

Date	Mintage		
2004	—	**PF63** 22.00	**PF65** 25.00

KM# 835   2 DOLLARS
8.80 g., 0.925 Silver, 0.26 oz. ASW 27.95mm. **Rev:** Proud Polar Bear advancing right

Date	Mintage		
2004	12,607	**PF63** 30.00	**PF65** 40.00

KM# 631   2 DOLLARS
7.30 g., Bi-Metallic, 28mm. **Subject:** 10th Anniversary of $2 coin **Obv.** Crowned head right **Edge:** Segmented reeding

Date	Mintage			MS63
2006(ml)	5,005,000			25.00
2006(ml)	—	**PF63** 37.00	**PF65** 40.00	

KM# 631a   2 DOLLARS
Bi-Metallic, **Subject:** 10th Anniversary of $2 coin **Obv.** Crowned head right **Rev:** Polar bear

Date	Mintage	
2006	2,068	**PF65** 400

KM# 836   2 DOLLARS
7.30 g., Bi-Metallic, 28mm. **Subject:** $2 coin, 10th Anniversary **Rev:** Churchill" Polar Bear, northern lights **Edge:** Segmented reeding

Date	Mintage	MS63
2006(ml)	31,636	7.50

KM# 837   2 DOLLARS
7.30 g., Bi-Metallic, **Obv.** Bust left, date at top **Rev:** Polar Bear advancing right

Date	Mintage	MS63
2006(ml)	—	7.50
2007(ml)	38,957,000	7.50

KM# 796   2 DOLLARS
8.83 g., 0.925 Silver, 0.26 oz. ASW 28.07mm. **Rev:** Bear, gold plated center

Date	Mintage	MS63
2008	—	25.00

KM# 1040   2 DOLLARS
7.30 g., Bi-Metallic, 28mm. **Subject:** Quebec 400th Anniversary **Rev:** Lis and small sailing ship **Edge:** Segmented reeding

Date	Mintage	MS63
2008	—	7.50

KM# 1020   2 DOLLARS
7.30 g., Bi-Metallic, 28mm. **Rev:** Two lynx cubs **Rev. Designer:** Christie Paquet **Edge:** Segmented reeding

Date	Mintage	
2010 Specimen	15,000	**PF63** 40.00

KM# 1088   2 DOLLARS
7.30 g., Bi-Metallic, 28mm. **Rev:** Elk Calf **Rev. Designer:** Christine Paquet **Edge:** Segmented reeding

Date	Mintage	MS63
2011	—	7.50

2 DOLLARS

KM# 1167   2 DOLLARS
7.30 g., Bi-Metallic, 28mm. **Subject:** Canada Parks **Obv.**
Bust right **Rev:** Stylized trees

Date	Mintage		MS63
2011	—		7.50

KM# 1257   2 DOLLARS
6.92 g., Bi-Metallic, 28mm. **Rev:** Polar bear with security
device above **Edge:** Lettered and segmented reeding

Date	Mintage		MS63
2012	—		7.50
2012	—	PF65	10.00
2013	—		7.50
2013	—	PF65	10.00

KM# 1258   2 DOLLARS
6.92 g., Bi-Metallic, 28mm. **Subject:** H.M.S. Shannon
Obv. Designer: Susana Blunt **Rev. Designer:** Christie
Paquet **Edge:** Lettered and segmented reeding

Date	Mintage	MS63
2012	—	10.00

KM# 1263   2 DOLLARS
7.30 g., Bi-Metallic, 28mm. **Rev:** Wolf cubs

Date	Mintage	MS63
2012	—	10.00

KM# 1463   2 DOLLARS
(No Composition), 28mm. **Rev:** Two black bear cubs
playing **Rev. Designer:** Glen Lontes

Date	Mintage			
2013	17,500	PF63 45.00	PF65 50.00

KM# 657   3 DOLLARS
11.72 g., 0.925 Silver, 0.35 oz. ASW 27x27mm. **Rev:**
Beaver within wreath **Shape:** Square

Date	Mintage		
2006	19,963	PF65	225

KM# 1051   3 DOLLARS
11.60 g., 0.925 Silver, 0.34 oz. ASW 27x27mm. **Subject:**
Wildlife conservation **Rev:** Stylized polar bear and
northern lights **Shape:** square

Date	Mintage	MS63
2010 Specimen	15,000	55.00

KM# 978   3 DOLLARS
7.96 g., Silver, 27mm. **Rev:** Return of the Tyee (giant
salmon)

Date	Mintage				
2010	15,000	PF63 40.00	PF65 50.00

KM# 1011   3 DOLLARS
11.60 g., 0.925 Silver, 0.34 oz. ASW 27x27mm. **Rev:**
Barn Owl **Rev. Designer:** Jason Bouwman **Shape:** Square

Date	Mintage				
2010	15,000	PF63 55.00	PF65 65.00

KM# 1089 3 DOLLARS
11.60 g., 0.925 Silver, 0.34 oz. ASW 27x27mm. **Rev:**
Orca Whale **Rev. Designer:** Jason Bouwman **Shape:**
Square

Date	Mintage		
2011	15,000	PF63 55.00	PF65 65.00

KM# 1090 3 DOLLARS
7.96 g., 0.999 Silver, 0.25 oz. ASW 27mm. **Obv.** Bust
right **Rev:** Eskimo mother kneeling, child on back, partially
gilt **Rev. Designer:** Andrew Oappik

Date	Mintage		
2011	10,000	PF63 55.00	PF65 65.00

KM# 1117 3 DOLLARS
7.96 g., 0.9999 Silver, 0.25 oz. ASW 27mm. **Subject:**
January birthstone, Garnet **Obv.** Bust left **Rev:** Birthstone
at cener of artistic sunburst **Edge:** Reeded

Date	Mintage		
2011	—	PF63 40.00	PF65 45.00

KM# 1118 3 DOLLARS
7.96 g., 0.9999 Silver, 0.25 oz. ASW 27mm. **Subject:**
February birthstone, Amythest **Obv.** Bust right **Rev:**
Birthstone at cener of artistic sunburst **Edge:** Reeded

Date	Mintage		
2011	—	PF63 40.00	PF65 45.00

KM# 1119 3 DOLLARS
7.96 g., 0.9999 Silver, 0.25 oz. ASW 27mm. **Subject:**
March birthstone, Aquamarine **Obv.** Bust right **Rev:**
Birthstone at cener of artistic sunburst **Edge:** Reeded

Date	Mintage		
2011	—	PF63 40.00	PF65 45.00

KM# 1120 3 DOLLARS
7.96 g., 0.9999 Silver, 0.25 oz. ASW 27mm. **Subject:**
April birthstone, diamond **Obv.** Bust right **Rev:** Birthstone
at cener of artistic sunburst **Edge:** Reeded

Date	Mintage		
2011	—	PF63 40.00	PF65 45.00

KM# 1121 3 DOLLARS
7.96 g., 0.9999 Silver, 0.25 oz. ASW 27mm. **Subject:**
May birthstone **Obv.** Bust right **Rev:** Birthstone at cener
of artistic sunburst **Edge:** Reeded

Date	Mintage		
2011	—	PF63 40.00	PF65 45.00

KM# 1122 3 DOLLARS
7.96 g., 0.9999 Silver, 0.25 oz. ASW 27mm. **Subject:**
June birthstone, Alexandrite **Obv.** Bust right **Rev:**
Birthstone at cener of artistic sunburst

Date	Mintage		
2011	—	PF63 40.00	PF65 45.00

KM# 1123 3 DOLLARS
7.96 g., 0.9999 Silver, 0.25 oz. ASW 27mm. **Subject:** July
birthstone, Ruby **Obv.** Bust right **Rev:** Birthstone at cener
of artistic sunburst

Date	Mintage		
2011	—	PF63 40.00	PF65 45.00

KM# 1124 3 DOLLARS
7.96 g., 0.9999 Silver, 0.25 oz. ASW 27mm. **Subject:**
August birthstone, Priedot **Obv.** Bust right **Rev:** Birthstone
at cener of artistic sunburst

Date	Mintage		
2011	—	PF63 40.00	PF65 45.00

KM# 1126 3 DOLLARS
7.96 g., 0.9999 Silver, 0.25 oz. ASW 27mm. **Subject:**
October birthstone **Obv.** Bust right **Rev:** Birthstone at
cener of artistic sunburst

Date	Mintage		
2011	—	PF63 40.00	PF65 45.00

KM# 1127 3 DOLLARS
7.96 g., 0.9999 Silver, 0.25 oz. ASW 27mm. **Subject:**
November birthstone **Obv.** Bust right **Rev:** Birthstone at
cener of artistic sunburst

Date	Mintage		
2011	—	PF63 40.00	PF65 45.00

KM# 1128 3 DOLLARS
7.96 g., 0.9999 Silver, 0.25 oz. ASW 27mm. **Subject:**
December birhtstone **Obv.** Bust right **Rev:** Birthstone at
cener of artistic sunburst

Date	Mintage		
2011	—	PF63 40.00	PF65 45.00

KM# 1151 3 DOLLARS
11.80 g., 0.925 Silver, 0.35 oz. ASW 27x27mm. **Obv.**
Bust right **Rev:** Black footed ferret

Date	Mintage		
2011	Est. 15000	PF63 55.00	PF65 65.00

KM# 1300 3 DOLLARS
7.96 g., 0.9999 Silver, 0.25 oz. ASW 27mm. **Subject:**
January birthstone, Garnet **Obv.** Bust right **Obv.**
Designer: Susana Blunt **Rev:** Birthstone at center of
wreath **Rev. Designer:** Maurice Gervias

Date	Mintage	
2013	—	PF65 50.00

KM# 1301 3 DOLLARS
7.96 g., 0.999 Silver, 0.25 oz. ASW 27mm. **Subject:**
February birthstone, Amythest **Obv.** Bust right **Obv.**
Designer: Susana Blunt **Rev:** Birthstone at center of
wreath **Rev. Designer:** Maurice Gervais

Date	Mintage	
2013	—	PF65 65.00

KM# 1302 3 DOLLARS
7.96 g., 0.999 Silver, 0.25 oz. ASW 27mm. **Subject:**
March birthstone, Aquamarine **Obv.** Bust right **Obv.**
Designer: Susana Blunt **Rev:** Birthstone at center of
wreath **Rev. Designer:** Maurice Gervais

Date	Mintage		
2013	—	PF65 50.00	

KM# 1303 3 DOLLARS
7.96 g., 0.999 Silver, 0.25 oz. ASW 27mm. **Subject:** April
birthstone, Diamond **Obv.** Bust right **Obv. Designer:**
Susana Blunt **Rev:** Birthstone at center of wreath **Rev.**
Designer: Maurice Gervais

Date	Mintage		
2013	—	PF65 50.00	

KM# 1304 3 DOLLARS
7.96 g., 0.999 Silver, 0.25 oz. ASW 27mm. **Subject:**
May birthstone **Obv.** Bust right **Obv. Designer:** Susana
Blunt **Rev:** Birthstone at center of wreath **Rev. Designer:**
Maurice Gervais

Date	Mintage		
2013	—	PF65 50.00	

KM# 1305 3 DOLLARS
7.96 g., 0.999 Silver, 0.25 oz. ASW 27mm. **Subject:** June
birthstone, Alexandrite **Obv.** Bust right **Obv. Designer:**
Susana Blunt **Rev:** Birthstone at center of wreath **Rev.**
Designer: Maurice Gervais

Date	Mintage		
2013	—	PF65 50.00	

KM# 1306 3 DOLLARS
7.96 g., 0.999 Silver, 0.25 oz. ASW 27mm. **Subject:** July
birthstone - Ruby **Obv.** Bust right **Obv. Designer:** Susana
Blunt **Rev:** Birthstone at center of wreath **Rev. Designer:**
Maurice Gervais

Date	Mintage		
2013	—	PF65 50.00	

KM# 1307 3 DOLLARS
7.96 g., 0.999 Silver, 0.25 oz. ASW 27mm. **Subject:**
August birthstone - Priedot **Obv.** Bust right **Obv.**
Designer: Susana Blunt **Rev:** Birthstone at center of
wreath **Rev. Designer:** Maurice Gervais

Date	Mintage		
2013	—	PF65 50.00	

KM# 1308 3 DOLLARS
7.96 g., 0.999 Silver, 0.25 oz. ASW 27mm. **Subject:**
September birthstone **Obv.** Bust right **Obv. Designer:**
Susana Blunt **Rev:** Birthstone at center of wreath **Rev.**
Designer: Maruice Gervais

Date	Mintage		
2013	—	PF65 50.00	

KM# 1309 3 DOLLARS
7.96 g., 0.999 Silver, 0.25 oz. ASW 27mm. **Subject:**
October birthstone **Obv.** Bust right **Obv. Designer:**
Susana Blunt **Rev:** Birthstone at center of wreath **Rev.**
Designer: Maurice Gervais

Date	Mintage		
2013	—	PF65 50.00	

KM# 1310 3 DOLLARS
7.96 g., 0.999 Silver, 0.25 oz. ASW 27mm. **Subject:**
November birthstone **Obv.** Bust right **Obv. Designer:**
Susana Blunt **Rev:** Birthstone at center of wreath **Rev.**
Designer: Maurice Gervais

Date	Mintage		
2013	—	PF65 50.00	

KM# 1311 3 DOLLARS
7.96 g., 0.999 Silver, 0.25 oz. ASW 27mm. **Subject:**
December birthstone **Obv.** Bust right **Obv. Designer:**
Susana Blunt **Rev:** Birthstone at center of wreath **Rev.**
Designer: Maurice Gervais

Date	Mintage		
2013	—	PF65 50.00	

KM# 1352 3 DOLLARS
7.96 g., 0.9999 Silver, 0.25 oz. ASW 27mm. **Rev:**
Hummingbirds around crystal **Rev. Designer:** Yves
Bérubé

Date	Mintage		
2013	20,000	PF63 65.00	PF65 70.00

KM# 1367 3 DOLLARS
7.96 g., 0.9999 Silver, 0.25 oz. ASW 27mm. **Subject:**
Animal Architects: Bee **Rev:** Bee and Hive in color **Rev.**
Designer: Yves Berube

Date	Mintage		
2013	Est. 10000	PF63 60.00	PF65 70.00

KM# 1451 3 DOLLARS
7.96 g., 0.9999 Silver, 0.25 oz. ASW 27mm. **Rev:** Large
maple leaf and many small maple leaves **Rev. Designer:**
Jose Osio

Date	Mintage		
2013	10,000	PF63 50.00	PF65 60.00

KM# 1481 3 DOLLARS
19.20 g., 0.950 Copper, 0.58 oz. 35.75mm. **Subject:**
Banknote Allegory **Rev:** Female seated **Rev. Designer:**
Laurie McGaw

Date	Mintage		
2013	15,000	PF63 35.00	PF65 40.00

KM# 1485 3 DOLLARS
31.11 g., 0.999 Silver, 0.99 oz. ASW 38mm. **Rev:** Gradfather and grandson fishing from lake dock, dog at their side

Date	Mintage		
2013	—	PF63 45.00	PF65 50.00

KM# 1492 3 DOLLARS
7.96 g., 0.9999 Silver, 0.25 oz. ASW 27mm. **Rev:** Hummingbird and morning glory - crystal insert **Rev. Designer:** Yves Berube

Date	Mintage		
2013	20,000	PF63 50.00	PF65 60.00

KM# 1617 3 DOLLARS
7.96 g., 0.999 Silver, 0.25 oz. ASW 27mm. **Subject:** Jewel of Life **Obv.** Bust right **Rev:** Tree and crystals **Rev. Designer:** Caroline Néron

Date	Mintage		
2014	15,000	PF63 50.00	PF65 60.00

KM# 728 4 DOLLARS
15.87 g., 0.925 Silver, 0.47 oz. ASW 34mm. **Subject:** Dinosaur fossil **Obv.** Bust right **Rev:** Parasaurolophus, selective enameling

Date	Mintage		
2007	14,946	PF63 115	PF65 125

KM# 797 4 DOLLARS
15.87 g., 0.999 Silver, 0.51 oz. ASW 34mm. **Subject:** Dinosaur fossil **Obv.** Bust right **Rev:** Triceratops, enameled **Rev. Designer:** Kerri Burnett

Date	Mintage		
2008	13,046	PF63 65.00	PF65 75.00

KM# 890 4 DOLLARS
15.87 g., 0.999 Silver, 0.51 oz. ASW 34mm. **Subject:** Tyrannosaurus Rex **Obv.** Bust right **Obv. Designer:** Susanna Blunt **Rev:** T-Rex skeleton in selective aging **Obv. Legend:** Elizabeth II DG Regina **Rev. Designer:** Kerri Burnette **Rev. Legend:** Canada 4 Dollars

Date	Mintage		
2009	13,572	PF63 50.00	PF65 60.00

KM# 942 4 DOLLARS
15.87 g., Silver, 34mm. **Rev:** Kids hanging stocking on fireplace, Christmas tree on right

Date	Mintage		
2009	6,011	PF63 40.00	PF65 45.00

KM# 1014 4 DOLLARS
15.87 g., 0.999 Silver, 0.51 oz. ASW 34mm. **Rev:** Euoplocephalus **Rev. Designer:** Kerri Burnett

Date	Mintage		
2010	Est. 13000	PF63 50.00	PF65 60.00

KM# 1022 4 DOLLARS
Silver, **Rev:** Dromaeosaurus

Date	Mintage		
2010	8,982	PF63 75.00	PF65 85.00

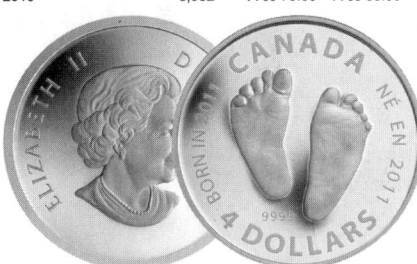

KM# 1129 4 DOLLARS
15.87 g., 0.9999 Silver, 0.51 oz. ASW 34mm. **Obv.** Bust right **Rev:** Baby's footprint **Edge:** Reeded

Date	Mintage		
2011	Est. 10000	PF63 50.00	PF65 60.00

KM# 1325 4 DOLLARS
7.96 g., 0.999 Silver, 0.25 oz. ASW 27mm. **Subject:** War of 1812 - Tecumseh **Rev:** Portrait at right, red maple leaf **Rev. Designer:** Bonnie Ross

Date	Mintage		
2012	10,000	PF63 45.00	PF65 50.00

4 DOLLARS

KM# 1323   4 DOLLARS
7.96 g., 0.999 Silver, 0.25 oz. ASW 27mm. **Subject:** War of 1812 - Brock **Rev:** Portrait at right, red maple leaf **Rev. Designer:** Bonnie Ross

Date	Mintage		
2012	10,000	PF63 45.00	PF65 50.00

KM# 1356   4 DOLLARS
7.96 g., 0.9999 Silver, 0.25 oz. ASW 27mm. **Subject:** War of 1812 - Salaberry **Rev:** Bust at right, red maple leaf **Rev. Designer:** Bonnie Ross

Date	Mintage		
2013	10,000	PF63 45.00	PF65 50.00

KM# 1452   4 DOLLARS
7.96 g., 0.999 Silver, 0.25 oz. ASW 27mm. **Subject:** Heroes of 1812 **Rev:** Bust at right, maple leaf in color

Date	Mintage		
2013	Est. 10000	PF63 40.00	PF65 50.00

KM# 14   SOVEREIGN
7.99 g., 0.917 Gold, 0.23 oz. AGW **Rev:** St. George slaying dragon, mint mark below horse's rear hooves

Date	Mintage	F12	VF20	XF40	AU50	MS60	MS63
1908C	636	1,800	2,500	3,500	4,000	4,500	5,500
1909C	16,273	BV	350	400	450	650	2,300
1910C	28,012	BV	350	400	450	650	2,900

KM# 20   SOVEREIGN
7.99 g., 0.917 Gold, 0.23 oz. AGW **Rev:** St. George slaying dragon, mint mark below horse's rear hooves

Date	Mintage	F12	VF20	XF40	AU50	MS60	MS63
1911C Specimen	—	—	—	—	—	—	3,000
1911C	256,946	—	BV	350	400	450	500
1913C	3,715	650	800	1,050	1,400	1,800	3,500
1914C	14,871	BV	400	450	500	650	1,150
1916C About 20 known	—	16,000	17,000	18,000	22,000	24,000	40,000
Note: Stacks' A.G. Carter Jr. Sale 12-89 Gem BU realized $82,500							
1917C	58,845	—	BV	350	400	450	700
1918C	106,514	—	BV	350	400	450	1,000
1919C	135,889	—	BV	350	400	450	800

KM# 26   5 DOLLARS
8.36 g., 0.900 Gold, 0.24 oz. AGW **Obv.** Crowned bust left **Obv. Designer:** E. B. MacKennal **Rev:** Arms within wreath, date and denomination below **Rev. Designer:** W. H. J. Blakemore

Date	Mintage	F12	VF20	XF40	AU50	MS60	MS63
1912	165,680	—	BV	350	400	450	650
1913	98,832	—	BV	350	400	450	800
1914	31,122	—	BV	450	600	900	3,000

KM# 84 5 DOLLARS

24.30 g., 0.925 Silver, 0.72 oz. ASW 38mm. **Subject:**
1976 Montreal Olympics **Obv.** Young bust right, small
maple below, date at right **Rev:** Sailboat "Kingston", date
at left, denomination below **Rev. Designer:** Georges Huel
Note: Series I.

Date	Mintage		MS63
1973	—		24.00
1973	165,203	PF60	24.00

KM# 85 5 DOLLARS

24.30 g., 0.925 Silver, 0.72 oz. ASW 38mm. **Subject:**
1976 Montreal Olympics **Obv.** Young bust right, small
maple leaf below, date at right **Rev:** North American map,
denomination below **Rev. Designer:** Georges Huel **Note:**
Series I.

Date	Mintage		MS63
1973	—		24.00
1973	165,203	PF60	24.00

KM# 89 5 DOLLARS

24.30 g., 0.925 Silver, 0.72 oz. ASW 38mm. **Subject:**

1976 Montreal Olympics **Obv.** Young bust right, small
maple leaf below, date at right **Rev:** Olympic rings,
denomination below **Rev. Designer:** Anthony Mann **Note:**
Series II.

Date	Mintage		MS63
1974	—		24.00
1974	97,431	PF60	24.00

KM# 90 5 DOLLARS

24.30 g., 0.925 Silver, 0.72 oz. ASW 38mm. **Subject:**
1976 Montreal Olympics **Obv.** Young bust right, small
maple leaf below, date at right **Rev:** Athlete with torch,
denomination below **Rev. Designer:** Anthony Mann **Note:**
Series II.

Date	Mintage		MS63
1974	—		24.00
1974	97,431	PF60	24.00

KM# 91 5 DOLLARS

24.30 g., 0.925 Silver, 0.72 oz. ASW 38mm. **Subject:**
1976 Montreal Olympics **Obv.** Young bust right, small
maple leaf below, date at right **Rev:** Rower, denomination
below **Rev. Designer:** Ken Danby **Note:** Series III.

Date	Mintage		MS63
1974	—		24.00
1974	104,684	PF60	24.00

KM# 92 5 DOLLARS

24.30 g., 0.925 Silver, 0.72 oz. ASW 38mm. **Subject:** 1976
Montreal Olympics **Obv.** Young bust right, small maple
leaf below, date at right **Rev:** Canoeing, denomination

below **Rev. Designer:** Ken Danby **Note:** Series III.

Date	Mintage		MS63
1974	—		24.00
1974	104,684	**PF60**	24.00

KM# 98   5 DOLLARS
24.30 g., 0.925 Silver, 0.72 oz. ASW 38mm. **Subject:** 1976 Montreal Olympics **Obv.** Young bust right, small maple leaf below, date at right **Rev:** Marathon, denomination below **Rev. Designer:** Leo Yerxa **Note:** Series IV.

Date	Mintage		MS63
1975	—		24.00
1975	89,155	**PF60**	24.00

KM# 99   5 DOLLARS
24.30 g., 0.925 Silver, 0.72 oz. ASW 38mm. **Subject:** Montreal 1976 - 21st Summer Olympic Games **Obv.** Young bust right, small maple leaf below, date at right **Rev:** Women's javelin event, denomination below **Rev. Designer:** Leo Yerxa **Note:** Series IV.

Date	Mintage		MS63
1975	—		24.00
1975	89,155	**PF60**	24.00

KM# 100   5 DOLLARS
24.30 g., 0.925 Silver, 0.72 oz. ASW 38mm. **Subject:** 1976 Montreal Olympics **Obv.** Young bust right, small maple leaf below, date at right **Rev:** Swimmer, denomination below **Rev. Designer:** Lynda Cooper **Note:** Series V.

Date	Mintage		MS63
1975	—		24.00
1975	89,155	**PF60**	24.00

KM# 101   5 DOLLARS
24.30 g., 0.925 Silver, 0.72 oz. ASW 38mm. **Subject:** Montreal 1976 - 21st Summer Olympic Games **Obv.** Young bust right, small maple leaf below, date at right **Rev:** Platform Diver, denomination below **Rev. Designer:** Lynda Cooper **Note:** Series V.

Date	Mintage		MS63
1975	—		24.00
1975	89,155	**PF60**	24.00

KM# 107   5 DOLLARS
24.30 g., 0.925 Silver, 0.72 oz. ASW 38mm. **Subject:** 1976 Montreal Olympics **Obv.** Young bust right, small maple leaf below, date at right **Rev:** Fencing, denomination below **Rev. Designer:** Shigeo Fukada **Note:** Series VI.

Date	Mintage		MS63
1976	—		24.00
1976	82,302	**PF60**	24.00

KM# 108   5 DOLLARS
24.30 g., 0.925 Silver, 0.72 oz. ASW 38mm. **Subject:** 1976 Montreal Olympics **Obv.** Young bust right, small maple leaf below, date at right **Rev:** Boxers, denomination below **Obv. Legend:** Boxing **Rev. Designer:** Shigeo Fukada **Note:** Series VI.

Date	Mintage		MS63
1976	—		24.00
1976	82,302	**PF60**	24.00

KM# 109 5 DOLLARS
24.30 g., 0.925 Silver, 0.72 oz. ASW 38mm. **Subject:**
1976 Montreal Olympics **Obv.** Young bust right, small
maple leaf below, date at right **Rev:** Olympic village,
denomination below **Rev. Designer:** Elliot John Morrison
Note: Series VII.

Date	Mintage		MS63
1976	—		24.00
1976	76,908	PF60 24.00	

KM# 110 5 DOLLARS
24.30 g., 0.925 Silver, 0.72 oz. ASW 38mm. **Subject:**
1976 Montreal Olympics **Obv.** Young bust right, maple
leaf below, date at right **Rev:** Olympic flame, denomination
below **Rev. Designer:** Elliot John Morrison **Note:** Series
VII.

Date	Mintage		MS63
1976	—	PF60 24.00	
1976	79,102		24.00

KM# 316 5 DOLLARS
31.39 g., 0.9999 Silver, 1.00 oz. ASW **Subject:** Dr.

Norman Bethune **Obv.** Young bust right **Rev:** Bethune and
party, date at upper right **Rev. Designer:** Harvey Chan

Date	Mintage	
1998	61,000	PF60 40.00

KM# 398 5 DOLLARS
Copper-Nickel-Zinc, **Obv.** Young bust right **Rev:** Viking
ship under sail **Rev. Designer:** Donald Curley **Note:** Sold
in sets with Norway 20 kroner, KM#465.

Date	Mintage	
1999	28,450	PF60 18.50

KM# 435 5 DOLLARS
16.86 g., 0.925 Silver, 0.50 oz. ASW 28.4mm. **Subject:**
Guglielmo Marconi **Obv.** Crowned head right **Rev:** Gold-
plated cameo portrait of Marconi **Rev. Designer:** Cosme
Saffioti **Edge:** Reeded **Note:** Only issued in two coin set
with British 2 pounds KM#1014a.

Date	Mintage		
2001	15,011	PF63 22.00	PF65 30.00

KM# 519 5 DOLLARS
8.36 g., 0.900 Gold, 0.24 oz. AGW 21.6mm. **Obv.**
Crowned head right **Rev:** National arms **Edge:** Reeded

Date	Mintage	
1912-2002	2,002	PF65 450

KM# 603 5 DOLLARS
31.11 g., 0.9999 Silver, 0.99 oz. ASW **Obv.** Head right
Rev: Loon splashing in the water, hologram

Date	Mintage	
2002 Satin Proof	30,000	PF65 50.00

KM# 518 5 DOLLARS
31.12 g., 0.9999 Silver, 0.99 oz. ASW 38mm. **Subject:**
F.I.F.A. World Cup Soccer , Germany 2006 **Obv.** Crowned
head right, denomination **Rev:** Goalie on knees **Edge:**
Reeded

Date	Mintage		
2003	21,542	PF63 35.00	PF65 40.00

5 DOLLARS

KM# 514   5 DOLLARS
31.12 g., 0.9999 Silver, 0.99 oz. ASW 38mm. **Obv.** Crowned head right **Rev:** Moose **Edge:** Reeded

Date	Mintage		
2004	12,822	**PF65** 175	

KM# 527   5 DOLLARS
31.12 g., 0.9999 Silver, 0.99 oz. ASW **Subject:** Golf, Championship of Canada, Centennial **Obv.** Head right

Date	Mintage		
2004	18,750	**PF63** 25.00	**PF65** 30.00

KM# 554   5 DOLLARS
31.12 g., 0.9999 Silver, 0.99 oz. ASW **Subject:** Alberta **Obv. Designer:** Head right **Rev. Designer:** Michelle Grant

Date	Mintage		
2005	20,000	**PF63** 30.00	**PF65** 35.00

KM# 555   5 DOLLARS
31.12 g., 0.9999 Silver, 0.99 oz. ASW **Subject:** Saskatchewan **Obv.** Head right **Obv. Designer:** Susanna Blunt **Rev. Designer:** Paulett Sapergia

Date	Mintage		
2005	20,000	**PF63** 30.00	**PF65** 35.00

KM# 556.1   5 DOLLARS
31.12 g., 0.999 Silver, 0.99 oz. ASW 38.02mm. **Subject:** 60th Anniversay Victory WWII - Veterans **Obv.** Bust right **Rev:** Large V and heads of sailor, soldier and aviator on large maple leaf **Edge:** Reeded

Date	Mintage	MS63
2005	25,000	32.00

KM# 556.2   5 DOLLARS
31.12 g., 0.9999 Silver, 0.99 oz. ASW 38.02mm. **Subject:** 60th Anniversary Victory WW II - Veterans **Obv.** Bust right **Rev:** Large V and heads of sailor, soldier and aviator on maple leaf with small maple leaf added at left and right **Edge:** Reeded

Date	Mintage	MS63
2005	10,000	125

KM# 557   5 DOLLARS
31.12 g., 0.9999 Silver, 0.99 oz. ASW 36mm. **Subject:** Walrus and calf **Obv.** Head right **Obv. Designer:** Susanna Blunt **Rev:** Two walrusus and calf **Rev. Designer:** Pierre Leduc

Date	Mintage		
2005	5,519	**PF63** 40.00	**PF65** 45.00

KM# 558   5 DOLLARS
31.12 g., 0.9999 Silver, 0.99 oz. ASW 36mm. **Subject:** White tailed deer **Obv.** Head right **Obv. Designer:** Susanna Blunt **Rev:** Two deer standing **Rev. Designer:** Xerxes Irani

Date	Mintage		
2005	6,439	**PF63** 40.00	**PF65** 45.00

5 DOLLARS

KM# 585   5 DOLLARS
31.12 g., 0.9999 Silver, 0.99 oz. ASW 36mm. **Obv.** Head right   **Obv. Designer:** Susanna Blunt **Rev:** Peregrine Falcon feeding young ones **Rev. Designer:** Dwayne Harty

Date	Mintage		
2006	7,226	**PF63** 45.00	**PF65** 50.00

KM# 586   5 DOLLARS
31.12 g., 0.9999 Silver, 0.99 oz. ASW 36mm. **Subject:** Sable Island horses **Obv.** Head right   **Obv. Designer:** Susanna Blunt **Rev:** Horse and foal standing   **Rev. Designer:** Christie Paquet

Date	Mintage		
2006	10,108	**PF63** 45.00	**PF65** 50.00

KM# 658   5 DOLLARS
31.12 g., 0.9999 Silver, 0.99 oz. ASW 36.07mm. **Subject:** Breast Cancer Awareness **Rev:** Colorized pink ribbon

Date	Mintage		
2006	11,048	**PF63** 45.00	**PF65** 50.00

KM# 659   5 DOLLARS
31.12 g., 0.9999 Silver, 0.99 oz. ASW **Subject:** C.A.F. Snowbirds Acrobatic Jet Flying Team **Rev:** Image of fighter jets and piolt

Date	Mintage		
2006	10,034	**PF63** 45.00	**PF65** 50.00

KM# 1036   5 DOLLARS
31.12 g., 0.999 Silver, 0.99 oz. ASW **Subject:** 80th Anniversary **Rev:** Two deer standing, one eating branch

Date	Mintage		
2009	27,872	**PF63** 60.00	**PF65** 70.00

KM# 1130   5 DOLLARS
8.50 g., Bi-Metallic, 28mm. **Subject:** Summer - Buck Moon **Obv.** Bust right **Rev:** Buck against summer moon

Date	Mintage		
2011	7,500	**PF63** 115	**PF65** 125

KM# 1131   5 DOLLARS
8.50 g., Bi-Metallic, 28mm. **Subject:** Fall Moon **Obv.** Bust right **Rev:** Native American hunter seated tracking prey before Harvest Moon

Date	Mintage		
2011	7,500	**PF63** 115	**PF65** 125

KM# 1149   5 DOLLARS
3.13 g., 0.9999 Gold, 0.10 oz. AGW 16mm. **Subject:** Norman Bethune **Obv.** Bust right **Rev:** Half-length figure at right, looking left

Date	Mintage	
2011	Est. 5000	**PF65** 300

KM# 1236   5 DOLLARS
8.36 g., 0.900 Gold, 0.24 oz. AGW 21.6mm. **Obv.** Bust
right **Rev:** Crowned monogram in wreath

Date	Mintage	
1952-2012	—	PF65 500

KM# 1132   5 DOLLARS
8.50 g., Bi-Metallic, 28mm. **Subject:** Winter Moon **Obv.**
Bust right **Rev:** Wolf howling before Winter Moon

Date	Mintage		
2012	7,500	PF63 115	PF65 125

KM# 1133   5 DOLLARS
8.50 g., Bi-Metallic, 28mm. **Subject:** Spring Moon **Rev:**
Phlox blossoming against a Spring Moon, field in color

Date	Mintage		
2012	—	PF63 115	PF65 125

KM# 1194   5 DOLLARS
3.13 g., 0.999 Gold, 0.10 oz. AGW 16mm. **Obv.** Bust
right **Rev:** Royal Cypher, wreath below

Date	Mintage	
2012	—	PF65 200

KM# 1220   5 DOLLARS
3.13 g., 0.9999 Gold, 0.10 oz. AGW 16mm. **Subject:** Year
of the Dragon **Obv.** Bust right **Rev:** Dragon forpart right

Date	Mintage	
2012 Specimen	—	PF65 225

KM# 1248   5 DOLLARS
31.12 g., 0.999 Silver, 0.99 oz. ASW 36mm. **Subject:**
Rick Hansen **Rev:** Wheelchair bound athlete

Date	Mintage		
2012	—	PF63 65.00	PF65 75.00

KM# 1281   5 DOLLARS
3.13 g., 0.999 Gold, 0.10 oz. AGW 16mm. **Subject:** Year
of the Dragon

Date	Mintage	
2012	—	PF65 200

KM# 1332   5 DOLLARS
31.11 g., 0.999 Silver, 0.99 oz. ASW 36mm. **Subject:**
Georgia Pope **Rev:** Four female soldiers

Date	Mintage		
2012	—	PF63 70.00	PF65 75.00

KM# 1298   5 DOLLARS
3.13 g., 0.999 Gold, 0.10 oz. AGW **Subject:** Year of the
Snake

Date	Mintage	
2013	—	PF65 225

5 DOLLARS

KM# 1395 5 DOLLARS
3.13 g., 0.9999 Gold, 0.10 oz. AGW 16mm. **Rev:** Beaver swimming with branch in mouth **Rev. Designer:** Pierre Le Duc

Date	Mintage	
2013	Est. 4000	PF65 280

KM# 1401 5 DOLLARS
3.13 g., 0.9999 Gold, 0.10 oz. AGW 16mm. **Rev:** Polar Bear head **Rev. Designer:** Pierre Le Duc

Date	Mintage	
2013	Est. 4000	PF65 275

KM# 1426 5 DOLLARS
23.17 g., 0.9999 Silver, 0.74 oz. ASW 36mm. **Subject:** Traditions: Hunting **Rev:** Deer and hunter teaching child **Rev. Designer:** Darleen Gait

Date	Mintage		
2013	Est. 10000	PF63 60.00	PF65 70.00

KM# 1453 5 DOLLARS
3.13 g., 0.999 Gold, 0.10 oz. AGW 16mm. **Rev:** Caribou head **Rev. Designer:** Pierre Leduc

Date	Mintage	
2013	4,000	PF65 275

KM# 1454 5 DOLLARS
3.13 g., 0.999 Gold, 0.10 oz. AGW 16mm. **Rev:** Wolf head **Rev. Designer:** Pierre Leduc

Date	Mintage	
2013	4,000	PF65 275

KM# 1461a 5 DOLLARS
23.17 g., 0.9999 Gilt, 0.74 oz. 36mm. **Subject:** Birth of Prince George **Rev:** W and C crowned in gilt center, infant toys around **Rev. Designer:** Laurie McCaw

Date	Mintage		
2013	Est. 15000	PF63 65.00	PF65 75.00

KM# 1461 5 DOLLARS
23.17 g., 0.9999 Silver, 0.74 oz. ASW 36mm. **Subject:** Birth of Prince George **Rev:** W and C crowned in gilt center, Infant toys around **Rev. Designer:** Laurie McCaw

Date	Mintage		
2013	Est. 15000	PF63 65.00	PF65 75.00

KM# 1475 5 DOLLARS
8.50 g., 0.9999 Silver, 0.27 oz. ASW 28mm. **Subject:** Father Ice **Rev. Designer:** Ulaayn Pilurtuut

Date	Mintage		
2013	6,500	PF63 130	PF65 140

KM# 1476 5 DOLLARS
8.50 g., 0.9999 Silver, 0.27 oz. ASW 28mm. **Subject:** Mother Ice **Rev. Designer:** Ulaayu Pilurtuut

Date	Mintage		
2013	6,500	PF63 130	PF65 140

KM# 1497 5 DOLLARS
7.80 g., 0.999 Gold, 0.25 oz. AGW 20mm. **Subject:** US / Canada Devil's Brigade **Rev:** Special Forces Emblem **Rev. Designer:** Ardell Bourgeois

Date	Mintage	
2013	2,000	PF65 650

KM# 1498 5 DOLLARS
23.17 g., 0.9999 Silver, 0.74 oz. ASW 36mm. **Subject:** US / Canada Devil's Brigade **Rev:** Special Forces Emblem **Rev. Designer:** Ardell Bourgeois

Date	Mintage		
2013	20,000	PF63 70.00	PF65 80.00

KM# 1559 5 DOLLARS
23.00 g., 0.9999 Silver, 0.73 oz. ASW 36mm. **Rev:** St. George slaying dragon

Date	Mintage		
2014	8,500	PF63 65.00	PF65 75.00

KM# 1611 5 DOLLARS
3.13 g., 0.999 Gold, 0.10 oz. AGW 16mm. **Obv.** Bust right **Rev:** Grizzly bear

Date	Mintage	
2014	4,000	PF65 280

5 DOLLARS

KM# 1615 5 DOLLARS
23.17 g., 0.999 Silver, 0.74 oz. ASW 36.07mm. **Subject:**
Traditions of the Hunt - Seal Spearing **Obv.** Bust right **Rev:**
Two men ready to spear seal **Rev. Designer:** Darlene Gait

Date	Mintage		
2014	10,000	PF63 60.00	PF65 70.00

KM# 515 8 DOLLARS
28.80 g., 0.925 Silver, 0.85 oz. ASW 39mm. **Obv.** Head
right **Obv. Designer:** Susanna Blunt **Rev:** Grizzly bear
walking left **Edge:** Reeded

Date	Mintage	
2004	12,942	PF65 85.00

KM# 597 8 DOLLARS
32.15 g., 0.9999 Silver, 1.03 oz. ASW **Subject:** Canadian
Pacific Railway, 120th Anniversary **Obv.** Head right **Obv.
Designer:** Susanna Blunt **Rev:** Railway bridge, center is gilt

Date	Mintage		
2005	9,892	PF63 60.00	PF65 65.00

KM# 598 8 DOLLARS
32.15 g., 0.9999 Silver, 1.03 oz. ASW **Subject:** Canadian
Pacific Railway, 120th Anniversary **Obv.** Head right **Rev:**
Railway memorial to the Chinese workers, center gilt

Date	Mintage		
2005	9,892	PF63 60.00	PF65 65.00

KM# 730 8 DOLLARS
25.18 g., 0.9999 Silver, 0.80 oz. ASW 36.07mm. **Obv.**
Queens's head at top in circle, three Chinese characters
Rev: Dragon and other creatures

Date	Mintage		
2007	19,996	PF63 45.00	PF65 50.00

KM# 731 8 DOLLARS
25.18 g., 0.999 Silver, 0.80 oz. ASW 36.1mm. **Rev:** Maple
leaf, long life hologram

Date	Mintage	
2007	15,000	PF65 55.00

KM# 943 8 DOLLARS
25.18 g., 0.925 Silver, 0.74 oz. ASW 36.1mm. **Rev:**
Hologram maple of wisdom at top left, crystal in center,
dragons around

Date	Mintage		
2009	7,273	PF63 85.00	PF65 90.00

KM# 1012 8 DOLLARS
25.30 g., 0.925 Silver, 0.75 oz. ASW 36.07mm. **Rev:**
Horses around central maple leaf hologram **Rev.
Designer:** Simon Ng

Date	Mintage		
2010	8,888	PF63 90.00	PF65 100

KM# 27   10 DOLLARS
16.72 g., 0.900 Gold, 0.48 oz. AGW 26.92mm. **Obv.** Crowned bust left **Obv. Designer:** E. B. MacKennal **Rev:** Arms within wreath, date and denomination below **Rev. Designer:** W. H. J. Blakemore

Date	Mintage	F12	VF20	XF40	AU50	MS60	MS63
1912	74,759	—	—	800	800	900	2,700
1912 Specimen	—	—	—	—	—	—	7,000
1913	149,232	—	—	800	800	900	3,000
1912 (1913) Specimen	—	—	—	—	—	—	—
1914	140,068	—	—	800	850	1,150	3,000
1914 Specimen	—	—	—	—	—	—	—

KM# 87   10 DOLLARS
48.60 g., 0.925 Silver, 1.44 oz. ASW 45mm. **Subject:** 1976 Montreal Olympics **Obv.** Young bust right, small maple leaf below, date at right **Rev:** Montreal skyline, denomination below **Rev. Designer:** Georges Huel **Note:** Series I.

Date	Mintage		MS63
1973	165,203	PF60 47.50	
1973	—		47.50

KM# 86.2   10 DOLLARS
48.60 g., 0.925 Silver, 1.44 oz. ASW 45mm. **Subject:** 1976 Montreal Olympics **Obv.** Young bust right, small maple leaf below, date at right **Rev:** World map **Rev. Designer:** Georges Huel **Note:** Series I.

Date	Mintage	MS63
1974	320	325

Note: Error: mule

KM# 86.1   10 DOLLARS
48.60 g., 0.925 Silver, 1.44 oz. ASW 45mm. **Subject:** 1976 Montreal Olympics **Obv.** Young bust right, maple leaf below, date at right **Rev:** World map, denomination below **Rev. Designer:** Georges Huel **Note:** Series I.

Date	Mintage		MS63
1973	103,426		47.50
1973	165,203	PF60 47.50	

KM# 93   10 DOLLARS
48.60 g., 0.925 Silver, 1.44 oz. ASW 45mm. **Subject:**

1976 Montreal Olympics **Obv.** Young bust right, small maple leaf below, date at right **Rev:** Head of Zeus, denomination below **Rev. Designer:** Anthony Mann **Note:** Series II.

Date	Mintage		MS63
1974	104,684	PF60 47.50	
1974	—		47.50

KM# 94   10 DOLLARS
48.60 g., 0.925 Silver, 1.44 oz. ASW 45mm. **Subject:** 1976 Montreal Olympics **Obv.** Young bust right, small maple leaf below, date at right **Rev:** Temple of Zeus, denomination below **Rev. Designer:** Anthony Mann **Note:** Series II.

Date	Mintage		MS63
1974	104,684	PF60 47.50	
1974	—		47.50

KM# 95   10 DOLLARS
48.60 g., 0.925 Silver, 1.44 oz. ASW 45mm. **Subject:** 1976 Montreal Olympics **Obv.** Young bust right, small maple leaf below, date at right **Rev:** Cycling, denomination below **Rev. Designer:** Ken Danby **Note:** Series III.

Date	Mintage		MS63
1974	97,431	PF60 47.50	
1974	—		47.50

KM# 96   10 DOLLARS
48.60 g., 0.925 Silver, 1.44 oz. ASW 45mm. **Subject:** 1976 Montreal Olympics **Obv.** Young bust right, small maple leaf below, date at right **Rev:** Lacrosse, denomination below **Rev. Designer:** Ken Danby **Note:** Series III.

Date	Mintage		MS63
1974	97,431	PF60 47.50	
1974	—		47.50

KM# 102   10 DOLLARS
48.60 g., 0.925 Silver, 1.44 oz. ASW 45mm. **Subject:** 1976 Montreal Olympics **Obv.** Young bust right, small maple leaf below, date at right **Rev:** Men's hurdles, denomination below **Rev. Designer:** Leo Yerxa **Note:** Series IV.

Date	Mintage		MS63
1975	82,302	PF60 47.50	
1975	—		47.50

KM# 103   10 DOLLARS
48.60 g., 0.925 Silver, 1.44 oz. ASW 45mm. **Subject:** Montreal 1976 - 21st Summer Olympic Games **Obv.** Young bust right, small maple leaf below, date at right **Rev:** Women's shot put, denomination below **Rev.**

Designer: Leo Yerxa **Note:** Series IV.

Date	Mintage		MS63
1975	82,302	PF60 47.50	
1975	—		47.50

KM# 104 10 DOLLARS
48.60 g., 0.925 Silver, 1.44 oz. ASW 45mm. **Subject:** 1976 Montreal Olympics **Obv.** Young bust right, small maple leaf below, date at right **Rev:** Sailing, denomination below **Rev. Designer:** Lynda Cooper **Note:** Series V.

Date	Mintage		MS63
1975	89,155	PF60 47.50	
1975	—		47.50

KM# 105 10 DOLLARS
48.60 g., 0.925 Silver, 1.44 oz. ASW 45mm. **Subject:** 1976 Montreal Olympics **Obv.** Young bust right, small maple leaf below, date at right **Rev:** Canoeing, denomination below **Rev. Designer:** Lynda Cooper **Note:** Series V.

Date	Mintage		MS63
1975	89,155	PF60 47.50	
1975	—		47.50

KM# 112 10 DOLLARS
48.60 g., 0.925 Silver, 1.44 oz. ASW 45mm. **Subject:** 1976 Montreal Olympics **Obv.** Young bust right, small maple leaf below, date at right **Rev:** Field hockey **Rev. Designer:** Shigeo Fukada **Note:** Series VI.

Date	Mintage		MS63
1976	76,908	PF60 47.50	
1976	—		47.50

KM# 111 10 DOLLARS
48.60 g., 0.925 Silver, 1.44 oz. ASW 45mm. **Subject:** 1976 Montreal Olympics **Obv.** Young bust right, small maple leaf below, date at right **Rev:** Football, denomination below **Rev. Designer:** Shigeo Fukada **Note:** Series VI.

Date	Mintage		MS63
1976	76,908	PF60 47.50	
1976	—		47.50

KM# 113 10 DOLLARS
48.60 g., 0.925 Silver, 1.44 oz. ASW 45mm. **Subject:** 1976 Montreal Olympics **Obv.** Young bust right, small maple leaf below, date at right **Rev:** Olympic Stadium, denomination below **Rev. Designer:** Elliot John Morrison **Note:** Series VII.

Date	Mintage		MS63
1976	79,102	PF60 47.50	
1976	—		47.50

10 DOLLARS

KM# 114   10 DOLLARS
48.60 g., 0.925 Silver, 1.44 oz. ASW 45mm. **Subject:** 1976 Montreal Olympics **Obv.** Young bust right, small maple leaf below, date at right **Rev:** Olympic Velodrome, denomination below **Rev. Designer:** Elliot John Morrison **Note:** Series VII.

Date	Mintage		MS63
1976	79,102	PF60 47.50	
1976	—		47.50

KM# 520   10 DOLLARS
16.72 g., 0.900 Gold, 0.48 oz. AGW 26.92mm. **Obv.** Crowned head right **Rev:** National arms **Edge:** Reeded

Date	Mintage		MS63
1912-2002	2,002	PF65 850	

KM# 559   10 DOLLARS
25.18 g., 0.9999 Silver, 0.80 oz. ASW 36mm. **Subject:** Pope John Paul II **Obv.** Head right

Date	Mintage		
2005	24,716	PF63 40.00	PF65 45.00

KM# 757   10 DOLLARS
25.18 g., 0.9999 Silver, 0.80 oz. ASW **Subject:** Year of the Veteran **Rev:** Profile left of young and old veteran

Date	Mintage	
2005	6,549	PF65 225

KM# 661   10 DOLLARS
25.18 g., 0.9999 Silver, 0.80 oz. ASW **Subject:** National Historic Sites **Obv.** Head right **Rev:** Fortress of Louisbourg

Date	Mintage		
2006	5,544	PF63 35.00	PF65 40.00

KM# 1010   10 DOLLARS
15.87 g., 0.999 Silver, 0.51 oz. ASW **Subject:** 75th Anniversary Canadian Bank Notes **Rev:** Female seated

Date	Mintage		
2010	7,500	PF63 45.00	PF65 50.00

KM# 1096   10 DOLLARS
27.78 g., 0.925 Silver, 0.82 oz. ASW 40mm. **Obv.** Bust right **Rev:** Blue whale diving in sea

Date	Mintage		
2010	10,000	PF63 75.00	PF65 85.00

KM# 1199   10 DOLLARS
15.87 g., 0.9999 Silver, 0.51 oz. ASW 34mm. **Subject:**

Winter Scene - Skating **Rev:** Three kids skating on pond, colored holly at left

Date	Mintage		
2011	Est. 8000	PF63 35.00	PF65 40.00

KM# 1198 10 DOLLARS
15.87 g., 0.999 Silver, 0.51 oz. ASW 34mm. **Subject:** Highway of Heroes **Obv.** Bust right **Obv. Designer:** Susanna Blunt **Rev:** Citizens on Highway 401 overpass with signs and flags, large maple leaf in background, Memorial Cross medal at top left. **Rev. Designer:** Stan Witten and Major Carl Gauthier **Edge:** Reeded

Date	Mintage		
2011	25,000	PF63 60.00	PF65 70.00

KM# 1200 10 DOLLARS
15.87 g., 0.9999 Silver, 0.51 oz. ASW 34mm. **Subject:** Winter scene - Two houses **Rev:** Two houses in snowy lane, colored holly flanking

Date	Mintage		
2011	—	PF63 35.00	PF65 40.00

KM# 1201 10 DOLLARS
15.87 g., 0.9999 Silver, 0.51 oz. ASW 34mm. **Obv.** Bust right **Rev:** Wood Bison **Rev. Designer:** Corrine Hunt

Date	Mintage		
2011	Est. 10000	PF63 40.00	PF65 50.00

KM# 1203 10 DOLLARS
15.87 g., 0.9999 Silver, 0.51 oz. ASW 34mm. **Subject:** Boreal Forest **Rev:** Bird and tree **Rev. Designer:** Corrine Hunt

Date	Mintage		
2011	Est. 10000	PF63 40.00	PF65 50.00

KM# 1205 10 DOLLARS
15.87 g., 0.9999 Silver, 0.51 oz. ASW 34mm. **Obv.** Bust

right **Rev:** Peregrine Falcon perched on branch **Rev. Designer:** Corrine Hunt

Date	Mintage		
2011	Est. 10000	PF63 40.00	PF65 50.00

KM# 1207 10 DOLLARS
15.87 g., 0.9999 Silver, 0.51 oz. ASW 34mm. **Obv.** Bust right **Rev:** Orca Whale **Rev. Designer:** Corrine Hunt

Date	Mintage		
2011	Est. 10000	PF63 40.00	PF65 50.00

KM# 1221 10 DOLLARS
15.87 g., 0.999 Silver, 0.51 oz. ASW 34mm. **Subject:** Year of the Dragon **Obv.** Bust right **Rev:** Dragon forepart right

Date	Mintage	MS63
2012 Specimen	58,888	40.00

KM# 1235 10 DOLLARS
25.18 g., 0.999 Silver, 0.80 oz. ASW 36mm. **Obv.** Bust right **Rev:** Titanic sailing at right, map of Eastern Canada at left

Date	Mintage		
2012	—	PF63 90.00	PF65 100

KM# 1249 10 DOLLARS
15.87 g., 0.999 Silver, 0.51 oz. ASW 34mm. **Subject:** H.M.S. Shannon

Date	Mintage		
2012	—	PF63 55.00	PF65 65.00

KM# 1259   10 DOLLARS
15.87 g., 0.999 Silver, 0.51 oz. ASW 34mm. **Subject:**
Praying Mantis

Date	Mintage		
2012	—	PF63 40.00	PF65 45.00

KM# 1282   10 DOLLARS
7.77 g., 0.999 Gold, 0.25 oz. AGW 20mm. **Subject:** Year
of the Dragon

Date	Mintage	
2012	—	PF65 450

KM# 1346   10 DOLLARS
15.55 g., 0.999 Silver, 0.50 oz. ASW 34mm. **Rev:** Baby's
feet

Date	Mintage	MS63
2012 Specimen	—	27.50
2013	—	27.50

KM# 1355   10 DOLLARS
30.00 g., 0.999 Silver, 0.96 oz. ASW 36.5mm. **Rev:**
Male and female mallards in color **Rev. Designer:** Trevor
Tennant

Date	Mintage		
2013	—	PF63 75.00	PF65 85.00

KM# 1357   10 DOLLARS
15.87 g., 0.999 Silver, 0.51 oz. ASW 34mm. **Subject:**
Year of the Snake **Rev:** Circular coiled snake **Rev.
Designer:** Simon Ng

Date	Mintage		
2013	18,888	PF63 40.00	PF65 45.00

KM# 1383   10 DOLLARS
15.87 g., 0.999 Silver, 0.51 oz. ASW 34mm. **Subject:** Ice
Skating on Frozen Lake **Rev:** Winter Scene in Color **Rev.
Designer:** Remi Clark

Date	Mintage		
2013	Est. 8000	PF63 55.00	PF65 65.00

KM# 1299   10 DOLLARS
31.11 g., 0.999 Silver, 0.99 oz. ASW 34mm. **Subject:**
Year of the Snake

Date	Mintage	
2013	—	PF65 50.00

KM# 1392 10 DOLLARS
15.87 g., 0.999 Silver, 0.51 oz. ASW 35mm. **Subject:** Oh Canada - R.C.M.P. **Rev:** Mountie on horseback

Date	Mintage		
2013	—	PF63 32.00	PF65 40.00

KM# 1392a 10 DOLLARS
15.87 g., 0.999 Silver, 0.51 oz. ASW 35mm. **Subject:** Oh Canada - R.C.M.P. **Rev:** Mountie on horseback

Date	Mintage		
2013	—	PF63 65.00	PF65 75.00

KM# 1393 10 DOLLARS
15.87 g., 0.999 Silver, 0.51 oz. ASW 34mm. **Rev:** Twelve Spotted Skimmer Dragonfly in color **Rev. Designer:** Celia Godkin

Date	Mintage		
2013	Est. 10000	PF63 70.00	PF65 80.00

KM# 1396 10 DOLLARS
15.87 g., 0.9999 Silver, 0.51 oz. ASW 34mm. **Rev:** Bever Felling Tree **Rev. Designer:** Pierre Le Duc

Date	Mintage		
2013	Est. 40000	PF63 35.00	PF65 40.00

KM# 1400 10 DOLLARS
15.87 g., 0.999 Silver, 0.51 oz. ASW 34mm. **Rev:** Stone formation at sea side **Rev. Designer:** Tony Bianco

Date	Mintage		
2013	40,000	PF63 35.00	PF65 40.00

KM# 1402 10 DOLLARS
15.57 g., 0.999 Silver, 0.50 oz. ASW 34mm. **Rev:** Polar Bear walking right **Rev. Designer:** Tony Bianco

Date	Mintage		
2013	—	PF63 35.00	PF65 40.00

KM# 1421 10 DOLLARS
15.87 g., 0.9999 Silver, 0.51 oz. ASW 34mm. **Rev:** Caribou

Date	Mintage		
2013	Est. 40000	PF63 25.00	PF65 30.00

KM# 1422 10 DOLLARS
15.87 g., 0.9999 Silver, 0.51 oz. ASW 34mm. **Rev:** Niagra Falls

Date	Mintage		
2013	Est. 40000	PF63 32.00	PF65 40.00

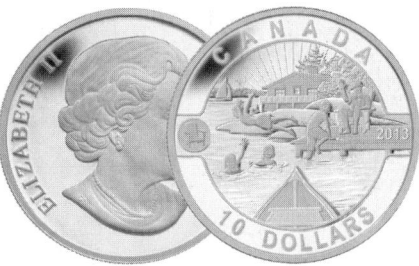

KM# 1423 10 DOLLARS
15.57 g., 0.9999 Silver, 0.50 oz. ASW 34mm. **Rev:** Summer lake swimming

Date	Mintage		
2013	Est. 40000	PF63 32.00	PF65 40.00

KM# 1424 10 DOLLARS
15.87 g., 0.9999 Silver, 0.51 oz. ASW 34mm. **Rev:** Hand holding three Fall colored maple leaves **Rev. Designer:** Emily S. Damstra

Date	Mintage		
2013	Est. 40000	PF63 32.00	PF65 40.00

10 DOLLARS

KM# 1425 10 DOLLARS
15.87 g., 0.9999 Silver, 0.51 oz. ASW 34mm. **Rev:** Outdoor ice hockey rink

Date	Mintage		
2013	Est. 40000	PF63 32.00	PF65 40.00

KM# 1442 10 DOLLARS
15.87 g., 0.999 Silver, 0.51 oz. ASW **Ruler:** Elizabeth II 34mm. **Obv.** Bust right **Obv. Designer:** Susana Blunt **Rev:** Dreamcatcher in color **Rev. Designer:** Darlene Gait **Edge:** Reeded **Mint:** Royal Canadian Mint

Date	Mintage		
2013	10,000	PF63 70.00	PF65 80.00

KM# 1445 10 DOLLARS
7.06 g., 0.999 Silver, 0.23 oz. ASW 27mm. **Subject:** 75th Anniversary of Superman **Rev:** Superman breaking chains **Rev. Legend:** Joe Shuster, DC Comics

Date	Mintage		
2013	Est. 15000	PF63 40.00	PF65 45.00

KM# 1455 10 DOLLARS
15.57 g., 0.999 Silver, 0.50 oz. ASW 34mm. **Rev:** Wolf standing right **Rev. Designer:** Pierre Leduc

Date	Mintage		
2013	Est. 40000	PF63 35.00	PF65 40.00

KM# 1517 10 DOLLARS
15.87 g., 0.9999 Silver, 0.51 oz. ASW 34mm. **Subject:** Year of the Horse **Rev:** Horse head left **Rev. Designer:** Simon Ng

Date	Mintage		
2014	58,888	PF63 35.00	PF65 40.00

KM# 1580 10 DOLLARS
15.87 g., 0.999 Silver, 0.51 oz. ASW 34mm. **Obv.** Bust right **Rev:** Igloo

Date	Mintage		
2014	—	PF63 55.00	PF65 65.00

KM# 1590 10 DOLLARS
15.87 g., 0.999 Silver, 0.51 oz. ASW 34mm. **Obv.** Bust right **Rev:** Adult teaching child how to ice skate, in color

Date	Mintage		
2014	—	PF63 50.00	PF65 60.00

KM# 1607 10 DOLLARS
15.87 g., 0.999 Silver, 0.51 oz. ASW 34mm. **Rev:** Pintail ducks in color **Rev. Designer:** Trevor Tennant

Date	Mintage	MS63
2014	10,000	35.00

KM# 1612 10 DOLLARS
15.87 g., 0.999 Silver, 0.51 oz. ASW 34mm. **Obv.** Bust right **Rev:** Grizzly bear left **Rev. Designer:** Glen Loates

Date	Mintage		
2014	40,000	PF63 35.00	PF65 40.00

KM# 1613 10 DOLLARS
0.999 Silver ASW 34mm. **Subject:** World War I -
Mobilization of a nation **Obv.** Bust right **Rev:** Soldier with
gear walking up ship's gangway **Rev. Designer:** Maskull
Lasserre

Date	Mintage		
2014	40,000	PF63 40.00	PF65 45.00

KM# 1625 10 DOLLARS
15.87 g., 0.999 Silver, 0.51 oz. ASW 34mm. **Obv.** Bust
right **Rev:** Downhill sking **Rev. Designer:** Kendra Dixon

Date	Mintage		
2014	40,000	PF63 35.00	PF65 40.00

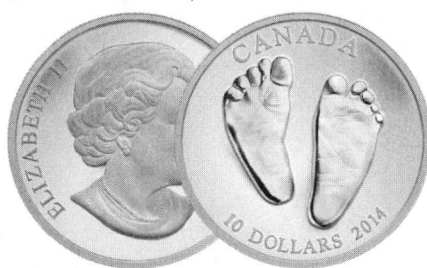

KM# 1629 10 DOLLARS
0.999 Silver ASW 34mm. **Obv.** Bust right **Rev:** Two
baby's feet

Date	Mintage		
2014	—	PF63 45.00	PF65 50.00

KM# 215 15 DOLLARS
33.63 g., 0.925 Silver, 0.99 oz. ASW 39mm. **Subject:**
1992 Olympics **Obv.** Crowned head right, date at left,
denomination below **Rev:** Coaching track **Rev. Designer:**
Stewart Sherwood

Date	Mintage	
1992	275,000	PF60 35.00

KM# 216 15 DOLLARS
33.63 g., 0.925 Silver, 0.99 oz. ASW **Subject:** 1992
Olympics **Obv.** Crowned head right, date at left,
denomination below **Rev:** High jump, rings, speed skating
Rev. Designer: David Craig

Date	Mintage	
1992	275,000	PF60 35.00

KM# 304 15 DOLLARS
33.63 g., 0.925 Silver, 0.99 oz. ASW 40mm. **Subject:**
Year of the Tiger **Obv.** Crowned head right **Rev:** Tiger
within octagon at center, animal figures surround **Rev.
Designer:** Harvey Chan

Date	Mintage	
1998	68,888	PF60 375

KM# 331 15 DOLLARS
33.63 g., 0.925 Silver, 0.99 oz. ASW **Subject:** Year
of the Rabbitt **Obv.** Crowned head right **Rev:** Rabbit
within octagon at center, animal figures surround **Rev.
Designer:** Harvey Chan

Date	Mintage	
1999	77,791	PF60 100

15 DOLLARS

KM# 387 15 DOLLARS
33.63 g., 0.925 Silver, 0.99 oz. ASW **Subject:** Year of the
Dragon **Obv.** Crowned head right **Rev. Designer:** Harvey
Chan

Date	Mintage	
2000	88,634	**PF60** 150

KM# 415 15 DOLLARS
33.63 g., 0.925 Silver, 0.99 oz. ASW 40mm. **Subject:**
Year of the Snake **Obv.** Crowned head right **Rev:** Snake
within circle of lunar calendar signs **Rev. Designer:**
Harvey Chain **Edge:** Reeded

Date	Mintage		
2001	—	**PF63** 75.00	**PF65** 85.00

KM# 463 15 DOLLARS
33.63 g., 0.925 Silver, 0.99 oz. ASW **Subject:** Year of the
Horse **Obv.** Crowned head right **Obv. Designer:** Dora
dePédery-Hunt **Rev:** Horse in center with Chinese Lunar
calendar around **Rev. Designer:** Harvey Chain

Date	Mintage		
2002	59,395	**PF63** 75.00	**PF65** 85.00

KM# 481 15 DOLLARS
33.63 g., 0.925 Silver, 0.99 oz. ASW 40mm. **Subject:**
Year of the Sheep **Obv.** Crowned head right **Rev:** Sheep
in center with Chinese Lunar calendar around **Rev.
Designer:** Harvey Chain

Date	Mintage		
2003	53,714	**PF63** 75.00	**PF65** 85.00

KM# 610 15 DOLLARS
33.63 g., 0.925 Silver, 0.99 oz. ASW **Subject:** Year of the
Monkey **Obv.** Crowned head right **Rev:** Monkey in center
with Chinese Lunar calendar around

Date	Mintage	
2004	46,175	**PF65** 150

KM# 560 15 DOLLARS
33.63 g., 0.925 Silver, 0.99 oz. ASW **Subject:** Year of the
Rooster **Obv.** Crowned head right **Rev:** Rooster in center
with Chinese Lunar calendar around

Date	Mintage	
2005	44,690	**PF65** 125

KM# 587 15 DOLLARS
33.63 g., 0.925 Silver, 0.99 oz. ASW **Subject:** Year of
the Dog **Obv.** Crowned head left **Rev:** Dog in center with
Chinese Lunar calendar around

Date	Mintage		
2006	41,617	**PF63** 85.00	**PF65** 100

KM# 732 15 DOLLARS
33.63 g., 0.925 Silver, 0.99 oz. ASW 40mm. **Subject:**
Year of the Pig **Rev:** Pig at center of lunar characters

Date	Mintage		
2007	48,888	**PF63** 90.00	**PF65** 100

KM# 801 15 DOLLARS
33.63 g., 0.925 Silver, 0.99 oz. ASW 40mm. **Subject:**
Year of the Rat **Rev:** Rat, gold octagonal insert at center

Date	Mintage		
2008	48,888	**PF63** 80.00	**PF65** 90.00

KM# 803 15 DOLLARS
30.00 g., 0.925 Silver, 0.89 oz. ASW 36.15mm. **Rev:**
Queen Victoria's coinage portrait

Date	Mintage	MS63
2008	3,442	100

KM# 804 15 DOLLARS
30.00 g., 0.925 Silver, 0.89 oz. ASW 36.15mm. **Rev:**
Edward VII coinage portrait **Rev. Designer:** G. W.
DeSaulles

Date	Mintage	MS63
2008	6,261	100

KM# 805   15 DOLLARS
20.00 g., 0.925 Silver, 0.59 oz. ASW 36.15mm. **Rev:**
George V coinage portrait

Date	Mintage		MS63
2008	—		100

KM# 806   15 DOLLARS
31.56 g., 0.925 Silver, 0.93 oz. ASW 49.8 x 28.6mm. **Rev:**
Queen of Spades, multicolor playing card

Date	Mintage		
2008	8,714	**PF63** 80.00	**PF65** 90.00

KM# 807   15 DOLLARS
31.56 g., 0.925 Silver, 0.93 oz. ASW 28.6x49.8mm. **Rev:**
Jack of Hearts, multicolor playing card

Date	Mintage		
2008	11,362	**PF63** 75.00	**PF65** 85.00

KM# 919   15 DOLLARS
31.56 g., 0.925 Silver, 0.93 oz. ASW 49.8 x 28.6mm.
Obv. Bust right **Obv. Designer:** Susanna Blunt **Rev:** Ten
of spades, multicolor **Shape:** rectangle

Date	Mintage		
2009	5,921	**PF63** 140	**PF65** 150

KM# 920   15 DOLLARS
31.56 g., 0.925 Silver, 0.93 oz. ASW 49.8 x 28.6mm. **Obv.**
Bust right **Obv. Designer:** Susanna Blunt **Rev:** King of
hearts, multicolor **Shape:** Rectangle

Date	Mintage		
2009	5,798	**PF63** 110	**PF65** 120

KM# 866   15 DOLLARS
33.63 g., 0.925 Silver, 0.99 oz. ASW 40mm. **Subject:**
Year of the Ox **Rev:** Ox, octagon gold insert

Date	Mintage		
2009	48,888	**PF63** 80.00	**PF65** 90.00

KM# 922   15 DOLLARS
30.00 g., 0.925 Silver, 0.89 oz. ASW 36.15mm. **Obv.**
Bust right **Obv. Designer:** Susanna Blunt **Rev:** Paget
portrait of George VI

Date	Mintage	MS63
2009(ml) Prooflike	—	100

KM# 923   15 DOLLARS
30.00 g., 0.925 Silver, 0.89 oz. ASW 36.15mm. **Obv.**
Bust right **Obv. Designer:** Susanna Blunt **Rev:** Gillick
portrait of Queen Elizabeth II

Date	Mintage	MS63
2009(ml) Prooflike	2,643	100

KM# 1038   15 DOLLARS
Silver, 38mm. **Subject:** Year of the tiger **Rev:** Tiger in
forest **Shape:** scalloped

Date	Mintage		
2009	10,268	PF63 75.00	PF65 85.00

KM# 980   15 DOLLARS
34.00 g., 0.925 Silver, 1.00 oz. ASW 40mm. **Rev:** Tiger
in gold insert

Date	Mintage		
2010	48,888	PF63 90.00	PF65 100

KM# 1032   15 DOLLARS
0.999 Silver, **Subject:** Year of the tiger **Rev:** Tiger walking
tiger

Date	Mintage		
2010	9,999	PF63 75.00	PF65 85.00

KM# 1055   15 DOLLARS
31.11 g., 0.999 Silver, 0.99 oz. ASW 38mm. **Rev:** Rabbit
sitting, head turned left **Shape:** scalloped

Date	Mintage		
2011	19,888	PF63 75.00	PF65 85.00

KM# 1091   15 DOLLARS
25.11 g., 0.925 Silver, 0.74 oz. ASW 36.15mm. **Rev:**
Prince Charles bust **Rev. Designer:** Laurie McGaw

Date	Mintage	MS63
2011 Prooflike	10,000	110

KM# 1092 15 DOLLARS
25.11 g., 0.925 Silver, 0.74 oz. ASW 36.15mm. **Rev:**
Prince William **Rev. Designer:** Laurie McGaw

Date	Mintage	MS63
2011 Prooflike	10,000	110

KM# 1093 15 DOLLARS
25.18 g., 0.925 Silver, 0.74 oz. ASW 36.15mm. **Rev:**
Prince Harry bust 1/4 right **Rev. Designer:** Laurie McGaw

Date	Mintage	MS63
2011 Prooflike	10,000	110

KM# 1094 15 DOLLARS
31.39 g., 0.999 Silver, 1.00 oz. ASW 38mm. **Rev:** Rabbit
bounding left **Rev. Designer:** Aries Cheung

Date	Mintage		
2011	9,999	PF63 90.00	PF65 100

KM# 1152 15 DOLLARS
31.39 g., 0.9999 Silver, 1.00 oz. ASW 38mm. **Obv.** Bust
right **Rev:** Magpie, bird of happyness in flight at top, lotus
flowers at bottom, maple leaf hologram at center

Date	Mintage		
2011	—	PF63 90.00	PF65 100

KM# 1183 15 DOLLARS
31.11 g., 0.999 Silver, 0.99 oz. ASW 36.5mm. **Subject:**
Year of the Dragon **Obv.** Bust right **Rev:** Dragon right

Date	Mintage		
2012	—	PF63 65.00	PF65 75.00

KM# 1186 15 DOLLARS
31.11 g., 0.999 Silver, 0.99 oz. ASW 36.5mm. **Subject:**
Year of the Dragon **Obv.** Bust right **Rev:** Dragon left
Shape: Scalloped

Date	Mintage		
2012	—	PF63 65.00	PF65 75.00

KM# 1260 15 DOLLARS
31.39 g., 0.999 Silver, 1.00 oz. ASW 36.5mm. **Subject:**
Good Fortune **Rev:** Deer and doe froclicking around
central hologram

Date	Mintage		
2012	—	PF63 65.00	PF65 75.00

KM# 1358 15 DOLLARS
31.39 g., 0.999 Silver, 1.00 oz. ASW 36.5mm. **Subject:**
Year of the Snake **Rev:** Snake vertically between two
Chinese characters **Rev. Designer:** Aries Cheung

Date	Mintage		
2013	28,888	**PF65** 100

KM# 1516 15 DOLLARS
26.70 g., 0.999 (No Composition), 0.85 oz. 38mm.
Subject: Year of the Horse **Rev:** Horse forepart right
Rev. Designer: Three Degrees Creative Group **Shape:**
Scalloped

Date	Mintage		
2014	2,888	**PF63** 90.00	**PF65** 100

KM# 1359 15 DOLLARS
26.70 g., 0.999 Silver, 0.85 oz. ASW 38mm. **Subject:**
Year of the Snake **Rev:** Snake under maple leaves **Rev.
Designer:** Three Degrees Creative Group **Shape:** Scalloped

Date	Mintage		
2013	28,888	**PF63** 65.00	**PF65** 75.00

KM# 1446 15 DOLLARS
15.87 g., 0.999 Silver, 0.51 oz. ASW 34mm. **Subject:**
75th Anniversary of Superman **Obv.** Superman in color
flying forward

Date	Mintage		
2013	15,000	**PF63** 60.00	**PF65** 70.00

KM# 71 20 DOLLARS
18.27 g., 0.900 Gold, 0.53 oz. AGW 27.05mm. **Subject:**
Centennial **Obv.** Crowned head right **Rev:** Crowned and
supported arms **Edge:** Reeded

Date	Mintage	MS63
1967 Specimen	334,288	900

KM# 1514 15 DOLLARS
31.11 g., 0.9999 Silver, 0.99 oz. ASW 38mm. **Subject:**
Year of the Horse **Rev:** Horse prancing left **Rev. Designer:**
Aries Cheung

Date	Mintage		
2014	28,888	**PF63** 90.00	**PF65** 100

KM# 145 20 DOLLARS
33.63 g., 0.925 Silver, 0.99 oz. ASW 40mm. **Subject:**
1988 Calgary Olympics **Obv.** Young bust right, maple leaf
below, date at right **Rev:** Downhill skier, denomination
below **Rev. Designer:** Ian Stewart **Edge:** Lettered

Date	Mintage	
1985	Inc. below	**PF60** 200
Note: Plain edge		
1985	406,360	**PF60** 35.00

KM# 146 20 DOLLARS
33.63 g., 0.925 Silver, 0.99 oz. ASW 40mm. **Subject:** 1988 Calgary Olympics **Obv.** Young bust right, small maple leaf below, date at right **Rev:** Speed skater, denomination below **Rev. Designer:** Friedrich Peter **Edge:** Lettered

Date	Mintage		
1985	Inc. below	PF60	200
Note: Plain edge			
1985	354,222	PF60	35.00

KM# 148 20 DOLLARS
33.63 g., 0.925 Silver, 0.99 oz. ASW 40mm. **Subject:** 1988 Calgary Olympics **Obv.** Young bust right, small maple leaf below, date at right **Rev:** Hockey, denomination below **Rev. Designer:** Ian Stewart **Edge:** Lettered

Date	Mintage		
1986	Inc. below	PF60	200
Note: Plain edge			
1986	396,602	PF60	35.00

KM# 150 20 DOLLARS
33.63 g., 0.925 Silver, 0.99 oz. ASW 40mm. **Subject:** Calgary 1988 - 15th Winter Olympic Games **Obv.** Young bust right, small maple leaf below, date at right **Rev:** Cross-country skier, denomination below **Rev. Designer:** Ian Stewart **Edge:** Lettered

Date	Mintage		
1986	303,199	PF60	35.00

KM# 151 20 DOLLARS
33.63 g., 0.925 Silver, 0.99 oz. ASW 40mm. **Subject:** 1988 Calgary Olympics **Obv.** Young bust right, small maple leaf below, date at right **Rev:** Free-style skier, denomination below **Rev. Designer:** Walter Ott **Edge:** Lettered

Date	Mintage		
1986	Inc. below	PF60	200
Note: Plain edge			
1986	294,322	PF60	35.00

KM# 147 20 DOLLARS
33.63 g., 0.925 Silver, 0.99 oz. ASW 40mm. **Subject:** 1988 Calgary Olympics **Obv.** Young bust right, small maple leaf below, date at right **Rev:** Biathlon, denomination below **Rev. Designer:** John Mardon **Edge:** Lettered

Date	Mintage		
1986	Inc. below	PF60	200
Note: Plain edge			
1986	308,086	PF60	35.00

KM# 155 20 DOLLARS
34.11 g., 0.925 Silver, 1.01 oz. ASW 40mm. **Subject:** Calgary 1988 - 15th Winter Olympic Games **Obv.** Young bust right, small maple leaf below, date at right **Rev:** Figure skating pairs event, denomination below **Rev. Designer:** Raymond Taylor **Edge:** Lettered

Date	Mintage		
1987	334,875	PF60	35.00

KM# 156   20 DOLLARS
34.11 g., 0.925 Silver, 1.01 oz. ASW 40mm. **Subject:**
1988 Calgary Olympics **Obv.** Young bust right, small
maple leaf below, date at right **Rev:** Curling, denomination
below **Rev. Designer:** Ian Stewart **Edge:** Lettered

Date	Mintage	
1987	286,457	PF60 35.00

KM# 159   20 DOLLARS
34.11 g., 0.925 Silver, 1.01 oz. ASW 40mm. **Subject:** 1988
Calgary Olympics **Obv.** Young bust right, small maple leaf
below, date at right **Rev:** Ski jumper, denomination below
Rev. Designer: Raymond Taylor **Edge:** Lettered

Date	Mintage	
1987	290,954	PF60 35.00

KM# 160   20 DOLLARS
34.11 g., 0.925 Silver, 1.01 oz. ASW 40mm. **Subject:**
1988 Calgary Olympics **Obv.** Young bust right, maple leaf
below, date at right **Rev:** Bobsled, denomination below
Rev. Designer: John Mardon **Edge:** Lettered

Date	Mintage	
1987	274,326	PF60 35.00

KM# 172   20 DOLLARS
31.10 g., 0.925 Silver, 0.92 oz. ASW 38mm. **Subject:**
Aviation **Obv.** Crowned head right, date below **Rev:**
Lancaster, Fauquier in cameo, denomination below **Rev.
Designer:** Robert R. Carmichael

Date	Mintage	
1990	43,596	PF60 125

KM# 173   20 DOLLARS
31.10 g., 0.925 Silver, 0.92 oz. ASW 38mm. **Subject:**
Aviation **Obv.** Crowned head right, date below **Rev:**
Anson and Harvard, Air Marshal Robert Leckie in cameo,
denomination below **Rev. Designer:** Geoff Bennett

Date	Mintage	
1990	41,844	PF60 45.00

KM# 196   20 DOLLARS
31.10 g., 0.925 Silver, 0.92 oz. ASW 38mm. **Subject:**
Aviation **Obv.** Crowned head right, date below **Rev:** Silver
Dart, John A. D. McCurdy and F. W. "Casey" Baldwin in
cameo, denomination below **Rev. Designer:** George
Velinger

Date	Mintage	
1991	28,791	PF60 45.00

KM# 197 20 DOLLARS
31.10 g., 0.925 Silver, 0.92 oz. ASW 38mm. **Subject:** Aviation **Obv.** Crowned head right, date below **Rev:** de Haviland Beaver, Philip C. Garratt in cameo, denomination below **Rev. Designer:** Peter Massman

Date	Mintage		
1991	—	PF60	45.00

KM# 224 20 DOLLARS
31.10 g., 0.925 Silver, 0.92 oz. ASW 38mm. **Subject:** Aviation **Obv.** Crowned head right, date below **Rev:** Curtiss JN-4 Canick ("Jenny"), Sir Frank W. Baillie in cameo, denomination below **Rev. Designer:** George Velinger

Date	Mintage		
1992	—	PF60	45.00

KM# 225 20 DOLLARS
31.10 g., 0.925 Silver, 0.92 oz. ASW 38mm. **Subject:** Aviation **Obv.** Crowned head right, date below **Rev:** de Haviland Gypsy Moth, Murton A. Seymour in cameo, denomination below **Rev. Designer:** John Mardon

Date	Mintage		
1992	—	PF60	45.00

KM# 236 20 DOLLARS
31.10 g., 0.925 Silver, 0.92 oz. ASW 38mm. **Subject:** Aviation **Obv.** Crowned head right, date below **Rev:** Fairchild 71C float plane, James A. Richardson, Sr. in cameo, denomination below **Rev. Designer:** Robert R. Carmichael

Date	Mintage		
1993	—	PF60	45.00

KM# 237 20 DOLLARS
31.10 g., 0.925 Silver, 0.92 oz. ASW 38mm. **Subject:** Aviation **Obv.** Crowned head right, date below **Rev:** Lockheed 14, Zebulon Lewis Leigh in cameo, denomination below **Rev. Designer:** Robert R. Carmichael

Date	Mintage		
1993	—	PF60	45.00

KM# 246 20 DOLLARS
31.10 g., 0.925 Silver, 0.92 oz. ASW 38mm. **Subject:** Aviation **Obv.** Crowned head right, date below **Rev:** Curtiss HS-2L seaplane, Stewart Graham in cameo, denomination below **Rev. Designer:** John Mardon

Date	Mintage		
1994	—	PF60	45.00

KM# 247   20 DOLLARS

31.10 g., 0.925 Silver, 0.92 oz. ASW 38mm. **Subject:**
Aviation **Obv.** Crowned head right, date below **Rev:**
Vickers Vedette, Wilfred T. Reid in cameo, denomination
below **Rev. Designer:** Robert R. Carmichael

Date	Mintage		
1994	30,880	PF60	45.00

KM# 271   20 DOLLARS

31.10 g., 0.925 Silver, 0.92 oz. ASW 38mm. **Subject:**
Aviation **Obv.** Crowned head right, date below **Rev:**
C-FEA1 Fleet Cannuck, denomination below **Rev.
Designer:** Robert Bradford

Date	Mintage		
1995	17,438	PF60	45.00

KM# 272   20 DOLLARS

31.10 g., 0.925 Silver, 0.92 oz. ASW 38mm. **Subject:**
Aviation **Obv.** Crowned head right, date below **Rev:** DHC-
1 Chipmunk, denomination below **Rev. Designer:** Robert
Bradford

Date	Mintage		
1995	17,722	PF60	45.00

KM# 276   20 DOLLARS

31.10 g., 0.925 Silver, 0.92 oz. ASW 38mm. **Subject:**
Aviation **Obv.** Crowned head right, date below **Rev:** CF-
100 Cannuck, denomination below **Rev. Designer:** Jim
Bruce

Date	Mintage		
1996	18,508	PF60	45.00

KM# 277   20 DOLLARS

31.10 g., 0.925 Silver, 0.92 oz. ASW 38mm. **Subject:**
Aviation **Obv.** Crowned head right, date below **Obv.
Legend:** CF-105 Arrow, denomination below **Rev.
Designer:** Jim Bruce

Date	Mintage		
1996	27,163	PF60	100

KM# 297   20 DOLLARS

31.10 g., 0.925 Silver, 0.92 oz. ASW 38mm. **Subject:**
Aviation **Obv.** Crowned head right, date below **Rev:**
Canadair F-86 Sabre, denomination below **Rev. Designer:**
Ross Buckland

Date	Mintage		
1997	14,389	PF60	45.00

KM# 298 20 DOLLARS
31.10 g., 0.925 Silver, 0.92 oz. ASW 38mm. **Subject:** Aviation **Obv.** Crowned head right, date below **Rev:** Canadair CT-114 Tutor, denomination below **Rev. Designer:** Ross Buckland

Date	Mintage		
1997	15,669	PF60	45.00

KM# 329 20 DOLLARS
31.10 g., 0.925 Silver, 0.92 oz. ASW 38mm. **Subject:** Aviation **Obv.** Crowned head, right, date below **Rev:** CP-107 Argus, denomination below **Rev. Inscription:** Peter Mossman

Date	Mintage		
1998	Est. 50000	PF60	50.00

KM# 330 20 DOLLARS
31.10 g., 0.925 Silver, 0.92 oz. ASW 38mm. **Subject:** Aviation **Obv.** Crowned head right, date below **Rev:** CP-215 Waterbomber, denomination below **Rev. Designer:** Peter Mossman

Date	Mintage		
1998	Est. 50000	PF60	75.00

KM# 339 20 DOLLARS
31.10 g., 0.925 Silver, 0.92 oz. ASW 38mm. **Subject:** Aviation **Obv.** Crowned head right, date below **Rev:** DHC-6 Twin Otter, denomination below **Rev. Designer:** Neil Aird

Date	Mintage		
1999	Est. 50000	PF60	95.00

KM# 340 20 DOLLARS
31.10 g., 0.925 Silver, 0.92 oz. ASW 38mm. **Subject:** Aviation **Obv.** Crowned head right, date below **Rev:** DHC-8 Dash 8, denomination below

Date	Mintage		
1999	50,000	PF60	100

KM# 395 20 DOLLARS
0.925 Silver, 38mm. **Subject:** First Canadian locomotive **Obv.** Crowned head right, date below **Rev:** Locomotive below multicolored cameo, denomination below

Date	Mintage		
2000	—	PF60	50.00

20 DOLLARS

KM# 428 20 DOLLARS
31.10 g., 0.925 Silver, 0.92 oz. ASW 38mm. **Obv.**
Crowned head right **Rev:** Russell touring car with
hologram cameo **Series:** Transportation - Russell Touring
Car **Rev. Designer:** John Mardon **Edge:** Segmented
reeding

Date	Mintage		
2001	15,000	PF63 35.00	PF65 45.00

KM# 396 20 DOLLARS
0.925 Silver, 38mm. **Subject:** First Canadian self-
propelled car **Obv.** Crowned head right, date below **Rev:**
Car below multicolored cameo, denomination below

Date	Mintage	
2000	—	PF60 50.00

KM# 397 20 DOLLARS
0.925 Silver, 38mm. **Subject:** Bluenose sailboat **Obv.**
Crowned head right, date below **Rev:** Bluenose sailing left
below multicolored cameo, denomination below

Date	Mintage	
2000	—	PF60 150

KM# 427 20 DOLLARS
31.10 g., 0.925 Silver, 0.92 oz. ASW 38mm. **Obv.**
Crowned head right **Rev:** Sailship with hologram cameo
Series: Transportation - The Marco Polo **Rev. Designer:**
J. Franklin Wright **Edge:** Segmented reeding

Date	Mintage		
2001	15,000	PF63 35.00	PF65 45.00

KM# 464 20 DOLLARS
31.10 g., 0.925 Silver, 0.92 oz. ASW **Obv.** Crowned head
right **Obv. Designer:** Dora dePédery-Hunt **Rev:** Gray-Dort
Model 25-SM with cameo hologram **Rev. Designer:** John
Mardon

Date	Mintage		
2002	15,000	PF63 35.00	PF65 45.00

KM# 465 20 DOLLARS
31.10 g., 0.925 Silver, 0.92 oz. ASW **Obv.** Crowned head
right **Obv. Designer:** Dora dePédery-Hunt **Rev:** Sailing
ship William D. Lawrence **Rev. Designer:** Bonnie Ross

Date	Mintage		
2002	15,000	PF63 35.00	PF65 45.00

KM# 411 20 DOLLARS
31.10 g., 0.925 Silver, 0.92 oz. ASW 38mm. **Subject:**
Transportation - Steam Locomotive **Obv.** Crowned head
right **Obv. Designer:** Dora dePédery-Hunt **Rev:** First
Canadian Steel Steam Locomotive and cameo hologram
Rev. Designer: Don Curely **Edge:** Segmented reeding

Date	Mintage		
2001	15,000	PF63 35.00	PF65 45.00

KM# 482 20 DOLLARS
31.39 g., 0.9999 Silver, 1.00 oz. ASW 38mm. **Obv.**
Crowned head right **Obv. Designer:** Dora dePédery-
Hunt **Rev:** Niagara Falls hologram **Rev. Designer:** Gary
Corcoran

Date	Mintage		
2003	29,967	PF63 65.00	PF65 75.00

KM# 483 20 DOLLARS
31.10 g., 0.925 Silver, 0.92 oz. ASW **Subject:** The HMCS
Bras d'or (FHE-400) **Obv.** Crowned head right **Obv.**
Designer: Dora dePédery-Hunt **Rev:** Ship in water **Rev.**
Designer: Donald Curley, Stan Witten

Date	Mintage		
2003	15,000	PF63 35.00	PF65 45.00

KM# 523 20 DOLLARS
31.39 g., 0.999 Silver, 1.00 oz. ASW 38mm. **Obv.**
Crowned head right **Obv. Designer:** Dora dePédery-Hunt
Rev: Canadian Rockies, multicolor

Date	Mintage		
2003	29,967	PF63 45.00	PF65 50.00

KM# 484 20 DOLLARS
31.10 g., 0.925 Silver, 0.92 oz. ASW **Subject:** Canadian
National FA-1 diesel-electric locomotive **Obv.** Crowned
head right **Obv. Designer:** Dora dePédery-Hunt **Rev.**
Designer: John Mardon, William Woodruff

Date	Mintage		
2003	15,000	PF63 35.00	PF65 45.00

KM# 485 20 DOLLARS
31.10 g., 0.925 Silver, 0.92 oz. ASW **Obv.** Crowned
head right **Obv. Designer:** Dora dePédery-Hunt **Rev:** The
Bricklin SV-1 **Rev. Designer:** Brian Hughes, José Oslo

Date	Mintage		
2003	15,000	PF63 35.00	PF65 45.00

KM# 611 20 DOLLARS
31.39 g., 0.9999 Silver, 1.00 oz. ASW 38mm. **Obv.**
Head right **Obv. Designer:** Susanna Blunt **Rev:** Iceberg,
hologram

Date	Mintage		
2004	24,879	PF63 40.00	PF65 45.00

KM# 838 20 DOLLARS
31.39 g., 0.9999 Silver, 1.00 oz. ASW 38mm. **Rev:**
Hopewell Rocks, gilt

Date	Mintage		
2004	16,918	PF63 35.00	PF65 45.00

KM# 561 20 DOLLARS
31.39 g., 0.9999 Silver, 1.00 oz. ASW 38mm. **Obv.** Head
right **Obv. Designer:** Susanna Blunt **Rev:** Three-masted
sailing ship, hologram of the sea **Rev. Designer:** Bonnie
Ross

Date	Mintage		
2005	18,276	PF63 50.00	PF65 55.00

KM# 562 20 DOLLARS
31.39 g., 0.9999 Silver, 1.00 oz. ASW 38mm. **Subject:**
Northwest Territories Diamonds **Obv.** Head right **Obv.**
Designer: Susanna Blunt **Rev:** Multicolor diamond
hologram on landscape **Rev. Designer:** José Oslo **Edge:**
Reeded

Date	Mintage		
2005	35,000	PF63 45.00	PF65 50.00

KM# 563   20 DOLLARS
31.39 g., 0.9999 Silver, 1.00 oz. ASW **Subject:** Mingan Archepelago **Obv.** Head right **Obv. Designer:** Susanna Blunt **Rev:** Cliffs with whale tail out of water **Rev. Designer:** Pierre Leduc

Date	Mintage		
2005	—	PF63 470	PF65 45.00

KM# 564   20 DOLLARS
31.39 g., 0.9999 Silver, 1.00 oz. ASW **Subject:** Rainforests of the Pacific Northwest **Obv.** Head right **Rev:** Open winged bird **Designer:** Susanna Blunt

Date	Mintage		
2005	—	PF63 40.00	PF65 45.00

KM# 663   20 DOLLARS
31.39 g., 0.9999 Silver, 1.00 oz. ASW 38mm. **Subject:** Nahanni National Park **Obv.** Head right **Rev:** Bear walking along sream, cliff in background

Date	Mintage		
2006	—	PF63 55.00	PF65 60.00

KM# 565   20 DOLLARS
31.39 g., 0.9999 Silver, 1.00 oz. ASW 38mm. **Subject:** Toronto Island National Park **Obv.** Head right **Rev:** Toronto Island Lighthouse, Toronto skyline in background

Date	Mintage		
2005	—	PF63 50.00	PF65 55.00

KM# 588   20 DOLLARS
31.39 g., 0.9999 Silver, 1.00 oz. ASW **Subject:** Georgian Bay National Park **Obv.** Head right **Rev:** Canoe and small trees on island

Date	Mintage		
2006	—	PF63 50.00	PF65 60.00

KM# 664   20 DOLLARS
31.39 g., 0.9999 Silver, 1.00 oz. ASW 38mm. **Subject:** Jasper National Park **Obv.** Head right **Rev:** Cowboy on horseback in majestic scene

Date	Mintage		
2006	—	PF63 55.00	PF65 60.00

KM# 589   20 DOLLARS
31.10 g., 0.9999 Silver, 0.99 oz. ASW 38mm. **Obv.** Head right **Rev:** Notre Dame Basilica, Montreal, as a hologram

Date	Mintage		
2006	15,000	PF63 45.00	PF65 50.00

KM# 665   20 DOLLARS
31.10 g., 0.9999 Silver, 0.99 oz. ASW 38mm. **Obv.** Head right **Rev:** Holographic rendering of CN Tower

Date	Mintage		
2006	15,000	PF63 55.00	PF65 60.00

KM# 666 20 DOLLARS
31.10 g., 0.9999 Silver, 0.99 oz. ASW **Obv.** Head right
Rev: Holographic view of Pengrowth Saddledome in
Calgary

Date	Mintage		
2006	15,000	**PF63** 50.00	**PF65** 55.00

KM# 735 20 DOLLARS
31.10 g., 0.999 Silver, 0.99 oz. ASW 38mm. **Rev:**
Snowflake, aquamarine crystal

Date	Mintage	
2007	4,989	**PF65** 175

KM# 737 20 DOLLARS
31.10 g., 0.999 Silver, 0.99 oz. ASW 38mm. **Subject:**
International Polar Year

Date	Mintage		
2007	9,164	**PF63** 60.00	**PF65** 65.00

KM# 667 20 DOLLARS
31.39 g., 0.9999 Silver, 1.00 oz. ASW **Subject:** Tall Ship
Obv. Head right **Rev:** Ketch and holographic image of
thunderstorm in sky

Date	Mintage		
2006	10,299	**PF63** 55.00	**PF65** 60.00

KM# 737a 20 DOLLARS
27.78 g., 0.925 Silver, 0.82 oz. ASW 40mm. **Subject:**
International Polar Year **Rev:** Blue plasma coating

Date	Mintage	
2007	3,005	**PF65** 250

KM# 734 20 DOLLARS
31.10 g., 0.999 Silver, 0.99 oz. ASW 38mm. **Rev:** Holiday
sleigh ride

Date	Mintage		
2007	6,804	**PF63** 65.00	**PF65** 70.00

KM# 738 20 DOLLARS
31.39 g., 0.9999 Silver, 1.00 oz. ASW 38mm. **Subject:**
Tall ships **Rev:** Brigantine in harbor, hologram

Date	Mintage		
2007	16,000	**PF63** 55.00	**PF65** 60.00

20 DOLLARS

KM# 839   20 DOLLARS
31.39 g., 0.9999 Silver, 1.00 oz. ASW **Rev:** Northern lights
in hologram

Date	Mintage	MS63
2007	—	35.00

KM# 808   20 DOLLARS
31.50 g., 0.925 Silver, 0.93 oz. ASW 38mm. **Subject:**
Agriculture trade **Rev:** Team of horses plowing

Date	Mintage		
2008	5,802	PF63 65.00	PF65 70.00

KM# 809   20 DOLLARS
31.11 g., 0.999 Silver, 0.99 oz. ASW 38mm. **Rev:** Royal
Hudson Steam locomotive

Date	Mintage		
2008	8,345	PF63 65.00	PF65 70.00

KM# 810   20 DOLLARS
31.39 g., 0.999 Silver, 1.00 oz. ASW 38mm. **Rev:** Green
leaf and crystal raindrop **Rev. Designer:** Stanley Witten

Date	Mintage		
2008	15,000	PF63 165	PF65 175

KM# 811   20 DOLLARS
31.11 g., 0.999 Silver, 0.99 oz. ASW **Rev:** Snowflake,
amethyst crystal

Date	Mintage		
2008	7,172	PF63 90.00	PF65 95.00

KM# 813   20 DOLLARS
31.11 g., 0.999 Silver, 0.99 oz. ASW 38mm. **Rev:**
Carolers around tree

Date	Mintage		
2008	10,000	PF63 60.00	PF65 70.00

KM# 872 20 DOLLARS
31.11 g., 0.999 Silver, 0.99 oz. ASW 38mm. **Rev:**
Snowflake, sapphire crystal

Date	Mintage		
2008	7,765	**PF63** 90.00	**PF65** 95.00

KM# 891 20 DOLLARS
31.39 g., 0.999 Silver, 1.00 oz. ASW 38mm. **Subject:**
Great Canadian Locomotives - Jubilee **Obv.** Bust right
Obv. Designer: Susanna Blunt **Rev:** Jubilee locomotive
side view **Obv. Legend:** Elizabeth II DG Regina **Rev.**
Legend: Canada 20 Dollars **Edge Lettering:** Jubilee

Date	Mintage		
2009	6,036	**PF63** 65.00	**PF65** 70.00

KM# 893 20 DOLLARS
31.39 g., 0.999 Silver, 1.00 oz. ASW 38mm. **Subject:** Coal
mining trade **Obv.** Bust right **Obv. Designer:** Susanna
Blunt **Rev:** Miner pushing cart with coal **Obv. Legend:**
Elizabeth II DG Regina **Rev. Designer:** John Marder **Rev.**
Legend: Canada 20 Dollars

Date	Mintage		
2009	10,000	**PF63** 65.00	**PF65** 75.00

KM# 870 20 DOLLARS
27.78 g., 0.925 Silver, 0.82 oz. ASW 40mm. **Rev:** Calgary
Flames goalie mask multicolor on goal net

Date	Mintage		
2009	10,000	**PF63** 60.00	**PF65** 70.00

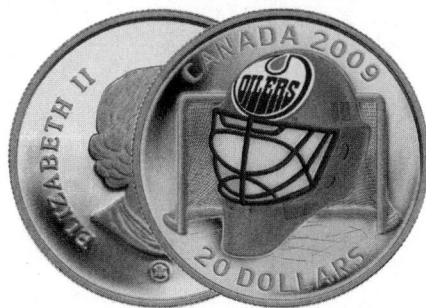

KM# 871 20 DOLLARS
27.78 g., 0.925 Silver, 0.82 oz. ASW 40mm. **Rev:**
Edmonton Oilers goalie mask, multicolor on goal net

Date	Mintage		
2009	10,000	**PF63** 60.00	**PF65** 70.00

KM# 872A 20 DOLLARS
27.78 g., 0.925 Silver, 0.82 oz. ASW 40mm. **Rev:**
Montreal Canadians goalie mask multicolor

Date	Mintage		
2009	10,000	**PF63** 60.00	**PF65** 70.00

KM# 873 20 DOLLARS
27.78 g., 0.925 Silver, 0.82 oz. ASW 40mm. **Rev:** Ottawa
Senators goalie mask on goal net

Date	Mintage		
2009	10,000	**PF63** 60.00	**PF65** 70.00

20 DOLLARS

KM# 874   20 DOLLARS
27.78 g., 0.925 Silver, 0.82 oz. ASW 40mm. **Rev:** Toronto
Maple Leafs goalie mask, multicolor on goal net

Date	Mintage		
2009	10,000	PF63 60.00	PF65 70.00

KM# 875   20 DOLLARS
27.78 g., 0.925 Silver, 0.82 oz. ASW 40mm. **Rev:**
Vancouver Canucks goalie mask, multicolor on goal net

Date	Mintage		
2009	10,000	PF63 60.00	PF65 70.00

KM# 876   20 DOLLARS
31.50 g., 0.925 Silver, 0.93 oz. ASW 40mm. **Rev:**
Summer moon mask

Date	Mintage	
2009	2,834	PF65 225

KM# 944   20 DOLLARS
31.11 g., 0.999 Silver, 0.99 oz. ASW 38mm. **Rev:**
Snowflake - light blue crystal

Date	Mintage		
2009	7,477	PF63 95.00	PF65 100

KM# 945   20 DOLLARS
31.11 g., 0.999 Silver, 0.99 oz. ASW 38mm. **Rev:**
Snowflake - light red crystal

Date	Mintage		
2009	7,004	PF63 95.00	PF65 100

KM# 892   20 DOLLARS
31.39 g., 0.999 Silver, 1.00 oz. ASW 38mm. **Subject:**
Crystal raindrop **Obv.** Bust right **Rev:** Maple leaf and rain
drop - fall colors **Rev. Designer:** Celia Godkin

Date	Mintage		
2009	9,998	PF63 75.00	PF65 85.00

KM# 987   20 DOLLARS
31.39 g., 0.9999 Silver, 1.00 oz. ASW 38mm. **Rev:** Lotus
Water Lilly in multicolor and crystal **Rev. Designer:**
Cladio D'Angelo

Date	Mintage		
2010	10,000	PF63 110	PF65 120

KM# 1009   20 DOLLARS
31.39 g.,   0.999 Silver, 1.00 oz. ASW **Subject:** 75th Anniversary of Canadian Bank Notes **Rev:** Female and farmer seated

Date	Mintage		
2010	7,500	PF63 65.00	PF65 70.00

KM# 1048   20 DOLLARS
31.11 g.,   0.9999 Silver, 0.99 oz. ASW 38mm.   **Rev:** Snowflake, blue crystals

Date	Mintage		
2010	7,500	PF63 85.00	PF65 95.00

KM# 1049   20 DOLLARS
31.11 g.,   0.9999 Silver, 0.99 oz. ASW 38mm.   **Rev:** Snowflake, tanzanite crystals

Date	Mintage		
2010	7,500	PF63 85.00	PF65 95.00

KM# 1013   20 DOLLARS
31.39 g., 0.999 Silver, 1.00 oz. ASW 38mm.   **Rev:** Maple leaf and crystal **Rev. Designer:** Celia Godkin

Date	Mintage		
2010	10,000	PF63 90.00	PF65 100

KM# 1066   20 DOLLARS
31.99 g.,   0.999 Silver, 1.02 oz. ASW 38mm.   **Rev:** Pinecone with ruby crystals **Rev. Designer:** Susan Taylor

Date	Mintage		
2010	5,000	PF63 110	PF65 120

KM# 1067   20 DOLLARS
31.99 g.,   0.999 Silver, 1.02 oz. ASW 38mm.   **Rev:** Pinecone with moonlight blue crystals **Rev. Designer:** Susan Taylor

Date	Mintage		
2010	5,000	PF63 110	PF65 120

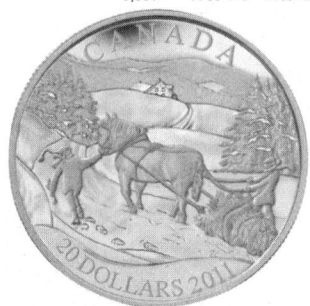

KM# 1018   20 DOLLARS
31.39 g.,   0.999 Silver, 1.00 oz. ASW 38mm.   **Rev:** Steam Locomotive Selkirk

Date	Mintage	
2010	10,000	PF65 80.00

KM# 1075   20 DOLLARS
27.78 g.,   0.925 Silver, 0.82 oz. ASW 40mm.   **Subject:** Winter Scene **Rev:** Horse pulling cut Christmas Tree **Rev. Designer:** Rene Clark

Date	Mintage		
2011	8,000	PF63 60.00	PF65 70.00

20 DOLLARS

KM# 1111   20 DOLLARS
31.39 g., 0.999 Silver, 1.00 oz. ASW 40mm. **Subject:**
Royal Wedding **Rev:** Portraits of Katherine and William
facing each other, crystal insert

Date	Mintage		
2011	—	PF63 70.00	PF65 80.00

KM# 1134   20 DOLLARS
31.39 g., 0.9999 Silver, 1.00 oz. ASW 38mm. **Subject:**
Canadian Pacific's D-10 Steam Locomotive **Obv.** Bust
right **Rev:** Steam locomotive right **Edge:** Lettered

Date	Mintage		
2011	10,000	PF63 70.00	PF65 80.00

KM# 1135   20 DOLLARS
31.39 g., 0.9999 Silver, 1.00 oz. ASW 38mm. **Obv.** Bust
right **Rev:** Tulip in color and Vienitian glass lady bug

Date	Mintage	
2011	5,000	PF65 1,000

KM# 1145   20 DOLLARS
31.39 g., 0.9999 Silver, 1.00 oz. ASW 38mm. **Obv.** Bust
right **Rev:** Wild rose in color, swarovski crystrals

Date	Mintage		
2011	Est. 10000	PF63 125	PF65 135

KM# 1147   20 DOLLARS
31.39 g., 0.9999 Silver, 1.00 oz. ASW 38mm. **Obv.** Bust
right **Rev:** Maple leaves, seeds in color, swarovski crystal
drop

Date	Mintage		
2011	—	PF63 100	PF65 110

KM# 1181   20 DOLLARS
31.39 g., 0.999 Silver, 1.00 oz. ASW 38mm. **Obv.** Bust
right **Rev:** Winnipeg Jets Logo, jet over maple leaf

Date	Mintage		
2011	15,000	PF63 85.00	PF65 95.00

KM# 1182 20 DOLLARS
31.99 g., 0.9999 Silver, 1.02 oz. ASW 38mm. **Obv.** Bust
right **Rev:** Christmas tree with six crystals

Date	Mintage		
2011	—	PF63 65.00	PF65 75.00

KM# 1187 20 DOLLARS
31.39 g., 0.999 Silver, 1.00 oz. ASW 38mm. **Obv.** Bust
right **Rev:** Snowflake with emerald crystals

Date	Mintage		
2011	15,000	PF63 75.00	PF65 85.00

KM# 1188 20 DOLLARS
31.89 g., 0.999 Silver, 1.02 oz. ASW 38mm. **Obv.** Bust
right **Rev:** Snowflake with topaz crystals

Date	Mintage		
2011	15,000	PF63 75.00	PF65 85.00

KM# 1189 20 DOLLARS
31.89 g., 0.999 Silver, 1.02 oz. ASW 38mm. **Obv.** Bust
right **Rev:** Three snowflakes with three Hyacinth red
crystals

Date	Mintage		
2011	15,000	PF63 75.00	PF65 85.00

KM# 1190 20 DOLLARS
31.89 g., 0.999 Silver, 1.02 oz. ASW 38mm. **Obv.** Bust
right **Rev:** Three snowflakes with three Montana blue
crystals

Date	Mintage		
2011	15,000	PF63 75.00	PF65 85.00

KM# 1137 20 DOLLARS
31.39 g., 0.999 Silver, 1.00 oz. ASW 38mm. **Subject:**
Elizabeth II, 60th Anniversary of reign **Obv.** Bust right
Rev: Crowned bust right with swarovski crystal insert
Edge: Reeded

Date	Mintage		
1952-2012	15,000	PF63 70.00	PF65 80.00

KM# 1177 20 DOLLARS
27.78 g., 0.925 Silver, 0.82 oz. ASW 38mm. **Obv.** Bust
right **Rev:** Youthful busts right of Elizabeth II and Prince
Philip

Date	Mintage		
1952-2012	—	PF63 75.00	PF65 85.00

KM# 1178 20 DOLLARS
27.78 g., 0.925 Silver, 0.82 oz. ASW 38mm. **Obv.** Bust
right **Rev:** Royal cypher, wreath below

Date	Mintage		
1952-2012	—	PF63 75.00	PF65 85.00

20 DOLLARS

KM# 1238   20 DOLLARS
30.75 g., 0.9999 Silver, 0.98 oz. ASW 36mm. **Subject:** Elizabeth II, Diamond Jubilee **Obv.** Bust right **Rev:** Elizabeth II profile left, high releif **Rev. Designer:** Laurie McGaw

Date	Mintage		
2012	7,500	**PF63** 65.00	**PF65** 75.00

KM# 1239   20 DOLLARS
7.96 g., 0.999 Silver, 0.25 oz. ASW 27mm. **Subject:** Royal visit to Canada **Obv.** Young portrait right **Rev:** Elizabeth II with Mountie and horse

Date	Mintage		
1952-2012	25,000	**PF63** 25.00	**PF65** 30.00

KM# 1246   20 DOLLARS
27.78 g., 0.925 Silver, 0.82 oz. ASW 38mm. **Subject:** Coast Guard, 50th Anniversary

Date	Mintage		
2012	—	**PF63** 90.00	**PF65** 100

KM# 1250   20 DOLLARS
27.78 g., 0.925 Silver, 0.82 oz. ASW 38mm. **Subject:** F.H. Varley

Date	Mintage		
2012	—	**PF63** 65.00	**PF65** 75.00

KM# 1251   20 DOLLARS
27.78 g., 0.925 Silver, 0.82 oz. ASW 38mm. **Subject:** Arthur Lismer

Date	Mintage		
2012	—	**PF63** 65.00	**PF65** 75.00

KM# 1266   20 DOLLARS
31.10 g., 0.999 Silver, 0.99 oz. ASW 38mm. **Subject:** Aster and bee

Date	Mintage		
2012	—	**PF63** 90.00	**PF65** 100

KM# 1269   20 DOLLARS
31.39 g., 0.999 Silver, 1.00 oz. ASW 38mm. **Subject:** Sugar Maple Leaf **Rev:** Leaves in color, crystal

Date	Mintage	
2012	—	**PF65** 130

KM# 1270 20 DOLLARS
31.39 g., 0.999 Silver, 1.00 oz. ASW 38mm. **Rev:**
Rhododendron

Date	Mintage		
2012	—	**PF65** 125	

KM# 1280 20 DOLLARS
31.11 g., 0.999 Silver, 0.99 oz. ASW 38mm. **Subject:**
Bateman Moose

Date	Mintage		
2012	—	**PF65** 135	

KM# 1283 20 DOLLARS
15.55 g., 0.999 Gold, 0.50 oz. AGW 25mm. **Subject:** Year
of the Dragon

Date	Mintage		
2012	—	**PF65** 900	

KM# 1333 20 DOLLARS
31.11 g., 0.999 Silver, 0.99 oz. ASW 38mm. **Rev:**
Snowstorm

Date	Mintage		
2012	—	**PF63** 45.00	**PF65** 50.00

KM# 1334 20 DOLLARS
28.02 g., 0.999 Silver, 0.89 oz. ASW **Subject:** Christmas
Play **Rev:** Three childred as the Magi, crystal **Rev.**
Designer: Jason Bouwman

Date	Mintage		
2012	10,000	**PF63** 110	**PF65** 115

KM# 1335 20 DOLLARS
27.78 g., 0.925 Silver, 0.82 oz. ASW 38mm. **Subject:**
Franklin Carmichael **Rev:** Snowy Landscape

Date	Mintage		
2012	—	**PF63** 70.00	**PF65** 75.00

KM# 1347 20 DOLLARS
31.39 g., 0.999 Silver, 1.00 oz. ASW 38mm. **Rev:** Blue
flag iris in color with three crystals **Rev. Designer:** Celia
Godkin

Date	Mintage		
2013	10,000	**PF63** 110	**PF65** 120

KM# 1361 20 DOLLARS
31.39 g., 0.999 Silver, 1.00 oz. ASW 35mm. **Rev:**
Purple cone flower, butterfly in color and high relief **Rev.**
Designer: Maurice Gervais

Date	Mintage		
2013	—	**PF63** 50.00	**PF65** 60.00

20 DOLLARS

KM# 1363   20 DOLLARS
31.39 g., 0.9999 Silver, 1.00 oz. ASW 38mm. **Subject:** Canadian Maple Canopy - Spring **Rev:** Forest Canopy in Spring, Colorized **Rev. Designer:** Emily Damstra

Date	Mintage		
2013	Est. 7500	PF63 90.00	PF65 100

KM# 1374   20 DOLLARS
31.40 g., 0.999 Silver, 1.00 oz. ASW 38mm. **Subject:** Baseball **Rev:** Baseball Batter **Rev. Designer:** Steve Hepburn

Date	Mintage		
2013	Est. 7500	PF63 110	PF65 115

KM# 1375   20 DOLLARS
31.39 g., 0.999 Silver, 1.00 oz. ASW 38mm. **Subject:** Baseball **Rev:** Baseball Fielder **Rev. Designer:** Steve Hepburn

Date	Mintage		
2013	Est. 7500	PF63 110	PF65 115

KM# 1376   20 DOLLARS
31.39 g., 0.999 Silver, 1.00 oz. ASW 38mm. **Subject:** Baseball **Rev:** Baseball Pitcher **Rev. Designer:** Steve Hepburn

Date	Mintage		
2013	—	PF63 110	PF65 115

KM# 1377   20 DOLLARS
31.39 g., 0.999 Silver, 1.00 oz. ASW 38mm. **Subject:** Baseball **Rev:** Baseball Runner **Rev. Designer:** Steve Hepburn

Date	Mintage		
2013	Est. 7500	PF63 110	PF65 115

KM# 1381   20 DOLLARS
31.11 g., 0.999 Silver, 0.99 oz. ASW 38mm. **Subject:** Snow Flake With Crystal

Date	Mintage		
2013	—	PF63 110	PF65 120

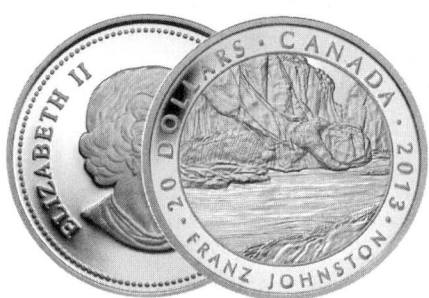

KM# 1384   20 DOLLARS
31.39 g., 0.999 Silver, 1.00 oz. ASW 38mm. **Subject:**
Frank Johnston - Painter **Rev:** Painting: Guardian of the
Gorge **Rev. Designer:** F.H. Varley

Date	Mintage		
2013	Est. 7000	PF63 80.00	PF65 90.00

KM# 1385   20 DOLLARS
31.39 g., 0.999 Silver, 1.00 oz. ASW 38mm. **Subject:**
Lauren S. Harris - Painter **Rev:** Painting: Toronto Street,
Winter Morning **Rev. Designer:** F.H. Varley

Date	Mintage		
2013	Est. 7000	PF63 80.00	PF65 90.00

KM# 1397   20 DOLLARS
31.39 g., 0.9999 Silver, 1.00 oz. ASW 38mm. **Rev:** Beaver
gnawing on tree **Rev. Designer:** Glen Loates

Date	Mintage		
2013	8,500	PF63 90.00	PF65 100

KM# 1404   20 DOLLARS
28.20 g., 0.9999 Silver, 0.90 oz. ASW 40mm. **Rev:** Arctic
Fox and Northern lights in background **Rev. Designer:**
Tivadar Bote

Date	Mintage		
2013	—	PF63 75.00	PF65 85.00

KM# 1447   20 DOLLARS
31.39 g., 0.999 Silver, 1.00 oz. ASW 38mm. **Rev:**
Superman standing right, cape blowing **Rev. Designer:**
Jim Lee, DC Comics

Date	Mintage		
2013	Est. 10000	PF63 100	PF65 110

KM# 1448   20 DOLLARS
31.39 g., 0.999 Silver, 1.00 oz. ASW 38mm. **Subject:** 75th
Anniversary of Superman **Rev:** Superman flying forward,
multi-color background hologram **Rev. Designer:** Jim
Lee, DC Comics

Date	Mintage		
2013	Est. 10000	PF63 120	PF65 130

KM# 1449   20 DOLLARS
31.39 g., 0.999 Silver, 1.00 oz. ASW 38mm. **Subject:**
75th Anniversary of Superman **Rev:** 'S' shield logo in color

Date	Mintage		
2013	Est. 10000	PF63 110	PF65 120

KM# 1451a   20 DOLLARS
7.96 g., 0.9999 Silver, 0.25 oz. ASW **Ruler:** Elizabeth
II 38mm. **Rev:** Red maple leaf in center of many small
maple leaves **Rev. Designer:** Jose Osio **Mint:** Royal
Canadian Mint

Date	Mintage		
2013	Est. 10000	PF63 100	PF65 115

KM# 1459   20 DOLLARS
31.39 g., 0.999 Silver, 1.00 oz. ASW 38mm. **Rev:**
Pronghorn Antelope with northern lights in the background
Rev. Designer: Pierre Leduc

Date	Mintage		
2013	Est. 8500	PF63 80.00	PF65 90.00

KM# 1466   20 DOLLARS
31.39 g., 0.9999 Silver, 1.00 oz. ASW 38mm. **Subject:**
Birth of Prince George **Rev:** Baby sleeping in crib **Rev.
Designer:** Laurie McGaw

Date	Mintage		
2013	7,500	PF63 70.00	PF65 80.00

KM# 1467   20 DOLLARS
31.39 g., 0.9999 Silver, 1.00 oz. ASW 38mm. **Subject:**
Birth of Prince George **Rev:** Parents hands holding baby's
head **Rev. Designer:** Laurie McGaw

Date	Mintage		
2013	7,500	PF63 70.00	PF65 80.00

KM# 1468   20 DOLLARS
31.39 g., 0.9999 Silver, 1.00 oz. ASW 38mm. **Subject:**
Birth of Prince George **Rev:** Mint Mascot Moose and
Beaver Mountie plush dolls in crib with sleeping baby
Rev. Designer: Laurie McGaw

Date	Mintage		
2013	7,500	PF63 70.00	PF65 80.00

KM# 1470   20 DOLLARS
31.39 g., 0.9999 Silver, 1.00 oz. ASW 38mm. **Subject:**
A.Y. Jackson, painter **Rev:** Detail of painting, Sant Tile de
Caps

Date	Mintage		
2013	7,000	PF63 90.00	PF65 100

20 DOLLARS

KM# 1471   20 DOLLARS
31.39 g., 0.9999 Silver, 1.00 oz. ASW 38mm. **Subject:**
J.E.H. MacDonald, painter **Rev:** Detail of painting, Sumacs

Date	Mintage		
2013	7,000	**PF63** 90.00	**PF65** 100

KM# 1474   20 DOLLARS
31.39 g., 0.999 Silver, 1.00 oz. ASW 38mm. **Subject:**
Dinosaurs of Canada **Rev:** Bathygnathus advancing left
Rev. Designer: Julius Cstonyi

Date	Mintage		
2013	8,500	**PF63** 80.00	**PF65** 90.00

KM# 1479   20 DOLLARS
31.39 g., 0.999 Silver, 1.00 oz. ASW 38mm. **Rev:** Eagle
in flight left

Date	Mintage		
2013	—	**PF63** 80.00	**PF65** 90.00

KM# 1484   20 DOLLARS
31.11 g., 0.999 Silver, 0.99 oz. ASW 38mm. **Subject:**
Louisburg Settlement **Rev:** Colonial sea-side scene **Rev.**
Designer: John Horton

Date	Mintage		
2013	8,500	**PF63** 80.00	**PF65** 90.00

KM# 1507   20 DOLLARS
0.999 Silver, 38mm. **Subject:** Carlito Dalceggio, artist

Date	Mintage		
2013	7,500	**PF63** 80.00	**PF65** 90.00

KM# 1510   20 DOLLARS
31.39 g., 0.9999 Silver, 1.00 oz. ASW 38mm. **Rev:** Two
eagles standing on rock **Rev. Designer:** Claudio d'Angelo

Date	Mintage		
2013	7,500	**PF63** 75.00	**PF65** 80.00

KM# 1513   20 DOLLARS
31.39 g., 0.9999 Silver, 1.00 oz. ASW 38mm. **Subject:**
Northern Lights, the great Hare **Rev:** Hare seated watching
hologram of Northern Lights **Rev. Designer:** Nathalie
Bertin

Date	Mintage		
2013	8,500	**PF63** 100	**PF65** 110

KM# 1553   20 DOLLARS
Silver ASW 38mm. **Subject:** Pond Hockey in color **Rev.
Designer:** Richard D. Wolfe

Date	Mintage		
2014	8,500	PF63 90.00	PF65 100

KM# 1556   20 DOLLARS
31.39 g., 0.9999 Silver, 1.00 oz. ASW 38mm. **Rev:** Polar
bear walking on rocks in color **Rev. Designer:** Glen Loates

Date	Mintage		
2014	8,500	PF63 90.00	PF65 100

KM# 1558   20 DOLLARS
31.39 g., 0.999 Silver, 1.00 oz. ASW 38mm. **Rev:**
Canadian UN Peacekeeper with binoculars, blue beret
Rev. Designer: Selvia Pecota

Date	Mintage	
2014	8,500	PF65 115

KM# 1565   20 DOLLARS
31.39 g., 0.9999 Silver, 1.00 oz. ASW 38mm. **Rev:** Lake
Superior in blue color

Date	Mintage		
2014	10,000	PF63 110	PF65 115

KM# 1566   20 DOLLARS
31.39 g., 0.999 Silver, 1.00 oz. ASW 38mm. **Rev:** Lake
Huron in color

Date	Mintage		
2014	10,000	PF63 110	PF65 115

KM# 1567   20 DOLLARS
31.39 g., 0.999 Silver, 1.00 oz. ASW 38mm. **Rev:** Lake
Michigan in color

Date	Mintage		
2014	10,000	PF63 110	PF65 115

KM# 1568   20 DOLLARS
31.39 g., 0.999 Silver, 1.00 oz. ASW 38mm. **Rev:** Lake
Erie in color

Date	Mintage		
2014	10,000	PF63 110	PF65 115

KM# 1569   20 DOLLARS
31.39 g., 0.999 Silver, 1.00 oz. ASW 38mm. **Rev:** Lake
Ontario in color

Date	Mintage		
2014	10,000	PF63 110	PF65 115

KM# 1570   20 DOLLARS
31.39 g., 0.9999 Silver, 1.00 oz. ASW 38mm. **Rev:**
Caribou in color **Rev. Designer:** Trevor Tennant

Date	Mintage		
2014	8,500	PF63 90.00	PF65 100

20 DOLLARS

KM# 1609 20 DOLLARS
31.39 g., 0.999 Silver, 1.00 oz. ASW 38mm. **Obv.** Bust right **Rev:** Bison head facing **Rev. Designer:** Doug Comeau

Date	Mintage		
2014	7,500	**PF63** 90.00	**PF65** 100

KM# 1610 20 DOLLARS
31.39 g., 0.999 Silver ASW 38mm. **Obv.** Bust right **Rev:** Bison pair advancing left **Rev. Designer:** Trevor Tennant

Date	Mintage		
2014	7,500	**PF63** 90.00	**PF65** 100

KM# 1614 20 DOLLARS
31.11 g., 0.999 Silver, 0.99 oz. ASW 40mm. **Obv.** Bust right **Rev:** Wolverine with northern lights in background **Rev. Designer:** Tivadar Bote

Date	Mintage		
2014	8,500	**PF63** 80.00	**PF65** 90.00

KM# 742 25 DOLLARS
27.78 g., 0.925 Silver, 0.82 oz. ASW 40mm. **Subject:** Vancouver Olympics **Rev:** Alpine skiing, hologram

Date	Mintage		
2007	45,000	**PF63** 45.00	**PF65** 50.00

KM# 743 25 DOLLARS
27.78 g., 0.925 Silver, 0.82 oz. ASW 40mm. **Subject:** Vancouver Olympics **Rev:** Athletics pride hologram

Date	Mintage		
2007	45,000	**PF63** 60.00	**PF65** 65.00

KM# 744 25 DOLLARS
27.75 g., 0.925 Silver, 0.82 oz. ASW 40mm. **Subject:** Vancouver Olympics **Rev:** Biathleon hologram

Date	Mintage		
2007	45,000	**PF63** 45.00	**PF65** 50.00

KM# 745 25 DOLLARS
27.78 g., 0.925 Silver, 0.82 oz. ASW 40mm. **Subject:**
Vancouver Olympics **Rev:** Curling hologram

Date	Mintage		
2007	—	PF63 45.00	PF65 50.00

KM# 746 25 DOLLARS
27.78 g., 0.925 Silver, 0.82 oz. ASW 40mm. **Subject:**
Vancouver Olympics **Rev:** Hockey, hologram

Date	Mintage		
2007	45,000	PF63 45.00	PF65 50.00

KM# 814 25 DOLLARS
27.78 g., 0.925 Silver, 0.82 oz. ASW 40mm. **Subject:**
Vancouver Olympics **Rev:** Bobsleigh, hologram

Date	Mintage		
2008	45,000	PF63 40.00	PF65 50.00

KM# 815 25 DOLLARS
27.78 g., 0.925 Silver, 0.82 oz. ASW 40mm. **Subject:**
Vancouver Olympics **Rev:** Figure skating, hologram

Date	Mintage		
2008	45,000	PF63 40.00	PF65 50.00

KM# 816 25 DOLLARS
27.78 g., 0.925 Silver, 0.82 oz. ASW 40mm. **Subject:**
Vancouver Olympics **Rev:** Freestyle skating, hologram

Date	Mintage		
2008	45,000	PF63 40.00	PF65 50.00

KM# 817 25 DOLLARS
27.78 g., 0.925 Silver, 0.82 oz. ASW 40mm. **Subject:**
Vancouver Olympics **Rev:** Snowboarding, hologram

Date	Mintage		
2008	45,000	PF63 40.00	PF65 50.00

KM# 818 25 DOLLARS
27.78 g., 0.925 Silver, 0.82 oz. ASW 40mm. **Subject:** Vancouver Olympics **Rev:** Home of the 2010 Olympics

Date	Mintage		
2008	45,000	PF63 40.00	PF65 50.00

KM# 903 25 DOLLARS
27.78 g., 0.925 Silver, 0.82 oz. ASW 40mm. **Subject:** 2010 Vancouver Olympics **Obv.** Bust right **Obv. Designer:** Susanna Blunt **Rev:** Cross Country Skiing and hologram at left

Date	Mintage		
2009	45,000	PF63 45.00	PF65 50.00

KM# 904 25 DOLLARS
27.78 g., 0.925 Silver, 0.82 oz. ASW 40mm. **Subject:** 2010 Vancouver Olympics **Obv.** Bust right **Obv. Designer:** Susanna Blunt **Rev:** Olympians holding torch, hologram at left

Date	Mintage		
2009	45,000	PF63 45.00	PF65 50.00

KM# 905 25 DOLLARS
27.78 g., 0.925 Silver, 0.82 oz. ASW 40mm. **Subject:** 2010 Vancouver Olympics **Obv.** Bust right **Obv. Designer:** Susanna Blunt **Rev:** Sled, hologram at left

Date	Mintage		
2009	45,000	PF63 45.00	PF65 50.00

KM# 906 25 DOLLARS
27.78 g., 0.925 Silver, 0.82 oz. ASW 40mm. **Subject:** 2010 Vancouver Olympics **Obv.** Bust right **Obv. Designer:** Susanna Blunt **Rev:** Ski Jumper, hologram at left

Date	Mintage		
2009	45,000	PF63 45.00	PF65 50.00

KM# 907 25 DOLLARS
27.78 g., 0.925 Silver, 0.82 oz. ASW 40mm. **Subject:** 2010 Vancouver Olympics **Obv.** Bust right **Obv. Designer:** Susanna Blunt **Rev:** Speed Skaters, hologram at left

Date	Mintage		
2009	45,000	PF63 45.00	PF65 50.00

KM# 1146 25 DOLLARS
62.41 g., 0.9999 Silver, 1.99 oz. ASW 60mm. **Obv.** Bust right **Rev:** Toronto map and skyline, partilly gilt **Edge:** Reeded

Date	Mintage		
2011	Est. 7500	PF63 170	PF65 180

KM# 1173   25 DOLLARS
31.39 g., 0.9999 Silver, 1.00 oz. ASW 38mm. **Obv.** Bust right **Rev:** Wayne Greskey skating right, father's portrait in circle at right, 99 in hologram at lower right

Date	Mintage		
2011	—	PF63 75.00	PF65 85.00

KM# 1330   25 DOLLARS
31.11 g., 0.999 Silver, 0.99 oz. ASW 38mm. **Rev:** Grandmother Moon Mask **Rev. Designer:** Richard Cochrane

Date	Mintage		
2012	—	PF63 70.00	PF65 75.00

KM# 1398   25 DOLLARS
31.39 g., 0.9999 Silver, 1.00 oz. ASW 38mm. **Rev:** Beaver with two kits **Rev. Designer:** Pierre Le Duc

Date	Mintage		
2013	Est. 8500	PF63 80.00	PF65 90.00

KM# 1403   25 DOLLARS
31.39 g., 0.999 Silver, 1.00 oz. ASW 38mm. **Rev:** Polar Bear and two cubs **Rev. Designer:** Pierre Le Duc

Date	Mintage		
2013	Est. 8500	PF63 80.00	PF65 90.00

KM# 1405   25 DOLLARS
7.77 g., 0.999 Gold, 0.25 oz. AGW 20mm. **Rev:** Arctic Fox with Northern lights in the background **Rev. Designer:** Tivadar Bote

Date	Mintage	
2013	Est. 1500	PF65 650

KM# 1456   25 DOLLARS
31.39 g., 0.999 Silver, 1.00 oz. ASW 38mm. **Rev:** Caribou mother and calf **Rev. Designer:** Pierre Leduc

Date	Mintage		
2013	Est. 8500	PF63 80.00	PF65 90.00

KM# 1457   25 DOLLARS
31.39 g., 0.999 Silver, 1.00 oz. ASW 38mm. **Rev:** Wolf mother and two pups **Rev. Designer:** Pierre Leduc

Date	Mintage		
2013	Est. 8500	PF63 80.00	PF65 90.00

KM# 1458   25 DOLLARS
7.77 g., 0.999 Gold, 0.25 oz. AGW 20mm. **Rev:** Pronghorn Antelope with northern lights in background **Rev. Designer:** Tony Bianco

Date	Mintage	
2013	Est. 1500	PF65 650

KM# 1482   25 DOLLARS
BANKNOTE ALLEGORY 31.11 g., 0.999 Silver, 0.99 oz. ASW **Ruler:** Elizabeth II 38mm. **Rev:** Female seated **Rev. Designer:** Laurie McGaw **Mint:** Royal Canadian Mint

Date	Mintage	MS63
2013 Proof	8,500	90.00

KM# 1483   25 DOLLARS
7.80 g., 0.9999 Gold, 0.25 oz. AGW 20mm. **Subject:** Banknote Allegory **Rev:** Seated female **Rev. Designer:** Laurie McGaw

Date	Mintage	
2013	2,000	PF65 650

KM# 1508   25 DOLLARS
30.76 g., 0.9999 Silver, 0.98 oz. ASW 36.15mm. **Subject:** Grandmother Moon Mask **Rev:** Mask carving **Rev. Designer:** Richard Cochrane

Date	Mintage		
2013	6,000	PF63 140	PF65 150

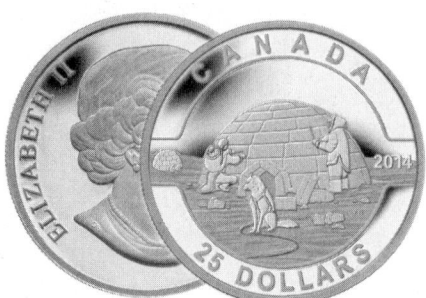

KM# 1581   25 DOLLARS
31.39 g., 0.999 Silver, 1.00 oz. ASW 38mm. **Obv.** Bust
right **Rev:** Igloo

Date	Mintage		
2014	—	PF63 65.00	PF65 75.00

KM# 1608   25 DOLLARS
7.97 g., 0.999 Gold 20mm. **Obv.** Bust right **Rev:**
Wolverine with northern lights in background **Rev.
Designer:** Tivadar Bote

Date	Mintage	
2014	1,500	PF65 650

KM# 1626   25 DOLLARS
31.39 g., 0.999 Silver, 1.00 oz. ASW 38mm. **Obv.** Bust
right **Rev:** Downhill skiing **Rev. Designer:** Kendra Dixon

Date	Mintage		
2014	—	PF63 80.00	PF65 90.00

KM# 590   30 DOLLARS
31.50 g., 0.925 Silver, 0.93 oz. ASW **Subject:** Pacific
Northwest Wood Carvings **Obv.** Head right **Rev:** Welcome
figure totem pole

Date	Mintage		
2006	9,904	PF63 65.00	PF65 75.00

KM# 668   30 DOLLARS
31.50 g., 0.925 Silver, 0.93 oz. ASW **Subject:** Canadarm

and Col. C. Hadfield **Obv.** Head right **Rev:** Hologram of
Canadarm

Date	Mintage		
2006	9,357	PF63 85.00	PF65 90.00

KM# 669   30 DOLLARS
31.50 g., 0.925 Silver, 0.93 oz. ASW **Subject:** National
War Memorial **Obv.** Head right **Rev:** Statue of three
soldiers

Date	Mintage		
2006	8,876	PF63 80.00	PF65 85.00

KM# 670   30 DOLLARS
31.50 g., 0.925 Silver, 0.93 oz. ASW **Subject:** Beaumont
Hamel Newfoundland **Obv.** Head right **Rev:** Caribou statue
on rock outcrop

Date	Mintage		
2006	15,325	PF63 90.00	PF65 95.00

KM# 671   30 DOLLARS
31.50 g., 0.925 Silver, 0.93 oz. ASW **Obv.** Head right **Rev:**
Dog Sled Team in color

Date	Mintage		
2006	7,384	PF63 80.00	PF65 85.00

KM# 739   30 DOLLARS
31.50 g., 0.925 Silver, 0.93 oz. ASW 40mm. **Rev:** Niagra
Falls panoramic hologram

Date	Mintage		
2007	7,384	PF63 75.00	PF65 85.00

KM# 741 30 DOLLARS
31.50 g., 0.925 Silver, 0.93 oz. ASW 40mm. **Rev:** War Memorial, Vimy Ridge

Date	Mintage	
2007	5,335	PF65 85.00

KM# 819 30 DOLLARS
31.50 g., 0.925 Silver, 0.93 oz. ASW 40mm. **Subject:** IMAX **Rev:** Youth reaching out to shark on large screen

Date	Mintage		
2008	3,861	PF63 65.00	PF65 75.00

KM# 895 30 DOLLARS
33.75 g., 0.925 Silver, 1.00 oz. ASW 40mm. **Subject:** International year of astronomy **Obv.** Bust right **Obv. Designer:** Susanna Blunt **Rev:** Observatory with planets and colored sky **Obv. Legend:** Elizabeth II 30 Dollars DG Regina **Rev. Designer:** Colin Mayne **Rev. Legend:** Canada

Date	Mintage		
2009	7,174	PF63 80.00	PF65 90.00

KM# 1623 30 DOLLARS
62.70 g., 0.999 Silver, 2.00 oz. ASW 54mm. **Subject:**

Canada thru the eyes of Tim Barnard **Obv.** Bust right **Rev:** Multitude of designs

Date	Mintage	
2014	5,000	PF65 250

KM# 566 50 DOLLARS
12.00 g., 0.5833 Gold, 0.22 oz. AGW 27mm. **Subject:** End of World War II, 60th Anniversary **Obv.** Head right **Rev:** Large V and three portraits

Date	Mintage	
2005 Specimen	4,000	PF65 375

KM# 672 50 DOLLARS
31.16 g., 0.9995 Palladium, 0.99 oz. APW **Subject:** Constellation in Spring sky position **Rev:** Large Bear at top

Date	Mintage	
2006	297	PF65 1,250

KM# 673 50 DOLLARS
31.16 g., 0.9995 Palladium, 0.99 oz. APW **Subject:** Constellation in Summer sky position **Rev:** Large Bear at left

Date	Mintage	
2006	296	PF65 1,250

KM# 674 50 DOLLARS
31.16 g., 0.9995 Palladium, 0.99 oz. APW **Subject:** Constellation in Autumn sky position **Rev:** Large Bear towards bottom

Date	Mintage	
2006	296	PF65 1,250

KM# 675   50 DOLLARS
31.16 g., 0.9995 Palladium, 0.99 oz. APW **Subject:** Constellation in Winter sky position **Rev:** Large Bear towards right

Date	Mintage	
2006	293	PF65 1,250

KM# 709   50 DOLLARS
155.50 g., 0.9999 Silver, 4.97 oz. ASW **Subject:** Queen's 60th Wedding Anniversary **Rev:** Coat of Arms and Mascots of Elizabeth and Philip

Date	Mintage	
2007	1,957	PF65 350

KM# 783   50 DOLLARS
156.77 g., 0.999 Silver, 5.00 oz. ASW 65mm. **Subject:** Ottawa Mint Centennial 1908-2008 **Rev:** Mint building facade **Note:** Photo reduced.

Date	Mintage	
2008	2,078	PF65 400

KM# 896   50 DOLLARS
156.77 g., 0.999 Silver, 5.00 oz. ASW 65.25mm. **Subject:** 150 Anniversary of the start of construction of the parliament buildings **Obv.** Bust right **Obv. Designer:** Susanna Blunt **Rev:** Incomplete west block, original architecture **Obv. Legend:** Elizabeth II Canada DG Regina **Rev. Legend:** 50 Dollars 1859-2009

Date	Mintage	
2009	910	PF65 450

KM# 1008   50 DOLLARS
157.60 g., 0.999 Silver, 5.03 oz. ASW 65.25mm. **Subject:** 75th Anniverary of Canadian Bank Notes **Rev:** Female seated speaking into microphone **Note:** Photo reduced.

Date	Mintage	
2010	2,000	PF65 400

KM# 1243 50 DOLLARS

156.77 g., 0.925 Silver, 4.63 oz. ASW 65.25mm. **Subject:** Calgary Stampede

Date	Mintage	
2012	—	PF65 400

KM# 1284 50 DOLLARS

31.11 g., 0.999 Gold, 0.99 oz. AGW 30mm. **Subject:** Year of the Dragon

Date	Mintage	
2012	—	PF65 1,750

KM# 1296 50 DOLLARS

33.17 g., 0.999 Gold, 33.13 g. AGW **Obv.** Bust right **Obv. Designer:** Susana Blunt **Rev:** High relief bust **Note:** Ultra high relief

Date	Mintage	
2012	500	PF65 3,000

KM# 1399 50 DOLLARS

155.55 g., 0.999 Silver, 4.96 oz. ASW 65mm. **Rev:** Beaver gnawing standing tree, two others with felled tree

Date	Mintage	
2013	—	PF65 450

KM# 1417 50 DOLLARS

155.55 g., 0.9999 Silver, 4.97 oz. ASW 65.25mm. **Obv.** Four Seasons: Spring/Fall Scene **Rev:** Winter/Summer/Large Tree

Date	Mintage	
2013	—	PF65 250

KM# 1557 50 DOLLARS

157.60 g., 0.999 Silver, 5.03 oz. ASW 65mm. **Rev:** Beaver swimming with birch branch in mouth **Rev. Designer:** Emily Damstra

Date	Mintage	
2014	1,500	PF65 520

KM# 567 75 DOLLARS

31.44 g., 0.4166 Gold, 0.42 oz. AGW 36.07mm. **Subject:** Pope John Paul II **Obv.** Head right **Rev:** Pope giving blessing

Date	Mintage	
2005	1,870	PF65 825

75 DOLLARS

KM# 747   75 DOLLARS
12.00 g.,   0.583 Gold, 0.22 oz. AGW 27mm.   **Subject:**
Vancouver Olympics - Athletics Pride **Rev:** Athletics
celebrating, holding flag aloft

Date	Mintage		
2007	4,524	PF65 440	

KM# 748   75 DOLLARS
12.00 g., 0.583 Gold, 0.22 oz. AGW 27mm. **Obv.** Bust
right **Obv. Designer:** Susanna Blunt **Rev:** Canada geese in
flight left, multicolor

Date	Mintage		
2007	4,418	PF65 440	

KM# 749   75 DOLLARS
12.00 g.,   0.583 Gold, 0.22 oz. AGW 27mm.   **Rev:**
Mountie, multicolor

Date	Mintage		
2007	6,687	PF65 440	

KM# 820   75 DOLLARS
12.00 g., 0.583 Gold, 0.22 oz. AGW 27mm. **Rev:** 2010
Olympic Inukshuk Stone man, partially silver plated

Date	Mintage		
2008	—	PF65 420	

KM# 821   75 DOLLARS
12.00 g.,   0.583 Gold, 0.22 oz. AGW 27mm.   **Rev:** Four
Host Nations mask emblems, colored **Rev. Designer:**
Jody Broomfield

Date	Mintage		
2008	8,000	PF65 440	

KM# 947   75 DOLLARS
12.00 g.,   0.583 Gold, 0.22 oz. AGW 27mm.   **Subject:**
Vancouver Olympics **Rev:** Tent building at Olympic site,
color

Date	Mintage		
2008	8,000	PF63 430	PF65 440

KM# 908   75 DOLLARS
12.00 g., 0.583 Gold, 0.22 oz. AGW 27mm. **Subject:** 2010
Vancouver Olympics **Obv.** Bust right **Obv. Designer:**
Susana Blunt **Rev:** Multicolor moose

Date	Mintage		
2009	4,075	PF65 440	

KM# 909   75 DOLLARS
12.00 g., 0.583 Gold, 0.22 oz. AGW 27mm. **Subject:** 2010
Vancouver Olympics **Obv.** Bust right **Obv. Designer:**
Susanna Blunt **Rev:** Multicolor athletics and torch

Date	Mintage		
2009	4,479	PF65 440	

KM# 910 75 DOLLARS
12.00 g., 0.583 Gold, 0.22 oz. AGW 27mm. **Subject:** 2010
Vancouver Olympics **Obv.** Bust right **Obv. Designer:**
Susanna Blunt **Rev:** Wolf, multicolor

Date	Mintage	
2009	4,161	PF65 440

KM# 1005 75 DOLLARS
12.00 g., 0.583 Gold, 0.22 oz. AGW 27mm. **Rev:** Winter
color maple leaves

Date	Mintage	
2010	1,000	PF65 500

KM# 1002 75 DOLLARS
12.00 g., 0.583 Gold, 0.22 oz. AGW 27mm. **Rev:** Spring
color maple leaves

Date	Mintage	
2010	1,000	PF65 500

KM# 1378 75 DOLLARS
7.77 g., 0.999 Gold, 0.25 oz. AGW 20mm. **Subject:**
Baseball **Rev:** Baseball Diamond and Crossed Bats **Rev.
Designer:** Steve Hepburn

Date	Mintage	
2013	—	PF65 900

KM# 1379 75 DOLLARS
7.77 g., 0.999 Gold, 0.25 oz. AGW 20mm. **Subject:**
Baseball **Rev:** Baseball **Rev. Designer:** Steve Hepburn

Date	Mintage	
2013	Est. 3500	PF65 900

KM# 1003 75 DOLLARS
12.00 g., 0.583 Gold, 0.22 oz. AGW 27mm. **Rev:** Summer
color maple leaves

Date	Mintage	
2010	1,000	PF65 500

KM# 1450 75 DOLLARS
12.00 g., 0.583 Gold, 0.22 oz. AGW 27mm. **Subject:**
75th Anniversary of Superman **Rev:** Superman in color,
jumping on rooftop, logo name above **Rev. Designer:** Joe
Schuster, DC Comics

Date	Mintage	
2013	Est. 2000	PF65 750

KM# 1004 75 DOLLARS
12.00 g., 0.583 Gold, 0.22 oz. AGW 27mm. **Rev:** Fall
color maple leaves

Date	Mintage	
2010	1,000	PF65 500

KM# 115 100 DOLLARS
13.34 g., 0.583 Gold, 0.25 oz. AGW 27mm. **Subject:**
1976 Montreal Olympics **Obv.** Young bust right, maple

100 DOLLARS

leaf below, date at right, beaded borders **Rev:** Past and present Olympic figures, denomination at right **Rev. Designer:** Dora dePedery-Hunt

Date	Mintage	MS63
1976	650,000	475

KM# 116   100 DOLLARS

16.97 g., 0.917 Gold, 0.50 oz. AGW 25mm. **Subject:** 1976 Montreal Olympics **Obv.** Young bust right, maple leaf below, date at right, plain borders **Rev:** Past and present Olympic figures, denomination at right **Rev. Designer:** Dora dePedery-Hunt

Date	Mintage	
1976	350,000	**PF60** 950

KM# 119   100 DOLLARS

16.97 g., 0.917 Gold, 0.50 oz. AGW **Subject:** Queen's silver jubilee **Obv.** Young bust right **Rev:** Bouquet of provincial flowers, denomination below **Rev. Designer:** Raymond Lee

Date	Mintage	
1952-1977	180,396	**PF60** 950

KM# 122   100 DOLLARS

16.97 g., 0.917 Gold, 0.50 oz. AGW **Subject:** Canadian unification **Obv.** Young bust right, denomination at left, date upper right **Rev:** Geese (representing the provinces) in flight formation **Rev. Designer:** Roger Savage

Date	Mintage	
1978	200,000	**PF60** 950

KM# 126   100 DOLLARS

16.97 g., 0.917 Gold, 0.50 oz. AGW **Subject:** International

Year of the Child **Obv.** Young bust right **Rev:** Children with hands joined divide denomination and date **Rev. Designer:** Carola Tietz

Date	Mintage	
1979	250,000	**PF60** 950

KM# 129   100 DOLLARS

16.97 g., 0.917 Gold, 0.50 oz. AGW **Subject:** Arctic Territories **Obv.** Young bust right, denomination at left, date above right **Rev:** Kayaker **Rev. Designer:** Arnaldo Marchetti

Date	Mintage	
1980	130,000	**PF60** 950

KM# 131   100 DOLLARS

16.97 g., 0.917 Gold, 0.50 oz. AGW **Subject:** National anthem **Obv.** Young bust right, denomination at left, date above right **Rev:** Music score on map **Rev. Designer:** Roger Savage

Date	Mintage	
1981	102,000	**PF60** 950

KM# 137   100 DOLLARS

16.97 g., 0.917 Gold, 0.50 oz. AGW **Subject:** New Constitution **Obv.** Young bust right, denomination at left **Rev:** Open book, maple leaf on right page, date below **Rev. Designer:** Friedrich Peter

Date	Mintage	
1982	121,708	**PF60** 950

KM# 139   100 DOLLARS

16.97 g., 0.917 Gold, 0.50 oz. AGW **Subject:** 400th Anniversary of St. John's, Newfoundland **Obv.** Young bust right **Rev:** Anchor divides building and ship, denomination below, dates above **Rev. Designer:** John Jaciw

Date	Mintage	
1583-1983	83,128	PF60 950

KM# 142 100 DOLLARS

16.97 g., 0.917 Gold, 0.50 oz. AGW **Subject:** Jacques Cartier **Obv.** Young bust right **Rev:** Cartier head on right facing left, ship on left, date lower right, denomination above **Rev. Designer:** Carola Tietz

Date	Mintage	
1534-1984	67,662	PF60 950

KM# 144 100 DOLLARS

16.97 g., 0.917 Gold, 0.50 oz. AGW **Subject:** National Parks **Obv.** Young bust right **Rev:** Bighorn sheep, denomination divides dates below **Rev. Designer:** Hector Greville

Date	Mintage	
1885-1985	58,520	PF60 950

KM# 152 100 DOLLARS

16.97 g., 0.917 Gold, 0.50 oz. AGW **Subject:** Peace **Obv.** Young bust right **Rev:** Maple leaves and letters intertwined, date at right, denomination below **Rev. Designer:** Dora dePedery-Hunt

Date	Mintage	
1986	76,255	PF60 950

KM# 158 100 DOLLARS

13.34 g., 0.583 Gold, 0.25 oz. AGW **Subject:** 1988 Calgary Olympics **Obv.** Young bust right, maple leaf below, date at right **Rev:** Torch and logo, denomination below **Rev. Designer:** Friedrich Peter **Edge Lettering:** In English and French

Date	Mintage	
1987 Proof, plain edge	Inc. above	PF60 475
1987 Proof, letter edge	145,175	PF60 475

KM# 162 100 DOLLARS

13.34 g., 0.583 Gold, 0.25 oz. AGW **Subject:** Bowhead Whales, balaera mysticetus **Rev:** Whales left, date below, within circle, denomination below **Rev. Designer:** Robert R. Carmichael

Date	Mintage	
1988	52,239	PF60 475

KM# 169 100 DOLLARS

13.34 g., 0.583 Gold, 0.25 oz. AGW **Subject:** Sainte-Marie **Obv.** Young bust right **Rev:** Huron Indian, Missionary and Mission building, denomination below, dates above **Rev. Designer:** D. J. Craig

Date	Mintage	
1639-1989	63,881	PF60 475

KM# 171 100 DOLLARS

13.34 g., 0.583 Gold, 0.25 oz. AGW **Subject:** International Literacy Year **Obv.** Crowned head right, date below **Rev:** Woman with children, denomination below **Rev. Designer:** John Mardon

Date	Mintage	
1990	49,940	PF60 475

KM# 180 100 DOLLARS

13.34 g., 0.583 Gold, 0.25 oz. AGW **Subject:** S.S. Empress of India **Obv.** Crowned head right, date below **Rev:** Ship,"SS Empress", denomination below **Rev. Designer:** Karsten Smith

Date	Mintage	
1991	33,966	PF60 475

KM# 211 100 DOLLARS
13.34 g., 0.583 Gold, 0.25 oz. AGW **Subject:** Montreal **Obv.** Crowned head right, date below **Rev:** Half figure in foreground with paper, buildings in back, denomination below **Rev. Designer:** Stewart Sherwood

Date	Mintage		
1992	28,190	PF60	475

KM# 245 100 DOLLARS
13.34 g., 0.583 Gold, 0.25 oz. AGW **Subject:** Antique Automobiles **Obv.** Crowned head right, date below **Rev:** German Bene Victoria; Simmonds Steam Carriage; French Panhard-Levassor's Daimler; American Duryea; Canadian Featherston Haugh in center, denomination below **Rev. Designer:** John Mardon

Date	Mintage		
1993	25,971	PF60	475

KM# 249 100 DOLLARS
13.34 g., 0.583 Gold, 0.25 oz. AGW **Subject:** World War II Home Front **Obv.** Crowned head right, date below **Rev:** Kneeling figure working on plane, denomination below **Rev. Designer:** Paraskeva Clark

Date	Mintage		
1994	17,603	PF60	475

KM# 260 100 DOLLARS
13.34 g., 0.583 Gold, 0.25 oz. AGW **Subject:** Louisbourg **Obv.** Crowned head right, date below **Rev:** Ship and buildings, dates and denomination above **Rev. Designer:** Lewis Parker

Date	Mintage		
1995	16,916	PF60	475

KM# 273 100 DOLLARS
13.34 g., 0.583 Gold, 0.25 oz. AGW **Subject:** Klondike Gold Rush Centennial **Obv.** Crowned head right, date below **Rev:** Scene of Kate Carmack panning for gold, dates above, denomination lower left **Rev. Designer:** John Mantha

Date	Mintage		
1896-1996	17,973	PF60	450

KM# 287 100 DOLLARS
13.34 g., 0.583 Gold, 0.25 oz. AGW **Subject:** Alexander Graham Bell **Obv.** Crowned head right, date below **Rev:** A. G. Bell head right, globe and telephone, denomination upper right **Rev. Designer:** Donald H. Carley

Date	Mintage		
1997	14,775	PF60	475

KM# 307 100 DOLLARS
13.34 g., 0.583 Gold, 0.25 oz. AGW **Subject:** Discovery of Insulin **Obv.** Crowned head right, date below **Rev:** Nobel prize award figurine, dates at left, denomination at right **Rev. Designer:** Robert R. Carmichael

Date	Mintage		
1998	11,220	PF60	475

KM# 341 100 DOLLARS
13.34 g., 0.583 Gold, 0.25 oz. AGW **Subject:** 50th Anniversary Newfoundland Unity With Canada **Obv.** Crowned head right, date below **Rev:** Two designs at front, mountains in back, denomination below **Rev. Designer:** Jackie Gale-Vaillancourt

Date	Mintage		
1999	10,242	PF60	475

100 DOLLARS

KM# 402 100 DOLLARS
13.34 g., 0.583 Gold, 0.25 oz. AGW 27mm. **Subject:** McClure's Arctic expedition **Obv.** Crowned head right, date below **Rev:** Six men pulling supply sled to an icebound ship, denomination below **Rev. Designer:** John Mardon **Edge:** Reeded

Date	Mintage		
2000	10,547	PF60	475

KM# 416 100 DOLLARS
13.34 g., 0.583 Gold, 0.25 oz. AGW 27mm. **Subject:** Library of Parliament **Obv.** Crowned head right **Obv. Designer:** Dora dePedery-Hunt **Rev:** Statue in domed building **Rev. Designer:** Robert R. Carmichael **Edge:** Reeded

Date	Mintage		
2001	8,080	PF65	475

KM# 452 100 DOLLARS
13.34 g., 0.583 Gold, 0.25 oz. AGW 27mm. **Subject:** Discovery of Oil in Alberta **Obv.** Crowned head right **Rev:** Oil well with black oil spill on ground **Rev. Designer:** John Marden **Edge:** Reeded

Date	Mintage		
2002	9,994	PF65	475

KM# 486 100 DOLLARS
13.34 g., 0.583 Gold, 0.25 oz. AGW **Subject:** 100th Anniversary of the Discovery of Marquis Wheat **Obv.** Head right

Date	Mintage		
2003	9,993	PF65	475

KM# 528 100 DOLLARS
12.00 g., 0.583 Gold, 0.22 oz. AGW **Subject:** St. Lawrence Seaway, 50th Anniversary **Obv.** Head right

Date	Mintage		
2004	7,454	PF65	425

KM# 593 100 DOLLARS
12.00 g., 0.5833 Gold, 0.22 oz. AGW **Subject:** 130th Anniversary, Supreme Court **Obv.** Head right

Date	Mintage		
2005	5,092	PF65	425

KM# 591 100 DOLLARS
12.00 g., 0.5833 Gold, 0.22 oz. AGW **Subject:** 75th Anniversary, Hockey Classic between Royal Military College and U.S. Military Academy **Obv.** Head right

Date	Mintage		
2006	5,439	PF65	425

KM# 689 100 DOLLARS
12.00 g., 0.5833 Gold, 0.22 oz. AGW 27mm. **Subject:** 140th Anniversary Dominion **Obv.** Head right

Date	Mintage		
2007	4,453	PF65	425

KM# 823 100 DOLLARS
12.00 g., 0.583 Gold, 0.22 oz. AGW 27mm. **Rev:** Fraser River

Date	Mintage		
2008	3,089	PF65	425

KM# 898 100 DOLLARS
12.00 g., 0.583 Gold, 0.22 oz. AGW 27mm. **Subject:** 10th Anniversary of Nunavut **Obv.** Bust right **Obv. Designer:** Susanna Blunt **Rev:** Inuit dancer with 3 faces behind **Obv. Legend:** Elizabeth II DG Regina **Rev. Legend:** Canada 100 Dollars 1999-2009

Date	Mintage		
2009	2,309	PF65	425

KM# 997 100 DOLLARS

12.00 g., 0.583 Gold, 0.22 oz. AGW 27mm. **Rev:** Henry Hudson, Map of Hudson's Bay **Rev. Designer:** John Mantha

Date	Mintage	
2010	Est. 5000	PF65 425

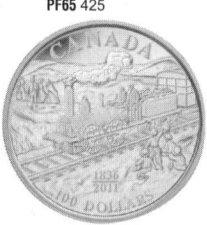

KM# 1073 100 DOLLARS

12.00 g., 0.583 Gold, 0.22 oz. AGW 27mm. **Subject:** Canadian Railroads, 175th Anniversary **Rev:** Early steam locomotive

Date	Mintage	
2011	3,000	PF65 425

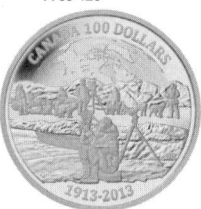

KM# 1389 100 DOLLARS

12.00 g., 0.5833 Gold, 0.22 oz. AGW 27mm. **Subject:** Arctic Exploration - 100th Anniversary **Rev:** Map of the North Pole, Explorers **Rev. Designer:** Bonnie Ross

Date	Mintage	
2013	—	PF65 600

KM# 1582 100 DOLLARS

13.34 g., 0.999 Gold, 0.43 oz. AGW 27mm. **Subject:** Charlottetown Quebec, 1864 **Obv.** Bust right **Rev:** Building views

Date	Mintage	
2014	—	PF65 475

KM# 388 150 DOLLARS

13.61 g., 0.750 Gold, 0.33 oz. AGW **Subject:** Year of the Dragon **Obv.** Crowned head right **Rev. Designer:** Harvey Chan

Date	Mintage	
2000	8,874	PF60 625

KM# 417 150 DOLLARS

13.61 g., 0.750 Gold, 0.33 oz. AGW 28mm. **Subject:** Year of the Snake **Obv.** Crowned head right **Obv. Designer:** Dora dePedery-Hunt **Rev:** Multicolor snake hologram **Edge:** Reeded

Date	Mintage	
2001	6571	PF65 625

KM# 604 150 DOLLARS

13.61 g., 0.750 Gold, 0.33 oz. AGW **Obv.** Head right **Rev:** Stylized horse left

Date	Mintage	
2002	6,843	PF65 625

KM# 487 150 DOLLARS

13.61 g., 0.750 Gold, 0.33 oz. AGW 28mm. **Subject:** Year of the Ram **Obv.** Crowned head right **Rev:** Stylized ram left, hologram **Rev. Designer:** Harvey Chan

Date	Mintage	
2003	3,927	PF65 625

KM# 614 150 DOLLARS

13.61 g., 0.750 Gold, 0.33 oz. AGW **Obv.** Head right **Rev:** Year of the Monkey, hologram

Date	Mintage	
2004	3,392	PF65 625

KM# 568 150 DOLLARS

13.61 g., 0.750 Gold, 0.33 oz. AGW **Subject:** Year of the Rooster **Obv.** Head right **Rev:** Rooster left, hologram

Date	Mintage	
2005	3,731	PF65 625

KM# 592 150 DOLLARS

13.61 g., 0.750 Gold, 0.33 oz. AGW 28mm. **Subject:** Year of the Dog, hologram **Obv.** Head right **Rev:** Stylized dog left

Date	Mintage	
2006	2,604	PF65 625

KM# 733 150 DOLLARS

11.84 g., 0.750 Gold, 0.28 oz. AGW 28mm. **Subject:** Year of the Pig **Obv.** Head right **Rev:** Pig in center with Chinese lunar calendar around, hologram

Date	Mintage	
2007	826	PF65 675

KM# 802 150 DOLLARS
11.84 g., 0.750 Gold, 0.28 oz. AGW 28mm. **Subject:** Year of the Rat **Rev:** Rat, hologram

Date	Mintage	
2008	582	PF65 675

KM# 899 150 DOLLARS
10.40 g., 0.999 Gold, 0.33 oz. AGW 22.5mm. **Subject:** Blessings of wealth **Obv.** Bust right **Obv. Designer:** Susanna Blunt **Rev:** Three goldfish surround peony, clouds **Obv. Legend:** Elizabeth II, DG Regina, Fine Gold 99999 or PUR **Rev. Designer:** Harvey Chan **Rev. Legend:** Canada 150 Dollars (Chinese symbols of good fortune) **Edge:** Scalloped

Date	Mintage	
2009	1,273	PF65 650

KM# 867 150 DOLLARS
11.84 g., 0.750 Gold, 0.28 oz. AGW 28mm. **Subject:** Year of the Ox **Rev:** Ox, hologram

Date	Mintage	
2009	486	PF65 550

KM# 979 150 DOLLARS
11.84 g., 0.750 Gold, 0.28 oz. AGW 28mm. **Subject:** Year of the Tiger **Rev:** Tiger in hologram

Date	Mintage	
2010	1,507	PF65 550

KM# 1030 150 DOLLARS
10.40 g., 0.9999 Gold, 0.33 oz. AGW **Subject:** Blessing of Wealth **Shape:** Scalloped

Date	Mintage	
2010	1,388	PF65 650

KM# 1031 150 DOLLARS
Gold, AGW **Subject:** Year of the Tiger **Rev:** Tiger walking

Date	Mintage	
2010	2,500	PF65 600

KM# 1053 150 DOLLARS
13.61 g., 0.750 Gold, 0.33 oz. AGW 28mm. **Subject:** Year of the rabbit **Rev:** Rabbit hologram

Date	Mintage	
2011	—	PF65 600

KM# 1184 150 DOLLARS
13.61 g., 0.750 Gold, 0.33 oz. AGW 28mm. **Subject:** Year of the Dragon **Obv.** Bust right **Rev:** Dragon left

Date	Mintage	
2012	—	PF65 650

KM# 1262 150 DOLLARS
10.40 g., 0.999 Gold, 0.33 oz. AGW 22.5mm. **Subject:** Good Fortune Panda

Date	Mintage	
2012	—	PF65 650

KM# 1362 150 DOLLARS
11.84 g., 0.750 Gold, 0.28 oz. AGW 28mm. **Subject:** Year of the Snake **Rev:** Snake vertical between two Chinese characters **Rev. Designer:** Aries Cheung

Date	Mintage	
2013	2,500	PF65 700

KM# 1418 150 DOLLARS
15.59 g., Gold, AGW 25mm. **Subject:** Baseball **Rev:** Runner with hands raised **Rev. Designer:** Steve Hepburn

Date	Mintage	
2013	Est. 3500	PF65 1,550

KM# 1515 150 DOLLARS
11.84 g., 0.750 Gold, 0.28 oz. AGW 28mm. **Subject:** Year of the Horse **Rev:** Horse prancing left **Rev. Designer:** Aries Cheung

Date	Mintage	
2014	2,500	PF65 700

KM# 217 175 DOLLARS
16.97 g., 0.917 Gold, 0.50 oz. AGW **Subject:** 1992 Olympics **Obv.** Crowned head right, date at left, denomination below **Rev:** Passing the torch **Rev. Designer:** Stewart Sherwood **Edge:** Lettered

Date	Mintage	
1992	22,092	PF60 950

KM# 178 200 DOLLARS
17.14 g., 0.9166 Gold, 0.50 oz. AGW 29mm. **Subject:** Canadian flag silver jubilee **Obv.** Crowned head right, date below **Rev:** People with flag, denomination above **Rev. Designer:** Stewart Sherwood

Date	Mintage	
1990	20,980	PF60 975

KM# 202 200 DOLLARS
17.14 g., 0.9166 Gold, 0.50 oz. AGW 29mm. **Subject:** Hockey **Obv.** Crowned head right **Rev:** Hockey players, denomination above **Rev. Designer:** Stewart Sherwood

Date	Mintage	
1991	10,215	PF60 975

KM# 230 200 DOLLARS
17.14 g., 0.9166 Gold, 0.50 oz. AGW 29mm. **Subject:** Niagara Falls **Obv.** Crowned head right **Rev:** Niagara Falls, denomination above **Rev. Designer:** John Mardon

Date	Mintage	
1992	9465	PF60 975

KM# 244 200 DOLLARS
17.14 g., 0.9166 Gold, 0.50 oz. AGW 29mm. **Subject:** Mounted police **Obv.** Crowned head right, date below **Rev:** Mountie with children, denomination above **Rev. Designer:** Stewart Sherwood

Date	Mintage	
1993	10,807	PF60 975

KM# 250 200 DOLLARS
17.14 g., 0.9166 Gold, 0.50 oz. AGW 29mm. **Subject:** Interpretation of 1908 novel by Lucy Maud Montgomery, 1874-1942, Anne of Green Gables **Obv.** Crowned head right **Rev:** Figure sitting in window, denomination above **Rev. Designer:** Phoebe Gilman

Date	Mintage	
1994	10,655	PF60 975

KM# 265   200 DOLLARS
17.14 g., 0.9166 Gold, 0.50 oz. AGW 29mm. **Subject:**
Maple-syrup production **Obv.** Crowned head right, date
below **Rev:** Maple syrup making, denomination at right
Rev. Designer: J. D. Mantha

Date	Mintage		
1995	9,579	**PF60**	975

KM# 275   200 DOLLARS
17.14 g., 0.9166 Gold, 0.50 oz. AGW 29mm. **Subject:**
Transcontinental Canadian Railway **Obv.** Crowned head
right, date below **Rev:** Train going through mountains,
denomination below **Rev. Designer:** Suzanne Duranceau

Date	Mintage		
1996	8,047	**PF60**	975

KM# 288   200 DOLLARS
17.14 g., 0.9166 Gold, 0.50 oz. AGW 29mm. **Subject:**
Haida mask **Obv.** Crowned head right, date below **Rev:**
Haida mask **Rev. Designer:** Robert Davidson

Date	Mintage		
1997	11,610	**PF60**	975

KM# 317   200 DOLLARS
17.14 g., 0.9166 Gold, 0.50 oz. AGW 29mm. **Subject:**
Legendary white buffalo **Obv.** Crowned head right, date
below **Rev:** Buffalo **Rev. Designer:** Alex Janvler

Date	Mintage		
1998	7,149	**PF60**	975

KM# 358   200 DOLLARS
17.14 g., 0.9166 Gold, 0.50 oz. AGW 29mm. **Subject:**
Mikmaq butterfly **Obv.** Crowned head right **Rev:** Butterfly
within design **Rev. Designer:** Alan Syliboy

Date	Mintage		
1999	6,510	**PF60**	975

KM# 403   200 DOLLARS
17.14 g., 0.9166 Gold, 0.50 oz. AGW 29mm. **Subject:**
Motherhood **Obv.** Crowned head right, date above,
denomination at right **Rev:** Inuit mother with infant **Rev.
Designer:** Germaine Arnaktauyak **Edge:** Reeded

Date	Mintage		
2000	7,410	**PF60**	975

KM# 418   200 DOLLARS
17.14 g., 0.9166 Gold, 0.50 oz. AGW 29mm. **Subject:**
Cornelius D. Krieghoff's "The Habitant farm **Obv.** Queens
head right **Edge:** Reeded

Date	Mintage		
2001	5,406	**PF65**	975

KM# 466   200 DOLLARS
17.14 g., 0.9166 Gold, 0.50 oz. AGW 29mm. **Subject:**
Thomas Thompson "The Jack Pine" (1916-17) **Obv.**
Crowned head right

Date	Mintage		
2002	5,264	**PF65**	975

KM# 488   200 DOLLARS
17.14 g., 0.9166 Gold, 0.50 oz. AGW **Subject:** Fitzgerald's "Houses" (1929) **Obv.** Crowned head right **Rev:** House with trees

Date	Mintage		
2003	4,118	PF65	975

KM# 516   200 DOLLARS
16.00 g., 0.9166 Gold, 0.47 oz. AGW 29mm. **Subject:** Fragments **Obv.** Crowned head right **Rev:** Fragmented face **Edge:** Reeded

Date	Mintage		
2004	3,917	PF65	900

KM# 569   200 DOLLARS
16.00 g., 0.9166 Gold, 0.47 oz. AGW **Subject:** Fur traders **Obv.** Head right **Rev:** Men in canoe riding wave

Date	Mintage		
2005	3,669	PF65	900

KM# 594   200 DOLLARS
16.00 g., 0.9166 Gold, 0.47 oz. AGW **Subject:** Timber trade **Obv.** Head right **Rev:** Lumberjacks felling tree

Date	Mintage		
2006	3,218	PF65	900

KM# 691   200 DOLLARS
16.00 g., 0.9166 Gold, 0.47 oz. AGW 29mm. **Subject:** Fishing Trade **Obv.** Head right **Rev:** Two fishermen hauling net

Date	Mintage		
2007	2,137	PF65	900

KM# 824   200 DOLLARS
16.00 g., 0.917 Gold, 0.47 oz. AGW 29mm. **Subject:** Commerce **Rev:** Horse drawn plow

Date	Mintage		
2008	1,951	PF65	900

KM# 894   200 DOLLARS
16.00 g., 0.916 Gold, 0.47 oz. AGW 29mm. **Subject:** Coal mining trade **Obv.** Bust right **Obv. Designer:** Susanna Blunt **Rev:** Miner pushing cart with black coal **Obv. Legend:** Elizabeth II DG Regina **Rev. Designer:** John Marder **Rev. Legend:** Canada 200 Dollars

Date	Mintage		
2009	2,241	PF65	900

KM# 1000   200 DOLLARS
16.00 g., 0.916 Gold, 0.47 oz. AGW 29mm. **Subject:** Petroleum and Oil Trade **Rev:** Oil railcar and well head

Date	Mintage		
2010	Est. 4000	PF65	900

KM# 1060   200 DOLLARS
16.00 g., 0.9167 Gold, 0.47 oz. AGW 29mm. **Rev:** Olympic athletics with medal, flag and flowers

Date	Mintage		
2010	—	PF65	900

KM# 1074   200 DOLLARS
16.00 g., 0.9167 Gold, 0.47 oz. AGW 29mm. **Rev:** SS Beaver - Seam Sail ship **Rev. Designer:** John Mardon

Date	Mintage		
2011	2,800	PF65	900

KM# 1143   200 DOLLARS
16.00 g., 0.9167 Gold, 0.47 oz. AGW 27mm. **Subject:** Wedding, Prince William and Katherine Middleton **Obv.** Bust right **Rev:** Half-length figures facing, swarovski crystal **Edge:** Reeded

Date	Mintage		
2011	2,000	PF65	900

KM# 1174   200 DOLLARS
16.00 g., 0.916 Gold, 0.47 oz. AGW 29mm. **Obv.** Bust right **Rev:** Wayne Greskey skating right, father's portrait in circle at right, 99 in color at lower right **Rev. Designer:** Glen Green

Date	Mintage		
2011	999	PF65	900

KM# 1219   200 DOLLARS
16.00 g., 0.9167 Gold, 0.47 oz. AGW 29mm. **Obv.** Bust right **Rev:** Prospector panning for gold in stream

Date	Mintage		
2012	—	PF65	900

KM# 1223   200 DOLLARS
16.00 g., 0.9167 Gold, 0.47 oz. AGW 29mm. **Obv.** Bust right **Rev:** Vikings and ship

Date	Mintage		
2012	—	PF65	900

KM# 1279   200 DOLLARS
31.11 g., 0.999 Gold, 0.99 oz. AGW 30mm. **Subject:** Bateman Moose

Date	Mintage		
2012	—	PF65	1,850

KM# 1331   200 DOLLARS
33.33 g., 0.999 Gold, 1.06 oz. AGW 30mm. **Rev:** Grandmother Moon Mask **Rev. Designer:** Richard Cochrane

Date	Mintage		
2012	500	PF65	3,000

KM# 1390   200 DOLLARS
15.43 g., 0.999 Gold, 0.49 oz. AGW 29mm. **Subject:** Explorer Jacques Cartier **Rev. Designer:** Laurie McGaw

Date	Mintage		
2013	Est. 2000	PF65	1,200

KM# 1480   200 DOLLARS
31.11 g., 0.999 Gold, 0.99 oz. AGW **Ruler:** Elizabeth II 30mm. **Rev:** Eagle in nest with two chicks **Rev. Designer:** Claudio d'Angelo **Mint:** Royal Canadian Mint

Date	Mintage	MS63
2013 Proof	350	2,750

KM# 1500   200 DOLLARS
33.33 g., 0.9999 Gold, 1.06 oz. AGW 30mm. **Subject:** Grandmother Moon Mask **Rev:** Mask carving **Rev. Designer:** Richard Cochrane

Date	Mintage		
2013	500	PF65	3,000

200 DOLLARS

KM# 1583   200 DOLLARS
16.00 g., 0.9167 Gold, 0.47 oz. AGW 29mm. **Obv.** Bust
right **Rev:** Indian and explorer standing next to canoes

Date	Mintage	
2014	—	PF65 900

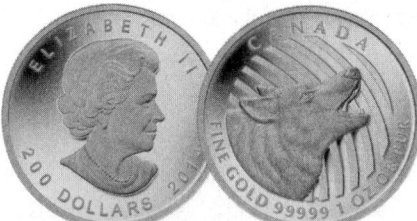

KM# 1616   200 DOLLARS
31.11 g., 0.999 Gold, 0.99 oz. AGW 30mm. **Obv.** Bust
right **Rev:** Howling wolf **Rev. Designer:** Pierre Leduc

Date	Mintage	
2014	2,000	PF65 2,800

KM# 677   250 DOLLARS
45.00 g., 0.5833 Gold, 0.84 oz. AGW 40mm. **Rev:** Dog
Sled Team

Date	Mintage	
2006	953	PF65 1,625

KM# 751   250 DOLLARS
1000.00 g., 0.9999 Silver, 31.94 oz. ASW 101.6mm.
Subject: Vancouver Olympics, 2010 **Rev:** Early Canada
motif **Note:** Illustration reduced.

Date	Mintage	
2007	2,500	PF65 1,250

KM# 833   250 DOLLARS
1000.00 g., 0.999 Silver, 31.91 oz. ASW 101.6mm.
Subject: Vancouver Olympics 2010 **Rev:** Towards
confederation **Note:** Illustration reduced.

Date	Mintage	
2008	2,500	PF65 1,350

KM# 913   250 DOLLARS
1000.00 g., 0.9999 Silver, 31.94 oz. ASW 101.5mm. **Obv.**

Bust right **Obv. Designer:** Susanna Blunt **Rev:** Mask with fish - Surviving the flood **Note:** Illustration reduced.

Date	Mintage	
2009	815	**PF65** 1,350

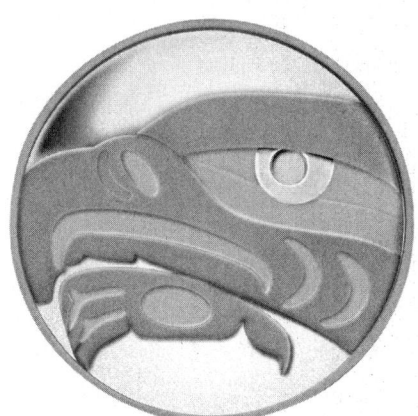

KM# 949 250 DOLLARS
1000.00 g., 0.999 Silver, 31.91 oz. ASW 101.6mm. **Rev:** Modern Canada

Date	Mintage	
2009	905	**PF65** 1,350

KM# 981 250 DOLLARS
1000.00 g., 0.999 Silver, 31.91 oz. ASW 101.6mm. **Rev:** Eagle head

Date	Mintage		
2010 Antique Patina	500		1,350
2010	500	**PF65** 1,400	

KM# 981a 250 DOLLARS
1000.00 g., 0.999 Silver, 31.91 oz. ASW 101.6mm. **Rev:** Eagle head, blue enamel

Date	Mintage	
2010	500	**PF65** 1,400

KM# 1044 250 DOLLARS
1000.00 g., 0.999 Silver, 31.91 oz. ASW 101.6mm. **Subject:** Baniff, 125th Anniversary of resort founding **Rev:** Features of Baniff

Date	Mintage	
2010	750	**PF65** 1,650

KM# 1285 250 DOLLARS
1000.00 g., 0.999 Silver, 31.91 oz. ASW 101mm. **Subject:** Olympic views

Date	Mintage	
2010	—	**PF65** 1,350

KM# 1150 250 DOLLARS
1000.00 g., 0.9999 Silver, 31.94 oz. ASW 100mm. **Rev:** Lacrosse

Date	Mintage	
2011	—	**PF65** 1,350

250 DOLLARS

KM# 1185   250 DOLLARS
1000.00 g.,   0.999 Silver, 31.91 oz. ASW 101.6mm.
Subject: Year of the Dragon **Obv.** Bust left **Rev:** Dragon
left

Date	Mintage		
2012	—	PF65	1,550

KM# 1277   250 DOLLARS
1000.00 g.,   0.999 Silver, 31.91 oz. ASW 101mm.
Subject: Bateman Moose

Date	Mintage		
2012	—	PF65	1,650

KM# 1340   250 DOLLARS
1000.00 g.,   0.9999 Silver, 31.94 oz. ASW 102mm.
Subject: War of 1812, Battle of Queenstown Heights **Rev:**
Battle scene

Date	Mintage		
2012	7,000	PF65	2,250

KM# 1366   250 DOLLARS
1000.00 g., 0.9999 Silver, 31.94 oz. ASW **Subject:** Year of
the Snake **Rev:** Snake under maple leaves **Rev. Designer:**
Three Degrees Creative Group

Date	Mintage		
2013	Est. 888	PF65	2,250

KM# 1369   250 DOLLARS
1000.00 g., 0.999 Silver, 31.91 oz. ASW **Subject:** End of 7
Years War **Rev:** Map of North America with Arms of France
and Great Britain **Rev. Designer:** Luc Normandin

Date	Mintage		
2013	Est. 500	PF65	2,250

KM# 1371   250 DOLLARS
1000.00 g.,   0.999 Silver, 31.91 oz. ASW 101mm.
Subject: Arctic Coastline **Rev. Designer:** W. David Ward

Date	Mintage		
2013	Est. 750	PF65	2,250

KM# 1477 250 DOLLARS
1000.00 g., 0.9999 Silver, 31.94 oz. ASW 102.1mm.
Subject: Battle of Chateauguay **Rev:** Henri Julien's painting of the battle

Date	Mintage		
2013	500	PF65	2,250

KM# 1579 250 DOLLARS
1000.00 g., 0.9999 Silver, 31.94 oz. ASW 101mm.
Subject: Year of the Horse

Date	Mintage		
2014	—	PF65	1,350

KM# 1502 250 DOLLARS
1000.00 g., 0.9999 Silver, 31.94 oz. ASW 102.1mm. **Rev:** Two caribou advancing left **Rev. Designer:** Trevor Tennant

Date	Mintage		
2013	500	PF65	2,500

KM# 1518 250 DOLLARS
1000.00 g., 0.9999 Silver, 31.94 oz. ASW 102.1mm.
Subject: Year of the Horse **Rev:** Horse rearing up left **Rev. Designer:** Three Degrees Creative Group

Date	Mintage		
2014	388	PF65	2,250

KM# 1605 250 DOLLARS
1000.00 g., 0.9999 Silver, 31.94 oz. ASW 101mm. **Obv.** Bust right **Rev:** Snowy owl, yellow eyes

Date	Mintage		
2014	—	PF65	1,650

KM# 1622   250 DOLLARS
62.34 g., 0.999 Gold, 1.99 oz. AGW 42mm. **Subject:**
Canada thru the eyes of Tim Barnard **Obv.** Bust right **Rev:**
Multitude of designs

Date	Mintage	
2014	300	PF65 5,200

KM# 501   300 DOLLARS
60.00 g., 0.5833 Gold, 1.12 oz. AGW 50mm. **Obv.** Triple
cameo portraits of Queen Elizabeth II by Gillick, Machin
and de Pedery-Hunt, each in 14K gold, rose in center **Rev:**
Dates "1952-2002" and denomination in legend, rose in
center **Note:** Housed in anodized gold-colored aluminum
box with cherrywood stained siding

Date	Mintage	
1952-2002	999	PF65 2,150

KM# 517   300 DOLLARS
60.00 g., 0.5833 Gold, 1.12 oz. AGW 50mm. **Obv.** Four
coinage portraits of Elizabeth II **Rev:** Canadian arms above
value **Edge:** Plain

Date	Mintage	
2004	998	PF65 2,150

KM# 600   300 DOLLARS
60.00 g., 0.5833 Gold, 1.12 oz. AGW 40mm. **Subject:**
Welcome Figure Totem Pole **Obv.** Head right **Rev:** Men
with totem pole

Date	Mintage	
2005	948	PF65 2,150

KM# 570.1   300 DOLLARS
45.00 g., 0.5833 Gold, 0.84 oz. AGW 40mm. **Subject:**
Standard Time - 4 AM Pacific **Obv.** Head right **Rev:**
Roman numeral clock with world inside

Date	Mintage	
2005	200	PF65 1,650

KM# 570.2   300 DOLLARS
45.00 g., 0.583 Gold, 0.84 oz. AGW 40mm. **Subject:**
Standard Time - Mountian 5 AM **Obv.** Head right **Rev:**
Roman numeral clock with world inside.

Date	Mintage	
2005	200	PF65 1,650

KM# 570.3   300 DOLLARS
45.00 g., 0.583 Gold, 0.84 oz. AGW 40mm. **Subject:**
Standard Time - Central 6 PM **Obv.** Head right **Rev:**
Roman numeral clock with world inside

Date	Mintage	
2005	200	PF65 1,650

KM# 570.4   300 DOLLARS
45.00 g., 0.583 Gold, 0.84 oz. AGW 40mm. **Subject:**
Standard Time - Eastern 7 AM **Obv.** Head right **Rev:**
Roman numeral clock with world inside

Date	Mintage	
2005	200	PF65 1,650

KM# 570.5   300 DOLLARS
45.00 g., 0.583 Gold, 0.84 oz. AGW 40mm. **Subject:**
Standard Time - Atlantic 8 AM **Obv.** Head right **Rev:**
Roman numeral clock with world inside

Date	Mintage	
2005	200	PF65 1,650

KM# 570.6   300 DOLLARS
45.00 g., 0.583 Gold, 0.84 oz. AGW 40mm. **Subject:**
Standard Time - Newfoundland 8:30 **Obv.** Head right **Rev:**
Roman numeral clock with world inside

Date	Mintage	
2005	200	PF65 1,650

KM# 596   300 DOLLARS
60.00 g., 0.5833 Gold, 1.12 oz. AGW 50mm. **Subject:**
Shinplaster **Obv.** Head right **Rev:** Britannia bust, spear
over shoulder

Date	Mintage	
2005	994	PF65 2,150

KM# 678 300 DOLLARS
45.00 g., 0.5833 Gold, 0.84 oz. AGW 40mm. **Rev:** Hologram of Canadarm, Col. C. Hadfield in spacewalk

Date	Mintage	
2006	581	PF65 1,650

KM# 679 300 DOLLARS
60.00 g., 0.5833 Gold, 1.12 oz. AGW 50mm. **Subject:** Queen Elizabeth's 80th Birthday **Rev:** State Crown, colorized

Date	Mintage	
2006	996	PF65 2,150

KM# 680 300 DOLLARS
60.00 g., 0.5833 Gold, 1.12 oz. AGW 50mm. **Subject:** Crystal Snowflake

Date	Mintage	
2006	998	PF65 2,150

KM# 595 300 DOLLARS
60.00 g., 0.5833 Gold, 1.12 oz. AGW 50mm. **Subject:** Shinplaster **Obv.** Head right **Rev:** Seated Britannia with shield

Date	Mintage	
2006	940	PF65 2,150

KM# 692 300 DOLLARS
60.00 g., 0.5833 Gold, 1.12 oz. AGW 50mm. **Subject:** Shinplaster **Rev:** 1923 25 cent bank note

Date	Mintage	
2007	778	PF65 2,150

KM# 740 300 DOLLARS
45.00 g., 0.583 Gold, 0.84 oz. AGW 40mm. **Rev:** Canadian Rockies panoramic hologram

Date	Mintage	
2007	511	PF65 1,750

KM# 752 300 DOLLARS
60.00 g., 0.583 Gold, 1.12 oz. AGW 50mm. **Subject:** Vancouver Olympics **Rev:** Olympic ideals, classic figures and torch

Date	Mintage	
2007	953	PF65 2,150

KM# 825 300 DOLLARS
45.00 g., 0.583 Gold, 0.84 oz. AGW 50mm. **Rev:** Alberta Coat of Arms

Date	Mintage	
2008	344	PF65 1,750

KM# 826 300 DOLLARS
60.00 g., 0.583 Gold, 1.12 oz. AGW 50mm. **Rev:** Newfoundland and Labrador Coat of Arms

Date	Mintage	
2008	472	PF65 2,150

300 DOLLARS

KM# 827 300 DOLLARS
45.00 g., 0.583 Gold, 0.84 oz. AGW 40mm. **Subject:** Canadian achievements IMAX **Rev:** Kid in audience reaching out to shark on big screen

Date	Mintage	
2008	—	**PF65** 1,650

KM# 828 300 DOLLARS
60.00 g., 0.583 Gold, 1.12 oz. AGW 50mm. **Rev:** Four seasons moon mask in color, blue design in border

Date	Mintage	
2008	544	**PF65** 3,800

KM# 830 300 DOLLARS
60.00 g., 0.583 Gold, 1.12 oz. AGW 50mm. **Subject:** Vancouver Olympics **Rev:** Olympic competition, athletics and torch

Date	Mintage	
2008	334	**PF65** 2,250

KM# 900 300 DOLLARS
60.00 g., 0.583 Gold, 1.12 oz. AGW 50mm. **Subject:** Yukon Coat of Arms **Obv.** Bust right **Obv. Designer:** Susanna Blunt **Rev:** Yukon Coat of Arms **Obv. Legend:** Elizabeth II DG Regina **Rev. Legend:** Canada 300 Dollars

Date	Mintage	
2009	325	**PF65** 2,150

KM# 877 300 DOLLARS
60.00 g., 0.583 Gold, 1.12 oz. AGW 50mm. **Rev:** Summer moon mask, enameled

Date	Mintage	
2009	—	**PF65** 2,250

KM# 911 300 DOLLARS
60.00 g., 0.583 Gold, 1.12 oz. AGW 50mm. **Subject:** 2010 Vancouver Olympics **Obv.** Bust right **Obv. Designer:** Susanna Blunt **Rev:** Athletics with torch - Olympic firendship

Date	Mintage	
2009	880	**PF65** 2,150

KM# 999 300 DOLLARS
54.00 g., 0.583 Gold, 1.01 oz. AGW 50mm. **Rev:** British Columbia Arms

Date	Mintage	
2010	500	**PF65** 1,900

KM# 1095 300 DOLLARS
60.00 g., 0.9167 Gold, 1.76 oz. AGW 50mm. **Rev:** Manitoba Coat of arms

Date	Mintage	
2011	500	**PF65** 3,300

KM# 1047 300 DOLLARS
60.00 g., 0.583 Gold, 1.12 oz. AGW 50mm. **Rev:** Snowflake, white crystals

Date	Mintage	
2010	750	**PF65** 2,150

KM# 1215 300 DOLLARS
60.00 g., 0.917 Gold, 1.76 oz. AGW 50mm. **Obv.** Bust right **Rev:** Arms of Nova Scotia

Date	Mintage	
2011	—	**PF65** 3,300

KM# 1078 300 DOLLARS
60.00 g., 0.583 Gold, 1.12 oz. AGW 50mm. **Rev:** New Brunswick Coat of arms

Date	Mintage	
2010	500	**PF65** 2,150

KM# 1195 300 DOLLARS
45.00 g., 0.583 Gold, 0.84 oz. AGW 40mm. **Subject:** Elizabeth II, Diamond Jubilee **Obv.** Bust right **Rev:** Youthful bust with crown right, insert crystal at right

Date	Mintage	
1952-2012	—	PF65 1,600

KM# 1224 300 DOLLARS
60.00 g., 0.9167 Gold, 1.76 oz. AGW 50mm. **Obv.** Bust right **Rev:** Shield of Quebec

Date	Mintage	
2012	—	PF65 3,300

KM# 1242 300 DOLLARS
16.00 g., 0.916 Gold, 0.47 oz. AGW 29mm. **Subject:** Calgary Stampede

Date	Mintage	
2012	—	PF65 900

KM# 1278 300 DOLLARS
31.11 g., 0.999 Platinum, 0.99 oz. APW 30mm. **Subject:** Bateman Moose

Date	Mintage	
2012	—	PF65 1,750

KM# 1338 300 DOLLARS
60.00 g., 0.917 Gold, 1.76 oz. AGW 50mm. **Subject:** Nunavut Province **Rev:** Provincial Arms

Date	Mintage	
2012	—	PF65 4,000

KM# 1571 300 DOLLARS
60.00 g., 0.917 Gold, 1.76 oz. AGW 50mm. **Obv.** Bust right **Rev:** Arms of Ontario

Date	Mintage	
2013 Proof	—	PF65 3,300

KM# 1592 300 DOLLARS
60.00 g., 0.999 Gold, 1.91 oz. AGW **Obv.** Bust right **Rev:** Saskashawan coat of arms

Date	Mintage	
2014	—	PF65 3,300

KM# 308 350 DOLLARS
38.05 g., 0.9999 Gold, 1.22 oz. AGW **Subject:** Flowers of Canada's Coat of Arms **Obv.** Crowned head right, date behind, denomination at bottom **Rev:** Flowers **Rev. Designer:** Pierre Leduc

Date	Mintage	
1998	—	PF60 2,350

KM# 370 350 DOLLARS
38.05 g., 0.9999 Gold, 1.22 oz. AGW **Rev:** Lady's slipper
Rev. Designer: Henry Purdy

Date	Mintage		
1999	1,990	PF60	2,350

KM# 404 350 DOLLARS
38.05 g., 0.9999 Gold, 1.22 oz. AGW 34mm. **Obv.** Crowned head right **Rev:** Three Pacific Dogwood flowers **Rev. Designer:** Caren Heine **Edge:** Reeded

Date	Mintage		
2000	1,506	PF60	2,350

KM# 433 350 DOLLARS
38.05 g., 0.9999 Gold, 1.22 oz. AGW 34mm. **Subject:** The Mayflower Flower **Obv.** Crowned head right **Rev:** Two flowers **Rev. Designer:** Bonnie Ross **Edge:** Reeded

Date	Mintage		
2001	1,988	PF65	2,350

KM# 502 350 DOLLARS
38.05 g., 0.9999 Gold, 1.22 oz. AGW 34mm. **Subject:** The Wild Rose **Obv. Designer:** Dora de Pedery-Hunt **Rev:** Wild rose plant **Rev. Designer:** Dr. Andreas Kare Hellum

Date	Mintage		
2002	2,001	PF65	2,350

KM# 504 350 DOLLARS
38.05 g., 0.9999 Gold, 1.22 oz. AGW 34mm. **Subject:** The White Trillium **Obv.** Crowned head right **Obv. Designer:** Dora de Pedery-Hunt **Rev:** White Trillium

Date	Mintage		
2003	1,865	PF65	2,350

KM# 601 350 DOLLARS
38.05 g., 0.9999 Gold, 1.22 oz. AGW **Subject:** Western Red Lilly **Obv.** Head right **Rev:** Western Red Lilies

Date	Mintage		
2005	1,634	PF65	2,350

KM# 626 350 DOLLARS
38.05 g., 0.9999 Gold, 1.22 oz. AGW 34mm. **Subject:** Iris Vericolor **Obv.** Crowned head right **Rev:** Iris

Date	Mintage		
2006	1,995	PF65	2,350

KM# 754 350 DOLLARS
35.00 g., 0.9999 Gold, 1.12 oz. AGW 34mm. **Rev:** Purple violet

Date	Mintage		
2007	1,392	PF65	2,200

KM# 832 350 DOLLARS
35.00 g., 0.9999 Gold, 1.12 oz. AGW 34mm. **Rev:** Purple saxifrage

Date	Mintage		
2008	1,313	PF65	2,200

KM# 901 350 DOLLARS
35.00 g., 1.000 Gold, 1.12 oz. AGW 34mm. **Subject:** Pitcher plant **Obv.** Bust right **Obv. Designer:** Susana Blunt **Rev:** Cluster of pitcher flowers **Obv. Legend:** Elizabeth II Canada DG Regina Fine Gold 350 Dollars or PUR 99999 **Rev. Legend:** Julie Wilson

Date	Mintage		
2009	1,003	PF65	2,200

350 DOLLARS

KM# 1019 350 DOLLARS
35.00 g., 0.999 Gold, 1.12 oz. AGW 34mm. **Rev:** Prairie
Crocus **Rev. Designer:** Celia Godkin

Date	Mintage	
2010	Est. 1400	PF65 2,200

KM# 1136 350 DOLLARS
35.00 g., 0.9999 Gold, 1.12 oz. AGW 34mm. **Obv.** Bust
right **Rev:** Mountain Avens in bloom **Edge:** Reeded

Date	Mintage	
2011	1,300	PF65 2,200

KM# 1327 350 DOLLARS
35.00 g., 0.999 Gold, 1.12 oz. AGW 34mm. **Subject:** War
of 1812 - Sir Issac Brock **Rev:** Putti crowning funeral urn,
design of 1816 Half-penny token

Date	Mintage	
2012	1,000	PF65 2,800

KM# 1499 350 DOLLARS
35.00 g., 0.9999 Gold, 1.12 oz. AGW 34mm. **Rev:** Polar
Bear **Rev. Designer:** Glen Loates

Date	Mintage	
2013	600	PF65 2,800

KM# 710 500 DOLLARS
156.50 g., 0.9999 Gold, 5.00 oz. AGW 60mm. **Subject:**
Queen's 60th Wedding **Rev:** Coat of Arms and Mascots of
Elizabeth and Philip

Date	Mintage	MS63
2007	198	9,150

KM# 782 500 DOLLARS
155.76 g., 0.999 Gold, 4.97 oz. AGW 60mm. **Subject:**
Ottawa Mint Centennial 1908-2008 **Rev:** Mint building
facade **Note:** Illustration reduced.

Date	Mintage	MS63
2008	248	9,150

KM# 897 500 DOLLARS
156.05 g., 0.999 Gold, 4.98 oz. AGW 60mm. **Subject:**
150th Anniversary of the start of construction of the
Parliament Buildings **Obv.** Bust right **Rev:** Incomplete
west block, original architecture **Rev. Legend:** 500 Dollars
1859-2009

Date	Mintage	
2009	77	PF65 9,150

KM# 1007 500 DOLLARS
156.50 g., 0.999 Gold, 4.99 oz. AGW 60mm. **Subject:**
75th Anniversary of Canadian Bank Notes **Rev:** Abundance
seated under tree

Date	Mintage	
2010	200	PF65 9,150

KM# 1179 500 DOLLARS
156.50 g., 0.9999 Gold, 5.00 oz. AGW 60mm. **Obv.**
Crowned bust of George V **Rev:** Arms of Canada, dual
dates and denomination below **Edge:** Serially numbered

Date	Mintage	
1912-2012	200	PF65 9,150

KM# 1495 500 DOLLARS
156.00 g., 0.9999 Gold, 4.98 oz. AGW 60.15mm. **Subject:**
Aboriginal art **Rev:** Artic animals, aboriginal in canoe **Rev.**
Designer: Raymond Weizineau

Date	Mintage	
2013	1,000	PF65 12,000

KM# 681 2500 DOLLARS
1000.00 g., 0.9999 Gold, 31.94 oz. AGW 101.6mm.
Subject: Kilo **Rev:** Common Characters, Early Canada

Date	Mintage	MS63
2007 (2006)	20	57,000

KM# 1288 2500 DOLLARS
1000.00 g., 0.999 Gold, 31.91 oz. AGW 101mm. **Subject:**
Old town view

Date	Mintage	
2008	—	PF65 57,000

KM# 902 2500 DOLLARS
1000.00 g., 0.999 Silver, 31.91 oz. ASW 101.6mm.
Subject: Modern Canada **Obv.** Bust right **Obv. Designer:**
Susanna Blunt **Rev:** Canadian landscape with modern

elements **Series:** History and Culture Collection **Obv.**
Legend: Vancouver 2010, 2500 Dollars, Elizabeth II

Date	Mintage		
2009	2,500	**PF65** 1,250	

KM# 902a   2500 DOLLARS
1000.00 g.,   0.999 Gold, 31.91 oz. AGW 101.6mm.
Subject: Modern Canada **Obv.** Bust right **Obv. Designer:**
Susana Blunt **Rev:** Canadian landscape with modern
elements **Series:** History and Culture Collection **Obv.**
Legend: Vancouver 2010, 2500 Dollars, Elizabeth II

Date	Mintage		
2009	50	**PF65** 57,000	

KM# 912   2500 DOLLARS
1000.00 g., 0.9999 Gold, 31.94 oz. AGW 101mm. **Obv.**
Bust right **Obv. Designer:** Susanna Blunt **Rev:** Mask with
fish - Surviving the flood

Date	Mintage		
2009	40	**PF65** 58,000	

KM# 1045   2500 DOLLARS
1000.00 g.,   0.9999 Gold, 31.94 oz. AGW 101mm.
Subject: Baniff, 125th Anniversary **Rev:** Highlights of
Baniff

Date	Mintage		
2010	—	**PF65** 60,000	

KM# 1286   2500 DOLLARS
1000.00 g., 0.999 Gold, 31.91 oz. AGW 101mm. **Subject:**
Olympic views

Date	Mintage		
2010	—	**PF65** 60,000	

KM# 984   2500 DOLLARS
1000.00 g., 0.999 Gold, 31.91 oz. AGW 101mm.

Date	Mintage		
2010	20	**PF65** 60,000	

KM# 1197   2500 DOLLARS
1000.00 g.,   0.9999 Gold, 31.94 oz. AGW 101mm. **Obv.**
Bust right **Rev:** Early lacrosse game

Date	Mintage		
2011	35	**PF65** 60,000	

KM# 1276 2500 DOLLARS
1000.00 g., 0.999 Gold, 31.91 oz. AGW 101mm. **Subject:**
Bateman Moose

Date	Mintage	
2012	—	PF65 58,000

KM# 1339 2500 DOLLARS
1000.00 g., 0.9999 Gold, 31.94 oz. AGW 101mm.
Subject: War of 1812, Battle of Queenston Heights **Rev:**
Battle scene

Date	Mintage	
2012	20	PF65 69,000

KM# 1364 2500 DOLLARS
1000.00 g., 0.9999 Gold, 31.94 oz. AGW 101.6mm.
Subject: Year of the Snake **Rev:** Snake under maple leaves
Rev. Designer: Three Degrees Creative Group

Date	Mintage	
2013	Est. 25	PF65 69,000

KM# 1372 2500 DOLLARS
1000.00 g., 0.999 Gold, 31.91 oz. AGW 101.6mm.
Subject: Arctic Coastline **Rev. Designer:** W. David Ward

Date	Mintage	
2013	Est. 20	PF65 69,000

KM# 1478 2500 DOLLARS
1000.00 g., 0.9999 Gold, 31.94 oz. AGW 101mm.
Subject: Battle of Chateauguay and Crysler's Farm

Date	Mintage	
2013	20	PF65 69,000

KM# 1501   2500 DOLLARS
1000.00 g., 0.9999 Gold, 31.94 oz. AGW 101.6mm. **Rev:**
Two caribou advancing left **Rev. Designer:** Trevor Tennant

Date	Mintage		
2013	20	PF65	69,000

KM# 1519   2500 DOLLARS
1000.00 g., 0.9999 Gold, 31.94 oz. AGW 101.6mm.
Subject: Year of the Horse **Rev:** Horse rearing up left **Rev.
Designer:** Three Degrees Creative Group

Date	Mintage		
2014	18	PF65	69,000

KM# 1606   2500 DOLLARS
1000.00 g., 0.9999 Gold, 31.94 oz. AGW 101mm. **Obv.**
Bust right **Rev:** Snowy owl, colored eyes

Date	Mintage		
2014	—	PF65	60,000

KM# 1370   2500 DOLLARS
1000.00 g., 0.999 Gold, 31.91 oz. AGW 102mm. **Rev:**
Map of North America and Arms of France and Great
Britain. **Series:** End of 7 Years War - 250th Anniversary
Rev. Designer: Luc Normandin

Date	Mintage		
2013	Est. 20	PF65	69,000

SILVER BULLION COINAGE

KM# 617   DOLLAR
1.56 g., 0.9999 Silver, 0.05 oz. ASW 16mm. **Obv.**
Crowned head right **Rev:** Holographic Maple leaf **Edge:**
Reeded

Date	Mintage		
2003	—	PF65	4.50

KM# 621   DOLLAR
1.56 g., 0.9999 Silver, 0.05 oz. ASW 17mm. **Obv.**
Crowned head right **Rev:** Maple leaf **Edge:** Reeded

Date	Mintage				
2004 Mint logo privy mark	13,859	PF63	3.50	PF65	4.50

KM# 718 DOLLAR
15.55 g., 0.999 Silver, 0.50 oz. ASW 32mm. **Obv.** Bust right **Rev:** Grey Wolf standing with moon in background **Rev. Designer:** William Woodruff **Edge:** Reeded

Date	Mintage	MS63
2005	106,800	40.00
2006	—	40.00
2007	—	40.00

KM# 1489 DOLLAR
1.000 Silver, **Rev:** Maple leaf tilted left **Note:** Thick planchet.

Date	Mintage		
2010	—	PF63 65.00	PF65 75.00

KM# 1406 DOLLAR
1.55 g., 0.9999 Silver, 0.05 oz. ASW 17mm. **Obv. Designer:** Arnold Machin **Rev:** Three Maple Leaves **Rev. Designer:** Arnold Nogy

Date	Mintage		
2013	—	PF63 18.00	PF65 20.00

KM# 1593 DOLLAR
1.56 g., 0.9999 Silver, 0.05 oz. ASW 16mm. **Obv.** Bust right **Rev:** Two maple leaves, one gilt

Date	Mintage	MS63
2014	—	5.00

KM# 618 2 DOLLARS
3.11 g., 0.9999 Silver, 0.10 oz. ASW 20.1mm. **Obv.** Crowned head right **Rev:** Holographic Maple leaf **Edge:** Reeded

Date	Mintage	
2003	—	PF65 7.50

KM# 622 2 DOLLARS
3.11 g., 0.9999 Silver, 0.10 oz. ASW 21mm. **Obv.** Crowned head right **Rev:** Maple leaf **Edge:** Reeded

Date	Mintage		
2004 Mint logo privy mark	13,859	PF63 6.50	PF65 7.50

KM# 571 2 DOLLARS
3.11 g., 0.9999 Silver, 0.10 oz. ASW 21mm. **Obv.** Head right **Rev:** Lynx

Date	Mintage		
2005	—	PF63 6.50	PF65 7.50

KM# 1407 2 DOLLARS
3.11 g., 0.999 Silver, 0.10 oz. ASW **Obv. Designer:** Arnold Machin **Rev:** Three Maple Leaves **Rev. Designer:** Arnold Nogy

Date	Mintage		
2013	—	PF63 25.00	PF65 30.00

KM# 1594 2 DOLLARS
3.11 g., 0.9999 Silver, 0.10 oz. ASW 20.1mm. **Obv.** Bust right **Rev:** Two maple leaves, one gilt

Date	Mintage	MS63
2014	—	10.00

KM# 619 3 DOLLARS
7.78 g., 0.9999 Silver, 0.25 oz. ASW 26.9mm. **Obv.** Crowned head right **Rev:** Holographic Maple leaf **Edge:** Reeded

Date	Mintage	
2003	—	PF65 15.00

KM# 623 3 DOLLARS
7.78 g., 0.9999 Silver, 0.25 oz. ASW 27mm. **Obv.** Crowned head right **Rev:** Maple leaf **Edge:** Reeded

Date	Mintage		
2004 Mint logo privy mark	13,859	PF63 11.00	PF65 12.50

KM# 1415 3 DOLLARS
7.77 g., 0.999 Silver, 0.25 oz. ASW 27mm. **Rev:** Fox

Date	Mintage		
2004	—	PF63 30.00	PF65 35.00

SILVER BULLION COINAGE

KM# 572   3 DOLLARS
7.78 g., 0.9999 Silver, 0.25 oz. ASW 27mm. **Obv.** Head right **Rev:** Lynx

Date	Mintage		
2005	—	PF63 11.00	PF65 12.50

KM# 1408   3 DOLLARS
7.78 g., 0.9999 Silver, 0.25 oz. ASW 27mm. **Obv. Designer:** Arnold Machin **Rev:** Three Maple Leaves **Rev. Designer:** Arnold Nogy

Date	Mintage		
2012	—	PF63 35.00	PF65 40.00

KM# 1595   3 DOLLARS
7.77 g., 0.9999 Silver, 0.25 oz. ASW 27mm. **Obv.** Bust right **Rev:** Two maple leaves, one gilt

Date	Mintage	MS63
2014	—	15.00

KM# 620   4 DOLLARS
15.55 g., 0.9999 Silver, 0.50 oz. ASW 33.9mm. **Obv.** Crowned head right **Rev:** Holographic Maple leaf **Edge:** Reeded

Date	Mintage		
2003	—	PF63 22.00	PF65 25.00

KM# 624   4 DOLLARS
15.55 g., 0.9999 Silver, 0.50 oz. ASW 34mm. **Obv.** Crowned head right **Rev:** Maple leaf **Edge:** Reeded

Date	Mintage	
2004 Mint logo privy mark Reverse Proof	13,859	PF65 22.50

KM# 573   4 DOLLARS
15.55 g., 0.9999 Silver, 0.50 oz. ASW 34mm. **Obv.** Head right **Rev:** Lynx

Date	Mintage		
2005	—	PF63 20.00	PF65 22.50

KM# 1409   4 DOLLARS
15.55 g., 0.9999 Silver, 0.50 oz. ASW 33.9mm. **Obv. Designer:** Arnold Machin **Rev:** Three maple leaves **Rev. Designer:** Arnold Nogy

Date	Mintage		
2013	—	PF63 35.00	PF65 40.00

KM# 1596   4 DOLLARS
15.55 g., 0.9999 Silver, 0.50 oz. ASW 34mm. **Obv.** Bust right **Rev:** Two maple leaves, one gilt

Date	Mintage	MS63
2014	—	22.50

KM# 163 5 DOLLARS

31.10 g., 0.9999 Silver, 0.99 oz. ASW **Obv.** Young bust right, denomination and date below **Obv. Designer:** Arnold Machin **Rev:** Maple leaf flanked by 9999

Date	Mintage		MS63
1988	1,155,931		35.00
1989	—	PF60 40.00	
1989	3,332,200		35.00

KM# 187 5 DOLLARS

31.10 g., 0.9999 Silver, 0.99 oz. ASW **Obv.** Crowned head right, date and denomination below **Obv. Designer:** Dora de Pedery-Hunt **Rev:** Maple leaf flanked by 9999

Date	Mintage		MS63
1990	1,708,800		35.00
1991	644,300		35.00
1992	343,800		35.00
1993	889,946		35.00
1994	1,133,900		35.00
1995	326,244		35.00
1996	250,445		42.50
1997	100,970		35.00
1998 90th Anniversary R.C.M. privy mark	13,025		35.00
1998 R.C.M.P. privy mark	25,000		35.00
1998 Tiger privy mark	25,000		35.00
1998 Titanic privy mark	26,000		85.00
1998	591,359		35.00
1999 Rabbit privy mark	25,000		35.00
1999	1,229,442		35.00
1999 Y2K privy mark	9,999		37.50
2000 Dragon privy mark	25,000		35.00
2000 Expo Hanover privy mark	—		45.00
2000	403,652		35.00
2001	398,563		35.00
2001 Reverse proof, Snake privy mark	25,000	PF63 35.00	PF65 45.00

Date	Mintage		MS63
2002	576,196		35.00
2002 Reverse proof, Horse privy mark	25,000	PF63 35.00	PF65 45.00
2003	—		35.00
2003 Reverse proof, sheep privy mark	25,000	PF63 35.00	PF65 45.00

KM# 363 5 DOLLARS

31.10 g., 0.9999 Silver, 0.99 oz. ASW **Obv.** Crowned head right, date and denomination below **Rev:** Maple leaf flanked by 9999

Date	Mintage	MS63
1999/2000 (1999) Fireworks privy mark	298,775	35.00

KM# 437 5 DOLLARS

31.10 g., 0.9999 Silver, 0.99 oz. ASW 38mm. **Obv.** Crowned head right, date and denomination below **Rev:** Radiant maple leaf hologram **Edge:** Reeded

Date	Mintage	MS63
2001 Good fortune privy mark	29,906	75.00

KM# 436 5 DOLLARS

31.10 g., 0.9999 Silver, 0.99 oz. ASW 38mm. **Obv.** Crowned head right, date and denomination below **Rev:** Three maple leaves in autumn colors, 9999 flanks **Rev. Designer:** Debbie Adams **Edge:** Reeded

Date	Mintage		
2001	49,709	PF63 30.00	PF65 40.00

KM# 505   5 DOLLARS
31.10 g., 0.9999 Silver, 0.99 oz. ASW 38mm. **Obv.**
Crowned head right, date and denomination below **Rev:**
Two maple leaves in spring color (green) **Edge:** Reeded

Date	Mintage	MS63
2002	29,509	37.50

KM# 521   5 DOLLARS
31.10 g., 0.9999 Silver, 0.99 oz. ASW **Obv.** Head right
Rev: Maple leaf, summer colors **Rev. Designer:** Stan
Witten

Date	Mintage	MS63
2003	29,416	37.50

KM# 508   5 DOLLARS
31.10 g., 0.9999 Silver, 0.99 oz. ASW 38mm. **Obv.**
Crowned head right, date and denomination below **Obv.**
Designer: Dora de Pedery-Hunt **Rev:** Holographic Maple
leaf flanked by 9999 **Edge:** Reeded

Date	Mintage		
2003 (2004)	—	PF63 35.00	PF65 37.50

KM# 607   5 DOLLARS
31.12 g., 0.9999 Silver, 0.99 oz. ASW **Obv.** Head right
Rev: Maple leaf, winter colors

Date	Mintage	MS63
2004	—	37.50

KM# 625   5 DOLLARS
31.10 g., 0.99 oz. ASW 38mm. **Obv.** Bust
right **Obv. Designer:** Susanna Blunt **Rev:** Maple leaf
Edge: Reeded

Date	Mintage	MS63
2004 Mint logo privy mark Specimen	13,859	PF65 37.50
2004 Monkey privy mark Specimen	25,000	PF65 37.50
2004 D-Day privy mark Specimen	11,698	PF65 37.50
2004 Desjardins privy mark	15,000	37.50
2004 Capricorn privy Mark Reverse proof	5,000	PF65 37.50
2004 Aquarius privy mark Reverse proof	5,000	PF65 37.50
2004 Pisces privy mark Reverse proof	5,000	PF65 37.50
2004 Aries privy mark Reverse proof	5,000	PF65 37.50
2004 Taurus privy mark Reverse proof	5,000	PF65 37.50
2004 Gemini privy mark Reverse proof	5,000	PF65 37.50
2004 Cancer privy mark Reverse proof	5,000	PF65 37.50
2004 Leo privy mark Reverse proof	5,000	PF65 37.50
2004 Virgo privy mark Reverse proof	5,000	PF65 37.50
2004 Libra privy mark Reverse proof	5,000	PF65 37.50
2004 Scorpio privy mark Reverse proof	5,000	PF65 37.50
2004 Sagittarius privy mark Reverse proof	5,000	PF65 50.00
2005	—	35.00
2005 Tulip privy mark Reverse proof	3,500	PF65 50.00
2005 Tank privy mark Reverse proof	7,000	PF65 60.00
2005 USS Missouri privy mark Reverse proof	7,000	PF65 60.00
2005 Rooster privy mark Reverse proof	15,000	PF65 50.00
2006	—	35.00
2006 Dog privy mark Reverse proof	—	PF65 50.00
2007	—	35.00
2007 F12 privy mark Reverse proof	—	PF65 130
2007 Pig privy mark Reverse proof	—	PF65 50.00
2008	—	35.00
2008 F12 privy mark Reverse proof	—	PF65 130
2008 Rat privy mark Reverse proof	—	PF65 50.00
2009	—	35.00
2009 Brandenberg Gate privy mark Reverse proof	—	PF65 50.00
2009 Tower Bridge privy mark Reverse proof	—	PF65 50.00
2009 Ox Privy mark Reverse proof	—	PF65 50.00
2010	—	35.00
2010 Fabulous 15 privy mark Reverse proof	—	PF65 50.00
2011	—	35.00
2012	—	35.00
2012 Dragon privy mark Reverse proof	—	PF65 50.00
2012 Titanic privy mark Reverse proof	—	PF65 50.00
2012 Pisa privy mark	—	35.00
2012 Fabulous 15 privy mark Reverse proof	—	PF65 75.00
2013	—	35.00
2014	—	35.00

KM# 522 5 DOLLARS
31.11 g., 0.9999 Silver, 0.99 oz. ASW **Obv.** Head right **Rev:** Maple leaf, winter color **Rev. Designer:** Stan Witten

Date	Mintage	MS63
2004	26,763	35.00

KM# 574 5 DOLLARS
31.10 g., 0.9999 Silver, 0.99 oz. ASW 38mm. **Obv.** Head right **Rev:** Lynx

Date	Mintage		
2005	—	PF63 35.00	PF65 37.50

KM# 924 5 DOLLARS
31.11 g., 0.9999 Silver, 0.99 oz. ASW **Rev:** Maple Leaf, laser engraved **Rev. Designer:** Joan Nguyen

Date	Mintage		
2005	25,000	PF63 50.00	PF65 60.00

KM# 550 5 DOLLARS
31.10 g., 0.9999 Silver, 0.99 oz. ASW 38mm. **Obv.** Head right **Rev:** Big Leaf Maple and seed pod, color **Rev. Designer:** Stan Witten

Date	Mintage	MS63
2005	21,233	35.00

KM# 660 5 DOLLARS
31.10 g., 0.999 Silver, 0.99 oz. ASW **Obv.** Bust right **Obv. Designer:** Susanna Blunt **Rev:** Silver maple, colorized **Rev. Designer:** Stan Witten

Date	Mintage	MS63
2006	14,157	37.50

KM# 625a 5 DOLLARS
31.11 g., 0.9999 Silver, 0.99 oz. ASW 38mm. **Rev:** Maple leaf, gilt

Date	Mintage	MS63
2007	—	75.00
2008	—	75.00
2009	—	75.00
2009 Tower Bridge Privy Mark	—	75.00
2010	—	75.00

KM# 729 5 DOLLARS
31.11 g., 0.999 Silver, 0.99 oz. ASW 38mm. **Obv.** Bust right **Rev:** Maple leaf orange multicolor

Date	Mintage		
2007	—	PF63 40.00	PF65 45.00

KM# 925 5 DOLLARS
31.11 g., 0.999 Silver, 0.99 oz. ASW **Obv.** Bust right **Obv. Designer:** Susanna Blunt **Rev:** Sugar maple, colorized **Rev. Designer:** Stan Witten

Date	Mintage	MS63
2007	11,495	37.50

KM# 928   5 DOLLARS
31.39 g., 0.999 Silver, 1.00 oz. ASW 38mm. **Rev:** Orange
sugar maple leaf **Rev. Designer:** Stan Witten

Date	Mintage	MS63
2007 Specimen	20,000	100

KM# 798   5 DOLLARS
31.11 g., 0.999 Silver, 0.99 oz. ASW 38mm. **Subject:**
Maple Leaf 20th Anniversary **Rev:** Maple Leaf, selective
gold plating

Date	Mintage		
2008	10,000	PF63 65.00	PF65 75.00

KM# 799   5 DOLLARS
31.11 g., 0.999 Silver, 0.99 oz. ASW 38mm. **Subject:**
Breast Cancer Awareness **Rev:** Multicolor, green maple
leaf and pink ribbon

Date	Mintage	MS63
2008	11,048	85.00

KM# 800   5 DOLLARS
31.11 g., 0.999 Silver, 0.99 oz. ASW 38mm. **Subject:**
Vancouver Olympics **Obv.** Bust right **Obv. Designer:**
Susanna Blunt **Rev:** Maple leaf, Olympic logo at left, turtle

Date	Mintage	MS63
2008	—	37.50
2009	—	37.50
2010	—	37.50

KM# 800a   5 DOLLARS
31.11 g., 0.9999 Silver, 0.99 oz. ASW 38mm. **Rev:** Maple
leaf gilt, olympic logo at left

Date	Mintage	MS63
2008	—	50.00

KM# 1056   5 DOLLARS
31.11 g., 0.9999 Silver, 0.99 oz. ASW 38mm. **Rev:** Maple
leaf in brown color, card diamond

Date	Mintage	MS63
2008	—	50.00

KM# 1057   5 DOLLARS
31.11 g., 0.9999 Silver, 0.99 oz. ASW 38mm. **Rev:** Maple
Leaf in green color, card heart

Date	Mintage	MS63
2008	—	50.00

KM# 1058 5 DOLLARS
31.11 g., 0.9999 Silver, 0.99 oz. ASW 38mm. **Rev:** Maple leaf in green color, card club

Date	Mintage	MS63
2008	—	50.00

KM# 1059 5 DOLLARS
31.11 g., 0.9999 Silver, 0.99 oz. ASW 38mm. **Rev:** Maple Leaf in red color, card spade

Date	Mintage	MS63
2008	—	50.00

KM# 863 5 DOLLARS
31.11 g., 0.9999 Silver, 0.99 oz. ASW 38mm. **Subject:** Vancouver Olympics **Rev:** Thunderbird Totem **Rev. Designer:** Rick Harry

Date	Mintage	MS63
2009	—	50.00

KM# 863a 5 DOLLARS
31.11 g., 0.9999 Silver, 0.99 oz. ASW 38mm. **Rev:** Thunderbird, gilt

Date	Mintage	MS63
2009	—	60.00

KM# 1061 5 DOLLARS
31.11 g., 0.9999 Silver, 0.99 oz. ASW 38mm. **Rev:** Maple leaf in red color, support our troops yellow ribbon

Date	Mintage	MS63
2009	—	70.00

KM# 998 5 DOLLARS
31.12 g., 0.999 Silver, 0.99 oz. ASW 38mm. **Rev:** Olympic Hockey

Date	Mintage		
2010	—	PF63 38.00	PF65 42.00

KM# 998a 5 DOLLARS
31.11 g., 0.9999 Silver, 0.99 oz. ASW 38mm. **Rev:** Hockey player, gilt maple leaves flanking

Date	Mintage	MS63
2010	—	50.00

KM# 1077 5 DOLLARS
31.39 g., 0.999 Silver, 1.00 oz. ASW 34mm. **Rev:** Maple leaf on 45 degree angle left **Note:** Piedfort.

Date	Mintage	
2010 Reverse Proof	9,000	PF65 80.00

KM# 1289 5 DOLLARS
31.11 g., 0.9999 Silver, 0.99 oz. ASW 38mm. **Rev:** Maple leaf in green with crystal

Date	Mintage	MS63
2010	—	65.00

KM# 1290 5 DOLLARS
31.11 g., 0.999 Silver, 0.99 oz. ASW 38mm. **Rev:** Maple leaf in red with crystal

Date	Mintage	MS63
2010	—	65.00

KM# 1291 5 DOLLARS
31.11 g., 0.9999 Silver, 0.99 oz. ASW 38mm. **Rev:** Maple leaf in dark green with crystal

Date	Mintage	MS63
2010	—	65.00

KM# 1292 5 DOLLARS
31.11 g., 0.9999 Silver, 0.99 oz. ASW **Ruler:** Elizabeth II 38mm. **Rev:** Maple leaf in color with crystal **Mint:** Royal Canadian Mint

Date	Mintage	MS63
2010	—	65.00

KM# 1052 5 DOLLARS
31.11 g., 0.9999 Silver, 0.99 oz. ASW 38mm. **Rev:** Wolf standing with moonlight in background

Date	Mintage	MS63
2011	1,000,000	42.00

KM# 1109 5 DOLLARS
31.11 g., 0.999 Silver, 0.99 oz. ASW 38mm. **Rev:** Grizzly Bear walking right

Date	Mintage	MS63
2011	1,000,000	40.00

KM# 1164 5 DOLLARS
31.11 g., 0.999 Silver, 0.99 oz. ASW 38mm. **Obv.
Designer:** Susanna Blunt **Rev:** Cougar **Rev. Designer:**
William Woodruff

Date	Mintage	MS63
2012	1,000,000	40.00

KM# 1241 5 DOLLARS
31.14 g., 0.9999 Silver, 0.99 oz. ASW 38mm. **Obv.** Bust
right **Obv. Designer:** Susana Blunt **Rev:** Moose left **Rev.
Designer:** William Woodruff **Edge:** Reeded

Date	Mintage	MS63
2012	1,000,000	42.00

KM# 1297 5 DOLLARS
31.11 g., 0.999 Silver, 0.99 oz. ASW 38mm. **Obv.** Bust
right **Rev:** Antelope

Date	Mintage	MS63
2013	—	42.00

KM# 1350 5 DOLLARS
31.11 g., 0.999 Silver, 0.99 oz. ASW 38mm. **Rev:**
Antelope

Date	Mintage	MS63
2013	—	35.00

KM# 1382 5 DOLLARS
31.11 g., 0.999 Silver, 0.99 oz. ASW 38mm. **Subject:**
Silver Maple Leaf - 25th Anniversary **Rev:** Maple leaf and
gilt shadow of maple leaf **Rev. Designer:** Jean-Louis
Sirois

Date	Mintage		
2013	Est. 10000	PF63 100	PF65 110

KM# 1410 5 DOLLARS
31.11 g., 0.9999 Silver, 0.99 oz. ASW 38mm. **Obv.
Designer:** Arnold Machin **Rev:** Three maple leaves **Rev.
Designer:** Arnold Nogy

Date	Mintage	MS63
2013	—	45.00

KM# 1597 5 DOLLARS
31.10 g., 0.9999 Silver, 0.99 oz. ASW 38mm. **Obv.** Bust
right **Rev:** Two maple leaves, one gilt

Date	Mintage	MS63
2014	—	40.00

KM# 1601 5 DOLLARS
31.11 g., 0.9999 Silver, 0.99 oz. ASW 38mm. **Obv.** Bust right, rays in field **Rev:** Maple leaf, rays in field

Date	Mintage	MS63
2014	—	50.00

KM# 1604 5 DOLLARS
31.11 g., 0.9999 Silver, 0.99 oz. ASW 38mm. **Obv.** Bust right **Rev:** Peregrine falcon in flight left

Date	Mintage			MS63
2014 Matte fields	—			40.00
2014		PF63 45.00	PF65 50.00	

KM# 1158 10 DOLLARS
31.11 g., 0.9999 Silver, 0.99 oz. ASW 38mm. **Obv.** Bust right **Rev:** Branch with three maple leaves

Date	Mintage		
2011	—	PF63 45.00	PF65 50.00

KM# 1268 10 DOLLARS
31.11 g., 0.999 Silver, 0.99 oz. ASW 38mm. **Subject:** Maple Leaf Forever

Date	Mintage		
2012	—	PF63 40.00	PF65 50.00

KM# 1473 10 DOLLARS
15.87 g., 0.9999 Silver, 0.51 oz. ASW 34mm. **Rev:** Two maple leaves **Rev. Designer:** Piere Ledec

Date	Mintage		
2013	5,000	PF63 35.00	PF65 40.00

KM# 1062 20 DOLLARS
7.96 g., 0.9999 Silver, 0.25 oz. ASW 27mm. **Rev:** Five Maple leaves at left **Note:** Thick planchet

Date	Mintage	MS63
2011	200,000	25.00

KM# 1176 20 DOLLARS
7.96 g., 0.9999 Silver, 0.25 oz. ASW 27mm. **Obv.** Bust right **Rev:** Canoe and reflection **Rev. Designer:** Jason Bouwman **Edge:** Reeded **Note:** Thick planchet.

Date	Mintage	MS63
2011	200,000	30.00

KM# 1226 20 DOLLARS
7.96 g., 0.9999 Silver, 0.25 oz. ASW 27mm. **Obv.** Bust right **Rev:** Waterline view of polar bear swimming **Edge:** Reeded

Date	Mintage	MS63
2012	250,000	25.00

SILVER BULLION COINAGE

KM# 1237   20 DOLLARS
7.96 g.,   0.9999 Silver, 0.25 oz. ASW 27mm. **Subject:**
Commemorating the end of the Canadian Cent **Obv.** Bust
right **Rev:** Maple leaves floating on water

Date	Mintage	MS63
2012	—	20.00

KM# 1337   20 DOLLARS
7.96 g., 0.999 Silver, 0.25 oz. ASW 27mm. **Rev:** Reindeer

Date	Mintage	MS63
2012	—	27.50

KM# 1554   20 DOLLARS
7.96 g., 0.999 Silver, 0.25 oz. ASW 27mm. **Rev:** Santa
Rev. Designer: Jesse Koreck

Date	Mintage	MS63
2013	225,000	20.00

KM# 1365   20 DOLLARS
7.96 g., 0.999 Silver, 0.25 oz. ASW 27mm. **Subject:** Year
of the Snake **Rev:** Snake in Tree

Date	Mintage		
2013	Est. 128888	PF63 25.00	PF65 30.00

KM# 1511   20 DOLLARS
7.96 g., 0.999 Silver, 0.25 oz. ASW 27mm. **Rev:** Wolf
Rev. Designer: Glen Loates

Date	Mintage	MS63
2013	250,000	25.00

KM# 1512   20 DOLLARS
7.70 g., 0.9999 Silver, 0.25 oz. ASW 27mm. **Rev:** Iceberg
and whale **Rev. Designer:** Emily Damstra

Date	Mintage	MS63
2013	225,000	25.00

KM# 1561   20 DOLLARS
7.96 g., 0.999 Silver, 0.25 oz. ASW **Rev:** Goose in flight
right **Rev. Designer:** Trevor Tennant

Date	Mintage	MS63
2014	225,000	20.00

KM# 1562   20 DOLLARS
7.96 g., 0.999 Silver, 0.25 oz. ASW 27mm. **Rev:** Bobcat

Date	Mintage	MS63
2014	225,000	20.00

KM# 1563   20 DOLLARS
7.96 g.,   0.999 Silver, 0.25 oz. ASW 27mm. **Rev:**
Summertime

Date	Mintage	MS63
2014	225,000	20.00

KM# 1564   20 DOLLARS
7.96 g., 0.999 Silver, 0.25 oz. ASW 27mm. **Rev:** Holiday
Candles

Date	Mintage	MS63
2014	225,000	20.00

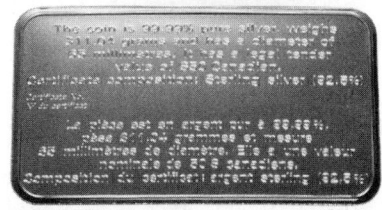

KM# 326   50 DOLLARS
311.04 g.,   0.9999 Silver, 9.93 oz. ASW **Subject:** 10th
Anniversary Silver Maple Leaf **Obv.**   Crowned head
right **Rev:** Maple leaf flanked by 9999 **Edge:** 10th
ANNIVERSARY 10e ANNIVERSAIRE

Date	Mintage		
1998	—	PF60 350	

KM# 1509   50 DOLLARS
157.60 g., 0.9999 Silver, 5.03 oz. ASW 65mm. **Subject:**
Maple Leaf Bullion, 25th Anniversary **Rev:** Three maple
leaves **Rev. Designer:** Arnold Nogy

Date	Mintage		
2013	2,500	PF65 500	

KM# 1624   50 DOLLARS
157.60 g., 0.999 Silver, 5.03 oz. ASW 65.25mm. **Obv.**
Bust right **Rev:** Three maple leaves **Rev. Designer:** Luc
Normandin

Date	Mintage		
2014	2,500	PF65 520	

KM# 1555   100 DOLLARS
31.60 g., 0.9999 Silver, 1.01 oz. ASW 40mm. **Rev:** Bear
eating salmon in river **Rev. Designer:** Claudio D'Angelo

Date	Mintage	MS63
2014	50,000	100

KM# 1620   100 DOLLARS
31.60 g., 0.999 Silver, 1.01 oz. ASW 40mm. **Obv.** Bust
right **Rev:** Eagle in flight **Rev. Designer:** Claudio D'Angelo

Date	Mintage		
2014 Matte Proof	50,000	PF63 115	

KM# 1621   100 DOLLARS
31.60 g.,   0.999 Silver, 1.01 oz. ASW 40mm.   **Obv.**
Bust right **Rev:** Two big horn sheep butting heads   **Rev.**
Designer: Claudio D'Angelo

Date	Mintage	
2014 Matte Proof	50,000	**PF63** 115

KM# 676   250 DOLLARS
1000.00 g.,   0.9999 Silver, 31.94 oz. ASW **Subject:** Kilo

Date	Mintage	MS63
2006	—	1,350

KM# 1160   250 DOLLARS
1000.00 g.,   0.9999 Silver, 31.94 oz. ASW 101mm.   **Obv.**
Bust right **Obv. Designer:** Susana Blunt **Rev:** Three maple
leaves on branch **Rev. Designer:** Debbie Adams

Date	Mintage	
2011	999	**PF65** 2,000

KM# 1272   250 DOLLARS
1000.00 g.,   0.999 Silver, 31.91 oz. ASW 101mm.
Subject: Maple Leaf Forever

Date	Mintage	
2012	—	**PF65** 1,450

KM# 1472   250 DOLLARS
1000.00 g., 0.999 Silver, 31.91 oz. ASW 102.1mm.   **Rev:**
Two maple leaves, gilt **Rev. Designer:** Emily Damstra

Date	Mintage	
2013	600	**PF65** 2,300

KM# 1245   500 DOLLARS
5000.00 g.,   0.9999 Silver, 159.70 oz. ASW 101mm.
Subject: Haida sculpture

Date	Mintage	
2012	100	**PF65** 7,500

GOLD BULLION COINAGE

KM# 542   50 CENTS
1.27 g.,   0.999 Gold, 0.04 oz. AGW 13.92mm.   **Rev:**
Voyagers with northern lights above   **Rev. Designer:**
Emanuel Hahn

Date	Mintage	
2005	—	**PF65** 100

KM# 717   50 CENTS
1.24 g.,   0.999 Gold, 0.04 oz. AGW 13.9mm.   **Rev:** Wolf

Date	Mintage		
2006	—	**PF63** 90.00	**PF65** 100

KM# 926   50 CENTS
1.24 g., 0.999 Gold, 0.04 oz. AGW 13.9mm. **Rev:** Cowboy
and bronco rider

Date	Mintage		
2006	—	**PF63** 90.00	**PF65** 100

SILVER BULLION COINAGE

KM# 927 50 CENTS
1.24 g., 0.999 Gold, 0.04 oz. AGW 13.9mm. **Subject:**
Gold Louis

Date	Mintage		
2007	—	PF63 90.00	PF65 100

KM# 777 50 CENTS
1.24 g., 0.999 Gold, 0.04 oz. AGW 13.9mm. **Subject:**
DeHavilland beaver

Date	Mintage		
2008	20,000	PF63 90.00	PF65 100

KM# 888 50 CENTS
1.27 g., 0.999 Gold, 0.04 oz. AGW 13.92mm. **Subject:**
Red maple **Obv.** Bust right **Obv. Designer:** Susanna Blunt
Rev: Two maple leaves **Obv. Legend:** Elizabeth II 50 cents
Rev. Legend: Canada, Fine gold 1/25 oz or PUR 9999

Date	Mintage		
2009	150,000	PF63 75.00	PF65 90.00

KM# 985 50 CENTS
1.24 g., 0.999 Gold, 0.04 oz. AGW 13.92mm. **Subject:**
RCMP **Obv.** Bust right **Rev:** Mountie on horseback **Rev.**
Designer: Janet Griffin-Scott

Date	Mintage		
2010	Est. 14000	PF63 90.00	PF65 100

KM# 1085 50 CENTS
1.27 g., 0.999 Gold, 0.04 oz. AGW 13.92mm. **Rev:** Geese
in flight left **Rev. Designer:** Emily Damstra

Date	Mintage		
2011	10,000	PF63 80.00	PF65 90.00

KM# 1214 50 CENTS
1.27 g., 1.000 Gold, 0.04 oz. AGW 13.92mm. **Obv.** Bust
right **Rev:** Three maple leaves, 2007-2012 above

Date	Mintage		
2012	—	PF63 80.00	PF65 90.00

KM# 1218 50 CENTS
1.27 g., 0.9999 Gold, 0.04 oz. AGW 13.92mm. **Obv.** Bust
right **Rev:** Schooner sailing left

Date	Mintage	
2012	—	PF65 90.00

KM# 1348 50 CENTS
1.27 g., 0.9999 Gold, 0.04 oz. AGW 13.92mm. **Rev:** Bald
eagle head left **Rev. Designer:** Trevor Tennant

Date	Mintage		
2013	10,000	PF63 120	PF65 130

KM# 1349 50 CENTS
1.27 g., 0.9999 Gold, 0.04 oz. AGW 13.92mm. **Subject:**
Inuit Art by Joanassie Nowkawalk

Date	Mintage		
2013	10,000	PF63 120	PF65 130

KM# 238 DOLLAR
1.56 g., 0.9999 Gold, 0.05 oz. AGW **Obv.** Crowned
head right, denomination and date below **Rev:** Maple leaf
flanked by 9999

Date	Mintage	MS63
1993	37,080	BV+25%

Date	Mintage	MS63
1994	78,860	BV+25%
1995	85,920	BV+25%
1996	56,520	BV+25%
1997	59,720	BV+25%
1998	44,260	BV+25%
1999 oval "20 YEARS ANS" privy mark	—	BV+30%
2000 oval "2000" privy mark	—	BV+30%
2001	—	BV+30%

KM# 365 DOLLAR
1.56 g., 0.999 Gold, 0.05 oz. AGW **Obv.** Crowned head
right **Rev:** Maple leaf hologram

Date	Mintage	MS63
1999	500	115

KM# 438 DOLLAR
1.58 g., 0.999 Gold, 0.05 oz. AGW 14.1mm. **Subject:**
Holographic Maple Leaves **Obv.** Crowned head right **Rev:**
Three maple leaves multicolor hologram **Edge:** Reeded

Date	Mintage	MS63
2001	600	85.00

KM# 1416 DOLLAR
1.55 g., 0.9999 Gold, 0.05 oz. AGW 14mm. **Obv.** Bust
right **Obv. Designer:** Susanna Blunt **Rev:** Maple Leaf

Date	Mintage		
2009	—	PF63 115	PF65 125

KM# 1490 DOLLAR
1.000 Gold, AGW **Rev:** Maple leaf tilted left **Note:** Thick
planchet.

Date	Mintage	MS63
2010 Proof	—	—

KM# 1138 DOLLAR
1.56 g., 0.9999 Gold, 0.05 oz. AGW 14mm. **Obv.** Bust
right **Rev:** Maple leaf

Date	Mintage	MS63
1911-2011	—	100

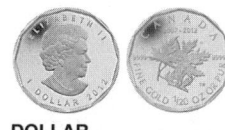

KM# 1213 DOLLAR
1.58 g., 1.000 Gold, 0.05 oz. AGW 14.1mm. **Obv.** Bust
right **Rev:** Three maple leaves, 2007-2012 above

Date	Mintage		
2012	—	PF63 100	PF65 110

KM# 1411 DOLLAR
1.55 g., 0.999 Gold, 0.05 oz. AGW **Ruler:** Elizabeth II
Obv. Designer: Susanna Blunt **Rev:** Two maple leaves
Rev. Designer: Claudio D'Angelo **Mint:** Royal Canadian
Mint

Date	Mintage		
2013	—	PF63 115	PF65 125

KM# 1506   DOLLAR
1.58 g., 0.9999 Gold, 0.05 oz. AGW 14.1mm. **Rev:** Two maple leaves **Rev. Designer:** Claudio d'Angelo

Date	Mintage		
2013 Reverse proof	—	PF65	150

KM# 256   2 DOLLARS
2.07 g., 0.9999 Gold, 0.07 oz. AGW **Obv.** Crowned head right, denomination and date below **Rev:** Maple leaf flanked by 9999

Date	Mintage	MS63
1994	5,493	140

KM# 135   5 DOLLARS
3.12 g., 0.9999 Gold, 0.10 oz. AGW **Obv.** Young bust right, date and denomination below **Obv. Designer:** Arnold Machin **Rev:** Maple leaf flanked by 9999

Date	Mintage		MS63
1982	246,000		BV+14%
1983	304,000		BV+14%
1984	262,000		BV+14%
1985	398,000		BV+14%
1986	529,516		BV+14%
1987	459,000		BV+14%
1988	506,500		BV+14%
1989	16,992	PF60 200	
1989	539,000		BV+14%

KM# 188   5 DOLLARS
3.12 g., 0.9999 Gold, 0.10 oz. AGW **Obv.** Elizabeth II effigy **Obv. Designer:** Dora dePedery-Hunt **Rev:** Maple leaf

Date	Mintage	MS63
1990	476,000	BV+14%
1991	322,000	BV+14%
1992	384,000	BV+14%
1993	248,630	BV+14%
1994	313,150	BV+14%
1995	294,890	BV+14%
1996	179,220	BV+14%
1997	188,540	BV+14%
1998	301,940	BV+14%
1999 oval "20 Years ANS" privy mark	—	BV+19%
2000 oval "2000" privy mark	—	BV+19%
2001	—	BV+14%

KM# 366   5 DOLLARS
3.12 g., 0.9999 Gold, 0.10 oz. AGW **Rev:** Maple leaf hologram

Date	Mintage	MS63
1999	500	210

KM# 439   5 DOLLARS
3.13 g., 0.9999 Gold, 0.10 oz. AGW 16mm. **Subject:** Holographic Maple Leaves **Obv.** Crowned head right **Rev:** Three maple leaves multicolor hologram **Edge:** Reeded

Date	Mintage	MS63
2001	600	200

KM# 929   5 DOLLARS
3.13 g., 0.999 Gold, 0.10 oz. AGW 16mm. **Obv. Designer:** Susan Blunt **Rev:** Maple leaf **Rev. Designer:** Walter Ott

Date	Mintage		
2007	—	PF65	200
2008	—	PF65	200
2009	—	PF65	200

Date	Mintage		
2010	—	PF65	200
2011	—	PF65	200

KM# 1139   5 DOLLARS
3.13 g., 0.999 Gold, 0.10 oz. AGW 16mm. **Obv.** Bust right **Rev:** Maple leaf

Date	Mintage	MS63
1911-2011	—	225

KM# 1212   5 DOLLARS
3.13 g., 1.000 Gold, 0.10 oz. AGW 16mm. **Obv.** Bust right **Rev:** Three maple leaves, 2007-2012 above

Date	Mintage		
2012	—	PF65	200

KM# 1267   5 DOLLARS
3.13 g., 0.999 Gold, 0.10 oz. AGW 16mm. **Subject:** Maple Leaf Forever

Date	Mintage		
2012	—	PF65	200

KM# 1412   5 DOLLARS
3.11 g., 0.9999 Gold, 0.10 oz. AGW **Obv. Designer:** Susanna Blunt **Rev:** Two maple leaves **Rev. Designer:** Claudia D'Angelo

Date	Mintage		
2013	—	PF65	250

KM# 1505   5 DOLLARS
3.13 g., 0.9999 Gold, 0.10 oz. AGW 16mm. **Rev:** Two maple leaves **Rev. Designer:** Claudio d'Angelo

Date	Mintage		
2013 Reverse Proof	—	PF65	225

KM# 1598   5 DOLLARS
3.11 g., 0.9999 Gold, 0.10 oz. AGW 16mm. **Obv.** Bust right **Rev:** Three maple leaves

Date	Mintage		
2014	—	PF65	200

KM# 136   10 DOLLARS
7.79 g., 0.9999 Gold, 0.25 oz. AGW **Obv.** Young bust right, date and denomination below **Obv. Designer:** Arnold Machin **Rev:** Maple leaf flanked by 9999

Date	Mintage	MS63
1982	184,000	BV+10%
1983	308,800	BV+10%
1984	242,400	BV+10%
1985	620,000	BV+10%
1986	915,200	BV+10%
1987	376,000	BV+10%

Date	Mintage	MS63
1988	436,000	BV+10%
1989	— PF60 500	
1989	328,800	BV+10%

KM# 189 10 DOLLARS
7.79 g., 0.9999 Gold, 0.25 oz. AGW **Obv.** Crowned head right, date and denomination below **Obv. Designer:** Dora dePedery-Hunt **Rev:** Maple leaf flanked by 9999

Date	Mintage	MS63
1990	253,600	BV+10%
1991	166,400	BV+10%
1992	179,600	BV+10%
1993	158,452	BV+10%
1994	148,792	BV+10%
1995	127,596	BV+10%
1996	89,148	BV+10%
1997	98,104	BV+10%
1998	85,472	BV+10%
1999 oval "20 Years ANS" privy mark	—	BV+15%
2000 oval "2000" privy mark	—	BV+15%
2001	—	BV+15%

KM# 367 10 DOLLARS
7.79 g., 0.9999 Gold, 0.25 oz. AGW **Rev:** Maple leaf hologram

Date	Mintage	MS63
1999	—	485

KM# 440 10 DOLLARS
7.80 g., 0.9999 Gold, 0.25 oz. AGW 20mm. **Subject:** Holographic Maples Leaves **Obv.** Crowned head right **Rev:** Three maple leaves multicolor hologram **Edge:** Reeded

Date	Mintage	MS63
2001	15,000	475

KM# 1140 10 DOLLARS
7.80 g., 0.9999 Gold, 0.25 oz. AGW 20mm. **Obv.** Bust right **Rev:** Maple leaf

Date	Mintage	MS63
1911-2011	—	485

KM# 1312 10 DOLLARS
6.22 g., 0.999 Gold, 0.20 oz. AGW **Obv.** Bust right **Rev:** Maple leaf **Note:** Piedfort

Date	Mintage	MS63
2011	—	400

KM# 1211 10 DOLLARS
7.80 g., 1.000 Gold, 0.25 oz. AGW 20mm. **Obv.** Bust right **Rev:** Three maple leaves, 2007-2012 above

Date	Mintage	
2012	—	PF65 475

KM# 1275 10 DOLLARS
7.77 g., 0.9999 Gold, 0.25 oz. AGW 20mm. **Subject:** War of 1812

Date	Mintage	
2012	—	PF65 500

KM# 1413 10 DOLLARS
7.77 g., 0.9999 Gold, 0.25 oz. AGW **Obv. Designer:** Susanna Blunt **Rev:** Two maple leaves **Rev. Designer:** Claudio D'Angelo

Date	Mintage	
2013	—	PF65 500

KM# 1504 10 DOLLARS
7.77 g., 0.999 Gold, 0.25 oz. AGW 20mm. **Rev:** Two maple leaves **Rev. Designer:** Claudio d'Angelo

Date	Mintage	
2013 Reverse proof	600	PF65 400

KM# 1599 10 DOLLARS
7.77 g., 0.9999 Gold, 0.25 oz. AGW 20mm. **Obv.** Bust right **Rev:** Three maple leaves

Date	Mintage	
2014	—	PF65 475

KM# 153 20 DOLLARS
15.55 g., 0.9999 Gold, 0.50 oz. AGW 32mm. **Obv.** Young bust right, date and denomination below **Obv. Designer:** Arnold Machin **Rev:** Maple leaf flanked by 9999

Date	Mintage	MS63
1986	529,200	BV+7%
1987	332,800	BV+7%
1988	538,400	BV+7%
1989	— PF60 935	
1989	259,200	BV+7%

KM# 190 20 DOLLARS
15.55 g., 0.9999 Gold, 0.50 oz. AGW **Obv.** Crowned head right, date and denomination below **Obv. Designer:** Dora dePedery-Hunt **Rev:** Maple leaf flanked by 9999

Date	Mintage	MS63
1990	174,400	BV+7%
1991	96,200	BV+7%
1992	108,000	BV+7%

Date	Mintage	MS63
1993	99,492	BV+7%
1994	104,766	BV+7%
1995	103,162	BV+7%
1996	66,246	BV+7%
1997	63,354	BV+7%
1998	65,366	BV+7%
1999 oval "20 Years ANS" privy mark	—	BV+12%
2000 oval "2000" privy mark	—	BV+12%
2001	—	BV+12%

KM# 368 20 DOLLARS
15.55 g., 0.9999 Gold, 0.50 oz. AGW **Rev:** Maple leaf hologram

Date	Mintage	MS63
1999	500	935

KM# 441 20 DOLLARS
15.58 g., 0.9999 Gold, 0.50 oz. AGW 25mm. **Subject:** Holographic Maples Leaves **Obv.** Crowned head right **Rev:** Three maple leaves multicolor hologram **Edge:** Reeded

Date	Mintage	MS63
2001	600	925

KM# 125.1 50 DOLLARS
31.10 g., 0.999 Gold, 0.99 oz. AGW **Obv.** Young bust right, denomination and date below **Rev:** Maple leaf flanked by .999

Date	Mintage	MS63
1979	1,000,000	BV+4%
1980	1,251,500	BV+4%
1981	863,000	BV+4%
1982	883,000	BV+4%

KM# 125.2 50 DOLLARS
31.10 g., 0.9999 Gold, 0.99 oz. AGW **Obv.** Young bust right, date and denomination below **Rev:** Maple leaf flanked by .9999

Date	Mintage	MS63
1983	843,000	BV+4%
1984	1,067,500	BV+4%
1985	1,908,000	BV+4%
1986	779,115	BV+4%
1987	978,000	BV+4%
1988	826,500	BV+4%
1989	17,781	PF60 1,900
1989	856,000	BV+4%

KM# 191 50 DOLLARS
31.10 g., 0.9999 Gold, 0.99 oz. AGW **Obv.** Crowned head right, date and denomination below **Obv. Designer:** Dora dePedery-Hunt **Rev:** Maple leaf flanked by .9999

Date	Mintage	MS63
1990	815,000	BV+4%
1991	290,000	BV+4%
1992	368,900	BV+4%
1993	321,413	BV+4%
1994	180,357	BV+4%
1995	208,729	BV+4%
1996	143,682	BV+4%
1997	478,211	BV+4%
1998	593,704	BV+4%
1999 oval "20 Years ANS" privy mark	—	BV+7%
2000 oval "2000" privy mark	—	BV+7%
2000 oval fireworks privy mark	—	BV+7%
2001	—	BV+7%

KM# 305 50 DOLLARS
31.10 g., 0.9999 Gold, 0.99 oz. AGW **Obv.** Crowned head denomination below, within circle, dates below **Rev:** Mountie at gallop right, within circle **Rev. Designer:** Ago Aarand **Shape:** 10-sided

Date	Mintage	MS63
1997	12,913	1,850

KM# 369 50 DOLLARS
31.10 g., 0.9999 Gold, 0.99 oz. AGW **Obv.** Crowned head right, date and denomination below **Rev:** Maple leaf hologram flanked by 9999, with fireworks privy mark

Date	Mintage	MS63
2000 (1999)	500	1,850

KM# 442 50 DOLLARS
31.15 g., 0.9999 Gold, 0.99 oz. AGW 30mm. **Subject:** Holographic Maples Leaves **Obv.** Crowned head right **Rev:** Three maple leaves multicolor hologram **Edge:** Reeded

Date	Mintage	MS63
2001	600	1,850

KM# 1042 50 DOLLARS
31.11 g., 0.999 Gold, 0.99 oz. AGW 30mm. **Rev:** Vancouver logo and maple leaf **Edge:** Reeded

Date	Mintage	MS63
2008P	—	1,850

KM# 1042a 50 DOLLARS
31.11 g., 0.9999 Gold, 0.99 oz. AGW 30mm. **Rev:** Maple leaf in red enamel, olympic logo at left

Date	Mintage	MS63
2008	—	1,850

KM# 1037 50 DOLLARS
31.11 g., 0.9999 Gold, 0.99 oz. AGW 30mm. **Rev:** Thunderbird **Edge:** Reeded

Date	Mintage	MS63
2009	—	1,850

KM# 1037a 50 DOLLARS
31.11 g., 0.9999 Gold, 0.99 oz. AGW 30mm. **Rev:** Thunderbird, stars in red enamel highlights

Date	Mintage	MS63
2009	—	1,850

KM# 1029 50 DOLLARS
31.11 g., 0.9999 Gold, 0.99 oz. AGW 30mm. **Rev:** Hockey player flanked by maple leaves

Date	Mintage	MS63
2010	—	1,850

KM# 1029a 50 DOLLARS
31.11 g., 0.9999 Gold, 0.99 oz. AGW 30mm. **Rev:** Hockey player, red enameled maple leaves flanking

Date	Mintage	MS63
2010	—	1,850

KM# 1141 50 DOLLARS
31.11 g., 0.9999 Gold, 0.99 oz. AGW 30mm. **Obv.** Bust right **Rev:** Maple leaf

Date	Mintage	MS63
1911-2011	—	1,850

KM# 1210 50 DOLLARS
31.11 g., 1.000 Gold, 0.99 oz. AGW 30mm. **Obv.** Bust right **Rev:** Three maple leaves, 2007-2012 above

Date	Mintage		MS63
2012	—	PF65 1,850	

KM# 1414 50 DOLLARS
31.10 g., 0.9999 Gold, 0.99 oz. AGW 30mm. **Obv. Designer:** Susanna Blunt **Rev:** Two Maple Leaves **Rev. Designer:** Claudio D'Angelo

Date	Mintage	MS63
2013	—	1,800

KM# 1488   50 DOLLARS
31.11 g., 0.9999 Gold, 0.99 oz. AGW 30mm. **Rev:** Maple Leaf, security feature added

Date	Mintage		MS63
2013	—		BV+3%
2014	—		BV+3%

KM# 1503   50 DOLLARS
31.11 g., 0.9999 Gold, 0.99 oz. AGW 30mm. **Rev:** Two maple leaves **Rev. Designer:** Claudio d'Angelo

Date	Mintage		
2013 Reverse Proof	600	PF65	1,800

KM# 1600   50 DOLLARS
31.11 g., 0.9999 Gold, 0.99 oz. AGW 30mm. **Obv.** Bust right **Rev:** Three maple leaves

Date	Mintage		
2014	—	PF65	1,500

KM# 750   200 DOLLARS
31.11 g., 1.000 Gold, 0.99 oz. AGW 30mm. **Rev:** Three maple leaves

Date	Mintage		
2007 Proof, T/E privy mark	500	PF65	1,850

KM# 786   200 DOLLARS
31.11 g., 1.000 Gold, 0.99 oz. AGW 30mm. **Obv.** Bust right on lathe-work background **Rev:** Two maple leaves on lathe-work background

Date	Mintage		
2008	—	PF65	1,850

KM# 1162   200 DOLLARS
31.11 g., 1.000 Gold, 0.99 oz. AGW **Rev:** Maple leaf with lathe backgound

Date	Mintage		
2009	—	PF65	1,850

KM# 1163   200 DOLLARS
31.11 g., 0.999 Gold, 0.99 oz. AGW **Subject:** Celebrating win **Rev:** Three athletics with hands raised

Date	Mintage		
2010	—	PF65	1,850

KM# 1165   200 DOLLARS
31.11 g., 1.000 Gold, 0.99 oz. AGW 30mm. **Obv. Designer:** Susanna Blunt **Rev:** Mountie on horseback, lathe backgound **Rev. Designer:** Ago Aarand

Date	Mintage		MS63
2011	—		1,850

KM# 1487   200 DOLLARS
31.11 g., 0.9999 Gold, 0.99 oz. AGW 30mm. **Rev:** Three maple leaves, engine turned background

Date	Mintage		
2012	—	PF65	1,800

KM# 1328   500 DOLLARS
155.55 g., 0.9999 Gold, 4.97 oz. AGW 55mm. **Rev:** Three Maple Leaves

Date	Mintage		
2012	—	PF65	10,000

KM# 1161   2500 DOLLARS
1000.00 g., 0.9999 Gold, 31.94 oz. AGW 101mm. **Rev:** Three maple leaves on branch

Date	Mintage		
2011	—	PF65	56,000

GOLD BULLION COINAGE

KM# 1271 2500 DOLLARS
1000.00 g., 0.999 Gold, 31.91 oz. AGW 101mm. **Subject:** Maple Leaf Forever

Date	Mintage	
2012	—	PF65 56,000

KM# 1486 2500 DOLLARS
1000.00 g., 0.9999 Gold, 31.94 oz. AGW 101mm. **Rev:** Three maple leaves

Date	Mintage	
2012	—	PF65 69,000

KM# 755 1000000 DOLLARS
100000.00 g., 0.9999 Gold, 3194.06 oz. AGW **Obv.** Bust right **Rev:** Three maple leaves **Note:** Cast

Date	Mintage	MS63
2007	10	5,630,000

PLATINUM BULLION COINAGE

KM# 239 DOLLAR
1.56 g., 0.9995 Platinum, 0.05 oz. APW **Obv.** Crowned head right, date and denomination below **Rev:** Maple leaf flanked by 9995

Date	Mintage	MS63
1993	2,120	BV+30%
1994	4,260	BV+30%
1995	460	150
1996	1,640	BV+30%
1997	1,340	BV+30%
1998	2,000	BV+30%
1999	2,000	BV+30%

KM# 257 2 DOLLARS
2.07 g., 0.9995 Platinum, 0.07 oz. APW **Obv.** Crowned head right, date and denomination below **Rev:** Maple leaf flanked by 9995

Date	Mintage	MS63
1994	1,470	240

KM# 164 5 DOLLARS
3.12 g., 0.9995 Platinum, 0.10 oz. APW **Obv.** Young bust right, date and denomination below **Obv. Designer:** Arnold Machin **Rev:** Maple leaf flanked by 9995

Date	Mintage		MS63
1988	74,000		BV+18%
1989	11,999	PF60 250	
1989	18,000		BV+18%

KM# 1209 100000 DOLLARS
10000.00 g., 1.000 Gold, 319.43 oz. AGW **Obv.** Bust right **Rev:** Bill Reid's sculpture: Spirit of Haida Gwaii **Note:** The sculpture is at the Canadian Embassy in Washington, D.C.

Date	Mintage	
2011	—	PF65 565,000

KM# 192 5 DOLLARS
3.12 g., 0.9995 Platinum, 0.10 oz. APW **Obv. Designer:** dePedery-Hunt **Rev:** Maple leaf

Date	Mintage	MS63
1990	9,000	BV+18%
1991	13,000	BV+18%
1992	16,000	BV+18%
1993	14,020	BV+18%
1994	19,190	BV+18%
1995	8,940	BV+18%
1996	8,820	BV+18%
1997	7,050	BV+18%
1998	5,710	BV+18%
1999	2,000	BV+18%

KM# 165 10 DOLLARS
7.79 g., 0.9995 Platinum, 0.25 oz. APW **Obv.** Young bust right, date and denomination below **Obv. Designer:** Machin **Rev:** Maple leaf flanked by 9995

Date	Mintage		MS63
1988	93,600		BV+13%
1989	1,999	PF60 550	
1989	3,200		BV+13%

KM# 193 10 DOLLARS
7.79 g., 0.9995 Platinum, 0.25 oz. APW **Obv. Designer:** dePedery-Hunt **Rev:** Maple leaf

Date	Mintage	MS63
1990	1,600	BV+13%
1991	7,200	BV+13%
1992	11,600	BV+13%
1993	8,048	BV+13%
1994	9,456	BV+13%
1995	6,524	BV+13%
1996	6,160	BV+13%
1997	4,552	BV+13%
1998	3,816	BV+13%
1999	2,000	BV+13%

KM# 166 20 DOLLARS
15.55 g., 0.9995 Platinum, 0.50 oz. APW **Obv.** Young bust right, denomination and date below **Obv. Designer:** Machin **Rev:** Maple leaf flanked by 9995

Date	Mintage		MS63
1988	23,600		BV+9%
1989	1,999	PF60 1,000	
1989	4,800		BV+9%

KM# 194 20 DOLLARS
15.55 g., 0.9995 Platinum, 0.50 oz. APW **Obv. Designer:** dePedery-Hunt **Rev:** Maple leaf

Date	Mintage	MS63
1990	2,600	BV+9%
1991	5,600	BV+9%
1992	12,800	BV+9%
1993	6,022	BV+9%
1994	6,710	BV+9%
1995	6,308	BV+9%
1996	5,490	BV+9%
1997	3,990	BV+9%

Date	Mintage	MS63
1998	5,486	BV+9%
1999	500	BV+15%

KM# 174 30 DOLLARS
3.11 g., 0.999 Platinum, 0.10 oz. APW **Obv.** Crowned head right **Rev:** Polar bear swimming, denomination below **Rev. Designer:** Robert Bateman

Date	Mintage	
1990	2,629	PF60 210

KM# 198 30 DOLLARS
3.11 g., 0.999 Platinum, 0.10 oz. APW **Obv.** Crowned head right **Rev:** Snowy owl, denomination below **Rev. Designer:** Glen Loates

Date	Mintage	
1991	3,500	PF60 210

KM# 226 30 DOLLARS
3.11 g., 0.999 Platinum, 0.10 oz. APW **Obv.** Crowned head right **Rev:** Cougar head and shoulders, denomination below **Rev. Designer:** George McLean

Date	Mintage	
1992	3,500	PF60 210

KM# 240 30 DOLLARS
3.11 g., 0.999 Platinum, 0.10 oz. APW **Obv.** Crowned head right **Rev:** Arctic fox, denomination below **Rev. Designer:** Claude D'Angelo

Date	Mintage	
1993	3,500	PF60 210

KM# 252 30 DOLLARS
3.11 g., 0.999 Platinum, 0.10 oz. APW **Obv.** Crowned head right, date below **Rev:** Sea otter, denomination below **Rev. Designer:** Ron S. Parker

Date	Mintage	
1994	1,500	PF60 210

KM# 266 30 DOLLARS
3.11 g., 0.999 Platinum, 0.10 oz. APW **Obv.** Crowned head right, date below **Rev:** Canadian lynx, denomination below **Rev. Designer:** Michael Dumas

Date	Mintage	
1995	620	PF60 210

KM# 278 30 DOLLARS
3.11 g., 0.999 Platinum, 0.10 oz. APW **Obv.** Crowned head right, date below **Rev:** Falcon portrait, denomination below **Rev. Designer:** Dwayne Harty

Date	Mintage	
1996	489	PF60 210

KM# 300 30 DOLLARS
3.11 g., 0.9995 Platinum, 0.10 oz. APW **Obv.** Crowned head right, date below **Rev:** Bison head, denomination below **Rev. Designer:** Chris Bacon

Date	Mintage	
1997	5,000	PF60 210

KM# 322 30 DOLLARS
3.11 g., 0.999 Platinum, 0.10 oz. APW **Obv.** Crowned head right, date below **Rev:** Grey wolf **Rev. Designer:** Kerr Burnett

Date	Mintage	
1998	2,000	PF60 210

KM# 359 30 DOLLARS
3.11 g., 0.9995 Platinum, 0.10 oz. APW **Obv.** Crowned head right, date below **Rev:** Musk ox **Rev. Designer:** Mark Hobson

Date	Mintage	
1999	1,500	PF60 210

KM# 405 30 DOLLARS
3.11 g., 0.9995 Platinum, 0.10 oz. APW 16mm. **Obv.** Crowned head right, date below **Rev:** Pronghorn antelope head, denomination below **Rev. Designer:** Mark Hobson **Edge:** Reeded

Date	Mintage	
2000	600	PF60 210

KM# 429 30 DOLLARS
3.11 g., 0.9995 Platinum, 0.10 oz. APW 16mm. **Obv.** Crowned head right **Rev:** Harlequin duck's head **Rev. Designer:** Cosme Saffioti and Susan Taylor **Edge:** Reeded

Date	Mintage	
2001	448	PF65 200

KM# 1097 30 DOLLARS
3.11 g., 0.9995 Platinum, 0.10 oz. APW 16mm. **Rev:** Great Blue Heron

Date	Mintage	
2002	344	PF65 200

KM# 1101 30 DOLLARS
3.11 g., 0.9995 Platinum, 0.10 oz. APW 16mm. **Rev:** Atlantic Walrus

Date	Mintage	
2003	365	PF65 250

KM# 1105 30 DOLLARS
3.11 g., 0.9995 Platinum, 0.10 oz. APW 16mm. **Rev:** Grizzly Bear

Date	Mintage	
2004	380	PF65 250

KM# 167 50 DOLLARS
31.10 g., 0.9995 Platinum, 0.99 oz. APW **Obv.** Young bust right, denomination and date below **Obv. Designer:** Machin **Rev:** Maple leaf flanked by 9995

Date	Mintage		MS63
1988	37,500		BV+4%
1989	5,965	PF60 1,900	
1989	10,000		BV+4%

KM# 195 50 DOLLARS
31.10 g., 0.9995 Platinum, 0.99 oz. APW **Obv. Designer:** dePedery-Hunt **Rev:** Maple leaf

Date	Mintage	MS63
1990	15,100	BV+4%

Date	Mintage	MS63
1991	31,900	BV+4%
1992	40,500	BV+4%
1993	17,666	BV+4%
1994	36,245	BV+4%
1995	25,829	BV+4%
1996	62,273	BV+4%
1997	25,480	BV+4%
1998	10,403	BV+4%
1999	1,300	BV+10%

KM# 175 75 DOLLARS
7.78 g., 0.999 Platinum, 0.25 oz. APW **Obv.** Crowned head right **Rev:** Polar bear resting, denomination below **Rev. Designer:** Robert Bateman

Date	Mintage	
1990	2,629	PF60 520

KM# 199 75 DOLLARS
7.78 g., 0.999 Platinum, 0.25 oz. APW **Obv.** Crowned head right **Rev:** Snowy owls perched on branch, denomination below **Rev. Designer:** Glen Loates

Date	Mintage	
1991	3,500	PF60 520

KM# 227 75 DOLLARS
7.78 g., 0.999 Platinum, 0.25 oz. APW **Obv.** Crowned head right **Rev:** Cougar prowling, denomination below **Rev. Designer:** George McLean

Date	Mintage	
1992	3,500	PF60 520

KM# 241 75 DOLLARS
7.78 g., 0.999 Platinum, 0.25 oz. APW **Obv.** Crowned head right **Rev:** Two Arctic foxes, denomination below **Rev. Designer:** Claude D'Angelo

Date	Mintage	
1993	3,500	PF60 520

KM# 253 75 DOLLARS
7.78 g., 0.999 Platinum, 0.25 oz. APW **Obv.** Crowned head right, date below **Rev:** Sea otter eating urchin, denomination below **Rev. Designer:** Ron S. Parker

Date	Mintage	
1994	1,500	PF60 520

KM# 267 75 DOLLARS
7.78 g., 0.999 Platinum, 0.25 oz. APW **Obv.** Crowned head right, date below **Rev:** Two lynx kittens, denomination below **Rev. Designer:** Michael Dumas

Date	Mintage	
1995	1,500	PF60 520

PLATINUM BULLION COINAGE

KM# 279   75 DOLLARS
7.78 g., 0.999 Platinum, 0.25 oz. APW **Obv.** Crowned head right, date below **Rev:** Peregrine falcon, denomination below **Rev. Designer:** Dwayne Harty

Date	Mintage		
1996	1,500	PF60	520

KM# 301   75 DOLLARS
7.78 g., 0.999 Platinum, 0.25 oz. APW **Obv.** Crowned head right, date below **Rev:** Two bison calves, denomination below **Rev. Designer:** Chris Bacon

Date	Mintage		
1997	1,500	PF60	520

KM# 323   75 DOLLARS
7.78 g., 0.999 Platinum, 0.25 oz. APW **Obv.** Crowned head right, date below **Rev:** Gray wolf **Rev. Designer:** Kerr Burnett

Date	Mintage		
1998	1,000	PF60	520

KM# 360   75 DOLLARS
7.78 g., 0.999 Platinum, 0.25 oz. APW **Obv.** Crowned head right, date below **Rev:** Musk ox **Rev. Designer:** Mark Hobson

Date	Mintage		
1999	500	PF60	520

KM# 406   75 DOLLARS
7.78 g., 0.999 Platinum, 0.25 oz. APW 20mm. **Obv.** Crowned head right **Rev:** Standing pronghorn antelope, denomination below **Rev. Designer:** Mark Hobson **Edge:** Reeded

Date	Mintage		
2000	600	PF60	520

KM# 430   75 DOLLARS
7.78 g., 0.9995 Platinum, 0.25 oz. APW 20mm. **Obv.** Crowned head right **Rev:** Harlequin duck in flight **Rev. Designer:** Cosme Saffioti and Susan Taylor **Edge:** Reeded

Date	Mintage		
2001	448	PF65	500

KM# 1098   75 DOLLARS
7.77 g., 0.9995 Platinum, 0.25 oz. APW 20mm. **Rev:** Great Blue Heron

Date	Mintage		
2002	344	PF65	525

KM# 1102   75 DOLLARS
7.77 g., 0.9995 Platinum, 0.25 oz. APW 20mm. **Rev:** Atlantic Walrus

Date	Mintage		
2003	365	PF65	550

KM# 1106   75 DOLLARS
7.77 g., 0.9995 Platinum, 0.25 oz. APW 20mm. **Rev:** Grizzly Bear

Date	Mintage		
2004	380	PF65	550

KM# 176   150 DOLLARS
15.55 g., 0.999 Platinum, 0.50 oz. APW **Obv.** Crowned head right **Rev:** Polar bear walking, denomination below **Rev. Designer:** Robert Bateman

Date	Mintage		
1990	2,629	PF60	1,000

KM# 200   150 DOLLARS
15.55 g., 0.999 Platinum, 0.50 oz. APW **Obv.** Crowned head right **Rev:** Snowy owl flying, denomination below **Rev. Designer:** Glen Loates

Date	Mintage		
1991	3,500	PF60	1,000

KM# 228   150 DOLLARS
15.55 g., 0.999 Platinum, 0.50 oz. APW **Obv.** Crowned head right **Rev:** Cougar mother and cub, denomination below **Rev. Designer:** George McLean

Date	Mintage		
1992	3,500	PF60	1,000

KM# 242   150 DOLLARS
15.55 g., 0.999 Platinum, 0.50 oz. APW **Obv.** Crowned head right **Rev:** Arctic fox by lake, denomination below **Rev. Designer:** Claude D'Angelo

Date	Mintage		
1993	3,500	PF60	1,000

KM# 254   150 DOLLARS
15.55 g., 0.999 Platinum, 0.50 oz. APW **Obv.** Crowned head right, date below **Rev:** Sea otter mother carrying pup, denomination below **Rev. Designer:** Ron S. Parker

Date	Mintage		
1994	1,500	PF60	1,000

KM# 268   150 DOLLARS
15.55 g., 0.999 Platinum, 0.50 oz. APW **Obv.** Crowned head right, date below **Rev:** Prowling lynx, denomination below **Rev. Designer:** Michael Dumas

Date	Mintage		
1995	226	PF60	1,000

KM# 280   150 DOLLARS
15.55 g., 0.999 Platinum, 0.50 oz. APW **Obv.** Crowned head right, date below **Rev:** Peregrine falcon on branch, denomination below **Rev. Designer:** Dwayne Harty

Date	Mintage		
1996	100	PF60	1,000

KM# 302   150 DOLLARS
15.55 g., 0.999 Platinum, 0.50 oz. APW **Obv.** Crowned head right, date below **Rev:** Bison bull, denomination below **Rev. Designer:** Chris Bacon

Date	Mintage		
1997	4,000	PF60	1,000

KM# 324   150 DOLLARS
15.55 g., 0.999 Platinum, 0.50 oz. APW **Obv.** Crowned head right, date below **Rev:** Two gray wolf cubs, denomination below **Rev. Designer:** Kerr Burnett

Date	Mintage		
1998	2,000	PF60	1,000

KM# 361   150 DOLLARS
15.55 g., 0.999 Platinum, 0.50 oz. APW **Obv.** Crowned head right **Rev:** Musk ox, denomination below **Rev. Designer:** Mark Hobson

Date	Mintage		
1999	500	PF60	1,000

KM# 407   150 DOLLARS
15.55 g., 0.999 Platinum, 0.50 oz. APW 25mm. **Obv.** Crowned head right **Rev:** Two pronghorn antelope, denomination below **Rev. Designer:** Mark Hobson **Edge:** Reeded

Date	Mintage		
2000	600	PF60	1,000

KM# 431   150 DOLLARS
15.55 g., 0.9995 Platinum, 0.50 oz. APW 25mm. **Obv.** Crowned head right **Rev:** Two harlequin ducks **Rev. Designer:** Cosme Saffioti and Susan Taylor **Edge:** Reeded

Date	Mintage		
2001	448	PF65	1,000

KM# 1099   150 DOLLARS
15.55 g., 0.9995 Platinum, 0.50 oz. APW 25mm. **Rev:** Great Blue Heron

Date	Mintage		
2002	344	PF65	1,000

KM# 1103   150 DOLLARS
15.55 g., 0.9995 Platinum, 0.50 oz. APW 25mm. **Rev:** Atlantic Walrus

Date	Mintage		
2003	365	PF65	1,000

KM# 1107   150 DOLLARS
15.55 g., 0.9995 Platinum, 0.50 oz. APW 25mm. **Rev:** Grizzly Bear

Date	Mintage		
2004	380	PF65	1,000

KM# 177   300 DOLLARS
31.10 g., 0.999 Platinum, 0.99 oz. APW **Obv.** Crowned head right **Rev:** Polar bear mother and cub, denomination below **Rev. Designer:** Robert Bateman

Date	Mintage		
1990	2,629	PF60	1,950

KM# 201   300 DOLLARS
31.10 g., 0.999 Platinum, 0.99 oz. APW **Obv.** Crowned head right **Rev:** Snowy owl with chicks, denomination below **Rev. Designer:** Glen Loates

Date	Mintage		
1991	3,500	PF60	1,950

KM# 229   300 DOLLARS
31.10 g., 0.999 Platinum, 0.99 oz. APW **Obv.** Crowned head right **Rev:** Cougar resting in tree, denomination below **Rev. Designer:** George McLean

Date	Mintage		
1992	3,500	PF60	1,950

PLATINUM BULLION COINAGE

KM# 243 300 DOLLARS
31.10 g., 0.999 Platinum, 0.99 oz. APW **Obv.** Crowned head right **Rev:** Mother fox and three kits, denomination below **Rev. Designer:** Claude D'Angelo

Date	Mintage		
1993	3,500	PF60	1,950

KM# 255 300 DOLLARS
31.10 g., 0.999 Platinum, 0.99 oz. APW **Obv.** Crowned head right, date below **Rev:** Two otters swimming, denomination below **Rev. Designer:** Ron S. Parker

Date	Mintage		
1994	1,500	PF60	1,950

KM# 269 300 DOLLARS
31.10 g., 0.999 Platinum, 0.99 oz. APW **Obv.** Crowned head right, date below **Rev:** Female lynx and three kittens, denomination below **Rev. Designer:** Michael Dumas

Date	Mintage		
1995	1,500	PF60	1,950

KM# 281 300 DOLLARS
31.10 g., 0.999 Platinum, 0.99 oz. APW **Obv.** Crowned head right, date below **Rev:** Peregrine falcon feeding nestlings, denomination below **Rev. Designer:** Dwayne Harty

Date	Mintage		
1996	1,500	PF60	1,950

KM# 303 300 DOLLARS
31.10 g., 0.999 Platinum, 0.99 oz. APW **Obv.** Crowned head right, date below **Rev:** Bison family, denomination below **Rev. Designer:** Chris Bacon

Date	Mintage		
1997	1,500	PF60	1,950

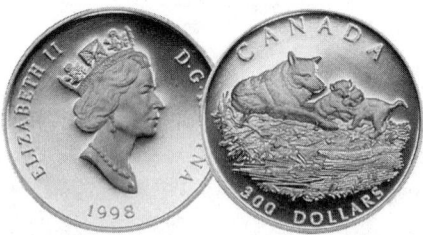

KM# 325 300 DOLLARS
31.10 g., 0.999 Platinum, 0.99 oz. APW **Obv.** Crowned head right, date below **Rev:** Gray wolf and two cubs, denomination below **Rev. Designer:** Kerr Burnett

Date	Mintage		
1998	—	PF60	1,950

KM# 362 300 DOLLARS
31.10 g., 0.999 Platinum, 0.99 oz. APW **Obv.** Crowned head right, date below **Rev:** Musk ox **Rev. Designer:** Mark Hobson

Date	Mintage		
1999	500	PF60	1,950

KM# 408 300 DOLLARS
31.10 g., 0.999 Platinum, 0.99 oz. APW 30mm. **Obv.** Crowned head right, date below **Rev:** Four pronghorn antelope, denomination below **Rev. Designer:** Mark Hobson **Edge:** Reeded

Date	Mintage		
2000	600	PF60	1,950

KM# 432 300 DOLLARS
31.10 g., 0.9995 Platinum, 0.99 oz. APW 30mm. **Obv.** Crowned head right **Rev:** Two standing harlequin ducks **Rev. Designer:** Cosme Saffioti and Susan Taylor **Edge:** Reeded

Date	Mintage	
2001	448	PF65 1,900

KM# 1100 300 DOLLARS
31.11 g., 0.9995 Platinum, 0.99 oz. APW 30mm. **Rev:** Great Blue Heron

Date	Mintage	
2002	344	PF65 1,950

KM# 1104 300 DOLLARS
31.11 g., 0.9995 Platinum, 0.99 oz. APW 30mm. **Rev:** Atlantic Walrus

Date	Mintage	
2003	365	PF65 1,950

KM# 1108 300 DOLLARS
31.11 g., 0.9995 Platinum, 0.99 oz. APW 30mm. **Rev:** Grizzly Bear

Date	Mintage	
2004	380	PF65 1,950

KM# 753 300 DOLLARS
31.11 g., 0.9999 Platinum, 0.99 oz. APW **Rev:** Wooly mammoth

Date	Mintage	
2007	400	PF65 3,200

KM# 831 300 DOLLARS
31.11 g., 0.999 Platinum, 0.99 oz. APW **Rev:** Saber Tooth Scimitar cat

Date	Mintage	
2008	200	PF65 3,500

KM# 951 300 DOLLARS
31.16 g., 0.999 Platinum, 0.99 oz. APW 30mm. **Rev:** Steppe Bison

Date	Mintage	
2009	200	PF65 3,500

KM# 1159 300 DOLLARS
31.11 g., 0.999 Platinum, 0.99 oz. APW 30mm. **Rev:** Ground Sloth

Date	Mintage	
2010	200	PF65 1,900

KM# 1175 300 DOLLARS
31.11 g., 0.9995 Platinum, 0.99 oz. APW 30mm. **Obv.** Bust right **Rev:** Cougar head left

Date	Mintage	
2011	200	PF65 1,950

KM# 1273 300 DOLLARS
31.11 g., 0.999 Platinum, 0.99 oz. APW 30mm. **Subject:** Maple Leaf Forever

Date	Mintage	
2012	—	PF65 1,950

KM# 1386 300 DOLLARS
31.11 g., 0.999 Platinum, 0.99 oz. APW 30mm. **Subject:** Maple Leaf - 25th Anniversary **Rev:** Maple Leaf - Gilt Shadow **Rev. Designer:** John Louis Sirois

Date	Mintage	
2013	Est. 250	PF65 3,000

KM# 1391 300 DOLLARS
31.11 g., 0.999 Platinum, 0.99 oz. APW 30mm. **Rev:** The Bald Eagles at Nest

Date	Mintage	
2013	—	PF65 2,250

KM# 1560 300 DOLLARS
31.16 g., 0.9995 Platinum, 0.99 oz. APW 30mm. **Rev:** Bighorn Sheep **Rev. Designer:** Emily Damstra

Date	Mintage	
2014	250	PF65 3,000

PLATINUM BULLION COINAGE

CUSTOM PROOF-LIKE SETS (CPL)

KM#	Date	Mintage	Identification	Issue Price	Mkt Val
CPL1	1971 (7)	33,517	KM59.1 (2 pcs.), 60.1, 62b, 75.1, 77.1 ,79	6.50	5.00
CPL2	1971 (6)	38,198	KM59.1 (2 pcs.), 60.1, 62b, 75.1, 77.1	6.50	5.00
CPL3	1973 (6)	35,676	KM59.1 (2 pcs.), 60.1, 75.1, 77.1, 81.1 obv. 120 beads, 82	6.50	6.50
CPL4	1973 (7)	Inc. above	KM59.1 (2 pcs.), 60.1, 75.1, 77.1, 81.1 obv. 132 beads, 82	6.50	200
CPL5	1974 (5)	44,296	KM59.1 (2 pcs.), 60.1, 62b-75.1, 88	8.00	5.00
CPL6	1975 (6)	36,851	KM59.1 (2 pcs.), 60.1, 62b-75.1, 76.2, 77.1	8.00	5.00
CPL7	1976 (6)	28,162	KM59.1 (2 pcs.), 60.1, 62b-75.1, 76.2, 77.1	8.00	5.50
CPL8	1977 (6)	44,198	KM59.1 (2 pcs.), 60.1, 62b-75.2, 77.1, 117	8.15	7.50
CPL9	1978 (6)	41,000	KM59.1 (2 pcs.), 60.1, 62b-75.3, 77.1, 120.1	—	5.00
CPL10	1979 (6)	31,174	KM59.2 (2 pcs.), 60.2, 74, 75.3, 77.2, 120.1	10.75	5.00
CPL11	1980 (7)	41,447	KM60.2, 74, 75.3, 77.2, 120.1, 127 (2 pcs.)	10.75	6.00

MINT SETS

KM#	Date	Mintage	Identification	Issue Price	Mkt Val
MS1	1973 (4)	Inc. above	KM84, 85, 86.1, 87; Olympic Commemoratives, Series I	45.00	135
MS2	1974 (4)	Inc. above	KM89, 90, 93, 94; Olympic Commemoratives, Series II	48.00	135
MS3	1974 (4)	Inc. above	KM91-92, 95-96; Olympic Commemorative, Series III	48.00	135
MS4	1975 (4)	Inc. above	KM98, 99, 102, 103; Olympic Commemoratives, Series IV	48.00	135
MS5	1975 (4)	Inc. above	KM100, 101, 104, 105; Olympic Commemoratives, Series V	60.00	135
MS6	1976 (4)	Inc. above	KM107, 108, 111, 112; Olympic Commemoratives, Series VI	60.00	135
MS7	1976 (4)	Inc. above	KM109, 110, 113, 114; Olympic Commemoratives, Series VII	60.00	135
MS8	2001 (5)	600	KM438-442	1,996	2,950
MS9	2002 (7)	135,000	Double-dated 1952-2002, KM#444-449, 467	11.75	16.00
MS10	2002 (7)	—	KM#444-449, 467, Oh! Canada! 135th Birthday Gift set.	17.00	16.00
MS11	2002 (7)	—	KM#444-449, 467, Tiny Treasures Uncirculated Gift Set	17.00	16.00
MS12	2003 (7)	135,000	KM#289, 182b, 183b, 184b, 290, 186, 270	12.00	16.00
MS13	2003 (7)	75,000	KM490-496	13.25	20.00
MS14	2003 (7)	—	KM289, 182-184, 290, 186, 270, Oh! Canada!	17.75	16.00
MS15	2003 (7)	—	KM289, 182-184, 290, 186, 270, Tiny Treasures Uncirculated Gift Set	17.75	16.00

OLYMPIC COMMEMORATIVES (OCP)

KM#	Date	Mintage	Identification	Issue Price	Mkt Val
OCP1	1973 (4)	Inc. above	KM84-87, Series I	78.50	135
OCP2	1974 (4)	Inc. above	KM89-90, 93-94, Series II	88.50	135
OCP3	1974 (4)	Inc. above	KM91-92, 95-96, Series III	88.50	135
OCP4	1975 (4)	Inc. above	KM98-99, 102-103, Series IV	88.50	135
OCP5	1975 (4)	Inc. above	KM100-101, 104-105, Series V	88.50	135
OCP6	1976 (4)	Inc. above	KM107-108, 111-112, Series VI	88.50	135
OCP7	1976 (4)	Inc. above	KM109-110, 113-114, Series VII	88.50	135

PROOF SETS

KM#	Date	Mintage	Identification	Issue Price	Mkt Val
PS1	1981 (7)	199,000	KM60.2, 74, 75.3, 77.2, 120.1, 127, 130	36.00	30.00
PS2	1982 (7)	180,908	KM60.2a, 74, 75.3, 77.2, 120.1, 132, 133	36.00	37.50
PS3	1983 (7)	166,779	KM60.2a, 74, 75.3, 77.2, 120.1, 132, 138	36.00	27.50
PS4	1984 (7)	161,602	KM60.2a, 74, 75.3, 77.2, 120.1, 132, 140	30.00	27.50
PS5	1985 (7)	157,037	KM60.2a, 74, 75.3, 77.2, 120.1, 132, 143	30.00	30.00
PS6	1986 (7)	175,745	KM60.2a, 74, 75.3, 77.2, 120.1, 132, 149	30.00	29.00
PS7	1987 (7)	179,004	KM60.2a, 74, 75.3, 77.2, 120.1, 132, 154	34.00	30.00
PS8	1988 (7)	175,259	KM60.2a, 74, 75.3, 77.2, 132, 157, 161	37.50	34.00
PS9	1989 (7)	170,928	KM60.2a, 74, 75.3, 77.2, 132, 157, 168	40.00	34.00
PS10	1989 (4)	6,823	KM125.2, 135-136, 153	1,190	2,900
PS11	1989 (4)	1,995	KM164-167	1,700	3,750
PS12	1989 (3)	2,550	KM125.2, 163, 167	1,530	3,500
PS13	1989 (3)	9,979	KM135, 163, 164	165	475
PS14	1990 (7)	158,068	KM170, 181, 182, 183, 184, 185, 186	41.00	42.50
PS15	1990 (4)	2,629	KM174-177	1,720	3,700
PS16	1991 (7)	14,629	KM179, 181, 182, 183, 184, 185, 186	—	80.00
PS17	1991 (4)	873	KM198-201	1,760	3,700
PS18	1992 (11)	84,397	KM203a, 212a-214a, 218, 220a-223a, 231a-234a	—	92.50
PS19	1992 (7)	147,061	KM204-210	42.75	65.00
PS20	1992 (4)	3,500	KM226-229	1,680	3,700
PS21	1993 (7)	143,065	KM181, 182, 183, 184, 185, 186, 235	42.75	40.00
PS22	1993 (4)	3,500	KM240-243	1,329	3,700
PS23	1994 (7)	47,303	KM181-186, 248	47.50	30.00
PS24	1994 (7)	99,121	KM181-186, 251	43.00	45.00
PS25	1994 (4)	1,500	KM252-255	915	3,700
PS26	1995 (7)	Inc. above	KM181-186, 259	37.45	52.00
PS27	1995 (7)	50,000	KM181-185, 258, 259	49.45	52.00
PS28	1995 (4)	Inc. above	KM261-264	42.00	95.00
PS29	1995 (4)	682	KM266-269	1,555	3,700
PS30	1995 (2)	Inc. above	KM261-262	22.00	48.00
PS31	1995 (2)	Inc. above	KM263-264	22.00	46.00
PS32	1996 (4)	423	KM278-281	1,555	3,700

KM#	Date	Mintage	Identification	Issue Price	Mkt Val
PS33	1996 (7)	Inc. above	KM181, 182a, 183a, 184a, 185a, 186, 274	49.00	60.00
PS34	1996 (4)	Inc. above	KM283-286	44.45	80.00
PS35	1997 (7)	Inc. above	KM182a, 183a, 184a, 270c, 282, 289, 290	60.00	75.00
PS36	1997 (4)	Inc. above	KM292-295	44.45	68.00
PS37	1997 (4)	Inc. above	KM300-303	1,530	3,700
PS38	1998 (8)	Inc. above	KM182a, 183a, 184a, 186, 270b, 289, 290a, 306	59.45	80.00
PS39	1998 (5)	25,000	KM309-313	73.50	55.00
PS40	1998 (2)	61,000	KM316 w/China Y-727	72.50	40.00
PS41	1998 (4)	Inc. above	KM318-321	44.45	68.00
PS42	1998 (4)	1,000	KM322-325	1,552	3,700
PS43	1998 (5)	25,000	KM310-313, 332	73.50	68.00
PS44	1999 (7)	Inc. above	KM182a-184a, 186, 270c, 289, 290a,	59.45	55.00
PS45	1999 (4)	Inc. above	KM335-338	39.95	140
PS46	1999 (12)	Inc. above	KM342a-353a	99.45	115
PS47	1999 (4)	Inc. above	KM359-362	1,425	3,700
PS48	2000 (12)	—	KM373a-383a, 384.2a	101	110
PS49	2000 (4)	—	KM389-392	44.00	80.00
PS50	2000 (4)	600	KM405-408	1,416	3,700
PS51	2001 (4)	—	KM429, 430, 431, 432	—	3,600
PS52	2002 (8)	100,000	KM#443, 444a,445,446a-449a, 467	60.00	125
PS53	2002 (3)	—	KM#459-461	57.50	35.00
PS54	2002 (2)	—	KM#519, 520	750	1,125
PS55	2003 (8)	100,000	KM#182a,183a,184a, 186, 270d, 289, 290a, 450	62.50	125
PS56	2003 (6)	30,000	KM#468-473	75.00	100
PS57	2004 (8)	—	KM#490, 491a-494a, 495, 496a, 512	—	115
PS58	2004 (5)	25,000	KM#621-625	—	100

PROOF-LIKE DOLLARS

KM#	Date	Mintage	Identification	Issue Price	Mkt Val
D1.1	1951 (1)	—	KM46, Canoe	—	200
D1.2	1951 (1)	—	KM46, Arnprior	—	1,300
D2.1	1952 (1)	—	KM46, water lines	—	1,150
D2.2	1952 (1)	—	KM46, without water lines	—	200
D3	1953 (1)	1,200	KM54, Canoe w/shoulder fold	—	500
D4	1954 (1)	5,300	KM54, Canoe	1.25	175
D5	1955 (1)	7,950	KM54, Canoe	1.25	125
D5a	1955 (1)	Inc. above	KM54, Arnprior	1.25	225
D6	1956 (1)	10,212	KM54, Canoe	1.25	95.00
D7	1957 (1)	16,241	KM54, Canoe	1.25	50.00
D8	1958 (1)	33,237	KM55, British Columbia	1.25	30.00
D9	1959 (1)	45,160	KM54, Canoe	1.25	24.00
D10	1960 (1)	82,728	KM54, Canoe	1.25	22.00
D11	1961 (1)	120,928	KM54, Canoe	1.25	22.00
D12	1962 (1)	248,901	KM54, Canoe	1.25	22.00
D13	1963 (1)	963,525	KM54, Canoe	1.25	22.00
D14	1964 (1)	2,862,441	KM58, Charlottetown	1.25	22.00
D15	1965 (1)	2,904,352	KM64.1, Canoe	—	22.00
D16	1966 (1)	672,514	KM64.1, Canoe	—	22.00
D17	1967 (1)	1,036,176	KM70, Confederation	—	22.00

PROOF-LIKE SETS (PL)

KM#	Date	Mintage	Identification	Issue Price	Mkt Val
PL1	1953 (6)	1,200	KM49 w/o shoulder fold, 50-54	2.20	2,000
PL3	1954 (6)	3,000	KM49-54	2.50	650
PL4	1954 (6)	Inc. above	KM49 w/o shoulder fold, 50-54	2.50	1,600
PL5	1955 (6)	6,300	KM49, 50a, 51-54	2.50	400
PL6	1955 (6)	Inc. above	KM49, 50a, 51-54, Arnprior	2.50	500
PL7	1956 (5)	6,500	KM49, 50a, 51-54	2.50	200
PL8	1957 (6)	11,862	KM49, 50a, 51-54	2.50	150
PL9	1958 (6)	18,259	KM49, 50a, 51-53, 55	2.50	125
PL10	1959 (6)	31,577	KM49, 50a, 51, 52, 54, 56	2.50	60.00
PL11	1960 (6)	64,097	KM49, 50a, 51, 52, 54, 56	3.00	45.00
PL12	1961 (6)	98,373	KM49, 50a, 51, 52, 54, 56	3.00	45.00
PL13	1962 (6)	200,950	KM49, 50a, 51, 52, 54, 56	3.00	40.00
PL14	1963 (6)	673,006	KM49, 51, 52, 54, 56, 57	3.00	35.00
PL15	1964 (5)	1,653,162	KM49, 51, 52, 56-58	3.00	35.00
PL16	1965 (4)	2,904,352	KM59.1-60.1, 61-63, 64.1	4.00	35.00
PL17	1966 (6)	672,514	KM59.1-60.1, 61-63, 64.1	4.00	35.00
PL18	1967 (6)	961,887	KM65-70 (pliofilm flat pack)	4.00	35.00
PL18A	1967 (6)	70,583	KM65-70 Specimen Quality and Silver Medal (red box)	12.00	55.00
PL18B	1967 (7)	337,688	KM65-71 Specimen Quality (black box)	40.00	850
PL19	1968 (6)	521,641	KM59.1-60.1, 62b, 72a, 75.1-76.1	4.00	2.25
PL20	1969 (4)	326,203	KM59.1-60.1, 62b, 75.1-77.1	4.00	3.00
PL21	1970 (4)	349,120	KM59.1-60.1, 62b, 75.1, 77.1, 78	4.00	3.50
PL22	1971 (4)	253,311	KM59.1-60.1, 62b, 75.1, 77.1, 79	4.00	3.00
PL23	1972 (3)	224,275	KM59.1-60.1, 62b-77.1	4.00	3.00

KM#	Date	Mintage	Identification	Issue Price	Mkt Val
PL24	1973 (6)	243,695	KM59.1-60.1, 62b-75.1 obv. 120 beads, 77.1, 81.1, 82	4.00	4.00
PL25	1973 (3)	Inc. above	KM59.1-60.1, 62b-75.1 obv. 132 beads, 77.1, 81.2, 82	4.00	250
PL26	1974 (6)	213,589	KM59.1-60.1, 62b-75.1, 77.1, 88	5.00	3.00
PL27.1	1975 (4)	197,372	KM59.1, 60.1, 62b-75.1, 76.2, 77.1	5.00	3.50
PL27.2	1975 (6)	Inc. above	KM59.1, 60.1, 62b-75.1, 76.3, 77.1	5.00	5.00
PL28	1976 (4)	171,737	KM59.1, 60.1, 62b-75.1, 76.2, 77.1	5.15	3.00
PL29	1977 (4)	225,307	KM59.1-60.1, 62b, 75.2, 77.1, 117.1	5.15	3.00
PL30	1978 (6)	260,000	KM59.1-60.1, 62b, 75.3, 77.1, 120.1	5.25	4.25
PL31	1979 (6)	187,624	KM59.2-60.2, 74, 75.3, 77.2, 120.1	6.25	4.25
PL32	1980 (6)	410,842	KM60.2, 74, 75.3, 77.2, 120.1, 127	6.50	4.50
PL33	1981 (5)	186,250	KM60.2, 74, 75.3, 77.2, 120.1, 123	5.00	4.00
PL34	1982 (5)	203,287	KM60.2, 74, 75.3, 77.2, 120.1, 123	6.00	4.00
PL36	1983 (6)	190,838	KM60.2a, 74, 75.3, 77.2, 120.1, 132	5.00	5.00
PL36.1	1983 (6)	Inc. above	KM60.2a, 74, 75.3, 77.2, 120.1, 132; set in folder packaged by British Royal Mint Coin Club	—	10.00
PL37	1984 (6)	181,249	KM60.2a, 74, 75.3, 77.2, 120.1, 132	5.25	5.00
PL38	1985 (6)	173,924	KM60.2a, 74, 75.3, 77.2, 120.1, 132	5.25	24.00
PL39	1986 (6)	167,338	KM60.2a, 74, 75.3, 77.2, 120.1, 132	5.25	6.50
PL40	1987 (6)	212,136	KM60.2a, 74, 75.3, 77.2, 120.1, 132	5.25	7.00
PL41	1988 (6)	182,048	KM60.2a, 74, 75.3, 77.2, 132, 157	6.05	5.50
PL42	1989 (6)	173,622	KM60.2a, 74, 75.3, 77.2, 132, 157	6.60	8.00
PL43	1990 (6)	170,791	KM181-186	7.40	8.00
PL44	1991 (6)	147,814	KM181-186	7.40	25.00
PL45	1992 (6)	217,597	KM204-209	8.25	17.50
PL46	1993 (6)	171,680	KM181-186	8.25	5.00
PL47	1994 (6)	141,676	KM181-185, 258	8.50	5.50
PL48	1994 (6)	18,794	KM181-185, 258 (Oh Canada holder)	—	8.50
PL49	1995 (6)	143,892	KM181-186	6.95	5.50
PL50	1995 (6)	50,927	KM181-186 (Oh Canada holder)	14.65	8.50
PL51	1995 (6)	36,443	KM181-186 (Baby Gift holder)	—	9.00
PL52	1996 (4)	116,736	KM181-186	—	27.00
PL53	1996 (6)	29,747	KM181-186 (Baby Gift holder)	—	14.00
PL54	1996 (10)	Inc. above	KM181a-185a, 186	8.95	65.00
PL55	1996 (6)	Inc. above	KM181a-185a, 186 (Oh Canada holder)	14.65	12.00
PL56	1996 (6)	Inc. above	KM181a-185a, 186 (Baby Gift holder)	—	12.00
PL57	1997 (7)	Inc. above	KM182a-184a, 209, 270, 289-290	10.45	8.00
PL58	1997 (7)	Inc. above	KM182a-184a, 270, 289-291 (Oh Canada holder)	16.45	30.00
PL59	1997 (5)	Inc. above	KM182a-184a, 209, 270, 289-290 (Baby Gift holder)	18.50	25.00
PL60	1998 (7)	Inc. above	KM182-184, 186, 270, 289-290	10.45	25.00
PL61	1998 (7)	Inc. above	KM182-184, 186, 270, 289-290 (Oh Canada holder)	16.45	25.00
PL62	1998 (7)	Inc. above	KM182-184, 186, 270, 289-290 (Tiny Treasures holder)	16.45	25.00
PL63	1999 (12)	Inc. above	KM342-353	16.95	10.00
PL64	2000 (12)	—	KM373-384	16.95	10.00

SPECIMEN SETS (SS)

KM#	Date	Mintage	Identification	Issue Price	Mkt Val
SS1	1858 (4)	Inc. above	KM1-4, Reeded edge	—	12,000
SS2	1858 (4)	Inc. above	KM1-4, Plain edge	—	10,000
SS3	1858 (4)	Inc. above	KM1-4; Double Set	—	20,000
SS4	1858 (1)	Inc. above	KM1 (overdate), 2-4; Double Set	—	20,000
SS5	1870 (1)	100	KM2, 3, 5, 6 (reeded edges)	—	40,000
SS6	1870 (1)	Inc. above	KM2, 3, 5, 6; Double Set (plain edges)	—	80,000
SS7	1872 (4)	Inc. above	KM2, 3, 5, 6	—	12,500
SS8	1875 (2)	Inc. above	KM2 (Large date), 3, 5	—	100,000
SS9	1880 (2)	Inc. above	KM2, 3, 5 (Narrow 0)	—	55,000
SS10	1881 (5)	Inc. above	KM7, 2, 3, 5, 6	—	35,000
SS11	1892 (2)	Inc. above	KM3, 5	—	10,000
SS12	1902 (5)	100	KM8-12	—	60,000
SS13	1902 (3)	Inc. above	KM9 (Large H), 10, 11	—	40,000
SS14	1903 (3)	Inc. above	KM10, 12, 13	—	7,000
SS15	1908 (5)	1,000	KM8, 10-13	—	3,500
SS16	1911 (5)	1,000	KM15-19	—	5,500
SS17	1911/12 (7)	5	KM15-20, 26-27	—	75,000
SS18	1921 (5)	Inc. above	KM22a-25a, 28	—	225,000
SS19	1922 (2)	Inc. above	KM28, 29	—	2,500
SS20	1923 (2)	Inc. above	KM28, 29	—	5,000
SS21	1924 (2)	Inc. above	KM28, 29	—	4,000
SS22	1925 (2)	Inc. above	KM28, 29	—	7,000
SS23	1926 (2)	Inc. above	KM28, 29 (Near 6)	—	5,000
SS24	1927 (3)	Inc. above	KM24a, 28, 29	—	8,000
SS25	1928 (4)	Inc. above	KM23a, 24a, 28, 29	—	12,000
SS26	1929 (5)	Inc. above	KM23a,-25a, 28, 29	—	35,000
SS27	1930 (4)	Inc. above	KM23a, 24a, 28, 29	—	35,000
SS28	1931 (5)	Inc. above	KM23a-25a, 28, 29	—	60,000
SS29	1932 (5)	Inc. above	KM23a-25a, 28, 29	—	20,000
SS30	1934 (2)	Inc. above	KM23-25, 28, 29	—	50,000

KM#	Date	Mintage	Identification	Issue Price	Mkt Val
SS31	1936 (5)	Inc. above	KM23a-25a, 28, 29	—	12,000
SS32	1936 (5)	Inc. above	KM23a(dot), 24a(dot), 25a, 28(dot), 29, 30	—	550,000
SS33	1937 (6)	1,025	KM32-37, Matte Finish	—	1,600
SS34	1937 (4)	Inc. above	KM32-35, Mirror Fields	—	1,200
SS35	1937 (6)	75	KM32-37, Mirror Fields	—	3,000
SS36	1938 (6)	Inc. above	KM32-37	—	40,000
SS37	1944 (5)	3	KM32, 34-37, 40a	—	20,000
SS38	1945 (5)	6	KM32, 34-37, 40a	—	12,500
SS39	1946 (5)	15	KM32, 34-37, 39a	—	9,000
SS40	1947 (6)	Inc. above	KM32, 34-36(7 curved), 37(7 pointed),	—	12,500
SS41	1947 (6)	Inc. above	KM32, 34-36(7 curved), 37(blunt 7), 39a	—	14,000
SS42	1947 (6)	Inc. above	KM32, 34-36(7 curved right), 37, 39a	—	10,000
SS43	1948 (6)	30	KM41-46	—	10,000
SS44	1949 (4)	20	KM41-45, 47	—	8,000
SS44A	1949 (2)	Inc. above	KM47 (Proof)	—	2,600
SS45	1950 (4)	12	KM41-46	—	5,500
SS46	1950 (4)	Inc. above	KM41-45, 46 (Arnprior)	—	7,000
SS47	1951 (5)	12	KM41, 48, 42a, 43-46 (w/water lines)	—	6,500
SS48	1952 (5)	2,317	KM41, 42a, 43-46 (water lines)	—	6,500
SS48A	1952 (5)	Inc. above	KM41, 42a, 43-46 (w/o water lines)	—	6,500
SS49	1953 (6)	28	KM49 w/o straps, 50-54	—	6,500
SS50	1953 (6)	Inc. above	KM49 w/ straps, 50-54	—	6,500
SS51	1964 (5)	Inc. above	KM49, 51, 52, 56-58	—	2,400
SS52	1965 (4)	Inc. above	KM59.1-60.1, 61-63, 64.1	—	2,400
SS56	1971 (6)	66,860	KM59.1-60.1, 62b-75.1, 77.1, 79 (2 pcs.); Double Dollar Prestige Sets	12.00	14.50
SS57	1972 (5)	36,349	KM59.1,-60.1, 62b-75.1, 76.1 (2 pcs.)	12.00	18.00
SS58	1973 (6)	119,819	KM59.1-60.1, 75.1, 77.1, 81.1, 82, 83	12.00	16.00
SS59	1973 (6)	Inc. above	KM59.1-60.1, 75.1, 77.1, 81.2, 82, 83	—	1,600
SS60	1974 (6)	85,230	KM59.1-60.1, 62b-75.1, 77.1, 88, 88a	15.00	12.50
SS61	1975 (5)	97,263	KM59.1-60.1, 62b-75.1, 76.2, 77.1, 97	15.00	12.50
SS62	1976 (5)	87,744	KM59.1-60.1, 62b-75.1, 76.2, 77.1, 106	16.00	14.00
SS63	1977 (5)	142,577	KM59.1-60.1, 62b, 75.2, 77.1, 117.1, 118	16.50	14.50
SS64	1978 (6)	147,000	KM59.1-60.1, 62b, 75.3, 77.1, 120.1, 121	16.50	10.00
SS65	1979 (6)	155,698	KM59.2-60.2, 74, 75.3, 77.2, 120, 124	18.50	15.50
SS66	1980 (6)	162,875	KM60.2, 74-75.3, 77.2, 120, 127, 128	30.50	25.00
SS67	1981 (6)	71,300	KM60.2, 74, 75.3, 77.2, 120.1, 127; Regular Specimen Sets	10.00	5.50
SS68	1982 (10)	62,298	KM60.2a, 74, 75.3, 77.2, 120.1, 132	11.50	100
SS69	1983 (6)	60,329	KM60.2a, 74, 75.3, 77.2, 120.1, 132	12.75	9.00
SS70	1984 (2)	60,400	KM60.2a, 74, 75.3, 77.2, 120.1, 132	10.00	5.50
SS71	1985 (6)	61,553	KM60.2a, 74, 75.3, 77.2, 120.1, 132	10.00	23.50
SS72	1986 (6)	67,152	KM60.2a, 74, 75.3, 77.2, 120.1, 132	10.00	9.00
SS72A	1987 (6)	75,194	KM60.2a, 74, 75.3, 77.2, 120.1, 132	11.00	7.50
SS73	1988 (6)	70,205	KM60.2a, 74, 75.3, 77.2, 132, 157	12.30	7.50
SS74	1989 (6)	75,306	KM60.2a, 74, 75.3, 77.2, 132, 157	14.50	9.50
SS75	1990 (6)	76,611	KM181-186	15.50	8.50
SS76	1991 (6)	68,552	KM181-186	15.50	17.50
SS77	1992 (6)	78,328	KM204-209	16.25	17.50
SS78	1993 (6)	77,351	KM181-186; Regular Specimen Sets Resumed	16.25	13.00
SS79	1994 (6)	77,349	KM181-186	16.50	9.50
SS80	1995 (6)	Inc. above	KM181-186	13.95	9.50
SS82	1996 (6)	Inc. above	KM181a-185a, 186	18.95	35.00
SS83	1997 (7)	Inc. above	KM182a-184a, 270, 289-291	19.95	47.50
SS84	1998 (7)	Inc. above	KM182-184, 186, 270, 289, 290	19.95	18.00
SS85	1999 (7)	Inc. above	KM182-184, 186, 270, 289a, 290	19.95	20.00
SS90	2002 (7)	75,000	KM#444-449,462	30.00	65.00
SS91	2003 (3)	75,000	KM#(uncertain), 270, 289, 290	30.00	50.00
SS-A36	1939 (5)	Inc. above	KM32-35, 38, Matte Finish	—	—
SS-A37	1944 (2)	Inc. above	KM32, 40a	—	1,000
SS-A38	1945 (2)	Inc. above	KM32, 40a	—	1,000
SS-B36	1939 (5)	Inc. above	KM32-35, 38, Mirror Fields	—	12,000
SS-C36	1942 (2)	Inc. above	KM32, 33	—	1,000
SS-D36	1943 (2)	Inc. above	KM32, 40	—	1,000

V.I.P. SPECIMEN SETS (VS)

KM#	Date	Mintage	Identification	Issue Price	Mkt Val
VS1	1969 (0)	4		—	2,000
VS2	1970 (0)	100	KM59.1-60.1, 74.1-75.1, 77.1, 78	—	525
VS3	1971 (0)	69	KM59.1-60.1, 74.1-75.1, 77.1, 79(2 pcs.)	—	525
VS4	1972 (0)	25	KM59.1-60.1, 74.1-75.1, 76.1, (2 pcs.), 77.1	—	650
VS5	1973 (0)	26	KM59.1-60.1, 75.1, 77.1, 81.1, 82, 83	—	650
VS6	1974 (0)	72	KM59.1-60.1, 74.1-75.1, 77.1, 88, 88a	—	525
VS7	1975 (0)	94	KM59.1-60.1, 74.1-75.1, 76.2, 77.1, 97	—	525
VS8	1976 (0)	Inc. above	KM59.1-60.1, 74.1-75.1, 76.2, 77.1, 106	—	525

NEW BRUNSWICK
PROVINCE
STERLING COINAGE

KM# 1 HALFPENNY TOKEN
Copper, **Obv.** Crowned head left **Rev:** Three masted ship **Obv. Legend:** VICTORIA DEI GRATIA REGINA **Rev. Legend:** NEW BRUNSWICK

Date	Mintage	VG8	F12	VF20	XF40	AU50	MS60	MS63
1843	480,000	4.00	7.50	15.00	45.00	200	300	400
1843	— PF60 750							

KM# 3 HALFPENNY TOKEN
Copper, **Obv.** Head left **Rev:** Three masted ship **Obv. Legend:** VICTORIA DEI GRATIA REGINA **Rev. Legend:** NEW BRUNSWICK

Date	Mintage	VG8	F12	VF20	XF40	AU50	MS60	MS63
1854	864,000	4.00	7.50	15.00	45.00	200	300	400

KM# 3a HALFPENNY TOKEN
Bronze, **Obv.** Head left **Rev:** Three masted ship **Obv. Legend:** VICTORIA DEI GRATIA REGINA **Rev. Legend:** NEW BRUNSWICK

Date	Mintage	VG8	F12	VF20	XF40	AU50	MS60	MS63
1854	— PF60 400							

KM# 2 1 PENNY TOKEN
Copper, **Obv.** Crowned head left **Rev:** Three masted ship **Obv. Legend:** VICTORIA DEI GRATIA REGINA **Rev. Legend:** NEW BRUNSWICK

Date	Mintage	VG8	F12	VF20	XF40	AU50	MS60	MS63
1843	480,000	5.00	9.50	23.00	65.00	175	250	350
1843	— PF60 800							

KM# 4 1 PENNY TOKEN

Copper, **Obv.** Head left **Rev:** Three masted ship **Obv. Legend:** VICTORIA DEI GRATIA REGINA **Rev. Legend:** NEW BRUNSWICK

Date	Mintage	VG8	F12	VF20	XF40	AU50	MS60	MS63
1854	432,000	3.75	7.50	22.00	65.00	200	300	400

DECIMAL COINAGE

KM# 5 HALF CENT

Bronze, **Obv.** Laureate bust left **Rev:** Crown and date within beaded circle, wreath surrounds **Obv. Legend:** VICTORIA D:G: BRITT: REG: F:D:

Date	Mintage	VG8	F12	VF20	XF40	AU50	MS60	MS63
1861	222,800	125	175	225	350	500	650	1,500
1861	—	PF60 2,200						

KM# 6 CENT

Bronze, **Obv.** Laureate bust left **Rev:** Crown and date within beaded circle, wreath surrounds **Obv. Legend:** VICTORIA D:G: BRITT: REG: F:D: **Rev. Legend:** NEW BRUNSWICK

Date	Mintage	VG8	F12	VF20	XF40	AU50	MS60	MS63
1861	1,000,000	3.50	6.00	9.00	14.00	60	100	450
1861	—	PF60 450						
1864 short 6	1,000,000	3.50	6.00	9.00	20.00	75	125	550
1864 long 6	Inc. above	4.00	6.50	13.00	24.00	100	175	650

KM# 7 5 CENTS

1.16 g., 0.925 Silver, 0.03 oz. ASW **Obv.** Laureate head left **Rev:** Denomination and date within wreath, crown above **Obv. Legend:** VICTORIA D: G: REG: / NEW BRUNSWICK

Date	Mintage	VG8	F12	VF20	XF40	AU50	MS60	MS63
1862	100,000	65.00	100	225	500	1,000	1,700	3,200
1862	—	PF60 3,500						
1864 small 6	100,000	65.00	100	225	1,000	1,500	2,200	4,900
1864 large 6	Inc. above	75.00	125	300	600	1,600	2,500	5,000

NEW BRUNSWICK

KM# 8   10 CENTS
2.32 g., 0.925 Silver, 0.07 oz. ASW **Obv.** Laureate head left **Rev:** Denomination and date within wreath, crown above **Obv.**
Legend: VICTORIA D: G: REG: / NEW BRUNSWICK

Date	Mintage	VG8	F12	VF20	XF40	AU50	MS60	MS63
1862	150,000	65.00	100	225	450	950	1,600	3,000
1862 recut 2	Inc. above	95.00	175	350	750	1,800	2,900	6,700
1862	—	PF60 2,850						
1864	100,000	65.00	100	225	450	1,600	2,700	6,300

KM# 9   20 CENTS
4.65 g., 0.925 Silver, 0.14 oz. ASW **Obv.** Laureate head left **Rev:** Denomination and date within wreath, crown above **Obv.**
Legend: VICTORIA D: G: REG: / NEW BRUNSWICK

Date	Mintage	VG8	F12	VF20	XF40	AU50	MS60	MS63
1862	150,000	29.00	50.00	100	225	625	1,050	4,400
1862	—	PF60 2,850						
1864	150,000	29.00	50.00	100	225	825	1,600	4,600

NEWFOUNDLAND
PROVINCE
CIRCULATION COINAGE

KM# 1   LARGE CENT
Bronze, **Obv.** Laureate bust left **Rev:** Crown and date within circle, florals surround **Obv. Legend:** VICTORIA D:G: BRITT: REG:F:D: **Rev. Legend:** NEWFOUNDLAND

Date	Mintage	VG8	F12	VF20	XF40	AU50	MS60	MS63
1865	240,000	3.50	5.50	12.00	30.00	100	175	900
1872 H	200,000	2.50	4.00	7.00	17.00	60.00	125	250
1872 H	—	PF60 800						
1873	200,025	4.00	6.50	20.00	40.00	200	500	1,600
1873	—	PF60 3,000						
1876 H	200,000	3.50	7.00	15.00	60.00	200	500	1,600
1876 H Proof, reported not confirmed	—	—	—	—	—	—	—	—
1880 round 0, even date	400,000	3.00	3.50	7.00	20.00	80.00	200	500
1880 round and low 0	Inc. above	4.50	12.00	20.00	50.00	300	900	2,600
1880 oval 0	Inc. above	200	300	500	950	1,850	3,000	6,000
1880 oval 0 Proof	—	PF60 2,500						
1885	40,000	27.50	50.00	75.00	125	450	900	2,400
1885	—	PF60 2,500						
1888	50,000	30.00	55.00	80.00	175	650	1,350	4,800
1890	200,000	3.00	6.00	15.00	45.00	150	300	1,200
1894	200,000	3.00	5.00	10.00	25.00	125	300	1,200
1894	—	PF60 1,500						
1896	200,000	3.00	3.50	7.00	27.00	90.00	175	500
1896	—	PF60 1,500						

KM# 9   LARGE CENT
Bronze, **Obv.** Crowned bust right **Obv. Designer:** G.W. DeSaulles **Rev:** Crown and date within center circle, wreath surrounds, denomination above **Rev. Designer:** Horace Morehen

Date	Mintage	VG8	F12	VF20	XF40	AU50	MS60	MS63
1904 H	100,000	10.00	18.00	30.00	75.00	175	400	1,300
1904 H	—	PF60 6,000						
1907	200,000	3.00	5.00	11.00	35.00	125	250	1,000
1909	200,000	3.00	5.00	9.00	27.50	65.00	125	250
1909	—	PF60 600						

KM# 16 LARGE CENT
Bronze, **Obv.** Crowned bust left **Obv. Designer:** E.B. MacKennal **Rev:** Crown and date within center circle, wreath surrounds, denomination above **Rev. Designer:** Horace Morehen

Date	Mintage	VG8	F12	VF20	XF40	AU50	MS60	MS63
1913	400,000	1.50	2.50	3.50	9.00	30.00	60.00	125
1917 C	702,350	1.50	2.50	3.50	8.00	30.00	100	400
1917 C	—	PF60 950						
1919 C	300,000	1.50	2.50	4.00	14.00	50.00	225	750
1919 C	—	PF60 2,500						
1920 C	302,184	1.50	2.50	6.00	24.00	90.00	350	1,900
1929	300,000	1.50	2.50	3.50	7.00	30.00	85.00	175
1929 C	—	PF60 3,000						
1936	300,000	1.50	2.00	2.50	5.00	18.00	40.00	100

KM# 18 SMALL CENT
3.20 g., Bronze, 19mm. **Obv.** Crowned head left **Obv. Designer:** Percy Metcalfe **Rev:** Pitcher plant divides date, denomination below **Rev. Designer:** Walter J. Newman

Date	Mintage	VG8	F12	VF20	XF40	AU50	MS60	MS63
1938	500,000	0.45	0.95	1.25	3.50	9.00	24.00	70.00
1938	—	PF60 6,000						
1940	300,000	1.25	2.25	4.50	14.00	40.00	95.00	600
1940 Re-engraved date	Inc. above	45.00	60.00	85.00	150	300	650	2,400
1940	—	PF60 2,500						
1941 C	827,662	0.45	0.70	0.95	2.50	9.00	29.00	200
1941 C Re-engraved date	Inc. above	16.00	24.00	40.00	95.00	175	400	2,000
1942	1,996,889	0.45	0.70	0.95	2.50	13.50	40.00	250
1943 C	1,239,732	0.45	0.70	0.95	2.50	9.00	22.50	100
1944 C	1,328,776	1.50	2.50	9.00	35.00	100	300	2,000
1947 C	313,772	1.25	1.75	4.00	19.00	45.00	100	350
1947 C	—	PF60 3,000						

KM# 2 5 CENTS
1.18 g., 0.925 Silver, 0.03 oz. ASW **Obv.** Laureate head left **Rev:** Denomination and date within ornamental circle **Obv. Legend:** VICTORIA D: G: REG: / NEWFOUNDLAND **Edge:** Reeded

Date	Mintage	VG8	F12	VF20	XF40	AU50	MS60	MS63
1865	80,000	35.00	50.00	150	300	800	1,800	3,000
1865	—	PF60 4,000						
1870	40,000	65.00	125	225	500	1,500	2,500	3,500
1870	—	PF60 4,000						
1872 H	40,000	40.00	70.00	125	175	700	1,250	2,400
1873	44,260	125	200	450	1,100	4,500	6,000	—
1873 H	Inc. above	950	1,400	2,000	3,700	9,500	16,000	22,000
1873	—	PF60 10,000						
1876 H	20,000	125	200	350	650	1,000	1,350	2,750
1880	40,000	45.00	65.00	150	300	1,100	2,250	2,400
1880	—	PF60 5,000						
1881	40,000	45.00	65.00	150	300	1,100	1,900	2,500

Date	Mintage	VG8	F12	VF20	XF40	AU50	MS60	MS63
1881	—	PF60 5,000						
1882 H	60,000	23.00	45.00	90.00	200	650	1,800	3,000
1882 H	—	PF60 2,000						
1885	16,000	130	210	335	750	1,550	2,400	4,500
1885	—	PF60 7,500						
1888	40,000	40.00	75.00	225	350	1,600	4,000	8,000
1888	—	PF60 7,500						
1890	160,000	11.00	21.00	45.00	125	700	1,300	2,000
1890	—	PF60 5,000						
1894	160,000	10.00	19.00	30.00	100	500	1,100	2,500
1894	—	PF60 5,000						
1896	400,000	4.00	8.00	20.00	50.00	450	900	2,700
1896	—	PF60 5,000						

KM# 7   5 CENTS
1.18 g., 0.925 Silver, 0.03 oz. ASW **Obv.** Crowned bust right **Rev:** Denomination and date within circle **Designer:** G.W. DeSaulles

Date	Mintage	VG8	F12	VF20	XF40	AU50	MS60	MS63
1903	100,000	5.00	11.00	29.00	70.00	175	450	1,700
1903	—	PF60 3,000						
1904 H	100,000	4.00	7.00	19.00	45.00	90.00	225	450
1904 H	—	PF60 1,800						
1908	400,000	4.00	7.00	18.00	45.00	100	250	1,100

KM# 13   5 CENTS
1.18 g., 0.925 Silver, 0.03 oz. ASW **Obv.** Crowned bust left **Obv. Designer:** E.B. MacKennal **Rev:** Denomination and date within circle **Rev. Designer:** G.W. DeSaulles

Date	Mintage	VG8	F12	VF20	XF40	AU50	MS60	MS63
1912	300,000	2.00	3.00	6.00	24.00	55.00	125	250
1912	—	PF60 2,400						
1917 C	300,319	2.00	5.00	8.00	27.00	100	350	1,200
1917 C	—	PF60 2,400						
1919 C	100,844	6.00	11.00	27.00	100	450	1,200	3,500
1919 C	—	PF60 2,400						
1929	300,000	2.00	3.00	4.00	14.00	65.00	175	400

KM# 19   5 CENTS
1.18 g., 0.925 Silver, 0.03 oz. ASW **Obv.** Crowned head left **Obv. Designer:** Percy Metcalfe **Rev:** Denomination and date within circle **Rev. Designer:** G.W. DeSaulles

Date	Mintage	VG8	F12	VF20	XF40	AU50	MS60	MS63
1938	100,000	1.50	2.50	3.00	11.00	30.00	100	300
1938	—	PF60 1,600						
1940 C	200,000	1.50	2.50	3.00	11.00	30.00	100	350
1940 C	—	PF60 3,200						
1941 C	621,641	BV	1.75	2.50	4.00	9.00	22.00	35.00
1942 C	298,348	BV	1.75	2.50	5.00	13.50	28.00	60.00
1943 C	351,666	BV	1.50	2.50	5.00	10.50	22.00	45.00

KM# 19a   5 CENTS
1.17 g., 0.800 Silver, 0.03 oz. ASW 15.67mm. **Obv.** Crowned head left **Obv. Designer:** Percy Metcalfe **Rev:** Denomination and date within circle **Rev. Designer:** G.W. DeSaulles **Edge:** Reeded

Date	Mintage	VG8	F12	VF20	XF40	AU50	MS60	MS63
1944 C	286,504	1.50	1.75	2.50	9.00	22.00	70.00	150
1945 C	203,828	1.50	1.75	2.50	4.00	9.00	22.50	35.00
1946 C	2,041	PF60 3,000						
1946 C Prooflike	—	—	—	—	—	—	—	4,000
1946 C	—	PF60 3,500						
1947 C	38,400	3.00	5.00	8.00	30.00	45.00	100	250
1947 C Prooflike	—	—	—	—	—	—	—	2,100

KM# 3 10 CENTS
2.36 g., 0.925 Silver, 0.07 oz. ASW **Obv.** Laureate head left **Rev:** Denomination and date within ornamental circle **Obv. Legend:** VICTORIA D: G: REG: / NEWFOUNDLAND

Date	Mintage	VG8	F12	VF20	XF40	AU50	MS60	MS63
1865	80,000	27.00	45.00	75.00	250	650	1,100	2,250
1865 Proof, plain edge	—	PF60 5,500						
1870	30,000	150	250	450	750	1,250	2,500	5,000
1870	—	PF60 10,000						
1872 H	40,000	22.00	35.00	80.00	200	500	800	1,700
1873 flat 3	23,614	55.00	70.00	250	650	2,000	4,000	5,000
1873 round 3	Inc. above	55.00	70.00	250	650	2,000	4,000	5,000
1873	—	PF60 12,000						
1876 H	10,000	55.00	70.00	225	350	850	1,400	2,500
1880	10,000	55.00	100	250	400	800	1,800	3,000
1880	—	PF60 7,500						
1882 H	20,000	30.00	55.00	150	700	1,150	2,800	4,000
1882 H	—	PF60 3,000						
1885	8,000	70.00	130	300	800	1,100	2,200	4,500
1885	—	PF60 8,000						
1888	30,000	35.00	70.00	200	700	2,000	4,000	5,000
1888	—	PF60 8,000						
1890	100,000	9.00	19.00	35.00	150	550	1,100	3,500
1890	—	PF60 5,000						
1894	100,000	8.50	12.00	25.00	125	550	1,200	3,000
1894	—	PF60 5,000						
1896	230,000	5.00	10.00	25.00	90.00	600	1,200	3,500
1896	—	PF60 5,000						

KM# 8 10 CENTS
2.36 g., 0.925 Silver, 0.07 oz. ASW **Obv.** Crowned bust right **Rev:** Denomination and date within circle **Designer:** G.W. DeSaulles

Date	Mintage	VG8	F12	VF20	XF40	AU50	MS60	MS63
1903	100,000	11.00	30.00	90.00	250	650	2,400	5,500
1903	—	PF60 3,750						
1904 H	100,000	6.00	14.00	35.00	100	200	350	600
1904 H	—	PF60 2,250						

KM# 14 10 CENTS
2.36 g., 0.925 Silver, 0.07 oz. ASW **Obv.** Crowned bust left **Obv. Designer:** E.B. MacKennal **Rev. Designer:** G.W. DeSaulles

Date	Mintage	VG8	F12	VF20	XF40	AU50	MS60	MS63
1912	150,000	4.00	5.50	14.00	45.00	100	225	350
1917 C	250,805	3.50	5.00	14.00	45.00	175	450	1,350
1919 C	54,342	4.00	11.00	22.00	70.00	125	250	350

KM# 20   10 CENTS

2.36 g., 0.925 Silver, 0.07 oz. ASW **Obv.** Crowned head left **Obv. Designer:** Percy Metcalfe **Rev:** Denomination and date within circle **Rev. Designer:** G.W. DeSaulles

Date	Mintage	VG8	F12	VF20	XF40	AU50	MS60	MS63
1938	100,000	3.50	4.00	4.50	18.00	100	200	800
1938	—	PF60 3,200						
1940	100,000	3.00	3.50	4.50	14.00	45.00	100	400
1940	—	PF60 4,000						
1941 C	483,630	BV	3.00	3.50	7.00	18.00	50.00	125
1942 C	293,736	BV	3.00	3.50	7.00	22.00	70.00	200
1943 C	104,706	BV	3.00	3.50	9.00	30.00	250	800
1944 C	151,471	BV	3.50	11.00	27.00	65.00	350	1,300

KM# 20a   10 CENTS

2.33 g., 0.800 Silver, 0.06 oz. ASW **Obv.** Crowned head left **Obv. Designer:** Percy Metcalfe **Rev. Designer:** G.W. DeSaulles

Date	Mintage	VG8	F12	VF20	XF40	AU50	MS60	MS63
1945 C	175,833	BV	2.50	3.00	7.00	22.00	100	400
1946 C	—	PF60 1,200						
1946 C	38,400	3.50	4.50	9.00	30.00	60.00	125	300
1947 C	61,988	3.00	3.50	7.00	20.00	45.00	100	350

KM# 4   20 CENTS

4.71 g., 0.925 Silver, 0.14 oz. ASW 23.19mm. **Obv.** Laureate head left **Rev:** Denomination and date within ornamental circle

Date	Mintage	VG8	F12	VF20	XF40	AU50	MS60	MS63
1865	100,000	16.00	30.00	60.00	225	550	950	2,600
1865 Proof, plain edge	—	PF60 6,500						
1865 Proof, reeded edge	—	PF60 10,000						
1870	50,000	21.00	45.00	100	250	750	1,250	2,600
1870 Proof, plain edge	—	PF60 6,500						
1870 Proof, reeded edge	—	PF60 6,500						
1872 H	90,000	12.00	25.00	60.00	150	400	750	1,800
1873	45,797	21.00	65.00	175	550	2,700	5,500	8,000
1873	—	PF60 12,000						
1876 H	50,000	25.00	50.00	80.00	300	800	1,350	2,700
1880	30,000	27.00	55.00	100	350	1,000	2,000	3,000
Note: No longer recognized as 1880/70 overdate								
1880	—	PF60 8,000						
1881	60,000	12.00	25.00	80.00	300	750	1,200	2,900
1881	—	PF60 8,000						
1882 H	100,000	9.00	19.00	50.00	175	1,150	2,250	3,500
1882 H	—	PF60 3,500						
1885	40,000	14.00	30.00	80.00	300	1,350	2,900	4,500
1885	—	PF60 10,000						
1888	75,000	12.00	25.00	70.00	225	800	1,400	4,500
1888	—	PF60 10,000						
1890	100,000	9.00	15.00	45.00	225	800	1,400	3,500
1890	—	PF60 6,500						
1894	100,000	12.00	24.00	50.00	175	600	1,200	3,500
1894	—	PF60 6,500						
1896 small 96	125,000	6.00	12.00	35.00	150	750	1,400	4,000
1896 large 96	Inc. above	7.00	15.00	50.00	200	800	1,700	4,500
1896 large 96, Proof	—	PF60 6,500						
1899 hook 99	125,000	27.00	50.00	125	350	1,050	1,800	5,000
1899 large 99	Inc. above	5.00	12.00	30.00	125	600	1,400	4,000
1900	125,000	5.00	8.00	25.00	80.00	450	1,100	4,500
1900	—	PF60 6,500						

KM# 10 20 CENTS
4.71 g., 0.925 Silver, 0.14 oz. ASW **Obv.** Crowned bust right **Obv. Designer:** G.W. DeSaulles **Rev:** Denomination and date within circle **Rev. Designer:** W.H.J. Blakemore

Date	Mintage	VG8	F12	VF20	XF40	AU50	MS60	MS63
1904 H	75,000	13.00	35.00	65.00	300	900	2,700	7,000
1904 H	—	PF60 2,400						

KM# 15 20 CENTS
4.71 g., 0.925 Silver, 0.14 oz. ASW **Obv.** Crowned bust left **Obv. Designer:** E.B. MacKennal **Rev:** Denomination and date within circle **Rev. Designer:** W.H.J. Blakemore

Date	Mintage	VG8	F12	VF20	XF40	AU50	MS60	MS63
1912	350,000	5.50	8.00	18.00	65.00	175	300	750
1912	—	PF60 2,500						

KM# 17 25 CENTS
5.83 g., 0.925 Silver, 0.17 oz. ASW **Obv.** Crowned bust left **Obv. Designer:** E.B. MacKennal **Rev:** Denomination and date within circle **Rev. Designer:** W.H.J. Blakemore

Date	Mintage	VG8	F12	VF20	XF40	AU50	MS60	MS63
1917 C	464,779	7.00	8.00	10.00	18.00	50.00	200	400
1917 C	—	PF60 3,000						
1919 C	163,939	7.00	8.00	15.00	35.00	125	450	2,000
1919 C	—	PF60 3,000						

KM# 6 50 CENTS
11.78 g., 0.925 Silver, 0.35 oz. ASW 29.85mm. **Obv.** Laureate head left **Rev:** Denomination and date within ornamental circle **Obv. Legend:** VICTORIA DEI GRATIA REGINA NEWFOUNDLAND

Date	Mintage	VG8	F12	VF20	XF40	AU50	MS60	MS63
1870	50,000	26.00	50.00	150	600	1,800	3,500	8,500
1870 Proof, plain edge	—	PF60 25,000						
1870 Proof, reeded edge	—	PF60 25,000						
1872 H	48,000	18.00	35.00	90.00	400	950	1,600	4,000
1873	37,675	40.00	75.00	200	650	2,700	9,500	13,000
1873	—	PF60 40,000						
1874	80,000	25.00	45.00	125	550	2,700	13,000	17,500
1874	—	PF60 40,000						
1876 H	28,000	35.00	85.00	150	450	1,350	2,250	5,500

Date	Mintage	VG8	F12	VF20	XF40	AU50	MS60	MS63
1880	24,000	45.00	95.00	250	900	3,000	6,500	16,000
1880	—	PF60 40,000						
1881	50,000	20.00	35.00	135	400	1,800	3,500	8,000
1881	—	PF60 40,000						
1882 H	100,000	12.00	30.00	95.00	350	950	1,600	5,500
1882 H	—	PF60 8,000						
1885	40,000	30.00	60.00	175	650	1,700	2,800	7,500
1885	—	PF60 40,000						
1888	20,000	50.00	90.00	250	1,350	4,500	11,000	13,000
1888	—	PF60 40,000						
1894	40,000	12.00	28.00	75.00	300	1,350	4,000	8,000
1896	60,000	8.50	16.00	65.00	300	1,350	3,000	8,500
1896	—	PF60 25,000						
1898	76,607	8.50	13.00	60.00	200	1,050	3,500	6,500
1899 wide 9's	150,000	8.50	13.00	60.00	200	1,350	2,800	7,500
1899 narrow 9's	Inc. above	8.50	13.00	45.00	150	900	2,600	7,000
	150,000	8.50	13.00	45.00	175	800	2,600	5,500

KM# 11   50 CENTS
11.78 g., 0.925 Silver, 0.35 oz. ASW 30mm. **Obv.** Crowned bust right **Obv. Designer:** G.W. DeSaulles **Rev. Designer:** W.H.J. Blakemore

Date	Mintage	VG8	F12	VF20	XF40	AU50	MS60	MS63
1904 H	140,000	14.00	16.00	20.00	60.00	175	350	1,000
1904 H	—	PF60 2,900						
1907	100,000	14.00	16.00	25.00	75.00	225	400	1,200
1908	160,000	14.00	16.00	20.00	60.00	125	300	800
1909	200,000	14.00	16.00	22.00	60.00	150	350	1,000

KM# 12   50 CENTS
11.78 g., 0.925 Silver, 0.35 oz. ASW 30mm. **Obv.** Crowned bust left **Obv. Designer:** E.B. MacKennal **Rev:** Denomination and date within circle **Rev. Designer:** W.H.J. Blakemore

Date	Mintage	VG8	F12	VF20	XF40	AU50	MS60	MS63
1911	200,000	13.50	15.00	15.00	45.00	100	300	750
1917 C	375,560	13.00	14.00	15.00	40.00	80.00	175	500
1917 C	—	PF60 3,250						
1918 C	294,824	13.00	14.00	15.00	40.00	80.00	175	500
1919 C	306,267	13.00	14.00	15.00	40.00	100	300	1,200
1919 C	—	PF60 3,250						

KM# 5   2 DOLLARS
3.33 g., 0.917 Gold, 0.10 oz. AGW **Obv.** Laureate head left **Rev:** Denomination and date within circle **Obv. Legend:** VICTORIA D: G: REG: / NEWFOUNDLAND

Date	Mintage	F12	VF20	XF40	AU50	MS60	MS63
1865	10,000	150	225	300	400	1,100	8,500
1865 plain edge, Specimen-63, $15,000.	Est. 10	—	—	—	—	—	—
1870	10,000	150	225	300	450	1,500	7,500

Date	Mintage	F12	VF20	XF40	AU50	MS60	MS63
1870 reeded edge, Specimen-63 20,000.	—	—	—	—	—	—	—
1872	6,050	220	400	500	900	2,200	9,000
1872 Specimen-63 $12,500.	Est. 10	—	—	—	—	—	—
1880	2,500	800	1,000	1,200	2,300	3,000	14,500
1880/70	—	—	—	—	—	—	—
Note: Specimen. Bowers and Merena Norweb sale 11-96, specimen 64 realized $70,400.							
1881	10,000	150	200	250	350	1,600	2,500
1881 Specimen; Rare	—	—	—	—	—	—	—
1882 H	25,000	150	200	250	300	700	2,200
1882 H Specimen 4,250.	—	—	—	—	—	—	—
1885	10,000	150	200	250	300	850	2,750
1885 Specimen	—	—	—	—	—	—	—
Note: Bowers and Merena Norweb sale 11-96, specimen 66 realized $44,000							
1888	25,000	150	175	200	250	600	2,000
1888 Specimen; Rare	—	—	—	—	—	—	—

NOVA SCOTIA
PROVINCE
STERLING COINAGE

KM# 1 HALFPENNY TOKEN
Copper, **Obv.** Laureate head left **Rev:** Thistle **Obv. Legend:** PROVINCE OF NOVA SCOTIA

Date	Mintage	VG8	F12	VF20	XF40	AU50	MS60	MS63
1823	400,000	3.00	6.00	13.00	60.00	150	275	—
1823 without hyphen	Inc. above	5.00	10.00	35.00	125	225	325	—
1824	118,636	6.00	12.00	27.00	65.00	250	450	—
1832	800,000	3.00	5.00	13.50	40.00	125	225	—

KM# 1a HALFPENNY TOKEN
Copper, **Obv.** Laureate head left, draped collar **Rev:** Thistle **Obv. Legend:** PROVINCE OF NOVA SCOTIA

Date	Mintage	VG8	F12	VF20	XF40	AU50	MS60	MS63
1382 1382 (error)	—	500	700	1,650	—	—	—	—
1832 (imitation)	—	3.00	9.00	27.00	75.00	95.00	125	200
1832/1382	—	10.00	15.00	50.00	150	—	—	—

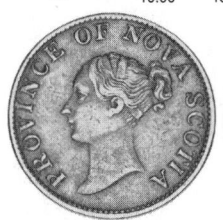

KM# 3 HALFPENNY TOKEN
Copper, **Obv.** Head left **Rev:** Thistle **Obv. Legend:** PROVINCE OF NOVA SCOTIA

Date	Mintage	VG8	F12	VF20	XF40	AU50	MS60	MS63
1840 small 0	300,000	3.50	10.00	25.00	65.00	125	185	—
1840 large 0	Inc. above	4.00	10.00	40.00	125	185	250	—
1840 medium 0	Inc. above	3.50	9.00	25.00	65.00	125	185	—
1843	300,000	3.00	6.00	24.00	65.00	125	185	—

KM# 5   HALFPENNY TOKEN
Copper,

Date	Mintage	VG8	F12	VF20	XF40	AU50	MS60	MS63
1856 without LCW	720,000	3.00	4.00	7.50	23.00	85.00	175	—
1856 without LCW, Proof	—	PF60 600						
1856 without LCW, inverted A for V in PROVINCE, Proof	—	PF60 600						

KM# 5a   HALFPENNY TOKEN
Bronze,

Date	Mintage	VG8	F12	VF20	XF40	AU50	MS60	MS63
1856 with LCW, Proof	—	PF60 600						

KM# 2   1 PENNY TOKEN
Copper, **Obv.** Laureate head left **Rev:** Thistle **Obv. Legend:** PROVINCE OF NOVA SCOTIA

Date	Mintage	VG8	F12	VF20	XF40	AU50	MS60	MS63
1824	217,776	4.00	10.00	26.00	85.00	240	400	—
1832	200,000	4.00	8.00	15.00	55.00	190	350	—

KM# 2a   1 PENNY TOKEN
Copper, **Obv.** Laureate head left **Rev:** Thistle **Obv. Legend:** PROVINCE OF NOVA SCOTIA

Date	Mintage	VG8	F12	VF20	XF40	AU50	MS60	MS63
1832 (imitation)	—	3.75	7.50	22.50	85.00	—	—	—

KM# 4   1 PENNY TOKEN
Copper, 32mm. **Obv.** Head left **Rev:** Thistle **Obv. Legend:** PROVINCE OF NOVA SCOTIA

Date	Mintage	VG8	F12	VF20	XF40	AU50	MS60	MS63
1840	150,000	3.50	9.00	23.00	65.00	250	450	—
1843/0	150,000	45.00	75.00	250	—	—	—	—
1843	Inc. above	4.00	12.00	24.00	65.00	250	450	—

NOVA SCOTIA

KM# 6   1 PENNY TOKEN

Copper, **Obv.** Crowned head left **Rev:** Plant **Obv. Legend:** VICTORIA D: G: BRITANNIA R: REG: F: D: **Rev. Legend:** PROVINCE OF NOVA SCOTIA

Date	Mintage	VG8	F12	VF20	XF40	AU50	MS60	MS63
1856 without LCW	360,000	4.00	7.50	13.00	35.00	150	300	—
1856 with LCW	Inc. above	2.50	5.00	12.00	35.00	200	350	—

KM# 6a   1 PENNY TOKEN

Bronze, **Obv.** Crowned head left **Rev:** Plant **Obv. Legend:** VICTORIA D: G: BRITANNIA R: REG: F: D: **Rev. Legend:** PROVINCE OF NOVA SCOTIA

Date	Mintage	VG8	F12	VF20	XF40	AU50	MS60	MS63
1856	—	PF60 400						

DECIMAL COINAGE

KM# 7   HALF CENT

Bronze, **Obv.** Laureate bust left **Rev:** Crown and date within beaded circle, wreath of roses surrounds **Obv. Legend:** VICTORIA D:G: BRITT: REG:F:D: **Rev. Legend:** NOVA SCOTIA

Date	Mintage	VG8	F12	VF20	XF40	AU50	MS60	MS63
1861	400,000	5.00	7.00	8.00	13.00	35.00	60.00	300
1864	400,000	5.00	7.00	8.00	13.00	30.00	55.00	250
1864	—	PF60 300						

KM# 8.2   CENT

Bronze, **Obv.** Laureate bust left **Rev:** Crown and date within beaded circle, wreath of roses surrounds **Obv. Legend:** VICTORIA D:G: BRITT: REG:F:D: **Rev. Legend:** NOVA SCOTIA **Note:** Prev. KM#8. Small rosebud right of SCOTIA. The Royal Mint report records mintage of 1 million for 1862, which is considered incorrect.

Date	Mintage	VG8	F12	VF20	XF40	AU50	MS60	MS63
1861	800,000	3.00	4.50	5.00	11.00	60.00	125	400
1862	Est. 1000000	45.00	75.00	150	300	650	1,300	—
1864	800,000	3.00	4.50	5.00	16.00	75.00	150	450

PRINCE EDWARD ISLAND
PROVINCE
DECIMAL COINAGE

KM# 4 CENT
Bronze, **Obv.** Crowned head left within beaded circle **Rev:** Trees within beaded circle **Obv. Legend:** VICTORIA QUEEN **Rev. Legend:** PRINCE EDWARD ISLAND

Date	Mintage	VG8	F12	VF20	XF40	AU50	MS60	MS63
1871	2,000,000	2.50	4.00	6.50	20.00	50.00	100	185
1871	—	PF60 2,000						

CUT & COUNTERMARKED COINAGE

KM# 1 SHILLING
Silver, **Note:** Countermark on center plug of Spanish or Spanish Colonial 8 Reales.

Date	Mintage	VG8	F12	VF20	XF40	AU50	MS60	MS63
ND (1813)	1,000	2,500	4,500	7,500	—	—	—	—

KM# 3 5 SHILLING
Silver, **Note:** Countermark on holed Lima 8 Reales, KM#106.2.

Date	Mintage	VG8	F12	VF20	XF40	AU50	MS60	MS63
ND1809-11	1,000	2,500	4,500	7,500	—	—	—	—

KM# 2.1 5 SHILLING
Silver, **Note:** Countermark on holed Mexico City 8 Reales, KM#109.

Date	Mintage	VG8	F12	VF20	XF40	AU50	MS60	MS63
1791-1808	—	1,500	2,250	3,750	—	—	—	—

KM# 2.2 5 SHILLING
Silver, **Note:** Countermark on holed Mexico City 8 Reales, KM#110.

Date	Mintage	VG8	F12	VF20	XF40	AU50	MS60	MS63
ND1808-11	—	1,500	2,250	3,750	—	—	—	—

MEXICO

The United States of Mexico, located immediately south of the United States has an area of 759,529 sq. mi. (1,967,183 sq. km.) and an estimated population of 100 million. Capital: Mexico City. The economy is based on agriculture, manufacturing and mining. Oil, cotton, silver, coffee, and shrimp are exported.

Mexico was the site of highly advanced Indian civilizations 1,500 years before conquistador Hernando Cortes conquered the wealthy Aztec empire of Montezuma, 1519-21, and founded a Spanish colony, which lasted for nearly 300 years. During the Spanish period, Mexico, then called New Spain, stretched from Guatemala to the present states of Wyoming and California, its present northern boundary having been established by the secession of Texas during 1836 and the war of 1846-48 with the United States.

Independence from Spain was declared by Father Miguel Hidalgo on Sept. 16, 1810, (Mexican Independence Day) and was achieved by General Agustin de Iturbide in1821. Iturbide became emperor in 1822 but was deposed when a republic was established a year later. For more than fifty years following the birth of the republic, the political scene of Mexico was characterized by turmoil, which saw two emperors (including the unfortunate Maximilian), several dictators and an average of one new government every nine months passing swiftly from obscurity to oblivion. The land, social, economic and labor reforms promulgated by the Reform Constitution of Feb. 5, 1917 established the basis for sustained economic development and participative democracy that have made Mexico one of the most politically stable countries of modern Latin America.

SPANISH COLONY

COB COINAGE

KM# 24 1/2 REAL
1.69 g., 0.931 Silver, 0.05 oz. ASW **Ruler:** Philip V **Obv.** Legend around crowned PHILIPVS monogram **Rev:** Legend around cross, lions and castles **Mint:** Mexico City **Note:** Mint mark M, Mo. For this series completeness of date is a stronger determining factor of price than grade. The values listed below reflect a range for examples with an average amount of date visible.

Date	Mintage	VG8	F12	VF20	XF40
ND(1701-28) Date off flan	—	25.00	40.00	65.00	—
1701 L	—	125	200	300	—
1702 L	—	125	200	300	—
1703 L	—	125	200	300	—
1704 L	—	125	200	300	—
1705 L	—	125	200	300	—
1706 J	—	125	200	300	—
1707 J	—	125	200	300	—
1708 J	—	125	200	285	—
1709 J	—	125	200	285	—
1710 J	—	125	200	285	—
1711 J	—	125	200	285	—
1712 J	—	125	200	285	—
1713 J	—	125	200	285	—
1714 J	—	125	200	285	—
1715 J	—	125	200	285	—
1716 J	—	125	200	285	—
1717 J	—	125	200	285	—
1718/7	—	—	—	—	—
1718 J	—	125	200	285	—
1719 J	—	125	200	285	—
1720 J	—	125	200	285	—
1721 J	—	125	200	285	—
1722 J	—	125	200	285	—
1723 J	—	125	200	285	—
1724 J	—	125	200	285	—
1724 D	—	125	200	285	—
1725 D	—	125	200	285	—
1726 D	—	125	200	285	—
1727 D	—	125	200	285	—
1728 D	—	125	200	285	—

KM# 25 1/2 REAL
1.69 g., 0.931 Silver, 0.05 oz. ASW **Ruler:** Luis I **Obv.** Legend around crowned LVDOVICVS monogram **Rev:** Legend around cross, lions and castles **Note:** Mint mark M, Mo.

Date	Mintage	VG8	F12	VF20	XF40
ND(1724-25) Date off flan	—	125	200	250	—
1724 D Rare	—	—	—	—	—
1725 D Rare	—	—	—	—	—

KM# 24a 1/2 REAL
1.69 g., 0.916 Silver, 0.05 oz. ASW **Ruler:** Philip V **Obv.** Legend around crowned PHILIPVS monogram **Rev:** Legend around cross, lions and castles **Mint:** Mexico City **Note:** Mint mark M, Mo.

Date	Mintage	VG8	F12	VF20	XF40
ND(1729-33) Date off flan	—	25.00	40.00	65.00	—
1729 R	—	90.00	120	150	—
1730 F Rare	—	—	—	—	—
1730 R	—	90.00	120	150	—
1731 F	—	90.00	120	150	—
1732/1 F	—	90.00	120	150	—
1732 F	—	90.00	120	150	—
1733/2 F	—	90.00	120	150	—
1733 F	—	90.00	120	150	—

KM# 30 REAL
3.38 g., 0.931 Silver, 0.10 oz. ASW **Ruler:** Philip V **Obv.** Legend and date around crowned arms **Rev:** Lions and castles in angles of cross **Obv. Legend:** PHILIPVS V DEI G **Mint:** Mexico City **Note:** Mint mark M, Mo. For this series completeness of date is a stronger determining factor of price than grade. The values listed below reflect a range for examples with an average amount of date visible.

Date	Mintage	VG8	F12	VF20	XF40
ND(1701-28) Date off flan	—	35.00	55.00	75.00	—
1701 L	—	165	275	400	—
1702 L	—	165	275	400	—
1703 L	—	165	275	400	—
1704 L	—	165	275	400	—
1705 L	—	165	275	400	—
1706 J	—	165	275	400	—
1707 J	—	165	275	400	—
1708 J	—	165	275	400	—
1709 J	—	165	275	400	—
1710 J	—	165	275	400	—
1711 J	—	165	275	400	—
1712 J	—	165	275	400	—
1713 J	—	165	275	400	—
1714 J	—	165	275	400	—
1715 J	—	150	275	400	—
1716 J	—	150	275	400	—
1717 J	—	150	275	400	—
1718 J	—	150	275	400	—

Date	Mintage	VG8	F12	VF20	XF40
1719 J	—	150	275	400	—
1720/19 J Rare	—	—	—	—	—
1720 J	—	150	275	400	—
1721 J	—	150	275	400	—
1722 J	—	150	275	400	—
1723 J	—	150	275	400	—
1726 D	—	150	275	400	—
1727 D	—	150	275	400	—
1728 D	—	150	275	400	—

KM# A31 REAL
3.38 g., 0.931 Silver, 0.10 oz. ASW **Ruler:** Luis I **Mint:** Mexico City **Note:** A significant portion of the legend must be visibile for proper attribution. Mint mark M, Mo.

Date	Mintage	G4	VG8	F12	VF20	XF40
1724 D Rare	—	—	—	—	—	—
1725 D Rare	—	—	—	—	—	—

KM# 30a REAL
3.38 g., 0.916 Silver, 0.10 oz. ASW **Ruler:** Philip V **Obv.** Legend and date around crowned arms **Rev:** Lions and castles in angles of cross **Obv. Legend:** PHILIPVS V DEI G **Mint:** Mexico City **Note:** Mint mark M, Mo.

Date	Mintage	VG8	F12	VF20	XF40
ND(1729-32) Date off flan	—	30.00	50.00	70.00	—
1729 R	—	90.00	125	175	
1730 R	—	90.00	125	175	
1730 F	—	90.00	125	175	
1730 G	—	90.00	125	175	
1731 F	—	90.00	125	175	
1732 F	—	90.00	125	175	

KM# 35 2 REALES
6.77 g., 0.931 Silver, 0.20 oz. ASW **Ruler:** Philip V **Obv.** Legend and date around crowned arms **Rev:** Lions and castles in angles of cross **Obv. Legend:** PHILIPVS V DEI G **Mint:** Mexico City **Note:** Mint mark M, Mo. For this series completeness of date is a stronger determining factor of price than grade. The values listed below reflect a range for examples with an average amount of date visible.

Date	Mintage	G4	VG8	F12	VF20	XF40
ND(1701-28) Date off flan	—	—	45.00	65.00	90.00	—
1701 L	—	—	175	300	450	—
1702 L	—	—	175	300	450	—
1703 L	—	—	175	300	450	—
1704 L	—	—	175	300	450	—
1705 L	—	—	175	300	450	—
1706 J	—	—	175	300	450	—
1707 J	—	—	175	300	450	—
1708 J	—	—	175	300	450	—
1710 J	—	—	175	300	450	—
1711 J	—	—	175	300	450	—
1712 J	—	—	175	300	450	—
1713 J	—	—	175	300	450	—
1714 J	—	—	185	325	475	—
1715 J	—	—	185	325	475	—
1716 J	—	—	185	325	475	—
1717 J	—	—	185	325	475	—
1718 J	—	—	185	325	475	—
1719 J	—	—	185	325	475	—
1720 J	—	—	185	325	475	—
1721 J	—	—	185	325	475	—
1722 J	—	—	185	325	475	—
1723 J	—	—	185	325	475	—
1724 J	—	—	185	325	475	—
1725 D Rare	—	—	—	—	—	—
1726 D	—	—	185	325	475	—
1727 D	—	—	185	325	475	—
1728 D	—	—	185	325	475	—

KM# 35a 2 REALES
6.77 g., 0.916 Silver, 0.20 oz. ASW **Ruler:** Philip V **Obv.** Legend and date around crowned arms **Rev:** Lions and castles in angles of cross **Obv. Legend:** PHILIPVS V DEI G **Mint:** Mexico City **Note:** Mint mark M, Mo.

Date	Mintage	VG8	F12	VF20	XF40
ND(1729-32) Date off flan	—	40.00	60.00	90.00	—
1729 R	—	125	175	225	—
1730 G/R Rare	—	—	—	—	—
1730 G Rare	—	—	—	—	—
1730 R	—	125	175	225	—
1731 F	—	125	175	225	—
1731/0 F Requires Confirmation	—	—	—	—	—
1732 F	—	125	175	225	—
1733 F Rare	—	—	—	—	—

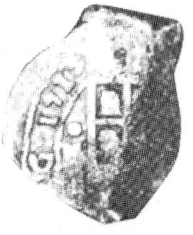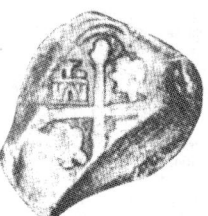

KM# 40 4 REALES
13.54 g., 0.931 Silver, 0.40 oz. ASW **Ruler:** Philip V **Obv.** Legend and date around crowned arms **Rev:** Lions and castles in angles of cross **Obv. Legend:** PHILIPVS V DEI G **Mint:** Mexico City **Note:** Mint mark M, Mo. For this series completeness of date is a stronger determining factor of price than grade. The values listed below reflect a range for examples with an average amount of date visible.

Date	Mintage	G4	VG8	F12	VF20
ND ND (1701-28) Date off flan	—	—	50.00	75.00	100
1701 L	—	—	225	475	800
1702 L	—	—	225	475	800
1703 L	—	—	225	475	800
1704 L	—	—	225	475	800
1705 L	—	—	225	475	800
1706 J	—	—	225	475	800
1707 J	—	—	225	475	800
1708 J	—	—	225	475	800
1709 J	—	—	225	475	800
1710 J	—	—	225	475	800
1711 J	—	—	200	425	700
1712 J	—	—	200	425	700
1713 J	—	—	200	425	700
1714 J	—	—	200	425	700
1715 J Rare	—	—	—	—	—
1716 J	—	—	250	600	1,000
1717 J	—	—	250	600	1,000
1718 J	—	—	250	600	1,000
1719 J	—	—	250	600	1,000
1720 J	—	—	250	600	1,000
1721 J	—	—	250	600	1,000
1722 J	—	—	250	600	1,000
1723 J	—	—	250	600	1,000
1726 D	—	—	250	600	1,000
1727 D	—	—	250	600	1,000
1728 D	—	—	250	600	1,000

KM# 42 4 REALES

13.54 g., 0.931 Silver, 0.40 oz. ASW **Ruler:** Luis I **Obv.** Legend around crowned arms **Rev:** Lions and castles in angles of cross, legend around **Obv. Legend:** LVDOVICVS I DEI G **Mint:** Mexico City **Note:** A significant portion of the legend must be visible for proper attribution. Mint mark M, Mo.

Date	Mintage	G4	VG8	F12	VF20	XF40
1724 D Rare	—	—	—	—	—	—
1725 D Rare	—	—	—	—	—	—

KM# 40a 4 REALES

13.54 g., 0.916 Silver, 0.40 oz. ASW **Ruler:** Philip V **Obv.** Legend around crowned arms **Rev:** Lions and castles in angles of cross **Obv. Legend:** PHILIPVS V DEI G **Mint:** Mexico City **Note:** Mint mark M, Mo.

Date	Mintage	G4	VG8	F12	VF20	XF40
ND(1729-33)	—	—	50.00	75.00	100	—
Date off flan						
1729 R	—	—	150	250	350	—
1730 R	—	—	150	250	350	—
1730 F/G	—	—	150	250	375	—
1730 G	—	—	150	250	350	—
1731/0 F	—	—	150	250	375	—
1731 F	—	—	150	250	350	—
1732/1 F	—	—	150	250	350	—
1732 F	—	—	150	250	350	—
1733/2 F Rare	—	—	—	—	—	—
1733 F Rare	—	—	—	—	—	—

KM# 41 4 REALES

13.54 g., 0.916 Silver, 0.40 oz. ASW **Ruler:** Philip V **Obv.** Legend and date around crowned arms **Rev:** Lions and castles in angles of cross, legend around **Obv. Legend:** PHILIPVS V DEI G **Mint:** Mexico City **Note:** Klippe. Similar to KM#40a. Mint mark M, Mo.

Date	Mintage	G4	VG8	F12	VF20	XF40
1733 MF	—	—	450	600	750	—
1734 MF Rare	—	—	—	—	—	—
1734/3 MF	—	—	450	600	750	—

KM# 46 8 REALES

27.07 g., 0.931 Silver, 0.81 oz. ASW **Ruler:** Charles II **Obv.** Legend around crowned arms **Rev:** Legend around cross, lions and castles **Obv. Legend:** CAROLVS II DEI G **Note:** Struck at Mexico City Mint, mint mark M, Mo.

Date	Mintage	G4	VG8	F12	VF20
ND(1667-1701) Date	—	—	90.00	110	150
off flan					
1701 L Rare	—	—	—	—	—

KM# 47 8 REALES

27.07 g., 0.931 Silver, 0.81 oz. ASW **Ruler:** Philip V **Obv.** Legend and date around crowned arms **Rev:** Lions and castles in angles of cross, legend around **Obv. Legend:** PHILIPVS V DEI G **Mint:** Mexico City **Note:** Mint mark M, Mo. For this series completeness of date is a stronger determining factor of price than grade. The values listed below reflect a range for examples with an average amount of date visible.

Date	Mintage	G4	VG8	F12	VF20
ND(1701-28) Date off flan	—	—	70.00	90.00	120
1701 L Rare	—	—	—	—	—

Date	Mintage	G4	VG8	F12	VF20
1702 L Rare	—	—	—	—	—
1703 L Rare	—	—	—	—	—
1704 L Rare	—	—	—	—	—
1705 L Rare	—	—	—	—	—
1706 J Rare	—	—	—	—	—
1707 J Rare	—	—	—	—	—
1708 J Rare	—	—	—	—	—
1709 J Rare	—	—	—	—	—
1710 J Rare	—	—	—	—	—
1711 J	—	—	200	1,100	2,000
1712 J	—	—	200	1,100	2,000
1713 J	—	—	200	1,100	2,000
1714 J	—	—	200	1,100	2,000
1715 J	—	—	200	1,200	2,250
1716 J	—	—	575	2,300	4,500
1717 J	—	—	575	2,300	4,500
1718/7 J	—	—	575	2,300	4,500
1718 J	—	—	525	2,000	4,000
1719 J	—	—	525	2,000	4,000
1720 J	—	—	525	2,000	4,000
1721 J	—	—	525	2,000	4,000
1722 J	—	—	525	2,000	4,000
1723 J	—	—	525	2,000	4,000
1724 D	—	—	525	2,000	4,000
1725 D	—	—	525	2,000	4,000
1726 D	—	—	525	2,000	4,000
1727 D	—	—	525	2,000	4,000
1728 D	—	—	600	2,400	5,000

KM# 49   8 REALES

27.07 g., 0.931 Silver, 0.81 oz. ASW **Ruler:** Luis I **Obv.** Legend and date around crowned arms **Rev:** Lions and castles in angles of cross, legend around **Obv. Legend:** LVDOVICVS I DEI G **Rev. Legend:** INDIARVM * REX HISPANIARV ... **Mint:** Mexico City **Note:** A significant portion of the legend must be visible for proper attribution. Mint mark M, Mo.

Date	Mintage	G4	VG8	F12	VF20
ND(1724-25) Date off flan; Rare	—	—	—	—	—
1724 D Rare	—	—	—	—	—
1725 D Rare	—	—	—	—	—

KM# 47a   8 REALES

27.07 g., 0.916 Silver, 0.79 oz. ASW **Ruler:** Philip V **Obv.** Legend and date around crowned arms **Rev:** Lions and castles in angles of cross, legend around **Obv. Legend:** PHILIPVS V DEI G **Mint:** Mexico City **Note:** Mint mark M, Mo.

Date	Mintage	G4	VG8	F12	VF20
ND(1729-33) Date off flan	—	—	70.00	100	125
1729 R	—	—	150	225	350
1730 G/R	—	—	150	225	350
1730 R	—	—	150	225	350
1730 G	—	—	150	225	350
1730 F Requires Confirmation	—	—	—	—	—
1731/0 F	—	—	150	225	350
1731/0 F/G Rare	—	—	—	—	—
1731 F	—	—	135	210	325
1732/1 F	—	—	135	210	325
1732 F	—	—	135	210	350
1733/2 F	—	—	200	300	400
1733 F	—	—	200	300	400

KM# 48   8 REALES

0.92 g., Silver, **Ruler:** Philip V **Obv.** Legend around crowned arms **Rev:** Lions and castles in angles of cross, legend around **Mint:** Mexico City **Note:** Klippe. Similar to KM#47a. Mint mark M, Mo.

Date	Mintage	G4	VG8	F12	VF20
ND(1733-34) Date off flan	—	—	200	350	500
1733 F	—	—	550	750	1,150
1733 MF	—	—	450	600	750
1734/3 MF	—	—	500	750	1,000
1734 MF	—	—	500	750	1,000

KM# 50   ESCUDO

3.38 g., 0.917 Gold, 0.10 oz. AGW **Ruler:** Charles II **Obv.** Legend and date around crowned arms **Rev:** Lions and castles in angles of cross, legend around **Obv. Legend:** CAROLVS II DEI G **Mint:** Mexico City

Date	Mintage	VG8	F12	VF20	XF40
ND(1679-1701) Date off flan	—	—	1,200	1,500	2,000
1701/0 MXo L Rare	—	—	—	—	—

KM# 51.1   ESCUDO

3.38 g., 0.917 Gold, 0.10 oz. AGW **Ruler:** Philip V **Obv.** Legend and date around crowned arms **Rev:** Lions and castles in angles of cross, legend around **Obv. Legend:** PHILIPVS V DEI G **Mint:** Mexico City

Date	Mintage	VG8	F12	VF20	XF40
ND(1702-13) Date off flan	—	—	1,000	1,350	1,500
1702 MXo L Rare	—	—	—	—	—
1703/2 MXo L Rare	—	—	—	—	—
1704 MXo L Rare	—	—	—	—	—
1707 MXo J Rare	—	—	—	—	—
1708 MXo J Rare	—	—	—	—	—
1709 MXo J Rare	—	—	—	—	—
1710 MXo J Rare	—	—	—	—	—

Date	Mintage	VG8	F12	VF20	XF40
1711 MXo J	—	—	1,500	2,500	3,500
1712 MXo J	—	—	1,500	2,500	3,500
1713 MXo J	—	—	1,500	2,500	3,500

KM# 51.2 ESCUDO
3.38 g., 0.917 Gold, 0.10 oz. AGW **Ruler:** Philip V **Obv.** Legend and date around crowned arms **Rev:** Lions and castles in angles of cross, legend around **Obv. Legend:** PHILIPVS V DEI G **Mint:** Mexico City

Date	Mintage	VG8	F12	VF20	XF40
1712 Mo J	—	—	2,000	3,000	4,000
1714 Mo J	—	—	1,400	2,000	3,000
1714 Mo J J's 1's (J7J4J) Rare	—	—	—	—	—
1715 Mo J	—	—	2,000	3,000	4,000
1727 Mo J Rare	—	—	—	—	—
1728 Mo J Rare	—	—	—	—	—
1731 F Rare	—	—	—	—	—

Note: Die-struck counterfeits of 1731 F exist

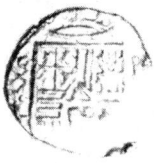 

KM# 52 2 ESCUDOS
6.77 g., 0.917 Gold, 0.20 oz. AGW **Ruler:** Philip V **Obv.** Legend and date around crowned arms **Rev:** Legend around cross **Obv. Legend:** CAROLVS II DEI G **Mint:** Mexico City

Date	Mintage	VG8	F12	VF20	XF40
ND(1679-1701) Date off flan	—	—	1,300	1,750	2,500
1701 MXo L Rare	—	—	—	—	—

KM# 53.1 2 ESCUDOS
6.77 g., 0.917 Gold, 0.20 oz. AGW **Ruler:** Philip V **Obv.** Legend and date around crowned arms **Rev:** Legend around cross **Obv. Legend:** PHILIPVS V DEI G **Mint:** Mexico City

Date	Mintage	VG8	F12	VF20	XF40
ND(1704-13) Date off flan	—	—	1,250	1,500	2,000
1704 MXo L Rare	—	—	—	—	—
1708 MXo J Rare	—	—	—	—	—
1710 MXo J Rare	—	—	—	—	—
1711 MXo J	—	—	2,500	3,500	4,500
1712 MXo J	—	—	2,500	3,500	4,500
1713 MXo J	—	—	2,500	3,500	4,500

KM# 53.2 2 ESCUDOS
6.77 g., 0.917 Gold, 0.20 oz. AGW **Ruler:** Philip V **Obv.** Legend and date around crowned arms **Rev:** Legend around

cross **Obv. Legend:** PHILIPVS V DEI G **Mint:** Mexico City
Note: Struck counterfeits exist for 1731.

Date	Mintage	VG8	F12	VF20	XF40
ND(1714-31) Date off flan	—	—	1,500	1,750	2,500
1714 Mo J	—	—	—	2,500	3,500
1715 Mo J	—	—	—	3,000	4,000
1717 Mo J Rare	—	—	—	—	—
1722 Mo J Rare	—	—	—	—	—
1729 Mo R Rare	—	—	—	—	—
1731 Mo F Rare	—	—	—	—	—

KM# A54 2 ESCUDOS
6.77 g., 0.917 Gold, 0.20 oz. AGW **Ruler:** Luis I **Obv.** Legend and date around crowned arms **Rev:** Legend around cross **Obv. Legend:** LVDOVICVS I DEI G. **Mint:** Mexico City
Note: A significant portion of the legend must be visible for proper attribution.

Date	Mintage	VG8	F12	VF20	XF40
ND (1724)Mo D Rare	—	—	—	—	—

 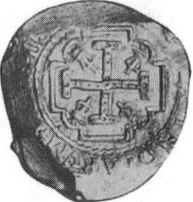

KM# 54 4 ESCUDOS
13.54 g., 0.917 Gold, 0.40 oz. AGW **Ruler:** Charles II **Obv.** Legend and date around crowned arms **Rev:** Legend around cross **Obv. Legend:** CAROLVS II DEI G **Mint:** Mexico City

Date	Mintage	VG8	F12	VF20	XF40	MS60
ND(1679-1701) Date off flan	—	—	2,500	3,500	4,750	—
1701 MXo L Rare	—	—	—	—	—	—

KM# 55.1 4 ESCUDOS
13.54 g., 0.917 Gold, 0.40 oz. AGW **Ruler:** Philip V **Obv.** Legend and date around crowned arms **Rev:** Legend around cross **Obv. Legend:** PHILIPVS V DEI G **Mint:** Mexico City

Date	Mintage	VG8	F12	VF20	XF40
ND(1705-13) Date off flan	—	—	2,500	3,000	4,000
1705 MXo J Rare	—	—	—	—	—
1706 MXo L Rare	—	—	—	—	—
1711 MXo J	—	—	3,500	4,750	6,000
1712 MXo J	—	—	3,500	4,750	6,000
1713 MXo J	—	—	3,500	4,750	6,000

KM# 55.2 4 ESCUDOS

13.54 g., 0.917 Gold, 0.40 oz. AGW **Ruler:** Philip V **Obv.**
Legend and date around crowned arms **Rev:** Legend around
cross **Obv. Legend:** PHILIPVS V DEI G **Mint:** Mexico City

Date	Mintage	VG8	F12	VF20	XF40
ND(1714-20) Date off flan	—	—	2,500	3,500	4,500
1714 Mo J	—	—	—	5,500	7,000
1715 Mo J	—	—	—	5,500	7,000
1720 Mo J Rare	—	—	—	—	—

KM# 57.1 8 ESCUDOS

27.07 g., 0.917 Gold, 0.79 oz. AGW **Ruler:** Philip V **Obv.**
Legend and date around crowned arms **Rev:** Legend around
cross **Obv. Legend:** PHILIPVS V DEI G **Mint:** Mexico City

Date	Mintage	VG8	F12	VF20	XF40
ND(1701-13) Date off flan	—	—	2,500	3,500	4,500
1701 MXo L Rare	—	—	—	—	—
1703 MXo L Rare	—	—	—	—	—
1706 MXo J Rare	—	—	—	—	—
1708 MXo J Rare	—	—	—	—	—
1709 MXo J Rare	—	—	—	—	—
1710 MXo J Rare	—	—	—	—	—
1711 MXo J	—	—	3,500	4,500	6,000
1712 MXo J	—	—	3,500	4,500	6,000
1713 MXo J	—	—	3,500	4,500	6,000

KM# 57.2 8 ESCUDOS

27.07 g., 0.917 Gold, 0.79 oz. AGW **Ruler:** Philip V **Obv.**
Legend and date around crowned arms **Rev:** Legend around
cross **Obv. Legend:** PHILIPVS V DEI G **Mint:** Mexico City

Date	Mintage	VG8	F12	VF20	XF40
ND(1714-32) Mo Date off flan	—	—	2,750	3,750	5,000
1714 Mo J	—	—	4,000	5,500	7,500
1714 Mo Date over GRAT on obverse	—	—	6,000	7,500	9,000
1715 Mo J	—	—	5,000	6,500	8,000
1717/6 Mo J Rare	—	—	—	—	—
1720/19 Mo J Rare	—	—	—	—	—
1723 Mo J Rare	—	—	—	—	—

Date	Mintage	VG8	F12	VF20	XF40
1727/6 Mo D Rare	—	—	—	—	—
1728/7 Mo D Rare	—	—	—	—	—
1729 Mo R Rare	—	—	—	—	—
1730 Mo R Rare	—	—	—	—	—
1730 Mo F Rare	—	—	—	—	—
1731 Mo F Rare	—	—	—	—	—
1732 Mo F Rare	—	—	—	—	—

KM# 57.3 8 ESCUDOS

27.07 g., 0.917 Gold, 0.79 oz. AGW **Ruler:** Philip V **Obv.**
Date around crowned arms **Rev:** Legend and date around
cross **Obv. Legend:** PHILIPVS V DEI G **Mint:** Mexico City

Date	Mintage	VG8	F12	VF20	XF40
1714 Mo J Date on reverse	—	—	6,000	7,500	9,000

KM# 58 8 ESCUDOS

27.07 g., 0.917 Gold, 0.79 oz. AGW **Ruler:** Luis I **Obv.**
Legend and date around crowned arms **Rev:** Legend around
cross **Obv. Legend:** LVDOVICVS I DEI G **Mint:** Mexico City
Note: A significant portion of the legend must be visible for
proper attribution.

Date	Mintage	VG8	F12	VF20	XF40
ND(1724-25) Mo D Rare	—	—	—	—	—

ROYAL COINAGE

Struck on specially prepared round planchets using
well centered dies in excellent condition to prove the quality
of the minting to the Viceroy or even to the King.

KM# R24 1/2 REAL

1.69 g., 0.931 Silver, 0.05 oz. ASW **Ruler:** Philip V **Mint:**
Mexico City **Note:** Normally found holed. Mint mark Mo.

Date	Mintage	G4	VG8	F12	VF20	XF40
1715Mo J	—	—	250	400	575	750
1719Mo J	—	—	250	400	575	750
1721Mo J	—	—	250	400	575	750
1722Mo J	—	—	250	400	575	750
1726Mo D	—	—	250	400	575	750
1727Mo D	—	—	250	400	575	750

KM# R25 1/2 REAL

1.69 g., 0.931 Silver, 0.05 oz. ASW **Ruler:** Luis I **Obv.**
Legend around crowned LVDOVICVS monogram **Rev:**
Lions and castles in angles of cross, legend around **Mint:**
Mexico City **Note:** Mint mark Mo.

Date	Mintage	G4	VG8	F12	VF20
1724Mo D Rare	—	—	—	—	—

KM# R24a 1/2 REAL

1.69 g., 0.917 Silver, 0.05 oz. ASW **Ruler:** Philip V **Mint:**
Mexico City **Note:** Normally found holed. Mint mark Mo.

Date	Mintage	G4	VG8	F12	VF20	XF40
1730Mo D	—	—	250	400	575	750

KM# R30 REAL

3.38 g., 0.931 Silver, 0.10 oz. ASW **Ruler:** Philip V **Obv.**
Legend: PHILIPVS V DEI G **Mint:** Mexico City **Note:** Mint
mark Mo.

Date	Mintage	G4	VG8	F12	VF20
1715Mo J Rare	—	—	—	—	—
1716Mo J Rare	—	—	—	—	—
1718Mo J Rare	—	—	—	—	—

KM# R35 2 REALES
6.77 g., 0.931 Silver, 0.20 oz. ASW **Ruler:** Philip V **Obv. Legend:** PHILIPVS V DEI G **Mint:** Mexico City **Note:** Mint mark Mo.

Date	Mintage	G4	VG8	F12	VF20
1715Mo J Rare	—	—	—	—	—

KM# R35a 2 REALES
6.77 g., 0.917 Silver, 0.20 oz. ASW **Ruler:** Philip V **Mint:** Mexico City **Note:** Mint mark Mo.

Date	Mintage	G4	VG8	F12	VF20
1730Mo R Rare	—	—	—	—	—

KM# R40 4 REALES
13.53 g., 0.931 Silver, 0.40 oz. ASW **Ruler:** Philip V **Obv. Legend:** PHILIPVS V DEI G **Mint:** Mexico City **Note:** Mint mark Mo.

Date	Mintage	G4	VG8	F12	VF20	XF40
1716Mo J Rare	—	—	—	—	—	—
1719Mo J Rare	—	—	—	—	—	—
1721Mo J Rare	—	—	—	—	—	—
1722Mo J Rare	—	—	—	—	—	—
1723Mo J Rare	—	—	—	—	—	—

KM# R47 8 REALES
27.07 g., 0.931 Silver, 0.80 oz. ASW **Ruler:** Philip V **Obv. Legend:** PHILIPVS V DEI G **Mint:** Mexico City **Note:** Struck at Mexico City Mint, mint mark Mo.

Date	Mintage	G4	VG8	F12	VF20	XF40
1702Mo L Rare	—	—	—	—	—	—
1703Mo L Rare	—	—	—	—	—	—
1705Mo J Rare	—	—	—	—	—	—
1706Mo J Rare	—	—	—	—	—	—
1709Mo J Rare	—	—	—	—	—	—
1711Mo J Rare	—	—	—	—	—	—
1714Mo J Rare	—	—	—	—	—	—
1715Mo J Rare	—	—	—	—	—	—
1716Mo J Rare	—	—	—	—	—	—
1717Mo J Rare	—	—	—	—	—	—
1719Mo J Rare	—	—	—	—	—	—
1721Mo J Rare	—	—	—	—	—	—
1722Mo J Rare	—	—	—	—	—	—
1723Mo J Rare	—	—	—	—	—	—
1724Mo D Rare	—	—	—	—	—	—
1725Mo D Rare	—	—	—	—	—	—
1726/5Mo D Rare	—	—	—	—	—	—
1726Mo D Rare	—	—	—	—	—	—
1727Mo D Rare	—	—	—	—	—	—

KM# R49 8 REALES
27.07 g., 0.931 Silver, 0.80 oz. ASW **Ruler:** Luis I **Note:** Mint mark Mo.

Date	Mintage	G4	VG8	F12	VF20	XF40
1724 D Rare	—	—	—	—	—	—
1725 D Rare	—	—	—	—	—	—

KM# R47a 8 REALES
27.07 g., 0.917 Silver, 0.79 oz. ASW **Ruler:** Philip V **Mint:** Mexico City **Note:** Mint mark Mo.

Date	Mintage	G4	VG8	F12	VF20	XF40
1729Mo R Rare	—	—	—	—	—	—
1730Mo R/D Rare	—	—	—	—	—	—
1730Mo G Rare	—	—	—	—	—	—

KM# R51.2 ESCUDO
3.38 g., 0.917 Gold, 0.10 oz. AGW **Ruler:** Philip V **Mint:** Mexico City

Date	Mintage	G4	VG8	F12	VF20	XF40
1714Mo J Rare	—	—	—	—	—	—
1715Mo J Rare	—	—	—	—	—	—

KM# R53.1 2 ESCUDOS
6.77 g., 0.917 Gold, 0.20 oz. AGW **Ruler:** Philip V **Mint:** Mexico City

Date	Mintage	G4	VG8	F12	VF20	XF40
1711MXo J Rare	—	—	—	—	—	—
1712MXo J Rare	—	—	—	—	—	—

KM# R55.1 4 ESCUDOS
13.53 g., 0.917 Gold, 0.40 oz. AGW **Ruler:** Philip V **Mint:** Mexico City **Note:** Mint mark M, Mo.

Date	Mintage	G4	VG8	F12	VF20	XF40
1711 Rare	—	—	—	—	—	—

KM# R55.2 4 ESCUDOS
13.53 g., 0.917 Gold, 0.40 oz. AGW **Ruler:** Philip V **Mint:** Mexico City **Note:** Mint mark M, Mo.

Date	Mintage	G4	VG8	F12	VF20	XF40
1714 Rare	—	—	—	—	—	—

KM# R57.1 8 ESCUDOS
27.07 g., 0.917 Gold, 0.79 oz. AGW **Ruler:** Philip V **Mint:** Mexico City

Date	Mintage	G4	VG8	F12	VF20	XF40
1702MXo L Rare	—	—	—	—	—	—
1711MXo J Rare	—	—	—	—	—	—
1712MXo J Rare	—	—	—	—	—	—
1713MXo J Rare	—	—	—	—	—	—

KM# R57.3 8 ESCUDOS
27.07 g., 0.917 Gold, 0.79 oz. AGW **Ruler:** Philip V **Mint:** Mexico City

Date	Mintage	G4	VG8	F12	VF20	XF40
1714Mo J Rare	—	—	—	—	—	—
1715Mo J Rare	—	—	—	—	—	—
1717Mo J Rare	—	—	—	—	—	—
1718Mo J Rare	—	—	—	—	—	—
1723Mo J Rare	—	—	—	—	—	—

MILLED COINAGE

KM# 59 1/8 PILON (1/16 REAL)
Copper, **Ruler:** Ferdinand VII **Obv.** Crowned monogram **Rev:** Castles and lions in wreath **Mint:** Mexico City **Note:** Mint mark Mo.

Date	Mintage	VG8	F12	VF20	XF40	MS60
1814	—	12.00	25.00	55.00	145	—
1815	—	12.00	25.00	55.00	145	—

KM# 63 1/4 TLACO (1/8 REAL)

Copper, **Ruler:** Ferdinand VII **Obv.** Crowned monogram flanked by value and mint mark **Rev:** Arms without shield within wreath **Obv. Legend:** FERDIN. VII... **Mint:** Mexico City **Note:** Mint mark Mo.

Date	Mintage	VG8	F12	VF20	XF40	MS60
1814	—	14.00	30.00	60.00	180	—
1815	—	14.00	30.00	60.00	180	—
1816	—	14.00	30.00	60.00	180	—

KM# 62 1/4 REAL

0.85 g., 0.896 Silver, **Ruler:** Charles IV **Obv.** Crowned rampant lion, left **Rev:** Castle **Mint:** Mexico City **Note:** Mint mark Mo.

Date	Mintage	VG8	F12	VF20	XF40	MS60
1796	—	35.00	65.00	125	200	—
1797	—	35.00	65.00	125	200	—
1798	—	35.00	65.00	125	200	—
1799/8	—	35.00	65.00	125	200	—
1799	—	35.00	65.00	125	200	—
1800	—	35.00	65.00	125	200	—
1801/0	—	10.00	20.00	40.00	70.00	—
1801	—	10.00	20.00	40.00	70.00	—
1802	—	10.00	20.00	40.00	70.00	—
1803	—	10.00	20.00	40.00	70.00	—
1804	—	10.00	20.00	40.00	75.00	—
1805/4	—	12.50	25.00	55.00	85.00	—
1805	—	10.00	22.00	50.00	75.00	—
1806	—	10.00	22.00	50.00	80.00	—
1807/797	—	15.00	30.00	55.00	85.00	—
1807	—	12.50	25.00	50.00	80.00	—
1808	—	12.50	25.00	50.00	80.00	—
1809/8	—	12.50	25.00	50.00	80.00	—
1809	—	12.50	25.00	50.00	80.00	—
1810	—	12.50	25.00	50.00	75.00	—
1811	—	12.50	25.00	50.00	75.00	—
1812	—	12.50	25.00	50.00	75.00	—
1813	—	10.00	20.00	40.00	70.00	—
1815	—	12.50	22.00	50.00	75.00	—
1816	—	10.00	20.00	40.00	70.00	—

KM# 64 2/4 SENAL (1/4 REAL)

Copper, **Ruler:** Ferdinand VII **Obv.** Legend around crowned monogram flanked by mint mark and value **Rev:** Arms without shield within wreath **Obv. Legend:** FERDIN. VII... **Mint:** Mexico City **Note:** Mint mark Mo.

Date	Mintage	VG8	F12	VF20	XF40	MS60
1814	—	14.00	30.00	60.00	180	—
1815/4	—	18.00	36.00	70.00	200	—
1815	—	14.00	30.00	60.00	180	—
1816	—	14.00	30.00	60.00	180	—
1821	—	25.00	48.00	90.00	240	—

KM# 65 1/2 REAL

1.69 g., 0.917 Silver, 0.05 oz. ASW **Ruler:** Philip V **Obv.** Crowned shield flanked by M F, rosettes and small cross **Rev:** Crowned globes flanked by crowned pillars with banner, date below **Obv. Legend:** PHILIP • V • D • G • HISPAN • ET IND • REX **Mint:** Mexico City **Note:** Mint mark M, Mo, MX.

Date	Mintage	VG8	F12	VF20	XF40	MS60
1732 Rare	—	—	—	—	—	—
1732 F	—	500	800	1,200	2,000	—
1733 MF (MX)	—	400	600	1,000	1,500	—
1733 F	—	200	325	550	800	—
1733/2 MF	—	300	400	600	800	—
1733 MF	—	300	400	600	800	—
1734/3 MF	—	20.00	50.00	100	150	—
1734 MF	—	20.00	50.00	100	150	—
1735/4 MF	—	20.00	50.00	100	150	—
1735 MF	—	20.00	50.00	100	150	—
1736/5 MF	—	20.00	50.00	100	150	—
1736 MF	—	20.00	50.00	100	150	—
1737/6 MF	—	20.00	50.00	100	150	—
1737 MF	—	20.00	50.00	100	150	—
1738/7 MF	—	20.00	50.00	100	150	—
1738 MF	—	20.00	50.00	100	150	—
1739 MF	—	20.00	50.00	100	150	—
1740/30 MF	—	20.00	50.00	100	150	—
1740 MF	—	20.00	50.00	100	150	—
1741 MF	—	20.00	50.00	100	150	—

KM# 66 1/2 REAL

1.69 g., 0.917 Silver, 0.05 oz. ASW **Ruler:** Philip V **Obv.** Crowned shield flanked by stars **Rev:** Crowned globes flanked by crowned pillars with banner, date below **Obv. Legend:** PHS • V • D • G • HISP • ET IND • R **Mint:** Mexico City **Note:** Mint mark M, Mo.

Date	Mintage	VG8	F12	VF20	XF40	MS60
1742 M	—	15.00	40.00	75.00	125	—
1743 M	—	15.00	40.00	75.00	125	—
1744/3 M	—	15.00	40.00	75.00	125	—
1744 M	—	15.00	40.00	75.00	125	—
1745 M Rare	—	—	—	—	—	—

Note: Legend variation: PHS. V. D. G. HISP. EST IND. R

Date	Mintage	VG8	F12	VF20	XF40	MS60
1745 M	—	15.00	40.00	75.00	125	—
1746/5 M	—	15.00	40.00	75.00	125	—
1746 M	—	15.00	40.00	75.00	125	—
1747 M	—	15.00	40.00	75.00	125	—

KM# 67.1 1/2 REAL

1.69 g., 0.917 Silver, 0.05 oz. ASW **Ruler:** Ferdinand VI **Obv.** Royal crown **Obv. Legend:** FRD • VI • D • G • HIPS • ET IND • R **Mint:** Mexico City **Note:** Mint mark M, Mo.

Date	Mintage	VG8	F12	VF20	XF40	MS60
1747/6 M	—	15.00	40.00	75.00	125	—
1747 M	—	15.00	40.00	75.00	125	—
1748/7 M	—	15.00	40.00	75.00	125	—
1748 M	—	15.00	40.00	75.00	125	—
1749 M	—	15.00	40.00	75.00	125	—
1750 M	—	15.00	40.00	75.00	125	—
1751 M	—	15.00	40.00	75.00	125	—
1752 M	—	15.00	40.00	75.00	125	—
1753 M	—	15.00	40.00	75.00	125	—
1754 M	—	15.00	40.00	75.00	125	—
1755/6 M	—	15.00	40.00	75.00	125	—
1755 M	—	15.00	40.00	75.00	125	—

Date	Mintage	VG8	F12	VF20	XF40	MS60
1756/5 M	—	15.00	40.00	75.00	125	—
1756 M	—	15.00	40.00	75.00	125	—
1757/6 M	—	15.00	40.00	75.00	125	—
1757 M	—	15.00	40.00	75.00	125	—

KM# 67.2 1/2 REAL
1.69 g., 0.917 Silver, 0.05 oz. ASW **Ruler:** Ferdinand VI **Obv.** Different crown **Mint:** Mexico City **Note:** Mint mark M, Mo.

Date	Mintage	VG8	F12	VF20	XF40	MS60
1757 M	—	15.00	40.00	75.00	125	—
1758/7 M	—	15.00	40.00	75.00	125	—
1758 M	—	15.00	40.00	75.00	125	—
1759 M	—	15.00	40.00	75.00	125	—
1760/59 M	—	15.00	40.00	75.00	125	—
1760 M	—	15.00	40.00	75.00	125	—

KM# 68 1/2 REAL
1.69 g., 0.917 Silver, 0.05 oz. ASW **Ruler:** Charles III **Obv.** Crowned shield flanked by stars **Rev:** Crowned globes flanked by crowned pillars with banner, date below **Obv. Legend:** CAR • III • D • G • HISP • ET IND • R **Mint:** Mexico City **Note:** Mint mark M, Mo.

Date	Mintage	VG8	F12	VF20	XF40	MS60
1760/59 M	—	15.00	40.00	75.00	125	—
1760 M	—	15.00	40.00	75.00	125	—
1761 M	—	15.00	40.00	75.00	125	—
1762 M	—	15.00	40.00	75.00	125	—
1763/2 M	—	15.00	40.00	75.00	125	—
1763 M	—	15.00	40.00	75.00	125	—
1764 M	—	15.00	40.00	75.00	125	—
1765/4 M	—	15.00	40.00	75.00	125	—
1765 M	—	15.00	40.00	75.00	125	—
1766 M	—	15.00	40.00	75.00	125	—
1767 M	—	15.00	40.00	75.00	125	—
1768/6 M	—	15.00	40.00	75.00	125	—
1768 M	—	15.00	40.00	75.00	125	—
1769 M	—	15.00	40.00	75.00	125	—
1770 M	—	15.00	40.00	75.00	125	—
1770 F	—	15.00	40.00	75.00	125	—
1771 F	—	15.00	40.00	75.00	125	—

KM# 69.1 1/2 REAL
1.69 g., 0.903 Silver, 0.05 oz. ASW **Ruler:** Charles III **Rev:** Inverted FM and mint mark **Obv. Legend:** CAROLUS • III • DEI • GRATIA **Mint:** Mexico City **Note:** Mint mark Mo.

Date	Mintage	VG8	F12	VF20	XF40	MS60
1772 Mo FM	—	12.00	35.00	60.00	100	—
1773 Mo FM	—	10.00	25.00	50.00	90.00	—

KM# 69.2 1/2 REAL
1.69 g., 0.903 Silver, 0.05 oz. ASW **Ruler:** Charles III **Obv.** Armored bust of Charles III, right **Rev:** Crown above shield flanked by pillars with banner, normal initials and mint mark **Obv. Legend:** CAROLUS • III • DEI • GRATIA **Mint:** Mexico City **Note:** Mint mark Mo.

Date	Mintage	VG8	F12	VF20	XF40
1772 Mo FF	—	15.00	40.00	70.00	110
1773 Mo FM	—	12.00	35.00	60.00	100
1773 Mo FM CAROLS (error)	—	75.00	150	250	400
1774 Mo FM	—	10.00	25.00	50.00	90.00
1775 Mo FM	—	10.00	25.00	50.00	90.00
1776 Mo FM	—	20.00	40.00	70.00	110

Date	Mintage	VG8	F12	VF20	XF40
1777/6 Mo FM	—	10.00	25.00	50.00	90.00
1777 Mo FM	—	10.00	25.00	50.00	90.00
1778 Mo FF	—	10.00	25.00	50.00	90.00
1779 Mo FF	—	10.00	25.00	50.00	90.00
1780/79 Mo FF	—	10.00	25.00	50.00	90.00
1780 Mo FF	—	10.00	25.00	50.00	90.00
1781 Mo FF	—	10.00	25.00	50.00	90.00
1782/1 Mo FF	—	10.00	25.00	50.00	90.00
1782 Mo FF	—	10.00	25.00	50.00	90.00
1783 Mo FF	—	10.00	25.00	50.00	90.00
1783 Mo FM	—	10.00	25.00	50.00	90.00
1784 Mo FF	—	10.00	25.00	50.00	90.00
1784 Mo FM	—	10.00	25.00	50.00	90.00

KM# 69.2a 1/2 REAL
1.69 g., 0.896 Silver, 0.05 oz. ASW **Ruler:** Charles III **Rev:** Normal initials and mint mark **Note:** Mint mark M, Mo.

Date	Mintage	VG8	F12	VF20	XF40	MS60
1785/4 FM	—	10.00	25.00	50.00	90.00	—
1785 FM	—	10.00	25.00	50.00	90.00	—
1786 FM	—	10.00	25.00	50.00	90.00	—
1787 FM	—	10.00	25.00	50.00	90.00	—
1788 FM	—	10.00	25.00	50.00	90.00	—
1789 FM	—	12.00	35.00	60.00	100	—

KM# 70 1/2 REAL
1.69 g., 0.896 Silver, 0.05 oz. ASW **Ruler:** Charles IV **Obv.** Armored bust of Charles IV, right **Rev:** Crown above shield flanked by pillars with banner **Obv. Legend:** CAROLUS • IV •... **Mint:** Mexico City **Note:** Mint mark M, Mo.

Date	Mintage	VG8	F12	VF20	XF40	MS60
1789 FM	—	12.00	35.00	60.00	100	—
1790 FM	—	12.00	35.00	60.00	100	—

KM# 71 1/2 REAL
1.69 g., 0.896 Silver, 0.05 oz. ASW **Ruler:** Charles IV **Obv.** Armored bust of Charles IIII, right **Rev:** Crown above shield flanked by pillars with banner **Obv. Legend:** CAROLUS • IIII •... **Mint:** Mexico City **Note:** Mint mark M, Mo.

Date	Mintage	VG8	F12	VF20	XF40	MS60
1790 FM	—	12.00	35.00	60.00	100	—

KM# 72 1/2 REAL
1.69 g., 0.903 Silver, 0.05 oz. ASW **Ruler:** Charles IV **Obv.** Armored bust of Charles IIII, right **Rev:** Crowned shield flanked by pillars with banner **Obv. Legend:** CAROLUS • IIII • ... **Rev. Legend:** IND • R • .... **Mint:** Mexico City **Note:** Mint mark Mo.

Date	Mintage	VG8	F12	VF20	XF40	MS60
1792 FM	—	10.00	20.00	55.00	85.00	—
1793 FM	—	10.00	20.00	55.00	85.00	—
1794/3 FM	—	10.00	20.00	55.00	85.00	—
1794 FM	—	10.00	20.00	55.00	85.00	—
1795 FM	—	10.00	20.00	55.00	85.00	—
1796 FM	—	10.00	20.00	55.00	85.00	—
1797 FM	—	10.00	20.00	55.00	85.00	—

Date	Mintage	VG8	F12	VF20	XF40	MS60
1798/7 FM	—	10.00	20.00	55.00	85.00	—
1798 FM	—	10.00	20.00	55.00	85.00	—
1799 FM	—	10.00	20.00	55.00	85.00	—
1800/799 FM	—	10.00	20.00	55.00	85.00	—
1800 FM	—	10.00	20.00	55.00	85.00	—
1801 FM	—	8.00	17.00	33.00	85.00	—
1801 FT	—	4.00	11.00	25.00	50.00	—
1802 FT	—	4.00	11.00	25.00	50.00	—
1803 FT	—	6.00	13.00	27.50	55.00	—
1804 TH	—	4.00	11.00	25.00	50.00	—
1805 TH	—	4.00	11.00	25.00	50.00	—
1806 TH	—	4.00	11.00	25.00	50.00	—
1807/6 TH	—	6.00	13.00	27.50	55.00	—
1807 TH	—	4.00	11.00	25.00	50.00	—
1808/7 TH	—	6.00	13.00	27.50	55.00	—
1808 TH	—	4.00	11.00	25.00	50.00	—

KM# 73 1/2 REAL
1.69 g., 0.903 Silver, 0.05 oz. ASW **Ruler:** Ferdinand VII **Obv.** Armored laureate bust right **Rev:** Crowned shield flanked by pillars **Obv. Legend:** FERDIN.VII... **Rev. Legend:** IND.R.... **Mint:** Mexico City **Note:** Mint mark Mo.

Date	Mintage	VG8	F12	VF20	XF40	MS60
1808 TH	—	4.00	9.00	22.50	40.00	—
1809 TH	—	4.00	9.00	22.50	40.00	—
1810 TH	—	6.00	11.00	25.00	50.00	—
1810 HJ	—	4.00	9.00	22.50	40.00	—
1811 HJ	—	4.00	9.00	22.50	40.00	—
1812/1 HJ	—	8.00	17.00	38.50	85.00	—
1812 HJ	—	4.00	9.00	22.50	40.00	—
1812 JJ	—	13.00	27.50	49.50	105	—
1813/2 JJ	—	13.00	27.50	49.50	105	—
1813 TH	—	4.00	9.00	22.50	40.00	—
1813 JJ	—	7.00	13.00	27.50	80.00	—
1813 HJ	—	8.00	17.00	38.50	95.00	—
1814/3 JJ	—	8.00	17.00	38.50	95.00	—
1814 JJ	—	6.00	11.00	25.00	50.00	—

KM# 74 1/2 REAL
1.69 g., 0.903 Silver, 0.05 oz. ASW **Ruler:** Ferdinand VII **Obv.** Draped laureate bust right **Rev:** Crowned shield flanked by pillars **Obv. Legend:** FERDIN.VII.... **Rev. Legend:** IND.R.... **Mint:** Mexico City **Note:** Mint mark Mo.

Date	Mintage	VG8	F12	VF20	XF40	MS60
1815 JJ	—	4.00	9.00	22.50	45.00	—
1816 JJ	—	4.00	9.00	22.50	45.00	—
1817/6 JJ	—	13.00	27.50	55.00	125	—
1817 JJ	—	4.00	9.00	30.75	50.00	—
1818/7 JJ	—	4.00	9.00	27.50	55.00	—
1818 JJ	—	4.00	9.00	27.50	55.00	—
1819/8 JJ	—	7.00	13.00	38.50	95.00	—
1819 JJ	—	4.00	9.00	22.50	45.00	—
1820 JJ	—	4.00	9.00	27.50	55.00	—
1821 JJ	—	4.00	9.00	22.50	45.00	—

KM# 75.1 REAL
3.38 g., 0.917 Silver, 0.10 oz. ASW **Ruler:** Philip V **Obv.** Crowned shield flanked by MF I ** **Rev:** Crowned globes flanked by crowned pillars with banner, date below **Obv. Legend:** PHILIP • V • D • G • HISPAN • ET IND • REX **Mint:** Mexico City **Note:** Mint mark M, Mo, (MX).

Date	Mintage	VG8	F12	VF20	XF40	MS60
1732 Rare	—	—	—	—	—	—
1732 F	—	—	—	—	—	—
1733 F (MX)	—	150	350	425	750	—
1733 MF (MX)	—	150	350	425	750	—
1733 F Rare	—	—	—	—	—	—
1733 MF	—	100	200	300	500	—
1734/3 MF	—	35.00	60.00	125	175	—
1734 MF	—	35.00	60.00	125	175	—
1735 MF	—	35.00	60.00	125	175	—
1736 MF	—	35.00	60.00	125	175	—
1737 MF	—	35.00	60.00	125	175	—
1738 MF	—	35.00	60.00	125	175	—
1739 MF	—	35.00	60.00	125	175	—
1740 MF	—	35.00	60.00	125	175	—
1741 MF	—	35.00	60.00	125	175	—

KM# 75.2 REAL
3.38 g., 0.917 Silver, 0.10 oz. ASW **Ruler:** Philip V **Obv. Legend:** PHS • V • D • G • HISP • ET • IND • R **Note:** Mint mark M, Mo.

Date	Mintage	VG8	F12	VF20	XF40	MS60
1742 M	—	35.00	60.00	110	165	—
1743 M	—	35.00	60.00	110	165	—
1744/3 M	—	35.00	60.00	110	165	—
1744 M	—	35.00	60.00	110	165	—
1745 M	—	35.00	60.00	110	165	—
1746/5 M	—	35.00	60.00	110	165	—
1746 M	—	35.00	60.00	110	165	—
1747 M	—	35.00	60.00	110	165	—

KM# 76.1 REAL
3.38 g., 0.917 Silver, 0.10 oz. ASW **Ruler:** Ferdinand VI **Obv.** Crowned shield flanked by R I **Rev:** Crowned globes flanked by crowned pillars with banner, date below **Obv. Legend:** FRD • VI • D • G • HISP • ET IND • R **Mint:** Mexico City **Note:** Mint mark M, Mo.

Date	Mintage	VG8	F12	VF20	XF40	MS60
1747 M	—	30.00	50.00	100	150	—
1748/7 M	—	30.00	50.00	100	150	—
1748 M	—	30.00	50.00	100	150	—
1749 M	—	30.00	50.00	100	150	—
1750/40 M	—	30.00	50.00	100	150	—
1750 M	—	30.00	50.00	100	150	—
1751 M	—	30.00	50.00	100	150	—
1752 M	—	30.00	50.00	100	150	—
1753 M	—	30.00	50.00	100	150	—
1754 M	—	30.00	50.00	100	150	—
1755/4 M	—	30.00	50.00	100	150	—
1755 M	—	30.00	50.00	100	150	—
1756 M	—	30.00	50.00	100	150	—
1757 M	—	30.00	50.00	100	150	—
1758/5 M	—	30.00	50.00	100	150	—
1758 M	—	30.00	50.00	100	150	—

KM# 76.2 REAL
3.38 g., 0.917 Silver, 0.10 oz. ASW **Ruler:** Ferdinand VI **Obv.** Royal and Imperial crowns **Note:** Mint mark M, Mo.

Date	Mintage	VG8	F12	VF20	XF40	MS60
1757 M	—	30.00	50.00	100	150	—
1758/7 M	—	30.00	50.00	100	150	—
1758 M	—	30.00	50.00	100	150	—
1759 M	—	30.00	50.00	100	150	—
1760 M	—	30.00	50.00	100	150	—

KM# 77 REAL

3.38 g., 0.917 Silver, 0.10 oz. ASW **Ruler:** Charles III **Obv.** Crowned shield flanked by R I **Rev:** Crowned globes flanked by crowned pillars with banner, date below **Obv. Legend:** CAR • III • D • G • HISP • ET IND • R **Mint:** Mexico City **Note:** Mint mark M, Mo.

Date	Mintage	VG8	F12	VF20	XF40	MS60
1760 M	—	30.00	50.00	100	150	—
1761/0 M	—	30.00	50.00	100	150	—
1761 M	—	30.00	50.00	100	150	—
1762 M	—	30.00	50.00	100	150	—
1763/2 M	—	30.00	50.00	100	150	—
1763 M	—	30.00	50.00	100	150	—
1764 M	—	30.00	50.00	100	150	—
1765 M	—	30.00	50.00	100	150	—
1766 M	—	30.00	50.00	100	150	—
1767 M	—	30.00	50.00	100	150	—
1768 M	—	30.00	50.00	100	150	—
1769 M	—	30.00	50.00	100	150	—
1769/70 M	—	30.00	50.00	100	150	—
1770 M	—	30.00	50.00	100	150	—
1770 F	—	30.00	50.00	100	200	—
1771 F	—	30.00	50.00	100	200	—

KM# 78.1 REAL

3.38 g., 0.903 Silver, 0.10 oz. ASW **Ruler:** Charles III **Rev:** Inverted FM and mint mark **Obv. Legend:** CAROLUS • III • DEI • GRATIA **Note:** Mint mark M, Mo.

Date	Mintage	VG8	F12	VF20	XF40	MS60
1772 FM	—	25.00	40.00	80.00	125	—
1773 FM	—	25.00	40.00	80.00	125	—

KM# 78.2 REAL

3.38 g., 0.903 Silver, 0.10 oz. ASW **Ruler:** Charles III **Obv.** Armored bust of Charles III, right **Obv. Legend:** CAROLUS • III • DEI • GRATIA **Rev. Legend:** Crowned shield flanked by pillars with banner, normal initials and mint mark **Mint:** Mexico City **Note:** Mint mark M, Mo.

Date	Mintage	VG8	F12	VF20	XF40	MS60
1774 FM	—	20.00	35.00	65.00	100	—
1775/4 FM	—	20.00	35.00	65.00	100	—
1775 FM	—	20.00	35.00	65.00	100	—
1776 FM	—	20.00	35.00	65.00	100	—
1777 FM	—	20.00	35.00	65.00	100	—
1778 FF/M	—	20.00	35.00	65.00	100	—
1778 FF	—	20.00	35.00	65.00	100	—
1779 FF	—	20.00	35.00	65.00	100	—
1780 FF	—	20.00	35.00	65.00	100	—
1780 F F/M	—	20.00	35.00	65.00	100	—
1781 FF	—	20.00	35.00	65.00	100	—
1782 FF	—	20.00	35.00	65.00	100	—
1783 FF	—	20.00	35.00	65.00	100	—
1784 FF	—	20.00	35.00	65.00	100	—

KM# 78.2a REAL

3.38 g., 0.896 Silver, 0.10 oz. ASW **Ruler:** Charles III **Rev:** Normal initials and mint mark **Note:** Mint mark M, Mo.

Date	Mintage	VG8	F12	VF20	XF40	MS60
1785 FF	—	20.00	35.00	65.00	100	—
1785 FM	—	20.00	35.00	65.00	100	—
1786 FM	—	20.00	35.00	65.00	100	—
1787 FF	—	20.00	35.00	65.00	125	—
1787 FM	—	20.00	35.00	65.00	100	—
1788 FF	—	50.00	100	200	—	—
1788 FM	—	20.00	35.00	65.00	100	—
1789 FM	—	20.00	35.00	65.00	100	—

KM# 79 REAL

3.38 g., 0.903 Silver, 0.10 oz. ASW **Ruler:** Charles IV **Obv.** Armored bust of Charles III, right **Rev:** Crown above shield flanked by pillars with banner **Obv. Legend:** CAROLUS • IV • ... **Mint:** Mexico City **Note:** Mint mark M, Mo.

Date	Mintage	VG8	F12	VF20	XF40	MS60
1789 FM	—	20.00	35.00	65.00	150	—
1790 FM	—	20.00	35.00	65.00	150	—

KM# 80 REAL

3.38 g., 0.903 Silver, 0.10 oz. ASW **Ruler:** Charles IV **Obv.** Armored bust of Charles IIII, right **Rev:** Crowned shield flanked by pillars with banner **Obv. Legend:** CAROLUS • IIII • ... **Mint:** Mexico City **Note:** Mint mark M, Mo.

Date	Mintage	VG8	F12	VF20	XF40	MS60
1790 FM	—	20.00	35.00	70.00	165	—

KM# 81 REAL

3.38 g., 0.896 Silver, 0.10 oz. ASW **Ruler:** Charles IV **Obv.** Armored bust of Charles IIII, right **Rev:** Crowned shield flanked by pillars with banner **Obv. Legend:** CAROLUS • IIII • ... **Rev. Legend:** IND • REX ... **Mint:** Mexico City **Note:** Mint mark Mo.

Date	Mintage	VG8	F12	VF20	XF40	MS60
1792 FM	—	15.00	30.00	60.00	90.00	—
1793 FM	—	15.00	30.00	60.00	150	—
1794 FM	—	25.00	50.00	100	250	—
1795 FM	—	15.00	30.00	60.00	150	—
1796 FM	—	15.00	30.00	60.00	90.00	—
1797/6 FM	—	15.00	30.00	60.00	90.00	—
1797 FM	—	15.00	30.00	60.00	90.00	—
1798/7 FM	—	15.00	30.00	60.00	90.00	—
1798 FM	—	15.00	30.00	60.00	90.00	—
1799 FM	—	15.00	30.00	60.00	90.00	—
1800 FM	—	15.00	30.00	60.00	90.00	—
1801 FT/M	—	6.00	11.00	27.50	65.00	—
1801 FM	—	9.00	17.00	30.75	65.00	—
1801 FT	—	6.00	11.00	27.50	65.00	—
1802 FM	—	6.00	11.00	27.50	65.00	—
1802 FT	—	6.00	11.00	27.50	65.00	—
1802/1 FT	—	6.00	11.00	27.50	65.00	—
1802 FT/M	—	6.00	11.00	27.50	65.00	—
1803 FT	—	6.00	11.00	27.50	65.00	—
1804 TH	—	6.00	11.00	27.50	65.00	—
1805 TH	—	6.00	11.00	27.50	65.00	—
1806 TH	—	6.00	11.00	27.50	65.00	—
1807/6 TH	—	6.00	11.00	27.50	65.00	—
1807 TH	—	6.00	11.00	27.50	65.00	—
1808/7 TH	—	6.00	11.00	27.50	65.00	—
1808 FM	—	6.00	11.00	27.50	65.00	—

KM# 82   REAL

3.38 g., 0.903 Silver, 0.10 oz. ASW **Ruler:** Ferdinand VII **Obv.** Armored laureate bust right **Rev:** Crowned shield flanked by pillars **Obv. Legend:** FERDIN.VII... **Rev. Legend:** IND.REX.... **Mint:** Mexico City **Note:** Mint mark Mo.

Date	Mintage	VG8	F12	VF20	XF40	MS60
1809 TH	—	10.00	18.00	32.00	95.00	—
1810/09 TH	—	10.00	18.00	32.00	95.00	—
1810 TH	—	10.00	18.00	32.00	95.00	—
1811 TH	—	27.50	38.50	65.00	250	—
1811 HJ	—	10.00	18.00	32.00	95.00	—
1812 HJ	—	6.00	12.00	32.00	85.00	—
1812 JJ	—	12.00	22.50	45.00	135	—
1813 HJ	—	12.00	22.50	45.00	135	—
1813 JJ	—	55.00	110	165	250	—
1814 HJ	—	17.00	33.00	165	155	—
1814 JJ	—	55.00	110	195	300	—

KM# 83   REAL

3.38 g., 0.903 Silver, 0.10 oz. ASW **Ruler:** Ferdinand VII **Obv.** Draped laureate bust right **Rev:** Crowned shield flanked by pillars **Obv. Legend:** FERDIN.VII... **Rev. Legend:** IND.REX... **Mint:** Mexico City **Note:** Mint mark Mo.

Date	Mintage	VG8	F12	VF20	XF40	MS60
1814 JJ	—	27.50	55.00	110	350	—
1815 HJ	—	17.00	33.00	65.00	150	—
1815 JJ	—	12.00	22.50	45.00	125	—
1816 JJ	—	6.00	12.00	27.50	75.00	—
1817 JJ	—	6.00	12.00	27.50	75.00	—
1818 JJ	—	33.00	65.00	140	500	—
1819 JJ	—	6.00	12.00	27.50	75.00	—
1820 JJ	—	6.00	12.00	27.50	75.00	—
1821/0 JJ	—	10.00	18.00	33.00	115	—
1821 JJ	—	6.00	12.00	27.50	55.00	—

KM# 84   2 REALES

6.77 g., 0.917 Silver, 0.20 oz. ASW **Ruler:** Philip V **Obv.** Crowned shield flanked by M F 2 **Rev:** Crowned globes flanked by crowned pillars with banner, date below **Obv. Legend:** PHILIP • V • D • G • HISPAN • ET IND • REX **Rev. Legend:** VTRAQUE VNUM **Mint:** Mexico City **Note:** Mint mark M, Mo, (MX).

Date	Mintage	VG8	F12	VF20	XF40	MS60
1732 Rare	—	—	—	—	—	—
1732 F	—	800	1,300	1,750	2,750	—
1733 F	—	600	800	1,350	2,250	—
1733 MF (MX)	—	350	600	1,000	1,650	—
1733 MF	—	600	900	1,500	2,500	—
1734/3 MF	—	45.00	75.00	135	200	—
1734 MF	—	45.00	75.00	135	200	—

Date	Mintage	VG8	F12	VF20	XF40	MS60
1735/3 MF	—	45.00	75.00	135	200	—
1735/4 MF	—	45.00	75.00	135	200	—
1735 MF	—	45.00	75.00	135	200	—
1736/3 MF	—	45.00	75.00	135	200	—
1736/4 MF	—	45.00	75.00	135	200	—
1736/5 MF	—	45.00	75.00	135	200	—
1736 MF	—	45.00	75.00	135	200	—
1737/3 MF	—	45.00	75.00	135	200	—
1737 MF	—	45.00	75.00	135	200	—
1738/7 MF	—	45.00	75.00	135	200	—
1738 MF	—	45.00	75.00	135	200	—
1739 MF	—	45.00	75.00	135	200	—
1740/30 MF	—	45.00	75.00	135	200	—
1740 MF	—	45.00	75.00	135	200	—
1741 MF	—	45.00	75.00	135	200	—

KM# 85   2 REALES

6.77 g., 0.917 Silver, 0.20 oz. ASW **Ruler:** Philip V **Obv.** Crowned shield flanked by R 2 **Rev:** Crowned globes flanked by crowned pillars with banner, date below **Obv. Legend:** PHS • V • D • G • HISP • ET IND • R * **Rev. Legend:** VTRA QUE VNUM **Mint:** Mexico City **Note:** Mint mark M, Mo.

Date	Mintage	F12	VF20	XF40	MS60	MS63
1742 M	—	70.00	125	185	—	—
1743/2 M	—	70.00	125	185	—	—
1743 M	—	70.00	125	185	—	—
1744/3 M	—	70.00	125	185	—	—
1744 M	—	70.00	125	185	—	—
1745/4 M	—	70.00	125	185	—	—
1745 M	—	70.00	125	185	—	—
1745 M HIP Rare	—	—	—	—	—	—
1746/5 M	—	70.00	125	185	—	—
1746 M	—	70.00	125	185	—	—
1747 M	—	70.00	125	185	—	—
1750 M Rare	—	—	—	—	—	—

Note: Posthumous mule.

KM# 86.1   2 REALES

6.77 g., 0.917 Silver, 0.20 oz. ASW **Ruler:** Ferdinand VI **Obv.** Crowned shield flanked by R 2 **Rev:** Crowned globes flanked by crowned pillars with banner, date below **Obv. Legend:** FRD • VI • D • G • HISP • ET IND • R **Rev. Legend:** VTRA QUE VNUM **Mint:** Mexico City **Note:** Mint mark M, Mo.

Date	Mintage	VG8	F12	VF20	XF40	MS60
1747 M	—	35.00	60.00	110	175	—
1748/7 M	—	35.00	60.00	110	175	—
1748 M	—	35.00	60.00	110	175	—
1749 M	—	35.00	60.00	110	175	—
1750 M	—	35.00	60.00	110	175	—
1751/41 M	—	35.00	60.00	110	175	—
1751 M	—	35.00	60.00	110	175	—
1752 M	—	35.00	60.00	110	175	—
1753/2 M	—	35.00	60.00	110	175	—
1753 M	—	35.00	60.00	110	175	—
1754 M	—	35.00	60.00	110	175	—
1755/4 M	—	35.00	60.00	110	175	—

Date	Mintage	VG8	F12	VF20	XF40	MS60
1755 M	—	35.00	60.00	110	175	—
1756/55 M	—	35.00	60.00	110	175	—
1756 M	—	35.00	60.00	110	175	—
1757/6 M	—	35.00	60.00	110	175	—
1757 M	—	35.00	60.00	110	175	—

KM# 86.2 2 REALES
6.77 g., 0.917 Silver, 0.20 oz. ASW **Ruler:** Ferdinand VI **Obv.** Royal and Imperial crowns **Note:** Mint mark M, Mo.

Date	Mintage	VG8	F12	VF20	XF40	MS60
1757 M	—	35.00	60.00	110	175	—
1758 M	—	35.00	60.00	110	175	—
1759/8 M	—	35.00	60.00	110	175	—
1759 M	—	35.00	60.00	110	175	—
1760 M	—	35.00	60.00	110	175	—

KM# 87 2 REALES
6.77 g., 0.917 Silver, 0.20 oz. ASW **Ruler:** Charles III **Obv.** Crowned shield flanked by R 2 **Rev:** Crowned globes flanked by crowned pillars with banner, date below **Obv. Legend:** CAR • III • D • G • HISP • ET IND • R **Rev. Legend:** VTRA QUE VNUM **Mint:** Mexico City **Note:** Mint mark M, Mo.

Date	Mintage	VG8	F12	VF20	XF40	MS60
1760 M	—	35.00	60.00	110	175	—
1761 M	—	35.00	60.00	110	175	—
1762/1 M	—	35.00	60.00	110	175	—
1762 M	—	35.00	60.00	110	175	—
1763/2 M	—	35.00	60.00	110	175	—
1763 M	—	35.00	60.00	110	175	—
1764 M	—	35.00	60.00	110	175	—
1765 M	—	35.00	60.00	110	175	—
1766 M	—	35.00	60.00	110	175	—
1767 M	—	35.00	60.00	110	175	—
1768/6 M	—	35.00	60.00	110	175	—
1768 M	—	35.00	60.00	110	175	—
1769 M	—	35.00	60.00	110	175	—
1770 M	—	350	550	—	—	—
1770 F Rare	—	—	—	—	—	—
1771 F	—	35.00	60.00	110	175	—

KM# 88.1 2 REALES
6.77 g., 0.903 Silver, 0.20 oz. ASW **Ruler:** Charles III **Obv.** Armored bust of Charles III, right **Rev:** Inverted FM and mint mark **Obv. Legend:** CAROLUS • III • DEI • GRATIA **Note:** Mint mark M, Mo.

Date	Mintage	VG8	F12	VF20	XF40	MS60
1772 FM	—	30.00	50.00	100	150	—
1773 FM	—	30.00	50.00	100	150	—

KM# 88.2 2 REALES
6.77 g., 0.903 Silver, 0.20 oz. ASW **Ruler:** Charles III **Obv.** Armored bust of Charles III, right **Rev:** Crowned shield flanked by pillars with banner, normal initials and mint mark **Obv. Legend:** CAROLUS • III • DEI • GRATIA • **Rev. Legend:** • HISPAN • ET IND • REX • ... **Mint:** Mexico City **Note:** Mint mark M, Mo.

Date	Mintage	VG8	F12	VF20	XF40
1773 FM	—	25.00	40.00	80.00	125
1774 FM	—	25.00	40.00	80.00	125
1775 FM	—	25.00	40.00	80.00	125
1776 FM	—	25.00	40.00	80.00	125
1777 FM	—	25.00	40.00	80.00	125
1778/7 FF	—	25.00	40.00	80.00	125
1778 FF	—	25.00	40.00	80.00	125
1778 F F/M	—	25.00	40.00	80.00	125
1779/8 FF	—	25.00	40.00	80.00	125
1779 FF	—	25.00	40.00	80.00	125
1780 FF	—	25.00	40.00	80.00	125
1781 FF	—	25.00	40.00	80.00	125
1782/1 FF	—	25.00	40.00	80.00	125
1782 FF	—	25.00	40.00	80.00	125
1783 FF	—	25.00	40.00	80.00	125
1784 FF	—	25.00	40.00	80.00	125
1784 FF DEI GRTIA (error)	—	100	150	250	600
1784 FM	—	70.00	120	225	575

KM# 88.2a 2 REALES
6.77 g., 0.896 Silver, 0.19 oz. ASW **Ruler:** Charles III **Obv.** Armored bust of Charles III, right **Rev:** Crowned shield flanked by pillars with banner **Mint:** Mexico City **Note:** Mint mark Mo.

Date	Mintage	VG8	F12	VF20	XF40	MS60
1785 Mo FM	—	25.00	40.00	80.00	125	—
1786 Mo FF	—	200	350	550	950	—
1786 Mo FM	—	25.00	40.00	80.00	125	—
1787 Mo FM	—	25.00	40.00	80.00	125	—
1788/98 Mo FM	—	25.00	40.00	80.00	125	—
1788 Mo FM	—	25.00	40.00	80.00	125	—
1789 Mo FM	—	25.00	40.00	80.00	150	—

KM# 89 2 REALES
6.77 g., 0.903 Silver, 0.20 oz. ASW **Ruler:** Charles IV **Obv.** Armored bust of Charles IV, right **Rev:** Crowned shield flanked by pillars with banner **Obv. Legend:** CAROLUS • IV • DEI • GRATIA • **Rev. Legend:** • HISPAN • ET IND • REX • ... **Mint:** Mexico City **Note:** Mint mark M, Mo.

Date	Mintage	VG8	F12	VF20	XF40	MS60
1789 FM	—	25.00	40.00	75.00	200	—
1790 FM	—	25.00	40.00	75.00	200	—

KM# 90   2 REALES

6.77 g., 0.903 Silver, 0.20 oz. ASW **Ruler:** Charles IV **Obv.** Armored bust of Charles IIII, right **Rev:** Crowned shield flanked by pillars with banner **Obv. Legend:** CAROLUS • IIII • DEI • GRATIA • **Rev. Legend:** • HISPAN • ET IND REX • ... **Mint:** Mexico City **Note:** Mint mark M, Mo.

Date	Mintage	VG8	F12	VF20	XF40	MS60
1790 FM	—	25.00	40.00	80.00	200	—

KM# 91   2 REALES

6.77 g., 0.896 Silver, 0.19 oz. ASW **Ruler:** Charles IV **Obv.** Armored bust of Charles IIII, right **Rev:** Crowned shield flanked by pillars with banner **Obv. Legend:** CAROLUS • IIII • DEI • GRATIA • **Rev. Legend:** • HISPAN • ET IND REX • ... **Mint:** Mexico City **Note:** Mint mark Mo.

Date	Mintage	VG8	F12	VF20	XF40	MS60
1792 FM	—	20.00	35.00	60.00	200	—
1793 FM	—	20.00	35.00	60.00	200	—
1794/3 FM	—	50.00	100	200	450	—
1794 FM	—	40.00	75.00	150	400	—
1795 FM	—	20.00	35.00	70.00	100	—
1796 FM	—	20.00	35.00	70.00	100	—
1797 FM	—	20.00	35.00	70.00	100	—
1798 FM	—	20.00	35.00	70.00	100	—
1799/8 FM	—	20.00	35.00	70.00	100	—
1799 FM	—	20.00	35.00	70.00	100	—
1800 FM	—	20.00	35.00	70.00	100	—
1801 FT/M	—	8.00	18.00	36.00	100	—
1801 FT	—	8.00	18.00	36.00	100	—
1801 FM	—	25.00	48.00	90.00	300	—
1802 FT	—	8.00	18.00	36.00	100	—
1803 FT	—	8.00	18.00	36.00	100	—
1804/3 TH	—	8.00	18.00	36.00	100	—
1804 TH	—	8.00	18.00	36.00	100	—
1805 TH	—	8.00	18.00	36.00	100	—
1806/5 TH	—	8.00	18.00	38.50	110	—
1806 TH	—	8.00	18.00	36.00	100	—
1807/5 TH	—	8.00	18.00	38.50	110	—
1807/6 TH	—	18.00	36.00	70.00	240	—
1807 TH	—	8.00	18.00	36.00	100	—
1808/7 TH	—	8.00	18.00	38.50	110	—
1808 TH	—	8.00	18.00	36.00	100	—

KM# 92   2 REALES

6.77 g., 0.903 Silver, 0.20 oz. ASW **Ruler:** Ferdinand VII **Obv.** Armored laureate bust right **Rev:** Crowned shield flanked by pillars **Obv. Legend:** FERDIN.VII... **Rev. Legend:** IND.REX... **Mint:** Mexico City **Note:** Mint mark Mo.

Date	Mintage	VG8	F12	VF20	XF40	MS60
1809 TH	—	15.00	30.00	75.00	200	—
181/00 TH	—	15.00	30.00	75.00	200	—
1810 TH	—	15.00	30.00	75.00	200	—
181/00 HJ/TH	—	15.00	30.00	75.00	200	—
181/00 HJ	—	15.00	30.00	75.00	200	—
1810 HJ	—	15.00	30.00	75.00	200	—
1811 TH	—	150	250	350	750	—
1811/0 HJ/TH	—	40.00	80.00	150	300	—
1811 HJ/TH	—	40.00	80.00	150	300	—
1811 HJ	—	15.00	30.00	75.00	200	—

KM# 93   2 REALES

6.77 g., 0.903 Silver, 0.20 oz. ASW **Ruler:** Ferdinand VII **Obv.** Draped laureate bust right **Rev:** Crowned shield flanked by pillars **Obv. Legend:** FERDIN.VII... **Rev. Legend:** IND.REX... **Mint:** Mexico City **Note:** Mint mark Mo.

Date	Mintage	VG8	F12	VF20	XF40	MS60
1812 TH	—	60.00	125	250	550	—
1812 HJ	—	40.00	100	200	500	—
1812 JJ	—	10.00	20.00	60.00	200	—
1813 TH	—	15.00	30.00	100	400	—
1813 JJ	—	20.00	60.00	125	350	—
1813 HJ	—	40.00	100	200	500	—
1814/2 JJ	—	15.00	30.00	100	400	—
1814/3 JJ	—	15.00	30.00	100	400	—
1814 JJ	—	15.00	30.00	100	400	—
1815 JJ	—	7.00	15.00	30.00	85.00	—
1816 JJ	—	7.00	15.00	30.00	85.00	—
1817 JJ	—	7.00	15.00	30.00	85.00	—
1818 JJ	—	7.00	15.00	30.00	85.00	—
1819/8 JJ	—	7.00	15.00	30.00	85.00	—
1819 JJ	—	7.00	15.00	30.00	85.00	—
1820 JJ	—	175	—	—	—	—
1821/0 JJ	—	8.00	16.00	32.00	90.00	—
1821 JJ	—	7.00	15.00	30.00	85.00	—

KM# 94   4 REALES

13.53 g., 0.917 Silver, 0.40 oz. ASW **Ruler:** Philip V **Obv.** Crowned shield flanked by F 4 **Rev:** Crowned globes flanked by crowned pillars with banner, date below **Obv. Legend:** PHILLIP • V • D • G • HISPAN • ET IND • REX **Rev. Legend:** VTRAQUE VNUM **Mint:** Mexico City **Note:** Mint mark M, Mo, MX.

Date	Mintage	VG8	F12	VF20	XF40
1732 Rare; Specimen	—	—	—	—	—
1732 F	—	2,000	3,000	5,000	10,000
1733/2 F	—	1,500	2,000	4,000	6,500
1733 MF	—	1,100	1,650	2,250	4,250

Date	Mintage	VG8	F12	VF20	XF40
1733 MF (MX)	—	1,500	2,200	3,250	5,500
1733 MX/XM	—	1,500	2,200	3,250	5,500
1734/3 MF	—	150	300	600	1,200
1734 MF	—	150	300	600	1,200
1735/4 MF	—	125	200	300	600
1735 MF	—	125	200	300	600
1736 MF	—	125	200	300	600
1737 MF	—	125	200	300	600
1738/7 MF	—	125	200	300	600
1738 MF	—	125	200	300	600
1739 MF	—	125	200	300	600
1740/30 MF	—	125	200	325	625
1740 MF	—	125	200	300	600
1741 MF	—	125	200	300	600
1742/1 MF	—	125	200	300	600
1742/32 MF	—	125	200	300	600
1742 MF	—	110	185	300	600
1743 MF	—	110	185	300	600
1744/3 MF	—	125	200	325	625
1744 MF	—	110	185	300	600
1745 MF	—	110	185	300	600
1746 MF	—	110	185	300	600
1747 MF	—	150	275	400	650

KM# 95 4 REALES
13.54 g., 0.917 Silver, 0.40 oz. ASW **Ruler:** Ferdinand VI **Obv.** Crowned shield flanked by M F 4 **Rev:** Crowned globes flanked by crowned pillars with banner, date below **Obv. Legend:** FERDND • VI • D • G • HISPAN • ET IND • REX **Rev. Legend:** ...QUE VNUM **Mint:** Mexico City **Note:** Struck at Mexico City Mint, mint mark M, Mo.

Date	Mintage	VG8	F12	VF20	XF40	MS60
1747 MF	—	125	175	300	550	—
1748/7 MF	—	125	175	300	550	—
1748 MF	—	125	175	250	500	—
1749 MF	—	150	225	350	650	—
1750/40 MF	—	125	175	250	500	—
1751/41 MF	—	125	175	250	500	—
1751 MF	—	125	175	250	500	—
1752 MF	—	125	175	250	500	—
1753 MF	—	125	175	300	550	—
1754 MF	—	250	375	500	850	—
1755 MM	—	125	175	250	500	—
1756 MM	—	125	175	300	550	—
1757 MM	—	125	175	300	550	—
1758 MM	—	125	175	250	500	—
1759 MM	—	125	175	250	500	—
1760/59 MM	—	125	175	350	600	—
1760 MM	—	125	175	350	600	—

KM# 96 4 REALES
13.54 g., 0.917 Silver, 0.40 oz. ASW **Ruler:** Charles III **Obv.** Crowned shield flanked by F M 4 **Rev:** Crowned globes flanked by crowned pillars with banner, date below **Obv. Legend:** CAROLVS • III • D • G • HISPAN • ET IND • REX **Rev. Legend:** ...AQUE VNUM **Mint:** Mexico City **Note:** Mint mark M, Mo.

Date	Mintage	VG8	F12	VF20	XF40
1760 MM	—	125	175	250	900
1761 MM	—	125	175	250	900
1761 MM Cross between H and I	—	125	175	250	900
1762 MM	—	125	175	250	500
1763/1 MM	—	125	175	300	600
1763 MM	—	125	175	300	600
1764 MM	—	400	600	1,000	2,000
1764 MF	—	350	500	1,000	2,000
1765 MF	—	350	500	1,000	2,000
1766 MF	—	250	350	550	1,250
1767 MF	—	125	175	300	600
1768 MF	—	125	175	250	500
1769 MF	—	125	175	250	500
1770 MF	—	125	175	250	500
1771 MF	—	125	200	325	700

KM# 97.1 4 REALES
13.53 g., 0.903 Silver, 0.39 oz. ASW **Ruler:** Charles III **Obv.** Armored bust of Charles III, right **Rev:** Crowned shield flanked by pillars with banner, inverted FM and mint mark **Obv. Legend:** CAROLUS • III • DEI • GRATIA • **Rev. Legend:** • HISPAN • ET IND REX • ... **Mint:** Mexico City **Note:** Mint mark M, Mo.

Date	Mintage	VG8	F12	VF20	XF40	MS60
1772 FM	—	100	125	250	500	—
1773 FM	—	100	175	300	650	—

KM# 97.2 4 REALES
13.54 g., 0.903 Silver, 0.39 oz. ASW **Ruler:** Charles III **Obv.** Armored bust of Charles III, right **Rev:** Crowned shield flanked by pillars with banner, normal initials and mint mark **Obv. Legend:** CAROLUS • III • DEI • GRATIA • **Rev. Legend:** • HISPAN • ET IND REX • ... **Mint:** Mexico City **Note:** Mint mark M, Mo.

Date	Mintage	VG8	F12	VF20	XF40	MS60
1774 FM	—	70.00	100	200	500	—
1775 FM	—	70.00	100	200	500	—
1776 FM	—	70.00	100	200	500	—
1777 FM	—	70.00	100	200	500	—
1778 FF	—	70.00	100	200	500	—
1779 FF	—	70.00	100	200	500	—
1780 FF	—	70.00	100	200	500	—
1781 FF	—	70.00	100	200	500	—
1782 FF	—	70.00	100	200	500	—
1783 FF	—	70.00	100	200	500	—
1784 FF	—	70.00	100	200	500	—
1784 FM	—	100	200	350	600	—

SPANISH COLONIAL · MILLED COINAGE

KM# 97.2a 4 REALES

13.53 g., 0.896 Silver, 0.39 oz. ASW **Ruler:** Charles III
Obv. Armored bust of Charles III, right **Rev:** Crowned shield
flanked by pillars with banner, normal initials and mint mark
Obv. Legend: CAROLUS • III • DEI • GRATIA • **Rev. Legend:**
• HISPAN • ET IND REX • ... **Note:** Mint mark M, Mo.

Date	Mintage	VG8	F12	VF20	XF40	MS60
1785 FM	—	100	200	350	600	—
1786 FM	—	70.00	100	200	500	—
1787 FM	—	70.00	100	200	500	—
1788 FM	—	70.00	100	200	500	—
1789 FM	—	70.00	100	200	500	—

KM# 98 4 REALES

13.54 g., 0.903 Silver, 0.39 oz. ASW **Ruler:** Charles IV
Obv. Armored bust of Charles III, right **Rev:** Crowned shield
flanked by pillars with banner **Obv. Legend:** CAROLUS •
IV • DEI • GRATIA • **Rev. Legend:** • HISPAN • ET IND REX
• ... **Mint:** Mexico City **Note:** Mintint mark M, Mo, using old
bust punch.

Date	Mintage	VG8	F12	VF20	XF40	MS60
1789 FM	—	75.00	125	250	550	—
1790 FM	—	70.00	100	200	500	—

KM# 99 4 REALES

13.54 g., 0.903 Silver, 0.39 oz. ASW **Ruler:** Charles IV
Obv. Armored bust of Charles III, right **Rev:** Crowned shield
flanked by pillars with banner **Obv. Legend:** CAROLUS •
IIII • DEI • GRATIA • **Rev. Legend:** • HISPAN • ET IND •
REX • ... **Mint:** Mexico City **Note:** Mint mark M, Mo, using
old bust punch.

Date	Mintage	VG8	F12	VF20	XF40	MS60
1790 FM	—	75.00	125	250	550	—

KM# 100 4 REALES

13.53 g., 0.896 Silver, 0.39 oz. ASW **Ruler:** Charles IV
26.5mm. **Obv.** Armored bust of Charles IIII, right **Rev:**
Crowned shield flanked by pillars with banner **Obv. Legend:**
CAROLUS • IIII • DEI • GRATIA • **Rev. Legend:** • HISPAN
• ET IND • REX • ... **Mint:** Mexico City **Note:** Mint mark Mo.

Date	Mintage	VG8	F12	VF20	XF40	MS60
1792 FM	—	65.00	95.00	165	450	—
1793 FM	—	85.00	140	220	550	—
1794/3 FM	—	65.00	95.00	165	450	—
1794 FM	—	65.00	95.00	165	450	—
1795 FM	—	65.00	95.00	165	450	—
1796 FM	—	165	275	450	875	—
1797 FM	—	75.00	130	220	550	—
1798/7 FM	—	65.00	95.00	165	450	—
1798 FM	—	65.00	95.00	165	450	—
1799 FM	—	65.00	95.00	165	450	—
1800 FM	—	65.00	95.00	165	450	—
1801 FM	—	38.50	70.00	165	475	—
1801 FT	—	65.00	130	220	575	—
1802 FT	—	220	325	550	1,100	—
1803 FT	—	85.00	150	250	625	—
1803 FM	—	220	325	550	1,100	—
1804 TH	—	44.00	85.00	195	525	—
1805 TH	—	38.50	70.00	165	475	—
1806 TH	—	38.50	70.00	165	475	—
1807 TH	—	38.50	70.00	165	475	—
1808/7 TH	—	44.00	85.00	195	525	—
1808 TH	—	44.00	85.00	195	525	—

KM# 101 4 REALES

13.54 g., 0.903 Silver, 0.39 oz. ASW **Ruler:** Ferdinand
VII **Obv.** Armored laureate bust right **Rev:** Crowned shield
flanked by pillars **Obv. Legend:** FERDIN.VII... **Rev. Legend:**
IND.REX... **Mint:** Mexico City **Note:** Mint mark Mo.

Date	Mintage	VG8	F12	VF20	XF40	MS60
1809 HJ	—	75.00	135	250	775	—
1810 HJ	—	75.00	135	250	775	—
1811 HJ	—	75.00	135	250	775	—
1812 HJ	—	400	650	900	1,850	—

KM# 102 4 REALES
13.54 g., 0.903 Silver, 0.39 oz. ASW **Ruler:** Ferdinand VII **Obv.** Draped laureate bust right **Rev:** Crowned shield flanked by pillars **Obv. Legend:** FERDIN.VII... **Rev. Legend:** IND.REX... **Mint:** Mexico City **Note:** Mint mark Mo.

Date	Mintage	VG8	F12	VF20	XF40	MS60
1816 JJ	—	150	200	325	800	—
1817 JJ	—	250	400	500	1,000	—
1818/7 JJ	—	250	400	500	1,000	—
1819 JJ	—	175	250	325	800	—
1820 JJ	—	175	250	325	800	—
1821 JJ	—	75.00	135	250	700	—

Date	Mintage	VG8	F12	VF20	XF40
1738/6 MF	—	100	150	250	475
1738/7 MF	—	100	150	250	475
1738 MF	—	100	150	250	475
1739/6 MF 9 over inverted 6	—	100	150	250	475
1739 MF	—	100	150	250	475
1740/30 MF	—	100	150	275	600
1740/39 MF	—	100	150	275	600
1740 MF	—	100	150	250	475
1741/31 MF	—	100	150	250	475
1741 MF	—	100	150	250	475
1742/32 MF	—	100	150	250	600
1742/1 MF	—	100	150	250	475
1742 MF	—	100	150	250	475
1743/2 MF	—	100	150	250	475
1743 MF	—	100	150	250	475
1744/34 MF	—	100	150	250	475
1744/3 MF	—	100	150	250	475
1744 MF	—	100	150	250	475
1745/4 MF	—	100	150	250	500
1745 MF	—	100	150	250	475
1746/5 MF	—	100	150	275	700
1746 MF	—	100	150	250	475
1747 MF	—	100	150	250	475

KM# 103 8 REALES
27.07 g., 0.917 Silver, 0.79 oz. ASW **Ruler:** Philip V **Obv.** Crowned shield flanked by M F 8 **Rev:** Crowned globes flanked by crowned pillars with banner, date below **Obv. Legend:** PHILIP • V • D • G • HISPAN • ET IND • REX **Rev. Legend:** ...VNUM **Mint:** Mexico City **Note:** Mint mark M, Mo, MX.

Date	Mintage	VG8	F12	VF20	XF40
1732 F	—	2,750	4,750	8,500	18,000
1733/2 F (MX)	—	3,000	5,250	9,500	—
1733 F	—	2,000	3,000	5,500	11,000
1733 MF Large crown; Rare	—	—	—	—	—
1733 F (MX) Rare	—	—	—	—	—

Note: Bonhams Patterson sale 7-96 VF 1733 F (MX) realized $11,710.

Date	Mintage	VG8	F12	VF20	XF40
1733 MF (MX) Rare	—	—	—	—	—
1733 MF Small crown	—	700	1,500	2,250	4,200
1734/3 MF	—	125	175	275	700
1734 MF	—	125	175	250	550
1735 MF	—	125	175	250	550
1736/5 MF	—	125	175	275	700
1736 MF Small planchet	—	125	175	250	550
1736 MF	—	125	175	250	550
1737 MF	—	100	150	250	475

KM# 104.1 8 REALES
27.07 g., 0.917 Silver, 0.79 oz. ASW **Ruler:** Ferdinand VI **Obv.** Crowned shield flaned by M F 8 **Rev:** Crowned globes flanked by crowned pillars with banner, date below **Obv. Legend:** FERDND • VI • D • G • HISPAN • ET IND • REX **Rev. Legend:** ...VNUM M **Mint:** Mexico City **Note:** Mint mark M, Mo.

Date	Mintage	VG8	F12	VF20	XF40	MS60
1747 MF	—	100	140	200	350	—
1748/7 MF	—	100	140	200	550	—
1748 MF	—	100	140	200	350	—
1749 MF	—	100	140	200	350	—
1749/8 MF	—	100	140	200	350	—
1750 MF	—	100	140	200	350	—
1751/0 MF	—	100	140	200	350	—
1751 MF	—	100	140	200	350	—
1752/1 MF	—	100	140	200	350	—
1752 MF	—	100	140	200	350	—
1753/2 MF	—	100	140	200	350	—
1753 MF	—	100	140	200	350	—
1754/3 MF	—	100	140	200	400	—
1754 MF	—	100	140	200	350	—
1754 MM/MF	—	300	700	1,500	4,200	—
1754 MM	—	300	700	1,500	4,200	—

KM# 104.2 8 REALES
27.07 g., 0.917 Silver, 0.79 oz. ASW **Ruler:** Ferdinand VI
Obv. Crowned shield flanked by M M 8 **Rev:** Imperial crown
on left pillar **Obv. Legend:** FERDND • VI • D • G • HISPAN •
ET IND • REX **Rev. Legend:** ...VNUM M **Mint:** Mexico City
Note: Mint mark M, Mo.

Date	Mintage	VG8	F12	VF20	XF40	MS60
1754 MM	—	100	140	200	450	—
1754 MM/MF	—	100	140	250	600	—
1754 MF	—	150	285	550	1,150	—
1755/4 MM	—	100	140	200	400	—
1755 MM	—	100	140	200	350	—
1756/5 MM	—	100	140	200	350	—
1756 MM	—	100	140	200	350	—
1757/6 MM	—	100	140	200	350	—
1757 MM	—	100	140	200	400	—
1758 MM	—	100	140	200	350	—
1759 MM	—	100	140	200	350	—
1760/59 MM	—	100	140	200	350	—
1760 MM	—	100	140	200	350	—

KM# 105 8 REALES
27.07 g., 0.917 Silver, 0.79 oz. ASW **Ruler:** Charles III **Obv.**
Crowned shield flanked by M M 8 **Rev:** Crowned globes
flanked by crowned pillars with banner, date below **Obv.**
Legend: CAROLUS • III • D • G • HISPAN • ET IND • REX
Rev. Legend: ...E VNUM M **Mint:** Mexico City **Note:** Mint
mark M, Mo.

Date	Mintage	VG8	F12	VF20	XF40	MS60
1760/59 MM	—	450	700	—	—	—
Note: CAROLUS. III/Ferdin. Vi						
1760 MM	—	100	140	200	400	—
Note: CAROLUS. III/FERDIN. VI. recut die						
1760 MM	—	100	140	200	350	—
1761/50 MM	—	100	140	200	400	—
Note: Tip of cross between I and S in legend						
1761/51 MM	—	100	140	200	400	—
Note: Tip of cross between I and S in legend						
1761/0 MM	—	100	140	200	400	—
Note: Tip of cross between H and I in legend						

Date	Mintage	VG8	F12	VF20	XF40	MS60
1761 MM	—	100	140	200	325	—
Note: Cross under I in legend						
1761 MM	—	100	140	200	325	—
Note: Tip of cross between H and I in legend						
1761 MM	—	100	140	200	400	—
Note: Tip of cross between I and S in legend						
1762/1 MM	—	100	140	200	550	—
Note: Tip of cross between H and I in legend						
1762/1 MM	—	100	140	200	550	—
1762 MM	—	100	140	200	325	—
Note: Tip of cross between H and I in legend						
1762 MM	—	100	140	200	300	—
Note: Tip of cross between I and S in legend						
1762 MF	—	500	750	1,250	2,750	—
1763/2 MM	—	300	450	750	1,600	—
1763 MM	—	450	650	1,150	2,700	—
1763/1 MF	—	100	140	200	300	—
1763/2 MF	—	100	140	200	300	—
1763 MF	—	100	140	200	300	—
1764 MF	—	100	140	200	325	—
Note: CAR/CRA						
1764 MF	—	100	140	200	300	—
1765 MF	—	100	140	200	300	—
1766/5 MF	—	100	150	200	700	—
1766 MF	—	100	140	200	300	—
1767/6 MF	—	100	140	200	300	—
1767 MF	—	100	140	200	300	—
1768/7 MF	—	100	165	250	725	—
1768 MF	—	100	140	200	300	—
1769 MF	—	100	140	200	300	—
1770/60 MF	—	100	185	300	775	—
1770 MF	—	100	140	200	300	—
1770/60 FM	—	100	185	300	775	—
1770/69 FM	—	100	185	300	775	—
1770 FM/F	—	100	140	200	300	—
1770 FM	—	100	140	200	300	—
1771/0 FM	—	100	140	200	300	—
1771 FM	—	100	140	200	300	—

KM# 106.1 8 REALES
27.07 g., 0.903 Silver, 0.78 oz. ASW **Ruler:** Charles III
Obv. Armored bust of Charles III, right **Rev:** Crowned shield
flanked by pillars with banner, Assayer initials and mint mark
inverted from remainder of legend **Obv. Legend:** CAROLUS
• III • DEI • GRATIA • **Rev. Legend:** • HISPAN • ET IND • REX
• ... **Mint:** Mexico City **Note:** Mint mark M, Mo. Mintmark and
assayer initials bottom facing rim.

Date	Mintage	VG8	F12	VF20	XF40	MS60
1772 FM	—	100	150	225	425	—
1772 MF	—	150	350	750	1,500	—
1773 FM	—	75.00	100	160	290	—

KM# 106.2 8 REALES

27.07 g., 0.903 Silver, 0.78 oz. ASW **Ruler:** Charles III **Obv.** Armored bust of Charles III, right **Rev:** Crowned shield flanked by pillars with banner, normal initials and mint mark **Obv. Legend:** CAROLUS • III • DEI • GRATIA • **Rev. Legend:** • HISPAN • ET IND • REX • ... **Note:** Mint mark M, Mo.

Date	Mintage	VG8	F12	VF20	XF40	MS60
1773 FM	—	75.00	100	150	270	—
1774 FM	—	75.00	100	150	270	—
1775 FM	—	75.00	100	150	270	—
1776 FM	—	100	150	225	425	—
1776 FF	—	75.00	100	150	270	—
1777/6 FM	—	75.00	100	150	270	—
1777 FM	—	75.00	100	150	270	—
1777 FF	—	75.00	100	150	270	—
1778 FM	—	—	—	—	—	—

Note: Superior Casterline sale 5-89 VF realized $17,600

Date	Mintage	VG8	F12	VF20	XF40	MS60
1778/7 FF	—	75.00	100	150	270	—
1778 FF	—	75.00	100	150	270	—
1779 FF	—	75.00	100	150	270	—
1780 FF	—	75.00	100	150	270	—
1781 FF	—	75.00	100	150	270	—
1782 FF	—	75.00	100	150	270	—
1783 FF	—	75.00	100	150	270	—
1783 FM	—	4,000	6,000	9,000	—	—
1784 FF	—	150	300	600	1,500	—
1784 FM	—	75.00	100	150	270	—

KM# 106.2a 8 REALES

27.07 g., 0.896 Silver, 0.77 oz. ASW **Ruler:** Charles III **Obv.** Armored bust of Charles III, right **Rev:** Crowned shield flanked by pillars with banner, normal initials and mint mark **Obv. Legend:** CAROLUS • III • DEI • GRATIA • **Rev. Legend:** • HISPAN • ET IND • REX • ... **Note:** Mint mark M, Mo.

Date	Mintage	VG8	F12	VF20	XF40	MS60
1785 FM	—	75.00	100	140	200	—
1786/5 FM	—	75.00	100	200	400	—
1786 FM	—	75.00	100	140	200	—
1787/6 FM	—	100	250	450	1,200	—
1787 FM	—	75.00	100	140	200	—
1788 FM	—	75.00	100	140	200	—
1789 FM	—	75.00	100	150	225	—

KM# 107 8 REALES

27.07 g., 0.903 Silver, 0.78 oz. ASW **Ruler:** Charles IV **Obv.** Armored bust of Charles III, right **Rev:** Crowned shield flanked by pillars with banner **Obv. Legend:** CAROLUS • IV • DEI • GRATIA • **Rev. Legend:** • HISPAN • ET IND • REX • ... **Mint:** Mexico City **Note:** Mint mark M, Mo, using old bust punch.

Date	Mintage	VG8	F12	VF20	XF40	MS60
1789 FM	—	75.00	100	160	300	—
1790 FM	—	75.00	100	150	270	—

KM# 108 8 REALES

27.07 g., 0.903 Silver, 0.78 oz. ASW **Ruler:** Charles IV **Obv.** Armored bust of Charles III, right **Rev:** Crowned shield flanked by pillars with banner **Obv. Legend:** CAROLUS • IIII • DEI • GRATIA • **Rev. Legend:** • HISPAN • ET IND • REX • ... **Mint:** Mexico City **Note:** Mint mark M, Mo, using old portait punch.

Date	Mintage	VG8	F12	VF20	XF40	MS60
1790 FM	—	75.00	100	150	270	—

KM# 109 8 REALES

27.07 g., 0.896 Silver, 0.77 oz. ASW **Ruler:** Charles IV **Obv.** Armored bust of Charles IIII, right **Rev:** Crowned shield flanked by pillars with banner **Obv. Inscription:** CAROLUS • IIII • DEI • GRATIA • **Rev. Legend:** • HISPAN • ET IND • REX • ... **Mint:** Mexico City **Note:** Mint mark Mo.

Date	Mintage	VG8	F12	VF20	XF40	MS60
1791 FM	—	60.00	90.00	135	210	—
1792 FM	—	60.00	90.00	135	210	—

Date	Mintage	VG8	F12	VF20	XF40	MS60
1793 FM	—	60.00	90.00	135	210	—
1794 FM	—	60.00	90.00	135	210	—
1795/4 FM	—	60.00	90.00	135	210	—
1795 FM	—	60.00	90.00	135	210	—
1796 FM	—	60.00	90.00	135	210	—
1797 FM	—	60.00	90.00	135	210	—
1798 FM	—	60.00	90.00	135	210	—
1799 FM	—	60.00	90.00	135	210	—
1800/700 FM	—	60.00	90.00	135	210	—
1800 FM	—	60.00	90.00	135	210	—
1801/0 FT/FM	—	60.00	90.00	135	210	—
1801/791 FM	—	46.25	80.00	130	400	—
1801/0 FM	—	46.25	80.00	130	400	—
1801 FM	—	27.50	55.00	135	400	—
1801 FT/M	—	46.25	80.00	150	425	—
1801 FT	—	27.50	46.25	65.00	170	—
1802/1 FT	—	46.25	80.00	150	425	—
1802 FT	—	27.50	46.25	65.00	170	—
1802 FT/M	—	27.50	46.25	65.00	170	—
1803 FT	—	27.50	46.25	65.00	180	—
1803 FT/M	—	27.50	46.25	65.00	170	—
1803 TH	—	100	200	325	725	—
1804/3 TH	—	46.25	80.00	150	425	—
1804 TH	—	27.50	46.25	65.00	170	—
Note: CARLUS (error)						
1805/4 TH	—	55.00	110	175	450	—
1805 TH	—	27.50	46.25	65.00	170	—
Note: Narrow date						
1805 TH	—	27.50	46.25	65.00	170	—
Note: Wide date						
1806 TH	—	27.50	46.25	65.00	170	—
1807/6 TH	—	200	325	475	1,100	—
1807 TH	—	27.50	46.25	65.00	170	—
1808/7 TH	—	27.50	46.25	65.00	170	—
1808 TH	—	27.50	46.25	65.00	170	—

KM# 110   8 REALES
27.07 g., 0.896 Silver, 0.77 oz. ASW **Ruler:** Ferdinand VII **Obv.** Armored laureate bust right **Rev:** Crowned shield flanked by pillars **Obv. Legend:** FERDIN • VII... **Rev. Legend:** IND • REX... **Mint:** Mexico City **Note:** Mint mark Mo.

Date	Mintage	VG8	F12	VF20	XF40	MS60
1808 TH	—	33.00	55.00	100	240	—
1809/8 TH	—	33.00	55.00	100	240	—
1809 TH	—	27.50	47.50	70.00	200	—
1809 HJ	—	33.00	55.00	100	240	—
1809 HJ/TH	—	27.50	47.50	70.00	200	—
1810/09 HJ	—	33.00	55.00	100	240	—
1810 TH	—	100	200	400	950	—
1810 HJ/TH	—	33.00	55.00	100	240	—
1810 HJ	—	33.00	55.00	100	240	—
1811/0 HJ	—	27.50	47.50	70.00	200	—
1811 HJ	—	27.50	47.50	70.00	200	—
1811 HJ/TH	—	27.50	45.00	65.00	170	—

KM# 111   8 REALES
27.07 g., 0.903 Silver, 0.78 oz. ASW **Ruler:** Ferdinand VII **Obv.** Draped laureate bust right **Rev:** Crowned shield flanked by pillars **Obv. Legend:** FERDIN • VII... **Rev. Legend:** IND • REX... **Mint:** Mexico City **Note:** Mint mark Mo.

Date	Mintage	VG8	F12	VF20	XF40	MS60
1811 HJ	—	27.50	55.00	80.00	210	—
1812 HJ	—	65.00	100	170	425	—
1812 JJ/HJ	—	27.50	45.00	65.00	170	—
1812 JJ	—	27.50	45.00	65.00	170	—
1813 HJ	—	65.00	100	170	425	—
1813 JJ	—	27.50	45.00	65.00	170	—
1814/3 HJ	—	1,550	3,300	6,600	—	—
1814/3 JJ	—	27.50	45.00	65.00	170	—
1814 JJ	—	27.50	45.00	65.00	170	—
1815/4 JJ	—	27.50	45.00	65.00	170	—
1815 JJ	—	27.50	45.00	65.00	170	—
1816/5 JJ	—	27.50	45.00	65.00	150	—
1816 JJ	—	27.50	45.00	65.00	150	—
1817 JJ	—	27.50	45.00	65.00	150	—
1818 JJ	—	27.50	45.00	65.00	150	—
1819 JJ	—	27.50	45.00	65.00	150	—
1820 JJ	—	27.50	45.00	65.00	150	—
1821 JJ	—	27.50	45.00	65.00	150	—

KM# 112   1/2 ESCUDO
1.69 g., 0.875 Gold, 0.05 oz. AGW **Ruler:** Ferdinand VII **Obv.** Laureate head right **Rev:** Crowned oval shield **Obv. Legend:** FERD • VII • D • G • HISP • ET IND **Mint:** Mexico City **Note:** Mint mark Mo.

Date	Mintage	VG8	F12	VF20	XF40	MS60
1814 JJ	—	100	150	225	375	550
1815/4 JJ	—	150	200	250	400	875
1815 JJ	—	150	200	250	400	—
1816 JJ	—	100	150	225	375	550
1817 JJ	—	150	200	250	400	—
1818 JJ	—	150	200	250	400	—
1819 JJ	—	150	200	250	400	—
1820 JJ	—	200	300	400	550	—

KM# 113   ESCUDO
3.38 g., 0.917 Gold, 0.10 oz. AGW **Ruler:** Philip V **Obv.** Armored bust right **Rev:** Crowned shield flanked by M F I **Obv. Legend:** PHILIP • V • D • G • HISPAN • ET IND • REX **Mint:** Mexico City

Date	Mintage	VG8	F12	VF20	XF40	MS60
1732 F	—	1,000	2,000	3,000	4,000	—
1733/2 F	—	1,000	2,000	3,000	4,000	—
1734/3 MF	—	200	300	400	850	—
1735/4 MF	—	200	300	400	850	—
1735 MF	—	200	300	400	850	—
1736/5 MF	—	200	300	400	850	—
1736 MF	—	200	300	400	850	—
1737 MF	—	200	300	600	1,200	—
1738/7 MF	—	200	300	600	1,200	—
1738 MF	—	200	300	600	1,200	—
1739 MF	—	200	300	600	1,200	—
1740/30 MF	—	200	300	600	1,200	—
1741 MF	—	200	300	600	1,200	—
1742 MF	—	200	300	600	1,200	—
1743/2 MF	—	200	300	450	800	—
1743 MF	—	200	300	400	700	—
1744/3 MF	—	200	300	400	700	—
1744 MF	—	200	300	400	700	—
1745 MF	—	200	300	400	700	—
1746/5 MF	—	200	300	400	700	—
1747 MF Rare	—	—	—	—	—	—

KM# 114 ESCUDO

3.38 g., 0.917 Gold, 0.10 oz. AGW **Ruler:** Ferdinand VI **Obv.** Armored bust right **Rev:** Crowned shield flanked by M F I **Obv. Legend:** FERD • VI • D • G • HISPAN • ET IND • REX **Mint:** Mexico City **Note:** Mint mark M, Mo.

Date	Mintage	VG8	F12	VF20	XF40	MS60
1747 MF	—	1,650	3,000	5,000	7,500	—

KM# 115.1 ESCUDO

3.38 g., 0.917 Gold, 0.10 oz. AGW **Ruler:** Ferdinand VI **Obv.** Short armored bust right **Rev:** Crowned shield **Obv. Legend:** FERD • VI • D • G • HISPAN • ET IND • REX **Mint:** Mexico City **Note:** Mint mark M, Mo.

Date	Mintage	VG8	F12	VF20	XF40	MS60
1748 MF	—	250	350	550	950	—
1749 MF	—	300	450	700	1,150	—
1750 MF	—	200	300	400	800	—
1751 MF	—	200	300	400	800	—

KM# 115.2 ESCUDO

3.38 g., 0.917 Gold, 0.10 oz. AGW **Ruler:** Ferdinand VI **Obv.** Short armored bust right **Rev:** Without 1 S flanking crowned shield **Obv. Legend:** FERD • VI • D • G • HISPAN • ET IND • REX **Mint:** Mexico City

Date	Mintage	VG8	F12	VF20	XF40	MS60
1752 MF	—	200	300	375	750	—
1753/2 MF	—	200	300	400	800	—
1753 MF	—	200	300	400	800	—
1754 MF	—	200	300	400	800	—
1755 MM	—	200	300	400	800	—
1756 MM	—	200	300	400	800	—

KM# A116 ESCUDO

3.38 g., 0.917 Gold, 0.10 oz. AGW **Ruler:** Ferdinand VI **Obv.** Armored bust right **Rev:** Crowned shield **Obv. Legend:** FERDIND • VI • D • G • HISPAN • ETIND • REX • **Rev. Legend:** M • NOMINA MAGNA SEQUOR • M **Mint:** Mexico City

Date	Mintage	VG8	F12	VF20	XF40	MS60
1757 MM	—	200	300	400	800	—
1759 MM	—	200	300	400	800	—

KM# 116 ESCUDO

3.38 g., 0.917 Gold, 0.10 oz. AGW **Ruler:** Charles III **Obv.** Armored bust right **Rev:** Crowned shield **Obv. Legend:** CAROLVS • III • D • G • HISPAN • ET IND • REX **Rev. Legend:** M • NOMINA MAGNA SEQUOR • M • **Mint:** Mexico City **Note:** Mint mark M, Mo.

Date	Mintage	VG8	F12	VF20	XF40	MS60
1760 MM	—	400	800	1,500	2,500	—
1761/0 MM	—	400	800	1,500	2,500	—
1761 MM	—	400	800	1,500	2,500	—

KM# 117 ESCUDO

3.38 g., 0.917 Gold, 0.10 oz. AGW **Ruler:** Charles III **Obv.** Large armored bust right **Rev:** Crowned shield **Obv. Legend:** CAR • III • D • G • HISP • ET IND • R **Rev. Legend:** IN • UTROQ • FELIX • **Mint:** Mexico City **Note:** Mint mark M, Mo.

Date	Mintage	VG8	F12	VF20	XF40	MS60
1762 MM	—	250	375	600	1,000	—
1763 MM	—	275	425	700	1,100	—
1764 MM	—	250	375	600	1,000	—
1765 MF	—	250	375	600	1,000	—
1766 MF	—	250	375	600	1,000	—
1767 MF	—	250	375	600	1,000	—
1768 MF	—	250	375	600	1,000	—
1769 MF	—	250	375	600	1,000	—
1770 MF	—	250	375	600	1,000	—
1771 MF	—	250	375	600	1,000	—

KM# 118.1 ESCUDO

3.38 g., 0.901 Gold, 0.10 oz. AGW **Ruler:** Charles III **Obv.** Large armored bust right **Rev:** Crowned shield flanked by 1 S within order chain **Obv. Legend:** CAROL • III • D • G • HISPAN • ET IND • R **Rev. Legend:** FELIX • A • D • ... **Mint:** Mexico City **Note:** Mint mark M, Mo.

Date	Mintage	VG8	F12	VF20	XF40	MS60
1772 MF	—	175	250	350	475	—
1772 FM	—	175	250	275	475	—
1773 FM	—	175	250	275	475	—

KM# 118.2 ESCUDO
3.38 g., 0.901 Gold, 0.10 oz. AGW **Ruler:** Charles III **Obv.** Large armored bust right **Rev:** crowned shield in order chain, initials and mint mark inverted **Obv. Legend:** CAROL • III • D • G • HISPAN • ET IND • R **Rev. Legend:** FELIX • A • D • ... **Mint:** Mexico City **Note:** Mint mark M, Mo.

Date	Mintage	VG8	F12	VF20	XF40	MS60
1773 FM	—	175	250	350	475	—
1774 FM	—	175	250	350	475	—
1775 FM	—	175	250	350	475	—
1776 FM	—	225	300	400	575	—
1777 FM	—	175	250	350	475	—
1778 FF	—	175	250	350	475	—
1779 FF	—	175	250	350	475	—
1780 FF	—	175	250	350	475	—
1781 FF	—	175	250	350	475	—
1782 FF	—	175	250	350	475	—
1783/2 FF	—	175	250	350	475	—
1783 FF	—	175	250	350	475	—
1784/3 FF	—	175	250	350	475	—
1784/3 FM/F	—	175	250	350	475	—

KM# 118.2a ESCUDO
3.38 g., 0.875 Gold, 0.09 oz. AGW **Ruler:** Charles III **Obv.** Large armored bust right **Rev:** Crowned shield in order chain, initials and mint mark inverted **Obv. Legend:** CAROL • III • D • G • HISPAN • ET IND • R • **Rev. Legend:** FELIX • A • D • ... **Mint:** Mexico City **Note:** Mint mark M, Mo.

Date	Mintage	VG8	F12	VF20	XF40	MS60
1785 FM	—	175	250	350	475	—
1786 FM	—	175	250	350	475	—
1787 FM	—	175	250	350	475	—
1788 FM	—	175	250	350	475	—

KM# 118.1a ESCUDO
3.38 g., 0.875 Gold, 0.09 oz. AGW **Ruler:** Charles III **Obv.** Large armored bust right **Rev:** Crowned shield in order chain, initial letters and mint mark upright **Obv. Legend:** CAROL • III • D • G • HISPAN • ET IND • R **Rev. Legend:** FELIX • A • D • ... **Mint:** Mexico City **Note:** Mint mark M, Mo.

Date	Mintage	VG8	F12	VF20	XF40	MS60
1788 FM	—	175	250	350	475	—

KM# 119 ESCUDO
3.38 g., 0.875 Gold, 0.09 oz. AGW **Ruler:** Charles IV **Obv.** Armored bust of Charles III, right **Rev:** Crowned shield in order chain, initial letters and mint mark upright **Obv. Legend:** CAROL • IV • D • G • ... **Rev. Legend:** FELIX • A • D • ... **Mint:** Mexico City **Note:** Mint mark M, Mo, using old portrait punch.

Date	Mintage	VG8	F12	VF20	XF40	MS60
1789 FM	—	300	550	1,000	2,000	—
1790 FM	—	300	550	1,000	2,000	—

KM# 120 ESCUDO
3.38 g., 0.875 Gold, 0.09 oz. AGW **Ruler:** Charles IV **Obv.** Armored bust right **Rev:** Crowned shield in order chain, initial letters and mint mark upright **Obv. Legend:** CAROL • IIII • D • G • ... **Rev. Legend:** FELIX • A • D • ... **Mint:** Mexico City **Note:** Mint mark Mo.

Date	Mintage	VG8	F12	VF20	XF40	MS60
1792 MF	—	150	225	300	375	—
1793 FM	—	150	225	300	375	—
1794 FM	—	150	225	300	375	—
1795 FM	—	150	225	300	375	—
1796 FM	—	150	225	300	375	—
1797 FM	—	150	225	300	375	—
1798 FM	—	150	225	300	375	—
1799 FM	—	150	225	300	375	—
1800 FM	—	150	225	300	375	—
1801 FM	—	155	185	265	375	—
1801 FT	—	155	185	265	375	700
1802 FT	—	155	185	265	375	—
1803 FT	—	155	185	265	375	—
1804/3 TH	—	155	185	265	375	800
1804 TH	—	155	185	265	375	800
1805 TH	—	155	185	265	375	—
1806/5 TH	—	155	185	265	375	—
1806 TH	—	155	185	265	375	—
1807 TH	—	155	185	265	375	—
1808 TH	—	155	185	265	375	—

KM# 121 ESCUDO
3.38 g., 0.875 Gold, 0.09 oz. AGW **Ruler:** Ferdinand VII **Obv.** Armored bust right **Rev:** Crowned shield divides designed wreath **Obv. Legend:** FERDIN.VII... **Rev. Legend:** FELIX. A. D, initial letters and mint mark upright **Mint:** Mexico City **Note:** Mint mark Mo.

Date	Mintage	VG8	F12	VF20	XF40	MS60
1809 HJ/TH	—	150	180	235	400	750
1809 HJ	—	150	180	235	400	750
1811/0 HJ	—	150	180	235	400	—
1812 HJ	—	165	250	300	500	—

KM# 122 ESCUDO
3.38 g., 0.875 Gold, 0.09 oz. AGW **Ruler:** Ferdinand VII **Obv.** Laureate head right **Rev:** Crowned shield divides designed wreath, initial letters and mint mark upright **Obv. Legend:** FERDIN • VII • D • G... **Rev. Legend:** FELIX • A • D... **Mint:** Mexico City **Note:** Mint mark Mo.

Date	Mintage	VG8	F12	VF20	XF40	MS60
1814 HJ	—	165	250	300	500	900
1815 HJ	—	165	250	300	500	900
1815 JJ	—	165	250	300	500	900
1816 JJ	—	180	275	325	550	950
1817 JJ	—	165	250	300	500	900
1818 JJ	—	165	250	300	500	900

Date	Mintage	VG8	F12	VF20	XF40	MS60
1819 JJ	—	165	250	300	500	900
1820 JJ	—	165	250	300	500	900

KM# 124 2 ESCUDOS
6.77 g., 0.917 Gold, 0.20 oz. AGW **Ruler:** Philip V **Obv.** Armored bust right **Rev:** Crowned shield flanked by M F 2 **Obv. Legend:** PHILIP • V • D • G • HISPAN • ET IND • REX **Rev. Legend:** INITIUM SAPIENTIAE TIMOR DOMINI **Mint:** Mexico City

Date	Mintage	VG8	F12	VF20	XF40	MS60
1732 F	—	1,000	1,500	2,000	3,000	—
1733 F	—	750	1,000	1,500	2,500	—
1734/3 MF	—	400	500	900	1,400	—
1735 MF	—	400	500	900	1,400	—
1736/5 MF	—	400	500	900	1,400	—
1736 MF	—	400	500	900	1,400	—
1737 MF	—	400	500	900	1,400	—
1738/7 MF	—	400	500	900	1,400	—
1739 MF	—	400	500	900	1,400	—
1740/30 MF	—	400	500	900	1,400	—
1741 MF	—	400	500	900	1,400	—
1742 MF	—	400	500	900	1,400	—
1743 MF	—	400	500	900	1,400	—
1744/2 MF	—	400	500	900	1,400	—
1744 MF	—	400	500	900	1,400	—
1745 MF	—	400	500	900	1,400	—
1746/5 MF	—	400	500	900	1,400	—
1747 MF	—	400	500	900	1,400	—

KM# 125 2 ESCUDOS
6.77 g., 0.917 Gold, 0.20 oz. AGW **Ruler:** Ferdinand VI **Obv.** Large armored bust right **Rev:** Crowned shield flanked by M F 2 **Obv. Legend:** FERD • VI • D • G • ... **Rev. Legend:** INITIUM... **Mint:** Mexico City

Date	Mintage	VG8	F12	VF20	XF40	MS60
1747 MF	—	3,000	5,500	9,000	15,000	—

KM# 126.1 2 ESCUDOS
6.77 g., 0.917 Gold, 0.20 oz. AGW **Ruler:** Ferdinand VI **Obv.** Head right **Rev:** Crowned shield **Obv. Legend:** FERD • VI • D • G • ... **Rev. Legend:** NOMINA MAGNA SEQUOR **Mint:** Mexico City **Note:** Mint mark M, Mo.

Date	Mintage	VG8	F12	VF20	XF40	MS60
1748 MF	—	450	750	1,500	3,000	—
1749/8 MF	—	450	750	1,500	3,000	—
1750 MF	—	400	700	1,400	2,850	—
1751 MF	—	400	700	1,400	2,850	—

KM# 126.2 2 ESCUDOS
6.77 g., 0.917 Gold, 0.20 oz. AGW **Ruler:** Ferdinand VI **Obv.** Head right **Rev:** Without 2 S by crowned shield **Obv. Legend:** FERD • VI • D • G • ... **Rev. Legend:** NOMINA MAGNA SEQUOR **Mint:** Mexico City **Note:** Mint mark M, Mo.

Date	Mintage	VG8	F12	VF20	XF40	MS60
1752 MF	—	400	700	1,400	2,850	—
1753 MF	—	400	700	1,400	2,850	—
1754 MF	—	600	850	1,750	3,500	—
1755 MM	—	400	700	1,400	2,850	—
1756 MM	—	600	850	1,750	3,500	—

KM# 127 2 ESCUDOS
6.77 g., 0.917 Gold, 0.20 oz. AGW **Ruler:** Ferdinand VI **Obv.** Armored bust right **Rev:** Without 2 S by crowned shield **Obv. Legend:** FERDIND • VI • D • G • ... **Rev. Legend:** NOMINA MAGNA SEQUOR **Mint:** Mexico City **Note:** Mint mark M, Mo.

Date	Mintage	VG8	F12	VF20	XF40	MS60
1757 MM	—	450	750	1,500	3,000	—
1759 MM	—	450	750	1,500	3,000	—

KM# 128 2 ESCUDOS
6.77 g., 0.917 Gold, 0.20 oz. AGW **Ruler:** Charles III **Obv.** Armored bust right **Rev:** Without 2 S by crowned shield **Obv. Legend:** CAROLVS • III • D • G • ... **Rev. Legend:** NOMINA MAGNA SEQUOR **Mint:** Mexico City **Note:** Mint mark M, Mo.

Date	Mintage	VG8	F12	VF20	XF40	MS60
1760 MM	—	550	1,000	2,000	4,000	—
1761 MM	—	550	1,000	2,000	4,000	—

KM# 129 2 ESCUDOS
6.77 g., 0.917 Gold, 0.20 oz. AGW **Ruler:** Charles III **Obv.** Large armored bust right **Rev:** Without 2 S by crowned shield **Obv. Legend:** CAROLUS • III • D • G • ... **Rev. Legend:** IN • UTROQ • FELIX • AUSPICE • DEO **Mint:** Mexico City **Note:** Mint mark M, Mo.

Date	Mintage	VG8	F12	VF20	XF40	MS60
1762 MF	—	500	900	1,850	3,750	—

Date	Mintage	VG8	F12	VF20	XF40	MS60
1763 MF	—	500	900	1,850	3,750	—
1764/3 MF	—	500	900	1,850	3,750	—
1765 MF	—	500	900	1,850	3,750	—
1766 MF	—	500	900	1,850	3,750	—
1767 MF	—	500	900	1,850	3,750	—
1768 MF	—	500	900	1,850	3,750	—
1769 MF	—	500	900	1,850	3,750	—
1770 MF	—	500	900	1,850	3,750	—
1771 MF	—	500	900	1,850	3,750	—

KM# 130.1 2 ESCUDOS
6.77 g., 0.901 Gold, 0.19 oz. AGW **Ruler:** Charles III **Obv.** Older, armored bust right **Rev:** Crowned shield in order chain, initials and mint mark upright **Obv. Legend:** CAROLUS • III • D • G • ... **Rev. Legend:** IN • UTROQ • FELIX • AUSPICE • DEO **Mint:** Mexico City **Note:** Mint mark M, Mo.

Date	Mintage	VG8	F12	VF20	XF40	MS60
1772 FM	—	300	400	550	1,000	—
1773 FM	—	300	400	550	1,000	—

KM# 130.2 2 ESCUDOS
6.77 g., 0.901 Gold, 0.19 oz. AGW **Ruler:** Charles III **Obv.** Older, armored bust right **Rev:** Crowned shield in order chain, initials and mint mark inverted **Obv. Legend:** CAROLUS • III • D • G • ... **Rev. Legend:** IN • UTROQ • FELIX • AUSPICE • DEO **Mint:** Mexico City **Note:** Mint mark M, Mo.

Date	Mintage	VG8	F12	VF20	XF40	MS60
1773 FM	—	300	400	550	1,000	—
1774 FM	—	300	400	550	1,000	—
1775 FM	—	300	400	550	1,000	—
1776 FM	—	350	500	675	1,000	—
1777 FM	—	300	400	500	900	—
1778 FF	—	300	400	500	900	—
1779 FF	—	300	400	500	900	—
1780 FF	—	300	400	500	900	—
1781 FM/M	—	300	400	500	900	—
1781 FF	—	300	400	500	900	—
1782 FF	—	300	400	500	900	—
1783 FF	—	300	400	500	900	—
1784 FF	—	300	400	500	900	—
1784 FM/F	—	300	400	500	900	—

KM# 130.2a 2 ESCUDOS
6.77 g., 0.875 Gold, 0.19 oz. AGW **Ruler:** Charles III **Obv.** Older, armored bust right **Rev:** Crowned shield in order chain, initials and mint mark inverted **Obv. Legend:** CAROLUS • III • D • G • ... **Rev. Legend:** IN • UTROQ • FELIX • AUSPICE • DEO **Mint:** Mexico City **Note:** Mint mark M, Mo.

Date	Mintage	VG8	F12	VF20	XF40	MS60
1785 FM	—	300	400	500	900	—
1786 FM	—	300	400	500	900	—
1787 FM	—	300	400	500	900	—
1788 FM	—	300	400	500	900	—

KM# 130.1a 2 ESCUDOS
6.77 g., 0.875 Gold, 0.19 oz. AGW **Ruler:** Charles III **Obv.** Older, armored bust right **Rev:** Crowned shield in order chain, initials and mint mark upright **Obv. Legend:** CAROLUS • III • D • G • ... **Rev. Legend:** IN • UTROQ • FELIX • AUSPICE • DEO **Mint:** Mexico City **Note:** Mint mark M, Mo.

Date	Mintage	VG8	F12	VF20	XF40	MS60
1788 FM	—	300	400	500	900	—

KM# 131 2 ESCUDOS
6.77 g., 0.875 Gold, 0.19 oz. AGW **Ruler:** Charles IV **Obv.** Armored bust of Charles III, right **Rev:** Crowned shield in order chain, initials and mint mark upright **Obv. Legend:** CAROL • IV • D • G • ... **Rev. Legend:** IN • UTROQ • FELIX • AUSPICE • DEO **Mint:** Mexico City **Note:** Mint mark M, Mo, using old portrait punch.

Date	Mintage	VG8	F12	VF20	XF40	MS60
1789 FM	—	650	1,200	2,000	3,500	—
1790 FM	—	650	1,200	2,000	3,500	—

KM# 132 2 ESCUDOS
6.77 g., 0.875 Gold, 0.19 oz. AGW **Ruler:** Charles IV **Obv.** Armored bust of Charles IIII, right **Rev:** Crowned shield flanked by 2 S in order chain **Obv. Legend:** CAROL • IIII • D • G • ... **Rev. Legend:** IN • UTROQ • FELIX • AUSPICE • DEO; initials and mint mark upright **Mint:** Mexico City **Note:** Mint mark Mo.

Date	Mintage	VG8	F12	VF20	XF40	MS60
1791 FM Mo over inverted Mo	—	300	400	600	950	—
1792 FM	—	250	350	450	575	—
1793 FM	—	250	350	450	575	—
1794 FM	—	250	350	450	575	—
1795 FM	—	250	350	450	575	—
1796 FM	—	250	350	450	575	—
1797 FM	—	250	350	450	575	—
1798 FM	—	250	350	450	575	—
1799 FM	—	250	350	450	575	—
1800 FM	—	250	350	450	575	—
1801 FT	—	300	350	425	600	—
1802 FT	—	300	350	425	600	1,000
1803 FT	—	300	350	425	600	—
1804 TH	—	300	350	425	600	—
1805 TH	—	300	350	425	600	—
1806/5 TH	—	300	350	425	600	—
1807 TH	—	300	350	425	600	—
1808 TH	—	300	350	425	600	1,500

KM# 134 2 ESCUDOS
6.77 g., 0.875 Gold, 0.19 oz. AGW **Ruler:** Ferdinand VII **Obv.** Laureate head right **Rev:** Crowned shield divides designed wreath, initials and mint mark upright **Obv. Legend:** FERDIN • VII • D • G... **Rev. Legend:** IN • UTROQ • FELIX • AUSPICE • DEO **Mint:** Mexico City **Note:** Mint mark Mo.

Date	Mintage	VG8	F12	VF20	XF40	MS60
1814 Mo HJ	—	300	450	750	1,250	—
1815 JJ	—	300	450	750	1,250	—
1816 JJ	—	300	450	750	1,250	—
1817 JJ	—	300	450	750	1,250	—
1818 JJ	—	300	450	750	1,250	3,750
1819 JJ	—	300	450	750	1,250	—
1820 JJ	—	300	450	750	1,250	—
1821 JJ	—	300	450	750	1,250	—

KM# 135 4 ESCUDOS

13.53 g., 0.917 Gold, 0.40 oz. AGW **Ruler:** Philip V **Obv.**
Armored bust right **Rev:** Crowned shield flanked by F 4
Obv. Legend: PHILIP • V • D • G • HISPAN • ET IND • REX
Rev. Legend: INITIUM SAPIENTIAE TIMOR DOMINI **Mint:**
Mexico City

Date	Mintage	VG8	F12	VF20	XF40	MS60
1732 Rare	—	—	—	—	—	—
1732 F Rare	—	—	—	—	—	—
1733 F Rare	—	—	—	—	—	—
1734/3 F	—	1,200	1,800	3,350	5,400	—
1734 MF	—	1,000	1,600	3,000	5,100	—
1735 MF	—	1,000	1,600	3,000	5,400	—
1736 MF	—	1,000	1,600	3,000	5,400	—
1737 MF	—	900	1,500	2,900	4,800	—
1738/7 MF	—	900	1,500	2,900	4,800	—
1738 MF	—	900	1,500	2,900	4,800	—
1739 MF	—	900	1,500	2,900	4,800	—
1740/30 MF	—	900	1,500	2,900	4,800	—
1740 MF	—	900	1,500	2,900	4,800	—
1741 MF	—	900	1,500	2,900	4,800	—
1742/32 MF	—	900	1,500	2,900	4,800	—
1743 MF	—	900	1,500	2,900	4,800	—
1744 MD	—	900	1,500	2,900	4,800	—
1745 MF	—	900	1,500	2,900	4,800	—
1746 MF	—	900	1,500	2,900	4,800	—
1747 MF	—	900	1,500	2,900	4,800	—
1746/5 MF	—	900	1,500	2,900	4,800	—

KM# 136 4 ESCUDOS

13.53 g., 0.917 Gold, 0.40 oz. AGW **Ruler:** Ferdinand
VI **Obv.** Large, armored bust right **Rev:** Crowned shield
flanked by F 4 **Obv. Legend:** FERDND • VI • D • G • ...
Rev. Legend: INITIUM SAPIENTIAE TIMOR DOMINI **Mint:**
Mexico City **Note:** Mint mark M, Mo.

Date	Mintage	VG8	F12	VF20	XF40	MS60
1747 MF	—	7,500	13,500	20,000	30,000	—

KM# 137 4 ESCUDOS

13.53 g., 0.917 Gold, 0.40 oz. AGW **Ruler:** Ferdinand VI
Obv. Armored bust right **Rev:** Crowned shield flanked by

4 S **Obv. Legend:** FERDND • VI • D • G • ... **Rev. Legend:**
NOMINA MAGNA SEQUOR **Mint:** Mexico City **Note:** Mint
mark M, Mo.

Date	Mintage	VG8	F12	VF20	XF40	MS60
1748 MF	—	1,500	3,000	5,000	8,000	—
1749 MF	—	1,500	3,000	5,000	8,000	—
1750/48 MF	—	1,500	3,000	5,000	8,000	—
1750 MF	—	1,500	3,000	5,000	8,000	—
1751 MF	—	1,500	3,000	5,000	8,000	—

KM# 138 4 ESCUDOS

13.53 g., 0.917 Gold, 0.40 oz. AGW **Ruler:** Ferdinand
VI **Obv.** Small, armored bust right **Rev:** Crowned shield,
without value **Obv. Legend:** FERDND • VI • D • G • ... **Rev.
Legend:** NOMINA MAGNA... **Mint:** Mexico City **Note:** Mint
mark M, Mo.

Date	Mintage	VG8	F12	VF20	XF40	MS60
1752 MF	—	1,000	2,000	3,500	6,000	—
1753 MF	—	1,000	2,000	3,500	6,000	—
1754 MF	—	1,000	2,000	3,500	6,000	—
1755 MM	—	1,000	2,000	3,500	6,000	—
1756 MM	—	1,000	2,000	3,500	6,000	—

KM# 139 4 ESCUDOS

13.53 g., 0.917 Gold, 0.40 oz. AGW **Ruler:** Ferdinand VI **Obv.**
Armored bust right **Rev:** Crowned shield, without value **Obv.
Legend:** FERDND • VI • D • G • ... **Rev. Legend:** NOMINA
MAGNA... **Mint:** Mexico City **Note:** Mint mark M, Mo.

Date	Mintage	VG8	F12	VF20	XF40	MS60
1757 MM	—	1,250	2,500	4,000	6,500	—
1759 MM	—	1,250	2,500	4,000	6,500	—

KM# 140 4 ESCUDOS

13.53 g., 0.917 Gold, 0.40 oz. AGW **Ruler:** Charles III **Obv.**
Armored bust right **Rev:** Crowned shield, without value **Obv.
Legend:** CAROLVS • III • D • G • ... **Rev. Legend:** NOMINA
MAGNA SEQUOR **Mint:** Mexico City **Note:** Mint mark M, Mo.

Date	Mintage	VG8	F12	VF20	XF40	MS60
1760 MM	—	3,500	6,500	10,000	20,000	—
1761 MM	—	3,500	6,500	10,000	20,000	—

KM# 141   4 ESCUDOS
13.53 g., 0.917 Gold, 0.40 oz. AGW **Ruler:** Charles III **Obv.** Large, armored bust right **Rev:** Crowned shield in order chain, without value **Obv. Legend:** CAROLUS • III • D • G • ... **Rev. Legend:** IN • UTROQ • FELIX • AUSPICE • DEO **Mint:** Mexico City **Note:** Mint mark M, Mo.

Date	Mintage	VG8	F12	VF20	XF40	MS60
1762 MF	—	2,500	4,500	7,500	15,000	—
1763 MF	—	2,500	4,500	7,500	15,000	—
1764 MF	—	2,500	4,500	7,500	15,000	—
1765 MF	—	2,500	4,500	7,500	15,000	—
1766/5 MF	—	2,500	4,500	7,500	15,000	—
1767 MF	—	2,500	4,500	7,500	15,000	—
1768 MF	—	2,500	4,500	7,500	15,000	—
1769 MF	—	2,500	4,500	7,500	15,000	—
1770 MF	—	2,500	4,500	7,500	15,000	—
1771 MF	—	2,500	4,500	7,500	15,000	—

KM# 142.1   4 ESCUDOS
13.53 g., 0.901 Gold, 0.39 oz. AGW **Ruler:** Charles III **Obv.** Large, armored bust right **Rev:** Crowned shield in order chain, initials and mint mark upright **Obv. Legend:** CAROL • III • D • G • ... **Rev. Legend:** IN • UTROQ • FELIX • AUSPICE • DEO **Mint:** Mexico City **Note:** Mint mark M, Mo.

Date	Mintage	VG8	F12	VF20	XF40	MS60
1772 FM	—	600	975	1,500	3,000	—
1773 FM	—	600	975	1,500	3,000	—

KM# 142.2   4 ESCUDOS
13.53 g., 0.901 Gold, 0.39 oz. AGW **Ruler:** Charles III **Obv.** Large, armored bust right **Rev:** Crowned shield flanked by 4 S in order chain, initials and mint mark inverted **Obv. Legend:** CAROL • III • D • G • ... **Rev. Legend:** IN • UTROQ • FELIX • AUSPICE • DEO **Mint:** Mexico City **Note:** Mint mark M, Mo.

Date	Mintage	VG8	F12	VF20	XF40	MS60
1773 FM	—	525	725	1,100	2,200	—
1774 FM	—	525	725	1,100	2,200	—
1775 FM	—	525	725	1,100	2,200	—
1776 FM	—	525	725	1,100	2,200	—
1777 FM	—	525	725	1,100	2,200	—
1778 FF	—	525	725	1,100	2,200	—
1779 FF	—	525	725	1,100	2,200	—
1780 FF	—	525	725	1,100	2,200	—
1781 FF	—	525	725	1,100	2,200	—
1782 FF	—	525	725	1,100	2,200	—
1783 FF	—	525	725	1,100	2,200	—
1784 FF	—	525	725	1,100	2,200	—
1784/3 FM/F	—	525	725	1,100	2,200	—

KM# 142.2a   4 ESCUDOS
13.53 g., 0.875 Gold, 0.38 oz. AGW **Ruler:** Charles III **Obv.** Large, armored bust right **Rev:** Crowned shield in order chain, initials and mint mark inverted **Obv. Legend:** CAROL • III • D • G • ... **Rev. Legend:** IN • UTROQ • FELIX • AUSPICE • DEO **Mint:** Mexico City **Note:** Mint mark M, Mo.

Date	Mintage	VG8	F12	VF20	XF40	MS60
1785 FM	—	525	725	1,100	2,200	—
1786 FM/F	—	525	725	1,100	2,200	—
1786 FM	—	525	725	1,100	2,200	—
1787 FM	—	525	725	1,100	2,200	—
1788 FM	—	525	725	1,100	2,200	—

KM# 142.1a   4 ESCUDOS
13.53 g., 0.875 Gold, 0.38 oz. AGW **Ruler:** Charles III **Obv.** Large, armored bust right **Rev:** Crowned shield in order chain, initials and mint mark upright **Obv. Legend:** CAROL • III • D • G • ... **Rev. Legend:** IN • UTROQ • FELIX • AUSPICE • DEO **Mint:** Mexico City **Note:** Mint mark M, Mo.

Date	Mintage	VG8	F12	VF20	XF40	MS60
1788 FM	—	600	975	1,500	3,000	—

KM# 143.1   4 ESCUDOS
13.53 g., 0.875 Gold, 0.38 oz. AGW **Ruler:** Charles IV **Obv.** Armored bust of Charles III, right **Rev:** Crowned shield in order chain, initials and mint mark upright **Obv. Legend:** CAROL • IV • D • G • ... **Rev. Legend:** IN • UTROQ • FELIX • AUSPICE • DEO **Mint:** Mexico City **Note:** Mint mark M, Mo, using old portrait punch.

Date	Mintage	VG8	F12	VF20	XF40	MS60
1789 FM	—	550	750	1,100	2,150	—
1790 FM	—	550	750	1,100	2,150	—

KM# 143.2   4 ESCUDOS
13.53 g., 0.875 Gold, 0.38 oz. AGW **Ruler:** Charles IV **Obv.** Armored bust of Charles III, right **Rev:** Crowned shield in order chain, initials and mint mark upright **Obv. Legend:** CAROL • IIII • D • G • ... **Rev. Legend:** IN • UTROQ • FELIX • AUSPICE • DEO **Mint:** Mexico City **Note:** Mint mark M, Mo, using old portrait punch.

Date	Mintage	VG8	F12	VF20	XF40	MS60
1790 FM	—	600	1,000	1,800	3,000	—

KM# 144   4 ESCUDOS
13.53 g., 0.875 Gold, 0.38 oz. AGW **Ruler:** Charles IV **Obv.** Armored bust of Charles IIII, right **Rev:** Crowned shield flanked by 4 S in order chain **Obv. Legend:** CAROL • IIII • D • G • ... **Rev. Legend:** IN • UTROQ • FELIX • AUSPICE • DEO; initials and mint mark upright **Mint:** Mexico City **Note:** Mint mark Mo.

Date	Mintage	VG8	F12	VF20	XF40	MS60
1792 FM	—	525	600	750	1,500	—
1793 FM	—	525	600	750	1,500	—
1794/3 FM	—	525	600	750	1,500	—
1795 FM	—	525	600	750	1,500	—
1796 FM	—	525	600	750	1,500	—
1797 FM	—	525	600	750	1,500	—
1798/7 FM	—	525	600	750	1,500	—
1798 FM	—	525	600	750	1,500	—
1799 FM	—	525	600	750	1,500	—
1800 FM	—	525	600	750	1,500	—
1801 FM	—	600	650	800	1,500	—
1801 FT	—	600	650	800	1,500	—
1802 FT	—	600	700	800	1,650	—
1803 FT	—	600	650	800	1,500	—
1803/2	—	600	750	900	1,500	—
1804/3 TH	—	600	650	800	1,500	—

Date	Mintage	VG8	F12	VF20	XF40	MS60
1804 TH	—	600	650	800	1,500	—
1805 TH	—	600	650	800	1,500	—
1806/5 TH	—	600	650	800	1,500	—
1807 TH	—	600	700	900	1,650	—
1808/0 TH	—	600	650	800	1,500	—
1808 TH	—	600	650	800	1,500	—

KM# 145 4 ESCUDOS
13.53 g., 0.875 Gold, 0.38 oz. AGW **Ruler:** Ferdinand VII **Obv.** Armored bust right **Rev:** Crowned shield divides designed wreath, initials and mint mark upright **Obv. Legend:** FERDIN • VII D • G... **Rev. Legend:** IN • UTROQ • FELIX • AUSPICE • DEO **Mint:** Mexico City **Note:** Mint mark Mo.

Date	Mintage	VG8	F12	VF20	XF40	MS60
1810 HJ	—	650	750	1,150	2,500	—
1811 HJ	—	650	750	1,150	2,500	—
1812 HJ	—	650	750	1,150	2,500	—

KM# 146 4 ESCUDOS
13.53 g., 0.875 Gold, 0.38 oz. AGW **Ruler:** Ferdinand VII **Obv.** Laureate head right **Rev:** Crowned shield designed wreath **Obv. Legend:** FERDIN. VII D. G... **Rev. Legend:** IN. UTROQ. FELIX. AUSPICE. DEO; initials and mint mark upright **Mint:** Mexico City **Note:** Mint mark Mo.

Date	Mintage	VG8	F12	VF20	XF40	MS60
1814 HJ	—	675	800	1,250	2,700	—
1815 HJ	—	675	800	1,250	2,700	—
1815 JJ	—	675	800	1,250	2,700	—
1816 JJ	—	675	800	1,250	2,700	—
1817 JJ	—	675	800	1,250	2,700	—
1818 JJ	—	675	800	1,250	2,700	—
1819 JJ	—	675	800	1,250	2,700	—
1820 JJ	—	675	800	1,250	2,700	—

KM# 148 8 ESCUDOS
27.07 g., 0.917 Gold, 0.79 oz. AGW **Ruler:** Philip V **Obv.** Large, armored bust right **Rev:** Crowned shield flanked by M F 8 in order chain **Obv. Legend:** PHILIP • V • D • G • HISPAN

• ET IND • REX **Rev. Legend:** INITIUM SAPIENTIAE TIMOR DOMINI **Mint:** Mexico City **Note:** Mint mark M, Mo.

Date	Mintage	VG8	F12	VF20	XF40	MS60
1732 Rare	—	—	—	—	—	—
1732 F Rare	—	—	—	—	—	—
1733 F Rare	—	—	—	—	—	—

Note: Heritage World Coin Auctions #3004, 1-09, MS64 realized $54,625

Date	Mintage	VG8	F12	VF20	XF40	MS60
1734 MF	—	1,500	2,000	3,300	5,800	—
1734 MF/F	—	1,500	2,000	3,300	5,800	—
1735 MF	—	1,500	1,800	3,000	5,400	—
1736 MF	—	1,500	1,800	3,000	5,400	—
1737 MF	—	1,500	1,800	3,000	5,400	—
1738/7 MF	—	1,500	1,800	3,000	5,400	—
1738 MF	—	1,500	1,800	3,000	5,400	—
1739 MF	—	1,500	1,800	3,000	5,400	—
1740 MF	—	1,500	1,800	3,000	5,400	—
1740/30 MF	—	1,500	1,800	3,000	5,400	—
1741 MF	—	1,500	1,800	3,000	5,400	—
1742 MF	—	1,500	1,800	3,000	5,400	—
1743 MF	—	1,500	1,800	3,000	5,400	—
1744 MF	—	1,500	1,800	3,000	5,400	—
1744/3 MF	—	1,500	1,800	3,000	5,400	—
1745 MF	—	1,500	1,800	3,000	5,400	—
1745/4 MF	—	1,500	1,800	3,000	5,400	—
1746 MF	—	1,500	1,800	3,000	5,400	—
1746/5 MF	—	1,500	1,800	3,000	5,400	—
1747 MF	—	1,500	2,100	3,400	6,000	—

KM# 149 8 ESCUDOS
27.07 g., 0.917 Gold, 0.79 oz. AGW **Ruler:** Ferdinand VI **Obv.** Large, armored bust right **Rev:** Crowned shield flanked by M F 8 in order chain **Obv. Legend:** FERDND • VI • D • G • ... **Rev. Legend:** INITIUM SAPIENTIAE TIMOR DOMINI **Mint:** Mexico City **Note:** Mint mark M, Mo.

Date	Mintage	VG8	F12	VF20	XF40	MS60
1747 MF	—	9,000	15,000	22,000	35,000	—

KM# 150 8 ESCUDOS
27.07 g., 0.917 Gold, 0.79 oz. AGW **Ruler:** Ferdinand VI **Obv.** Small, armored bust right **Rev:** Crowned shield flanked by 8 S in order chain **Obv. Legend:** FERDND • VI • D • G • ... **Rev. Legend:** NOMINA MAGNA SEQUOR **Mint:** Mexico City **Note:** Mint mark M, Mo.

Date	Mintage	VG8	F12	VF20	XF40	MS60
1748 MF	—	1,500	2,400	4,200	7,200	—

Date	Mintage	VG8	F12	VF20	XF40	MS60
1749/8 MF	—	1,500	2,400	4,200	7,200	—
1749 MF	—	1,500	2,400	4,200	7,200	—
1750 MF	—	1,500	2,400	4,200	7,200	—
1751/0 MF	—	1,800	2,400	4,200	7,200	—
1751 MF	—	1,500	2,400	4,200	7,200	—

KM# 151   8 ESCUDOS

27.07 g., 0.917 Gold, 0.79 oz. AGW **Ruler:** Ferdinand VI **Obv.** Armored bust right **Rev:** Crowned shield in order chain **Obv. Legend:** FERDND • VI • D • G • ... **Rev. Legend:** NOMINA MAGNA SEQUOR **Mint:** Mexico City **Note:** Mint mark M, Mo.

Date	Mintage	VG8	F12	VF20	XF40	MS60
1752 MF	—	1,500	2,400	4,200	7,200	—
1753 MF	—	1,500	2,400	4,200	7,200	—
1754 MF	—	1,500	2,400	4,200	7,200	—
1755 MM	—	1,500	2,400	4,200	7,200	—
1756 MM	—	1,500	2,400	4,200	7,200	—

KM# 152   8 ESCUDOS

27.07 g., 0.917 Gold, 0.79 oz. AGW **Ruler:** Ferdinand VI **Obv.** Armored bust right **Rev:** Crowned shield in order chain **Obv. Legend:** FERDND • VI • D • G • ... **Rev. Legend:** NOMINA MAGNA SEQUOR **Mint:** Mexico City **Note:** Mint mark M, Mo.

Date	Mintage	VG8	F12	VF20	XF40	MS60
1757 MM	—	1,500	2,400	4,200	7,200	—
1758 MM	—	1,500	2,400	4,200	7,200	—
1759 MM	—	1,500	2,400	4,200	7,200	—

KM# 153   8 ESCUDOS

27.07 g., 0.917 Gold, 0.79 oz. AGW **Ruler:** Charles III **Obv.** Armored bust right **Rev:** Crowned shield in order chain **Obv. Legend:** CAROLVS • III • D • G • ... **Rev. Legend:** NOMINA

MAGNA SEQUOR **Mint:** Mexico City **Note:** Mint mark M, Mo.

Date	Mintage	VG8	F12	VF20	XF40	MS60
1760 MM	—	2,100	3,600	6,000	11,000	—
1761/0 MM	—	2,400	4,200	6,600	12,000	—
1761 MM	—	2,400	4,200	6,600	12,000	—

KM# 154   8 ESCUDOS

27.07 g., 0.917 Gold, 0.79 oz. AGW **Ruler:** Charles III **Obv.** Armored bust right **Rev:** Crowned shield in order chain **Obv. Legend:** CAROLVS • III • D • G • ... **Rev. Legend:** NOMINA MAGNA SEQUOR **Mint:** Mexico City **Note:** Mint mark M, Mo.

Date	Mintage	VG8	F12	VF20	XF40	MS60
1761 MM	—	2,100	3,600	6,300	11,500	—

KM# 155   8 ESCUDOS

27.07 g., 0.917 Gold, 0.79 oz. AGW **Ruler:** Charles III **Obv.** Large, armored bust right **Rev:** Crowned shield in order chain **Obv. Legend:** CAROLUS • III • D • G • ... **Rev. Legend:** IN • UTROQ • FELIX • AUSPICE • DEO • **Mint:** Mexico City **Note:** Mint mark M, Mo.

Date	Mintage	VG8	F12	VF20	XF40	MS60
1762 MM	—	2,000	3,450	5,600	10,500	—
1763 MM	—	2,000	3,450	5,600	10,500	—
1764 MF	—	2,200	3,750	6,300	11,500	—
1764/2 MF	—	2,200	3,750	6,300	11,500	—
1764 MM	—	2,200	3,750	6,300	11,500	—
1765/4 MF	—	2,200	3,750	6,300	11,500	—
1765/4 MM	—	2,200	3,750	6,300	11,500	—
1765 MF	—	2,200	3,750	6,300	11,500	—
1765 MM	—	1,900	3,150	5,000	9,400	—
1766 MF	—	1,900	3,150	5,000	9,400	—
1767/6 MF	—	1,900	3,150	5,000	9,400	—
1767 MF	—	1,900	3,150	5,000	9,400	—
1768/7 MF	—	1,900	3,150	5,000	9,400	—
1768 MF	—	1,900	3,150	5,000	9,400	—
1769 MF	—	1,900	3,150	5,000	9,400	—
1770 MF	—	1,900	3,150	5,000	9,400	—
1771 MF	—	2,200	3,750	6,300	11,500	—

SPANISH COLONIAL · MILLED COINAGE

KM# 156.1 8 ESCUDOS

27.07 g., 0.901 Gold, 0.78 oz. AGW **Ruler:** Charles III **Obv.** Large, armored bust right **Rev:** Crowned shield flanked by 8 S in order chain, initials and mint mark upright **Obv. Legend:** CAROL • III • D • G • ... **Rev. Legend:** ... AUSPICE • DEO • **Mint:** Mexico City **Note:** Mint mark M, Mo.

Date	Mintage	VG8	F12	VF20	XF40	MS60
1772 FM	—	1,100	1,500	2,000	2,750	—
1773 FM	—	1,100	1,500	2,000	2,750	—

KM# 156.2 8 ESCUDOS

27.07 g., 0.901 Gold, 0.78 oz. AGW **Ruler:** Charles III **Obv.** Large, armored bust right **Rev:** Crowned shield flanked by 8 S in order chain, initials and mint mark inverted **Obv. Legend:** CAROL • III • D • G • ... **Rev. Legend:** ... AUSPICE • DEO • **Mint:** Mexico City **Note:** Mint mark M, Mo.

Date	Mintage	VG8	F12	VF20	XF40	MS60
1773 FM	—	1,100	1,350	1,800	2,400	—
1774 FM	—	1,100	1,350	1,800	2,400	—
1775 FM	—	1,100	1,350	1,800	2,400	—
1776 FM	—	1,500	1,850	2,250	3,000	—
1777/6 FM	—	1,100	1,350	1,500	2,400	—
1777 FM	—	1,100	1,350	1,500	2,400	—
1778 FF	—	1,100	1,350	1,500	2,400	—
1779 FF	—	1,100	1,350	1,500	2,400	—
1780 FF	—	1,100	1,350	1,500	2,400	—
1781 FF	—	1,100	1,350	1,500	2,400	—
1782 FF	—	1,100	1,350	1,500	2,400	—
1783 FF	—	1,100	1,350	1,500	2,400	—
1784 FF	—	1,100	1,350	1,500	2,400	—
1784 FM/F	—	1,100	1,350	1,500	2,400	—
1784 FM	—	1,100	1,350	1,500	2,400	—
1785 FM	—	1,100	1,350	1,500	2,400	—

KM# 156.2a 8 ESCUDOS

27.07 g., 0.875 Gold, 0.76 oz. AGW **Ruler:** Charles III **Obv.** Large, armored bust right **Rev:** Crowned shield flanked by 8 S in order chain, initials and mint mark inverted **Obv. Legend:** CAROL • III • D • G • ... **Rev. Legend:** ... AUSPICE • DEO • **Mint:** Mexico City **Note:** Mint mark M, Mo.

Date	Mintage	VG8	F12	VF20	XF40	MS60
1786 FM	—	1,100	1,350	1,800	2,400	—
1787 FM	—	1,100	1,350	1,800	2,400	—
1788 FM	—	1,100	1,350	1,800	2,400	—

KM# 156.1a 8 ESCUDOS

27.07 g., 0.875 Gold, 0.76 oz. AGW **Ruler:** Charles III **Obv.** Large, armored bust right **Rev:** Crowned shield flanked by 8 S in order chain, initials and mint mark upright **Obv. Legend:** CAROL • III • D • G • ... **Rev. Legend:** ... AUSPICE • DEO • **Mint:** Mexico City **Note:** Mint mark M, Mo.

Date	Mintage	VG8	F12	VF20	XF40	MS60
1788 FM	—	1,100	1,300	1,500	2,400	—

KM# 157 8 ESCUDOS

27.07 g., 0.875 Gold, 0.76 oz. AGW **Ruler:** Charles IV **Obv.** Armored bust of Charles III, right **Rev:** Crowned shield

flanked by 8 S in order chain **Obv. Legend:** CAROL • IV •
D • G • ... **Rev. Legend:** IN • UTROQ • ... **Mint:** Mexico City
Note: Mint mark M, Mo, using old portrait punch.

Date	Mintage	VG8	F12	VF20	XF40	MS60
1789 FM	—	1,100	1,500	2,000	2,750	—
1790 FM	—	1,100	1,500	2,000	2,750	—

KM# 158   8 ESCUDOS

27.07 g.,   0.875 Gold, 0.76 oz. AGW **Ruler:**   Charles IV
Obv. Armored bust of Charles III, right **Rev:** Crowned shield
flanked by 8 S in order chain **Obv. Legend:** CAROL • IIII •
D • G • ... **Rev. Legend:** IN • UTROQ • ... **Mint:** Mexico City
Note: Mint mark M, Mo, using old portrait punch.

Date	Mintage	VG8	F12	VF20	XF40	MS60
1790 FM	—	1,100	1,500	2,000	2,750	—

KM# 159   8 ESCUDOS

27.07 g.,   0.875 Gold, 0.76 oz. AGW **Ruler:**   Charles IV **Obv.**
Armored bust right **Rev:** Crowned shield flanked by 8 S in order
chain **Obv. Legend:** CAROL • IIII • D • G • ... **Rev. Legend:** IN •
UTROQ • ... **Mint:** Mexico City **Note:** Mint mark Mo.

Date	Mintage	VG8	F12	VF20	XF40	MS60
1791 FM	—	1,100	1,250	1,500	2,000	—
1792 FM	—	1,100	1,250	1,500	2,000	—
1793 FM	—	1,100	1,250	1,500	2,000	—
1794 FM	—	1,100	1,250	1,500	2,000	—
1795 FM	—	1,100	1,250	1,500	2,000	—
1796/5 FM	—	1,100	1,250	1,500	2,000	—
1796 FM	—	1,100	1,250	1,500	2,000	—
1797 FM EPLIX	—	1,100	1,250	1,500	2,000	—
1797 FM	—	1,100	1,250	1,500	2,000	—
1798 FM	—	1,100	1,250	1,500	2,000	—
1799 FM	—	1,100	1,250	1,500	2,000	—
1800 FM	—	1,100	1,250	1,500	2,000	—
1801/0 FT	—	1,225	1,275	1,375	1,950	—
1801 FM	—	1,225	1,275	1,350	1,700	—
1801 FT	—	1,225	1,275	1,350	1,700	—
1802 FT	—	1,225	1,275	1,350	1,700	—
1803 FT	—	1,225	1,275	1,350	1,700	—
1804/3 TH	—	1,225	1,275	1,375	1,950	—
1804 TH	—	1,225	1,275	1,350	1,700	5,300
1805 TH	—	1,225	1,275	1,350	1,700	—
1806 TH	—	1,225	1,275	1,350	1,700	5,300
1807 TH Mo over inverted Mo	—	1,225	1,275	1,375	1,950	—
1807/6 TH	—	1,225	1,275	1,375	1,950	—
1808/7 TH	—	1,225	1,275	1,350	2,100	—
1807 TH	—	1,225	1,275	1,450	1,700	—
1808 TH	—	1,225	1,275	1,450	2,100	—

KM# 160   8 ESCUDOS

27.07 g.,   0.875 Gold, 0.76 oz. AGW **Ruler:** Ferdinand VII **Obv.**
Armored bust right **Rev:** Crowned shield divides designed
wreath **Obv. Legend:** FERDIN • VII • D • G... **Rev. Legend:**
IN UTROQ • FELIX **Mint:** Mexico City **Note:** Mint mark Mo.

Date	Mintage	VG8	F12	VF20	XF40	MS60
1808 TH	—	1,225	1,250	1,400	2,250	—
1809 HJ	—	1,225	1,250	1,400	2,250	—
1810 HJ	—	1,225	1,250	1,400	2,250	—
1811/0 HJ	—	1,225	1,250	1,400	2,250	—
1811 HJ H/T	—	1,225	1,250	1,400	2,250	—
1811 HJ	—	1,225	1,250	1,400	2,250	—
1811 JJ	—	1,225	1,250	1,400	2,250	—
1812 JJ	—	1,225	1,250	1,400	2,250	—

KM# 161   8 ESCUDOS

27.07 g.,   0.875 Gold, 0.76 oz. AGW **Ruler:**   Ferdinand VII
Obv.   Laureate head right **Rev:** Crowned shield divides
designed wreath **Obv. Legend:** FERDIN • VII • D • G... **Rev.
Legend:** IN UTROQ • FELIX **Mint:** Mexico City **Note:** Mint
mark Mo.

Date	Mintage	VG8	F12	VF20	XF40	MS60
1814 JJ	—	1,225	1,275	1,400	2,000	—
1815/4 JJ	—	1,225	1,275	1,400	2,150	—
1815/4 HJ	—	1,225	1,275	1,400	2,150	—
1815 JJ	—	1,225	1,275	1,400	2,000	—
1815 HJ	—	1,225	1,275	1,400	2,000	—
1816 JJ	—	1,225	1,275	1,400	2,000	—
1817 JJ	—	1,225	1,275	1,400	2,150	—
1818/7 JJ	—	1,225	1,275	1,400	2,100	—
1818 JJ	—	1,225	1,275	1,400	2,100	—
1819 JJ	—	1,225	1,275	1,400	2,100	—
1820 JJ	—	1,225	1,275	1,400	2,100	—
1821 JJ	—	1,225	1,275	1,400	2,250	—

PROCLAMATION MEDALLIC COINAGE

KM# Q22   1/2 REAL

1.60 g., Silver **Issuer:** Mexico City **Obv.** Crowned shield
flanked by crowned pillars with banner **Rev:** Legend,
date within wreath **Obv. Legend:** A CARLOS IV REY DE

ESPANA Y DE LAS YNDIAS **Rev. Legend:** PROCLAMADO
EN MEXICO ANO DE 1789

Date	Mintage	F12	VF20	XF40	MS60	MS63
1789	—	40.00	70.00	120	—	—

KM# Q22a 1/2 REAL
Bronze **Issuer:** Mexico City **Obv.** Crowned shield flanked
by crowned pillars with banner **Rev:** Legend, date within
wreath **Obv. Legend:** A CARLOS IV REY DE ESPANA Y DE
LAS YNDIAS **Rev. Legend:** PROCLAMADO EN MEXICO
ANO DE 1789

Date	Mintage	F12	VF20	XF40	MS60	MS63
1789	—	45.00	90.00	150	—	—

KM# Q23 1/2 REAL
Silver **Issuer:** Mexico City **Obv.** Crowned arms in double-
lined circle **Obv. Legend:** A CARLOS IV REY DE ESPANA
Y DE LAS YNDIAS **Rev. Legend:** PROCLAMADO EN
MEXICO ANO DE 1789

Date	Mintage	F12	VF20	XF40	MS60	MS63
1789	—	40.00	70.00	120	—	—

KM# Q23a 1/2 REAL
Bronze **Issuer:** Mexico City **Obv.** Crowned arms in double-
lined circle **Obv. Legend:** A CARLOS IV REY DE ESPANA
Y DE LAS YNDIAS **Rev. Legend:** PROCLAMADO EN
MEXICO ANO DE 1789

Date	Mintage	F12	VF20	XF40	MS60	MS63
1789	—	45.00	90.00	150	—	—

KM# Q24 REAL
Silver **Issuer:** Mexico City **Obv.** Crowned shield flanked by
crowned pillars with banner **Rev:** Legend, date, value within
wreath **Obv. Legend:** A CARLOS IV REY DE ESPANA Y DE
LAS YNDIAS **Rev. Legend:** PROCLAMADO EN MEXICO
ANO DE 1789

Date	Mintage	F12	VF20	XF40	MS60	MS63
1789	—	40.00	70.00	120	—	—

KM# Q24a REAL
Bronze **Issuer:** Mexico City **Obv.** Crowned shield flanked by
crowned pillars with banner **Rev:** Legend, date, value within
wreath **Obv. Legend:** A CARLOS IV REY DE ESPANA Y DE
LAS YNDIAS **Rev. Legend:** PROCLAMADO EN MEXICO
ANO DE 1789

Date	Mintage	F12	VF20	XF40	MS60	MS63
1789	—	45.00	90.00	150	—	—

KM# Q-A24 REAL
Silver **Issuer:** Mexico City **Obv.** Crowned arms in double-
lined circle **Obv. Legend:** A CARLOS IV REY DE ESPANA
Y DE LAS YNDIAS **Rev. Legend:** PROCLAMADO EN
MEXICO ANO DE 1789

Date	Mintage	F12	VF20	XF40	MS60	MS63
1789	—	40.00	70.00	120	—	—

KM# Q-A24a REAL
Copper **Issuer:** Mexico City **Obv.** Crowned arms in double-
lined circle **Obv. Legend:** A CARLOS IV REY DE ESPANA
Y DE LAS YNDIAS **Rev. Legend:** PROCLAMADO EN
MEXICO ANO DE 1789

Date	Mintage	F12	VF20	XF40	MS60	MS63
1789	—	45.00	90.00	150	—	—

KM# Q8 REAL
Silver **Issuer:** Chiapa **Obv.** Crowned shield flanked by pillars
Rev: Legend within wreath **Obv. Legend:** FERNANDO. VII.
REY DE ESPAÑA. Y DE SUS IND. **Rev. Legend:** PROCLA/
MADO ENCUID•R•DE/ CHIAPA•/•A1808•

Date	Mintage	F12	VF20	XF40	MS60	MS63
1808	—	25.00	40.00	70.00	125	—

KM# Q25 2 REALES
6.70 g., Silver **Issuer:** Mexico City **Obv.** Crowned shield
flanked by crowned pillars with banner **Rev:** Legend, date,
value within wreath **Obv. Legend:** A CARLOS IV REY DE
ESPANA Y DE LAS YNDIAS **Rev. Legend:** PROCLAMADO
EN MEXICO ANO DE 1789

Date	Mintage	F12	VF20	XF40	MS60	MS63
1789	—	70.00	125	225	—	—

KM# Q25a 2 REALES
6.70 g., Bronze **Issuer:** Mexico City **Obv.** Crowned shield
flanked by crowned pillars with banner **Rev:** Legend, date,
value within wreath **Obv. Legend:** A CARLOS IV REY DE
ESPANA Y DE LAS YNDIAS **Rev. Legend:** PROCLAMADO
EN MEXICO ANO DE 1789

Date	Mintage	F12	VF20	XF40	MS60	MS63
1789	—	60.00	115	180	—	—

KM# Q10 2 REALES
Silver **Issuer:** Chiapa **Obv.** Crowned shield flanked by
pillars **Rev:** Legend, date within wreath **Obv. Legend:**
FERNANDO VII REY DE ESPANA Y DE SUS INDIAS

Date	Mintage	F12	VF20	XF40	MS60	MS63
1808	—	45.00	70.00	100	175	—

KM# Q64 2 REALES
Silver **Issuer:** Queretaro **Obv.** Crowned shield flanked
by pillars **Rev:** Legend, date within wreath **Obv. Legend:**
FERNANDO VII REY DE ESPANA

Date	Mintage	F12	VF20	XF40	MS60	MS63
1808	—	25.00	45.00	90.00	150	—

KM# Q27 4 REALES
13.60 g., Silver **Issuer:** Mexico City **Obv.** Crowned shield flanked by crowned pillars with banner **Rev:** Legend, date, value within wreath **Obv. Legend:** A CARLOS IV REY DE ESPANA Y DE LAS YNDIAS **Rev. Legend:** PROCLAMADO EN MEXICO ANO DE 1789

Date	Mintage	F12	VF20	XF40	MS60	MS63
1789	—	200	375	675	1,150	—

KM# Q27a 4 REALES
13.60 g., Bronze **Issuer:** Mexico City **Obv.** Crowned shield flanked by crowned pillars with banner **Rev:** Legend, date, value within wreath **Obv. Legend:** A CARLOS IV REY DE ESPANA Y DE LAS YNDIAS **Rev. Legend:** PROCLAMADO EN MEXICO ANO DE 1789

Date	Mintage	F12	VF20	XF40	MS60	MS63
1789	—	140	250	450	—	—

KM# Q-A66 4 REALES
Silver **Issuer:** Queretaro **Obv.** Crowned shield flanked by pillars **Rev:** Legend, date within wreath **Obv. Legend:** FERNANDO VII REY DE ESPANA

Date	Mintage	F12	VF20	XF40	MS60	MS63
1808	—	100	160	295	475	—

KM# Q28 8 REALES
27.00 g., Silver **Issuer:** Mexico City **Obv.** Crowned shield flanked by crowned pillars with banner **Rev:** Legend, date, value within wreath **Obv. Legend:** A CARLOS IV REY DE ESPANA Y DE LAS YNDIAS **Rev. Legend:** PROCLAMADO EN MEXICO ANO DE 1789

Date	Mintage	F12	VF20	XF40	MS60	MS63
1789	—	400	700	1,200	2,000	—

KM# Q28a 8 REALES
27.00 g., Bronze **Issuer:** Mexico City **Obv.** Crowned shield flanked by crowned pillars with banner **Rev:** Legend, date, value within wreath **Obv. Legend:** A CARLOS IV REY DE ESPANA Y DE LAS YNDIAS **Rev. Legend:** PROCLAMADO EN MEXICO ANO DE 1789

Date	Mintage	F12	VF20	XF40	MS60	MS63
1789	—	140	250	450	—	—

KM# Q68 8 REALES
Silver **Issuer:** Queretaro **Obv.** Crowned shield flanked by pillars **Rev:** Legend, date within wreath **Obv. Legend:** FERNANDO VII REY DE ESPANA

Date	Mintage	F12	VF20	XF40	MS60	MS63
1808	—	220	425	575	950	—

WAR OF INDEPENDENCE

CHIHUAHUA

The Chihuahua Mint was established by a decree of October 8, 1810 as a temporary mint. Their first coins were cast 8 Reales using Mexico City coins as patterns and obliterating/changing the mint mark and moneyer initials. Two c/m were placed on the obverse - on the left, a T designating receipt by the Royal Treasurer, crowned pillars of Hercules on the right with pomegranate beneath, the comptrollers symbol.

In 1814, standard dies were made available, thus machine struck 8 Reales were produced until 1822. Only the one denomination was made at Chihuahua.

Mint mark: CA.

ROYALIST COINAGE

KM# 123 8 REALES
Cast Silver, **Ruler:** Ferdinand VII **Obv.** Armored bust right **Rev:** Crowned shield flanked by pillars **Obv. Legend:** FERDIN• VII • DEI • GRATIA **Mint:** Chihuahua

Date	Mintage	G4	VG8	F12	VF20	XF40
1810CA RP	—	—	—	—	—	—
Rare						
1811CA RP	—	45.00	70.00	120	200	—
1812CA RP	—	40.00	65.00	90.00	175	—
1813CA RP	—	35.00	50.00	70.00	120	—

KM# 111.1 8 REALES
27.07 g., 0.903 Silver, 0.78 oz. ASW **Ruler:** Ferdinand VII **Obv.** Draped bust right **Rev:** Crowned shield flanked by pillars **Obv. Legend:** FERDIN • VII • DEI • GRATIA

Date	Mintage	VG8	F12	VF20	XF40	MS60
1815 RP	—	220	300	525	750	—
1816 RP	—	90.00	140	225	425	—
1817 RP	—	110	165	280	425	—
1818 RP	—	110	165	280	425	—
1819/8 RP	—	140	195	375	525	—
1819 RP	—	140	195	375	525	—
1820 RP	—	220	300	525	750	—
1821 RP	—	220	300	525	750	—
1822 RP	—	450	650	1,200	1,650	—

Note: KM#111.1 is normally found struck over earlier cast 8 Reales, KM#123 and Monclova (MVA) 1812 cast countermark 8 Reales, KM#202 and Zacatecas 8 Reales, KM#190

DURANGO

The Durango mint was authorized as a temporary mint on the same day as the Chihuahua Mint, October 8, 1810. The mint opened in 1811 and made coins of 6 denominations between 1811 and 1822.

Mint mark: D.

ROYALIST COINAGE

KM# 60 1/8 REAL
Copper, **Ruler:** Ferdinand VII **Obv.** Crowned monogram **Rev:** EN DURANGO, value, date **Mint:** Durango

Date	Mintage	VG8	F12	VF20	XF40	MS60
1812 D	—	40.00	75.00	125	250	—
1813 D	—	65.00	135	185	375	—
1814 D Rare	—	—	—	—	—	—

KM# 61 1/8 REAL
Copper, **Ruler:** Ferdinand VII **Obv.** Crowned monogram **Rev:** Value within spray, date below **Rev. Legend:** ENDURANGO. **Mint:** Durango

Date	Mintage	VG8	F12	VF20	XF40	MS60
1814 D	—	18.00	32.50	55.00	95.00	—
1815 D	—	18.00	35.00	60.00	100	—
1816 D	—	18.00	35.00	60.00	100	—
1817 D	—	15.00	30.00	50.00	95.00	—
1818 D	—	15.00	30.00	50.00	95.00	—
1818 D	—	45.00	80.00	125	225	—

Note: OCTAVO DD REAL, error

KM# 74.1 1/2 REAL
1.69 g., 0.903 Silver, 0.05 oz. ASW **Ruler:** Ferdinand VII **Obv.** Draped laureate bust right **Rev:** Crowned shield flanked by pillars **Mint:** Durango

Date	Mintage	VG8	F12	VF20	XF40	MS60
1813 D RM	—	275	500	825	2,050	—
1814 D MZ	—	275	500	825	2,050	—
1816 D MZ	—	275	500	825	2,050	—

KM# 83.1 REAL
3.38 g., 0.903 Silver, 0.10 oz. ASW **Ruler:** Ferdinand VII **Obv.** Draped laureate bust right **Rev:** Crowned shield flanked by pillars **Obv. Legend:** FERDIN • VII... **Rev. Legend:** IND • REX... **Mint:** Durango

Date	Mintage	VG8	F12	VF20	XF40	MS60
1813 D RM	—	275	500	725	1,800	—
1814 D MZ	—	275	500	725	1,800	—
1815 D MZ	—	275	500	725	1,800	—

KM# 92.2 2 REALES
6.77 g., 0.903 Silver, 0.20 oz. ASW **Ruler:** Ferdinand VII **Obv.** Armored bust right **Rev:** Crowned shield flanked by pillars **Rev. Legend:** MON PROV DE DURANGO... **Mint:** Durango

Date	Mintage	VG8	F12	VF20	XF40	MS60
1811 D RM	—	700	800	1,550	3,200	—

KM# 92.3 2 REALES
6.77 g., 0.903 Silver, 0.20 oz. ASW **Ruler:** Ferdinand VII **Obv.** Armored bust right **Rev:** Crowned shield flanked by pillars **Rev. Legend:** HISPAN ET IND REX...

Date	Mintage	VG8	F12	VF20	XF40	MS60
1812 RM	—	425	650	1,250	2,750	—

KM# 93.1 2 REALES
6.77 g., 0.903 Silver, 0.20 oz. ASW **Ruler:** Ferdinand VII **Obv.** Draped laureate bust right **Rev:** Crowned shield flanked by pillars **Obv. Legend:** FERDIN • VII... **Rev. Legend:** IND • REX... **Mint:** Durango

Date	Mintage	VG8	F12	VF20	XF40	MS60
1812 D RM	—	375	600	1,150	2,550	—
1813 D RM	—	475	925	1,550	4,250	—
1813 D MZ	—	475	925	1,550	4,250	—
1814 D MZ	—	475	925	1,550	4,250	—
1815 D MZ	—	475	925	1,550	4,250	—
1816 D MZ	—	475	925	1,550	4,250	—
1817 D MZ	—	475	925	1,550	4,250	—

KM# 102.1 4 REALES
13.54 g., 0.903 Silver, 0.39 oz. ASW **Ruler:** Ferdinand VII **Obv.** Draped laureate bust right **Rev:** Crowned shield flanked by pillars **Obv. Legend:** FERDIN • VII... **Rev. Legend:** IND • REX... **Mint:** Durango

Date	Mintage	VG8	F12	VF20	XF40	MS60
1814 D MZ	—	850	1,550	2,550	6,900	—
1816 D MZ	—	700	1,400	2,150	6,200	—
1817 D MZ	—	700	1,400	2,150	6,200	—

KM# 110.1 8 REALES

27.07 g., 0.903 Silver, 0.78 oz. ASW **Ruler:** Ferdinand VII
Obv. Armored bust right **Rev:** Crowned shield flanked by
pillars **Obv. Legend:** FERD • VII... **Rev. Legend:** DURANGO
• 8R R • M... **Mint:** Durango

Date	Mintage	VG8	F12	VF20	XF40	MS60
1811 D RM	—	2,800	5,500	9,000	—	—
1812 D RM	—	450	825	1,250	4,400	—
1814 D MZ	—	450	825	1,250	4,400	—

KM# 111.2 8 REALES

27.07 g., 0.903 Silver, 0.78 oz. ASW **Ruler:** Ferdinand
VII **Obv.** Draped laureate bust right **Rev:** Crowned shield
flanked by pillars **Obv. Legend:** FERDIN • VII... **Rev.
Legend:** IND • REX... **Mint:** Durango

Date	Mintage	VG8	F12	VF20	XF40	MS60
1812 D RM	—	175	245	375	1,150	—
1813 D RM	—	210	280	450	1,250	—
1813 D MZ	—	175	245	375	1,100	—
1814/2 D MZ	—	210	280	425	1,100	—
1814 D MZ	—	210	280	425	1,100	—
1815 D MZ	—	105	175	325	875	—
1816 D MZ	—	70.00	105	175	500	—
1817 D MZ	—	42.00	70.00	125	375	—

Date	Mintage	VG8	F12	VF20	XF40	MS60
1818 D MZ	—	70.00	105	175	525	—
1818 D RM	—	70.00	105	175	500	—
1818 D CG/RM	—	140	175	210	525	—
1818 D CG	—	70.00	105	175	500	—
1819 D CG/RM	—	70.00	140	210	450	—
1819 D CG	—	42.00	85.00	140	375	—
1820 D CG	—	42.00	85.00	140	375	—
1821 D CG	—	42.00	55.00	110	325	—
1822 D CG	—	42.00	70.00	125	375	—

Note: Occasionally these are found struck over cast Chihuahua
8 reales and are very rare in general, specimens dated prior to
1816 are rather crudely struck

GUADALAJARA

The Guadalajara Mint made its first coins in 1812 and
the mint operated until April 30, 1815. It was to reopen in 1818
and continue operations until 1822. It was the only Royalist
mint to strike gold coins, both 4 and 8 Escudos. In addition to
these it struck the standard 5 denominations in silver.
Mint mark: GA.

ROYALIST COINAGE

KM# 74.2 1/2 REAL

1.69 g., 0.903 Silver, 0.05 oz. ASW **Ruler:** Ferdinand
VII **Obv.** Draped laureate bust right **Rev:** Crowned shield
flanked by pillars **Obv. Legend:** FERDIN • VII... **Rev.
Legend:** IND... **Mint:** Guadalajara

Date	Mintage	VG8	F12	VF20	XF40
1812 GA MR Rare	—	—	—	—	—
1814 GA MR	—	60.00	145	290	425
1815 GA MR	—	290	500	725	1,450

KM# 83.2 REAL

3.38 g., 0.903 Silver, 0.10 oz. ASW **Ruler:** Ferdinand
VII **Obv.** Draped laureate bust right **Rev:** Crowned shield
flanked by pillars **Obv. Legend:** FERDIN • VII... **Rev.
Legend:** IND • REX... **Mint:** Guadalajara

Date	Mintage	VG8	F12	VF20	XF40	MS60
1813 GA MR	—	425	725	1,150	—	—
1814 GA MR	—	215	290	500	925	—
1815 GA MR	—	425	725	1,150	—	—

KM# 93.2 2 REALES

6.77 g., 0.903 Silver, 0.20 oz. ASW **Ruler:** Ferdinand
VII **Obv.** Draped laureate bust right **Rev:** Crowned shield
flanked by pillars **Obv. Legend:** FERDIN • VII... **Rev.
Legend:** IND • REX.... **Mint:** Guadalajara

Date	Mintage	VG8	F12	VF20	XF40	MS60
1812 GA MR	—	350	600	950	3,000	—
1814/2 GA MR	—	90.00	150	300	775	—
1814 GA MR	—	90.00	150	300	775	—
1815/4 GA MR	—	500	875	1,300	4,300	—
1815 GA MR	—	475	850	1,200	4,200	—
1821 GA FS	—	240	300	425	1,150	—

KM# 102.2 4 REALES
13.54 g., 0.903 Silver, 0.39 oz. ASW **Ruler:** Ferdinand
VII **Obv.** Draped laureate bust right **Rev:** Crowned shield
flanked by pillars **Obv. Legend:** FERDIN • VII... **Rev.**
Legend: IND • REX... **Mint:** Guadalajara

Date	Mintage	VG8	F12	VF20	XF40	MS60
1814 GA MR	—	65.00	105	245	425	—
1815 GA MR	—	130	245	500	825	—

KM# 102.3 4 REALES
13.54 g., 0.903 Silver, 0.39 oz. ASW **Ruler:** Ferdinand
VII **Obv.** Draped laureate bust right **Rev:** Crowned shield
flanked by pillars **Obv. Legend:** FERDIN • VII... **Rev.**
Legend: IND • REX... **Mint:** Guadalajara

Date	Mintage	VG8	F12	VF20	XF40	MS60
1814 GA MR	—	85.00	165	325	650	—

KM# 102.4 4 REALES
13.54 g., 0.903 Silver, 0.39 oz. ASW **Ruler:** Ferdinand
VII **Obv.** Draped laureate bust right **Rev:** Crowned shield
flanked by pillars **Obv. Legend:** FERDIN • VII... **Rev.**
Legend: IND • REX... **Mint:** Guadalajara

Date	Mintage	VG8	F12	VF20	XF40	MS60
1814 GA MR	—	100	195	425	750	—

KM# 111.3 8 REALES
27.07 g., 0.903 Silver, 0.78 oz. ASW **Ruler:** Ferdinand
VII **Obv.** Draped laureate bust right **Rev:** Crowned shield
flanked by pillars **Obv. Legend:** FERDIN • VII... **Rev.**
Legend: IND • REX... **Mint:** Guadalajara

Date	Mintage	VG8	F12	VF20	XF40	MS60
1812 GA MR	—	2,700	4,500	6,500	9,500	—
1813/2 GA MR	—	110	180	270	725	—
1813 GA MR	—	110	180	270	725	—
1814 GA MR	—	36.00	65.00	110	325	—
Note: Several bust varieties exist for the 1814 issue						
1815 GA MR	—	230	300	550	1,150	—
1818 GA FS	—	55.00	90.00	140	350	—
1821/18 GA FS	—	55.00	90.00	140	350	—
1821 GA FS	—	45.00	65.00	110	300	—
1821/2 GA FS	—	55.00	90.00	140	350	—
1822/1 GA FS	—	55.00	90.00	140	350	—
1822 GA FS	—	45.00	80.00	115	300	—

Note: Die varieties exist. Early dates are also encountered
struck over other types

KM# 147 4 ESCUDOS
13.54 g., 0.875 Gold, 0.38 oz. AGW **Ruler:** Ferdinand VII
Obv. Uniformed bust right **Rev:** Crowned shield divides
designed wreath **Mint:** Guadalajara

Date	Mintage	VG8	F12	VF20	XF40	MS60
1812 GA MR Rare	—	—	—	—	—	—

KM# 162 8 ESCUDOS
27.07 g., 0.875 Gold, 0.76 oz. AGW **Ruler:** Ferdinand
VII **Obv.** Large uniformed bust right **Rev:** Crowned shield
divides designed wreath **Obv. Legend:** FERDIN • VII • D
• G... **Rev. Legend:** UTROQ • FELIX... **Mint:** Guadalajara

Date	Mintage	VG8	F12	VF20	XF40	MS60
1812 GA MR Rare	—	—	—	—	—	—
1813 GA MR	—	6,000	9,000	15,000	25,000	—

Note: Heritage Long Beach sale 5-08, Choice AU realized
$37,500. American Numismatic Rarities Eliasberg sale 4-05,
VF-30 realized $23,000.

KM# 163   8 ESCUDOS
27.07 g.,   0.875 Gold, 0.76 oz. AGW **Ruler:** Ferdinand
VII **Obv.** Small uniformed bust right **Rev:** Crowned shield
divides designed wreath **Obv. Legend:** FERDIN • VII... **Rev.
Legend:** UTROQ • FELIX... **Mint:** Guadalajara

Date	Mintage	VG8	F12	VF20	XF40	MS60
1813 GA MR	— 10,000	16,000	30,000	45,000	—

Note: Spink America Gerber sale 6-96 VF or better realized
$46,200

KM# 161.1   8 ESCUDOS
27.07 g.,   0.875 Gold, 0.76 oz. AGW **Ruler:** Ferdinand VII
Obv. Laureate head right **Rev:** Crowned shield divides
designed wreath **Obv. Legend:** FERDIN • VII • D • G... **Rev.
Legend:** UTROQ • FELIX... **Mint:** Guadalajara

Date	Mintage	VG8	F12	VF20	XF40	MS60
1821 GA FS	— 2,000	4,000	10,000	17,000	—

Note: American Numismatic Rarities Eliasberg sale 4-05, AU-
55 realized $20,700.

KM# 164   8 ESCUDOS
27.07 g.,   0.875 Gold, 0.76 oz. AGW **Ruler:** Ferdinand
VII **Obv.** Draped laureate bust right **Rev:** Crowned shield
flanked by pillars **Mint:** Guadalajara

Date	Mintage	VG8	F12	VF20	XF40	MS60
1821 GA FS	— 5,500	8,000	14,500	23,500	—

GUANAJUATO

The Guanajuato Mint was authorized December 24,
1812 and started production shortly thereafter; closing for
unknown reasons on May 15, 1813. The mint was reopened
in April, 1821 by the insurgents, who struck coins of the
old royal Spanish design to pay their army, even after
independence, well into 1822.

Only the 2 and 8 Reales coins were made.
Mint mark: Go.

ROYALIST COINAGE

KM# 93.3   2 REALES
6.77 g.,   0.903 Silver, 0.20 oz. ASW **Ruler:** Ferdinand
VII **Obv.** Draped laureate bust right **Rev:** Crowned shield
flanked bu pillars **Obv. Legend:** FERDIN • VII... **Rev.
Legend:** IND • REX... **Mint:** Guanajuato

Date	Mintage	VG8	F12	VF20	XF40	MS60
1821 Go JM	—	50.00	95.00	145	265	—
1822 Go JM	—	43.25	70.00	110	210	—

KM# 111.4   8 REALES
27.07 g.,   0.903 Silver, 0.78 oz. ASW **Ruler:** Ferdinand
VII **Obv.** Draped laureate bust right **Rev:** Crowned shield
flanked by pillars **Obv. Legend:** FERDIN • VII... **Rev.
Legend:** IND • REX... **Mint:** Guanajuato

Date	Mintage	VG8	F12	VF20	XF40	MS60
1812 Go JJ	—	3,700	6,500	—	—	—
1813 Go JJ	—	180	250	400	875	—
1821 Go JM	—	36.00	70.00	110	290	—
1822 Go JM	—	30.00	50.00	85.00	265	—

NUEVA GALICIA

(Later became Jalisco State)

In early colonial times, Nueva Galicia was an extensive province which substantially combined later provinces of Zacatecas and Jalisco. These are states of Mexico today although the name was revived during the War of Independence. The only issue was 2 Reales of rather enigmatic origin. No decrees or other authorization to strike this coin has yet been located or reported.

INSURGENT COINAGE

KM# 218 2 REALES

0.903 Silver **Obv.** N. G. in center, date **Rev:** 2R in center **Obv. Legend:** PROVYCIONAL... **Rev. Legend:** ... A. JUNIANA...

Date	Mintage	G4	VG8	F12	VF20	XF40
1813	—	1,250	3,150	5,600	—	—

Note: Excellent struck counterfeits exist

NUEVA VISCAYA

(Later became Durango State)

This 8 Reales, intended for the province of Nueva Viscaya, was minted in the newly-opened Durango Mint during February and March of 1811, before the regular coinage of Durango was started.

ROYALIST COINAGE

KM# 181 8 REALES

27.07 g., 0.903 Silver, 0.78 oz. ASW **Ruler:** Ferdinand VII **Obv.** Crowned shield within sprays **Rev:** Crowned shield flanked by pillars **Obv. Legend:** MON • PROV • DE NUEV • VIZCAYA

Date	Mintage	G4	VG8	F12	VF20	XF40
1811 RM	—	1,250	2,800	3,550	6,900	—

Note: Several varieties exist.

OAXACA

The city of Oaxaca was in the midst of a coin shortage when it became apparent the city would be taken by the Insurgents. Royalist forces under Lt. Gen. Saravia had coins made. They were cast in a blacksmith shop. 1/2, 1, and 8 Reales were made only briefly in 1812 before the Royalists surrendered the city.

ROYALIST COINAGE

KM# 166 1/2 REAL

0.903 Silver, **Ruler:** Ferdinand VII **Obv.** Cross separating castle, lion, Fo, 7o **Rev:** Legend around shield **Rev. Legend:** PROV • D • OAXACA

Date	Mintage	G4	VG8	F12	VF20	XF40
1812	—	1,250	1,900	3,150	4,400	—

KM# 167 REAL

0.903 Silver, **Ruler:** Ferdinand VII **Obv.** Cross separating castle, lion, Fo, 7o **Rev:** Legend around shield **Rev. Legend:** PROV • D • OAXACA

Date	Mintage	G4	VG8	F12	VF20	XF40
1812	—	450	825	1,500	3,150	—

KM# 168 8 REALES

0.903 Silver **Obv.** Cross separating castle, lion, Fo, 7o **Rev:** Shield, authorization mark above **Obv. Legend:** OAXACA 1812... **Note:** These issues usually display a second mark 'O' between the crowned pillars on the obverse. Varieties of large and small lion in shield also exist.

Date	Mintage	G4	VG8	F12	VF20	XF40
1812 A	—	1,500	2,100	3,500	5,700	—
1812 B	—	1,500	2,100	3,500	5,700	—
1812 C	—	1,500	2,100	3,500	5,700	—
1812 D	—	1,500	2,100	3,500	5,700	—
1812 K	—	1,500	2,100	3,500	5,700	—

Date	Mintage	G4	VG8	F12	VF20	XF40
1812 L	—	1,500	2,100	3,500	5,700	—
1812 Mo	—	1,500	2,100	3,500	5,700	—
1812 N	—	1,500	2,100	3,500	5,700	—
1812 O	—	1,500	2,100	3,500	5,700	—
1812 R	—	1,500	2,100	3,500	5,700	—
1812 V	—	1,500	2,100	3,500	5,700	—
1812 Z	—	1,500	2,100	3,500	5,700	—

INSURGENT COINAGE

Oaxaca was the hub of Insurgent activity in the south where coinage started in July 1811 and continued until October 1814. The Oaxaca issues represent episodic strikings, usually under dire circumstances by various individuals. Coins were commonly made of copper due to urgency and were intended to be redeemed at face value in gold or silver once silver was available to the Insurgents. Some were later made in silver, but most appear to be of more recent origin, to satisfy collectors.

KM# 219 1/2 REAL

Struck Copper **Obv.** Bow, arrow, SUD **Rev:** Morelos monogram Mo, date

Date	Mintage	G4	VG8	F12	VF20	XF40
1811	—	6.75	11.50	20.00	35.00	—
1812	—	6.75	11.50	20.00	35.00	—
1813	—	5.50	9.00	17.50	30.00	—
1814	—	9.00	16.50	25.00	40.00	—

Note: Uniface strikes exist of #219

KM# 220.1 1/2 REAL

Struck Silver **Obv.** Bow, arrow, SUD **Rev:** Morelos monogram Mo, date

Date	Mintage	G4	VG8	F12	VF20	XF40
1811	—	—	—	—	—	—
1812	—	—	—	—	—	—
1813	—	—	—	—	—	—

KM# 220.2 1/2 REAL

Struck Silver **Obv.** Bow, arrow, SUD **Rev:** Morelos monogram Mo, date

Date	Mintage	G4	VG8	F12	VF20	XF40
1811	—	—	—	—	—	—
1812	—	—	—	—	—	—
1813	—	33.00	65.00	130	200	—

Note: Use caution as silver specimens appear questionable and may be considered spurious

KM# 221 1/2 REAL

Struck Silver **Obv.** Bow, arrow **Rev:** Lion **Obv. Legend:** PROVICIONAL DE OAXACA **Rev. Legend:** AMERICA MORELOS

Date	Mintage	G4	VG8	F12	VF20	XF40
1812	—	46.25	80.00	130	200	—
1813	—	46.25	80.00	130	200	—

KM# 221a 1/2 REAL

Struck Copper **Obv.** Bow, arrow **Rev:** Lion **Obv. Legend:** PROVICIONAL DE OAXACA **Rev. Legend:** AMERICA MORELOS

Date	Mintage	G4	VG8	F12	VF20	XF40
1812	—	36.25	55.00	90.00	130	—
1813	—	27.50	46.25	80.00	115	—

KM# 243 1/2 REAL

Struck Copper **Obv.** Bow, T.C., SUD **Rev:** Morelos monogram, value, date

Date	Mintage	G4	VG8	F12	VF20	XF40
1813	—	49.50	90.00	170	265	—

KM# A222 1/2 REAL

Struck Copper **Obv.** Similar to KM#220 **Rev:** Similar to KM#221 but with 1/2 at left of lion **Rev. Legend:** AMERICA MORELOS

Date	Mintage	G4	VG8	F12	VF20	XF40
1813	—	36.25	55.00	90.00	130	—

KM# 222 REAL

Struck Copper **Obv.** Bow, arrow, SUD **Rev:** Morelos monogram, 1 R., date

Date	Mintage	G4	VG8	F12	VF20	XF40
1811	—	6.00	12.00	25.00	50.00	—
1812	—	5.00	10.00	18.00	39.50	—
1813	—	5.00	10.00	18.00	39.50	—

KM# 222a REAL

Struck Silver **Obv.** Bow, arrow, SUD **Rev:** Morelos monogram, 1 R., date

Date	Mintage	G4	VG8	F12	VF20	XF40
1812	—	—	—	—	—	—
1813	—	—	—	—	—	—

KM# 223 REAL

Cast Silver **Obv.** Bow, arrow, SUD with floral ornaments **Rev:** Morelos monogram, 1 R., date

Date	Mintage	G4	VG8	F12	VF20	XF40
1812	—	—	—	—	—	—
1813	—	36.25	80.00	150	210	—

Note: Use caution as many silver specimens appear questionable and may be considered spurious

KM# 224 REAL

Struck Copper **Obv.** Bow, arrow/SUD **Rev:** Lion **Rev.**

Legend: AMERICA MORELOS

Date	Mintage	G4	VG8	F12	VF20	XF40
1813	—	36.25	55.00	100	145	—

KM# 225 REAL
Silver **Obv.** Bow, arrow/SUD **Rev:** Lion **Rev. Legend:** AMERICA MORELOS

Date	Mintage	G4	VG8	F12	VF20	XF40
1813 Rare	—	—	—	—	—	—

KM# 244 REAL
Struck Copper **Obv.** Bow, T.C., SUD **Rev:** Morelos monogram, value, date

Date	Mintage	G4	VG8	F12	VF20	XF40
1813	—	18.00	33.00	65.00	110	—

KM# 226.1 2 REALES
Struck Copper **Obv.** Bow, arrow/SUD **Rev:** Morelos monogram, .2.R., date

Date	Mintage	G4	VG8	F12	VF20	XF40
1811	—	17.00	33.00	70.00	130	—
1811 inverted 2	—	20.00	39.50	80.00	155	—
1812	—	3.00	5.00	8.00	16.00	—
1813	—	4.00	7.00	11.00	20.00	—
1814	—	18.00	37.00	85.00	155	—

KM# 226.1a 2 REALES
Struck Silver **Obv.** Bow, arrow/SUD **Rev:** Morelos monogram, .2.R., date

Date	Mintage	G4	VG8	F12	VF20	XF40
1812	—	215	350	600	900	—

KM# 229 2 REALES
Cast Silver **Obv.** Bow, arrow, SUD **Rev:** Morelos monogram, value, date in center with ornamentation around

Date	Mintage	G4	VG8	F12	VF20	XF40
1812 Filled in D in SUD	—	80.00	130	200	300	—

Note: Use caution as many silver specimens appear questionable and may be considered spurious

Date	Mintage	G4	VG8	F12	VF20	XF40
1812	—	80.00	130	200	300	—

KM# 227 2 REALES
Struck Silver **Obv.** Bow, arrow **Rev:** Morelos monogram, value, date **Obv. Legend:** SUD-OXA

Date	Mintage	G4	VG8	F12	VF20	XF40
1813	—	80.00	130	265	400	—
1814	—	80.00	130	265	400	—

KM# 245 2 REALES
Struck Copper **Obv.** Bow, T.C., SUD **Rev:** Morelos monogram, value, date

Date	Mintage	G4	VG8	F12	VF20	XF40
1813	—	12.00	30.00	46.25	65.00	—

KM# 226.2 2 REALES
Struck Silver **Obv.** Three large stars added **Rev:** Morelos monogram, .2.R., date

Date	Mintage	G4	VG8	F12	VF20	XF40
1814	—	13.00	27.50	55.00	80.00	—

KM# 228 2 REALES
Struck Silver **Obv.** Bow, arrow **Rev:** Morelos monogram, value, date **Obv. Legend:** SUD. OAXACA

Date	Mintage	G4	VG8	F12	VF20	XF40
1814	—	80.00	130	265	425	—

KM# 246 2 REALES
Struck Copper **Obv.** Bow, T.C., SUD **Rev:** Morelos monogram, value, date

Date	Mintage	G4	VG8	F12	VF20	XF40
1814	—	33.00	70.00	145	250	—

KM# 234 8 REALES
Copper **Obv.** Bow, arrow, SUD in floral ornamentation **Rev:** Morelos monogram, .8.R., date surrounded by ornate flowery fields

Date	Mintage	G4	VG8	F12	VF20	XF40
1811	—	115	190	225	350	—
1812	—	10.00	15.00	25.00	50.00	—
1813	—	10.00	15.00	25.00	50.00	—
1814	—	19.00	27.50	47.00	95.00	—

KM# 234a   8 REALES
Struck Silver **Obv.** Bow, arrow, SUD in floral ornamentation **Rev:** Morelos monogram, .8.R., date surrounded by ornate flowery fields

Date	Mintage	G4	VG8	F12	VF20	XF40
1811	—	—	—	3,150	5,000	—
1812	—	—	—	1,500	2,500	—

KM# 235   8 REALES
Cast Silver **Obv.** Bow, arrow, SUD in floral ornamentation **Rev:** Morelos monogram, value, date surrounded by ornate flowery fields

Date	Mintage	G4	VG8	F12	VF20	XF40
1811	—	—	—	—	—	—
1812	—	115	190	300	525	—
1813	—	90.00	150	265	450	—
1814	—	—	—	—	—	—

Note: Most silver specimens available in today's market are considered spurious

KM# 233.1   8 REALES
Copper **Obv.** Bow, arrow, SUD **Rev:** Morelos monogram, 8.R., date, plain fields

Date	Mintage	G4	VG8	F12	VF20	XF40
1812	—	27.50	55.00	115	170	—

KM# 233.2   8 REALES
Copper **Obv.** Bow, arrow, SUD **Rev:** Morelos monogram, 8 R, date, plain fields

Date	Mintage	G4	VG8	F12	VF20	XF40
1812	—	15.00	20.00	31.25	37.50	—
1813	—	15.00	20.00	31.25	37.50	—
1814	—	25.00	31.25	37.50	50.00	—

Note: Similar to KM#233.4 but lines below bow slant left

KM# 236   8 REALES
0.903 Struck Silver **Obv.** M monogram **Rev:** Lion shield with or without bow above **Obv. Legend:** PROV • D • OAXACA

Date	Mintage	G4	VG8	F12	VF20	XF40
1812 Rare	—	—	—	—	—	—

KM# 242   8 REALES
Copper **Obv.** Legend around bow, arrow/SUD **Obv. Legend:** MONEDA PROVI • CIONAL PS • ES • **Rev. Legend:** FABRICADO EN HUAUTLA

Date	Mintage	G4	VG8	F12	VF20	XF40
1812	—	1,250	1,900	2,500	—	—

KM# 233.1a   8 REALES
Struck Silver **Obv.** Bow, arrow, SUD **Rev:** Morelos monogram, 8.R., date, plain fields

Date	Mintage	G4	VG8	F12	VF20	XF40
1812	—	150	225	375	700	—

KM# 233.5a   8 REALES
Silver **Obv.** 8 dots below bow, SUD, plain fields **Rev:** Morelos monogram, 8.R., date

Date	Mintage	G4	VG8	F12	VF20	XF40
1812	—	—	—	1,500	2,500	—

KM# 233.3   8 REALES
Struck Copper **Obv.** Bow, arrow, SUD, with left slant lines below bow **Rev:** Morelos monogram, 8.R., date, plain fields

Date	Mintage	G4	VG8	F12	VF20	XF40
1813	—	19.00	34.50	55.00	95.00	—

KM# 233.4 8 REALES
Struck Copper **Obv.** Bow, arrow, SUD, with right slant lines below bow **Rev:** Morelos monogram, 8.R., date, plain fields

Date	Mintage	G4	VG8	F12	VF20	XF40
1813	—	19.00	34.50	55.00	95.00	—

KM# 237 8 REALES
0.925 Silver **Obv.** M monogram, without legend **Rev:** Lion shield with or without bow above

Date	Mintage	G4	VG8	F12	VF20	XF40
1813 Rare	—	—	—	—	—	—

KM# 238 8 REALES
0.903 Struck Silver **Obv.** Bow/M/SUD **Rev:** PROV. DE. ... arms

Date	Mintage	G4	VG8	F12	VF20	XF40
1813 Rare	—	—	—	—	—	—

KM# 248 8 REALES
Struck Copper **Obv.** Bow, T.C., SUD **Rev:** Morelos monogram, value, date

Date	Mintage	G4	VG8	F12	VF20	XF40
1813	—	18.00	37.50	75.00	145	—

KM# 249 8 REALES
Cast Silver **Obv.** Bow, T.C., SUD **Rev:** Morelos monogram, value, date

Date	Mintage	G4	VG8	F12	VF20	XF40
1813	—	—	—	—	—	—

Note: Use caution as many silver specimens appear questionable and may be considered spurious

KM# 233.2a 8 REALES
Silver **Obv.** bow, arrow, SUD **Rev:** Morelos monogram, 8R, date, plain fields

Date	Mintage	G4	VG8	F12	VF20	XF40
1813	—	—	—	1,500	2,500	—

KM# 239 8 REALES
Cast Silver **Obv.** Bow, arrow **Rev:** Morelos monogram **Obv. Legend:** SUD-OXA

Date	Mintage	G4	VG8	F12	VF20	XF40
1814 Rare	—	—	—	—	—	—

KM# 240 8 REALES
Copper **Obv.** Bow, arrow **Rev:** Morelos monogram, 8.R., date **Obv. Legend:** SUD-OXA

Date	Mintage	G4	VG8	F12	VF20	XF40
1814	—	55.00	105	225	375	—

KM# 241 8 REALES
Copper **Obv.** Bow, arrow **Rev:** Morelos monogram, 8.R., date **Obv. Legend:** SUD-OAXACA

Date	Mintage	G4	VG8	F12	VF20	XF40
1814	—	125	250	450	700	—

PUEBLA

INSURGENT COINAGE

KM# 250 1/2 REAL
Copper **Obv.** Osorno monogram, ZACATLAN, date **Rev:** Crossed arrows, wreath, value

Date	Mintage	G4	VG8	F12	VF20	XF40
1813 Rare	—	—	—	—	—	—

KM# 251   REAL
Copper **Obv.** Osorno monogram, ZACATLAN, date **Rev:**
Crossed arrows, wreath, value

Date	Mintage	G4	VG8	F12	VF20	XF40
1813	—	140	210	300	625	—

KM# 252   2 REALES
Copper **Obv.** Osorno monogram, ZACATLAN, date **Rev:**
Crossed arrows, wreath, value

Date	Mintage	G4	VG8	F12	VF20	XF40
1813	—	170	240	375	700	—

REAL DEL CATORCE

(City in San Luis Potosi)
    Real del Catorce is an important mining center in the
Province of San Luis Potosi. In 1811 an 8 Reales coin was
issued under very primitive conditions while the city was still
in Royalist hands. Few survive.

ROYALIST COINAGE

KM# 169   8 REALES
0.903 Silver, **Ruler:** Ferdinand VII **Obv. Legend:** EL R • D
• CATORC • POR FERNA • VII **Rev. Legend:** MONEDA •
PROVISIONAL • VALE • 8R

Date	Mintage	VG8	F12	VF20	XF40	MS60
1811	—	8,400	18,000	42,000	78,000	—

    Note: Spink America Gerber Sale 6-96 VF or XF realized
$63,800

SAN FERNANDO DE BEXAR

TOKEN COINAGE

KM# Tn1   1/2 REAL (JOLA)
Copper, **Ruler:** Ferdinand VII **Note:** Prev. KM#170.

Date	Mintage	G4	VG8	F12	VF20	XF40
1818	8,000	—	—	—	28,000	32,000

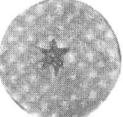

KM# Tn2   1/2 REAL (JOLA)
Copper, **Ruler:** Ferdinand VII **Note:** Prev. KM#171.

Date	Mintage	G4	VG8	F12	VF20	XF40
1818	Inc. above	—	—	—	25,000	30,000

SAN LUIS POTOSI

Sierra de Pinos

ROYALIST COINAGE

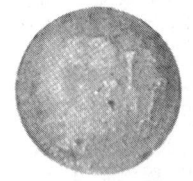

KM# A172   1/4 REAL
Copper, **Ruler:** Ferdinand VII

Date	Mintage	G4	VG8	F12	VF20	XF40
1814	—	125	190	325	500	—

KM# A172a   1/4 REAL
Silver, **Ruler:** Ferdinand VII

Date	Mintage	G4	VG8	F12	VF20	XF40
1814 Rare	—	—	—	—	—	—

SOMBRERETE

(Under Royalist Vargas)
    The Sombrerete Mint opened on October 8, 1810 in
an area that boasted some of the richest mines in Mexico.
The mint operated only until July 16, 1811, only to reopen in
1812 and finally close for good at the end of the year. Mines
Administrator Fernando Vargas, was also in charge of the
coining, all coins bear his name.

ROYALIST COINAGE

KM# 172   1/2 REAL
0.903 Silver, **Ruler:** Ferdinand VII **Obv.** Legend around
crowned globes **Rev:** Legend above lys in oval, sprays, date

below **Obv. Legend:** FERDIN • VII • SOMBRERETE... **Rev.
Legend:** VARGAS

Date	Mintage	G4	VG8	F12	VF20	XF40
1811	—	55.00	85.00	180	325	—
1812	—	60.00	110	210	350	—

KM# 173 REAL
0.903 Silver, **Ruler:** Ferdinand VII **Obv.** Legend around
crowned globes **Rev:** Legend above lys in oval with
denomination flanking, sprays, date below **Obv. Legend:**
FERDIN • VII • SOMBRERETE... **Rev. Legend:** VARGAS

Date	Mintage	G4	VG8	F12	VF20	XF40
1811	—	55.00	85.00	180	325	—

Note: For 1811, denomination reads as '1R' or 'R1'

| 1812 | — | 60.00 | 110 | 210 | 350 | — |

KM# 174 2 REALES
0.903 Silver, **Ruler:** Ferdinand VII **Obv.** Royal arms **Rev:**
1811, S between crowned pillars **Obv. Legend:** R • CAXA •
DE • SOMBRERETE

Date	Mintage	G4	VG8	F12	VF20	XF40
1811 SE	—	120	300	550	900	—

KM# 175 4 REALES
0.903 Silver, **Ruler:** Ferdinand VII **Obv.** Crowned Royal
arms **Rev:** Large legend **Obv. Legend:** R • CAXA • DE •
SOMBRERETE **Rev. Legend:** VARGAS / 1812 **Note:** Prev.
KM#172.

Date	Mintage	G4	VG8	F12	VF20	XF40
1812	—	60.00	120	240	600	—

KM# 176 8 REALES
0.903 Silver, **Ruler:** Ferdinand VII **Obv.** Royal arms
Rev: Several countermarks between crowned pillars **Obv.
Legend:** R • CAXA • DE SOMBRERETE

Date	Mintage	G4	VG8	F12	VF20	XF40
1810	—	1,200	2,100	3,300	5,400	10,500
1811	—	270	400	550	725	—

KM# 177 8 REALES
0.903 Silver, **Ruler:** Ferdinand VII **Obv.** Crowned Royal
arms **Obv. Legend:** R • CAXA • DE SOMBRETE **Rev.
Legend:** VARGAS / date /3, S between crowned pillars

Date	Mintage	G4	VG8	F12	VF20	XF40
1811	—	170	240	475	950	—
1812	—	150	220	450	925	—

VALLADOLID MICHOACAN

ROYALIST COINAGE

KM# 178 8 REALES
0.903 Silver, **Ruler:** Ferdinand VII **Obv.** Royal arms in
wreath, value at sides **Rev. Legend:** PROVISIONAL / DE
VALLADOLID / 1813

Date	Mintage	G4	VG8	F12	VF20	XF40
1813 Rare	—	—	—	—	—	—

KM# 179 8 REALES
0.903 Silver, **Ruler:** Ferdinand VII **Obv.** Draped laureate
bust right **Rev:** Crowned shield flanked by pillars, P. D. V. in
legend **Obv. Legend:** FERDIN • VII •... **Rev. Legend:** REX
• P • D • V...

Date	Mintage	G4	VG8	F12	VF20	XF40
1813 Rare	—	—	—	—	—	—

Note: Spink America Gerber sale 6-96 good realized $23,100

VERACRUZ

In Zongolica, in the province of Veracruz, 2 priests and a lawyer decided to raise an army to fight for independence. Due to isolation from other Insurgent forces, they decided to make their own coins. Records show that they intended to mint coins of 1/2, 1, 2, 4, and 8 Reales, but specimens are extant of only the three higher denominations.

INSURGENT COINAGE

KM# 253   2 REALES

0.903 Silver **Obv.** Bow and arrow **Rev:** Value, crossed palm branch, sword, date **Obv. Legend:** VIVA FERNANDO VII Y AMERICA **Rev. Legend:** ZONGOLICA

Date	Mintage	G4	VG8	F12	VF20	XF40
1812	—	120	240	425	775	—

KM# 255   8 REALES

0.903 Silver **Obv.** Bow and arrow **Rev:** Value, crossed palm branch, sword, date **Obv. Legend:** VIVA FERNANDO VII Y AMERICA **Rev. Legend:** ZONGOLICA **Note:** Similar to 2 Reales, KM#253.

Date	Mintage	G4	VG8	F12	VF20	XF40
1812 Rare	—	—	—	—	—	—

Note: Spink America Gerber sale 6-96 VF to XF realized $57,200

ZACATECAS

The city of Zacatecas, in a rich mining region has provided silver for the world since mid-1500. On November 14, 1810 a mint began production for the Royalist cause. Zacatecas was the most prolific during the War of Independence. Four of the 5 standard silver denominations were made here, 4 Reales were not. The first, a local type showing mountains of silver on the coins were made only in 1810 and 1811. Some 1811 coins were made by the Insurgents who took the city on April 15, 1811, later retaken by the Royalists on May 21, 1811. Zacatecas struck the standard Ferdinand VII bust type until 1822.

Mint marks: Z, ZS, Zs.

ROYALIST COINAGE

KM# 180   1/2 REAL

0.903 Silver, **Ruler:** Ferdinand VII **Obv.** Crowned shield flanked by pillars **Rev:** Mountain within beaded circle **Obv. Legend:** FERDIN • VII... **Mint:** Zacatecas **Note:** Mint marks: Z, ZS, Zs.

Date	Mintage	G4	VG8	F12	VF20	XF40
1810	—	90.00	150	240	475	—
1811	—	36.00	60.00	110	240	—

Note: Date aligned with legend

KM# 181   1/2 REAL

0.903 Silver, **Ruler:** Ferdinand VII **Obv.** Crowned shield flanked by pillars **Rev:** Mountain within beaded circle **Rev. Legend:** MONEDA PROVISIONAL DE ZACATECAS **Mint:** Zacatecas **Note:** Mint marks: Z, ZS, Zs.

Date	Mintage	G4	VG8	F12	VF20	XF40
1811	—	36.00	60.00	110	240	—

KM# 182   1/2 REAL

0.903 Silver, **Ruler:** Ferdinand VII **Obv.** Provincial bust right **Rev:** Crowned shield flanked by pillars **Obv. Legend:** FERDIN • VII **Rev. Legend:** MONEDA PROVISIONAL DE ZACATECAS **Mint:** Zacatecas **Note:** Mint marks: Z, ZS, Zs.

Date	Mintage	G4	VG8	F12	VF20	XF40
1811	—	36.00	48.00	80.00	170	—
1812	—	30.00	42.00	70.00	150	—

KM# 73.1   1/2 REAL

1.69 g., 0.903 Silver, 0.05 oz. ASW **Ruler:** Ferdinand VII **Obv.** Armored laureate bust right **Rev:** Crowned shield flanked by pillars **Obv. Legend:** FERDIN • VII... **Rev. Legend:** IND... **Mint:** Zacatecas **Note:** Mint marks: Z, ZS, Zs.

Date	Mintage	G4	VG8	F12	VF20	XF40
1813 AG	—	25.00	48.00	70.00	130	—
1813 FP	—	30.00	55.00	100	220	—
1814 AG	—	18.00	36.00	70.00	130	—
1815 AG	—	15.00	30.00	48.00	85.00	—
1816 AG	—	12.00	18.00	30.00	65.00	—
1817 AG	—	12.00	18.00	30.00	65.00	—
1818 AG	—	12.00	18.00	30.00	65.00	—
1819 AG	—	12.00	18.00	30.00	65.00	—

KM# 74.3   1/2 REAL

1.69 g., 0.903 Silver, 0.05 oz. ASW **Ruler:** Ferdinand VII **Obv.** Draped laureate bust right **Rev:** Crowned shield flanked by pillars **Obv. Legend:** FERDIN • VII... **Rev. Legend:** IND... **Mint:** Zacatecas **Note:** Mint marks: Z, ZS, Zs.

Date	Mintage	VG8	F12	VF20	XF40	MS60
1819 AG	—	10.00	14.00	30.00	60.00	—

Date	Mintage	VG8	F12	VF20	XF40	MS60
1820 AG	—	10.00	14.00	30.00	60.00	—
1820 RG	—	6.00	12.00	25.00	55.00	—
1821 AG	—	180	300	550	1,000	—
1821 RG	—	6.00	12.00	25.00	55.00	—

KM# 183 REAL
0.903 Silver, **Ruler:** Ferdinand VII **Obv.** Crowned shield flanked by pillars **Rev:** Mountain within beaded circle **Mint:** Zacatecas **Note:** Mint marks: Z, ZS, Zs.

Date	Mintage	G4	VG8	F12	VF20	XF40
1810	—	120	180	350	600	—
1811	—	25.00	48.00	90.00	180	—

Note: Date aligned with legend

KM# 184 REAL
0.903 Silver, **Ruler:** Ferdinand VII **Obv.** Crowned shield flanked by pillars **Rev:** Mountain within beaded circle **Rev. Legend:** MONEDA PROVISIONAL DE ZACATECAS **Mint:** Zacatecas **Note:** Mint marks: Z, ZS, Zs.

Date	Mintage	G4	VG8	F12	VF20	XF40
1811	—	18.00	36.00	70.00	160	—

KM# 185 REAL
0.903 Silver, **Ruler:** Ferdinand VII **Obv.** Provincial bust right **Rev:** Crowned shield flanked by pillars **Obv. Legend:** FERDIN • VII... **Rev. Legend:** MONEDA PROVISIONAL DE ZACATECAS **Mint:** Zacatecas **Note:** Mint marks: Z, ZS, Zs.

Date	Mintage	G4	VG8	F12	VF20	XF40
1811	—	60.00	100	155	265	—
1812	—	48.00	85.00	130	235	—

KM# 82.1 REAL
3.38 g., 0.903 Silver, 0.10 oz. ASW **Ruler:** Ferdinand VII **Obv.** Armored laureate bust right **Rev:** Crowned shield flanked by pillars **Obv. Legend:** FERDIN • VII... **Rev. Legend:** IND • REX... **Mint:** Zacatecas **Note:** Mint marks: Z, ZS, Zs.

Date	Mintage	G4	VG8	F12	VF20	XF40
1813 FP	—	60.00	120	180	300	—
1814 FP	—	25.00	42.00	60.00	100	—
1814 AG	—	25.00	42.00	60.00	100	—
1815 AG	—	25.00	42.00	60.00	100	—
1816 AG	—	14.00	25.00	36.00	80.00	—
1817 AG	—	10.00	15.00	25.00	55.00	—
1818 AG	—	10.00	15.00	25.00	55.00	—
1819 AG	—	7.00	13.00	22.50	42.00	—

KM# 83.3 REAL
3.38 g., 0.903 Silver, 0.10 oz. ASW **Ruler:** Ferdinand VII **Obv.** Draped laureate bust right **Rev:** Crowned shield flanked by pillars **Obv. Legend:** FERDIN • VII... **Rev. Legend:** REX • Z... **Mint:** Zacatecas **Note:** Mint marks: Z, ZS, Zs.

Date	Mintage	VG8	F12	VF20	XF40	MS60
1820 AG	—	7.00	14.00	25.00	70.00	—
1820 RG	—	7.00	14.00	25.00	70.00	—
1821 AG	—	22.50	36.00	55.00	110	—
1821 AZ	—	14.00	25.00	48.00	100	—
1821 RG	—	8.00	15.00	30.00	80.00	—
1822 AZ	—	8.00	15.00	30.00	80.00	—
1822 RG	—	22.50	36.00	55.00	110	—

KM# 186 2 REALES
0.903 Silver, **Ruler:** Ferdinand VII **Obv.** Crowned shield flanked by pillars **Rev:** Mountain within beaded circle **Obv. Legend:** FERDIN • VII... **Rev. Legend:** MONEDA • PROVISION... **Mint:** Zacatecas **Note:** Mint marks: Z, ZS, Zs.

Date	Mintage	G4	VG8	F12	VF20	XF40
1810 Rare	—	—	—	—	—	—
1811	—	36.00	60.00	100	175	—

Note: Date aligned with legend

KM# 187 2 REALES
0.903 Silver, **Ruler:** Ferdinand VII **Obv.** Crowned shield flanked by pillars **Rev:** Mountain above L. V. O within beaded circle **Rev. Legend:** MONEDA PROVISIONAL DE ZACATECAS **Mint:** Zacatecas **Note:** Mint marks: Z, ZS, Zs.

Date	Mintage	G4	VG8	F12	VF20	XF40
1811	—	22.50	43.25	85.00	145	—

KM# 188 2 REALES
0.903 Silver, **Ruler:** Ferdinand VII **Obv.** Armored bust

right **Rev:** Crowned shield flanked by pillars **Obv. Legend:** FERDIN • VII... **Rev. Legend:** MONEDA PROVISIONAL DE ZACATECAS **Mint:** Zacatecas **Note:** Mint marks: Z, ZS, Zs.

Date	Mintage	G4	VG8	F12	VF20	XF40
1811	—	46.25	85.00	180	300	—
1812	—	39.50	80.00	170	265	—

KM# 92.1 2 REALES

6.77 g., 0.903 Silver, 0.20 oz. ASW **Ruler:** Ferdinand VII **Obv.** Large armored bust right **Rev:** Crowned shield flanked by pillars **Obv. Legend:** FERDIN • VII **Rev. Inscription:** MONEDA • PROVISION... **Mint:** Zacatecas **Note:** Mint marks: Z, ZS, Zs.

Date	Mintage	G4	VG8	F12	VF20	XF40
1813 FP	—	42.00	60.00	90.00	150	—
1814 FP	—	42.00	60.00	90.00	150	—
1814 AG	—	42.00	60.00	90.00	150	—
1815 AG	—	9.00	18.00	36.00	65.00	—
1816 AG	—	9.00	18.00	36.00	65.00	—
1817 AG	—	9.00	18.00	36.00	65.00	—
1818 AG	—	9.00	18.00	36.00	65.00	—

KM# 93.4 2 REALES

6.77 g., 0.903 Silver, 0.20 oz. ASW **Ruler:** Ferdinand VII **Obv.** Draped laureate bust right **Rev:** Crowned shield flanked by pillars **Obv. Legend:** FERDIN • VII **Rev. Legend:** IND • REX... **Mint:** Zacatecas **Note:** Mint marks: Z, ZS, Zs.

Date	Mintage	VG8	F12	VF20	XF40	MS60
1818 AG	—	9.00	18.00	36.00	65.00	—
1819 AG	—	12.00	25.00	48.00	100	—
1819 AG	—	12.00	25.00	48.00	100	—
Note: Reversed 'S' in HISPAN						
1820 AG	—	12.00	25.00	48.00	100	—
1820 RG	—	12.00	25.00	48.00	100	—
1821 AG	—	12.00	25.00	48.00	100	—
1821 AZ/RG	—	12.00	25.00	48.00	100	—
1821 AZ	—	12.00	25.00	48.00	100	—
1821 RG	—	12.00	25.00	48.00	100	—
1822 AG	—	12.00	25.00	48.00	100	—
1822 RG	—	12.00	25.00	48.00	100	—

KM# A92 2 REALES

6.77 g., 0.903 Silver, 0.20 oz. ASW **Ruler:** Ferdinand VII **Obv.** Small armored bust right **Rev:** Crowned shield flanked by pillars **Obv. Legend:** FERDIN • VII **Rev. Legend:** IND •

REX... **Mint:** Zacatecas **Note:** Mint marks: Z, ZS, Zs.

Date	Mintage	G4	VG8	F12	VF20	XF40
1819 AG	—	55.00	120	240	475	—

KM# 189 8 REALES

0.903 Silver, **Ruler:** Ferdinand VII **Obv.** Crowned shield flanked by pillars **Rev:** Mountain above L.V.O. within beaded circle **Rev. Legend:** MONEDA.PROVISION... **Mint:** Zacatecas **Note:** Mint Zacatecas.

Date	Mintage	G4	VG8	F12	VF20	XF40
1810	—	350	600	900	1,500	—
1811	—	120	180	270	425	—

Note: Date aligned with legend. Also exists with incomplete date

KM# 190 8 REALES

0.903 Silver, **Ruler:** Ferdinand VII **Obv.** Crowned shield flanked by pillars **Rev:** Mountain above L. V. O within beaded circle **Obv. Legend:** FERDIN • VII • DEI... **Rev. Legend:** MONEDA PROVISIONAL DE ZACATECAS **Mint:** Zacatecas

Date	Mintage	G4	VG8	F12	VF20	XF40
1811	—	80.00	120	160	425	775
Note: Date aligned with legend						
1811 Error FERDIN • VI	—	—	—	—	3,600	6,000

Date	Mintage	VG8	F12	VF20	XF40	MS60
1814 AG	—	150	210	270	400	—
Note: D over horizontal D in IND						
1814 AG/FP	—	120	180	240	350	—
1815 AG	—	60.00	120	180	300	—
1816 AG	—	42.00	60.00	80.00	150	—
1817 AG	—	42.00	60.00	80.00	150	—
1818 AG	—	36.00	48.00	60.00	120	—
1819 AG	—	36.00	48.00	60.00	120	—
1819 AG	—	120	240	350	475	—
'GRATIA' error						
1820 AG	—	120	240	350	475	—
18/11 error						
1820 AG	—	36.00	48.00	60.00	120	600
1820 RG	—	36.00	48.00	60.00	120	—
1821/81 RG	—	90.00	180	270	350	—
1821 RG	—	18.00	30.00	42.00	80.00	—
1821 AZ/RG	—	60.00	120	180	240	—
1821 AZ	—	60.00	120	180	240	—
1822 RG	—	48.00	70.00	120	210	775

KM# 191 8 REALES
0.903 Silver, **Ruler:** Ferdinand VII **Obv.** Armored bust right **Rev:** Crowned shield flanked by pillars **Obv. Legend:** FERDIN • VII • 8 •R • DEI... **Rev. Legend:** MONEDA PROVISIONAL DE ZACATECAS **Mint:** Zacatecas

Date	Mintage	G4	VG8	F12	VF20	XF40
1811	—	55.00	90.00	175	325	—
1812	—	60.00	100	190	350	—

KM# 192 8 REALES
0.903 Silver, **Ruler:** Ferdinand VII **Obv.** Draped laureate bust right **Rev:** Crowned shield flanked by pillars **Obv. Legend:** FERDIN • VII • DEI... **Rev. Legend:** MONEDA PROVISIONAL DE ZACATECAS **Mint:** Zacatecas

Date	Mintage	G4	VG8	F12	VF20	XF40
1812	—	90.00	180	325	550	—

KM# 111.6 8 REALES
27.07 g., 0.903 Silver, 0.78 oz. ASW **Ruler:** Ferdinand VII **Obv.** Draped laureate bust right **Rev:** Crowned shield flanked by pillars **Obv. Legend:** FERDIN • VII • DEI • GRATIA **Rev. Legend:** HISAV • ET IND • REX **Mint:** Zacatecas

Date	Mintage	VG8	F12	VF20	XF40	MS60
1821 Zs	—	190	375	650	900	—

ROYALIST COUNTERMARKED COINAGE

LCM - LA COMANDANCIA MILITAR
Crown and Flag
This countermark exists in 15 various sizes.

KM# 111.5 8 REALES
27.07 g., 0.903 Silver, 0.78 oz. ASW **Ruler:** Ferdinand VII **Obv.** Draped laureate bust right **Rev:** Crowned shield flanked by pillars **Obv. Legend:** FERDIN • VII • DEI • GRATIA **Rev. Legend:** HISPAN • ET IND • REX **Mint:** Zacatecas **Note:** Mint mark: Zs. Several bust types exist for the 1821 issues.

Date	Mintage	VG8	F12	VF20	XF40	MS60
1813 FP	—	90.00	150	210	325	—
1814 FP	—	180	300	425	550	—
1814 AG	—	120	180	240	350	—

KM# 193.1 2 REALES
0.903 Silver **Note:** Countermark on Mexico KM#92.

Date	Mintage	G4	VG8	F12	VF20	XF40
1809 TH	—	100	200	300	550	

KM# 193.2 2 REALES
0.903 Silver **Note:** Countermark on Mexico KM#186.

Date	Mintage	G4	VG8	F12	VF20	XF40
1811	—	100	200	300	550	—

KM# 194.1 8 REALES
Cast Silver **Note:** Countermark on Chihuahua KM#123.

Date	Mintage	G4	VG8	F12	VF20	XF40
1811 RP	—	120	240	350	600	—
1812 RP	—	120	240	350	600	—

KM# 194.2 8 REALES
0.903 Silver **Note:** Countermark on Chihuahua KM#111.1 struck over KM#123.

Date	Mintage	G4	VG8	F12	VF20	XF40
1815 RP	—	240	325	475	725	—
1817 RP	—	150	210	270	425	—
1820 RP	—	150	210	270	425	—
1821 RP	—	150	210	270	425	—

KM# 194.3 8 REALES
0.903 Silver **Note:** Countermark on Durango KM#111.2.

Date	Mintage	G4	VG8	F12	VF20	XF40
1812 RM	—	85.00	150	240	350	—
1821 CG	—	85.00	150	240	350	—

KM# 194.4 8 REALES
0.903 Silver **Note:** Countermark on Guadalajara KM#111.3.

Date	Mintage	G4	VG8	F12	VF20	XF40
1813 MR	—	180	270	350	600	—

KM# 194.5 8 REALES
0.903 Silver **Note:** Countermark on Guanajuato KM#111.4.

Date	Mintage	G4	VG8	F12	VF20	XF40
1813 JJ	—	270	425	575	850	—

KM# 194.6 8 REALES
0.903 Silver **Note:** Countermark on Nueva Viscaya KM#165.

Date	Mintage	G4	VG8	F12	VF20	XF40
1811 RM Rare	—	—	—	—	—	—

KM# 194.7 8 REALES
0.903 Silver **Note:** Countermark on Mexico KM#111.

Date	Mintage	G4	VG8	F12	VF20	XF40
1811 HJ	—	150	270	425	775	—
1812 JJ	—	130	160	240	425	—
1817 JJ	—	60.00	80.00	100	210	—
1818 JJ	—	60.00	80.00	100	210	—
1820 JJ	—	—	—	—	—	—

KM# 194.8 8 REALES
0.903 Silver **Note:** Countermark on Sombrerete KM#176.

Date	Mintage	G4	VG8	F12	VF20	XF40
1811 Rare	—	—	—	—	—	—
1812 Rare	—	—	—	—	—	—

KM# 194.9 8 REALES
0.903 Silver **Note:** Countermark on Zacatecas KM#190.

Date	Mintage	G4	VG8	F12	VF20	XF40
1811	—	270	425	600	—	—

KM# 194.10 8 REALES
0.903 Silver **Note:** Countermark on Zacatecas KM#111.5.

Date	Mintage	G4	VG8	F12	VF20	XF40
1813 FP	—	—	—	—	—	—
1814 AG	—	—	—	—	—	—
1822 RG	—	—	—	—	—	—

LCV - LAS CAJAS DE VERACRUZ
The Royal Treasury of the City of Veracruz

KM# 195 7 REALES
Silver **Note:** Countermark and 7 on underweight 8 Reales.

Date	Mintage	G4	VG8	F12	VF20	XF40
ND (1813) Rare	—	—	—	—	—	—

Note: Most examples are counterfeit

KM# 196 7-1/4 REALES
Silver **Note:** Countermark and 7-1/4 on underweight 8 Reales.

Date	Mintage	G4	VG8	F12	VF20	XF40
ND (1813) Rare	—	—	—	—	—	—

Note: Most examples are counterfeit

KM# 197 7-1/2 REALES
Silver **Note:** Countermark and 7-1/2 on underweight 8 Reales.

Date	Mintage	G4	VG8	F12	VF20	XF40
ND (1813) Rare	—	—	—	—	—	—

Note: Most examples are counterfeit

KM# 198 7-3/4 REALES
Silver **Note:** Countermark and 7-3/4 on underweight 8 Reales.

Date	Mintage	G4	VG8	F12	VF20	XF40
ND (1813)	—	350	450	550	850	—

Note: Many examples are counterfeit

KM# A198 8 REALES
Cast Silver **Note:** Countermark on Chihuahua KM#123.

Date	Mintage	G4	VG8	F12	VF20	XF40
1811 RP	—	180	300	475	725	—

KM# 199 8 REALES
Silver **Note:** Countermark on Zacatecas KM#191.

Date	Mintage	G4	VG8	F12	VF20	XF40
1811	—	210	270	325	450	—
1812	—	210	270	325	450	—

MS (MONOGRAM) - MANUEL SALCEDO

KM# 200   8 REALES
Silver **Note:** Countermark on Mexico KM#110.

Date	Mintage	G4	VG8	F12	VF20	XF40
1809 TH	—	180	300	475	725	—
1810 HJ	—	180	300	475	725	—
1811 HJ	—	180	300	475	725	—

MVA - MONCLOVA

KM# 202.3   8 REALES
Silver **Note:** Countermark on cast Mexico KM#110.

Date	Mintage	G4	VG8	F12	VF20	XF40
1809 HJ	—	120	180	300	450	—
1809 TH	—	120	180	300	450	—
1810 HJ	—	120	180	300	450	—

KM# 201   8 REALES
Silver **Note:** Countermark on Chihuahua KM#111.1; struck over cast Mexico KM#110.

Date	Mintage	G4	VG8	F12	VF20	XF40
1809	—	300	550	850	1,200	—
1816 RP	—	300	550	850	1,200	—
1821 RP	—	300	550	850	1,200	—

KM# 202.1   8 REALES
Silver **Note:** Countermark on Chihuahua KM#111.1; struck over cast Mexico KM#109.

Date	Mintage	G4	VG8	F12	VF20	XF40
1810	—	150	210	300	450	—

KM# 202.5   8 REALES
Silver **Note:** Countermark on Zacatecas KM#189.

Date	Mintage	G4	VG8	F12	VF20	XF40
1813	—	350	425	550	850	—

KM# 202.2   8 REALES
Silver **Note:** Countermark on cast Mexico KM#109.

Date	Mintage	G4	VG8	F12	VF20	XF40
1798 FM	—	120	180	300	450	—
1802 FT	—	120	180	300	450	—

INSURGENT COINAGE

AMERICAN CONGRESS

KM# 216   REAL
0.903 Silver **Obv.** Eagle on cactus **Rev:** F. 7 on spread mantle **Obv.** **Legend:** CONGRESO AMERICANO **Rev.** **Legend:** DEPOSIT D.L. AUCTORI J **Mint:** Mexico City

Date	Mintage	G4	VG8	F12	VF20	XF40
ND(1813)	—	42.00	90.00	150	270	—

KM# 217 REAL
0.903 Silver **Obv.** Eagle on cactus **Rev:** F. 7 on spread mantle **Obv. Legend:** CONGR. AMER. **Rev. Legend:** DEPOS. D. L. AUT. D. **Mint:** Mexico City

Date	Mintage	G4	VG8	F12	VF20	XF40
ND(1813)	—	42.00	90.00	150	270	—

NATIONAL CONGRESS

KM# 209 1/2 REAL
Struck Copper **Obv.** Eagle on bridge **Rev:** Value, bow quiver, etc **Obv. Legend:** VICE FERD. VII DEI GRATIA ET **Rev. Legend:** S. P. CONG. NAT. IND.

Date	Mintage	G4	VG8	F12	VF20	XF40
1811	—	55.00	100	180	300	—
1812	—	33.00	70.00	120	210	—
1813	—	33.00	70.00	120	210	—
1814	—	55.00	100	180	300	—

KM# 210 1/2 REAL
0.903 Silver **Obv.** Eagle on bridge **Rev:** Value, bow quiver, etc **Obv. Legend:** VICE FERD. VII DEI GRATIA ET **Rev. Legend:** S. P. CONG. NAT. IND.

Date	Mintage	G4	VG8	F12	VF20	XF40
1812	—	33.00	70.00	120	210	—
1813	—	55.00	110	210	325	—

Note: 1812 exists with the date reading inwards and outwards

KM# 211 REAL
0.903 Silver **Obv.** Eagle on bridge **Rev:** Value, bow quiver, etc **Obv. Legend:** VICE FERD. VII DEI GRATIA ET **Rev. Legend:** S. P. CONG. NAT. IND.

Date	Mintage	G4	VG8	F12	VF20	XF40
1812	—	27.50	55.00	95.00	180	—
1813	—	27.50	55.00	95.00	180	—

Note: 1812 exists with the date reading either inward or outward

KM# 212 2 REALES
Struck Copper **Obv.** Eagle on bridge **Rev:** Value, bow quiver, etc **Obv. Legend:** VICE FERD. VII DEI GRATIA ET **Rev. Legend:** S. P. CONG. NAT. IND.

Date	Mintage	G4	VG8	F12	VF20	XF40
1812	—	120	180	270	425	—
1813	—	27.50	60.00	90.00	180	—
1814	—	39.00	90.00	130	220	—

KM# 213 2 REALES
0.903 Silver **Obv.** Eagle on bridge in shield, denomination at sides **Rev:** Canon, quiver, arm, etc **Obv. Legend:** VICE FERD. VII DEI GRATIA ET

Date	Mintage	G4	VG8	F12	VF20	XF40
1813	—	95.00	200	350	500	—

Note: These dies were believed to be intended for the striking of 2 Escudos

KM# A213 2 REALES
Struck Silver **Obv.** Eagle on bridge **Rev:** Value, bow, quiver, etc **Obv. Legend:** VICE FERD. VII DEI GRATIA ET **Rev. Legend:** S. P. CONG. NAT. IND.

Date	Mintage	G4	VG8	F12	VF20	XF40
1813	—	1,050	1,950	3,300	5,500	—

KM# 214 4 REALES
0.903 Silver **Obv.** Eagle on bridge **Rev:** Value, bow, quiver, etc **Obv. Legend:** VICE FERD. VII DEI GRATIA ET **Rev. Legend:** S. P. CONG. NAT. IND. **Mint:** Mexico City

Date	Mintage	G4	VG8	F12	VF20	XF40
1813	—	650	1,300	2,700	5,200	—

WAR OF INDEPENDENCE

KM# 215.1 8 REALES

0.903 Silver **Obv.** Small crowned eagle **Rev:** Value, bow, quiver, etc **Obv. Legend:** VICE FERD. VII DEI GRATIA ET **Rev. Legend:** S. P. CONG. NAT. IND. **Mint:** Mexico City

Date	Mintage	G4	VG8	F12	VF20	XF40
1812Mo	—	650	1,250	2,600	4,950	—

KM# 215.2 8 REALES

0.903 Silver **Obv.** Large crowned eagle **Rev:** Value, bow, quiver, etc **Obv. Legend:** VICE FERD. VII DEI GRATIA ET **Rev. Legend:** S. P. CONG. NAT. IND. **Mint:** Mexico City

Date	Mintage	G4	VG8	F12	VF20	XF40
1813Mo	—	650	1,250	2,600	4,950	—

SUPREME NATIONAL CONGRESS OF AMERICA

PDV - Provisional de Valladolid
VTIL - Util = useful
(Refer to Multiple countermarks)

KM# 203 1/2 REAL

Struck Copper **Obv.** Eagle on bridge **Rev:** Value, bow, quiver, etc **Obv. Legend:** FERDIN. VII DEI GRATIA **Rev. Legend:** S. P. CONG. NAT. IND. GUV.T.

Date	Mintage	G4	VG8	F12	VF20	XF40
1811	—	34.50	55.00	80.00	150	—
1812	—	34.50	55.00	80.00	150	—
1813	—	34.50	55.00	80.00	150	—
1814	—	34.50	55.00	80.00	150	—

KM# 204 REAL

Struck Copper **Obv.** Eagle on bridge **Rev:** Value, bow, quiver, etc **Obv. Legend:** FERDIN. VII DEI GRATIA **Rev. Legend:** S. P. CONG. NAT. IND. GUV.T.

Date	Mintage	G4	VG8	F12	VF20	XF40
1811	—	55.00	95.00	155	250	—

KM# 205 2 REALES

Struck Copper **Obv.** Eagle on bridge **Rev:** Value, bow, quiver, etc **Obv. Legend:** FERDIN. VII DEI GRATIA

Date	Mintage	G4	VG8	F12	VF20	XF40
1812	—	280	400	600	950	—

KM# 206 8 REALES

Cast Silver **Obv.** Eagle on bridge **Rev:** Value, bow, quiver, etc **Obv. Legend:** FERDIN. VII DEI GRATIA

Date	Mintage	G4	VG8	F12	VF20	XF40
1811	—	190	325	450	700	—
1812	—	190	325	475	700	—

KM# 207 8 REALES

Struck Silver **Obv.** Eagle on bridge **Rev:** Value, bow, quiver, etc **Obv. Legend:** FERDIN. VII DEI GRATIA

Date	Mintage	G4	VG8	F12	VF20	XF40
1811	—	—	—	—	—	—

Note: Ira & Larry Goldberg Millennia Sale 5-08, QU-55 realized $55,000.

1812	—	625	1,250	1,900	3,150	—

KM# 208 8 REALES

Struck Copper **Obv.** Eagle on bridge **Rev:** Bow, sword and quiver **Obv. Legend:** FERDIN. VII... **Rev. Legend:** PROVICIONAL POR LA SUPREMA JUNTA DE AMERICA

Date	Mintage	G4	VG8	F12	VF20	XF40
1811	—	125	190	280	600	—
1812	—	125	190	280	600	—

INSURGENT COUNTERMARKED COINAGE

CONGRESS OF CHILPANZINGO

Type A: Hand holding bow and arrow between quiver
with arrows, sword and bow.

Type B: Crowned eagle on bridge.Congress of
Chilpanzingo

KM# 256.1 1/2 REAL
Silver **Note:** Countermark on cast Mexico City KM#72.

Date	Mintage	G4	VG8	F12	VF20	XF40
1812	—	50.00	85.00	110	170	—

KM# 256.2 1/2 REAL
Silver **Note:** Countermark on Zacatecas KM#181.

Date	Mintage	G4	VG8	F12	VF20	XF40
1811	—	60.00	90.00	120	180	—

KM# A257 REAL
Cast Silver **Note:** Countermark on cast Mexico City KM#81.

Date	Mintage	G4	VG8	F12	VF20	XF40
1803	—	22.50	36.00	60.00	100	—

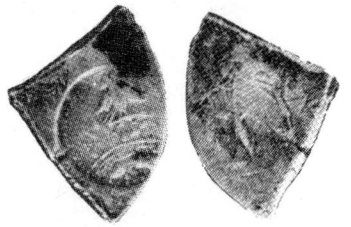

KM# 257.1 2 REALES
Silver **Mint:** (no Mint Information) **Note:** Countermark on
1/4 cut of 8 Reales.

Date	Mintage	G4	VG8	F12	VF20	XF40
ND Unique	—	—	—	—	—	—

KM# 257.2 2 REALES
Silver **Note:** Countermark on Zacatecas KM#186.

Date	Mintage	G4	VG8	F12	VF20
1811 Unique	—	—	—	—	—

KM# 258.1 8 REALES
Silver **Note:** Countermark on cast Mexico City KM#109.

Date	Mintage	G4	VG8	F12	VF20	XF40
1805	—	55.00	80.00	100	180	—

Note: A countermark appears on coins dated 1805 TH

KM# 258.2 8 REALES
Silver **Note:** Countermark on cast Mexico City KM#110.

Date	Mintage	G4	VG8	F12	VF20	XF40
1810 HJ	—	60.00	90.00	120	210	—

KM# 258.3 8 REALES
Silver **Note:** Countermark on cast Mexico City KM#111.

Date	Mintage	G4	VG8	F12	VF20	XF40
1812 HJ	—	120	150	210	325	—
1811 HJ	—	55.00	80.00	100	180	—

KM# 259.1 8 REALES
Silver **Note:** Countermark on Chihuahua KM#111.1.

Date	Mintage	G4	VG8	F12	VF20	XF40
1816 RP	—	240	300	350	475	—

KM# 259.2 8 REALES
Silver **Note:** Countermark on cast Mexico City KM#111.

Date	Mintage	G4	VG8	F12	VF20	XF40
1811 HJ	—	155	180	210	300	—

KM# 259.3 8 REALES
Silver **Note:** Countermark on Valladolid KM#178.

Date	Mintage	G4	VG8	F12	VF20	XF40
1813	—	1,250	2,500	3,750	6,300	—

KM# 259.4 8 REALES
Silver **Note:** Countermark on Zacatecas KM#190.

Date	Mintage	G4	VG8	F12	VF20	XF40
1810	—	500	625	750	975	—

DON JOSE MARIA DE LINARES

KM# 263.1 8 REALES
Silver **Note:** Countermark on Mexico City KM#110.

Date	Mintage	G4	VG8	F12	VF20	XF40
1808 TH	—	325	375	475	700	—

KM# 263.2 8 REALES
Silver **Note:** Countermark on Zacatecas KM#190.

Date	Mintage	G4	VG8	F12	VF20	XF40
1811	—	375	475	575	825	—

KM# 263.3 8 REALES
Silver **Note:** Countermark on Zacatecas KM#191.

Date	Mintage	G4	VG8	F12	VF20	XF40
1812	—	325	375	475	700	—

KM# 263.4 8 REALES
Silver, **Issuer:** Don Jose Maria De Linares **Note:** Countermark on Zacatecas KM#190.

Date	Mintage	F12	VF20	XF40	MS60	MS63
1811	—	—	—	—	—	—

KM# 263.5 8 REALES
Silver, **Issuer:** Don Jose Maria De Linares **Note:** Countermark on Zacatecas KM#192.

Date	Mintage	F12	VF20	XF40	MS60	MS63
1812	—	—	—	—	—	—

ENSAIE

KM# 260.3 8 REALES
Silver **Note:** Countermark on Zacatecas KM#190.

Date	Mintage	G4	VG8	F12	VF20	XF40
1810	—	—	—	—	—	—
1811	—	120	180	240	400	—

KM# 260.4 8 REALES
Silver **Note:** Countermark on Zacatecas KM#191.

Date	Mintage	G4	VG8	F12	VF20	XF40
1810	—	600	850	1,100	1,500	—
1811	—	300	350	450	650	—
1812	—	240	300	350	550	—

KM# 260.1 8 REALES
Silver **Note:** Countermark on Mexico City KM#110.

Date	Mintage	G4	VG8	F12	VF20	XF40
1811 HJ	—	180	240	325	450	—

KM# 260.2 8 REALES
Silver **Note:** Countermark on Zacatecas KM#189.

Date	Mintage	G4	VG8	F12	VF20	XF40
1811	—	240	475	725	1,000	—

GENERAL VICENTE GUERRERO

The countermark of an eagle facing left within a pearled oval has been attributed by some authors as that of General Vicente Guerrero, a leader of the insurgents in the south, 1816-1821.

KM# 276 1/2 REAL
Silver **Note:** Countermark on Mexico City KM#72.

Date	Mintage	G4	VG8	F12	VF20	XF40
ND	—	48.00	70.00	95.00	210	—

KM# 277 REAL
Silver **Note:** Countermark on Mexico City KM#78.

Date	Mintage	G4	VG8	F12	VF20	XF40
1772 FM	—	43.75	65.00	95.00	205	—

KM# 278.1 2 REALES
Silver **Note:** Countermark on Mexico City KM#88.

Date	Mintage	G4	VG8	F12	VF20	XF40
1784 FM	—	40.00	60.00	100	225	—
1798	—	40.00	60.00	100	225	—

KM# 278.2 2 REALES
Silver **Note:** Countermark on Mexico City KM#91.

Date	Mintage	G4	VG8	F12	VF20	XF40
1807 PJ	—	36.00	60.00	95.00	240	—

KM# 279 8 REALES
Silver **Note:** Countermark on Zacatecas KM#191.

Date	Mintage	G4	VG8	F12	VF20	XF40
1811	—	120	180	240	425	—

JOSE MARIA LICEAGA
J.M.L. with banner on cross, crossed olive branches.
(J.M.L./V., D.s, S.M., S.Y.S.L., Ve, A.P., s.r.a., Sea, P.G.,
S., S.M., El)

KM# A260 1/2 REAL
Silver **Note:** Countermark on cast Mexico City 1/2 Real.

Date	Mintage	G4	VG8	F12	VF20	XF40
ND	—	125	190	250	375	—

KM# 261.6 2 REALES
Silver **Note:** Countermark on Zacatecas KM#187.

Date	Mintage	G4	VG8	F12	VF20	XF40
1811	—	250	280	325	400	—

KM# 261.7 2 REALES
Silver **Note:** Countermark on Zacatecas KM#187.

Date	Mintage	G4	VG8	F12	VF20	XF40
1811	—	250	295	350	450	—

KM# 261.8 2 REALES
Silver **Note:** Countermark on Zacatecas KM#187.

Date	Mintage	G4	VG8	F12	VF20	XF40
1811	—	240	280	325	425	—

KM# 261.9 2 REALES
Silver **Note:** Countermark on Zacatecas KM#187.

Date	Mintage	G4	VG8	F12	VF20	XF40
1811	—	240	280	325	425	—

KM# 261.1 2 REALES
Silver **Note:** Countermark on 1/4 cut of 8 Reales.

Date	Mintage	G4	VG8	F12	VF20	XF40
ND	—	210	270	400	—	—

KM# 261.2 2 REALES
Silver **Note:** Countermark on Zacatecas KM#186.

Date	Mintage	G4	VG8	F12	VF20	XF40
1811	—	250	280	325	400	—

KM# 261.3 2 REALES
Silver **Note:** Countermark on Zacatecas KM#186.

Date	Mintage	G4	VG8	F12	VF20	XF40
1811	—	250	295	350	450	—

KM# 261.4 2 REALES
Silver **Note:** Countermark on Zacatecas KM#186.

Date	Mintage	G4	VG8	F12	VF20	XF40
1811	—	250	295	350	450	—

KM# 261.5 2 REALES
Silver **Note:** Countermark on Zacatecas KM#186.

Date	Mintage	G4	VG8	F12	VF20	XF40
1811	—	250	295	350	450	—

KM# 262.1 8 REALES
Silver **Note:** Countermark on Zacatecas KM#190.

Date	Mintage	G4	VG8	F12	VF20	XF40
1811	—	325	400	525	775	—

KM# 262.4 8 REALES
Silver **Note:** Countermark on Zacatecas KM#190.

Date	Mintage	G4	VG8	F12	VF20	XF40
1811	—	250	350	475	725	—

KM# 262.2 8 REALES
Silver **Note:** Countermark on Zacatecas KM#190.

Date	Mintage	G4	VG8	F12	VF20	XF40
1811	—	280	375	500	750	—

KM# 262.3   8 REALES
Silver   **Note:** Countermark on Durango KM#111.2.

Date	Mintage	G4	VG8	F12	VF20	XF40
1813 RM	—	250	350	475	725	—

KM# 262.5   8 REALES
Silver   **Note:** Countermark on Zacatecas KM#190.

Date	Mintage	G4	VG8	F12	VF20	XF40
1811	—	250	350	475	700	—

KM# 262.10   8 REALES
Silver   **Note:** Countermark on Zacatecas KM#190.

Date	Mintage	G4	VG8	F12	VF20	XF40
1811	—	—	—	—	—	

KM# 262.6   8 REALES
Silver   **Note:** Countermark on Zacatecas KM#190.

Date	Mintage	G4	VG8	F12	VF20	XF40
1811	—	250	350	475	700	—

KM# 262.12   8 REALES
Silver   **Mint:** (no Mint Information) **Note:** Countermark on Guanajuato 8 Reales, KM#111.4.

Date	Mintage	G4	VG8	F12	VF20	XF40
ND1813	—	190	325	575	—	—

KM# 262.7   8 REALES
Silver   **Note:** Countermark on Zacatecas KM#190.

Date	Mintage	G4	VG8	F12	VF20	XF40
1811	—	—	—	—	—	

KM# 262.9   8 REALES
Silver   **Note:** Countermark on Zacatecas KM#190.

Date	Mintage	G4	VG8	F12	VF20	XF40
1811	—	—	—	—	—	

KM# 262.11   8 REALES
Silver   **Note:** Countermark on Zacatecas KM#190.

Date	Mintage	G4	VG8	F12	VF20	XF40
1811	—	—	—	—	—	

KM# 262.8   8 REALES
Silver   **Note:** Countermark on Zacatecas KM#190.

Date	Mintage	G4	VG8	F12	VF20	XF40
1811	—	—	—	—	—	

L.V.S. - LABOR VINCIT SEMPER

Some authorities believe L.V.S. is for La Villa de Sombrerete.

KM# 264.1   8 REALES
Cast Silver   **Note:** Countermark on Chihuahua KM#123.

Date	Mintage	G4	VG8	F12	VF20	XF40
1811 RP	—	350	450	575	750	—
1812 RP	—	250	325	375	500	—

KM# 264.2   8 REALES
Silver   **Note:** Countermark on Chihuahua KM#111.1 overstruck on KM#123.

Date	Mintage	G4	VG8	F12	VF20	XF40
1816 RP	—	325	375	400	525	—
1817 RP	—	325	375	400	525	—
1818 RP	—	325	375	400	525	—
1819 RP	—	500	575	625	875	—
1820 RP	—	575	625	700	450	—

KM# 264.3 8 REALES
Silver **Note:** Countermark on Guadalajara KM#111.3.

Date	Mintage	G4	VG8	F12	VF20	XF40
1817	—	230	275	325	450	—

KM# 264.4 8 REALES
Silver **Note:** Countermark on Nueva Vizcaya KM#165.

Date	Mintage	G4	VG8	F12	VF20	XF40
1811 RM	—	1,250	3,450	5,800	9,100	—

KM# 264.5 8 REALES
Silver **Note:** Countermark on Sombrerete KM#177.

Date	Mintage	G4	VG8	F12	VF20	XF40
1811	—	375	450	575	825	—
1812	—	375	450	575	825	—

KM# 264.6 8 REALES
Silver **Note:** Countermark on Zacatecas KM#190.

Date	Mintage	G4	VG8	F12	VF20	XF40
1811	—	450	500	575	825	—

KM# 264.7 8 REALES
Silver **Note:** Countermark on Zacatecas KM#192.

Date	Mintage	G4	VG8	F12	VF20	XF40
1813	—	450	500	575	825	—

KM# 264.8 8 REALES
Cast Silver, **Issuer:** Labor Vincit Semper **Note:** Countermark on Zacatecas KM#190.

Date	Mintage	F12	VF20	XF40	MS60	MS63
1811	—	—	—	—	—	—

MORELOS
Morelos monogram

Type A: Stars above and below monogram in circle.

Type B: Dots above and below monogram in oval.

Type C: Monogram in rectangle.
Note: Many specimens of Type C available in todays market are considered spurious.

KM# A265 2 REALES
Copper **Note:** Countermark on Oaxaca Sud, KM#226.1.

Date	Mintage	G4	VG8	F12	VF20	XF40
1812	—	—	—	—	—	—

KM# 265.1 8 REALES
Silver **Note:** Countermark on Mexico City KM#109.

Date	Mintage	G4	VG8	F12	VF20	XF40
1797 FM	—	55.00	65.00	75.00	120	—
1798 FM	—	55.00	65.00	75.00	120	—
1800 FM	—	55.00	65.00	75.00	120	—
1807 TH	—	55.00	65.00	75.00	120	—

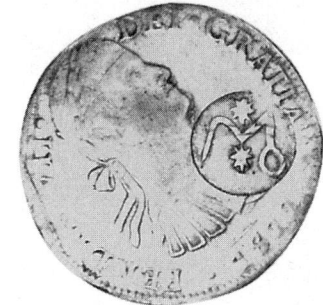

KM# 265.2 8 REALES
Silver **Note:** Countermark on Mexico City KM#110.

Date	Mintage	G4	VG8	F12	VF20	XF40
1809 TH	—	70.00	95.00	150	250	—
1811 HJ	—	70.00	95.00	150	250	—

KM# 265.3 8 REALES
Silver **Note:** Countermark on Mexico City KM#111.

Date	Mintage	G4	VG8	F12	VF20	XF40
1812 JJ	—	65.00	75.00	95.00	155	—

KM# 265.5 8 REALES
Cast Silver   **Note:** Countermark on Supreme National Congress KM#206.

Date	Mintage	G4	VG8	F12	VF20	XF40
1811	—	250	325	475	750	—

KM# 266.1 8 REALES
Silver **Note:** Countermark on Guatamala 8 Reales, C#67.

Date	Mintage	G4	VG8	F12	VF20	XF40
1810 M Rare	—	—	—	—	—	—

KM# 266.2 8 REALES
Silver **Note:** Countermark on Mexico City KM#110.

Date	Mintage	G4	VG8	F12	VF20	XF40
1809 TH	—	55.00	70.00	80.00	125	—

KM# 267.1 8 REALES
Silver   **Note:** Countermark on Zacatecas KM#189. Many specimens of Type C available in today's market are considered spurious.

Date	Mintage	G4	VG8	F12	VF20	XF40
1811	—	375	450	575	950	—

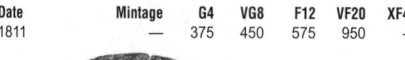

KM# 265.4 8 REALES
Copper **Note:** Countermark on Oaxaca Sud KM#233.2.

Date	Mintage	G4	VG8	F12	VF20	XF40
1812	—	25.00	35.75	48.75	80.00	—
1813	—	25.00	35.75	48.75	80.00	—
1814	—	25.00	35.75	48.75	80.00	—

KM# 265.6 8 REALES
Silver **Note:** Countermark on Zacatecas KM#190.

Date	Mintage	G4	VG8	F12	VF20	XF40
1811	—	450	750	1,100	—	—

KM# 265.7 8 REALES
Silver **Note:** Countermark on Zacatecas KM#191.

Date	Mintage	G4	VG8	F12	VF20	XF40
1811	—	240	300	450	725	—

KM# 265.8 8 REALES
Silver, **Issuer:** Morelos **Note:** Countermark on Zacatecas KM#190.

Date	Mintage	F12	VF20	XF40	MS60	MS63
1811	—	—	—	—	—	—

KM# 267.2 8 REALES
Silver **Note:** Countermark Type C on Zacatecas KM#190. Many specimens of Type C available in today's market are considered spurious.

Date	Mintage	G4	VG8	F12	VF20	XF40
1811	—	375	450	575	950	—

NORTE
Issued by the Supreme National Congress and the Army of the North.

Countermark: Eagle on cactus; star to left; NORTE below.

KM# 268 1/2 REAL
Silver **Note:** Countermark on Zacatecas KM#180.

Date	Mintage	G4	VG8	F12	VF20	XF40
1811	—	275	325	425	550	—

WAR OF INDEPENDENCE

KM# 269 2 REALES
Silver **Note:** Countermark on Zacatecas KM#187.

Date	Mintage	G4	VG8	F12	VF20	XF40
1811	—	250	300	350	500	—

KM# A269 2 REALES
Silver **Note:** Countermark on Zacatecas KM#188.

Date	Mintage	G4	VG8	F12	VF20	XF40
1812	—	—	—	—	—	—

KM# B269 4 REALES
Silver **Note:** Countermark on Sombrerete KM#175.

Date	Mintage	G4	VG8	F12	VF20	XF40
1812	—	110	165	220	325	—

KM# 270.1 8 REALES
Silver **Note:** Countermark on Chihuahua KM#111.1.

Date	Mintage	G4	VG8	F12	VF20	XF40
1813 RP	—	275	375	500	600	—

KM# 270.2 8 REALES
Silver **Note:** Countermark on Guanajuato KM#111.4.

Date	Mintage	G4	VG8	F12	VF20	XF40
1813 JM	—	450	625	800	975	—

KM# 270.3 8 REALES
Silver **Note:** Countermark on Zacatecas KM#190.

Date	Mintage	G4	VG8	F12	VF20	XF40
1811	—	350	450	575	775	—

KM# 270.4 8 REALES
Silver **Note:** Countermark on Zacatecas KM#191.

Date	Mintage	G4	VG8	F12	VF20	XF40
1811	—	220	325	450	600	—
1811	—	220	325	450	600	—
1812	—	220	325	450	600	—

KM# 270.5 8 REALES
Silver, **Note:** Countermark on Zacatecas KM#190.

Date	Mintage	G4	VG8	F12	VF20	XF40
1811	—	—	—	—	—	—

KM# 270.6 8 REALES
Silver, **Mint:** (no Mint Information) **Note:** Countermark on Sombrerete KM# 177.

Date	Mintage	G4	VG8	F12	VF20	XF40
1812	—	1,250	1,600	2,000	—	—

OSORNO

Countermark: Osorno monogram.
(Jose Francisco Osorno)

KM# 271.1 1/2 REAL
Silver **Note:** Countermark on Mexico City KM#72.

Date	Mintage	G4	VG8	F12	VF20	XF40
1798 FM	—	80.00	120	180	270	—
1802 FT	—	80.00	120	180	270	—
1806	—	80.00	120	180	270	—

KM# 271.2 1/2 REAL
Silver **Note:** Countermark on Mexico City KM#73.

Date	Mintage	G4	VG8	F12	VF20	XF40
1809 TH	—	80.00	120	180	270	—

KM# 272.1 REAL
Silver **Note:** Countermark on Mexico City KM#81.

Date	Mintage	G4	VG8	F12	VF20	XF40
1803 FT	—	80.00	120	180	300	—

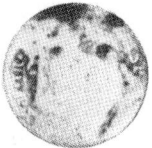

KM# 272.2 REAL
Silver **Note:** Countermark on Potosi KM#70.

Date	Mintage	G4	VG8	F12	VF20	XF40
ND (1814)	—	90.00	140	210	325	—

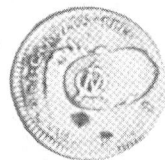

KM# 272.3 REAL
Silver **Note:** Countermark on Guatemala KM#54.

Date	Mintage	G4	VG8	F12	VF20	XF40
1804	—	90.00	140	210	325	—

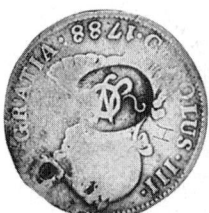

KM# A272.1 2 REALES
Silver **Note:** Countermark on Mexico City KM#88.2.

Date	Mintage	G4	VG8	F12	VF20	XF40
1788 FM	—	90.00	150	210	325	—

KM# A272.2 2 REALES
Silver **Note:** Countermark on Mexico City KM#91.

Date	Mintage	G4	VG8	F12	VF20	XF40
1808 TH	—	90.00	150	210	325	—

KM# A272.3 2 REALES
Silver **Note:** Countermark on Mexico City KM#92.

Date	Mintage	G4	VG8	F12	VF20	XF40
1809 TH	—	90.00	150	210	325	—

KM# A272.4 2 REALES
Silver **Note:** Countermark on Zacatlian KM#252.

Date	Mintage	G4	VG8	F12	VF20	XF40
1813	—	180	240	425	600	—

KM# 273.1 4 REALES
Silver **Note:** Countermark on Mexico City KM#97.2.

Date	Mintage	G4	VG8	F12	VF20	XF40
1782 FF	—	100	180	240	350	—

KM# 273.2 4 REALES
Silver **Note:** Countermark on Mexico City KM#100.

Date	Mintage	G4	VG8	F12	VF20	XF40
1799 FM	—	100	180	240	350	—

KM# 274.1 8 REALES
Silver **Note:** Countermark on Lima 8 Reales, C#101.

Date	Mintage	G4	VG8	F12	VF20	XF40
1811 JP	—	240	270	300	425	—

KM# 274.2 8 REALES
Silver **Note:** Countermark on Mexico City KM#110.

Date	Mintage	G4	VG8	F12	VF20	XF40
1809 TH	—	150	180	270	450	—
1810 HJ	—	150	180	270	450	—
1811 HJ	—	150	180	270	450	—

VILLA / GRAN

(Julian Villagran)

KM# 298 2 REALES
Cast Silver **Note:** Countermark on cast Mexico City KM#91.

Date	Mintage	G4	VG8	F12	VF20	XF40
1799 FM	—	180	240	300	425	—
1802 FT	—	180	240	300	425	—

KM# 275 8 REALES
Cast Silver **Note:** Countermark on cast Mexico City KM#109.

Date	Mintage	G4	VG8	F12	VF20	XF40
1796 FM	—	240	300	425	600	—
1806 TH	—	240	300	425	600	—

ZMY

KM# 286 8 REALES
Silver **Note:** Countermark on Zacatecas KM#191.

Date	Mintage	G4	VG8	F12	VF20	XF40
1812	—	120	180	240	425	—

MULTIPLE COUNTERMARKS

Many combinations of Royalist and Insurgent countermarks are usually found on the cast copies produced by Chihuahua and Mexico City and on the other crude provisional issues of this period. Struck Mexico City coins were used to make molds for casting necessity issues and countermarked afterwards to show issuing authority. Some were marked again by either both or separate opposing friendly forces to authorize circulation in their areas of occupation. Some countermarks are only obtainable with companion markings.

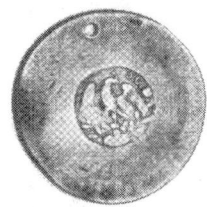 

KM# 289 2 REALES
Silver **Note:** Countermark on Mexico City KM#91.

Date	Mintage	G4	VG8	F12	VF20	XF40
ND (1811)	—	—	—	—	—	—

KM# 295 2 REALES
Silver **Note:** Countermark on Mexico City KM#91.

Date	Mintage	G4	VG8	F12	VF20	XF40
ND (1811)	—	180	300	550	—	—

KM# 296 2 REALES
Silver **Note:** Countermark on cast Mexico City KM#110.

Date	Mintage	G4	VG8	F12	VF20	XF40
1809 TH	—	—	—	—	—	—

KM# A286 2 REALES
Silver **Note:** Countermark on Zacatecas KM#186.

Date	Mintage	G4	VG8	F12	VF20	XF40
1811	—	90.00	150	210	325	—

KM# B286 2 REALES
Silver **Note:** Countermark on Zacatecas KM#186.

Date	Mintage	G4	VG8	F12	VF20	XF40
1810	—	90.00	150	210	325	—
1811	—	90.00	150	210	325	—

WAR OF INDEPENDENCE

KM# 285.2   8 REALES
Silver **Note:** Countermark on cast Mexico City KM#110.

Date	Mintage	G4	VG8	F12	VF20	XF40
1810 HJ	—	42.00	55.00	70.00	180	—
1811 HJ	—	42.00	55.00	70.00	180	—

KM# C286   8 REALES
Silver

Date	Mintage	G4	VG8	F12	VF20	XF40
1809 HJ	—	60.00	90.00	150	400	—

KM# A298   8 REALES
Silver

Date	Mintage	G4	VG8	F12	VF20	XF40
ND (1810)	—	42.00	60.00	90.00	240	—

KM# A297   8 REALES
Silver **Note:** Countermark on Zacatecas KM#189.

Date	Mintage	G4	VG8	F12	VF20	XF40
ND (1811)	—	210	300	425	—	—

KM# 297   8 REALES
Silver **Note:** Countermark on Mexico City KM#109.

Date	Mintage	G4	VG8	F12	VF20	XF40
1805 TH	—	55.00	90.00	175	350	—

KM# 281   8 REALES
Silver **Note:** Countermark on cast Mexico City KM#110.

Date	Mintage	G4	VG8	F12	VF20	XF40
1809 HJ	—	55.00	80.00	160	350	—

KM# 288.2   8 REALES
Silver **Note:** Countermark on Zacatecas KM#190. Prev. KM#288.

Date	Mintage	G4	VG8	F12	VF20	XF40
1811	—	—	—	—	—	—

KM# 290.2   8 REALES
Silver **Note:** Countermark on Zacatecas KM#190. Prev. KM#290.

Date	Mintage	G4	VG8	F12	VF20	XF40
1811	—	125	220	350	475	—

KM# 291   8 REALES
Silver   **Note:** Countermark on Mexico City KM#110.

Date	Mintage	G4	VG8	F12	VF20	XF40
1810 HJ	—	105	190	325	575	—

KM# 282   8 REALES
Silver   **Note:** Countermark on cast Mexico City KM#109.

Date	Mintage	G4	VG8	F12	VF20	XF40
1792 FM	—	—	—	—	—	—

KM# 283   8 REALES
Silver   **Note:** Countermark on cast Mexico City KM#109.

Date	Mintage	G4	VG8	F12	VF20	XF40
1806 TH	—	—	—	—	—	—

KM# 285.1   8 REALES
Silver   **Note:** Countermark on struck Mexico City KM#110.

Date	Mintage	G4	VG8	F12	VF20	XF40
1809 TH	—	55.00	80.00	170	375	—

KM# 285.3   8 REALES
Silver   **Note:** Countermark on cast Mexico City KM#111.

Date	Mintage	G4	VG8	F12	VF20	XF40
1811 HJ	—	95.00	150	220	450	—

KM# A290   8 REALES
Silver   **Note:** Countermark on Zacatecas KM#190.

Date	Mintage	G4	VG8	F12	VF20	XF40
1811	—	125	220	350	600	—

KM# 294   8 REALES
Silver   **Note:** Countermark on cast Mexico City KM#110.

Date	Mintage	G4	VG8	F12	VF20	XF40
ND HJ	—	55.00	95.00	170	375	—

KM# 280.1   8 REALES
Silver   **Note:** Countermark on Zacatecas KM#189.

Date	Mintage	G4	VG8	F12	VF20	XF40
1811	—	—	—	—	—	—

KM# 288.1   8 REALES
Silver   **Note:** Countermark on Zacatecas KM#189.

Date	Mintage	G4	VG8	F12	VF20	XF40
1811	—	—	—	—	—	—

KM# 290.1   8 REALES
Silver   **Note:** Countermark on Zacatecas KM#189.

Date	Mintage	G4	VG8	F12	VF20	XF40
1811	—	125	220	350	600	—

KM# 284   8 REALES
Silver   **Note:** Countermark on cast Mexico City KM#109.

Date	Mintage	G4	VG8	F12	VF20	XF40
1806 TH	—	43.75	65.00	125	280	—
1807 TH	—	43.75	65.00	125	280	—

KM# 280.2   8 REALES
Silver   **Note:** Countermark on Zacatecas KM#190.

Date	Mintage	G4	VG8	F12	VF20	XF40
1811	—	—	—	—	—	—

KM# 287   8 REALES
Silver   **Note:** Countermark on Valladolid KM#178.

Date	Mintage	G4	VG8	F12	VF20	XF40
1813	—	—	—	—	—	—

EMPIRE OF ITURBIDE
MILLED COINAGE

KM# 299   1/8 REAL
Copper, **Ruler:** Augustin I Iturbide **Obv.** Crowned shield within sprays **Rev:** Inscription, date **Rev. Inscription:** DE LA PROVINCIA DE NUEVA VISCAYA **Mint:** Durango

Date	Mintage	G4	VG8	F12	VF20	XF40
1821D	—	22.50	50.00	150	—	
1822D	—	7.50	13.50	28.50	60.00	—
1823D	—	9.00	13.50	26.50	55.00	—

KM# 300   1/4 REAL
Copper, **Ruler:** Augustin I Iturbide **Obv.** Crowned shield within sprays **Rev:** Inscription, date **Rev. Inscription:** DE LA PROVINCIA DE NUEVA VISCAYA **Mint:** Durango

Date	Mintage	G4	VG8	F12	VF20	XF40
1822D	—	160	275	400	550	—

KM# 301   1/2 REAL
0.903 Silver, **Ruler:** Augustin I Iturbide **Obv.** Head right **Rev:** Crowned eagle **Obv. Legend:** AUGUSTINUS DEI... **Rev. Legend:** I.M.E.X.I... **Mint:** Mexico City

Date	Mintage	F12	VF20	XF40	MS60	MS63
1822Mo JM	—	22.50	55.00	110	375	700
1823Mo JM	—	17.00	42.00	85.00	325	—

KM# 302   REAL
0.903 Silver, **Ruler:** Augustin I Iturbide **Obv.** Head right **Rev:** Crowned eagle **Obv. Legend:** AUGUSTINUS DEI... **Rev. Legend:** MEX.I.IMPERATOR... **Mint:** Mexico City

Date	Mintage	VG8	F12	VF20	XF40	MS60
1822 Mo JM	—	100	175	350	550	1,150

KM# 303   2 REALES
6.77 g., 0.903 Silver, 0.20 oz. ASW **Ruler:** Augustin I

Iturbide **Obv.** Head right **Rev:** Crowned eagle **Obv. Legend:** AUGUSTINUS DEI... **Rev. Legend:** MEX • I • IMPERATOR... **Mint:** Mexico City

Date	Mintage	F12	VF20	XF40	MS60	MS63
1822Mo JM	—	60.00	120	350	1,000	—
1823Mo JM	—	40.00	80.00	250	850	1,600

KM# 304   8 REALES
27.07 g., 0.903 Silver, 0.78 oz. ASW **Ruler:** Augustin I Iturbide **Obv.** Head right **Rev:** Crowned eagle **Obv. Legend:** AUGUST.... **Rev. Legend:** ...MEX • I • IMPERATOR... **Mint:** Mexico City

Date	Mintage	F12	VF20	XF40	MS60	MS63
1822Mo JM	—	75.00	150	375	1,300	—
1822Mo JM Proof, 3 known	—	—	—	—	—	—

Note: Ponterio & Associates Sale #86, 04-97, choice AU Proof realized $12,650

KM# 305   8 REALES
0.903 Silver, **Ruler:** Augustin I Iturbide **Obv.** Bust similar to 8 Escudos, KM#131 **Rev:** Crowned eagle **Mint:** Mexico City

Date	Mintage	F12	VF20	XF40	MS60	MS63
1822Mo JM Rare	—	—	—	—	—	—

KM# 306.1   8 REALES
0.903 Silver, **Ruler:** Augustin I Iturbide **Obv.** Head right **Rev:** Crowned eagle, 8 R.J.M. at upper left of eagle **Obv. Legend:** AUGUST... **Rev. Legend:** MEX • I • IMPERATOR... **Mint:** Mexico City **Note:** Type I.

Date	Mintage	F12	VF20	XF40	MS60	MS63
1822Mo JM	—	100	200	475	1,800	—

KM# 306.2 8 REALES

0.903 Silver, **Ruler:** Augustin I Iturbide **Obv.** Head right **Rev:** Cross on crown **Mint:** Mexico City **Note:** Type I.

Date	Mintage	F12	VF20	XF40	MS60	MS63
1822Mo JM	—	650	1,100	—	—	—

KM# 307 8 REALES

0.903 Silver, **Ruler:** Augustin I Iturbide **Obv.** Head right **Rev:** Crowned eagle **Mint:** Mexico City **Note:** Type II.

Date	Mintage	F12	VF20	XF40	MS60	MS63
1822Mo JM	—	150	350	850	3,750	—

KM# 308 8 REALES

0.903 Silver, **Ruler:** Augustin I Iturbide **Obv.** Head right, continuous legend with long smooth truncation **Rev:** Crowned eagle **Obv. Legend:** AUGUSTINUS DEI... **Mint:** Mexico City **Note:** Type III.

Date	Mintage	F12	VF20	XF40	MS60	MS63
1822Mo JM	—	175	500	1,150	3,750	—

Note: Variety with long, straight truncation is valued at $5,000 in uncirculated condition

KM# 309 8 REALES

0.903 Silver, **Ruler:** Augustin I Iturbide **Obv.** Head right **Rev:** Crowned eagle **Obv. Legend:** AUGUSTINUS DEI... **Rev. Legend:** MEX • I • IMPERATOR... **Mint:** Mexico City **Note:** Type IV.

Date	Mintage	F12	VF20	XF40	MS60	MS63
1822Mo JM	—	50.00	120	300	1,300	—

KM# 310 8 REALES

0.903 Silver, **Ruler:** Augustin I Iturbide **Obv.** Head right,

continuous legend with short irregular truncation **Rev:** Crowned eagle, 8 R.J.M. below eagle **Obv. Legend:** AUGUSTINUS DEI... **Rev. Legend:** MEX • I • IMPERATOR... **Mint:** Mexico City **Note:** Type V.

Date	Mintage	F12	VF20	XF40	MS60	MS63
1822Mo JM	—	50.00	120	300	1,500	—
1823Mo JM	—	50.00	120	300	1,500	—

KM# 311 8 REALES

0.903 Silver, **Ruler:** Augustin I Iturbide **Obv.** Head right, long truncation **Rev:** Crowned eagle **Mint:** Mexico City **Note:** Type VI.

Date	Mintage	F12	VF20	XF40	MS60	MS63
1822Mo JM Rare	—	—	—	—	—	—

KM# 312 4 SCUDOS

13.53 g., 0.875 Gold, 0.38 oz. AGW **Ruler:** Augustin I Iturbide **Obv.** Head right **Rev:** Crowned eagle within ornate shield **Obv. Legend:** AUGUSTINUS DEI... **Rev. Legend:** CONSTITUT.4.S.I.M... **Mint:** Mexico City

Date	Mintage	F12	VF20	XF40	MS60	MS63
1823Mo JM	—	1,350	2,750	6,250	12,000	—

KM# 313.1 8 SCUDOS

27.07 g., 0.875 Gold, 0.76 oz. AGW **Ruler:** Augustin I Iturbide **Obv.** Head right **Rev:** Crowned eagle **Obv. Legend:** AUGUSTINUS . DEI... **Rev. Legend:** CONSTITUT.8.S.I.M... **Mint:** Mexico City

Date	Mintage	F12	VF20	XF40	MS60	MS63
1822Mo JM	—	1,500	3,500	6,500	12,000	15,000

Note: American Numismatic Rarities Eliasberg sale 4-05, MS-62 realized $20,700. Superior Casterline sale 5-89 choice AU realized $11,000

KM# 313.2 8 SCUDOS

0.875 Gold, AGW **Ruler:** Augustin I Iturbide **Obv.** Head

right, error in legend **Rev:** Crowned eagle **Obv. Legend:**
AUGSTINUS • DEI... **Rev. Legend:** CONSTITUT • 8 • S • I •
M... **Mint:** Mexico City

Date	Mintage	F12	VF20	XF40	MS60	MS63
1822Mo JM	—	1,350	3,650	6,750	12,500	16,000

KM# 314 8 SCUDOS
0.875 Gold, AGW **Ruler:** Augustin I Iturbide **Obv.** Head
right **Rev:** Crowned eagle within ornate shield **Obv. Legend:**
AUGUSTINUS DEI... **Rev. Legend:** CONSTITUT • 8 • S • I •
M... **Mint:** Mexico City

Date	Mintage	F12	VF20	XF40	MS60	MS63
1823Mo JM	—	1,300	2,700	6,000	11,000	—

REPUBLIC
FIRST

MINT MARKS
A, AS - Alamos
CE - Real de Catorce
CA,CH - Chihuahua
C, Cn, Gn(error) - Culiacan
D, Do - Durango
EoMo - Estado de Mexico
Ga - Guadalajara
GC - Guadalupe y Calvo
G, Go - Guanajuato
H, Ho - Hermosillo
M, Mo - Mexico City
O, OA - Oaxaca
SLP, PI, P, I/P - San Luis Potosi
Z, Zs – Zacatecas

ASSAYERS' INITIALS

ALAMOS MINT

PG	1862-68	Pascual Gaxiola
DL, L	1866-79	Domingo Larraguibel
AM	1872-74	Antonio Moreno
ML, L	1878-95	Manuel Larraguibel

REAL DE CATORCE MINT

ML	1863	Mariano Cristobal Ramirez

CHIHUAHUA MINT

MR	1831-34	Mariano Cristobal Ramirez
AM	1833-39	Jose Antonio Mucharraz
MJ	1832	Jose Mariano Jimenez
RG	1839-56	Rodrigo Garcia
JC	1856-65	Joaquin Campa
BA	1858	Bruno Arriada
FP	1866	Francisco Potts
JC	1866-1868	Jose Maria Gomez del Campo
MM, M	1868-95	Manuel Merino
AV	1873-80	Antonio Valero
EA	1877	Eduardo Avila
JM	1877	Jacobo Mucharraz
GR	1877	Guadalupe Rocha
MG	1880-82	Manuel Gameros

CULIACAN MINT

CE	1846-70	Clemente Espinosa de los Monteros
C	1870	???
PV	1860-61	Pablo Viruega
MP, P	1871-76	Manuel Onofre Parodi
GP	1876	Celso Gaxiola & Manuel Onofre Parodi
CG, G	1876-78	Celso Gaxiola
JD, D	1878-82	Juan Dominguez
AM, M	1882-1899	Antonio Moreno
F	1870	Fernando Ferrari
JQ, Q	1899-1903	Jesus S. Quiroz

DURANGO MINT

RL	1825-1832	???
RM	1830-48	Ramon Mascarenas
OMC	1840	Octavio Martinez de Castro
CM	1848-76	Clemente Moron
JMR	1849-52	Jose Maria Ramirez
CP, P	1853-64, 1867-73	Carlos Leon de la Pena
LT	1864-65	???
JMP, P	1877	Carlos Miguel de la Palma
PE, E	1878	Pedro Espejo
TB, B	1878-80	Trinidad Barrera
JP	1880-94	J. Miguel Palma
MC, C,	1882-90	Manuel M. Canseco or Melchor Calderon
JB	1885	Jocobo Blanco
ND, D	1892-95	Norberto Dominguez

ESTADO DE MEXICO MINT

L	1828-30	Luis Valazquez de la Cadena
F	1828-30	Francisco Parodi

GUADALAJARA MINT

FS	1818-35	Francisco Suarez
JM	1830-32	???
JG	1836-39, 1842-67	Juan de Dios Guzman
MC	1839-46	Manuel Cueras
JM	1867-69	Jesus P. Manzano
IC, C	1869-77	Ignacio Canizo y Soto
MC	1874-75	Manuel Contreras
JA, A	1877-81	Julio Arancivia
FS, S	1880-82	Fernando Sayago
TB, B	1883-84	Trinidad Barrera
AH, H	1884-85	Antonio Hernandez y Prado
JS, S	1885-95	Jose S. Schiafino

GUADALUPE Y CALVO MINT

MP	1844-52	Manuel Onofre Parodi

GUANAJUATO MINT

JJ	1825-26	Jose Mariano Jimenez
MJ, MR, JM, PG, PJ, PF		???
PM	1841-48, 1853-61	Patrick Murphy
YF	1862-68	Yldefonso Flores
YE	1862-63	Ynocencio Espinoza
FR	1870-78	Faustino Ramirez
SB, RR		???
RS	1891-1900	Rosendo Sandoval

HERMOSILLO MINT

PP	1835-36	Pedro Peimbert
FM	1871-76	Florencio Monteverde
MP	1866	Manuel Onofre Parodi
PR	1866-75	Pablo Rubio
R	1874-75	Pablo Rubio

GR	1877	Guadalupe Rocha
AF, F	1876-77	Alejandro Fourcade
JA, A	1877-83	Jesus Acosta
FM, M	1883-86	Fernando Mendez
FG, G	1886-95	Fausto Gaxiola

MEXICO CITY MINT

Because of the great number of assayers for this mint (Mexico City is a much larger mint than any of the others) there is much confusion as to which initial stands for which assayer at any one time. Therefore we feel that it would be of no value to list the assayers.

OAXACA MINT

AE	1859-91	Agustin Endner
E	1889-90	Agustin Endner
FR	1861-64	Francisco de la Rosa
EN	1890	Eduardo Navarro Luna
N	1890	Eduardo Navarro Luna

POTOSI MINT

JS	1827-42	Juan Sanabria
AM	1838, 1843-49	Jose Antonio Mucharraz
PS	1842-43, 1848-49, 1857-61, 1867-70	Pompaso Sanabria
S	1869-70	Pomposo Sanabria
MC	1849-59	Mariano Catano
RO	1859-65	Romualdo Obregon
MH, H	1870-85	Manuel Herrera Razo
O	1870-73	Juan R. Ochoa
CA, G	1867-70	Carlos Aguirre Gomez
BE, E	1879-81	Blas Escontria
LC, C	1885-86	Luis Cuevas
MR, R	1886-93	Mariano Reyes

ZACATECAS MINT

A	1825-29	Adalco
Z	1825-26	Mariano Zaldivar
V	1824-31	Jose Mariano Vela
O	1829-67	Manuel Ochoa
M	1831-67	Manuel Miner
VL	1860-66	Vicente Larranaga
JS	1867-68, 1876-86	J.S. de Santa Ana
YH	1868-74	Ygnacio Hierro
JA	1874-76	Juan H. Acuna
FZ	18861905	Francisco de P. Zarate

DIE VARIETIES

Similar basic designs were utilized by all the Mexican mints, but many variations are noticeable, particularly in the eagle, cactus and sprays.

1835 Durango, 8 Escudos
Illustration enlarged.
A large winged eagle was portrayed on the earlier coinage of the new republic.

1849 Mexico City, 8 Escudos
Illustration enlarged.
The later eagle featured undersized wings.

1844 Durango, 8 Escudos
Illustration enlarged.
The early renditions of the hand held Liberty cap over open book were massive in the gold escudo series.

1864 Durango, 8 Escudos
Illustration enlarged.
A finer, more petite style was adopted later on in the gold escudo series.

PROFILE EAGLE COINAGE

The first coins of the Republic were of the distinctive Profile Eagle style, sometimes called the "Hooked Eagle". They were struck in the Mexico City in 1823 in denominations of eight reales and eight escudos. In 1824, they were produced at the Durango and Guanajuato mints in addition to Mexico City. Denominations included the one half, one, two and eight reales. no gold escudos of this design were struck n 1824. In 1825, only the eight reales were struck briefly at the Guanajuato mint.

Note: For a more extensive examination of Profile Eagle Coinage, please refer to *Hookneck - El Aguila de Perfil* by Clyde Hubbard and David O Harrow.

KM# 369   1/2 REAL

1.69 g., 0.903 Silver, 0.05 oz. ASW **Obv.** Full breast Profile eagle **Rev:** Cap and rays **Mint:** Mexico City **Note:** Die varieties exist.

Date	Mintage	F12	VF20	XF40	MS60	MS63
1824Mo JM	—	45.00	75.00	175	750	—

KM# 371.1   REAL

3.38 g., 0.903 Silver, 0.10 oz. ASW **Obv.** Thin Profile eagle **Rev:** Superscript S reversed **Mint:** Durango

Date	Mintage	F12	VF20	XF40	MS60	MS63
1824Do RL	—	5,500	9,500	13,000	—	—

KM# 371.2   REAL

3.38 g., 0.903 Silver, 0.10 oz. ASW **Obv.** Thin Profile eagle **Rev:** Superscript S normal **Mint:** Durango

Date	Mintage	F12	VF20	XF40	MS60
1824Do RL 3 known	—	—	—	—	—

Mint mark: Do

KM# 373.1   2 REALES

6.76 g., 0.903 Silver, 0.19 oz. ASW **Obv.** Profile eagle, snake in beak **Rev:** Radiant cap **Obv. Legend:** REPUBLICA • MEXICANA **Mint:** Durango **Note:** Die varieties exist.

Date	Mintage	F12	VF20	XF40	MS60	MS63
1824Do RL	—	60.00	135	850	2,200	—

KM# 373.2   2 REALES

6.76 g., 0.903 Silver, 0.19 oz. ASW **Obv.** Profile eagle, snake in beak **Rev:** Radiant cap **Obv. Legend:** Thin profile **Rev. Legend:** Type 1, dot before 2R in legend **Mint:** Durango

Date	Mintage	F12	VF20	XF40	MS60	MS63
1824D RL	—	120	250	1,000	3,000	—

KM# 373.3   2 REALES

6.76 g., 0.903 Silver, 0.19 oz. ASW **Obv.** Profile eagle, snake in beak **Rev:** Radiant cap **Obv. Legend:** Thin profile **Rev. Legend:** Type II, no dot before 2R in legend **Mint:** Durango

Date	Mintage	F12	VF20	XF40	MS60	MS63
1824D RL	—	120	250	1,000	3,000	—

KM# 373.4   2 REALES

6.76 g., 0.903 Silver, 0.19 oz. ASW **Obv.** Profile eagle, snake in beak **Rev:** Radiant cap **Obv. Legend:** REPUBLICA • MEXICANA **Mint:** Mexico City **Note:** Varieties exist.

Date	Mintage	F12	VF20	XF40	MS60	MS63
1824Mo JM	—	40.00	90.00	450	2,000	—

Note: No coins are known with visible feather details on the eagle's breast

KM# A376.1   8 REALES

27.07 g., 0.903 Silver, 0.78 oz. ASW **Obv.** Full breast profile eagle, snake in beak **Rev:** Radiant cap **Obv. Legend:** REPUBLICA MEXICANA. **Mint:** Guanajuato

Date	Mintage	F12	VF20	XF40	MS60	MS63
1824 Go JM	—	250	400	1,100	3,500	—
1825/4Go JJ	—	600	1,200	2,750	7,000	—
1825Go JJ	—	500	750	1,400	5,500	—

KM# A376.2 8 REALES
27.07 g., 0.903 Silver, 0.78 oz. ASW **Obv.** Full breast profile eagle, snake in beak **Rev:** Radiant cap **Obv. Legend:** REPUBLICA MEXICANA **Edge:** Standard or Republic **Mint:** Mexico City

Date	Mintage	F12	VF20	XF40	MS60	MS63
1823Mo JM	—	150	300	800	4,500	—
1824Mo JM	—	125	250	700	4,000	—

KM# A376.3 8 REALES
27.07 g., 0.903 Silver, 0.78 oz. ASW **Obv.** Full breast profile eagle, snake in beak **Rev:** Radiant cap **Edge:** Colonial or circle and rectangle **Mint:** Mexico City

Date	Mintage	F12	VF20	XF40	MS60	MS63
1823Mo JM Rare	—	—	—	—	—	—

The Round-Topped Three

KM# A376.4 8 REALES
27.07 g., 0.903 Silver, 0.78 oz. ASW **Obv.** Full breast profile eagle, snake in beak **Rev:** Radiant cap, round topped three **Edge:** Standard or Republic **Mint:** Mexico City

Date	Mintage	F12	VF20	XF40	MS60	MS63
1823Mo JM	—	2,000	4,000	6,000	8,000	—

Note: Many die varieties exist; Illustrations of one of the die differences is the size of the snake loop at the eagle's beak; This difference is not apparent except on the 1824 Mo 8 Reales

KM# A376.5 8 REALES
27.07 g., 0.903 Silver, 0.78 oz. ASW **Obv.** Full breast profile eagle, snake in beak, REPULICA (error) **Rev:** Radiant cap **Mint:** Mexico City

Date	Mintage	F12	VF20	XF40	MS60	MS63
1824 Mo JM	—	6,000	9,000	11,000	—	—

Note: Legible Libertads on the cap are not as prevalent on the Mexico City 8 Reales as on the Durango 8 Reales; They are much more numerous than on the Guanajuato 8 Reales

Typical Submissive
Snake Obverse

Typical Folded
Snake Obverse

NOTE: Legible Libertads on the Cap are common on Durango eight reales.

Med. Libertad　　**Small Libertad**　　**Large Libertad**
Cap Reverse　　　**Cap Reverse**　　　**Cap Reverse**

NOTE: The three styles of obverses and the three styles of reverses were combined to make six distinct varieties of coins.

KM# 376.1 8 REALES
27.07 g., 0.903 Silver, 0.78 oz. ASW **Obv.** Thin profile

eagle, defiant snake **Rev:** Radiant cap, medium Libertad
Mint: Durango

Date	Mintage	F12	VF20	XF40	MS60	MS63
1824Do RL	—	500	1,200	5,400	10,500	—

Note: Five die varieties are known, all are rare. Ira &
Larry Goldberg Millennia Sale 5-08, MS-64 realized $25,000.

KM# 376.2 8 REALES
27.07 g., 0.903 Silver, 0.78 oz. ASW **Obv.** Thin profile
eagle, defiant snake **Rev:** Radiant cap, small Libertad **Obv.
Legend:** REPUBLICA MEXICANA **Mint:** Durango

Date	Mintage	F12	VF20	XF40	MS60	MS63
1824Do RL	—	300	500	1,900	5,300	—

Note: Eleven die varieties are known, some are rare

KM# 376.3 8 REALES
27.07 g., 0.903 Silver, 0.78 oz. ASW **Obv.** Thin profile
eagle, submissive snake **Rev:** Radiant cap, small Libertad
Obv. Legend: REPUBLICA • MEXICANA **Mint:** Durango

Date	Mintage	F12	VF20	XF40	MS60	MS63
1824Do RL	—	200	400	1,500	4,150	—

Note: Seven die varieties are known, some are rare

KM# 376.4 8 REALES
27.07 g., 0.903 Silver, 0.78 oz. ASW **Obv.** Thin profile
eagle, submissive snake **Rev:** Radiant cap, large Libertad
Mint: Durango

Date	Mintage	F12	VF20	XF40	MS60	MS63
1824Do RL	—	200	400	1,500	4,150	—

Note: Twelve die varieties known, some are rare

KM# 376.5 8 REALES
27.07 g., 0.903 Silver, 0.78 oz. ASW **Obv.** Thin profile
eagle, folded snake **Rev:** Radiant cap, small Libertad **Mint:**
Durango

Date	Mintage	F12	VF20	XF40	MS60	MS63
1824Do RL	—	200	400	1,450	3,750	—

Note: Only one die variety is known

KM# 376.6 8 REALES
27.07 g., 0.903 Silver, 0.78 oz. ASW **Obv.** Thin profile
eagle, folded snake **Rev:** Radiant cap, large Libertad **Mint:**
Durango

Date	Mintage	F12	VF20	XF40	MS60	MS63
1824Do RL	—	200	450	1,800	4,500	—

Note: Eleven die varieties are known, some are rare

Type I Obverse/Reverse

NOTE: The cap on the reverse of the curved tail Type I
points to the "A" of LIBERTAD.

KM# 382.1 8 ESCUDOS
27.07 g., 0.875 Gold, 0.76 oz. AGW **Obv.** Profile eagle,
snake's tail curved **Rev:** Open book, hand holding stick
with cap, cap points to "A" of LIBERTAD **Obv. Legend:**
REPUBLICA MEXICANA **Rev. Legend:** LIBERTAD EN...
Mint: Mexico City

Date	Mintage	F12	VF20	XF40	MS60	MS63
1823Mo JM	—	7,000	10,000	20,000	35,000	—

Note: American Numismatic Rarities Eliasberg sale
4-05, MS-61 realized $55,200.

Type II Obverse/Reverse

NOTE: The cap on the reverse of the looped tail Type II
points to the "T" of LIBERTAD.

KM# 382.2 8 ESCUDOS
27.07 g., 0.875 Gold, 0.76 oz. AGW **Obv.** Profile eagle,
snake's tail looped **Rev:** Open book, hand holding stick
with cap, cap points to "T" of LIBERTAD **Obv. Legend:**
REPUBLICA MEXICANA **Rev. Legend:** LIBERTAD EN...
Mint: Mexico City

Date	Mintage	F12	VF20	XF40	MS60	MS63
1823Mo JM	—	6,000	9,000	18,000	35,000	—

Note: The quality of the strikes of Type I coins is almost
always superior to that of the Type II; Details of the
eagle feathers, cactus and lettering on the open
book are better on most Type I coins but the Type
II coins are scarcer; Type I coins outnumber Type
II coins by about two to one

STATE COINAGE

KM# 316 1/16 REAL (MEDIO OCTAVO)
4.75 g., Copper 21mm. **Obv.** Bow, quiver and flag **Rev:** Seated figure, left, cap on pole **Obv. Legend:** DEPARTAMENTO DE JALISCO **Edge:** Oblique reeding **Mint:** Guadalajara

Date	Mintage	G4	VG8	F12	VF20	XF40
1860	—	5.00	12.00	27.50	85.00	—

KM# 317 1/16 REAL (MEDIO OCTAVO)
4.75 g., Copper 21mm. **Obv. Legend:** ESTADO LIBRE DE JALISCO **Edge:** Oblique reeding **Mint:** Guadalajara

Date	Mintage	G4	VG8	F12	VF20	XF40
1861	—	4.00	9.00	20.00	48.75	—

KM# 320 1/8 REAL (OCTAVO REAL)
Copper **Obv.** Facing eagle, snake in beak, value at lower left **Rev:** Radiant Libertad above date within wreath **Rev. Legend:** LIBERTAD **Edge:** Oblique reeding **Mint:** Durango **Note:** Size varies 17-18mm. Weight varies 2.5-4 g. These pieces were frequently struck over 1/8 Real, dated 1821-23 of Nueva Vizcaya. All known examples struck over these coins are believed to be contemporary counterfeits.

Date	Mintage	G4	VG8	F12	VF20	XF40
1824D	—	8.00	19.00	55.00	130	—
1828D	—	225	375	600	1,500	—

KM# 338 1/8 REAL (OCTAVO REAL)
4.00 g., Brass 21mm. **Obv.** Monument **Rev:** Floating angel holding radiant cap **Obv. Legend:** ESTo LIBe FEDo DE ZACATECAS **Edge:** Oblique reeding **Mint:** Zacatecas

Date	Mintage	G4	VG8	F12	VF20
1825	—	5.00	8.00	18.00	37.50
1827	—	5.00	8.00	18.00	37.50
1827	—	18.00	30.00	60.00	150
Note: Inverted A for V in OCTAVO					
1827	—	22.50	37.50	75.00	180
Note: OCTAVA (error)					
1827 Inverted 1	—	18.00	30.00	60.00	150
1829 Rare	—	—	—	—	—
1830	—	4.00	8.00	12.00	30.00
1831	—	7.00	10.00	20.00	41.25
1832	—	4.00	8.00	12.00	30.00
1833	—	4.00	8.00	12.00	30.00
1835	—	5.00	9.00	15.00	37.50
1846	—	5.00	9.00	15.00	37.50
1851	—	55.00	105	175	325
1852	—	5.00	9.00	15.00	37.50
1858	—	4.00	8.00	12.00	30.00
1859	—	4.00	8.00	12.00	30.00
1862	—	4.00	8.00	12.00	30.00
1863 Reversed 6 in date	—	4.00	8.00	12.00	30.00

KM# 321 1/8 REAL (OCTAVO REAL)
3.30 g., Copper **Obv.** Child holding bow, right, small tree **Rev:** Radiant cap **Rev. Legend:** OCTo. DE. R. DE DO **Edge:** Oblique reeding **Mint:** Durango **Note:** Size varies 18-19mm.

Date	Mintage	G4	VG8	F12	VF20	XF40
1828D	—	11.00	27.50	60.00	175	—

KM# 329 1/8 REAL (OCTAVO REAL)
4.80 g., Copper 21mm. **Obv.** Bow, quiver and flag **Rev:** Seated figure, left, cap on pole **Obv. Legend:** ESTADO LIBRE DE JALISCO **Edge:** Oblique reeding **Mint:** Guadalajara

Date	Mintage	G4	VG8	F12	VF20	XF40
1828	—	5.00	8.00	12.00	33.75	—
1831	—	95.00	150	280	425	—
1832/28	—	7.00	10.00	17.00	41.25	—
1832	—	7.00	9.00	15.00	37.50	—
1833	—	5.00	8.00	14.00	35.25	—
1834	—	55.00	120	225	350	—

KM# 335 1/8 REAL (OCTAVO REAL)
Copper **Obv. Legend:** ESTADO DE OCCIDENTE **Edge:** Oblique reeding **Mint:** Alamos **Note:** Size varies: 17-18mm, weight varies: 2-3 g. The C before date on reverse may be a mint mark standing for Concepcion de Alamos.

Date	Mintage	G4	VG8	F12	VF20	XF40
1828 Reverse S	—	55.00	100	180	—	—
1829	—	45.00	90.00	165	—	—

KM# 326 1/8 REAL (OCTAVO REAL)
3.50 g., Copper 21mm. **Obv.** Seated figure **Rev:** Cap within center wreath of stylized rays, date below **Obv. Legend:** ESTADO LIBRE DE GUANAJUATO **Edge:** Ornamented with incuse dots **Mint:** Guanajuato

Date	Mintage	G4	VG8	F12	VF20	XF40
1829	—	5.00	8.00	15.00	39.75	—
1829	—	6.00	10.00	19.00	42.75	—
Note: Error with GUANJUATO						
1830	—	12.00	20.00	42.75	100	—

KM# 336 1/8 REAL (OCTAVO REAL)
Copper 21mm. **Obv.** Value above divides wreath, open book within **Rev:** Seated figure **Obv. Legend:** ESTADO LIBRE DE SAN LUIS POTOSI **Edge:** Oblique reeding **Mint:**

San Luis Potosi **Note:** Weight varies (1829-31) 4.5-5.5 g; (1859) 4-4.5 g.

Date	Mintage	G4	VG8	F12	VF20	XF40
1829	—	9.00	17.00	39.75	95.00	—
1830	—	13.00	22.50	45.00	105	—
1831	—	9.00	14.00	27.50	70.00	—
1859	—	8.00	12.00	25.00	70.00	—
1865/1	—	—	—	—	—	—

Note: Requires Confirmation

KM# 318 1/8 REAL (OCTAVO REAL)

3.54 g., Copper 20mm. **Obv. Legend:** ESTADO SOBERANO DE CHIHUAHUA **Edge:** Plain **Mint:** Chihuahua

Date	Mintage	G4	VG8	F12	VF20	XF40
1833	—	525	1,150	—	—	—
1834	—	525	1,150	—	—	—
1835/3	—	525	1,150	—	—	—

KM# 322 1/8 REAL (OCTAVO REAL)

3.50 g., Copper 20mm. **Obv.** Profile eagle, snake in beak **Rev:** Value and date within circle and wreath **Obv. Legend:** ESTADO DE DURANGO **Mint:** Durango

Date	Mintage	G4	VG8	F12	VF20	XF40
1833	—	525	—	—	—	—

KM# 339 1/8 REAL (OCTAVO REAL)

4.00 g., Copper 21mm. **Obv.** Monument **Rev:** Floating angel holding radiant cap **Obv. Legend:** DEPARTAMENTO DE ZACATECAS **Edge:** Oblique reeding **Mint:** Zacatecas

Date	Mintage	G4	VG8	F12	VF20	XF40
1836	—	8.00	13.00	27.50	60.00	—
1845	—	11.00	19.00	33.75	75.00	—
1846	—	13.00	15.00	30.00	70.00	—

KM# 323 1/8 REAL (OCTAVO REAL)

3.50 g., Copper **Obv.** Facing eagle, snake in beak **Rev:** Value and date within circle and wreath **Obv. Legend:** REPUBLICA MEXICANA **Mint:** Durango **Note:** Size varies: 19-23mm.

Date	Mintage	G4	VG8	F12	VF20	XF40
1842/33	—	19.00	33.75	65.00	175	—
1842	—	13.00	22.50	48.75	150	—

KM# 324 1/8 REAL (OCTAVO REAL)

Copper 19mm. **Obv.** Facing eagle, snake in beak **Rev:** Value within circle **Obv. Legend:** REPUBLICA MEXICANA **Rev. Legend:** DEPARTAMENTO DE DURANGO **Edge:** Ornamented with arc and dot pattern **Mint:** Durango **Note:** Weight varies: 3.5-3.8 g.

Date	Mintage	G4	VG8	F12	VF20	XF40
1845	—	33.75	85.00	175	375	—
1846 Rare	—	—	—	—	—	—
1847	—	5.00	11.00	27.50	55.00	—

KM# 325 1/8 REAL (OCTAVO REAL)

Copper 19mm. **Obv.** Facing eagle, snake in beak **Rev:** Value within circle **Obv. Legend:** REPUBLICA MEXICANA **Rev. Legend:** ESTADO DE DURANGO **Edge:** Ornamented with arc and dot pattern **Mint:** Durango **Note:** Weight varies: 3.5-3.8 g.

Date	Mintage	G4	VG8	F12	VF20	XF40
1851	—	5.00	12.00	19.00	50.00	—
1852/1	—	5.00	10.00	17.00	50.00	—
1852	—	5.00	8.00	12.00	45.00	—
1854	—	11.00	20.00	42.75	95.00	—

KM# 319 1/8 REAL (OCTAVO REAL)

3.54 g., Copper 20mm. **Obv.** Standing figure facing holding bow and arrow **Rev:** Date and value within wreath **Obv. Legend:** ESTADO DE CHIHUAHUA **Edge:** Plain **Mint:** Chihuahua

Date	Mintage	G4	VG8	F12	VF20	XF40
1855	—	8.00	13.00	37.50	115	—

KM# 327 1/8 REAL (OCTAVO REAL)

7.20 g., Brass 29mm. **Obv.** Facing eagle, snake in beak **Rev:** Oval arms within sprays below radiant cap **Obv. Legend:** ESTADO LIBRE DE GUANAJUATO **Edge:** Plain **Mint:** Guanajuato

Date	Mintage	G4	VG8	F12	VF20	XF40
1856	—	11.00	18.00	30.00	115	—

KM# 328 1/8 REAL (OCTAVO REAL)

Brass 25mm. **Obv.** Facing eagle, snake in beak **Rev:** Oval arms within sprays below radiant cap **Obv. Legend:** ESTADO LIBRE DE GUANAJUATO **Edge:** Plain **Mint:** Guanajuato **Note:** Weight varies: 7.1-7.2 g.

Date	Mintage	G4	VG8	F12	VF20	XF40
1856	—	6.00	11.00	19.00	55.00	—
1857	—	5.00	9.00	15.00	45.00	—

KM# 328a 1/8 REAL (OCTAVO REAL)
Copper 25mm. **Obv.** Facing eagle, snake in beak **Rev:** Oval arms within sprays below radiant cap **Obv. Legend:** ESTADO LIBRE DE GUANAJUATO **Edge:** Plain **Mint:** Guanajuato **Note:** Weight varies: 7.1-7.2 g.

Date	Mintage	G4	VG8	F12	VF20	XF40
1857	—	11.00	25.00	48.75	85.00	—

KM# 330 1/8 REAL (Octavo Real)
9.50 g., Copper 28mm. **Rev:** Seated figure, left, cap on pole **Obv. Legend:** ESTADO LIBRE DE JALISCO **Edge:** Oblique reeding **Mint:** Guadalajara

Date	Mintage	G4	VG8	F12	VF20	XF40
1856	—	5.00	9.00	14.00	27.50	—
1857	—	5.00	9.00	14.00	27.50	—
1858	—	5.00	9.00	14.00	27.50	—
1861	—	115	205	300	450	—
1862/1	—	6.00	11.00	15.00	33.75	—
1862	—	6.00	11.00	15.00	33.75	—

KM# 331 1/8 REAL (OCTAVO REAL)
9.50 g., Copper 28mm. **Obv.** Bow, quiver and flag **Obv. Legend:** DEPARTAMENTO DE JALISCO **Edge:** Oblique reeding **Mint:** Guadalajara

Date	Mintage	G4	VG8	F12	VF20	XF40
1858	—	6.00	11.00	20.00	42.75	—
1859	—	5.00	9.00	12.00	30.00	—
1860/59	—	5.00	9.00	14.00	33.75	—
1860	—	5.00	9.00	14.00	33.75	—
1862	—	6.00	12.00	27.50	55.00	—

KM# 337 1/8 REAL (OCTAVO REAL)
6.70 g., Copper 28mm. **Obv. Legend:** ESTO LIBE Y SOBO DE SONORA **Edge:** Reeded **Mint:** Hermosillo

Date	Mintage	G4	VG8	F12	VF20	XF40
1859 Rare	—	—	—	—	—	—

KM# 366 1/4 REAL (UN QUARTO/UNA QUARTILLA)
8.00 g., Brass **Obv.** Monument **Rev:** Floating angel with radiant cap on tip of arrow **Obv. Legend:** ESTO LIBE FEDO DE ZACATECAS **Edge:** Oblique reeding **Mint:** Zacatecas **Note:** Size varies: 28-29mm.

Date	Mintage	G4	VG8	F12	VF20	XF40
1824 Rare	—	—	—	—	—	—
1825	—	4.00	8.00	15.00	30.00	—
1826	—	115	195	325	500	—
1827/17	—	4.00	8.00	14.00	30.00	—
1829	—	4.00	8.00	14.00	30.00	—
1830	—	4.00	8.00	13.00	30.00	—
1831	—	60.00	130	210	325	—
1832	—	4.00	8.00	14.00	30.00	—
1833	—	4.00	8.00	14.00	30.00	—
1834 Rare	—	—	—	—	—	—
1835	—	4.00	8.00	14.00	30.00	—
1846	—	4.00	8.00	13.00	30.00	—
1847	—	4.00	8.00	13.00	30.00	—
1852	—	4.00	8.00	13.00	30.00	—
1853	—	4.00	8.00	13.00	30.00	—
1855	—	7.00	15.00	37.50	100	—
1858	—	4.00	8.00	13.00	30.00	—
1859	—	4.00	8.00	13.00	30.00	—
1860	—	115	190	300	475	—
1862/57	—	4.00	8.00	13.00	30.00	—
1862/59/7	—	12.00	27.50	55.00	115	—
1862	—	4.00	8.00	12.00	30.00	—
1863/2	—	4.00	8.00	12.00	30.00	—
1863	—	4.00	8.00	12.00	30.00	—
1864	—	6.00	17.00	37.50	90.00	—

KM# 351 1/4 REAL (UN QUARTO/UNA QUARTILLA)
7.00 g., Copper 27mm. **Obv.** Seated figure with head right **Rev:** Cap within radiant wreath **Obv. Legend:** ESTADO LIBRE DE GUANAJUATO **Edge:** Ornamented with incuse dots **Mint:** Guanajuato

Date	Mintage	G4	VG8	F12	VF20	XF40
1828	—	6.00	12.00	27.50	60.00	—
1828	—	6.00	14.00	30.00	65.00	—

Note: Error with GUANJUATO

Date	Mintage	G4	VG8	F12	VF20	XF40
1829	—	8.00	18.00	33.75	70.00	—

KM# 353 1/4 REAL (UN QUARTO/UNA QUARTILLA)
9.35 g., Copper 28mm. **Obv.** Oblique reeding **Rev:** Seated figure, left, cap on pole **Obv. Legend:** ESTADO LIBRE DE JALISCO **Mint:** Guadalajara

Date	Mintage	G4	VG8	F12	VF20	XF40
1828	—	6.00	11.00	22.50	55.00	—
1829/8	—	5.00	9.00	20.00	49.50	—
1829	—	5.00	9.00	20.00	49.50	—
1830/20	—	5.00	8.00	15.00	42.75	—
1830/29	—	5.00	8.00	15.00	42.75	—
1830	—	5.00	8.00	15.00	42.75	—
1831 Rare	—	—	—	—	—	—
1832/20	—	5.00	8.00	15.00	42.75	—
1832/28	—	5.00	8.00	15.00	42.75	—
1832	—	4.00	8.00	14.00	41.25	—

Date	Mintage	G4	VG8	F12	VF20	XF40
1833/2	—	5.00	8.00	14.00	41.25	—
1834	—	4.00	8.00	14.00	41.25	—
1835/3	—	5.00	8.00	14.00	41.25	—
1835	—	4.00	8.00	14.00	41.25	—
1836 Rare	—	—	—	—	—	—

KM# 359 1/4 REAL (UN QUARTO/UNA QUARTILLA)
Copper **Obv.** Value above divides wreath, open book within **Rev:** Seated figure with cap on tip of arrow **Obv. Legend:** ESTADO LIBRE DE SAN LUIS POTOSI **Rev. Legend:** MEXICO LIBRE **Edge:** Oblique reeding **Mint:** San Luis Potosi **Note:** Size varies: 25-31mm, weight varies: (1828-32) 9-10 g.; (1859-60) 8-9 g.

Date	Mintage	G4	VG8	F12	VF20
1828	—	3.00	6.00	14.00	27.50
1829	—	5.00	8.00	14.00	30.00
1830	—	3.00	6.00	12.00	25.00
1832	—	6.00	9.00	15.00	33.75
1859 Large LIBRE	—	4.00	6.00	12.00	27.50
1859 Small LIBRE	—	4.00	6.00	12.00	27.50
1860	—	4.00	6.00	12.00	27.50

KM# 364 1/4 REAL (UN QUARTO/UNA QUARTILLA)
Copper **Obv.** Arrow divides quivers **Rev:** Stylized radiant cap **Obv. Legend:** EST. D. SONORA UNA CUART **Edge:** Oblique reeding **Mint:** Hermosillo **Note:** Size varies: 21-22mm. Weight varies: 2.3-5.5 g.

Date	Mintage	G4	VG8	F12	VF20	XF40
1831 L.S. Rare	—	—	—	—	—	—
1832 L.S.	—	4.00	8.00	22.50	75.00	—
1833/2 L.S.	—	3.00	6.00	19.00	55.00	—
1833 L.S.	—	3.00	6.00	19.00	55.00	—
1834 L.S.	—	3.00	6.00	19.00	55.00	—
1835/3 L.S.	—	4.00	8.00	22.50	60.00	—
1835 L.S.	—	3.00	6.00	19.00	55.00	—
1836 L.S.	—	3.00	6.00	19.00	55.00	—

KM# 340 1/4 REAL (UN QUARTO/UNA QUARTILLA)
Copper 27mm. **Obv.** Child facing, holding bow and arrow **Rev:** Value and date within palm wreath **Obv. Legend:** ESTADO SOBERANO DE CHIHUAHUA **Edge:** Herringbone pattern **Mint:** Chihuahua

Date	Mintage	G4	VG8	F12	VF20	XF40
1833	—	11.00	25.00	55.00	130	—

Date	Mintage	G4	VG8	F12	VF20	XF40
1834	—	10.00	20.00	42.00	85.00	—
1835	—	8.00	15.00	33.00	75.00	—
1835 Plain edge	—	8.00	12.00	18.00	75.00	—

KM# 354 1/4 REAL (UN QUARTO/UNA QUARTILLA)
9.35 g., Copper 28mm. **Obv. Legend:** DEPARTAMENTO DE JALISCO **Edge:** Oblique reeding **Mint:** Guadalajara

Date	Mintage	G4	VG8	F12	VF20	XF40
1836	—	180	300	525	—	—

KM# 367 1/4 REAL (UN QUARTO/UNA QUARTILLA)
8.00 g., Brass **Obv.** Monument **Rev:** Floating angel with radiant cap on tip of arrow **Obv. Legend:** DEPARTAMENTO DE ZACATECAS **Edge:** Oblique reeding **Mint:** Zacatecas **Note:** Size varies: 28-29mm.

Date	Mintage	G4	VG8	F12	VF20	XF40
1836	—	6.00	13.00	20.00	37.50	—
1845 Rare	—	—	—	—	—	—
1846	—	5.00	10.00	14.00	30.00	—

KM# 345 1/4 REAL (UN QUARTO/UNA QUARTILLA)
7.00 g., Copper 27mm. **Obv.** Facing eagle, snake in beak **Rev:** Value and date within circle, DURANGO above in wreath **Obv. Legend:** REPUBLICA MEXICANA **Mint:** Durango

Date	Mintage	G4	VG8	F12	VF20	XF40
1845 Rare	—	—	—	—	—	—

KM# 341 1/4 REAL (UN QUARTO/UNA QUARTILLA)
7.08 g., Copper 27mm. **Obv.** Stylized figure facing, holding bow and arrow **Rev:** Value and date within designed wreath **Obv. Legend:** ESTADO LIBRE DE CHIHUAHUA **Edge:** Plain **Mint:** Chihuahua

Date	Mintage	G4	VG8	F12	VF20	XF40
1846	—	5.00	9.00	18.00	55.00	—
Note: With fraction bar						
1846	—	8.00	13.00	22.50	70.00	—
Note: Without fraction bar						

KM# 363 1/4 REAL (UN QUARTO/UNA QUARTILLA)
Copper 27mm. **Obv.** Head left within wreath **Rev:** Value and date within wreath **Obv. Legend:** ESTADO LIBRE Y SOBERANO DE SINALOA **Edge:** Reeded **Mint:** Culiacan

Date	Mintage	G4	VG8	F12	VF20	XF40
1847	—	5.00	8.00	18.00	35.25	—
1848	—	5.00	8.00	17.00	33.00	—
1859	—	5.00	7.00	11.00	25.00	—
1861	—	2.75	5.00	6.00	15.00	—
1862	—	2.75	5.00	6.00	17.00	—
1863	—	4.00	6.00	8.00	17.00	—
1864/3	—	4.00	6.00	8.00	17.00	—
1864	—	2.75	5.00	7.00	15.00	—
1865	—	5.00	8.00	13.00	27.50	—
1866/5	7,401,000	4.00	5.00	8.00	17.00	—
1866	Inc. above	2.75	5.00	6.00	15.00	—

KM# 363a 1/4 REAL (UN QUARTO/UNA QUARTILLA)
7.00 g., Brass 27mm. **Obv.** Head left within wreath **Rev:** Value and date within wreath **Obv. Legend:** ESTADO LIBRE Y SOBERANO DE SINALOA **Edge:** Reeded **Mint:** Culiacan

Date	Mintage	G4	VG8	F12	VF20	XF40
1847	—	8.00	15.00	27.50	60.00	—

KM# 342 1/4 REAL (UN QUARTO/UNA QUARTILLA)
7.08 g., Copper 27mm. **Obv.** Stylized figure facing, holding bow and arrow **Rev:** Value and date within designed wreath **Obv. Legend:** ESTADO DE CHIHUAHUA **Edge:** Plain **Mint:** Chihuahua

Date	Mintage	G4	VG8	F12	VF20	XF40
1855	—	4.00	9.00	20.00	60.00	—
1856	—	4.00	9.00	20.00	60.00	—

KM# 343 1/4 REAL (UN QUARTO/UNA QUARTILLA)
7.08 g., Copper 27mm. **Obv.** Stylized figure facing, holding bow and arrow **Rev:** Value and date within designed wreath **Obv. Legend:** DEPARTAMENTO DE CHIHUAHUA **Edge:** Plain **Mint:** Chihuahua

Date	Mintage	G4	VG8	F12	VF20
1855	—	5.00	9.00	20.00	55.00
1855 DE (reversed D)	—	7.00	13.00	27.50	60.00

KM# 352 1/4 REAL (UN QUARTO/UNA QUARTILLA)
14.00 g., Copper 32mm. **Obv.** Facing eagle, snake in beak **Rev:** Oval arms within sprays below radiant cap **Obv. Legend:** EST. LIB. DE GUANAXUATO **Rev. Legend:** OMNIA VINCIT LABOR **Edge:** Plain **Mint:** Guanajuato

Date	Mintage	G4	VG8	F12	VF20	XF40
1856	—	11.00	27.50	55.00	105	—
1857	—	10.00	20.00	41.25	75.00	—

KM# 352a 1/4 REAL (UN QUARTO/UNA QUARTILLA)
14.00 g., Brass 32mm. **Obv.** Facing eagle, snake in beak **Rev:** Oval arms within sprays below radiant cap **Obv. Legend:** EST. LIB. DE GUANAXUATO **Rev. Legend:** OMNIA VINCIT LABOR **Edge:** Plain **Mint:** Guanajuato

Date	Mintage	G4	VG8	F12	VF20	XF40
1856	—	5.00	10.00	20.00	45.00	—
1857	—	5.00	10.00	20.00	45.00	—

KM# 346 1/4 REAL (UN QUARTO/UNA QUARTILLA)
7.50 g., Copper 27mm. **Obv.** Facing eagle, snake in beak **Rev:** Date, value **Obv. Legend:** REPUBLICA MEXICANA **Rev. Legend:** DURANGO **Edge:** Ornamented with arc and dot pattern **Mint:** Durango

Date	Mintage	G4	VG8	F12	VF20	XF40
1858 Rare	—	—	—	—	—	—

KM# 347 1/4 REAL (UN QUARTO/UNA QUARTILLA)
7.50 g., Copper 27mm. **Obv.** Facing eagle, snake in beak **Rev:** Radiant cap above value and date within stylized sprays **Obv. Legend:** ESTADO DE DURANGO **Rev. Legend:** CONSTITUCION **Edge:** Ornamented with arc and dot pattern **Mint:** Durango **Note:** Brass examples have been reported, but not confirmed.

Date	Mintage	G4	VG8	F12	VF20	XF40
1858	—	6.00	13.00	33.00	75.00	—

KM# 355 1/4 REAL (UN QUARTO/UNA QUARTILLA)
19.00 g., Copper 32mm. **Obv.** Bow, quiver and flag **Rev:** Seated figure, left, cap on pole **Obv. Legend:** ESTADO LIBRE DE JALISCO **Edge:** Oblique reeding **Mint:** Guadalajara

Date	Mintage	G4	VG8	F12	VF20	XF40
1858	—	5.00	9.00	17.00	37.50	—
1861	—	6.00	12.00	25.00	49.50	—
1862	—	5.00	9.00	17.00	37.50	—

KM# 356 1/4 REAL (UN QUARTO/UNA QUARTILLA)
19.00 g., Copper 32mm. **Obv.** Bow, quiver and flag **Rev:** Seated figure, left, cap on pole **Obv. Legend:** DEPARTAMENTO DE JALISCO **Edge:** Oblique reeding **Mint:** Guadalajara

Date	Mintage	G4	VG8	F12	VF20	XF40
1858	—	5.00	9.00	14.00	30.00	—
1859/8	—	5.00	9.00	14.00	30.00	—
1859	—	5.00	9.00	14.00	30.00	—
1860	—	5.00	9.00	14.00	30.00	—

KM# 365 1/4 REAL (UN QUARTO/UNA QUARTILLA)
14.30 g., Copper 32mm. **Obv.** Facing eagle, snake in beak **Rev:** Seated figure, left, cap on pole **Obv. Legend:** ESTO. LIBE. Y SOBO. DE SONORA **Edge:** Reeded **Mint:** Hermosillo

Date	Mintage	G4	VG8	F12	VF20	XF40
1859	—	5.00	12.00	18.00	45.00	—
1861/59	—	6.00	15.00	25.00	55.00	—

Date	Mintage	G4	VG8	F12	VF20	XF40
1861	—	5.00	12.00	18.00	45.00	—
1862	—	5.00	12.00	18.00	45.00	—
1863/2	—	12.00	27.50	55.00	130	—

KM# 344 1/4 REAL (UN QUARTO/UNA QUARTILLA)
Copper 28mm. **Obv.** Seated figure, right **Rev:** Value and date within wreath **Obv. Legend:** E. CHIHA LIBERTAD **Edge:** Plain **Mint:** Chihuahua **Note:** Weight varies 11-11.5 g.

Date	Mintage	G4	VG8	F12	VF20	XF40
1860	—	3.00	6.00	17.00	37.50	—
1861	—	3.00	6.00	17.00	37.50	—
1865/1	—	4.00	8.00	20.00	45.00	—
1865	—	9.00	20.00	42.75	100	—
1866/5	—	8.00	14.00	37.50	90.00	—
1866	—	3.00	6.00	17.00	37.50	—
Note: Coin rotation						
1866	—	3.00	6.00	17.00	37.50	—
Note: Medal rotation						

KM# 348 1/4 REAL (UN QUARTO/UNA QUARTILLA)
Copper 27mm. **Obv.** Facing eagle, snake in beak **Rev:** Value and date within circular legend and wreath **Obv. Legend:** DEPARTAMENTO DE DURANGO **Rev. Legend:** LIBERTAD EN EL ORDEN **Edge:** Ornamented with arc and dot pattern **Mint:** Durango **Note:** Weight varies: 7-7.5 g.

Date	Mintage	G4	VG8	F12	VF20	XF40
1860	—	4.00	11.00	25.00	65.00	—
1866	—	5.00	12.00	27.50	70.00	—

KM# 360 1/4 REAL (UN QUARTO/UNA QUARTILLA)
Copper **Obv.** Value above divides wreath, open book within **Rev:** Seated figure with cap on tip of arrow **Obv. Legend:** ESTADO LIBRE DE SAN LUIS POTOSI **Rev. Legend:** REPUBLICA MEXICANA **Edge:** Oblique reeding **Mint:** San Luis Potosi **Note:** Size varies: 25-31mm.

Date	Mintage	G4	VG8	F12	VF20	XF40
1862	1,367	4.00	6.00	12.00	25.00	—
1862 LIBR	Inc. above	6.00	9.00	14.00	27.50	—

KM# 349 1/4 REAL (UN QUARTO/UNA QUARTILLA)

7.00 g., Copper **Obv.** Facing eagle, snake in beak **Rev:** Value and date above sprays **Obv. Legend:** ESTADO DE DURANGO **Rev. Legend:** INDEPENDENCIA Y LIBERTAD **Edge:** Ornamented with arc and dot pattern **Mint:** Durango **Note:** Size varies: 26-27mm.

Date	Mintage	G4	VG8	F12	VF20	XF40
1866	—	6.00	14.00	37.50	85.00	—

KM# 362 1/4 REAL (UN QUARTO/UNA QUARTILLA)

Copper **Obv. Legend:** ESTADO LIBRE Y SOBERANO DE S.L. POTOSI **Rev. Legend:** LIBERTAD Y REFORMA **Edge:** Plain **Mint:** San Luis Potosi

Date	Mintage	G4	VG8	F12	VF20	XF40
1867	Inc. above	4.00	6.00	11.00	25.00	—
1867 AFG	Inc. above	4.00	6.00	11.00	25.00	—

Note: AFG" are the coin designer/engraver initials

KM# 361 1/4 REAL (UN QUARTO/UNA QUARTILLA)

Copper **Rev:** Radiant cap and value within wrath, date below **Obv. Legend:** ESTADO LIBRE Y SOBERANO DE S.L. POTOSI **Rev. Legend:** LIBERTAD Y REFORMA **Edge:** Reeded or plain **Mint:** San Luis Potosi **Note:** Size varies: 27-28mm. Weight varies: 9-10 g.

Date	Mintage	G4	VG8	F12	VF20	XF40
1867	3,177,000	4.00	6.00	11.00	25.00	—
1867 AFG	Inc. above	4.00	6.00	11.00	25.00	—

Note: AFG" are the coin designer/engraver initials

KM# 350 1/4 REAL (UN QUARTO/UNA QUARTILLA)

7.50 g., Copper 27mm. **Obv.** Facing eagle, snake in beak **Rev:** Date and circular legend, value within **Obv. Legend:** ESTADO DE DURANGO **Rev. Legend:** SUFRAGIO LIBRE **Edge:** Ornamented with arc and dot pattern **Mint:** Durango **Note:** Brass examples have been reported, but not confirmed.

Date	Mintage	G4	VG8	F12	VF20	XF40
1872	—	3.00	6.00	14.00	30.00	—

FEDERAL COINAGE

KM# 315 1/16 REAL (MEDIO OCTAVO)

1.75 g., Copper 17mm. **Obv. Legend:** REPUBLICA MEXICANA **Edge:** Ornamented with small incuse rectangles **Mint:** Mexico City

Date	Mintage	VG8	F12	VF20	XF40	MS60
1831	—	10.00	20.00	50.00	100	—
1832/1	—	12.00	22.00	55.00	125	—
1832	—	10.00	20.00	50.00	100	—
1833	—	10.00	20.00	50.00	100	—

KM# 315a 1/16 REAL (MEDIO OCTAVO)

1.75 g., Brass 17mm. **Obv. Legend:** REPUBLICA MEXICANA **Edge:** Ornamented with small incuse rectangles **Mint:** Mexico City

Date	Mintage	VG8	F12	VF20	XF40	MS60
1832	—	13.50	22.50	65.00	175	650
1833	—	10.00	17.50	50.00	150	—
1835	—	400	800	1,250	2,500	—

KM# 332 1/8 REAL (OCTAVO REAL)

7.00 g., Copper 27mm. **Obv. Legend:** REPUBLICA MEXICANA **Edge:** Ornamented with small incuse rectangles **Mint:** Mexico City

Date	Mintage	VG8	F12	VF20	XF40	MS60
1829	—	450	900	1,500	2,500	—

KM# 333 1/8 REAL (OCTAVO REAL)

3.50 g., Copper 21mm. **Obv.** Facing eagle, snake in beak **Rev:** Value and date within wreath **Obv. Legend:** REPUBLICA MEXICANA **Edge:** Ornamented with small incuse rectangles **Mint:** Mexico City

Date	Mintage	G4	VG8	F12	VF20	XF40
1829	—	7.50	12.00	25.00	55.00	—
1830	—	1.00	2.00	6.00	20.00	—
1831	—	1.50	3.50	7.00	25.00	—
1832	—	1.50	3.50	7.00	25.00	—
1833/2	—	1.50	3.50	7.00	25.00	—
1833	—	1.50	2.75	6.00	20.00	—
1834	—	1.50	2.75	6.00	20.00	—
1835	—	1.50	2.75	6.00	20.00	—
1835/4	—	1.75	3.50	7.00	25.00	—

KM# 334 1/8 REAL (OCTAVO REAL)

14.00 g., Copper **Obv.** Seated figure, right **Rev:** Value and date within wreath **Obv. Legend:** LIBERTAD **Edge:** Lettered (1841-42); Plain (1850-61) **Edge Lettering:** REPUBLICA MEXICANA **Mint:** Mexico City **Note:** Size varies: 29-30mm.

Date	Mintage	G4	VG8	F12	VF20	XF40
1841	—	6.00	15.00	30.00	75.00	—
1842	—	2.50	5.00	10.00	30.00	—
1850	—	12.50	20.00	30.00	80.00	175
1861	—	5.00	12.00	25.00	70.00	—

KM# 357   1/4 REAL (UN QUARTO/UNA QUARTILLA)
14.00 g., Copper 33mm. **Obv.** Facing eagle, snake in beak **Rev:** Value and date within wreath **Obv. Legend:** REPUBLICA MEXICANA **Edge:** Ornamented with small incuse rectangles **Mint:** Mexico City

Date	Mintage	VG8	F12	VF20	XF40	MS60
1829	—	12.00	36.00	90.00	275	—

KM# 358   1/4 REAL (UN QUARTO/UNA QUARTILLA)
7.00 g., Copper 27mm. **Obv.** Facing eagle, snake in beak **Rev:** Value and date within wreath **Obv. Legend:** REPUBLICA MEXICANA **Edge:** Ornamented with small incuse rectangles **Mint:** Mexico City **Note:** Reduced size.

Date	Mintage	VG8	F12	VF20	XF40	MS60
1829	—	12.00	25.00	50.00	180	—
1830	—	1.50	2.75	5.00	12.00	—
1831	—	1.50	2.75	5.00	12.00	—
1832	—	5.50	10.00	20.00	42.00	—
1833	—	1.50	2.75	5.00	12.00	—
1834/3	—	1.75	3.00	6.00	14.00	—
1834	—	1.50	2.75	5.00	12.00	—
1835	—	1.50	2.75	5.00	12.00	—
1836/5	—	1.75	3.00	6.00	14.00	—
1836	—	1.50	2.75	5.00	12.00	—
1837	—	6.50	13.50	22.50	55.00	—

KM# 358a.1   1/4 REAL (UN QUARTO/UNA QUARTILLA)
7.00 g., Brass 27mm. **Obv. Legend:** REPUBLICA MEXICANA **Edge:** Ornamented with small incuse rectangles **Mint:** Mexico City **Note:** Reduced size.

Date	Mintage	VG8	F12	VF20	XF40	MS60
1831	—	8.00	13.50	27.50	60.00	—

KM# 358a.2   1/4 REAL (UN QUARTO/UNA QUARTILLA)
7.00 g., Brass 27mm. **Obv. Legend:** REPUBLICA MEXICANA **Edge:** Ornamented with small incuse rectangles **Mint:** Mexico City **Note:** Without countermark.

Date	Mintage	VG8	F12	VF20	XF40	MS60
1831	—	—	—	—	—	—

KM# 368   1/4 REAL (UN QUARTO/UNA QUARTILLA)
0.85 g., 0.903 Silver **Obv.** Head left **Rev:** Value **Mint:** Chihuahua **Note:** Mint mark CA.

Date	Mintage	VG8	F12	VF20	XF40	MS60
1843 CA RG	—	75.00	125	300	550	—

KM# 368.1   1/4 REAL (UN QUARTO/UNA QUARTILLA)
0.85 g., 0.903 Silver **Mint:** Culiacan **Note:** Mint mark C.

Date	Mintage	VG8	F12	VF20	XF40	MS60
1855 C LR	—	50.00	100	225	525	—

KM# 368.2   1/4 REAL (UN QUARTO/UNA QUARTILLA)
0.85 g., 0.903 Silver **Mint:** Durango **Note:** Struck at Durango Mint, mint mark Do.

Date	Mintage	VG8	F12	VF20	XF40	MS60
1842 Do LR	—	12.00	20.00	40.00	140	—
1843 Do	—	20.00	40.00	90.00	220	—

KM# 368.3   1/4 REAL (UN QUARTO/UNA QUARTILLA)
0.85 g., 0.903 Silver **Mint:** Guadalajara **Note:** Mint mark Ga.

Date	Mintage	VG8	F12	VF20	XF40	MS60
1842 Ga JG	—	3.00	7.00	10.00	25.00	—
1843/2 Ga JG	—	—	—	—	—	—
1843 Ga JG	—	7.00	11.00	15.00	36.00	—
1843 Ga MC	—	5.00	8.00	11.00	30.00	—
1844 Ga MC	—	5.00	8.00	11.00	30.00	—
1844 Ga LR	—	3.00	6.00	12.00	25.00	—
1845 Ga LR	—	10.00	25.00	48.00	90.00	—
1846 Ga LR	—	12.00	30.00	48.00	70.00	—
1847 Ga LR	—	10.00	25.00	48.00	70.00	—
1848 Ga LR Rare	—	—	—	—	—	—
1850 Ga LR Rare	—	—	—	—	—	—
1851 Ga LR	—	7.00	12.00	25.00	60.00	—
1852 Ga LR	—	60.00	120	160	240	—
1854/3 Ga LR	—	60.00	120	160	240	—
1854 Ga LR	—	12.00	25.00	60.00	120	—
1855 Ga LR	—	12.00	25.00	60.00	120	—
1857 Ga LR	—	12.00	25.00	60.00	120	—
1862 Ga LR	—	12.00	25.00	60.00	120	—

KM# 368.4   1/4 REAL (UN QUARTO/UNA QUARTILLA)
0.85 g., 0.903 Silver **Mint:** Guadalupe y Calvo **Note:** Mint mark GC.

Date	Mintage	VG8	F12	VF20	XF40	MS60
1844 GC LR	—	50.00	75.00	200	500	—

KM# 368.5   1/4 REAL (UN QUARTO/UNA QUARTILLA)
0.85 g., 0.903 Silver **Mint:** Guanajuato **Note:** Mint mark Go.

Date	Mintage	VG8	F12	VF20	XF40	MS60
1842 Go PM	—	5.00	15.00	35.00	90.00	—
1842 Go LR	—	2.00	4.00	8.00	18.00	—
1843/2 Go LR	—	4.00	6.00	10.00	25.00	—
1843 Go LR	—	2.00	4.00	8.00	18.00	—
1844/3 Go LR	—	—	—	—	—	—
1844 Go LR	—	10.00	25.00	60.00	150	—
1845 Go LR	—	8.00	17.00	40.00	95.00	—
1846/5 Go LR	—	—	—	—	—	—
1846 Go LR	—	6.00	15.00	30.00	70.00	—
1847 Go LR	—	2.00	4.00	8.00	18.00	—
1848/7 Go LR	—	2.00	4.00	8.00	18.00	—
1848 Go LR	—	2.00	4.00	8.00	18.00	—
1849/7 Go LR	—	8.00	15.00	30.00	70.00	—
1849 Go LR	—	2.00	4.00	8.00	18.00	—
1850 Go LR	—	2.00	4.00	8.00	15.00	—
1851 Go LR	—	2.00	4.00	8.00	18.00	—
1852 Go LR	—	2.00	4.00	8.00	18.00	—
1853 Go LR	—	2.00	4.00	8.00	18.00	—
1855 Go LR	—	4.00	8.00	15.00	36.00	—
1856/4 Go LR	—	20.00	40.00	60.00	120	—
1856 Go LR	—	5.00	10.00	20.00	42.00	—
1862/1 Go LR	—	3.00	5.00	10.00	25.00	—
1862 Go LR	—	2.00	4.00	8.00	18.00	—
1863 Go	—	2.00	4.00	8.00	18.00	—

KM# 368.6   1/4 REAL (UN QUARTO/UNA QUARTILLA)
0.85 g., 0.903 Silver **Mint:** Mexico City **Note:** Mint mark Mo.

Date	Mintage	VG8	F12	VF20	XF40	MS60
1842 Mo LR	—	2.00	4.00	8.00	18.00	—

Date	Mintage	VG8	F12	VF20	XF40	MS60
1843 Mo LR	—	2.00	4.00	8.00	18.00	—
1844/3 Mo LR	—	20.00	30.00	75.00	150	—
1844 Mo LR	—	4.00	6.00	10.00	25.00	—
1845 Mo LR	—	6.00	15.00	35.00	85.00	—
1846 Mo LR	—	10.00	20.00	35.00	80.00	—
1850 Mo LR Rare	—	—	—	—	—	—
1858 Mo LR	—	4.00	8.00	15.00	36.00	—
1859 Mo LR	—	4.00	6.00	10.00	25.00	—
1860 Mo LR	—	4.00	6.00	10.00	25.00	—
1861 Mo LR	—	4.00	6.00	10.00	25.00	—
1862 Mo LR	—	4.00	6.00	10.00	25.00	—
1863/53 Mo LR	—	4.00	6.00	10.00	25.00	—
1863 Mo LR	—	4.00	6.00	10.00	25.00	—

KM# 368.7 1/4 REAL (UN QUARTO/UNA QUARTILLA)
0.85 g., 0.903 Silver **Mint:** San Luis Potosi **Note:** Mint mark SLP, PI, P, I/P.

Date	Mintage	VG8	F12	VF20	XF40	MS60
1842 S.L.Pi	—	2.00	5.00	10.00	25.00	—
1843/2 S.L.Pi	—	4.00	6.00	10.00	25.00	—
1843 S.L.Pi	—	2.00	4.00	8.00	25.00	—
1844 S.L.Pi	—	2.00	4.00	8.00	25.00	—
1845/3 S.L.Pi	—	4.00	6.00	10.00	30.00	—
1845/4 S.L.Pi	—	4.00	6.00	10.00	30.00	—
1845 S.L.Pi	—	2.00	4.00	8.00	25.00	—
1847/5 S.L.Pi	—	4.00	9.00	20.00	48.00	—
1847 S.L.Pi	—	3.00	6.00	12.00	30.00	—
1851/47 S.L.Pi	—	10.00	20.00	35.00	70.00	—
1854 S.L.Pi	—	125	200	275	475	—
1856 S.L.Pi	—	10.00	20.00	35.00	70.00	—
1857 S.L.Pi	—	30.00	60.00	100	210	—
1862/57 S.L.Pi	—	10.00	20.00	40.00	100	—

KM# 368.8 1/4 REAL (UN QUARTO/UNA QUARTILLA)
0.85 g., 0.903 Silver **Mint:** Zacatecas **Note:** Mint mark Zs.

Date	Mintage	VG8	F12	VF20	XF40	MS60
1842/1 Zs LR	—	4.00	8.00	15.00	36.00	—
1842 Zs LR	—	4.00	8.00	15.00	36.00	—

KM# 370 1/2 REAL
1.69 g., 0.903 Silver, 0.05 oz. ASW **Obv.** Hooked-neck eagle **Mint:** Alamos

Date	Mintage	F12	VF20	XF40	MS60	MS63
1862 A PG Rare	—	—	—	—	—	—

KM# 370.1 1/2 REAL
1.69 g., 0.903 Silver, 0.05 oz. ASW **Obv.** Facing eagle **Mint:** Chihuahua

Date	Mintage	F12	VF20	XF40	MS60
1844 Ca RG	—	75.00	125	195	325
1845Ca RG	—	75.00	125	165	300

KM# 370.2 1/2 REAL
1.69 g., 0.903 Silver, 0.05 oz. ASW **Obv.** Facing eagle, snake in beak **Rev:** Radiant cap **Obv. Legend:** REPUBLICA MEXICANA **Mint:** Culiacan **Note:** Mint mark C.

Date	Mintage	F12	VF20	XF40	MS60
1846 CE	—	30.00	50.00	85.00	165
1848/7 CE	—	15.00	25.00	49.50	100
1849/8 CE	—	15.00	25.00	49.50	100
1849 CE	—	—	—	—	—
1852 CE	—	12.50	20.00	44.00	90.00
1853/1 CE	—	12.50	20.00	44.00	90.00
1854 CE	—	20.00	35.00	55.00	110
1856 CE	—	12.50	20.00	44.00	90.00
1857/6 CE	—	20.00	35.00	55.00	110
1857 CE	—	15.00	25.00	49.50	100
1858 CE Error 1 for 1/2	—	12.50	20.00	44.00	90.00
1860/59 PV	—	20.00	35.00	55.00	110
1860 PV	—	12.50	20.00	44.00	90.00
1861 PV	—	12.50	20.00	44.00	90.00
1863 CE Error 1 for 1/2	—	15.00	25.00	49.50	100
1867 CE	—	12.50	20.00	44.00	90.00
1869 6/5 CE Error 1 for 1/2	—	12.50	20.00	44.00	90.00

KM# 370.3 1/2 REAL
1.69 g., 0.903 Silver, 0.05 oz. ASW **Obv.** Facing eagle, snake in beak **Mint:** Durango **Note:** Mint mark D, Do.

Date	Mintage	F12	VF20	XF40	MS60
1832 RM	—	125	225	375	650
1832 RM/L	—	—	—	—	—
1833/2 RM/L	—	75.00	100	165	250
1833/1 RM/L	—	12.50	20.00	44.00	90.00
1833 RM	—	25.00	40.00	85.00	165
1834/1 RM	—	25.00	40.00	85.00	165
1834 RM	—	12.50	20.00	44.00	90.00
1837/1 RM	—	12.50	30.00	65.00	220
1837/4 RM	—	12.50	30.00	65.00	220
1837/6 RM	—	12.50	30.00	65.00	220
1841/33 RM	—	15.00	30.00	65.00	275
1842/32 RM	—	12.50	20.00	44.00	90.00
1842 RM	—	12.50	20.00	44.00	90.00
1842 RM 8R Error	—	12.50	20.00	44.00	90.00
1842 1/2 RM 8R Error	—	12.50	20.00	44.00	90.00
1843/33 RM	—	15.00	25.00	55.00	110
1843 RM	—	15.00	25.00	55.00	110
1845/31 RM	—	12.50	20.00	44.00	90.00
1845/34 RM	—	12.50	20.00	44.00	90.00
1845/35 RM	—	12.50	20.00	44.00	90.00
1845 RM	—	15.00	25.00	55.00	110
1846 RM	—	30.00	50.00	90.00	220
1848/5 RM	—	35.00	55.00	120	275
1848/36 RM	—	25.00	40.00	85.00	220
1849 JMR	—	25.00	40.00	85.00	220
1850 RM Rare	—	—	—	—	—
1850 JMR	—	25.00	40.00	85.00	220
1851 JMR	—	20.00	35.00	55.00	110
1852/1 JMR	—	65.00	125	275	650
1852 JMR	—	30.00	50.00	90.00	220
1853 CP	—	12.50	20.00	44.00	90.00
1854 CP	—	25.00	40.00	85.00	220
1855 CP	—	25.00	40.00	65.00	165
1856/5 CP	—	20.00	35.00	55.00	110
1857 CP	—	20.00	35.00	55.00	110
1858/7 CP	—	20.00	35.00	55.00	110
1859 CP	—	20.00	35.00	55.00	110
1860/59 CP	—	40.00	65.00	150	325
1861 CP	—	125	250	450	775
1862 CP	—	25.00	40.00	65.00	140
1864 LT	—	100	300	550	1,100
1869 CP	—	40.00	65.00	140	300

KM# 370.4 1/2 REAL
1.69 g., 0.903 Silver, 0.05 oz. ASW **Obv.** Facing eagle, snake in beak **Mint:** Estado de Mexico

Date	Mintage	F12	VF20	XF40	MS60	MS63
1829 EoMo LF	—	175	300	550	1,650	—

KM# 370.5 1/2 REAL
1.69 g., 0.903 Silver, 0.05 oz. ASW **Obv.** Facing eagle, snake in beak **Mint:** Guadalajara

Date	Mintage	F12	VF20	XF40	MS60
1825Ga FS	—	25.00	40.00	85.00	220
1826Ga FS	—	10.00	15.00	38.50	90.00
1828/7Ga FS	—	12.50	20.00	40.00	90.00
1829Ga FS	—	7.50	15.00	33.00	75.00
1830/29Ga FS	—	40.00	60.00	110	220
1831Ga LP	—	350	—	—	—
1832Ga FS	—	10.00	20.00	38.50	90.00
1834/3Ga FS	—	65.00	100	195	275

Date	Mintage	F12	VF20	XF40	MS60
1834Ga FS	—	10.00	20.00	38.50	90.00
1835/4/3 Ga FS/LP	—	15.00	25.00	44.00	100
1837/6Ga JG	—	100	250	550	1,100
1838/7Ga JG	—	15.00	25.00	44.00	100
1839/8Ga JG/FS	—	35.00	75.00	165	275
1839Ga MC	—	10.00	20.00	38.50	90.00
1840/39Ga MC/JG	—	—	—	—	—
1840Ga MC	—	15.00	25.00	44.00	100
1841Ga MC	—	20.00	35.00	55.00	110
1842/1Ga JG	—	15.00	25.00	44.00	100
1842Ga JG	—	10.00	20.00	38.50	90.00
1843/2Ga JG	—	15.00	30.00	55.00	110
1843Ga JG	—	10.00	20.00	38.50	90.00
1843Ga MC/JG	—	10.00	20.00	38.50	90.00
1843Ga MC	—	10.00	20.00	38.50	90.00
1844Ga MC	—	10.00	20.00	38.50	90.00
1845Ga MC	—	10.00	20.00	38.50	90.00
1845Ga JG	—	10.00	20.00	38.50	90.00
1846Ga MC	—	10.00	20.00	38.50	90.00
1846Ga JG	—	10.00	20.00	38.50	90.00
1847Ga JG	—	10.00	20.00	38.50	90.00
1848/7Ga JG	—	10.00	20.00	38.50	90.00
1849Ga JG	—	10.00	20.00	38.50	90.00
1850/49Ga JG	—	—	—	—	—
1850Ga JG	—	10.00	20.00	38.50	90.00
1851/0Ga JG	—	10.00	20.00	38.50	90.00
1852Ga JG	—	10.00	20.00	38.50	90.00
1853Ga JG	—	10.00	20.00	38.50	90.00
1854Ga JG	—	10.00	20.00	38.50	90.00
1855/4Ga JG	—	10.00	20.00	38.50	90.00
1855Ga JG	—	10.00	20.00	38.50	90.00
1856Ga JG	—	10.00	20.00	38.50	90.00
1857Ga JG	—	10.00	20.00	38.50	90.00
1858/7Ga JG	—	10.00	20.00	38.50	90.00
1858Ga JG	—	10.00	20.00	38.50	90.00
1859/7Ga JG	—	10.00	20.00	38.50	90.00
1860/59Ga JG	—	10.00	20.00	38.50	90.00
1861Ga JG	—	5.00	12.50	27.50	65.00
1862/1Ga JG	—	15.00	25.00	44.00	100

KM# 370.6 1/2 REAL
1.69 g., 0.903 Silver, 0.05 oz. ASW **Obv.** Facing eagle, snake in beak **Mint:** Guadalupe y Calvo

Date	Mintage	F12	VF20	XF40	MS60	MS63
1844 GC MP	—	50.00	100	165	425	—
1845GC MP	—	25.00	50.00	110	240	—
1846GC MP	—	25.00	50.00	110	240	—
1847GC MP	—	25.00	50.00	110	350	—
1848GC MP	—	20.00	40.00	85.00	180	—
1849GC MP	—	25.00	50.00	110	240	—
1850GC MP	—	30.00	60.00	140	300	—
1851GC MP	—	25.00	50.00	110	240	—

KM# 370.7 1/2 REAL
1.69 g., 0.903 Silver, 0.05 oz. ASW **Obv.** Facing eagle, snake in beak **Mint:** Guanajuato **Note:** Varieties exist.

Date	Mintage	F12	VF20	XF40	MS60
1826 Go MJ	—	125	250	450	1,100
1827/6Go MJ	—	7.50	15.00	33.00	85.00
1828/7Go MJ	—	7.50	15.00	33.00	85.00
1828Go MJ	—	—	—	—	—
Note: Denomination 2/1					
1828Go JG	—	—	—	—	—
1828Go MR	—	50.00	100	165	275
1829/8Go MJ	—	5.00	10.00	27.50	55.00
1829Go MJ	—	5.00	10.00	27.50	55.00
Note: Reversed N in MEXICANA					
1830Go MJ	—	5.00	10.00	27.50	55.00
1831/29Go MJ	—	15.00	30.00	65.00	165
1831Go MJ	—	10.00	20.00	44.00	90.00
1832/1Go MJ	—	7.50	15.00	33.00	85.00
1832Go MJ	—	7.50	15.00	33.00	85.00
1833Go MJ Round top 3	—	10.00	20.00	44.00	90.00
1833Go MJ Flat top 3	—	10.00	20.00	44.00	90.00
1834Go PJ	—	5.00	10.00	27.50	55.00
1835Go PJ	—	5.00	10.00	27.50	55.00

Date	Mintage	F12	VF20	XF40	MS60
1836/5Go PJ	—	7.50	15.00	33.00	85.00
1836Go PJ	—	5.00	10.00	27.50	55.00
1837Go PJ	—	5.00	10.00	27.50	55.00
1838/7Go PJ	—	5.00	10.00	27.50	55.00
1839Go PJ	—	5.00	10.00	27.50	55.00
1839Go PJ	—	5.00	10.00	27.50	55.00
Note: Error: REPUBLIGA					
1840/39Go PJ	—	7.50	10.00	27.50	85.00
1840Go PJ Straight J	—	5.00	10.00	27.50	55.00
1840Go PJ Curved J	—	5.00	10.00	27.50	55.00
1841/31Go PJ	—	5.00	10.00	27.50	55.00
1841Go PJ	—	5.00	10.00	27.50	55.00
1842/1Go PJ	—	5.00	10.00	27.50	55.00
1842/1Go PM	—	5.00	10.00	27.50	55.00
1842Go PM/J	—	5.00	10.00	27.50	55.00
1842Go PJ	—	5.00	10.00	27.50	55.00
1842Go PM	—	5.00	10.00	27.50	55.00
1843/33Go PM 1/2 over 8	—	5.00	10.00	27.50	55.00
1843Go PM	—	5.00	10.00	27.50	55.00
Note: Convex wings					
1843Go PM	—	5.00	10.00	27.50	55.00
Note: Concave wings					
1844/3Go PM	—	5.00	10.00	27.50	55.00
1844Go PM	—	10.00	20.00	44.00	100
1845/4Go PM	—	5.00	10.00	27.50	55.00
1845Go PM	—	5.00	10.00	27.50	55.00
1846/4Go PM	—	5.00	10.00	27.50	55.00
1846/5Go PM	—	5.00	10.00	27.50	55.00
1846Go PM	—	5.00	10.00	27.50	55.00
1847/6Go PM	—	7.50	15.00	33.00	65.00
1847Go PM	—	7.50	15.00	33.00	65.00
1848/35Go PM	—	5.00	10.00	27.50	55.00
1848Go PM	—	5.00	10.00	27.50	55.00
1848Go PF/M	—	5.00	10.00	27.50	55.00
1849/39Go PF	—	5.00	10.00	27.50	55.00
1849Go PF	—	5.00	10.00	27.50	55.00
1849Go PF	—	5.00	10.00	27.50	55.00
Note: Error: MEXCANA					
1850Go PF	—	5.00	10.00	27.50	55.00
1851Go PF	—	5.00	10.00	27.50	55.00
1852/1Go PF	—	5.00	10.00	27.50	55.00
1852Go PF	—	2.50	7.50	19.00	44.00
1853Go PF/R	—	5.00	10.00	27.50	55.00
1853Go PF	—	5.00	10.00	27.50	55.00
1854Go PF	—	5.00	10.00	27.50	55.00
1855Go PF	—	5.00	10.00	27.50	55.00
1856/4Go PF	—	5.00	10.00	27.50	55.00
1856/5Go PF	—	5.00	10.00	27.50	55.00
1856Go PF	—	5.00	10.00	27.50	55.00
1857/6Go PF	—	5.00	10.00	27.50	55.00
1857Go PF	—	5.00	10.00	27.50	55.00
1858/7Go PF	—	7.50	15.00	33.00	65.00
1858Go PF	—	5.00	10.00	27.50	55.00
1859Go PF	—	5.00	10.00	27.50	55.00
1860Go PF Small 1/2	—	5.00	10.00	27.50	55.00
1860Go PF Large 1/2	—	5.00	10.00	27.50	55.00
1860/59Go PF	—	5.00	10.00	27.50	55.00
1861Go PF Small 1/2	—	5.00	10.00	27.50	55.00
1861Go PF Large 1/2	—	5.00	10.00	27.50	55.00
1862/1Go YE	—	5.00	10.00	27.50	55.00
1862Go YE	—	2.50	7.50	19.00	44.00
1862Go YF	—	5.00	10.00	27.50	55.00
1867Go YF	—	2.50	7.50	19.00	44.00
1868Go YF	—	2.50	7.50	19.00	44.00

KM# 370.8 1/2 REAL
1.69 g., 0.903 Silver, 0.05 oz. ASW **Obv.** Facing eagle, snake in beak **Mint:** Hermosillo

Date	Mintage	F12	VF20	XF40	MS60	MS63
1839 Ho PP Unique	—	—	—	—	—	—
1862Ho FM	—	500	650	1,100	—	—
1867Ho PR/ FM Inverted 6, and 7/1	—	100	175	275	600	—

KM# 370.9 1/2 REAL
1.69 g., 0.903 Silver, 0.05 oz. ASW **Obv.** Facing eagle, snake in beak **Mint:** Mexico City

Date	Mintage	F12	VF20	XF40	MS60
1825Mo JM Short top 5	—	10.00	20.00	44.00	90.00
1825Mo JM Long top 5	—	10.00	20.00	44.00	90.00
1826/5Mo JM	—	10.00	20.00	44.00	90.00
1826Mo JM	—	5.00	10.00	22.50	65.00
1827/6Mo JM	—	5.00	10.00	22.50	65.00
1827Mo JM	—	5.00	10.00	22.50	65.00
1828/7Mo JM	—	7.50	15.00	27.50	95.00
1828Mo JM	—	10.00	20.00	44.00	100
1829Mo JM	—	7.50	15.00	27.50	85.00
1830Mo JM	—	5.00	10.00	22.50	65.00
1831Mo JM	—	5.00	10.00	22.50	65.00
1832Mo JM	—	7.50	12.50	30.25	65.00
1833Mo MJ	—	7.50	12.50	30.25	65.00
1834Mo ML	—	5.00	10.00	22.50	65.00
1835Mo ML	—	5.00	10.00	22.50	65.00
1836/5Mo ML/MF	—	7.50	15.00	27.50	70.00
1836Mo ML	—	7.50	15.00	27.50	70.00
1838Mo ML	—	5.00	10.00	22.50	65.00
1839/8Mo ML	—	5.00	10.00	27.50	70.00
1839Mo ML	—	5.00	10.00	22.50	55.00
1840Mo ML	—	5.00	10.00	22.50	55.00
1841Mo ML	—	5.00	10.00	22.50	55.00
1842Mo ML	—	15.00	35.00	90.00	220
1842Mo MM	—	5.00	10.00	22.50	55.00
1843Mo MM	—	10.00	20.00	44.00	90.00
1844Mo MF	—	5.00	10.00	22.50	55.00
1845/4Mo MF	—	5.00	10.00	27.50	65.00
1845Mo MF	—	5.00	10.00	22.50	55.00
1846Mo MF	—	5.00	10.00	22.50	55.00
1847Mo RC	—	10.00	20.00	44.00	90.00
1847Mo RC R/M	—	10.00	20.00	44.00	90.00
1848/7Mo GC/RC	—	5.00	10.00	22.50	55.00
1849Mo GC	—	5.00	10.00	22.50	55.00
1850Mo GC	—	5.00	10.00	22.50	55.00
1851Mo GC	—	5.00	10.00	22.50	55.00
1852Mo GC	—	5.00	10.00	22.50	55.00
1853Mo GC	—	5.00	10.00	22.50	55.00
1854Mo GC	—	5.00	10.00	22.50	55.00
1855Mo GC	—	5.00	10.00	22.50	55.00
1855Mo GF/GC	—	7.50	12.50	27.50	70.00
1856/5Mo GF	—	7.50	12.50	27.50	70.00
1857Mo GF	—	5.00	10.00	22.50	55.00
1858Mo FH	—	3.00	5.00	14.00	44.00
1858Mo FH F/G	—	5.00	10.00	22.50	55.00
1858/9Mo FH	—	5.00	10.00	22.50	55.00
1859Mo FH/GC	—	5.00	10.00	22.50	55.00
1859Mo FH	—	3.00	6.00	17.00	55.00
1860Mo FH/GC	—	5.00	10.00	22.50	55.00
1860Mo FH	—	3.00	6.00	17.00	55.00
1860Mo TH	—	25.00	50.00	110	220
1860/59Mo FH	—	7.50	12.50	27.50	70.00
1861Mo CH	—	3.00	6.00	17.00	49.50
1862/52Mo CH	—	5.00	10.00	22.50	55.00
1862Mo CH	—	3.00	6.00	17.00	49.50
1863/55Mo TH/GC	—	5.00	10.00	22.50	55.00
1863Mo CH/GC	—	5.00	10.00	22.50	55.00
1863Mo CH	—	3.00	6.00	17.00	49.50

KM# 370.10 1/2 REAL
1.69 g., 0.903 Silver, 0.05 oz. ASW **Obv.** Facing eagle, snake in beak **Mint:** San Luis Potosi

Date	Mintage	F12	VF20	XF40	MS60
1831 Pi JS	—	7.50	12.50	27.50	70.00
1841/36Pi JS	—	20.00	40.00	85.00	140
1842/1Pi PS	—	20.00	40.00	85.00	140
1842/1Pi PS P/J	—	60.00	80.00	165	325
1842Pi PS/PJ	—	50.00	75.00	140	275
1842 PS	—	60.00	80.00	165	325
1842Pi JS	—	20.00	40.00	85.00	140
1843/2Pi PS	—	17.50	25.00	44.00	90.00
1843Pi PS	—	15.00	25.00	38.50	75.00
1843Pi AM	—	10.00	15.00	27.50	65.00
1844Pi AM	—	10.00	15.00	33.00	70.00
1845Pi AM	—	250	375	550	1,650
1846/5Pi AM	—	40.00	75.00	140	220
1847/6Pi AM	—	15.00	25.00	44.00	90.00
1848Pi AM	—	15.00	25.00	44.00	90.00
1849Pi MC/AM	—	15.00	25.00	44.00	90.00
1849Pi MC	—	12.50	20.00	38.50	75.00
1850/49Pi MC	—	—	—	—	—
1850Pi MC	—	10.00	15.00	27.50	65.00
1850P MC	—	—	—	—	—
1851Pi MC	—	10.00	15.00	27.50	65.00
1852Pi MC	—	10.00	20.00	33.00	70.00
1853Pi MC	—	7.50	12.50	22.50	65.00
1854Pi MC	—	7.50	12.50	22.50	65.00
1855Pi MC	—	15.00	20.00	38.50	75.00
1856Pi MC	—	15.00	25.00	55.00	110
1856Pi (no I)	—	—	—	—	—
1857Pi MC	—	7.50	12.50	22.50	65.00
1857Pi PS	—	10.00	15.00	33.00	70.00
1858Pi MC	—	12.50	20.00	38.50	75.00
1858Pi PS	—	12.50	20.00	38.50	75.00
1859Pi MC Rare	—	—	—	—	—
1860/59Pi PS	—	125	200	650	—
1861Pi RO	—	10.00	15.00	33.00	65.00
1862/1Pi RO	—	15.00	25.00	55.00	140
1862Pi RO	—	15.00	25.00	55.00	140
1863/2Pi RO	—	15.00	25.00	49.50	110

KM# 370.11 1/2 REAL
1.69 g., 0.903 Silver, 0.05 oz. ASW **Obv.** Facing eagle, snake in beak **Mint:** Zacatecas **Note:** Mint mark Z, Zs.

Date	Mintage	F12	VF20	XF40	MS60
1826 AZ	—	5.00	10.00	22.50	65.00
1826 AO	—	5.00	10.00	22.50	65.00
1827 AO	—	5.00	10.00	22.50	65.00
1828/7 AO	—	5.00	10.00	22.50	65.00
1829 AO	—	5.00	10.00	22.50	65.00
1830 OV	—	5.00	10.00	22.50	65.00
1831 OV	—	25.00	50.00	85.00	165
1831 OM	—	5.00	10.00	22.50	65.00
1832 OM	—	5.00	10.00	22.50	65.00
1833 OM	—	5.00	10.00	22.50	65.00
1834 OM	—	5.00	10.00	22.50	65.00
1835/4 OM	—	5.00	10.00	22.50	65.00
1835 OM	—	5.00	10.00	22.50	65.00
1836 OM	—	5.00	10.00	22.50	65.00
1837 OM	—	10.00	20.00	44.00	90.00
1838 OM	—	5.00	10.00	22.50	65.00
1839 OM	—	7.50	15.00	33.00	70.00
1840 OM	—	10.00	25.00	49.50	100
1841 OM	—	10.00	25.00	49.50	100
1842/1 OM	—	5.00	10.00	22.50	65.00
1842 OM	—	5.00	10.00	22.50	65.00
1843 OM	—	40.00	75.00	125	275
1844 OM	—	5.00	10.00	22.50	65.00
1845 OM	—	5.00	10.00	22.50	65.00
1846 OM	—	7.50	15.00	33.00	70.00
1847 OM	—	5.00	10.00	22.50	55.00
1848 OM	—	5.00	10.00	22.50	55.00
1849 OM	—	5.00	10.00	22.50	55.00
1850 OM	—	5.00	10.00	22.50	55.00
1851 OM	—	5.00	10.00	22.50	55.00
1852 OM	—	5.00	10.00	22.50	55.00
1853 OM	—	5.00	10.00	22.50	55.00
1854/3 OM	—	5.00	10.00	22.50	55.00
1854 OM	—	5.00	10.00	22.50	55.00
1855/3 OM	—	7.50	15.00	33.00	70.00
1855 OM	—	5.00	10.00	22.50	55.00
1856 OM	—	5.00	10.00	22.50	55.00

Date	Mintage	F12	VF20	XF40	MS60
1857 MO	—	5.00	10.00	22.50	55.00
1858 MO	—	5.00	10.00	22.50	55.00
1859 MO	—	6.00	8.50	19.00	38.50
1859 VL	—	6.00	8.50	19.00	44.00
1860/50 VL Inverted A for V	—	5.00	10.00	22.50	55.00
1860/59 VL Inverted A for V	—	5.00	10.00	22.50	55.00
1860 MO	—	5.00	10.00	22.50	55.00
1860 VL	—	5.00	10.00	22.50	55.00
1861/0 VL Inverted A for V	—	7.50	15.00	33.00	70.00
1861 VL Inverted A for V	—	5.00	10.00	22.50	55.00
1862 VL Inverted A for V	—	5.00	10.00	22.50	55.00
1863/1 VL Inverted A for V	—	7.50	15.00	33.00	70.00
1863 VL Inverted A for V	—	5.00	10.00	22.50	55.00
1869 YH	—	5.00	10.00	22.50	55.00

KM# 372 REAL

3.38 g., 0.903 Silver, 0.10 oz. ASW **Obv.** Facing eagle, snake in beak **Mint:** Chihuahua

Date	Mintage	F12	VF20	XF40	MS60	MS63
1844 Ca RG	—	600	1,200	1,800	3,300	—
1845Ca RG	—	600	1,200	1,800	3,300	—
1855Ca RG	—	120	180	270	575	—

KM# 372.1 REAL

3.38 g., 0.903 Silver, 0.10 oz. ASW **Obv.** Facing eagle, snake in beak **Mint:** Culiacan

Date	Mintage	F12	VF20	XF40	MS60	MS63
1846 C CE	—	14.00	27.50	44.00	120	—
1848C CE	—	14.00	27.50	44.00	120	—
1850C CE	—	14.00	27.50	44.00	120	—
1851/0C CE	—	14.00	27.50	44.00	120	—
1852/1C CE	—	8.00	17.00	33.00	110	—
1853/2C CE	—	8.00	17.00	33.00	110	—
1854C CE	—	8.00	17.00	33.00	110	—
1856C CE	—	44.00	70.00	110	250	—
1857/4C CE	—	11.00	22.50	38.50	110	—
1857/6C CE	—	11.00	22.50	38.50	110	—
1858C CE	—	6.00	8.00	17.00	110	—
1859C CE	—	—	—	—	—	—
1860/9C PV/N	—	7.00	11.00	19.00	130	—
1860C PV	—	6.00	8.00	17.00	110	—
1861C PV	—	6.00	8.00	17.00	110	—
1863C CE	—	—	1,800	2,500		—
Note: 3 known						
1869C CE	—	6.00	8.00	17.00	110	—

KM# 372.3 REAL

3.38 g., 0.903 Silver, 0.10 oz. ASW **Obv.** Facing eagle, snake in beak **Mint:** Estado de Mexico

Date	Mintage	F12	VF20	XF40	MS60	MS63
1828 EoMo LF	—	240	350	550	1,900	—

KM# 372.2 REAL

3.38 g., 0.903 Silver, 0.10 oz. ASW **Obv.** Facing eagle, snake in beak **Mint:** Durango

Date	Mintage	F12	VF20	XF40	MS60	MS63
1832/1 Do RM	—	6.00	11.00	22.50	100	—
1832 Do RM/RL	—	11.00	17.00	33.00	110	—
1832 Do RM	—	6.00	11.00	22.50	110	—
1834/24Do RM/RL	—	17.00	27.50	55.00	165	—
1834/3Do RM/RL	—	17.00	27.50	55.00	165	—
1834Do RM	—	11.00	22.50	44.00	120	—
1836/4Do RM	—	6.00	8.00	17.00	110	—
1836Do RM	—	6.00	8.00	17.00	110	—
1837Do RM 3/2	—	14.00	22.50	44.00	120	—
1837Do RM	—	14.00	22.50	44.00	120	—
1841Do RM	—	8.00	17.00	33.00	110	—
1842/32Do RM	—	11.00	22.50	44.00	120	—
1842Do RM	—	8.00	17.00	33.00	110	—
1843/37Do RM	—	11.00	22.50	44.00	120	—

Date	Mintage	F12	VF20	XF40	MS60	MS63
1843Do RM	—	6.00	8.00	17.00	110	—
1844/34Do RM	—	17.00	27.50	49.50	140	—
1845Do RM	—	6.00	8.00	17.00	110	—
1846Do RM	—	8.00	17.00	33.00	110	—
1847Do RM	—	11.00	17.00	38.50	110	—
1848/31Do RM	—	11.00	17.00	38.50	110	—
1848/33Do RM	—	11.00	17.00	38.50	110	—
1848/5Do RM	—	11.00	17.00	38.50	110	—
1848Do RM	—	8.00	14.00	22.50	110	—
1849/8Do CM	—	11.00	17.00	33.00	110	—
1850Do JMR	—	22.50	44.00	85.00	195	—
1851Do JMR	—	22.50	44.00	85.00	195	—
1852Do JMR	—	22.50	44.00	85.00	195	—
1853Do CP	—	14.00	22.50	38.50	110	—
1854/1Do CP	—	11.00	17.00	27.50	110	—
1854Do CP	—	8.00	14.00	22.50	110	—
1855Do CP	—	11.00	17.00	27.50	110	—
1856Do CP	—	14.00	22.50	38.50	110	—
1857Do CP	—	14.00	22.50	38.50	110	—
1858Do CP	—	14.00	22.50	38.50	110	—
1859Do CP	—	8.00	14.00	22.50	110	—
1860/59Do CP	—	11.00	17.00	27.50	110	—
1861Do CP	—	17.00	27.50	44.00	120	—
1862/1Do CP	—	250	325	500	1,400	—
1864Do LT	—	17.00	27.50	44.00	120	—

KM# 372.4 REAL

3.38 g., 0.903 Silver, 0.10 oz. ASW **Obv.** Facing eagle, snake in beak **Mint:** Guadalajara

Date	Mintage	F12	VF20	XF40	MS60	MS63
1826 Ga FS	—	17.00	33.00	55.00	140	—
1828/7Ga FS	—	17.00	33.00	55.00	140	—
1829/8/7 Ga FS	—	—	—	—	—	—
1829Ga FS	—	17.00	33.00	55.00	140	—
1830Ga FS	—	275	475	650	—	—
1831Ga LP	—	17.00	33.00	55.00	140	—
1831Ga LP/FS	—	325	500	650	—	—
1832Ga FS	—	275	375	550	—	—
1833/2Ga G FS	—	110	165	300	600	—
1833Ga FS	—	85.00	140	250	550	—
1834/3Ga FS	—	85.00	140	250	550	—
1835Ga FS	—	—	—	—	—	—
1837/6Ga JG/FS	—	14.00	22.50	38.50	110	—
1838/7Ga JG/FS	—	110	220	450	—	—
1839Ga JG	—	275	375	550	—	—
1840Ga JG	—	14.00	22.50	38.50	110	—
1840Ga MC	—	8.00	14.00	27.50	75.00	—
1841Ga MC	—	55.00	85.00	140	275	—
1842/0Ga JG/MC	—	11.00	17.00	33.00	110	—
1842Ga JG	—	8.00	14.00	22.50	110	—
1843Ga JG	—	165	220	325	825	—
1843Ga MC	—	6.00	8.00	17.00	110	—
1844Ga MC	—	8.00	14.00	22.50	110	—
1845Ga MC	—	11.00	17.00	27.50	110	—
1845Ga JG	—	6.00	8.00	22.50	110	—
1846Ga JG	—	14.00	22.50	38.50	110	—
1847/6Ga JG	—	11.00	17.00	27.50	110	—
1847Ga JG	—	11.00	17.00	27.50	110	—
1848Ga JG	—	450	600	775	—	—
1849Ga JG	—	8.00	14.00	22.50	110	—
1850Ga JG	—	195	300	450	—	—
1851Ga JG	—	11.00	17.00	27.50	110	—
1852Ga JG	—	11.00	17.00	27.50	110	—
1853/2Ga JG	—	11.00	17.00	27.50	110	—
1854Ga JG	—	11.00	17.00	27.50	110	—
1855Ga JG	—	17.00	27.50	44.00	110	—
1856Ga JG	—	8.00	14.00	22.50	110	—
1857/6Ga JG	—	14.00	22.50	38.50	110	—
1858/7Ga JG	—	17.00	27.50	44.00	120	—
1859/8Ga JG	—	27.50	55.00	85.00	165	—
1860/59Ga JG	—	33.00	65.00	100	250	—
1861/0Ga JG	—	22.50	33.00	55.00	140	—
1861Ga JG	—	27.50	55.00	110	275	—
1862Ga JG	—	8.00	14.00	22.50	110	—

KM# 372.5 REAL
3.38 g., 0.903 Silver, 0.10 oz. ASW **Obv.** Facing eagle, snake in beak **Rev:** Radiant cap **Obv. Legend:** REPUBLICA MEXICANA **Mint:** Guadalupe y Calvo

Date	Mintage	F12	VF20	XF40	MS60	MS63
1844 GC MP	—	40.00	60.00	110	325	—
1845GC MP	—	40.00	60.00	110	325	—
1846GC MP	—	40.00	60.00	110	325	—
1847GC MP	—	40.00	60.00	110	325	—
1848GC MP	—	40.00	60.00	110	325	—
1849/7GC MP	—	40.00	60.00	110	325	—
1849/8GC MP	—	40.00	60.00	110	325	—
1849GC MP	—	40.00	60.00	110	325	—
1850GC MP	—	40.00	60.00	110	325	—
1851GC MP	—	40.00	60.00	110	325	—

KM# 372.6 REAL
3.38 g., 0.903 Silver, 0.10 oz. ASW **Obv.** Facing eagle, snake in beak **Mint:** Guanajuato

Date	Mintage	F12	VF20	XF40	MS60
1826/5 Go JJ	—	6.00	8.00	17.00	95.00
1826 Go MJ	—	4.00	7.00	17.00	95.00
1827Go MJ	—	4.00	7.00	17.00	70.00
1827Go JM	—	11.00	17.00	27.50	85.00
1828/7Go MR	—	4.00	7.00	17.00	95.00
1828Go MJ	—	4.00	7.00	17.00	95.00
Note: Straight J, small 8					
1828Go MJ	—	4.00	7.00	17.00	95.00
Note: Full J, large 8					
1828/6G MR/JJ	—	4.00	7.00	17.00	95.00
1828G MR/JJ	—	4.00	7.00	17.00	95.00
1828Go MR	—	4.00	7.00	17.00	95.00
1829/8Go MG Small eagle	—	4.00	7.00	17.00	95.00
1829Go MJ Small eagle	—	4.00	7.00	17.00	95.00
1829Go MJ Large eagle	—	4.00	7.00	17.00	95.00
1830Go MJ Small initials	—	4.00	7.00	17.00	95.00
1830Go MJ Medium initials	—	4.00	7.00	17.00	95.00
1830Go MJ Large initials	—	4.00	7.00	17.00	95.00
1830Go MJ	—	4.00	7.00	17.00	95.00
Note: Reversed N in MEXICANA					
1830 MJ 3/2	—	4.00	7.00	17.00	95.00
1831/0Go MJ	—	4.00	7.00	17.00	95.00
Note: Reversed N in MEXICANA					
1831Go MJ	—	4.00	7.00	17.00	95.00
1832/1Go MJ	—	17.00	33.00	55.00	140
1832Go MJ	—	17.00	33.00	55.00	140
1833Go MJ Top of 3 round	—	4.00	7.00	17.00	95.00
1833Go MJ Top of 3 flat	—	4.00	7.00	17.00	95.00
1834Go PJ	—	4.00	7.00	17.00	95.00
1835Go PJ	—	8.00	14.00	22.50	95.00
1836Go PJ	—	4.00	7.00	17.00	95.00
1837Go PJ	—	17.00	33.00	55.00	140
1838/7Go PJ	—	11.00	22.50	38.50	95.00
1839Go PJ	—	4.00	7.00	17.00	95.00
1840/39Go PJ	—	4.00	7.00	17.00	95.00
1840Go PJ	—	4.00	7.00	17.00	95.00
1841/31Go PJ	—	11.00	22.50	38.50	95.00
1841Go PJ	—	4.00	7.00	17.00	95.00
1842Go PJ	—	4.00	7.00	17.00	95.00
1842Go PM	—	4.00	7.00	17.00	95.00
1843Go PM Convex wings	—	4.00	7.00	17.00	95.00
1843Go PM Concave wings	—	4.00	7.00	17.00	95.00
1844Go PM	—	4.00	7.00	17.00	95.00
1845/4Go PM	—	4.00	7.00	17.00	95.00
1845Go PM	—	4.00	7.00	17.00	95.00
1846/5Go PM	—	8.00	14.00	22.50	95.00

Date	Mintage	F12	VF20	XF40	MS60
1846Go PM	—	4.00	7.00	17.00	95.00
1847/6Go PM	—	4.00	7.00	17.00	95.00
1847Go PM	—	4.00	7.00	17.00	95.00
1848Go PM	—	4.00	7.00	17.00	95.00
1849Go PF	—	11.00	22.50	38.50	95.00
1850Go PF	—	4.00	7.00	17.00	95.00
1851Go PF	—	11.00	22.50	38.50	110
1853/2Go PF	—	8.00	14.00	22.50	85.00
1853Go PF	—	4.00	7.00	17.00	85.00
1853Go PF/M 5/4	—	8.00	14.00	22.50	85.00
1854/3Go PF	—	4.00	7.00	17.00	85.00
1854Go PF Large eagle	—	4.00	7.00	17.00	85.00
1854Go PF Small eagle	—	4.00	7.00	17.00	85.00
1855/3Go PF	—	4.00	7.00	17.00	85.00
1855/4Go PF	—	4.00	7.00	17.00	85.00
1855Go PF	—	4.00	7.00	17.00	85.00
1856/5Go PF	—	4.00	7.00	17.00	85.00
1856Go PF	—	4.00	7.00	17.00	85.00
1857/6Go PF	—	4.00	7.00	17.00	85.00
1857Go PF	—	4.00	7.00	17.00	85.00
1858Go PF	—	4.00	7.00	17.00	85.00
1859Go PF	—	4.00	7.00	17.00	85.00
1860/50Go PF	—	4.00	7.00	17.00	85.00
1860Go PF	—	4.00	7.00	17.00	85.00
1861Go PF	—	4.00	7.00	17.00	85.00
1862Go YE	—	4.00	7.00	17.00	85.00
1862/1Go YF	—	8.00	14.00	22.50	85.00
1862Go YF	—	4.00	7.00	17.00	85.00
1867Go YF	—	4.00	7.00	17.00	85.00
1868/7Go YF	—	4.00	7.00	17.00	85.00

KM# 372.7 REAL
3.38 g., 0.903 Silver, 0.10 oz. ASW **Obv.** Facing eagle, snake in beak **Mint:** Hermosillo

Date	Mintage	F12	VF20	XF40	MS60	MS63
1867 Ho PR	—	46.25	90.00	145	300	—
Note: Small 7/1						
1867 Ho PR	—	46.25	90.00	145	300	—
Note: Large 7/ small 7						
1868Ho PR	—	46.25	90.00	145	300	—

KM# 372.8 REAL
3.38 g., 0.903 Silver, 0.10 oz. ASW **Obv.** Facing eagle, snake in beak **Mint:** Mexico City

Date	Mintage	F12	VF20	XF40	MS60	MS63
1825Mo JM	—	11.00	22.50	44.00	140	—
1826Mo JM	—	8.00	17.00	33.00	125	—
1827/6Mo JM	—	8.00	17.00	33.00	95.00	—
1827Mo JM	—	6.00	11.00	22.50	90.00	—
1828Mo JM	—	8.00	17.00	33.00	120	—
1830/29Mo JM	—	6.00	11.00	22.50	120	—
1830Mo JM	—	6.00	14.00	27.50	120	—
1831Mo JM	—	110	220	325	875	—
1832Mo JM	—	6.00	11.00	22.50	120	—
1833/2Mo MJ	—	6.00	11.00	22.50	120	—
1850Mo GC	—	6.00	11.00	22.50	120	—
1852Mo GC	—	300	475	625	—	—
1854Mo GC	—	11.00	22.50	44.00	120	—
1855Mo GF	—	6.00	11.00	22.50	100	—
1856Mo GF	—	110	220	450	1,100	—
1857Mo GF	—	6.00	11.00	22.50	100	—
1858Mo FH	—	6.00	11.00	22.50	100	—
1859Mo FH	—	6.00	11.00	22.50	100	—
1861Mo CH	—	6.00	11.00	22.50	100	—
1862Mo CH	—	6.00	11.00	22.50	100	—
1863/2Mo CH	—	8.00	14.00	27.50	100	—

KM# 372.9 REAL
3.38 g., 0.903 Silver, 0.10 oz. ASW **Obv.** Facing eagle, snake in beak **Mint:** San Luis Potosi

Date	Mintage	F12	VF20	XF40	MS60	MS63
1831 Pi JS	—	6.00	11.00	22.50	140	—
1837Pi JS	—	650	825	1,100	—	—
1838/7Pi JS	—	275	325	425	—	—
1838Pi JS	—	22.50	38.50	65.00	140	—
1840/39Pi JS	—	8.00	17.00	33.00	140	—
1840Pi JS	—	8.00	17.00	33.00	140	—

Date	Mintage	F12	VF20	XF40	MS60	MS63
1841Pi JS	—	8.00	17.00	33.00	140	—
1842Pi JS	—	17.00	33.00	60.00	165	—
1842Pi PS	—	6.00	11.00	22.50	140	—
1843Pi PS	—	14.00	22.50	38.50	140	—
1843Pi AM	—	44.00	65.00	90.00	165	—
1844Pi AM	—	44.00	65.00	90.00	165	—
1845Pi AM	—	8.00	17.00	33.00	140	—
1846/5Pi AM	—	8.00	17.00	33.00	140	—
1847/6Pi AM	—	8.00	17.00	33.00	140	—
1847Pi AM	—	8.00	17.00	33.00	140	—
1848/7Pi AM	—	8.00	17.00	33.00	140	—
1849Pi PS	—	8.00	17.00	33.00	140	—
1849/8Pi SP	—	65.00	110	165	—	—
1849Pi SP	—	17.00	27.50	44.00	140	—
1850Pi MC	—	6.00	11.00	22.50	140	—
1851/0Pi MC	—	8.00	17.00	33.00	140	—
1851Pi MC	—	8.00	17.00	33.00	140	—
1852/1/0 Pi MC	—	11.00	22.50	38.50	140	—
1852Pi MC	—	8.00	17.00	33.00	140	—
1853/1Pi MC	—	14.00	22.50	38.50	140	—
1853Pi MC	—	11.00	22.50	38.50	140	—
1854/2Pi MO	—	33.00	65.00	110	—	—
1854/3Pi MC	—	22.50	44.00	65.00	165	—
1855Pi MC	—	17.00	27.50	49.50	140	—
1855/4Pi MC	—	22.50	44.00	65.00	165	—
1856Pi MC	—	17.00	27.50	49.50	140	—
1857Pi PS	—	22.50	38.50	60.00	150	—
1857Pi MC	—	22.50	44.00	65.00	165	—
1858Pi MC	—	14.00	22.50	38.50	140	—
1859Pi PS	—	11.00	17.00	33.00	140	—
1860/59Pi PS	—	11.00	17.00	33.00	140	—
1861Pi PS	—	8.00	14.00	22.50	140	—
1861Pi RO	—	14.00	22.50	38.50	140	—
1862/1Pi RO	—	14.00	22.50	38.50	100	—
1862Pi RO	—	8.00	14.00	22.50	140	—

KM# 372.10 REAL
3.38 g., 0.903 Silver, 0.10 oz. ASW **Obv.** Facing eagle, snake in beak **Mint:** Zacatecas

Date	Mintage	F12	VF20	XF40	MS60
1826 Zs AZ	—	6.00	14.00	38.50	130
1826 Zs AO	—	6.00	14.00	38.50	130
1827Zs AO	—	6.00	14.00	38.50	130
1828/7Zs AO	—	6.00	14.00	38.50	130
1828Zs AO	—	6.00	14.00	38.50	130
1828Zs AO Inverted V for A	—	6.00	14.00	38.50	130
1829Zs AO	—	6.00	14.00	38.50	130
1830Zs ZsOV	—	6.00	14.00	38.50	130
1830Zs ZOV	—	6.00	14.00	38.50	130
1831Zs OV	—	6.00	14.00	38.50	130
1831Zs OM	—	6.00	14.00	33.00	130
1832Zs OM	—	6.00	14.00	33.00	130
1833/2Zs OM	—	6.00	14.00	33.00	130
1833/2Zs OM/V	—	6.00	14.00	33.00	130
1833Zs OM	—	6.00	14.00	33.00	130
1834/3Zs OM	—	6.00	14.00	33.00	130
1834Zs OM	—	6.00	14.00	33.00	130
1835/4Zs OM	—	22.50	38.50	65.00	165
1835Zs OM	—	4.00	9.00	22.50	70.00
1836/5Zs OM	—	4.00	9.00	22.50	95.00
1836Zs OM	—	4.00	9.00	22.50	95.00
1837Zs OM	—	4.00	9.00	22.50	95.00
1838Zs OM	—	4.00	9.00	22.50	95.00
1839Zs OM	—	4.00	9.00	22.50	95.00
1840Zs OM	—	4.00	9.00	22.50	95.00
1841Zs OM	—	22.50	44.00	65.00	165
1842/1Zs OM	—	4.00	9.00	22.50	95.00
1842Zs OM	—	4.00	9.00	22.50	95.00
1843Zs OM	—	4.00	9.00	22.50	95.00
1844Zs OM	—	4.00	9.00	22.50	95.00
1845/4Zs OM	—	6.00	14.00	33.00	110
1845Zs OM	—	4.00	9.00	22.50	95.00
1846Zs OM	—	4.00	9.00	22.50	95.00
Note: Old font and obverse					
1846Zs OM	—	4.00	9.00	22.50	95.00
Note: New font and obverse					

Date	Mintage	F12	VF20	XF40	MS60
1847Zs OM	—	4.00	9.00	22.50	95.00
1848Zs OM	—	4.00	9.00	22.50	95.00
1849Zs OM	—	11.00	27.50	55.00	140
1850Zs OM	—	4.00	7.00	17.00	95.00
1851Zs OM	—	4.00	7.00	17.00	95.00
1852Zs OM	—	4.00	7.00	17.00	95.00
1853Zs OM	—	4.00	7.00	17.00	95.00
1854/2Zs OM	—	4.00	7.00	17.00	95.00
1854/3Zs OM	—	4.00	7.00	17.00	95.00
1854Zs OM	—	4.00	7.00	17.00	95.00
1855/4Zs OM	—	4.00	7.00	17.00	95.00
1855Zs OM	—	4.00	7.00	17.00	95.00
1855Zs MO	—	4.00	7.00	17.00	95.00
1856Zs MO	—	4.00	7.00	17.00	95.00
1856Zs MO/OM	—	4.00	7.00	17.00	95.00
1857Zs MO	—	4.00	7.00	17.00	95.00
1858Zs MO	—	4.00	7.00	17.00	95.00
1859Zs MO	—	4.00	7.00	17.00	85.00
1860 MO	—	275	—	—	—
1860Zs VL	—	4.00	7.00	17.00	85.00
1860Zs VL Inverted A for V	—	4.00	7.00	17.00	85.00
1861Zs VL	—	4.00	7.00	17.00	85.00
1861Zs VL Inverted A for V	—	4.00	7.00	17.00	85.00
1862Zs VL	—	6.00	14.00	33.00	110
1868Zs JS	—	27.50	49.50	100	195
1869Zs YH	—	4.00	9.00	22.50	85.00

KM# 374 2 REALES
6.76 g., 0.903 Silver, 0.19 oz. ASW **Obv.** Facing eagle, snake in beak **Edge:** Reeded **Mint:** Alamos

Date	Mintage	F12	VF20	XF40	MS60	MS63
1872 A AM	15,000	70.00	145	290	700	—

KM# 374.1 2 REALES
6.76 g., 0.903 Silver, 0.19 oz. ASW **Obv.** Facing eagle, snake in beak **Edge:** Reeded **Mint:** Real de Catorce

Date	Mintage	F12	VF20	XF40	MS60	MS63
1863 Ce ML	—	145	230	375	800	—

KM# 374.2 2 REALES
6.76 g., 0.903 Silver, 0.19 oz. ASW **Obv.** Facing eagle, snake in beak **Edge:** Reeded **Mint:** Chihuahua

Date	Mintage	F12	VF20	XF40	MS60	MS63
1832 Ca MR	—	34.50	70.00	115	230	—
1833Ca MR	—	34.50	70.00	145	575	—
1834Ca MR	—	40.25	85.00	145	575	—
1834Ca AM	—	40.25	85.00	145	575	—
1835Ca AM	—	40.25	85.00	145	575	—
1836Ca AM	—	22.50	46.00	90.00	230	—
1844Ca AM Rare	—	—	—	—	—	—
1844Ca RG Unique	—	—	—	—	—	—
1845Ca RG	—	22.50	46.00	90.00	230	—
1855Ca RG	—	22.50	46.00	90.00	230	—

KM# 374.3 2 REALES
6.76 g., 0.903 Silver, 0.19 oz. ASW **Obv.** Facing eagle, snake in beak **Edge:** Reeded **Mint:** Culiacan

Date	Mintage	F12	VF20	XF40	MS60	MS63
1846/1146 C CE	—	30.00	60.00	115	260	—
1847C CE	—	14.00	22.50	46.00	230	—
1848C CE	—	14.00	22.50	46.00	230	—
1850C CE	—	30.00	60.00	85.00	230	—
1851C CE	—	14.00	22.50	46.00	230	—

Date	Mintage	F12	VF20	XF40	MS60	MS63
1852/1C CE	—	14.00	22.50	46.00	230	—
1853/2C CE	—	14.00	22.50	46.00	230	—
1854C CE	—	17.00	34.50	60.00	230	—
1856C CE	—	22.50	40.25	80.00	230	—
1857C CE	—	14.00	22.50	46.00	230	—
1860C PV	—	14.00	22.50	46.00	230	—
1861C PV	—	14.00	22.50	46.00	230	—
1869C CE	—	14.00	22.50	46.00	230	—

KM# 374.4 2 REALES
6.76 g., 0.903 Silver, 0.19 oz. ASW **Obv.** Facing eagle, snake in beak **Edge:** Reeded **Mint:** Durango

Date	Mintage	F12	VF20	XF40	MS60	MS63
1826 Do RL	—	22.50	46.00	70.00	230	—
1832Do RM	—	22.50	46.00	70.00	230	—
Note: Style of pre-1832						
1832Do RM	—	22.50	46.00	70.00	230	—
Note: Style of post-1832						
1834/2Do RM	—	22.50	46.00	70.00	230	—
1834/3Do RM	—	22.50	46.00	70.00	230	—
1835/4Do RM/RL	—	230	350	575	—	—
1841/31Do RM	—	60.00	85.00	145	290	—
1841Do RM	—	60.00	85.00	145	290	—
1842/32Do RM	—	14.00	22.50	46.00	230	—
1843Do RM/RL	—	14.00	22.50	46.00	230	—
1844Do RM	—	40.25	60.00	90.00	230	—
1845/34Do RM/RL	—	14.00	22.50	46.00	230	—
1846/36Do RM	—	115	175	230	400	—
1848/36Do RM	—	14.00	22.50	46.00	230	—
1848/37Do RM	—	14.00	22.50	46.00	230	—
1848/7Do RM	—	14.00	22.50	46.00	230	—
1848Do RM	—	14.00	22.50	46.00	230	—
1849Do CM/RM	—	14.00	22.50	46.00	230	—
1849Do CM	—	14.00	22.50	46.00	230	—
1851Do JMR/RL	—	14.00	22.50	46.00	230	—
1852Do JMR	—	14.00	22.50	46.00	230	—
1854Do CP/CR	—	34.50	60.00	90.00	230	—
1855Do CP	—	290	400	575	—	—
1856Do CP	—	115	175	290	575	—
1858Do CP	—	14.00	22.50	46.00	230	—
1859/8Do CP	—	14.00	22.50	46.00	230	—
1861Do CP	—	14.00	22.50	46.00	230	—

KM# 374.5 2 REALES
6.76 g., 0.903 Silver, 0.19 oz. ASW **Obv.** Facing eagle, snake in beak **Edge:** Reeded **Mint:** Estado de Mexico

Date	Mintage	F12	VF20	XF40	MS60	MS63
1828 EoMo LF	—	375	600	1,050	2,900	—

KM# 374.6 2 REALES
6.76 g., 0.903 Silver, 0.19 oz. ASW **Obv.** Facing eagle, snake in beak **Edge:** Reeded **Mint:** Guadalajara

Date	Mintage	F12	VF20	XF40	MS60	MS63
1825Ga FS	—	22.50	46.00	90.00	230	—
1826Ga FS	—	22.50	46.00	90.00	230	—
1828/7Ga FS	—	115	175	260	450	—
1829Ga FS Rare	—	—	—	—	—	—
1832/0Ga FS/LP	—	115	175	260	400	—
1832Ga FS	—	14.00	22.50	46.00	230	—
1833/2Ga FS/LP	—	14.00	22.50	46.00	230	—
1834/27Ga FS Rare	—	—	—	—	—	—
1834Ga FS	—	14.00	22.50	46.00	230	—
1835Ga FS	—	2,400	—	—	—	—
1837Ga JG	—	14.00	22.50	46.00	230	—

Date	Mintage	F12	VF20	XF40	MS60	MS63
1838Ga JG	—	14.00	22.50	46.00	230	—
1840/30Ga MC	—	14.00	22.50	46.00	230	—
1841Ga MC	—	34.50	60.00	230	575	—
1842/32Ga JG/MC	—	40.25	60.00	115	230	—
1842Ga JG	—	22.50	46.00	90.00	230	—
1843Ga JG	—	14.00	22.50	46.00	230	—
1843Ga MC/JG	—	14.00	22.50	46.00	230	—
1844Ga MC	—	14.00	22.50	46.00	230	—
1845/3Ga MC/JG	—	14.00	22.50	46.00	230	—
1845/4Ga MC/JG	—	14.00	22.50	46.00	230	—
1845Ga JG	—	14.00	22.50	46.00	230	—
1846Ga JG	—	14.00	22.50	46.00	230	—
1847/6Ga JG	—	30.00	46.00	90.00	230	—
1848/7Ga JG	—	14.00	22.50	46.00	230	—
1849Ga JG	—	14.00	22.50	46.00	230	—
1850/40Ga JG	—	14.00	22.50	46.00	230	—
1851Ga JG	—	290	400	575	—	—
1852Ga JG	—	14.00	22.50	46.00	230	—
1853/1Ga JG	—	14.00	22.50	46.00	230	—
1854/3Ga JG	—	290	400	575	—	—
1855Ga JG	—	40.25	60.00	90.00	230	—
1856Ga JG	—	14.00	22.50	46.00	230	—
1857Ga JG	—	290	400	575	—	—
1859/8Ga JG	—	14.00	22.50	46.00	230	—
1859Ga JG	—	14.00	22.50	46.00	230	—
1862/1Ga JG	—	14.00	22.50	46.00	230	—

KM# 374.7 2 REALES
6.76 g., 0.903 Silver, 0.19 oz. ASW **Obv.** Facing eagle, snake in beak **Edge:** Reeded **Mint:** Guadalupe y Calvo

Date	Mintage	F12	VF20	XF40	MS60	MS63
1844 GC MP	—	46.00	70.00	145	325	—
1845GC MP	—	46.00	70.00	145	325	—
1846GC MP	—	60.00	115	175	350	—
1847GC MP	—	40.25	60.00	115	290	—
1848GC MP	—	60.00	115	175	350	—
1849GC MP	—	60.00	115	175	350	—
1850GC MP	—	145	290	—	—	—
1851/0GC MP	—	60.00	115	175	350	—
1851GC MP	—	60.00	115	175	350	—

KM# 374.8 2 REALES
6.76 g., 0.903 Silver, 0.19 oz. ASW **Obv.** Facing eagle, snake in beak **Edge:** Reeded **Mint:** Guanajuato **Note:** Varieties exist.

Date	Mintage	F12	VF20	XF40	MS60	MS63
1825Go JJ	—	9.00	17.00	34.50	175	—
1826/5Go JJ	—	9.00	17.00	34.50	175	—
1826Go JJ	—	9.00	12.00	30.00	175	—
1826Go MJ	—	9.00	12.00	30.00	175	—
1827/6Go MJ	—	9.00	12.00	30.00	175	—
1827Go MJ	—	9.00	12.00	30.00	175	—
1828/7Go MR	—	9.00	17.00	34.50	175	—
1828Go MJ	—	9.00	12.00	22.50	175	—
1828Go JM	—	9.00	12.00	22.50	175	—
1829Go MJ	—	9.00	12.00	22.50	175	—
1831Go MJ	—	9.00	12.00	22.50	175	—
1832Go MJ	—	9.00	12.00	22.50	175	—
1833Go MJ	—	9.00	12.00	22.50	175	—
1834Go PJ	—	9.00	12.00	22.50	175	—
1835/4Go PJ	—	9.00	17.00	34.50	175	—
1835Go PJ	—	9.00	12.00	22.50	175	—
1836Go PJ	—	9.00	12.00	22.50	175	—
1837/6Go PJ	—	9.00	12.00	22.50	175	—
1837Go PJ	—	9.00	12.00	22.50	175	—
1838/7Go PJ	—	9.00	12.00	22.50	175	—
1838Go PJ	—	9.00	12.00	22.50	175	—
1839/8Go PJ	—	9.00	17.00	34.50	175	—
1839Go PJ	—	9.00	12.00	22.50	175	—
1840Go PJ	—	9.00	12.00	22.50	175	—
1841Go PJ	—	9.00	12.00	22.50	175	—
1842Go PJ	—	9.00	12.00	22.50	175	—
1842Go PJ/PJ	—	9.00	12.00	22.50	175	—
1842Go PM	—	9.00	12.00	22.50	175	—
1843/2Go PM	—	9.00	12.00	22.50	175	—

Note: Concave wings, thin rays, small letters

Date	Mintage	F12	VF20	XF40	MS60	MS63
1843Go PM	—	9.00	12.00	22.50	175	—

Note: Convex wings, thick rays, large letters

Date	Mintage	F12	VF20	XF40	MS60	MS63
1844Go PM	—	9.00	12.00	22.50	175	—
1845/4Go PM	—	9.00	12.00	22.50	175	—
1845Go PM	—	9.00	12.00	22.50	175	—
1846/5Go PM	—	12.00	17.00	40.25	175	—
1846Go PM	—	9.00	12.00	22.50	175	—
1847Go PM	—	9.00	12.00	22.50	175	—
1848/7Go PM	—	9.00	17.00	34.50	175	—
1848Go PM	—	9.00	17.00	34.50	175	—
1848Go PF	—	115	175	290	575	—
1849/8Go PF/PM	—	9.00	12.00	22.50	175	—
1849Go PF	—	9.00	12.00	22.50	175	—
1850/40Go PF	—	9.00	12.00	22.50	175	—
1850Go PF	—	9.00	12.00	22.50	175	—
1851Go PF	—	9.00	12.00	22.50	175	—
1852/1Go PF	—	9.00	12.00	22.50	175	—
1852Go PF	—	9.00	12.00	22.50	175	—
1853Go PF	—	9.00	12.00	22.50	175	—
1854/3Go PF	—	9.00	12.00	22.50	175	—
1854Go PF	—	9.00	12.00	22.50	175	—

Note: Old font and obverse

Date	Mintage	F12	VF20	XF40	MS60	MS63
1854Go PF	—	9.00	12.00	22.50	175	—

Note: New font and obverse

Date	Mintage	F12	VF20	XF40	MS60	MS63
1855Go PF	—	9.00	12.00	22.50	175	—
1855Go PF	—	9.00	12.00	22.50	175	—

Note: Star in G of mint mark

Date	Mintage	F12	VF20	XF40	MS60	MS63
1856/5Go PF	—	12.00	17.00	40.25	175	—
1856Go PF	—	12.00	17.00	30.00	175	—
1857/6Go PF	—	9.00	12.00	22.50	175	—
1857Go PF	—	9.00	12.00	22.50	175	—
1858/7Go PF	—	9.00	12.00	22.50	175	—
1858Go PF	—	9.00	12.00	22.50	175	—
1859/7Go PF	—	9.00	12.00	22.50	175	—
1859Go PF	—	9.00	12.00	22.50	175	—
1860/7Go PF	—	9.00	12.00	22.50	175	—
1860/50Go PF	—	9.00	12.00	22.50	175	—
1860/59Go PF	—	9.00	12.00	22.50	175	—
1860Go PF	—	9.00	12.00	22.50	175	—
1861/51Go PF	—	9.00	12.00	22.50	175	—
1861/57Go PF	—	9.00	12.00	22.50	175	—
1861/0Go PF	—	9.00	12.00	22.50	175	—
1861Go PF	—	9.00	12.00	22.50	175	—
1862/1Go YE	—	9.00	12.00	22.50	145	—
1862Go YE	—	9.00	12.00	22.50	145	—
1862/57Go YE	—	9.00	12.00	22.50	145	—
1862Go YE/PF	—	9.00	12.00	22.50	145	—
1862/57Go YF/E	—	9.00	12.00	22.50	145	—
1862/57Go YF	—	9.00	12.00	22.50	145	—
1862Go YF	—	9.00	12.00	22.50	145	—
1863/52Go YF/PE	—	9.00	12.00	22.50	145	—
1863/52Go YF	—	9.00	12.00	22.50	145	—
1863Go YF	—	9.00	12.00	22.50	145	—
1867/57Go YF	—	9.00	12.00	22.50	145	—
1868/57Go YF	—	12.00	17.00	30.00	145	—

KM# 374.9 2 REALES
6.76 g., 0.903 Silver, 0.19 oz. ASW **Obv.** Facing eagle, snake in beak **Edge:** Reeded **Mint:** Hermosillo

Date	Mintage	F12	VF20	XF40	MS60	MS63
1861 Ho FM	—	230	350	450	750	—
1862/52Ho FM/C. CE	—	290	400	625	—	—
1867/1Ho PR/FM	—	85.00	175	290	575	—

KM# 374.10 2 REALES
6.76 g., 0.903 Silver, 0.19 oz. ASW **Obv.** Facing eagle, snake in beak **Rev:** Radiant cap **Obv. Legend:** REPUBLICA MEXICANA. **Edge:** Reeded **Mint:** Mexico City **Note:** Varieties exist.

Date	Mintage	F12	VF20	XF40	MS60
1825Mo JM	—	12.00	17.00	34.50	200
1826Mo JM	—	12.00	17.00	34.50	200
1827Mo JM	—	12.00	17.00	34.50	200
1828Mo JM	—	12.00	17.00	34.50	200
1829/8Mo JM	—	12.00	17.00	34.50	200
1829Mo JM	—	12.00	17.00	34.50	200
1830Mo JM	—	46.00	70.00	145	290
1831Mo JM	—	12.00	17.00	34.50	200
1832Mo JM	—	115	230	450	—
1833/2Mo MJ/JM	—	12.00	17.00	34.50	200
1834Mo ML	—	60.00	115	230	450
1836Mo MF	—	12.00	17.00	34.50	200
1837Mo ML	—	12.00	17.00	34.50	200
1840/7Mo ML	—	175	260	400	—
1840Mo ML	—	175	260	400	—
1841Mo ML	—	17.00	46.00	115	290
1842 ML Rare	—	—	—	—	—
1847Mo RC Narrow date	—	12.00	17.00	34.50	200
1847Mo RC Wide date	—	12.00	17.00	34.50	200
1848Mo GC	—	12.00	17.00	34.50	200
1849Mo GC	—	12.00	17.00	34.50	200
1850Mo GC	—	12.00	17.00	34.50	200
1851Mo GC	—	46.00	70.00	145	290
1852Mo GC	—	12.00	17.00	34.50	200
1853Mo GC	—	12.00	17.00	34.50	200
1854/44Mo GC	—	12.00	17.00	34.50	200
1855Mo GC	—	12.00	17.00	34.50	200
1855Mo GF/GC	—	12.00	17.00	34.50	200
1855Mo GF	—	12.00	17.00	34.50	200
1856/5Mo GF/GC	—	12.00	17.00	34.50	200
1857Mo GF	—	12.00	17.00	34.50	200
1858Mo FH	—	9.00	14.00	30.00	175
1858Mo FH/GF	—	9.00	14.00	30.00	175
1859Mo FH	—	9.00	14.00	30.00	175
1860Mo FH	—	9.00	14.00	30.00	175
1860Mo TH	—	9.00	14.00	30.00	175
1861Mo CH	—	9.00	14.00	30.00	175
1862Mo CH	—	9.00	14.00	30.00	175
1863Mo CH	—	9.00	14.00	30.00	175
1863Mo TH	—	9.00	14.00	30.00	175
1867Mo CH	—	9.00	14.00	30.00	175
1868Mo CH	—	12.00	17.00	34.50	175
1868Mo PH	—	9.00	14.00	30.00	175

KM# 374.11 2 REALES
6.76 g., 0.903 Silver, 0.19 oz. ASW **Obv.** Facing eagle, snake in beak **Edge:** Reeded **Mint:** San Luis Potosi

Date	Mintage	F12	VF20	XF40	MS60	MS63
1829 Pi JS	—	12.00	17.00	34.50	230	—
1830/20Pi JS	—	22.50	34.50	70.00	230	—
1837Pi JS	—	12.00	17.00	34.50	230	—
1841Pi JS	—	12.00	17.00	34.50	230	—
1842/1Pi JS	—	12.00	17.00	34.50	230	—
1842Pi JS	—	12.00	17.00	34.50	230	—
1842Pi PS	—	22.50	40.25	70.00	230	—
1843Pi PS	—	14.00	22.50	46.00	230	—
1843Pi AM	—	12.00	17.00	34.50	230	—
1844Pi AM	—	12.00	17.00	34.50	230	—
1845Pi AM	—	12.00	17.00	34.50	230	—
1846Pi AM	—	12.00	17.00	34.50	230	—
1849Pi MC	—	12.00	17.00	34.50	230	—
1850Pi MC	—	12.00	17.00	34.50	230	—
1856Pi MC	—	46.00	70.00	145	290	—
1857Pi MC	—	—	—	—	—	—
1858Pi MC	—	14.00	22.50	46.00	230	—
1859Pi MC	—	60.00	80.00	115	230	—
1861Pi PS	—	12.00	17.00	34.50	230	—
1862Pi RO	—	14.00	22.50	46.00	230	—
1863Pi RO	—	115	290	400	575	—
1868Pi PS	—	12.00	17.00	34.50	230	—
1869/8Pi PS	—	12.00	17.00	34.50	230	—
1869Pi PS	—	12.00	17.00	34.50	230	—

KM# 374.12 2 REALES
6.76 g., 0.903 Silver, 0.19 oz. ASW **Obv.** Facing eagle, snake in beak **Edge:** Reeded **Mint:** Zacatecas **Note:** Varieties exist.

Date	Mintage	F12	VF20	XF40	MS60	MS63
1825Zs AZ	—	12.00	17.00	34.50	175	—
1826Zs AV	—	9.00	12.00	30.00	175	—
Note: A is inverted V						
1826Zs AZ	—	9.00	12.00	30.00	175	—
Note: A is inverted V						
1826Zs AO	—	12.00	17.00	34.50	175	—
1827Zs AO	—	7.00	9.00	14.00	175	—
Note: A is inverted V						
1827Zs AO	—	7.00	9.00	14.00	175	—
1828/7Zs AO	—	17.00	34.50	70.00	200	—
1828Zs AO	—	9.00	12.00	30.00	115	—
1828Zs AO	—	9.00	12.00	30.00	175	—
Note: A is inverted V						
1829Zs AO	—	9.00	12.00	30.00	175	—
1829Zs OV	—	9.00	12.00	30.00	175	—
1830Zs OV	—	9.00	12.00	30.00	175	—
1831Zs OV	—	9.00	12.00	30.00	175	—
1831Zs OM/OV	—	9.00	12.00	30.00	175	—
1831Zs OM	—	9.00	12.00	30.00	175	—
1832/1Zs OM	—	17.00	34.50	70.00	175	—
1832Zs OM	—	9.00	12.00	30.00	175	—
1833/27Zs OM	—	9.00	12.00	30.00	175	—
1833/2Zs OM	—	9.00	12.00	30.00	175	—
1833Zs OM	—	9.00	12.00	30.00	175	—
1834Zs OM	—	46.00	70.00	145	230	—
1835Zs OM	—	9.00	12.00	30.00	175	—
1836Zs OM	—	9.00	12.00	30.00	175	—
1837Zs OM	—	9.00	12.00	30.00	175	—
1838Zs OM	—	17.00	34.50	70.00	175	—
1839Zs OM	—	9.00	12.00	22.50	175	—
1840Zs OM	—	9.00	12.00	22.50	175	—
1841/0Zs OM	—	9.00	12.00	22.50	175	—
1841Zs OM	—	9.00	12.00	22.50	175	—
1842Zs OM Narrow date	—	9.00	12.00	22.50	175	—
1842Zs OM Wide date	—	9.00	12.00	22.50	175	—
1843Zs OM	—	9.00	12.00	22.50	175	—
1844Zs OM	—	9.00	12.00	22.50	175	—
1845Zs OM	—	9.00	12.00	22.50	175	—
Note: Small letters with leaves						
1845Zs OM	—	9.00	12.00	22.50	175	—
Note: Large letters with leaves						
1846Zs OM	—	9.00	12.00	22.50	175	—
1847Zs OM	—	9.00	12.00	22.50	175	—
1848Zs OM	—	9.00	12.00	22.50	175	—
1849Zs OM	—	9.00	12.00	22.50	175	—
1850Zs OM	—	9.00	12.00	22.50	175	—
1851Zs OM	—	9.00	12.00	22.50	175	—
1852Zs OM	—	9.00	12.00	22.50	175	—
1853Zs OM	—	9.00	12.00	22.50	175	—
1854/3 Zs OM	—	9.00	12.00	22.50	175	—
1854Zs OM	—	9.00	12.00	22.50	175	—
1855/4Zs OM	—	9.00	12.00	22.50	175	—
1855Zs OM	—	9.00	12.00	22.50	175	—
1855Zs MO	—	9.00	12.00	22.50	175	—
1856/5Zs MO	—	9.00	12.00	22.50	175	—
1856Zs MO	—	9.00	12.00	22.50	175	—
1857Zs MO	—	9.00	12.00	22.50	175	—
1858Zs MO	—	9.00	12.00	22.50	175	—
1859Zs MO	—	9.00	12.00	22.50	175	—
1860/59Zs MO	—	9.00	12.00	22.50	175	—
1860Zs MO	—	9.00	12.00	22.50	115	—
1860Zs VL	—	9.00	12.00	22.50	175	—
1861Zs VL	—	9.00	12.00	22.50	175	—
1862Zs VL	—	9.00	12.00	22.50	115	—
1863Zs MO	—	14.00	22.50	46.00	175	—
1863Zs VL	—	9.00	12.00	22.50	175	—
1864Zs MO	—	9.00	12.00	22.50	175	—
1864Zs VL	—	9.00	12.00	22.50	175	—
1865Zs MO	—	9.00	12.00	22.50	175	—
1867Zs JS	—	9.00	12.00	22.50	175	—

Date	Mintage	F12	VF20	XF40	MS60	MS63
1868Zs JS	—	12.00	17.00	40.25	175	—
1868Zs YH	—	9.00	12.00	22.50	175	—
1869Zs YH	—	9.00	12.00	22.50	175	—
1870Zs YH	—	9.00	12.00	22.50	175	—

KM# 375 4 REALES
13.54 g., 0.903 Silver, 0.39 oz. ASW **Obv.** Facing eagle, snake in beak **Rev:** Radiant cap **Obv. Legend:** REPUBLICA MEXICANA. **Mint:** Real de Catorce

Date	Mintage	F12	VF20	XF40	MS60	MS63
1863 Ce ML Large C	—	250	625	1,050	—	—
1863 Ce ML Small C	—	280	825	1,900	—	—

KM# 375.1 4 REALES
13.54 g., 0.903 Silver, 0.39 oz. ASW **Obv.** Facing eagle, snake in beak **Mint:** Culiacan

Date	Mintage	F12	VF20	XF40	MS60	MS63
1846 C CE	—	500	700	1,200	—	—
1850C CE	—	95.00	155	325	—	—
1852C CE	—	250	375	625	—	—
1857C CE Rare	—	—	—	—	—	—
1858C CE	—	125	250	450	—	—
1860C PV	—	31.25	65.00	155	—	—

KM# 375.2 4 REALES
13.54 g., 0.903 Silver, 0.39 oz. ASW **Obv.** Facing eagle, snake in beak **Mint:** Guadalajara

Date	Mintage	F12	VF20	XF40	MS60	MS63
1843 Ga MC	—	25.00	50.00	100	—	—
1844/3Ga MC	—	37.50	75.00	155	—	—
1844Ga MC	—	25.00	50.00	100	—	—
1845Ga MC	—	25.00	50.00	100	—	—
1845Ga JG	—	25.00	50.00	100	—	—
1846Ga JG	—	25.00	50.00	100	—	—
1847Ga JG	—	50.00	100	190	—	—
1848/7Ga JG	—	50.00	100	190	—	—
1849Ga JG	—	50.00	100	190	—	—
1850Ga JG	—	80.00	155	325	—	—
1852Ga JG Rare	—	—	—	—	—	—
1854Ga JG Rare	—	—	—	—	—	—
1855Ga JG	—	125	250	500	—	—
1856Ga JG Rare	—	—	—	—	—	—
1857/6Ga JG	—	80.00	155	325	—	—
1858Ga JG	—	155	325	575	—	—
1859/8Ga JG	—	155	325	575	—	—
1860Ga JG	—	1,050	1,800	—	—	—
1863/2Ga JG	—	190	375	1,550	—	—
1863Ga JG	—	190	375	1,550	—	—

KM# 375.3 4 REALES
13.54 g., 0.903 Silver, 0.39 oz. ASW **Obv.** Facing eagle, snake in beak **Mint:** Guadalupe y Calvo

Date	Mintage	F12	VF20	XF40	MS60	MS63
1844 GC MP	—	3,750	6,300	—	—	—
1845GC MP	—	8,100	10,000	—	—	—
1846GC MP	—	2,150	3,500	—	—	—
1847GC MP	—	1,900	3,150	—	—	—
1849GC MP	—	3,750	5,000	—	—	—
1850GC MP	—	1,900	3,150	—	—	—

KM# 375.4 4 REALES
13.54 g., 0.903 Silver, 0.39 oz. ASW **Obv.** Facing eagle, snake in beak **Rev:** Radiant cap **Obv. Legend:** REPUBLICA MEXICANA **Mint:** Guanajuato **Note:** Varieties exist. Some 1862 dates appear to be 1869 because of weak dies.

Date	Mintage	F12	VF20	XF40	MS60	MS63
1835 Go PJ	—	16.00	31.25	75.00	—	—
1836/5Go PJ	—	19.00	37.50	95.00	—	—
1836Go PJ	—	19.00	37.50	95.00	—	—
1837Go PJ	—	16.00	31.25	75.00	—	—
1838/7Go PJ	—	19.00	37.50	95.00	—	—
1838Go PJ	—	16.00	37.50	95.00	—	—
1839Go PJ	—	16.00	31.25	75.00	—	—
1840/30Go PJ	—	25.00	65.00	125	—	—
1840 PJ	—	25.00	65.00	125	—	—
1841/30 PJ	—	250	400	750	—	—
1841/31Go PJ	—	190	325	575	—	—
1842Go PJ Rare	—	—	—	—	—	—
1842Go PM	—	19.00	37.50	95.00	—	—
1843/2Go PM	—	16.00	31.25	75.00	—	—
Note: Eagle with convex wings, thick rays						
1843Go PM	—	16.00	31.25	75.00	—	—
Note: Eagle with concave wings, thin rays						
1844/3Go PM	—	19.00	37.50	95.00	—	—
1844Go PM	—	25.00	65.00	125	—	—
1845/4Go PM	—	25.00	65.00	125	—	—
1845Go PM	—	25.00	65.00	125	—	—
1846/5Go PM	—	19.00	37.50	95.00	—	—
1846Go PM	—	19.00	37.50	95.00	—	—
1847/6Go PM	—	19.00	37.50	95.00	—	—
1847Go PM	—	19.00	37.50	95.00	—	—
1848/7Go PM	—	25.00	65.00	125	—	—
1848Go PM	—	25.00	65.00	125	—	—
1849Go PF	—	25.00	65.00	125	—	—
1850Go PF	—	16.00	31.25	75.00	—	—
1851Go PF	—	16.00	31.25	75.00	—	—
1852Go PF	—	19.00	37.50	95.00	—	—
1852Go PF 5/4	—	25.00	65.00	125	—	—
1853Go PF	—	19.00	37.50	95.00	—	—
1854Go PF	—	19.00	37.50	95.00	—	—
Note: Large eagle						
1854Go PF	—	19.00	37.50	95.00	—	—
Note: Small eagle						
1855/4Go PF	—	19.00	37.50	95.00	—	—
1855Go PF	—	16.00	31.25	75.00	—	—
1856Go PF	—	16.00	31.25	75.00	—	—
1857Go PF	—	25.00	65.00	125	—	—
1858Go PF	—	25.00	65.00	125	—	—
1859Go PF	—	25.00	65.00	125	—	—
1860/59Go PF	—	19.00	37.50	95.00	—	—
1860Go PF	—	19.00	37.50	95.00	—	—
1861/51Go PF	—	19.00	37.50	95.00	—	—
1861Go PF	—	25.00	65.00	125	—	—

Date	Mintage	F12	VF20	XF40	MS60	MS63
1862/1Go YE	—	19.00	37.50	95.00	—	—
1862/1Go YF	—	19.00	37.50	95.00	—	—
1862Go YE/PF	—	19.00	37.50	95.00	—	—
1862Go YE	—	19.00	37.50	95.00	—	—
1862Go YF	—	19.00	37.50	95.00	—	—
1863/53Go YF	—	19.00	37.50	95.00	—	—
1863Go YF/PF	—	19.00	37.50	95.00	—	—
186/53 Go YF	—	19.00	37.50	95.00	—	—
1863Go YF	—	19.00	37.50	95.00	—	—
1867/57Go YF/PF	—	19.00	37.50	95.00	—	—
1868/58Go YF/PF	—	19.00	37.50	95.00	—	—
1870Go FR	—	19.00	37.50	95.00	—	—

KM# 375.5 4 REALES
13.54 g., 0.903 Silver, 0.39 oz. ASW **Obv.** Facing eagle, snake in beak **Mint:** Hermosillo

Date	Mintage	F12	VF20	XF40	MS60
1861 Ho FM	—	250	450	625	—
1867/1Ho PR/FM	—	190	350	500	—

KM# 375.6 4 REALES
13.54 g., 0.903 Silver, 0.39 oz. ASW **Obv.** Facing eagle, snake in beak **Mint:** Mexico City

Date	Mintage	F12	VF20	XF40	MS60	MS63
1827/6Mo JM	—	250	500	1,000	—	—
1850Mo GC Rare	—	—	—	—	—	—
1852Mo GC Rare	—	—	—	—	—	—
1854Mo GC Rare	—	—	—	—	—	—
1855Mo GF/GC	—	65.00	125	250	—	—
1855Mo GF	—	125	250	450	—	—
1856Mo GF/GC	—	65.00	155	500	—	—
1856Mo GF Rare	—	—	—	—	—	—
1859Mo FH	—	25.00	65.00	190	—	—
1861Mo CH	—	19.00	43.75	155	—	—
1862Mo CH	—	25.00	65.00	190	—	—
1863/2Mo CH	—	25.00	65.00	190	—	—
1863Mo CH	—	95.00	190	375	—	—
1867Mo CH	—	25.00	65.00	190	—	—
1868Mo CH/PH	—	37.50	95.00	190	—	—
1868Mo CH	—	25.00	65.00	190	—	—
1868Mo PH	—	37.50	95.00	250	—	—

KM# 375.7 4 REALES
13.54 g., 0.903 Silver, 0.39 oz. ASW **Obv.** Facing eagle, snake in beak **Rev:** Radiant cap **Obv. Legend:** REPUBLICA MEXICANA. **Mint:** Oaxaca

Date	Mintage	F12	VF20	XF40	MS60
1861 O FR	—	280	575	950	—
Note: Ornamental edge					
1861 O FR		375	700	1,050	—
Note: Herringbone edge					

Date	Mintage	F12	VF20	XF40	MS60
1861 O FR	—	250	500	875	—

Note: Obliquely reeded edge

KM# 375.8 4 REALES
13.54 g., 0.903 Silver, 0.39 oz. ASW **Obv.** Facing eagle, snake in beak **Mint:** San Luis Potosi

Date	Mintage	F12	VF20	XF40	MS60	MS63
1837 Pi JS	—	250	450	—	—	—
1838Pi JS	—	190	325	500	—	—
1842Pi PS	—	65.00	125	250	—	—
1843/2Pi PS	—	65.00	125	250	—	—
1843/2Pi PS	—	65.00	125	250	—	—
Note: 3 cut from 8 punch						
1843Pi AM	—	37.50	95.00	190	—	—
1843Pi PS	—	65.00	125	250	—	—
1844Pi AM	—	37.50	95.00	190	—	—
1845/4Pi AM	—	25.00	65.00	125	—	—
1845Pi AM	—	25.00	65.00	125	—	—
1846Pi AM	—	25.00	65.00	125	—	—
1847Pi AM	—	95.00	190	325	—	—
1848Pi AM Rare	—	—	—	—	—	—
1849Pi MC/AM	—	25.00	65.00	125	—	—
1849Pi MC	—	25.00	65.00	125	—	—
1849Pi PS	—	25.00	65.00	125	—	—
1850Pi MC	—	25.00	65.00	125	—	—
1851Pi MC	—	25.00	65.00	125	—	—
1852Pi MC	—	25.00	65.00	125	—	—
1853Pi MC	—	25.00	65.00	125	—	—
1854Pi MC	—	125	250	500	—	—
1855Pi MC	—	220	375	950	—	—
1856Pi MC	—	325	500	875	—	—
1857Pi MC Rare	—	—	—	—	—	—
1857Pi PS Rare	—	—	—	—	—	—
1858Pi MC	—	125	250	500	—	—
1859Pi MC	—	2,500	3,750	—	—	—
1860Pi PS	—	375	575	875	—	—
1861Pi PS	—	190	375	750	—	—
1861/0Pi PS	—	375	750	—	—	—
1861Pi RO/PS	—	37.50	95.00	190	—	—
1861Pi RO	—	65.00	125	250	—	—
1862Pi RO	—	37.50	95.00	190	—	—
1863Pi RO	—	37.50	95.00	190	—	—
1864Pi RO	—	3,150	4,400	—	—	—
1868Pi PS	—	37.50	95.00	190	—	—
1869/8Pi PS	—	37.50	95.00	190	—	—
1869Pi PS	—	37.50	95.00	190	—	—

KM# 375.9 4 REALES
13.54 g., 0.903 Silver, 0.39 oz. ASW **Obv.** Facing eagle, snake in beak **Mint:** Zacatecas

Date	Mintage	F12	VF20	XF40	MS60	MS63
1830 Zs OM	—	25.00	65.00	125	—	—
1831Zs OM	—	19.00	37.50	95.00	—	—
1832/1Zs OM	—	25.00	65.00	125	—	—
1832Zs OM	—	25.00	65.00	125	—	—
1833/2Zs OM	—	25.00	65.00	125	—	—
1833/27Zs OM	—	19.00	37.50	95.00	—	—
1833Zs OM	—	19.00	37.50	95.00	—	—
1834/3Zs OM	—	25.00	65.00	125	—	—
1834Zs OM	—	19.00	37.50	95.00	—	—
1835Zs OM	—	19.00	37.50	95.00	—	—
1836Zs OM	—	19.00	37.50	95.00	—	—
1837/5Zs OM	—	25.00	65.00	125	—	—
1837/6Zs OM	—	25.00	65.00	125	—	—
1837Zs OM	—	25.00	65.00	125	—	—
1838/7Zs OM	—	19.00	37.50	95.00	—	—
1839Zs OM	—	325	475	625	—	—
1840Zs OM	—	625	1,650	—	—	—
1841Zs OM	—	19.00	37.50	95.00	—	—
1842Zs OM	—	19.00	50.00	105	—	—
Small letters						
1842Zs OM	—	19.00	37.50	95.00	—	—
Large letters						
1843Zs OM	—	19.00	37.50	95.00	—	—
1844Zs OM	—	25.00	65.00	125	—	—
1845Zs OM	—	25.00	65.00	125	—	—
1846/5Zs OM	—	31.25	75.00	155	—	—

Date	Mintage	F12	VF20	XF40	MS60	MS63
1846Zs OM	—	25.00	65.00	125	—	—
1847Zs OM	—	19.00	37.50	95.00	—	—
1848/6Zs OM	—	65.00	95.00	155	—	—
1848Zs OM	—	25.00	65.00	125	—	—
1849Zs OM	—	25.00	65.00	125	—	—
1850Zs OM	—	25.00	65.00	125	—	—
1851Zs OM	—	19.00	37.50	95.00	—	—
1852Zs OM	—	19.00	37.50	95.00	—	—
1853Zs OM	—	25.00	65.00	125	—	—
1854/3Zs OM	—	37.50	95.00	190	—	—
1855/4Zs OM	—	25.00	65.00	125	—	—
1855Zs OM	—	19.00	37.50	95.00	—	—
1856Zs OM	—	19.00	37.50	95.00	—	—
1856Zs MO	—	25.00	65.00	125	—	—
1857/5Zs MO	—	25.00	65.00	125	—	—
1857Zs O/M	—	25.00	65.00	125	—	—
1857Zs MO	—	19.00	37.50	95.00	—	—
1858Zs MO	—	25.00	65.00	125	—	—
1859Zs MO	—	19.00	37.50	95.00	—	—
1860/59Zs MO	—	25.00	65.00	125	—	—
1860Zs MO	—	19.00	37.50	95.00	—	—
1860Zs VL	—	25.00	65.00	125	—	—
1861/0Zs VL	—	25.00	65.00	125	—	—
1861Zs VL	—	19.00	37.50	95.00	—	—
1861Zs VL 6/5	—	25.00	65.00	125	—	—
1862/1Zs VL	—	25.00	65.00	125	—	—
1862Zs VL	—	25.00	65.00	125	—	—
1863Zs VL	—	25.00	65.00	125	—	—
1863Zs MO	—	25.00	65.00	125	—	—
1864Zs VL	—	19.00	37.50	95.00	—	—
1868Zs JS	—	25.00	65.00	125	—	—
1868Zs YH	—	19.00	37.50	95.00	—	—
1869Zs YH	—	19.00	37.50	95.00	—	—
1870Zs YH	—	19.00	37.50	95.00	—	—

KM# 377 8 REALES
27.07 g., 0.903 Silver, 0.78 oz. ASW **Obv.** Facing eagle, snake in beak **Rev:** Radiant cap **Obv. Legend:** REPUBLICA MEXICANA. **Mint:** Alamos **Note:** Mint mark A, As. Varieties exist.

Date	Mintage	F12	VF20	XF40	MS60
1864 PG	—	825	1,400	2,600	—
1865/4 PG Rare	—	—	—	—	—
1865 PG	—	550	825	1,300	—
1866/5 PG Rare	—	—	—	—	—
1866 PG	—	1,400	2,500	—	—
1866 DL Rare	—	—	—	—	—
1867 DL	—	1,250	2,350	—	—
1868 DL	—	65.00	110	210	650
1869/8 DL	—	65.00	110	210	—
1869 DL	—	65.00	100	170	650
1870 DL	—	45.00	75.00	170	650
1871 DL	—	33.00	49.50	110	450
1872 AM/DL	—	38.50	65.00	145	650
1872 AM	—	38.50	65.00	145	550

Date	Mintage	F12	VF20	XF40	MS60
1873 AM	509,000	30.00	38.50	80.00	350
1874/3As DL	—	38.50	65.00	145	550
1874 DL	—	30.00	38.50	80.00	350
1875A DL 7/7	—	55.00	100	170	650
1875A DL	—	30.25	38.50	80.00	350
1875As DL	—	45.00	75.00	155	550
1876 DL	—	30.00	38.50	80.00	350
1877 DL	515,000	30.00	38.50	80.00	350
1878 DL	513,000	30.00	38.50	80.00	350
1879 DL	—	33.00	50.00	110	400
1879 ML	—	44.00	75.00	175	750
1880 ML	—	27.50	30.00	50.00	325
1881 ML	966,000	27.50	30.00	50.00	325
1882 ML	480,000	27.50	30.00	50.00	325
1883 ML	464,000	27.50	30.00	50.00	325
1884 ML	—	27.50	30.00	50.00	325
1885 ML	280,000	27.50	30.00	50.00	325
1886 ML	857,000	27.50	30.00	45.50	270
1886/0As/Cn ML/JD	Inc. above	30.00	33.00	60.00	350
1887 ML	650,000	27.50	30.00	45.50	270
1888/7 ML	508,000	44.00	75.00	145	850
1888 ML	Inc. above	27.50	30.00	45.50	270
1889 ML	427,000	27.50	30.00	45.50	270
1890 ML	450,000	27.50	30.00	45.50	270
1891 ML	533,000	27.50	30.00	45.50	270
1892/0 ML	—	33.00	44.00	90.00	350
1892 ML	465,000	27.50	30.00	45.50	270
1893 ML	734,000	27.50	30.00	42.50	230
1894 ML	725,000	27.50	30.00	42.50	230
1895 ML	477,000	27.50	30.00	42.50	230

KM# 377.1 8 REALES
27.07 g., 0.903 Silver, 0.78 oz. ASW **Obv.** Facing eagle, snake in beak **Rev:** Radiant cap **Obv. Legend:** REPUBLICA MEXICANA. **Mint:** Real de Catorce

Date	Mintage	F12	VF20	XF40	MS60	MS63
1863 Ce ME	—	575	975	2,200	7,500	—
1863 Ce /PI ML/MC	—	575	1,050	2,450	8,000	—

KM# 377.3 8 REALES
27.07 g., 0.903 Silver, 0.78 oz. ASW **Obv.** Facing eagle, snake in beak **Rev:** Radiant cap **Obv. Legend:** REPUBLICA MEXICANA **Mint:** Culiacan **Note:** Mint mark C, Cn. Varieties exist.

Date	Mintage	F12	VF20	XF40	MS60	MS63
1846 CE	—	165	325	1,050	3,000	—
1846 CE	—	195	425	1,150	3,300	—
Note: Dot after G						
1846 CE	—	140	290	975	2,900	—
Note: No dot after G						
1847 CE	—	450	775	1,950	—	—
1848 CE	—	140	275	575	2,000	—
1849 CE C/G	—	85.00	140	260	800	—
1849 CE	—	85.00	140	260	800	—
1850 CE	—	85.00	140	260	800	—
1851 CE	—	140	275	575	2,000	—
1852/1 CE	—	110	165	325	1,000	—
1852 CE	—	110	220	400	1,200	—
1853/0 CE	—	220	375	900	2,600	—
1853/2/0	—	220	450	975	2,800	—
1853 CE	—	110	195	400	1,200	—
Note: Thick rays						
1853 CE	—	220	375	850	—	—
Note: Error: MEXIGANA						
1854 CE	—	825	1,400	—	—	—
1854 CE	—	195	375	975	2,400	—
Note: Large eagle and hat						
1855/6 CE	—	55.00	75.00	145	450	—
1855 CE	—	38.50	55.00	110	350	—
1856 CE	—	65.00	120	240	750	—
1857 CE	—	33.00	49.50	110	350	—
1858 CE	—	44.00	55.00	110	350	—
1859 CE	—	33.00	49.50	110	350	—
1860/9 PV/CV	—	65.00	90.00	145	450	—
1860/9 PV/E	—	65.00	90.00	145	450	—
1860 CE	—	38.50	55.00	110	350	—
1860/9 PV	—	55.00	75.00	130	400	—
1860 PV	—	55.00	75.00	130	400	—
1861/0 CE	—	65.00	100	170	550	—
1861 PV/CE	—	95.00	150	275	750	—
1861 CE	—	33.00	49.50	90.00	350	—
1862 CE	—	33.00	49.50	90.00	350	—
1863/2 CE	—	44.00	65.00	110	450	—
1863 CE	—	33.00	44.00	90.00	350	—
1864 CE	—	44.00	75.00	145	650	—
1865 CE	—	150	230	425	1,350	—
1866 CE	—	450	825	1,650	4,500	—
1867 CE	—	150	230	450	1,450	—
1868/7 CE	—	44.00	55.00	110	350	—
1868/8	—	65.00	120	210	650	—
1868 CE	—	44.00	55.00	110	350	—
1869 CE	—	44.00	55.00	110	400	—
1870 CE	—	65.00	120	210	750	—
1873 MP	—	65.00	120	210	650	—
1874/3 MP	—	44.00	55.00	110	350	—
1874C MP	—	33.00	44.00	70.00	290	—
1874CN MP	—	150	230	400	1,250	—
1875 MP	—	27.50	30.00	41.50	230	—
1876 GP	—	27.50	30.00	50.00	240	—
1876 CG	—	27.50	30.00	41.50	230	—
1877 CG	339,000	27.50	30.00	41.50	230	—
1877Gn CG Error	—	85.00	150	275	850	—
1877 JA	Inc. above	49.50	95.00	175	550	—
1878/7 CG	483,000	49.50	95.00	175	550	—
1878 CG	Inc. above	30.00	38.50	60.00	290	—
1878 JD/CG	—	38.50	49.50	80.00	350	—
1878 JD	Inc. above	30.00	35.00	50.00	290	—
1878 JD	Inc. above	33.00	44.00	65.00	350	—
Note: D over retrograde D						
1879 JD	—	27.50	30.00	50.00	300	—
1880/70 JD	—	30.00	35.00	50.00	240	—
1880 JD	—	27.50	30.00	41.50	280	—
1881/0 JD	1,032,000	30.25	33.00	50.00	240	—
1881C JD	Inc. above	27.50	30.00	41.50	230	—
1881Cn JD	Inc. above	55.00	75.00	130	350	—

Date	Mintage	F12	VF20	XF40	MS60	MS63
1882 JD	397,000	27.50	30.00	41.50	230	—
1882 AM	Inc. above	27.50	30.00	41.50	230	—
1883 AM	333,000	27.50	30.00	41.50	290	—
1884 AM	—	27.50	30.00	41.50	230	—
1885/6 AM	227,000	33.00	44.00	70.00	290	—
1885C AM	Inc. above	49.50	90.00	210	750	—
1885Cn AM	Inc. above	27.50	30.00	41.50	230	—
1885Gn AM	Inc. above	38.50	65.00	145	600	—
Error						
1886 AM	571,000	27.50	30.00	41.50	230	—
1887 AM	732,000	27.50	30.00	41.50	230	—
1888 AM	768,000	27.50	30.00	41.50	230	—
1889 AM	1,075,000	27.50	30.00	41.50	230	520
1890 AM	874,000	27.50	29.50	39.00	220	—
1891 AM	777,000	27.50	29.50	39.00	220	—
1892 AM	681,000	27.50	29.50	39.00	220	—
1893 AM	1,144,000	27.50	29.50	39.00	220	—
1894 AM	2,118,000	27.50	29.50	39.00	220	—
1895 AM	1,834,000	27.50	29.50	39.00	220	—
1896 AM	2,134,000	27.50	29.50	39.00	220	—
1897 AM	1,580,000	27.50	29.50	39.00	220	—

KM# 377.4   8 REALES
27.07 g., 0.903 Silver, 0.78 oz. ASW **Obv.** Facing eagle, snake in beak **Mint:** Durango **Note:** Varieties exist.

Date	Mintage	F12	VF20	XF40	MS60
1825 Do RL	—	44.00	85.00	210	800
1826Do RL	—	55.00	105	275	1,000
1827/6Do RL	—	49.50	75.00	125	450
1827/8Do RL	—	175	325	650	—
1827Do RL	—	44.00	65.00	130	450
1828/7Do RL	—	49.50	75.00	130	450
1828Do RL	—	38.50	65.00	115	400
1829Do RL	—	38.50	65.00	115	400
1830Do RM	—	38.50	65.00	130	450
Note: B on eagle's claw					
1831Do RM	—	33.00	44.00	90.00	350
Note: B on eagle's claw					
1832Do RM	—	49.50	75.00	170	650
Note: Mexican dies, B on eagle's claw					
1832/1Do RM/RL	—	38.50	49.50	110	375
Note: French dies, REPUB MEX spaced					
1833/2Do RM/RL	—	33.00	49.50	110	375
1833Do RM	—	30.00	44.00	90.00	350
1834/3/2 Do	—	33.00	49.50	110	375
RM/RL					
1834Do RM	—	30.00	38.50	80.00	350
1835/4Do RM/RL	—	33.00	49.50	100	350
1835Do RM	—	33.00	49.50	100	350
Note: Mexican dies, REPUBMEX not spaced					
1836/1Do RM	—	33.00	49.50	100	350
1836/4Do RM	—	33.00	49.50	100	350

Date	Mintage	F12	VF20	XF40	MS60
1836/5/4 Do	—	95.00	175	350	1,050
RM/RL					
1836Do RM	—	33.00	44.00	85.00	350
1836Do RM	—	33.00	44.00	85.00	350
Note: M on snake					
1837/1Do RM	—	33.00	44.00	85.00	350
1837Do RM	—	33.00	44.00	85.00	350
1838/1Do RM	—	33.00	44.00	90.00	375
1838/7Do RM	—	33.00	44.00	90.00	375
1838Do RM	—	33.00	44.00	85.00	350
1839/1Do RM/RL	—	33.00	44.00	85.00	350
1839/1Do RM	—	33.00	44.00	85.00	350
1839Do RM	—	33.00	44.00	85.00	350
1840/38/31 Do RM	—	33.00	44.00	85.00	350
1840/39Do RM	—	33.00	44.00	85.00	350
1840Do RM	—	33.00	44.00	85.00	350
1841/31Do RM	—	85.00	150	375	950
1841/39Do RM/L	—	38.50	65.00	125	450
1841/39Do RM	—	38.50	65.00	125	450
1842/31Do RM	—	150	285	525	1,550
Note: B below cactus					
1842/31Do RM	—	55.00	100	175	550
1842/32Do RM	—	55.00	100	175	550
1842Do RM	—	33.00	44.00	85.00	350
Note: Eagle of 1832-41					
1842Do RM	—	33.00	44.00	85.00	350
Note: Pre-1832 eagle resumed					
1842Do RM	—	55.00	100	175	550
1843/33Do RM	—	65.00	110	210	550
1843Do RM	—	65.00	110	210	550
1844/34Do RM	—	120	230	400	1,050
1844/35Do RM	—	120	230	400	1,050
1844/43Do RM	—	75.00	145	300	900
1845/31Do RM	—	120	230	400	1,050
1845/34Do RM	—	49.50	95.00	175	550
1845/35Do RM	—	49.50	95.00	175	550
1845Do RM	—	33.00	44.00	85.00	350
1846/31Do RM	—	33.00	44.00	85.00	350
1846/36Do RM	—	33.00	44.00	85.00	350
1846Do RM	—	33.00	44.00	85.00	350
1847Do RM	—	38.50	65.00	115	400
1848/7Do RM	—	150	285	525	1,550
1848/7Do CM/RM	—	120	230	450	1,450
1848Do CM/RM	—	120	230	450	1,450
1848Do RM	—	120	230	400	1,250
1848Do CM	—	65.00	120	275	850
1849/39Do CM	—	120	230	450	1,450
1849Do CM	—	85.00	150	350	1,150
1849Do JMR/CM	—	230	450	575	1,650
Oval 0					
1849Do JMR	—	230	350	575	1,650
Oval 0					
1849Do JMR	—	230	450	775	2,000
Round 0					
1850Do JMR	—	120	175	350	1,050
1851/0Do JMR	—	85.00	150	300	1,000
1851Do JMR	—	120	175	350	1,050
1852Do CP/JMR	—	500	900	1,950	—
1852Do CP	—	825	1,350	2,950	—
1852Do JMR	—	205	285	500	1,350
1853Do CP/JMR	—	150	270	450	1,250
1853Do CP	—	230	375	775	2,400
1854Do CP	—	38.50	49.50	100	650
1855Do CP	—	65.00	120	240	750
Note: Eagle type of 1854					
1855Do CP	—	65.00	120	240	750
Note: Eagle type of 1856					
1856Do CP	—	65.00	120	240	750
1857Do CP	—	49.50	85.00	175	550
1858/7Do CP	—	38.50	49.50	105	375
1858Do CP	—	33.00	44.00	90.00	375
1859Do CP	—	33.00	44.00	90.00	375
1860/59Do CP	—	44.00	65.00	145	450
1860Do CP	—	33.00	44.00	90.00	375
1861/0Do CP	—	33.00	44.00	90.00	375
1861Do CP	—	33.00	44.00	80.00	290

Date	Mintage	F12	VF20	XF40	MS60
1862/1Do CP	—	38.50	49.50	90.00	290
1862Do CP	—	33.00	44.00	90.00	400
1863/1Do CP	—	44.00	75.00	130	450
1863/2Do CP	—	38.50	65.00	110	400
1863/53Do CP	—	44.00	75.00	130	450
1863Do CP	—	38.50	65.00	110	400
1864Do CP	—	120	175	350	1,050
1864Do LT	—	38.50	55.00	115	400
1864Do LT/T	—	38.50	55.00	115	400
1864Do LT/CP	—	65.00	120	240	750
1865Do LT Rare	—	—	—	—	—
1866/4Do CM	—	3,050	6,100	—	—
1866Do CM	—	1,950	3,600	7,200	17,000
1867Do CM	—	3,850	—	—	—
1867/6Do CP	—	220	450	775	2,400
1867Do CP	—	195	325	650	2,000
1867Do CP/CM	—	140	275	525	1,800
1867Do CP/LT	—	220	450	850	2,500
1868Do CP	—	38.50	55.00	115	400
1869Do CP	—	33.00	44.00	80.00	300
1870/69Do CP	—	33.00	44.00	80.00	290
1870/9Do CP	—	33.00	44.00	80.00	290
1870Do CP	—	33.00	44.00	80.00	290
1873Do CP	—	150	260	425	1,250
1873Do CM	—	44.00	65.00	145	450
1874/3Do CM	—	27.50	30.00	45.50	290
1874Do CM	—	27.50	30.00	45.50	290
1874Do JH	—	1,250	1,950	3,600	—
1875Do CM	—	27.50	30.00	45.50	290
1875Do JH	—	100	175	350	950
1876Do CM	—	27.50	30.00	45.50	290
1877Do CM	431,000	1,600	2,750	—	—
1877Do CP	Inc. above	27.50	30.00	45.50	290
1877Do JMP	825	1,400	2,600	—	
1878Do PE	409,000	30.00	38.50	65.00	290
1878Do TB	Inc. above	27.50	30.00	45.50	290
1879Do TB	—	27.50	30.00	45.50	290
1880/70Do TB	—	75.00	120	240	750
1880/70Do TB/JP	—	175	285	500	1,350
1880/70Do JP	—	30.00	38.50	65.00	290
1880Do TB	—	175	285	500	1,350
1880Do JP	—	27.50	30.00	45.50	290
1881Do JP	928,000	27.50	30.00	45.50	290
1882Do JP	414,000	27.50	30.00	45.50	290
1882Do MC/JP	Inc. above	44.00	75.00	145	450
1882Do MC	Inc. above	38.50	65.00	110	350
1883/73Do MC	452,000	30.00	38.50	65.00	290
1883Do MC	Inc. above	27.50	30.00	45.50	290
1884/3Do MC	—	30.00	38.50	65.00	290
1884Do MC	—	27.50	30.00	45.50	290
1885Do MC M/J	—	30.00	38.50	65.00	290
1885Do JB	Inc. above	38.50	49.50	80.00	300
1885Do MC	547,000	27.50	29.50	41.50	290
1886/5Do MC	—	30.00	38.50	65.00	240
1886/3Do MC	955,000	30.00	38.50	65.00	240
1886Do MC	Inc. above	27.50	29.50	41.50	220
1887Do MC	1,004,000	27.50	29.50	41.50	220
1888/7Do MC	—	85.00	150	350	950
1888Do MC	996,000	27.50	29.50	41.50	220
1889Do MC	874,000	27.50	29.50	41.50	220
1890Do MC	1,119,000	27.50	29.50	41.50	220
1890Do JP	Inc. above	27.50	29.50	41.50	220
1891Do JP	1,487,000	27.50	29.50	41.50	220
1892Do JP	1,597,000	27.50	29.50	41.50	220
1892Do ND	Inc. above	38.50	65.00	145	450
1893Do ND	1,617,000	27.50	29.50	41.50	220
1894Do ND	1,537,000	27.50	29.50	41.50	220
1895/3Do ND	761,000	30.00	38.50	65.00	240
1895Do ND	Inc. above	27.50	29.50	41.50	220
1895Do ND/P	—	30.00	38.50	65.00	240

KM# 377.5   8 REALES
27.07 g., 0.903 Silver, 0.78 oz. ASW **Obv.** Facing eagle,
snake in beak **Rev:** Radiant cap **Mint:** Estado de Mexico

Date	Mintage	F12	VF20	XF40	MS60	MS63
1828 EoMo	—	375	925	2,850	—	—
1828 EoMo LF LF/LP	—	375	925	2,850	9,600	—
1829EoMo LF	—	325	825	2,400	7,700	—
1830/20EoMo LF	—	1,400	3,050	5,900	—	—
1830EoMo LF	—	1,100	2,200	4,250	10,500	—

KM# 377.6   8 REALES
27.07 g., 0.903 Silver, 0.78 oz. ASW **Obv.** Facing eagle,
snake in beak **Rev:** Radiant cap **Obv. Legend:** REPUBLICA
MEXICANA. **Mint:** Guadalajara **Note:** Varieties exist.

Date	Mintage	F12	VF20	XF40	MS60
1825 Ga FS	—	165	300	625	2,000
1826/5Ga FS	—	140	275	575	2,000
1826Ga FS	—	140	275	575	2,000
1827/87Ga FS	—	140	275	575	2,000
1827Ga FS	—	140	275	575	2,000
1287 Ga FS Error	—	9,400	10,500	—	—
1828Ga FS	—	220	425	725	2,400
1829/8Ga FS	—	220	425	725	2,400
1829Ga FS	—	195	350	625	1,900
1830/29Ga FS	—	110	195	400	1,200
1830Ga FS	—	110	195	400	1,200
1830Ga LP/FS	—	875	1,600	—	—
Note: The 1830 LP/FS is currently only known with a Philippine countermark					
1831Ga LP	—	220	450	775	2,400
1831Ga FS/LP	—	325	550	975	3,000
1831Ga FS	—	140	300	525	—
1832/1Ga FS	—	65.00	120	240	650
1832/1Ga FS/LP	—	65.00	120	240	650
1832Ga FS/LP	—	95.00	175	375	1,150
1832Ga FS	—	38.50	65.00	145	500
1833/2/1 Ga FS/LP	—	60.00	95.00	175	550
1833/2Ga FS	—	38.50	65.00	145	500
1834/2Ga FS	—	75.00	150	275	750
1834/3Ga FS	—	75.00	150	275	750
1834/0Ga FS	—	65.00	120	210	650
1834Ga FS	—	65.00	120	210	650
1835Ga FS	—	38.50	65.00	145	500

Date	Mintage	F12	VF20	XF40	MS60
1836/5Ga FS	—	205	375	—	—
1836/1Ga JG/FS	—	55.00	100	175	550
1836Ga FS	—	325	500	975	—
1836Ga JG/FS	—	38.50	65.00	145	500
1836Ga JG	—	38.50	65.00	145	500
1837/6Ga JG/FS	—	65.00	120	240	650
1837/6Ga JG	—	60.00	110	220	600
1837Ga JG	—	55.00	100	175	550
1838/7Ga JG	—	120	205	400	1,150
1838Ga JG	—	120	175	375	1,050
1839Ga MC	—	120	230	450	1,250
1839Ga MC/JG	—	120	230	400	1,150
1839Ga JG	—	75.00	150	275	750
1840/30Ga MC	—	65.00	95.00	210	600
1840Ga MC	—	44.00	75.00	175	550
1841Ga MC	—	44.00	75.00	175	550
1842/1Ga JG/MG	—	120	175	350	950
1842/1Ga JG/MC	—	120	175	350	950
1842Ga JG	—	38.50	65.00	145	500
1842Ga JG/MG	—	38.50	65.00	145	500
1843/2Ga MC/JG	—	38.50	65.00	145	500
1843Ga MC/JG	—	38.50	65.00	145	500
1843Ga JG	—	450	650	1,150	3,600
1843Ga MC	—	65.00	120	210	650
1844Ga MC	—	65.00	120	210	650
1845Ga MC	—	95.00	175	400	1,450
1845Ga JG	—	550	925	1,650	3,700
1846Ga JG	—	55.00	100	210	650
1847Ga JG	—	120	175	300	850
1848/7Ga JG	—	70.00	105	175	550
1848Ga JG	—	65.00	95.00	145	500
1849Ga JG	—	110	150	240	700
1849/39Ga JG	—	275	550	—	—
1850Ga JG	—	65.00	120	210	650
1851Ga JG	—	140	220	450	1,300
1852Ga JG	—	110	165	325	900
1853/2Ga JG	—	140	195	325	950
1853Ga JG	—	110	150	240	650
1854/3Ga JG	—	85.00	110	175	550
1854Ga JG	—	65.00	95.00	155	500
1855Ga JG	—	65.00	120	210	600
1855Ga JG	—	38.50	65.00	145	500
1856/4Ga JG	—	75.00	150	240	650
1856/5Ga 56	—	75.00	150	240	650
1856Ga JG	—	65.00	120	210	600
1857Ga JG	—	65.00	120	300	950
1858Ga JG	—	120	175	400	1,050
1859/7Ga JG	—	38.50	65.00	155	500
1859/8Ga JG	—	38.50	65.00	145	450
1859Ga JG	—	33.00	55.00	115	400
1860Ga JG	—	375	825	1,550	4,500
Without dot					
1860Ga JG	—	2,200	3,600	5,900	—
Note: Dot in loop of snake's tail, base alloy					
1861Ga JG	—	2,400	6,300	—	—
1862Ga JG	—	925	1,500	3,600	9,000
1863/52Ga JG	—	—	—	—	—
1863/59Ga JG	—	60.00	65.00	125	325
1863/2Ga JG	—	44.00	65.00	130	400
1863/4Ga JG	—	55.00	95.00	210	550
1863Ga JG	—	38.50	60.00	110	350
1863Ga FV Rare	—	—	—	—	—
1867Ga JM Rare	—	—	—	—	—
1868/7Ga JM	—	65.00	95.00	175	450
1868Ga JM	—	65.00	95.00	175	450
1869Ga JM	—	65.00	95.00	175	450
1869Ga IC	—	95.00	150	275	800
1870/60Ga IC	—	75.00	110	210	600
1870Ga IC	—	75.00	110	210	600
1873Ga IC	—	27.50	38.50	80.00	300
1874Ga IC	—	27.50	29.50	41.50	220
1874Ga MC	—	38.50	65.00	145	450
1875Ga IC	—	30.00	44.00	90.00	300
1875Ga MC	—	27.50	29.50	41.50	290
1876Ga IC	559,000	30.00	44.00	80.00	290
1876Ga MC	Inc. above	150	205	350	800

Date	Mintage	F12	VF20	XF40	MS60
1877Ga IC	928,000	27.50	30.00	45.50	290
1877/6Ga JA	—	27.50	30.00	45.50	290
1877Ga JA	Inc. above	27.50	30.00	45.50	290
1878Ga JA	764,000	27.50	30.00	45.50	290
1879Ga JA	—	27.50	30.00	45.50	290
1880/70Ga FS	—	30.00	38.50	80.00	300
1880Ga JA	—	27.50	30.00	45.50	290
1880Ga FS	—	27.50	30.00	45.50	290
1881Ga FS	1,300,000	27.50	30.00	45.50	290
1882/1Ga FS	537,000	30.00	38.50	80.00	300
1882Ga FS	Inc. above	27.50	30.00	45.50	290
1882Ga TB/FS	Inc. above	65.00	120	240	650
1882Ga TB	Inc. above	65.00	120	240	650
1883Ga TB	561,000	30.00	38.50	65.00	300
1884Ga TB	—	27.50	29.50	41.50	290
1884Ga AH	—	27.50	29.50	41.50	290
1885Ga AH	443,000	27.50	29.50	41.50	290
1885Ga JS	Inc. above	27.50	29.50	145	450
1886Ga JS/H	—	27.50	29.50	41.50	290
1886Ga JS	1,038,999	27.50	29.50	41.50	290
1887Ga JS	878,000	27.50	29.50	41.50	290
1888Ga JS	1,159,000	27.50	29.50	41.50	290
1889Ga JS	1,583,000	27.50	29.50	41.50	290
1890Ga JS	1,658,000	27.50	29.50	41.50	260
1891Ga JS	1,507,000	27.50	29.50	41.50	260
1892/1Ga JS	1,627,000	30.00	38.50	80.00	290
1892Ga JS	Inc. above	27.50	29.50	41.50	260
1893Ga JS	1,952,000	27.50	29.50	41.50	260
1894Ga JS	2,045,999	27.50	29.50	41.50	260
1895/3Ga JS	—	27.50	33.00	60.00	270
1895Ga JS	1,146,000	27.50	29.50	41.50	260

KM# 377.7 8 REALES

27.07 g., 0.903 Silver, 0.78 oz. ASW **Obv.** Facing eagle, snake in beak **Rev:** Radiant cap **Obv. Legend:** REPUBLICA MEXICANA. **Mint:** Guadalupe y Calvo

Date	Mintage	F12	VF20	XF40	MS60
1844 GC MP	—	425	600	1,450	3,850
1844 GC MP	—	500	725	1,700	4,300
Note: Error, reversed S in Ds, Gs					
1845GC MP	—	155	240	450	1,350
Note: Eagle's tail square					
1845GC MP	—	215	425	950	2,300
Note: Eagle's tail round					
1846GC MP	—	215	425	1,050	3,200
Note: Eagle's tail square					
1846GC MP	—	155	240	500	1,450
Note: Eagle's tail round					
1847GC MP	—	180	300	575	1,500
1848GC MP	—	215	350	725	1,750
1849GC MP	—	215	350	750	1,900
1850GC MP	—	215	350	825	2,100
1851GC MP	—	350	600	1,300	3,050
1852GC MP	—	425	725	1,800	4,800

KM# 377.8   8 REALES
27.07 g.,   0.903 Silver, 0.78 oz. ASW **Obv.** Facing eagle, snake in beak **Rev:** Radiant cap **Obv. Legend:** REPUBLICA MEXICANA. **Mint:** Guanajuato **Note:** Varieties exist.

Date	Mintage	F12	VF20	XF40	MS60
1825 Go JJ	—	55.00	90.00	210	650
1825 G JJ	1,400	1,800	—	—	—
Note: Error mint mark G					
1826Go JJ	—	55.00	100	240	750
Note: Straight J's					
1826Go JJ	—	44.00	75.00	175	550
Note: Full J's					
1826Go MJ	—	275	500	1,100	—
1827Go MJ	—	55.00	95.00	175	550
1827Go MJ/JJ	—	—	—	—	—
1827Go MR	—	120	230	450	1,250
1828Go MJ	—	—	—	—	—
Note: Error mint mark Goo					
1828Go MJ	—	44.00	75.00	175	550
1828/7Go MR	—	165	325	775	2,400
1828Go MR	—	165	325	775	2,400
1829Go MJ	—	33.00	49.50	85.00	375
1830Go MJ	—	33.00	44.00	85.00	375
Note: Oblong beading and narrow J					
1830Go MJ	—	33.00	44.00	85.00	375
Note: Regular beading and wide J					
1831Go MJ	—	27.50	33.00	65.00	350
Note: Colon after date					
1831Go MJ	—	27.50	33.00	65.00	350
Note: 2 stars after date					
1832Go MJ	—	27.50	33.00	65.00	300
1832Go MJ	—	33.00	49.50	100	400
Note: 1 of date over inverted 1					
1833Go MJ/1	—	33.00	49.50	100	400
1833Go MJ	—	27.50	33.00	65.00	350
1833Go JM	—	450	825	1,650	5,000
1834Go PJ	—	27.50	33.00	65.00	350
1835Go PJ	—	27.50	33.00	65.00	350
Note: Star on cap					
1835Go PJ	—	27.50	33.00	65.00	350
Note: Dot on cap					
1836Go PJ	—	27.50	33.00	65.00	350
1837Go PJ	—	27.50	33.00	65.00	350
1838Go PJ	—	27.50	33.00	65.00	350
1839Go PJ/JJ	—	27.50	33.00	65.00	350
1839Go PJ	—	27.50	33.00	65.00	350
1840/30Go PJ	—	33.00	44.00	80.00	350
1840Go PJ	—	27.50	33.00	60.00	290
1841/31Go PJ	—	27.50	33.00	60.00	290
1841Go PJ	—	27.50	33.00	60.00	290
1842/1Go PM	—	33.00	44.00	80.00	290

Date	Mintage	F12	VF20	XF40	MS60
1842/31Go PM/PJ	—	38.50	49.50	90.00	350
1842/1Go PJ	—	33.00	44.00	80.00	290
1842Go PJ	—	33.00	44.00	80.00	290
1842Go PM/PJ	—	27.50	33.00	60.00	290
1842Go PM	—	27.50	33.00	60.00	290
1843Go PM	—	27.50	33.00	60.00	290
Note: Dot after date					
1843Go PM	—	27.50	33.00	60.00	290
Note: Triangle of dots after date					
1844Go PM	—	27.50	33.00	60.00	290
1845Go PM	—	27.50	33.00	60.00	290
1846/5Go PM	—	33.00	44.00	80.00	350
Note: Eagle type of 1845					
1846Go PM	—	33.00	44.00	80.00	350
Note: Eagle type of 1845					
1846Go PM	—	30.25	38.50	65.00	300
Note: Eagle type of 1847					
1847Go PM Narrow date	—	27.50	33.00	60.00	290
1847Go PM Wide date	—	27.50	33.00	60.00	290
1848/7Go PM	—	27.50	49.50	100	350
1848Go PM	—	33.00	49.50	100	350
1848Go PF	—	27.50	33.00	60.00	290
1849Go PF	—	27.50	33.00	60.00	290
1850Go PF	—	27.50	33.00	60.00	290
1851/0Go PF	—	33.00	44.00	80.00	350
1851Go PF	—	27.50	33.00	60.00	290
1852/1Go PF	—	33.00	44.00	80.00	350
1852Go PF	—	27.50	33.00	60.00	290
1853/2Go PF	—	33.00	44.00	80.00	350
1853Go PF	—	27.50	33.00	60.00	290
1854Go PF	—	27.50	33.00	60.00	290
1855Go PF Large letters	—	27.50	33.00	60.00	290
1855Go PF Small letters	—	27.50	33.00	60.00	290
1856/5Go PF	—	33.00	44.00	80.00	350
1856Go PF	—	27.50	33.00	60.00	290
1857/5Go PF	—	33.00	44.00	80.00	350
1857/6Go PF	—	33.00	49.50	105	450
1857Go PF	—	27.50	30.00	41.50	220
1858/7Go PI Narrow date	—	27.50	33.00	60.00	290
1858Go PF Wide date	—	27.50	33.00	60.00	290
1859/7Go PF	—	27.50	33.00	60.00	290
1859/8Go PF	—	33.00	44.00	80.00	350
1859Go PF	—	27.50	33.00	60.00	290
1860/50Go PF	—	33.00	44.00	80.00	350
1860/59Go PF	—	27.50	30.00	45.50	230
1860Go PF	—	27.50	30.00	41.50	220
1861/51Go PF	—	27.50	33.00	50.00	240
Note: Narrow and wide dates exist					
1861/0Go PF	—	27.50	30.00	41.50	220
1861Go PF	—	27.50	30.00	41.50	220
186/52 Go YE	—	30.00	33.00	50.00	240
1862Go YE/PF	—	27.50	30.00	41.50	220
186/52 Go YF	—	30.00	33.00	50.00	240
1862Go YE	—	27.50	30.00	41.50	220
1862Go YF	—	27.50	30.00	41.50	220
1862Go YF/PF	—	27.50	30.00	41.50	220
1863/53Go YF	—	27.50	30.00	45.50	220
1863/54Go YF	—	30.00	33.00	50.00	240
1863Go YE Rare	—	—	—	—	—
1863Go YF	—	27.50	30.00	41.50	220
1867/57Go YF	—	30.00	33.00	50.00	240
1867Go YF	—	27.50	30.00	41.50	220
1868/58Go YF	—	30.00	33.00	50.00	240
1868/7Go YF	—	30.00	33.00	50.00	240
1868Go YF	—	27.50	30.00	41.50	220
1870/60Go FR	—	33.00	44.00	80.00	350
1870Go YF	2,000	3,300	6,500	15,000	
1870Go FR/YF	—	33.00	49.50	105	450
1870Go FR	—	27.50	30.00	41.50	220
1873Go FR	—	27.50	30.00	41.50	220

Date	Mintage	F12	VF20	XF40	MS60
1874/3Go FR	—	30.00	33.00	50.00	230
1874Go FR	—	30.00	38.50	60.00	240
1875/3Go FR	—	30.00	33.00	50.00	230
1875/6Go FR	—	30.00	33.00	50.00	230
1875Go FR	—	27.50	30.00	41.50	220
Note: Small circle with dot on eagle					
1876/5Go FR	—	30.00	33.00	50.00	230
1876Go FR	—	27.50	30.00	41.50	220
1877Go FR Narrow date	—	27.50	30.00	41.50	220
1877Go FR Wide date	2,477,000	27.50	30.00	41.50	220
1878/7Go FR	2,273,000	30.00	33.00	50.00	220
1878/7Go SM, S/F	—	30.00	33.00	50.00	220
1878/7Go SM	—	30.00	33.00	50.00	220
1878Go FR	Inc. above	27.50	30.00	41.50	220
1878Go SM, S/F	—	30.25	33.00	45.50	220
1878Go SM	—	27.50	30.00	41.50	220
1879/7Go SM	—	30.00	33.00	50.00	220
1879/8Go SM	—	30.00	33.00	50.00	220
1879/8Go SM/FR	—	30.00	33.00	50.00	220
1879Go SM	—	27.50	30.00	41.50	220
1879Go SM/FR	—	30.00	33.00	50.00	220
1880/70Go SB	—	30.00	33.00	50.00	220
1880Go SB/SM	—	27.50	30.00	41.50	220
1880Go SB	—	27.50	30.00	41.50	220
1881/71Go SB	3,974,000	30.00	33.00	50.00	220
1881/0Go SB	Inc. above	30.00	33.00	50.00	220
1881Go SB	Inc. above	27.50	30.00	41.50	220
1882Go SB	2,015,000	27.50	30.00	41.50	220
1883Go SB	2,100,000	49.50	95.00	175	550
1883Go BR	Inc. above	27.50	30.00	41.50	220
1883Go BR/SR	—	27.50	30.00	41.50	220
1883Go BR/SB	Inc. above	27.50	30.00	41.50	220
1884/73Go BR	—	33.00	44.00	65.00	240
1884/74Go BR	—	33.00	44.00	65.00	240
1884/3Go BR	—	33.00	44.00	90.00	350
1884Go BR	—	27.50	30.00	41.50	220
1884/74Go RR	—	65.00	120	240	750
1884Go RR	—	38.50	65.00	145	550
1885/75Go RR/BR	—	30.00	33.00	400	220
1885/75Go RR	2,363,000	30.00	33.00	50.00	220
1885Go RR	Inc. above	27.50	30.00	41.50	220
1886/75Go RR/BR	—	30.00	33.00	45.50	220
1886/75Go RR	4,127,000	30.00	33.00	45.50	220
1886/76Go RR/BR	—	27.50	30.00	41.50	220
1886/76Go RR	Inc. above	27.50	30.00	41.50	220
1886/5Go RR/BR	Inc. above	27.50	30.00	41.50	220
1886Go RR	Inc. above	27.50	30.00	41.50	220
1887Go RR	4,205,000	27.50	30.00	41.50	220
1888Go RR	3,985,000	27.50	30.00	41.50	220
1889Go RR	3,646,000	27.50	30.00	41.50	220
1890Go RR	3,615,000	27.50	30.00	41.50	220
1891Go RS/R	—	27.50	30.00	41.50	220
1891Go RS	3,197,000	27.50	30.00	41.50	220
1892/0Go/A RS	—	27.50	30.00	41.50	220
1892/0Go RS	—	27.50	30.00	41.50	220
1892Go RS	3,672,000	27.50	30.00	41.50	220
1892Go/A RS	—	27.50	30.00	41.50	220
1893Go RS	3,854,000	27.50	30.00	41.50	220
1894Go RS	4,127,000	27.50	30.00	41.50	220
1895/1Go RS	3,768,000	30.00	33.00	41.50	220
1895/3Go RS	Inc. above	30.00	33.00	45.50	220
1895Go RS	Inc. above	27.50	30.00	41.50	220
1896/1Go/As RS/ML	5,229,000	30.00	33.00	45.50	220
1896/1Go RS	Inc. above	27.50	30.00	41.50	220
1896Go/Ga RS	Inc. above	—	—	—	—
1896Go RS	Inc. above	27.50	29.50	39.00	220
1897Go RS	4,344,000	27.50	29.50	39.00	220

KM# 377.9 8 REALES
27.07 g., 0.903 Silver, 0.78 oz. ASW **Obv.** Facing eagle, snake in beak **Rev:** Radiant cap **Mint:** Hermosillo **Note:** Varieties exist.

Date	Mintage	F12	VF20	XF40	MS60	MS63
1835 Ho PP Rare	—	—	—	—	—	—
1836Ho PP Rare	—	—	—	—	—	—
1839Ho PR Unique	—	—	—	—	—	—
1861Ho FM	—	4,950	8,300	—	—	—
Note: Reeded edge						
1862Ho FM Rare						
Note: Plain edge, snakes tail left, long ray over *8R						
1862Ho FM	—	1,700	2,950	—	—	—
Note: Plain edge, snake's tail left						
1862Ho FM	—	1,800	3,050	—	—	—
Note: Reeded edge, snakes tail right						
1863Ho FM	—	165	325	1,050	—	—
1864Ho FM	—	925	1,800	3,600	—	—
1864Ho PR/FM	—	1,300	2,400	—	—	—
1864Ho PR	—	725	1,400	2,800	6,700	—
1865Ho FM	—	275	550	1,250	3,700	—
1866Ho FM	—	1,250	2,350	4,550	11,000	—
1866Ho MP	—	1,050	1,950	3,900	9,300	—
1867Ho PR	—	110	195	350	1,000	—
1868Ho PR	—	33.00	49.50	100	400	—
1869Ho PR	—	55.00	75.00	175	550	—
1870Ho PR	—	120	205	375	1,150	—
1871/0Ho PR	—	65.00	95.00	175	550	—
1871Ho PR	—	44.00	65.00	130	450	—
1872/1Ho PR	—	49.50	75.00	130	450	—
1872Ho PR	—	44.00	65.00	110	400	—
1873Ho PR	351,000	44.00	65.00	125	350	—
1874Ho PR	—	30.00	35.00	65.00	290	—
1875Ho PR	—	30.00	35.00	65.00	290	—
1876Ho AF	—	30.00	35.00	65.00	290	—
1877Ho AF	410,000	33.00	44.00	80.00	350	—
1877Ho GR	Inc. above	120	175	300	850	—
1877Ho JA	Inc. above	38.50	65.00	125	400	—
1878Ho JA	451,000	30.00	35.00	65.00	280	—
1879Ho JA	—	30.00	35.00	65.00	280	—
1880Ho JA	—	30.00	35.00	65.00	280	—
1881Ho JA	586,000	30.00	35.00	65.00	280	—
1882Ho JA	240,000	38.50	55.00	100	290	—
Note: O above H						
1882Ho JA	Inc. above	38.50	55.00	100	290	—
Note: O after H						
1883/2Ho JA	204,000	230	400	675	2,050	—
1883/2Ho FM/JA	Inc. above	38.50	55.00	110	350	—
1883Ho FM/JA	—	40.00	60.00	125	375	—
1883Ho FM	Inc. above	33.00	44.00	90.00	290	—
1883Ho JA	Inc. above	325	500	1,050	3,050	—
1884/3Ho FM	—	33.00	38.50	80.00	290	—
1884Ho FM	—	30.00	35.00	65.00	280	—
1885Ho FM	132,000	30.00	35.00	65.00	280	—
1886Ho FM	225,000	33.00	44.00	70.00	290	—

Date	Mintage	F12	VF20	XF40	MS60	MS63
1886Ho FG	Inc. above	33.00	44.00	70.00	290	—
1887/6Ho FG	—	33.00	49.50	100	350	—
1887Ho FG	150,000	33.00	49.50	100	350	—
1888Ho FG	364,000	27.50	33.00	50.00	260	—
1889Ho FG	490,000	27.50	33.00	50.00	260	—
1890Ho FG	565,000	27.50	33.00	50.00	260	—
1891Ho FG	738,000	27.50	33.00	50.00	260	—
1892Ho FG	643,000	27.50	33.00	50.00	260	—
1893Ho FG	518,000	27.50	33.00	50.00	260	—
1894Ho FG	504,000	27.50	33.00	50.00	260	—
1895Ho FG	320,000	27.50	33.00	50.00	260	—

KM# 377.10 8 REALES

27.07 g., 0.903 Silver, 0.78 oz. ASW **Obv.** Facing eagle, snake in beak **Rev:** Radiant cap **Obv. Legend:** REPUBLICA MEXICANA. **Mint:** Mexico City **Note:** Varieties exist. 1874 CP is a die struck counterfeit.

Date	Mintage	F12	VF20	XF40	MS60	MS63
1824Mo JM	—	95.00	150	350	1,050	—
Round tail						
1824Mo JM	—	95.00	150	350	1,050	—
Square tail						
1825Mo JM	—	38.50	55.00	110	450	—
1826/5Mo JM	—	38.50	55.00	110	450	—
1826Mo JM	—	33.00	44.00	85.00	375	—
1827Mo JM	—	38.50	49.50	90.00	400	—
Note: Medal alignment						
1827Mo JM	—	38.50	49.50	90.00	400	—
Note: Coin alignment						
1828Mo JM	—	44.00	75.00	145	550	—
1829Mo JM	—	33.00	45.00	130	475	—
1830/20Mo JM	—	49.50	85.00	210	650	—
1830Mo JM	—	44.00	65.00	130	475	—
1831Mo JM	—	44.00	65.00	145	525	—
1832/1Mo JM	—	38.50	55.00	100	400	—
1832Mo JM	—	33.00	44.00	85.00	375	—
1833Mo MJ	—	38.50	55.00	115	450	—
1833Mo ML	—	500	725	1,250	4,000	—
1834/3Mo ML	—	38.50	49.50	90.00	400	—
1834Mo ML	—	33.00	44.00	85.00	375	—
1835Mo ML	—	33.00	44.00	85.00	375	—
Narrow date						
1835Mo ML	—	33.00	44.00	85.00	375	—
Wide date						
1836Mo ML	—	65.00	120	210	700	—
1836Mo ML/ MF	—	65.00	120	210	700	—
1836Mo MF	—	44.00	65.00	130	475	—
1836Mo MF/ ML	—	49.50	75.00	145	525	—
1837/6Mo ML	—	44.00	65.00	115	450	—
1837/6Mo MM	—	44.00	65.00	115	450	—
1837/6Mo MM/ML	—	44.00	65.00	115	450	—
1837/6Mo MM/MF	—	44.00	65.00	115	450	—
1837Mo ML	—	44.00	65.00	115	450	—
1837Mo MM	—	95.00	150	240	700	—
1838Mo MM	—	44.00	65.00	115	450	—
1838Mo ML	—	33.00	49.50	90.00	400	—

Date	Mintage	F12	VF20	XF40	MS60	MS63
1838Mo ML/ MM	—	33.00	49.50	90.00	400	—
1839Mo ML	—	30.00	38.50	80.00	375	—
Narow date						
1839Mo ML	—	30.00	38.50	80.00	375	—
Wide date						
1840Mo ML	—	30.00	38.50	80.00	375	—
1841Mo ML	—	30.00	38.50	70.00	350	—
1842Mo ML	—	30.00	38.50	70.00	350	—
1842Mo MM	—	30.00	38.50	70.00	350	—
1843Mo MM	—	30.00	38.50	70.00	350	—
1844Mo MF/ MM	—	—	—	—	—	—
1844Mo MF	—	30.00	38.50	70.00	350	—
1845/4Mo MF	—	30.00	38.50	70.00	350	—
1845Mo MF	—	30.00	38.50	70.00	350	—
1846/5Mo MF	—	30.00	38.50	80.00	375	—
1846Mo MF	—	30.00	38.50	80.00	375	—
1847/6Mo MF	2,200	3,900	—	—	—	—
1847Mo MF	1,650	3,050	6,500	15,000		—
1847Mo RC	—	33.00	44.00	85.00	375	—
1847Mo RC/ MF	—	30.00	38.50	70.00	350	—
1848Mo GC	—	30.00	38.50	70.00	350	—
1849/8Mo GC	—	33.00	49.50	90.00	400	—
1849Mo GC	—	30.00	38.50	70.00	350	—
1850/40Mo GC	—	38.50	65.00	145	525	—
1850/49Mo GC	—	38.50	65.00	145	525	—
1850Mo GC	—	33.00	55.00	110	450	—
1851Mo GC	—	33.00	55.00	90.00	400	—
1852Mo GC	—	33.00	55.00	110	450	—
1853Mo GC	—	30.00	38.50	80.00	350	—
1854Mo GC	—	27.50	30.00	50.00	290	—
1855Mo GC	—	33.00	49.50	100	400	—
1855Mo GF	—	27.50	30.00	50.00	290	—
1855Mo GF/ GC	—	27.50	30.00	50.00	290	—
1856/4Mo GF	—	30.00	38.50	70.00	325	—
1856/5Mo GF	—	30.00	38.50	70.00	325	—
1856Mo GF	—	27.50	30.00	50.00	290	—
1857Mo GF	—	27.50	30.00	50.00	290	—
1858Mo FH	—	27.50	30.00	50.00	290	—
Narrow date						
1858/7Mo FH/GF	—	27.50	30.00	50.00	290	—
1858Mo FH	—	27.50	30.00	50.00	290	—
Wide date						
1859Mo FH	—	27.50	30.00	50.00	290	—
1859/8Mo FH	—	38.50	65.00	145	525	—
1860/59Mo FH	—	30.00	33.00	50.00	290	—
1860Mo FH	—	27.50	30.00	50.00	290	—
1860Mo TH	—	27.50	30.00	65.00	325	—
1861Mo TH	—	27.50	30.00	65.00	325	—
1861Mo CH	—	27.50	30.00	41.50	220	—
1862Mo CH	—	27.50	30.00	41.50	220	—
1863Mo CH	—	27.50	30.00	41.50	220	—
1863Mo CH/ TH	—	27.50	30.00	41.50	220	—
1863Mo TH	—	27.50	30.00	41.50	220	—
1867Mo CH	—	27.50	30.00	41.50	220	—
1867Mo CH/ TH	—	33.00	60.00	105	400	—
1868Mo CH	—	27.50	30.00	41.50	220	—
1868Mo PH	—	27.50	30.00	41.50	220	—
1868Mo CH/ PH	—	27.50	30.00	41.50	220	—
1868Mo PH	—	27.50	30.00	41.50	220	—
Narrow date						
1868Mo PH	—	27.50	30.00	41.50	220	—
Wide date						
1869Mo CH	—	27.50	30.00	41.50	220	—
1873Mo MH	—	27.50	30.00	41.50	220	—
1873Mo MH/ HH	—	27.50	30.00	45.50	230	—

Date	Mintage	F12	VF20	XF40	MS60	MS63
1874/69Mo MH	—	33.00	60.00	105	400	—
1874Mo MH	—	27.50	30.00	45.50	230	—
1874Mo BH/MH	—	27.50	30.00	45.50	230	—
1874Mo BH	—	27.50	30.00	45.50	230	—
1875Mo BH	—	27.50	30.00	41.50	220	—
1876/4Mo BH	—	27.50	30.00	45.50	230	—
1876/5Mo BH	—	27.50	30.00	45.50	230	—
1876Mo BH	—	27.50	30.00	41.50	220	—
1877Mo MH	898,000	27.50	30.00	41.50	220	—
1877Mo MH/BH	Inc. above	27.50	30.00	45.50	230	—
1878Mo MH	2,154,000	27.50	30.00	41.50	220	—
1879/8Mo MH	—	27.50	30.00	41.50	230	—
1879Mo MH	—	27.50	30.00	41.50	220	—
1880/79Mo MH	—	30.00	33.00	50.00	240	—
1880Mo MH	—	27.50	30.00	41.50	220	—
1881Mo MH	5,712,000	27.50	30.00	41.50	220	—
1882/1Mo MH	2,746,000	27.50	30.00	41.50	220	—
1882Mo MH	Inc. above	27.50	30.00	41.50	220	—
1883/2Mo MH	2,726,000	27.50	30.00	45.50	230	—
1883Mo MH Narrow date	Inc. above	27.50	30.00	41.50	220	—
1883Mo MH Wide date	—	27.50	30.00	41.50	220	—
1884/3Mo MH	—	30.00	33.00	50.00	240	—
1884Mo MH	—	27.50	30.00	41.50	220	—
1885Mo MH	3,649,000	27.50	30.00	41.50	220	—
1886Mo MH	7,558,000	27.50	29.50	39.00	220	—
1887Mo MH	7,681,000	27.50	29.50	39.00	220	—
1888Mo MH Narrow date	7,179,000	27.50	29.50	39.00	220	—
1888Mo MH Wide date	—	27.50	29.50	39.00	220	—
1889Mo MH	7,332,000	27.50	30.00	41.50	220	—
1890Mo MH Narrow date	7,412,000	27.50	29.50	39.00	220	—
1890Mo AM Wide date	—	27.50	29.50	39.00	220	—
1890Mo AM	Inc. above	27.50	29.50	39.00	220	—
1891Mo AM	8,076,000	27.50	29.50	39.00	220	—
1892Mo AM	9,392,000	27.50	29.50	39.00	220	—
1893Mo AM	10,773,000	27.50	29.50	39.00	220	—
1894Mo AM	12,394,000	27.50	29.50	39.00	220	—
1895Mo AM	10,474,000	27.50	29.50	39.00	220	—
1895Mo AB	Inc. above	27.50	29.50	39.00	220	—
1896Mo AB	9,327,000	27.50	29.50	39.00	220	—
1896Mo AM	Inc. above	27.50	29.50	39.00	220	—
1897Mo AM	8,621,000	27.50	29.50	39.00	220	—

Date	Mintage	F12	VF20	XF40	MS60	MS63
1860 AE	—	220	500	1,050	—	—
Note: A in O of mint mark						
1861O FR	—	140	275	725	2,700	—
1861Oa FR	—	165	375	975	—	—
1862O FR	—	55.00	100	275	800	—
1862Oa FR	—	85.00	150	350	950	—
1863O FR	—	45.00	75.00	145	550	—
1863O AE	—	45.00	75.00	145	550	—
1863Oa AE	—	120	175	350	950	—
Note: A in O of mint mark						
1863Oa AE	—	1,100	1,950	3,600	—	—
Note: A above O in mint mark						
1864 FR	—	38.50	65.00	110	450	—
1865 AE	—	2,050	3,300	—	—	—
1867 AE	—	55.00	100	210	850	—
1868 AE	—	55.00	100	210	850	—
1869 AE	—	45.00	75.00	145	550	—
1873 AE	—	220	325	725	2,700	—
1874 AE	142,000	32.00	44.00	80.00	450	—
1875/4 AE	131,000	38.50	65.00	110	450	—
1875 AE	Inc. above	32.00	44.00	65.00	300	—
1876 AE	140,000	33.00	49.50	85.00	450	—
1877 AE	139,000	33.00	44.00	80.00	450	—
1878 AE	125,000	33.00	44.00	80.00	450	—
1879 AE	153,000	33.00	44.00	80.00	450	—
1880 AE	143,000	32.00	44.00	70.00	350	—
1881 AE	134,000	33.00	49.50	90.00	350	—
1882 AE	100,000	33.00	49.50	90.00	350	—
1883 AE	122,000	32.00	44.00	70.00	350	—
1884 AE	142,000	32.00	44.00	80.00	350	—
1885 AE	158,000	30.00	38.50	65.00	300	—
1886 AE	120,000	32.00	44.00	70.00	350	—
1887/6 AE	115,000	38.50	65.00	115	450	—
1887 AE	Inc. above	30.00	38.50	65.00	300	—
1888 AE	145,000	30.00	38.50	65.00	300	—
1889 AE	150,000	33.00	45.00	90.00	400	—
1890 AE	181,000	33.00	45.00	90.00	400	—
1891 EN	160,000	30.00	38.50	65.00	300	—
1892 EN	120,000	30.00	38.50	65.00	300	—
1893 EN	66,000	60.00	95.00	165	650	—

KM# 377.12 8 REALES

27.07 g., 0.903 Silver, 0.78 oz. ASW **Obv.** Facing eagle, snake in beak **Rev:** Radiant cap **Obv. Legend:** REPUBLICA MEXICANA **Mint:** San Luis Potosi **Note:** Varieties exist.

Date	Mintage	F12	VF20	XF40	MS60
1827 Pi JS	—	4,200	—	—	—
Note: Heritage World Coin Auction #3004, 1-09, MS63 realized $63,250					
1827 Pi SA	—	6,600	9,900	—	—
1828/7Pi JS	—	300	475	850	2,700
1828Pi JS	—	250	425	725	2,400
1829Pi JS	—	49.50	85.00	175	550
1830Pi JS	—	44.00	65.00	145	450

KM# 377.11 8 REALES

27.07 g., 0.903 Silver, 0.78 oz. ASW **Obv.** Facing eagle, snake in beak **Rev:** Radiant cap **Mint:** Oaxaca **Note:** Mint mark O, Oa. Varieties exist.

Date	Mintage	F12	VF20	XF40	MS60	MS63
1858 O AE	—	2,750	4,400	—	—	—
1858 Oa AE Unique	—	—	—	—	—	—
1859 AE	—	550	1,000	2,300	—	—
Note: A in O of mint mark						

FIRST REPUBLIC

Date	Mintage	F12	VF20	XF40	MS60
Note: Varities with low cap or centered cap					
1831/0Pi JS	—	49.50	95.00	275	750
1831Pi JS	—	38.50	49.50	110	450
1832/22Pi JS	—	38.50	49.50	100	375
18/032 Pi JS	—	55.00	100	240	650
1832Pi JS	—	38.50	49.50	100	375
1833/2Pi JS	—	44.00	60.00	115	550
1833Pi JS Narrow date	—	33.00	44.00	80.00	350
Note: Planchet diameter 37.5 mm					
1833Pi JS Wide date	—	33.00	44.00	80.00	350
Note: Planchet diameter 38.5 mm					
1834/3Pi JS	—	49.50	85.00	175	650
1834Pi JS	—	30.00	38.50	80.00	350
Note: Varieties with low cap or centered cap					
1835/4Pi JS	—	75.00	150	350	1,050
1835Pi JS	—	33.00	44.00	100	400
Note: Denomination as 8R					
1835Pi JS	—	30.00	38.50	80.00	350
Note: Denomination as 8Rs					
1836Pi JS	—	33.00	44.00	85.00	350
1837Pi JS	—	44.00	65.00	125	450
1838Pi JS	—	33.00	44.00	85.00	350
1839Pi JS	—	33.00	55.00	105	350
Note: Varieties with small low cap or large high cap					
1840Pi JS	—	33.00	44.00	90.00	350
184/31 Pi JS	—	38.50	55.00	125	450
1841Pi JS	—	38.50	55.00	125	450
1841iP JS Error	—	230	400	725	—
1842/1Pi JS	—	55.00	85.00	175	650
1842/1Pi JS/PS	—	49.50	70.00	130	450
1842Pi JS	—	44.00	65.00	115	400
Note: Eagle type of 1843					
1842Pi PS	—	44.00	65.00	115	400
1842Pi PS/JS	—	44.00	65.00	115	400
Note: Eagle type of 1841					
1843/2Pi PS Round-top 3	—	65.00	95.00	210	650
1843Pi PS Flat-top 3	—	75.00	120	275	1,000
1843Pi AM Round-top 3	—	33.00	44.00	85.00	350
1843Pi AM Flat-top 3	—	33.00	44.00	85.00	350
1844Pi AM	—	33.00	44.00	85.00	350
1845/4Pi AM	—	49.50	70.00	170	550
1845Pi AM	—	38.50	65.00	145	500
1846/5Pi AM	—	55.00	85.00	175	650
1846Pi AM	—	30.00	38.50	80.00	350
1847Pi AM	—	44.00	65.00	125	400
1848/7Pi AM	—	44.00	75.00	145	450
1848Pi AM	—	44.00	65.00	125	400
1849/8Pi PS/AM	—	1,050	1,950	—	—
1849Pi PS	—	1,050	1,950	—	—
1849Pi MC/PS	—	75.00	150	350	1,050
1849Pi AM	—	2,050	3,600	6,500	—
1849Pi MC	—	75.00	150	350	1,050
1850Pi MC	—	55.00	100	210	650
185/41 Pi MC	—	95.00	175	375	1,150
1851Pi MC	—	95.00	175	375	1,150
1852Pi MC	—	95.00	150	275	850
1853Pi MC	—	175	325	525	1,750
1854Pi MC	—	120	175	350	1,050
1855Pi MC	—	120	175	350	1,050
1856Pi MC	—	85.00	120	275	850
1857Pi MC	—	450	775	1,650	—
1857Pi PS/MC	—	165	275	575	2,000
1857Pi PS	—	140	220	450	1,300
1858Pi MC/PS	—	275	450	850	2,400
1858Pi MC	—	275	450	850	2,400
1858Pi PS	—	725	1,250	2,300	—
1859/8Pi MC/PS	—	4,000	6,300	—	—
1859Pi MC/PS	—	1,000	1,950	—	—
1859Pi MC	—	2,200	3,850	6,500	—
1859Pi PS/MC	—	875	1,650	3,250	—
1860Pi FC Rare	—	—	—	—	—

Date	Mintage	F12	VF20	XF40	MS60
1860Pi FE Rare	—	—	—	—	—
1860Pi MC	—	1,950	3,050	7,800	—
1860Pi PS/FE	—	550	1,100	—	—
1860Pi RO Rare	—	—	—	—	—
Note: Spink America Gerber sale 6-96 cleaned VF or better realized $33,000					
1860Pi PS	—	450	650	1,150	3,500
1861Pi PS	—	44.00	75.00	130	400
1861Pi RO	—	38.50	49.50	85.00	300
1862/1Pi RO	—	33.00	38.50	80.00	300
1862Pi RO	—	30.00	35.00	70.00	280
Note: Round O/M					
1862Pi RO	—	30.00	35.00	70.00	280
Note: Oval O in RO					
1862Pi RO	—	33.00	44.00	80.00	300
Note: Round O in RO, 6 is an inverted 9					
1863/2Pi RO	—	38.50	49.50	100	350
1863Pi RO/MO/FC	—	33.00	44.00	80.00	350
1863/5Pi RO	—	33.00	38.50	70.00	350
1863Pi RO	—	30.25	33.00	65.00	300
1863	—	38.50	49.50	85.00	300
Note: 6 over inverted 6					
1863Pi FC	—	3,050	5,200	—	—
1864Pi RO Rare	—	—	—	—	—
1867Pi CA	—	325	550	—	—
1867Pi LR	—	275	450	850	—
1867Pi PS/CA	—	925	—	—	—
1867Pi PS	—	44.00	75.00	175	600
1868/7Pi PS	—	44.00	75.00	175	550
1868Pi PS	—	33.00	44.00	80.00	300
1869/8Pi PS	—	33.00	38.50	70.00	300
1869Pi PS	—	30.00	35.00	70.00	300
1870/69Pi PS	—	825	1,600	4,550	—
1870Pi PS	—	725	1,400	3,250	—
1873Pi MH	—	30.00	38.50	70.00	350
1874/3Pi MH	—	38.50	65.00	170	550
1874Pi MH	—	27.50	29.50	41.50	280
1875Pi MH	—	27.50	29.50	41.50	260
1876/5Pi MH	—	30.00	38.50	70.00	350
1876Pi MH	—	27.50	29.50	41.50	260
1877/6Pi MH	—	195	375	725	—
1877Pi MH	1,018,000	27.50	29.50	41.50	280
1878Pi MH	1,046,000	30.00	44.00	145	500
1879/8Pi MH	—	30.00	35.00	50.00	290
1879Pi MH	—	27.50	29.50	41.50	260
1879Pi BE	—	38.50	65.00	110	350
1879Pi MR	—	44.00	65.00	145	450
1880Pi MR	—	285	425	1,000	—
1880/70Pi MH/R	—	27.50	29.50	41.50	260
1880Pi MH/R	—	27.50	29.50	41.50	260
1880Pi MH	—	27.50	29.50	41.50	260
1881/71Pi MH/R	—	27.50	29.50	41.50	260
1881Pi MH/R	—	27.50	29.50	41.50	260
1881Pi MH	2,100,000	27.50	29.50	41.50	260
1882/1Pi MH	1,602,000	30.00	35.00	50.00	290
1882Pi MH	Inc. above	27.50	29.50	41.50	260
1883/2Pi MH	—	30.00	35.00	50.00	290
1883Pi MH	1,545,000	27.50	29.50	41.50	260
1884/3Pi MH	—	30.00	35.00	50.00	290
1884Pi MH/MM	—	27.50	30.00	41.50	230
1884Pi MH	—	27.50	29.50	39.00	220
1885/4Pi MH	1,736,000	30.00	35.00	50.00	290
1885/8Pi MH	Inc. above	30.00	35.00	50.00	290
1885Pi MH	Inc. above	27.50	29.50	39.00	220
1885Pi LC	Inc. above	27.50	33.00	45.50	260
1886Pi LC	3,347,000	27.50	29.50	39.00	220
1886Pi MH	Inc. above	27.50	29.50	39.00	220
1887Pi MR	2,922,000	27.50	29.50	39.00	220
1888/7Pi MR	—	30.00	35.00	50.00	290
1888Pi MR	2,438,000	27.50	29.50	39.00	220
1889Pi MR	2,103,000	27.50	29.50	39.00	220
1890Pi MR	1,562,000	27.50	29.50	39.00	220
1891Pi MR	1,184,000	27.50	29.50	39.00	220
1892Pi MR	1,336,000	27.50	29.50	39.00	220
1893Pi MR	530,000	27.50	29.50	39.00	220

KM# 377.13 8 REALES
27.07 g., 0.903 Silver, 0.78 oz. ASW **Obv.** Facing eagle, snake in beak **Rev:** Radiant cap **Obv. Legend:** REPUBLICA MEXICANA. **Mint:** Zacatecas **Note:** Varieties exist.

Date	Mintage	F12	VF20	XF40	MS60
1825 Zs AZ	—	38.50	49.50	100	400
1826/5Zs AZ	—	38.50	60.00	125	450
1826Zs AZ	—	110	220	525	1,600
1826Zs AV	—	195	375	775	3,000
1826/5Zs AO/AZ	—	325	650	1,300	4,000
1826Zs AO	—	220	375	975	4,000
1827Zs AO/AZ	—	49.50	65.00	175	550
1827Zs AO	—	38.50	60.00	125	450
1828Zs AO	—	30.00	35.00	70.00	375
Note: Wide and narrow date varieties exist					
1829Zs AO	—	30.00	35.00	70.00	375
1829Zs OV	—	65.00	110	210	650
1830Zs OM	—	—	—	—	—
1830Zs OV	—	30.00	35.00	70.00	375
1831Zs OV	—	38.50	65.00	130	450
1831Zs OM	—	30.00	38.50	85.00	375
1832/1Zs OM	—	33.00	38.50	70.00	375
1832Zs OM	—	30.00	35.00	65.00	350
1833/2Zs OM	—	33.00	44.00	70.00	375
1833Zs OM/MM	—	30.00	38.50	65.00	350
1833Zs OM	—	30.00	35.00	60.00	350
1834Zs OM	—	30.00	35.00	60.00	350
Note: Known with large, medium and small "34" in date					
1835Zs OM	—	30.00	35.00	65.00	350
1836/4Zs OM	—	33.00	44.00	80.00	375
1836/5Zs OM	—	33.00	44.00	80.00	375
1836Zs OM	—	30.00	35.00	60.00	350
1837Zs OM	—	30.00	35.00	60.00	350
1838/7Zs OM	—	33.00	44.00	70.00	375
1838Zs OM	—	30.00	35.00	60.00	350
1839Zs OM	—	30.00	35.00	60.00	350
1840Zs OM	—	30.00	35.00	60.00	350
1841Zs OM	—	30.00	35.00	60.00	350
1842Zs OM	—	30.00	35.00	60.00	350
Note: Eagle type of 1841					
1842Zs OM	—	30.00	35.00	60.00	350
Note: Eagle type of 1843					
1843Zs OM	—	30.00	35.00	60.00	350
1844Zs OM	—	30.00	35.00	60.00	350
1845Zs OM	—	30.00	35.00	60.00	350
1846Zs OM	—	30.00	35.00	60.00	350
1847Zs OM	—	30.00	35.00	60.00	350
1848/7Zs OM	—	33.00	44.00	70.00	375
1848Zs OM	—	30.00	35.00	60.00	350
1849Zs OM	—	30.00	35.00	60.00	350
1850Zs OM	—	30.00	35.00	60.00	350
1851Zs OM	—	30.00	35.00	60.00	350
1852Zs OM	—	30.00	35.00	60.00	350
1853Zs OM	—	44.00	60.00	110	450
1854/3Zs OM	—	33.00	44.00	90.00	400
1854Zs OM	—	30.00	38.50	70.00	375

Date	Mintage	F12	VF20	XF40	MS60
1855Zs OM	—	33.00	44.00	90.00	400
1855Zs MO	—	44.00	75.00	130	450
1856/5Zs MO	—	33.00	44.00	70.00	375
1856Zs MO	—	30.00	35.00	60.00	350
1857/5Zs MO	—	33.00	44.00	70.00	375
1857Zs MO	—	30.00	35.00	60.00	350
1858/7Zs MO	—	30.00	35.00	60.00	350
1858Zs MO	—	30.00	35.00	60.00	350
1859/8Zs MO	—	30.00	35.00	60.00	350
1859Zs MO	—	30.00	35.00	60.00	350
1859Zs VL/MO	—	38.50	65.00	110	400
1859Zs VL	—	33.00	55.00	90.00	375
1860/50Zs MO	—	27.50	29.50	41.50	220
1860/59Zs MO	—	27.50	29.50	41.50	220
1860Zs MO	—	27.50	29.50	41.50	220
1860Zs VL/MO	—	27.50	29.50	41.50	220
1860Zs VL	—	27.50	29.50	41.50	220
1861/0Zs VL/MO	—	27.50	29.50	41.50	220
1861Zs VL	—	27.50	29.50	41.50	220
1861/0Zs VL	—	27.50	29.50	41.50	220
1862/1Zs VL	—	27.50	29.50	60.00	260
1862Zs VL	—	27.50	29.50	41.50	220
1863Zs VL	—	27.50	29.50	41.50	220
1863Zs MO	—	27.50	29.50	41.50	220
1864/3Zs VL	—	27.50	29.50	60.00	260
1864Zs VL	—	27.50	29.50	41.50	220
1864Zs MO	—	27.50	35.00	60.00	260
1865/4Zs MO	—	220	500	1,050	3,100
1865Zs MO	—	165	325	775	2,500
1866Zs VL	—	—	—	—	—
Note: Contemporary counterfeit					
1867Zs JS Rare	—	—	—	—	—
1868Zs JS	—	27.50	29.50	41.50	220
1868Zs YH	—	27.50	29.50	41.50	220
1869Zs YH	—	27.50	29.50	41.50	220
1870Zs YH Rare	—	—	—	—	—
1873Zs YH	—	27.50	29.50	41.50	220
1874Zs YH	—	27.50	29.50	41.50	220
1874Zs JA/YA	—	27.50	29.50	41.50	220
1874Zs JA	—	27.50	29.50	41.50	220
1875Zs JA	—	27.50	29.50	41.50	220
1876Zs JA	—	27.50	29.50	41.50	220
1876Zs JS	—	27.50	29.50	41.50	220
1877Zs JS	2,700,000	27.50	29.50	41.50	220
1878Zs JS	2,310,000	27.50	29.50	41.50	220
1879/8Zs JS	—	30.00	35.00	60.00	260
1879Zs JS	—	27.50	29.50	41.50	220
1880Zs JS	—	27.50	29.50	41.50	220
1881Zs JS	5,592,000	27.50	29.50	41.50	220
1882/1Zs JS	2,485,000	30.00	35.00	60.00	260
1882Zs JS Straight J	Inc. above	27.50	29.50	41.50	220
1882Zs JS Full J	Inc. above	27.50	29.50	41.50	220
1883/2Zs JS	2,563,000	30.00	35.00	60.00	260
1883Zs JS	Inc. above	27.50	29.50	41.50	220
1884Zs JS	—	27.50	29.50	41.50	220
1885Zs JS	2,252,000	27.50	29.50	41.50	220
1886/5Zs JS	5,303,000	30.00	35.00	60.00	260
1886/8Zs JS	Inc. above	30.00	35.00	60.00	260
1886Zs JS	Inc. above	27.50	29.50	41.50	220
1886Zs FZ	Inc. above	27.50	29.50	41.50	220
1887Zs FZ	4,733,000	27.50	29.50	41.50	220
1887Z FZ	Inc. above	33.00	44.00	80.00	260
1888/7Zs FZ	5,132,000	27.50	30.00	45.50	230
1888Zs FZ	Inc. above	27.50	29.50	41.50	220
1889Zs FZ	4,344,000	27.50	29.50	41.50	220
1890Zs FZ	3,887,000	27.50	29.50	41.50	220
1891Zs FZ	4,114,000	27.50	29.50	41.50	220
1892/1Zs FZ	4,238,000	27.50	30.00	45.50	230
1892Zs FZ Narrow date	Inc. above	27.50	29.50	41.50	220
1892Zs FZ Wide date	—	27.50	29.50	41.50	220
1893Zs FZ	3,872,000	27.50	29.50	41.50	220
1894Zs FZ	3,081,000	27.50	29.50	41.50	220
1895Zs FZ	4,718,000	27.50	29.50	41.50	220
1896Zs FZ	4,226,000	27.50	29.50	41.50	220
1897Zs FZ	4,877,000	27.50	29.50	41.50	220

KM# 377.2   8 REALES
27.07 g., 0.903 Silver, 0.78 oz. ASW **Obv.** Facing eagle, snake in beak **Rev:** Radiant cap **Obv. Legend:** REPUBLICA MEXICANA. **Mint:** Chihuahua **Note:** Varieties exist.

Date	Mintage	F12	VF20	XF40	MS60
1831 Ca MR	—	1,100	1,950	2,950	6,500
1832Ca MR	—	140	220	400	1,200
1833Ca MR	—	275	600	1,300	—
1834Ca MR	—	325	650	1,500	—
1834Ca AM	—	375	550	900	—
1835Ca AM	—	165	275	625	1,800
1836Ca AM	—	110	220	400	1,200
1837Ca AM	—	600	1,250	—	—
1838Ca AM	—	110	220	400	1,200
1839Ca RG	—	825	1,400	3,250	—
1840Ca RG	—	325	550	1,050	3,000
Note: 1 dot after date					
1840Ca RG	—	325	550	1,050	3,000
Note: 3 dots after date					
1841Ca RG	—	65.00	120	210	650
1842Ca RG	—	38.50	55.00	110	350
1843Ca RG	—	55.00	100	175	550
1844/1Ca RG	—	49.50	90.00	145	450
1844Ca RG	—	38.50	55.00	110	350
1845Ca RG	—	38.50	55.00	110	350
1846Ca RG	—	44.00	75.00	145	550
1847Ca RG	—	55.00	100	175	550
1848Ca RG	—	49.50	90.00	175	550
1849Ca RG	—	44.00	75.00	145	450
1850/40Ca RG	—	55.00	100	175	550
1850Ca RG	—	44.00	75.00	145	450
1851/41Ca RG	—	120	230	400	1,050
1851Ca RG	—	175	285	525	1,550
1852/42Ca RG	—	175	285	525	1,550
1852Ca RG	—	175	285	525	1,550
1853/43Ca RG	—	175	285	525	1,550
1853Ca RG	—	175	285	450	1,450
1854/44Ca RG	—	120	230	400	1,050
1854Ca RG	—	65.00	120	210	650
1855/45Ca RG	—	120	230	450	1,350
1855Ca RG	—	65.00	120	210	650
1856/45Ca RG	—	325	500	975	2,500
1856/5Ca RG	—	450	775	1,950	7,000
1857Ca JC/RG	—	55.00	100	175	550
1857Ca JC	—	65.00	120	210	550
1858Ca JC	—	49.50	90.00	175	550
1858Ca BA	—	2,200	3,850	—	—
1859Ca JC	—	55.00	100	175	550
1860Ca JC	—	33.00	55.00	130	400
1861Ca JC	—	30.00	38.50	85.00	300
1862Ca JC	—	30.00	38.50	85.00	300
1863Ca JC	—	33.00	49.50	110	350
1864Ca JC	—	33.00	49.50	110	350
1865Ca JC	—	120	230	450	1,250
1865Ca FP	—	1,400	2,350	4,250	—
1866Ca JC	—	825	1,250	2,950	—
1866Ca FP	—	1,100	2,200	4,250	10,000
1866Ca JG	—	925	1,800	3,600	8,500
1867Ca JG	—	110	220	450	1,200
1868Ca JG	—	85.00	165	325	800
1868Ca MM	—	70.00	140	260	700

Date	Mintage	F12	VF20	XF40	MS60
1869Ca MM	—	33.00	49.50	100	325
1870Ca MM	—	33.00	49.50	100	325
1871/0Ca MM	—	30.00	38.50	85.00	300
1871Ca MM	—	30.00	38.50	85.00	300
1871Ca MM	—	33.00	49.50	100	325
Note: Known with first M over inverted M and second M over inverted M					
1873/5Ca MM	—	33.00	49.50	100	325
1873Ca MM	—	33.00	49.50	100	325
1873Ca MM/T	—	30.00	38.50	85.00	300
1874 Ca MM	—	27.50	30.00	50.00	260
1875Ca MM	—	27.50	30.00	50.00	260
1876Ca MM	—	27.50	30.00	50.00	260
1877Ca EA E/G	—	33.00	55.00	125	450
1877Ca EA	472,000	33.00	55.00	125	450
1877Ca GR	Inc. above	38.50	60.00	100	350
1877Ca JM	Inc. above	27.50	30.00	50.00	260
1877Ca AV	Inc. above	120	230	450	1,550
1878Ca AV	439,000	27.50	30.00	45.50	220
1879Ca AV	—	27.50	30.00	45.50	220
1880Ca AV	—	220	375	775	2,500
1880Ca PM	—	550	875	1,650	5,000
1880Ca MG	—	27.50	30.00	45.50	260
Note: Normal initials					
1880Ca MG	—	27.50	30.00	45.50	260
Note: Tall initials					
1880Ca MM	—	27.50	30.00	45.50	260
1881Ca MG	1,085,000	27.50	29.50	41.50	220
1882Ca MG	779,000	27.50	29.50	41.50	220
1882Ca MM	Inc. above	27.50	29.50	41.50	220
1882Ca MM	—	33.00	60.00	145	400
Note: Second M over sideways M					
1883Ca MM	818,000	—	—	—	—
Note: Sideways M					
1883/2Ca MM/G	—	27.50	30.00	50.00	230
1883Ca MM	Inc. above	27.50	29.50	41.50	220
1884/3Ca MM	—	27.50	30.00	50.00	220
1884Ca MM	—	27.50	29.50	41.50	220
1885/4Ca MM	1,345,000	30.00	38.50	85.00	300
1885/6Ca MM	Inc. above	30.00	38.50	85.00	300
1885Ca MM	Inc. above	27.50	29.50	41.50	220
1886Ca MM	2,483,000	27.50	29.50	41.50	220
1887Ca MM	2,625,000	27.50	29.50	41.50	220
1888/7Ca MM	2,434,000	30.00	38.50	100	325
1888Ca MM	Inc. above	27.50	29.50	41.50	220
1889Ca MM	2,681,000	27.50	29.50	41.50	220
1890/89Ca MM	—	30.00	38.50	85.00	300
1890Ca MM	2,137,000	27.50	29.50	41.50	220
1891/0Ca MM	2,268,000	30.00	38.50	85.00	300
1891Ca MM	Inc. above	27.50	29.50	41.50	230
1892Ca MM	2,527,000	27.50	29.50	41.50	220
1893Ca MM	2,632,000	27.50	29.50	41.50	220
1894Ca MM	2,642,000	27.50	29.50	41.50	220
1895Ca MM	1,112,000	27.50	29.50	41.50	220

KM# 378   1/2 ESCUDO
1.69 g., 0.875 Gold, 0.05 oz. AGW **Obv.** Facing eagle, snake in beak **Rev:** Hand holding cap on stick, open book **Obv. Legend:** REPUBLICA MEXICANA **Rev. Legend:** LIBERTAD... **Mint:** Culiacan

Date	Mintage	VG8	F12	VF20	XF40	MS60
1848 C CE	—	85.00	95.00	125	215	375
1853 C CE	—	85.00	95.00	125	215	—
1854 C CE	—	85.00	95.00	125	215	—
Revised eagle						
Note: Dates 1854-1870 of this type display the revised eagle						
1856 C CE	—	95.00	155	215	325	—
1857 C CE	—	85.00	95.00	125	215	300
1859 C CE	—	85.00	95.00	125	215	—

Date	Mintage	VG8	F12	VF20	XF40	MS60
1860 C CE	—	85.00	95.00	125	215	300
1862 C CE	—	85.00	95.00	125	185	—
1863 C CE	—	85.00	95.00	125	185	375
1866 C CE	—	85.00	95.00	125	185	—
1867 C CE	—	85.00	95.00	125	185	325
1870 C CE	—	125	215	350	575	1,850

KM# 378.1 1/2 ESCUDO
1.69 g., 0.875 Gold, 0.05 oz. AGW **Obv.** Facing eagle, snake in beak **Rev:** Hand holding cap on stick, open book **Mint:** Durango

Date	Mintage	VG8	F12	VF20	XF40	MS60
1833 Do RM/RL	—	85.00	95.00	125	215	—
1834/1 Do RM	—	85.00	95.00	125	215	900
1834/3 Do RM	—	85.00	95.00	125	215	—
1835/2 Do RM	—	85.00	95.00	125	215	—
1835/3 Do RM	—	85.00	95.00	125	215	—
1835/4 Do RM	—	85.00	95.00	125	215	—
1836/5/4 Do RM/L	—	90.00	105	155	245	575
1836/4 Do RM	—	85.00	95.00	125	215	—
1837 Do RM	—	85.00	95.00	125	215	—
1838 Do RM	—	90.00	105	155	245	—
1843 Do RM	—	90.00	105	155	245	—
1844/33 Do RM	—	90.00	105	155	245	—
1844/33 Do R,/RL	—	115	185	350	575	—
1845 Do CM	—	90.00	105	155	245	—
1846 Do RM	—	90.00	105	155	245	—
1848 Do RM	—	90.00	105	155	245	—
1850/33 Do JMR	—	90.00	105	155	245	600
1851 Do JMR	—	90.00	105	155	275	—
1852 Do JMR	—	90.00	105	155	245	—
1853/33 Do CP	—	125	215	375	625	—
1853 Do CP	—	95.00	120	215	325	675
1854 Do CP	—	85.00	95.00	125	215	—
1855 Do CP	—	85.00	95.00	125	215	—
1859 Do CP	—	85.00	95.00	125	215	—
1861 Do CP	—	85.00	95.00	125	215	—
1862 Do CP	—	85.00	95.00	125	215	—
1864 Do LT	—	125	185	325	500	—

KM# 378.2 1/2 ESCUDO
1.69 g., 0.875 Gold, 0.05 oz. AGW **Obv.** Facing eagle, snake in beak **Rev:** Hand holding cap on stick, open book **Obv. Legend:** REPUBLICA MEXICANA **Rev. Legend:** LIBERTAD... **Mint:** Guadalajara

Date	Mintage	VG8	F12	VF20	XF40	MS60
1825 Ga FS	—	90.00	105	155	245	600
1829 Ga FS	—	90.00	105	155	245	—
1831 Ga FS	—	90.00	105	155	245	—
1834 Ga FS	—	100	125	200	450	2,500
1835 Ga FS	—	90.00	105	155	245	—
1837 Ga JG	—	90.00	105	155	245	—
1838 Ga JG	—	90.00	105	155	245	—
1839 Ga JG	—	—	—	—	—	—
1840 Ga MC						
Unique						

Note: Ponterio & Associates Sale 157, 1-11, AU realized $12,000

1842 Ga JG	—	—	—	—	—	—
1847 Ga JG	—	90.00	105	155	245	—
1850 Ga JG	—	90.00	115	185	300	—
1852 Ga JG	—	85.00	115	125	215	—
1859 Ga JG	—	90.00	105	155	245	—
1861 Ga JG	—	85.00	100	125	215	600

KM# 378.3 1/2 ESCUDO
1.69 g., 0.875 Gold, 0.05 oz. AGW **Obv.** Facing eagle, snake in beak **Rev:** Hand holding cap on stick, open book **Obv. Legend:** REPUBLICA MEXICANA. **Rev. Legend:** LIBERTAD... **Mint:** Guadalupe y Calvo

Date	Mintage	VG8	F12	VF20	XF40	MS60
1846 GC MP	—	95.00	125	155	245	—
1847 GC MP	—	95.00	125	155	245	600
1848/7 GC MP	—	95.00	125	155	275	800
1850 GC MP	—	95.00	125	155	245	—
1851 GC MP	—	95.00	125	155	245	—
Revised eagle						

KM# 378.4 1/2 ESCUDO
1.69 g., 0.875 Gold, 0.05 oz. AGW **Obv.** Facing eagle, snake in beak **Rev:** Hand holding cap on stick, open book **Mint:** Guanajuato

Date	Mintage	VG8	F12	VF20	XF40	MS60
1845 Go PM	—	75.00	90.00	115	185	—
1849 Go PF	—	75.00	95.00	145	245	775
1851/41 Go PF	—	75.00	90.00	115	185	—
1851 Go PF	—	75.00	90.00	115	185	—
1852 Go PF	—	75.00	90.00	115	185	—
1852 Go PF/FF	—	—	—	—	—	—
1853 Go PF	—	75.00	90.00	115	185	—
1855 Go PF	—	75.00	95.00	130	215	—
1857 Go PF	—	75.00	90.00	115	185	—
1858/7 Go PF	—	75.00	90.00	115	185	—
1859 Go PF	—	75.00	90.00	115	185	450
1860 Go PF	—	75.00	90.00	115	185	—
1861 Go PF	—	75.00	90.00	115	185	—
1862/1 Go YE	—	75.00	90.00	150	220	—
1863 Go PF	—	75.00	95.00	130	215	—
1863 Go YF	—	75.00	90.00	115	185	—

KM# 378.5 1/2 ESCUDO
1.69 g., 0.875 Gold, 0.05 oz. AGW **Obv.** Facing eagle, snake in beak **Rev:** Hand holding cap on stick, open book **Obv. Legend:** REPUBLICA MEXICANA. **Rev. Legend:** LIBERTAD... **Mint:** Mexico City

Date	Mintage	VG8	F12	VF20	XF40	MS60
1825/1 Mo JM	—	90.00	120	180	270	—
1825/4 Mo JM	—	90.00	120	180	270	—
1825 Mo JM	—	75.00	90.00	125	210	450
1827/6 Mo JM	—	75.00	90.00	125	210	—
1827 Mo JM	—	75.00	90.00	125	210	450
1829 Mo JM	—	75.00	90.00	125	210	—
1831/0 Mo JM	—	75.00	90.00	125	210	—
1831 Mo JM	—	75.00	85.00	110	180	—
1832 Mo	—	75.00	85.00	110	180	—
1833 Mo MJ	—	90.00	100	140	240	575
Note: Olive and oak branches reversed						
1834 Mo ML	—	75.00	85.00	120	210	500
1835 Mo ML	—	75.00	85.00	125	210	500
1838 Mo ML	—	70.00	85.00	140	240	—
1839 Mo ML	—	75.00	90.00	140	240	—
1840 Mo ML	—	75.00	85.00	110	180	—
1841 Mo ML	—	75.00	85.00	110	180	—
1842 Mo ML	—	75.00	85.00	125	210	—
1842 Mo MM	—	75.00	85.00	125	210	—
1843 Mo MM	—	75.00	85.00	110	180	400
1844 Mo MF	—	75.00	85.00	110	180	325
1845 Mo MF	—	75.00	85.00	110	180	350
1846/5 Mo MF	—	75.00	85.00	110	180	—
1846 Mo MF	—	75.00	85.00	110	180	—
1848 Mo GC	—	75.00	90.00	140	240	575
1850 Mo GC	—	75.00	85.00	110	180	—
1851 Mo GC	—	75.00	85.00	110	180	—
1852 Mo GC	—	75.00	85.00	110	180	350
1853 Mo GC	—	80.00	100	150	270	800
1854 Mo GC	—	75.00	85.00	110	180	600

Date	Mintage	VG8	F12	VF20	XF40	MS60
1855 Mo GF	—	75.00	85.00	120	210	450
1856/4 Mo GF	—	75.00	85.00	110	180	350
1857 Mo GF	—	75.00	85.00	110	180	—
1858/7 Mo FH/GF	—	75.00	90.00	120	210	—
1858 Mo FH	—	75.00	85.00	110	180	—
1859 Mo FH	—	75.00	85.00	110	180	—
1860/59 Mo FH	—	75.00	85.00	110	180	325
1861 Mo CH/FH	—	75.00	85.00	125	210	—
1862 Mo CH	—	75.00	85.00	110	180	270
1863/57 Mo CH/GF	—	75.00	85.00	110	180	325
1868/58 Mo PH	—	75.00	85.00	125	210	—
1869/59 Mo CH	—	75.00	85.00	125	210	—

KM# 378.6 1/2 ESCUDO
1.69 g., 0.875 Gold, 0.05 oz. AGW **Obv.** Facing eagle, snake in beak **Rev:** Hand holding cap on stick, open book **Obv. Legend:** REPUBLICA MEXICANA. **Rev. Legend:** LIBERTAD... **Mint:** Zacatecas

Date	Mintage	VG8	F12	VF20	XF40	MS60
1860 Zs VL	—	85.00	95.00	125	215	350
1862/1 Zs VL	—	85.00	95.00	125	215	350
1862 Zs VL	—	75.00	90.00	115	185	325

KM# 379 ESCUDO
3.38 g., 0.875 Gold, 0.09 oz. AGW **Obv.** Facing eagle, snake in beak **Rev:** Hand holding cap on stick, open book **Mint:** Culiacan

Date	Mintage	VG8	F12	VF20	XF40	MS60
1846 C CE	—	170	190	290	475	—
1847 C CE	—	150	160	200	260	—
1848 C CE	—	150	160	200	260	850
1849/8 C CE	—	155	190	230	325	—
1850 C CE	—	150	160	200	260	—
1851 C CE	—	155	190	230	325	—
1853/1 C CE	—	155	190	230	325	—
1854 C CE	—	150	160	200	260	—
1856/5/4 C CE	—	155	190	230	325	—
1856 C CE	—	150	160	200	260	—
1857/1 C CE	—	155	190	230	325	—
1857 C CE	—	150	160	200	260	—
1861 C PV	—	150	160	200	260	—
1862 C CE	—	150	160	200	260	—
1863 C CE	—	150	160	200	260	—
1866 C CE	—	150	160	200	260	—
1870 C CE	—	150	160	200	260	—

KM# 379.1 ESCUDO
3.38 g., 0.875 Gold, 0.09 oz. AGW **Obv.** Facing eagle, snake in beak **Rev:** Hand holding cap on stick, open book **Obv. Legend:** REPUBLICA MEXICANA. **Rev. Legend:** LIBERTAD... **Mint:** Durango

Date	Mintage	VG8	F12	VF20	XF40	MS60
1832 Do R.L.	—	—	—	—	—	—
1833/2 Do RM/R.L.	—	170	220	290	400	—

Date	Mintage	VG8	F12	VF20	XF40	MS60
1834 Do RM	—	155	190	230	350	—
1835 Do RM	—	—	—	—	—	—
1836 Do RM/RL	—	155	190	230	350	—
1838 Do RM	—	155	190	230	350	—
1846/38 Do RM	—	170	220	290	400	—
1850 Do JMR	—	170	220	260	375	—
1851/31 Do JMR	—	170	220	290	400	—
1851 Do JMR	—	170	220	260	375	—
1853 Do CP	—	170	220	260	375	—
1854/34 Do CP	—	170	220	260	375	—
1854/44 Do CP/RP	—	170	220	260	375	—
1855 Do CP	—	170	220	260	375	—
1859 Do CP	—	170	220	260	375	—
1861 Do CP	—	170	220	260	375	—
1864 Do LT/CP Rare	—	—	—	—	—	—

KM# 379.2 ESCUDO
3.38 g., 0.875 Gold, 0.09 oz. AGW **Obv.** Facing eagle, snake in beak **Rev:** Hand holding cap on stick, open book **Obv. Legend:** REPUBLICA MEXICANA. **Mint:** Guadalajara

Date	Mintage	VG8	F12	VF20	XF40	MS60
1825 Ga FS	—	155	180	200	290	—
1826 Ga FS	—	155	180	200	290	—
1829 Ga FS	—	—	—	—	—	—
1831 Ga FS	—	155	180	200	290	—
1834 Ga FS	—	155	180	200	290	—
1835 Ga JG	—	155	180	200	290	—
1842 Ga JG/MC	—	155	180	200	290	—
1843 Ga MC	—	155	180	200	290	—
1847 Ga JG	—	155	180	200	290	—
1848/7 Ga JG	—	155	180	200	290	—
1849 Ga JG	—	155	180	200	290	—
1850/40 Ga JG	—	160	220	325	450	—
1850 Ga JG	—	155	180	200	290	—
1852/1 Ga JG	—	155	180	200	290	1,150
1856 Ga JG	—	155	180	200	290	—
1857 Ga JG	—	155	180	200	290	—
1859/7 Ga JG	—	155	180	200	290	—
1860/59 Ga JG	—	160	190	260	375	—
1860 Ga	—	155	180	200	290	—

KM# 379.3 ESCUDO
3.38 g., 0.875 Gold, 0.09 oz. AGW **Obv.** Facing eagle, snake in beak **Rev:** Hand holding cap on stick, open book **Obv. Legend:** REPUBLICA MEXICANA. **Mint:** Guadalupe y Calvo

Date	Mintage	VG8	F12	VF20	XF40	MS60
1844 GC MP	—	170	190	260	350	—
1845 GC MP	—	170	190	260	350	—
1846 GC MP	—	170	190	260	350	—
1847 GC MP	—	170	190	260	350	—
1848 GC MP	—	170	190	260	350	—
1849 GC MP	—	170	190	260	350	—
1850 GC MP	—	200	250	350	650	2,400
1851 GC MP Revised eagle	—	170	190	260	350	—

KM# 379.4 ESCUDO
3.38 g., 0.875 Gold, 0.09 oz. AGW **Obv.** Facing eagle, snake in beak **Rev:** Hand holding cap on stick, open book **Mint:** Guanajuato

Date	Mintage	VG8	F12	VF20	XF40	MS60
1845 Go PM	—	155	165	200	290	—
1849 Go PF	—	155	165	200	290	—
1851 Go PF	—	155	165	200	290	—
1853 Go PF	—	155	165	200	290	—
1860 Go PF	—	170	220	290	400	—
1862 Go YE	—	155	165	200	290	725

KM# 379.5 ESCUDO
3.38 g., 0.875 Gold, 0.09 oz. AGW **Obv.** Facing eagle, snake in beak **Rev:** Hand holding cap on stick, open book **Obv. Legend:** REPUBLICA MEXICANA. **Mint:** Mexico City

Date	Mintage	VG8	F12	VF20	XF40	MS60
1825 Mo JM/FM	—	150	155	170	230	475
1825 Mo JM	—	150	155	170	230	—
1827/6 Mo JM	—	150	155	170	230	—
1827 Mo JM	—	150	155	170	230	—
1830/29 Mo JM	—	150	155	170	230	—
1831 Mo JM	—	150	160	200	260	650
1832 Mo JM	—	150	160	200	260	—
1833 Mo MJ	—	150	155	170	230	—
1834 Mo ML	—	150	160	200	260	—
1841 Mo ML	—	150	160	200	260	—
1843 Mo MM	—	150	160	200	260	1,050
1845 Mo MF	—	150	155	170	230	—
1846/5 Mo MF	—	150	155	170	230	—
1848 Mo GC	—	150	160	200	260	—
1850 Mo GC	—	150	160	200	260	—
1856/4 Mo GF	—	150	155	170	230	—
1856/5 Mo GF	—	150	155	170	230	—
1856 Mo GF	—	150	155	170	230	—
1858 Mo FH	—	150	160	200	260	—
1859 Mo FH	—	150	160	200	260	900
1860 Mo TH	—	150	160	200	260	—
1861 Mo CH	—	150	160	200	260	1,200
1862 Mo CH	—	150	160	200	260	—
1863 Mo TH	—	150	155	170	230	475
1869 Mo CH	—	150	160	200	260	775

KM# 379.6 ESCUDO
3.38 g., 0.875 Gold, 0.09 oz. AGW **Obv.** Facing eagle, snake in beak **Rev:** Hand holding cap on stick, open book **Mint:** Zacatecas **Note:** Struck at Zacatecas Mint, mint mark Zs.

Date	Mintage	VG8	F12	VF20	XF40	MS60
1853 Zs OM	—	200	220	290	400	—
1860/59 Zs VL V is inverted A	—	170	190	290	475	—
1860 Zs VL	—	170	190	230	290	—
1862 Zs VL	—	170	190	230	290	—

KM# 380 2 ESCUDOS
6.77 g., 0.875 Gold, 0.19 oz. AGW **Obv.** Facing eagle, snake in beak **Rev:** Hand holding cap on stick, open book

Obv. Legend: REPUBLICA MEXICANA. **Mint:** Culiacan

Date	Mintage	VG8	F12	VF20	XF40	MS60
1846 C CE	—	325	350	400	525	—
1847 C CE	—	325	350	400	525	—
1848 C CE	—	325	350	400	525	—
1852 C CE	—	325	350	400	525	—
1854 C CE	—	325	350	425	575	—
1856/4 C CE	—	325	350	425	575	—
1857 C CE	—	325	350	400	525	—

KM# 380.1 2 ESCUDOS
6.77 g., 0.875 Gold, 0.19 oz. AGW **Obv.** Facing eagle, snake in beak **Rev:** Hand holding cap on stick, open book **Obv. Legend:** REPUBLICA MEXICANA. **Rev. Legend:** LIBERTAD... **Mint:** Durango

Date	Mintage	VG8	F12	VF20	XF40	MS60
1833 Do RM	—	550	700	975	1,600	—
1837/4 Do RM	—	—	—	—	—	—
1837 Do RM	—	—	—	—	—	—
1844 Do RM	—	500	625	850	1,350	—

KM# 380.2 2 ESCUDOS
6.77 g., 0.875 Gold, 0.19 oz. AGW **Obv.** Facing eagle, snake in beak **Rev:** Hand holding cap on stick, open book **Obv. Legend:** REPUBLICA MEXICANA. **Rev. Legend:** LIBERTAD... **Mint:** Estado de Mexico

Date	Mintage	VG8	F12	VF20	XF40	MS60
1828 EoMo LF	—	1,000	1,350	2,200	3,700	—

KM# 380.3 2 ESCUDOS
6.77 g., 0.875 Gold, 0.19 oz. AGW **Obv.** Facing eagle, snake in beak **Rev:** Hand holding cap on stick, open book **Obv. Legend:** REPUBLICA MEXICANA. **Rev. Legend:** LIBERTAD... **Mint:** Guadalajara

Date	Mintage	VG8	F12	VF20	XF40	MS60
1835 Ga FS	—	325	350	400	525	—
1836/5 Ga JG	—	350	400	600	725	—
1839/5 Ga JG	—	—	—	—	—	—
1839 Ga JG	—	325	325	375	475	—
1840 Ga MC	—	325	325	375	475	—
1841 Ga MC	—	325	350	425	600	—
1847/6 Ga JG	—	325	350	400	475	—
1848/7 Ga JG	—	325	350	400	475	—
1850/40 Ga JG	—	325	325	375	475	—
1851 Ga JG	—	325	325	375	475	—
1852 Ga JG	—	325	350	400	525	—
1853 Ga JG	—	325	325	375	475	—
1854/2 Ga JG	—	—	—	—	—	—
1858 Ga JG	—	325	325	375	475	—
1859/8 Ga JG	—	325	350	400	475	—
1859 Ga JG	—	325	350	400	475	—

Date	Mintage	VG8	F12	VF20	XF40	MS60
1860/50 Ga JG	—	325	350	400	475	—
1860 Ga JG	—	325	350	400	475	950
1861/59 Ga JG	—	325	325	375	475	—
1861/0 Ga JG	—	325	325	375	475	—
1863/2 Ga JG	—	325	350	400	475	975
1863/1 Ga JG	—	325	325	375	475	—
1870 Ga IC	—	325	325	375	475	—

KM# 380.4 2 ESCUDOS
6.77 g., 0.875 Gold, 0.19 oz. AGW **Obv.** Facing eagle, snake in beak **Rev:** Hand holding cap on stick, open book **Mint:** Guadalupe y Calvo

Date	Mintage	VG8	F12	VF20	XF40	MS60
1844 GC MP	—	450	700	1,300	2,500	—
1845 GC MP	—	1,050	1,650	2,500	3,700	—
1846 GC MP	—	1,050	1,650	2,500	3,700	—
1847 GC MP	—	750	1,350	2,500	3,700	—
1848 GC MP	—	350	400	575	825	—
1849 GC MP	—	1,050	1,650	—	—	—
1850 GC MP	—	450	700	1,300	2,500	—

KM# 380.5 2 ESCUDOS
6.77 g., 0.875 Gold, 0.19 oz. AGW **Obv.** Facing eagle, snake in beak **Rev:** Hand holding cap on stick, open book **Mint:** Guanajuato

Date	Mintage	VG8	F12	VF20	XF40	MS60
1845 Go PM	—	325	350	425	600	—
1849 Go PF	—	325	350	425	600	—
1853 Go PF	—	350	500	900	1,350	—
1856 Go PF	—	—	—	—	—	—
1859 Go PF	—	350	500	900	1,350	—
1860/59 Go PF	—	—	—	—	—	—
1860 Go PF	—	325	350	425	600	—
1862 Go YE	—	325	350	425	600	—

KM# 380.6 2 ESCUDOS
6.77 g., 0.875 Gold, 0.19 oz. AGW **Obv.** Facing eagle, snake in beak **Rev:** Hand holding cap on stick, open book **Mint:** Hermosillo

Date	Mintage	VG8	F12	VF20	XF40	MS60
1861 Ho FM	—	750	1,350	1,950	2,800	—

KM# 380.7 2 ESCUDOS
6.77 g., 0.875 Gold, 0.19 oz. AGW **Obv.** Facing eagle, snake in beak **Rev:** Hand holding cap on stick, open book **Obv. Legend:** REPUBLICA MEXICANA **Rev. Legend:** LIBERTAD... **Mint:** Mexico City

Date	Mintage	VG8	F12	VF20	XF40	MS60
1825 Mo JM	—	315	325	375	475	—
1827/6 Mo JM	—	315	325	375	475	—
1827 Mo JM	—	315	325	375	475	—
1830/29 Mo JM	—	315	325	375	475	—
1831 Mo JM	—	315	325	375	475	—
1833 Mo ML	—	315	325	375	475	—
1841 Mo ML	—	315	325	375	475	—
1844 Mo MF	—	315	325	375	475	—
1845 Mo MF	—	315	325	375	475	—
1846 Mo MF	—	315	400	600	850	—
1848 Mo GC	—	315	325	375	475	—
1850 Mo GC	—	315	325	375	475	—
1856/5 Mo GF	—	315	325	375	475	—
1856 Mo GF	—	315	325	375	475	—
1858 Mo FH	—	315	325	375	475	—
1859 Mo FH	—	315	325	375	475	—
1861 Mo TH	—	315	325	375	475	—
1861 Mo CH	—	315	325	375	475	—
1862 Mo CH	—	315	325	375	475	—

Date	Mintage	VG8	F12	VF20	XF40	MS60
1863 Mo TH	—	315	325	375	475	950
1868 Mo PH	—	315	325	375	475	—
1869 Mo CH	—	315	325	375	475	—

KM# 380.8 2 ESCUDOS
6.77 g., 0.875 Gold, 0.19 oz. AGW **Obv.** Facing eagle, snake in beak **Rev:** Hand holding cap on stick, open book **Obv. Legend:** REPUBLICA MEXICANA. **Rev. Legend:** LA LIBERTAD... **Mint:** Zacatecas

Date	Mintage	VG8	F12	VF20	XF40	MS60
1860 Zs VL	—	350	500	850	1,600	—
1862 Zs VL	—	475	750	1,100	1,600	—
1864 Zs MO	—	350	500	850	1,600	—

KM# 381 4 ESCUDOS
13.54 g., 0.875 Gold, 0.38 oz. AGW **Obv.** Facing eagle, snake in beak **Rev:** Hand holding cap on stick, open book **Obv. Legend:** REPUBLICA MEXICANA. **Rev. Legend:** LA LIBERTAD... **Mint:** Culiacan

Date	Mintage	VG8	F12	VF20	XF40	MS60
1846 C CE	—	1,650	2,350	—	—	—
1847 C CE	—	750	1,050	1,250	2,050	—
1848 C CE	—	900	1,300	1,700	2,650	—

KM# 381.1 4 ESCUDOS
13.54 g., 0.875 Gold, 0.38 oz. AGW **Obv.** Facing eagle, snake in beak **Rev:** Hand holding cap on stick, open book **Obv. Legend:** REPUBLICA MEXICANA. **Rev. Legend:** LA LIBERTAD.... **Mint:** Durango

Date	Mintage	VG8	F12	VF20	XF40
1832 Do RM/LR Rare	—	—	—	—	—
1832 Do RM	—	900	1,300	1,700	2,650
1833 Do RM/RL Rare	—	—	—	—	—
1852 Do JMR Rare	—	—	—	—	—

KM# 381.2 4 ESCUDOS
13.54 g., 0.875 Gold, 0.38 oz. AGW **Obv.** Facing eagle, snake in beak **Rev:** Hand holding cap on stick, open book **Obv. Legend:** REPUBLICA MEXICANA. **Rev. Legend:** LA LIBERTAD... **Mint:** Guadalajara

Date	Mintage	VG8	F12	VF20	XF40	MS60
1844 Ga MC	—	875	1,200	1,450	2,150	—
1844 Ga JG	—	750	1,050	1,250	1,850	—

KM# 381.3 4 ESCUDOS
13.54 g., 0.875 Gold, 0.38 oz. AGW **Obv.** Facing eagle, snake in beak **Rev:** Hand holding cap on stick, open book **Obv. Legend:** REPUBLICA MEXICANA **Rev. Legend:** LA LIBERTAD... **Mint:** Guadalupe y Calvo

Date	Mintage	VG8	F12	VF20	XF40	MS60
1844 GC MP	—	750	1,050	1,250	1,850	—
1845 GC MP	—	700	875	1,100	1,450	—
1846 GC MP	—	750	1,050	1,250	1,850	—
1848 GC MP	—	750	1,050	1,250	1,850	—
1850 GC MP	—	825	1,100	1,450	2,150	—

KM# 381.4 4 ESCUDOS
13.54 g., 0.875 Gold, 0.38 oz. AGW **Obv.** Facing eagle, snake in beak **Rev:** Hand holding cap on stick, open book **Obv. Legend:** REPUBLICA MEXICANA. **Rev. Legend:** LA LIBERTAD... **Mint:** Guanajuato

Date	Mintage	VG8	F12	VF20	XF40	MS60
1829/8 Go MJ	—	625	700	800	1,250	—
1829 Go JM	—	625	700	800	1,250	—
1829 Go MJ	—	625	700	800	1,250	—
1831 Go MJ	—	625	700	800	1,250	—
1832 Go MJ	—	625	700	800	1,250	—
1833 Go MJ	—	625	725	850	1,350	—
1834 Go PJ	—	650	900	1,050	1,450	—
1835 Go PJ	—	650	900	1,050	1,450	—
1836 Go PJ	—	625	725	850	1,350	—
1837 Go PJ	—	625	725	850	1,350	3,500
1838 Go PJ	—	625	725	850	1,350	—
1839 Go PJ	—	650	900	1,050	1,450	—
1840 Go PJ	—	625	725	900	1,450	—

Date	Mintage	VG8	F12	VF20	XF40	MS60
1841 Go PJ	—	650	900	1,050	1,450	—
1845 Go PM	—	625	725	850	1,350	—
1847/5 Go YE	—	650	900	1,050	1,450	—
1847 Go PM	—	650	900	1,050	1,450	—
1849 Go PF	—	650	900	1,050	1,450	—
1851 Go PF	—	650	900	1,050	1,450	—
1852 Go PF	—	625	725	850	1,350	—
1855 Go PF	—	625	725	850	1,350	—
1857/5 Go PF	—	625	725	850	1,350	—
1858/7 Go PF	—	625	725	850	1,350	—
1858 Go PF	—	625	725	850	1,350	—
1859/7 Go PF	—	650	900	1,050	1,450	—
1860 Go PF	—	650	950	1,150	1,700	—
1862 Go YE	—	625	725	850	1,350	—
1863 Go YF	—	625	725	850	1,350	—

KM# 381.5 4 ESCUDOS
13.54 g., 0.875 Gold, 0.38 oz. AGW **Obv.** Facing eagle, snake in beak **Rev:** Hand holding cap on stick, open book **Mint:** Hermosillo

Date	Mintage	VG8	F12	VF20	XF40	MS60
1861 Ho FM	—	1,400	2,000	3,250	5,000	—

KM# 381.6 4 ESCUDOS
13.54 g., 0.875 Gold, 0.38 oz. AGW **Obv.** Facing eagle, snake in beak **Rev:** Hand holding cap on stick, open book **Obv. Legend:** REPUBLICA MEXICANA. **Rev. Legend:** LA LIBERTAD... **Mint:** Mexico City

Date	Mintage	VG8	F12	VF20	XF40	MS60
1825 Mo JM	—	625	725	875	1,400	—
1827/6 Mo JM	—	625	725	850	1,350	—
1829 Mo JM	—	625	775	1,050	1,450	—
1831 Mo JM	—	625	775	1,050	1,450	—
1832 Mo JM	—	650	950	1,150	1,700	—
1844 Mo MF	—	625	775	1,050	1,450	—
1850 Mo GC	—	625	775	1,050	1,450	—
1856 Mo GF	—	625	725	850	1,350	—
1857/6 Mo GF	—	625	725	850	1,350	—
1857 Mo GF	—	625	725	850	1,350	—
1858 Mo FH	—	625	775	1,050	1,450	—
1859/8 Mo FH	—	625	775	1,050	1,450	—
1861 Mo CH	—	750	1,300	1,650	2,300	—
1863 Mo CH	—	625	775	1,450	1,450	2,500
1868 Mo PH	—	625	725	850	1,350	—
1869 Mo CH	—	625	725	850	1,350	1,950

KM# 381.7 4 ESCUDOS
13.54 g., 0.875 Gold, 0.38 oz. AGW **Obv.** Facing eagle, snake in beak **Rev:** Hand holding cap on stick, open book **Obv. Legend:** REPUBLICA MEXICANA. **Rev. Legend:** LA LIBERTAD EN LA LEY... **Mint:** Oaxaca **Note:** Mint mark O, Oa.

Date	Mintage	VG8	F12	VF20	XF40	MS60
1861 O FR	—	2,000	3,250	5,000	9,000	—

FIRST REPUBLIC

KM# 381.8   4 ESCUDOS
13.54 g., 0.875 Gold, 0.38 oz. AGW **Obv.** Facing eagle,
snake in beak **Rev:** Hand holding cap on stick, open book
Obv. Legend: REPUBLICA MEXICANA. **Rev. Legend:** LA
LIBERTAD... **Mint:** Zacatecas

Date	Mintage	VG8	F12	VF20	XF40	MS60
1860 Zs VL Rare	—	—	—	—	—	—
1862 Zs VL	—	1,000	1,650	2,850	4,800	—

Note: American Numismatic Rarities Eliasberg sale
4-05, MS-64 realized $18,400.

KM# 383   8 ESCUDOS
27.07 g., 0.875 Gold, 0.76 oz. AGW **Obv.** Facing eagle,
snake in beak **Rev:** Hand holding cap on stick, open book
Obv. Legend: REPUBLICA MEXICANA **Rev. Legend:** LA
LIBERTAD... **Mint:** Alamos

Date	Mintage	F12	VF20	XF40	MS60	MS63
1864 A PG	—	1,400	2,050	3,000	—	—
1866A DL	—	—	—	9,000	—	—
1868/7A DL	—	2,500	4,400	6,600	—	—
1869A DL	—	—	5,000	7,200	—	—
1870A DL	—	—	3,150	6,000	—	—
1872A AM Rare	—	—	—	—	—	—

KM# 383.1   8 ESCUDOS
27.07 g., 0.875 Gold, 0.76 oz. AGW **Obv.** Facing eagle,
snake in beak **Rev:** Hand holding cap on stick, open book
Obv. Legend: REPUBLICA MEXICANA **Rev. Legend:** LA
LIBERTAD.... **Mint:** Chihuahua

Date	Mintage	F12	VF20	XF40	MS60	MS63
1841 Ca RG	—	1,300	1,600	1,950	2,700	—
1842Ca RG	—	1,250	1,400	1,650	2,350	—
1843Ca RG	—	1,250	1,400	1,650	2,350	—
1844Ca RG	—	1,250	1,400	1,650	2,350	—
1845Ca RG	—	1,250	1,400	1,650	2,350	—
1846Ca RG	—	1,450	2,300	2,300	3,000	—

Date	Mintage	F12	VF20	XF40	MS60	MS63
1847Ca RG	—	1,950	4,150	—	—	—
1848Ca RG	—	1,250	1,400	1,650	2,350	—
1849Ca RG	—	1,250	1,400	1,650	2,350	—
1850/40Ca RG	—	1,250	1,400	1,650	2,350	—
1851/41Ca RG	—	1,250	1,400	1,650	2,350	—
1852/42Ca RG	—	1,250	1,400	1,650	2,350	—
1853/43Ca RG	—	1,250	1,400	1,650	2,350	—
1854/44Ca RG	—	1,250	1,400	1,650	2,350	—
1855/43Ca RG	—	1,250	1,400	1,650	2,350	—
1856/46Ca RG	—	1,250	1,450	1,950	2,700	—
1857Ca JC/RG	—	1,250	1,300	1,400	2,050	—
1858Ca JC	—	1,250	1,300	1,400	2,050	—
1858Ca BA/RG	—	1,250	1,300	1,400	2,050	—
1859Ca JC/RG	—	1,250	1,300	1,400	2,050	—
1860Ca JC/RG	—	1,250	1,400	1,650	2,350	—
1861Ca JC	—	1,250	1,300	1,400	2,050	—
1862Ca JC	—	1,250	1,300	1,400	2,050	—
1863Ca JC	—	1,400	1,950	2,600	3,350	—
1864Ca JC	—	1,300	1,600	1,950	2,700	—
1865Ca JC	—	1,600	2,700	3,550	4,950	—
1866Ca JC	—	1,250	1,300	1,650	2,350	—
1866Ca FP	—	1,450	2,300	2,900	3,650	—
1866Ca JG	—	1,250	1,400	1,650	2,350	—
1867Ca JG	—	1,250	1,300	1,400	2,050	—
1868Ca JG	—	1,250	1,300	1,400	2,050	—
Concave wings						
1869Ca MM	—	1,250	1,300	1,400	2,050	—
Regular eagle						
1870/60Ca MM	—	1,250	1,300	1,400	2,050	—
1871/61Ca MM	—	1,250	1,300	1,400	2,050	—

KM# 383.2   8 ESCUDOS
27.07 g., 0.875 Gold, 0.76 oz. AGW **Obv.** Facing eagle,
snake in beak **Rev:** Hand holding cap on stick, open book
Obv. Legend: REPUBLICA MEXICANA. **Rev. Legend:** LA
LIBERTAD... **Mint:** Culiacan

Date	Mintage	F12	VF20	XF40	MS60	MS63
1846 C CE	—	1,250	1,400	1,650	2,700	—
1847C CE	—	1,250	1,300	1,400	2,050	—
1848C CE	—	1,250	1,400	1,650	2,700	—
1849C CE	—	1,250	1,300	1,400	2,050	—
1850C CE	—	1,250	1,300	1,400	2,050	—
1851C CE	—	1,250	1,300	1,400	2,050	—
1852C CE	—	1,250	1,300	1,400	2,050	—
1853/1C CE	—	1,250	1,300	1,350	1,950	—
1854C CE	—	1,250	1,300	1,350	1,950	—
1855/4C CE	—	1,250	1,250	1,650	2,700	—
1855C CE	—	1,250	1,300	1,400	2,050	—
1856C CE	—	1,250	1,300	1,350	1,950	—
1857C CE	—	1,250	1,300	1,350	1,950	—
1857C CE	—	—	—	—	—	—
Note: Without periods after C's						
1858C CE	—	1,250	1,300	1,350	1,950	—
1859C CE	—	1,250	1,300	1,350	1,950	—
1860/58C CE	—	1,250	1,300	1,400	2,050	—
1860C CE	—	1,250	1,300	1,400	2,050	—

Date	Mintage	F12	VF20	XF40	MS60	MS63
1860C PV	—	1,250	1,300	1,350	1,950	—
1861C PV	—	1,250	1,300	1,400	2,050	—
1861C CE	—	1,250	1,300	1,400	2,050	—
1862C CE	—	1,250	1,300	1,400	2,050	—
1863C CE	—	1,250	1,300	1,400	2,050	—
1864C CE	—	1,250	1,300	1,350	1,950	—
1865C CE	—	1,250	1,300	1,350	1,950	—
1866/5C CE	—	1,250	1,300	1,350	1,950	—
1866C CE	—	1,250	1,300	1,350	1,950	—
1867C CB Error	—	1,250	1,300	1,350	1,950	—
1867C CE/CB	—	1,250	1,300	1,350	1,950	—
1868C CB Error	—	1,250	1,300	1,350	1,950	—
1869C CE	—	1,250	1,300	1,350	1,950	—
1870C CE	—	1,250	1,300	1,400	2,050	—

KM# 383.3   8 ESCUDOS
27.07 g., 0.875 Gold, 0.76 oz. AGW **Obv.** Facing eagle, snake in beak **Rev:** Hand holding cap on stick, open book **Obv. Legend:** REPUBLICA MEXICANA **Rev. Legend:** LA LIBERTAD.... **Mint:** Durango

Date	Mintage	F12	VF20	XF40	MS60	MS63
1832 Do RM	—	1,250	1,300	2,900	4,300	—
1833Do RM/RL	—	1,250	1,300	1,400	2,050	—
1834Do RM	—	1,250	1,300	1,400	2,050	—
1835Do RM	—	1,250	1,300	1,400	2,050	—
1836Do RM/RL	—	1,250	1,300	1,400	2,050	—
1836Do RM	—	1,250	1,300	1,400	2,050	—
Note: M on snake						
1837Do RM	—	1,250	1,300	1,400	2,050	—
1838/6Do RM	—	1,250	1,300	1,400	2,050	—
1838Do RM	—	1,250	1,300	1,400	2,050	—
1839Do RM	—	1,250	1,300	1,400	2,050	2,600
1840/30Do RM/RL	—	1,250	1,450	1,650	2,700	—
1841/30Do RM	—	1,300	1,600	1,400	3,000	—
1841/0Do RM	—	1,250	1,300	1,350	2,050	—
1841/31Do RM	—	1,250	1,300	1,400	2,050	—
1841/34Do RM	—	1,250	1,300	1,400	2,050	—
1841Do RM/RL	—	1,250	1,300	1,400	2,050	—
1842/32Do RM	—	1,250	1,300	1,400	2,050	—
1843/33Do RM	—	1,300	1,600	1,950	3,000	—
1843/1Do RM	—	1,250	1,300	1,400	2,050	—
1843Do RM	—	1,250	1,300	1,400	2,050	—
1844/34Do RM/RL	—	1,400	1,950	2,300	3,650	—
1844Do RM	—	1,300	1,650	1,950	3,000	—
1845/36Do RM	—	1,250	1,450	1,650	2,700	—
1845Do RM	—	1,250	1,450	1,650	2,700	—
1846Do RM	—	1,250	1,300	1,400	2,050	—
1847/37Do RM	—	1,250	1,300	1,400	2,050	—
1848/37Do RM	—	—	—	—	—	—
1848/38Do CM	—	1,250	1,300	1,400	2,050	—
1849/39Do CM	—	1,250	1,300	1,400	2,050	—
1849Do J.M.R. Rare	—	—	—	—	—	—
1850Do .JMR.	—	1,250	1,600	1,950	3,000	—
1851Do JMR	—	1,250	1,600	1,950	3,000	—
1852/1Do JMR	—	1,250	1,650	1,950	3,000	—
1852Do CP	—	1,250	1,650	1,950	3,000	—
1853Do CP	—	1,250	1,650	1,950	3,000	—
1854Do CP	—	1,250	1,450	1,650	2,700	—
1855/4Do CP	—	1,250	1,300	1,400	2,050	—

Date	Mintage	F12	VF20	XF40	MS60	MS63
1855Do CP	—	1,250	1,300	1,400	2,050	—
1856Do CP	—	1,250	1,400	1,550	2,550	—
1857Do CP	—	1,250	1,300	1,400	2,050	—
Note: French style eagle, 1832-57						
1857Do CP	—	1,250	1,300	1,400	2,050	—
Note: Mexican style eagle						
1858Do CP	—	1,250	1,400	1,550	2,550	—
1859Do CP	—	1,250	1,300	1,400	2,050	—
1860/59Do CP	—	1,250	1,600	1,950	3,250	—
1861/0Do CP	—	1,250	1,450	1,650	2,700	—
1862/52Do CP	—	1,250	1,300	1,400	2,050	—
1862/1Do CP	—	1,250	1,300	1,400	2,050	—
1862Do CP	—	1,250	1,300	1,400	2,050	—
1863/53Do CP	—	1,250	1,300	1,400	2,050	—
1864Do LT	—	1,250	1,300	1,400	2,050	3,000
1865/4Do LT	—	1,400	1,950	2,450	4,000	—
1866/4Do CM	—	2,300	3,400	3,550	—	—
1866Do CM	—	1,250	1,450	1,650	2,700	—
1867/56Do CP	—	1,250	1,450	1,650	2,700	—
1867/4Do CP	—	1,250	1,300	1,400	2,050	—
1868/4Do CP/LT	—	—	—	—	—	—
1869Do CP	—	1,450	2,300	2,600	4,000	—
1870Do CP	—	1,250	1,450	1,650	2,700	—

KM# 383.4   8 ESCUDOS
27.07 g., 0.875 Gold, 0.76 oz. AGW **Obv.** Facing eagle, snake in beak **Rev:** Hand holding cap on stick, open book **Obv. Legend:** REPUBLICA MEXICANA **Rev. Legend:** LA LIBERTAD... **Mint:** Estado de Mexico

Date	Mintage	F12	VF20	XF40	MS60	MS63
1828 EoMo LF Rare	—	—	—	—	—	—
1829EoMo LF	—	4,850	7,600	11,500	—	—

KM# 383.5   8 ESCUDOS
27.07 g., 0.875 Gold, 0.76 oz. AGW **Obv.** Facing eagle, snake in beak **Rev:** Hand holding cap on stick, open book **Obv. Legend:** REPUBLICA MEXICANA **Rev. Legend:** LA LIBERTAD... **Mint:** Guadalajara

Date	Mintage	F12	VF20	XF40	MS60	MS63
1825 Ga FS	—	1,400	1,800	1,950	2,700	—
1826Ga FS	—	1,400	1,800	1,950	2,700	—
1830Ga FS	—	1,400	1,800	1,950	2,700	—
1836Ga FS	—	1,600	2,700	2,900	4,300	—
1836Ga JG	—	1,950	4,150	4,800	—	—
1837Ga JG	—	1,950	4,150	4,800	—	—
1840Ga MC Rare	—	—	—	—	—	—

Date	Mintage	F12	VF20	XF40	MS60	MS63
1841/31Ga MC	—	1,950	4,150	—	—	—
1841Ga MC	—	1,750	2,900	3,100	—	—
1842Ga JG Rare	—	—	4,850	6,900	—	—
1843Ga MC	—	—	4,150	8,900	—	—
1845Ga MC	—	—	—	—	—	—
Rare						
1847Ga JG	—	3,250	—	—	—	—
1849Ga JG	—	1,400	1,800	1,950	2,700	—
1850Ga JG	—	1,300	1,700	1,800	2,550	—
1851Ga JG	—	1,950	4,150	4,800	—	—
1852/1Ga JG	—	1,400	1,800	1,950	2,700	—
1855Ga JG	—	1,950	4,150	4,800	—	—
1856Ga JG	—	1,300	1,700	1,800	2,550	—
1857Ga JG	—	1,300	1,700	1,800	2,550	—
1861/0Ga JG	—	1,400	1,800	1,950	2,700	—
1861Ga JG	—	1,250	1,500	1,900	2,700	—
1863/1Ga JG	—	1,400	1,800	1,950	2,700	—
1866Ga JG	—	1,300	1,700	1,800	2,550	—

KM# 383.6 8 ESCUDOS

27.07 g., 0.875 Gold, 0.76 oz. AGW **Obv.** Facing eagle, snake in beak **Rev:** Hand holding cap on stick, open book **Obv. Legend:** REPUBLICA MEXICANA **Rev. Legend:** LA LIBERTAD... **Mint:** Guadalupe y Calvo

Date	Mintage	F12	VF20	XF40	MS60	MS63
1844 GC MP	—	1,300	1,600	1,950	3,000	—
1845GC MP	—	1,300	1,600	1,950	3,000	—
Note: Eagle's tail square						
1845GC MP	—	1,300	1,600	1,950	3,000	—
Note: Eagle's tail round						
1846GC MP	—	1,250	1,450	1,650	2,700	—
Note: Eagle's tail square						
1846GC MP	—	1,250	1,450	1,650	2,700	—
Note: Eagle's tail round						
1847GC MP	—	1,250	1,450	1,650	2,700	—
1848GC MP	—	1,300	1,600	1,950	3,000	—
1849GC MP	—	1,300	1,600	1,950	3,000	—
1850GC MP	—	1,250	1,450	1,650	2,700	—
1851GC MP	—	1,250	1,450	1,650	2,700	—
1852GC MP	—	1,300	1,600	1,950	3,000	—

KM# 383.7 8 ESCUDOS

27.07 g., 0.875 Gold, 0.76 oz. AGW **Obv.** Facing eagle, snake in beak **Rev:** Hand holding cap on stick, open book **Obv. Legend:** REPUBLICA MEXICANA **Rev. Legend:** LA LIBERTAD... **Mint:** Guanajuato

Date	Mintage	F12	VF20	XF40	MS60	MS63
1828 Go MJ	—	1,600	3,050	3,200	4,300	—
1829Go MJ	—	1,450	2,700	2,900	4,000	—
1830Go MJ	—	1,250	1,300	1,350	1,700	—
1831Go MJ	—	1,450	2,700	2,900	4,000	—
1832Go MJ	—	1,300	1,950	2,300	3,650	—
1833Go MJ	—	1,250	1,300	1,350	1,700	—
1834Go PJ	—	1,250	1,300	1,350	1,700	—
1835Go PJ	—	1,250	1,300	1,350	1,700	—
1836Go PJ	—	1,250	1,450	1,550	2,050	—
1837Go PJ	—	1,250	1,450	1,550	2,050	—
1838/7Go PJ	—	1,250	1,300	1,350	1,700	—
1838Go PJ	—	1,250	1,300	1,400	1,950	—
1839/8Go PJ	—	1,250	1,300	1,350	1,700	—
1839Go PJ	—	1,250	1,300	1,400	1,950	—
Note: Regular eagle						
1840Go PJ	—	1,250	1,300	1,350	1,700	—
Note: Concave wings						
1841Go PJ	—	1,250	1,300	1,350	1,700	—
1842Go PJ	—	1,250	1,300	1,350	1,550	—
1842Go PM	—	1,250	1,300	1,350	1,700	—
1843Go PM	—	1,250	1,300	1,350	1,700	—
Note: Small eagle						
1844/3Go PM	—	1,250	1,450	1,550	2,050	—
1844Go PM	—	1,250	1,300	1,350	1,700	—
1845Go PM	—	1,250	1,300	1,350	1,700	—
1846/5Go PM	—	1,250	1,300	1,400	1,950	—
1846Go PM	—	1,250	1,300	1,350	1,700	—
1847Go PM	—	1,250	1,450	1,550	2,050	—
1848/7Go PM	—	1,250	1,300	1,350	1,700	—
1848Go PM	—	1,250	1,300	1,350	1,700	—
1848Go PF	—	1,250	1,300	1,350	1,700	—
1849Go PF	—	1,250	1,300	1,350	1,650	—
1850Go PF	—	1,250	1,300	1,350	1,650	—
1851Go PF	—	1,250	1,300	1,350	1,700	—
1852Go PF	—	1,250	1,300	1,350	1,700	—
1853Go PF	—	1,250	1,300	1,350	1,700	—
1854Go PF	—	1,250	1,300	1,350	1,700	—
Note: Eagle of 1853						
1854Go PF	—	1,250	1,300	1,350	1,700	—
Note: Eagle of 1855						
1855/4Go PF	—	1,250	1,300	1,350	1,700	—
1855Go PF	—	1,250	1,300	1,350	1,700	—
1856Go PF	—	1,250	1,300	1,350	1,700	—
1857Go PF	—	1,250	1,300	1,350	1,700	—
1858Go PF	—	1,250	1,300	1,350	1,700	—
1859Go PF	—	1,250	1,300	1,350	1,550	—
1860/50Go PF	—	1,250	1,300	1,350	1,550	—
1860/59Go PF	—	1,250	1,300	1,350	1,850	—
1860Go PF	—	1,250	1,300	1,350	1,850	—
1861/0Go PF	—	1,250	1,300	1,350	1,500	—
1861Go PF	—	1,250	1,300	1,350	1,500	—
1862/1Go YE	—	1,250	1,300	1,350	1,700	—
1862Go YE	—	1,250	1,300	1,350	1,650	—
1862Go YF	—	—	—	—	—	—
1863/53Go YF	—	1,250	1,300	1,350	1,700	3,650
1863Go PF	—	1,250	1,300	1,350	1,700	—
1867/57Go YF/PF	—	1,250	1,300	1,350	1,700	—
1867Go YF	—	1,250	1,300	1,350	1,650	—
1868/58Go YF	—	1,250	1,300	1,350	1,700	2,700
1870Go FR	—	1,250	1,300	1,350	1,550	—

KM# 383.8 8 ESCUDOS

27.07 g., 0.875 Gold, 0.76 oz. AGW **Obv.** Facing eagle, snake in beak **Rev:** Hand holding cap on stick, open book **Obv. Legend:** REPUBLICA MEXICANA. **Rev. Legend:** LA LIBERTAD... **Mint:** Hermosillo

Date	Mintage	F12	VF20	XF40	MS60	MS63
1863 Ho FM	—	1,300	1,500	1,650	3,000	—
1864Ho FM	—	1,450	2,300	2,600	4,000	—
1864Ho PR/FM	—	1,300	1,500	1,650	3,000	—
1865Ho FM/PR	—	1,400	1,650	1,950	3,650	—
1867/57Ho PR	—	1,300	1,500	1,650	3,000	—
1868Ho PR	—	1,400	1,650	1,950	3,650	—
1868Ho PR/FM	—	1,400	1,650	1,950	3,650	—
1869Ho PR/FM	—	1,300	1,500	1,650	3,000	—
1869Ho PR	—	1,300	1,500	1,650	3,000	—
1870Ho PR	—	1,400	1,650	1,950	4,000	7,600
1871/0Ho PR	—	1,400	1,650	1,950	3,650	—
1871Ho PR	—	1,400	1,650	1,950	3,650	—
1872/1Ho PR	—	1,450	2,300	2,600	4,000	—
1873Ho PR	—	1,300	1,500	1,650	3,000	—

KM# 383.9 8 ESCUDOS

27.07 g., 0.875 Gold, 0.76 oz. AGW **Obv.** Facing eagle, snake in beak **Rev:** Hand holding cap on stick, open book **Obv. Legend:** REPUBLICA MEXICANA **Rev. Legend:** LA LIBERTAD... **Mint:** Mexico City **Note:** Formerly reported 1825/3 JM is merely a reworked 5.

Date	Mintage	F12	VF20	XF40	MS60	MS63
1824Mo JM	—	1,400	1,750	1,950	3,000	—
Note: Large book reverse						
1825Mo JM	—	1,250	1,300	1,350	1,700	3,000
Note: Small book reverse						
1826/5Mo JM	—	1,600	2,850	3,200	4,300	—
1827/6Mo JM	—	1,250	1,300	1,350	1,700	—
1827Mo JM	—	1,250	1,300	1,350	1,700	—
1828Mo JM	—	1,250	1,300	1,350	1,700	—
1829Mo JM	—	1,250	1,300	1,350	1,700	—
1830Mo JM	—	1,250	1,300	1,350	1,700	—
1831Mo JM	—	1,250	1,300	1,350	1,700	—
1832/1Mo JM	—	1,250	1,300	1,350	1,700	—
1832Mo JM	—	1,250	1,300	1,350	1,700	—
1833Mo MJ	—	1,300	1,600	1,700	2,350	—
1833Mo ML	—	1,250	1,300	1,350	1,700	—
1834Mo ML	—	1,300	1,600	1,700	2,350	—
1835/4Mo ML	—	1,400	1,750	1,950	3,000	—
1836Mo ML	—	1,250	1,300	1,250	1,700	—
1836Mo MF	—	1,300	1,600	1,900	3,000	—
1837/6Mo ML	—	1,250	1,300	1,350	1,700	—
1838Mo ML	—	1,250	1,300	1,350	1,700	—
1839Mo ML	—	1,250	1,300	1,350	1,700	—
1840Mo ML	—	1,250	1,300	1,350	1,700	—
1841Mo ML	—	1,250	1,300	1,350	1,700	—
1842/1Mo ML	—	—	—	—	—	—
1842Mo ML	—	1,250	1,300	1,350	1,700	—
1842Mo MM	—	—	—	—	—	—
1843Mo MM	—	1,250	1,300	1,350	1,700	—
1844Mo MF	—	1,250	1,300	1,350	1,700	—
1845Mo MF	—	1,250	1,300	1,350	1,700	—
1846Mo MF	—	1,400	1,750	1,950	3,000	—
1847Mo MF	—	1,950	3,750	—	—	—
1847Mo RC	—	1,250	1,400	1,550	2,050	—
1848Mo GC	—	1,250	1,300	1,350	1,700	—
1849Mo GC	—	1,250	1,300	1,350	1,700	—

Date	Mintage	F12	VF20	XF40	MS60	MS63
1850Mo GC	—	1,250	1,300	1,350	1,700	3,000
1851Mo GC	—	1,250	1,300	1,350	1,700	—
1852Mo GC	—	1,250	1,300	1,350	1,700	—
1853Mo GC	—	1,250	1,300	1,350	1,700	—
1854/44Mo GC	—	1,250	1,300	1,350	1,700	—
1854/3Mo GC	—	1,250	1,300	1,350	1,700	—
1855Mo GF	—	1,250	1,300	1,350	1,700	—
1856/5Mo GF	—	1,250	1,300	1,350	1,650	—
1856Mo GF	—	1,250	1,300	1,350	1,650	—
1857Mo GF	—	1,250	1,300	1,350	1,650	—
1858Mo FH	—	1,250	1,300	1,350	1,650	—
1859Mo FH	—	1,300	1,600	1,700	2,350	—
1860Mo FH	—	1,250	1,300	1,350	1,650	—
1860Mo TH	—	1,250	1,300	1,350	1,650	—
1861/51Mo CH	—	1,250	1,300	1,350	1,650	—
1862Mo CH	—	1,250	1,300	1,350	1,650	—
1863/53Mo CH	—	1,250	1,300	1,350	1,650	6,600
1863/53Mo TH	—	1,250	1,300	1,350	1,650	—
1867Mo CH	—	1,250	1,300	1,350	1,650	—
1868Mo CH	—	1,250	1,300	1,350	1,650	—
1868Mo PH	—	1,250	1,300	1,350	1,650	—
1869Mo CH	—	1,250	1,300	1,350	1,650	—

KM# 383.10 8 ESCUDOS

27.07 g., 0.875 Gold, 0.76 oz. AGW **Obv.** Facing eagle, snake in beak **Rev:** Hand holding cap on stick, open book **Obv. Legend:** REPUBLICA MEXICANA **Rev. Legend:** LA LIBERTAD... **Mint:** Oaxaca

Date	Mintage	F12	VF20	XF40	MS60
1858 Oa AE	—	3,200	4,800	5,500	8,600
1859O AE	—	1,950	4,150	5,100	7,600
1860O AE	—	1,950	4,150	5,100	7,600
1861O FR	—	1,400	1,750	1,950	4,000
1862O FR	—	1,400	1,750	1,950	4,000
1863O FR	—	1,400	1,750	1,950	4,000
1864O FR	—	1,400	1,750	1,950	4,000
1867O AE	—	1,400	1,750	1,950	4,000
1868O AE	—	1,400	1,750	1,950	4,000
1869O AE	—	1,400	1,750	1,950	4,000

KM# 383.11 8 ESCUDOS

27.07 g., 0.875 Gold, 0.76 oz. AGW **Obv.** Facing eagle, snake in beak **Rev:** Hand holding cap on stick, open book **Obv. Legend:** REPUBLICA MEXICANA **Rev. Legend:** LA LIBERTAD... **Mint:** Zacatecas

Date	Mintage	F12	VF20	XF40	MS60	MS63
1858 Zs MO	—	1,300	1,600	1,650	3,000	—

Date	Mintage	F12	VF20	XF40	MS60	MS63
1859Zs MO	—	1,250	1,300	1,350	1,700	—
1860/59Zs VL/MO	—	3,200	4,800	5,500	—	—
1860/9Zs MO	—	1,300	1,600	1,650	3,000	—
1860Zs MO	—	1,250	1,300	1,400	1,850	—
1861/0Zs VL	—	1,250	1,300	1,400	1,850	—
1861Zs VL	—	1,250	1,300	1,400	1,850	4,300
1862Zs VL	—	1,250	1,300	1,400	1,900	—
1863Zs VL	—	1,250	1,300	1,400	1,950	—
1863Zs MO	—	1,250	1,300	1,400	1,850	—
1864Zs MO	—	1,600	1,950	2,300	4,950	—
1865Zs MO	—	1,600	1,950	2,400	5,300	—
1868Zs JS	—	1,250	1,400	1,550	2,050	—
1868Zs YH	—	1,250	1,400	1,550	2,050	—
1869Zs YH	—	1,250	1,400	1,550	2,050	—
1870Zs YH	—	1,250	1,400	1,550	2,050	—
1871Zs YH	—	1,250	1,400	1,550	2,050	—

EMPIRE OF MAXIMILIAN

RULER
Maximilian, Emperor, 1864-1867

MINT MARKS
Refer To Republic Coinage

MONETARY SYSTEM
100 Centavos = 1 Peso (8 Reales)

MILLED COINAGE

KM# 384   CENTAVO
Copper, **Ruler:** Maximilian **Obv.** Crowned facing eagle, snake in beak **Rev:** Value and date within wreath **Obv. Legend:** IMPERIO MEXICANO **Edge:** Coarsely reeded **Mint:** Mexico City

Date	Mintage	F12	VF20	XF40	MS60	MS63
1864M	—	50.00	100	250	1,250	1,850

KM# 385   5 CENTAVOS
1.35 g., 0.903 Silver, 0.04 oz. ASW **Ruler:** Maximilian **Mint:** Guanajuato

Date	Mintage	F12	VF20	XF40	MS60	MS63
1864G	90,000	17.50	35.00	85.00	320	—
1865G	—	20.00	30.00	65.00	300	—
1866G	—	75.00	150	300	2,000	—

KM# 385.1   5 CENTAVOS
1.35 g., 0.903 Silver, 0.04 oz. ASW **Ruler:** Maximilian **Mint:** Mexico City

Date	Mintage	F12	VF20	XF40	MS60	MS63
1864M	—	12.50	20.00	55.00	300	—
1866/4M	—	25.00	40.00	75.00	425	—
1866M	—	20.00	35.00	65.00	400	—

KM# 385.2   5 CENTAVOS
1.35 g., 0.903 Silver, 0.04 oz. ASW **Ruler:** Maximilian **Mint:** San Luis Potosi

Date	Mintage	F12	VF20	XF40	MS60	MS63
1864P	—	150	400	1,500	2,500	—

KM# 385.3   5 CENTAVOS
1.35 g., 0.903 Silver, 0.04 oz. ASW **Ruler:** Maximilian **Obv.** Crowned facing eagle, snake in beak **Rev:** Value and date within wreath **Obv. Legend:** IMPERIO MEXICANO **Mint:** Zacatecas

Date	Mintage	F12	VF20	XF40	MS60	MS63
1865Z	—	25.00	45.00	150	450	650

KM# 386   10 CENTAVOS
2.71 g., 0.903 Silver, 0.08 oz. ASW **Ruler:** Maximilian **Obv.** Crowned facing eagle, snake in beak **Rev:** Value and date within wreath **Obv. Legend:** IMPERIO MEXICANO **Mint:** Guanajuato

Date	Mintage	F12	VF20	XF40	MS60	MS63
1864G	45,000	20.00	45.00	90.00	325	—
1865G	—	30.00	60.00	110	375	—

KM# 386.1   10 CENTAVOS
2.71 g., 0.903 Silver, 0.08 oz. ASW **Ruler:** Maximilian **Obv.** Crowned facing eagle, snake in beak **Rev:** Value and date within wreath **Obv. Legend:** IMPERIO MEXICANO **Mint:** Mexico City **Note:** Struck at Mexico City Mint, mint mark M.

Date	Mintage	F12	VF20	XF40	MS60	MS63
1864M	—	15.00	25.00	55.00	285	—
1866/4M	—	25.00	35.00	70.00	320	—
1866/5M	—	25.00	40.00	85.00	375	—
1866M	—	25.00	35.00	75.00	375	—

KM# 386.2   10 CENTAVOS
2.71 g., 0.903 Silver, 0.08 oz. ASW **Ruler:** Maximilian **Mint:** San Luis Potosi

Date	Mintage	F12	VF20	XF40	MS60	MS63
1864P	—	70.00	150	300	700	—

KM# 386.3   10 CENTAVOS
2.71 g., 0.903 Silver, 0.08 oz. ASW **Ruler:** Maximilian **Mint:** Zacatecas

Date	Mintage	F12	VF20	XF40	MS60	MS63
1865Z	—	22.50	55.00	165	525	750

KM# 387 50 CENTAVOS

13.54 g., 0.903 Silver, 0.39 oz. ASW **Ruler:** Maximilian **Obv.** Head right, with beard **Rev:** Crowned oval shield **Obv. Legend:** MAXIMILIANO EMPERADOR **Rev. Legend:** IMPERIO MEXICANO **Designer:** S. Navalon **Mint:** Mexico City

Date	Mintage	F12	VF20	XF40	MS60	MS63
1866Mo	31,000	40.00	95.00	225	850	2,250

KM# 388 PESO

27.07 g., 0.903 Silver, 0.78 oz. ASW **Ruler:** Maximilian **Obv.** Head right, with beard **Rev:** Crowned arms with supporters **Obv. Legend:** MAXIMILIANO EMPERADOR **Rev. Legend:** IMPERIO MEXICANO **Designer:** S. Navalon **Mint:** Guanajuato

Date	Mintage	F12	VF20	XF40	MS60	MS63
1866Go	—	375	575	1,200	3,750	—

KM# 388.1 PESO

27.07 g., 0.903 Silver, 0.78 oz. ASW **Ruler:** Maximilian **Obv.** Head right, with beard **Rev:** Crowned arms with supporters **Obv. Legend:** MAXIMILIANO EMPERADOR **Rev. Legend:** IMPERIO MEXICANO **Designer:** S. Navalon **Mint:** Mexico City

Date	Mintage	F12	VF20	XF40	MS60	MS63
1866Mo	2,148,000	36.00	55.00	175	400	—
1867Mo	1,238,000	48.00	80.00	240	450	—

KM# 388.2 PESO

27.07 g., 0.903 Silver, 0.78 oz. ASW **Ruler:** Maximilian **Obv.** Head right, with beard **Rev:** Crowned arms with supporters **Obv. Legend:** MAXIMILIANO EMPERADOR **Rev. Legend:** IMPERIO MEXICANO **Designer:** S. Navalon **Mint:** San Luis Potosi

Date	Mintage	F12	VF20	XF40	MS60	MS63
1866Pi	—	55.00	110	350	800	—

KM# 389 20 PESOS

33.84 g., 0.875 Gold, 0.95 oz. AGW **Ruler:** Maximilian **Obv.** Head right, with beard **Rev:** Crowned arms with supporters **Obv. Legend:** MAXIMILIANO EMPERADOR **Rev. Legend:** IMPERIO MEXICANO **Designer:** S. Navalon **Mint:** Mexico City

Date	Mintage	F12	VF20	XF40	MS60	MS63
1866Mo	8,274	1,650	2,000	3,200	5,000	—

REPUBLIC
SECOND

DECIMAL COINAGE

KM# 390 CENTAVO

Copper 25mm. **Obv.** Seated Liberty **Rev:** Thick wreath. **Mint:** Mexico City

Date	Mintage	F12	VF20	XF40	MS60	MS63
1863Mo	—	13.50	32.50	75.00	500	—
Note: Round-top 3, reeded edge						
1863Mo	—	13.50	32.50	75.00	500	—
Note: Round-top 3, plain edge						
1863Mo	—	10.00	30.00	70.00	500	—
Note: Flat-top 3, reeded edge						

KM# 390.1 CENTAVO

Copper 26.5mm. **Obv.** Seated liberty **Rev:** Value and date within wreath **Obv. Legend:** LIBERTAD V REFORMA. **Mint:** San Luis Potosi

Date	Mintage	F12	VF20	XF40	MS60	MS63
1863SLP	1,024,999	15.00	32.50	75.00	425	—

KM# 391 CENTAVO

Copper **Obv.** Facing eagle, snake in beak **Rev:** Value and date within wreath **Edge:** Reeded. **Mint:** Alamos

Date	Mintage	F12	VF20	XF40	MS60	MS63
1875 As Rare	—	—	—	—	—	—
1876As	50,000	100	200	300	650	—
1880As	—	25.00	50.00	200	500	—
1881As	—	30.00	60.00	125	350	—

KM# 391.1 CENTAVO
Copper **Obv.** Facing eagle, snake in beak **Rev:** Value and date within wreath **Obv. Legend:** REPUBLICA MEXICANA **Edge:** Plain **Mint:** Culiacan

Date	Mintage	F12	VF20	XF40	MS60	MS63
1874 Cn	266,000	12.50	17.50	35.00	250	—
1875/4Cn	153,000	15.00	20.00	45.00	250	—
1875Cn	Inc. above	10.00	15.00	25.00	250	—
1876Cn	154,000	5.00	8.00	15.00	200	—
1877/6Cn	993,000	7.50	11.50	17.50	200	—
1877Cn	Inc. above	6.00	9.00	15.00	200	—
1880Cn	142,000	7.50	10.00	12.50	200	—
1881Cn	167,000	7.50	10.00	25.00	200	—
1897Cn	300,000	2.50	5.00	12.00	50.00	—
Note: Large N in mint mark						
1897Cn	Inc. above	2.50	5.00	9.00	45.00	—
Note: Small N in mint mark						

KM# 391.2 CENTAVO
Copper **Obv.** Facing eagle, snake in beak **Rev:** Value and date within wreath **Mint:** Durango

Date	Mintage	F12	VF20	XF40	MS60	MS63
1879 Do	110,000	10.00	35.00	60.00	200	—
1880Do	69,000	40.00	90.00	175	500	—
1891Do	—	8.00	25.00	50.00	200	—
1891Do/Mo	—	8.00	25.00	50.00	200	—

KM# 391.3 CENTAVO
Copper **Obv.** Facing eagle, snake in beak **Rev:** Value and date within wreath **Obv. Legend:** REPUBLICA MEXICANA **Mint:** Guadalajara

Date	Mintage	F12	VF20	XF40	MS60	MS63
1872 Ga	263,000	15.00	30.00	60.00	225	—
1873Ga	333,000	6.00	9.00	25.00	200	—
1874Ga	76,000	15.00	25.00	50.00	200	—
1875Ga	—	10.00	15.00	30.00	200	—
1876Ga	303,000	3.00	6.00	17.50	200	—
1877Ga	108,000	4.00	6.00	20.00	200	—
1878Ga	543,000	4.00	6.00	15.00	200	—
1881/71Ga	975,000	7.00	9.00	20.00	—	—
1881Ga	Inc. above	7.00	9.00	20.00	200	—
1889Ga/Mo	—	3.50	5.00	25.00	200	—
1890Ga	—	4.00	7.50	20.00	200	—

KM# 391.4 CENTAVO
Copper **Obv.** Facing eagle, snake in beak **Rev:** Value and date within wreath **Mint:** Guanajuato

Date	Mintage	F12	VF20	XF40	MS60	MS63
1874 Go	—	20.00	40.00	80.00	250	—
1875Go	190,000	11.50	20.00	60.00	200	—
1876Go	—	125	200	350	750	—
1877Go Rare	—	—	—	—	—	—
1878Go	576,000	8.00	11.00	30.00	200	—
1880Go	890,000	6.00	10.00	25.00	200	—

KM# 391.5 CENTAVO
Copper **Obv.** Facing eagle, snake in beak **Rev:** Value and date within wreath **Obv. Inscription:** REPUBLICA MEXICANA **Mint:** Hermosillo

Date	Mintage	F12	VF20	XF40	MS60
1875 Ho	3,500	450	—	—	—
1876Ho	8,508	50.00	100	225	500
1880Ho Short H, round O	102,000	7.50	15.00	50.00	200
1880Ho Tall H, oval O	Inc. above	7.50	15.00	50.00	200
1881Ho	459,000	5.00	10.00	50.00	200

KM# 391.6 CENTAVO
7.40 g., Copper **Obv.** Facing eagle, snake in beak **Rev:** Value and date within wreath **Obv. Legend:** REPUBLICA MEXICANA **Mint:** Mexico City **Note:** Varieties exist.

Date	Mintage	F12	VF20	XF40	MS60
1869Mo	1,874,000	7.50	25.00	60.00	200
1870/69Mo	1,200,000	10.00	25.00	60.00	225
1870Mo	Inc. above	8.00	20.00	50.00	200
1871Mo	918,000	8.00	15.00	40.00	200
1872/1Mo	1,625,000	6.50	10.00	30.00	200
1872Mo	Inc. above	6.00	9.00	25.00	200
1873Mo	1,605,000	4.00	7.50	20.00	200
1874/3Mo	1,700,000	5.00	7.00	15.00	100
1874Mo	Inc. above	3.00	5.50	15.00	100
1874Mo	Inc. above	5.00	10.00	25.00	200
1875Mo	1,495,000	6.00	8.00	30.00	100
1876Mo	1,600,000	3.00	5.50	12.50	100
1877Mo	1,270,000	3.00	5.50	13.50	100
1878/5Mo	1,900,000	7.50	11.00	22.50	125
1878/6Mo	Inc. above	7.50	11.00	22.50	125
1878/7Mo	Inc. above	7.50	11.00	20.00	125
1878Mo	Inc. above	6.00	9.00	13.50	100
1879/8Mo	1,505,000	4.50	6.50	13.50	100
1879Mo	Inc. above	3.00	5.50	12.50	75.00
1880/70Mo	1,130,000	5.50	7.50	15.00	100
1880/72Mo	Inc. above	20.00	50.00	100	250
1880/79Mo	Inc. above	15.00	35.00	75.00	175
1880Mo	Inc. above	4.25	6.00	12.50	75.00
1881Mo	1,060,000	4.50	7.00	15.00	75.00
1886Mo	12,687,000	1.50	2.00	10.00	40.00
1887Mo	7,292,000	1.50	2.00	10.00	35.00
1888/78Mo	9,984,000	2.50	3.00	10.00	30.00
1888/7Mo	Inc. above	2.50	3.00	10.00	30.00
1888Mo	Inc. above	1.50	2.00	10.00	30.00
1889Mo	19,970,000	2.00	3.00	10.00	30.00
1890/89Mo	18,726,000	2.50	3.00	12.00	40.00
1890/990 Mo	Inc. above	2.50	3.00	12.00	40.00
1890Mo	Inc. above	1.50	2.00	10.00	30.00
1891Mo	14,544,000	1.50	2.00	10.00	30.00
1892Mo	12,908,000	1.50	2.00	10.00	30.00
1893/2Mo	5,078,000	2.50	3.00	12.00	35.00
1893Mo	Inc. above	1.50	2.00	10.00	30.00
1894/3Mo	1,896,000	3.00	6.00	15.00	50.00

Date	Mintage	F12	VF20	XF40	MS60
1894Mo	Inc. above	2.00	3.00	12.00	35.00
1895/3Mo	3,453,000	3.00	4.50	12.50	35.00
1895/85Mo	Inc. above	3.00	6.00	15.00	50.00
1895Mo	Inc. above	2.00	3.00	10.00	30.00
1896Mo	3,075,000	2.00	3.00	10.00	30.00
1897Mo	4,150,000	1.50	2.00	10.00	30.00

KM# 391.7 CENTAVO
Copper **Obv.** Facing eagle, snake in beak **Rev:** Value and date within wreath **Obv. Legend:** REPUBLICA MEXICANA **Mint:** Oaxaca

Date	Mintage	F12	VF20	XF40	MS60
1872 Oa	16,000	300	500	1,200	—
1873Oa	11,000	350	600	—	—
1874Oa	4,835	450	—	—	—
1875Oa	2,860	500	—	—	—

KM# 391.8 CENTAVO
Copper **Obv.** Facing eagle, snake in beak **Rev:** Value and date within wreath **Obv. Legend:** REPUBLICA MEXICANA **Mint:** San Luis Potosi

Date	Mintage	F12	VF20	XF40	MS60
1871 Pi Rare	—	—	—	—	—
1877Pi	249,000	15.00	50.00	200	—
1878Pi	751,000	12.50	25.00	50.00	200
1878	—	—	—	—	—
Note: Pp error mintmark - rare					
1891Pi/Mo	—	10.00	50.00	150	300
1891Pi	—	8.00	25.00	125	250

KM# 391.9 CENTAVO
Copper **Obv.** Facing eagle, snake in beak **Rev:** Value and date within wreath **Mint:** Zacatecas **Note:** Struck at Zacatecas Mint, mint mark Zs.

Date	Mintage	F12	VF20	XF40	MS60
1872 Zs	55,000	22.50	30.00	100	300
1873Zs	1,460,000	4.00	8.00	25.00	150
1874/3Zs	685,000	5.50	11.00	30.00	250
1874Zs	Inc. above	4.00	8.00	25.00	200
1875/4Zs	200,000	8.50	17.00	45.00	250
1875Zs	Inc. above	7.00	14.00	35.00	200
1876Zs	—	5.00	10.00	25.00	200
1877Zs	—	50.00	125	300	750
1878Zs	—	4.50	9.00	25.00	200
1880Zs	100,000	5.00	10.00	30.00	200
1881Zs	1,200,000	4.25	8.00	25.00	150

KM# 392 CENTAVO
Copper-Nickel **Obv.** Crossed bow and quiver above date **Rev:** Value within wreath **Obv. Legend:** REPUBLICA

MEXICANA **Mint:** Mexico City

Date	Mintage	F12	VF20	XF40	MS60	MS63
1882Mo	99,955,000	7.50	12.50	17.50	35.00	—
1883Mo	Inc. above	0.50	0.75	1.50	2.50	4.00

KM# 393 CENTAVO
Copper **Obv.** Facing eagle, snake in beak **Rev:** Value and date within wreath **Obv. Legend:** REPUBLICA MEXICANA **Mint:** Mexico City **Note:** Varieties exist.

Date	Mintage	F12	VF20	XF40	MS60	MS63
1898Mo	1,529,000	4.00	6.00	15.00	50.00	—

KM# 394.1 CENTAVO
2.61 g., Copper **Obv.** Facing eagle, snake in beak **Rev:** Value below date within wreath **Obv. Legend:** REPUBLICA MEXICANA **Mint:** Mexico City **Note:** Reduced size. Varieties exist.

Date	Mintage	F12	VF20	XF40	MS60
1899M	51,000	150	175	300	800
1900M Wide date	4,010,000	2.50	4.00	8.00	28.00
1900M Narrow date	Inc. above	2.50	4.00	8.00	28.00
1901M	1,494,000	3.00	8.00	25.00	100
1902/899 M	2,090,000	30.00	75.00	200	600
1902M	Inc. above	2.25	4.00	10.00	40.00
1903M	8,400,000	1.50	3.00	7.00	20.00
1904/3M	10,250,000	1.50	10.00	20.00	55.00
1904M	Inc. above	1.50	3.00	8.00	25.00
1905M	3,643,000	2.25	4.00	10.00	40.00

KM# 394 CENTAVO
Copper **Obv.** National arms **Rev:** Value below date within wreath **Mint:** Culiacan **Note:** Reduced size. Varieties exist.

Date	Mintage	F12	VF20	XF40	MS60	MS63
1901C	220,000	15.00	22.50	60.00	150	—
1902C	320,000	15.00	22.50	50.00	90.00	—
1903C	536,000	7.50	12.50	20.00	50.00	—
1904/3C	148,000	35.00	50.00	150	350	—
1905C	110,000	100	150	300	600	—

KM# 395 2 CENTAVOS
Copper-Nickel **Obv.** Crossed bow and quiver above date **Rev:** Value within wreath **Obv. Legend:** REPUBLICA MEXICANA **Mint:** Mexico City

Date	Mintage	F12	VF20	XF40	MS60	MS63
1882	50,023,000	2.00	3.00	7.50	15.00	—
1883/2	Inc. above	2.00	3.00	7.50	15.00	—
1883	Inc. above	0.50	0.75	1.00	2.50	—

KM# 396.1 5 CENTAVOS
1.35 g., 0.903 Silver, 0.04 oz. ASW **Obv.** Facing eagle, snake in beak **Rev:** Value within wreath **Mint:** San Luis Potosi

Date	Mintage	F12	VF20	XF40	MS60	MS63
1863SLP	—	37.50	135	350	1,200	—

KM# 397 5 CENTAVOS
1.35 g., 0.903 Silver, 0.04 oz. ASW **Obv.** Facing eagle, snake in beak **Rev:** Radiant cap **Obv. Legend:** REPUBLICA MEXICANA **Mint:** Mexico City **Note:** Varieties exist.

Date	Mintage	F12	VF20	XF40	MS60	MS63
1867Mo	—	20.00	45.00	110	400	—
1867/3Mo	—	22.50	50.00	125	425	—
1868/7Mo	—	22.50	50.00	150	500	—
1868Mo	—	18.50	42.50	100	400	—

KM# 396 5 CENTAVOS
1.35 g., 0.903 Silver, 0.04 oz. ASW **Obv.** Facing eagle, snake in beak **Rev:** Value within wreath **Obv. Legend:** REPUBLICA MEXICANA **Mint:** Chihuahua

Date	Mintage	F12	VF20	XF40	MS60	MS63
1868Ca	—	40.00	65.00	125	450	—
1869Ca	30,000	25.00	40.00	100	400	—
1870/69Ca	—	35.00	55.00	120	425	—
1870Ca	35,000	30.00	50.00	100	400	—

KM# 397.1 5 CENTAVOS
1.35 g., 0.903 Silver, 0.04 oz. ASW **Obv.** Facing eagle, snake in beak **Rev:** Radiant cap **Mint:** San Luis Potosi

Date	Mintage	F12	VF20	XF40	MS60	MS63
1868P	Inc. above	20.00	45.00	100	400	—
1868/7P	34,000	25.00	50.00	125	450	—
1869P	14,000	150	300	600	—	—

KM# 398.4 5 CENTAVOS
1.35 g., 0.903 Silver, 0.04 oz. ASW **Obv.** Facing eagle, snake in beak **Rev:** Value within 1/2 wreath **Mint:** Guadalajara

Date	Mintage	F12	VF20	XF40	MS60
1877 Ga A	—	15.00	30.00	60.00	150
1881Ga S	156,000	4.00	7.50	15.00	60.00
1886Ga S	87,000	2.00	4.00	7.50	25.00
1888Ga S Large G	262,000	2.00	4.00	10.00	30.00
1888Ga S Small G	Inc. above	2.00	4.00	10.00	30.00
1889Ga S	178,000	1.50	3.00	7.50	25.00
1890Ga S	68,000	4.00	7.50	12.50	35.00
1891Ga S	50,000	4.00	6.50	10.00	35.00
1892Ga S	78,000	2.00	4.00	7.50	25.00
1893Ga S	44,000	4.00	7.50	15.00	45.00

KM# 398 5 CENTAVOS
1.35 g., 0.903 Silver, 0.04 oz. ASW **Obv.** Facing eagle, snake in beak **Rev:** Value within 1/2 wreath **Mint:** Alamos

Date	Mintage	F12	VF20	XF40	MS60
1874 As DL	—	10.00	20.00	40.00	150
1875As DL	—	10.00	20.00	40.00	150
1876As L	—	22.00	45.00	70.00	160
1878As L	—	250	350	650	950
Note: Mule, gold peso reverse					
1879As L	—	40.00	65.00	120	275

Date	Mintage	F12	VF20	XF40	MS60
Note: Mule, gold peso obverse					
1880As L	12,000	55.00	85.00	165	325
Note: Mule, gold peso obverse					
1886As L	43,000	12.00	25.00	50.00	165
1886As L	Inc. above	55.00	85.00	165	300
Note: Mule, gold peso obverse					
1887As L	20,000	25.00	50.00	75.00	165
1888As L	32,000	12.00	25.00	50.00	125
1889As L	16,000	25.00	50.00	100	200
1890As L	30,000	25.00	50.00	85.00	175
1891As L	8,000	65.00	125	200	400
1892As L	13,000	20.00	40.00	60.00	125
1893As L	24,000	10.00	20.00	45.00	90.00
1895As L	20,000	10.00	20.00	45.00	90.00

KM# 398.1 5 CENTAVOS
1.35 g., 0.903 Silver, 0.04 oz. ASW **Obv.** Facing eagle, snake in beak **Rev:** Value within 1/2 wreath **Mint:** Chihuahua **Note:** Mint mark: *Ca or Ch*.

Date	Mintage	F12	VF20	XF40	MS60
1871* M	14,000	20.00	40.00	100	250
1873* M Crude date	—	100	150	250	500
1874* M Crude date	—	25.00	50.00	75.00	150
1886* M	25,000	7.50	15.00	30.00	100
1887* M	37,000	7.50	15.00	30.00	100
1887* Ca/MoM	Inc. above	10.00	20.00	40.00	125
1888* M	145,000	1.50	3.00	6.00	25.00
1889* M	44,000	5.00	10.00	20.00	50.00
1890* M	102,000	1.50	3.00	6.00	25.00
1891* M	164,000	1.50	3.00	6.00	25.00
1892* M	85,000	1.50	3.00	6.00	25.00
1892* M/U		2.00	4.00	7.50	30.00
1892* M 9/ inverted 9	Inc. above	2.00	4.00	7.50	30.00
1893* M	133,000	1.50	3.00	6.00	25.00
1894* M	108,000	1.50	3.00	6.00	25.00
1895* M	74,000	2.00	4.00	7.50	30.00

KM# 398.2 5 CENTAVOS
1.35 g., 0.903 Silver, 0.04 oz. ASW **Obv.** Facing eagle, snake in beak **Rev:** Value within 1/2 wreath **Mint:** Culiacan

Date	Mintage	F12	VF20	XF40	MS60
1871 Cn P	—	125	200	350	—
1873Cn P	4,992	50.00	100	200	400
1874Cn P	—	25.00	50.00	100	200
1875Cn P Rare	—	—	—	—	—
1876Cn P	—	25.00	50.00	100	200
1886Cn M	10,000	25.00	50.00	100	200
1887Cn M	10,000	25.00	50.00	100	200
1888Cn M	119,000	1.50	3.00	6.00	30.00
1889Cn M	66,000	4.00	7.50	15.00	50.00
189/80 Cn M	—	2.00	4.00	8.00	40.00
1890Cn M	180,000	1.50	3.00	6.00	25.00
1890/9Cn M	—	2.00	4.00	8.00	40.00
1890Cn D Error	Inc. above	175	275	400	—
1891Cn M	87,000	2.00	4.00	7.50	25.00
1894Cn M	24,000	4.00	7.50	15.00	40.00
1896Cn M	16,000	7.50	12.50	25.00	75.00
1897Cn M	223,000	1.50	2.50	5.00	20.00

KM# 398.3 5 CENTAVOS
1.35 g., 0.903 Silver, 0.04 oz. ASW **Obv.** Facing eagle, snake in beak **Rev:** Value within 1/2 wreath **Mint:** Durango

Date	Mintage	F12	VF20	XF40	MS60	MS63
1874 Do M	—	100	150	225	500	—
1877Do P	4,795	75.00	125	225	450	—
1878/7Do E/P	4,300	200	300	450	—	—
1879Do B	—	125	200	350	—	—

Date	Mintage	F12	VF20	XF40	MS60	MS63
1880Do B Rare	—	—	—	—	—	—
1881Do P	3,020	300	500	800	—	—
1887Do C	42,000	5.00	8.00	17.50	60.00	—
1888/9Do C	91,000	6.00	10.00	20.00	70.00	—
1888Do C	Inc. above	4.00	7.50	15.00	55.00	125
1889Do C	49,000	3.50	6.00	12.50	50.00	—
1890Do C	136,000	4.00	7.50	15.00	55.00	—
1890Do P	Inc. above	5.00	8.00	17.50	60.00	—
1891/0Do P	48,000	3.50	6.00	12.50	50.00	—
1891Do P	Inc. above	3.00	5.00	10.00	45.00	—
1894Do D	38,000	3.50	6.00	12.50	50.00	—

KM# 398.5 5 CENTAVOS
1.35 g., 0.903 Silver, 0.04 oz. ASW **Obv.** Facing eagle, snake in beak **Rev:** Value within 1/2 wreath **Obv. Legend:** REPUBLICA MEXICANA **Mint:** Guanajuato

Date	Mintage	F12	VF20	XF40	MS60	MS63
1869Go S	80,000	15.00	30.00	75.00	175	—
1871Go S	100,000	5.00	10.00	25.00	75.00	—
1872Go S	30,000	30.00	60.00	125	250	—
1873Go S	40,000	30.00	60.00	125	250	—
1874Go S	—	7.00	12.00	25.00	75.00	—
1875Go S	—	8.00	15.00	30.00	75.00	—
1876Go S	—	8.00	15.00	30.00	75.00	—
1877Go S	—	7.00	12.00	20.00	75.00	—
1878/7Go S	20,000	8.00	15.00	25.00	75.00	—
1879Go S	—	8.00	15.00	25.00	75.00	—
1880Go S	55,000	15.00	30.00	60.00	200	—
1881/0Go S	160,000	5.00	8.00	17.50	60.00	150
1881Go S	Inc. above	4.00	6.00	12.00	45.00	110
1886Go R	230,000	1.50	3.00	6.00	30.00	75.00
1887Go R/S	—	1.50	3.00	6.00	30.00	75.00
1887Go R	230,000	1.50	2.50	5.00	30.00	75.00
1888Go R	320,000	1.50	2.50	5.00	20.00	60.00
1889Go R/S	—	4.00	6.00	12.00	45.00	110
1889Go R	60,000	4.00	6.00	12.00	45.00	110
1890/5Go R/S	—	1.50	3.00	6.00	30.00	75.00
1890Go R	250,000	1.50	2.50	5.00	20.00	60.00
1891/0Go R	168,000	1.80	3.00	6.00	30.00	75.00
1891Go R	Inc. above	1.50	2.50	5.00	20.00	60.00
1892Go R	138,000	1.50	3.00	6.00	25.00	65.00
1893Go R	200,000	1.25	2.50	5.00	20.00	60.00
1894Go R	200,000	1.25	2.50	5.00	20.00	60.00
1896Go R	525,000	1.25	2.00	4.00	15.00	50.00
1896Go R/S	—	1.50	3.00	6.00	25.00	65.00
1897Go R	596,000	1.50	2.00	4.00	15.00	50.00
1898Go R	—	—	—	—	—	—

KM# 398.7 5 CENTAVOS
1.35 g., 0.903 Silver, 0.04 oz. ASW **Obv.** Facing eagle, snake in beak **Rev:** Value within 1/2 wreath **Obv. Legend:** REPUBLICA MEXICANA **Mint:** Mexico City **Note:** Mint mark Mo. Varieties exist.

Date	Mintage	F12	VF20	XF40	MS60
1869/8Mo C	40,000	8.00	15.00	40.00	120
1870Mo C	140,000	4.00	7.00	20.00	60.00
1871Mo C	103,000	9.00	20.00	40.00	100
1871Mo M	Inc. above	7.50	12.50	25.00	60.00
1872Mo M	266,000	5.00	8.00	20.00	55.00
1873Mo M	20,000	40.00	60.00	100	225
1874/69Mo M	—	7.50	15.00	30.00	75.00
1874Mo M	—	4.00	7.00	17.50	50.00
1874/3Mo B	—	5.00	8.00	22.50	55.00
1874Mo B	—	5.00	8.00	22.50	55.00

Date	Mintage	F12	VF20	XF40	MS60
1875Mo B	—	4.00	7.00	15.00	50.00
1875Mo B/M	—	6.00	9.00	17.50	60.00
1876/5Mo B	—	4.00	7.00	15.00	50.00
1876Mo B	—	4.00	7.00	12.50	50.00
1877/6Mo M	80,000	4.00	7.00	15.00	60.00
1877Mo M	Inc. above	4.00	7.00	12.50	60.00
1878/7Mo M	100,000	4.00	7.00	15.00	55.00
1878Mo M	Inc. above	2.50	5.00	12.50	45.00
1879/8Mo M	—	8.00	12.50	22.50	55.00
1879Mo M	—	4.50	7.00	15.00	50.00
1879Mo M 9/ inverted 9	—	10.00	15.00	25.00	75.00
1880/76Mo M/B	—	5.00	7.50	15.00	50.00
1880/76Mo M	—	5.00	7.50	15.00	50.00
1880Mo N	—	4.00	6.00	12.00	40.00
1881/0Mo M	180,000	4.00	6.00	10.00	35.00
1881Mo M	Inc. above	3.00	4.50	9.00	35.00
1886/0Mo M	398,000	2.00	2.75	7.50	25.00
1886/1Mo M	Inc. above	2.00	2.75	7.50	25.00
1886Mo M	Inc. above	1.75	2.25	6.00	20.00
1887Mo m	720,000	1.75	2.00	5.00	20.00
1887Mo M/m	Inc. above	1.75	2.00	6.00	20.00
1888/7Mo M	1,360,000	2.25	2.50	6.00	20.00
1888Mo M	Inc. above	1.75	2.00	5.00	20.00
1889/8Mo M	1,242,000	2.25	2.50	6.00	20.00
1889Mo M	Inc. above	1.75	2.00	5.00	20.00
1890/00Mo M	1,694,000	1.75	2.75	6.00	20.00
1890Mo M	Inc. above	1.50	2.00	5.00	20.00
1891Mo M	1,030,000	1.75	2.00	5.00	20.00
1892Mo M	1,400,000	1.75	2.00	5.00	20.00
1892Mo M 9/ inverted 9	Inc. above	2.00	2.75	7.50	20.00
1893Mo M	220,000	1.75	2.00	5.00	15.00
1894Mo M	320,000	1.75	2.00	5.00	15.00
1895Mo M	78,000	3.00	5.00	8.00	25.00
1896Mo B	80,000	1.75	2.00	5.00	20.00
1897Mo B	160,000	1.75	2.00	5.00	15.00

KM# 398.8 5 CENTAVOS
1.35 g., 0.903 Silver, 0.04 oz. ASW **Obv.** Facing eagle, snake in beak **Rev:** Value within 1/2 wreath **Obv. Legend:** REPUBLICA MEXICANA **Mint:** Oaxaca

Date	Mintage	F12	VF20	XF40	MS60
1890 Oa E Rare	48,000	—	—	—	—
1890 Oa N	Inc. above	65.00	125	200	350

KM# 398.9 5 CENTAVOS
1.35 g., 0.903 Silver, 0.04 oz. ASW **Obv.** Facing eagle, snake in beak **Rev:** Value within 1/2 wreath **Mint:** San Luis Potosi **Note:** Varieties exist.

Date	Mintage	F12	VF20	XF40	MS60
1869Pi S	—	375	500	625	—
1870Pi G/MoC	20,000	190	325	500	—
1870Pi O	Inc. above	250	375	575	—
1871Pi O Rare	5,400	—	—	—	—
1872Pi O	—	75.00	100	175	400
1873Pi Rare	5,000	—	—	—	—
1874Pi H	—	30.00	50.00	100	225
1875Pi H	—	7.50	12.50	30.00	75.00
1876Pi H	—	10.00	20.00	45.00	100
1877Pi H	—	7.50	12.50	20.00	60.00
1878/7Pi H Rare	—	—	—	—	—
1878Pi H	—	60.00	90.00	150	300
1879 H	—	200	400	—	—
1880Pi H Rare	6,200	—	—	—	—
1881Pi H Rare	4,500	—	—	—	—
1886Pi R	33,000	12.50	25.00	50.00	125
1887/0Pi R	169,000	4.00	7.50	15.00	45.00
1887Pi R	Inc. above	3.00	5.00	10.00	32.00
1888Pi R	210,000	2.00	4.00	9.00	30.00
1889/7Pi R	197,000	2.50	5.00	10.00	32.00

Date	Mintage	F12	VF20	XF40	MS60
1889Pi R	Inc. above	2.00	4.00	9.00	30.00
1890Pi R	221,000	2.00	3.00	6.00	25.00
1891/89Pi R/B	176,000	2.00	4.00	8.00	25.00
1891/0Pi R/B	—	2.00	4.00	8.00	25.00
1891Pi R	Inc. above	2.00	3.00	6.00	20.00
1892/89Pi R	182,000	2.00	4.00	8.00	25.00
1892/0Pi R	Inc. above	2.00	4.00	8.00	25.00
1892Pi R	Inc. above	2.00	3.00	6.00	20.00
1893Pi R	41,000	5.00	10.00	20.00	60.00

KM# 398.10   5 CENTAVOS
1.35 g., 0.903 Silver, 0.04 oz. ASW **Obv.** Facing eagle, snake in beak **Rev:** Value within 1/2 wreath **Mint:** Zacatecas

Date	Mintage	F12	VF20	XF40	MS60
1870 Zs H	40,000	12.50	25.00	50.00	125
1871Zs H	40,000	12.50	25.00	50.00	125
1872Zs H	40,000	12.50	25.00	50.00	125
1873/2Zs H	20,000	35.00	65.00	125	275
1873Zs H	Inc. above	25.00	50.00	100	250
1874Zs H	—	7.50	12.50	25.00	75.00
1874Zs A	40,000	75.00	—	150	300
1875Zs A	—	7.50	12.50	25.00	75.00
1876Zs A	—	50.00	75.00	100	500
1876/5Zs S	—	15.00	30.00	60.00	150
1876Zs S	—	12.50	25.00	50.00	125
1877Zs S	—	3.00	6.00	12.00	40.00
1878Zs S	60,000	3.00	6.00	12.00	40.00
1879/8Zs S	—	3.00	6.00	15.00	50.00
1879Zs S	—	3.00	6.00	12.00	40.00
1880/79Zs S	130,000	6.00	10.00	20.00	60.00
1880Zs S	Inc. above	5.00	8.00	16.00	45.00
1881Zs S	210,000	2.50	5.00	10.00	35.00
1886/4Zs S	360,000	6.00	10.00	20.00	60.00
1886Zs S	Inc. above	2.00	3.00	6.00	20.00
1886Zs Z	Inc. above	5.00	10.00	25.00	65.00
1887Zs Z	400,000	2.00	3.00	6.00	25.00
1888/7Zs Z	500,000	2.00	3.00	6.00	25.00
1888Zs Z	Inc. above	2.00	3.00	6.00	25.00
1889Zs Z	520,000	2.00	3.00	6.00	25.00
1889Zs Z 9/inverted 9	Inc. above	2.00	3.00	6.00	25.00
1889Zs Z/MoM	Inc. above	2.00	3.00	6.00	25.00
1890Zs Z	580,000	1.75	2.50	5.00	20.00
1890Zs Z/MoM	Inc. above	2.00	3.00	6.00	25.00
1890Zs ZsZ 9/8	—	2.00	3.00	6.00	25.00
1890Zs ZsZ 0/9 Z/M	—	2.00	3.00	6.00	25.00
1891Zs Z	420,000	1.75	2.50	5.00	20.00
1892Zs Z	346,000	1.75	2.50	5.00	20.00
1893Zs Z	258,000	1.75	2.50	5.00	20.00
1894Zs ZoZ Error	Inc. above	2.00	4.00	8.00	30.00
1894Zs Z	228,000	1.75	2.50	5.00	20.00
1895Zs Z	260,000	1.75	2.50	5.00	20.00
1895/4Zs ZsZ	—	2.00	3.00	6.00	25.00
1896Zs Z	200,000	1.75	2.50	5.00	20.00
1896Zs 6/inverted 6	Inc. above	2.00	3.00	6.00	25.00
1897/6Zs Z	200,000	2.00	3.00	6.00	25.00
1897Zs Z	Inc. above	1.75	2.50	5.00	20.00

KM# 398.6   5 CENTAVOS
1.35 g., 0.903 Silver, 0.04 oz. ASW **Obv.** Facing eagle, snake in beak **Rev:** Value within 1/2 wreath **Mint:** Hermosillo

Date	Mintage	F12	VF20	XF40	MS60
1874/69 Ho R	—	125	225	350	—
1874 Ho R	—	100	200	325	—
1878/7Ho A Rare	22,000	—	—	—	—
1878Ho A	Inc. above	20.00	40.00	80.00	175
1878Ho A	Inc. above	40.00	80.00	150	300
Note: Mule, gold peso obverse					
1880Ho A	43,000	7.50	15.00	30.00	75.00
1886Ho G	44,000	5.00	10.00	20.00	75.00
1887Ho G	20,000	5.00	10.00	20.00	75.00
1888Ho G	12,000	7.50	15.00	30.00	85.00

Date	Mintage	F12	VF20	XF40	MS60
1889Ho G	67,000	3.00	6.00	12.50	40.00
1890Ho G	50,000	3.00	6.00	12.50	40.00
1891Ho G	46,000	3.00	6.00	12.50	40.00
1893Ho G	84,000	2.50	5.00	10.00	30.00
1894Ho G	68,000	2.00	4.00	10.00	30.00

KM# 399   5 CENTAVOS
Copper-Nickel **Obv.** Crossed bow and quiver above date **Rev:** Value within wreath **Obv. Legend:** REPUBLICA MEXICANA **Mint:** Mexico City

Date	Mintage	F12	VF20	XF40	MS60	MS63
1882	Inc. above	0.50	1.00	2.50	7.50	—
1883	Inc. above	25.00	50.00	80.00	250	—

KM# 400.1   5 CENTAVOS
1.35 g., 0.9027 Silver, 0.04 oz. ASW **Obv.** Facing eagle, snake in beak **Rev:** Value within 1/2 wreath **Mint:** Guanajuato **Note:** Varieties exist.

Date	Mintage	F12	VF20	XF40	MS60	MS63
1898Go R	180,000	7.50	15.00	30.00	75.00	—
Note: Mule, gold peso obverse						
1899Go R	260,000	1.75	2.50	4.50	15.00	—
1900Go R	200,000	1.75	2.50	4.50	15.00	—

KM# 400.2   5 CENTAVOS
1.35 g., 0.9027 Silver, 0.04 oz. ASW 15mm. **Obv.** Facing eagle, snake in beak **Rev:** Value within 1/2 wreath **Edge:** Reeded **Mint:** Mexico City

Date	Mintage	F12	VF20	XF40	MS60	MS63
1898Mo M	80,000	2.50	5.00	8.00	30.00	—
1899Mo M	168,000	2.00	3.00	5.00	18.00	—
1900/800 Mo M	300,000	5.00	8.00	12.00	36.00	—
1900Mo M	Inc. above	2.00	3.00	5.00	18.00	—
1901Mo M	100,000	2.00	3.00	8.00	23.00	25.00
1902/1Mo MoM	—	2.00	4.00	10.00	23.00	25.00
1902Mo M	144,000	1.50	2.50	7.00	18.00	20.00
1903Mo M	500,000	1.50	2.50	6.00	15.00	18.00
1904/804 Mo M	1,090,000	2.00	4.00	7.00	18.00	18.00
1904Mo M	Inc. above	2.00	4.00	7.00	15.00	20.00
1905Mo M	344,000	2.00	4.00	8.00	18.00	20.00

KM# 400.3   5 CENTAVOS
1.35 g., 0.9027 Silver, 0.04 oz. ASW **Obv.** Facing eagle, snake in beak **Rev:** Value within 1/2 wreath **Mint:** Zacatecas

Date	Mintage	F12	VF20	XF40	MS60	MS63
1898Zs Z	100,000	2.00	2.75	5.00	15.00	—
1899Zs Z	50,000	2.50	4.00	8.00	25.00	—
1900Zs Z	55,000	2.00	3.00	6.00	20.00	—
1901Zs Z	40,000	2.50	5.00	11.00	30.00	35.00
1902/1Zs Z	34,000	2.50	5.00	11.00	28.00	30.00
1902Zs Z	Inc. above	2.00	5.00	11.00	35.00	40.00
1903Zs Z	217,000	1.50	2.50	7.00	18.00	22.00
1904Zs Z	191,000	2.00	3.00	7.00	18.00	22.00
1904Zs M	Inc. above	4.00	10.00	18.00	60.00	75.00
1905Zs M	46,000	10.00	25.00	50.00	200	250
1905Zs M	Inc. above	75.00	125	250	600	900
Repullica; Rare						

KM# 400   5 CENTAVOS
1.35 g., 0.9027 Silver, 0.04 oz. ASW 14mm. **Obv.** Facing

eagle, snake in beak **Rev:** Value within 1/2 wreath **Obv. Legend:** REPUBLICA MEXICANA **Mint:** Culiacan **Note:** Varieties exist.

Date	Mintage	F12	VF20	XF40	MS60	MS63
1898Cn M	44,000	2.00	5.00	10.00	25.00	—
1899Cn M	111,000	7.00	10.00	25.00	60.00	—
1899Cn Q	Inc. above	2.00	3.00	5.00	18.00	—
1900/800	239,000	4.00	6.00	15.00	36.00	—
Cn Q						
1900Cn Q	Inc. above	2.00	4.00	7.00	20.00	—
Note: Round Q, single tail						
1900Cn Q	Inc. above	2.00	4.00	7.00	20.00	—
Note: Narrow C, oval Q						
1900Cn Q	Inc. above	2.00	4.00	7.00	20.00	—
Note: Wide C, oval Q						
1901Cn Q	148,000	2.00	4.00	7.00	25.00	30.00
1902Cn Q	262,000	2.00	4.00	7.00	20.00	25.00
Note: Narrow C, heavy serifs						
1902Cn Q	Inc. above	2.00	4.00	7.00	20.00	25.00
Note: Wide C, light serifs						
1903/1Cn Q	331,000	2.50	4.00	7.00	20.00	25.00
1903Cn Q	Inc. above	2.00	3.00	5.00	18.00	23.00
1903Cn V	Inc. above	2.00	3.00	5.00	18.00	23.00
1904Cn H	352,000	2.00	2.75	6.00	20.00	25.00
1904Cn H/C	—	2.00	3.00	6.00	20.00	25.00
(1901/801)	Inc. above	3.00	5.00	12.00	40.00	50.00
Cn Q						

KM# 402 10 CENTAVOS
2.71 g., 0.903 Silver, 0.08 oz. ASW **Obv.** Facing eagle, snake in beak **Rev:** Radiant cap **Mint:** Mexico City

Date	Mintage	F12	VF20	XF40	MS60	MS63
1867/3Mo	—	50.00	100	200	550	—
1867Mo	—	20.00	50.00	150	450	—
1868/7Mo	—	20.00	50.00	175	500	—
1868Mo	—	20.00	55.00	175	500	—

KM# 401.1 10 CENTAVOS
2.71 g., 0.903 Silver, 0.08 oz. ASW **Obv.** Facing eagle, snake in beak **Rev:** Value within wreath **Mint:** Chihuahua **Note:** Previous KM#401.

Date	Mintage	F12	VF20	XF40	MS60	MS63
1868/7Ca	—	30.00	60.00	150	550	—
1868Ca	—	30.00	60.00	150	550	—
1869Ca	15,000	25.00	50.00	125	600	—
1870Ca	17,000	22.50	45.00	100	550	—

KM# 402.1 10 CENTAVOS
2.71 g., 0.903 Silver, 0.08 oz. ASW **Obv.** Facing eagle, snake in beak **Rev:** Radiant cap **Obv. Legend:** REPUBLICA MEXICANA **Mint:** San Luis Potosi

Date	Mintage	F12	VF20	XF40	MS60	MS63
1868/7P	38,000	50.00	95.00	200	675	—
1868P	Inc. above	25.00	45.00	125	575	—
1869/7P	4,900	60.00	130	275	825	—

KM# 401.2 10 CENTAVOS
2.71 g., 0.903 Silver, 0.08 oz. ASW **Obv.** Facing eagle, snake in beak **Rev:** Value and date within wreath **Obv. Legend:** REPUBLICA MEXICANA **Mint:** San Luis Potosi

Date	Mintage	F12	VF20	XF40	MS60	MS63
1863 SLP	—	75.00	150	275	900	—

KM# 403 10 CENTAVOS
2.71 g., 0.903 Silver, 0.08 oz. ASW **Obv.** Facing eagle, snake in beak **Rev:** Value within 1/2 wreath **Mint:** Alamos **Note:** Varieties exist.

Date	Mintage	F12	VF20	XF40	MS60	MS63
1874 As DL	—	20.00	40.00	80.00	175	—
1875As L	—	5.00	10.00	25.00	90.00	—
1876As L	—	10.00	18.00	40.00	110	—
1878As L	—	5.00	10.00	30.00	100	—
1878/7As L	—	10.00	18.00	45.00	120	—
1879As L	—	10.00	18.00	40.00	110	—
1880As L	13,000	10.00	18.00	40.00	110	—
1882As L	22,000	10.00	18.00	40.00	110	—
1883As L	8,520	25.00	50.00	100	225	—
1884As L	—	7.50	12.50	35.00	100	—
1885As L	15,000	7.50	12.50	35.00	100	—
1886As L	45,000	7.50	12.50	35.00	100	—
1887As L	15,000	7.50	12.50	35.00	100	—
1888As L	38,000	7.50	12.50	35.00	100	—
1889As L	20,000	7.50	12.50	35.00	100	—
1890As L	40,000	7.50	12.50	35.00	100	—
1891As L	38,000	7.50	12.50	35.00	100	—
1892As L	57,000	5.00	10.00	25.00	90.00	—
1893As L	70,000	10.00	18.00	40.00	110	—

Note: An 1891 As L over 1889 HoG exists which was evidently produced at the Alamos Mint using dies sent from the Hermosillo Mint

KM# 403.2 10 CENTAVOS
2.71 g., 0.903 Silver, 0.08 oz. ASW **Obv.** Facing eagle, snake in beak **Rev:** Value within 1/2 wreath **Mint:** Culiacan

Date	Mintage	F12	VF20	XF40	MS60	MS63
1871 Cn P	—	—	—	—	—	—
Rare						
1873Cn P	8,732	20.00	50.00	100	225	—
1881Cn D	9,440	75.00	175	325	500	—
1882Cn D	12,000	75.00	125	200	400	—
1885Cn M	18,000	25.00	50.00	100	200	—
Note: Mule, gold 2-1/2 peso obverse						
1886Cn M	13,000	50.00	100	150	300	—
Note: Mule, gold 2-1/2 peso obverse						
1887Cn M	11,000	20.00	40.00	75.00	175	—
1888Cn M	56,000	5.00	10.00	25.00	125	—
1889Cn M	42,000	5.00	10.00	20.00	75.00	—
1890Cn M	132,000	4.00	6.00	12.00	75.00	—
1891Cn M	84,000	5.00	10.00	20.00	75.00	—
1892/1Cn M	37,000	5.00	9.00	17.00	75.00	—
1892Cn M	Inc. above	4.00	7.00	14.00	75.00	—
1894Cn M	43,000	4.00	7.00	14.00	75.00	—
1895Cn M	23,000	4.00	7.00	14.00	60.00	—
1896Cn M	121,000	3.00	5.00	9.00	50.00	—

KM# 403.3 10 CENTAVOS
2.71 g., 0.903 Silver, 0.08 oz. ASW **Obv.** Facing eagle, snake in beak **Rev:** Value within 1/2 wreath **Mint:** Durango

Date	Mintage	F12	VF20	XF40	MS60
1878 Do E	2,500	100	175	300	600
1879Do B Rare	—	—	—	—	—
1880/70Do B Rare	—	—	—	—	—
1880/79Do B Rare	—	—	—	—	—
1884Do C	—	30.00	60.00	100	225
1886Do C	13,000	75.00	150	300	500
1887Do C	81,000	5.00	9.00	17.00	100
1888Do C	31,000	7.00	13.00	32.00	100
1889Do C	55,000	5.00	9.00	17.00	100
1890Do C	50,000	5.00	9.00	17.00	100
1891Do P	139,000	3.00	5.00	10.00	80.00
1892Do P	212,000	3.00	5.00	10.00	80.00
1892Do D	Inc. above	3.00	5.00	10.00	80.00
1893Do D	258,000	3.00	5.00	10.00	80.00
1893Do D/C	Inc. above	4.00	6.00	12.00	80.00
1894Do D	184,000	2.50	4.00	8.00	80.00
1894Do D/C	Inc. above	3.00	5.00	10.00	80.00
1895Do D	142,000	2.50	4.00	8.00	80.00

KM# 403.4 10 CENTAVOS
2.71 g., 0.903 Silver, 0.08 oz. ASW **Obv.** Facing eagle, snake in beak **Rev:** Value within 1/2 wreath **Mint:** Guadalajara **Note:** Varieties exist.

Date	Mintage	F12	VF20	XF40	MS60
1871 Ga C	4,734	75.00	125	200	500
1873/1Ga C	25,000	10.00	15.00	35.00	150
1873Ga C	Inc. above	10.00	15.00	35.00	150
1874Ga C	—	10.00	15.00	35.00	150
1877Ga A	—	10.00	15.00	30.00	150
1881Ga S	115,000	6.00	11.00	27.50	150
1883Ga B	90,000	5.00	9.00	17.00	90.00
1884Ga B	—	6.00	11.00	22.50	90.00
1884Ga H	—	4.00	6.00	12.00	90.00
1884Ga B/S	—	7.00	14.00	27.50	90.00
1885Ga H	93,000	4.00	6.00	12.00	90.00
1886Ga S	151,000	4.00	5.00	11.00	90.00
1887Ga S	162,000	2.50	4.00	8.00	90.00
1888Ga S	225,000	2.50	4.00	8.00	90.00
1888Ga GaS/HoG	Inc. above	2.50	4.00	8.00	90.00
1889Ga S	310,000	2.50	4.00	8.00	40.00
1890Ga S	303,000	2.50	4.00	8.00	40.00
1891Ga S	199,000	6.00	11.00	22.50	45.00
1892Ga S	329,000	2.50	4.00	8.00	40.00
1893Ga S	225,000	2.50	4.00	8.00	40.00
1894Ga S	243,000	4.00	7.00	14.00	40.00
1895Ga S	80,000	2.50	4.00	8.00	40.00

KM# 403.5 10 CENTAVOS
2.71 g., 0.903 Silver, 0.08 oz. ASW **Obv.** Facing eagle, snake in beak **Rev:** Value within 1/2 wreath **Mint:** Guanajuato **Note:** Varieties exist.

Date	Mintage	F12	VF20	XF40	MS60
1869Go S	7,000	20.00	40.00	80.00	200
1871/0Go S	60,000	15.00	25.00	50.00	125
1872Go S	60,000	15.00	25.00	50.00	125
1873Go S	50,000	15.00	25.00	50.00	125
1874Go S	—	15.00	25.00	50.00	125
1875Go S	—	250	350	500	800
1876Go S	—	10.00	20.00	40.00	100
1877Go S	—	80.00	120	200	400
1878/7Go S	10,000	10.00	20.00	45.00	110
1878Go S	Inc. above	7.50	12.00	20.00	75.00
1879Go S	—	7.50	12.00	20.00	75.00
1880Go S	—	100	200	300	450
1881/71Go S	100,000	4.00	6.00	12.00	75.00
1881/0Go S	Inc. above	5.00	6.00	12.00	75.00
1881Go S	Inc. above	4.00	6.00	12.00	75.00
1882/1Go S	40,000	4.00	7.00	14.00	75.00
1883Go B	—	4.00	6.00	12.00	75.00
1884Go B	—	2.50	4.00	8.00	75.00
1884Go S	—	7.00	14.00	27.50	90.00
1885Go R	100,000	2.50	4.00	8.00	75.00
1886Go R	95,000	4.00	6.00	12.00	75.00
1887Go R	330,000	4.00	6.00	12.00	75.00
1888Go R	270,000	2.50	4.00	8.00	75.00
1889Go R	205,000	3.00	5.00	10.00	75.00
1889Go GoR/HoG	Inc. above	4.00	6.00	12.00	75.00
1890Go R	270,000	2.50	4.00	8.00	35.00
1890Go GoR/Cn M	Inc. above	2.50	4.00	8.00	35.00
1891Go R	523,000	2.50	4.00	8.00	35.00
1891Go R/G	—	2.50	4.00	8.00	35.00
1891Go GoR/HoG	Inc. above	2.50	4.00	8.00	35.00
1892Go R	440,000	2.50	4.00	8.00	35.00
1893/1Go R	389,000	4.00	6.00	12.00	35.00
1893Go R	Inc. above	2.50	4.00	8.00	35.00
1894Go R	400,000	2.50	4.00	7.00	35.00
1895Go R	355,000	2.50	4.00	7.00	35.00
1896Go R	190,000	2.50	4.00	7.00	35.00
1897Go R	205,000	2.50	4.00	7.00	35.00

KM# 403.6 10 CENTAVOS
2.71 g., 0.903 Silver, 0.08 oz. ASW **Obv.** Facing eagle, snake in beak **Rev:** Value within 1/2 wreath **Mint:** Hermosillo

Date	Mintage	F12	VF20	XF40	MS60
1874 Ho R	—	30.00	60.00	100	200
1876Ho F	3,140	200	300	450	750
1878Ho A	—	6.00	11.00	17.00	85.00

Date	Mintage	F12	VF20	XF40	MS60
1879Ho A	—	25.00	50.00	90.00	175
1880Ho A	—	5.00	8.00	16.00	85.00
1881Ho A	28,000	5.00	9.00	19.00	85.00
1882/1Ho A	25,000	6.00	11.00	22.50	85.00
1882/1Ho a	Inc. above	7.00	14.00	27.50	85.00
1882Ho A	Inc. above	5.00	9.00	19.00	85.00
1883Ho	7,000	65.00	100	200	400
1884/3Ho M	—	10.00	20.00	40.00	90.00
1884Ho A	—	35.00	75.00	150	300
1884/3Ho M	—	7.50	15.00	30.00	85.00
1884Ho M	—	7.50	15.00	30.00	85.00
1885Ho M	21,000	12.50	25.00	50.00	100
1886Ho M Rare	10,000	—	—	—	—
1886Ho G	Inc. above	7.50	12.50	25.00	85.00
1887Ho G	—	25.00	50.00	75.00	150
1888Ho G	25,000	7.00	14.00	27.50	85.00
1889Ho G	42,000	5.00	8.00	14.00	85.00
1890Ho G	48,000	5.00	8.00	14.00	85.00
1891/80Ho G	136,000	5.00	8.00	14.00	85.00
1891/0Ho G	Inc. above	5.00	8.00	14.00	85.00
1891Ho G	Inc. above	5.00	8.00	14.00	85.00
1892Ho G	67,000	5.00	8.00	14.00	85.00
1893Ho G	67,000	5.00	8.00	14.00	85.00

KM# 403.7 10 CENTAVOS
2.71 g., 0.902 Silver, 0.08 oz. ASW **Obv.** Facing eagle, snake in beak **Rev:** Value within 1/2 wreath **Obv. Legend:** REPUBLICA MEXICANA **Mint:** Mexico City **Note:** Varieties exist.

Date	Mintage	F12	VF20	XF40	MS60
1869/8Mo C	30,000	10.00	20.00	40.00	100
1869Mo C	Inc. above	8.00	17.50	35.00	90.00
1870Mo C	110,000	5.00	9.00	17.00	50.00
1871Mo C	84,000	50.00	75.00	125	250
1871Mo M	Inc. above	12.00	17.50	45.00	125
1872/69Mo M	198,000	10.00	20.00	35.00	100
1872Mo M	Inc. above	5.00	9.00	17.00	65.00
1873Mo M	40,000	10.00	15.00	30.00	75.00
1874Mo M	—	6.00	11.00	22.50	65.00
1874Mo M/C	—	6.00	11.00	22.50	65.00
1874/64Mo B	—	6.00	11.00	22.50	65.00
1874Mo B/M	—	20.00	40.00	60.00	125
1874Mo B	—	6.00	11.00	17.00	65.00
1875Mo B	—	20.00	40.00	60.00	125
1876/5Mo B	—	5.00	7.00	12.00	65.00
1876/5Mo B/M	—	5.00	7.00	12.00	65.00
1877/6Mo M	—	5.00	7.00	12.00	65.00
1877/6Mo M/B	—	5.00	7.00	12.00	65.00
1877Mo M	—	5.00	7.00	12.00	65.00
1878/7Mo M	100,000	5.00	7.00	12.00	65.00
1878Mo M	Inc. above	5.00	7.00	12.00	65.00
1879/69Mo M	—	5.00	7.00	12.00	65.00
1879Mo M/C	—	5.00	7.00	12.00	65.00
1880/79Mo M	—	5.00	7.00	12.00	65.00
1881/0Mo M	510,000	5.00	7.00	12.00	35.00
1881Mo M	Inc. above	5.00	7.00	12.00	35.00
1882/1Mo M	550,000	5.00	7.00	12.00	35.00
1882Mo M	Inc. above	5.00	7.00	12.00	35.00
1883/2Mo M	250,000	5.00	7.00	12.00	35.00
1884Mo M	—	5.00	7.00	12.00	35.00
1885Mo M	470,000	5.00	7.00	12.00	35.00
1886Mo M	603,000	5.00	7.00	12.00	35.00
1887/6Mo M	—	5.00	7.00	12.00	35.00
1887Mo M	580,000	5.00	7.00	12.00	35.00
1888/7Mo MoM	710,000	5.00	7.00	12.00	35.00
1888Mo MoM	Inc. above	5.00	7.00	12.00	35.00
1888Mo MOM	Inc. above	5.00	7.00	12.00	35.00
1889/8Mo M	622,000	5.00	7.00	12.00	35.00
1889Mo M	Inc. above	5.00	7.00	12.00	35.00
1890/89Mo M	815,000	5.00	7.00	12.00	35.00

Date	Mintage	F12	VF20	XF40	MS60
1890Mo M	Inc. above	5.00	7.00	12.00	35.00
1891Mo M	859,000	3.00	5.00	10.00	25.00
1892Mo M	1,030,000	3.00	5.00	10.00	25.00
1893Mo M	310,000	3.00	5.00	10.00	25.00
1893Mo M/C	Inc. above	3.00	5.00	10.00	25.00
1893Mo Mo/ Ho M/G	—	3.00	5.00	10.00	25.00
1894/3Mo M	—	6.00	11.00	22.50	60.00
1894Mo M	350,000	6.00	11.00	22.50	60.00
1895Mo M	320,000	3.00	5.00	10.00	25.00
1896Mo B/G	340,000	3.00	5.00	10.00	25.00
1896Mo M	Inc. above	35.00	70.00	100	150
1897Mo M	170,000	3.00	5.00	8.00	22.00

KM# 403.8 10 CENTAVOS
2.71 g., 0.903 Silver, 0.08 oz. ASW **Obv.** Facing eagle, snake in beak **Rev:** Value within 1/2 wreath **Mint:** Oaxaca

Date	Mintage	F12	VF20	XF40	MS60
1889 Oa E	21,000	225	425	650	—
1890Oa N Rare	Inc. above	—	—	—	—
1890Oa E	31,000	125	175	275	550

KM# 403.9 10 CENTAVOS
2.71 g., 0.903 Silver, 0.08 oz. ASW **Obv.** Facing eagle, snake in beak **Rev:** Value within 1/2 wreath **Mint:** San Luis Potosi **Note:** Varieties exist.

Date	Mintage	F12	VF20	XF40	MS60
1869/8Pi S Rare	4,000	—	—	—	—
1870/69Pi O Rare	18,000	—	—	—	—
1870Pi G	Inc. above	125	200	325	600
1871Pi O	21,000	50.00	100	150	300
1872Pi O	16,000	150	225	350	650
1873Pi O Rare	4,750	—	—	—	—
1874Pi H	—	25.00	50.00	100	200
1875Pi H	—	75.00	125	200	400
1876Pi H	—	75.00	125	200	400
1877Pi H	—	75.00	125	200	400
1878Pi H	—	250	500	750	—
1879Pi H	—	—	—	—	—
1880Pi H	—	150	250	350	—
1881Pi H	7,600	250	350	500	—
1882Pi H Rare	4,000	—	—	—	—
1883Pi H	—	125	200	300	500
1884Pi H	—	25.00	50.00	100	200
1885Pi H	51,000	25.00	50.00	100	200
1885Pi C Rare	Inc. above	—	—	—	—
1886Pi C	52,000	15.00	30.00	60.00	150
1886Pi R	Inc. above	6.00	11.00	22.50	65.00
1887Pi R	118,000	4.00	7.00	14.00	50.00
1888Pi R	136,000	4.00	7.00	14.00	50.00
1889/8Pi R/G	—	9.00	14.00	22.50	60.00
1889/7Pi R	131,000	9.00	14.00	22.50	60.00
1890Pi R/G	—	4.00	6.00	12.00	40.00
1890Pi R	204,000	3.00	5.00	11.00	40.00
1891/89Pi R	163,000	4.00	7.00	14.00	40.00
1891Pi R	Inc. above	3.00	6.00	10.00	30.00
1892/0Pi R/G	—	4.00	6.00	12.00	40.00
1892/0Pi R	200,000	4.00	6.00	12.00	40.00
1892Pi R	Inc. above	3.00	4.00	7.00	40.00
1892Pi R/G	—	4.00	6.00	12.00	40.00
1893Pi R	48,000	9.00	11.00	20.00	60.00
1893Pi R/G	—	3.00	11.00	20.00	60.00

KM# 403.10 10 CENTAVOS
2.71 g., 0.903 Silver, 0.08 oz. ASW **Obv.** Facing eagle, snake in beak **Rev:** Value within 1/2 wreath **Obv. Legend:** REPUBLICA MEXICANA **Mint:** Zacatecas **Note:** Varieties exist.

Date	Mintage	F12	VF20	XF40	MS60
1870Zs H	20,000	100	150	200	400
1871Zs H	Inc. above	—	—	—	—
1871/0Zs H	10,000	—	—	—	—
1872Zs H	10,000	150	200	275	500
1873Zs H	10,000	250	350	600	—
1874/3Zs H	—	50.00	75.00	150	300
1874Zs A	—	200	300	500	—
1875Zs A	—	6.00	11.00	27.50	100
1876Zs A	—	6.00	11.00	27.50	100
1876Zs S	—	100	200	300	500
1877Zs S Small S	—	7.50	12.50	25.00	100
1877Zs Regular S over small S	—	7.50	12.50	25.00	100
1877Zs S Regular S	—	7.50	12.50	25.00	100
1878Zs S	Inc. above	6.00	11.00	22.50	80.00
1878/7Zs S	30,000	6.00	11.00	22.50	80.00
1879Zs S	—	6.00	11.00	22.50	80.00
1880Zs S	—	6.00	11.00	22.50	80.00
1881/0Zs S	120,000	5.00	8.00	15.00	50.00
1881Zs S	Inc. above	5.00	8.00	15.00	50.00
1882/1Zs S	64,000	12.50	25.00	50.00	125
1882Zs S	Inc. above	12.50	25.00	50.00	125
1883/73Zs S	102,000	4.00	6.00	12.00	50.00
1883Zs S	Inc. above	4.00	6.00	12.00	50.00
1884/3Zs S	—	4.00	6.00	12.00	50.00
1884Zs S	—	4.00	6.00	12.00	50.00
1885Zs S Small S in mint mark	Inc. above	4.00	6.00	12.00	50.00
1885Zs S	297,000	3.00	5.00	9.00	50.00
1885Zs Z	Inc. above	5.00	10.00	19.00	65.00
Note: Without assayers initials, error					
1886Zs S	274,000	3.00	5.00	9.00	30.00
1886Zs Z	Inc. above	12.50	25.00	50.00	125
1887Zs Z Z Error	Inc. above	5.00	11.00	27.50	100
1887Zs ZsZ	233,000	3.00	5.00	9.00	30.00
1888Zs Z Z Error	Inc. above	5.00	11.00	27.50	100
1888Zs ZsZ	270,000	3.00	5.00	9.00	30.00
1889/7Zs Z/S	240,000	6.00	9.00	15.00	40.00
1889Zs ZS	Inc. above	3.00	6.00	12.00	30.00
1889Zs Z/G	—	3.00	6.00	12.00	30.00
1889Zs Z	Inc. above	3.00	5.00	9.00	30.00
1890Zs Z Z Error	Inc. above	5.00	11.00	27.50	100
1890Zs ZsZ	410,000	3.00	5.00	9.00	30.00
1891Zs ZsZ Double s	Inc. above	4.00	6.00	11.00	30.00
1891Zs Z	1,105,000	3.00	5.00	9.00	30.00
1892Zs Z	1,102,000	3.00	5.00	9.00	30.00
1892Zs Z/G	—	4.00	6.00	11.00	30.00
1893/2Zs Z	—	4.00	6.00	12.00	40.00
1893Zs Z	1,010,999	3.00	5.00	9.00	25.00
1894Zs Z	892,000	3.00	5.00	9.00	30.00
1895Zs Z 9/5	—	4.00	6.00	12.00	30.00
1895Zs Z	920,000	3.00	5.00	9.00	30.00
1896/5Z S/O Z/G	—	4.00	6.00	12.00	30.00
1896/5Zs Z/G	—	3.00	5.00	9.00	30.00
1896Zs Z/G	—	3.00	5.00	9.00	30.00
1896/5Zs ZsZ	700,000	3.00	5.00	9.00	30.00
1896Zs ZsZ	Inc. above	3.00	5.00	9.00	30.00
1896Zs Z Z Error	Inc. above	5.00	11.00	27.50	100
1897/6Zs Z Z Error	Inc. above	5.00	11.00	27.50	100
1897/6Zs ZsZ	900,000	4.00	7.00	12.00	30.00
1897Zs Z	Inc. above	3.00	5.00	9.00	30.00

KM# 403.1 10 CENTAVOS
2.71 g., 0.903 Silver, 0.08 oz. ASW **Obv.** Facing eagle, snake in beak **Rev:** Value within 1/2 wreath **Mint:** Chihuahua **Note:** Mint mark CH, Ca. Varieties exist.

Date	Mintage	F12	VF20	XF40	MS60
1871 M	8,150	15.00	30.00	60.00	150
1873 M Crude date	—	35.00	75.00	125	175
1874 M	—	10.00	17.50	35.00	100
1880/70 G	7,620	20.00	40.00	80.00	175
1880 G/g	Inc. above	15.00	25.00	50.00	125
1881 Rare	340	—	—	—	—

Date	Mintage	F12	VF20	XF40	MS60
1883 M	9,000	10.00	20.00	40.00	125
1884/73	—	5.00	30.00	60.00	150
1884 M	—	10.00	20.00	40.00	125
1886 M	45,000	7.50	12.50	30.00	100
1887/3 M/G	96,000	5.00	10.00	20.00	75.00
1887 M/G		4.00	6.00	12.00	75.00
1887 M	Inc. above	4.00	6.00	12.00	75.00
1888 M/G		4.00	6.00	12.00	75.00
1888 M	299,000	3.00	5.00	9.00	75.00
1888 Ca/Mo	Inc. above	3.00	5.00	9.00	75.00
1889 M	Inc. above	4.00	6.00	12.00	75.00
Note: Small 89 (5 Centavo font)					
1889/8 M	115,000	4.00	6.00	12.00	75.00
1890/80 M	140,000	4.00	6.00	12.00	75.00
1890/89 M	Inc. above	4.00	6.00	12.00	75.00
1890 M	Inc. above	3.00	5.00	11.00	75.00
1891 M	163,000	3.00	5.00	11.00	75.00
1892 M 9/ inverted 9	Inc. above	4.00	6.00	12.00	75.00
1892 M	169,000	3.00	5.00	11.00	75.00
1893 M	246,000	3.00	5.00	11.00	75.00
1894 M	163,000	3.00	5.00	11.00	75.00
1895 M	127,000	3.00	5.00	11.00	75.00

KM# 404 10 CENTAVOS
2.71 g., 0.903 Silver, 0.08 oz. ASW **Obv.** Facing eagle, snake in beak **Rev:** Value within 1/2 wreath **Mint:** Culiacan **Note:** Varieties exist.

Date	Mintage	F12	VF20	XF40	MS60	MS63
1898Cn M	9,870	50.00	100	200	500	—
1899Cn Q Oval Q, double tail	Inc. above	5.00	7.50	25.00	100	—
1899Cn Q Round Q, single tail	80,000	5.00	7.50	25.00	100	—
1900Cn Q	160,000	3.75	4.25	9.50	30.00	—
1901Cn Q	235,000	2.75	3.25	7.00	25.00	28.00
1902Cn Q	186,000	2.75	3.25	7.00	25.00	28.00
1903Cn Q	256,000	2.75	3.25	7.00	25.00	28.00
1903Cn V	Inc. above	2.75	3.25	7.00	25.00	28.00
1904Cn H	307,000	2.75	3.25	7.00	25.00	28.00

KM# 404.2 10 CENTAVOS
2.71 g., 0.903 Silver, 0.08 oz. ASW **Obv.** Facing eagle, snake in beak **Rev:** Value within 1/2 wreath **Obv. Legend:** REPUBLICA MEXICANA **Mint:** Mexico City

Date	Mintage	F12	VF20	XF40	MS60	MS63
1898Mo M	130,000	3.75	6.00	10.00	27.50	—
1899Mo M	190,000	3.75	6.00	10.00	27.50	—
1900Mo M	311,000	3.75	6.00	10.00	27.50	—
1901Mo M	80,000	2.75	3.50	8.00	27.00	30.00
1902Mo M	181,000	2.75	3.50	8.00	25.00	28.00
1903Mo M	581,000	2.75	3.50	8.00	22.00	25.00
1904Mo MM (Error)	Inc. above	3.00	7.00	14.00	35.00	40.00
1904Mo M	1,266,000	2.75	3.50	6.00	22.00	25.00
1905Mo M	266,000	3.00	5.00	10.00	25.00	28.00

KM# 404.3 10 CENTAVOS
2.71 g., 0.902 Silver, 0.08 oz. ASW **Obv.** Facing eagle, snake in beak **Rev:** Value within 1/2 wreath **Mint:** Zacatecas

Date	Mintage	F12	VF20	XF40	MS60	MS63
1898Zs Z	240,000	3.75	6.00	15.00	30.00	—
1899Zs Z	105,000	3.75	6.00	18.00	35.00	—
1900Zs Z	219,000	10.00	14.00	27.50	60.00	—
1901Zs Z	70,000	3.00	7.00	18.00	45.00	60.00
1902Zs Z	120,000	3.00	7.00	14.00	30.00	35.00
1903Zs Z	228,000	2.75	4.00	12.00	25.00	28.00

Date	Mintage	F12	VF20	XF40	MS60	MS63
1904Zs Z	368,000	2.75	4.00	12.00	25.00	28.00
1904Zs M	Inc. above	2.75	4.00	15.00	60.00	85.00
1905Zs M	66,000	10.00	27.50	70.00	200	275

KM# 404.1 10 CENTAVOS
2.71 g., 0.903 Silver, 0.08 oz. ASW **Obv.** Facing eagle, snake in beak **Rev:** Value within 1/2 wreath **Mint:** Guanajuato

Date	Mintage	F12	VF20	XF40	MS60	MS63
1898Go R	435,000	3.00	4.50	9.00	20.00	—
1899Go R	270,000	3.00	4.50	9.00	25.00	—
1900Go R	130,000	7.50	12.50	25.00	60.00	—

KM# 405 20 CENTAVOS
5.42 g., 0.903 Silver, 0.16 oz. ASW **Obv.** Facing eagle, snake in beak **Rev:** Value within 1/2 wreath **Mint:** Culiacan

Date	Mintage	F12	VF20	XF40	MS60	MS63
1898Cn M	114,000	5.50	11.50	36.00	145	—
1899Cn M	44,000	12.00	20.00	45.00	225	—
1899Cn Q	Inc. above	20.00	35.00	100	250	—
1900Cn Q	68,000	6.50	12.50	35.00	140	—
1901Cn Q	185,000	6.00	12.00	25.00	130	150
1902/802 Cn Q	98,000	6.00	12.00	25.00	130	150
1902Cn Q	Inc. above	6.00	12.00	25.00	130	150
1903Cn Q	93,000	6.00	12.00	25.00	130	150
1904Cn H	258,000	6.00	12.00	25.00	130	150

KM# 405.1 20 CENTAVOS
5.42 g., 0.9027 Silver, 0.16 oz. ASW **Obv.** Facing eagle, snake in beak **Rev:** Value within 1/2 wreath **Obv. Legend:** REPUBLICA MEXICANA **Mint:** Guanajuato

Date	Mintage	F12	VF20	XF40	MS60	MS63
1898Go R	135,000	7.00	12.00	25.00	115	—
1899Go R	215,000	7.00	12.00	25.00	115	—
1900/800 Go R	38,000	12.00	22.00	65.00	265	—

KM# 405.2 20 CENTAVOS
5.42 g., 0.903 Silver, 0.16 oz. ASW **Obv.** Facing eagle, snake in beak **Rev:** Value within 1/2 wreath **Mint:** Mexico City **Note:** Varieties exist.

Date	Mintage	F12	VF20	XF40	MS60	MS63
1898Mo M	150,000	7.50	12.00	25.00	140	—
1899Mo M	425,000	7.50	12.00	25.00	140	—
1900/800 Mo M	295,000	7.50	12.00	25.00	140	—
1901Mo M	110,000	6.00	12.00	25.00	110	125
1902Mo M	120,000	6.00	12.00	25.00	110	125
1903Mo M	213,000	6.00	12.00	25.00	110	125
1904Mo M	276,000	6.00	12.00	25.00	110	125
1905Mo M	117,000	6.00	20.00	45.00	160	190

KM# 405.3 20 CENTAVOS
5.42 g., 0.9027 Silver, 0.16 oz. ASW **Obv.** Facing eagle, snake in beak **Rev:** Value within 1/2 wreath **Obv. Legend:** REPUBLICA MEXICANA **Mint:** Zacatecas

Date	Mintage	F12	VF20	XF40	MS60	MS63
1898Zs Z	195,000	8.00	14.00	30.00	115	—
1899Zs Z	210,000	8.00	14.00	30.00	115	—

Date	Mintage	F12	VF20	XF40	MS60	MS63
1900/800 Zs Z	97,000	8.00	14.00	50.00	215	—
1901Zs Z	Inc. above	6.00	12.00	25.00	130	150
1901/0Zs Z	130,000	50.00	75.00	175	500	600
1902Zs Z	105,000	6.00	12.00	50.00	400	550
1903Zs Z	143,000	6.00	12.00	25.00	130	150
1904Zs Z	246,000	6.00	12.00	25.00	130	150
1904Zs M	Inc. above	6.00	15.00	40.00	300	350
1904/804 Zs	—	20.00	50.00	125	350	500
1905Zs M	59,000	12.00	85.00	125	1,100	1,400

KM# 406 25 CENTAVOS
6.77 g., 0.903 Silver, 0.20 oz. ASW **Obv.** Facing eagle, snake in beak **Rev:** Radiant cap above scales **Mint:** Alamos **Note:** Mint mark A, As.

Date	Mintage	F12	VF20	XF40	MS60
1874 L	—	20.00	40.00	90.00	200
1875 L	—	15.00	30.00	70.00	200
1876 L	—	30.00	50.00	100	200
1877 L	11,000	200	300	500	—
1877.	Inc. above	10.00	25.00	60.00	200
1878 L	25,000	10.00	25.00	60.00	200
1879 L	—	10.00	25.00	60.00	200
1880 L	—	10.00	25.00	60.00	200
1880. L	—	10.00	25.00	60.00	200
1881 L	8,800	500	700	—	—
1882 L	7,777	15.00	35.00	80.00	200
1883 L	28,000	10.00	25.00	60.00	200
1884 L	—	10.00	25.00	60.00	200
1885 L	—	20.00	40.00	90.00	200
1886 L	46,000	15.00	30.00	70.00	200
1887 L	12,000	12.50	27.50	65.00	200
1888 L	20,000	12.50	27.50	65.00	200
1889 L	14,000	12.50	27.50	65.00	200
1890 L	23,000	10.00	25.00	60.00	200

KM# 406.1 25 CENTAVOS
6.77 g., 0.903 Silver, 0.20 oz. ASW **Obv.** Facing eagle, snake in beak **Rev:** Radiant cap above scales **Mint:** Chihuahua **Note:** Mint mark CA, CH, Ca.

Date	Mintage	F12	VF20	XF40	MS60
1871 M	18,000	25.00	50.00	100	200
1872 M Very crude date	24,000	50.00	100	150	300
1883 M	12,000	10.00	25.00	50.00	175
1885/3 M	35,000	10.00	25.00	50.00	175
1885 M	Inc. above	10.00	25.00	50.00	175
1886 M	22,000	10.00	25.00	50.00	175
1887/6 M	26,000	10.00	15.00	30.00	175
1887 M	Inc. above	10.00	15.00	30.00	175
1888 M	14,000	10.00	25.00	50.00	175
1889 M	50,000	10.00	15.00	30.00	175

KM# 406.2 25 CENTAVOS
6.77 g., 0.903 Silver, 0.20 oz. ASW **Obv.** Facing eagle, snake in beak **Rev:** Radiant cap above scales **Mint:** Culiacan

Date	Mintage	F12	VF20	XF40	MS60
1871 Cn P	—	250	500	750	—
1872Cn P	2,780	300	550	800	—
1873Cn P	20,000	100	150	250	500
1874Cn P	—	20.00	50.00	125	250
1875Cn P	—	250	500	750	—
1876Cn P Rare	—	—	—	—	—
1878/7Cn D/S	—	100	150	250	500
1878Cn Cn/Go D/S	—	100	150	250	500
1878Cn D	—	100	150	250	500
1879Cn D	—	15.00	35.00	70.00	175

Date	Mintage	F12	VF20	XF40	MS60
1880Cn D	—	250	500	750	—
1881/0Cn D	18,000	15.00	30.00	60.00	175
1882Cn D	—	200	350	600	—
1882Cn M Rare	—	—	—	—	—
1883Cn M	15,000	50.00	100	150	300
1884Cn M	—	20.00	40.00	80.00	175
1885/4Cn M	19,000	20.00	40.00	80.00	175
1886Cn M	22,000	12.50	20.00	50.00	175
1887Cn M	32,000	12.50	20.00	50.00	175
1888Cn M	86,000	8.00	15.00	30.00	175
1888Cn M Cn/Mo	—	—	—	—	—
1889Cn M	50,000	10.00	25.00	50.00	175
1890Cn M 9/8	—	9.00	17.50	40.00	175
1890Cn M	91,000	9.00	17.50	40.00	175
1892/0Cn M	16,000	20.00	40.00	80.00	200
1892Cn M	Inc. above	20.00	40.00	80.00	200

KM# 406.3 25 CENTAVOS
6.77 g., 0.903 Silver, 0.20 oz. ASW **Obv.** Facing eagle, snake in beak **Rev:** Radiant cap above scales **Mint:** Durango

Date	Mintage	F12	VF20	XF40	MS60
1873 Do P Rare	892	—	—	—	—
1877Do P	—	25.00	50.00	100	200
1878/7Do E	—	250	500	750	—
1878Do B Rare	—	—	—	—	—
1879Do B	—	50.00	75.00	125	250
1880Do B Rare	—	—	—	—	—
1882Do C	17,000	25.00	50.00	100	225
1884/3Do C	—	25.00	50.00	100	200
1885Do C	15,000	20.00	40.00	80.00	200
1885Do C/S	—	20.00	40.00	80.00	200
1886Do C	33,000	15.00	30.00	60.00	200
1887Do C	27,000	10.00	20.00	50.00	200
1888Do C	25,000	10.00	20.00	50.00	200
1889Do C	29,000	10.00	20.00	50.00	200
1890Do C	68,000	8.00	15.00	40.00	200

KM# 406.4 25 CENTAVOS
6.77 g., 0.903 Silver, 0.20 oz. ASW **Obv.** Facing eagle, snake in beak **Rev:** Radiant cap above scales **Mint:** Guadalajara

Date	Mintage	F12	VF20	XF40	MS60
1880 Ga A	38,000	25.00	50.00	100	200
1881/0Ga S	39,000	25.00	50.00	100	200
1881Ga S	Inc. above	25.00	50.00	100	200
1882Ga S	18,000	25.00	50.00	100	200
1883/2Ga B/S	—	50.00	100	150	300
1884Ga B	—	20.00	40.00	80.00	150
1889Ga S	30,000	20.00	40.00	80.00	150

KM# 406.5 25 CENTAVOS
6.77 g., 0.903 Silver, 0.20 oz. ASW **Obv.** Facing eagle, snake in beak **Rev:** Radiant cap above scales **Mint:** Guanajuato **Note:** Varieties exist.

Date	Mintage	F12	VF20	XF40	MS60
1870 Go S	128,000	10.00	20.00	50.00	125
1871Go S	172,000	10.00	20.00	50.00	125
1872/1Go S	178,000	10.00	20.00	50.00	125
1872Go S	Inc. above	10.00	20.00	50.00	125
1873Go S	120,000	10.00	20.00	50.00	125
1874Go S	—	15.00	30.00	60.00	150
1875/4Go S	—	15.00	30.00	60.00	150
1875Go S	—	10.00	20.00	50.00	125
1876Go S	—	20.00	40.00	80.00	175
1877Go S	124,000	10.00	20.00	50.00	125
1878Go S	146,000	10.00	20.00	50.00	125
1879Go S	—	10.00	20.00	50.00	125
1880Go S	—	20.00	40.00	80.00	175
1881Go S	408,000	9.00	17.50	45.00	125
1882Go S	204,000	9.00	17.50	45.00	125
1883Go B	168,000	9.00	17.50	45.00	125
1884/69Go B	—	9.00	17.50	45.00	125
1884/3Go B	—	9.00	17.50	45.00	125
1884/3Go B/R	—	9.00	17.50	45.00	125
1884Go B	—	9.00	17.50	45.00	125
1885/65Go R	300,000	9.00	17.50	45.00	125
1885/69Go R	Inc. above	9.00	17.50	45.00	125

Date	Mintage	F12	VF20	XF40	MS60
1885Go R	Inc. above	9.00	17.50	45.00	125
1886/65Go R	—	9.00	17.50	45.00	125
1886/66Go R	322,000	9.00	17.50	45.00	125
1886/69Go R/S	Inc. above	9.00	17.50	45.00	125
1886/5/69 Go R	Inc. above	9.00	15.00	45.00	125
1886Go R	Inc. above	9.00	15.00	45.00	125
1887Go R	254,000	9.00	15.00	45.00	125
1887Go/Cn R/D	Inc. above	9.00	15.00	45.00	125
1888Go R	312,000	8.00	15.00	45.00	125
1889/8Go R RS inverted B	—	—	—	—	—
1889/8Go R	304,000	8.00	15.00	45.00	125
1889/8Go/Cn R/D	Inc. above	8.00	15.00	45.00	125
1889Go R	Inc. above	8.00	15.00	45.00	125
1890Go R	236,000	8.00	15.00	45.00	125

KM# 406.6 25 CENTAVOS
6.77 g., 0.903 Silver, 0.20 oz. ASW **Obv.** Facing eagle, snake in beak **Rev:** Radiant cap above scales **Mint:** Hermosillo **Note:** Varieties exist.

Date	Mintage	F12	VF20	XF40	MS60
1874/64 Ho R	Inc. above	10.00	20.00	40.00	125
1874/69 Ho R	—	10.00	20.00	40.00	125
1874 Ho R	23,000	10.00	20.00	40.00	125
1875Ho R Rare	—	—	—	—	—
1876/4Ho F/R	34,000	10.00	20.00	50.00	150
1876Ho F/R	Inc. above	10.00	25.00	60.00	150
1876Ho F	Inc. above	10.00	25.00	55.00	135
1877Ho F	—	10.00	20.00	50.00	125
1878Ho A	23,000	10.00	20.00	50.00	125
1879Ho A	—	10.00	20.00	50.00	125
1880Ho A	—	15.00	30.00	60.00	125
1881Ho A	19,000	15.00	30.00	60.00	125
1882Ho A	8,120	20.00	40.00	80.00	150
1883Ho M	2,000	100	200	300	600
1884Ho M	—	12.50	25.00	50.00	150
1885Ho M	—	10.00	20.00	50.00	125
1886Ho G	6,400	30.00	60.00	125	250
1887Ho G	12,000	10.00	20.00	40.00	125
1888Ho G	20,000	10.00	20.00	40.00	125
1889Ho G	28,000	10.00	20.00	40.00	125
1890/80Ho G	18,000	25.00	50.00	100	125
1890Ho G	Inc. above	25.00	50.00	100	125

KM# 406.7 25 CENTAVOS
6.77 g., 0.9027 Silver, 0.20 oz. ASW **Obv.** Facing eagle, snake in beak **Rev:** Radiant cap above scales **Obv. Legend:** REPUBLICA MEXICANA **Mint:** Mexico City **Note:** Varieties exist.

Date	Mintage	F12	VF20	XF40	MS60
1869Mo C	76,000	10.00	25.00	50.00	125
1870/69Mo C	—	6.50	12.00	30.00	125
1870/9Mo C	136,000	6.50	12.00	30.00	125
1870Mo C	Inc. above	6.50	12.00	30.00	125
1871Mo M	138,000	6.50	12.00	30.00	125
1872Mo M	220,000	6.50	12.00	30.00	125
1873/1Mo M	48,000	10.00	25.00	50.00	125
1873Mo M	Inc. above	10.00	25.00	50.00	125
1874/69Mo B/M	—	10.00	25.00	50.00	125
1874/3Mo M	—	10.00	25.00	50.00	125
1874/3Mo B	—	10.00	25.00	50.00	125
1874/3Mo B/M	—	10.00	25.00	50.00	125
1874Mo M	—	6.50	12.00	30.00	125
1874Mo B/M	—	10.00	25.00	50.00	125
1875Mo B	—	6.50	12.00	30.00	125
1876/5Mo B	—	8.00	15.00	40.00	125
1876Mo B	—	6.50	12.00	30.00	125

Date	Mintage	F12	VF20	XF40	MS60
1877Mo M	56,000	10.00	25.00	50.00	125
1878/1Mo M	120,000	10.00	25.00	50.00	125
1878/7Mo M	Inc. above	10.00	25.00	50.00	125
1878Mo M	Inc. above	6.50	12.00	30.00	125
1879Mo M	—	10.00	20.00	40.00	125
1880Mo M	—	8.00	15.00	35.00	125
1881/0Mo M	300,000	10.00	25.00	50.00	125
1881Mo M	Inc. above	10.00	25.00	50.00	125
1882Mo M	212,000	8.00	15.00	35.00	125
1883Mo M	108,000	8.00	15.00	35.00	125
1884/3Mo M	—	10.00	25.00	50.00	125
1884Mo M	—	10.00	20.00	40.00	125
1885Mo M	216,000	8.00	15.00	40.00	125
1886/5Mo M	436,000	8.00	15.00	35.00	125
1886Mo M	Inc. above	8.00	15.00	35.00	125
1887Mo M	376,000	8.00	15.00	35.00	125
1888Mo M	192,000	8.00	15.00	35.00	125
1889Mo M	132,000	8.00	15.00	35.00	125
1890Mo M	60,000	10.00	20.00	40.00	125

KM# 406.8 25 CENTAVOS
6.77 g., 0.903 Silver, 0.20 oz. ASW **Obv.** Facing eagle, snake in beak **Rev:** Radiant cap above scales **Mint:** San Luis Potosi **Note:** Varieties exist.

Date	Mintage	F12	VF20	XF40	MS60
1869Pi S	—	25.00	75.00	150	300
1870Pi G	50,000	10.00	30.00	75.00	150
1870Pi O	Inc. above	15.00	35.00	85.00	175
1871Pi O	30,000	10.00	30.00	75.00	150
1872Pi O	46,000	10.00	30.00	75.00	150
1873Pi O	13,000	15.00	40.00	90.00	175
1874Pi H	—	15.00	40.00	90.00	200
1875Pi H	—	10.00	20.00	60.00	150
1876/5Pi H	—	15.00	30.00	80.00	175
1876Pi H	—	10.00	25.00	65.00	150
1877Pi H	19,000	10.00	25.00	65.00	150
1878Pi H	—	15.00	30.00	60.00	150
1879/8Pi H	—	10.00	25.00	60.00	150
1879Pi H	—	10.00	25.00	60.00	150
1879Pi E	—	100	200	300	600
1880Pi H	—	20.00	40.00	100	200
1880Pi H/M	—	20.00	40.00	100	200
1881Pi H	50,000	20.00	40.00	80.00	175
1881Pi E Rare	Inc. above	—	—	—	—
1882Pi H	20,000	10.00	20.00	60.00	150
1883Pi H	17,000	10.00	25.00	65.00	150
1884Pi H	—	10.00	25.00	65.00	150
1885/4Pi H	—	10.00	20.00	60.00	150
1885Pi H	43,000	10.00	20.00	60.00	150
1886Pi C	78,000	10.00	25.00	65.00	150
1886Pi R	Inc. above	9.00	20.00	50.00	150
1886Pi R 6/inverted 6	Inc. above	9.00	20.00	50.00	150
1887Pi/ZsR	92,000	9.00	20.00	50.00	150
1887Pi/ZsB	Inc. above	100	150	300	500
1887Pi R	—	9.00	20.00	50.00	150
1888Pi R	106,000	9.00	20.00	50.00	150
1888Pi/ZsR	Inc. above	10.00	20.00	50.00	150
1888Pi R/B	Inc. above	10.00	20.00	50.00	150
1889Pi R	115,000	8.00	15.00	40.00	150
1889Pi/ZsR	Inc. above	10.00	20.00	50.00	150
1889Pi R/B	Inc. above	10.00	20.00	50.00	150
1890Pi R	64,000	10.00	20.00	50.00	150
1890Pi/ZsR/B	Inc. above	8.00	15.00	40.00	150
1890Pi R/B	Inc. above	10.00	20.00	50.00	150

KM# 406.9 25 CENTAVOS
6.77 g., 0.903 Silver, 0.20 oz. ASW **Obv.** Facing eagle, snake in beak **Rev:** Radiant cap above scales **Mint:** Zacatecas **Note:** Varieties exist.

Date	Mintage	F12	VF20	XF40	MS60	MS63
1870 Zs H	152,000	8.00	15.00	50.00	125	—
1871Zs H	250,000	8.00	15.00	50.00	125	—
1872Zs H	260,000	8.00	15.00	50.00	125	—
1872Zs/Cn H	—	—	—	—	—	—
1872Zs H	—	—	—	—	—	—
1873Zs H	132,000	8.00	15.00	50.00	125	—
1874Zs H	—	10.00	20.00	60.00	125	—

Date	Mintage	F12	VF20	XF40	MS60	MS63
1874Zs A	—	10.00	20.00	60.00	125	—
1875Zs A	—	9.00	20.00	60.00	125	—
1876Zs A	—	8.00	15.00	50.00	125	—
1876Zs S	—	8.00	15.00	50.00	125	—
1877Zs S	350,000	8.00	15.00	50.00	125	—
1878Zs S	252,000	8.00	15.00	50.00	125	—
1878/7Zs S	—	9.00	20.00	60.00	125	—
1878/1Zs S	—	9.00	20.00	60.00	125	—
1879Zs S	—	8.00	15.00	50.00	125	—
1880Zs S	—	8.00	15.00	50.00	125	—
1881/0Zs S	570,000	8.00	15.00	50.00	125	—
1881Zs S	Inc. above	8.00	15.00	50.00	125	—
1882/1Zs S	300,000	10.00	17.50	55.00	125	—
1882Zs S	Inc. above	8.00	15.00	50.00	125	—
1883/2Zs S	193,000	10.00	17.50	55.00	125	—
1883Zs S	Inc. above	8.00	15.00	50.00	125	—
1884/3Zs S	—	10.00	17.50	55.00	125	—
1884Zs S	—	8.00	15.00	50.00	125	—
1885Zs S	309,000	8.00	15.00	50.00	125	—
1886/2Zs S	—	10.00	17.50	55.00	125	—
1886/5Zs S	613,000	8.00	15.00	50.00	125	—
1886Zs S	Inc. above	8.00	15.00	50.00	125	—
1886Zs Z	Inc. above	8.00	15.00	55.00	125	—
1887Zs Z	389,000	8.00	15.00	50.00	125	—
1888Zs Z	408,000	8.00	15.00	50.00	125	—
1889Zs Z	400,000	8.00	15.00	50.00	125	—
1890Zs Z	269,000	8.00	15.00	50.00	125	—

KM# 407.7 50 CENTAVOS
13.54 g., 0.903 Silver, 0.39 oz. ASW **Obv.** Facing eagle, snake in beak **Rev:** Radiant cap above scales **Mint:** San Luis Potosi

Date	Mintage	F12	VF20	XF40	MS60
1870 Pi G	Inc. above	22.50	42.00	105	450
1870/780 Pi G	50,000	27.50	47.00	115	500
1870 Pi O	Inc. above	22.50	42.00	105	450
1871Pi O	—	17.00	32.00	85.00	400
1871Pi O/G	64,000	17.00	32.00	85.00	400
1872Pi O	52,000	17.00	32.00	85.00	400
1872Pi O/G	Inc. above	17.00	32.00	85.00	400
1873Pi O	32,000	22.50	42.00	105	450
1873Pi H	Inc. above	27.50	52.00	130	550
1874Pi H/O	—	17.00	32.00	85.00	400
1875/3Pi H	—	17.00	32.00	85.00	400
1875Pi H	—	17.00	32.00	85.00	400
1876Pi H	—	32.00	62.00	155	700
1877Pi H	34,000	22.50	42.00	105	450
1878Pi H	9,700	22.50	42.00	105	450
1879/7Pi H	—	17.00	37.00	95.00	450
1879Pi H	—	17.00	37.00	95.00	400
1880Pi H	—	22.50	42.00	105	450
1881Pi H	28,000	22.50	42.00	105	450
1882Pi H	22,000	17.00	32.00	85.00	400
1883Pi H 8/8	29,000	50.00	100	200	750
1883Pi H	Inc. above	17.00	32.00	85.00	400
1884Pi H	—	50.00	100	175	600
1885/3Pi H	—	22.50	42.00	105	450
1885/0Pi H	45,000	22.50	42.00	105	450
1885/4Pi H	Inc. above	22.50	42.00	105	450
1885Pi H	Inc. above	27.50	52.00	130	450
1885Pi C	Inc. above	17.00	32.00	85.00	400
1886/1Pi R	92,000	50.00	100	175	600
1886/1Pi C	—	27.50	42.00	105	450
1886Pi C	Inc. above	17.00	32.00	85.00	400
1886Pi R	Inc. above	17.00	32.00	85.00	400
1887Pi R	32,000	17.00	32.00	95.00	450

KM# 407 50 CENTAVOS
13.54 g., 0.903 Silver, 0.39 oz. ASW **Obv.** Facing eagle, snake in beak **Rev:** Radiant cap above scales **Mint:** Alamos **Note:** Mint mark A, As.

Date	Mintage	F12	VF20	XF40	MS60
1875 L	—	14.00	27.50	75.00	400
1876/5 L	—	27.50	50.00	125	450
1876 L	—	14.00	27.50	75.00	400
1876. L	—	14.00	27.50	75.00	400
1877 L	26,000	17.00	32.00	90.00	450

Date	Mintage	F12	VF20	XF40	MS60
1878 L	—	14.00	27.50	75.00	400
1879 L	—	27.50	52.00	125	450
1880 L	57,000	14.00	27.50	75.00	400
1881 L	18,000	17.00	32.00	85.00	450
1884 L	6,286	65.00	120	250	650
1885As/HoL	21,000	17.00	37.00	95.00	450
1888 L	—	4,000	5,000	7,000	—

KM# 407.1 50 CENTAVOS
13.54 g., 0.903 Silver, 0.39 oz. ASW **Obv.** Facing eagle, snake in beak **Rev:** Radiant cap above scales **Mint:** Chihuahua **Note:** Mint mark Ca, CHa.

Date	Mintage	F12	VF20	XF40	MS60	MS63
1883 M	12,000	32.00	62.00	130	500	—
1884 M	—	27.50	52.00	130	500	—
1885 M	13,000	17.00	37.00	95.00	400	—
1886 M	18,000	22.50	42.00	105	450	—
1887 M	26,000	27.50	67.00	155	500	—

KM# 407.2 50 CENTAVOS
13.54 g., 0.903 Silver, 0.39 oz. ASW **Obv.** Facing eagle, snake in beak **Rev:** Radiant cap above scales **Obv. Legend:** REPUBLICA MEXICANA **Mint:** Culiacan

Date	Mintage	F12	VF20	XF40	MS60
1871 Cn P	—	400	550	750	1,500
1873Cn P	—	400	550	750	1,500
1874Cn P	—	200	300	500	1,000
1875/4Cn P	—	22.50	42.00	80.00	450
1875Cn P	—	14.00	27.50	55.00	450
1876Cn P	—	17.00	32.00	65.00	450
1877/6Cn G	—	17.00	32.00	65.00	450
1877Cn G	—	14.00	27.50	55.00	450
1878Cn G	18,000	22.50	42.00	80.00	450
1878Cn/Mo D	Inc. above	32.00	62.00	105	450
1878Cn D	Inc. above	17.00	37.00	80.00	450
1879Cn D	—	14.00	27.50	55.00	450
1879Cn D/G	—	14.00	27.50	55.00	450
1880/8Cn D	—	17.00	32.00	65.00	450
1880Cn D	—	17.00	32.00	65.00	450
1881/0Cn D	188,000	17.00	32.00	65.00	450
1881Cn D	Inc. above	17.00	32.00	65.00	450
1881Cn G	Inc. above	125	175	275	550
1882Cn D	—	175	300	500	2,000
1882Gn G	—	100	250	300	1,000
1883 D	19,000	27.50	82.00	110	500
1885Cn M/M/G	—	32.00	62.00	110	500
1885/3Cn M/H	9,254	32.00	62.00	110	500
1886Cn M/G	7,030	50.00	100	300	1,500
1886Cn M	Inc. above	42.00	82.00	160	800
1887Cn M	76,000	22.50	42.00	110	450
1888Cn M	—	4,000	6,000	—	—
1892Cn M	-	42.00	82.00	155	650

KM# 407.3 50 CENTAVOS
13.54 g., 0.903 Silver, 0.39 oz. ASW **Obv.** Facing eagle, snake in beak **Rev:** Radiant cap above scales **Obv. Legend:** REPUBLICA MEXICANA **Mint:** Durango

Date	Mintage	F12	VF20	XF40	MS60
1871 Do P Rare	591	—	—	—	—
1873Do P	4,010	150	250	500	1,250
1873Do M/P	Inc. above	150	250	500	1,250
1874Do M	—	22.50	42.00	180	750
1875Do M	—	22.50	42.00	85.00	350
1875Do H	—	150	250	450	1,000
1876/5Do M	—	37.00	72.00	155	500
1876Do M	—	37.00	72.00	155	500
1877Do P	2,000	32.00	47.00	155	1,250
1878Do B Rare	—	—	—	—	—
1879Do B Rare	—	—	—	—	—
1880Do P	—	32.00	62.00	130	500
1881Do P	10,000	42.00	82.00	155	550
1882Do C	8,957	32.00	77.00	205	800
1884/2Do C	—	22.50	52.00	130	600
1884Do C	—	—	—	—	—
1885Do B	—	17.00	42.00	110	500
1885Do B/P	—	17.00	42.00	110	500
1886Do C	16,000	17.00	42.00	110	500
1887Do C	—	17.00	42.00	110	500
1887Do/Mo C	28,000	17.00	42.00	110	500

KM# 407.4 50 CENTAVOS
13.54 g., 0.903 Silver, 0.39 oz. ASW **Obv.** Facing eagle, snake in beak **Rev:** Radiant cap above scales **Mint:** Guanajuato **Note:** Struck at Guanajuato Mint, mitn mark Go. Varieties exist.

Date	Mintage	F12	VF20	XF40	MS60
1869Go S	—	17.00	37.00	80.00	550
1870Go S	166,000	14.00	27.50	55.00	450
1871Go S	148,000	14.00	27.50	55.00	450
1872/1Go S	144,000	17.00	32.00	65.00	500
1872Go S	Inc. above	14.00	27.50	55.00	450
1873Go S	50,000	14.00	27.50	55.00	450
1874Go S	—	14.00	27.50	55.00	450
1875Go S	—	17.00	37.00	80.00	450
1876/5Go S	—	14.00	27.50	55.00	450
1877Go S	76,000	14.00	27.50	65.00	450
1878Go S	37,000	17.00	32.00	80.00	550
1879/8Go S	—	17.00	32.00	65.00	500
1879Go S	—	14.00	27.50	55.00	450
1880Go S	—	14.00	27.50	55.00	450
1881/79Go S	32,000	17.00	32.00	65.00	500
1881Go S	Inc. above	14.00	27.50	55.00	450
1882Go S	18,000	14.00	27.50	55.00	450
1883/2Go B/S	—	17.00	32.00	65.00	500
1883Go B	—	14.00	27.50	55.00	450
1883Go S Rare	—	—	—	—	—
1884Go B/S	—	17.00	32.00	65.00	500
1885/4Go R/B	—	17.00	32.00	65.00	500
1885Go R	53,000	14.00	27.50	55.00	450
1886/5Go R	59,000	17.00	32.00	65.00	500
1886/5Go R/S	Inc. above	22.50	42.00	80.00	500
1886Go R	Inc. above	22.50	42.00	80.00	450
1887Go R	18,000	22.50	42.00	80.00	550
1888Go R 1 known; Rare	—	—	—	—	—

KM# 407.5 50 CENTAVOS
13.54 g., 0.903 Silver, 0.39 oz. ASW **Obv.** Facing eagle, snake in beak **Rev:** Radiant cap above scales **Mint:** Hermosillo **Note:** With and without dot after 50 of denomination, in medal and coin alignment.

Date	Mintage	F12	VF20	XF40	MS60	MS63
1874 Ho R	—	22.50	42.00	110	600	—
1875/4Ho R	—	22.50	52.00	135	600	—
1875Ho R	—	22.50	52.00	135	600	—
1876/5Ho F/R	—	17.00	37.00	110	550	—
1876Ho F	—	17.00	37.00	110	550	—
1877Ho F	—	52.00	77.00	160	650	—
1880/70Ho A	—	17.00	37.00	110	550	—
1880Ho A	—	17.00	37.00	110	550	—
1881Ho A	13,000	17.00	37.00	110	550	—

Date	Mintage	F12	VF20	XF40	MS60	MS63
1882Ho A	—	75.00	150	250	750	—
1888Ho G	—	2,000	3,000	6,000	—	—
1894Ho G	59,000	17.00	32.00	110	450	—
1895Ho G	8,000	250	350	700	1,500	—

KM# 407.6 50 CENTAVOS
13.54 g., 0.9027 Silver, 0.39 oz. ASW **Obv.** Facing eagle, snake in beak **Rev:** Radiant cap above scales **Obv. Legend:** REPUBLICA MEXICANA **Mint:** Mexico City

Date	Mintage	F12	VF20	XF40	MS60
1869Mo C	46,000	17.00	37.00	100	600
1870Mo C	52,000	17.00	32.00	95.00	550
1871Mo C	14,000	42.00	77.00	155	650
1871Mo M/C	Inc. above	37.00	77.00	155	600
1872/1Mo M	60,000	37.00	77.00	155	550
1872Mo M	Inc. above	37.00	77.00	155	550
1873Mo M	6,000	37.00	77.00	155	600
1874/3Mo M	—	200	400	600	1,250
1874/2Mo B	—	17.00	32.00	80.00	500
1874/2Mo B/M	—	17.00	32.00	80.00	500
1874/3Mo B/M	—	17.00	32.00	80.00	500
1874Mo B	—	17.00	32.00	80.00	500
1875Mo B	—	17.00	32.00	80.00	550
1876Mo B	—	14.00	27.50	80.00	500
1876/5Mo B	—	17.00	32.00	80.00	500
1877Mo M	—	17.00	32.00	95.00	500
1877/2Mo M	—	22.50	42.00	105	550
1878Mo M	—	17.00	37.00	105	500
1878/7Mo M	8,000	27.50	52.00	130	600
1879Mo M	—	27.50	52.00	130	550
1880Mo M	—	100	150	250	750
1881Mo M	16,000	27.50	52.00	130	600
1881/0Mo M	—	32.00	52.00	130	600
1882/1Mo M	2,000	32.00	62.00	155	750
1883/2Mo M	4,000	150	225	350	1,000
1884Mo M	—	150	225	350	1,000
1885Mo M	12,000	32.00	62.00	155	600
1886/5Mo M	66,000	17.00	37.00	95.00	475
1886Mo M	Inc. above	14.00	27.50	80.00	450
1887Mo M	Inc. above	17.00	37.00	80.00	475
1887/6Mo M	88,000	17.00	37.00	95.00	475
1888Mo M	—	3,000	4,000	6,000	—

KM# 407.8 50 CENTAVOS
13.54 g., 0.903 Silver, 0.39 oz. ASW **Obv.** Facing eagle, snake in beak **Rev:** Radiant cap above scales **Mint:** Zacatecas **Note:** Varieties exist.

Date	Mintage	F12	VF20	XF40	MS60
1870 Zs H	86,000	14.00	27.50	65.00	450
1871Zs H	146,000	14.00	27.50	55.00	400
1872Zs H	132,000	14.00	27.50	55.00	400

Date	Mintage	F12	VF20	XF40	MS60
1873Zs H	56,000	14.00	27.50	55.00	400
1874Zs A Rare	—	—	—	—	—
1874Zs H	—	14.00	27.50	55.00	400
1875Zs A	—	14.00	27.50	55.00	400
1876Zs S	—	100	200	350	750
1876/5Zs A	—	17.00	32.00	65.00	450
1876Zs A	—	14.00	27.50	55.00	400
1877Zs S	100,000	14.00	27.50	55.00	400
1878/7Zs S	254,000	17.00	32.00	65.00	450
1878Zs S	Inc. above	17.00	32.00	65.00	400
1879Zs S	—	14.00	27.50	55.00	400
1880Zs S	—	14.00	27.50	55.00	400
1881Zs S	201,000	14.00	27.50	55.00	400
1882/1Zs S	2,000	60.00	110	260	660
1882Zs S	Inc. above	60.00	110	260	660
1883Zs S	Inc. above	27.50	52.00	105	450
1883Zs/Za S	31,000	32.00	62.00	105	450
1884/3Zs S	—	17.00	32.00	65.00	450
1884Zs S	—	14.00	27.50	55.00	400
1885Zs S	Inc. above	27.50	52.00	130	450
1885/4Zs S	2,000	27.50	52.00	130	450
1886Zs Z	2,000	150	275	400	1,000
1887Zs Z	63,000	32.00	62.00	130	450

KM# 408 PESO
27.07 g., 0.903 Silver, 0.78 oz. ASW **Obv.** Facing eagle, snake in beak **Rev:** Radiant cap above scales **Mint:** Chihuahua

Date	Mintage	F12	VF20	XF40	MS60
1872 CH P/M	747,000	750	1,500	3,500	—
1872 CH P	Inc. above	350	700	1,500	—
1872/1 CH M	Inc. above	35.00	55.00	100	525
1872CH M	Inc. above	27.50	38.50	70.00	325
1873CH M	320,000	30.00	44.00	85.00	350
1873CH M/P	Inc. above	35.00	55.00	100	450

KM# 410 PESO
1.69 g., 0.875 Gold, 0.05 oz. AGW **Obv.** Facing eagle, snake in beak **Rev:** Value within 1/2 wreath **Obv. Legend:** REPUBLICA MEXICANA **Mint:** Alamos

Date	Mintage	F12	VF20	XF40	MS60
1888 AsL/MoM Rare	—	—	—	—	—
1888 As L Rare	—	—	—	—	—

KM# 410.1 PESO
1.69 g., 0.875 Gold, 0.05 oz. AGW **Obv.** Facing eagle, snake in beak **Rev:** Value within 1/2 wreath **Obv. Legend:** REPUBLICA MEXICANA **Mint:** Chihuahua

Date	Mintage	F12	VF20	XF40	MS60
1888 Ca/MoM Rare	104	—	—	—	—

KM# 410.2 PESO
1.69 g., 0.875 Gold, 0.05 oz. AGW **Obv.** Facing eagle, snake in beak **Rev:** Value within 1/2 wreath **Obv. Legend:** REPUBLICA MEXICANA **Mint:** Culiacan

Date	Mintage	F12	VF20	XF40	MS60	MS63
1873 Cn P	1,221	105	125	165	250	—
1875Cn P	—	115	150	165	250	—
1878Cn G	248	130	200	240	500	—
1879Cn D	—	130	175	215	475	—

Date	Mintage	F12	VF20	XF40	MS60	MS63
1881/0Cn D	338	130	175	215	475	—
1882Cn D	340	130	175	215	475	—
1883Cn D	—	130	175	215	475	—
1884Cn M	—	130	175	215	475	—
1886/4Cn M	277	130	175	240	500	—
1888/7Cn M	2,586	130	175	215	450	—
1888Cn M	Inc. above	95.00	125	165	265	—
1889Cn M Rare	—	—	—	—	—	—
1891/89Cn M	969	105	125	165	275	—
1892Cn M	780	105	125	165	275	—
1893Cn M	498	115	150	165	275	—
1894Cn M	493	110	150	165	275	—
1895Cn M	1,143	95.00	125	165	250	350
1896/5Cn M	1,028	95.00	125	165	250	350
1897Cn M	785	95.00	125	165	250	350
1898Cn M	3,521	95.00	125	165	225	325
1898Cn/MoM	Inc. above	95.00	125	165	250	350
1899Cn Q	2,000	95.00	125	165	225	325
1901Cn Q	Inc. above	90.00	110	150	225	325
1901/0Cn Q	2,350	90.00	110	150	225	325
1902Cn Q	2,480	90.00	110	150	225	325
1902Cn/MoQ/C	Inc. above	90.00	110	150	225	325
1904Cn H	3,614	90.00	110	150	225	325
1904Cn/Mo/ H	Inc. above	90.00	110	150	250	350
1905Cn P	1,000	—	—	—	—	—

Note: Requires Confirmation

KM# 408.1 PESO
27.07 g., 0.903 Silver, 0.78 oz. ASW **Obv.** Facing eagle, snake in beak **Rev:** Radiant cap above scales **Mint:** Culiacan

Date	Mintage	F12	VF20	XF40	MS60
1870 Cn E	—	49.50	95.00	185	650
1871/11Cn P	478,000	33.00	55.00	125	575
1871Cn P	Inc. above	27.50	49.50	95.00	400
1872/1Cn P	—	27.50	49.50	95.00	400
1872Cn P	209,000	27.50	49.50	95.00	400
1873Cn P Narrow date	527,000	27.50	49.50	95.00	400
1873Cn P Wide date	Inc. above	27.50	49.50	95.00	400

KM# 410.3 PESO
1.69 g., 0.875 Gold, 0.05 oz. AGW **Obv.** Facing eagle, snake in beak **Rev:** Value within 1/2 wreath **Obv. Legend:** REPUBLICA MEXICANA **Mint:** Guanajuato

Date	Mintage	F12	VF20	XF40	MS60	MS63
1870 Go S	—	130	150	165	265	—
1871Go S	500	130	200	240	475	—
1888Go R	210	165	225	265	550	—
1890Go R	1,916	100	125	165	265	—
1892Go R	533	130	175	190	350	—
1894Go R	180	195	225	265	550	—
1895Go R	676	130	175	190	325	—
1896/5Go R	4,671	85.00	125	165	250	—
1897/6Go R	4,280	85.00	125	165	250	—
1897Go R	Inc. above	85.00	125	165	250	—
1898Go R	5,193	85.00	125	165	250	750

Note: Regular obverse

1898Go R	Inc. above	100	125	165	250	750

Note: Mule, 5 Centavos obverse, normal reverse

1899Go R	2,748	85.00	125	165	250	—
1900/800 Go R	864	100	150	165	285	—

KM# 408.2 PESO

27.07 g., 0.9027 Silver, 0.78 oz. ASW **Obv.** Facing eagle, snake in beak **Rev:** Radiant cap above scales **Obv. Legend:** REPUBLICA MEXICANA **Mint:** Durango

Date	Mintage	F12	VF20	XF40	MS60	MS63
1870 Do P	—	60.00	115	215	575	—
1871Do P	427,000	35.00	65.00	100	400	—
1872Do P	296,000	30.00	50.00	100	450	—
1872Do PT	Inc. above	110	195	300	1,100	—
1873Do P	203,000	35.00	60.00	115	450	—

KM# 409.2 PESO

27.07 g., 0.9027 Silver, 0.78 oz. ASW 39mm. **Obv.** Facing eagle, snake in beak **Rev:** Radiant cap **Obv. Legend:** REPUBLICA MEXICANA **Mint:** Mexico City **Note:** Varieties exist.

Date	Mintage	F12	VF20	XF40	MS60
1898 Mo AM	10,250,000	28.00	30.00	35.00	75.00
Note: Restrike (1949) - reverse with 134 beads					
1898 Mo AM	10,156,000	28.00	30.00	35.00	85.00
Note: Original strike - reverse with 139 beads					
1899Mo AM	7,930,000	28.00	30.00	37.00	95.00
1900Mo AM	8,226,000	28.00	30.00	37.00	95.00
1901Mo AM	14,505,000	28.00	30.00	37.00	80.00
1902/1Mo AM	16,224,000	240	475	875	1,800
1902Mo AM	Inc. above	28.00	30.00	37.00	130
1903Mo AM	22,396,000	28.00	30.00	37.00	130
1903Mo MA (Error)	Inc. above	1,500	2,500	3,850	9,000
1904Mo AM	14,935,000	28.00	30.00	37.00	130
1905Mo AM	3,557,000	28.00	40.00	100	240
1908Mo AM	7,575,000	28.00	30.00	37.00	115
1908Mo GV	Inc. above	28.00	30.00	37.00	80.00
1909Mo GV	2,924,000	28.00	30.00	37.00	80.00

KM# 410.4 PESO

1.69 g., 0.875 Gold, 0.05 oz. AGW **Obv.** Facing eagle,

snake in beak **Rev:** Value within 1/2 wreath **Obv. Legend:** REPUBLICA MEXICANA **Mint:** Hermosillo

Date	Mintage	F12	VF20	XF40	MS60
1875 Ho R Rare	310	—	—	—	—
1876Ho F Rare	—	—	—	—	—
1888Ho G/MoM Rare	—	—	—	—	—

KM# 408.3 PESO

27.07 g., 0.903 Silver, 0.78 oz. ASW **Obv.** Facing eagle, snake in beak **Rev:** Radiant cap above scales **Obv. Legend:** REPUBLICA MEXICANA **Mint:** Guadalajara

Date	Mintage	F12	VF20	XF40	MS60
1870 Ga C	—	850	1,100	—	—
1871Ga C	829,000	37.00	85.00	175	775
1872Ga C	485,000	50.00	110	220	850
1873/2Ga C	277,000	50.00	110	220	900
1873Ga C	Inc. above	37.00	85.00	175	775

KM# 410.5 PESO

1.69 g., 0.875 Gold, 0.05 oz. AGW **Obv.** Facing eagle, snake in beak **Rev:** Value within 1/2 wreath **Obv. Legend:** REPUBLICA MEXICANA **Mint:** Mexico City

Date	Mintage	F12	VF20	XF40	MS60	MS63
1870 Mo C	2,540	85.00	95.00	110	185	250
1871Mo M/C	1,000	95.00	120	165	250	250
1872Mo M/C	3,000	85.00	95.00	110	185	300
1873/1Mo M	2,900	85.00	95.00	115	200	250
1873Mo M	Inc. above	85.00	95.00	110	185	250
1874Mo M	—	85.00	95.00	110	185	250
1875Mo B/M	—	85.00	95.00	110	185	250
1876/5Mo B/M	—	85.00	95.00	110	185	250
1877Mo M	—	85.00	95.00	110	185	250
1878Mo M	2,000	85.00	95.00	110	185	250
1879Mo M	—	85.00	95.00	110	185	250
1880/70Mo M	—	85.00	95.00	110	185	250
1881/71Mo M	1,000	85.00	95.00	110	185	250
1882/72Mo M	—	85.00	95.00	110	185	250
1883/72Mo M	1,000	85.00	95.00	110	185	250
1884Mo M	—	85.00	95.00	110	185	250
1885/71Mo M	—	85.00	95.00	110	185	250
1885Mo M	—	85.00	95.00	110	185	250
1886Mo M	1,700	85.00	95.00	110	185	250
1887Mo M	2,200	85.00	95.00	110	185	250
1888Mo M	1,000	85.00	95.00	110	185	250
1889Mo M	500	125	170	215	285	—
1890Mo M	570	125	170	215	285	—
1891Mo M	746	125	170	215	285	—
1892/0Mo M	2,895	85.00	95.00	110	185	250
1893Mo M	5,917	85.00	95.00	110	185	250
1894/3M Mo	—	85.00	95.00	110	185	250
1894Mo M	6,244	85.00	95.00	110	185	250
1895Mo M	8,994	85.00	95.00	110	185	250
1895Mo B	Inc. above	85.00	95.00	110	185	250
1896Mo B	7,166	85.00	95.00	110	185	250
1896Mo M	Inc. above	85.00	95.00	110	185	250
1897Mo M	5,131	85.00	95.00	110	185	250
1898/7Mo M	5,368	85.00	95.00	110	185	250

Date	Mintage	F12	VF20	XF40	MS60	MS63
1899Mo M	9,515	85.00	95.00	110	185	250
1900/800 Mo M	9,301	85.00	95.00	110	185	250
1900/880 Mo M	Inc. above	85.00	95.00	110	185	250
1900/890 Mo M	Inc. above	85.00	95.00	110	185	250
1900Mo M	Inc. above	85.00	95.00	110	185	250
1901Mo M Small date	Inc. above	90.00	100	115	205	270
1901/801 Mo M Large date	8,293	90.00	100	115	205	270
1902Mo M Large date	11,000	90.00	100	115	205	270
1902Mo M Small date	Inc. above	90.00	100	115	205	270
1903Mo M Large date	10,000	90.00	100	115	205	270
1903Mo M Small date	Inc. above	90.00	100	145	220	325
1904Mo M	9,845	90.00	100	115	205	270
1905Mo M	3,429	90.00	100	115	205	270

KM# 410.6 PESO
1.69 g., 0.875 Gold, 0.05 oz. AGW **Obv.** Facing eagle, snake in beak **Rev:** Value within 1/2 wreath **Obv. Legend:** REPUBLICA MEXICANA **Mint:** Zacatecas

Date	Mintage	F12	VF20	XF40	MS60	MS63
1872 Zs H	2,024	155	175	190	295	—
1875/3Zs A	—	155	175	215	350	—
1878Zs S	—	155	175	190	295	—
1888Zs Z	280	205	250	350	725	—
1889Zs Z	492	180	200	240	475	—
1890Zs Z	738	180	200	240	475	—

KM# 408.4 PESO
27.07 g., 0.9027 Silver, 0.78 oz. ASW **Obv.** Facing eagle, snake in beak **Rev:** Radiant cap above scales **Obv. Legend:** REPUBLICA MEXICANA **Mint:** Guanajuato

Date	Mintage	F12	VF20	XF40	MS60
1871/0 Go S	3,946,000	35.00	60.00	115	450
1871/3 Go S	Inc. above	26.00	44.00	90.00	350
1871 Go S	Inc. above	BV	27.50	55.00	285
1872Go S	4,067,000	BV	27.50	55.00	325
1873/2Go S	1,560,000	26.00	33.00	65.00	325
1873Go S	Inc. above	BV	27.50	60.00	325
1873Go/Mo/S/M	Inc. above	BV	27.50	60.00	325

KM# 408.5 PESO
27.07 g., 0.903 Silver, 0.78 oz. ASW **Obv.** Facing eagle, snake in beak **Rev:** Radiant cap above scales **Mint:** Mexico City

Date	Mintage	F12	VF20	XF40	MS60
1869Mo C	—	50.00	90.00	180	775
1870Mo M/C	Inc. above	30.00	47.25	100	400
1870/69Mo C	5,115,000	27.50	42.00	85.00	350
1870Mo C	Inc. above	26.00	36.00	65.00	325
1870Mo M	Inc. above	30.00	47.25	100	400
1871/0Mo M	6,974,000	27.50	42.00	85.00	350
1871Mo M	Inc. above	26.00	36.00	65.00	325
1872/1Mo M	—	27.50	41.50	80.00	350
1872/1Mo M/C	4,801,000	27.50	41.50	80.00	350
1872Mo M	Inc. above	26.00	36.00	65.00	325
1873Mo M	1,765,000	26.00	36.00	65.00	325

Note: The 1869 C with large LEY on the scroll is a pattern

KM# 408.6 PESO
27.07 g., 0.903 Silver, 0.78 oz. ASW **Obv.** Facing eagle, snake in beak **Rev:** Radiant cap above scales **Obv. Legend:** REPUBLICA MEXICANA **Mint:** Oaxaca

Date	Mintage	F12	VF20	XF40	MS60
1869Oa E	—	300	450	725	2,600
1870Oa E Small A	Inc. above	26.00	44.00	100	525
1870OA E Large A	Inc. above	110	165	350	1,150
1871/69Oa E	140,000	42.00	65.00	160	725
1871Oa E Small A	Inc. above	27.50	44.00	85.00	400
1871Oa E Large A	Inc. above	27.50	44.00	100	525
1872Oa E Small A	180,000	27.50	44.00	100	525
1872Oa E Large A	Inc. above	60.00	110	240	575
1873Oa E	105,000	27.50	44.00	100	450

KM# 408.7 PESO
27.07 g., 0.903 Silver, 0.78 oz. ASW **Obv.** Facing eagle, snake in beak **Rev:** Radiant cap above scales **Mint:** San Luis Potosi **Note:** Varieties exist.

Date	Mintage	F12	VF20	XF40	MS60
1870 Pi S	1,967,000	220	375	600	1,300
1870 Pi S/A	Inc. above	220	375	650	1,550
1870 Pi G	Inc. above	37.00	55.00	100	725
1870 Pi H	Inc. above	—	—	—	—
Note: Contemporary counterfeits					
1870 Pi O/G	Inc. above	37.00	55.00	100	725
1870 Pi O	Inc. above	30.00	44.00	130	525
1871/69Pi O	2,103,000	90.00	120	265	650

Date	Mintage	F12	VF20	XF40	MS60
1871Pi O/G	Inc. above	27.50	44.00	85.00	650
1871Pi O	—	27.50	44.00	85.00	650
1872Pi O	1,873,000	27.50	44.00	85.00	650
1873Pi H	Inc. above	27.50	44.00	85.00	650
1873Pi O	893,000	27.50	44.00	85.00	650

KM# 408.8 PESO
27.07 g., 0.903 Silver, 0.78 oz. ASW **Obv.** Facing eagle, snake in beak **Rev:** Radiant cap above scales **Mint:** Zacatecas **Note:** Varieties exist.

Date	Mintage	F12	VF20	XF40	MS60	MS63
1870 Zs H	4,519,000	27.00	47.00	65.00	285	—
1871Zs H	4,459,000	26.00	36.00	65.00	285	—
1872Zs H	4,039,000	26.00	36.00	65.00	285	—
1873/1Zs H	Inc. above	26.00	36.00	65.00	285	—
1873Zs H	1,782,000	26.00	36.00	65.00	285	—

KM# 409 PESO
27.07 g., 0.903 Silver, 0.78 oz. ASW 39mm. **Obv.** Facing eagle, snake in beak **Rev:** Radiant cap **Mint:** Culiacan

Date	Mintage	F12	VF20	XF40	MS60
1898 Cn/MoAM	Inc. above	28.00	40.00	110	185
1898 Cn AM	1,720,000	28.00	30.00	55.00	120
1899Cn AM	1,722,000	32.50	55.00	110	215
1899Cn JQ	Inc. above	28.00	30.00	70.00	155
1900Cn JQ	1,804,000	28.00	30.00	55.00	120
1901Cn JQ	1,473,000	28.00	30.00	65.00	160
1902Cn JQ	1,194,000	28.00	30.00	75.00	240
1903Cn JQ	1,514,000	28.00	30.00	55.00	160
1903Cn FV	Inc. above	40.00	80.00	175	425
1904Cn MH	1,554,000	28.00	30.00	44.00	145
1904Cn RP	Inc. above	80.00	160	265	650
1905Cn RP	598,000	40.00	80.00	175	475

KM# 409.1 PESO
27.07 g., 0.903 Silver, 0.78 oz. ASW 39mm. **Obv.** Facing eagle, snake in beak **Rev:** Radiant cap **Mint:** Guanajuato **Note:** Varieties exist.

Date	Mintage	F12	VF20	XF40	MS60
1898 Go/MoRS	Inc. above	27.50	35.00	70.00	150
1898 Go RS	4,256,000	BV	26.00	47.00	100
1899Go RS	3,207,000	BV	26.00	42.00	95.00
1900Go RS	1,489,000	32.50	55.00	120	300

KM# 409.3 PESO
27.07 g., 0.903 Silver, 0.78 oz. ASW 39mm. **Obv.** Facing eagle, snake in beak **Rev:** Radiant cap **Mint:** Zacatecas **Note:** Mint mark Zs. Varieties exist.

Date	Mintage	F12	VF20	XF40	MS60
1898 Zs FZ	5,714,000	27.50	32.50	49.50	130
1899Zs FZ	5,618,000	27.50	32.50	49.50	140
1900Zs FZ	5,357,000	27.50	32.50	49.50	140
1901Zs FZ	Inc. above	28.00	30.00	36.00	110
1901Zs AZ	5,706,000	4,000	6,000	11,000	—
1902Zs FZ	7,134,000	28.00	30.00	36.00	110
1903/2Zs FZ	3,080,000	28.00	30.00	90.00	240
1903Zs FZ	Inc. above	28.00	30.00	37.00	125
1904Zs FZ	2,423,000	28.00	30.00	50.00	160
1904Zs FM	Inc. above	28.00	30.00	45.00	145
1905Zs FM	995,000	32.00	65.00	110	290

KM# 411 2-1/2 PESOS
4.23 g., 0.875 Gold, 0.12 oz. AGW **Obv.** Facing eagle, snake in beak **Rev:** Value within 1/2 wreath **Obv. Legend:** REPUBLICA MEXICANA **Mint:** Alamos

Date	Mintage	F12	VF20	XF40	MS60	MS63
1888 As/MoL Rare	—	—	—	—	—	—

KM# 411.1 2-1/2 PESOS
4.23 g., 0.875 Gold, 0.12 oz. AGW **Obv.** Facing eagle, snake in beak **Rev:** Value within 1/2 wreath **Mint:** Culiacan

Date	Mintage	F12	VF20	XF40	MS60
1893 Cn M	141	1,500	2,000	2,500	3,500

KM# 411.2 2-1/2 PESOS
4.23 g., 0.875 Gold, 0.12 oz. AGW **Obv.** Facing eagle, snake in beak **Rev:** Value within 1/2 wreath **Mint:** Durango

Date	Mintage	F12	VF20	XF40	MS60
1888 Do C Rare	—	—	—	—	—

KM# 411.3 2-1/2 PESOS
4.23 g., 0.875 Gold, 0.12 oz. AGW **Obv.** Facing eagle, snake in beak **Rev:** Value within 1/2 wreath **Obv. Legend:** REPUBLICA MEXICANA **Mint:** Guanajuato

Date	Mintage	F12	VF20	XF40	MS60
1871 Go S	600	1,250	2,000	2,500	3,250
1888Go/MoR	110	1,750	2,250	2,750	3,500

KM# 411.4 2-1/2 PESOS
4.23 g., 0.875 Gold, 0.12 oz. AGW **Obv.** Facing eagle, snake in beak **Rev:** Value within 1/2 wreath **Obv. Legend:** REPUBLICA MEXICANA **Mint:** Hermosillo

Date	Mintage	F12	VF20	XF40	MS60
1874 Ho R Rare	—	—	—	—	—
1888Ho G Rare	—	—	—	—	—

KM# 411.5 2-1/2 PESOS
4.23 g., 0.875 Gold, 0.12 oz. AGW **Obv.** Facing eagle, snake in beak **Rev:** Value within 1/2 wreath **Mint:** Mexico City

Date	Mintage	F12	VF20	XF40	MS60	MS63
1870 Mo C	820	215	300	400	800	—
1872 Mo M/C	800	215	300	400	800	—
1873/2Mo M	—	250	400	800	1,400	—
1874Mo M	—	250	400	800	1,400	—
1874Mo B/M	—	250	400	800	1,400	—
1875Mo B	—	250	400	800	1,400	—
1876Mo B	—	300	550	1,050	1,900	—
1877Mo M	—	250	400	800	1,400	—
1878Mo M	400	250	400	800	1,400	—
1879Mo M	—	250	400	800	1,400	—
1880/79Mo M	—	250	400	800	1,400	—
1881Mo M	400	250	400	800	1,400	—
1882Mo M	—	275	450	900	1,550	2,000
1883/73Mo M	400	250	400	800	1,400	—
1884Mo M	—	300	550	1,050	1,650	—
1885Mo M	—	450	900	1,800	3,050	—
1886Mo M	400	250	400	800	1,400	—
1887Mo M	400	250	400	800	1,400	—
1888Mo M	540	250	400	800	1,400	—
1889Mo M	240	200	350	575	1,000	—
1890Mo M	420	250	400	800	1,400	—
1891Mo M	188	250	400	800	1,400	—
1892Mo M	240	250	400	800	1,400	—

KM# 411.6   2-1/2 PESOS
4.23 g., 0.875 Gold, 0.12 oz. AGW **Obv.** Facing eagle, snake in beak **Rev:** Value within 1/2 wreath **Obv. Legend:** REPUBLICA MEXICANA **Mint:** Zacatecas

Date	Mintage	F12	VF20	XF40	MS60
1872 Zs H	1,300	250	400	550	1,250
1873Zs H	—	225	375	525	950
1875/3Zs A	—	250	400	800	1,400
1877Zs S	—	250	400	800	1,400
1878Zs S	300	250	400	800	1,400
1888Zs/MoS	80	350	550	1,050	1,850
1889Zs/Mo Z	184	300	500	1,000	1,650
1890Zs Z	326	250	400	800	1,400

KM# 412   5 PESOS
8.46 g., 0.875 Gold, 0.24 oz. AGW **Obv.** Facing eagle, snake in beak **Rev:** Radiant cap above scales **Obv. Legend:** REPUBLICA MEXICANA **Mint:** Alamos

Date	Mintage	F12	VF20	XF40	MS60
1875 As L	—	—	—	—	—
1878As L	383	900	1,700	3,000	4,500

KM# 412.1   5 PESOS
8.46 g., 0.875 Gold, 0.24 oz. AGW **Obv.** Facing eagle, snake in beak **Rev:** Radiant cap above scales **Obv. Legend:** REPUBLICA MEXICANA **Mint:** Chihuahua

Date	Mintage	F12	VF20	XF40	MS60	MS63
1888 Ca M Rare	120	—	—	—	—	—

KM# 412.2   5 PESOS
8.46 g., 0.875 Gold, 0.24 oz. AGW **Obv.** Facing eagle, snake in beak **Rev:** Radiant cap above scales **Obv. Legend:** REPUBLICA MEXICANA **Mint:** Culiacan

Date	Mintage	F12	VF20	XF40	MS60	MS63
1873 Cn P	—	450	750	1,200	2,200	—
1874Cn P	—	—	—	—	—	—
1875Cn P	—	450	650	1,000	1,950	—
1876Cn P	—	450	650	1,000	1,950	—
1877Cn G	—	450	650	1,000	1,950	—
1882Cn Rare	174	—	—	—	—	—
1888Cn M	—	650	1,150	1,450	2,200	—
1890Cn M	435	475	650	950	1,800	—
1891Cn M	1,390	450	550	750	1,200	—
1894Cn M	484	475	650	950	1,800	—
1895Cn M	142	650	900	1,500	2,700	—
1900Cn Q	1,536	450	500	675	1,100	—
1903 Cn Q	1,000	450	475	550	1,000	—

KM# 412.3   5 PESOS
8.46 g., 0.875 Gold, 0.24 oz. AGW **Obv.** Facing eagle, snake in beak **Rev:** Radiant cap above scales **Obv. Legend:** REPUBLICA MEXICANA **Mint:** Durango

Date	Mintage	F12	VF20	XF40	MS60	MS63
1873/2 Do P	—	750	1,250	1,850	3,000	—
1877Do P	—	750	1,250	1,850	3,000	—
1878Do E	—	750	1,250	1,850	3,000	—
1879Do B	—	750	1,250	1,850	3,000	—
1879/7Do B	—	750	1,250	1,850	3,000	—

KM# 412.4   5 PESOS
8.46 g., 0.875 Gold, 0.24 oz. AGW **Obv.** Facing eagle, snake in beak **Rev:** Radiant cap above scales **Obv. Legend:** REPUBLICA MEXICANA **Mint:** Guanajuato

Date	Mintage	F12	VF20	XF40	MS60	MS63
1871 Go S	1,600	550	950	1,450	2,450	—
1887Go R	140	750	1,350	1,750	3,200	—
1888Go R Rare	65	—	—	—	—	—
1893Go R Rare	16	—	—	—	—	—

KM# 412.6   5 PESOS
8.46 g., 0.875 Gold, 0.24 oz. AGW **Obv.** Facing eagle, snake in beak **Rev:** Radiant cap above scales **Obv. Legend:** REPUBLICA MEXICANA **Mint:** Mexico City

Date	Mintage	F12	VF20	XF40	MS60	MS63
1870 Mo C	550	475	550	750	1,650	—
1871/69Mo M	1,600	475	525	600	850	—
1871Mo M	Inc. above	475	525	600	850	—
1872Mo M	1,600	475	525	600	850	—
1873/2Mo M	—	475	550	700	1,000	—
1874Mo M	—	475	550	700	1,000	—
1875/3Mo B/M	—	475	550	700	1,100	—
1875Mo B	—	475	550	700	1,100	—
1876/5Mo B/M	—	475	550	700	1,150	—
1877Mo M	—	475	600	900	1,800	—
1878/7Mo M	400	475	550	700	1,400	—
1878Mo M	Inc. above	475	550	700	1,400	—
1879/8Mo M	—	475	550	700	1,400	—
1880Mo M	—	475	550	700	1,400	—
1881Mo M	—	475	550	700	1,400	—
1882Mo M	200	475	600	900	1,800	—
1883Mo M	200	475	600	900	1,800	—
1884Mo M	—	475	600	900	1,800	—
1886Mo M	200	475	600	900	1,800	—
1887Mo M	200	475	600	900	1,800	—
1888Mo M	250	475	550	700	1,800	—
1889Mo M	190	475	600	900	1,800	—
1890Mo M	149	475	600	900	1,800	—
1891Mo M	156	475	600	900	1,800	—
1892Mo M	214	475	600	900	1,800	—
1893Mo M	1,058	450	550	650	950	—
1897Mo M	370	475	550	700	1,150	—
1898Mo M	376	475	550	700	1,150	—
1900Mo M	1,014	450	475	500	850	1,200
1901Mo M	1,071	450	475	500	850	1,300
1902Mo M	1,478	450	475	500	850	1,300
1903Mo M	1,162	450	475	500	850	1,300
1904Mo M	1,415	450	475	500	850	1,300
1905Mo M	563	450	500	600	1,550	2,050

KM# 412.7 5 PESOS
8.46 g., 0.875 Gold, 0.24 oz. AGW **Obv.** Facing eagle, snake in beak **Rev:** Radiant cap above scales **Obv. Legend:** REPUBLICA MEXICANA **Mint:** Zacatecas

Date	Mintage	F12	VF20	XF40	MS60	MS63
1874 Zs A	—	475	650	900	1,650	—
1875Zs A	—	450	550	650	1,150	—
1877Zs S/A	—	450	550	700	1,150	—
1878/7Zs S/A	—	450	550	700	1,150	—
1883Zs S	—	425	450	600	900	—
1888Zs Z	70	1,150	1,650	2,150	3,150	—
1889Zs Z	373	425	450	650	1,000	—
1892Zs Z	1,229	425	450	600	900	1,400

KM# 412.5 5 PESOS
8.46 g., 0.875 Gold, 0.24 oz. AGW **Obv.** Facing eagle, snake in beak **Rev:** Radiant cap above scales **Obv. Legend:** REPUBLICA MEXICANA **Mint:** Hermosillo

Date	Mintage	F12	VF20	XF40	MS60
1874Ho R	—	1,950	2,700	3,200	4,700
1877Ho R	990	800	1,150	1,800	2,800
1877Ho A	Inc. above	700	1,350	1,950	2,950
1888Ho G Rare	—	—	—	—	—

KM# 413   10 PESOS
16.92 g., 0.875 Gold, 0.47 oz. AGW **Obv.** Facing eagle, snake in beak **Rev:** Radiant cap above scales **Obv. Legend:** REPUBLICA MEXICANA **Mint:** Alamos

Date	Mintage	F12	VF20	XF40	MS60	MS63
1874 As DL Rare	—	—	—	—	—	—
1875As L	642	950	1,500	2,750	3,850	—
1878As L	977	900	1,250	2,250	3,350	—
1879As L	1,078	900	1,250	2,250	3,350	—
1880As L	2,629	900	1,250	2,250	3,350	—
1881As L	2,574	900	1,250	2,250	3,350	—
1882As L	3,403	900	1,250	2,250	3,350	—
1883As L	3,597	900	1,250	2,250	3,350	—
1884As L Rare	—	—	—	—	—	—
1885As L	4,562	900	1,250	2,250	3,350	—
1886As L	4,643	900	1,250	2,250	3,350	—
1887As L	3,667	900	1,250	2,250	3,350	—
1888As L	4,521	900	1,250	2,250	3,350	—
1889As L	5,615	900	1,250	2,250	3,350	—
1890As L	4,920	900	1,250	2,250	3,350	—
1891As L	568	900	1,250	2,250	3,350	—
1892As L	—	—	—	—	—	—
1893As L	817	900	1,250	2,250	3,350	—
1894/3As L	1,658	—	—	—	—	—
1894As L	Inc. above	900	1,250	2,250	3,350	—
1895As L	1,237	900	1,250	2,250	3,350	—

KM# 413.1   10 PESOS
16.92 g., 0.875 Gold, 0.47 oz. AGW **Obv.** Facing eagle, snake in beak **Rev:** Radiant cap above scales **Obv. Legend:** REPUBLICA MEXICANA **Mint:** Chihuahua

Date	Mintage	F12	VF20	XF40	MS60	MS63
1888 Ca M	175	—	—	7,500	—	—

KM# 413.2   10 PESOS
16.92 g., 0.875 Gold, 0.47 oz. AGW **Obv.** Facing eagle, snake in beak **Rev:** Radiant cap above scales **Obv. Legend:** REPUBLICA MEXICANA **Mint:** Culiacan

Date	Mintage	F12	VF20	XF40	MS60	MS63
1881 Cn D	—	875	900	1,300	2,050	—
1882Cn D	874	875	900	1,300	2,050	—
1882Cn E	Inc. above	875	900	1,300	2,050	—
1883Cn D	221	—	—	—	—	—
1883Cn M	Inc. above	875	900	1,300	2,050	—

Date	Mintage	F12	VF20	XF40	MS60	MS63
1884Cn D	—	875	900	1,300	2,050	—
1884Cn M	—	875	900	1,300	2,050	—
1885Cn M	1,235	875	900	1,300	2,050	—
1886Cn M	981	875	900	1,300	2,050	—
1887Cn M	2,289	875	900	1,300	2,050	—
1888Cn M	767	875	900	1,300	2,050	—
1889Cn M	859	875	900	1,300	2,050	—
1890Cn M	1,427	875	900	1,300	2,050	—
1891Cn M	670	875	900	1,300	2,050	—
1892Cn M	379	875	900	1,300	2,050	—
1893Cn M	1,806	875	900	1,300	2,050	—
1895Cn M	179	900	1,300	1,800	2,800	—
1903 Cn Q	774	875	950	1,100	2,100	—

KM# 413.3   10 PESOS
16.92 g., 0.875 Gold, 0.47 oz. AGW **Obv.** Facing eagle, snake in beak **Rev:** Radiant cap above scales **Obv. Legend:** REPUBLICA MEXICANA **Mint:** Durango

Date	Mintage	F12	VF20	XF40	MS60	MS63
1872 Do P	1,755	875	950	1,100	1,550	—
1873/2Do P	1,091	875	950	1,150	1,650	—
1873/2Do M/P	Inc. above	875	950	1,200	1,750	—
1874Do M	—	875	950	1,200	1,750	—
1875Do M	—	875	950	1,200	1,750	—
1876Do M	—	900	1,050	1,550	2,300	—
1877Do P	—	875	950	1,200	1,750	—
1878Do E	582	875	950	1,200	1,750	—
1879/8Do B	—	875	950	1,200	1,750	—
1879Do B	—	875	950	1,200	1,750	—
1880Do P	2,030	875	950	1,200	1,750	4,050
1881/79Do P	2,617	875	950	1,200	1,750	—
1882Do P Rare	1,528	—	—	—	—	—
1882Do C	Inc. above	875	950	1,200	1,750	—
1883Do C	793	900	1,050	1,550	2,300	—
1884Do C	108	900	1,050	1,550	2,300	—

KM# 413.4   10 PESOS
16.92 g., 0.875 Gold, 0.47 oz. AGW **Obv.** Facing eagle, snake in beak **Rev:** Radiant cap above scales **Obv. Legend:** REPUBLICA MEXICANA **Mint:** Guadalajara

Date	Mintage	F12	VF20	XF40	MS60
1870 Ga C	490	875	1,100	1,250	2,100
1871Ga C	1,910	875	1,100	1,500	2,600
1872Ga C	780	900	1,250	2,250	2,850
1873Ga C	422	900	1,250	2,250	3,350
1874/3Ga C	477	900	1,250	2,250	3,350
1875Ga C	710	900	1,250	2,250	3,350
1878Ga A	183	925	1,450	2,750	3,850
1879Ga A	200	925	1,450	2,750	3,850
1880Ga S	404	900	1,250	2,250	3,350
1881Ga S	239	925	1,450	2,750	3,850
1891Ga S	196	925	1,450	2,750	3,850

KM# 413.5   10 PESOS
16.92 g., 0.875 Gold, 0.47 oz. AGW **Obv.** Facing eagle, snake in beak **Rev:** Radiant cap above scales **Obv. Legend:** REPUBLICA MEXICANA **Mint:** Guanajuato

Date	Mintage	F12	VF20	XF40	MS60
1872 Go S	1,400	2,000	4,000	6,500	10,000
1887Go R Rare	80	—	—	—	—

Note: Stack's Rio Grande Sale 6-93, P/L AU realized, $12,650

| 1888Go R Rare | 68 | — | — | — | — |

KM# 413.6   10 PESOS
16.92 g., 0.875 Gold, 0.47 oz. AGW **Obv.** Facing eagle, snake in beak **Rev:** Radiant cap above scales **Obv. Legend:** REPUBLICA MEXICANA **Mint:** Hermosillo

Date	Mintage	F12	VF20	XF40	MS60
1874 Ho R Rare	—	—	—	—	—
1876Ho F Rare	357	—	—	—	—
1878Ho A	814	1,750	3,000	3,500	5,500
1879Ho A	—	1,000	2,000	2,500	4,000
1880Ho A	—	1,000	2,000	2,500	4,000
1881Ho A Rare	—	—	—	—	—

Note: American Numismatic Rarities Eliasberg sale 4-05, MS-62 realized $34,500.

KM# 413.7   10 PESOS
16.92 g., 0.875 Gold, 0.47 oz. AGW **Obv.** Facing eagle, snake in beak **Rev:** Radiant cap above scales **Obv. Legend:** REPUBLICA MEXICANA **Mint:** Mexico City

Date	Mintage	F12	VF20	XF40	MS60	MS63
1870 Mo C	480	875	1,200	1,500	2,300	—
1872/1Mo M/C	2,100	875	900	1,200	1,650	—
1873Mo M	—	875	900	1,250	1,750	—
1874/3Mo M	—	875	900	1,250	1,750	—
1875Mo B/M	—	875	900	1,250	1,750	—
1876Mo B Rare	—	—	—	—	—	—
1878Mo M	300	875	900	1,250	1,750	—
1879Mo M	—	—	—	—	—	—
1881Mo M	100	900	1,300	1,900	2,800	—
1882Mo M	—	875	900	1,250	1,750	—
1883Mo M	100	900	1,300	1,900	2,800	—
1884Mo M	—	900	1,300	1,900	2,800	—
1885Mo M	—	875	900	1,250	1,750	—
1886Mo M	100	900	1,300	1,900	2,800	—
1887Mo M	100	900	1,300	1,950	3,050	—

Date	Mintage	F12	VF20	XF40	MS60	MS63
1888Mo M	144	875	1,050	1,500	2,300	—
1889Mo M	88	900	1,300	1,900	2,800	—
1890Mo M	137	900	1,300	1,900	2,800	—
1891Mo M	133	900	1,300	1,900	2,800	—
1892Mo M	45	900	1,300	1,900	2,800	—
1893Mo M	1,361	875	900	1,200	1,650	—
1897Mo M	239	875	900	1,250	1,750	—
1898/7Mo M	244	875	925	1,300	2,050	—
1900Mo M	733	875	900	1,250	1,750	—
1901Mo M	562	875	900	950	1,600	—
1902Mo M	719	875	900	950	1,600	2,800
1903Mo M	713	875	900	950	1,600	2,800
1904Mo M	694	875	900	950	1,600	—
1905Mo M	401	875	900	1,100	1,800	—

KM# 413.8 10 PESOS

16.92 g., 0.875 Gold, 0.47 oz. AGW **Obv.** Facing eagle, snake in beak **Rev:** Radiant cap above scales **Obv. Legend:** REPUBLICA MEXICANA **Mint:** Oaxaca

Date	Mintage	F12	VF20	XF40	MS60	MS63
1870 Oa E	4,614	850	900	1,200	1,900	—
1871Oa E	2,705	850	900	1,250	1,950	—
1872Oa E	5,897	850	900	1,150	1,800	—
1873Oa E	3,537	850	900	1,150	1,800	—
1874Oa E	2,205	875	950	1,500	2,150	—
1875Oa E	312	875	1,050	1,700	2,550	—
1876Oa E	766	875	1,050	1,700	2,550	—
1877Oa E	463	875	1,050	1,700	2,550	—
1878Oa E	229	875	1,050	1,700	2,550	—
1879Oa E	210	875	1,050	1,700	2,550	—
1880Oa E	238	875	1,050	1,700	2,550	—
1881Oa E	961	875	950	1,500	2,300	—
1882Oa E	170	900	1,300	1,800	2,800	—
1883Oa E	111	900	1,300	1,800	2,800	—
1884Oa E	325	875	1,050	1,700	2,550	—
1885Oa E	370	875	1,050	1,700	2,550	—
1886Oa E	400	875	1,050	1,700	2,550	—
1887Oa E	—	1,000	1,550	2,550	4,300	—
1888Oa E	—	—	—	—	—	—

KM# 413.9 10 PESOS

16.92 g., 0.875 Gold, 0.47 oz. AGW **Obv.** Facing eagle, snake in beak **Rev:** Radiant cap above scales **Obv. Legend:** REPUBLICA MEXICANA **Mint:** Zacatecas

Date	Mintage	F12	VF20	XF40	MS60	MS63
1871 Zs H	2,000	850	900	1,100	1,550	—
1872Zs H	3,092	850	900	1,050	1,450	—
1873Zs H	936	875	925	1,250	1,750	—
1874Zs H	—	875	925	1,250	1,750	—
1875/3Zs A	—	875	950	1,300	2,050	—
1876/5Zs S	—	875	950	1,300	2,050	—
1877Zs S/H	506	875	950	1,300	2,050	—
1878Zs S	711	875	950	1,300	2,050	—
1879/8Zs S	—	900	1,050	1,700	2,550	—
1879Zs S	—	900	1,050	1,700	2,550	—

Date	Mintage	F12	VF20	XF40	MS60	MS63
1880Zs S	2,089	875	925	1,250	1,750	—
1881Zs S	736	875	950	1,300	2,050	—
1882/1Zs Z	—	875	950	1,300	2,050	2,800
1882Zs S	1,599	875	925	1,250	1,750	—
1883/2Zs S	256	875	950	1,300	2,050	—
1884/3Zs S	—	875	925	1,250	1,900	—
1884Zs S	—	875	925	1,250	1,900	—
1885Zs S	1,588	875	925	1,250	1,750	—
1886Zs S	5,364	875	925	1,250	1,750	—
1887Zs Z	2,330	875	925	1,250	1,750	—
1888Zs Z	4,810	875	925	1,250	1,750	—
1889Zs Z	6,154	850	875	1,050	1,550	—
1890Zs Z	1,321	850	925	1,250	1,750	—
1891Zs Z	1,930	850	925	1,250	1,750	3,550
1892Zs Z	1,882	850	925	1,250	1,750	—
1893Zs Z	2,899	850	925	1,250	1,750	—
1894Zs Z	2,501	850	925	1,250	1,750	—
1895Zs Z	1,217	850	925	1,250	1,750	—

KM# 414 20 PESOS

33.84 g., 0.875 Gold, 0.95 oz. AGW **Obv.** Facing eagle, snake in beak **Rev:** Radiant cap above scales **Mint:** Alamos

Date	Mintage	F12	VF20	XF40	MS60
1876 As L Rare	276	—	—	—	—
1877As L Rare	166	—	—	—	—
1878As L	—	—	—	—	—
1888As L Rare	—	—	—	—	—

KM# 414.1 20 PESOS

33.84 g., 0.875 Gold, 0.95 oz. AGW **Obv.** Facing eagle, snake in beak **Rev:** Radiant cap above scales **Mint:** Chihuahua **Note:** Mint mark CH, Ca.

Date	Mintage	F12	VF20	XF40	MS60
1872 CH M	995	BV	1,750	1,850	3,500
1873CH M	950	BV	1,750	1,850	3,500
1874CH M	1,116	BV	1,750	1,850	3,500
1875CH M	750	BV	1,750	1,850	3,500
1876CH M	600	BV	1,800	2,000	3,750
1877CH Rare	55	—	—	—	—
1882CH M	1,758	BV	1,750	1,850	3,500
1883CH M	161	1,750	1,850	2,500	4,000
1884CH M	496	BV	1,750	1,850	3,500
1885CH M	122	1,750	1,850	2,500	4,000
1887Ca M	550	BV	1,750	1,850	3,500
1888Ca M	351	BV	1,750	1,850	3,500
1889Ca M	464	BV	1,750	1,850	3,500
1890Ca M	1,209	BV	1,750	1,850	3,500
1891Ca M	2,004	BV	1,750	1,800	3,250
1893Ca M	418	BV	1,750	1,850	3,500
1895Ca M	133	1,750	1,850	2,500	4,000

KM# 414.2 20 PESOS

33.84 g., 0.875 Gold, 0.95 oz. AGW **Obv.** Facing eagle, snake in beak **Rev:** Radiant cap above scales **Obv. Legend:** REPUBLICA MEXICANA **Mint:** Culiacan

Date	Mintage	F12	VF20	XF40	MS60	MS63
1870 Cn E	3,749	BV	1,750	1,850	2,950	—
1871Cn P	3,046	BV	1,750	1,850	2,950	—
1872Cn P	972	BV	1,750	1,850	2,950	—
1873Cn P	1,317	BV	1,750	1,850	2,950	—
1874Cn P	—	BV	1,750	1,850	2,950	—
1875Cn P	—	1,750	2,000	2,750	3,500	—
1876Cn P	—	BV	1,750	1,850	2,950	—

Date	Mintage	F12	VF20	XF40	MS60	MS63
1876Cn G	—	BV	1,750	1,850	2,950	—
1877Cn G	167	1,750	1,850	2,200	3,200	—
1878Cn Rare	842	—	—	—	—	—
1881/0Cn D	2,039	—	—	—	—	—
1881Cn D	Inc. above	BV	1,750	1,850	2,950	—
1882/1Cn D	736	BV	1,750	1,850	2,950	—
1883Cn M	1,836	BV	1,750	1,850	2,950	—
1884Cn M	—	BV	1,750	1,850	2,950	—
1885Cn M	544	BV	1,750	1,850	2,950	—
1886Cn M	882	BV	1,750	1,850	2,950	—
1887Cn M	837	BV	1,750	1,850	2,950	—
1888Cn M	473	BV	1,750	1,850	2,950	—
1889Cn M	1,376	BV	1,750	1,850	2,950	—
1890Cn M	—	1,750	2,450	4,600	11,500	—
1891Cn M	237	BV	1,800	2,000	3,200	—
1892Cn M	526	BV	1,750	1,850	2,950	—
1893Cn M	2,062	BV	1,750	1,850	2,950	—
1894Cn M	4,516	BV	1,750	1,850	2,950	—
1895Cn M	3,193	BV	1,750	1,850	2,950	—
1896Cn M	4,072	BV	1,750	1,850	2,950	—
1897/6Cn M	959	BV	1,750	1,850	2,950	—
1897Cn M	Inc. above	BV	1,750	1,850	2,950	—
1898Cn M	1,660	BV	1,750	1,850	2,950	—
1899Cn M	1,243	BV	1,750	1,850	2,950	—
1899Cn Q	Inc. above	BV	1,800	2,000	3,200	—
1900Cn Q	1,558	BV	1,750	1,850	2,950	—
1901Cn Q	1,496	BV	1,750	1,850	2,950	—
1901/0Cn Q	Inc. above	—	—	—	—	—
1902Cn Q	1,059	BV	1,750	1,850	2,950	—
1903Cn Q	1,121	BV	1,750	1,850	2,950	—
1904Cn H	4,646	BV	1,750	1,700	2,950	—
1905Cn P	1,738	BV	1,750	1,850	3,150	—

KM# 414.3 20 PESOS
33.84 g., 0.875 Gold, 0.95 oz. AGW **Obv.** Facing eagle, snake in beak **Rev:** Radiant cap above scales **Obv. Legend:** REPUBLICA MEXICANA **Mint:** Durango

Date	Mintage	F12	VF20	XF40	MS60	MS63
1870 Do P	416	1,800	2,100	2,950	3,600	—
1871Do P	Inc. above	1,800	2,100	2,950	3,600	—
1871/0Do P	1,073	1,800	2,400	3,250	3,900	—
1872/1Do PT	—	2,000	3,750	6,100	9,300	—
1876Do M	—	1,800	2,100	2,950	3,600	—
1877Do P	94	2,000	2,950	3,900	4,500	—
1878Do Rare	258	—	—	—	—	—

KM# 414.4 20 PESOS
33.84 g., 0.875 Gold, 0.95 oz. AGW **Obv.** Facing eagle, snake in beak **Rev:** Radiant cap above scales **Obv. Legend:**

REPUBLICA MEXICANA **Mint:** Guanajuato

Date	Mintage	F12	VF20	XF40	MS60	MS63
1870 Go S	3,250	BV	1,700	1,750	2,300	—
1871Go S	20,000	BV	1,700	1,750	2,300	2,950
1872Go S	18,000	BV	1,700	1,750	2,300	—
1873Go S	7,000	BV	1,700	1,750	2,300	—
1874Go S	—	BV	1,700	1,750	2,300	—
1875Go S	—	BV	1,700	1,750	2,300	—
1876Go S	—	BV	1,700	1,750	2,300	—
1876Go M/S	—	—	—	—	—	—
1877Go M/S Rare	15,000	—	—	—	—	—
1877Go R	Inc. above	BV	1,700	1,750	2,300	—
1877Go S Rare	Inc. above	—	—	—	—	—
1878/7Go M/S	13,000	1,500	2,150	2,900	3,900	—
1878Go M	Inc. above	1,500	2,150	2,900	3,900	—
1878Go S	Inc. above	BV	1,700	1,750	2,300	—
1879Go S	8,202	BV	1,700	1,750	3,300	—
1880Go S	7,375	BV	1,700	1,750	2,300	—
1881Go S	4,909	BV	1,700	1,750	2,300	—
1882Go S	4,020	BV	1,700	1,750	2,300	—
1883/2Go B	3,705	BV	1,700	1,950	3,200	—
1883Go B	Inc. above	BV	1,700	1,750	2,300	—
1884Go B	1,798	BV	1,700	1,750	2,300	—
1885Go R	2,660	BV	1,700	1,750	2,300	—
1886Go R	1,090	1,500	1,750	1,950	3,550	—
1887Go R	1,009	1,500	1,750	1,950	3,550	—
1888Go R	1,011	1,500	1,750	1,950	3,550	—
1889Go R	956	1,500	1,750	1,950	3,550	—
1890Go R	879	1,500	1,750	1,950	3,550	—
1891Go R	818	1,500	1,750	1,950	3,550	—
1892Go R	730	1,500	1,750	1,950	3,550	—
1893Go R	3,343	BV	1,700	1,850	2,700	—
1894/3Go R	6,734	BV	1,700	1,750	2,300	—
1894Go R	Inc. above	BV	1,700	1,750	2,300	—
1895/3Go R	7,118	BV	1,700	1,750	2,300	—
1895Go R	Inc. above	BV	1,700	1,750	2,300	—
1896Go R	9,219	BV	1,700	1,750	2,300	7,200
1897/6Go R	6,781	BV	1,700	1,750	2,300	—
1897Go R	Inc. above	BV	1,700	1,750	2,300	—
1898Go R	7,710	BV	1,700	1,750	2,300	—
1899Go R	8,527	BV	1,700	1,750	2,300	—
1900Go R	4,512	BV	1,750	1,950	3,350	—

KM# 414.5 20 PESOS
33.84 g., 0.875 Gold, 0.95 oz. AGW **Obv.** Facing eagle, snake in beak **Rev:** Radiant cap above scales **Obv. Legend:** REPUBLICA MEXICANA **Mint:** Hermosillo

Date	Mintage	F12	VF20	XF40	MS60
1874 Ho R Rare	—	—	—	—	—
Note: Stack's Bowers & Ponterio Sale 161, 8-11, AU55 realized $6,500.					
1875Ho R Rare	—	—	—	—	—
1876Ho F Rare	—	—	—	—	—
1888Ho g Rare	—	—	—	—	—

KM# 414.7 20 PESOS
33.84 g., 0.875 Gold, 0.95 oz. AGW **Obv.** Facing eagle, snake in beak **Rev:** Radiant cap above scales **Obv. Legend:** REPUBLICA MEXICANA **Mint:** Oaxaca

Date	Mintage	F12	VF20	XF40	MS60
1870 Oa E	1,131	1,800	2,500	3,600	6,800
1871Oa E	1,591	1,800	2,500	3,600	6,800
1872Oa E	255	1,800	2,200	4,200	9,300
1888Oa E	170	2,450	3,950	6,800	—

KM# 414.6 20 PESOS
33.84 g., 0.875 Gold, 0.95 oz. AGW **Obv.** Facing eagle, snake in beak **Rev:** Radiant cap above scales **Obv. Legend:** REPUBLICA MEXICANA **Mint:** Mexico City

Date	Mintage	F12	VF20	XF40	MS60	MS63
1870 Mo C	14,000	BV	1,750	1,850	2,450	—
1871Mo M	21,000	BV	1,750	1,850	2,450	—
1872/1Mo M	11,000	BV	1,750	1,850	2,550	—
1872Mo M	Inc. above	BV	1,750	1,850	2,450	—
1873Mo M	5,600	BV	1,750	1,850	2,450	—
1874/2Mo M	—	BV	1,750	1,850	2,450	—
1874/2Mo B	—	BV	1,750	1,950	2,550	—
1875Mo B	—	BV	1,750	1,950	2,500	—
1876Mo B	—	BV	1,750	1,950	2,500	—
1876Mo M						
Note: Requires Confirmation						
1877Mo M	2,000	BV	1,800	2,200	3,000	—
1878Mo M	7,000	BV	1,750	1,850	2,500	—
1879Mo M	—	BV	1,750	1,850	2,700	—
1880Mo M	—	BV	1,750	1,850	2,700	—
1881/0Mo M	11,000	BV	1,750	1,850	2,450	—
1881Mo M	Inc. above	BV	1,750	1,850	2,450	—
1882/1Mo M	5,800	BV	1,750	1,850	2,450	—
1882Mo M	Inc. above	BV	1,750	1,850	2,450	—
1883/1Mo M	4,000	BV	1,750	1,850	2,450	—
1883Mo M	Inc. above	BV	1,750	1,850	2,450	—
1884/3Mo M	—	BV	1,750	1,850	2,500	—
1884Mo M	—	BV	1,750	1,850	2,500	—
1885Mo M	6,000	BV	1,750	1,850	2,700	—
1886Mo M	10,000	BV	1,750	1,850	2,450	—
1887Mo M	12,000	BV	1,800	2,600	3,500	—
1888Mo M	7,300	BV	1,750	1,850	2,450	—
1889Mo M	6,477	BV	1,800	2,750	5,000	—
1890Mo M	7,852	BV	1,750	1,850	2,500	—
1891/0Mo M	8,725	BV	1,750	1,850	2,500	—
1891Mo M	Inc. above	BV	1,750	1,850	2,500	—
1892Mo M	11,000	BV	1,750	1,850	2,450	—
1893Mo M	15,000	BV	1,750	1,850	2,450	—
1894Mo M	14,000	BV	1,750	1,850	2,450	—
1895Mo M	13,000	BV	1,750	1,850	2,450	—
1896Mo B	14,000	BV	1,750	1,850	2,450	—
1897/6Mo M	12,000	BV	1,750	1,850	2,450	—
1897Mo M	Inc. above	BV	1,750	1,850	2,450	—
1898Mo M	20,000	BV	1,750	1,850	2,450	—
1899Mo M	23,000	BV	1,750	1,850	2,450	—
1900Mo M	21,000	BV	1,750	1,850	2,450	—
1901Mo M	29,000	BV	1,750	1,850	2,450	—
1902Mo M	38,000	BV	1,750	1,850	2,450	—
1903/2Mo M	31,000	BV	1,750	1,850	2,450	—
1903Mo M	Inc. above	BV	1,750	1,850	2,450	—
1904Mo M	52,000	BV	1,750	1,850	2,450	—
1905Mo M	9,757	BV	1,750	1,850	2,450	—

KM# 414.8 20 PESOS
33.84 g., 0.875 Gold, 0.95 oz. AGW **Obv.** Facing eagle, snake in beak **Rev:** Radiant cap above scales **Mint:** Zacatecas

Date	Mintage	F12	VF20	XF40	MS60
1871 Zs H	1,000	3,850	6,900	9,200	12,000
1875Zs A	—	4,350	6,400	9,800	12,500
1878Zs S	441	4,350	6,400	9,800	12,500
1888Zs Z Rare	50	—	—	—	—
1889Zs Z	640	3,900	5,900	9,200	12,000

ESTADOS UNIDOS

DECIMAL COINAGE
100 CENTAVOS = 1 PESO

KM# 415 CENTAVO
3.00 g., Bronze 20mm. **Obv.** National arms **Rev:** Value below date within wreath **Mint:** Mexico City **Note:** Mint mark Mo.

Date	Mintage	F12	VF20	XF40	MS60	MS63
1905 Narrow date	6,040,000	4.00	6.50	14.00	90.00	—
1905 Wide date	—	4.00	6.50	14.00	90.00	—
1906 Narrow date	Est. 67505000	0.50	0.75	1.25	14.00	25.00
Note: 50,000,000 pcs. were struck at the Birmingham Mint						
1906 Wide date	Inc. above	0.75	1.50	2.50	22.00	—
1910 Narrow date	8,700,000	2.00	3.00	6.50	85.00	100
1910 Wide date	—	2.00	3.00	6.50	85.00	100
1911 Narrow date	16,450,000	0.60	1.00	2.75	22.50	—
1911 Wide date	Inc. above	0.75	1.00	4.00	35.00	—
1912	12,650,000	1.00	1.35	3.25	35.00	—
1913	12,850,000	0.75	1.25	3.00	35.00	—
1914 Narrow date	17,350,000	0.75	1.00	3.00	15.00	20.00
1914 Wide date	Inc. above	0.75	1.00	3.00	15.00	20.00

Date	Mintage	F12	VF20	XF40	MS60	MS63
1915	2,277,000	11.00	25.00	67.50	250	—
1916	500,000	45.00	80.00	170	1,200	—
1920	1,433,000	22.00	50.00	115	400	—
1921	3,470,000	5.50	15.50	47.00	275	—
1922	1,880,000	9.00	17.00	50.00	250	—
1923	4,800,000	0.75	1.25	1.75	13.50	—
1924/3	2,000,000	65.00	170	275	525	—
1924	Inc. above	4.50	11.00	22.00	250	300
1925	1,550,000	4.50	10.00	25.00	220	—
1926	5,000,000	1.00	2.00	4.00	20.00	28.00
1927/6	6,000,000	30.00	45.00	70.00	175	—
1927	Inc. above	0.75	1.25	4.50	32.00	45.00
1928	5,000,000	0.75	1.00	3.25	16.50	25.00
1929	4,500,000	0.75	1.00	1.75	17.00	25.00
1930	7,000,000	0.75	1.00	2.50	20.00	—
1933	10,000,000	0.25	0.35	1.75	16.50	22.00
1934	7,500,000	0.25	0.95	3.25	40.00	—
1935	12,400,000	0.15	0.25	0.40	11.50	15.00
1936	20,100,000	0.15	0.20	0.30	9.00	—
1937	20,000,000	0.15	0.25	0.35	4.00	6.00
1938	10,000,000	0.10	0.15	0.30	2.00	3.00
1939	30,000,000	0.10	0.20	0.30	1.00	2.50
1940	10,000,000	0.20	0.30	0.60	5.50	8.50
1941	15,800,000	0.15	0.25	0.35	2.00	3.00
1942	30,400,000	0.15	0.20	0.30	1.25	2.00
1943	4,310,000	0.30	0.50	0.75	9.00	12.50
1944	5,645,000	0.15	0.25	0.50	6.00	8.50
1945	26,375,000	0.10	0.15	0.25	1.00	1.75
1946	42,135,000	—	0.15	0.20	0.60	1.50
1947	13,445,000	—	0.10	0.15	0.80	1.50
1948	20,040,000	0.10	0.15	0.30	1.10	2.25
1949	6,235,000	0.10	0.15	0.30	1.25	3.00

Note: Varieties exist

KM# 416 CENTAVO

1.50 g., Bronze 16mm. **Obv.** National arms **Rev:** Value below date within wreath **Mint:** Mexico City **Note:** Zapata issue. Struck at Mexico City Mint, mint mark Mo. Reduced size. Weight varies 1.39-1.5g.

Date	Mintage	F12	VF20	XF40	MS60	MS63
1915	179,000	18.00	30.00	60.00	85.00	—

KM# 417 CENTAVO

2.00 g., Brass 16mm. **Obv.** National arms, eagle left **Rev:** Oat sprigs **Mint:** Mexico City **Note:** Mint mark Mo.

Date	Mintage	F12	VF20	XF40	MS60	MS63
1950	12,815,000	—	0.15	0.35	1.65	2.25
1951	25,740,000	—	0.15	0.35	0.65	1.25
1952	24,610,000	—	0.10	0.25	0.40	0.85
1953	21,160,000	—	0.10	0.25	0.40	0.85
1954	25,675,000	—	0.10	0.15	0.85	1.50
1955	9,820,000	—	0.15	0.25	0.85	1.75
1956	11,285,000	—	0.15	0.25	0.80	1.75
1957	9,805,000	—	0.15	0.25	0.85	1.50
1958	12,155,000	—	0.10	0.25	0.45	0.75
1959	11,875,000	—	0.10	0.25	0.75	1.50
1960	10,360,000	—	0.10	0.15	0.40	0.65
1961	6,385,000	—	0.10	0.15	0.45	0.85
1962	4,850,000	—	0.10	0.15	0.55	0.90
1963	7,775,000	—	0.10	0.15	0.25	0.45
1964	4,280,000	—	0.10	0.15	0.20	0.30
1965	2,255,000	—	0.10	0.15	0.25	0.40
1966	1,760,000	—	0.10	0.25	0.60	1.00
1967	1,290,000	—	0.10	0.15	0.40	0.75
1968	1,000,000	—	0.10	0.20	0.85	1.45
1969	1,000,000	—	0.10	0.15	0.65	0.85

KM# 418 CENTAVO

1.50 g., Brass 13mm. **Obv.** National arms, eagle left **Rev:** Oat sprigs **Mint:** Mexico City **Note:** Reduced size.

Date	Mintage	F12	VF20	XF40	MS60	MS63
1970Mo	1,000,000	—	0.20	0.40	1.45	2.25
1972Mo	1,000,000	—	0.20	0.45	2.50	4.00
1972/2Mo	—	—	0.50	1.25	3.50	5.00
1973Mo	1,000,000	—	1.65	2.75	9.00	17.50

KM# 419 2 CENTAVOS

6.00 g., Bronze 25mm. **Obv.** National arms **Rev:** Value below date within wreath **Mint:** Mexico City **Note:** Mint mark Mo.

Date	Mintage	F12	VF20	XF40	MS60	MS63
1905	50,000	150	300	500	1,200	1,350
1906 Inverted 6	9,998,000	30.00	55.00	120	375	—
1906 Wide date	Inc. above	5.00	11.00	28.00	95.00	110
1906 Narrow date	Inc. above	6.50	14.00	30.00	95.00	—

Note: 5,000,000 pieces were struck at the Birmingham Mint

1920	1,325,000	6.50	17.50	75.00	350	—
1921	4,275,000	2.50	4.75	15.00	100	—
1922	—	225	550	1,750	5,500	—
1924	750,000	8.50	27.50	75.00	450	—
1925	3,650,000	2.50	3.50	7.50	35.00	40.00
1926	4,750,000	1.00	2.25	5.50	40.00	—
1927	7,250,000	0.60	1.00	4.50	22.00	35.00
1928	3,250,000	0.75	1.50	4.75	25.00	35.00
1929	250,000	85.00	225	550	1,200	—
1935	1,250,000	4.25	9.25	65.00	225	275
1939	5,000,000	0.60	0.90	2.25	20.00	30.00
1941	3,550,000	0.45	0.60	1.25	18.00	28.00

KM# 420 2 CENTAVOS

3.00 g., Bronze 20mm. **Obv.** National arms **Rev:** Value below date within wreath **Mint:** Mexico City **Note:** Zapata issue. Mint mark Mo. Reduced size. Weight varies 3-3.03g.

Date	Mintage	F12	VF20	XF40	MS60	MS63
1915	487,000	7.50	9.00	17.50	75.00	—

KM# 421 5 CENTAVOS

5.00 g., Nickel 20mm. **Obv.** National arms **Rev:** Value and date within beaded circle **Mint:** Mexico City **Note:** Mint mark Mo. Varieties exist.

Date	Mintage	F12	VF20	XF40	MS60	MS63
1905	1,420,000	7.00	10.00	28.00	325	375
1906/5	10,615,000	13.00	30.00	70.00	375	—
1906	Inc. above	0.75	1.35	3.25	55.00	75.00
1907	4,000,000	1.25	4.00	35.00	350	450
1909	2,052,000	3.25	10.00	50.00	360	—
1910	6,181,000	1.30	3.50	9.00	85.00	125
1911 Narrow date	4,487,000	1.00	3.00	7.00	95.00	135
1911 Wide date	Inc. above	2.50	5.00	9.00	110	170
1912 Small mint mark	420,000	90.00	100	230	725	—
1912 Large mint mark	Inc. above	70.00	95.00	200	575	—
1913	2,035,000	1.75	4.25	30.00	200	300

Note: Wide and narrow dates exist for 1913

| 1914 | 2,000,000 | 1.00 | 2.00 | 5.00 | 75.00 | 110 |

Note: 5,000,000 pieces appear to have been struck at the Birmingham Mint in 1914 and all of 1909-1911. The Mexican Mint report does not mention receiving the 1914 dated coins

KM# 422 5 CENTAVOS

9.00 g., Bronze 28mm. **Obv.** National arms **Rev:** Value below date within wreath **Mint:** Mexico City

Date	Mintage	F12	VF20	XF40	MS60	MS63
1914Mo	2,500,000	10.00	23.00	65.00	300	—
1915Mo	11,424,000	3.00	5.00	35.00	165	265
1916Mo	2,860,000	15.00	35.00	175	650	—
1917Mo	800,000	75.00	225	400	900	—
1918Mo	1,332,000	35.00	90.00	250	675	—
1919Mo	400,000	115	225	360	950	—
1920Mo	5,920,000	3.00	8.00	45.00	265	350
1921Mo	2,080,000	10.00	24.00	75.00	275	—
1924Mo	780,000	40.00	95.00	275	700	—
1925Mo	4,040,000	5.50	11.00	47.50	225	—
1926Mo	3,160,000	5.50	11.00	48.00	325	—
1927Mo	3,600,000	4.00	7.00	35.00	250	350
1928Mo Large date	1,740,000	11.00	18.00	65.00	250	325
1928Mo Small date	Inc. above	30.00	45.00	100	385	—
1929Mo	2,400,000	5.50	12.00	50.00	200	—
1930Mo	2,600,000	5.00	8.00	27.50	225	—

Note: Large oval O in date

| 1930Mo | Inc. above | 65.00 | 125 | 250 | 565 | — |

Note: Small square O in date

1931Mo	—	475	750	1,450	4,000	—
1933Mo	8,000,000	1.50	2.25	3.50	27.50	45.00
1934Mo	10,000,000	1.25	1.75	2.75	25.00	50.00
1935Mo	21,980,000	0.75	1.20	2.50	22.50	40.00

KM# 423 5 CENTAVOS

4.00 g., Copper-Nickel 20.5mm. **Obv.** National arms, eagle left **Rev:** Value and date within circle **Mint:** Mexico City

Date	Mintage	F12	VF20	XF40	MS60	MS63
1936M	46,700,000	—	0.65	1.25	7.50	8.50
1937M	49,060,000	—	0.50	1.00	7.00	8.00
1938M	3,340,000	—	4.00	10.00	80.00	200
1940M	22,800,000	—	0.75	1.25	8.00	10.00
1942M	7,100,000	—	1.50	3.00	35.00	50.00

KM# 424 5 CENTAVOS

6.50 g., Bronze 25.5mm. **Obv.** National arms, eagle left **Rev:** Head left **Mint:** Mexico City

Date	Mintage	F12	VF20	XF40	MS60	MS63
1942Mo	900,000	—	25.00	75.00	375	550
1943Mo	54,660,000	—	0.50	0.75	2.50	3.50
1944Mo	53,463,000	—	0.25	0.35	0.75	1.25
1945Mo	44,262,000	—	0.25	0.35	0.75	1.25
1946Mo	49,054,000	—	0.50	1.00	2.00	3.00
1951Mo	50,758,000	—	0.75	0.90	3.00	5.00
1952Mo	17,674,000	—	1.50	2.50	9.50	11.50
1953Mo	31,568,000	—	1.25	2.00	6.00	9.00
1954Mo	58,680,000	—	0.40	1.00	2.75	4.00
1955Mo	31,114,000	—	2.00	3.00	11.00	14.00

KM# 425 5 CENTAVOS

4.00 g., Copper-Nickel 20.5mm. **Obv.** National arms, eagle left **Rev:** Bust right flanked by date and value **Mint:** Mexico City

Date	Mintage	F12	VF20	XF40	MS60	MS63
1950Mo	5,700,000	—	0.75	1.50	6.00	7.00

Note: 5,600,000 pieces struck at Connecticut melted

KM# 426 5 CENTAVOS

4.00 g., Brass 20.4mm. **Obv.** National arms, eagle left **Rev:** Bust right **Mint:** Mexico City

Date	Mintage	F12	VF20	XF40	MS60	MS63
1954Mo Dot	—	—	10.00	50.00	300	375
1954Mo Without dot	—	—	15.00	35.00	275	325
1955Mo	12,136,000	—	0.75	1.50	9.00	12.50
1956Mo	60,216,000	—	0.20	0.30	0.75	1.25
1957Mo	55,288,000	—	0.15	0.20	0.90	1.50

Date	Mintage	F12	VF20	XF40	MS60	MS63
1958Mo	104,624,000	—	0.15	0.20	0.60	1.00
1959Mo	106,000,000	—	0.15	0.25	0.75	1.25
1960Mo	99,144,000	—	0.10	0.15	0.50	0.75
1961Mo	61,136,000	—	0.10	0.15	0.50	0.75
1962Mo	47,232,000	—	0.10	0.15	0.25	0.35
1963Mo	156,680,000	—	—	0.15	0.25	0.40
1964Mo	71,168,000	—	—	0.15	0.20	0.40
1965Mo	155,720,000	—	—	0.15	0.25	0.35
1966Mo	124,944,000	—	—	0.15	0.40	0.65
1967Mo	118,816,000	—	—	0.15	0.25	0.40
1968Mo	189,588,000	—	—	0.15	0.50	0.75
1969Mo	210,492,000	—	—	0.15	0.55	0.80

KM# 426a 5 CENTAVOS
Copper-Nickel 20.5mm. **Obv.** National arms, eagle left **Rev:** Bust right **Mint:** Mexico City

Date	Mintage	F12	VF20	XF40	MS60	MS63
1960Mo	—	—	250	300	375	—
1962Mo	19	—	250	300	375	—
1965Mo	—	—	250	300	375	—

KM# 427 5 CENTAVOS
2.75 g., Brass 18mm. **Obv.** National arms, eagle left **Rev:** Bust right **Note:** Due to some minor alloy variations this type is often encountered with a bronze-color toning. Reduced size.

Date	Mintage	F12	VF20	XF40	MS60	MS63
1970Mo	163,368,000	—	0.10	0.15	0.35	0.45
1971Mo	198,844,000	—	0.10	0.15	0.25	0.30
1972Mo	225,000,000	—	0.10	0.15	0.25	0.30
1973Mo Flat top 3	595,070,000	—	0.10	0.15	0.25	0.40
1973Mo Round top 3	Inc. above	—	0.10	0.15	0.20	0.30
1974Mo	401,584,000	—	0.10	0.15	0.30	0.40
1975Mo	342,308,000	—	0.10	0.15	0.25	0.35
1976Mo	367,524,000	—	0.10	0.15	0.40	0.60

KM# 428 10 CENTAVOS
2.50 g., 0.800 Silver, 0.06 oz. ASW 18mm. **Obv.** National arms **Rev:** Value and date within 3/4 wreath with Liberty cap above **Mint:** Mexico City **Note:** Mint mark Mo.

Date	Mintage	F12	VF20	XF40	MS60	MS63
1905	3,920,000	2.50	6.00	8.00	40.00	50.00
1906	8,410,000	2.50	5.50	7.50	27.00	40.00
1907/6	5,950,000	15.00	50.00	135	325	375
1907	Inc. above	2.50	5.50	6.25	35.00	50.00
1909	2,620,000	2.75	8.50	13.00	80.00	110
1910/00	3,450,000	3.00	10.00	40.00	75.00	85.00
1910	Inc. above	2.50	7.00	15.00	25.00	40.00
1911 Narrow date	2,550,000	3.00	11.00	17.00	88.00	125
1911 Wide date	Inc. above	2.50	7.50	10.00	45.00	65.00
1912	1,350,000	3.00	10.00	18.00	130	175
1912 Low 2	Inc. above	3.00	10.00	18.00	115	155
1913/2	1,990,000	3.00	10.00	25.00	40.00	70.00
1913	Inc. above	2.50	7.00	10.00	33.00	45.00
1914	3,110,000	2.50	5.50	7.00	15.00	25.00

Note: Wide and narrow dates exist for 1914

KM# 429 10 CENTAVOS
1.81 g., 0.800 Silver, 0.05 oz. ASW 15mm. **Obv.** National arms **Rev:** Value and date within 3/4 wreath with Liberty cap above **Mint:** Mexico City **Note:** Mint mark Mo. Reduced size.

Date	Mintage	F12	VF20	XF40	MS60	MS63
1919	8,360,000	3.00	10.00	15.00	95.00	125

KM# 430 10 CENTAVOS
12.00 g., Bronze 30.5mm. **Obv.** National arms **Rev:** Value below date within wreath **Mint:** Mexico City **Note:** Mint mark Mo.

Date	Mintage	F12	VF20	XF40	MS60	MS63
1919	1,232,000	7.00	25.00	85.00	475	550
1920	6,612,000	5.00	15.00	50.00	400	475
1921	2,255,000	10.00	35.00	95.00	650	800
1935	5,970,000	4.50	14.00	35.00	125	200

KM# 431 10 CENTAVOS
1.66 g., 0.720 Silver, 0.04 oz. ASW 15mm. **Obv.** National arms **Rev:** Value and date within wreath with Liberty cap above **Mint:** Mexico City **Note:** Mint mark Mo.

Date	Mintage	F12	VF20	XF40	MS60	MS63
1925/15	5,350,000	10.00	30.00	75.00	125	175
1925/3	Inc. above	8.00	20.00	40.00	125	175
1925	Inc. above	BV	2.00	5.00	40.00	50.00
1926/16	2,650,000	10.00	30.00	75.00	125	175
1926	Inc. above	1.80	3.50	7.50	65.00	95.00
1927	2,810,000	BV	2.25	3.00	17.50	25.00
1928	5,270,000	BV	2.00	2.75	13.50	20.00
1930	2,000,000	1.75	3.75	5.00	18.75	28.00
1933	5,000,000	BV	1.50	3.00	10.00	17.00
1934	8,000,000	BV	1.75	2.50	8.00	16.00
1935	3,500,000	1.50	2.75	5.00	11.00	18.00

KM# 432 10 CENTAVOS
5.50 g., Copper-Nickel 23.5mm. **Obv.** National arms, eagle left **Rev:** Value and date within circle **Mint:** Mexico City **Note:** Mint mark Mo.

Date	Mintage	F12	VF20	XF40	MS60	MS63
1936	33,030,000	—	0.75	2.50	10.00	12.00
1937	3,000,000	2.00	10.00	50.00	215	250
1938	3,650,000	1.25	2.00	7.00	70.00	85.00
1939	6,920,000	—	1.00	3.50	27.50	35.00

Date	Mintage	F12	VF20	XF40	MS60	MS63
1940	12,300,000	—	0.40	1.25	5.00	7.00
1942	14,380,000	—	0.60	1.50	7.00	10.00
1945	9,558,000	—	0.40	0.70	3.50	5.00
1946	46,230,000	—	0.40	0.60	2.50	4.00

KM# 433 10 CENTAVOS
5.50 g., Bronze 23.5mm. **Obv.** National arms, eagle left **Rev:** Bust left **Mint:** Mexico City **Note:** Mint mark Mo.

Date	Mintage	F12	VF20	XF40	MS60	MS63
1955	1,818,000	—	0.75	3.25	23.00	35.00
1956	5,255,000	—	0.75	3.25	23.00	32.00
1957	11,925,000	—	0.20	0.40	5.50	9.00
1959	26,140,000	—	0.30	0.45	0.75	1.25
1966	5,873,000	—	0.15	0.25	0.60	1.75
1967	32,318,000	—	0.10	0.15	0.30	0.40

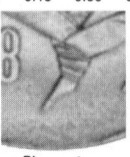

Sharp stem

KM# 434.1 10 CENTAVOS
1.50 g., Copper-Nickel **Obv.** National arms, eagle left **Rev:** Upright ear of corn **Edge:** Reeded **Mint:** Mexico City **Note:** Variety I- Sharp stem and wide date

Date	Mintage	F12	VF20	XF40	MS60	MS63
1974Mo	6,000,000	—	—	0.35	0.75	1.00
1975Mo	5,550,000	—	0.10	0.35	0.75	1.00
1976Mo	7,680,000	—	0.10	0.20	0.30	0.40
1977Mo	144,650,000	—	1.25	2.25	3.50	5.50
1978Mo	271,870,000	—	—	1.00	1.50	2.25
1979Mo	375,660,000	—	—	0.50	1.00	1.75
1980/79Mo	21,290,000	—	2.45	3.75	7.00	9.00
1980Mo	Inc. above	—	1.50	2.00	4.50	6.50

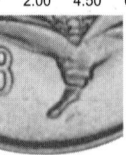

Blunt stem

KM# 434.2 10 CENTAVOS
1.50 g., Copper-Nickel **Obv.** National arms, eagle left **Rev:** Upright ear of corn **Edge:** Reeded **Mint:** Mexico City **Note:** Variety II- Blunt stem and narrow date

Date	Mintage	F12	VF20	XF40	MS60	MS63
1974Mo	Inc. above	—	0.10	0.20	0.30
1977Mo	Inc. above	—	0.15	0.50	1.25	2.25
1978Mo	Inc. above	—	—	0.10	0.30	0.40
1979Mo	Inc. above	—	0.15	0.35	0.85	1.50
1980Mo	Inc. above	—	—	0.10	0.20	0.30

KM# 434.3 10 CENTAVOS
1.50 g., Copper-Nickel **Obv.** National arms, eagle left **Rev:** Upright ear of corn **Edge:** Reeded **Mint:** Mexico City **Note:** Variety III- Blunt stem and wide date

Date	Mintage	F12	VF20	XF40	MS60	MS63
1980/79 Mo	—	—	—	2.50	7.00	9.00

KM# 434.4 10 CENTAVOS
1.50 g., Copper-Nickel **Obv.** National arms, eagle left **Rev:** Upright ear of corn **Edge:** Reeded **Mint:** Mexico City **Note:**

Variety IV- Sharp stem and narrow date

Date	Mintage	F12	VF20	XF40	MS60	MS63
1974Mo	—	—	—	—	1.50	2.50
1979Mo	—	—	—	—	1.50	2.50

KM# 435 20 CENTAVOS
5.00 g., 0.800 Silver, 0.13 oz. ASW 22mm. **Obv.** National arms **Rev:** Value and date within wreath with Liberty cap above **Mint:** Mexico City **Note:** Mint mark Mo.

Date	Mintage	F12	VF20	XF40	MS60	MS63
1905	2,565,000	5.00	12.00	25.00	175	195
1906	6,860,000	4.75	9.00	16.50	60.00	85.00
1907 Straight 7	4,000,000	5.00	11.50	22.00	75.00	125
1907 Curved 7	5,435,000	4.50	7.50	15.00	70.00	120
1908	350,000	50.00	95.00	250	1,800	—
1910	1,135,000	5.00	11.00	16.00	90.00	110
1911	1,150,000	12.00	15.00	40.00	145	175
1912	625,000	20.00	40.00	70.00	350	400
1913	1,000,000	5.00	14.50	30.00	100	125
1914	1,500,000	5.00	10.00	22.50	65.00	80.00

KM# 436 20 CENTAVOS
3.63 g., 0.800 Silver, 0.09 oz. ASW 19mm. **Obv.** National arms **Rev:** Value and date within wreath with Liberty cap above **Mint:** Mexico City **Note:** Mint mark Mo. Reduced size.

Date	Mintage	F12	VF20	XF40	MS60	MS63
1919	4,155,000	10.00	30.00	65.00	200	275

KM# 437 20 CENTAVOS
15.00 g., Bronze 32.5mm. **Obv.** National arms **Rev:** Value below date within wreath **Mint:** Mexico City **Note:** Mint mark Mo.

Date	Mintage	F12	VF20	XF40	MS60	MS63
1920	4,835,000	12.00	45.00	155	650	775
1935	20,000,000	2.00	6.00	10.00	95.00	145

KM# 438 20 CENTAVOS
3.33 g., 0.720 Silver, 0.08 oz. ASW 19mm. **Obv.** National arms **Rev:** Value and date within wreath with Liberty cap above **Mint:** Mexico City **Note:** Mint mark Mo.

ESTADOS UNIDOS - DECIMAL COINAGE

Date	Mintage	F12	VF20	XF40	MS60	MS63
1920	3,710,000	3.00	9.00	20.00	175	220
1921	6,160,000	3.00	7.00	14.00	100	150
1925	1,450,000	4.00	12.00	20.00	155	165
1926/5	1,465,000	7.00	20.00	70.00	350	375
1926	Inc. above	2.75	5.00	11.00	90.00	110
1927	1,405,000	2.75	5.00	12.00	95.00	115
1928	3,630,000	2.75	6.00	8.00	19.00	27.50
1930	1,000,000	2.75	8.00	12.00	30.00	42.00
1933	2,500,000	2.75	3.00	5.00	12.00	16.00
1934	2,500,000	2.75	3.00	6.00	13.00	20.00
1935	2,460,000	2.75	3.00	6.00	13.00	20.00
1937	10,000,000	BV	2.75	3.00	6.00	9.00
1939	8,800,000	BV	2.75	3.00	6.00	9.00
1940	3,000,000	BV	2.75	3.00	5.00	9.00
1941	5,740,000	BV	2.25	3.00	5.00	8.00
1942	12,460,000	BV	2.25	3.00	5.00	8.00
1943	3,955,000	BV	3.00	4.00	5.00	9.00

KM# 439 20 CENTAVOS
10.00 g., Bronze 28.5mm. **Obv.** National arms, eagle left **Rev:** Liberty cap divides value above Pyramid of the Sun at Teotihuacán, volcanos Ixtaccihuatl and Popocatepet in background **Edge:** Plain **Mint:** Mexico City **Note:** Mint mark Mo.

Date	Mintage	F12	VF20	XF40	MS60	MS63
1943	46,350,000	—	1.25	3.00	20.00	28.00
1944	83,650,000	—	0.40	0.65	8.00	12.00
1945	26,801,000	—	1.25	3.50	9.50	15.00
1946	25,695,000	—	1.10	2.25	6.00	9.00
1951	11,385,000	0.50	3.00	8.75	100	120
1952	6,560,000	0.50	3.00	5.00	25.00	35.00
1953	26,948,000	—	0.35	0.80	9.00	15.00
1954	40,108,000	—	0.35	0.80	9.00	15.00
1955	16,950,000	0.50	2.75	7.00	60.00	75.00

KM# 440 20 CENTAVOS
10.00 g., Bronze 28.5mm. **Obv.** National arms, eagle left **Rev:** Liberty cap divides value above Pyramid of the Sun at Teotihuacán, volcanos Ixtaccihuatl and Popocatepet in background **Edge:** Plain **Mint:** Mexico City **Note:** Mint mark Mo.

Date	Mintage	F12	VF20	XF40	MS60	MS63
1955 Inc. KM#439	Inc. above	—	0.75	1.75	17.00	22.00
1956	22,431,000	—	0.30	0.35	3.00	5.00
1957	13,455,000	—	0.45	1.25	9.00	13.00
1959	6,017,000	0.75	4.50	9.00	75.00	100
1960	39,756,000	—	0.15	0.25	0.75	1.00
1963	14,869,000	—	0.25	0.35	0.80	1.00
1964	28,654,000	—	0.25	0.40	0.90	1.25
1965	74,162,000	—	0.20	0.35	0.80	1.00
1966	43,745,000	—	0.15	0.25	0.75	1.00
1967	46,487,000	—	0.20	0.50	1.00	1.25
1968	15,477,000	—	0.30	0.55	1.35	1.65

Date	Mintage	F12	VF20	XF40	MS60	MS63
1969	63,647,000	—	0.20	0.35	0.80	1.00
1970	76,287,000	—	0.15	0.20	0.90	1.30
1971	49,892,000	—	0.30	0.50	1.25	2.00

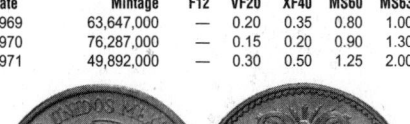

KM# 441 20 CENTAVOS
10.00 g., Bronze 28.5mm. **Obv.** National arms, eagle left **Rev:** Liberty cap divides value above Pyramid of the Sun at Teotihuacán, volcanos Ixtaccihuatl and Popocatepet in background **Edge:** Plain **Mint:** Mexico City

Date	Mintage	F12	VF20	XF40	MS60	MS63
1971Mo Inc. KM#440	Inc. above	—	0.20	0.35	1.85	2.50
1973Mo	78,398,000	—	0.25	0.35	0.95	1.65
1974Mo	34,200,000	—	0.20	0.35	1.25	2.00

KM# 442 20 CENTAVOS
3.00 g., Copper-Nickel 20mm. **Obv.** National arms, eagle left **Rev:** Bust 3/4 facing flanked by value and date **Edge:** Reeded **Mint:** Mexico City

Date	Mintage	F12	VF20	XF40	MS60	MS63
1974Mo	112,000,000	—	0.10	0.15	0.25	0.30
1975Mo	611,000,000	—	0.10	0.15	0.30	0.35
1976Mo	394,000,000	—	0.10	0.15	0.35	0.45
1977Mo	394,350,000	—	0.10	0.15	0.40	0.45
1978Mo	527,950,000	—	0.10	0.15	0.25	0.30
1979Mo	524,615,000	—	0.10	0.15	0.25	0.30
1979Mo	—	—	1.25	2.00	4.00	8.00
Note: Doubled die obv. small letters						
1979Mo	—	—	1.25	2.00	4.00	8.00
Note: Doubled die obv. large letters						
1980Mo	326,500,000	—	0.15	0.20	0.30	0.40
1981Mo Open 8	106,205,000	—	0.30	0.50	1.00	2.00
1981Mo Closed 8, high date	248,500,000	—	0.30	0.50	1.00	2.00
1981Mo Closed 8, low date	—	—	1.00	1.50	3.50	4.25
1981/1982 Mo	—	10.00	40.00	75.00	175	195
Note: The 1981/1982 overdate is often mistaken as 1982/1981						
1982Mo	286,855,000	—	0.40	0.60	0.90	1.10
1983Mo Round top 3	100,930,000	—	0.25	0.40	1.75	2.25
1983Mo Flat top 3	Inc. above	—	0.25	0.50	1.25	1.75
1983Mo	998	PF60 45.00				

KM# 491   20 CENTAVOS
3.00 g., Bronze 20mm. **Obv.** National arms, eagle left **Rev:** Mask 3/4 right with value below **Mint:** Mexico City

Date	Mintage	F12	VF20	XF40	MS60	MS63
1983Mo	53	PF60 185				
1983Mo	260,000,000	—	0.20	0.25	1.25	1.75
1984Mo	180,320,000	—	0.20	0.35	1.85	2.25

KM# 443   25 CENTAVOS
3.33 g., 0.300 Silver, 0.03 oz. ASW 21.5mm. **Obv.** National arms, eagle left **Rev:** Scale below Liberty cap **Edge:** Reeded **Mint:** Mexico City **Note:** Mint mark Mo.

Date	Mintage	F12	VF20	XF40	MS60	MS63
1950	77,060,000	—	1.25	1.50	2.00	2.50
1951	41,172,000	—	1.25	1.50	2.00	2.50
1952	29,264,000	—	1.25	1.50	2.25	2.75
1953	38,144,000	—	1.25	1.25	2.00	2.50

KM# 444   25 CENTAVOS
5.50 g., Copper-Nickel 23mm. **Obv.** National arms, eagle left **Rev:** Bust 3/4 facing **Edge:** Reeded **Mint:** Mexico City

Date	Mintage	F12	VF20	XF40	MS60	MS63
1964Mo	20,686,000	—	—	0.15	0.20	0.30
1966Mo Closed beak	180,000	—	0.75	1.25	3.00	4.50
1966Mo Open beak	Inc. above	—	2.00	4.00	12.00	15.00

KM# 445   50 CENTAVOS
12.50 g., 0.800 Silver, 0.32 oz. ASW 30mm. **Obv.** National arms **Rev:** Value and date within 3/4 wreath with Liberty cap above **Mint:** Mexico City **Note:** Mint mark Mo.

Date	Mintage	F12	VF20	XF40	MS60	MS63
1905	2,446,000	12.50	20.00	35.00	175	250
1906 Open 9	16,966,000	BV	12.00	15.00	55.00	85.00
1906 Closed 9	Inc. above	BV	11.50	14.00	48.00	70.00
1907 Straight 7	18,920,000	BV	11.50	14.00	36.00	42.00
1907 Curved 7	14,841,000	BV	11.50	14.00	36.00	45.50
1908	488,000	25.00	80.00	190	550	675
1912	3,736,000	12.00	22.50	20.00	55.00	85.00
1913/07	10,510,000	15.00	40.00	90.00	250	300

Date	Mintage	F12	VF20	XF40	MS60	MS63
1913/2	Inc. above	12.00	20.00	27.50	75.00	100
1913	Inc. above	BV	11.50	13.00	33.00	42.00
1914	7,710,000	BV	14.00	20.00	42.00	65.00
1916 Narrow date	480,000	20.00	60.00	85.00	250	350
1916 Wide date	Inc. above	20.00	60.00	85.00	250	350
1917	37,112,000	BV	12.00	14.00	27.50	33.00
1918	1,320,000	20.00	70.00	135	300	400

KM# 446   50 CENTAVOS
9.06 g., 0.800 Silver, 0.23 oz. ASW 27mm. **Obv.** National arms **Rev:** Value and date within 3/4 wreath with Liberty cap above **Mint:** Mexico City **Note:** Mint mark Mo. Reduced size.

Date	Mintage	F12	VF20	XF40	MS60	MS63
1918/7	2,760,000	175	525	700	1,450	—
1918	Inc. above	9.00	20.00	70.00	350	450
1919	29,670,000	BV	12.00	25.00	150	180

KM# 447   50 CENTAVOS
8.33 g., 0.720 Silver, 0.19 oz. ASW 27mm. **Obv.** National arms **Rev:** Value and date within 3/4 wreath with Liberty cap above **Edge Lettering:** INDEPENDENCIA Y LIBERTAD **Mint:** Mexico City **Note:** Mint mark Mo.

Date	Mintage	F12	VF20	XF40	MS60	MS63
1919	10,200,000	BV	12.00	22.00	100	130
1920	27,166,000	BV	9.00	17.00	75.00	90.00
1921	21,864,000	BV	9.00	17.00	95.00	120
1925	3,280,000	7.00	17.50	35.00	145	185
1937	20,000,000	BV	7.00	9.00	13.00	18.00
1938	100,000	15.00	50.00	95.00	245	350
1939	10,440,000	BV	7.00	9.00	16.00	25.00
1942	800,000	BV	7.00	10.00	18.00	22.00
1943	41,512,000	BV	7.00	9.00	12.00	15.00
1944	55,806,000	BV	7.00	9.00	12.00	15.00
1945	56,766,000	BV	7.00	9.00	12.00	15.00

KM# 448   50 CENTAVOS
7.97 g., 0.420 Silver, 0.11 oz. ASW 27mm. **Obv.** National arms **Rev:** Value and date within 3/4 wreath with Liberty cap above **Mint:** Mexico City **Note:** Mint mark Mo.

Date	Mintage	F12	VF20	XF40	MS60	MS63
1935	70,800,000	4.00	4.25	5.00	9.00	12.00

KM# 449 50 CENTAVOS
6.66 g., 0.300 Silver, 0.06 oz. ASW 26mm. **Obv.** National arms, eagle left **Rev:** Head with head covering right **Mint:** Mexico City **Note:** Mint mark Mo.

Date	Mintage	F12	VF20	XF40	MS60	MS63
1950	13,570,000	—	2.50	2.75	5.00	8.00
1951	3,650,000	—	3.00	4.00	6.00	9.00

KM# 450 50 CENTAVOS
14.00 g., Bronze 33mm. **Obv.** National arms, eagle left **Rev:** Head with headdress left **Edge:** Reeded **Mint:** Mexico City **Note:** Mint mark Mo.

Date	Mintage	F12	VF20	XF40	MS60	MS63
1955	3,502,000	—	1.50	3.00	4.00	8.00
1956	34,643,000	—	0.75	1.50	7.00	9.00
1957	9,675,000	—	1.00	2.00	6.50	8.00
1959	4,540,000	—	0.50	0.75	2.00	3.50

KM# 451 50 CENTAVOS
6.50 g., Copper-Nickel 25mm. **Obv.** National arms, eagle left **Rev:** Head with headdress left **Edge:** Reeded **Mint:** Mexico City

Date	Mintage	F12	VF20	XF40	MS60	MS63
1964Mo	43,806,000	—	0.15	0.20	0.40	0.60
1965Mo	14,326,000	—	0.20	0.25	0.45	0.65
1966Mo	1,726,000	—	0.20	0.40	1.50	2.00
1967Mo	55,144,000	—	0.20	0.30	0.75	1.25
1968Mo	80,438,000	—	0.15	0.30	0.65	1.00
1969Mo	87,640,000	—	0.20	0.35	0.80	1.25

KM# 452 50 CENTAVOS
6.50 g., Copper-Nickel 25mm. **Obv.** National arms, eagle left **Rev:** Head with headdress left **Edge:** Reeded **Mint:** Mexico City **Note:** Coins dated 1975 and 1976 exist with and without dots in centers of three circles on plumage on reverse. Edge varieties exist.

Date	Mintage	F12	VF20	XF40	MS60	MS63
1970Mo	76,236,000	—	0.15	0.20	0.80	1.35
1971Mo	125,288,000	—	0.15	0.20	0.90	1.45
1972Mo	16,000,000	—	1.25	2.00	3.50	5.50
1975Mo Dots	177,958,000	—	0.65	1.75	3.50	6.00
1975Mo No dots	Inc. above	—	0.15	0.20	0.75	1.25
1976Mo Dots	37,480,000	—	0.75	1.50	5.00	7.00

Date	Mintage	F12	VF20	XF40	MS60	MS63
1976Mo No dots	Inc. above	—	0.15	0.20	0.50	0.90
1977Mo	12,410,000	—	6.50	10.00	32.50	45.00
1978Mo	85,400,000	—	0.15	0.25	0.50	1.20
1979Mo Round 2nd 9 in date	229,000,000	—	0.15	0.25	0.50	1.00
1979Mo Square 9's in date	Inc. above	—	0.20	0.40	1.60	2.25
1980Mo Narrow date, square 9	89,978,000	—	0.45	0.75	1.75	2.50
1980Mo Wide date, round 9	178,188,000	—	0.20	0.25	1.00	2.25
1981Mo Rectangular 9, narrow date	142,212,000	—	0.50	0.75	1.75	2.50
1981Mo Round 9, wide date	Inc. above	—	0.30	0.50	1.25	1.75
1982Mo	45,474,000	—	0.20	0.40	1.95	1.75
1983Mo	90,318,000	—	0.50	0.75	1.75	2.50
1983Mo	998	PF60 45.00				

KM# 492 50 CENTAVOS
4.40 g., Stainless Steel 22mm. **Obv.** National arms, eagle left **Rev:** Head with headdress 3/4 left **Mint:** Mexico City

Date	Mintage	F12	VF20	XF40	MS60	MS63
1983Mo	99,540,000	—	—	0.30	1.50	2.50
1983Mo	53	PF60 195				

KM# 453 PESO
27.07 g., 0.903 Silver, 0.78 oz. ASW 39mm. **Obv.** National arms **Rev:** Horse and rider facing left among sun rays **Designer:** Charles Pillet **Mint:** Mexico City **Note:** Mint mark Mo. .

Date	Mintage	F12	VF20	XF40	MS60	MS63
1910	3,814,000	BV	45.00	50.00	200	275
1911	1,227,000	BV	45.00	75.00	200	300
Note: Long lower left ray on reverse						
1911	Inc. above	50.00	145	250	750	950
Note: Short lower left ray on reverse						

Date	Mintage	F12	VF20	XF40	MS60	MS63
1912	322,000	35.00	100	210	365	500
1913/2	2,880,000	BV	45.00	75.00	300	450
1913	Inc. above	BV	45.00	70.00	200	300
Note: 1913 coins exist with even and unevenly spaced date						
1914	120,000	300	700	1,200	4,000	—

KM# 454 PESO
18.13 g., 0.800 Silver, 0.46 oz. ASW 34mm. **Obv.** National arms **Rev:** Value and date within 3/4 wreath with Liberty cap above **Mint:** Mexico City **Note:** Mint mark Mo.

Date	Mintage	F12	VF20	XF40	MS60	MS63
1918/7	—	250	350	—	—	—
1918	3,050,000	20.00	45.00	150	1,350	2,500
1919	6,151,000	18.00	30.00	125	950	1,750

KM# 455 PESO
16.66 g., 0.720 Silver, 0.38 oz. ASW 34mm. **Obv.** National arms **Rev:** Value and date within 3/4 wreath with Liberty cap above **Edge Lettering:** INDEPENDENCIA Y LIBERTAD **Mint:** Mexico City **Note:** Mint mark Mo.

Date	Mintage	F12	VF20	XF40	MS60	MS63
1920/10	8,830,000	18.00	50.00	90.00	325	—
1920	Inc. above	BV	15.00	35.00	195	350
1921	5,480,000	BV	15.00	35.00	195	275
1922	33,620,000	—	BV	15.00	20.00	35.00
1923	35,280,000	—	BV	15.00	20.00	35.00
1924	33,060,000	—	BV	15.00	20.00	35.00
1925	9,160,000	—	BV	15.00	60.00	85.00
1926	28,840,000	—	BV	15.00	25.00	40.00
1927	5,060,000	BV	15.00	16.00	70.00	90.00
1932 Open 9	50,770,000	—	—	BV	14.00	16.00
1932 Closed 9	Inc. above	—	—	BV	14.00	16.00
1933/2	43,920,000	15.00	20.00	35.00	100	—
1933	Inc. above	—	BV	15.00	16.50	18.00
1934	22,070,000	—	—	BV	15.00	22.00
1935	8,050,000	—	BV	15.00	16.00	24.00
1938	30,000,000	—	—	BV	15.00	16.50
1940	20,000,000	—	—	BV	15.00	16.50
1943	47,662,000	—	—	BV	15.00	16.50
1944	39,522,000	—	—	BV	15.00	16.50
1945	37,300,000	—	—	BV	15.00	16.50

KM# 456 PESO
14.00 g., 0.500 Silver, 0.22 oz. ASW 32mm. **Obv.** National arms, eagle left **Rev:** Head with headcovering right **Edge:** Reeded **Mint:** Mexico City **Note:** Mint mark Mo.

Date	Mintage	F12	VF20	XF40	MS60	MS63
1947	61,460,000	—	—	BV	8.00	10.00
1948	22,915,000	—	—	BV	8.00	10.00
1949	—	PF60 4,500				
1949	4,000,000	350	650	1,300	1,700	2,700
Note: Not released for circulation						

KM# 457 PESO
13.33 g., 0.300 Silver, 0.13 oz. ASW 32mm. **Obv.** National arms, eagle left **Rev:** Armored bust 3/4 left **Mint:** Mexico City **Note:** Mint mark Mo.

Date	Mintage	F12	VF20	XF40	MS60	MS63
1950	3,287,000	—	5.00	6.00	10.00	15.00

KM# 458 PESO
16.00 g., 0.100 Silver, 0.05 oz. ASW 34.5mm. **Obv.** National arms, eagle left within wreath **Obv. Designer:** Manuel L. Negrete **Rev:** Head left **Edge Lettering:** INDEPENDENCIA Y LIBERTAD **Mint:** Mexico City **Note:** Mint mark Mo.

Date	Mintage	F12	VF20	XF40	MS60	MS63
1957	500,000	—	4.00	6.00	12.50	16.50

KM# 459 PESO

16.00 g., 0.100 Silver, 0.05 oz. ASW 34.5mm. **Obv.** National arms, eagle left within wreath **Rev:** Armored bust right within wreath **Edge Lettering:** INDEPENDENCIA Y LIBERTAD **Mint:** Mexico City **Note:** Mint mark Mo.

Date	Mintage	F12	VF20	XF40	MS60	MS63
1957	28,273,000	—	BV	2.00	3.00	10.00
1958	41,899,000	—	—	BV	2.00	3.00
1959	27,369,000	—	BV	2.00	5.50	8.00
1960	26,259,000	—	BV	3.00	3.50	6.00
1961	52,601,000	—	—	BV	2.50	5.00
1962	61,094,000	—	—	BV	2.00	4.00
1963	26,394,000	—	—	BV	2.00	2.50
1964	15,615,000	—	—	BV	2.00	2.50
1965	5,004,000	—	—	BV	2.00	2.50
1966	30,998,000	—	—	BV	2.00	2.25
1967	9,308,000	—	—	BV	2.75	4.50

Tall date

KM# 460 PESO

9.00 g., Copper-Nickel 29mm. **Obv.** National arms, eagle left **Rev:** Head left **Edge:** Reeded **Mint:** Mexico City

Date	Mintage	F12	VF20	XF40	MS60	MS63
1970Mo Narrow date	102,715,000	—	0.25	0.35	0.65	0.80
1970Mo Wide date	Inc. above	—	1.25	2.50	7.50	10.00
1971Mo	426,222,000	—	0.20	0.25	0.55	0.75
1972Mo	120,000,000	—	0.20	0.25	0.40	0.65
1974Mo	63,700,000	—	0.20	0.25	0.65	0.90
1975Mo Tall narrow date	205,979,000	—	0.25	0.45	1.00	1.35
1975Mo Short wide date	Inc. above	—	0.30	0.40	0.75	1.00
1976Mo	94,489,000	—	0.15	0.20	0.50	0.75
1977Mo Thick date close to rim	94,364,000	—	0.25	0.45	1.00	1.25
1977Mo Thin date, space between sideburns and collar	Inc. above	—	1.00	2.50	8.50	16.50
1978Mo Closed 8	208,300,000	—	0.20	0.30	1.00	1.50
1978Mo Open 8	55,140,000	—	1.00	2.50	14.00	20.00
1979Mo Thin date	117,884,000	—	0.20	0.30	1.15	1.50
1979Mo Thick date	Inc. above	—	0.20	0.30	1.25	1.75
1980Mo Closed 8	318,800,000	—	0.25	0.35	1.00	1.25
1980Mo Open 8	23,865,000	—	0.75	1.50	8.00	15.00
1981Mo Closed 8	413,349,000	—	0.20	0.30	0.75	0.90
1981Mo Open 8	58,616,000	—	0.50	1.25	6.50	9.00
1982Mo Closed 8	235,000,000	—	0.25	0.75	2.25	2.50
1982Mo Open 8	—	—	0.75	1.50	8.00	15.00
1983Mo Wide date	100,000,000	—	0.30	0.45	3.00	3.50
1983Mo Narrow date	Inc. above	—	0.30	0.45	3.00	4.50
1983Mo	1,051,000	PF60 38.00				

KM# 496 PESO

5.70 g., Stainless Steel 24.5mm. **Obv.** National arms, eagle left **Rev:** Armored bust right **Mint:** Mexico City

Date	Mintage	F12	VF20	XF40	MS60	MS63
1984Mo	722,802,000	—	0.10	0.25	0.65	1.45
1985Mo	985,000,000	—	0.10	0.25	0.50	1.25
1986Mo	740,000,000	—	0.10	0.25	0.50	1.25
1987Mo	250,000,000	—	0.10	0.25	0.50	1.25
1987Mo Proof; 2 known	—	PF60 1,000				

KM# 461 2 PESOS

1.67 g., 0.900 Gold, 0.05 oz. AGW 13mm. **Obv.** National arms **Rev:** Date above value within wreath **Mint:** Mexico City **Note:** Mint mark Mo.

Date	Mintage	F12	VF20	XF40	MS60
1919	1,670,000	—	BV	100	110
1920/10	—	BV	100	105	145
1920	4,282,000	—	BV	100	105
1944	10,000	BV	100	110	130
1945	Est. 140000	—	—	—	BV+20%
1946	168,000	BV	100	110	165
1947	25,000	BV	100	110	145
1948 No specimens known	45,000	—	—	—	—

Note: During 1951-1972 a total of 4,590,493 pieces were restruck, most likely dated 1945. In 1996 matte restrikes were produced. An additional 260,000 pieces dated 1945 were struck during 2000-2013

KM# 462   2 PESOS
26.67 g., 0.900 Silver, 0.77 oz. ASW 39mm. **Obv.** National arms, eagle left within wreath **Rev:** Winged Victory **Designer:** Emilio del Moral **Mint:** Mexico City **Note:** Mint mark Mo.

Date	Mintage	F12	VF20	XF40	MS60	MS63
1921	1,278,000	30.00	45.00	75.00	450	700

KM# 463   2-1/2 PESOS
2.08 g., 0.900 Gold, 0.06 oz. AGW 15.5mm. **Obv.** National arms **Rev:** Miguel Hidalgo y Costilla **Mint:** Mexico City **Note:** Mint mark Mo.

Date	Mintage	F12	VF20	XF40	MS60
1918	1,704,000	—	BV	110	130
1919	984,000	—	BV	110	130
1920/10	607,000	—	BV	110	180
1920	Inc. above	—	BV	110	125
1944	20,000	—	BV	115	145
1945	Est. 180000	—	—	—	BV+18%
1946	163,000	—	BV	115	145
1947	24,000	230	300	425	750
1948	63,000	—	BV	115	145

Note: During 1951-1972 a total of 5,025,087 pieces were restruck, most likely dated 1945. In 1996 matte restrikes were produced. An additional 539,000 pieces dated 1945 were struck during 2000-2013

KM# 464   5 PESOS
4.17 g., 0.900 Gold, 0.12 oz. AGW 19mm. **Obv.** National arms **Rev:** Miguel Hidalgo y Costilla **Mint:** Mexico City **Note:** Mint mark Mo.

Date	Mintage	F12	VF20	XF40	MS60
1905	18,000	220	230	325	700
1906	4,638,000	—	—	BV	200
1907/6	—	—	—	—	—
1907	1,088,000	—	—	BV	200
1910	100,000	—	—	BV	220
1918/7	609,000	—	—	BV	250
1918	Inc. above	—	—	BV	220
1919	506,000	—	—	BV	200
1920	2,385,000	—	—	BV	200
1955	—	—	—	—	BV+12%

Note: During 1955-1972 a total of 1,767,645 pieces were restruck, most likely dated 1955. In 1996 matte restrikes were produced. An additional 96,300 pieces dated 1955 were struck during 2000-2013

KM# 465   5 PESOS
30.00 g., 0.900 Silver, 0.86 oz. ASW 40mm. **Obv.** National arms, eagle left **Rev:** Head with headdress left **Edge:** Reeded **Mint:** Mexico City **Note:** Mint mark Mo.

Date	Mintage	F12	VF20	XF40	MS60	MS63
1947	5,110,000	—	—	BV	32.50	35.00
1948	26,740,000	—	—	BV	32.50	35.00

KM# 466   5 PESOS
27.78 g., 0.720 Silver, 0.64 oz. ASW 40mm. **Obv.** National arms, eagle left **Rev:** Radiant sun flanked by palm trees above train **Edge Lettering:** COMERCIO - AGRICULTURA - INDUSTRIA **Designer:** Manuel L. Negrete **Mint:** Mexico City **Note:** Mint mark Mo.

Date	Mintage	F12	VF20	XF40	MS60	MS63
1950	200,000	—	27.50	45.00	65.00	75.00

Note: It is recorded that 100,000 pieces were melted to be used for the 1968 Mexican Olympic 25 Pesos

KM# 467   5 PESOS
27.78 g., 0.720 Silver, 0.64 oz. ASW 40mm. **Obv.** National arms, eagle left **Rev:** Head left within wreath **Edge Lettering:** COMERCIO - AGRICULTURA - INDUSTRIA **Mint:** Mexico City **Note:** Mint mark Mo.

Date	Mintage	F12	VF20	XF40	MS60	MS63
1951	4,958,000	—	—	BV	22.50	25.00
1952	9,595,000	—	—	BV	22.50	25.00
1953	20,376,000	—	—	BV	22.50	25.00
1954	30,000	—	30.00	60.00	70.00	85.00

KM# 468 5 PESOS

27.78 g., 0.720 Silver, 0.64 oz. ASW 40mm. **Obv.** National arms, eagle left **Rev:** Half-length figure facing to right of building and dates **Edge Lettering:** COMERCIO - AGRICULTURA - INDUSTRIA **Designer:** Manuel L. Negrete **Mint:** Mexico City **Note:** Mint mark Mo.

Date	Mintage	F12	VF20	XF40	MS60	MS63
1953	1,000,000	—	—	BV	23.00	25.00

KM# 469 5 PESOS

18.05 g., 0.720 Silver, 0.42 oz. ASW 36mm. **Obv.** National arms, eagle left **Rev:** Head left **Mint:** Mexico City **Note:** Mint mark Mo.

Date	Mintage	F12	VF20	XF40	MS60	MS63
1955	4,271,000	—	—	BV	15.00	16.50
1956	4,596,000	—	—	BV	15.00	16.50
1957	3,464,000	—	—	BV	15.00	16.50

KM# 470 5 PESOS

18.05 g., 0.720 Silver, 0.42 oz. ASW 36mm. **Obv.** National arms, eagle left **Rev:** Head left **Edge Lettering:** INDEPENDENCIA Y LIBERTAD **Designer:** Manuel L. Negrete **Mint:** Mexico City **Note:** Mint mark Mo.

Date	Mintage	F12	VF20	XF40	MS60	MS63
1957	200,000	—	BV	15.00	16.00	18.00

KM# 471 5 PESOS

18.05 g., 0.720 Silver, 0.42 oz. ASW 36mm. **Obv.** National arms, eagle left **Rev:** Head left **Edge:** Plain **Designer:** Manuel L. Negrete **Mint:** Mexico City **Note:** Mint mark Mo.

Date	Mintage	F12	VF20	XF40	MS60	MS63
1959	1,000,000	—	—	BV	15.00	16.50

Large date

KM# 472 5 PESOS

14.00 g., Copper-Nickel 33mm. **Obv.** National arms, eagle left **Rev:** Armored bust right **Edge Lettering:** INDEPENDENCIA Y LIBERTAD **Mint:** Mexico City **Note:** Small date, large date varieties.

Date	Mintage	F12	VF20	XF40	MS60	MS63
1971Mo	28,457,000	—	0.50	0.95	2.50	3.25
1972Mo	75,000,000	—	0.60	1.25	2.00	2.50
1973Mo	19,405,000	—	1.25	2.00	4.50	5.50
1974Mo	34,500,000	—	0.50	0.80	1.75	2.25
1976Mo Small date	26,121,000	—	0.75	1.45	3.25	4.00
1976Mo Large date	121,550,000	—	0.35	0.50	1.50	1.75
1977Mo	102,000,000	—	0.35	0.50	1.50	1.75
1978Mo	25,700,000	—	1.00	1.50	4.50	6.25

KM# 485 5 PESOS

10.20 g., Copper-Nickel 27mm. **Obv.** National arms, eagle left **Rev:** Native sculpture to lower right of value and dollar sign **Edge Lettering:** LIBERTAD Y INDEPENDENCIA **Mint:** Mexico City **Note:** Inverted and normal edge legend varieties exist for the 1980 and 1981 dates.

Date	Mintage	F12	VF20	XF40	MS60	MS63
1980Mo	266,899,999	—	0.25	0.50	1.75	2.25
1981Mo	30,500,000	—	0.45	0.65	2.75	3.25
1982Mo	20,000,000	—	1.50	2.35	4.25	5.25
1982Mo	1,051	PF60 50.00				
1983Mo Proof; 7 known	—	PF60 1,200				
1984Mo	16,300,000	—	1.25	2.00	4.75	6.00
1985Mo	76,900,000	—	2.00	3.25	4.25	5.00

KM# 502 5 PESOS

3.10 g., Brass 17mm. **Obv.** National arms, eagle left **Rev:** Date and value **Edge:** Reeded **Mint:** Mexico City

Date	Mintage	F12	VF20	XF40	MS60	MS63
1985Mo	30,000,000	—	—	0.15	0.35	0.50
1987Mo	81,900,000	2.00	8.00	9.50	12.50	16.50
1988Mo	76,600,000	—	—	0.10	0.25	0.35

ESTADOS UNIDOS - DECIMAL COINAGE

Date	Mintage	F12	VF20	XF40	MS60	MS63
1988Mo Proof; 2 known	—	PF60 600				

KM# 473 10 PESOS
8.33 g., 0.900 Gold, 0.24 oz. AGW 22.5mm. **Obv.** National arms **Rev:** Miguel Hidalgo y Costilla **Mint:** Mexico City **Note:** Mint mark Mo.

Date	Mintage	F12	VF20	XF40	MS60	MS63
1905	39,000	—	BV	450	475	500
1906	2,949,000	—	BV	450	475	500
1907	1,589,000	—	BV	450	475	500
1908	890,000	—	BV	450	475	500
1910	451,000	—	BV	450	475	500
1916	26,000	—	BV	475	500	525
1917	1,967,000	—	BV	450	475	500
1919	266,000	—	BV	450	475	500
1920	12,000	—	BV	550	925	1,000
1959	Est. 50000	—	—	—BV+7%		—

Note: *During 1961-1972 a total of 954,983 pieces were restruck, most likely dated 1959. In 1996 matte restrikes were produced. An additional 67,300 pieces dated 1959 were struck during 2000-2013

KM# 474 10 PESOS
28.89 g., 0.900 Silver, 0.83 oz. ASW 40mm. **Obv.** National arms **Rev:** Head left **Edge:** Reeded **Mint:** Mexico City **Note:** Mint mark Mo.

Date	Mintage	F12	VF20	XF40	MS60	MS63
1955	585,000	—	—	BV	32.00	35.00
1956	3,535,000	—	—	BV	32.00	33.00

KM# 475 10 PESOS
28.88 g., 0.900 Silver, 0.83 oz. ASW 40mm. **Obv.** National arms, eagle left **Rev:** Head left **Edge Lettering:** INDEPENDENCIA Y LIBERTAD **Designer:** Manuel L. Negrete **Mint:** Mexico City **Note:** Mint mark Mo.

Date	Mintage	F12	VF20	XF40	MS60	MS63
1957	100,000	BV	32.00	40.00	55.00	60.00

KM# 476 10 PESOS
28.89 g., 0.900 Silver, 0.83 oz. ASW 40mm. **Obv.** National arms, eagle left **Rev:** Conjoined busts facing flanked by dates **Edge:** Reeded **Designer:** Manuel L. Negrete **Mint:** Mexico City **Note:** Mint mark Mo.

Date	Mintage	F12	VF20	XF40	MS60	MS63
1960	1,000,000	—	—	BV	32.00	34.00

KM# 477.1 10 PESOS
10.00 g., Copper-Nickel 30.5mm. **Obv.** National arms, eagle left **Rev:** Head left **Shape:** 7-sided **Mint:** Mexico City **Note:** Thin flan - 1.6mm

Date	Mintage	F12	VF20	XF40	MS60	MS63
1974Mo	3,900,000	—	0.50	1.00	3.00	4.50
1974Mo	—	PF60 650				
1975Mo	1,000,000	—	2.25	3.25	7.50	8.50
1976Mo	74,500,000	—	0.25	0.75	1.75	2.75
1977Mo	79,620,000	—	0.50	1.00	2.00	3.00

KM# 477.2 10 PESOS
11.50 g., Copper-Nickel 30.5mm. **Obv.** National arms, eagle left **Rev:** Head left **Shape:** 7-sided **Mint:** Mexico City **Note:** Thick flan - 2.3mm

Date	Mintage	F12	VF20	XF40	MS60	MS63
1978Mo	124,850,000	—	0.50	0.75	2.50	2.75
1979Mo	57,200,000	—	0.50	0.75	2.50	2.75
1980Mo	55,200,000	—	0.50	0.75	2.50	3.75
1981Mo	222,768,000	—	0.40	0.60	2.25	2.75
1982Mo	1,051	PF60 45.00				
1982Mo	151,770,000	—	0.50	0.80	2.50	3.50
1983Mo Proof; 3 known	—	PF60 1,800				
1985Mo	58,000,000	—	1.25	1.75	5.75	8.00

KM# 512 10 PESOS
3.84 g., Stainless Steel 19mm. **Obv.** National arms, eagle left **Rev:** Head facing with diagonal value at left **Mint:** Mexico City **Note:** Date varieties exist.

Date	Mintage	F12	VF20	XF40	MS60	MS63
1985Mo	257,000,000	—	—	0.15	0.50	0.75
1986Mo	392,000,000	—	—	0.15	0.50	1.50
1987Mo	305,000,000	—	—	0.15	0.35	0.50
1988Mo	500,300,000	—	—	0.15	0.25	0.35
1989Mo	336,900,000	—	0.20	0.25	0.75	1.50
1990Mo Proof; 2 known	—	PF60 550				
1990Mo	101,000,000	—	—	0.25	0.75	1.25

KM# 478 20 PESOS
16.67 g., 0.900 Gold, 0.48 oz. AGW 27.5mm. **Obv.** National arms, eagle left **Rev:** Aztec Sunstone with denomination below **Edge:** Lettered **Edge Lettering:** INDEPEDENCIA Y LIBERTAD **Mint:** Mexico City **Note:** Mint mark Mo.

Date	Mintage	F12	VF20	XF40	MS60	MS63
1917	852,000	—	—	BV	900	—
1918	2,831,000	—	—	BV	900	—
1919	1,094,000	—	—	BV	900	—
1920/10	462,000	—	—	BV	900	—
1920	Inc. above	—	—	BV	900	—
1921/11	922,000	—	—	BV	900	—
1921/10	—	—	—	—	—	—
1921	Inc. above	—	—	BV	925	—
1959	Est. 13000	—	—	—BV+4%		—

Note: During 1960-1971 a total of 1,158,414 pieces were restruck, most likely dated 1959. In 1996 matte re-strikes were produced. An additional 95,300 pieces dated 1959 were struck in 2000-2013

KM# 486 20 PESOS
15.20 g., Copper-Nickel 32mm. **Obv.** National arms, eagle left **Rev:** Figure with headdress facing left within circle **Edge Lettering:** INDEPENDENCIA Y LIBERTAD **Mint:** Mexico City

Date	Mintage	F12	VF20	XF40	MS60	MS63
1980Mo	84,900,000	—	0.50	0.85	2.25	3.25
1981Mo	250,573,000	—	0.60	0.80	2.25	3.25
1982Mo	236,892,000	—	1.00	1.75	2.50	3.75
1982Mo	1,051	PF60 50.00				

Date	Mintage	F12	VF20	XF40	MS60	MS63
1983Mo Proof; 3 known	—	PF60 575				
1984Mo	55,000,000	—	1.00	1.50	2.50	4.75

KM# 508 20 PESOS
6.00 g., Brass 21mm. **Obv.** National arms, eagle left **Rev:** Bust facing with diagonal value at left **Edge:** Reeded **Mint:** Mexico City

Date	Mintage	F12	VF20	XF40	MS60	MS63
1985Mo Wide date	25,000,000	—	0.10	0.20	1.00	1.50
1985Mo Narrow date	Inc. above	—	0.10	0.25	1.50	2.25
1986Mo	10,000,000	—	1.00	1.75	5.00	6.00
1988Mo	355,200,000	—	0.10	0.20	0.45	0.75
1989Mo	289,100,000	—	0.15	0.30	1.50	2.00
1990Mo	126,550,000	—	0.15	0.30	1.50	2.50
1990Mo Proof; 3 known	—	PF60 600				

Snake's tongue straight

KM# 479.1 25 PESOS
22.50 g., 0.720 Silver, 0.52 oz. ASW 38mm. **Obv.** National arms, eagle left **Rev:** Olympic rings below dancing native left, numeral design in background **Designer:** Lorenzo Rafael **Note:** Type I, Rings aligned.

Date	Mintage	F12	VF20	XF40	MS60	MS63
1968Mo	27,182,000	—	—	BV	19.00	21.00

KM# 479.2 25 PESOS
22.50 g., 0.720 Silver, 0.52 oz. ASW 38mm. **Obv.** National arms, eagle left **Rev:** Olympic rings below dancing native left, numeral design in background **Mint:** Mexico City **Note:** Type II, center ring low.

Date	Mintage	F12	VF20	XF40	MS60	MS63
1968Mo	Inc. above	—	BV	19.00	20.00	21.00

ESTADOS UNIDOS • DECIMAL COINAGE

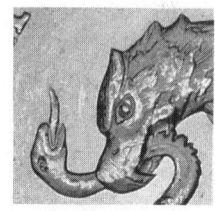

Snake's tongue curved

KM# 479.3 25 PESOS
22.50 g., 0.720 Silver, 0.52 oz. ASW 38mm. **Obv.** National arms, eagle left **Rev:** Olympic rings below dancing native left, numeral design in background **Mint:** Mexico City **Note:** Snake with long curved or normal tongue. Type III, center rings low.

Date	Mintage	F12	VF20	XF40	MS60	MS63
1968Mo	Inc. above	—	BV	19.00	20.00	22.50

KM# 480 25 PESOS
22.50 g., 0.720 Silver, 0.52 oz. ASW 38mm. **Obv.** National arms, eagle left **Rev:** Bust facing **Mint:** Mexico City

Date	Mintage	F12	VF20	XF40	MS60	MS63
1972Mo	2,000,000	—	BV	19.00	20.00	21.00

KM# 497 25 PESOS
7.78 g., 0.720 Silver, 0.18 oz. ASW **Obv.** National arms, eagle left **Rev:** Value above soccer ball with date below, with fineness **Mint:** Mexico City

Date	Mintage	F12	VF20	XF40	MS60	MS63
1985Mo	473,605	—	—	—	—	10.00

KM# 497a 25 PESOS
8.41 g., 0.925 Silver, 0.25 oz. ASW **Obv.** National arms, eagle left **Rev:** Value above soccerball with date below **Mint:** Mexico City **Note:** Without finess statement- reverse description

Date	Mintage	F12	VF20	XF40	MS60	MS63
1986Mo	22,552	PF60 15.00				

KM# 503 25 PESOS
8.41 g., 0.925 Silver, 0.25 oz. ASW **Obv.** National arms,

eagle left **Rev:** Pre-Columbian hieroglyphs, ojo de buey, and soccer ball **Mint:** Mexico City

Date	Mintage	F12	VF20	XF40	MS60	MS63
1985Mo	41,255	PF60 15.00				

KM# 514 25 PESOS
8.41 g., 0.925 Silver, 0.25 oz. ASW **Obv.** National arms, eagle left **Rev:** Value above soccer ball **Mint:** Mexico City

Date	Mintage	F12	VF20	XF40	MS60	MS63
1985Mo	21,260	PF60 15.00				

KM# 519 25 PESOS
8.41 g., 0.925 Silver, 0.25 oz. ASW **Obv.** National arms, eagle left **Rev:** Soccer ball within net, date and value to left **Mint:** Mexico City

Date	Mintage	F12	VF20	XF40	MS60	MS63
1986Mo	20,172	PF60 15.00				

KM# 481 50 PESOS
41.67 g., 0.900 Gold, 1.20 oz. AGW 37mm. **Obv.** National arms **Rev:** Winged Victory **Edge:** Reeded **Designer:** Emilio del Moral **Mint:** Mexico City **Note:** During 1949-1972 a total of 3,975,654 pieces were restruck, most likely dated 1947 and an additional 388,800 pieces dated 1947 were struck during 2000-2013. In 1996 matte restrikes were produced. Mint mark Mo.

Date	Mintage	F12	VF20	XF40	MS60	MS63
1921	180,000	—	—	BV	2,300	3,300
1922	463,000	—	—	BV	2,200	2,400
1923	432,000	—	—	BV	2,200	2,400
1924	439,000	—	—	BV	2,200	2,400
1925	716,000	—	—	BV	2,200	2,400
1926	600,000	—	—	BV	2,200	2,400
1927	606,000	—	—	BV	2,200	2,400
1928	538,000	—	—	BV	2,200	2,400
1929	458,000	—	—	BV	2,200	2,400
1930	372,000	—	—	BV	2,200	2,400
1931	137,000	—	—	BV	2,250	2,500
1944	593,000	—	—	BV	2,200	2,300
1945	1,012,000	—	—	BV	2,200	2,300
1946	1,588,000	—	—	BV	2,200	2,300

ESTADOS UNIDOS - DECIMAL COINAGE

Date	Mintage	F12	VF20	XF40	MS60	MS63
1947	309,000	—	—	— BV+5%	—
1947 Specimen	—	—	—	—	—	—
Note: Value, $6,500						

KM# 481a 50 PESOS
Platinum, APW **Obv.** National arms **Rev:** Winged Victory **Edge:** Reeded **Mint:** Mexico City

Date	Mintage	F12	VF20	XF40	MS60	MS63
1947Mo	Est. 5	—	—	—	—	13,500

KM# 482 50 PESOS
41.67 g., 0.900 Gold, 1.20 oz. AGW 37mm. **Obv.** National arms **Rev:** Winged Victory

Date	Mintage	F12	VF20	XF40	MS60	MS63
1943Mo	89,000	—	—	—	BV	2,300

KM# 490 50 PESOS
19.84 g., Copper-Nickel 39mm. **Obv.** National arms, eagle left **Rev:** Value to right of artistic designs **Edge:** Reeded **Mint:** Mexico City **Note:** Doubled die examples of 1982 and 1983 dates exist.

Date	Mintage	F12	VF20	XF40	MS60	MS63
1982Mo	222,890,000	—	1.00	2.50	5.00	6.50
1983Mo	45,000,000	—	1.50	3.00	6.00	7.00
1983Mo	1,051	PF60 55.00				
1984Mo	73,537,000	—	1.00	1.35	3.50	4.50
1984Mo	—	PF60 750				
Proof; 4 known						

KM# 495 50 PESOS
8.60 g., Copper-Nickel 23.5mm. **Obv.** National arms, eagle left **Rev:** Bust 1/4 left with diagonal value at left **Edge:** Reeded **Mint:** Mexico City

Date	Mintage	F12	VF20	XF40	MS60	MS63
1984Mo	94,216,000	—	0.65	1.25	2.70	3.25
1985Mo	296,000,000	—	0.25	0.45	1.25	2.25
1986Mo	50,000,000	—	6.00	10.00	12.00	14.00

Date	Mintage	F12	VF20	XF40	MS60	MS63
1987Mo	210,000,000	—	0.25	0.45	1.00	1.25
1988Mo	80,200,000	—	6.25	9.00	13.50	16.00

KM# 495a 50 PESOS
7.10 g., Stainless Steel 23.5mm. **Obv.** National arms, eagle left **Rev:** Bust 1/4 left with diagonal value at left **Edge:** Plain **Mint:** Mexico City

Date	Mintage	F12	VF20	XF40	MS60	MS63
1988 Mo	353,300,000	—	—	0.20	1.25	1.75
1989Mo	20,000	—	—	—	—	—
Note: Reported not confirmed.						
1990Mo	180,000,000	—	—	0.30	1.00	2.00
1992Mo	84,520,000	—	—	0.25	1.00	2.75

KM# 504 50 PESOS
16.83 g., 0.925 Silver, 0.50 oz. ASW **Obv.** National arms, eagle left **Rev:** Stiyilized athlete as soccer forerunner **Mint:** Mexico City

Date	Mintage	F12	VF20	XF40	MS60	MS63
1985Mo	41,255	PF60 25.00				

KM# 515 50 PESOS
16.83 g., 0.925 Silver, 0.50 oz. ASW **Obv.** National arms, eagle left **Rev:** Value to right of soccer player **Mint:** Mexico City

Date	Mintage	F12	VF20	XF40	MS60	MS63
1985Mo	24,907	PF60 25.00				

KM# 498 50 PESOS
15.55 g., 0.720 Silver, 0.36 oz. ASW **Obv.** National arms, eagle left **Rev:** Pair of feet and soccer ball, with fineness **Mint:** Mexico City

Date	Mintage	F12	VF20	XF40	MS60	MS63
1985Mo	439,763	—	—	—	—	16.50

KM# 498a 50 PESOS
16.83 g., 0.925 Silver, 0.50 oz. ASW **Obv.** National arms, eagle left **Rev:** Without fineness statement **Mint:** Mexico City

Date	Mintage	F12	VF20	XF40	MS60	MS63
1986Mo	19,564	**PF60** 25.00				

KM# 523 50 PESOS
16.83 g., 0.925 Silver, 0.50 oz. ASW **Obv.** National arms, eagle left **Rev:** Value to left of soccer balls **Mint:** Mexico City

Date	Mintage	F12	VF20	XF40	MS60	MS63
1986Mo	18,653	**PF60** 25.00				

KM# 532 50 PESOS
15.55 g., 0.999 Silver, 0.50 oz. ASW **Obv.** National arms, eagle left **Rev:** Monument **Mint:** Mexico City

Date	Mintage	F12	VF20	XF40	MS60	MS63
ND(1988)Mo	20,000	—	—	—	22.50	25.00

Low 7's

KM# 483.1 100 PESOS
27.77 g., 0.720 Silver, 0.64 oz. ASW 39mm. **Obv.** National arms, eagle left **Rev:** Bust facing, sloping right shoulder, round left shoulder with no clothing folds **Edge:** Reeded **Mint:** Mexico City

Date	Mintage	VF20	XF40	MS60	MS63
1977Mo Low 7's	5,225,000	—	BV	23.00	25.00
1977Mo High 7's	Inc. above	—	BV	23.00	25.00

High 7's

KM# 483.2 100 PESOS
27.77 g., 0.720 Silver, 0.64 oz. ASW 39mm. **Obv.** National arms, eagle left **Rev:** Bust facing, higher right shoulder, left shoulder with clothing folds. **Mint:** Mexico City **Note:** Mintage inc. KM#483.1

Date	Mintage	F12	VF20	XF40	MS60	MS63
1977Mo Date in line	—	—	—	BV	23.00	25.00
1978Mo	9,879,000	—	—	BV	23.00	25.00
1979Mo	784,000	—	—	BV	23.00	25.00
1979Mo	—	**PF60** 650				

KM# 493 100 PESOS
11.70 g., Aluminum-Bronze 26.5mm. **Obv.** National arms, eagle left **Rev:** Head 1/4 right with diagonal value at right **Edge:** Segmented reeding **Mint:** Mexico City

Date	Mintage	F12	VF20	XF40	MS60	MS63
1984Mo	227,809,000	—	0.45	0.60	2.50	4.00
1985Mo	377,423,000	—	0.30	0.50	2.00	3.00
1986Mo	43,000,000	—	1.00	2.50	4.75	7.50
1987Mo	165,000,000	—	0.60	1.25	2.25	3.00
1988Mo	433,100,000	—	0.30	0.50	2.00	2.75
1989Mo	135,630,000	—	0.35	0.65	2.00	2.75
1990Mo	248,350,000	—	0.15	0.40	1.50	2.50
1990Mo Proof; 1 known	—	**PF60** 650				
1991Mo	189,900,000	—	0.15	0.25	1.00	2.50
1992Mo	277,310,000	—	0.30	0.75	1.75	3.00

KM# 499 100 PESOS
31.10 g., 0.720 Silver, 0.72 oz. ASW **Obv.** National arms, eagle left **Rev:** Value above artistic designs and soccer ball **Mint:** Mexico City

Date	Mintage	F12	VF20	XF40	MS60	MS63
1985Mo	449,247	—	—	—	—	30.00

KM# 499a 100 PESOS
32.63 g., 0.925 Silver, 0.96 oz. ASW **Obv.** National arms, eagle left **Rev:** Without fineness statement **Mint:** Mexico City

Date	Mintage	F12	VF20	XF40	MS60	MS63
1985Mo	26,964	PF60 55.00				

KM# 505 100 PESOS
32.63 g., 0.925 Silver, 0.96 oz. ASW 38mm. **Obv.** National arms, eagle left **Rev:** Without fineness statement **Mint:** Mexico City

Date	Mintage	F12	VF20	XF40	MS60	MS63
1985Mo	71,718	PF60 50.00				

KM# 521 100 PESOS
32.63 g., 0.925 Silver, 0.96 oz. ASW **Obv.** National arms, eagle left **Rev:** Without fineness statement **Mint:** Mexico City

Date	Mintage	F12	VF20	XF40	MS60	MS63
1986Mo	19,279	PF60 55.00				

KM# 524 100 PESOS
32.63 g., 0.925 Silver, 0.96 oz. ASW **Obv.** National arms, eagle left **Rev:** Without fineness statement **Mint:** Mexico City

Date	Mintage	F12	VF20	XF40	MS60	MS63
1986Mo	18,510	PF60 55.00				

KM# 537 100 PESOS
32.63 g., 0.720 Silver, 0.75 oz. ASW **Obv.** National arms, eagle left **Rev:** Monarch butterflies **Mint:** Mexico City

Date	Mintage	F12	VF20	XF40	MS60	MS63
1987Mo	28,500	PF60 65.00				

ESTADOS UNIDOS • DECIMAL COINAGE

KM# 533 100 PESOS
31.10 g., 0.999 Silver, 0.99 oz. ASW **Obv.** National arms, eagle left **Rev:** Bust facing above sprigs and dates **Mint:** Mexico City

Date	Mintage	F12	VF20	XF40	MS60	MS63
1988Mo	20,000	—	—	—	40.00	55.00

KM# 539 100 PESOS
33.63 g., 0.925 Silver, 0.99 oz. ASW **Obv.** National arms, eagle left **Rev:** Child flying kite, two others sitting and playing **Mint:** Mexico City

Date	Mintage	F12	VF20	XF40	MS60	MS63
1991Mo	11,000	PF60 50.00				

KM# 566 100 PESOS
31.10 g., 0.999 Silver, 0.99 oz. ASW **Obv.** National arms, eagle left **Rev:** Swimming vaquita porpoise **Mint:** Mexico City

Date	Mintage	F12	VF20	XF40	MS60	MS63
1992Mo	28,007	PF60 60.00				

KM# 540 100 PESOS
27.00 g., 0.925 Silver, 0.80 oz. ASW 40mm. **Obv.** National arms, eagle left within center of assorted arms **Rev:** Maps within circles flanked by pillars above sailboats **Series:** Ibero - America **Mint:** Mexico City

Date	Mintage	F12	VF20	XF40	MS60	MS63
1991Mo	30,000	PF60 85.00				
1992Mo	20,000	PF60 40.00				

KM# 509 200 PESOS
Copper-Nickel 29.5mm. **Obv.** National arms, eagle left **Rev:** Conjoined busts left **Mint:** Mexico City

Date	Mintage	F12	VF20	XF40	MS60	MS63
1985Mo	75,000,000	—	—	2.00	3.50	5.50

KM# 510 200 PESOS
Copper-Nickel 29.5mm. **Obv.** National arms, eagle left **Rev:** Conjoined heads left below building **Mint:** Mexico City

Date	Mintage	F12	VF20	XF40	MS60	MS63
1985Mo	98,590,000	—	—	2.00	4.00	6.00

KM# 525 200 PESOS
Copper-Nickel 29.5mm. **Obv.** National arms, eagle left **Rev:** Soccer players **Edge:** Reeded **Mint:** Mexico City

Date	Mintage	F12	VF20	XF40	MS60	MS63
1986Mo	50,000,000	—	—	2.50	4.00	6.00

KM# 526   200 PESOS
62.21 g., 0.999 Silver, 1.99 oz. ASW **Obv.** National arms, eagle left **Rev:** Value above 3 soccer balls **Mint:** Mexico City

Date	Mintage	F12	VF20	XF40	MS60	MS63
1986Mo	23,489	—	—	—	80.00	90.00

KM# 500.1   250 PESOS
8.64 g., 0.900 Gold, 0.25 oz. AGW **Obv.** National arms, eagle left **Rev:** Soccer ball within top 1/2 of design with value, date, and state below **Mint:** Mexico City

Date	Mintage	F12	VF20	XF40	MS60	MS63
1985Mo	54,770	—	—	—	—	475
1986Mo	—	—	—	—	—	475

KM# 500.2   250 PESOS
8.64 g., 0.900 Gold, 0.25 oz. AGW **Obv.** National arms, eagle left **Rev:** Without fineness statement **Mint:** Mexico City

Date	Mintage	F12	VF20	XF40	MS60	MS63
1985Mo	4,506	PF60 500				
1986Mo	—	PF60 500				

KM# 506.1   250 PESOS
8.64 g., 0.900 Gold, 0.25 oz. AGW **Obv.** National arms, eagle left **Rev:** Equestrian left within circle **Mint:** Mexico City

Date	Mintage	F12	VF20	XF40	MS60	MS63
1985Mo	44,595	—	—	—	—	475

KM# 506.2   250 PESOS
8.64 g., 0.900 Gold, 0.25 oz. AGW **Obv.** National arms, eagle left **Rev:** Without fineness statement **Mint:** Mexico City

Date	Mintage	F12	VF20	XF40	MS60	MS63
1985Mo	Est. Inc. above	PF60 475				

KM# 501.1   500 PESOS
17.28 g., 0.900 Gold, 0.50 oz. AGW **Obv.** National arms, eagle left **Rev:** Soccer player to right within emblem **Mint:** Mexico City

Date	Mintage	F12	VF20	XF40	MS60	MS63
1985Mo	51,776	—	—	—	—	950
1986Mo	—	—	—	—	—	950

KM# 501.2   500 PESOS
17.28 g., 0.900 Gold, 0.50 oz. AGW **Obv.** National arms, eagle left **Rev:** Without fineness statement **Mint:** Mexico City

Date	Mintage	F12	VF20	XF40	MS60	MS63
1985Mo	5,506	PF60 950				
1986Mo	—	PF60 950				

KM# 507.1   500 PESOS
17.28 g., 0.900 Gold, 0.50 oz. AGW **Obv.** National arms, eagle left **Rev:** Soccer ball within emblem flanked by value and date **Mint:** Mexico City

Date	Mintage	F12	VF20	XF40	MS60	MS63
1985Mo	6,267	—	—	—	—	950

KM# 507.2   500 PESOS
17.28 g., 0.900 Gold, 0.50 oz. AGW **Obv.** National arms, eagle left **Rev:** Without fineness statement **Mint:** Mexico City

Date	Mintage	F12	VF20	XF40	MS60	MS63
1985Mo	Inc. above	PF60 950				

KM# 511   500 PESOS
33.45 g., 0.925 Silver, 0.99 oz. ASW **Obv.** National arms, eagle left **Rev:** Conjoined heads left below building **Mint:** Mexico City

Date	Mintage	F12	VF20	XF40	MS60	MS63
1985Mo	40,002	PF60 65.00				

KM# 529 500 PESOS
12.60 g., Copper-Nickel 28.5mm. **Obv.** National arms, eagle left **Rev:** Head 1/4 right **Edge:** Reeded **Mint:** Mexico City

Date	Mintage	F12	VF20	XF40	MS60	MS63
1986Mo	20,000,000	—	—	1.00	3.25	4.00
1987Mo	180,000,000	—	—	0.75	2.25	3.00
1988Mo	230,000,000	—	—	0.50	2.25	3.00
1988Mo Proof; 2 known	—	PF60 650				
1989Mo	40,000,000	—	—	0.75	2.25	3.50
1992Mo	20,000,000	—	—	1.00	2.25	4.00

KM# 534 500 PESOS
17.28 g., 0.900 Gold, 0.50 oz. AGW **Obv.** National arms, eagle left **Rev:** Monument **Mint:** Mexico City **Note:** Similar to 5000 Pesos, KM#531.

Date	Mintage	F12	VF20	XF40	MS60	MS63
1988Mo	611	—	—	—	—	950

KM# 513 1000 PESOS
17.28 g., 0.900 Gold, 0.50 oz. AGW **Obv.** National arms, eagle left **Rev:** Conjoined heads left below value **Mint:** Mexico City

Date	Mintage	F12	VF20	XF40	MS60	MS63
1985Mo	3,721	PF60 950				

KM# 527 1000 PESOS
31.11 g., 0.999 Gold, 0.99 oz. AGW **Obv.** National arms, eagle left **Rev:** Value above soccer ball and two hemispheres **Mint:** Mexico City

Date	Mintage	F12	VF20	XF40	MS60	MS63
1986Mo	1,279	—	—	—	—	2,000

KM# 535 1000 PESOS
34.56 g., 0.900 Gold, 0.99 oz. AGW **Obv.** National arms, eagle left **Rev:** Portrait of Cardenas **Mint:** Mexico City **Note:** Similar to 5000 Pesos, KM#531.

Date	Mintage	F12	VF20	XF40	MS60	MS63
1988Mo	657	PF60 2,000				

KM# 536 1000 PESOS
15.00 g., Aluminum-Bronze 30.5mm. **Obv.** National arms, eagle left **Rev:** Bust 1/4 left with diagonal value at left **Edge:** Reeded **Mint:** Mexico City

Date	Mintage	F12	VF20	XF40	MS60	MS63
1988Mo	229,300,000	—	0.85	2.00	4.25	5.75
1989Mo	215,716,000	—	0.85	2.00	4.25	5.75
1990Mo	41,291,000	—	0.85	2.00	4.00	5.50
1990Mo Proof; 2 known	—	PF60 550				
1991Mo	42,468,000	—	1.00	2.00	3.00	7.00
1992Mo	84,725,000	—	1.00	2.00	3.50	7.50

KM# 528 2000 PESOS
62.20 g., 0.999 Gold, 1.98 oz. AGW **Obv.** National arms, eagle left **Rev:** Value above soccer ball and two hemispheres **Mint:** Mexico City

Date	Mintage	F12	VF20	XF40	MS60	MS63
1986Mo	964	—	—	—	—	4,000

KM# 531 5000 PESOS
Copper-Nickel 33.5mm. **Obv.** National arms, eagle left **Rev:** Monument above dates with diagonal value at left **Mint:** Mexico City

Date	Mintage	F12	VF20	XF40	MS60	MS63
ND(1988)Mo	50,000,000	—	—	4.75	7.75	10.00

REFORM COINAGE
1 NEW PESO = 1000 OLD PESOS

KM# 546 5 CENTAVOS
1.58 g., Stainless Steel 15.5mm. **Obv.** National arms **Rev:** Large value **Edge:** Plain **Mint:** Mexico City

Date	Mintage	F12	VF20	XF40	MS60	MS63
1992Mo	136,800,000	—	—	0.15	0.20	0.50
1993Mo	234,000,000	—	—	0.15	0.20	0.50
1994Mo	125,000,000	—	—	0.15	0.20	0.50
1995Mo	195,000,000	—	—	0.15	0.20	0.50
1995Mo	6,981	PF60 2.00				
1996Mo	104,831,000	—	—	0.15	0.20	0.50
1997Mo	153,675,000	—	—	0.15	0.20	0.50
1998Mo	64,417,000	—	—	0.15	0.20	0.50
1999Mo	9,949,000	—	—	0.20	0.75	1.00
2000Mo	10,871,000	—	—	0.20	0.75	1.00
2001Mo	34,811,000	—	—	0.15	0.20	0.50
2002Mo	14,901,000	—	—	0.20	0.75	1.00

KM# 547 10 CENTAVOS
2.08 g., Stainless Steel 17mm. **Obv.** National arms, eagle left **Rev:** Large value **Mint:** Mexico City

Date	Mintage	F12	VF20	XF40	MS60	MS63
1992Mo	121,250,000	—	—	0.20	0.25	0.60
1993Mo	755,000,000	—	—	0.20	0.25	0.60
1994Mo	557,000,000	—	—	0.20	0.25	0.60
1995Mo	560,000,000	—	—	0.20	0.25	0.60
1995Mo	6,981	PF60 2.00				
1996Mo	594,216,000	—	—	0.20	0.25	0.60
1997Mo	581,622,000	—	—	0.20	0.25	0.60
1998Mo	602,667,000	—	—	0.20	0.25	0.60
1999Mo	488,346,000	—	—	0.20	0.25	0.60
2000Mo	577,546,000	—	—	0.20	0.30	0.75
2001Mo	618,061,000	—	—	0.20	0.25	0.30
2002Mo	463,968,000	—	—	0.20	0.25	0.30
2003Mo	378,938,000	—	—	0.20	0.25	0.30
2004Mo	393,705,000	—	—	0.20	0.25	0.30
2005Mo	488,594,000	—	—	0.20	0.25	0.30
2006Mo	473,261,000	—	—	0.20	0.25	0.30
2007Mo	498,735,000	—	—	0.20	0.25	0.30
2008Mo	433,951,000	—	—	0.20	0.25	0.30
2009Mo	90,968,000	—	—	0.20	0.25	0.30

KM# 548 20 CENTAVOS
3.04 g., Aluminum-Bronze 19.5mm. **Obv.** National arms, eagle left **Rev:** Value and date within 3/4 wreath **Shape:** 12-sided **Mint:** Mexico City

Date	Mintage	F12	VF20	XF40	MS60	MS63
1992Mo	95,000,000	—	—	0.25	0.35	1.00
1993Mo	95,000,000	—	—	0.25	0.35	1.00
1994Mo	105,000,000	—	—	0.25	0.35	11.00
1995Mo	180,000,000	—	—	0.25	0.35	1.00
1995Mo	6,981	PF60 3.00				
1996Mo	54,896,000	—	—	0.25	0.35	1.00
1997Mo	178,807,000	—	—	0.25	0.35	1.00

Date	Mintage	F12	VF20	XF40	MS60	MS63
1998Mo	223,847,000	—	—	0.25	0.35	1.00
1999Mo	233,753,000	—	—	0.25	0.35	1.00
2000Mo	223,973,000	—	—	0.25	0.35	1.00
2001Mo	234,360,000	—	—	0.25	0.35	0.40
2002Mo	229,256,000	—	—	0.25	0.35	0.40
2003Mo	149,518,000	—	—	0.25	0.35	0.40
2004Mo	174,351,000	—	—	0.25	0.35	0.40
2005Mo	204,426,000	—	—	0.25	0.35	0.40
2006Mo	234,263,000	—	—	0.25	0.35	0.40
2007Mo	234,301,000	—	—	0.25	0.35	0.40
2008Mo	214,313,000	—	—	0.25	0.35	0.40
2009Mo	41,167,000	—	—	0.25	0.35	0.40

KM# 549 50 CENTAVOS
4.39 g., Aluminum-Bronze 22mm. **Obv.** National arms, eagle left **Rev:** Value and date within 1/2 designed wreath **Shape:** 12-sided **Mint:** Mexico City

Date	Mintage	F12	VF20	XF40	MS60	MS63
1992Mo	120,150,000	—	—	0.45	0.85	1.75
1993Mo	330,000,000	—	—	0.45	0.75	1.50
1994Mo	100,000,000	—	—	0.45	0.75	1.50
1995Mo	60,000,000	—	—	0.45	0.75	1.50
1995Mo	6,981	PF60 5.00				
1996Mo	69,956,000	—	—	0.45	0.75	1.50
1997Mo	129,029,000	—	—	0.45	0.75	1.50
1998Mo	223,605,000	—	—	0.45	0.75	1.50
1999Mo	89,516,000	—	—	0.45	0.75	1.50
2000Mo	135,112,000	—	—	0.45	0.75	1.50
2001Mo	199,006,000	—	—	0.45	0.75	1.00
2002Mo	94,552,000	—	—	0.45	0.75	1.00
2003Mo	124,522,000	—	—	0.45	0.75	1.00
2004Mo	154,434,000	—	—	0.45	0.75	1.00
2005Mo	179,296,000	—	—	0.45	0.75	1.00
2006Mo	234,142,000	—	—	0.45	0.75	1.00
2007Mo	253,634,000	—	—	0.45	0.75	1.00
2008Mo	249,279,000	—	—	0.45	0.75	1.00
2009Mo	90,602,000	—	—	0.45	0.75	1.00

KM# 550 NUEVOS PESO
3.95 g., Bi-Metallic Aluminum-Bronze center in Stainless Steel ring, 21mm. **Obv.** National arms, eagle left **Rev:** Value

Date	Mintage	F12	VF20	XF40	MS60	MS63
1992Mo	144,000,000	—	—	0.60	1.50	2.75
1993Mo	329,860,000	—	—	0.60	1.50	2.75
1994Mo	221,000,000	—	—	0.60	1.50	2.75
1995Mo	125,000,000	—	—	0.60	1.50	2.75
Small date						
1995Mo	Inc. above	—	—	0.60	1.50	2.75
Large date						
1995Mo	6,981	PF60 6.00				

KM# 603   PESO

3.95 g., Bi-Metallic Aluminum-Bronze center in Stainless Steel ring, 21mm. **Obv.** National arms, eagle left within circle **Rev:** Value and date within circle **Note:** Similar to KM#550 but without N.

Date	Mintage	F12	VF20	XF40	MS60	MS63
1996Mo	169,510,000	—	—	—	1.25	2.25
1997Mo	222,870,000	—	—	—	1.25	2.25
1998Mo	261,942,000	—	—	—	1.25	2.25
1999Mo	99,168,000	—	—	—	1.25	2.25
2000Mo	158,379,000	—	—	—	1.25	2.25
2001Mo	208,576,000	—	—	—	1.25	2.75
2002Mo	119,514,000	—	—	—	1.25	2.75
2003Mo	169,320,000	—	—	—	1.25	2.75
2004Mo	208,611,000	—	—	—	1.25	2.75
2005Mo	253,923,000	—	—	—	1.25	2.75
2006Mo	289,834,000	—	—	—	1.25	2.75
2007Mo	368,408,000	—	—	—	1.25	2.75
2008Mo	363,878,000	—	—	—	1.25	2.75
2009Mo	239,229,000	—	—	—	1.25	2.75
2010Mo	209,313,000	—	—	—	0.75	1.25
2011Mo	199,283,000	—	—	—	0.75	1.00
2012Mo	383,908,000	—	—	—	0.75	1.00
2013Mo	Est. 265000000	—	—	—	0.75	1.00

KM# 551   2 NUEVOS PESOS

5.19 g., Bi-Metallic Aluminum-Bronze center in Stainless Steel ring, 23mm. **Obv.** National arms, eagle left within circle **Rev:** Value and date within circle with assorted emblems around border

Date	Mintage	F12	VF20	XF40	MS60	MS63
1992Mo	60,000,000	—	—	1.00	2.50	4.00
1993Mo	77,000,000	—	—	1.00	2.50	4.00
1994Mo	44,000,000	—	—	1.00	2.50	4.00
1995Mo	20,000,000	—	—	1.00	2.50	4.00
1995Mo	6,981	PF60 6.00				

KM# 604   2 PESOS

5.19 g., Bi-Metallic Aluminum-Bronze center in Stainless Steel ring, 23mm. **Obv.** National arms, eagle left within circle **Rev:** Value and date within center circle of assorted emblems **Note:** Similar to KM#551, but denomination without N.

Date	Mintage	F12	VF20	XF40	MS60	MS63
1996Mo	24,902,000	—	—	—	2.50	4.00
1997Mo	34,560,000	—	—	—	2.50	4.00
1998Mo	104,138,000	—	—	—	2.50	4.00
1999Mo	34,713,000	—	—	—	2.50	4.00
2000Mo	69,322,000	—	—	—	2.50	4.00
2001Mo	74,563,000	—	—	—	2.35	4.00
2002Mo	74,547,000	—	—	—	2.35	4.00
2003Mo	39,814,000	—	—	—	2.35	4.00
2004Mo	89,496,000	—	—	—	2.35	4.00
2005Mo	94,532,000	—	—	—	2.35	4.00
2006Mo	144,123,000	—	—	—	2.35	4.00
2007Mo	129,422,000	—	—	—	2.35	4.00
2008Mo	134,235,000	—	—	—	2.35	4.00
2009Mo	64,650,000	—	—	—	2.35	4.00
2010Mo	34,878,000	—	—	—	1.00	1.50

Date	Mintage	F12	VF20	XF40	MS60	MS63
2011Mo	114,522,000	—	—	—	1.00	1.50
2012Mo	134,445,000	—	—	—	1.00	1.25
2013Mo	Est. 105,000,000	—	—	—	1.00	1.25

KM# 552   5 NUEVOS PESOS

7.07 g., Bi-Metallic Aluminum-Bronze center in Stainless Steel ring, 25.5mm. **Obv.** National arms, eagle left within circle **Rev:** Value and date within circle with bow below

Date	Mintage	F12	VF20	XF40	MS60	MS63
1992Mo	70,000,000	—	—	2.00	6.00	8.50
1993Mo	168,240,000	—	—	2.00	6.00	8.50
1994Mo	58,000,000	—	—	2.00	6.00	8.50
1995Mo	6,981	PF60 25.00				

KM# 588   5 NUEVOS PESOS

27.00 g., 0.925 Silver, 0.80 oz. ASW **Subject:** Environmental Protection **Obv.** National arms, eagle left within center of past and present arms **Rev:** Pacific Ridley Sea Turtle **Series:** Ibero-America

Date	Mintage	F12	VF20	XF40	MS60	MS63
1994Mo	11,005	PF60 50.00				

KM# 605   5 PESOS

7.07 g., Bi-Metallic Aluminum-Bronze center in Stainless Steel ring, 25.5mm. **Obv.** National arms, eagle left within circle **Rev:** Value within circle **Note:** Similar to KM#552 but denomination without N.

Date	Mintage	F12	VF20	XF40	MS60	MS63
1997Mo	39,468,000	—	—	2.00	4.00	7.00
1998Mo	103,729,000	—	—	2.00	4.00	7.00
1999Mo	59,427,000	—	—	2.00	4.00	7.00
2000Mo	20,869,000	—	—	2.00	4.50	7.00
2001Mo	79,169,000	—	—	2.00	3.50	8.00
2002Mo	34,754,000	—	—	2.00	3.50	6.00
2003Mo	54,676,000	—	—	2.00	3.50	6.00
2004Mo	89,518,000	—	—	2.00	3.50	6.00
2005Mo	94,482,000	—	—	2.00	3.50	6.00
2006Mo	89,447,000	—	—	2.00	3.50	6.00
2007Mo	123,382,000	—	—	2.00	3.50	6.00
2008Mo	9,939,000	—	—	2.50	4.00	6.00

Date	Mintage	F12	VF20	XF40	MS60	MS63
2009Mo	9,898,000	—	—	2.50	4.00	6.00
2010Mo	6,929,000	—	—	2.50	3.00	3.50
2011Mo	209,214,000	—	—	1.00	2.00	2.50
2012Mo	159,398,000	—	—	—	2.00	2.50
2013Mo Est.	130,000,000	—	—	—	2.00	2.50

KM# 627 5 PESOS

31.10 g., 0.999 Silver, 0.99 oz. ASW **Subject:** World Wildlife Fund **Obv.** National arms, eagle left **Rev:** Wolf with pup

Date	Mintage	F12	VF20	XF40	MS60	MS63
1997Mo	—	—	—	—	—	—
1998Mo	13,004	PF60 95.00				

KM# 629 5 PESOS

27.00 g., 0.925 Silver, 0.80 oz. ASW 40mm. **Subject:** Jarabe Tapatio **Obv.** National arms, eagle left within center of assorted arms **Rev:** Mexican dancers **Series:** Ibero-America

Date	Mintage	F12	VF20	XF40	MS60	MS63
1997Mo	8,011	PF60 350				
1998Mo	3,000	PF60 350				

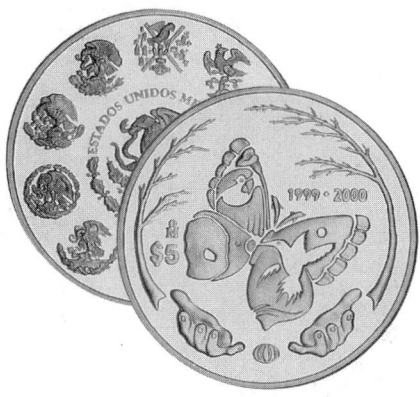

KM# 630 5 PESOS

31.18 g., 0.999 Silver, 1.00 oz. ASW **Subject:** Millennium Series **Obv.** National arms, eagle left within center of past and present arms **Rev:** Butterfly flanked by sprigs above hands **Rev. Designer:** Francisco Ortega Romero

Date	Mintage	F12	VF20	XF40	MS60	MS63
1999-2000 Mo	47,435	PF60 60.00				

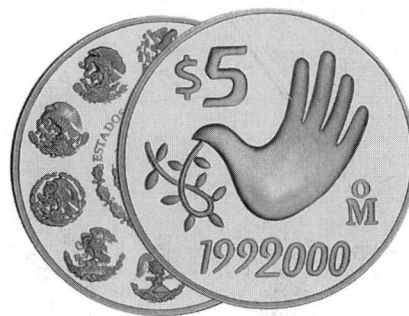

KM# 631 5 PESOS

31.18 g., 0.999 Silver, 1.00 oz. ASW **Subject:** Millennium Series **Obv.** National arms, eagle left within center of past and present arms **Rev:** Stylized dove as hand of peace **Rev. Designer:** Omar Jiminez Torres

Date	Mintage	F12	VF20	XF40	MS60	MS63
1999-2000 Mo	47,389	PF60 55.00				

KM# 632 5 PESOS

31.18 g., 0.999 Silver, 1.00 oz. ASW **Subject:** Millennium Series **Obv.** National arms, eagle left within center of past and present arms **Rev:** Aztec bird design and value eagle left within center of past and present arms **Rev:** Aztec bird design and value

Date	Mintage	F12	VF20	XF40	MS60	MS63
1999-2000 Mo	48,080	PF60 55.00				

KM# 635   5 PESOS
19.60 g., 0.925 Silver, 0.58 oz. ASW **Subject:** Millennium
Series **Obv.** National arms, eagle left **Rev:** Naval training
ship Cuauhtemoc sailing into world globe

Date	Mintage	F12	VF20	XF40	MS60	MS63
1999Mo	15,504	**PF60** 45.00				

KM# 640   5 PESOS
31.10 g., 0.999 Silver, 0.99 oz. ASW 40mm. **Subject:**
UNICEF **Obv.** National arms, eagle left **Rev:** Two children
flying kite **Edge:** Reeded **Mint:** Mexico City

Date	Mintage	F12	VF20	XF40	MS60	MS63
1999Mo	4,010	**PF60** 60.00				

KM# 652   5 PESOS
31.10 g., 0.999 Silver, 0.99 oz. ASW 40mm. **Obv.** National
arms, eagle left within center of past and present arms
Rev: Golden Eagle on branch, value and date **Series:**
Endangered Wildlife

Date	Mintage	F12	VF20	XF40	MS60	MS63
2000Mo	30,000	—	—	—	45.00	—

KM# 655   5 PESOS
31.10 g., 0.999 Silver, 0.99 oz. ASW 40mm. **Obv.** National
arms, eagle left within center of past and present arms **Rev:**
American Crocodile, value and date **Series:** Endangered
Wildlife

Date	Mintage	F12	VF20	XF40	MS60	MS63
2000Mo	30,000	—	—	—	45.00	55.00

KM# 656   5 PESOS
31.10 g., 0.999 Silver, 0.99 oz. ASW 40mm. **Obv.** National
arms, eagle left within center of past and present arms **Rev:**
Neotropical River Otter, value and date **Series:** Endangered
Wildlife

Date	Mintage	F12	VF20	XF40	MS60	MS63
2000Mo	30,000	—	—	—	45.00	55.00

KM# 670   5 PESOS
27.00 g., 0.925 Silver, 0.80 oz. ASW 40mm. **Obv.** National
arms, eagle left within center of past and present arms **Rev:**
Cowboy trick riding two horses **Series:** Ibero-American
Edge: Reeded **Mint:** Mexico City

Date	Mintage	F12	VF20	XF40	MS60	MS63
2000Mo	9,000	**PF60** 85.00				

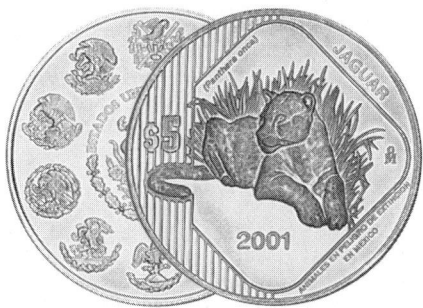

KM# 653   5 PESOS

31.10 g., 0.999 Silver, 0.99 oz. ASW 40mm. **Obv.** National arms in center of past and present arms **Rev:** Crowned Harpy Eagle perched on branch, value and date **Series:** Endangered Wildlife

Date	Mintage	F12	VF20	XF40	MS60	MS63
2001Mo	30,000	—	—	—	45.00	—

KM# 658   5 PESOS

31.10 g., 0.999 Silver, 0.99 oz. ASW 40mm. **Obv.** National arms in center of past and present arms **Rev:** Jaguar, value and date **Series:** Endangered Wildlife - Jaguar

Date	Mintage	F12	VF20	XF40	MS60	MS63
2001Mo	30,000	—	—	—	45.00	—

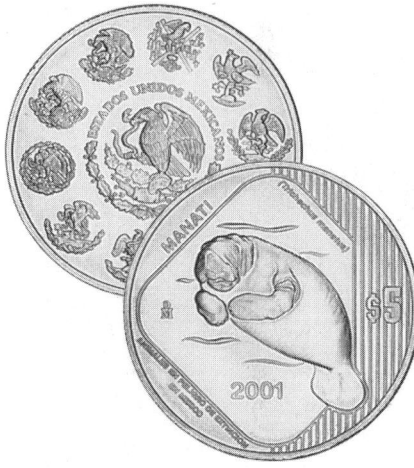

KM# 654   5 PESOS

31.10 g., 0.999 Silver, 0.99 oz. ASW 40mm. **Obv.** National arms in center of past and present arms **Rev:** Black bear, value and date **Series:** Endangered Wildlife

Date	Mintage	F12	VF20	XF40	MS60	MS63
2001Mo	30,000	—	—	—	45.00	—

KM# 651   5 PESOS

31.10 g., 0.999 Silver, 0.99 oz. ASW 40mm. **Obv.** National arms in center of past and present arms **Rev:** Manatee, value and date **Series:** Endangered Wildlife - Manatee **Edge:** Reeded **Mint:** Mexico City

Date	Mintage	F12	VF20	XF40	MS60	MS63
2001Mo	30,000	—	—	—	45.00	—

KM# 657   5 PESOS

31.10 g., 0.999 Silver, 0.99 oz. ASW 40mm. **Obv.** National arms, eagle left within center of past and present arms **Rev:** Peninsular Pronghorn, giant cardon cactus in back, value and date **Series:** Endangered Wildlife - American Antelope

Date	Mintage	F12	VF20	XF40	MS60	MS63
2000Mo	30,000	—	—	—	45.00	—

KM# 659   5 PESOS

31.10 g., 0.999 Silver, 0.99 oz. ASW 40mm. **Obv.** National arms in center of past and present arms **Rev:** Prairie dog, value and date **Series:** Endangered Wildlife - Prairie Dog

Date	Mintage	F12	VF20	XF40	MS60	MS63
2001Mo	30,000	—	—	—	45.00	—

KM# 660 5 PESOS
31.10 g., 0.999 Silver, 0.99 oz. ASW 40mm. **Obv.** National arms in center of past and present arms **Rev:** Volcano rabbit, value and date **Series:** Endangered Wildlife - Volcano Rabbit

Date	Mintage	F12	VF20	XF40	MS60	MS63
2001Mo	30,000	—	—	—	45.00	—

KM# 678 5 PESOS
27.00 g., 0.925 Silver, 0.80 oz. ASW 40mm. **Obv.** National arms in center of past and present arms **Rev:** Spanish galleon with Pacific Ocean background and trading scene in foreground **Series:** Ibero-America **Edge:** Reeded **Mint:** Mexico City

Date	Mintage	F12	VF20	XF40	MS60	MS63
2003Mo	17,015	**PF63** 60.00				

KM# 894 5 PESOS
7.07 g., Bi-Metallic Aluminum-bronze center in stainless steel ring, 25.5mm. **Subject:** Ignacio Rayon **Obv.** National Arms - Eagle left **Rev:** Ignacio Rayon bust left **Series:** Mexican Independence, 200th Anniversary

Date	Mintage	VF20	XF40	MS60	MS63
2008Mo	9,934,397	—	0.75	1.50	—
2008Mo Prooflike	4,267	—	—	—	7.50

KM# 895 5 PESOS
7.07 g., Bi-Metallic Aluminum-bronze center in stainless steel ring, 25.5mm. **Subject:** Alvaro Obregon **Obv.** National Arms - Eagle left **Rev:** Alvaro Obregon bust 3/4 facing left **Series:** Mexican Revolution 100th Anniversary

Date	Mintage	VF20	XF40	MS60	MS63
2008Mo	9,948,722	—	0.75	1.50	—
2008Mo Prooflike	4,727	—	—	—	7.50

KM# 896 5 PESOS
7.07 g., Bi-Metallic Aluninum-bronze center in stainless steel ring, 25.5mm. **Subject:** Carlos Maria de Bustamante **Obv.** National Arms - Eagle left **Rev:** Carlos Maria de Bustamante bust left **Series:** Mexican Independence 200th Anniversary

Date	Mintage	VF20	XF40	MS60	MS63
2008Mo	9,941,302	—	0.75	1.50	—
2008Mo Prooflike	4,852	—	—	—	7.50

KM# 897 5 PESOS
7.07 g., Bi-Metallic Aluminum-bronze center in stainless steel ring, 25.5mm. **Subject:** Jose Vasconcelos **Obv.** National Arms - Eagle left **Rev:** Jose Vasconcelos bust left **Series:** Mexican Revolution 100th Anniversary

Date	Mintage	VF20	XF40	MS60	MS63
2008Mo	9,939,839	—	0.75	1.50	—
2008Mo Prooflike	4,767	—	—	—	7.50

KM# 898 5 PESOS
7.07 g., Bi-Metallic Aluminum-bronze center in stainless steel ring, 25.5mm. **Subject:** Francisco Xavier Mina **Obv.** National Arms - Eagle left **Rev:** Francisco Mina bust 3/4 facing left **Series:** Mexican Independence 200th Anniversary

Date	Mintage	VF20	XF40	MS60	MS63
2008Mo	9,914,938	—	0.75	1.50	—
2008Mo Prooflike	4,523	—	—	—	7.50

KM# 899 5 PESOS
7.07 g., Bi-Metallic Aluminum-bronze center in stainless steel ring, 25.5mm. **Subject:** Francisco Villa **Obv.** National Arms - Eagle left **Rev:** Francisco Villa on horseback left **Series:** Mexican Revolution 100th Anniversary

Date	Mintage	VF20	XF40	MS60	MS63
2008Mo	9,917,084	—	0.75	1.50	—
2008Mo Prooflike	4,866	—	—	—	7.50

KM# 900.1 5 PESOS
7.07 g., Bi-Metallic Aluminum-Bronze center in Stainless Steel ring, 25.5mm. **Subject:** Francisco Primo de Verdad y Ramos **Obv.** National Arms - Eagle left **Rev:** Francisco Primode Verdad y Ramos bust right **Series:** Mexican Independence 200th Anniversary **Note:** Pellets at 4 and 7 o'clock in legend.

Date	Mintage	VF20	XF40	MS60	MS63
2008Mo	9,937,000	—	0.75	1.50	—
2008Mo Prooflike	4,279	—	—	—	7.50

KM# 901 5 PESOS
7.07 g., Bi-Metallic Aluminum-Bronze center in Stainless Steel ring, 25.5mm. **Subject:** Heriberto Jara **Obv.** National Arms - Eagle left **Rev:** Heriberto Jara bust 3/4 left **Series:** Mexican Revolution 100th Anniversary

Date	Mintage	VF20	XF40	MS60	MS63
2008Mo	9,936,333	—	0.75	1.50	—
2008Mo Prooflike	4,870	—	—	—	7.50

KM# 902 5 PESOS
7.07 g., Bi-Metallic Aluminum-Bronze center in Stainless Steel ring, 25.5mm. **Subject:** Mariano Matamoros **Obv.** National Arms - Eagle left **Rev:** Mariano Matamoros bust 3/4 facing right **Series:** Mexican Independence 200th Anniversary

Date	Mintage	VF20	XF40	MS60	MS63
2008Mo	9,947,802	—	0.75	1.50	—
2008Mo Prooflike	4,820	—	—	—	7.50

KM# 903 5 PESOS
7.07 g., Bi-Metallic Aluminum-Bronze center in Stainless Steel ring, 25.5mm. **Subject:** Ricardo Magon **Obv.** National Arms - Eagle left **Rev:** Ricardo Magon bust right **Series:** Mexican Revolution 100th Anniversary

Date	Mintage	VF20	XF40	MS60	MS63
2008Mo	9,940,278	—	0.75	1.50	—
2008Mo Prooflike	4,690	—	—	—	7.50

KM# 904 5 PESOS
7.07 g., Bi-Metallic Aluminum-Bronze center in Stainless Steel ring, 25.5mm. **Subject:** Miguel Ramos Arizpe **Obv.** National Arms - Eagle left **Rev:** Miguel Ramos Arizpe bust right **Series:** Mexican Independence 200th Anniversary

Date	Mintage	VF20	XF40	MS60	MS63
2008Mo	9,927,433	—	0.75	1.50	—
2008Mo Prooflike	4,863	—	—	—	7.50

KM# 905 5 PESOS
7.07 g., Bi-Metallic Aluminum-Bronze center in Stainless Steel ring, 25.5mm. **Subject:** Francisco J. Mugica **Obv.** National arms, eagle left **Rev:** Francisco J. Mugica bust 3/4 facing left **Series:** Mexican Revolution 100th Anniversary

Date	Mintage	VF20	XF40	MS60	MS63
2008Mo	9,926,537	—	0.75	1.50	—
2008Mo Prooflike	4,588	—	—	—	7.50

KM# 906 5 PESOS
7.07 g., Bi-Metallic Aluminum-Bronze center in Stainless Steel ring, 25.5mm. **Subject:** Hermenegildo Galeana **Obv.** National Arms, eagle left **Rev:** Hermenegildo Galeana bust 3/4 facing left **Series:** Mexican Independence 200th Anniversary

Date	Mintage	VF20	XF40	MS60	MS63
2008Mo	9,935,901	—	0.75	1.50	—
2008Mo Prooflike	4,966	—	—	—	7.50

KM# 907 5 PESOS
7.07 g., Bi-Metallic Aluminum-Bronze center in Stainless Steel ring, 25.5mm. **Subject:** Filomeno Mata **Obv.** National arms, eagle left **Rev:** Filomeno Mata bust facing left **Series:** Mexican Revolution, 100th Anniversary

Date	Mintage	VF20	XF40	MS60	MS63
2009Mo	9,935,689	—	0.75	1.50	—
2009Mo Prooflike	4,920	—	—	—	7.50

KM# 911 5 PESOS
7.07 g., Bi-Metallic Aluminum-Bronze center in Stainless Steel ring, 25.5mm. **Subject:** Andres Molina Enriquez **Obv.** National arms, eagle left **Rev:** Andres Molina Enriquez, bust 3/4 right **Series:** Mexican Revolution 100th Anniversary

Date	Mintage	VF20	XF40	MS60	MS63
2009Mo	6,942,763	—	0.75	1.50	—
2009Mo Prooflike	4,666	—	—	—	7.50

KM# 908 5 PESOS
7.07 g., Bi-Metallic Aluminum-Bronze cetner in Stainless Steel ring, 25.5mm. **Subject:** Jose Maria Cos **Obv.** National arms, eagle left. **Rev:** Jose Maria Cos bust right **Series:** Mexican Independence 200th Anniversary

Date	Mintage	VF20	XF40	MS60	MS63
2009Mo	9,935,040	—	0.75	1.50	—
2009Mo Prooflike	4,950	—	—	—	7.50

KM# 912 5 PESOS
7.07 g., Bi-Metallic Aluminum-Bronze center in Stainless Steel ring, 25.5mm. **Subject:** Agustin de Iturbide **Obv.** National arms, eagle left. **Rev:** Agustin de Iturbide bust left **Series:** Mexican Independence, 200th Anniversary

Date	Mintage	VF20	XF40	MS60	MS63
2009Mo	6,944,222	—	0.75	1.50	—
2009Mo Prooflike	4,838	—	—	—	7.50

KM# 909 5 PESOS
7.07 g., Bi-Metallic Aluminum-Bronze center in Stainless Steel ring, 25.5mm. **Subject:** Carmen Serdan **Obv.** National Amrs, Eagle left **Rev:** Carmen Serdan bust facing slightly right **Series:** Mexican Revolution 100th Anniversary

Date	Mintage	VF20	XF40	MS60	MS63
2009Mo	7,160,841	—	0.75	1.50	—
2009Mo Prooflike	4,787	—	—	—	7.50

KM# 913 5 PESOS
7.07 g., Bi-Metallic Aluminumn-Bronze center in Stainless Steel ring, 25.5mm. **Subject:** Luis Cabrera **Obv.** National Arms, eagle left **Rev:** Luis Cabrera bust 3/4 facing left **Series:** Mexican Revolution 100th Anniversary

Date	Mintage	VF20	XF40	MS60	MS63
2009Mo	6,902,593	—	0.75	1.50	—
2009Mo Prooflike	4,656	—	—	—	7.50

KM# 910 5 PESOS
7.07 g., Bi-Metallic Aluminum-Bronze center in Stainless Steel ring, 25.5mm. **Subject:** Pedro Moreno **Obv.** National arms, eagle left **Rev:** Pedro Moreno bust 3/4 right **Series:** Mexican Independence, 200th Anniversary

Date	Mintage	VF20	XF40	MS60	MS63
2009Mo	6,942,480	—	0.75	1.50	—
2009Mo Prooflike	4,940	—	—	—	7.50

KM# 914 5 PESOS
7.07 g., Bi-Metallic Aluminum-Bronze center Stainless Steel ring, 25.5mm. **Subject:** Nicolas Bravo **Obv.** National Arms, Eagle left **Rev:** Nicolas Bravo bust 3/4 facing left **Series:** Mexican Independence 200th Anniversary

Date	Mintage	VF20	XF40	MS60	MS63
2009Mo	6,930,174	—	0.75	0.50	—
2009Mo Prooflike	4,780	—	—	—	7.50

KM# 915 5 PESOS
7.07 g., Bi-Metallic Aluminum-bronze center in Stainless steel ring, 25.5mm. **Subject:** Eulalio Gutierrez **Obv.** National Arms, eagle left **Rev:** Eulalio Gutierrez bust 3/4 right **Series:** Mexican Revolution 100th Anniversary

Date	Mintage	VF20	XF40	MS60	MS63
2009Mo	6,908,760	—	0.75	1.50	—
2009Mo Prooflike	4,862	—	—	—	7.50

KM# 919 5 PESOS
7.07 g., Bi-Metallic Aluminum-Bronze center in Stainless Steel ring, 25.5mm. **Subject:** Leona Vicario **Obv.** National Arms, eagle left **Rev:** Leona Vicario bust left **Series:** Mexican Independence 200th Anniversary

Date	Mintage	VF20	XF40	MS60	MS63
2009Mo	6,937,872	—	0.75	1.50	—
2009Mo Prooflike	4,730	—	—	—	7.50

KM# 916 5 PESOS
7.07 g., Bi-Metallic Aluminum-Bronze center in Stainless Steel ring, 25.5mm. **Subject:** Servando Teresa de Mier **Obv.** National Arms, eagle left **Rev:** Servando Teresa de Mier bust left **Series:** Mexican Independence 200th Anniversary

Date	Mintage	VF20	XF40	MS60	MS63
2009Mo	6,937,421	—	0.75	1.50	—
2009Mo Prooflike	4,675	—	—	—	7.50

KM# 920 5 PESOS
7.07 g., Bi-Metallic Aluminum-Bronze center in Stainless Steel ring, 25.5mm. **Subject:** Miguel Hidalgo y Costilla **Obv.** National Arms, eagle left **Rev:** Miguel Hidalgo y Costilla bust **Series:** Mexican Independence 200th Anniversary

Date	Mintage	VF20	XF40	MS60	MS63
2010Mo	6,932,486	—	0.75	1.50	—
2010Mo Prooflike	4,763	—	—	—	7.50

KM# 962 5 PESOS
27.00 g., 0.925 Silver, 0.80 oz. ASW 40mm. **Obv.** National arms within circle of other national arms **Rev:** Horse Peso **Mint:** Mexico City

Date	Mintage	F12	VF20	XF40	MS60	MS63
2011Mo	8,000	PF63 80.00				

KM# 553 10 NUEVOS PESOS
11.18 g., Bi-Metallic 0.925 Silver center, .1667 oz. ASW within Aluminum-Bronze ring, 28mm. **Obv.** National arms **Rev:** Assorted shields within circle **Obv. Legend:** Estados Unidos Mexicanos **Edge:** Groved

Date	Mintage	F12	VF20	XF40	MS60	MS63
1992Mo	20,000,000	—	—	7.00	10.00	14.00
1993Mo	47,981,000	—	—	7.00	10.00	14.00
1994Mo	15,000,000	—	—	7.00	10.00	14.00
1995Mo	6,981	PF60 20.00				
1995Mo	15,000,000	—	—	7.00	10.00	14.00

KM# 917 5 PESOS
7.07 g., Bi-Metallic Aluminum-Bronze center in Stainless Steel ring, 25.5mm. **Subject:** Otilio Montano **Obv.** National Arms, eagle left **Rev:** Otilio Montano bust left **Series:** Mexican Revolution 100th Anniversary

Date	Mintage	VF20	XF40	MS60	MS63
2009Mo	6,890,052	—	0.75	1.50	—
2009Mo Prooflike	4,923	—	—	—	7.50

KM# 616 10 PESOS
10.33 g., Bi-Metallic Copper-Nickel-Zinc center in Aluminum-Bronze ring, 28mm. **Obv.** National arms **Rev:** Aztec design of Tonatiuh with the Fire Mask **Obv. Legend:** ESTADOS UNIDOS MEXICANOS

Date	Mintage	F12	VF20	XF40	MS60	MS63
1997Mo	44,837,000	—	—	2.50	4.00	8.00
1998Mo	203,735,000	—	—	2.50	4.00	8.00
1999Mo	29,842,000	—	—	2.50	4.00	8.00
2002Mo	44,721,000	—	—	2.50	4.00	8.00

KM# 918 5 PESOS
7.07 g., Bi-Metallic Aluminum-Bronze center in Stainless Steel ring, 25.5mm. **Subject:** Belisario Dominguez **Obv.** National Arms, eagle left **Rev:** Belisario Dominguez bust 3/4 left **Series:** Mexican Revolution 100th Anniversary

Date	Mintage	VF20	XF40	MS60	MS63
2009Mo	6,926,606	—	0.75	1.50	—
2009Mo Prooflike	4,773	—	—	—	7.50

Date	Mintage	F12	VF20	XF40	MS60	MS63
2004Mo	74,739,000	—	—	2.50	4.00	8.00
2005Mo	64,616,000	—	—	2.50	4.00	8.00
2006Mo	84,575,000	—	—	2.50	4.00	8.00
2007Mo	89,678,000	—	—	2.50	4.00	8.00
2008Mo	64,744,000	—	—	2.50	4.00	8.00
2009Mo	54,812,000	—	—	2.00	3.00	6.00
2010Mo	54,822,000	—	—	2.00	3.00	6.00
2011Mo	69,731,000	—	—	—	3.00	6.00
2012Mo	89,732,000	—	—	—	3.00	6.00
2013Mo	Est. 45,000,000	—	—	—	2.50	3.00

KM# 633   10 PESOS
62.03 g., 0.999 Silver, 1.98 oz. ASW **Obv.** National arms, eagle left within center of past and present arms **Rev:** Ancient and modern buildings within circle

Date	Mintage	F12	VF20	XF40	MS60	MS63
1999-2000 Mo	47,641	**PF60** 80.00				

KM# 636   10 PESOS
10.33 g., Bi-Metallic Copper-Nickel-Zinc center in Aluminum-Bronze ring, 28mm. **Obv.** National arms **Rev:** Aztec carving **Series:** Millennium **Obv. Legend:** ESTADOS UNIDOS MEXICANOS **Edge Lettering:** ANO (year) repeated 3 times

Date	Mintage	F12	VF20	XF40	MS60	MS63
2000Mo	24,839,000	—	—	3.50	4.50	8.50
2001Mo	44,768,000	—	—	3.00	4.00	8.00

KM# 679   10 PESOS
31.10 g., 0.999 Silver, 0.99 oz. ASW 39.9mm. **Obv.** National arms **Rev:** State Arms **Series:** First **Obv. Legend:** ESTADOS UNIDOS MEXICANOS **Rev. Legend:** ESTADO DE ZACATECAS **Edge:** Reeded **Mint:** Mexico City

Date	Mintage	F12	VF20	XF40	MS60	MS63
2003Mo	10,000	**PF63** 70.00				

KM# 680   10 PESOS
31.10 g., 0.999 Silver, 0.99 oz. ASW 39.9mm. **Obv.** National arms **Rev:** State arms **Series:** First **Obv. Legend:** ESTADO UNIDOS MEXICANOS **Rev. Legend:** ESTADO DE YUCATÁN **Edge:** Reeded **Mint:** Mexico City

Date	Mintage	F12	VF20	XF40	MS60	MS63
2003Mo	10,000	**PF63** 60.00				

KM# 681   10 PESOS
31.10 g., 0.999 Silver, 0.99 oz. ASW 39.9mm. **Obv.** National arms **Rev:** State arms **Series:** First **Obv. Legend:** ESTADOS UNIDOS MEXICANOS **Rev. Legend:** ESTADO DE VERACRUZ-LLAVE **Edge:** Reeded **Mint:** Mexico City

Date	Mintage	F12	VF20	XF40	MS60	MS63
2003Mo	10,000	**PF63** 60.00				

ESTADOS UNIDOS - REFORM COINAGE

KM# 682 10 PESOS
31.10 g., 0.999 Silver, 0.99 oz. ASW 39.9mm. **Obv.** National arms **Rev:** State arms **Series:** First **Obv. Legend:** ESTADOS UNIDOS MEXICANOS **Rev. Legend:** ESTADO DE TLAXCALA **Edge:** Reeded **Mint:** Mexico City

Date	Mintage	F12	VF20	XF40	MS60	MS63
2003Mo	10,000	**PF63** 60.00				

KM# 683 10 PESOS
31.10 g., 0.999 Silver, 0.99 oz. ASW 39.9mm. **Obv.** National arms **Rev:** State arms **Series:** First **Obv. Legend:** ESTADOS UNIDOS MEXICANOS **Rev. Legend:** ESTADO DE TAMAULIPAS **Edge:** Reeded **Mint:** Mexico City

Date	Mintage	F12	VF20	XF40	MS60	MS63
2004Mo	10,000	**PF63** 60.00				

KM# 684 10 PESOS
31.10 g., 0.999 Silver, 0.99 oz. ASW 39.9mm. **Obv.** National arms **Rev:** State arms **Series:** First **Obv. Legend:** ESTADOS UNIDOS DE MEXICANOS **Rev. Legend:** ESTADO DE TABASCO **Edge:** Reeded **Mint:** Mexico City

Date	Mintage	F12	VF20	XF40	MS60	MS63
2004Mo	10,000	**PF63** 60.00				

KM# 685 10 PESOS
31.10 g., 0.999 Silver, 0.99 oz. ASW 39.9mm. **Obv.** National arms **Rev:** State arms **Series:** First **Obv. Legend:** ESTADOS UNIDOS MEXICANOS **Rev. Legend:** ESTADO DE SONORA **Edge:** Reeded **Mint:** Mexico City **Note:** Mexican States: Sonora

Date	Mintage	F12	VF20	XF40	MS60	MS63
2004Mo	10,000	**PF63** 60.00				

KM# 686 10 PESOS
31.10 g., 0.999 Silver, 0.99 oz. ASW 39.9mm. **Obv.** National arms **Rev:** State arms **Series:** First **Obv. Legend:** ESTADOS UNIDOS DE MEXICANOS **Rev. Legend:** ESTADO DE SINALOA **Edge:** Reeded **Mint:** Mexico City **Note:** Mexican States: Sinaloa

Date	Mintage	F12	VF20	XF40	MS60	MS63
2004Mo	10,000	**PF63** 60.00				

KM# 687 10 PESOS
31.10 g., 0.999 Silver, 0.99 oz. ASW 39.9mm. **Obv.** National arms **Rev:** State arms **Series:** First **Obv. Legend:** ESTADOS UNIDOS MEXICANOS **Rev. Legend:** ESTADO DE SAN LUIS POTOSÍ **Edge:** Reeded **Mint:** Mexico City

Date	Mintage	F12	VF20	XF40	MS60	MS63
2004Mo	10,000	**PF63** 60.00				

KM# 735   10 PESOS
31.10 g.,   0.999 Silver, 0.99 oz. ASW 39.9mm.   **Obv.**
National arms **Rev:** State arms **Series:** First **Obv. Legend:**
ESTADOS UNIDOS MEXICANOS **Rev. Legend:** ESTADO
DE QUINTANA ROO

Date	Mintage	F12	VF20	XF40	MS60	MS63
2004Mo	10,000	PF63 60.00				

KM# 739   10 PESOS
31.10 g.,   0.999 Bi-Metallic, 0.99 oz. 39.9mm.   **Obv.**
National arms **Rev:** State arms **Series:** First **Obv. Legend:**
ESTADOS UNIDOS MEXICANOS **Rev. Legend:** ESTADO
DE OAXACA **Edge:** Reeded **Mint:** Mexico City

Date	Mintage	F12	VF20	XF40	MS60	MS63
2004Mo	10,000	PF63 60.00				

KM# 733   10 PESOS
31.10 g.,   0.999 Silver, 0.99 oz. ASW 39.9mm.   **Obv.**
National arms **Rev:** State arms **Series:** First **Obv. Legend:**
ESTADOS UNIDOS MEXICANOS **Rev. Legend:** ESTADO
DE QUERÉTARO ARTEAGA **Edge:** Reeded

Date	Mintage	F12	VF20	XF40	MS60	MS63
2004Mo	10,000	PF63 60.00				

KM# 741   10 PESOS
31.10 g.,   0.999 Silver, 0.99 oz. ASW 39.9mm.   **Obv.**
National arms **Rev:** State arms **Series:** First **Obv. Legend:**
ESTADOS UNIDOS MEXICANOS **Rev. Legend:** ESTADO
DE NUEVO LEÓN **Edge:** Reeded **Mint:** Mexico City

Date	Mintage	F12	VF20	XF40	MS60	MS63
2004Mo	10,000	PF63 60.00				

KM# 737   10 PESOS
31.10 g.,   0.999 Silver, 0.99 oz. ASW 39.9mm.   **Obv.**
National arms **Rev:** State arms **Series:** First **Obv. Legend:**
ESTADOS UNIDOS MEXICANOS **Rev. Legend:** ESTADO
DE PUEBLA **Edge:** Reeded **Mint:** Mexico City

Date	Mintage	F12	VF20	XF40	MS60	MS63
2004Mo	10,000	PF63 60.00				

KM# 743   10 PESOS
31.10 g.,   0.999 Silver, 0.99 oz. ASW 39.9mm.   **Obv.**
National arms **Rev:** State arms **Series:** First **Obv. Legend:**
ESTADOS UNIDOS MEXICANOS **Rev. Legend:** ESTADO
DE NAYARIT **Edge:** Reeded **Mint:** Mexico City

Date	Mintage	F12	VF20	XF40	MS60	MS63
2004Mo	10,000	PF63 60.00				

KM# 745 10 PESOS
31.10 g., 0.999 Silver, 0.99 oz. ASW 39.9mm. **Obv.**
National arms **Rev:** State arms **Series:** First **Obv. Legend:**
ESTADOS UNIDOS MEXICANOS **Rev. Legend:** ESTADO
DE MORELOS **Edge:** Reeded **Mint:** Mexico City

Date	Mintage	F12	VF20	XF40	MS60	MS63
2004Mo	10,000	PF63 60.00				

KM# 749 10 PESOS
31.10 g., 0.999 Silver, 0.99 oz. ASW 39.9mm. **Obv.**
National arms **Rev:** State arms **Series:** First **Obv. Legend:**
ESTADOS UNIDOS MEXICANOS **Rev. Legend:** ESTADO
DE JALISCO **Edge:** Reeded **Mint:** Mexico City

Date	Mintage	F12	VF20	XF40	MS60	MS63
2004Mo	10,000	PF63 60.00				

KM# 796 10 PESOS
31.10 g., 0.999 Silver, 0.99 oz. ASW 39.9mm. **Obv.**
National arms **Rev:** State arms **Series:** First **Obv. Legend:**
ESTADOS UNIDOS MEXICANOS **Rev. Legend:** ESTADO
DE MICHOACÁN DE OCAMPO **Edge:** Reeded **Mint:**
Mexico City

Date	Mintage	F12	VF20	XF40	MS60	MS63
2004Mo	10,000	PF63 60.00				

KM# 711 10 PESOS
31.10 g., 0.999 Silver, 0.99 oz. ASW 39.9mm. **Obv.**
National arms **Rev:** State arms **Series:** First **Obv. Legend:**
ESTADOS UNIDOS MEXICANOS **Rev. Legend:** ESTADO
DE HIDALGO **Edge:** Reeded **Mint:** Mexico City

Date	Mintage	F12	VF20	XF40	MS60	MS63
2005Mo	10,000	PF63 60.00				

KM# 747 10 PESOS
31.10 g., 0.999 Silver, 0.99 oz. ASW 39.9mm. **Obv.**
National arms **Rev:** State arms **Series:** First **Obv. Legend:**
ESTADOS UNIDOS MEXICANOS **Rev. Legend:** ESTADO
DE MÉXICO **Edge:** Reeded **Mint:** Mexico City

Date	Mintage	F12	VF20	XF40	MS60	MS63
2004Mo	10,000	PF63 60.00				

KM# 710 10 PESOS
31.10 g., 0.999 Silver, 0.99 oz. ASW 39.9mm. **Obv.**
National arms **Rev:** State arms **Series:** First **Obv. Legend:**
ESTADOS UNIDOS MEXICANOS **Rev. Legend:** ESTADO
DE GUERRERO **Edge:** Reeded **Mint:** Mexico City

Date	Mintage	F12	VF20	XF40	MS60	MS63
2005Mo	10,000	PF63 60.00				

KM# 709   10 PESOS
31.10 g.,   0.999 Silver, 0.99 oz. ASW 39.9mm.   **Obv.**
National arms **Rev:** State arms **Series:** First **Obv. Legend:**
ESTADOS UNIDOS MEXICANOS **Rev. Legend:** ESTADO
DE GUANAJUATO **Edge:** Reeded **Mint:** Mexico City

Date	Mintage	F12	VF20	XF40	MS60	MS63
2005Mo	10,000	PF63 60.00				

KM# 708   10 PESOS
31.10 g.,   0.999 Silver, 0.99 oz. ASW 39.9mm.   **Obv.**
National arms **Rev:** State arms **Series:** First **Obv. Legend:**
ESTADOS UNIDOS MEXICANOS **Rev. Legend:** ESTADO
DE DURANGO **Edge:** Reeded **Mint:** Mexico City

Date	Mintage	F12	VF20	XF40	MS60	MS63
2005Mo	10,000	PF63 60.00				

KM# 707   10 PESOS
31.10 g.,   0.999 Silver, 0.99 oz. ASW 39.9mm.   **Obv.**
National arms **Rev:** Federal District arms **Series:** First **Obv.**
Legend: ESTADOS UNIDOS MEXICANOS **Rev. Legend:**
DISTRITO FEDERAL **Edge:** Reeded **Mint:** Mexico City

Date	Mintage	F12	VF20	XF40	MS60	MS63
2005Mo	10,000	PF63 60.00				

KM# 753   10 PESOS
31.10 g.,   0.999 Silver, 0.99 oz. ASW 39.9mm.   **Obv.**
National arms **Rev:** State arms **Series:** First **Obv. Legend:**
ESTADOS UNIDOS MEXICANOS **Rev. Legend:** ESTADO
DE CHIHUAHUA **Edge:** Reeded **Mint:** Mexico City

Date	Mintage	F12	VF20	XF40	MS60	MS63
2005Mo	10,000	PF63 60.00				

KM# 706   10 PESOS
31.10 g.,   0.999 Silver, 0.99 oz. ASW 39.9mm.   **Obv.**
National arms **Rev:** State arms **Series:** First **Obv. Legend:**
ESTADOS UNIDOS MEXICANOS **Rev. Legend:** ESTADO
DE CHIAPAS **Edge:** Reeded **Mint:** Mexico City

Date	Mintage	F12	VF20	XF40	MS60	MS63
2005Mo	10,000	PF63 60.00				

KM# 728   10 PESOS
31.10 g.,   0.999 Silver, 0.99 oz. ASW 39.9mm.   **Obv.**
National arms **Rev:** State arms **Series:** First **Obv. Legend:**
ESTADOS UNIDOS MEXICANOS **Rev. Legend:** ESTADO
DE COLIMA **Edge:** Reeded **Mint:** Mexico City

Date	Mintage	F12	VF20	XF40	MS60	MS63
2005Mo	10,000	PF63 60.00				

KM# 751 10 PESOS
31.10 g., 0.999 Silver, 0.99 oz. ASW 39.9mm. **Obv.**
National arms **Rev:** State arms **Series:** First **Obv. Legend:**
ESTADOS UNIDOS MEXICANOS **Rev. Legend:** ESTADO
DE COAHUILA DE ZARAGOZA **Edge:** Reeded **Mint:**
Mexico City

Date	Mintage	F12	VF20	XF40	MS60	MS63
2005Mo	10,000	PF63 60.00				

KM# 722 10 PESOS
31.10 g., 0.999 Silver, 0.99 oz. ASW 39.9mm. **Obv.**
National arms **Rev:** State arms **Series:** First **Obv. Legend:**
ESTADOS UNIDOS MEXICANOS **Rev. Legend:** ESTADO
DE BAJA CALIFORNIA **Edge:** Reeded **Mint:** Mexico City

Date	Mintage	F12	VF20	XF40	MS60	MS63
2005Mo	10,000	PF63 60.00				

KM# 726 10 PESOS
31.10 g., 0.999 Silver, 0.99 oz. ASW 39.9mm. **Obv.**
National arms **Rev:** State arms **Series:** First **Obv. Legend:**
ESTADOS UNIDOS MEXICANOS **Rev. Legend:** ESTADO
DE CAMPECHE **Edge:** Reeded **Mint:** Mexico City

Date	Mintage	F12	VF20	XF40	MS60	MS63
2005Mo	10,000	PF63 60.00				

KM# 720 10 PESOS
31.10 g., 0.999 Silver, 0.99 oz. ASW 39.9mm. **Obv.**
National arms **Rev:** State arms **Series:** First **Obv. Legend:**
ESTADOS UNIDOS MEXICANOS **Rev. Legend:** ESTADO
DE AGUASCALIENTES **Edge:** Reeded **Mint:** Mexico City

Date	Mintage	F12	VF20	XF40	MS60	MS63
2005Mo	10,000	PF63 60.00				

KM# 724 10 PESOS
31.10 g., 0.999 Silver, 0.99 oz. ASW 39.9mm. **Obv.** National
arms **Rev:** State arms **Series:** First **Obv. Legend:** ESTADOS
UNIDOS MEXICANOS **Rev. Legend:** ESTADO DE BAJA
CALIFORNIA SUR **Edge:** Reeded **Mint:** Mexico City

Date	Mintage	F12	VF20	XF40	MS60	MS63
2005Mo	10,000	PF63 60.00				

KM# 718 10 PESOS
31.10 g., 0.999 Silver, 0.99 oz. ASW 40mm. **Obv.** National
arms **Rev:** Facade of the San Marcos garden above
sculpture of national emblem at left, San Antonio Temple
at right **Series:** Second **Obv. Legend:** ESTADOS UNIDOS
MEXICANOS **Rev. Legend:** AGUASCALIENTES **Edge:**
Reeded **Mint:** Mexico City

Date	Mintage	F12	VF20	XF40	MS60	MS63
2005Mo	6,000	PF63 65.00				

ESTADOS UNIDOS - REFORM COINAGE

KM# 757   10 PESOS
31.10 g.,   0.999 Silver, 0.99 oz. ASW 40mm.   **Obv.**
National arms **Rev:** Rams head, mountain outline in
background **Series:** Second **Obv. Legend:** ESTADOS
UNIDOS MEXICANOS **Rev. Legend:** BAJA CALIFORNIA -
GOBIERNO DEL ESTADO **Edge:** Reeded **Mint:** Mexico City

Date	Mintage	F12	VF20	XF40	MS60	MS63
2005Mo	6,000	PF63 65.00				

KM# 761   10 PESOS
31.10 g., 0.999 Silver, 0.99 oz. ASW 40mm. **Obv.** National
arms **Rev:** Outlined map of peninsula at center, cave
painting of deer behind, cactus at right **Series:** Second **Obv.
Legend:** ESTADOS UNIDOS MEXICANOS **Rev. Legend:**
ESTADO DE BAJA CALIFORNIA SUR **Edge:** Reeded **Mint:**
Mexico City

Date	Mintage	F12	VF20	XF40	MS60	MS63
2006Mo	6,000	PF63 65.00				

KM# 759   10 PESOS
31.10 g., 0.999 Silver, 0.99 oz. ASW 40mm. **Obv.** National
arms **Rev:** Jade mask - Calakmul, Campeche **Series:**
Second **Obv. Legend:** ESTADOS UNIDOS MEXICANOS
Rev. Legend: ESTADO DE CAMPECHE **Edge:** Reeded
Mint: Mexico City

Date	Mintage	F12	VF20	XF40	MS60	MS63
2006Mo	6,000	PF63 65.00				

KM# 780   10 PESOS
31.10 g., 0.999 Silver, 0.99 oz. ASW 40mm. **Obv.** National
arms **Rev:** Outlined map with turtle, mine cart above grapes
at center, Friendship dam above Christ of the Nodas at
left, chimneys above crucibles and bell tower of Santiago's
cathedral at right **Series:** Second **Obv. Legend:** ESTADOS
UNIDOS MEXICANOS   **Rev. Inscription:** COAHUILA DE
ZARAGOZA **Edge:** Reeded **Mint:** Mexico City

Date	Mintage	F12	VF20	XF40	MS60	MS63
2006Mo	6,000	PF63 65.00				

KM# 776   10 PESOS
31.10 g., 0.999 Silver, 0.99 oz. ASW 40mm. **Obv.** National
arms **Rev:** State arms at lower center, Nevado de Colima
and Volcan de Fuego volcanos in background **Series:**
Second **Obv. Legend:** ESTADOS UNIDOS MEXICANOS
Rev. Legend: Colima   **Rev. Inscription:** GENEROSO
Edge: Reeded **Mint:** Mexico City

Date	Mintage	F12	VF20	XF40	MS60	MS63
2006Mo	6,000	PF63 65.00				

KM# 772   10 PESOS
31.10 g., 0.999 Silver, 0.99 oz. ASW 40mm. **Obv.** National
arms **Rev:** Head of Pakal, ancient Mayan king, Palenque
Series: Second **Obv. Legend:** ESTADOS UNIDOS
MEXICANOS **Rev. Legend:** ESTADO DE CHIAPAS -
CABEZA MAYA DEL REY PAKAL, PALENQUE **Edge:**
Reeded **Mint:** Mexico City

Date	Mintage	F12	VF20	XF40	MS60	MS63
2006Mo	6,000	PF63 65.00				

KM# 774   10 PESOS
31.10 g., 0.999 Silver, 0.99 oz. ASW 40mm. **Obv.** National arms **Rev:** Angel of Liberty **Series:** Second **Obv. Legend:** ESTADOS UNIDOS MEXICANOS **Rev. Legend:** MÉXICO - ANGEL DE LA LIBERTAD, CHIHUAHUA **Edge:** Reeded **Mint:** Mexico City

Date	Mintage	F12	VF20	XF40	MS60	MS63
2006Mo	6,000	PF63 65.00				

KM# 778   10 PESOS
31.10 g., 0.999 Silver, 0.99 oz. ASW 40mm. **Obv.** National arms **Rev:** National Palace **Series:** Second **Obv. Legend:** ESTADOS UNIDOS MEXICANOS **Rev. Legend:** DISTRITO FEDERAL - ANTIGUO AYUNTAMIENTO **Edge:** Reeded **Mint:** Mexico City

Date	Mintage	F12	VF20	XF40	MS60	MS63
2006Mo	6,000	PF63 65.00				

KM# 786   10 PESOS
31.10 g., 0.999 Silver, 0.99 oz. ASW 40mm. **Obv.** National arms **Rev:** Tree **Series:** Second **Obv. Legend:** ESTADOS UNIDOS MEXICANOS **Rev. Legend:** PRIMERA RESERVA NACIONAL FORESTAL - DURANGO **Edge:** Reeded **Mint:** Mexico City

Date	Mintage	F12	VF20	XF40	MS60	MS63
2006Mo	6,000	PF63 65.00				

KM# 788   10 PESOS
31.10 g., 0.999 Silver, 0.99 oz. ASW 40mm. **Obv.** National arms **Rev:** State arms at center, statue of Miguel Hidalgo at left, monument to Pípila at lower right **Series:** Second **Obv. Legend:** ESTADOS UNIDOS MEXICANOS **Rev. Inscription:** Guanajuato **Edge:** Reeded **Mint:** Mexico City

Date	Mintage	F12	VF20	XF40	MS60	MS63
2006Mo	6,000	PF63 65.00				

KM# 790   10 PESOS
31.10 g., 0.999 Silver, 0.99 oz. ASW 40mm. **Obv.** National arms **Rev:** Stylized portrait of Vicente Guerrero at left, church of Taxco at upper center, Acapulco's la Quebrada with diver above Christmas Eve flower and mask **Series:** Second **Obv. Legend:** ESTADOS UNIDOS MEXICANOS **Rev. Legend:** GUERRERO **Edge:** Reeded **Mint:** Mexico City

Date	Mintage	F12	VF20	XF40	MS60	MS63
2006Mo	6,000	PF63 65.00				

KM# 792   10 PESOS
31.10 g., 0.999 Silver, 0.99 oz. ASW 40mm. **Obv.** National arms **Rev:** Monument of Pachuca Hidalgo **Series:** Second **Obv. Legend:** ESTADOS UNIDOS MEXICANOS **Rev. Inscription:** RELOJ / MONUMENTAL / DE / PACHUCA / HIDALGO - La / Bella / Airosa **Edge:** Reeded **Mint:** Mexico City

Date	Mintage	F12	VF20	XF40	MS60	MS63
2006Mo	6,000	PF63 65.00				

ESTADOS UNIDOS - REFORM COINAGE

KM# 794   10 PESOS
31.10 g., 0.999 Silver, 0.99 oz. ASW 40mm. **Obv.** National arms **Rev:** Hospicio Cabañas orphanage **Series:** Second **Obv. Legend:** ESTADOS UNIDOS MEXICANOS **Rev. Legend:** ESTADO DE JALISCCO **Edge:** Reeded **Mint:** Mexico City

Date	Mintage	F12	VF20	XF40	MS60	MS63
2006Mo	6,000	PF63 65.00				

KM# 832   10 PESOS
31.10 g., 0.999 Silver, 0.99 oz. ASW 40mm. **Obv.** National arms **Rev:** 1/2 length figure of Chinelo (local dancer) at right, Palacio de Cortes in background **Series:** Second **Obv. Legend:** ESTADOS UNIDOS MEXICANOS **Rev. Inscription:** ESTADO DE / MORELOS **Edge:** Reeded **Mint:** Mexico City

Date	Mintage	F12	VF20	XF40	MS60	MS63
2006Mo	6,000	PF63 65.00				

KM# 830   10 PESOS
31.10 g., 0.999 Silver, 0.99 oz. ASW 40mm. **Obv.** National arms **Rev:** Pyramid de la Loona (Moon) **Series:** Second **Obv. Legend:** ESTADOS UNIDOS MEXICANOS **Rev. Legend:** ESTADO DE MÉXICO **Edge:** Reeded **Mint:** Mexico City

Date	Mintage	F12	VF20	XF40	MS60	MS63
2006Mo	6,000	PF63 65.00				

KM# 833   10 PESOS
31.10 g., 0.999 Silver, 0.99 oz. ASW 40mm. **Obv.** National arms **Rev:** Isle de Mexcaltitlán **Series:** Second **Obv. Legend:** ESTADOS UNIDOS MEXICANOS **Rev. Legend:** ESTADO DE NAYARIT **Edge:** Reeded **Mint:** Mexico City

Date	Mintage	F12	VF20	XF40	MS60	MS63
2007Mo	6,000	PF63 65.00				

KM# 831   10 PESOS
31.10 g., 0.999 Silver, 0.99 oz. ASW 40mm. **Obv.** National arms **Rev:** Four Monarch butterflies **Series:** Second **Obv. Legend:** ESTADOS UNIDOS MEXICANOS **Rev. Legend:** ESTADO DE MICHOACÁN **Edge:** Reeded **Mint:** Mexico City

Date	Mintage	F12	VF20	XF40	MS60	MS63
2006Mo	6,000	PF63 65.00				

KM# 834   10 PESOS
31.10 g., 0.999 Silver, 0.99 oz. ASW 40mm. **Obv.** National arms **Rev:** Old foundry in Pargue Fundidora (public park) at right, Cerro de la Silla (Saddle Hill) in background **Series:** Second **Obv. Legend:** ESTADOS UNIDOS MEXICANOS **Rev. Legend:** ESTADO DE NUEVO LEÓN **Edge:** Reeded **Mint:** Mexico City

Date	Mintage	F12	VF20	XF40	MS60	MS63
2007Mo	6,000	PF63 65.00				

KM# 835   10 PESOS
31.10 g., 0.999 Silver, 0.99 oz. ASW 40mm. **Obv.** National arms **Rev:** Teatro Macedonio Alcala (theater) **Series:** Second **Obv. Legend:** ESTADOS UNIDOS MEXICANOS **Rev. Legend:** OAXACA **Edge:** Reeded **Mint:** Mexico City

Date	Mintage	F12	VF20	XF40	MS60	MS63
2007Mo	6,000	PF63 65.00				

KM# 836   10 PESOS
31.10 g., 0.999 Silver, 0.99 oz. ASW 40mm. **Obv.** National arms **Rev:** Talavera porcelain dish **Series:** Second **Obv. Legend:** ESTADOS UNIDOS MEXICANOS **Rev. Legend:** ESTADO DE PUEBLA **Edge:** Reeded **Mint:** Mexico City

Date	Mintage	F12	VF20	XF40	MS60	MS63
2007Mo	6,000	PF63 65.00				

KM# 837   10 PESOS
31.10 g., 0.999 Silver, 0.99 oz. ASW 40mm. **Obv.** National arms **Rev:** Mask at left, rays above state arms at center, Mayan ruins at right **Series:** Second **Obv. Legend:** ESTADOS UNIDOS MEXICANOS **Rev. Legend:** QUINTANA ROO **Edge:** Reeded **Mint:** Mexico City

Date	Mintage	F12	VF20	XF40	MS60	MS63
2007Mo	6,000	PF63 65.00				

KM# 838   10 PESOS
31.10 g., 0.999 Silver, 0.99 oz. ASW 40mm. **Obv.** National arms **Rev:** Acqueduct of Querétaro at left, church of Santa Rosa de Viterbo at right **Series:** Second **Obv. Legend:** ESTADOS UNIDOS MEXICANOS **Rev. Legend:** ESTADO DE QUERÉTARO ARTEAGA **Edge:** Reeded **Mint:** Mexico City

Date	Mintage	F12	VF20	XF40	MS60	MS63
2007Mo	6,000	PF63 65.00				

KM# 839   10 PESOS
31.10 g., Silver 40mm. **Obv.** National arms **Rev:** Facade of Caja Real **Series:** Second **Obv. Legend:** ESTADOS UNIDOS MEXICANOS **Rev. Legend:** • SAN LUIS POTOSÍ • **Edge:** Reeded **Mint:** Mexico City

Date	Mintage	F12	VF20	XF40	MS60	MS63
2007Mo	6,000	PF63 65.00				

KM# 840   10 PESOS
31.10 g., 0.999 Silver, 0.99 oz. ASW 40mm. **Obv.** National arms **Rev:** Shield on pile of cactus fruits **Series:** Second **Obv. Legend:** ESTADOS UNIDOS MEXICANOS **Rev. Legend:** ESTADO DE SINALOA - LUGAR DE PITAHAYAS **Edge:** Reeded **Mint:** Mexico City

Date	Mintage	F12	VF20	XF40	MS60	MS63
2007Mo	6,000	PF63 65.00				

KM# 841   10 PESOS
31.10 g., 0.999 Silver, 0.99 oz. ASW 40mm. **Obv.** National arms **Rev:** Local in Dance of the Deer at left, cactus at right, mountains in background **Series:** Second **Obv. Legend:** ESTADOS UNIDOS MEXICANOS **Rev. Legend:** ESTADO DE SONORA **Edge:** Reeded **Mint:** Mexico City

Date	Mintage	F12	VF20	XF40	MS60	MS63
2007Mo	6,000	PF63 65.00				

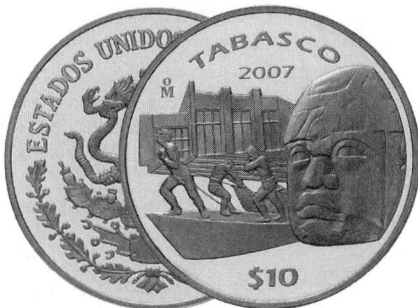

KM# 842   10 PESOS
31.10 g., 0.999 Silver, 0.99 oz. ASW 40mm. **Obv.** National arms **Rev:** Fuente de los Pescadores (fisherman fountain) at lower left, giant head from the Olmec-pre-Hispanic culture at right, Planetario Tabasco in background **Series:** Second **Obv. Legend:** ESTADOS UNIDOS MEXICANOS **Rev. Legend:** TABASCO **Edge:** Reeded **Mint:** Mexico City

Date	Mintage	F12	VF20	XF40	MS60	MS63
2007Mo	6,000	PF63 65.00				

KM# 843   10 PESOS
31.10 g., 0.999 Silver, 0.99 oz. ASW 40mm. **Obv.** National arms **Rev:** Ridge - Cerro Del Bernal, Gonzáles **Series:** Second **Obv. Legend:** ESTADOS UNIDOS MEXICANOS **Rev. Legend:** TAMAULIPAS **Edge:** Reeded **Mint:** Mexico City

Date	Mintage	F12	VF20	XF40	MS60	MS63
2007Mo	6,000	PF63 65.00				

KM# 844   10 PESOS
31.10 g., 0.999 Silver, 0.99 oz. ASW 40mm. **Obv.** National arms **Rev:** Basilica de Ocotlán at left, state arms above Capilla Abierta, Plaza de Toros Ranchero Aguilar below, Exconvento de San Francisco at right **Series:** Second **Obv. Legend:** ESTADOS UNIDOS MEXICANOS **Rev. Legend:** ESTADO DE TLAXCALA **Edge:** Reeded **Mint:** Mexico City

Date	Mintage	F12	VF20	XF40	MS60	MS63
2007Mo	6,000	PF63 65.00				

KM# 845   10 PESOS
31.10 g., 0.999 Silver, 0.99 oz. ASW 40mm. **Obv.** National arms **Rev:** Pyramid of El Tajín **Series:** Second **Obv. Legend:** ESTADOS UNIDOS MEXICANOS **Rev. Legend:** • VERACRUZ • - • DE IGNACIO DE LA LLAVE • **Edge:** Reeded **Mint:** Mexico City

Date	Mintage	F12	VF20	XF40	MS60	MS63
2007Mo	6,000	PF63 65.00				

KM# 846   10 PESOS
31.10 g., 0.999 Silver, 0.99 oz. ASW 40mm. **Obv.** National arms **Rev:** Stylized pyramid of Chichén-Itzá **Series:** Second **Obv. Legend:** ESTADOS UNIDOS MEXICANOS **Rev. Legend:** Castillo de Chichén Itzá **Rev. Inscription:** YUCATÁN **Edge:** Reeded **Mint:** Mexico City

Date	Mintage	F12	VF20	XF40	MS60	MS63
2007Mo	6,000	PF63 65.00				

Date	Mintage	F12	VF20	XF40	MS60	MS63
2000Mo	14,850,000	—	2.50	3.50	15.00	18.50
2001Mo	2,478,000	—	2.50	3.50	16.00	18.00

KM# 847   10 PESOS
31.10 g., 0.999 Silver, 0.99 oz. ASW 40mm. **Obv.** National arms **Rev:** Cable car above Monumento al Minero at left, Cathedral de Zacatecas at center right **Series:** Second **Obv. Legend:** ESTADOS UNIDOS MEXICANOS **Rev. Legend:** Zacatecas **Edge:** Reeded **Mint:** Mexico City

Date	Mintage	F12	VF20	XF40	MS60	MS63
2007Mo	6,000	PF63 65.00				

KM# 961   10 PESOS
31.10 g., 0.999 Silver, 0.99 oz. ASW 40mm.

Date	Mintage	F12	VF20	XF40	MS60	MS63
2010	—	PF63 100				

KM# 561   20 NUEVOS PESOS
16.92 g., Bi-Metallic 0.925 Silver (.250 oz. ASW) center within Aluminum-Bronze ring, 31.86mm. **Obv.** National arms **Rev:** Head of Hidalgo left within wreath **Obv. Legend:** ESTADOS UNIDOS MEXICANOS **Edge:** Reeded **Mint:** Mexico City

Date	Mintage	F12	VF20	XF40	MS60	MS63
1993Mo	25,000,000	—	—	10.00	12.00	15.00
1994Mo	5,000,000	—	—	10.00	12.00	15.00
1995Mo	5,000,000	—	—	10.00	12.00	15.00

KM# 641   20 PESOS
6.22 g., 0.999 Gold, 0.20 oz. AGW 21.9mm. **Obv.** National arms, eagle left **Rev:** Child playing with lasso **Edge:** Reeded **Mint:** Mexico City

Date	Mintage	F12	VF20	XF40	MS60	MS63
1999Mo	1,510	PF60 375				

KM# 637   20 PESOS
Bi-Metallic Copper-Nickel center within Brass ring, 32mm. **Subject:** Xiuhtecuhtli **Obv.** National arms, eagle left within circle **Rev:** Aztec with torch within spiked circle

KM# 638   20 PESOS
Bi-Metallic Copper-Nickel center within Brass ring, 32mm. **Subject:** Octavio Paz **Obv.** National arms, eagle left within circle **Rev:** Head 1/4 right within circle

Date	Mintage	F12	VF20	XF40	MS60	MS63
2000Mo	14,943,000	—	2.50	3.50	15.00	18.50
2001Mo	2,515,000	—	2.50	3.50	16.00	18.50

KM# 969   20 PESOS
15.95 g., Bi-Metallic Copper-Nickel center in Aluminum-Bronze ring, 32mm. **Subject:** Armed Forces, 100th Anniversary **Obv.** National arms **Rev:** Silhouette of soldier with a helmet **Edge:** Segmented reeding **Mint:** Mexico City

Date	Mintage	F12	VF20	XF40	MS60	MS63
2013Mo	Est. 5000000	—	—	—	3.50	4.00

KM# 970   20 PESOS
15.95 g., Bi-Metallic Copper-Nickel center in Aluminum-Bronze ring, 32mm. **Subject:** Belisario Dominguez Palencia, 150th Anniversary of Birth and 100th Anniversary of Death **Obv.** National arms **Rev:** Bust 1/4 right **Edge:** Segmented reeding **Mint:** Mexico City

Date	Mintage	F12	VF20	XF40	MS60	MS63
2013Mo	Est. 1000000	—	—	—	4.50	5.00

KM# 571   50 NUEVOS PESOS
34.11 g., Bi-Metallic 0.925 Silver .500 ASW center within Brass ring, 38.87mm. **Subject:** Nino Heroes **Obv.** National arms **Rev:** Six heads facing with date at upper right, all within circle and 1/2 wreath **Obv. Legend:** ESTADOS UNIDOS MEXICANOS **Edge:** Reeded **Mint:** Mexico City

Date	Mintage	F12	VF20	XF40	MS60	MS63
1993Mo	2,000,000	—	—	18.00	25.00	32.50
1994Mo	1,500,000	—	—	18.00	25.00	32.50
1995Mo	1,500,000	—	—	18.00	25.00	32.50

KM# 688   100 PESOS

33.94 g., Bi-Metallic .925 Silver 16.812g center in Aluminum-Bronze ring, 39.04mm. **Subject:** 180th Anniversary of Federation **Obv.** National arms **Rev:** State arms **Series:** First **Obv. Legend:** ESTADOS UNIDOS MEXICANOS **Rev. Legend:** ESTADO DE ZACATECAS **Edge:** Segmented reeding **Mint:** Mexico City

Date	Mintage	F12	VF20	XF40	MS60	MS63
2003Mo	244,900	—	—	—	40.00	50.00

KM# 696   100 PESOS

29.17 g., Bi-Metallic .999 Gold 17.154g center in .999 Silver 12.015g ring, 34.5mm. **Subject:** 180th Anniversary of Federation **Obv.** National arms **Rev:** State arms **Series:** First **Obv. Legend:** ESTADOS UNIDOS MEXICANOS **Rev. Legend:** ESTADO DE ZACATECAS **Edge:** Segmented reeding **Mint:** Mexico City

Date	Mintage	F12	VF20	XF40	MS60	MS63
2003Mo	1,000	PF65 1,200				

KM# 689   100 PESOS

33.94 g., Bi-Metallic .925 Silver 16.812g center in Aluminum-Bronze ring, 39.04mm. **Subject:** 180th Anniversary of Federation **Obv.** National arms **Rev:** State arms **Series:** First **Obv. Legend:** ESTADOS UNIDOS MEXICANOS **Rev. Legend:** ESTADO DE YUCATÁN **Edge:** Segmented reeding **Mint:** Mexico City

Date	Mintage	F12	VF20	XF40	MS60	MS63
2003Mo	235,763	—	—	—	40.00	50.00

KM# 697   100 PESOS

29.17 g., Bi-Metallic .999 Gold 17.154g center in .999 Silver 12.015g ring, 34.5mm. **Subject:** 180th Anniversary of Federation **Obv.** National arms **Rev:** State arms **Series:** First **Obv. Legend:** ESTADOS UNIDOS MEXICANOS **Rev. Legend:** ESTADO DE YUCATÁN **Edge:** Segmented reeding **Mint:** Mexico City

Date	Mintage	F12	VF20	XF40	MS60	MS63
2003Mo	1,000	PF65 1,200				

KM# 690   100 PESOS

33.94 g., Bi-Metallic .925 Silver 16.812g center in Aluminum-Bronze ring, 39.04mm. **Subject:** 180th Anniversary of Federation **Obv.** National arms **Rev:** State arms **Series:** First **Obv. Legend:** ESTADOS UNIDOS MEXICANOS **Rev. Legend:** ESTADO DE VERACRUZ-LLAVE **Edge:** Segmented reeding **Mint:** Mexico City

Date	Mintage	F12	VF20	XF40	MS60	MS63
2003Mo	248,810	—	—	—	40.00	50.00

KM# 698   100 PESOS

29.17 g., Bi-Metallic .999 Gold 17.154g center in .999 Silver 12.015g ring, 34.5mm. **Subject:** 180th Anniversary of Federation **Obv.** National arms **Rev:** State arms **Series:** First **Obv. Legend:** ESTADOS UNIDOS MEXICANOS **Rev. Legend:** ESTADO DE VERACRUZ-LLAVE **Edge:** Segmented reeding **Mint:** Mexico City

Date	Mintage	F12	VF20	XF40	MS60	MS63
2003Mo	1,000	PF65 1,200				

KM# 691   100 PESOS

33.94 g., Bi-Metallic .925 Silver 16.812g center in Aluminum-Bronze ring, 39.9mm. **Subject:** 180th Anniversary of Federation **Obv.** National arms **Rev:** State arms **Series:** First **Obv. Legend:** ESTADOS UNIDOS MEXICANOS **Rev. Legend:** ESTADO DE TLAXCALA **Edge:** Segmented reeding **Mint:** Mexico City

Date	Mintage	F12	VF20	XF40	MS60	MS63
2003Mo	248,976	—	—	—	35.00	40.00

KM# 699   100 PESOS

29.17 g., Bi-Metallic .999 Gold 17.154g center in .999 Silver 12.015g ring, 34.5mm. **Subject:** 180th Anniversary of Federation **Obv.** National arms **Rev:** State arms **Series:** First **Obv. Legend:** ESTADOS UNIDOS MEXICANOS **Rev. Legend:** ESTADO DE TLAXCALA **Edge:** Segmented reeding **Mint:** Mexico City

Date	Mintage	F12	VF20	XF40	MS60	MS63
2003Mo	1,000	PF65 1,200				

KM# 692 100 PESOS
33.94 g., Bi-Metallic .925 Silver 16.812g center in Aluminum-Bronze ring, 39.04mm. **Subject:** 180th Anniversay of Federation **Obv.** National arms **Rev:** State arms **Series:** First **Obv. Legend:** ESTADOS UNIDOS MEXICANOS **Rev. Legend:** ESTADO DE TAMAULIPAS **Edge:** Segmented reeding **Mint:** Mexico City

Date	Mintage	F12	VF20	XF40	MS60	MS63
2004Mo	249,398	—	—	—	35.00	40.00

KM# 700 100 PESOS
29.17 g., Bi-Metallic .999 Gold 17.154g center in .999 Silver 12.015g ring, 34.5mm. **Subject:** 180th Anniversary of Federation **Obv.** National arms **Rev:** State arms **Series:** First **Obv. Legend:** ESTADOS UNIDOS MEXICANOS **Rev. Legend:** ESTADO DE TAMAULIPAS **Edge:** Segmented reeding **Mint:** Mexico City

Date	Mintage	F12	VF20	XF40	MS60	MS63
2004Mo	1,000	PF65 1,200				

KM# 693 100 PESOS
33.94 g., Bi-Metallic .925 Silver 16.812g center in Aluminum-Bronze ring, 39.04mm. **Subject:** 180th Anniversary of Federation **Obv.** National arms **Rev:** State arms **Series:** First **Obv. Legend:** ESTADOS UNIDOS MEXICANOS **Rev. Legend:** ESTADO DE TABASCO **Edge:** Segmented reeding **Mint:** Mexico City

Date	Mintage	F12	VF20	XF40	MS60	MS63
2004Mo	249,318	—	—	—	35.00	40.00

KM# 701 100 PESOS
29.17 g., Bi-Metallic .999 Gold 17.154g center in .999 Silver 12.015g ring, 34.5mm. **Subject:** 180th Anniversary of Federation **Obv.** National arms **Rev:** State arms **Series:** First **Obv. Legend:** ESTADOS UNIDOS MEXICANOS **Rev. Legend:** ESTADO DE TABASCO **Edge:** Segmented reeding **Mint:** Mexico City

Date	Mintage	F12	VF20	XF40	MS60	MS63
2004Mo	1,000	PF65 1,200				

KM# 694 100 PESOS
33.94 g., Bi-Metallic .925 Silver 16.812g center in Aluminum-Bronze ring, 39.04mm. **Subject:** 180th Anniversary of Federation **Obv.** National arms **Rev:** State arms **Series:** First **Obv. Legend:** ESTADOS UNIDOS MEXICANOS **Rev. Legend:** ESTADO DE SONORA **Edge:** Segmented reeding **Mint:** Mexico City

Date	Mintage	F12	VF20	XF40	MS60	MS63
2004Mo	249,300	—	—	—	35.00	40.00

KM# 702 100 PESOS
29.17 g., Bi-Metallic .999 Gold 17.154g center in .999 Silver 12.015g ring, 34.5mm. **Subject:** 180th Anniversary of Federation **Obv.** National arms **Rev:** State arms **Series:** First **Obv. Legend:** ESTADOS UNIDOS MEXICANOS **Rev. Legend:** ESTADO DE SONORA **Edge:** Segmented reeding **Mint:** Mexico City

Date	Mintage	F12	VF20	XF40	MS60	MS63
2004Mo	1,000	PF65 1,200				

KM# 695 100 PESOS
33.94 g., Bi-Metallic .925 Silver 16.812g center in Aluminum-Bronze ring, 39.04mm. **Subject:** 180th Anniversary of Federation **Obv.** National arms **Rev:** State arms **Series:** First **Obv. Legend:** ESTADOS UNIDOS MEXICANOS **Rev. Legend:** ESTADO DE SINALOA **Edge:** Segmented reeding **Mint:** Mexico City

Date	Mintage	F12	VF20	XF40	MS60	MS63
2004Mo	244,722	—	—	—	35.00	40.00

KM# 703 100 PESOS
29.17 g., Bi-Metallic .999 Gold 17.154g center in .999 Silver 12.015g ring, 34.5mm. **Subject:** 180th Anniversary of Federation **Obv.** National arms **Rev:** State arms **Series:** First **Obv. Legend:** ESTADOS UNIDOS MEXICANOS **Rev. Legend:** ESTADO DE SINALOA **Edge:** Segmented reeding **Mint:** Mexico City

Date	Mintage	F12	VF20	XF40	MS60	MS63
2004Mo	1,000	PF65 1,200				

KM# 803   100 PESOS
33.94 g., Bi-Metallic .925 Silver 16.812g center in Aluminum-Bronze ring, 39.04mm. **Subject:** 180th Anniversary of Federation **Obv.** National arms **Rev:** State arms **Series:** First **Obv. Legend:** ESTADOS UNIDOS MEXICANOS **Rev. Legend:** ESTADO DE SAN LUIS POTOSÍ **Edge:** Segmented reeding **Mint:** Mexico City

Date	Mintage	F12	VF20	XF40	MS60	MS63
2004Mo	249,662	—	—	—	35.00	40.00

KM# 806   100 PESOS
29.17 g., Bi-Metallic .999 Gold 17.154g center in .999 silver 12.015 ring, 34.5mm. **Subject:** 180th Anniversary of Federation **Obv.** National arms **Rev:** State arms **Series:** First **Obv. Legend:** ESTADOS UNIDOS MEXICANOS **Rev. Legend:** ESTADO DE SAN LUIS POTOSÍ **Edge:** Segmented reeding **Mint:** Mexico City

Date	Mintage	F12	VF20	XF40	MS60	MS63
2004Mo	1,000	PF65 1,200				

KM# 736   100 PESOS
33.94 g., Bi-Metallic .925 Silver 16.812g center in Aluminum-Bronze ring, 39.04mm. **Subject:** 180th Anniversary of Federation **Obv.** National arms **Rev:** State arms **Series:** First **Obv. Legend:** ESTADOS UNIDOS MEXICANOS **Rev. Legend:** ESTADO DE QUINTANA ROO **Edge:** Segmented reeding **Mint:** Mexico City

Date	Mintage	F12	VF20	XF40	MS60	MS63
2004Mo	249,134	—	—	—	35.00	40.00

KM# 807   100 PESOS
29.17 g., Bi-Metallic .999 Gold 17.154g center in .999 Silver 12.015g ring, 34.5mm. **Subject:** 180th Anniversary of Federation **Obv.** National arms **Rev:** State arms **Series:** First **Obv. Legend:** ESTADOS UNIDOS MEXICANOS **Rev. Legend:** ESTADO DE QUINTANA ROO **Edge:** Segmented reeding **Mint:** Mexico City

Date	Mintage	F12	VF20	XF40	MS60	MS63
2004Mo	1,000	PF65 1,200				

KM# 734   100 PESOS
33.94 g., Bi-Metallic .925 Silver 16.812g center in Aluminum-Bronze ring, 39.04mm. **Subject:** 180th Anniversary of Federation **Obv.** National arms **Rev:** State arms **Series:** First **Obv. Legend:** ESTADOS UNIDOS MEXICANOS **Rev. Legend:** ESTADO DE QUERÉTARO ARTEAGA **Edge:** Segmented reeding **Mint:** Mexico City

Date	Mintage	F12	VF20	XF40	MS60	MS63
2004Mo	249,263	—	—	—	35.00	40.00

KM# 808   100 PESOS
29.17 g., Bi-Metallic .999 Gold 17.154g center in .999 Silver 12.015g ring, 34.5mm. **Subject:** 180th Anniversary of Federation **Obv.** National arms **Rev:** State arms **Series:** First **Obv. Legend:** ESTADOS UNIDOS MEXICANOS **Rev. Legend:** ESTADO DE QUERÉTARO ARTEAGA **Edge:** Segmented reeding **Mint:** Mexico City

Date	Mintage	F12	VF20	XF40	MS60	MS63
2004Mo	1,000	PF65 1,200				

KM# 738   100 PESOS
33.94 g., Bi-Metallic .925 Silver 16.812g center in Aluminum-Bronze ring, 39.04mm. **Subject:** 180th Anniversary of Federation **Obv.** National arms **Rev:** State arms **Series:** First **Obv. Legend:** ESTADOS UNIDOS MEXICANOS **Rev. Legend:** ESTADO DE PUEBLA **Edge:** Segmented reeding **Mint:** Mexico City

Date	Mintage	F12	VF20	XF40	MS60	MS63
2004Mo	248,850	—	—	—	35.00	40.00

KM# 809   100 PESOS
29.17 g., Bi-Metallic .999 Gold 17.154g center in .999 Silver 12.015g ring, 34.5mm. **Subject:** 180th Anniversary of Federation **Obv.** National arms **Rev:** State arms **Series:** First **Obv. Legend:** ESTADOS UNIDOS MEXICANOS **Rev. Legend:** ESTADO DE PUEBLA **Edge:** Segmented reeding **Mint:** Mexico City

Date	Mintage	F12	VF20	XF40	MS60	MS63
2004Mo	1,000	PF65 1,200				

ESTADOS UNIDOS - REFORM COINAGE

KM# 740 100 PESOS
33.94 g., Bi-Metallic .925 Silver 16.812g center in Aluminum-Bronze ring, 39.04mm. **Subject:** 180th Anniversary of Federation **Obv.** National arms **Rev:** State arms **Series:** First **Obv. Legend:** ESTADOS UNIDOS MEXICANOS **Rev. Legend:** ESTADO DE OAXACA **Edge:** Segmented reeding **Mint:** Mexico City

Date	Mintage	F12	VF20	XF40	MS60	MS63
2004Mo	249,589	—	—	—	35.00	40.00

KM# 810 100 PESOS
29.17 g., Bi-Metallic .999 Gold 17.154g center in .999 Silver 12.015g ring, 34.5mm. **Subject:** 180th Anniversary of Federation **Obv.** National arms **Rev:** State arms **Series:** First **Obv. Legend:** ESTADOS UNIDOS MEXICANOS **Rev. Legend:** ESTADO DE OAXACA **Edge:** Segmented reeding **Mint:** Mexico City

Date	Mintage	F12	VF20	XF40	MS60	MS63
2004Mo	1,000	PF65 1,200				

KM# 742 100 PESOS
33.94 g., Bi-Metallic .925 Silver 16.812g center in Aluminum-Bronze ring, 39.04mm. **Subject:** 180th Anniversary of Federation **Obv.** National arms **Rev:** State arms **Series:** First **Obv. Legend:** ESTADOS UNIDOS MEXICANOS **Rev. Legend:** ESTADO DE NUEVO LEÓN **Edge:** Segmented reeding **Mint:** Mexico City

Date	Mintage	F12	VF20	XF40	MS60	MS63
2004Mo	249,199	—	—	—	35.00	40.00

KM# 811 100 PESOS
29.17 g., Bi-Metallic .999 Gold 17.154g center in .999 Silver 12.015g ring, 34.5mm. **Subject:** 180th Anniversary of Federation **Obv.** National arms **Rev:** State arms **Series:** First **Obv. Legend:** ESTADOS UNIDOS MEXICANOS **Rev. Legend:** ESTADO DE NUEVO LEÓN **Edge:** Segmented reeding **Mint:** Mexico City

Date	Mintage	F12	VF20	XF40	MS60	MS63
2004Mo	1,000	PF65 1,200				

KM# 744 100 PESOS
33.94 g., Bi-Metallic .925 Silver 16.812g center in Aluminum-Bronze ring, 39.04mm. **Subject:** 180th Anniversary of Federation **Obv.** National arms **Rev:** State arms **Series:** First **Obv. Legend:** ESTADOS UNIDOS MEXICANOS **Rev. Legend:** ESTADO DE NAYARIT **Edge:** Segmented reeding **Mint:** Mexico City

Date	Mintage	F12	VF20	XF40	MS60	MS63
2004Mo	248,305	—	—	—	35.00	40.00

KM# 812 100 PESOS
29.17 g., Bi-Metallic .999 Gold 17.154g center in .999 Silver 12.015g ring, 34.5mm. **Subject:** 180th Anniversary of Federation **Obv.** National arms **Rev:** State arms **Series:** First **Obv. Legend:** ESTADOS UNIDOS MEXICANOS **Rev. Legend:** ESTADO DE NAYARIT **Edge:** Segmented reeding **Mint:** Mexico City

Date	Mintage	F12	VF20	XF40	MS60	MS63
2004Mo	1,000	PF65 1,200				

KM# 746 100 PESOS
33.94 g., Bi-Metallic .925 Silver 16.812g center in Aluminum-Bronze ring, 39.04mm. **Subject:** 180th Anniversary of Federation **Obv.** National arms **Rev:** State arms **Series:** First **Obv. Legend:** ESTADOS UNIDOS MEXICANOS **Rev. Legend:** ESTADO DE MORELOS **Edge:** Segmented reeding **Mint:** Mexico City

Date	Mintage	F12	VF20	XF40	MS60	MS63
2004Mo	249,260	—	—	—	35.00	40.00

KM# 813 100 PESOS
29.17 g., Bi-Metallic .999 Gold 17.154g center in .999 Silver 12.015g ring, 34.5mm. **Subject:** 180th Anniversary of Federation **Obv.** National arms **Rev:** State arms **Series:** First **Obv. Legend:** ESTADOS UNIDOS MEXICANOS **Rev. Legend:** ESTADO DE MORELOS **Edge:** Segmented reeding **Mint:** Mexico City

Date	Mintage	F12	VF20	XF40	MS60	MS63
2004Mo	1,000	PF65 1,200				

ESTADOS UNIDOS - REFORM COINAGE

KM# 804   100 PESOS
33.94 g., Bi-Metallic .925 Silver 16.812g center in Aluminum-Bronze ring, 39.04mm. **Subject:** 180th Anniversary of Federation **Obv.** National arms **Rev:** State arms **Series:** First **Obv. Legend:** ESTADOS UNIDOS MEXICANOS **Rev. Legend:** ESTADO DE MICHOACÁN DE OCAMPO **Edge:** Segmented reeding **Mint:** Mexico City

Date	Mintage	F12	VF20	XF40	MS60	MS63
2004Mo	249,492	—	—	—	35.00	40.00

KM# 814   100 PESOS
29.17 g., Bi-Metallic .999 Gold 17.154g center in .999 12.015g ring, 34.5mm. **Subject:** 180th Anniversary of Federation **Obv.** National arms **Rev:** State arms **Series:** First **Obv. Legend:** ESTADOS UNIDOS MEXICANOS **Rev. Legend:** ESTADO DE MICHOACÁN DE OCAMPO **Edge:** Segmented reeding **Mint:** Mexico City

Date	Mintage	F12	VF20	XF40	MS60	MS63
2004Mo	1,000	PF65 1,200				

KM# 748   100 PESOS
33.94 g., Bi-Metallic .925 Silver 16.812g center in Aluminum-Bronze ring, 39.04mm. **Subject:** 180th Anniversary of Federation **Obv.** National arms **Rev:** State arms **Series:** First **Obv. Legend:** ESTADOS UNIDOS MEXICANOS **Rev. Legend:** ESTADO DE MÉXICO **Edge:** Segmented reeding **Mint:** Mexico City

Date	Mintage	F12	VF20	XF40	MS60	MS63
2004Mo	249,800	—	—	—	35.00	40.00

KM# 815   100 PESOS
29.17 g., Bi-Metallic .999 Gold 17.154 center in .999 Silver 12.015 ring, 34.5mm. **Subject:** 180th Anniversary of Federation **Obv.** National arms **Rev:** State arms **Series:** First **Obv. Legend:** ESTADOS UNIDOS MEXICANOS **Rev. Legend:** ESTADO DE MÉXICO **Edge:** Segmented reeding **Mint:** Mexico City

Date	Mintage	F12	VF20	XF40	MS60	MS63
2004Mo	1,000	PF65 1,200				

KM# 750   100 PESOS
33.94 g., Bi-Metallic .925 Silver 16.812g center in Aluminum-Bronze ring, 39.04mm. **Subject:** 180th Anniversary of Federation **Obv.** National arms **Rev:** State arms **Series:** First **Obv. Legend:** ESTADOS UNIDOS MEXICANOS **Rev. Legend:** ESTADO DE JALISCO **Edge:** Segmented reeding

Date	Mintage	F12	VF20	XF40	MS60	MS63
2004Mo	249,115	—	—	—	35.00	40.00

KM# 816   100 PESOS
29.17 g., Bi-Metallic .999 Gold 17.154g center in .999 Silver 12.015g ring, 34.5mm. **Subject:** 180th Anniversary of Federation **Obv.** National arms **Rev:** State arms **Series:** First **Obv. Legend:** ESTADOS UNIDOS MEXICANOS **Rev. Legend:** ESTADO DE JALISCO **Edge:** Segmented reeding

Date	Mintage	F12	VF20	XF40	MS60	MS63
2004Mo	1,000	PF65 1,200				

KM# 705   100 PESOS
33.74 g., Bi-Metallic .925 16.812g Silver center in Aluminum-Bronze ring, 39mm. **Subject:** 400th Anniversary of Don Quijote de la Manchia **Obv.** National arms **Rev:** Skeletal figure on horseback with spear galloping right **Obv. Legend:** ESTADOS UNIDOS MEXICANOS **Edge:** Segmented reeding **Mint:** Mexico City

Date	Mintage	VF20	XF40	MS60	MS63
2005Mo	726,833	—	—	25.00	32.00
2005Mo Prooflike	3,761	—	—	—	75.00
2006Mo	5,201	PF63 60.00			

KM# 730 100 PESOS
33.83 g., Bi-Metallic .925 Silver 16.812g center in Aluminum-Bronze ring, 39.9mm. **Subject:** Monetary Reform Centennial **Obv.** National arms **Rev:** Radiant Liberty Cap divides date above value within circle **Edge:** Segmented reeding **Mint:** Mexico City

Date	Mintage	F12	VF20	XF40	MS60	MS63
2005Mo	49,716	—	—	—	40.00	45.00
2005Mo	—	PF63 75.00				

KM# 731 100 PESOS
33.83 g., Bi-Metallic .925 Silver 16.812g center in Aluminum-Bronze ring, 39.9mm. **Subject:** Mexico City Mint's 470th Anniversary **Obv.** National arms **Rev:** Screw press, value and date within circle **Edge:** Segmented reeding **Mint:** Mexico City

Date	Mintage	F12	VF20	XF40	MS60	MS63
2005Mo	49,895	—	—	—	40.00	45.00
2005Mo	—	PF63 95.00				

KM# 732 100 PESOS
33.83 g., Bi-Metallic .925 Silver 16.812g center in Aluminum-Bronze ring, 39.9mm. **Subject:** Bank of Mexico's 80th Anniversary **Obv.** National arms **Rev:** Back design of the 1925 hundred peso note **Edge:** Segmented reeding **Mint:** Mexico City

Date	Mintage	F12	VF20	XF40	MS60	MS63
2005Mo	49,712	—	—	—	40.00	45.00
2005Mo	—	PF63 95.00				

KM# 717 100 PESOS
33.94 g., Bi-Metallic .925 Silver 16.812g center in Brass ring, 39.04mm. **Subject:** 180th Anniversary of Federation **Obv.** National arms **Rev:** State arms **Series:** First **Obv. Legend:** ESTADOS UNIDOS MEXICANOS **Rev. Legend:** ESTADO DE HIDALGO **Edge:** Segmented reeding **Mint:** Mexico City

Date	Mintage	F12	VF20	XF40	MS60	MS63
2005Mo	249,820	—	—	—	35.00	40.00

KM# 817 100 PESOS
29.17 g., Bi-Metallic .999 Gold 17.154g center in .999 Silver 12.015g ring, 34.5mm. **Subject:** 180th Anniversary of Federation **Obv.** National arms **Rev:** State arms **Series:** First **Obv. Legend:** ESTADOS UNIDOS MEXICANOS **Rev. Legend:** ESTADO DE HIDALGO **Edge:** Segmented reeding **Mint:** Mexico City

Date	Mintage	F12	VF20	XF40	MS60	MS63
2005Mo	1,000	PF65 1,200				

KM# 716 100 PESOS
33.94 g., Bi-Metallic .925 Silver 16.812g center in Brass ring, 39.04mm. **Subject:** 180th Anniversary of Federation **Obv.** National arms **Rev:** State arms **Series:** First **Obv. Legend:** ESTADOS UNIDOS MEXICANOS **Rev. Legend:** ESTADO DE GUERRERO **Edge:** Segmented reeding **Mint:** Mexico City

Date	Mintage	F12	VF20	XF40	MS60	MS63
2005Mo	248,850	—	—	—	35.00	40.00

KM# 818 100 PESOS
29.17 g., Bi-Metallic .999 Gold 17.154g center in .999 Silver 12.015 ring, 34.5mm. **Subject:** 180th Anniversary of Federation **Obv.** National arms **Rev:** State arms **Series:** First **Obv. Legend:** ESTADOS UNIDOS MEXICANOS **Rev. Legend:** ESTADO DE GUERRERO **Edge:** Segmented reeding **Mint:** Mexico City

Date	Mintage	F12	VF20	XF40	MS60	MS63
2005Mo	1,000	PF65 1,200				

KM# 715 100 PESOS
33.94 g., Bi-Metallic .925 Silver 16.812g center in Brass ring, 39.04mm. **Subject:** 180th Anniversary of Federation **Obv.** National arms **Rev:** State arms **Series:** First **Obv. Legend:** ESTADOS UNIDOS MEXICANOS **Rev. Legend:** ESTADO DE GUANAJUATO **Edge:** Segmented reeding

Date	Mintage	F12	VF20	XF40	MS60	MS63
2005Mo	249,489	—	—	—	35.00	40.00

KM# 819   100 PESOS
29.17 g., Bi-Metallic .999 Gold 17.154g center in .999 Silver 12.015g ring, 34.5mm. **Subject:** 180th Anniversary of Federation **Obv.** National arms **Rev:** State arms **Series:** First **Obv. Legend:** ESTADOS UNIDOS MEXICANOS **Rev. Legend:** ESTADO DE GUANAJUATO **Edge:** Segmented reeding **Mint:** Mexico City

Date	Mintage	F12	VF20	XF40	MS60	MS63
2005Mo	1,000	PF65 1,200				

KM# 714   100 PESOS
33.94 g., Bi-Metallic .925 Silver 16.812g center in Brass ring, 39.04mm. **Subject:** 180th Anniversary of Federation **Obv.** National arms **Rev:** State arms **Series:** First **Obv. Legend:** ESTADOS UNIDOS MEXICANOS **Rev. Legend:** ESTADO DE DURANGO **Edge:** Segmented reeding

Date	Mintage	F12	VF20	XF40	MS60	MS63
2005Mo	249,774	—	—	—	35.00	40.00

KM# 820   100 PESOS
29.17 g., Bi-Metallic .999 Gold 17.154g center in .999 silver 12.015g ring, 34.5mm. **Subject:** 180th Anniversary of Federation **Obv.** National arms **Rev:** State arms **Series:** First **Obv. Legend:** ESTADOS UNIDOS MEXICANOS **Rev. Legend:** ESTADO DE DURANGO **Edge:** Segmented reeding **Mint:** Mexico City

Date	Mintage	F12	VF20	XF40	MS60	MS63
2005Mo	1,000	PF65 1,200				

KM# 754   100 PESOS
33.94 g., Bi-Metallic .925 Silver 16.812g center in Aluminum-Bronze ring, 39.04mm. **Subject:** 180th Anniversary of Federation **Obv.** National arms **Rev:** State arms **Series:** First **Obv. Legend:** ESTADOS UNIDOS MEXICANOS **Rev. Legend:** ESTADO DE CHIHUAHUA **Edge:** Segmented reeding **Mint:** Mexico City

Date	Mintage	F12	VF20	XF40	MS60	MS63
2005Mo	249,102	—	—	—	35.00	40.00

KM# 822   100 PESOS
29.17 g., Bi-Metallic .999 Gold 17.154g center in .999 Silver 12.015g ring, 34.5mm. **Subject:** 180th Anniversary of Federation **Obv.** National arms **Rev:** State arms **Series:** First **Obv. Legend:** ESTADOS UNIDOS MEXICANOS **Rev. Legend:** ESTADO DE CHIHUAHUA **Edge:** Segmented reeding **Mint:** Mexico City

Date	Mintage	F12	VF20	XF40	MS60	MS63
2005Mo	1,000	PF65 1,200				

KM# 713   100 PESOS
33.94 g., Bi-Metallic .925 Silver 16.812g center in Brass ring, 39.04mm. **Subject:** 180th Anniversary of Federation **Obv.** National arms **Rev:** Federal District arms **Series:** First **Obv. Legend:** ESTADOS UNIDOS MEXICANOS **Rev. Legend:** DISTRITO FEDERAL **Edge:** Segmented reeding

Date	Mintage	F12	VF20	XF40	MS60	MS63
2005Mo	249,461	—	—	—	35.00	40.00

KM# 821   100 PESOS
29.17 g., Bi-Metallic .999 Gold 17.154g center in .999 Silver 12.015g ring, 34.5mm. **Subject:** 180th Anniversary of Federation **Obv.** National arms **Rev:** Federal District arms **Series:** First **Obv. Legend:** ESTADOS UNIDOS MEXICANOS **Rev. Legend:** DISTRITO FEDERAL **Edge:** Segmented reeding **Mint:** Mexico City

Date	Mintage	F12	VF20	XF40	MS60	MS63
2005Mo	1,000	PF65 1,200				

KM# 712   100 PESOS
33.94 g., Bi-Metallic .925 Silver 16.812g center in Brass ring, 39.04mm. **Subject:** 180th Anniversary of Federation **Obv.** National arms **Rev:** State arms **Series:** First **Obv. Legend:** ESTADOS UNIDOS MEXICANOS **Rev. Legend:** ESTADO DE CHIAPAS **Edge:** Segmented reeding **Mint:** Mexico City

Date	Mintage	F12	VF20	XF40	MS60	MS63
2005Mo	249,417	—	—	—	35.00	40.00

KM# 823   100 PESOS
29.17 g., Bi-Metallic .999 Gold 17.154g center in .999 Silver 12.015g ring, 34.5mm. **Subject:** 180th Anniversary of Federation **Obv.** National arms **Rev:** State arms **Series:** First **Obv. Legend:** ESTADOS UNIDOS MEXICANOS **Rev. Legend:** ESTADO DE CHIAPAS **Edge:** Segmented reeding **Mint:** Mexico City

Date	Mintage	F12	VF20	XF40	MS60	MS63
2005Mo	1,000	PF65 1,200				

KM# 727 100 PESOS
33.94 g., Bi-Metallic .925 Silver 16.812g center in Aluminum-Bronze ring, 39.04mm. **Subject:** 180th Anniversary of Federation **Obv.** National arms **Rev:** State arms **Series:** First **Obv. Legend:** ESTADOS UNIDOS MEXICANOS **Rev. Legend:** ESTADO DE CAMPECHE **Edge:** Segmented reeding **Mint:** Mexico City

Date	Mintage	F12	VF20	XF40	MS60	MS63
2005Mo	249,040	—	—	—	35.00	40.00

KM# 729 100 PESOS
33.83 g., Bi-Metallic .925 Silver 16.812g center in Aluminum-Bronze ring, 39.04mm. **Subject:** 180th Anniversary of Federation **Obv.** National arms **Rev:** State arms **Series:** First **Obv. Legend:** ESTADOS UNIDOS MEXICANOS **Rev. Legend:** ESTADO DE COLIMA **Edge:** Segmented reeding **Mint:** Mexico City

Date	Mintage	F12	VF20	XF40	MS60	MS63
2005Mo	248,850	—	—	—	35.00	40.00

KM# 826 100 PESOS
29.17 g., Bi-Metallic .999 Gold 17.154g center in .999 Silver 12.015g ring, 34.5mm. **Subject:** 180th Anniversary of Federation **Obv.** National arms **Rev:** State arms **Series:** First **Obv. Legend:** ESTADOS UNIDOS MEXICANOS **Rev. Legend:** ESTADO DE CAMPECHE **Edge:** Segmented reeding **Mint:** Mexico City

Date	Mintage	F12	VF20	XF40	MS60	MS63
2005Mo	1,000	PF65 1,200				

KM# 824 100 PESOS
29.17 g., Bi-Metallic .999 Gold 17.154g center in .999 Silver 12.015g ring, 34.5mm. **Subject:** 180th Anniversary of Federation **Obv.** National arms **Rev:** State arms **Series:** First **Obv. Legend:** ESTADOS UNIDOS MEXICANOS **Rev. Legend:** ESTADO DE COLIMA **Edge:** Segmented reeding **Mint:** Mexico City

Date	Mintage	F12	VF20	XF40	MS60	MS63
2005Mo	1,000	PF65 1,200				

KM# 752 100 PESOS
33.94 g., Bi-Metallic .925 Silver 16.812g center in Aluminum-Bronze ring, 39.04mm. **Subject:** 180th Anniversary of Federation **Obv.** National arms **Rev:** State arms **Series:** First **Obv. Legend:** ESTADOS UNIDOS MEXICANOS **Rev. Legend:** ESTADO DE COAHUILA DE ZARAGOZA **Edge:** Segmented reeding **Mint:** Mexico City

Date	Mintage	F12	VF20	XF40	MS60	MS63
2005Mo	247,991	—	—	—	35.00	40.00

KM# 825 100 PESOS
29.17 g., Bi-Metallic .999 Gold 17.154g center in .999 Silver 12.015g ring, 34.5mm. **Subject:** 180th Anniversary of Federation **Obv.** National arms **Rev:** State arms **Series:** First **Obv. Legend:** ESTADOS UNIDOS MEXICANOS **Rev. Legend:** ESTADO DE COAHUILA DE ZARAGOZA **Edge:** Segmented reeding **Mint:** Mexico City

Date	Mintage	F12	VF20	XF40	MS60	MS63
2005Mo	1,000	PF65 1,200				

KM# 725 100 PESOS
33.94 g., Bi-Metallic .925 Silver 16.812g center in Aluminum-Bronze ring, 39.04mm. **Subject:** 180th Anniversary of Federation **Obv.** National arms **Rev:** State arms **Series:** First **Obv. Legend:** ESTADOS UNIDOS MEXICANOS **Rev. Legend:** ESTADO DE BAJA CALIFORNIA SUR **Edge:** Segmented reeding **Mint:** Mexico City

Date	Mintage	F12	VF20	XF40	MS60	MS63
2005Mo	249,585	—	—	—	35.00	40.00

KM# 827 100 PESOS
29.17 g., Bi-Metallic .999 Gold 17.154g center in .999 Silver 12.015g ring, 34.5mm. **Subject:** 180th Anniversary of Federation **Obv.** National arms **Rev:** State arms **Series:** First **Obv. Legend:** ESTADOS UNIDOS MEXICANOS **Rev. Legend:** ESTADO DE BAJA CALIFORNIA SUR **Edge:** Segmented reeding **Mint:** Mexico City

Date	Mintage	F12	VF20	XF40	MS60	MS63
2005Mo	1,000	PF65 1,200				

KM# 723   100 PESOS
33.94 g., Bi-Metallic .925 Silver 16.812g center in Aluminum-Bronze ring, 39.04mm. **Subject:** 180th Anniversary of Federation **Obv.** National arms **Rev:** State arms **Series:** First **Obv. Legend:** ESTADOS UNIDOS MEXICANOS **Rev. Legend:** ESTADO DE BAJA CALIFORNIA **Edge:** Segmented reeding **Mint:** Mexico City

Date	Mintage	F12	VF20	XF40	MS60	MS63
2005Mo	249,263	—	—	—	35.00	40.00

KM# 828   100 PESOS
29.17 g., Bi-Metallic .999 Gold 17.154g center in .999 Silver 12.015g ring, 34.5mm. **Subject:** 180th Anniversary of Federation **Obv.** National arms **Rev:** State arms **Series:** First **Obv. Legend:** ESTADOS UNIDOS MEXICANOS **Rev. Legend:** ESTADO DE BAJA CALIFORNIA **Edge:** Segmented reeding **Mint:** Mexico City

Date	Mintage	F12	VF20	XF40	MS60	MS63
2005Mo	1,000		PF65 1,200			

KM# 719   100 PESOS
33.83 g., Bi-Metallic .925 Silver 16.812g center in Aluminum-Bronze ring, 39.04mm. **Obv.** National arms **Rev:** Facade of the San Marcos garden above sculpture of national emblem at left, San Antonio Temple at right **Series:** Second **Obv. Legend:** ESTADOS UNIDOS MEXICANOS **Rev. Legend:** AGUASCALIENTES **Edge:** Segmented reeding **Mint:** Mexico City

Date	Mintage	F12	VF20	XF40	MS60	MS63
2005Mo	149,705	—	—	—	25.00	30.00

KM# 862   100 PESOS
29.17 g., Bi-Metallic .999 Gold 17.154g center in .999 Silver 12.015g ring, 34.5mm. **Obv.** National arms **Rev:** Facade of the San Marcos garden above sculpture of national emblem at left, San Antonio temple at right **Series:** Second **Obv. Legend:** ESTADOS UNIDOS MEXICANOS **Rev. Legend:** AGUASCALIENTES **Edge:** Segmented reeding **Mint:** Mexico City

Date	Mintage	F12	VF20	XF40	MS60	MS63
2005Mo	600		PF65 1,200			

KM# 721   100 PESOS
33.94 g., Bi-Metallic .925 Silver 16.812g center in Aluminum-Bronze ring, 39.04mm. **Subject:** 180th Anniversary of Federation **Obv.** National arms **Rev:** Estados de Aguascalientes state arms **Series:** First **Obv. Legend:** ESTADOS UNIDOS MEXICANOS **Rev. Legend:** ESTADO DE AGUASCALIENTES **Edge:** Segmented reeding **Mint:** Mexico City

Date	Mintage	F12	VF20	XF40	MS60	MS63
2005Mo	248,410	—	—	—	35.00	40.00

KM# 829   100 PESOS
29.17 g., Bi-Metallic .999 Gold 17.154g center in .999 Silver 12.015g ring, 34.5mm. **Subject:** 180th Anniversary of Federation **Obv.** National arms **Rev:** State arms **Series:** First **Obv. Legend:** ESTADOS UNIDOS MEXICANOS **Rev. Legend:** ESTADO DE AGUASCALIENTES **Edge:** Segmented reeding **Mint:** Mexico City

Date	Mintage	F12	VF20	XF40	MS60	MS63
2005Mo	1,000		PF65 1,200			

KM# 758   100 PESOS
33.94 g., Bi-Metallic .925 Silver 16.812g center in Aluminum-Bronze ring, 39.04mm. **Obv.** National arms **Rev:** Ram's head and value within circle **Series:** Second **Obv. Legend:** ESTADOS UNIDOS MEXICANOS **Rev. Legend:** BAJA CALIFORNIA - GOBIERNO DEL ESTADO **Edge:** Segmented reeding **Mint:** Mexico City

Date	Mintage	F12	VF20	XF40	MS60	MS63
2005Mo	149,771	—	—	—	25.00	30.00

KM# 863   100 PESOS
29.17 g., Bi-Metallic .999 Gold 17.154g center in .999 Silver 12.015g ring, 34.5mm. **Obv.** National arms **Rev:** Ram's head, mountain outline in background **Series:** Second **Obv. Legend:** ESTTUDOS UNIDOS MEXICANOS **Rev. Legend:** BAJA CALIFORNIA - GOBIERNO DEL ESTADO **Edge:** Segmented reeding **Mint:** Mexico City

Date	Mintage	F12	VF20	XF40	MS60	MS63
2005Mo	600		PF65 1,200			

KM# 762 100 PESOS
33.94 g., Bi-Metallic .925 Silver 16.812g center in Aluminum-Bronze ring, 39.04mm. **Obv.** National arms **Rev:** Outlined map of peninsula at center, cave painting of deer behind, cactus at right **Series:** Second **Obv. Legend:** ESTADOS UNIDOS MEXICANOS **Rev. Legend:** ESTADO DE BAJA CALIFORNIA SUR **Edge:** Segmented reeding **Mint:** Mexico City

Date	Mintage	F12	VF20	XF40	MS60	MS63
2005Mo	149,152	—	—	—	25.00	30.00

KM# 764 100 PESOS
33.70 g., Bi-Metallic .925 Silver 16.812g center in Aluminum-Bronze ring, **Subject:** 200th Anniversary Birth of Benito Juarez Garcia **Obv.** National arms **Rev:** Bust 1/4 left within circle **Mint:** Mexico City

Date	Mintage	F12	VF20	XF40	MS60	MS63
2006Mo	49,913	—	—	—	40.00	45.00

KM# 864 100 PESOS
29.17 g., Bi-Metallic .999 Gold 17.154g center in .999 Silver 12.015g ring, 34.5mm. **Obv.** National arms **Rev:** Outlined map of peninsula at center, cave painting of deer behind, cactus at right **Series:** Second **Obv. Legend:** ESTADOS UNIDOS MEXICANOS **Rev. Legend:** ESTADO DE BAJA CALIFORNIA SUR **Edge:** Segmented reeding **Mint:** Mexico City

Date	Mintage	F12	VF20	XF40	MS60	MS63
2006Mo	600	PF65 1,200				

KM# 760 100 PESOS
33.94 g., Bi-Metallic .925 Silver 16.812g center in Aluminum-Bronze ring, 39.04mm. **Subject:** Estado de Campeche **Obv.** National arms **Rev:** Jade mask - Calakmul, Campeche **Series:** Second **Obv. Legend:** ESTADOS UNIDOS MEXICANOS **Rev. Legend:** ESTADO DE CAMPECHE **Edge:** Segmented reeding **Mint:** Mexico City

Date	Mintage	F12	VF20	XF40	MS60	MS63
2006Mo	149,803	—	—	—	25.00	30.00

KM# 865 100 PESOS
29.17 g., Bi-Metallic .999 Gold 17.154g center in .999 Silver 12.015g ring, 34.5mm. **Obv.** National arms **Rev:** Jade mask - Calakmul, Campeche **Series:** Second **Obv. Legend:** ESTADOS UNIDOS MEXICANOS **Rev. Legend:** ESTADO DE CAMPECHE **Edge:** Segmented reeding **Mint:** Mexico City

Date	Mintage	F12	VF20	XF40	MS60	MS63
2006Mo	600	PF65 1,200				

KM# 781 100 PESOS
33.70 g., Bi-Metallic .925 Silver 16.812g center in Aluminum-Bronze ring, 39.04mm. **Obv.** National arms **Rev:** Outlined map with turtle, mine cart above grapes at center, Friendship Dam above Christ of the Nodas at left, chimneys above crucibles and bell tower of Santiago's cathedral at right **Series:** Second **Obv. Legend:** ESTADOS UNIDOS MEXICANOS **Rev. Legend:** COAHUILA DE ZARAGOZA **Edge:** Segmented reeding **Mint:** Mexico City

Date	Mintage	F12	VF20	XF40	MS60	MS63
2006Mo	149,560	—	—	—	25.00	30.00

KM# 866 100 PESOS
29.17 g., Bi-Metallic .999 Gold 17.154g center in .999 Silver 12.015g ring, 34.5mm. **Obv.** National arms **Rev:** Outlined map with turtle, mine cart above grapes at center, Friendship dam above Christ of the Nodas at left, chimneys above crucibles and bell tower of Santiago's cathedral at right **Series:** Second **Obv. Legend:** ESTADOS UNIDOS MEXICANOS **Rev. Inscription:** COAHUILA DE ZARAGOZA **Edge:** Segmented reeding **Mint:** Mexico City

Date	Mintage	F12	VF20	XF40	MS60	MS63
2006Mo	600	PF65 1,200				

KM# 777 100 PESOS
33.94 g., Bi-Metallic .925 Silver 16.812g center in Aluminum-Bronze ring, 39.04mm. **Obv.** National arms **Rev:** State

arms at lower center, Nevado de Colima and Volcan de Fuego volcanos in background **Series:** Second **Obv. Legend:** ESTADOS UNIDOS MEXICANOS **Rev. Legend:** Colima **Rev. Inscription:** GENEROSO **Edge:** Segmented reeding **Mint:** Mexico City

Date	Mintage	F12	VF20	XF40	MS60	MS63
2006Mo	149,041	—	—	—	25.00	30.00

KM# 867 100 PESOS
29.17 g., Bi-Metallic .999 Gold 17.154g center in .999 Silver 12.015 ring, 34.5mm. **Obv.** National arms **Rev:** State arms at lower center, Nevado de Colima and Volcan de Fuego volcanos in background **Series:** Second **Obv. Legend:** ESTADOS UNIDOS MEXICANOS **Rev. Legend:** Colima **Rev. Inscription:** GENEROSO **Edge:** Segmented reeding

Date	Mintage	F12	VF20	XF40	MS60	MS63
2006Mo	600	PF65 1,200				

KM# 773 100 PESOS
33.94 g., Bi-Metallic .925 Silver 16.812g center in Aluminum-Bronze ring, 39.04mm. **Obv.** National arms **Rev:** Head of Pakal, ancient Mayan king, Palenque **Series:** Second **Obv. Legend:** ESTADOS UNIDOS MEXICANOS **Rev. Legend:** ESTADO DE CHIAPAS - CABEZA MAYA DEL REY PAKAL, PALENQUE **Edge:** Segmented reeding **Mint:** Mexico City

Date	Mintage	F12	VF20	XF40	MS60	MS63
2006Mo	149,491	—	—	—	25.00	30.00

KM# 868 100 PESOS
29.17 g., Bi-Metallic .999 Gold 17.154g center in .999 Silver 12.015g ring, 34.5mm. **Obv.** National arms **Rev:** Head of Pakal, ancient Mayan king, Palenque **Series:** Second **Obv. Legend:** ESTADOS UNIDOS MEXICANOS **Rev. Legend:** ESTADO DE CHIAPAS - CABEZA MAYA DEL REY PAKAL, PALENQUE **Edge:** Segmented reeding **Mint:** Mexico City

Date	Mintage	F12	VF20	XF40	MS60	MS63
2006Mo	600	PF65 1,200				

KM# 775 100 PESOS
33.94 g., Bi-Metallic .925 Silver 16.812g center in Aluminum-Bronze ring, 39.04mm. **Obv.** National arms **Rev:** Angel of Liberty **Series:** Second **Obv. Legend:** ESTADOS UNIDOS MEXICANOS **Rev. Legend:** MÉXICO - ANGEL DE LA LIBERTAD, CHIHUAHUA **Edge:** Segmented reeding

Date	Mintage	F12	VF20	XF40	MS60	MS63
2006Mo	149,557	—	—	—	25.00	30.00

KM# 869 100 PESOS
29.17 g., Bi-Metallic .999 Gold 17.154g center in .999 Silver 12.015g ring, 34.5mm. **Obv.** National arms **Rev:** Angel of Liberty **Series:** Second **Obv. Legend:** ESTADOS UNIDOS MEXICANOS **Rev. Legend:** MÉXICO - ANGEL DE LA LIBERTAD, CHIHUAHUA **Edge:** Segmented reeding **Mint:** Mexico City

Date	Mintage	F12	VF20	XF40	MS60	MS63
2006Mo	600	PF65 1,200				

KM# 779 100 PESOS
33.94 g., Bi-Metallic .925 Silver 16.812g center in Aluminum-Bronze ring, 39.04mm. **Obv.** National arms **Rev:** National Palace **Series:** Second **Obv. Legend:** ESTADOS UNIDOS MEXICANOS **Rev. Legend:** DISTRITO FEDERAL - ANTIGUO AYUNTAMIENTO **Edge:** Segmented reeding **Mint:** Mexico City

Date	Mintage	F12	VF20	XF40	MS60	MS63
2006Mo	149,525	—	—	—	25.00	30.00

KM# 870 100 PESOS
29.17 g., Bi-Metallic .999 Gold 17.154g center in .999 Silver 12.015g ring, 34.5mm. **Obv.** National arms **Rev:** National palace **Series:** Second **Obv. Legend:** ESTADOS UNIDOS MEXICANOS **Rev. Legend:** DISTRITO FEDERAL - ANTIGUO AYUNTAMIENTO **Edge:** Segmented reeding

Date	Mintage	F12	VF20	XF40	MS60	MS63
2006Mo	600	PF65 1,200				

KM# 787 100 PESOS
33.94 g., Bi-Metallic .925 Silver 16.812g center in Brass ring, 39.04mm. **Obv.** National arms **Rev:** Tree **Series:** Second **Obv. Legend:** ESTADOS UNIDOS MEXICANOS **Rev. Legend:** PRIMERA RESERVA NACIONAL FORESTAL - DURANGO **Edge:** Segmented reeding **Mint:** Mexico City

Date	Mintage	F12	VF20	XF40	MS60	MS63
2006Mo	149,034	—	—	—	25.00	30.00

KM# 871 100 PESOS
29.17 g., Bi-Metallic .999 Gold 17.154g center in .999 Silver 12.015g ring, 34.5mm. **Obv.** National arms **Rev:** Tree **Series:** Second **Obv. Legend:** ESYADOS UNIDOS MEXICANOS **Rev. Legend:** PRIMERA RESERVA NACIONAL RORESTAL - DURANGO **Edge:** Segmented reeding **Mint:** Mexico City

Date	Mintage	F12	VF20	XF40	MS60	MS63
2006Mo	600	PF65 1,200				

KM# 789   100 PESOS
33.94 g., Bi-Metallic .925 Silver 16.812g center in Brass ring, 39.04mm. **Obv.** National arms **Rev:** State arms at center, statue of Miguel Hidalgo at left, monument to Pipla at lower right **Series:** Second **Obv. Legend:** ESTADOS UNIDOS MEXICANOS **Rev. Inscription:** Guanajuato **Edge:** Segmented reeding **Mint:** Mexico City

Date	Mintage	F12	VF20	XF40	MS60	MS63
2006Mo	149,921	—	—	—	25.00	30.00

KM# 872   100 PESOS
29.17 g., Bi-Metallic .999 Gold 17.154g center in .999 Silver 12.015g ring, 34.50mm. **Obv.** National arms **Rev:** State arms at lower center, statue of Miguel Hidalgo at left, monument to Pipila at lower right **Series:** Second **Obv. Legend:** ESTADOS UNIDOS MEXICANOS **Rev. Inscription:** Guanajauto **Edge:** Segmented reeding **Mint:** Mexico City

Date	Mintage	F12	VF20	XF40	MS60	MS63
2006Mo	600		PF65 1,200			

KM# 791   100 PESOS
33.94 g., Bi-Metallic .925 Silver 16.812g center in Brass ring, 39.04mm. **Obv.** National arms **Rev:** Stylized portrait of Vicente Guerrero at left, church of Taxco at upper center, Acapulco's la Quebrada with diver above Christmas Eve flower and mask **Series:** Second **Obv. Legend:** ESTADOS UNIDOS MEXICANOS **Rev. Legend:** GUERRERO **Edge:** Segmented reeding **Mint:** Mexico City

Date	Mintage	F12	VF20	XF40	MS60	MS63
2006Mo	149,675	—	—	—	25.00	30.00

KM# 873   100 PESOS
29.17 g., Bi-Metallic .999 Gold 17.154g center in .999 Silver 12.015g ring, 34.5mm. **Obv.** National arms **Rev:** Stylized portrait of Vicente Guerrero at left, church of Taxco at upper center, Acapulco's la Quebrada with diver over Christmas Eve flower and mask **Series:** Second **Obv. Legend:** ESTADOS UNIDOS MEXICANOS **Rev. Legend:** GUERRERO **Edge:** Segmented reeding **Mint:** Mexico City

Date	Mintage	F12	VF20	XF40	MS60	MS63
2006Mo	600		PF65 1,200			

KM# 793   100 PESOS
33.94 g., Bi-Metallic .925 Silver 16.812g center in Aluminum-Bronze ring, 39.04mm. **Obv.** National arms **Rev:** Monument of Pachuca Hidalgo **Series:** Second **Obv. Legend:** ESTADOS UNIDOS MEXICANOS **Rev. Inscription:** RELOJ / MONUMENTAL / DE / PACHUCA / HIDALGO - La / Bella / Airosa **Edge:** Segmented reeding

Date	Mintage	F12	VF20	XF40	MS60	MS63
2006Mo	149,273	—	—	—	25.00	30.00

KM# 874   100 PESOS
29.17 g., Bi-Metallic .999 Gold 17.154g center in .999 Silver 12.015g ring, 34.5mm. **Obv.** National arms **Rev:** Monument of Pachuca Hidalgo **Series:** Second **Obv. Legend:** ESTADOS UNIDOS MEXICANOS **Rev. Inscription:** RELOJ / MONUMENTAL / DE / PACHUCA / HIDALGO **Edge:** Segmented reeding **Mint:** Mexico City

Date	Mintage	F12	VF20	XF40	MS60	MS63
2006Mo	600		PF65 1,200			

KM# 795   100 PESOS
33.94 g., Bi-Metallic .925 Silver 16.812g center in Brass ring, 39.04mm. **Obv.** National arms **Rev:** Hospicio Cabañas orphanage **Series:** Second **Obv. Legend:** ESTADOS UNIDOS MEXICANOS **Rev. Legend:** ESTADO DE JALISCO **Edge:** Segmented reeding **Mint:** Mexico City

Date	Mintage	F12	VF20	XF40	MS60	MS63
2006Mo	149,750	—	—	—	25.00	30.00

KM# 875   100 PESOS
29.17 g., Bi-Metallic .999 Gold 17.154g center in .999 Silver 12.015g ring, 34.5mm. **Obv.** National arms **Rev:** Hospicio Cabañas orphanage **Series:** Second **Obv. Legend:** ESTADOS UNIDOS MEXICANOS **Rev. Legend:** ESTADO DE JALISCO **Edge:** Segmented reeding **Mint:** Mexico City

Date	Mintage	F12	VF20	XF40	MS60	MS63
2006Mo	600		PF65 1,200			

KM# 802   100 PESOS
33.94 g., Bi-Metallic .925 Silver 16.812g center in Aluminum-Bronze ring, 39.04mm. **Obv.** National arms **Rev:** Pyramid de la Loona (moon) **Series:** Second **Obv. Legend:** ESTADOS UNIDOS MEXICANOS **Rev. Legend:** ESTADO DE MÉXICO **Edge:** Segmented reeding **Mint:** Mexico City

Date	Mintage	F12	VF20	XF40	MS60	MS63
2006Mo	149,377	—	—	—	25.00	30.00

KM# 876   100 PESOS
29.17 g., Bi-Metallic .999 Gold 17.154g center in .999 Silver 12.015g ring, 34.5mm. **Obv.** National arms **Rev:** Pyramid de la Looona (moon) **Series:** Second **Obv. Legend:** ESTADOS UNIDOS MEXICANOS **Rev. Legend:** ESTADO DE MÉXICO **Edge:** Segmented reeding **Mint:** Mexico City

Date	Mintage	F12	VF20	XF40	MS60	MS63
2006Mo	600	PF65 1,200				

KM# 785   100 PESOS
33.94 g., Bi-Metallic .925 Silver 16.812g center in Aluminum-Bronze ring, 39.04mm. **Obv.** National arms **Rev:** Four Monarch butterflies **Series:** Second **Obv. Legend:** ESTADOS UNIDOS MEXICANOS **Rev. Legend:** ESTADO DE MICHOACÁN **Edge:** Segmented reeding **Mint:** Mexico City

Date	Mintage	F12	VF20	XF40	MS60	MS63
2006Mo	149,730	—	—	—	25.00	30.00

KM# 877   100 PESOS
29.17 g., Bi-Metallic .999 Gold 17.154g center in .999 Silver 12.015g ring, 34.5mm. **Obv.** National arms **Rev:** Four Monarch butterflies **Series:** Second **Obv. Legend:** ESTADOS UNIDOS MEXICANOS **Rev. Legend:** ESTADO DE MICHOACÁN **Edge:** Segmented reeding **Mint:** Mexico City

Date	Mintage	F12	VF20	XF40	MS60	MS63
2006Mo	600	PF65 1,200				

KM# 798   100 PESOS
33.94 g., Bi-Metallic .925 Silver 16.812g center in Aluminum-Bronze ring, 39.04mm. **Obv.** National arms **Rev:** Isle de Mexcaltitlán **Series:** Second **Obv. Legend:** ESTADOS UNIDOS MEXICANOS **Rev. Legend:** ESTADO DE NAYARIT **Edge:** Segmented reeding **Mint:** Mexico City

Date	Mintage	F12	VF20	XF40	MS60	MS63
2007Mo	149,560	—	—	—	25.00	30.00

KM# 879   100 PESOS
29.17 g., Bi-Metallic .999 Gold 17.154g center in .999 Silver 12.015g ring, 34.5mm. **Obv.** National arms **Rev:** Isle de Mexcaltitlán **Series:** Second **Obv. Legend:** ESTADOS UNIDOS MEXICANOS **Rev. Legend:** ESTADO DE NAYARIT **Edge:** Segmented reeding **Mint:** Mexico City

Date	Mintage	F12	VF20	XF40	MS60	MS63
2007Mo	600	PF65 1,200				

KM# 800   100 PESOS
33.94 g., Bi-Metallic .925 Silver 16.812g center in Aluminum-Bronze ring, 39.04mm. **Obv.** National arms **Rev:** 1/2 length figure of Chinelo (local dancer) at right, Palacio de Cortes in background **Series:** Second **Obv. Legend:** ESTADOS UNIDOS MEXICANOS **Rev. Inscription:** ESTADO DE / MORELOS **Edge:** Segmented reeding **Mint:** Mexico City

Date	Mintage	F12	VF20	XF40	MS60	MS63
2006Mo	149,648	—	—	—	25.00	30.00

KM# 878   100 PESOS
29.17 g., Bi-Metallic .999 Gold 17.154g center in .999 Silver 12.015g ring, 34.5mm. **Obv.** National arms **Rev:** 1/2 length figure of Chinelo (local dancer) at right, Palacio de Cortes in background **Series:** Second **Obv. Legend:** ESTADOS UNIDOS MEXICANOS **Rev. Inscription:** ESTADO DE / MORELOS **Edge:** Segmented reeding **Mint:** Mexico City

Date	Mintage	F12	VF20	XF40	MS60	MS63
2006Mo	600	PF65 1,200				

KM# 848   100 PESOS
33.94 g., Bi-Metallic .925 Silver 20.1753 center in Aluminum-Bronze ring, 39.04mm. **Obv.** National arms **Rev:** Old foundry in Parque Fundidora (public park) at right, Cerro de la Silla (Saddle Hill) in background **Series:** Second **Obv. Legend:** ESTADOS UNIDOS MEXICANOE **Rev. Legend:** ESTADO DE NUEVO LÉON **Edge:** Segmented reeding **Mint:** Mexico City

Date	Mintage	F12	VF20	XF40	MS60	MS63
2007Mo	149,425	—	—	—	25.00	30.00

KM# 880   100 PESOS
29.17 g., Bi-Metallic .999 Gold 17.154g center in .999 Silver 12.015g ring, 34.5mm. **Obv.** National arms **Rev:** Old foundry in Parque Fundidora (public park) at right, Cerro de la Silla (Saddle hill) in background **Series:** Second **Obv. Legend:** ESTADOS UNIDOS MEXICANOS **Rev. Legend:** ESTADO DE NUEVO LEÓN **Edge:** Segmented reeding **Mint:** Mexico City

Date	Mintage	F12	VF20	XF40	MS60	MS63
2007Mo	600	PF65 1,200				

ESTADOS UNIDOS - REFORM COINAGE

KM# 849 100 PESOS
33.94 g., Bi-Metallic .925 Silver 20.1753g center in Aluminum-Bronze ring, 39.04mm. **Obv.** National arms **Rev:** Teatro Macedonio Alcala (theater) **Series:** Second **Obv. Legend:** ESTADOS UNIDOS MEXICANOS **Rev. Legend:** OAXACA **Edge:** Segmented reeding **Mint:** Mexico City

Date	Mintage	F12	VF20	XF40	MS60	MS63
2007Mo	149,892	—	—	—	25.00	30.00

KM# 881 100 PESOS
29.17 g., Bi-Metallic .999 Gold 17.154g center in .999 Silver 12.015g ring, 34.50mm. **Obv.** National arms **Rev:** Teatro Macedonio Alcala (theater) **Series:** Second **Obv. Legend:** ESTADOS UNIDOS MEXICANOS **Rev. Legend:** OAXACA **Edge:** Segmented reeding **Mint:** Mexico City

Date	Mintage	F12	VF20	XF40	MS60	MS63
2007Mo	600	PF65 1,200				

KM# 850 100 PESOS
33.94 g., Bi-Metallic .925 Silver 20.1753g center in Aluminum-Bronze ring, 39.04mm. **Obv.** National arms **Rev:** Talavera porcelain dish **Series:** Second **Obv. Legend:** ESTADOS UNIDOS MEXICANOS **Rev. Legend:** ESTADO DE PUEBLA **Edge:** Segmented reeding **Mint:** Mexico City

Date	Mintage	F12	VF20	XF40	MS60	MS63
2007Mo	149,474	—	—	—	25.00	30.00

KM# 882 100 PESOS
29.17 g., Bi-Metallic .999 Gold 17.154g center in .999 Silver 12.015g ring, 34.5mm. **Obv.** National arms **Rev:** Talavera porcelain dish **Series:** Second **Obv. Legend:** ESTADOS UNIDOS MEXICANOS **Rev. Legend:** ESTADO DE PUEBLA **Edge:** Segmented reeding **Mint:** Mexico City

Date	Mintage	F12	VF20	XF40	MS60	MS63
2007Mo	600	PF65 1,200				

KM# 851 100 PESOS
33.94 g., Bi-Metallic .925 Silver 20.1753g center in Aluminum-Bronze ring, 39.04mm. **Obv.** National arms **Rev:** Mask at left, rays above state arms at center, Mayan ruins at right **Series:** Second **Obv. Legend:** ESTADOS UNIDOS MEXICANOS **Rev. Legend:** QUINTANA ROO **Edge:** Segmented reeding **Mint:** Mexico City

Date	Mintage	F12	VF20	XF40	MS60	MS63
2007Mo	149,582	—	—	—	25.00	30.00

KM# 883 100 PESOS
29.17 g., Bi-Metallic .999 Gold 17.154g center in .999 Silver 12.015g ring, 34.5mm. **Obv.** National arms **Rev:** Mask at left, rays above state arms at center, Mayan ruins at right **Series:** Second **Obv. Legend:** ESTADOS UNIDOS MEXICANOS **Rev. Legend:** QUINTANA ROO **Edge:** Segmented reeding **Mint:** Mexico City

Date	Mintage	F12	VF20	XF40	MS60	MS63
2007Mo	600	PF65 1,200				

KM# 852 100 PESOS
33.94 g., Bi-Metallic .925 Silver 20.1753 center in Aluminum-Bronze ring, 39.04mm. **Obv.** National arms **Rev:** Aqueduct of Querétaro at left, church of Santa Rosa de Viterbo at right **Series:** Second **Obv. Legend:** ESTADOS UNIDOS MEXICANOS **Rev. Legend:** ESTADO DE QUERÉTARO ARTEAGA **Edge:** Segmented reeding **Mint:** Mexico City

Date	Mintage	F12	VF20	XF40	MS60	MS63
2007Mo	149,127	—	—	—	25.00	30.00

KM# 884 100 PESOS
29.17 g., Bi-Metallic .999 Gold 17.154g center in .999 Silver 12.015g ring, 34.5mm. **Obv.** National arms **Rev:** Aqueduct of Querétaro at left, church of Santa Rosa de Viterbo at right **Series:** Second **Obv. Legend:** ESTADOS UNIDOS MEXICANOS **Rev. Legend:** ESTADO DE QUERÉTARO ARTEAGA **Edge:** Segmented reeding **Mint:** Mexico City

Date	Mintage	F12	VF20	XF40	MS60	MS63
2007Mo	600	PF65 1,200				

KM# 853   100 PESOS
33.94 g., Bi-Metallic .925 Silver 20.1753g center in Aluminum-Bronze ring, 39.04mm. **Obv.** National arms **Rev:** Facade of Caja Real **Series:** Second **Obv. Legend:** ESTADOS UNIDOS MEXICANOS **Rev. Legend:** • SAN LUIS POTOSÍ • **Edge:** Segmented reeding **Mint:** Mexico City

Date	Mintage	F12	VF20	XF40	MS60	MS63
2007Mo	148,750	—	—	—	25.00	30.00

KM# 885   100 PESOS
29.17 g., Bi-Metallic .999 Gold 17.154g center in .999 Silver 12.015 ring, 34.5mm. **Obv.** National arms **Rev:** Facade of Caja Real **Series:** Second **Obv. Legend:** ESTADOS UNIDOS MEXICANOS **Rev. Legend:** • SAN LUIS POTOSÍ • **Edge:** Segmented reeding **Mint:** Mexico City

Date	Mintage	F12	VF20	XF40	MS60	MS63
2007Mo	600	PF65 1,200				

KM# 854   100 PESOS
33.94 g., Bi-Metallic .925 Silver 20.1753g center in Aluminum-Bronze ring, 39.04mm. **Obv.** National arms **Rev:** Shield on pile of cactus fruits **Series:** Second **Obv. Legend:** ESTADOS UNIDOS MEXICANOS **Rev. Legend:** ESTADO DE SINALOA - LUGAR DE PITAHAYAS **Edge:** Segmented reeding **Mint:** Mexico City

Date	Mintage	F12	VF20	XF40	MS60	MS63
2007Mo	149,032	—	—	—	25.00	30.00

KM# 886   100 PESOS
29.17 g., Bi-Metallic .999 Gold 17.154 center in .999 Silver 12.015g ring, 34.5mm. **Obv.** National arms **Rev:** Shield on pile of cactus fruits **Series:** Second **Obv. Legend:** ESTADOS UNIDOS MEXICANOS **Rev. Legend:** ESTADO DE SINALOA - LUGAR DE PITAHAYES **Edge:** Segmented reeding **Mint:** Mexico City

Date	Mintage	F12	VF20	XF40	MS60	MS63
2007Mo	600	PF65 1,200				

KM# 855   100 PESOS
33.94 g., Bi-Metallic .925 Silver 20.1753g center in Aluminum-Bronze ring, 39.04mm. **Obv.** National arms **Rev:** Local in Dance of the Deer at left, cactus at right, mountains in background **Series:** Second **Obv. Legend:** ESTADOS UNIDOS MEXICANOS **Rev. Legend:** ESTADO DE SONORA **Edge:** Segmented reeding **Mint:** Mexico City

Date	Mintage	F12	VF20	XF40	MS60	MS63
2007Mo	149,891	—	—	—	25.00	30.00

KM# 887   100 PESOS
29.17 g., Bi-Metallic .999 Gold 17.154g center in .999 Silver 12.015g ring, 34.5mm. **Obv.** National arms **Rev:** Local in Dance of the Deer at left, cactus at right, mountains in background **Series:** Second **Obv. Legend:** ESTADOS UNIDOS MEXICANOS **Rev. Legend:** ESTADO DE SONORA **Edge:** Segmented reeding **Mint:** Mexico City

Date	Mintage	F12	VF20	XF40	MS60	MS63
2007Mo	600	PF65 1,200				

KM# 856   100 PESOS
33.94 g., Bi-Metallic .925 Silver 20.1753 center in Aluminum-Bronze ring, 39.04mm. **Obv.** National arms **Rev:** Fuente de los Pescadores (fisherman fountain) at lower left, giant head from the Olmec-pre-Hispanic culture at right, Planetario Tabasco in background **Series:** Second **Obv. Legend:** ESTADOS UNIDOS MEXICANOS **Rev. Legend:** TABASCO **Edge:** Segmented reeding **Mint:** Mexico City

Date	Mintage	F12	VF20	XF40	MS60	MS63
2007Mo	149,715	—	—	—	25.00	30.00

KM# 888   100 PESOS
29.17 g., Bi-Metallic .999 Gold 17.154 center in .999 Silver 12.015g ring, 34.5mm. **Obv.** National arms **Rev:** Fuente de los Pescadores (fisherman fountain) at lower left, giant head from the Olmec-pre-Hispanic culture at right, Planetario Tabasco in background **Series:** Second **Obv. Legend:** ESTADOS UNIDOS MEXICANOS **Rev. Legend:** TABASCO **Edge:** Segmented reeding **Mint:** Mexico City

Date	Mintage	F12	VF20	XF40	MS60	MS63
2007Mo	600	PF65 1,200				

KM# 857 100 PESOS
33.94 g., Bi-Metallic .925 Silver 20.1753g center in Aluminum-Bronze ring, 39.04mm. **Obv.** National arms **Rev:** Ridge - Cerro Del Bernal, Gonzáles **Series:** Second **Obv. Legend:** ESTADOS UNIDOS MEXICANOS **Rev. Legend:** TAMAULIPAS **Edge:** Segmented reeding **Mint:** Mexico City

Date	Mintage	F12	VF20	XF40	MS60	MS63
2007Mo	149,776	—	—	—	25.00	30.00

KM# 889 100 PESOS
29.17 g., Bi-Metallic .999 Gold 17.154g center in .999 Silver 12.015g ring, 34.5mm. **Obv.** National arms **Rev:** Ridge - Cerro Del Bernal, Gonzáles **Series:** Second **Obv. Legend:** ESTADOS DE MEXICANOS **Rev. Legend:** TAMAULIPAS **Edge:** Segmented reeding **Mint:** Mexico City

Date	Mintage	F12	VF20	XF40	MS60	MS63
2007Mo	600	PF65 1,200				

KM# 859 100 PESOS
33.94 g., Bi-Metallic .912 Silver 20.1753g center in Aluminum-Bronze ring, 39.04mm. **Obv.** National arms **Rev:** Pyramid of El Tajín **Series:** Second **Obv. Legend:** ESTADOS UNIDOS MEXICANOS **Rev. Legend:** • VERACRUZ • - • DE IGNACIO DE LA LLAVE • **Edge:** Segmented reeding **Mint:** Mexico City

Date	Mintage	F12	VF20	XF40	MS60	MS63
2007Mo	149,703	—	—	—	25.00	30.00

KM# 891 100 PESOS
29.17 g., Bi-Metallic .999 Gold 17.154g center in .999 Silver 12.015g ring, 34.5mm. **Obv.** National arms **Rev:** Pyramid of El Tajín **Series:** Second **Obv. Legend:** ESTADOS UNIDOS MEXICANOS **Rev. Legend:** • VERACRUZ • - • DE IGNACIO DE LA LLAVE • **Edge:** Segmented reeding **Mint:** Mexico City

Date	Mintage	F12	VF20	XF40	MS60	MS63
2007Mo	600	PF65 1,200				

KM# 858 100 PESOS
33.94 g., Bi-Metallic .925 Silver 20.1753g center in Aluminum-Bronze ring, 39.04mm. **Obv.** National arms **Rev:** Basilica de Ocotlán at left, state arms above Capilla Abierta, Plaza de Toros Ranchero Aguilar below, Exconvento de San Francisco at right **Series:** Second **Obv. Legend:** ESTADOS UNIDOS MEXICANOS **Rev. Legend:** ESTADO DE TLAXCALA **Edge:** Segmented reeding **Mint:** Mexico City

Date	Mintage	F12	VF20	XF40	MS60	MS63
2007Mo	149,465	—	—	—	25.00	30.00

KM# 890 100 PESOS
29.17 g., Bi-Metallic .999 Gold 17.154g center in .999 Silver 12.015g ring, 34.5mm. **Obv.** National arms **Rev:** Basilica de Ocotlán at left, state arms above Capilla Abierta, Plaza de Toros Ranchero Aguilar below, Exconvento de San Francisco at right **Series:** Second **Obv. Legend:** ESTADOS UNIDOS MEXICANOS **Rev. Legend:** ESTADO DE TLAXCALA **Edge:** Segmented reeding **Mint:** Mexico City

Date	Mintage	F12	VF20	XF40	MS60	MS63
2007Mo	600	PF65 1,200				

KM# 860 100 PESOS
33.94 g., Bi-Metallic .925 Silver 20.1753 center in Aluminum-Bronze ring, 39.04mm. **Obv.** National arms **Rev:** Stylized pyramid of Chichén Itzá **Series:** Second **Obv. Legend:** ESTADOS UNIDOS MEXICANOS **Rev. Legend:** Castillo de Chichén Itzá **Edge:** Segmented reeding **Mint:** Mexico City

Date	Mintage	F12	VF20	XF40	MS60	MS63
2007Mo	149,579	—	—	—	25.00	30.00

KM# 892 100 PESOS
29.17 g., Bi-Metallic .999 Gold 17.154g center in .999 Silver 12.015g ring, 34.5mm. **Obv.** National arms **Rev:** Stylized pyramid of Chichén-Itzá **Series:** Second **Obv. Legend:** ESTADOS UNIDOS MEXICANOS **Rev. Inscription:** YUCATÁN **Edge:** Segmented reeding **Mint:** Mexico City

Date	Mintage	F12	VF20	XF40	MS60	MS63
2007Mo	600	PF65 1,200				

ESTADOS UNIDOS - REFORM COINAGE

KM# 861   100 PESOS
33.94 g., Bi-Metallic .925 Silver 20.1753g center in Aluminum-Bronze ring, 39.04mm. **Obv.** National arms **Rev:** Cable car above Monumento al Minero at left, Cathedral de Zacatecas at center right **Series:** Second **Obv. Legend:** ESTADOS UNIDOS MEXICANOS **Rev. Legend:** ZACATECAS **Edge:** Segmented reeding **Mint:** Mexico City

Date	Mintage	F12	VF20	XF40	MS60	MS63
2007Mo	148,833	—	—	—	25.00	30.00

KM# 893   100 PESOS
29.17 g., Bi-Metallic .999 Gold 17.154g center in .999 Silver 12.015g ring, 34.5mm. **Obv.** National arms **Rev:** Cable car above Monumento al Minero at left, Cathedral de Zacatecas at center right **Series:** Second **Obv. Legend:** ESTADOS UNIDOS MEXICANOS **Rev. Legend:** Zacatecas **Edge:** Segmented reeding **Mint:** Mexico City

Date	Mintage	F12	VF20	XF40	MS60	MS63
2007Mo	600	PF65 1,200				

KM# 963   100 PESOS
33.97 g., Bi-Metallic .925 Silver .500 ASW center in Aluminum-Bronze ring, 39mm. **Subject:** Numismatic Heritage of Mexico **Obv.** National arms **Rev:** Obverse of 1804Mo 8 Reale coin with chopmarks **Edge:** Segmented reeding **Mint:** Mexico City

Date	Mintage	F12	VF20	XF40	MS60	MS63
2012Mo Prooflike	8,000	—	—	—	—	40.00

KM# 964   100 PESOS
Bi-Metallic .925 Silver .500 ASW center in Aluminum-Bronze ring 39mm. **Subject:** Numismatic Heritage of Mexico **Obv.** National arms **Rev:** 1608Mo 8 Reales Cob coin of Philip III **Edge:** Segmented reeding **Mint:** Mexico City

Date	Mintage	F12	VF20	XF40	MS60	MS63
2012Mo Prooflike	8,000	—	—	—	—	40.00

KM# 965   100 PESOS
33.97 g., Bi-Metallic .925 Silver .500 ASW center in Aluminum-Bronze ring, 39mm. **Subject:** Numismatic Heritage of Mexico **Obv.** National arms **Rev:** 1811Zs 8 Reale Royalist Provisional Coin **Edge:** Segmented reeding **Mint:** Mexico City

Date	Mintage	F12	VF20	XF40	MS60	MS63
2012Mo Prooflike	8,000	—	—	—	—	40.00

KM# 966   100 PESOS
33.97 g., Bi-Metallic .925 Silver .500 ASW center in Aluminum-Bronze ring, 39mm. **Subject:** Numismatic Heritage of Mexico **Obv.** National arms **Rev:** 1866Mo 1 Peso coin **Edge:** Segmented reeding **Mint:** Mexico City

Date	Mintage	F12	VF20	XF40	MS60	MS63
2012Mo Prooflike	8,000	—	—	—	—	40.00

KM# 967   100 PESOS
33.97 g., Bi-Metallic .925 Silver .500 ASW center in Aluminum-Bronze ring, 39mm. **Subject:** Numismatic Heritage of Mexico **Obv.** National arms **Rev:** 1828Mo 8 Escudo coin **Edge:** Segmented reeding **Mint:** Mexico City

Date	Mintage	F12	VF20	XF40	MS60	MS63
2012Mo Prooflike	8,000	—	—	—	—	40.00

KM# 968   100 PESOS
33.97 g., Bi-Metallic .925 Silver .500 ASW center in Aluminum-Bronze ring, 39mm. **Subject:** Numismatic Heritage of Mexico **Obv.** National arms **Rev:** 1950Mo 5 Peso Southeast Railway Inauguration coin **Edge:** Segmented reeding **Mint:** Mexico City

Date	Mintage	F12	VF20	XF40	MS60	MS63
2012Mo Prooflike	8,000	—	—	—	—	40.00

KM# 971   100 PESOS
33.97 g., Bi-Metallic .925 Silver .500 ASW center in Aluminum-Bronze ring, 39mm. **Subject:** Numismatic Heritage of Mexico **Obv.** National arms **Rev:** 1915Gro. 2 Peso Zapatista coin from Suriana **Edge:** Segmented reeding **Mint:** Mexico City

Date	Mintage	F12	VF20	XF40	MS60	MS63
2013Mo Prooflike	—	—	—	—	—	40.00

KM# 972   100 PESOS
33.97 g., Bi-Metallic .925 Silver .500 ASW center in Aluminum-Bronze ring, 39mm. **Subject:** Numismatic Heritage of Mexico **Obv.** National arms **Rev:** Early MoR Charles and Joanna 3 Reale coin **Edge:** Segmented reeding **Mint:** Mexico City

Date	Mintage	F12	VF20	XF40	MS60	MS63
2013Mo Prooflike	—	—	—	—	—	40.00

KM# 973   100 PESOS
33.97 g., Bi-Metallic .925 Silver .500 ASW center in Aluminum-Bronze ring, 39mm. **Subject:** Numismatic Heritage of Mexico **Obv.** National arms **Rev:** Zs 1 Peso Scale of Justice coin **Mint:** Mexico City

Date	Mintage	F12	VF20	XF40	MS60	MS63
2013Mo Prooflike	—	—	—	—	—	40.00

KM# 974   100 PESOS
33.97 g., Bi-Metallic .925 Silver .500 ASW center in Aluminum-Bronze ring, 39mm. **Subject:** Numismatic Heritage of Mexico **Obv.** National arms **Rev:** Ca M.M. 8 Reale Republican coin with counterstamp **Edge:** Segmented reeding **Mint:** Mexico City

Date	Mintage	F12	VF20	XF40	MS60	MS63
2013Mo Prooflike	—	—	—	—	—	40.00

KM# 975   100 PESOS
33.97 g., Bi-Metallic .925 Silver .500 ASW center in Aluminum-Bronze ring, 39mm. **Subject:** Numismatic Heritage of Mexico **Obv.** National arms **Rev:** 1811 8 Reale insurgent coin of the Supreme American Governing Board **Edge:** Segmented reeding **Mint:** Mexico City

Date	Mintage	F12	VF20	XF40	MS60	MS63
2013Mo Prooflike	—	—	—	—	—	40.00

KM# 976   100 PESOS
33.97 g., Bi-Metallic .925 Silver .500 ASW center in Aluminum-Bronze ring, 39mm. **Subject:** Numismatic Heritage of Mexico **Obv.** National arms **Rev:** 1822Mo 8 Escudo **Edge:** Segmented reeding **Mint:** Mexico City

Date	Mintage	F12	VF20	XF40	MS60	MS63
2013Mo Prooflike	—	—	—	—	—	40.00

KM# 771   50000 PESOS
7.77 g., 0.999 Gold, 0.25 oz. AGW 23mm. **Obv.** Mexican Eagle and Snake **Rev:** Kneeling Mayan Pelota player and soccer ball **Mint:** Mexico City

Date	Mintage	F12	VF20	XF40	MS60	MS63
2006Mo	9,505	PF63 600				

SILVER BULLION COINAGE

KM# 921 100 PESOS
1000.00 g., 0.999 Silver, 31.91 oz. ASW 110mm. **Obv.** National arms in center of past and present arms **Rev:** Aztec Calendar **Edge:** Plain **Mint:** Mexico City

Date	Mintage	F12	VF20	XF40	MS60	MS63
2007Mo Prooflike	303	—	—	—	—	2,000
2008Mo Prooflike	1,000	—	—	—	—	1,800
2009Mo Prooflike	1,500	—	—	—	—	1,500
2010Mo Prooflike	1,500	—	—	—	—	1,500
2011Mo Prooflike	1,500	—	—	—	—	1,500
2012Mo Prooflike	1,500	—	—	—	—	1,800
2013Mo Prooflike	500	—	—	—	—	1,500

KM# 542 1/20 ONZA (1/20 TROY OUNCE OF SILVER)
1.56 g., 0.999 Silver, 0.05 oz. ASW 16mm. **Obv.** National arms, eagle left **Rev:** Winged Victory **Mint:** Mexico City

Date	Mintage	F12	VF20	XF40	MS60	MS63
1991Mo	50,017	—	—	—	—	5.50
1992Mo	295,783	—	—	—	—	4.50
1992Mo	5,000	PF60 10.00				
1993Mo	100,000	—	—	—	—	4.50
1993Mo	5,002	PF60 10.00				
1994Mo	90,100	—	—	—	—	4.50
1994Mo	5,002	PF60 10.00				
1995Mo	50,000	—	—	—	—	5.50
1995Mo	2,000	PF60 12.00				

KM# 609 1/20 ONZA (1/20 TROY OUNCE OF SILVER)
1.56 g., 0.999 Silver, 0.05 oz. ASW 16mm. **Obv.** National arms, eagle left **Rev:** Winged Victory **Mint:** Mexico City

Date	Mintage	F12	VF20	XF40	MS60	MS63
1996Mo	50,000	—	—	—	—	20.00
1996Mo	1,000	PF63 30.00				
1997Mo	20,000	—	—	—	—	20.00
1997Mo	800	PF63 30.00				
1998Mo	6,400	—	—	—	—	30.00
1998Mo	300	PF63 37.00				
1999Mo	8,001	—	—	—	—	25.00
1999Mo	600	PF63 33.00				
2000Mo	57,500	—	—	—	—	25.00
2000Mo	900	PF63 33.00				
2001Mo	4,500	—	—	—	—	25.00
2001Mo	1,500	PF63 30.00				
2002Mo	50,000	—	—	—	—	16.00
2002Mo	2,800	PF63 25.00				
2003Mo	30,000	—	—	—	—	16.00
2003Mo	4,400	PF63 25.00				
2004Mo	30,000	—	—	—	—	16.00
2004Mo	2,700	PF63 25.00				
2005Mo	15,000	—	—	—	—	16.00
2005Mo	2,600	PF63 25.00				
2006Mo	20,000	—	—	—	—	16.00
2006Mo	3,300	PF63 25.00				
2007Mo	3,500	—	—	—	—	16.00
2007Mo	4,000	PF63 25.00				
2008Mo	7,000	—	—	—	—	16.00
2008Mo	3,300	PF63 25.00				
2009Mo	10,000	—	—	—	—	10.00
2009Mo	5,000	PF63 12.00				
2010Mo	12,000	—	—	—	—	10.00
2010Mo	10,000	PF63 12.00				

Date	Mintage	F12	VF20	XF40	MS60	MS63
2011Mo	15,000	—	—	—	—	10.00
2011Mo	10,000	PF63 12.00				
2013Mo	13,500	—	—	—	—	8.00
2013Mo	4,200	PF63 12.00				

KM# 543 1/10 ONZA (1/10 TROY OUNCE OF SILVER)
3.11 g., 0.999 Silver, 0.10 oz. ASW 20mm. **Obv.** National arms, eagle left **Rev:** Winged Victory **Mint:** Mexico City

Date	Mintage	F12	VF20	XF40	MS60	MS63
1991Mo	50,017	—	—	—	—	7.50
1992Mo	299,983	—	—	—	—	6.50
1992Mo	5,000	PF60 12.00				
1993Mo	100,000	—	—	—	—	6.50
1993Mo	5,002	PF60 12.00				
1994Mo	90,100	—	—	—	—	6.50
1994Mo	5,002	PF60 12.00				
1995Mo	50,000	—	—	—	—	7.50
1995Mo	2,000	PF60 13.50				

KM# 610 1/10 ONZA (1/10 TROY OUNCE OF SILVER)
3.11 g., 0.999 Silver, 0.10 oz. ASW 20mm. **Obv.** National arms, eagle left **Rev:** Winged Victory **Mint:** Mexico City

Date	Mintage	F12	VF20	XF40	MS60	MS63
1996Mo	50,000	—	—	—	—	25.00
1996Mo	1,000	PF63 35.00				
1997Mo	20,000	—	—	—	—	25.00
1997Mo	800	PF63 35.00				
1998Mo	6,400	—	—	—	—	33.00
1998Mo	300	PF63 45.00				
1999Mo	8,000	—	—	—	—	27.50
1999Mo	600	PF63 40.00				
2000Mo	27,500	—	—	—	—	27.50
2000Mo	1,000	PF63 40.00				
2001Mo	25,000	—	—	—	—	27.50
2001Mo	1,500	PF63 36.00				
2002Mo	35,000	—	—	—	—	20.00
2002Mo	2,800	PF63 30.00				
2003Mo	20,000	—	—	—	—	20.00
2003Mo	4,900	PF63 30.00				
2004Mo	15,000	—	—	—	—	20.00
2004Mo	2,500	PF63 30.00				
2005Mo	9,277	—	—	—	—	20.00
2005Mo	3,000	PF63 27.50				
2006Mo	15,000	—	—	—	—	20.00
2006Mo	3,000	PF63 27.50				
2007Mo	3,500	—	—	—	—	20.00
2007Mo	4,000	PF63 27.50				
2008Mo	10,000	—	—	—	—	20.00
2008Mo	5,000	PF63 27.50				
2009Mo	10,000	—	—	—	—	20.00
2009Mo	5,000	PF63 27.50				
2010Mo	12,000	—	—	—	—	12.00
2010Mo	10,000	PF63 15.00				
2011Mo	15,000	—	—	—	—	12.00
2011Mo	10,000	PF63 15.00				
2012Mo	3,300	—	—	—	—	15.00
2013Mo	18,900	—	—	—	—	10.00
2013Mo	4,100	PF63 15.00				

KM# 544   1/4 ONZA (1/4 TROY OUNCE OF SILVER)
7.78 g., 0.999 Silver, 0.25 oz. ASW 25mm. **Obv.** National arms, eagle left **Rev:** Winged Victory **Mint:** Mexico City

Date	Mintage	F12	VF20	XF40	MS60	MS63
1991Mo	50,017	—	—	—	—	11.50
1992Mo	104,000	—	—	—	—	10.00
1992Mo	5,000	PF60 16.50				
1993Mo	90,500	—	—	—	—	10.00
1993Mo	5,002	PF60 16.50				
1994Mo	90,100	—	—	—	—	10.00
1994Mo	5,002	PF60 16.50				
1995Mo	50,000	—	—	—	—	11.50
1995Mo	2,000	PF60 17.50				

KM# 611   1/4 ONZA (1/4 TROY OUNCE OF SILVER)
7.78 g., 0.999 Silver, 0.25 oz. ASW 27mm. **Obv.** National arms, eagle left **Rev:** Winged Victory **Mint:** Mexico City

Date	Mintage	F12	VF20	XF40	MS60	MS63
1996Mo	50,000	—	—	—	—	32.00
1996Mo	1,000	PF63 40.00				
1997Mo	20,000	—	—	—	—	32.00
1997Mo	800	PF63 40.00				
1998Mo	6,400	—	—	—	—	40.00
1998Mo	300	PF63 65.00				
1999Mo	7,000	—	—	—	—	36.00
1999Mo	600	PF63 50.00				
2000Mo	21,000	—	—	—	—	36.00
2000Mo	700	PF63 50.00				
2001Mo	25,000	—	—	—	—	36.00
2001Mo	1,000	PF63 44.00				
2002Mo	35,000	—	—	—	—	27.50
2002Mo	2,800	PF63 40.00				
2003Mo	22,000	—	—	—	—	27.50
2003Mo	3,900	PF63 40.00				
2004Mo	15,000	—	—	—	—	27.50
2004Mo	2,500	PF63 40.00				
2005Mo	15,000	—	—	—	—	27.50
2005Mo	2,400	PF63 37.00				
2006Mo	15,000	—	—	—	—	25.00
2006Mo	2,900	PF63 37.00				
2007Mo	3,500	—	—	—	—	25.00
2007Mo	3,000	PF63 37.00				
2008Mo	9,000	—	—	—	—	25.00
2008Mo	2,900	PF63 37.00				
2009Mo	10,000	—	—	—	—	25.00
2009Mo	3,000	PF63 37.00				
2010Mo	15,500	—	—	—	—	25.00
2010Mo	5,000	PF63 37.00				
2011Mo	15,500	—	—	—	—	25.00
2011Mo	5,000	PF63 37.00				
2012Mo	16,700	—	—	—	—	25.00
2013Mo	9,600	—	—	—	—	12.00
2013Mo	3,200	PF63 30.00				

KM# 545   1/2 ONZA (1/2 TROY OUNCE OF SILVER)
15.55 g., 0.999 Silver, 0.50 oz. ASW 30mm. **Obv.** National arms, eagle left **Rev:** Winged Victory **Mint:** Mexico City

Date	Mintage	F12	VF20	XF40	MS60	MS63
1991Mo	50,618	—	—	—	—	24.00
1992Mo	119,000	—	—	—	—	22.00
1992Mo	5,000	PF60 27.00				
1993Mo	90,500	—	—	—	—	22.00
1993Mo	5,002	PF60 27.00				
1994Mo	90,100	—	—	—	—	22.00
1994Mo	5,002	PF60 27.00				
1995Mo	50,000	—	—	—	—	22.00
1995Mo	2,000	PF60 28.00				

KM# 612   1/2 ONZA (1/2 TROY OUNCE OF SILVER)
15.55 g., 0.999 Silver, 0.50 oz. ASW 33mm. **Obv.** National arms, eagle left **Rev:** Winged Victory **Mint:** Mexico City

Date	Mintage	F12	VF20	XF40	MS60	MS63
1996Mo	50,000	—	—	—	—	40.00
1996Mo	1,000	PF63 60.00				
1997Mo	20,000	—	—	—	—	40.00
1997Mo	800	PF63 60.00				
1998Mo	6,400	—	—	—	—	60.00
1998Mo	2,500	PF63 90.00				
1999Mo	2,000	—	—	—	—	45.00
1999Mo	7,000	PF63 70.00				
2000Mo	20,000	—	—	—	—	45.00
2000Mo	700	PF63 70.00				
2001Mo	20,000	—	—	—	—	45.00
2001Mo	1,000	PF63 60.00				
2002Mo	35,000	—	—	—	—	37.00
2002Mo	2,800	PF63 50.00				
2003Mo	28,000	—	—	—	—	37.00
2003Mo	3,400	PF63 50.00				
2004Mo	20,000	—	—	—	—	37.00
2004Mo	2,500	PF63 50.00				
2005Mo	10,000	—	—	—	—	37.00
2005Mo	2,800	PF63 45.00				
2006Mo	15,000	—	—	—	—	37.00
2006Mo	2,900	PF63 45.00				
2007Mo	3,500	—	—	—	—	37.00
2007Mo	1,500	PF63 45.00				
2008Mo	9,000	—	—	—	—	37.00
2008Mo	2,500	PF63 45.00				
2009Mo	10,000	—	—	—	—	37.00
2009Mo	3,000	PF63 45.00				
2010Mo	20,000	—	—	—	—	37.00
2010Mo	5,000	PF63 45.00				

Date	Mintage	F12	VF20	XF40	MS60	MS63
2011Mo	30,000	—	—	—	—	37.00
2011Mo	5,000	PF63 45.00				
2012Mo	17,000	—	—	—	—	37.00
2013Mo	24,500	—	—	—	—	20.00
2013Mo Proof	3,000	—	—	—	—	—

Date	Mintage	F12	VF20	XF40	MS60	MS63
1991Mo	Inc. above	—	—	—	BV	50.00
1991Mo	10,000	PF60 85.00				
1992Mo	2,458,000	—	—	—	BV	50.00
1992Mo	10,000	PF60 85.00				

KM# 494.1 ONZA (TROY OUNCE OF SILVER)
31.10 g., 0.999 Silver, 0.99 oz. ASW 36mm. **Obv.** National arms, eagle left **Rev:** Winged Victory **Edge:** Plain **Mint:** Mexico City

Date	Mintage	F12	VF20	XF40	MS60	MS63
1982Mo	1,049,680	—	—	—	BV	35.00
1983Mo	1,001,768	—	—	—	BV	35.00
1983Mo	998	PF60 600				
1984Mo	1,014,000	—	—	—	BV	32.00
1985Mo	2,017,000	—	—	—	BV	32.00
1986Mo	1,699,426	—	—	—	BV	35.00
1986Mo	30,006	PF60 45.00				
1987Mo	500,000	—	—	—	BV	70.00
1987Mo	Inc. above	—	—	—	—	70.00
Doubled die						
1987Mo	12,000	PF60 60.00				
1988Mo	1,500,500	—	—	—	BV	80.00
1989Mo	1,396,500	—	—	—	BV	45.00
1989Mo	10,000	PF60 95.00				

KM# 494.2 ONZA (TROY OUNCE OF SILVER)
31.10 g., 0.999 Silver, 0.99 oz. ASW 36mm. **Obv.** National arms, eagle left **Rev:** Winged Victory **Edge:** Reeded **Mint:** Mexico City

Date	Mintage	F12	VF20	XF40	MS60	MS63
1988Mo	10,000	PF60 105				
1990Mo	1,200,000	—	—	—	BV	60.00
1990Mo	10,000	PF60 90.00				
1991Mo	1,650,518	—	—	—	BV	52.00

KM# 494.5 ONZA (TROY OUNCE OF SILVER)
31.10 g., 0.999 Silver, 0.99 oz. ASW **Obv.** National arms, eagle left, KM#494.3 **Rev:** Winged Victory, KM#494.2 **Edge:** Reeded **Mint:** Mexico City **Note:** Mule

Date	Mintage	F12	VF20	XF40	MS60	MS63
1991 Mo	10,000	PF60 85.00				

KM# 494.3 ONZA (TROY OUNCE OF SILVER)
31.10 g., 0.999 Silver, 0.99 oz. ASW 36mm. **Obv.** National arms, eight dots below eagle's left talons **Rev:** Winged Victory with revised design and lettering **Edge:** Reeded **Mint:** Mexico City

KM# 494.4 ONZA (TROY OUNCE OF SILVER)
31.10 g., 0.999 Silver, 0.99 oz. ASW 36mm. **Obv.** National arms, Seven dots below eagle's left talon, dull claws on right talon, thick lettering **Rev:** Winged Victory with revised design and lettering **Edge:** Reeded **Mint:** Mexico City

Date	Mintage	F12	VF20	XF40	MS60	MS63
1993Mo	1,000,000	—	—	—	BV	45.00
1993Mo	5,002	PF60 90.00				
1994Mo	400,000	—	—	—	BV	45.00
1994Mo	5,002	PF60 85.00				
1995Mo	500,000	—	—	—	BV	45.00
1995Mo	2,000	PF60 85.00				

KM# 613 ONZA (TROY OUNCE OF SILVER)
31.11 g., 0.999 Silver, 0.99 oz. ASW 40mm. **Obv.** National arms, eagle left **Rev:** Winged Victory **Mint:** Mexico City

Date	Mintage	F12	VF20	XF40	MS60	MS63
1996Mo	300,000	—	—	—	—	48.00
1996Mo	2,000	PF60 90.00				
1997Mo	100,000	—	—	—	—	80.00
1997Mo	1,500	PF60 70.00				
1998Mo	67,000	—	—	—	—	135
1998Mo	500	PF60 205				
1999Mo	95,000	—	—	—	—	140
1999Mo	600	PF60 95.00				

KM# 639   ONZA (TROY OUNCE OF SILVER)

31.10 g., 0.999 Silver, 0.99 oz. ASW 40mm. **Obv.** National arms, eagle left within center of past and present arms **Rev:** Winged Victory **Edge:** Reeded **Mint:** Mexico City

Date	Mintage	F12	VF20	XF40	MS60	MS63
2000Mo	340,000	—	—	—	—	55.00
2000Mo	1,600	PF63 140				
2001Mo	725,000	—	—	—	—	55.00
2001Mo	2,000	PF63 140				
2002Mo	854,000	—	—	—	—	55.00
2002Mo	3,800	PF63 150				
2003Mo	805,000	—	—	—	—	60.00
2003Mo	5,400	PF63 130				
2004Mo	450,000	—	—	—	—	50.00
2004Mo	3,000	PF63 130				
2005Mo	698,281	—	—	—	—	50.00
2005Mo	3,300	PF63 150				
2006Mo	300,000	—	—	—	—	50.00
2006Mo	4,000	PF63 140				
2007Mo	200,000	—	—	—	—	100
2007Mo	5,800	PF63 150				
2008Mo	950,000	—	—	—	—	60.00
2008Mo	11,000	PF63 150				
2009Mo	1,650,000	—	—	—	—	40.00
2009Mo	10,000	PF63 100				
2010Mo	1,000,000	—	—	—	—	50.00
2010Mo	10,000	PF63 140				
2011Mo	1,200,000	—	—	—	—	30.00
2011Mo	10,000	PF63 80.00				
2012Mo	746,400	—	—	—	—	30.00
2012Mo	4,200	PF63 80.00				
2013Mo	777,100	—	—	—	—	80.00
2013Mo	9,100	PF63 40.00				

KM# 614   2 ONZAS (2 TROY OUNCES OF SILVER)

62.21 g., 0.999 Silver, 1.99 oz. ASW 48mm. **Obv.** National arms, eagle left within center of past and present arms **Rev:** Winged Victory **Edge:** Reeded **Mint:** Mexico City

Date	Mintage	F12	VF20	XF40	MS60	MS63
1996Mo	50,000	—	—	—	—	90.00
1996Mo	1,200	PF63 275				
1997Mo	15,000	—	—	—	—	100
1997Mo	1,300	PF63 150				
1998Mo	7,000	—	—	—	—	100
1998Mo	400	PF63 450				
1999Mo	5,000	—	—	—	—	110
1999Mo	280	PF63 7,100				
2000Mo	7,500	—	—	—	—	100
2000Mo	500	PF63 300				
2001Mo	6,700	—	—	—	—	120
2001Mo	500	PF63 300				
2002Mo	8,700	—	—	—	—	110
2002Mo	1,000	PF63 225				
2003Mo	9,500	—	—	—	—	110
2003Mo	800	PF63 225				
2004Mo	8,000	—	—	—	—	100
2004Mo	1,000	PF63 175				
2005Mo	3,549	—	—	—	—	100
2005Mo	600	PF63 500				
2006Mo	5,800	—	—	—	—	100
2006Mo	1,100	PF63 175				
2007Mo	8,000	—	—	—	—	100
2007Mo	500	PF63 250				
2008Mo	17,000	—	—	—	—	110
2008Mo	1,000	PF63 170				
2009Mo	46,000	—	—	—	—	90.00
2009Mo	6,200	PF63 100				
2010Mo	14,000	—	—	—	—	75.00
2010Mo	1,300	PF63 120				
2011Mo	14,000	—	—	—	—	110
2011Mo	1,000	PF63 140				
2012Mo	18,600	—	—	—	—	70.00
2013Mo	17,400	—	—	—	—	60.00
2013Mo	1,300	PF63 110				

KM# 615   5 ONZAS (5 TROY OUNCES OF SILVER)

155.52 g., 0.999 Silver, 4.96 oz. ASW 65mm. **Obv.** National arms, eagle left within center of past and present arms **Rev:** Winged Victory **Edge:** Reeded **Mint:** Mexico City **Note:** Illustration reduced.

Date	Mintage	F12	VF20	XF40	MS60	MS63
1996Mo	20,000	—	—	—	—	265
1996Mo	1,200	PF63 295				
1997Mo	10,000	—	—	—	—	265
1997Mo	1,300	PF63 295				
1998Mo	3,500	—	—	—	—	325
1998Mo	400	PF63 1,000				
1999Mo	2,800	—	—	—	—	255
1999Mo	100	PF63 1,250				
2000Mo	4,000	—	—	—	—	255
2000Mo	500	PF63 375				
2001Mo	4,000	—	—	—	—	190
2001Mo	600	PF63 325				
2002Mo	5,200	—	—	—	—	190
2002Mo	1,000	PF63 325				
2003Mo	6,000	—	—	—	—	180
2003Mo	1,500	PF63 250				
2004Mo	3,923	—	—	—	—	180
2004Mo	800	PF63 225				
2005Mo	2,401	—	—	—	—	205
2005Mo	1,000	PF63 225				
2006Mo	3,000	—	—	—	—	180
2006Mo	700	PF63 265				
2007Mo	3,000	—	—	—	—	180
2007Mo	500	PF63 205				
2008Mo	9,000	—	—	—	—	205
2008Mo	900	PF63 270				
2009Mo	21,000	—	—	—	—	250
2009Mo	5,000	PF63 270				
2010Mo	9,500	—	—	—	—	220
2010Mo	2,000	PF63 230				
2011Mo	10,000	—	—	—	—	220
2011Mo	2,000	PF63 230				
2012Mo	9,500	—	—	—	—	220
2013Mo	10,400	—	—	—	—	150
2013Mo	1,600	PF63 220				

KM# 677 KILO (32.15 TROY OUNCES OF SILVER)

999.98 g., 0.999 Silver, 31.91 oz. ASW 110mm. **Obv.** National arms in center of past and present arms **Rev:** Winged Victory **Edge:** Reeded **Mint:** Mexico City

Date	Mintage	F12	VF20	XF40	MS60	MS63
2001Mo Prooflike	—	—	—	—	—	2,200
2002Mo Prooflike	1,820	—	—	—	—	1,750
2003Mo Prooflike	1,514	—	—	—	—	1,650
2004Mo Prooflike	1,501	—	—	—	—	1,800
2005Mo Prooflike	500	—	—	—	—	1,750
2006Mo Prooflike	874	—	—	—	—	1,650
2007Mo Prooflike	700	—	—	—	—	1,650
2008Mo	2,003	—	—	—	—	1,200
2008Mo Prooflike	1,700	—	—	—	—	1,500
2009Mo	4,000	—	—	—	—	1,200
2009Mo Prooflike	1,700	—	—	—	—	1,500
2010Mo	4,000	—	—	—	—	1,200
2010Mo Prooflike	1,500	—	—	—	—	1,500
2011Mo	6,000	—	—	—	—	1,200
2011Mo Prooflike	1,000	—	—	—	—	1,500
2012Mo Prooflike	500	—	—	—	—	1,500
2013 Mo	2,300	—	—	—	—	1,200
2013Mo Prooflike	400	—	—	—	—	1,500

GOLD BULLION COINAGE

KM# 530 1/20 ONZA (1/20 OUNCE OF PURE GOLD)

1.75 g., 0.900 Gold, 0.05 oz. AGW **Obv.** Winged Victory **Rev:** Calendar stone **Mint:** Mexico City

Date	Mintage	F12	VF20	XF40	MS60	MS63
1987Mo	—	—	—	—	—	275
1988Mo	—	—	—	—	—	—

KM# 589 1/20 ONZA (1/20 OUNCE OF PURE GOLD)

1.56 g., 0.999 Gold, 0.05 oz. AGW 13mm. **Obv.** Winged Victory **Rev:** National arms, eagle left **Mint:** Mexico City

Date	Mintage	F12	VF20	XF40	MS60	MS63
1991Mo	10,000	—	—	—	—	BV+30%
1992Mo	65,225	—	—	—	—	BV+30%

Date	Mintage	F12	VF20	XF40	MS60	MS63
Note: According to Mexican mint records combined mintages of 1991 and 1992 BU and proof coins are 73,858.						
1993Mo	10,000	—	—	—	—	BV+30%
1994Mo	10,000	—	—	—	—	BV+30%

KM# 642 1/20 ONZA (1/20 OUNCE OF PURE GOLD)

1.56 g., 0.999 Gold, 0.05 oz. AGW **Obv.** National arms, eagle left **Rev:** Native working **Mint:** Mexico City

Date	Mintage	F12	VF20	XF40	MS60	MS63
2000Mo	—	PF60 95.00				

KM# 671 1/20 ONZA (1/20 OUNCE OF PURE GOLD)

1.56 g., 0.999 Gold, 0.05 oz. AGW 13mm. **Obv.** National arms, eagle left **Rev:** Winged Victory **Edge:** Reeded **Mint:** Mexico City **Note:** Design similar to KM#609. Value estimates do not include the high taxes and surcharges added to the issue prices by the Mexican Government.

Date	Mintage	F12	VF20	XF40	MS60	MS63
2000Mo	5,300	—	—	—	—	BV+30%
2002Mo	5,000	—	—	—	—	BV+30%
2003Mo	800	—	—	—	—	BV+32%
2004Mo	4,000	—	—	—	—	BV+30%
2005Mo	3,200	—	—	—	—	BV+30%
2005Mo	400	PF63 BV+35%				
2006Mo	3,000	—	—	—	—	BV+30%
2006Mo	520	PF63 BV+35%				
2007Mo	500	PF63 BV+35%				
2007Mo	1,200	—	—	—	—	BV+30%
2008Mo	500	PF63 BV+35%				
2008Mo	800	—	—	—	—	BV+30%
2009Mo	600	PF63 BV+35%				
2009Mo	2,000	—	—	—	—	BV+30%
2010Mo	1,500	—	—	—	—	BV+30%
2010Mo	600	PF63 BV+35%				
2011Mo	2,500	—	—	—	—	BV+30%
2011Mo	1,100	PF63 BV+35%				
2013Mo	300	PF63 BV+35%				
2013Mo	650	—	—	—	—	BV+30%

KM# 628 1/15 ONZA (1/15 OUNCE OF PURE GOLD)

0.999 Gold, AGW **Obv.** Winged Victory above legend **Rev:** National arms, eagle left within circle **Mint:** Mexico City

Date	Mintage	F12	VF20	XF40	MS60	MS63
1987Mo	—	—	—	—	—	275

KM# 541 1/10 ONZA (1/10 OUNCE OF PURE GOLD)

3.11 g., 0.999 Gold, 0.10 oz. AGW 16mm. **Obv.** National arms, eagle left **Rev:** Winged Victory **Mint:** Mexico City

Date	Mintage	F12	VF20	XF40	MS60	MS63
1991Mo	10,000	—	—	—	—	BV+20%
1992Mo	50,777	—	—	—	—	BV+20%
1993Mo	10,000	—	—	—	—	BV+20%
1994Mo	10,000	—	—	—	—	BV+20%

Date	Mintage	F12	VF20	XF40	MS60	MS63

Note: According to Mexican mint records combined mintages of 1991 and 1992 coins are 60,592.

KM# 672 1/10 ONZA (1/10 OUNCE OF PURE GOLD)

3.11 g., 0.999 Gold, 0.10 oz. AGW 16mm. **Obv.** National arms, eagle left **Rev:** Winged Victory **Edge:** Reeded **Mint:** Mexico City **Note:** Design similar to KM#610. Value estimates do not include the high taxes and surcharges added to the issue prices by the Mexican Government.

Date	Mintage	F12	VF20	XF40	MS60	MS63
2000Mo	3,500	—	—	—	—	BV+20%
2002Mo	5,000	—	—	—	—	BV+20%
2003Mo	300	—	—	—	—	BV+22%
2004Mo	2,000	—	—	—	—	BV+20%
2005Mo	500	—	—	—	—	BV+20%
2005Mo	400	PF63 BV+22%				
2006Mo	2,500	—	—	—	—	BV+20%
2006Mo	520	PF63 BV+22%				
2007Mo	1,200	—	—	—	—	BV+20%
2007Mo	500	PF63 BV+22%				
2008Mo	2,500	—	—	—	—	BV+20%
2008Mo	500	PF63 BV+22%				
2009Mo	9,000	—	—	—	—	BV+20%
2009Mo	600	PF63 BV+22%				
2010Mo	4,500	—	—	—	—	BV+20%
2010Mo	600	PF63 BV+22%				
2011Mo	6,500	—	—	—	—	BV+20%
2011Mo	1,100	PF63 BV+22%				
2013Mo	300	PF63 BV+22%				
2013Mo	2,150	—	—	—	—	BV+20%

KM# 487 1/4 ONZA (1/4 OUNCE OF PURE GOLD)

8.64 g., 0.900 Gold, 0.25 oz. AGW **Obv.** National arms, eagle left **Rev:** Winged Victory **Mint:** Mexico City **Note:** Similar to KM#488.

Date	Mintage	F12	VF20	XF40	MS60	MS63
1981Mo	313,000	—	—	—	—	BV+11%
1982Mo	—	—	—	—	—	BV+11%

KM# 590 1/4 ONZA (1/4 OUNCE OF PURE GOLD)

7.78 g., 0.999 Gold, 0.25 oz. AGW 23mm. **Obv.** Winged Victory above legend **Rev:** National arms, eagle left **Mint:** Mexico City

Date	Mintage	F12	VF20	XF40	MS60	MS63
1991Mo	10,000	—	—	—	—	BV+11%
1992Mo	28,106	—	—	—	—	BV+11%
1993Mo	2,500	—	—	—	—	BV+11%
1994Mo	2,500	—	—	—	—	BV+11%

Note: According to Mexican mint records, combined mintages of 1991 and 1992 are 37,321.

KM# 673 1/4 ONZA (1/4 OUNCE OF PURE GOLD)

7.78 g., 0.999 Gold, 0.25 oz. AGW 23mm. **Obv.** National arms, eagle left **Rev:** Winged Victory **Edge:** Reeded **Mint:** Mexico City **Note:** Design similar to KM#611. Value estimates do not include the high taxes and surcharges added to the issue prices by the Mexican Government.

Date	Mintage	F12	VF20	XF40	MS60	MS63
2000Mo	2,500	—	—	—	—	BV+12%
2002Mo	5,000	—	—	—	—	BV+12%
2003Mo	300	—	—	—	—	BV+14%
2004Mo	1,500	—	—	—	—	BV+12%
2004Mo	1,000	PF63 BV+15%				
2005Mo	500	—	—	—	—	BV+14%
2005Mo	2,600	PF63 BV+15%				
2006Mo	1,500	—	—	—	—	BV+12%
2006Mo	2,120	PF63 BV+15%				
2007Mo	500	—	—	—	—	BV+14%
2007Mo	1,500	PF63 BV+15%				
2008Mo	800	—	—	—	—	BV+14%
2008Mo	800	PF63 BV+15%				
2009Mo	3,000	—	—	—	—	BV+12%
2009Mo	1,700	PF63 BV+15%				
2010Mo	1,500	—	—	—	—	BV+12%

Date	Mintage	F12	VF20	XF40	MS60	MS63
2010Mo	1,000	PF63 BV+15%				
2011Mo	1,500	—	—	—	—	BV+12%
2011Mo	2,000	PF63 BV+15%				
2013Mo	600	PF63 BV+15%				
2013Mo	750	—	—	—	—	BV+12%

KM# 488 1/2 ONZA (1/2 OUNCE OF PURE GOLD)

17.28 g., 0.900 Gold, 0.50 oz. AGW **Obv.** National arms, eagle left **Rev:** Winged Victory **Mint:** Mexico City

Date	Mintage	F12	VF20	XF40	MS60	MS63
1981Mo	193,000	—	—	—	—	BV+8%
1982Mo	—	—	—	—	—	BV+8%
1989Mo	704	PF60 850				

KM# 591 1/2 ONZA (1/2 OUNCE OF PURE GOLD)

15.55 g., 0.999 Gold, 0.50 oz. AGW 29mm. **Obv.** Winged Victory above legend **Rev:** National arms, eagle left **Mint:** Mexico City

Date	Mintage	F12	VF20	XF40	MS60	MS63
1991Mo	10,000	—	—	—	—	BV+8%
1992Mo	25,220	—	—	—	—	BV+8%
1993Mo	2,500	—	—	—	—	BV+8%
1994Mo	2,500	—	—	—	—	BV+8%

Note: According to Mexican mint records, combined mintages of 1981-1992 BU and proof coins are 35,047.

KM# 674 1/2 ONZA (1/2 OUNCE OF PURE GOLD)

15.55 g., 0.999 Gold, 0.50 oz. AGW 29mm. **Obv.** National arms, eagle left **Rev:** Winged Victory **Edge:** Reeded **Mint:** Mexico City **Note:** Design similar to KM#612. Value estimates do not include the high taxes and surcharges added to the issue prices by the Mexican Government.

Date	Mintage	F12	VF20	XF40	MS60	MS63
2000Mo	1,500	—	—	—	—	BV+8%
2002Mo	5,000	—	—	—	—	BV+8%
2003Mo	300	—	—	—	—	BV+10%
2004Mo	500	—	—	—	—	BV+8%
2005Mo	500	—	—	—	—	BV+10%
2005Mo	400	PF63 BV+12%				
2006Mo	500	—	—	—	—	BV+10%
2006Mo	520	PF63 BV+12%				
2007Mo	500	—	—	—	—	BV+10%
2007Mo	500	PF63 BV+12%				
2008Mo	300	—	—	—	—	BV+10%
2008Mo	500	PF63 BV+12%				
2009Mo	3,000	—	—	—	—	BV+8%
2009Mo	600	PF63 BV+12%				
2010Mo	1,500	—	—	—	—	BV+8%
2010Mo	600	PF63 BV+12%				
2011Mo	1,500	—	—	—	—	BV+8%
2011Mo	1,100	PF63 BV+12%				
2013Mo	300	PF63 BV+12%				
2013Mo	500	—	—	—	—	BV+8%

KM# 489 ONZA (OUNCE OF PURE GOLD)

34.56 g., 0.900 Gold, 0.99 oz. AGW **Obv.** National arms, eagle left **Rev:** Winged Victory **Mint:** Mexico City **Note:** Similar to KM#488.

Date	Mintage	F12	VF20	XF40	MS60	MS63
1981Mo	596,000	—	—	—	—	BV+3%
1985Mo	—	—	—	—	—	BV+3%
1988Mo	—	—	—	—	—	BV+3%

KM# 592 ONZA (OUNCE OF PURE GOLD)

31.10 g., 0.999 Gold, 0.99 oz. AGW 34.5mm. **Obv.** Winged Victory above legend **Rev:** National arms, eagle left **Mint:** Mexico City

Date	Mintage	F12	VF20	XF40	MS60	MS63
1991Mo	109,193	—	—	—	—BV+3%	
1992Mo	46,281	—	—	—	—BV+3%	
1993Mo	73,881	—	—	—	—BV+3%	
1994 Mo	1,000	—	—	—	—BV+5%	

Note: According to Mexican mint redords, combined mintages of 1981-1992 BU and proof coins are 90,384.

KM# 675 ONZA (OUNCE OF PURE GOLD)

31.10 g., 0.999 Gold, 0.99 oz. AGW 34.5mm. **Obv.** National arms, eagle left **Rev:** Winged Victory **Edge:** Reeded **Mint:** Mexico City **Note:** Design similar to KM#639. Value estimates do not include the high taxes and surcharges added to the issue prices by the Mexican Government.

Date	Mintage	F12	VF20	XF40	MS60	MS63
2000Mo	2,370	—	—	—	—BV+3%	
2002Mo	15,000	—	—	—	—BV+3%	
2003Mo	500	—	—	—	—BV+4%	
2004Mo	3,000	—	—	—	—BV+3%	
2005Mo	3,000	—	—	—	—BV+3%	
2005Mo	250	PF63 BV+5%				
2006Mo	4,000	—	—	—	—BV+3%	
2006Mo	520	PF63 BV+5%				
2007Mo	2,500	—	—	—	—BV+3%	
2007Mo	500	PF63 BV+5%				
2008Mo	800	—	—	—	—BV+3%	
2008Mo	500	PF63 BV+5%				
2009Mo	6,200	—	—	—	—BV+3%	
2009Mo	600	PF63 BV+5%				
2010Mo	4,000	—	—	—	—BV+3%	
2010Mo	600	PF63 BV+5%				
2011Mo	3,000	—	—	—	—BV+3%	
2011Mo	1,100	PF63 BV+5%				
2012Mo	3,000	—	—	—	—BV+3%	
2013Mo	400	PF63 BV+5%				
2013Mo	2,350	—	—	—	—BV+3%	

PLATINUM BULLION COINAGE

KM# 538 1/4 ONZA (1/4 OUNCE)

7.78 g., 0.999 Platinum, 0.25 oz. APW **Obv.** National arms, eagle left **Rev:** Winged Victory **Mint:** Mexico City

Date	Mintage	F12	VF20	XF40	MS60	MS63
1989Mo	3,500	PF60 550				

BULLION COINAGE AZTEC SERIES

KM# 644 NUEVOS PESO

7.77 g., 0.999 Silver, 0.25 oz. ASW 26.8mm. **Obv.** National arms, eagle left within D-shaped circle and dotted border **Rev:** Eagle warrior within D-shaped circle and dotted border **Edge:** Reeded **Mint:** Mexico City

Date	Mintage	F12	VF20	XF40	MS60	MS63
1993Mo	1,500	—	—	—	—	18.00
1993Mo	900	PF60 30.00				

KM# 645 2 NUEVOS PESOS

15.42 g., 0.999 Silver, 0.49 oz. ASW 32.9mm. **Obv.** National arms, eagle left **Rev:** Eagle warrior **Edge:** Reeded **Mint:** Mexico City

Date	Mintage	F12	VF20	XF40	MS60	MS63
1993Mo	1,500	—	—	—	—	20.00
1993Mo	800	PF60 40.00				

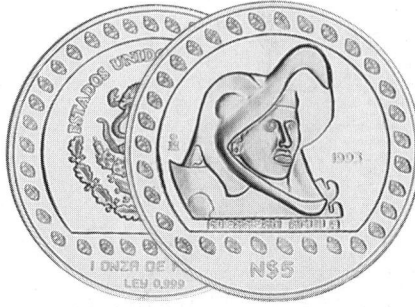

KM# 646 5 NUEVOS PESOS

31.05 g., 0.999 Silver, 0.99 oz. ASW 40mm. **Obv.** National arms, eagle left **Rev:** Eagle warrior **Edge:** Reeded **Mint:** Mexico City

Date	Mintage	F12	VF20	XF40	MS60	MS63
1993Mo	2,000	—	—	—	—	35.00
1993Mo	1,000	PF60 70.00				

KM# 647 5 NUEVOS PESOS

31.00 g., 0.999 Silver, 0.99 oz. ASW 40mm. **Obv.** National arms, eagle left within D-shaped circle and flower blossom border **Rev:** Seated figure sculpture within D-shaped circle and flower blossom border **Edge:** Reeded **Mint:** Mexico City

Date	Mintage	F12	VF20	XF40	MS60	MS63
1993Mo	2,000	—	—	—	35.00	—
1993Mo	800	PF60 75.00				

KM# 649   5 NUEVOS PESOS
31.00 g., 0.999 Silver, 0.99 oz. ASW 40mm. **Obv.** National arms, eagle left within D-shaped circle and designed border **Rev:** Aztec sculpture within D-shaped circle and designed border **Edge:** Reeded

Date	Mintage	F12	VF20	XF40	MS60	MS63
1993Mo	5,000	—	—	—	25.00	—
1993Mo	800	**PF60** 75.00				

KM# 650   10 NUEVOS PESOS
155.31 g., 0.999 Silver, 4.96 oz. ASW 65mm. **Obv.** National arms, eagle left **Rev:** Warrior capturing woman **Edge:** Reeded **Mint:** Mexico City **Note:** Illustration reduced, similar to 100 Pesos, KM# 557

Date	Mintage	F12	VF20	XF40	MS60	MS63
1992Mo	—	**PF60** 300				
1993Mo	1,000	**PF60** 200				
1993Mo	1,000	—	—	—	—	175

KM# 648   5 NUEVOS PESOS
31.00 g., 0.999 Silver, 0.99 oz. ASW 40mm. **Obv.** National arms, eagle left within D-shaped circle and designed border **Rev:** Sculpture within D-shaped circle and designed border **Edge:** Reeded

Date	Mintage	F12	VF20	XF40	MS60	MS63
1993Mo	2,000	—	—	—	35.00	—
1993Mo	500	**PF60** 75.00				

KM# 554   25 PESOS
7.78 g., 0.999 Silver, 0.25 oz. ASW **Obv.** National arms, eagle left within D-shaped circle and designed border **Rev:** Eagle warrior right within D-shaped circle and a designed border **Mint:** Mexico City

Date	Mintage	F12	VF20	XF40	MS60	MS63
1992Mo	50,000	—	—	—	15.00	—
1992Mo	3,000	**PF60** 30.00				

Note: Combined mintages of KM#554 and KM#644 through 2013 are 54,005 Unc. and 2,700 Proof.

KM# 555   50 PESOS
15.55 g., 0.999 Silver, 0.50 oz. ASW **Obv.** National arms, eagle left within D-shaped circle designed border **Rev:** Eagle warrior right within D-shaped circle and designed border **Mint:** Mexico City

Date	Mintage	F12	VF20	XF40	MS60	MS63
1992Mo	50,000	—	—	—	20.00	—
1992Mo	3,000	**PF60** 40.00				

Note: Combined mintages for KM#555 and #645 through 2013 are 52,000 Unc. and 4,300 Proof.

KM# 556 100 PESOS
31.10 g., 0.999 Silver, 0.99 oz. ASW 40mm. **Obv.** National arms, eagle left **Rev:** Eagle warrior **Mint:** Mexico City

Date	Mintage	F12	VF20	XF40	MS60	MS63
1992Mo	205,000	—	—	—	35.00	—
1992	4,000	**PF60** 75.00				

Note: KM#556 and #646 have a combined mintage through 2013 of 208,400 Unc and 7,000 Proof.

KM# 562 100 PESOS
31.10 g., 0.999 Silver, 0.99 oz. ASW 40mm. **Obv.** National arms, eagle left within D-shaped circle and designed border **Rev:** Seated figure sculpture within D-shaped circle and designed border **Mint:** Mexico City

Date	Mintage	F12	VF20	XF40	MS60	MS63
1992Mo	4,000	**PF60** 90.00				

Note: KM#562 and #647 have a combined mintage through 2013 of 3,511 Unc and 6,200 Proof.

KM# 563 100 PESOS
31.10 g., 0.999 Silver, 0.99 oz. ASW 40mm. **Obv.** National arms, eagle left within D-shaped circle and designed border **Rev:** Brasero Efigie - The God of Rain within D-shaped circle and designed border **Mint:** Mexico City

Date	Mintage	F12	VF20	XF40	MS60	MS63
1992Mo	4,000	**PF60** 60.00				

Note: KM#563 and #648 have combined mintage through 2013 of 4,580 Unc. and 6,400 Proof.

KM# 564 100 PESOS
31.10 g., 0.999 Silver, 0.99 oz. ASW **Obv.** National arms, eagle left within D-shaped circle and designed border **Rev:** Huehueteotl - The God of Fire within D-shaped circle and designed border **Mint:** Mexico City

Date	Mintage	F12	VF20	XF40	MS60	MS63
1992Mo	4,000	**PF60** 70.00				

Note: KM#564 and #649 have combined mintage through 2013 of 6,105 Unc. and 6,400 Proof.

KM# 558 250 PESOS
7.78 g., 0.999 Gold, 0.25 oz. AGW **Obv.** National arms, eagle left within D-shaped circle and designed border **Rev:** Sculpture of Jaguar head within D-shaped circle and designed border **Mint:** Mexico City

Date	Mintage	F12	VF20	XF40	MS60	MS63
1992Mo	12,000	—	—	—	—	475
1992Mo	2,000	**PF60** 450				

KM# 559 500 PESOS
15.55 g., 0.999 Gold, 0.50 oz. AGW **Obv.** National arms, eagle left within D-shaped circle and designed border **Rev:** Sculpture of Jaguar head within D-shaped circle and designed border **Mint:** Mexico City

Date	Mintage	F12	VF20	XF40	MS60	MS63
1992Mo	12,000	—	—	—	—	900
1992Mo	2,000	**PF60** 925				

KM# 560   1000 PESOS

31.10 g., 0.999 Gold, 0.99 oz. AGW **Obv.** National arms, eagle left within D-shaped circle and designed border **Rev:** Sculpture of Jaguar head within D-shaped circle and designed border **Mint:** Mexico City

Date	Mintage	F12	VF20	XF40	MS60	MS63
1992Mo	19,850	—	—	—	—	1,750
1992Mo	2,000	**PF60** 1,800				

KM# 557   10000 PESOS

155.52 g., 0.999 Silver, 4.96 oz. ASW 64mm. **Obv.** National arms, eagle left within D-shaped circle and designed border **Rev:** Native warriors within D-shaped circle and designed border **Mint:** Mexico City **Note:** Similar to 10 Nuevo Pesos, KM#650

Date	Mintage	F12	VF20	XF40	MS60	MS63
1992Mo	51,900	—	—	—	—	175
1992Mo	3,300	**PF60** 275				

Note: KM#557 and #650 have combined mintage through 2013 of 54,305 Unc. and 5,400 Proof.

CENTRAL VERACRUZ SERIES

KM# 567   NUEVOS PESO

7.76 g., 0.999 Silver, 0.25 oz. ASW 27mm. **Obv.** National arms, eagle left within D-shaped circle and designed border **Rev:** Design within D-shaped circle and designed border **Mint:** Mexico City

Date	Mintage	F12	VF20	XF40	MS60	MS63
1993Mo	100,005	—	—	—	—	20.00
1993Mo	4,305	**PF60** 35.00				

KM# 568   2 NUEVOS PESOS

15.55 g., 0.999 Silver, 0.50 oz. ASW 33mm. **Obv.** National arms, eagle left within D-shaped circle and designed border **Rev:** Design within D-shaped circle and designed border **Mint:** Mexico City

Date	Mintage	F12	VF20	XF40	MS60	MS63
1993Mo	100,005	—	—	—	—	25.00
1993Mo	3,005	**PF60** 35.00				

KM# 569   5 NUEVOS PESOS

31.10 g., 0.999 Silver, 0.99 oz. ASW 40mm. **Obv.** National arms, eagle left within D-shaped circle and designed border **Rev:** Design within D-shaped circle and designed border **Mint:** Mexico City

Date	Mintage	F12	VF20	XF40	MS60	MS63
1993Mo	101,005	—	—	—	—	37.50
1993Mo	4,405	**PF60** 70.00				

KM# 582   5 NUEVOS PESOS

31.10 g., 0.999 Silver, 0.99 oz. ASW 40mm. **Obv.** National arms, eagle left within D-shaped circle and designed border **Rev:** Aerial view of crocodile within D-shaped circle and designed border **Mint:** Mexico City

Date	Mintage	F12	VF20	XF40	MS60	MS63
1993Mo	5,105	—	—	—	—	37.50
1993Mo	3,855	**PF60** 75.00				

KM# 583 5 NUEVOS PESOS

31.10 g., 0.999 Silver, 0.99 oz. ASW 40mm. **Obv.** National arms, eagle left within D-shaped circle and designed border **Rev:** Kneeling figure sculpture within D-shaped circle and designed border **Mint:** Mexico City

Date	Mintage	F12	VF20	XF40	MS60	MS63
1993Mo	3,800	—	—	—	—	37.50
1993Mo	4,160	**PF60** 75.00				

KM# 584 5 NUEVOS PESOS

31.10 g., 0.999 Silver, 0.99 oz. ASW 40mm. **Obv.** National arms, eagle left **Rev:** Sculptured head **Mint:** Mexico City

Date	Mintage	F12	VF20	XF40	MS60	MS63
1993Mo	5,105	—	—	—	—	37.50
1993Mo	4,705	**PF60** 75.00				

KM# 570 10 NUEVOS PESOS

155.52 g., 0.999 Silver, 4.96 oz. ASW 65mm. **Obv.** National arms, eagle left within flat shaped circle and designed border **Rev:** Pyramid within flat shaped circle and designed border **Note:** Illustration reduced.

Date	Mintage	F12	VF20	XF40	MS60	MS63
1993Mo	50,905	—	—	—	—	175
1993Mo	4,148	**PF60** 190				

KM# 585 25 NUEVOS PESOS

7.78 g., 0.999 Gold, 0.25 oz. AGW **Obv.** National arms, eagle left **Rev:** Mask left **Note:** Similar to 100 New Pesos, KM#587.

Date	Mintage	F12	VF20	XF40	MS60	MS63
1993Mo	802	**PF60** 500				
1993Mo	15,508	—	—	—	—	475

KM# 586 50 NUEVOS PESOS

15.55 g., 0.999 Gold, 0.50 oz. AGW **Obv.** National arms, eagle left **Rev:** Mask left **Note:** Similar to 100 New Pesos, KM#587.

Date	Mintage	F12	VF20	XF40	MS60	MS63
1993Mo	15,508	—	—	—	—	900
1993Mo	802	**PF60** 925				

KM# 587 100 NUEVOS PESOS

31.10 g., 0.999 Gold, 0.99 oz. AGW **Obv.** National arms, eagle left **Rev:** Mask left

Date	Mintage	F12	VF20	XF40	MS60	MS63
1993Mo	7,160	—	—	—	—	1,800
1993Mo	500	**PF60** 1,850				

MAYAN SERIES

KM# 572 NUEVOS PESO

7.76 g., 0.999 Silver, 0.25 oz. ASW **Obv.** National arms, eagle left within six sided shield and designed border **Rev:** Reclining figure within six sided shield and designed border **Mint:** Mexico City

Date	Mintage	F12	VF20	XF40	MS60	MS63
1994Mo	53,505	—	—	—	—	20.00
1994Mo	2,700	**PF60** 35.00				

KM# 573 2 NUEVOS PESOS

15.55 g., 0.999 Silver, 0.50 oz. ASW **Obv.** National arms, eagle left within six sided shield and designed border **Rev:** Reclining figure within six sided shield and designed border **Mint:** Mexico City

Date	Mintage	F12	VF20	XF40	MS60	MS63
1994Mo	51,500	—	—	—	—	25.00
1994Mo	4,300	**PF60** 35.00				

ESTADOS UNIDOS - BULLION COINAGE

KM# 574   5 NUEVOS PESOS
31.10 g., 0.999 Silver, 0.99 oz. ASW 40mm. **Obv.** National arms, eagle left within six sided shield and designed border **Rev:** Reclining figure within six sided shield and designed border **Mint:** Mexico City

Date	Mintage	F12	VF20	XF40	MS60	MS63
1994Mo	208,300	—	—	—	—	37.00
1994Mo	6,700	**PF60** 70.00				

KM# 575   5 NUEVOS PESOS
31.10 g., 0.999 Silver, 0.99 oz. ASW 40mm. **Obv.** National arms, eagle left within six sided shield and designed border **Rev:** Tomb of Palenque Memorial Stone within six sided shield and designed border **Mint:** Mexico City

Date	Mintage	F12	VF20	XF40	MS60	MS63
1994Mo	5,905	—	—	—	—	37.00
1994Mo	6,300	**PF60** 70.00				

KM# 577   5 NUEVOS PESOS
31.10 g., 0.999 Silver, 0.99 oz. ASW 40mm. **Rev:** Elaborately carved wall segment **Mint:** Mexico City

Date	Mintage	F12	VF20	XF40	MS60	MS63
1994Mo	3,011	—	—	—	—	37.00
1994Mo	6,300	**PF60** 70.00				

KM# 578   5 NUEVOS PESOS
31.10 g., 0.999 Silver, 0.99 oz. ASW 40mm. **Obv.** National

---

arms, eagle left within six sided shield and designed border **Rev:** Two seated figures wall carving within six sided shield and designed border

Date	Mintage	F12	VF20	XF40	MS60	MS63
1994Mo	4,080	—	—	—	—	45.00
1994Mo	6,000	**PF60** 75.00				

KM# 676   10 NUEVOS PESOS
155.52 g., 0.999 Silver, 4.96 oz. ASW 65mm. **Obv.** National arms, eagle left above metal content statement **Rev:** Pyramid above two-line inscription **Rev. Inscription:** PIRAMIDE DEL CASTILLO / CHICHEN-ITZA **Edge:** Reeded **Mint:** Mexico City

Date	Mintage	F12	VF20	XF40	MS60	MS63
1993Mo	—	**PF60** 650				

KM# 576   10 NUEVOS PESOS
155.70 g., 0.999 Silver, 4.97 oz. ASW 64mm. **Obv.** National arms, eagle left **Rev:** Pyramid **Note:** Illustration reduced.

Date	Mintage	F12	VF20	XF40	MS60	MS63
1994Mo	54,305	—	—	—	—	175
1994Mo	5,500	**PF60** 225				

KM# 579   25 NUEVOS PESOS
7.78 g., 0.999 Gold, 0.25 oz. AGW **Rev:** Seated figure

Date	Mintage	F12	VF20	XF40	MS60	MS63
1994Mo	501	**PF60** 500				
1994Mo	2,000	—	—	—	—	475

KM# 580   50 NUEVOS PESOS
15.55 g., 0.999 Gold, 0.50 oz. AGW **Rev:** Seated figure

Date	Mintage	F12	VF20	XF40	MS60	MS63
1994Mo	1,000	—	—	—	—	900
1994Mo	501	**PF60** 925				

KM# 581 100 NUEVOS PESOS

31.10 g., 0.999 Gold, 0.99 oz. AGW **Obv.** National arms, eagle left within six sided shield and designed border **Rev:** Seated figure within six sided shield and designed border

Date	Mintage	F12	VF20	XF40	MS60	MS63
1994Mo	1,000	—	—	—	—	1,800
1994Mo	501	PF60 1,850				

OLMEC SERIES

KM# 593 PESO

7.78 g., 0.999 Silver, 0.25 oz. ASW **Obv.** National arms, eagle left within square and designed border **Rev:** Sitting figure facing within square and designed border **Mint:** Mexico City **Note:** Similar to 5 Pesos, KM#595.

Date	Mintage	F12	VF20	XF40	MS60	MS63
1996Mo	6,400	—	—	—	—	20.00
1996Mo	3,700	PF60 35.00				
1998Mo Matte	2,400	—	—	—	—	22.00

KM# 594 2 PESOS

15.55 g., 0.999 Silver, 0.50 oz. ASW **Obv.** National arms, eagle left within square and designed border **Rev:** Sitting figure facing within square and designed border **Mint:** Mexico City **Note:** Similar to 5 Pesos, KM#595.

Date	Mintage	F12	VF20	XF40	MS60	MS63
1996Mo	6,500	—	—	—	—	25.00
1996Mo	2,200	PF60 35.00				
1998Mo Matte	2,400	—	—	—	—	28.00

KM# 595 5 PESOS

31.10 g., 0.999 Silver, 0.99 oz. ASW 40mm. **Obv.** National arms, eagle left within square and designed border **Rev:** Seated figure facing within square and designed border

Date	Mintage	F12	VF20	XF40	MS60	MS63
1996Mo	9,200	—	—	—	—	37.50
1996Mo	4,100	PF60 70.00				
1998 Matte	3,400	—	—	—	—	40.00

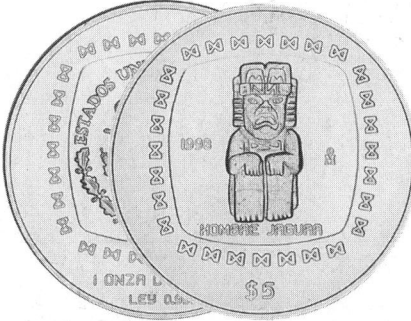

KM# 596 5 PESOS

31.10 g., 0.999 Silver, 0.99 oz. ASW 40mm. **Obv.** National arms, eagle left within square and designed border **Rev:** Statue facing within square and designed border

Date	Mintage	F12	VF20	XF40	MS60	MS63
1996Mo	6,000	—	—	—	—	90.00
1996Mo	4,200	PF60 70.00				
1998Mo Matte	6,000	—	—	—	—	37.50
1998Mo	4,800	PF60 75.00				

KM# 597 5 PESOS

31.10 g., 0.999 Silver, 0.99 oz. ASW 40mm. **Obv.** National arms, eagle left **Rev:** El Luchador

Date	Mintage	F12	VF20	XF40	MS60	MS63
1996Mo	7,100	—	—	—	—	37.50
1996Mo	3,800	PF60 70.00				
1998 Matte	2,000	—	—	—	—	40.00

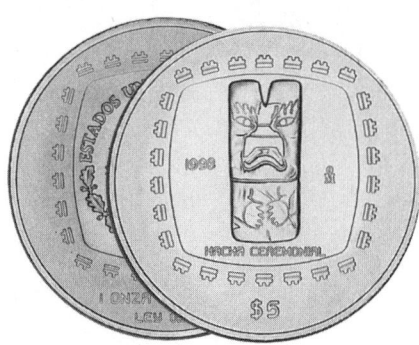

KM# 598   5 PESOS

31.10 g., 0.999 Silver, 0.99 oz. ASW 40mm. **Obv.** National arms, eagle left within square and designed border **Rev:** Statue within square and designed border

Date	Mintage	F12	VF20	XF40	MS60	MS63
1996Mo	3,700	—	—	—	—	37.50
1996Mo	7,500	PF60 70.00				
1998 Matte	2,000	—	—	—	—	40.00

KM# 599   10 PESOS

155.52 g., 0.999 Silver, 4.96 oz. ASW 64mm. **Obv.** National arms, eagle left **Rev:** Native mask **Note:** Illustration reduced.

Date	Mintage	F12	VF20	XF40	MS60	MS63
1996Mo	3,900	—	—	—	—	180
1996Mo	5,560	PF60 190				
1998 Matte	2,150	—	—	—	—	180

KM# 600   25 PESOS

7.78 g., 0.999 Gold, 0.25 oz. AGW **Obv.** National arms, eagle left **Rev:** Sculpture **Note:** Similar to 100 Pesos, KM#602.

Date	Mintage	F12	VF20	XF40	MS60	MS63
1996Mo	500	—	—	—	—	475
1996Mo	750	PF60 500				

KM# 601   50 PESOS

15.55 g., 0.999 Gold, 0.50 oz. AGW **Obv.** National arms, eagle left **Rev:** Sculpture **Note:** Similar to 100 Pesos, KM#602.

Date	Mintage	F12	VF20	XF40	MS60	MS63
1996Mo	500	PF60 925				
1996Mo	500	—	—	—	—	900

KM# 602   100 PESOS

31.10 g., 0.999 Gold, 0.99 oz. AGW **Obv.** National arms, eagle left within square and designed border **Rev:** Sculpture within square and designed border

Date	Mintage	F12	VF20	XF40	MS60	MS63
1996Mo	500	—	—	—	—	1,800
1996Mo	500	PF60 1,850				

TEOTIHUACAN SERIES

KM# 617   PESO

7.78 g., 0.999 Silver, 0.25 oz. ASW **Obv.** National arms, eagle left within oblong circle and designed border **Rev:** Sculpture within oblong circle and designed border **Mint:** Mexico City

Date	Mintage	F12	VF20	XF40	MS60	MS63
1997Mo	3,100	—	—	—	—	20.00
1997Mo	1,906	PF60 35.00				
1998Mo Matte	2,400	—	—	—	—	25.00
1998Mo	500	PF60 45.00				

KM# 618   2 PESOS

15.55 g., 0.999 Silver, 0.50 oz. ASW **Obv.** National arms,

eagle left within oblong circle and designed border **Rev:**
Sculpture within oblong circle and designed border **Mint:**
Mexico City

Date	Mintage	F12	VF20	XF40	MS60	MS63
1997Mo	1,606	—	—	—	—	25.00
1997Mo	3,500	**PF60** 35.00				
1998Mo	500	**PF60** 50.00				
1998Mo	2,400	—	—	—	—	30.00

KM# 621 5 PESOS
31.10 g., 0.999 Silver, 0.99 oz. ASW 40mm. **Obv.** National
arms, eagle left within oval and designed border **Rev:**
Seated woman joined to pottery vase within oval and
designed border

Date	Mintage	F12	VF20	XF40	MS60	MS63
1997Mo	Est. 1800	**PF60** 75.00				
1997Mo	5,300	—	—	—	—	42.00
1998Mo Matte	2,000	—	—	—	—	42.00
1998Mo	3,006	**PF60** 150				

KM# 622 5 PESOS
31.10 g., 0.999 Silver, 0.99 oz. ASW 40mm. **Obv.** National
arms, eagle left

Date	Mintage	F12	VF20	XF40	MS60	MS63
1997Mo	3,206	**PF60** 75.00				
1997Mo	5,400	—	—	—	—	37.50
1998Mo Matte	2,000	—	—	—	—	40.00
1998Mo	500	**PF60** 150				

KM# 619 5 PESOS
31.10 g., 0.999 Silver, 0.99 oz. ASW 40mm. **Obv.** National
arms, eagle left within oblong circle and designed border
Rev: Sculpture within oblong circle and designed border

Date	Mintage	F12	VF20	XF40	MS60	MS63
1997Mo	4,700	—	—	—	—	37.50
1997Mo	3,206	**PF60** 75.00				
1998Mo	3,400	—	—	—	—	40.00
1998Mo	500	**PF60** 150				

KM# 620 5 PESOS
31.10 g., 0.99 Silver, 0.99 oz. ASW 40mm. **Obv.** National
arms, eagle left within oblong circle and designed border
Rev: Face sculpture within oblong circle and designed
border

Date	Mintage	F12	VF20	XF40	MS60	MS63
1997Mo	5,200	—	—	—	—	37.50
1997Mo	2,906	**PF60** 75.00				
1998Mo	2,000	—	—	—	—	40.00
1998Mo	500	**PF60** 150				

KM# 623 10 PESOS
155.52 g., 0.999 Silver, 4.96 oz. ASW 64mm. **Obv.** National
arms, eagle left within oblong circle and designed border
Rev: Pyramid within oblong circle and designed border
Note: Illustration reduced.

Date	Mintage	F12	VF20	XF40	MS60	MS63
1997Mo	3,306	PF60 225				
1997Mo	3,136	—	—	—	—	200
1998Mo Matte	2,150	—	—	—	—	200

KM# 624 25 PESOS
7.78 g., 0.999 Gold, 0.25 oz. AGW **Obv.** National arms, eagle left **Note:** Similar to 100 Pesos, KM#626.

Date	Mintage	F12	VF20	XF40	MS60	MS63
1997Mo	500	—	—	—	—	475
1997Mo	206	PF60 525				

KM# 625 50 PESOS
15.55 g., 0.999 Gold, 0.50 oz. AGW **Obv.** National arms, eagle left **Note:** Similar to 100 Pesos, KM#626.

Date	Mintage	F12	VF20	XF40	MS60	MS63
1997Mo	206	PF60 950				
1997Mo	500	—	—	—	—	925

KM# 626 100 PESOS
31.10 g., 0.999 Gold, 0.99 oz. AGW **Obv.** National arms, eagle left

Date	Mintage	F12	VF20	XF40	MS60	MS63
1997Mo	206	PF60 1,900				
1997Mo	500	—	—	—	—	1,850

TOLTECA SERIES

KM# 661 PESO
7.78 g., 0.999 Silver, 0.25 oz. ASW 27mm. **Obv.** National arms, eagle left **Rev:** Jaguar carving **Edge:** Reeded **Mint:** Mexico City

Date	Mintage	F12	VF20	XF40	MS60	MS63
1998Mo	6,400	—	—	—	—	20.00
1998Mo	4,000	PF60 30.00				

KM# 662 2 PESOS
15.55 g., 0.999 Silver, 0.50 oz. ASW 33mm. **Obv.** National arms, eagle left **Rev:** Jaguar carving **Edge:** Reeded **Mint:** Mexico City

Date	Mintage	F12	VF20	XF40	MS60	MS63
1998Mo	6,600	—	—	—	—	25.00
1998Mo	2,200	PF60 35.00				

KM# 663 5 PESOS
31.10 g., 0.999 Silver, 0.99 oz. ASW 40mm. **Obv.** National arms, eagle left within shield and designed border **Rev:** Jaguar carving within shield and designed border **Edge:** Reeded **Mint:** Mexico City

Date	Mintage	F12	VF20	XF40	MS60	MS63
1998Mo	5,800	—	—	—	—	37.50
1998Mo	4,300	PF60 75.00				

KM# 664 5 PESOS
31.10 g., 0.999 Silver, 0.99 oz. ASW 40mm. **Obv.** National arms, eagle left **Rev:** Sacerdote sculpture **Edge:** Reeded **Mint:** Mexico City

Date	Mintage	F12	VF20	XF40	MS60	MS63
1998Mo	7,100	—	—	—	35.00	—
1998Mo	3,900	PF60 75.00				

KM# 665 5 PESOS
31.10 g., 0.999 Silver, 0.99 oz. ASW 40mm. **Obv.** National arms, eagle left **Rev:** Quetzalcoatl sculpture **Edge:** Reeded **Mint:** Mexico City

Date	Mintage	F12	VF20	XF40	MS60	MS63
1998Mo	6,600	—	—	—	—	37.50
1998Mo	3,600	PF60 75.00				

KM# 666 5 PESOS
31.10 g., 0.999 Silver, 0.99 oz. ASW 40mm. **Obv.** National arms, eagle left **Rev:** Large sculpture **Edge:** Reeded **Mint:** Mexico City

Date	Mintage	F12	VF20	XF40	MS60	MS63
1998Mo	8,700	—	—	—	—	37.50
1998Mo	3,800	PF60 75.00				

KM# 634   10 PESOS

155.73 g., 0.999 Silver, 4.97 oz. ASW **Obv.** National arms, eagle left within shield and designed border **Rev:** Three carved statues within shield and designed border

Date	Mintage	F12	VF20	XF40	MS60	MS63
1998Mo	5,560	—	—	—	—	180
1998Mo	3,650	PF60 200				

KM# 667   25 PESOS

7.78 g., 0.999 Gold, 0.25 oz. AGW 23mm. **Obv.** National arms, eagle left **Rev:** Eagle sculpture **Edge:** Reeded **Mint:** Mexico City

Date	Mintage	F12	VF20	XF40	MS60	MS63
1998Mo	303	PF60 525				
1998Mo	303	—	—	—	—	500

KM# 668   50 PESOS

15.55 g., 0.999 Gold, 0.50 oz. AGW 29mm. **Obv.** National arms, eagle left **Rev:** Eagle sculpture **Edge:** Reeded **Mint:** Mexico City

Date	Mintage	F12	VF20	XF40	MS60	MS63
1998Mo	303	PF60 950				
1998Mo	303	—	—	—	—	925

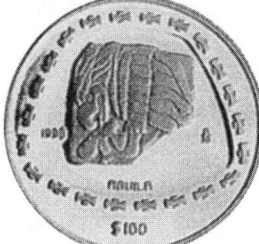

KM# 669   100 PESOS

31.10 g., 0.999 Gold, 0.99 oz. AGW 34.5mm. **Obv.** National arms, eagle left within designed shield **Rev:** Eagle sculpture within designed shield **Edge:** Reeded **Mint:** Mexico City

Date	Mintage	F12	VF20	XF40	MS60	MS63
1998Mo	303	PF60 1,900				
1998Mo	303	—	—	—	—	1,850

MEDALLIC SILVER BULLION COINAGE

KM# M49a   ONZA

33.63 g., 0.925 Silver, 0.99 oz. ASW 41mm. **Obv.** Mint mark above coin press

Date	Mintage	F12	VF20	XF40	MS60	MS63
1949	1,000,000	BV	36.50	40.00	45.00	60.00

KM# M49b.1   ONZA

33.63 g., 0.925 Silver, 0.99 oz. ASW 41mm. **Obv.** Wide spacing between DE MONEDA **Rev:** Mint mark below balance scale **Mint:** Mexico City **Note:** Type I

Date	Mintage	F12	VF20	XF40	MS60	MS63
1978Mo	280,000	—	—	BV	37.50	45.00

KM# M49b.2   ONZA

33.63 g., 0.925 Silver, 0.99 oz. ASW 41mm. **Obv.** Close spacing between DE MONEDA **Rev:** Mint mark below balance scale **Mint:** Mexico City **Note:** Type II

Date	Mintage	F12	VF20	XF40	MS60	MS63
1978Mo	Inc. above	—	—	BV	38.50	48.00

KM# M49b.3 ONZA
33.63 g., 0.925 Silver, 0.99 oz. ASW 41mm. **Obv.** Close spacing between DE MONEDA **Rev:** Left scale pan points to U in UNA **Mint:** Mexico City **Note:** Type III

Date	Mintage	F12	VF20	XF40	MS60	MS63
1979Mo	4,508,000	—	—	BV	37.50	42.00

KM# M49b.4 ONZA
33.63 g., 0.925 Silver, 0.99 oz. ASW 41mm. **Obv.** Close spacing between DE MONEDA **Rev:** Left scale pan points between U and N of UNA **Mint:** Mexico City **Note:** Type IV

Date	Mintage	F12	VF20	XF40	MS60	MS63
1979Mo	Inc. above	—	—	BV	37.50	42.00

KM# M49b.5 ONZA
33.63 g., 0.925 Silver, 0.99 oz. ASW 41mm. **Obv.** Close spacing between DE MONEDA **Rev:** Left scale pan points between U and N of UNA **Mint:** Mexico City **Note:** Type V

Date	Mintage	F12	VF20	XF40	MS60	MS63
1980/70Mo	Inc. above	—	—	BV	38.50	46.00
1980Mo	6,104,000	—	—	BV	37.50	42.00

MEDALLIC GOLD COINAGE

KM# M91a 10 PESOS
8.33 g., 0.900 Gold, 0.24 oz. AGW

Date	Mintage	F12	VF20	XF40	MS60	MS63
1953	—	—	—	—	BV	450

KM# M123a 10 PESOS
8.33 g., 0.900 Gold, 0.24 oz. AGW

Date	Mintage	F12	VF20	XF40	MS60	MS63
1957	—	—	—	—	BV	450

Note: Mintage includes #M122a

KM# M92a 20 PESOS
16.67 g., 0.900 Gold, 0.48 oz. AGW

Date	Mintage	F12	VF20	XF40	MS60	MS63
1953	—	—	—	—	BV	850

KM# M122a 50 PESOS
41.67 g., 0.900 Gold, 1.20 oz. AGW

Date	Mintage	F12	VF20	XF40	MS60	MS63
1957	—	—	—	—	BV	2,150

Note: Mintage included in total for KM#M123a

REVOLUTIONARY

AGUASCALIENTES

Aguascalientes is a state in central Mexico. Its coin issues, struck by authority of Pancho Villa, represent his deepest penetration into the Mexican heartland. Lack of silver made it necessary to make all denominations in copper.

FRANCISCO PANCHO VILLA

REVOLUTIONARY COINAGE

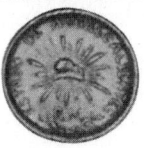

KM# 601 CENTAVO
3.55 g., Copper, 17mm. **Obv.** Liberty cap **Rev:** Value within 3/4 wreath below date **Note:** Large date weight 3.55g.

Date	Mintage	VG8	F12	VF20	XF40	MS60
1915	—	30.00	60.00	100	300	—
Note: Large date, reeded edge
1915	—	30.00	60.00	100	300	—
Note: Small date, plain edge
1915	—	250	350	450	—	—
Note: Large date, plain edge
1915	—	30.00	60.00	80.00	250	—
Note: Small date, reeded edge

KM# 602.1 2 CENTAVOS
4.28 g., Copper, **Obv.** Liberty cap **Rev:** Value within 3/4 wreath below date

Date	Mintage	VG8	F12	VF20	XF40	MS60
1915	—	40.00	100	300	450	—
Note: Round front 2, plain edge

KM# 602.2 2 CENTAVOS
3.35 g., Copper, 19mm. **Obv.** Liberty cap **Rev:** Value within 1/2 wreath below date

Date	Mintage	VG8	F12	VF20	XF40	MS60
1915 Plain edge	—	50.00	90.00	200	500	—
Note: Square front 2
1915	—	35.00	60.00	85.00	300	—
Note: Square front 2, reeded edge

KM# 603 5 CENTAVOS
Copper, 25mm. **Obv.** National arms **Rev:** Liberty cap and value above sprigs

Date	Mintage	VG8	F12	VF20	XF40
1915 Plain edge; Rare	—	—	—	—	—
1915 Reeded edge	—	10.00	20.00	30.00	75.00

KM# 604.1 5 CENTAVOS
7.13 g., Copper, 25mm. **Obv.** National arms **Rev:** Vertically shaded 5 within sprigs

Date	Mintage	VG8	F12	VF20	XF40	MS60
1915	—	20.00	40.00	50.00	175	—
Note: Reeded edge
1915	—	100	150	225	400	—
Note: Plain edge

KM# 604.2 5 CENTAVOS
Copper, 25mm. **Obv.** National arms **Rev:** Horizontally shaded 5 within sprigs

Date	Mintage	VG8	F12	VF20	XF40	MS60
1915	—	25.00	40.00	65.00	150	—
Note: Reeded edge
1915	—	35.00	60.00	90.00	275	—
Note: Plain edge

KM# 606 20 CENTAVOS
Copper, 29mm. **Obv.** National arms **Rev:** Value below Liberty cap within sprigs

Date	Mintage	VG8	F12	VF20	XF40
1915 Reeded edge	—	10.00	20.00	60.00	100

KM# 605　20 CENTAVOS
Copper, 29mm. **Obv.** National arms **Rev:** Value below Liberty cap within sprigs

Date	Mintage	VG8	F12	VF20	XF40
1915 Reeded edge	—	11.00	30.00	85.00	150

KM# 600　20 CENTAVOS
Copper, **Obv.** National arms **Rev:** Value below Liberty cap within sprigs **Edge:** Reeded

Date	Mintage	VG8	F12	VF20	XF40	MS60
1915	—	15.00	20.00	50.00	100	—

Note: Varieties exist with both plain and milled edges and many variations in the shading of the numerals

CHIHUAHUA

Chihuahua is a northern state of Mexico bordering the U.S. It was the arena that introduced Pancho Villa to the world. Villa, an outlaw, was given a title when asked by Madero to participate in maintaining order during Madero's presidency. After Madero's death in February 1913, Villa became a persuasive leader. Chihuahua was where he made his first coins - the Parral series. The Army of the North pesos also came from this state. This coin helped Villa recruit soldiers because of his ability to pay in silver while others were paying in worthless paper money.

ARMY OF THE NORTH

REVOLUTIONARY COINAGE

KM# 619　PESO
29.27 g., Silver, **Obv.** National arms **Rev:** Liberty cap

Date	Mintage	VG8	F12	VF20	XF40	MS60
1915	—	25.00	40.00	75.00	200	500

KM# 619a　PESO
Copper, **Obv.** National arms **Rev:** Liberty cap

Date	Mintage	VG8	F12	VF20	XF40	MS60
1915	—	500	1,000	1,500	2,500	—

KM# 619b　PESO
Brass, **Obv.** National arms **Rev:** Liberty cap **Note:** Uniface obverse

Date	Mintage	VG8	F12	VF20	XF40	MS60
1915 Rare	—	—	—	—	—	—

CONSTITUTIONALIST ARMY

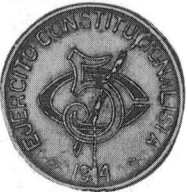

KM# 612　5 CENTAVOS
Copper, **Obv.** Liberty cap **Rev:** Value above date

Date	Mintage	VG8	F12	VF20	XF40	MS60
1914	—	25.00	45.00	100	250	—

KM# 613　5 CENTAVOS
6.60 g., Copper, 25mm. **Obv.** Liberty cap **Rev:** Value above date **Note:** Numerous varieties exist. Weight varies 6.3-6.93g.

Date	Mintage	VG8	F12	VF20	XF40	MS60
1914	—	1.00	2.50	4.00	10.00	—
1915	—	1.00	2.50	4.00	10.00	—

KM# 613a　5 CENTAVOS
Brass, **Obv.** Liberty cap **Rev:** Value above date **Note:** Numerous varieties exist.

Date	Mintage	VG8	F12	VF20	XF40	MS60
1914	—	2.00	3.00	8.00	10.00	—
1915	—	2.00	3.00	8.00	10.00	—

KM# 613b　5 CENTAVOS
Cast Copper, **Obv.** Liberty cap **Rev:** Value above date

Date	Mintage	VG8	F12	VF20	XF40	MS60
1914	—	75.00	200	300	450	—

KM# 614a　5 CENTAVOS
Copper, **Obv.** National arms **Rev:** Value below date within sprigs with solid V

Date	Mintage	VG8	F12	VF20	XF40	MS60
1915 Rare	—	—	—	—	—	—

KM# 614b　5 CENTAVOS
Copper, **Obv.** National arms **Rev:** Value above date **Note:** Mule.

Date	Mintage	VG8	F12	VF20	XF40	MS60
1915	—	—	500	—	—	—

KM# 614c　5 CENTAVOS
Copper, **Obv.** National arms **Rev:** Liberty cap **Note:** Mule.

Date	Mintage	VG8	F12	VF20	XF40	MS60
1915 Rare	—	—	—	—	—	—

KM# 614　5 CENTAVOS
Copper, **Obv.** National arms **Rev:** Value below date within sprigs with double-lined V

Date	Mintage	VG8	F12	VF20	XF40	MS60
1915 SS Unique	—	—	—	—	—	—

KM# 615 10 CENTAVOS
8.79 g., Copper, 27.5mm. **Obv.** Liberty cap **Rev:** Value above date

Date	Mintage	VG8	F12	VF20	XF40	MS60
1915	—	1.25	2.50	3.50	8.00	20.00

KM# 615a 10 CENTAVOS
8.89 g., Brass, 27.5mm. **Obv.** Liberty cap **Rev:** Value above date

Date	Mintage	VG8	F12	VF20	XF40	MS60
1915	—	5.00	10.00	30.00	50.00	—

Note: Many varieties exist

HIDALGO DEL PARRAL

KM# 607 2 CENTAVOS
6.85 g., Copper, 25mm. **Obv.** Liberty cap within circle flanked by sprigs **Rev:** Value flanked by sprigs within circle

Date	Mintage	VG8	F12	VF20	XF40	MS60
1913	—	5.00	10.00	25.00	50.00	—

KM# 607a 2 CENTAVOS
Brass, **Obv.** Liberty cap within circle flanked by sprigs **Rev:** Value flanked by sprigs within circle

Date	Mintage	VG8	F12	VF20	XF40	MS60
1913	—	95.00	150	200	400	—

KM# 608 50 CENTAVOS
12.65 g., Silver, **Obv.** Liberty cap **Rev:** Value flanked by sprigs below Liberty cap **Edge:** Reeded

Date	Mintage	VG8	F12	VF20	XF40	MS60
1913	—	18.00	40.00	80.00	150	—

KM# 609 50 CENTAVOS
12.17 g., Silver, 30mm. **Edge:** Plain

Date	Mintage	VG8	F12	VF20	XF40	MS60
1913	—	50.00	70.00	125	250	—

KM# 610 PESO
30.00 g., Silver, **Obv.** Inscription **Rev:** 1 through PESO and small circle above sprigs **Note:** Weight varies 29.18-30.9g.

Date	Mintage	VG8	F12	VF20	XF40	MS60
1913	—	1,200	2,000	3,000	6,500	14,000

KM# 611 PESO
Silver, 38mm. **Obv.** Inscription **Rev:** Value above sprigs **Note:** Well struck counterfeits of this coin exist with the dot at the end of the word Peso even with the bottom of the O. On legitimate pieces the dot is slightly higher. Weight varies 27.3-28.85g.

Date	Mintage	VG8	F12	VF20	XF40	MS60
1913	—	35.00	45.00	125	275	475
1913	—					
1914	—					
1914	—					

Note: Specimens exist in silver plated copper

1914	—					
1914 Unique	—					

Note: Silver or silver-plated copper pieces are modern fantasies

DURANGO

A state in north central Mexico. Another area of operation for Pancho Villa. The Muera Huerta peso originates in this state. The coins were made in Cuencame under the orders of Generals Cemceros and Contreras.

CUENCAME

REVOLUTIONARY COINAGE

KM# 620 PESO
Silver, 38mm. **Obv.** National arms **Rev:** Liberty cap with written value flanked by stars

Date	Mintage	VG8	F12	VF20	XF40	MS60
1914	—	1,000	2,000	4,000	8,000	12,000

KM# 621 PESO
23.20 g., Silver, 39mm. **Obv.** National arms with continuous border **Rev:** Liberty cap with continuous border

Date	Mintage	VG8	F12	VF20	XF40	MS60
1914	—	75.00	150	300	700	1,200

KM# 621a PESO
Copper, **Obv.** National arms with continuous border **Rev:** Liberty cap with continuous border **Note:** Varieties exist.

Date	Mintage	VG8	F12	VF20	XF40	MS60
1914	—	400	600	2,000	3,000	—

KM# 621b PESO
Brass, **Obv.** National arms **Rev:** Liberty cap

Date	Mintage	VG8	F12	VF20	XF40	MS60
1914	—	—	2,000	3,000	4,000	—

KM# 622 PESO
23.40 g., Silver, 38.5mm. **Obv.** National arms with dot and dash border **Rev:** Liberty cap with continuous border **Note:** The so-called 20 Pesos gold Muera Huerta pieces are modern fantasies. Refer to Unusual World Coins, 4th edition, ©2005, KP Books, Inc.

Date	Mintage	VG8	F12	VF20	XF40	MS60
1914	—	65.00	120	300	600	1,100

ESTADO DE DURANGO

KM# 624 CENTAVO
Lead, **Obv.** Date **Rev:** Value within wreath **Note:** Cast.

Date	Mintage	VG8	F12	VF20	XF40	MS60
1914	—	45.00	75.00	100	200	—

KM# 625 CENTAVO
3.29 g., Copper, 20mm. **Obv.** Large date in center **Rev:** Value within wreath

Date	Mintage	VG8	F12	VF20	XF40	MS60
1914	—	2.00	4.00	10.00	20.00	—

KM# 625a CENTAVO
Brass, **Obv.** Large date in center **Rev:** Value within wreath

Date	Mintage	VG8	F12	VF20	XF40	MS60
1914	—	75.00	200	400	500	—

KM# 625b CENTAVO
Lead, **Obv.** Large date in center **Rev:** Value within wreath

Date	Mintage	VG8	F12	VF20	XF40	MS60
1914	—	20.00	40.00	65.00	90.00	—

KM# 625c CENTAVO
Copper, **Obv.** Large date in center **Rev:** Value within wreath

Date	Mintage	VG8	F12	VF20	XF40	MS60
1914	—	25.00	50.00	80.00	125	—

REVOLUTIONARY COINAGE

KM# 626 CENTAVO
2.80 g., Copper, 20mm. **Obv.** Date **Rev:** Value within wreath **Note:** Weight varies 2.46-2.78g.

Date	Mintage	VG8	F12	VF20	XF40	MS60
1914	—	15.00	20.00	40.00	50.00	—

KM# 626a CENTAVO
Brass, **Obv.** Date **Rev:** Value within wreath

Date	Mintage	VG8	F12	VF20	XF40	MS60
1914	—	75.00	100	300	500	—

KM# 626b CENTAVO
Lead, **Obv.** Date **Rev:** Value within wreath

Date	Mintage	VG8	F12	VF20	XF40	MS60
1914	—	20.00	40.00	70.00	125	—

Note: Varieties in size exist

KM# 627 CENTAVO
Copper, 20mm. **Obv.** Stars below date **Rev:** Value with retrograde N

Date	Mintage	VG8	F12	VF20	XF40	MS60
1914	—	6.00	12.00	30.00	45.00	—

KM# 627a CENTAVO
Lead, 20mm. **Obv.** Stars below date **Rev:** Value with retrograde N

Date	Mintage	VG8	F12	VF20	XF40	MS60
1914	—	20.00	40.00	60.00	125	—

KM# 628 CENTAVO
Aluminum, **Obv.** National arms within sprigs **Rev:** Value

Date	Mintage	VG8	F12	VF20	XF40	MS60
1914	—	0.65	1.00	2.00	4.00	12.00

KM# 629 5 CENTAVOS
6.20 g., Copper, 24mm. **Obv.** Date above sprigs **Rev:** Value within designed wreath **Obv. Legend:** ESTADO DE DURANGO

Date	Mintage	VG8	F12	VF20	XF40	MS60
1914	—	2.00	3.00	8.00	15.00	—

KM# 630 5 CENTAVOS
Copper, **Obv.** Date above sprigs **Rev:** Value within designed wreath **Obv. Legend:** E. DE DURANGO

Date	Mintage	VG8	F12	VF20	XF40	MS60
1914	—	125	275	450	700	—

KM# 631 5 CENTAVOS
5.05 g., Copper, 23.5mm. **Obv.** Date above sprigs **Rev:** Value within designed wreath **Obv. Legend:** E. DE DURANGO

Date	Mintage	VG8	F12	VF20	XF40	MS60
1914	—	1.25	3.00	6.00	15.00	—

KM# 631a 5 CENTAVOS
Brass, **Obv.** Date above sprigs **Rev:** Value within designed wreath **Obv. Legend:** E. DE DURANGO

Date	Mintage	VG8	F12	VF20	XF40	MS60
1914	—	30.00	40.00	70.00	100	—

KM# 631b 5 CENTAVOS
Lead, **Obv.** Date above sprigs **Rev:** Value within designed wreath **Obv. Legend:** E. DE DURANGO

Date	Mintage	VG8	F12	VF20	XF40	MS60
1914	—	45.00	70.00	100	180	—

KM# 632 5 CENTAVOS
4.61 g., Copper, 23.5mm. **Obv.** Date above sprigs **Rev:** Roman numeral value **Obv. Legend:** E. DE DURANGO

Date	Mintage	VG8	F12	VF20	XF40	MS60
1914	—	4.00	8.00	20.00	50.00	—

KM# 632a 5 CENTAVOS
Lead, **Obv.** Date above sprigs **Rev:** Roman numeral value **Obv. Legend:** E. DE DURANGO

Date	Mintage	VG8	F12	VF20	XF40	MS60
1914	—	50.00	75.00	100	150	—

KM# 633 5 CENTAVOS
Lead, **Obv.** Three stars below 1914 **Rev:** 5 CVS **Note:** Counterfeits are prevalent in the market

Date	Mintage	VG8	F12	VF20	XF40	MS60
1914	—	—	600	2,000	—	—

REVOLUTIONARY COINAGE

KM# 634 5 CENTAVOS
Brass, **Obv.** National arms above sprigs **Rev:** Value **Obv. Legend:** REPUBLICA MEXICANA **Rev. Legend:** ESTADO DE DURANGO

Date	Mintage	VG8	F12	VF20	XF40	MS60
1914	—	0.50	1.00	2.50	6.00	12.00

KM# 634a 5 CENTAVOS
Copper, **Obv.** National arms above sprigs **Rev:** Value **Obv. Legend:** REPUBLICA MEXICANA **Rev. Legend:** ESTADO DE DURANGO **Note:** There are numerous varieties of these general types of the Durango 1 and 5 Centavo pieces.

Date	Mintage	VG8	F12	VF20	XF40	MS60
1914	—	75.00	125	175	250	—

KM# 634b 5 CENTAVOS
6.89 g., Copper-Nickel, 25.53mm. **Obv.** National arms above sprigs **Rev:** Value **Obv. Legend:** REPUBLICA MEXICANA **Rev. Legend:** ESTADO DE DURANGO **Edge:** Plain

Date	Mintage	F12	VF20	XF40	MS60	MS63
1914	—	25.00	50.00	85.00	135	200

GUERRERO

Guerrero is a state on the southwestern coast of Mexico. It was one of the areas of operation of Zapata and his forces in the south of Mexico. The Zapata forces operated seven different mints in this state. The date ranges were from 1914 to 1917 and denominations from 2 Centavos to 2 Pesos. Some were cast but most were struck and the rarest coin of the group was the Suriana 1915 2 Pesos.

EMILIANO ZAPATA

REVOLUTIONARY COINAGE

KM# 638 2 CENTAVOS
6.00 g., Copper, 22mm. **Obv.** National arms **Rev:** Value within wreath **Obv. Legend:** REPUBLICA ★ MEXICANA **Note:** Weight varies 5.4-6.03g.

Date	Mintage	VG8	F12	VF20	XF40	MS60
1915	—	75.00	125	175	250	—

KM# 635 3 CENTAVOS
Copper, 25mm. **Obv.** National arms **Rev:** Value within

wreath **Obv. Legend:** REPUBLICA MEXICANA **Note:** Weight varies 4.63-6.87g.

Date	Mintage	VG8	F12	VF20	XF40	MS60
1915	—	500	1,500	2,000	3,000	—

KM# 636 5 CENTAVOS
Copper, 26mm. **Obv.** National arms **Rev:** Value within wreath **Mint:** Guerrero

Date	Mintage	VG8	F12	VF20	XF40	MS60
1915 GRO	—	800	1,200	2,000	3,000	—

KM# 637.1 10 CENTAVOS
Copper, 27-28.5mm. **Obv.** National arms, snake head ends at L in REPUBLICA **Rev:** Date and value within wreath **Obv. Legend:** REPUBLICA MEXICANA **Mint:** Guerrero **Note:** Size varies.

Date	Mintage	VG8	F12	VF20	XF40	MS60
1915 GRO	—	600	1,000	1,500	2,000	—

KM# 637.2 10 CENTAVOS
Copper, 27-28.5mm. **Obv.** National arms, snake head ends at C in REPUBLICA **Rev:** Value within wreath **Obv. Legend:** REPUBLICA MEXICANA **Mint:** Guerrero **Note:** Size varies.

Date	Mintage	VG8	F12	VF20	XF40	MS60
1915 GRO	—	3.00	5.00	8.00	15.00	—

KM# 637.2a 10 CENTAVOS
8.23 g., Brass, 26mm. **Obv.** National arms, snake head ends at C in REPUBLICA **Rev:** Value within wreath **Obv. Legend:** REPUBLICA MEXICANA **Mint:** Guerrero

Date	Mintage	VG8	F12	VF20	XF40	MS60
1915 GRO	—	8.00	15.00	25.00	50.00	—

KM# 637.2b 10 CENTAVOS
Lead, **Obv.** National arms, snake head ends at C in REPUBLICA **Rev:** Value within wreath **Obv. Legend:** REPUBLICA MEXICANA **Mint:** Guerrero

Date	Mintage	VG8	F12	VF20	XF40	MS60
1915 GRO	—	50.00	75.00	175	275	—

KM# 637.3 10 CENTAVOS
Copper, **Obv.** National arms, snake head ends before A in REPUBLICA **Rev:** Date and value within wreath **Obv. Legend:** REPUBLICA MEXICANA **Mint:** Guerrero

Date	Mintage	VG8	F12	VF20	XF40	MS60
1915. GRO	—	3.00	5.00	8.00	15.00	—

KM# 637.3a 10 CENTAVOS
Brass, **Obv.** National arms, snake head ends before A in REPUBLICA **Rev:** Value and date within wreath **Obv. Legend:** REPUBLICA MEXICANA **Mint:** Guerrero

Date	Mintage	VG8	F12	VF20	XF40	MS60
1915. GRO	—	12.00	20.00	50.00	100	—

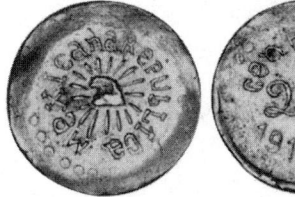

KM# 639 25 CENTAVOS
7.50 g., Silver, 25mm. **Obv.** Liberty cap **Rev:** Value above date **Obv. Legend:** Mexicana REPUbLICA **Note:** Weight varies 7.41-7.5g.

Date	Mintage	VG8	F12	VF20	XF40	MS60
1915	—	125	300	800	1,200	—

KM# 640 50 CENTAVOS
14.80 g., Silver, 34mm. **Obv.** Liberty cap **Rev:** Date and value within beaded border **Note:** Weight varies 14.5-14.8g.

Date	Mintage	VG8	F12	VF20	XF40	MS60
1915	—	1,000	2,000	6,000	12,000	—

KM# 641 PESO (UN)
Gold with Silver, 29-31mm. **Obv.** National arms **Rev:** Liberty cap and rays within sprigs **Obv. Legend:** REPUBLICA

MEXICANA - ★UN PESO **Rev. Legend:** REFORMA LIBERTAD JUSTICIA Y LEY **Rev. Inscription:** Oro:0,300 **Mint:** Guerrero **Note:** Many die varieties exist. Size varies. Weight varies 10.28-14.84g. Coin is 0.30g fine Gold.

Date	Mintage	VG8	F12	VF20	XF40	MS60
1914 GRO	—	20.00	30.00	40.00	85.00	—

KM# 642 PESO (UN)
Gold with Silver, 30.5-31mm. **Obv.** National arms **Rev:** Liberty cap and rays within sprigs **Obv. Legend:** REPUBLICA MEXICANA - ★UN PESO★ **Rev. Legend:** REFORMA. LIBERTAD.JUSTICIA Y LEY **Rev. Inscription:** Oro:0,300 **Mint:** Guerrero **Note:** Weight varies 12.93-14.66g. Coin is 0.300g fine Gold.

Date	Mintage	VG8	F12	VF20	XF40	MS60
1914 GRO	—	50.00	75.00	100	180	—
1915 GRO	—	600	1,000	1,500	1,850	—

KM# 643 2 PESOS (DOS)
Gold with Silver, 38.25-39.6mm. **Obv.** National arms **Rev:** Radiant sun face above high mountain peaks **Obv. Legend:** REPUBLICA MEXICANA **Rev. Legend:** REFORMA LIBERTAD, JUSTICIA Y LEY", **Rev. Inscription:** Oro:0,595 **Mint:** Guerrero **Note:** Many varieties exist. Coin is 0.595g fine Gold.

Date	Mintage	VG8	F12	VF20	XF40	MS60
1914 GRO	—	25.00	45.00	125	200	425

KM# 644 2 PESOS (DOS)
Gold with Silver, 39-40mm. **Obv.** National arms **Rev:** Radiant sun face above high and low mountain peaks **Obv. Legend:** REPUBLICA MEXICANA **Rev. Legend:** REFORMA, LIBERTAD, JUSTICIA Y LEY **Rev. Inscription:** Oro:0,595 **Mint:** Guerrero **Note:** Weight varies 21.71-26.54g. Coin is 0.595g fine Gold.

Date	Mintage	VG8	F12	VF20	XF40	MS60
1915 GRO	—	65.00	85.00	160	250	550

KM# 644a 2 PESOS (DOS)
Copper, **Obv.** National arms **Rev:** Radiant sun face above high and low mountain peaks **Obv. Legend:** REPUBLICA MEXICANA **Rev. Legend:** REFORMA, LIBERTAD, JUSTICIA Y LEY **Mint:** Guerrero

Date	Mintage	VG8	F12	VF20	XF40	MS60
1915 GRO	—	400	1,000	1,500	2,500	—

ATLIXTAC

KM# 645 10 CENTAVOS
Copper, 27.5-28mm. **Obv.** National arms **Rev:** Value within sprigs **Obv. Legend:** REPUBLICA MEXICANA **Note:** Size varies. Weight varies 4.76-9.74g.

Date	Mintage	VG8	F12	VF20	XF40	MS60
1915	—	3.00	5.00	8.00	15.00	—

KM# 646 10 CENTAVOS
Copper, 27.55-28mm. **Obv.** National arms **Rev:** Value within sprigs **Obv. Legend:** REPUBLICA ★ MEXICANA **Note:** Size varies. Weight varies 6.13-7.94g.

Date	Mintage	VG8	F12	VF20	XF40	MS60
1915	—	3.00	5.00	8.00	15.00	—

CACAHUATEPEC

KM# 648 5 CENTAVOS
12.19 g., Copper, 28mm. **Obv.** National arms **Rev:** Value within wreath **Obv. Legend:** ESTADOS UNIDOS MEXICANOS

Date	Mintage	VG8	F12	VF20	XF40	MS60
1917	—	12.00	25.00	40.00	75.00	—

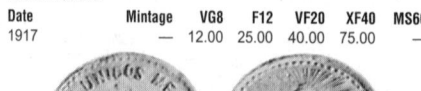

KM# 649 20 CENTAVOS
Silver, 21-23.8mm. **Obv.** National arms **Rev:** Value within sprigs below liberty cap and rays **Obv. Legend:** ESTADOS UNIDOS MEXICANOS **Note:** Size varies. Weight varies 3.99-6.2g.

Date	Mintage	VG8	F12	VF20	XF40	MS60
1917	—	100	200	350	400	—

KM# 650 50 CENTAVOS
13.80 g., Silver, 30-30.3mm. **Obv.** National arms **Rev:** Value and date within sprigs below Liberty cap **Obv. Legend:** ESTADOS UNIDOS MEXICANOS **Note:** Size varies. Weight varies 13.45-13.78g.

Date	Mintage	VG8	F12	VF20	XF40	MS60
1917	—	25.00	65.00	150	375	—

KM# 651 PESO (UN)
Silver, 38mm. **Obv.** National arms **Rev:** Liberty cap **Note:** Weight varies 26.81-32.05g.

Date	Mintage	VG8	F12	VF20	XF40	MS60
1917 L.V. Go	—	2,000	4,000	10,000	12,000	—

CACALOTEPEC

KM# 652 20 CENTAVOS
Silver, 22.5mm. **Obv.** National arms **Rev:** Date and value within sprigs below Liberty cap and rays **Obv. Legend:** ESTADOS UNIDOS MEXICANOS **Note:** Weight varies 3.89-5.73g.

Date	Mintage	VG8	F12	VF20	XF40	MS60
1917	—	1,000	1,800	4,000	8,000	—

CAMPO MORADO

KM# 653 5 CENTAVOS
4.37 g., Copper, 23.5-24mm. **Obv.** National arms **Rev:** Value within wreath **Note:** Size varies.

Date	Mintage	VG8	F12	VF20	XF40	MS60
1915 C.M.	—	9.00	15.00	22.50	50.00	—

KM# 654 10 CENTAVOS
Copper, 25.25-26mm. **Obv.** National arms **Rev:** Value and date within wreath **Note:** Size varies. Weight varies. 4.48-8.77g.

Date	Mintage	VG8	F12	VF20	XF40	MS60
1915 C.M. GRO	—	6.00	10.00	20.00	30.00	—

KM# 655 20 CENTAVOS
Copper, 28mm. **Obv.** National arms **Rev:** Date above star and value within wreath **Note:** Weight varies 4.48-9g.

Date	Mintage	VG8	F12	VF20	XF40	MS60
1915 C.M. GRO	—	15.00	25.00	35.00	50.00	—

KM# 656 50 CENTAVOS
Copper, 29-31mm. **Obv.** National arms **Rev:** Date and value within wreath **Note:** Size varies. Weight varies 9.81-16.77g.

Date	Mintage	VG8	F12	VF20	XF40	MS60
1915 C.M. GRO	—	12.00	20.00	30.00	60.00	—

KM# 657 50 CENTAVOS
Copper, 30-31mm. **Obv.** National arms **Rev:** Date and value within wreath **Note:** Regular obverse. Size varies. Weight varies 6.49-13.19g.

Date	Mintage	VG8	F12	VF20	XF40	MS60
1915 C.M. GRO	—	6.00	10.00	15.00	50.00	—

KM# 657a 50 CENTAVOS
Billon, **Obv.** National arms **Rev:** Date and value within wreath **Note:** Regular obverse.

Date	Mintage	VG8	F12	VF20	XF40	MS60
1915 C.M. GRO	—	200	300	500	1,000	—

KM# 658 PESO (UN)
Gold with Silver, 32-32.5mm. **Obv.** National arms **Rev:** Liberty cap **Rev. Inscription:** Oro:0,300 **Note:** Weight varies 12.42-16.5g. Coin is 0.300g fine Gold.

Date	Mintage	VG8	F12	VF20	XF40	MS60
1914 Co Mo Gro	—	500	600	1,000	1,200	—

KM# 658a PESO (UN)
Brass, **Obv.** National arms **Rev:** Liberty cap

Date	Mintage	VG8	F12	VF20	XF40	MS60
1914 Co Mo Gro Unique	—	—	—	—	10,000	—

KM# 659 PESO (UN)
Gold with Silver, 30-31mm. **Obv.** National arms **Rev:** Liberty cap within sprigs **Rev. Inscription:** Oro:0,300 **Note:** Weight varies 12.26-15.81g. Coin is 0.300g fine Gold.

Date	Mintage	VG8	F12	VF20	XF40
1914 CAMPO Mo	—	20.00	35.00	50.00	85.00

KM# 660a 2 PESOS (DOS)
Copper, **Obv.** National arms **Rev:** Sun over mountains

Date	Mintage	VG8	F12	VF20	XF40	MS60
1915 Co. Mo.	—	—	800	1,000	1,200	—

KM# 661   2 PESOS (DOS)
29.44 g., Gold with Silver, 39mm. **Obv.** National arms **Rev:** Sun and mountains **Rev. Inscription:** Oro:0,595 **Note:** Coin is 0.595g fine Gold.

Date	Mintage	VG8	F12	VF20	XF40	MS60
1915 Co. Mo.	—	2,500	5,000	9,000	15,000	—

KM# 662   2 PESOS (DOS)
0.60 g., 1.000 Gold with Silver, 34.5-35mm. **Obv.** National arms **Rev:** Liberty cap **Note:** Size varies. Weight varies 18.27-20.08g.

Date	Mintage	VG8	F12	VF20	XF40	MS60
1915 C. M. GRO	—	25.00	35.00	65.00	125	—

KM# 662a.1   2 PESOS (DOS)
Copper, **Obv.** National arms **Rev:** Liberty cap

Date	Mintage	VG8	F12	VF20	XF40	MS60
1915 C. M. GRO	—	—	—	—	1,200	—

KM# 662a.2   2 PESOS (DOS)
Copper, **Obv.** National arms **Rev:** Liberty cap

Date	Mintage	VG8	F12	VF20	XF40	MS60
1915 C. M. GRO Unique	—	—	—	—	—	—

KM# 660   2 PESOS (DOS)
Gold with Silver, 38.9-39mm. **Obv.** National arms **Rev:** Sun over mountains **Rev. Inscription:** Oro:0,595 **Note:** Weight varies 20.6-26.02g. Coin is 0.595g fine Gold.

Date	Mintage	VG8	F12	VF20	XF40	MS60
1915 Co. Mo.	—	18.00	22.00	40.00	85.00	425

CHILPANCINGO

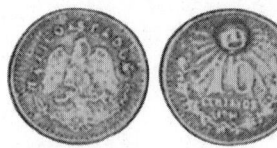

KM# 663   10 CENTAVOS
2.52 g., Cast Silver, 18mm. **Obv.** National arms **Rev:** Sun above value and sprigs

Date	Mintage	VG8	F12	VF20	XF40	MS60
1914	—	700	1,000	1,200	1,500	—

Note: Many counterfeits exist

KM# 664   20 CENTAVOS
4.94 g., Cast Silver, 21.5mm. **Obv.** National arms **Rev:** Sun above value and sprigs

Date	Mintage	VG8	F12	VF20	XF40	MS60
1914	—	700	1,000	1,200	1,500	—

Note: Many counterfeits exist

SURIANA

KM# 665   2 PESOS (DOS)
22.93 g., Gold with Silver, 39mm. **Obv.** National arms **Rev:** Sun over mountains **Rev. Inscription:** Oro:0,595 **Note:** Coin is 0.595g fine Gold.

Date	Mintage	VG8	F12	VF20	XF40	MS60
1915 Rare	—	—	—	20,000	35,000	—

Note: Ira & Larry Goldberg - Millenia sale, 5-08 AU-55 replica. Ponterio & Associates sale, 4-09 VF realized $17,000. Spink America Gerber sale part 2, 6-96 VF realized $16,500

TAXCO

KM# 667 2 CENTAVOS
Copper, 25.25-26mm. **Obv.** National arms **Rev:** Value within sprigs **Obv. Legend:** EDO.DE.GRO **Note:** Size varies. Weight varies 6.81-8.55g.

Date	Mintage	VG8	F12	VF20	XF40	MS60
1915 O/T	—	25.00	40.00	60.00	90.00	—

KM# 668 5 CENTAVOS
Copper, **Obv.** National arms **Rev:** Value within sprigs **Obv. Legend:** REPUBLICA ★MEXICANA **Note:** Weight varies 7.13-7.39g.

Date	Mintage	VG8	F12	VF20	XF40	MS60
1915	—	10.00	20.00	40.00	80.00	—

KM# 669 10 CENTAVOS
Copper, 27-28mm. **Obv.** National arms **Rev:** Date and value within sprigs **Obv. Legend:** REPUBLICA ★ MEXICANA **Note:** Size varies. Weight varies 7.51-8.67g.

Date	Mintage	VG8	F12	VF20	XF40	MS60
1915	—	9.00	20.00	35.00	50.00	—

KM# 670 50 CENTAVOS
5.45 g., Copper, 27-28mm. **Obv.** National arms with legend in large letters **Rev:** Value within sprigs **Note:** Size varies.

Date	Mintage	VG8	F12	VF20	XF40	MS60
1915	—	15.00	25.00	50.00	65.00	—

KM# 671 50 CENTAVOS
Silver, 27.6-28mm. **Obv.** National arms **Rev:** Sun above value and sprigs **Note:** Size varies. Weight varies 8.95-10.85g.

Date	Mintage	VG8	F12	VF20	XF40	MS60
1915	—	25.00	40.00	80.00	150	—

KM# 672 PESO (UN)
Gold with Silver, 30-31mm. **Obv.** National arms **Rev:** Liberty cap within sprigs **Rev. Inscription:** Oro:0,300 **Note:** Weight varies 30-31g. Coin is 0.300g fine Gold.

Date	Mintage	VG8	F12	VF20	XF40	MS60
1915	—	18.00	22.00	50.00	90.00	—

KM# 672a PESO (UN)
Brass, **Obv.** National arms **Rev:** Liberty cap within sprigs

Date	Mintage	VG8	F12	VF20	XF40	MS60
1915	—	300	500	700	1,000	—

KM# 672b PESO (UN)
Lead, **Obv.** National arms **Rev:** Liberty cap within sprigs

Date	Mintage	VG8	F12	VF20	XF40	MS60
1915	—	50.00	200	300	500	—

KM# 672c PESO (UN)
Copper, **Obv.** National arms **Rev:** Liberty cap within sprigs

Date	Mintage	VG8	F12	VF20	XF40	MS60
1915	—	200	300	400	650	—

KM# 673 PESO (UN)
11.60 g., Gold with Silver, 30mm. **Obv.** National arms **Rev:** Liberty cap within sprigs **Rev. Inscription:** Oro:0,300 **Note:** Coin is 0.300g fine Gold.

Date	Mintage	VG8	F12	VF20	XF40	MS60
1915	—	250	500	800	1,000	—

KM# 674 PESO (UN)
Gold with Silver, 30mm. **Obv.** National arms **Rev:** Liberty cap within sprigs **Rev. Inscription:** Oro:0,300 **Note:** Weight varies 10.51-12.79g. Coin is 0.300g fine Gold.

Date	Mintage	VG8	F12	VF20	XF40	MS60
1915	—	100	200	300	550	—
1914	—					
1914	—					

JALISCO

Jalisco is a state on the west coast of Mexico. The few coins made for this state show that the Army of the North did not restrict their operations to the northern border states. The coins were made in Guadalajara under the watchful eye of General Dieguez, commander of this segment of Villa's forces.

GUADALAJARA

REVOLUTIONARY COINAGE

KM# 675   CENTAVO
Copper, **Obv.** Liberty cap **Rev:** Value

Date	Mintage	VG8	F12	VF20	XF40	MS60
1915	—	9.50	15.00	20.00	30.00	—

KM# 675a   CENTAVO
Brass, **Obv.** Liberty cap **Rev:** Value

Date	Mintage	VG8	F12	VF20	XF40	MS60
1915	—	—	—	400	550	—

KM# A676   CENTAVO
Copper, **Obv.** Liberty cap **Rev:** Retrograde value **Note:** Varieties exist.

Date	Mintage	VG8	F12	VF20	XF40	MS60
1915	—	100	300	600	1,000	—

KM# 676.1   2 CENTAVOS
Copper, 20mm. **Obv.** Liberty cap **Rev:** Value

Date	Mintage	VG8	F12	VF20	XF40	MS60
1915	—	10.00	18.00	20.00	35.00	—

Note: Varieties exist.

KM# 676.2   2 CENTAVOS
Copper, **Obv.** Sm. Liberty cap **Rev:** Value

Date	Mintage	VG8	F12	VF20	XF40	MS60
1915	—	200	300	500	800	—

KM# 677   5 CENTAVOS
Copper, 24mm. **Obv.** Liberty cap **Rev:** Value

Date	Mintage	VG8	F12	VF20	XF40	MS60
1915	—	6.50	20.00	40.00	60.00	—

KM# 677a   5 CENTAVOS
Brass, **Obv.** Liberty cap **Rev:** Value

Date	Mintage	VG8	F12	VF20	XF40	MS60
1915 rare	—	—	—	—	—	—

KM# 678   10 CENTAVOS
Copper, **Obv.** Liberty cap above value and date **Rev:** Crowned shield

Date	Mintage	VG8	F12	VF20	XF40	MS60
1915	—	—	—	5,000	10,000	—

KM# A678   PESO
Copper, **Obv.** Liberty cap above value and date **Rev:** Crowned shield

Date	Mintage	VG8	F12	VF20	XF40	MS60
1915	—	—	—	—	20,000	—

MEXICO, ESTADO DE

Estado de Mexico is a state in central Mexico that surrounds the Federal District on three sides. The issues by the Zapata forces in this state have two distinctions – the Amecameca pieces are the crudest and the Toluca cardboard piece is the most unusual. General Tenorio authorized the crude incuse Amecameca pieces.

AMECAMECA

REVOLUTIONARY COINAGE

KM# 679   5 CENTAVOS
12.55 g., Brass, 24.5mm. **Obv.** Legend **Rev:** Value above cent sign **Obv. Legend:** EJERCITO CONVENCIONISTA

Date	Mintage	VG8	F12	VF20	XF40	MS60
ND unique	—	—	—	—	—	—

KM# 680   5 CENTAVOS
12.77 g., Brass, 24.6mm. **Obv.** National arms above RM **Rev:** Value above cent sign **Note:** Hand stamped.

Date	Mintage	VG8	F12	VF20	XF40	MS60
ND	—	300	500	800	1,000	—

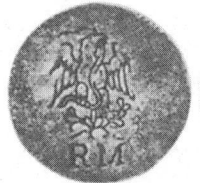

KM# 681 10 CENTAVOS
15.00 g., Brass, 24.5-24.8mm. **Obv.** National arms above RM **Rev:** Value above cent sign **Note:** Hand stamped. Varieties exist. Size varies.

Date	Mintage	VG8	F12	VF20	XF40	MS60
ND	—	60.00	90.00	150	200	—

KM# 681a 10 CENTAVOS
Copper, **Obv.** National arms above RM **Rev:** Value above cent sign **Note:** Hand stamped.

Date	Mintage	VG8	F12	VF20	XF40	MS60
ND	—	75.00	125	225	350	—

KM# 682 20 CENTAVOS
Brass, 24-25mm. **Obv.** National arms above RM **Rev:** Value above cent sign **Note:** Hand stamped. Varieties exist. Size varies. Weight varies 11.34-12.86g.

Date	Mintage	VG8	F12	VF20	XF40	MS60
ND	—	15.00	22.50	35.00	60.00	—

KM# 682a 20 CENTAVOS
Copper, **Obv.** National arms above RM **Rev:** Value above cent sign **Note:** Hand stamped.

Date	Mintage	VG8	F12	VF20	XF40	MS60
ND	—	25.00	50.00	175	250	—

KM# 683 20 CENTAVOS
Copper, 19-20mm. **Obv.** National arms above A. D. J. **Rev:** Value **Note:** Size varies. Weight varies 3.99-5.35g.

Date	Mintage	VG8	F12	VF20	XF40	MS60
ND	—	7.50	12.50	20.00	35.00	—

KM# 683a 20 CENTAVOS
Brass, **Obv.** National arms above A. D. J. **Rev:** Value

Date	Mintage	VG8	F12	VF20	XF40	MS60
ND	—	—	—	300	500	—

KM# 684 25 CENTAVOS
Brass, **Obv.** Legend **Rev:** Value above cent sign **Obv. Legend:** EJERCITO CONVENCIONISTA

Date	Mintage	VG8	F12	VF20	XF40	MS60
ND unique	—	—	—	—	—	—

KM# 685 25 CENTAVOS
Copper, 25mm. **Obv.** National arms above sprigs **Rev:** Large numeral value **Note:** Hand stamped. Many modern counterfeits exist in all metals. Weight varies 6.32-6.99g.

Date	Mintage	VG8	F12	VF20	XF40	MS60
ND	—	15.00	20.00	30.00	40.00	—

KM# 685a 25 CENTAVOS
7.92 g., Brass, 25mm. **Obv.** National arms above sprigs **Rev:** Large numeral value **Note:** Hand stamped.

Date	Mintage	VG8	F12	VF20	XF40	MS60
ND	—	—	—	100	300	—

KM# 685b 25 CENTAVOS
Silver, **Obv.** National arms above sprigs **Rev:** Large numeral value **Note:** Hand stamped.

Date	Mintage	VG8	F12	VF20	XF40	MS60
ND	—	—	—	300	500	—

KM# 686 50 CENTAVOS
Copper, 28-28.5mm. **Obv.** Eagle over sprays **Note:** Hand stamped. Size varies.

Date	Mintage	VG8	F12	VF20	XF40	MS60
ND	—	8.00	10.00	18.00	30.00	—

KM# 686a 50 CENTAVOS
16.04 g., Brass, 28.5mm. **Obv.** National arms above sprigs **Rev:** Large numeral value **Note:** Hand stamped.

Date	Mintage	VG8	F12	VF20	XF40	MS60
ND	—	100	200	300	400	—

Note: Stem of "¢" above the 5

KM# 687 50 CENTAVOS
Copper, 23.5-29mm. **Obv.** National arms above sprigs **Rev:** Large numeral value **Note:** Contemporary counterfeit, hand engraved. Size varies. Weight varies 8.8-10.8g.

Date	Mintage	VG8	F12	VF20	XF40	MS60
ND	—	12.00	30.00	50.00	80.00	—

Note: ¢" clears top of 5

TENANCINGO, TOWN

KM# 688.1 2 CENTAVOS
Copper, **Obv.** National arms **Rev:** Value within wreath without TM below value

Date	Mintage	VG8	F12	VF20	XF40	MS60
1915	—	—	400	2,000	6,000	—

KM# 688.2 2 CENTAVOS
Copper, **Obv.** National arms **Rev:** Value within wreath with TM below value

Date	Mintage	VG8	F12	VF20	XF40	MS60
1915	—	—	400	1,000	5,000	—

KM# 689.1 5 CENTAVOS
Copper, 19mm. **Obv.** National arms **Rev:** Numeral value over lined C within wreath **Note:** Weight varies 2.83-2.84g.

Date	Mintage	VG8	F12	VF20	XF40	MS60
1915	—	10.00	20.00	40.00	60.00	—

KM# 689.2 5 CENTAVOS
Copper, 19mm. **Obv.** National arms **Rev:** Numeral value over solid C within wreath **Note:** Weight varies 2.83-2.84g.

Date	Mintage	VG8	F12	VF20	XF40	MS60
1915	—	200	400	800	1,200	—

KM# 690.1 10 CENTAVOS
Copper, 25.25mm. **Obv.** National arms **Rev:** Value over lined C within wreath below date **Note:** Weight varies 4.27-5.64g.

Date	Mintage	VG8	F12	VF20	XF40	MS60
1916	—	10.00	20.00	40.00	80.00	—

KM# 690.2 10 CENTAVOS
Copper, 25.25mm. **Obv.** National arms **Rev:** Value over lined C within wreath **Note:** Weight varies 4.27-5.64g.

Date	Mintage	VG8	F12	VF20	XF40	MS60
1916	—	100	300	500	800	—

KM# 691 20 CENTAVOS
Copper, 27.5-28mm. **Obv.** National arms **Rev:** Value and date above sprigs **Note:** Size varies. Weight varies 8.51-11.39g.

Date	Mintage	VG8	F12	VF20	XF40	MS60
1915	—	25.00	40.00	55.00	85.00	—

TOLUCA, CITY

KM# 692.1 5 CENTAVOS
Cardboard, 27-28mm. **Obv.** Crowned shield within sprigs **Rev:** Banner accross large numeral value **Note:** Size varies. Weight varies 1.04-1.16g.

Date	Mintage	VG8	F12	VF20	XF40	MS60
1915	—	15.00	30.00	50.00	100	—

KM# 692.2 5 CENTAVOS
Cardboard, 27-28mm. **Obv.** Crowned shield within sprigs **Rev:** Banner accross large numeral value **Note:** Size varies. Weight varies 1.04-1.16g.

Date	Mintage	VG8	F12	VF20	XF40	MS60
1915	—	15.00	30.00	50.00	100	—

COUNTERMARKED COINAGE

KM# 693.1 20 CENTAVOS

Copper, 20mm. **Obv.** National arms **Rev:** Numeral 20 within C and inner circle within sprigs **Note:** Countermark on 1 Centavo, KM#415. Varieties exist. Weight varies 2.65-2.95g.

Date	Mintage	VG8	F12	VF20	XF40	MS60
ND	—	20.00	40.00	55.00	95.00	—

KM# 693.2 20 CENTAVOS

Copper, 20mm. **Obv.** National arms **Rev:** Numeral 20 within C and inner circle within 3/4 wreath **Note:** Countermark on 1 Centavo, KM#394.1. Weight varies 2.65-2.95g.

Date	Mintage	VG8	F12	VF20	XF40	MS60
1904	—	30.00	50.00	90.00	165	—

KM# 694 40 CENTAVOS

5.86 g., Copper, 24.75-25mm. **Obv.** National arms **Rev:** Numeral 40 within C and inner circle within wreath **Note:** Countermark on 2 Centavos, KM#419. Varieties exist. Size varies.

Date	Mintage	VG8	F12	VF20	XF40	MS60
ND	—	25.00	60.00	80.00	150	—

MORELOS

Morelos is a state in south central Mexico, adjoining the federal district on the south. It was the headquarters of Emiliano Zapata. His personal quarters were at Tlatizapan in Morelos. The Morelos coins from 2 Centavos to 1 Peso were all copper except one type of 1 Peso in silver. The two operating Zapatista mints in Morelos were Atlihuayan and Tlaltizapan.

EMILIANO ZAPATA

REVOLUTIONARY COINAGE

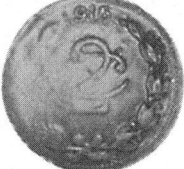

KM# 695 2 CENTAVOS

Copper, 23mm. **Obv.** National arms **Rev:** Value within wreath **Obv. Legend:** E.L. DE MORELOS

Date	Mintage	VG8	F12	VF20	XF40	MS60
1915	—	1,000	1,400	1,800	2,750	—

KM# 696 5 CENTAVOS

9.00 g., Copper, 25.9mm. **Obv.** National arms **Rev:** Value within 3/4 wreath **Rev. Legend:** E. DE MOR. 1915

Date	Mintage	VG8	F12	VF20	XF40	MS60
1915	—	300	800	2,000	5,000	—

KM# 697 10 CENTAVOS

8.69 g., Copper, 24mm. **Obv.** National arms **Rev:** Value within lined C and wreath

Date	Mintage	VG8	F12	VF20	XF40	MS60
1915	—	12.00	20.00	30.00	40.00	—

KM# 698 10 CENTAVOS

Copper, 24-24.5mm. **Obv.** National arms **Rev:** Value within lined C and wreath with date effaced from die **Note:** Size varies. Weight varies 4.83-6.8g.

Date	Mintage	VG8	F12	VF20	XF40	MS60
ND	—	12.00	20.00	35.00	55.00	—

KM# 699 10 CENTAVOS

Copper, **Obv.** National arms **Rev:** Date and value within wreath **Rev. Legend:** E. DE MOR

Date	Mintage	VG8	F12	VF20	XF40	MS60
1915	—	1,000	2,000	3,000	5,000	—

KM# 700   10 CENTAVOS
Copper, 28mm. **Obv.** National arms **Rev:** Date and value within wreath **Rev. Legend:** MOR **Note:** Weight varies 5.56-8.36g.

Date	Mintage	VG8	F12	VF20	XF40	MS60
1916	—	5.00	20.00	40.00	60.00	—

KM# 701   20 CENTAVOS
Copper, 23.75-24.75mm. **Obv.** National arms **Rev:** Value within lined C and 3/4 wreath **Note:** Size varies. Weight varies 3.88-4.15g.

Date	Mintage	VG8	F12	VF20	XF40	MS60
1915	—	9.00	15.00	25.00	35.00	—

KM# 702   50 CENTAVOS
Copper, 28.8mm. **Obv.** National arms with MOR beneath eagle **Rev:** 50C monogram

Date	Mintage	VG8	F12	VF20	XF40	MS60
1915	—	300	500	900	1,450	—

KM# 703   50 CENTAVOS
Copper, 28-29.5mm. **Obv.** National arms **Rev:** Numeral value within lined C and 1/2 wreath **Note:** This coin exists with a silver and also a brass wash. Size varies. Weight varies 5.73-13.77g.

Date	Mintage	VG8	F12	VF20	XF40	MS60
1915	—	12.50	17.50	30.00	50.00	—

KM# 703a   50 CENTAVOS
Brass, **Obv.** National arms above sprigs **Rev:** 50C monogram

Date	Mintage	VG8	F12	VF20	XF40	MS60
1915	—	100	200	400	600	—

KM# 706   50 CENTAVOS
Copper, 28mm. **Obv.** National arms **Rev:** Date above large numeral value **Rev. Legend:** REFORMA LIBERTAD JUSTICIA Y LEY

Date	Mintage	VG8	F12	VF20	XF40	MS60
1915	—	400	600	1,000	1,800	—

KM# 704   50 CENTAVOS
Copper, 29-30mm. **Obv.** National arms with Morelos written below **Rev:** Value within wreath **Note:** Size varies. Weight varies 8.56-11.47g.

Date	Mintage	VG8	F12	VF20	XF40	MS60
1916	—	12.50	20.00	40.00	60.00	—

KM# 708   PESO (UN)
Silver, **Obv.** National arms **Rev:** Liberty cap within wreath

Date	Mintage	VG8	F12	VF20	XF40	MS60
1916	—	450	750	1,150	1,850	—

KM# 708a   PESO (UN)
10.00 g., Copper, 30mm. **Obv.** National arms **Rev:** Liberty cap within wreath

Date	Mintage	VG8	F12	VF20	XF40	MS60
1916	—	500	1,000	1,200	2,300	—
1915	—					
1915	—					
191x	—					
191x	—					
1916	—					

OAXACA

Oaxaca is one of the southern states in Mexico. The coins issued in this state represent the most prolific series of the Revolution. Most of the coins bear the portrait of Benito Juarez, have corded or plain edges and were issued by a provisional government in the state. The exceptions are the rectangular 1 and 3 Centavos pieces that begin the series.

PROVISIONAL GOVERNMENT

REVOLUTIONARY COINAGE

 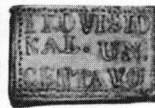

KM# 709   CENTAVO (UN)
Copper, 19mm. **Obv.** Legend within beaded rectangle **Rev:** Legend within beaded rectangle **Note:** Rectangular flan.

Date	Mintage	VG8	F12	VF20	XF40	MS60
1915	—	90.00	125	400	650	—

KM# 710   CENTAVO (UN)
Copper, 18mm. **Obv.** Bust left with date flanked by stars below **Rev:** Value within lined C and 1/2 wreath

Date	Mintage	VG8	F12	VF20	XF40	MS60
1915	—	12.00	17.50	25.00	40.00	—

KM# 710a   CENTAVO (UN)
Brass, **Obv.** Head left with date flanked by stars below **Rev:** Value within lined C and 1/2 wreath

Date	Mintage	VG8	F12	VF20	XF40	MS60
1915	—	50.00	100	200	350	—

KM# 711   3 CENTAVOS (TRES)
Copper, 24mm. **Obv.** Legend within rectangle with date below, stars in corners **Rev:** Legend within rectangle with stars in corners **Rev. Legend:** PROVISIO... **Note:** Rectangular flan.

Date	Mintage	VG8	F12	VF20	XF40	MS60
1915	—	100	200	400	600	—

 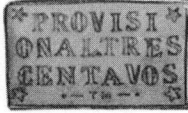

KM# 712   3 CENTAVOS (TRES)
Copper, **Obv.** Legend within rectangle with date below, stars in corners **Rev:** Legend within rectangle with stars in corners **Rev. Legend:** PROVISI... **Note:** Rectangular flan.

Date	Mintage	VG8	F12	VF20	XF40	MS60
1915	—	2,000	4,000	6,000	10,000	—

KM# 713.1   3 CENTAVOS (TRES)
2.25 g., Copper, 20mm. **Obv.** Bust left flanked by stars below **Rev:** Value above sprigs **Note:** Without TM below value

Date	Mintage	VG8	F12	VF20	XF40	MS60
1915	—	3.00	5.00	12.00	25.00	—

KM# 713.2   3 CENTAVOS (TRES)
2.25 g., Copper, 20mm. **Obv.** Bust left flanked by stars below **Rev:** Value above sprigs **Edge:** Plain **Note:** Without TM below value

Date	Mintage	VG8	F12	VF20	XF40	MS60
1915	—	—	—	70.00	100	—

KM# 713.3   3 CENTAVOS (TRES)
2.25 g., Copper, 20mm. **Obv.** Bust left flanked by stars below **Rev:** Value above sprigs **Note:** With TM below value

Date	Mintage	VG8	F12	VF20	XF40	MS60
1915	—	100	200	500	600	—

KM# 714   3 CENTAVOS (TRES)
Copper, 20mm. **Obv.** Bust left **Rev:** Value above sprigs **Note:** Small 3

Date	Mintage	VG8	F12	VF20	XF40	MS60
1915	—	6.00	10.00	15.00	30.00	—

KM# 715   5 CENTAVOS
Copper, **Note:** JAN. 15 1915. incuse lettering

Date	Mintage	VG8	F12	VF20	XF40	MS60
1915 Rare	—	—	—	—	—	—

KM# 716   5 CENTAVOS
Copper, **Obv.** Bust facing within circle **Rev:** Value above sprigs

Date	Mintage	VG8	F12	VF20	XF40	MS60
1915	—	—	—	—	12,000	—

KM# 717 5 CENTAVOS
Copper, 22mm. **Obv.** Low relief bust left with date flanked by stars below **Rev:** Value above sprigs **Note:** Low relief with long, pointed truncation

Date	Mintage	VG8	F12	VF20	XF40	MS60
1915	—	1.50	3.00	4.50	12.00	—

KM# 718 5 CENTAVOS
Copper, 22mm. **Obv.** Raised bust left with date flanked by stars below **Rev:** Value above sprigs **Note:** Heavy with short unfinished lapels

Date	Mintage	VG8	F12	VF20	XF40	MS60
1915	—	1.50	2.50	4.00	12.00	—

KM# 719 5 CENTAVOS
Copper, 22mm. **Obv.** Raised bust left with date flanked by stars below **Rev:** Value above sprigs **Note:** Curved bottom

Date	Mintage	VG8	F12	VF20	XF40	MS60
1915	—	1.50	2.50	4.00	12.00	—

KM# 720 5 CENTAVOS
Copper, 22mm. **Obv.** Bust left with date flanked by stars below **Rev:** Value above sprigs **Note:** Short truncation with closed lapels

Date	Mintage	VG8	F12	VF20	XF40	MS60
1915	—	1.50	3.00	4.50	12.00	—

KM# 721 5 CENTAVOS
Copper, 22mm. **Obv.** Bust left with date flanked by stars below **Rev:** Value above sprigs **Note:** Short curved truncation

Date	Mintage	VG8	F12	VF20	XF40	MS60
1915	—	1.50	2.50	5.00	12.00	—

KM# 722 10 CENTAVOS
Copper, **Obv.** Low relief bust left with date flanked by stars below **Rev:** Value above sprigs **Note:** Low relief with long pointed truncation

Date	Mintage	VG8	F12	VF20	XF40	MS60
1915	—	1.50	2.50	5.00	12.00	—

KM# 723 10 CENTAVOS
Copper, **Obv.** Bust left with date flanked by stars below **Rev:** Value above sprigs **Note:** Obverse and reverse legend retrograde.

Date	Mintage	VG8	F12	VF20	XF40	MS60
1915 Rare	—	—	—	—	—	—

KM# 724 10 CENTAVOS
Copper, 26.5mm. **Obv.** Raised bust left with date flanked by stars below **Rev:** Value above sprigs **Note:** Bold and unfinished truncation using 1 peso obverse die of km#740

Date	Mintage	VG8	F12	VF20	XF40	MS60
1915	—	3.00	5.00	8.00	12.00	—

KM# 725 10 CENTAVOS
Copper, 26.5mm. **Obv.** Bust left with date flanked by stars below **Rev:** Value above sprigs **Note:** Heavy with short unfinished lapels centered high

Date	Mintage	VG8	F12	VF20	XF40	MS60
1915	—	1.50	2.50	4.00	12.00	—

KM# 726 10 CENTAVOS
Copper, **Obv.** Raised bust left with date flanked by stars below **Rev:** Value above sprigs **Note:** Curved bottom

Date	Mintage	VG8	F12	VF20	XF40	MS60
1915	—	1.50	2.50	4.00	12.00	—

KM# 727.1 10 CENTAVOS
Copper, **Obv.** Raised bust left with date flanked by stars

below **Rev:** Value above sprigs **Note:** Short truncation with closed lapels

Date	Mintage	VG8	F12	VF20	XF40	MS60
1915	—	1.50	2.50	4.00	12.00	—

KM# 727.2 10 CENTAVOS
Copper, **Obv.** Bust left with date flanked by stars below **Rev:** Value above sprigs **Note:** At present, only four pieces of this type are known. All are VF or better; T below bow with M below first leaf

Date	Mintage	VG8	F12	VF20	XF40	MS60
1915	—	—	—	500	700	—

KM# 727.3 10 CENTAVOS
Copper, **Obv.** Raised bust left flanked by letters GV with date flanked by stars below **Rev:** Value above sprigs **Note:** This counterstamp appears on several different type host 10 cent coins.

Date	Mintage	VG8	F12	VF20	XF40	MS60
1915	—	100	200	400	500	—

Note: Letters GV correspond to General Garcia Vigil

KM# 728 20 CENTAVOS
Silver, 19mm. **Obv.** Low relief bust left with date flanked by stars below **Rev:** Value above sprigs **Note:** Low relief with long pointed truncation

Date	Mintage	VG8	F12	VF20	XF40	MS60
1915	—	800	2,000	4,000	6,000	—

KM# 728a 20 CENTAVOS
Copper, 19mm. **Obv.** Bust left with date flanked by stars below **Rev:** Value above sprigs **Note:** Low relief with long pointed truncation

Date	Mintage	VG8	F12	VF20	XF40	MS60
1915 Rare	—	—	—	—	—	—

KM# 729.1 20 CENTAVOS
Copper, **Obv.** Raised bust left with date flanked by stars below **Rev:** Value above sprigs **Note:** Unfinished truncation using 1 peso obverse die

Date	Mintage	VG8	F12	VF20	XF40	MS60
1915	—	1.50	3.00	4.50	12.00	—

KM# 729.2 20 CENTAVOS
Copper, **Obv.** Bust left with date flanked by stars below **Rev:** Value above sprigs **Note:** Counterstamp: Liberty cap and rays with bold unfinished truncation using 1 peso obverse die

Date	Mintage	VG8	F12	VF20	XF40	MS60
1915	—	100	150	300	375	—

KM# 730 20 CENTAVOS
Copper, **Obv.** Bust left with date flanked by stars below **Rev:** Value above sprigs **Note:** 5th bust, heavy with short unfinished lapels using 20 Pesos obverse die

Date	Mintage	VG8	F12	VF20	XF40	MS60
1915	—	5.00	7.00	10.00	15.00	—

KM# 731.1 20 CENTAVOS
Copper, 31mm. **Obv.** Raised bust left with date flanked by stars below **Rev:** Value above sprigs **Note:** Curved bottom

Date	Mintage	VG8	F12	VF20	XF40	MS60
1915	—	1.50	2.50	5.00	12.00	—

KM# 731.2 20 CENTAVOS
Copper, **Obv.** Raised bust left with date flanked by stars below **Rev:** Value above sprigs **Note:** Similar to KM#731.1 but with fourth bust.

Date	Mintage	VG8	F12	VF20	XF40	MS60
1915 Unique	—	—	—	—	—	—

KM# 732   20 CENTAVOS
Copper,   **Obv.** Raised bust left with date flanked by stars below **Rev:** Value above sprigs

Date	Mintage	VG8	F12	VF20	XF40	MS60
1915	—	1.50	2.50	4.00	12.00	—

KM# 733   20 CENTAVOS
Copper,   **Obv.** Bust left with date flanked by stars below **Rev:** Value above sprigs **Note:** 7th bust, short truncation with closed lapels

Date	Mintage	VG8	F12	VF20	XF40	MS60
1915	—	1.50	3.00	4.50	12.00	—

KM# 734   50 CENTAVOS
4.07 g., Silver, 22mm. **Obv.** Raised bust left with date flanked by stars below **Rev:** Value above sprigs **Note:** Heavy with short unfinished lapels

Date	Mintage	VG8	F12	VF20	XF40	MS60
1915	—	10.00	20.00	50.00	100	—

KM# 735   50 CENTAVOS
Silver, 22mm. **Obv.** Raised bust left with date flanked by stars below **Rev:** Value above sprigs **Note:** Curved bottom

Date	Mintage	VG8	F12	VF20	XF40	MS60
1915	—	8.00	15.00	30.00	75.00	—

KM# 736   50 CENTAVOS
Silver, **Obv.** Bust left with date flanked by stars below **Rev:** Value above sprigs **Note:** Short truncation with closed lapels

Date	Mintage	VG8	F12	VF20	XF40	MS60
1915	—	8.00	15.00	30.00	50.00	—

KM# 737   50 CENTAVOS
4.54 g., Silver, 22mm. **Obv.** Bust left with date flanked by stars below **Rev:** Value above sprigs **Note:** Short truncation with pronounced curve

Date	Mintage	VG8	F12	VF20	XF40	MS60
1915	—	10.00	15.00	25.00	50.00	—

KM# 739   50 CENTAVOS
Billon, 28mm. **Obv.** Raised bust left with date flanked by stars below **Rev:** Value above sprigs **Note:** Ninth bust, high nearly straight truncation

Date	Mintage	VG8	F12	VF20	XF40	MS60
1915	—	—	—	—	8,000	—

KM# 739a   50 CENTAVOS
Copper, 28mm. **Obv.** Raised bust left with date flanked by stars below **Rev:** Value above sprigs **Note:** Ninth bust, high nearly straight truncation

Date	Mintage	VG8	F12	VF20	XF40	MS60
1915	—	—	—	—	8,000	—

KM# 740.1   PESO (UN)
Silver, 26mm. **Obv.** Raised bust left with date flanked by stars below **Rev:** Written value above sprigs **Note:** Fourth bust with heavy unfinished truncation

Date	Mintage	VG8	F12	VF20	XF40	MS60
1915	—	7.00	12.00	30.00	50.00	—

KM# 740.2   PESO (UN)
Silver, 26mm. **Obv.** Raised bust left with date flanked by stars below **Rev:** Written value above sprigs **Note:** Fourth bust with heavy unfinished truncation w/TM.

Date	Mintage	VG8	F12	VF20	XF40	MS60
1915	—	150	300	400	800	—

KM# 741 PESO (UN)
Silver, **Obv.** Raised bust with date flanked by stars below **Rev:** Value above sprigs **Note:** Fifth bust, heavy with short unfinished lapels, centered high

Date	Mintage	VG8	F12	VF20	XF40	MS60
1915	—	8.00	10.00	35.00	45.00	—

KM# 742 PESO (UN)
Silver, **Obv.** Low relief bust left with date flanked by stars below **Rev:** Value above sprigs **Note:** Sixth bust; Curved bottom line

Date	Mintage	VG8	F12	VF20	XF40	MS60
1915	—	10.00	15.00	30.00	50.00	—

KM# 742a PESO (UN)
Copper, **Obv.** Low relief bust left with date flanked by stars below **Rev:** Value above sprigs **Note:** Sixth bust; Curved bottom line

Date	Mintage	VG8	F12	VF20	XF40	MS60
1915	—	—	—	—	600	—

KM# 743 PESO (UN)
Silver, **Obv.** Low relief bust left with date flanked by stars below **Rev:** Value above sprigs **Note:** Seventh bust, short truncation with closed lapels

Date	Mintage	VG8	F12	VF20	XF40	MS60
1915	—	10.00	20.00	30.00	50.00	—

KM# 743a PESO (UN)
Silver, **Obv.** Low relief bust left with date flanked by stars below **Rev:** Value above sprigs **Note:** Seventh bust, short truncation with closed lapels

Date	Mintage	VG8	F12	VF20	XF40	MS60
1915	—	35.00	75.00	150	200	—

KM# 744 2 PESOS (DOS)
Silver, 30mm. **Obv.** Raised bust left with date flanked by stars below **Rev:** Value above sprigs **Note:** Fourth bust, using 1 peso obverse die

Date	Mintage	VG8	F12	VF20	XF40	MS60
1915	—	18.00	28.00	45.00	75.00	—

KM# 744a 2 PESOS (DOS)
Copper, **Obv.** Raised bust left with date flanked by stars below **Rev:** Value above sprigs **Note:** Fourth bust, using 1 peso obverse die

Date	Mintage	VG8	F12	VF20	XF40	MS60
1915 Rare	—	—	—	—	—	—

KM# 745 2 PESOS (DOS)
Gold with Silver, 22mm. **Obv.** Low relief bust left with date flanked by stars below **Rev:** Value above sprigs **Note:** 0.902 Silver, 0.010 Gold. Fifth bust, curved bottom 2 over pesos

Date	Mintage	VG8	F12	VF20	XF40	MS60
1915	—	15.00	25.00	50.00	110	—

KM# 745a 2 PESOS (DOS)
Copper, **Obv.** Low relief bust left with date flanked by stars below **Rev:** Value above sprigs **Note:** Fifth bust, curved bottom 2 over pesos

Date	Mintage	VG8	F12	VF20	XF40	MS60
1915	—	75.00	100	200	400	—

KM# A746 2 PESOS (DOS)
Copper, **Obv.** Raised bust left with date flanked by stars below **Rev:** Balance scale below liberty cap **Note:** Seventh bust, short truncation with closed lapels

Date	Mintage	VG8	F12	VF20	XF40	MS60
1915 Unique	—	—	—	—	—	—

KM# 746 2 PESOS (DOS)
Silver, **Obv.** Raised bust left with date flanked by stars below **Rev:** Balance scale below liberty cap

Date	Mintage	VG8	F12	VF20	XF40	MS60
1915	—	22.00	28.00	50.00	75.00	—

KM# 746a 2 PESOS (DOS)
Copper, **Obv.** Bust left with date flanked by stars below **Rev:** Balance scale below liberty cap

Date	Mintage	G4	VG8	F12	VF20	XF40
1915	—	—	150	200	600	1,000

KM# A747 2 PESOS (DOS)
Silver, **Obv.** Bust left with date flanked by stars below **Rev:** Balance scale below liberty cap **Note:** Obverse die is free hand engraved.

Date	Mintage	VG8	F12	VF20	XF40	MS60
1915	—	—	—	185	275	—

KM# 747.1 2 PESOS (DOS)
13.44 g., Silver, 33mm. **Obv.** Bust left with date flanked by stars below **Rev:** Balance scale below liberty cap

Date	Mintage	VG8	F12	VF20	XF40	MS60
1915	—	20.00	25.00	55.00	95.00	—

KM# 747.2 2 PESOS (DOS)
13.44 g., Silver, 33mm. **Obv.** Bust left with date flanked by stars below **Rev:** Balance scale below liberty cap

Date	Mintage	VG8	F12	VF20	XF40	MS60
1915	—	22.00	28.00	60.00	100	—

KM# 747.3 2 PESOS (DOS)
13.44 g., Silver, 33mm. **Obv.** Bust left with date flanked by stars below **Rev:** Balance scale below liberty cap

Date	Mintage	VG8	F12	VF20	XF40	MS60
1915	—	20.00	30.00	60.00	100	—

KM# 748 2 PESOS (DOS)
0.902 Silver, 22mm. **Obv.** Bust left with date flanked by stars below **Rev:** Value above sprigs

Date	Mintage	VG8	F12	VF20	XF40	MS60
1915	—	20.00	30.00	60.00	100	—

KM# 749 2 PESOS (DOS)
Silver, **Obv.** Head left with date flanked by stars below **Rev:** Value above sprigs

Date	Mintage	VG8	F12	VF20	XF40	MS60
1915 Unique	—	—	—	—	5,000	—

KM# 750 5 PESOS
0.175 Gold, AGW 19mm. **Obv.** Bust left **Rev:** Value above sprigs **Note:** Third bust, heavy, with short unfinished lapels

Date	Mintage	VG8	F12	VF20	XF40	MS60
1915	—	175	225	350	550	900

KM# 750a 5 PESOS
Copper, **Obv.** Bust left **Rev:** Value above sprigs **Note:** Third bust, heavy, with short unfinished lapels

Date	Mintage	VG8	F12	VF20	XF40	MS60
1915 Unique	—	—	—	—	—	—

KM# 751 5 PESOS
16.77 g., Silver, 30mm. **Obv.** Low relief bust left with date flanked by stars below **Rev:** Value above sprigs **Note:** Seventh bust, short truncation with closed lapels

Date	Mintage	VG8	F12	VF20	XF40	MS60
1915	—	50.00	80.00	175	275	—

KM# 751a 5 PESOS
Copper, **Obv.** Low relief bust left with date flanked by stars below **Rev:** Value above sprigs **Note:** Seventh bust, short truncation with closed lapels

Date	Mintage	VG8	F12	VF20	XF40	MS60
1915	—	125	200	300	1,000	—

KM# 752 10 PESOS
0.175 Gold, AGW 23mm. **Obv.** Bust left with date flanked by stars below **Rev:** Value above sprigs

Date	Mintage	VG8	F12	VF20	XF40	MS60
1915	—	225	350	450	650	1,000

KM# 752a 10 PESOS
Copper, **Obv.** Bust left with date flanked by stars below **Rev:** Value above sprigs

Date	Mintage	VG8	F12	VF20	XF40	MS60
1915	—	800	1,500	2,000	4,000	—

KM# A752 10 PESOS
0.150 Gold, AGW **Obv.** Bust left with date flanked by stars below **Rev:** Value above sprigs

Date	Mintage	VG8	F12	VF20	XF40	MS60
1915 Rare	—	—	—	—	—	—

KM# 753 20 PESOS
0.175 Gold, AGW **Obv.** Bust left with date flanked by stars below **Rev:** Value above sprigs

Date	Mintage	VG8	F12	VF20	XF40	MS60
1915	—	400	500	800	1,000	1,500

KM# 754 20 PESOS
0.175 Gold, AGW 27mm. **Obv.** Bust left with date flanked by stars below **Rev:** Value above sprigs

Date	Mintage	VG8	F12	VF20	XF40	MS60
1915	—	250	450	650	950	1,700

KM# A753 20 PESOS
0.150 Gold, AGW **Obv.** Bust left with date flanked by stars below **Rev:** Value above sprigs **Note:** Fourth bust

Date	Mintage	VG8	F12	VF20	XF40	MS60
1915 Unique	—	—	—	—	—	—

KM# 755 60 PESOS
50.00 g., 0.859 Gold, 1.37 oz. AGW **Obv.** Head left within 3/4 wreath **Rev:** Balance scale below liberty cap **Edge:** Reeded

Date	Mintage	F12	VF20	XF40	MS60	MS63
1916 Rare	—	—	10,000	20,000	28,000	—

KM# 755a 60 PESOS
Silver, **Obv.** Head left within 3/4 wreath **Rev:** Balance scales below liberty cap **Edge:** Reeded

Date	Mintage	F12	VF20	XF40	MS60	MS63
1916	—	—	—	—	15,000	—

KM# 755b 60 PESOS
Copper, **Obv.** Head left within 3/4 wreath **Rev:** Balance scales below liberty cap **Edge:** Plain

Date	Mintage	F12	VF20	XF40	MS60	MS63
1916	—	—	—	2,000	5,000	—

PUEBLA

A state of central Mexico. Puebla was a state that occasionally saw Zapata forces active within its boundaries. Also active, and an issuer of coins, was the Madero brigade who issued coins with their name two years after Madero's death. The state issue of 2, 5, 10 and 20 Centavos saw limited circulation and recent hoards have been found of some values.

CHICONCUAUTLA

REVOLUTIONARY COINAGE

KM# 756 10 CENTAVOS
6.73 g., Copper, 27mm. **Obv.** Date below national arms **Rev:** Letters X and C entwined

Date	Mintage	VG8	F12	VF20	XF40	MS60
1915	—	7.50	12.50	17.50	25.00	—

KM# 757 20 CENTAVOS
Copper, 28mm. **Obv.** Date below national arms **Rev:** Value
Note: Varieties exist.

Date	Mintage	VG8	F12	VF20	XF40	MS60
1915	—	2.50	4.00	6.50	12.00	—

KM# 758 20 CENTAVOS
Copper, 28mm. **Obv.** Date below national arms **Rev:** Value

Date	Mintage	VG8	F12	VF20	XF40	MS60
1915	—	2.50	4.00	6.50	12.00	—

TETELA DEL ORO Y OCAMPO

KM# 759 2 CENTAVOS
Copper, 16mm. **Obv.** National arms above date **Rev:** Value

Date	Mintage	VG8	F12	VF20	XF40	MS60
1915	—	12.50	20.00	28.00	45.00	—
1915 Restrikes	—	—	1.00	1.50	2.00	—

KM# 760 2 CENTAVOS
Copper, 20mm. **Obv.** National arms within beaded circle
Rev: Value within beaded circle **Rev. Legend:** E. DE PU.

Date	Mintage	VG8	F12	VF20	XF40	MS60
1915	—	15.00	25.00	35.00	90.00	—

KM# 761 2 CENTAVOS
Copper, 20mm. **Obv.** National arms within beaded circle

Rev: Value within beaded circle **Rev. Legend:** E. DE PUE.

Date	Mintage	VG8	F12	VF20	XF40	MS60
1915	—	9.00	20.00	25.00	50.00	—

KM# 762 5 CENTAVOS
Copper, 21mm. **Obv.** National arms within beaded circle
Rev: Value within beaded circle

Date	Mintage	VG8	F12	VF20	XF40	MS60
1915	—	100	200	300	400	—

KM# 764 20 CENTAVOS
Copper, 24mm. **Obv.** National arms **Rev:** Value above
sprigs

Date	Mintage	VG8	F12	VF20	XF40	MS60
1915	—	50.00	100	150	225	—

SINALOA

A state along the west coast of Mexico. The cast pieces
of this state have been attributed to two people - Generals
Rafael Buelna and Juan Carrasco. The cap and rays 8
Reales is usually attributed to General Buelna and the rest
of the series to Carrasco. Because of their crude nature it
is questionable whether separate series or mints can be
determined.

BUELNA / CARRASCO

CAST COINAGE
Revolutionary

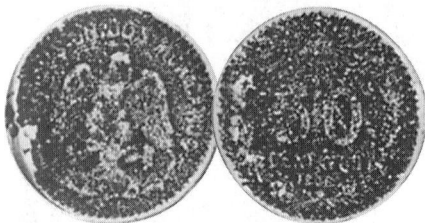

KM# 766 50 CENTAVOS
Cast Silver, 29-31mm. **Obv.** National arms **Rev:** Numeral
value within wreath **Note:** Sand molded using regular 50
Centavos, KM#445. Size varies. Weight varies 12.81-14.8g.

Date	Mintage	G4	VG8	F12	VF20	XF40
ND(1905-1918)	—	200	300	—	—	—

COUNTERMARKED COINAGE

These are all crude sand cast coins using regular coins to prepare the mold. Prices below give a range for how much of the original coin from which the mold was prepared is visible.Revolutionary

KM# 765 20 CENTAVOS

Cast Silver, **Obv.** National arms within beaded circle **Rev:** Value within beaded circle **Note:** Sand molded using regular 20 Centavos.

Date	Mintage	G4	VG8	F12	VF20	XF40
ND(1898-1905)	—	200	300	—	—	—

KM# 767 50 CENTAVOS

Cast Silver, **Obv.** National arms with additional countermark **Rev:** Value and date within wreath with liberty cap above **Note:** Sand molded using regular 50 Centavos, KM#445.

Date	Mintage	G4	VG8	F12	VF20	XF40
ND(1905-1918)	—	100	150	200	300	—

KM# 768.1 PESO

Cast Silver, 38.8-39mm. **Note:** Sand molded using regular 8 Reales, KM#377. Size varies. Weight varies 26-33.67g.

Date	Mintage	G4	VG8	F12	VF20	XF40
ND(1824-97)	—	20.00	35.00	45.00	60.00	—

KM# 768.2 PESO

Cast Silver, 38.5-39mm. **Obv.** With additional countermark **Note:** Sand molded using regular 8 Reales, KM#377. Size varies. Weight varies 26-33.67g.

Date	Mintage	G4	VG8	F12	VF20	XF40
ND(1824-97)	—	25.00	45.00	100	150	—

KM# 769 PESO

Cast Silver, **Note:** Sand molded using regular Peso, KM#409.

Date	Mintage	G4	VG8	F12	VF20	XF40
ND(1898-1909)	—	15.00	25.00	40.00	55.00	—

KM# 770 PESO

Cast Silver, 38.5mm. **Obv.** National arms with additional countermark **Rev:** Liberty cap with additional countermark **Note:** Sand molded using regular Peso, KM#409.

Date	Mintage	G4	VG8	F12	VF20	XF40
ND(1898-1909)	—	35.00	65.00	150	185	—

Note: Many C/S counterfeits exist

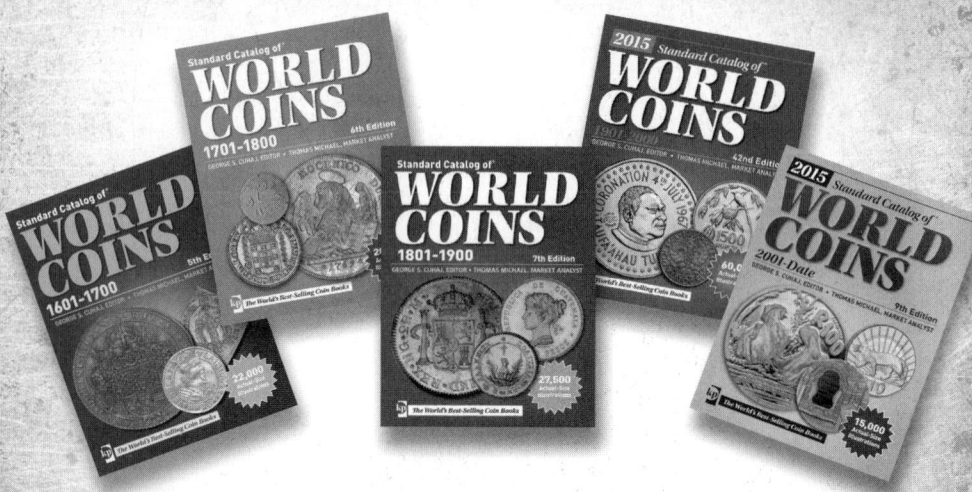